HARVARD DICTIONARY OF MUSIC

HARVARD
Dictionary of Music

By

WILLI APEL

1953

HARVARD UNIVERSITY PRESS

Cambridge, Massachusetts

First printing, November 1944
Second printing, December 1944
Third printing, 1945
Fourth printing, 1946
Fifth printing, 1947
Sixth printing, 1950
Seventh printing, 1951
Eighth printing, 1953

PRINTED IN THE UNITED STATES OF AMERICA

PREFACE

Nowhere in literature is a preface more clearly out of place than in a book which, like the present one, is predestined to be read without leisure and to be consulted (somewhat like a dentist) in the case of an emergency only. Moreover it seems incongruous to write a wordy preface for a book which by its very nature aims at the utmost conciseness. In the way of general description it will suffice to say that this book is designed to provide accurate and pertinent information on all musical topics and that it is addressed to the musical amateur as well as to the student and the scholar. To reconcile the different, if not conflicting, interests of these three groups of readers has been one of the chief concerns of the author. In the majority of the articles this has been no problem, since an article on "Major and Minor" or "Eroica," for instance, falls just as clearly within the province of the first group as does one on "Lai" or "Oktoechos" within that of the last. In the case of articles which are of interest to the amateur as well as to the musicologist the difficulty has been solved — successfully, it is hoped — by clearly dividing the material into two paragraphs, one of which treats the subject from the present-day point of view, the other, from that of the historian. The articles on "Sonata" and "Fugue" may be cited as examples. A special feature of this book, not to be found in any other music dictionary in the English language, is the bibliography, which covers book publications as well as the periodical literature — the latter more completely than any other music dictionary in any language.

The most distinctive trait of the present work is the restriction to musical topics, which has entailed the omission of biographical articles. The reason for this restriction is that the biographical field is adequately covered in a considerable number of recent reference books, several of which are devoted exclusively to biography, while exactly the opposite is true of the information on the various aspects of music itself. In this respect even the best dictionaries fail even to approximate the standard which has long been established in the biographical field. This situation indicates the point of departure and the *raison d'être* for the present publication.

The restriction of subject matter means the exclusion not only of individual composers, but also of individual organizations, orchestras, publishers. There are, however, general articles on "Societies," "Orchestras," "Publishers," which supply information about the most important mem-

[v]

bers of such groups. For the purpose of orientation the list of general articles ("Synoptic Guide") given on p. 2 may be consulted.

There remains the pleasant duty of acknowledging gratefully the assistance which the author has received from many sides. A complete list of those scholars who have contributed original articles is found on p. x. Less obvious, but hardly less important, is the collaboration of others who have given valuable advice or other assistance, as follows:

Mrs. Willi Apel, Boston: Final check of the periodical literature.

Mr. Artur Bogen, Cambridge: Preparatory work for the articles on individual operas.

Dr. Manfred F. Bukofzer, University of California: Reading of articles on Medieval and Oriental music.

Mr. Leonard Burkat, Boston Public Library: Reading of the articles on Periodicals and Publishers.

Dr. Yuen Ren Chao, Harvard University: Reading of the articles on Chinese and Japanese music.

Dr. Alfred Einstein, Smith College: Reading of various articles on 16th- and 17th-century music.

Mr. Klaus Goetze, Cambridge: Material for the article on Pianoforte playing.

Dr. Lloyd Hibberd, Graham-Eckes School, Palm Beach: Reading of the entire manuscript.

Prof. Edward B. Hill, Cambridge: Reading of articles on modern instruments.

Dom Anselm Hughes, O.S.B.: Reading of articles on liturgical music.

Dr. Otto Kinkeldey, Cornell University: See below.

Mrs. Edward B. Lawton, Berkeley, California: Material for the article on the Mass.

Dr. Curt Sachs, New York University: Reading of articles on ancient instruments.

Mr. Nicolas Slonimsky, Boston: Proofreading of the entire manuscript, with particular regard to "Music Since 1900."

Dr. Harold Spivacke, Library of Congress: Reading of articles on Orchestras, Periodicals, Publishers, and others.

Mr. David Stone, Howard University: Material for the article on Piano playing; final check of the periodical literature.

I am particularly indebted to Professor Kinkeldey, who not only has read the entire sections A and B of the Dictionary, but also numerous articles (e.g., Aufführungspraxis; Binary and ternary form; Character piece; Choral, chorale; Classicism; Expression; Figural, figurate, figured;

Folk song; Modern music; Plainsong notation; Song form) which the author would have been hesitant to publish in their present form without the backing of the authority which Professor Kinkeldey, the dean of American musicology, so justly enjoys.

I also wish to express my gratitude to the members of the staff of the Music Department of the Boston Public Library whose kind coöperation has greatly facilitated the completion of the book.

Grateful acknowledgment is made to Mr. W. W. Norton, New York, for permission to reproduce a number of illustrations of instruments, taken from C. Sachs, *The History of Musical Instruments* (1940); and to the Macmillan Company, London, to reproduce from *Grove's Dictionary* the illustrations for the article "Bow" and the drawing of the *colascione* for the article "Lute."

In conclusion the author wishes to say that he will appreciate suggestions for corrections to be used in a second edition which may be forthcoming sooner or later.

W. A.

Boston, Massachusetts
May 1944

NOTE

Addenda and corrigenda will be found on page 825 and following pages.

LIST OF ABBREVIATIONS

I. *Periodicals*

Reference is usually made by annual volume numbers (i, ii, iii, . . .), if a list of contents is given with the volume. Otherwise, copy numbers are added (e.g., ii, no. 4). Special methods of reference (e.g., when the volume numbering is inconsistently used) are indicated below. In the case of articles the title of which is essentially identical with that of the subject under consideration, this title is usually omitted.

AM   *Acta Musicologica* (quarterly, 1928–).
AMF   *Archiv für Musikforschung* (quarterly, 1936–).
AMW   *Archiv für Musikwissenschaft* (quarterly, 1918–28).
BAMS   *Bulletin of the American Musicological Society* (annual, 1936–).
BJ   *Bach Jahrbuch* (annual, 1904–).
BSIM   Abbreviation for a monthly publication which appeared from 1905 to 1914 under five different titles, as follows: i–iii: *Le Mercure musical*; iv–v: *Bulletin français de la Société Internationale de Musique*; vi–vii: *S.I.M. Revue musicale mensurelle*; viii–ix: *Revue musicale S.I.M.*; x: *La Revue musicale S.I.M.* See also *RMC*.
BUM   *Bulletin de la société "Union musicologique"* (semiannual, 1921–26).
DM   *Die Musik* (1901–15 in 24 copies per year, numbered i.1–i.24, . . ., xiv.1–xiv.24; 1922 to date in 12 copies per year, numbered xv.1–xv.12, etc.).
JMP   *Jahrbuch der Musikbibliothek Peters* (annual, 1894–).
JMW   *Jahrbücher für musikalische Wissenschaft* (two volumes, 1863 and 1867).
KIM   *Kongress der Internationalen Musikgesellschaft* (Leipzig, 1904; Basel, 1906; Vienna, 1909; London, 1911). Also included under this sign are: *Bericht über den Musikwissenschaftlichen Kongress*, Basel, 1924; *Bericht über den 1. musikwissenschaftlichen Kongress der Deutschen Musikgesellschaft*, Leipzig, 1925; *Kongressbericht (Compte rendu, Report)*, Internationale Gesellschaft für Musikwissenschaft, Liége, 1930. Cf. R. S. Angell, in *Music Library Association Notes*, 1944, no. 2.
KJ   *Kirchenmusikalisches Jahrbuch* (1885–1932); preceded by *Cäcilien-Kalender* (1876–84).
LRM   *La Rassegna Musicale* (monthly, 1928–).
MA   *Musical Antiquary, The* (quarterly, 1909–13).
MfM   *Monatshefte für Musikgeschichte* (monthly, 1869–1905).
ML   *Music and Letters* (quarterly, 1920–).
MM   *Modern Music* (quarterly, 1924–).
MQ   *Musical Quarterly* (quarterly, 1915–).
MR   *Music Review* (quarterly, 1940–).
PAMS   *Papers Read by Members of the American Musicological Society* (annual, 1936–).
PMA   *Proceedings of the Musical Association* (annual, 1874–).
RdM   *Revue de musicologie* (quarterly, 1922–), preceded by *Bulletin de la société française de musicologie* (quarterly, 1917–21). Reference by year

and continuous numbering of copies, e.g., 1922, no. 1; 1937, no. 64, etc.

RM   *Revue musicale, La* (ed. by Prunières, monthly, 1920–).

RMC   *Revue musicale, La* (ed. by Combarieu, monthly, 1901–10). Merged in 1911 with *BSIM.*

RMI   *Rivista musicale italiana* (quarterly, 1870–).

SIM   *Sammelbände der Internationalen Musikgesellschaft* (quarterly, 1900–14).

StM   *Studien zur Musikwissenschaft* (Beihefte der Denkmäler der Tonkunst in Oesterreich; annual, 1913–34).

TG   *Tribune de St. Gervais* (monthly, 1895–?).

VMW   *Vierteljahrsschrift für Musikwissenschaft* (quarterly, 1884–94).

ZIM   *Zeitschrift der Internationalen Musikgesellschaft* (monthly, 1900–14).

ZMW   *Zeitschrift für Musikwissenschaft* (quarterly, 1918–35).

II. Books

AdHM   G. Adler, *Handbuch der Musikgeschichte*, 2 vols., 1930.

ApMZ   W. Apel, *Musik aus früher Zeit*, 2 vols.

ApNPM   W. Apel, *Notation of Polyphonic Music*, 1942 (2d ed., 1944).

AR   *Antiphonale Sacrosanctae Romanae Ecclesiae*, 1924 (No. 820, edition in neumatic signs).

BeMMR   H. Besseler, *Musik des Mittelalters und der Renaissance*, 1931.

BüHM   E. Bücken, *Handbuch der Musikwissenschaft*, 7 vols., 1928–32.

CS   H. Coussemaker, *Scriptorum de musica medii aevi nova series*, 4 vols., 1864–76.

DdT   *Denkmäler deutscher Tonkunst*, 65 vols., 1892–1931.

DTB   *Denkmäler der Tonkunst in Bayern*, 36 vols., 1900–31.

DTOe   *Denkmäler der Tonkunst in Oesterreich*, 83 vols., 1894–1938.

EiBM   A. Einstein, *Beispielsammlung zur Musikgeschichte*, 1930 (incorporated in his *A Short History of Music*, 2d edition, 1938).

GD   Grove, *Dictionary of Music and Musicians*, 5 vols., 1938; supplementary vol., 1940.

GéHM   Th. Gérold, *Histoire de la musique des origines à la fin du xive siècle*, 1936.

GR   *Graduale Sacrosanctae Romanae Ecclesiae*, 1924 (No. 696, edition in neumatic signs).

GS   M. Gerbert, *Scriptores ecclesiastici de musica sacra potissimum*, 3 vols., 1784; facsimile edition, 1931.

HAM   *Historical Anthology of Music,* ed. by A. T. Davison and W. Apel, Harvard University Press.

LaMWC   P. Lang, *Music in Western Civilization*, 1941.

LavE   Lavignac, *Encyclopédie de la musique*, 1913ff; Histoire: i.1–5; Technique: ii.1–6.

LU   *Liber Usualis Missae et Officii*, 1937 (No. 780, edition in neumatic signs).

MoML   H. J. Moser, *Musik-Lexikon*, 1935.

OH   *Oxford History of Music* (mainly vol. i of the first ed., 1901).

ReMMA   G. Reese, *Music in the Middle Ages*, 1940.

RiHM   H. Riemann, *Handbuch der Musikgeschichte*, 5 vols., 1904–13.

RiMB   H. Riemann, *Musikgeschichte in Beispielen*, 1925.

RiML   H. Riemann, *Musik Lexikon*, 2 vols., 1929.

SaHMI   C. Sachs, *History of Musical Instruments*, 1940.

SaRM   C. Sachs, *Reallexikon der Musikinstrumente*, 1913.
SchGMB A. Schering, *Geschichte der Musik in Beispielen*, 1931.
TaAM   G. Tagliapietra, *Antologia di musica . . . per pianoforte*, 18 vols., 1931/2.
WoGM   J. Wolf, *Geschichte der Mensuralnotation*, 3 vols., 1904.
WoHN   J. Wolf, *Handbuch der Notationskunde*, 2 vols., 1913–19.

III. *Contributors of Articles*

A. E.   Alfred Einstein, Smith College (Madrigal comedy).

A. T. D.   Archibald T. Davison, Harvard University (Anglican chant; Conducting; Glee; Just note and accent; Music education; Psalter).

A. T. M. A. Tillman Merritt, Harvard University (Counterpoint; Harmonic analysis; Harmony I).

D. D.   Dorothea Doig, Longy School of Music, Cambridge (Tests).

D. J. G. Donald J. Grout, University of Texas (Opera; Comic opera; Ballet in opera; and related articles).

E. B. H. Everett B. Helm (Composition; Degrees; Profession; Scholarships; Societies I).

E. C.   Eunice Crocker, Radcliffe College (Canzona).

E. P.   Ernest La Prade, National Broadcasting Company (Electronic musical instruments; Radio broadcasting of music).

G. C.   Gilbert Chase, Library of Congress (Latin American countries).

G. D. H. G. Donald Harrison, Aeolian-Skinner Company (Organ I–IX).

H. A.   Hans Abraham, Cambridge (Copyright).

H. G. M. Henry G. Mishkin, Amherst College (Accademia; Bologna School).

H. J. S. Helen Joy Sleeper, Wellesley College (Fancy).

H. L.   Hugo Leichtentritt, Cambridge (Music criticism).

H. N.   Hugo Norden, Boston (Bowing).

J. F. O. John F. Ohl, Fisk University (Recorder).

J. T. H. John Tasker Howard, Glen Ridge, New Jersey (American music; American Indian music).

L. H.   Lloyd Hibberd, Graham-Eckes School, Palm Beach (Dictionaries; Jazz).

L. S.   Leo Schrade, Yale University (Maniera).

N. S.   Nicolas Slonimsky, Boston (Russian music II).

P. A.   Putnam Aldrich, University of Texas (Ornamentation and related articles).

P. L. M. Philip Lieson Miller, New York Public Library (Phonograph and recorded music).

R. S. A. Richard S. Angell, Columbia University (Libraries).

R. Y. R. Rulon Y. Robison, Boston University (Register; Voice).

W. D. D. William D. Denny, Vassar College (Orchestra; various instruments).

W. P.   Walter Piston, Harvard University (Harmonic rhythm).

V. Z.   Victor Zuckerkandl, Princeton, N. J. (Urlinie).

IV. *Signs*

* indicates reference to other articles.

† indicates publications consisting mainly or exclusively of music.

If you want to understand the invisible, look carefully at the visible. [See *Aesthetics III (b).]

SYNOPTIC GUIDE

*List of articles of a general character and of master articles
containing reference to others*

Acoustics
Aesthetics
Analysis
Appreciation
Arrangement
Chamber music
Church music
Color and music
Composition
Concert
Conducting
Copyright
Counterpoint
Dance music
Degrees
Dictionaries
Editions, Historical
Electronic musical instruments
Exotic music
Expression
Festivals

Folk music
Form
Gregorian chant
Harmonic analysis
Harmony
History of music
Improvisation
Instrumental music
Instruments
Libraries
Mechanical instruments
Melody
Modern music
Music criticism
Music education
Musicology
Notation
Opera houses
Orchestras and concert halls
Oriental music
Ornamentation

Periodicals
Phonograph and recorded music
Poetic meter
Primitive music
Printing of music
Profession of music
Publishers
Radio broadcasting
Rhythm
Scholarships
Singing
Societies
Sources prior to 1450
Style
Tests and measurements
Text and music
Texture
Theory
Tonality
Vocal music
Wind instruments

Articles on Nations and Races: American Indian; American; Arabian; Argentina;
Armenian; Australian; Babylonian; Belgian; Brazilian; Bulgarian; Byzantine; Canadian; Central America; Chile; Chinese; Colombia; Cuba; Czech; Danish; Egyptian;
English; Eskimo; Ethiopian; Finnish; French; German; Greek; Hindu; Hungarian;
Icelandic; Irish; Italian; Japanese; Javanese; Jewish; Mexico; Negro; Netherlands;
Norwegian; Oriental; Peru; Polish; Portuguese; Roman; Rumanian; Russian; Scottish; Spanish; Swedish; Swiss; Syrian; Tibetan; Turkish; Venezuela; Yugoslavian.

HARVARD DICTIONARY OF MUSIC

A

A. See *Pitch names; *Letter notation; *Hexachord; *Pitch. On the title page of *part-books of the 16th century A stands for *altus*. In liturgical books it stands for *antiphon*.

Ab [G.]. Off, chiefly with reference to the discontinuation of an organ stop.

Abandonné [F.]. With abandon; unrestrained.

A battuta [It.]. See *Battuta.

Abbandono, Con; abbandonasi [It.]. With abandon, unrestrained.

Abbellimenti [It.]. Embellishments, *ornaments.

Abbreviations. The most important abbreviations used in musical notation are indicated in the accompanying table.

A – b – c – dieren [G.]. The use of pitch-letters, a, b, c . . . , rather than of *solmization syllables, in singing and elementary instruction. This system prevails in Germany.

Abdämpfen [G.]. To *mute.

Abduction from the Seraglio. See *Entführung aus dem Serail.

Abegg Variations. R. Schumann's op. 1, dedicated to his friend Meta Abegg. The first five notes of the theme a – bb – e' – g' – g' read, in German pitch names, A – B – E – G – G.

Abendlied [G.]. Evening song.

Abendmusik [G.]. Evening musical performances, usually of a religious or contemplative character. The term applies particularly to the famous concerts started in 1673 by Dietrich Buxtehude in the Marienkirche of Lübeck in North Germany. These took place annually on the five Sundays before Christmas, following the afternoon service, and consisted of concerted pieces of sacred music for orchestra and chorus and of organ music [see *DdT* 14]. They continued throughout the 18th and 19th centuries. In 1705 J. S. Bach walked 200 miles from Arnstadt to Lübeck to hear the *Abendmusik*.

Lit.: W. Maxton, in *ZMW* x; C. Stiehl, *Die Organisten an der St. Marienkirche und die Abendmusiken zu Lübeck* (1885).

A bene placito [It., at pleasure]. An indication permitting a certain freedom in performance, equivalent to *ad libitum*.

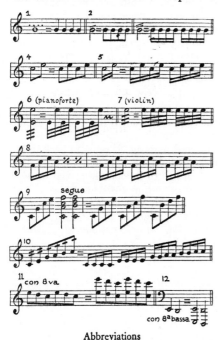

Abbreviations

Abgesang [G.]. See *Barform.

Abgestossen [G., detached]. *Détaché [see *Bowing (b)].

Abnehmend [G.]. Diminuendo.

Abschieds-symphonie [G.]. *Farewell Symphony.

Abschnitt [G.]. Section.

Absetzen [G.]. (1) To separate, either notes [*Détaché] or phrases. — (2) In 16th-century parlance, *absetzen in die Tabulatur* means to transcribe (vocal music) into *tablature.

Absolute music [L. *absolutus*, separated]. Music which is dissociated from extramusical implications. The term is used most frequently in contradistinction to *program music, i.e., music in which pictorial or poetic ideas are portrayed. It also excludes vocal music, especially that type of vocal music in which the text clearly influences the musical language and structure (e.g., a song by Schubert). In German usage the term is employed in a stricter sense, excluding not only program and vocal music but also music of a definite emotional character (*Romantic music), so that Bach and, to some extent, Mozart become the main representatives of absolute music.

Absolute pitch. Properly, "the position of a tone in reference to the whole range of pitch . . . , conceived as independently determined by its rate of vibration" (Webster). The German term for this is *absolute Tonhöhe*. Usually, however, the term is used to denote what should be termed more accurately "absolute judgment of (absolute) pitch," i.e., the capacity of a person to identify a musical sound immediately by name, without reference to a previously sounded note of different pitch [see *Relative pitch]. This faculty, called in German *absolutes Gehör*, is a tonal memory which is inborn with certain individuals but can also be acquired by practice, as recent experiments have shown. The faculty, whether inborn or acquired, is found chiefly in persons possessing some

degree of musical experience or aptitude, but it can by no means be considered a measuring stick of musical talent. In fact, it is just as frequent (perhaps more so) among mediocre orchestral players as among great composers and outstanding artists. While Mozart had an extremely acute sense of absolute pitch, Wagner and Schumann are reputed to have lacked it.

Absolute pitch is in various respects a valuable asset to a musician, particularly to a conductor, but it may prove a real inconvenience when music for one reason or another must be transposed in performance to another key, as is frequently the case in vocal music, in order to accommodate the range of the singer [see remark under *chiavette]. It is questionable, indeed, whether it is an advantage or a disadvantage to hear a composition "all wrong" simply because it is a half tone higher or lower. Needless to say, all the discussions about the "true pitch" of Beethoven's C minor Symphony, for example, are entirely pointless unless the standard pitch of Beethoven's day is taken into account. Since this pitch has considerably changed (still more so in the case of Bach), it can be definitely said that, from the standpoint of absolute pitch, all present-day performances of music written prior to the general acceptance of the modern concert pitch [see *Pitch (2)] are "wrong." Generally speaking, they are higher than the composer wanted them to be. A musician with absolute pitch who lived one hundred years ago if brought back to life today would be horrified to hear Beethoven's Fifth Symphony played in what would be to him C-sharp minor.

Lit.: C. H. Wedell, *The Nature of the Absolute Judgment of Pitch* (1934); L. A. Petrau, *An Experimental Study of Pitch Recognition* (1932); A. Wellek, *Das absolute Gehör und seine Typen* (1938, bibl.); C. E. Seashore, *The Measurement of Musical Memory* (1917); O. Abraham, in *SIM* iii, viii; F. Auerbach, in *SIM* viii; H. Riemann, in *ZIM* xiii; J. Kobelt, in *AMW* ii (bibl.); G. Révész, "Über die beiden Arten des absoluten Gehörs" (*ZIM* xiv); N. Slonimsky, in *American Mercury* xxi.

Abstossen [G.]. (1) In violin playing, same as *abgestossen*. — (2) In organ playing, to take off a stop [see *Ab].

Abstract music. Same as *absolute music.

Abstrich [G.]. Down-bow.

Abzug [G.]. *Scordatura.

Academic Festival Overture (*Akademische Festouvertüre*). The title of Brahms's op. 80, an orchestral composition written for the University of Breslau as a recompense for the degree of Doctor of Philosophy conferred upon him (1879). It is a presentation of various German student songs, much in the manner of a *potpourri.

Académie [F.]. *Academy. In the early part of the 19th century the term was used for concerts or recitals. Beethoven in one of his letters says: "Heute keine Akademie," i.e., "No concert to-night."

Academy [Gr., derived from the olive grove of Academe, the meeting place of Plato and his disciples near Athens]. A term applied to scholarly or artistic societies and to musical organizations of various types. The movement started in Italy around 1600 [see *Accademia]. The societies outside of Italy include: (*a*) *Learned associations*, part of whose activity is the promoting of musical studies. They usually have a membership limited to those of demonstrable ability, maintain periodic discussions and proceedings which are often gathered into publications, and generally offer honors, medals, or prizes for achievement in composition or research. Many of these are state-supported: Paris, Institut de France, division Académie des Beaux Arts; Berlin, Akademie der Künste; Brussels, Académie Royale; others in Stockholm and Moscow. (*b*) *Organizations for the giving of operas and concerts:* Paris, Académie de Musique; London, Royal Academy of Music

and Academy of Ancient Music; Munich, Akademie der Tonkunst; New York, Academy of Music (today the Metropolitan Opera); Brooklyn, Academy of Music (founded 1861), etc. [see *Concert halls; *Opera houses]. (*c*) *Institutions of musical education:* London, Royal Academy of Music; Berlin, Staatliche Akademie für Kirchen- und Schulmusik; Munich, Königliche Akademie der Tonkunst (founded 1846); Philadelphia, Academy of Music (1870); New York, Academy of Allied Arts (School of Music, 1928). See also *Societies.

A cappella [It. *cappella*, chapel]. Music written "for the choir of a chapel," i.e., choral music without instrumental accompaniment. The music of Palestrina [see *Palestrina style] is usually considered the model of *a cappella* music. An *a cappella* choir is one formed for the cultivation of unaccompanied singing. Historians of the 19th century held the idea that all "early music" — i.e., music before 1600 — was *a cappella*. Such a statement is correct, however, only with respect to strictly liturgical music, such as masses and motets. Secular music, whether for a soloist or a choral group, was frequently accompanied or duplicated by instruments, particularly in the period 1300–1450 [see *Ars nova; *Burgundian School].
   Lit.: J. Handschin, *Die Grundlagen des a-cappella-Stils* (1929); Th. Kroyer, in *Kretzschmar Festschrift* (1918), *AMW* ii; *AM* vi, no. 4.

Acathistus [Gr., not seated]. A hymn of praise of the Byzantine Church, sung in honor of the Virgin upon the Saturday of the fifth week in Lent by the whole congregation standing. Both text and music were written by the patriarch Sergios in A.D. 626, on the occasion of the deliverance of Constantinople from the Persians. The poem consists of 24 stanzae the initial letters of which represent the alphabet (acrostic). It belongs to the general species of Byzantine poetry known as *kontakion* [see *Byzantine chant II].
   Lit.: H. J. W. Tillyard, *Byzantine*

Music and Hymnography (1923), p. 16; *AdHM* i, 131.

Accademia [It.]. Italian learned association, named after Plato's Academy [see *Academy]. An *A. di Platone* was founded in 1470 at the court of Lorenzo de' Medici in Florence. With the beginning of the 17th century, the movement spread enormously in Italy; every place of some repute had its *accademia*, and larger cities had numbers of them. They were of two types: (a) *Learned societies* founded for the promotion of science, literature, and arts, part of whose activity was the encouragement and cultivation of music. The most famous of these was the *A. dei Arcadi* of Rome (founded 1692), which included among its members the musicians Marcello, Corelli, Alessandro Scarlatti, Gluck. Handel attended many meetings, but as a foreigner was not eligible for membership. Other institutions of the same type existed, in Florence: *A. della Crusca* (1588), *A. dei Filarmonici*; in Bologna: *A. dei Gelati* (1588), *A. dei Concordi* (1615), *A. dei Filomusi* (1622), *A. dei Filarmonici* (1675); in Venice: *A. Pellegrina* (1550), *A. degli Olimpici*; and elsewhere. (b) *Organizations* of professional and amateur musicians which had the cultivation of music as their sole purpose. The activities of these groups were varied; they gave public and private concerts, conducted research investigations in the history of music and in the science of sound, founded music schools, and even launched operatic enterprises. The most important of these is the *A. Filarmonica* of Bologna, founded in 1666 by Count Vincenzo Carrati, which included among its members such distinguished figures as Bassani (1657–1716), Corelli (1653–1713), Torelli (d. 1708), Domenico Gabrielli (1640–90), Padre Martini (1706–84), Mozart (1756–91), Rossini (1792–1868), and Busoni (1866–1924). Cf. N. Morini, *La Reale Accademia filarmonica di Bologna* (1930); A. Einstein, in *BAMS* vii.   H. G. M.

Accarezzevole [It.]. Caressing.

Accelerando [It.]. Becoming faster.

Accent. (1) The stress of one tone over others. According to the position of the stressed note within the measure, one may distinguish between regular (natural) accent, which falls on the first and, in compound meters, also on other beats (secondary accent); and irregular (unnatural) accent, which falls on a normally weak beat. According to the means of achieving stress, the following distinctions are usually made: dynamic accent, which results from reinforcement; *tonic accent, which results from higher

pitch; and *agogic accent, which results from longer duration of the stressed note. Of these, the dynamic accent is by far the most important, the other two being largely subsidiary or incidental. Irregular dynamic accent is usually indicated by signs such as *sf*, >, —. Ex. 1 (Mozart, Symphony in G minor) shows an irregular dynamic accent which, at the same time, is tonic and agogic also. Frequently, the emphasis on the weak beat is enhanced by means of striking dissonances, as in Ex. 2. The *tonic accent has played a role in the discussions on Gregorian chant and on other types of medieval monophonic music.

(2) [F.]. In French music of the 17th and 18th centuries, an ornamentation belonging to the class of *Nachschläge.

(3) Signs used in ancient Greek literature (probably also in Hebrew poetry, e.g., Psalms, Book of Job) to indicate a change of pitch of the voice in recitation: *accentus acutus* ´, for a raising; *a. gravis* `, for a lowering; *a. circumflexus* ^, for an inflection (raising followed by lowering) of the voice. These signs are considered today as the origin of the neumes (accent neumes; see *Neumes II) and of certain other related systems

of notation, called *ekphonetic notation. Cf. *WoHN* i, 61.

(4) The notational signs used in Jewish chant [see *Jewish music II].

Accentuation. The proper placement of accents, especially in music set to a text. See *Declamation; *Text and music.

Accentus, concentus. The terms are used in liturgical music in two different though related meanings: (a) liturgically, as referring to the chanting of the priest (*accentus*) and to that of the *schola,* i.e., the choir, the soloists, or both (*concentus*); (b) stylistically, as referring to two opposite types of plainsong, the syllabic recitation, largely on a monotone with slight inflections, as in the psalm tones (*accentus*), and the melismatic type found in the alleluias, graduals, etc. (*concentus*). The chant of the priest is usually of the simpler type; that of the *schola* of the more elaborate. See P. Wagner, *Einführung in die Gregorianischen Melodien,* iii (1921), p. 4.

Acciaccato [It.]. "Crushed," i.e., brusquely, forcibly.

Acciaccatura [It. *acciaccare,* to crush]. Italian name for an ornament of harpsichord music (*c.* 1675–1725) which calls

for the lower second of the normal note to be simultaneously struck and immediately released. It usually occurs in con-

nection with chords; either written out as an ordinary note, but to be played as described above [Ex. 1, Domenico Scarlatti, Sonata; Ex. 2, Scherzo in Bach's Partita no. 3]; or indicated by a diagonal dash, in which case arpeggio execution is usually intended, particularly in slow tempo. The direction of the dash indicates the direction of the arpeggio [Ex. 3]. The French name for this ornamentation was *arpègement figuré.* For an erroneous usage, frequent in modern writings, of the term acciaccatura, see under *Appoggiatura III.

Accidentals. I. *General.* The signs of chromatic alteration momentarily introduced for single notes or measures, as opposed to those given in the *signature. The signs of chromatic alteration together with their names in English, French, German, and Italian are given in the following table:

	♯	♭	✕
E:	sharp	flat	double-sharp
F:	dièse	bémol	double dièse
G:	Kreuz	Be	Doppelkreuz
It:	diesis	bemolle	doppio diesis
	♭♭		♮
E:	double-flat		natural
F:	double bémol		bécarre
G:	Doppel-Be		Auflösungszeichen
It:	doppio bemolle		bequadro

The sharp raises the pitch one semitone, the flat lowers it one semitone; the double-sharp and double-flat raise and lower two semitones respectively; the natural cancels any of the other signs. The use of the compound signs ♮♯, ♮♭, ♮♮ to cancel partly or entirely a previous ✕ or ♭♭ is quite frequent but unnecessary. The simple signs ♯, ♭, ♮ answer the purpose [Ex. 1]. In modern practice a sign affects the note immediately following and is valid for all the notes of the same pitch (but not in different octaves) within the same measure. Recent composers frequently add bracketed ac-

cidentals to those demanded by this rule, in order to clarify complicated passages or chords.

II. *History*. All the signs used for chromatic alteration developed from the same sign, namely, the letter b which indicates the whole tone above a. The fact that in the diatonic scale c – d – e . . . no perfect fourth above f is available necessitated, as early as the 10th century, the introduction of another b, a semitone lower than the diatonic b [see *Hexachord]. These two b's were distinguished by their shape, the higher one being written in a square form and called *b durum* (*durus*, hard, angular), the lower in a round form and called

Early shapes
{
♮ B durum
♭ B molle
✕ Sharp
𝄪 Double sharp
✳ Double sharp
}

b molle (*mollis*, soft, round). It is from these designations that the German names *Dur* and *Moll* for major and minor mode are derived. When in the ensuing period the introduction of other chromatic tones became necessary, the sign *b durum* and its later modifications ♮, ♯ were used to indicate the higher of two semitones; the sign *b molle* or ♭, the

D D♭ C C♭   C♯ C

lower one. Thus, in early music, ♮ f is not F-natural (canceled), but F-sharp; likewise, ♭ f is not F-flat, but F (in distinction from a previous F-sharp); [see Ex. 2, from Frescobaldi's *Canzone* (1628)]. Bach continued to use the sign ♭ for the cancellation of a previous f♯. In Germany, during the 16th century, the sign *b durum* was erroneously interpreted as the letter h, to which it bears some visual resemblance. Hence, in German terminology h denotes the B-natural, and b the B-flat.

In the printed books of the 16th century the sharp sign usually occurs in a diagonal position. The double-sharp (introduced in the early 18th century; cf. Bach's *Well-tempered Clavier*, 1722, and J. G. Walther's *Musik Lexikon*, 1732) originally appeared as a sharp with

doubled lines, either in a straight or in a diagonal position. The present sign is a simplification of the latter.

In music prior to 1700 an accidental is not valid for the entire measure, but only for the next note and immediate repetitions of the same note. See Ex. 3.

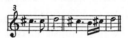

For the problem of accidentals in music of the 13th to the 16th centuries, see *Musica ficta. Cf. F. Niecks, "The Flat, Sharp, and Natural" (*PMA* xvi).

Acclamation. A type of Byzantine poetry and music which served as a salutation for the emperor in the ceremonial of the Byzantine court of the 9th and 10th centuries. The acclamations are practically the only type of non-liturgical Byzantine music known to us. Acclamations are still used today in Russia and the Balkans for welcoming high dignitaries of the church. Those beginning with the traditional phrase "Many be the years" were called *polychronion* [cf. the examples in *ReMMA*, 77 and in *MQ* xxiii, 207].

Lit.: *AdHM* i, 128; E. Wellesz, *Byzantinische Musik* (1927); H. Tillyard, in *The Annual of the British School of Athens*, xviii.

Accolade [F.]. *Brace.

Accompagnato. Accompanied. See *Recitative II (c).

Accompaniment. I. The musical background provided by a less important for a more important part. For instance, in piano music, the chords or other subsidiary material of the left hand, as against the melody of the right hand. The term also refers to the support given to a soloist (singer, violinist) by a pianist or an orchestra. The auxiliary role of the accompaniment frequently leads to an underestimation of its musical and artistic importance, on the part of the soloist as well as the audience. Vocalists, especially, are inclined to demand an undue subordination of their accompanists, condemning them to complete slavery in questions of interpretation, of tempo, of dynamics, etc. This situation is the more dangerous, since the possession of an outstanding voice and vocal technique is no guarantee of musical taste and artistic discrimination.

The modern church organist as well as the leader of a choir is frequently confronted with the problem of providing suitable accompaniment for the singing of the congregation or the chorus, either improvised or written out. Following are a number of books on this subject: J. F. Bridge, *Organ Accompaniment* (1886); D. Buck, *Illustrations in Choir Accompaniment* (1877); C. Forsyth, *Choral Orchestration* (1920); W. Hickin, *Pianoforte Accompaniment*; A. H. Lindo, *The Art of Accompanying* (1916); Ch. W. Pearce, *The Organist's Directory to the Accompaniment of the Church Service* (1908); A. M. Richardson, *Modern Organ Accompaniment* (1907). See also *Vamp.

II. References to instrumental accompaniment of songs are not infrequently found in the Bible (harp-accompaniment is suggested by the remark "on eight strings," given with Psalms 6 and 12) and in the writings of the ancient Greeks. Pictorial reproductions and literary documents of the Middle Ages show the use of harps, fiddles, bells, small drums, trumpets, etc., in connection with the monophonic songs of the troubadours and Minnesinger, and in conjunction with dance music. Neither in ancient nor in medieval music was this improvised type of accompaniment ever of a harmonic nature; it was merely a unison- (or octave-) doubling of the voice part, with occasional *heterophonic elements. The same type of accompaniment is to be found with the Oriental nations, especially in *China, *India, *Arabia. While the polyphonic music of the 9th to the 13th centuries (organa, motets) does not admit the separation of the polyphonic fabric into parts of greater or lesser importance, such a separation takes place in the French secular compositions of the 14th and early 15th

centuries (ballades, virelais by G. de Machaut and his successors, see *Ars Nova; chansons of Dufay and his contemporaries, see *Burgundian School). It disappears again with the rise of Flemish sacred music and of Flemish counterpoint (Ockeghem, Obrecht), which is essentially opposed to any distinction between principal and auxiliary parts. The instrumental doubling of vocal parts, such as was occasionally practiced in this period, can scarcely be considered an accompaniment. In the 16th century the renewed shift to secular things immediately led to a revival of accompanied melody, e.g., in the lute-songs of the German Schlick (1512), of the Spanish Valderrabano (1547), and of the English Dowland (1597).

III. A new era of accompaniment began with the period of thorough-bass (Baroque period, 1600–1750), which calls for a harmonic accompaniment to be improvised upon the notes of the bass. Moreover, the growing interest in florid and singable melody brought about a gradually increasing separation of the musical substance into a predominant melody with subordinate accompaniment (e.g., in the aria). Whereas, throughout the Baroque period, the written-out accompaniment (and, consequently, the improvised one, too) shows many traits of contrapuntal and harmonic interest, it degenerated, in the second half of the 18th century, into a stereotyped pattern of plain chords, arpeggios, *Alberti-bass figures, etc. As a curiosity it may be mentioned that, about 1760, sonatas were frequently written for the "pianoforte with the accompaniment of a violin or flute" (Mondonville, 1734, see *Editions XXIV, 9; Schobert, see *DdT* 34), that is, with the violin or flute merely duplicating the upper part of the pianoforte. In this connection it is interesting to note that Samuel Wesley speaks of J. S. Bach's "Six sonatas for harpsichord with an obbligato violin accompaniment."

IV. About 1780 Haydn and Mozart evolved a new type of accompaniment known as *accompanimento obbligato*, characterized by a greater individuality of the lower parts, by the occasional introduction of fugal elements, by the occasional shift of the melody from the higher part into a lower part, etc. This style is particularly evident in the quartets written in this period. Because of these efforts Beethoven was able to say of himself: "Ich bin mit einem obligaten Accompaniment auf die Welt gekommen." What Haydn and Mozart did in the field of instrumental music, Schubert achieved in the field of song, by freeing the pianoforte accompaniment from the slavery of mere chord-filling and making it an independent, sometimes the most interesting, part of the composition. Composers such as Schumann, Brahms, and H. Wolf adopted his method, whereas others (e.g., Tchaikovsky) rarely went beyond a chordal accompaniment in lush harmonies of a rather ephemeral interest. More recent composers (Mahler, Strauss) have repeatedly used the whole orchestra as an instrumental background for a solo singer.

V. The extraordinary growth of accompanied melody as it occurs in the songs of the 19th century has had a deplorable effect upon the minds of musical scholars and editors engaged in the study and publication of early monophonic music, such as Greek music, exotic melodies, Gregorian chant, the songs of the trouvères, Minnesinger, etc. Numerous volumes have been published in which the melodies of the pre-Christian era or of the Middle Ages are coupled with cheap accompaniments in the styles of Schumann, Brahms, or Debussy. Even well-known scholars have not withstood this temptation [cf., e.g., O. Fleischer, *Reste der altgriechischen Tonkunst* (1899)]. More recent attempts to give these accompaniments an "antique" air [see reference under *Quartal harmony] are only more dangerous and misleading. For literature on the 17th-century accompaniment see *Thorough-bass. See also *Additional accompaniment.

Accord [F.]. (1) Chord. — (2) Manner of tuning, especially that of instruments such as the lute for which various systems of tuning were in use during the 17th century [cf. *WoHN* ii, 91; *ApNPM*, 71f]. See *Scordatura.

Accordare [It.], **accorder** [F.]. To tune.

Accordatura [It.]. See *Accord (2).

Accordion. A portable musical instrument consisting of a rather large rectangular bellows with reeds in the two headboards. It has pushed-out and drawn-in reeds, the former sounding by expiration, the latter by inspiration. The modern accordion has a piano keyboard at the right side for the playing of melody notes, while buttons on the left side operate bass notes and full chords. The earliest instruments of this type were made by Buschmann (1822), Buffet (1827), and Damian (1829).

A similar instrument, preferred to the accordion in England, is the *concertina* invented by Wheatstone in 1829. This is of hexagonal shape and is provided at each side with a number of studs. It possesses a full chromatic scale and produces the same note whether the bellows are pressed or drawn. Artistically, this instrument is superior to the accordion. A good deal of solo music has been written for it by virtuosos such as G. Regondi, W. B. Molique, G. A. Macfarren, and E. Solas, and it has occasionally been used in the orchestra (Tchaikovsky, Orchestral Suite op. 53). The *bandoneon* is an Argentine variety of the accordion with buttons on each side, each of them for a single tone.

Accordo [It.]. Chord.

Accusé [F.]. With emphasis.

Achromatic. *Diatonic.

Achtel, Achtelnote, Achtelpause [G. *achtel*, one-eighth]. See *Notes and rests.

Achtfuss [G.]. Eight-foot (stop) [see *Foot (2)].

Acoustic bass (also called resultant bass). On organs, a 32-foot stop which is obtained as a differential tone of a 16-foot stop and a 10⅔-foot stop. According to the acoustic phenomenon of the differential tones [see *Combination tones] the simultaneous sounding of C (produced by the 16-foot) and of G (produced by the 10⅔-foot) produces the tone C_1 (32-foot). The acoustic bass is frequently used where the great expense of the large 32-foot pipes is prohibitive.

Acoustics. The science which treats of sounds. From the standpoint of the musician the most important problems of acoustics are: (1) the nature of the musical sound; (2) *intervals; (3) *consonance and dissonance; (4) *resonance; (5) *architectural acoustics. Only the first problem will be treated here; for the others, see the respective entries.

I. *Vibration.* The generation of sound is invariably bound up with the vibration of an elastic body, i.e., of a body which, when its equilibrium is disturbed, develops inner forces which try to restore the equilibrium. Such a process does not end at once, since the body upon returning to its initial position still has a certain amount of kinetic energy which causes it to go beyond this position so that a new contrary disturbance results. This leads to a repetition of the whole movement in the reverse direction and, in fact, to a succession of movements back and forth which would continue indefinitely were it not for friction, which causes them to diminish and finally to stop. A tongue of steel fastened at one end may serve as an example [Ex. 1].

The movement A − B − A (or A − C − A or B − A − C) is called "single vibration" (half-vibration); the movement A − B − A − C − A (or B − A − C − A − B) is called "double vibration" or simply "vibration" or "cycle" (in modern writings usually the double vibration is used as the unit of measurement). The distance B − C is called "amplitude." The number of vibrations made in one second is called "frequency." Example 2 represents a vibration of 3 cycles.

(In order to understand the relation of this graph to the vibration it is meant to

represent, one may imagine the lowest point of the tongue, A, to be made luminous and then photographed. If for this purpose a single exposure of film is used, a horizontal dash (—) will appear. If,

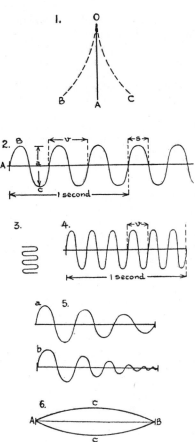

Ex. 1: Vibration of Elastic Body; O, fixed end; A, position of equilibrium; B, position of initial disturbance; C, reverse position. *Ex. 2:* Vibration of 3 Cycles; a = amplitude; v = (double) vibration; s = single vibration. *Ex. 3:* Path of Vibrating Tongue. *Ex. 4:* Vibration of 6 Cycles. *Ex. 5:* Fading Sound. *Ex. 6:* Vibrating String; A, B, fastened ends of the string; C, point of plucking.

however, a quickly moving film is used, this dash will appear drawn out into an oscillating curve [Ex. 3]).

If the same tongue is plucked with different degrees of force, the ear will notice different intensities of sound, and the vibration curve will show different amplitudes, corresponding to the different magnitudes of the initial disturbance. This leads to the first law of acoustics: *The intensity of a sound depends upon the amplitude of the vibration* [see *Bel]. Therefore a fading sound will show a vibration curve of gradually diminishing elongations [see below].

Still more important is another element of variety, namely, that which enters if sounds of different pitch are studied. If the photographic experiment described above is repeated with a shorter tongue, a higher tone will be heard and the resulting curve will show vibrations of narrower width (provided that the speed of the moving film remains unaltered) [Ex. 4]. This means that the single vibration of the higher-pitched tongue takes a shorter time than that of the lower-pitched one. In other words, the higher sound makes more vibrations per second, i.e., has a greater frequency, than the lower sound. This is the basis of the second law of acoustics: *The pitch of a sound depends only upon the frequency of the vibration*. A sound is audible if its frequency is approximately between 16 and 20,000 cycles; the tones of the piano vary from about 30 to 4,000, those of the violin from about 300 to 3,000. The frequency of a middle A (a′), i.e., of concert pitch, is 440 (or 880, if single vibrations are counted).

In the above law, the word *only* is of particular importance. It expresses the fact, known to every musician, that the pitch of a vibrating string is not altered by the greater or lesser force with which the string is plucked, or, in other words, that the pitch does not depend upon the amplitude. The piano player obtains a tone of the same pitch regardless of whether he uses a pianissimo or a fortissimo touch. The same principle is borne out by the fact that a sound does not alter its pitch when it gradually decreases in intensity. This means that a curve representing a fading sound [Ex. 5] will always have the form *a*, not the form *b*.

II. *Vibrating Strings.* If a violin is plucked or bowed, each single point of the string will make an up-and-down

vibration comparable to that made by the lowest point of the steel tongue previously described. All these vibrations have the same frequency, but differ in amplitude. For the purpose of our explanations, the vibration of the string can be considered as being represented by that of its point of highest vibration amplitude, i.e., of the point at which the string is plucked. If this is the middle point of the string, the resulting phenomenon can be roughly illustrated by Example 6.

III. *Frequency, Vibrating Length, and Pitch.* The pitch produced by a vibrating string depends upon its material (steel, copper, etc.), its diameter, its tension, and its length. For the present purpose it is sufficient to consider only the latter factor, the others being regarded as constant. These conditions are realized in the case of a single string whose vibrating length can be changed by stopping (violin) or by means of a movable fret (*monochord). The following fundamental law results: *The frequency is in inverse proportion to the vibrating length*. This means that if the whole string (e.g., one yard) gives a sound of the frequency 600, the string of the half length (one-half yard) gives a sound of the double frequency, 1200, while a string of two-thirds of a yard produces the frequency $600 \times \frac{3}{2} = 900$, etc. More important from the musical point of view is the relation between a given vibration and the pitch of the sound it produces. This problem was investigated and solved by Pythagoras, who established the law relating the pitch of a note to the length of the string by which it is obtained. The results have a more general application, however, if they are expressed in frequencies rather than in vibrating lengths. Thus expressed, they remain unchanged regardless of whether the sound is produced by a pipe or by a string, and they do not depend upon additional factors such as the tension, thickness, or material of the string. The fundamental principle is as follows: *If the frequency of a tone is* n, *that of the octave is* 2n, *that of the fifth,* $\frac{3}{2}$n, *and that of the major third,* $\frac{5}{4}$n. From these tones, all the others of the diatonic scale can be derived [see *Intervals, Calculation of, II]. The result is as follows:

	c	d	e	f	g	a	b	c'
Frequency ($n=1$):	1	9/8	5/4	4/3	3/2	5/3	15/8	2
Frequency ($n=24$):	24	27	30	32	36	40	45	48
Vibrating length:	1	8/9	4/5	3/4	2/3	3/5	9/15	1/2

The illustration [Ex. 7] shows a number of frequencies calculated for the tone $f' = 360$ (the correct frequency for f' is 352). It must be noted that these frequencies give the tones of *just intonation, not of equal temperament [see *Temperament].

IV. *Harmonics.* The acoustic effect produced by a single vibration of the type described above is called a pure sound; but practically no vibrating body produces a pure sound. All the musical instruments produce composite sounds,

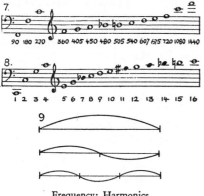

Frequency; Harmonics

consisting of the main sound, or fundamental, plus a number of additional pure sounds, the so-called overtones, which, however, are not heard distinctly because their intensity (amplitude) is much less than that of the main sound. The frequencies of the overtones are exact multiples of the frequency of the fundamental. In other words, an instrument which produces the tone of the frequency n actually produces vibrations (pure sounds) of the frequencies n, $2n$, $3n$, $4n$, . . . (up to $20n$ and more). The illustration [Ex. 8] shows the first 15 overtones of the tone C. A more common designation for these tones is partials or harmonics. It should be noted,

however, that these terms (if properly used) include the fundamental, while the term overtone (if properly used) excludes it. Thus, the first overtone is the second harmonic, etc. Although the terms harmonics and partials are frequently used as interchangeable, the latter has, in scientific studies, a wider significance, since it includes also non-harmonic overtones, such as occur in noises, also in bells. With the exception of the octaves (2,4,8) none of the harmonics are tones of equal temperament. Those which result from the factors 3 and 5 (3,5,6,9,10,12, etc.) are tones of *just intonation (see the above table of frequencies) whereas the harmonics 7, 11 and 13 (indicated by black notes) can only approximately be identified with tones available in our system of tuning and notation. As can easily be seen, the 7th harmonic, which is $7 = 6 3/8$, is lower than the B-flat of just intonation which is $16/9 \times 4 = 6 4/9$; this, in turn, is slightly lower than the B-flat of equal temperament (in *cents, the three tones are: 972, 996, 1000, respectively). Similarly, the 11th harmonic, which is $11 = 4 4/4$, is lower than the F-sharp of just intonation ($15/2 \times 3/2 = 45/4$) and, in fact, nearer to the F than to the F-sharp of equal temperament. Finally, the 13th harmonic is $13 = 3 9/3$, whereas the A of just intonation is $5/3 \times 8 = 4 0/3$.

The physical cause of the harmonics is to be found in the fact that a vibrating body, such as a string, vibrates simultaneously as a whole and in sections of one-half, one-third, one-fourth, etc., of the entire length. The secondary vibrations, however, have a much smaller amplitude, approximately between one-fifth and one-fiftieth of that of the fundamental [Ex. 9].

The existence of these additional tones in what the ear believes to be a single sound was shown first by Helmholtz (1821–94), by means of *resonators of various sizes which reinforce one frequency and eliminate all the others. The harmonics can easily be demonstrated by the following simple experiment on the pianoforte: Depress the key of C without producing a sound, i.e., merely raise the damper of the key of C; then strike forcefully the key of C_1 and release it at once; the higher C, corresponding to the tone of the depressed key, will clearly be heard. The experiment can be repeated by depressing the keys of G, c, e, g, etc., and striking each time the key of C_1. In every case, the tone corresponding to the depressed key will be heard. The explanation of the phenomenon is found in the fact that the harmonics C, G, c, . . . produced by the fundamental tone C_1 generate, by way of resonance, sympathetic vibrations in the shorter strings corresponding to these tones. The harmonics are the cause of three important musical phenomena, namely, *timbre, the *natural tones of wind instruments, and the *harmonics of the violin.

V. *Pipes.* In pipes (organ pipes, and all wind instruments) an enclosed air column is caused to vibrate in what is technically termed "stationary waves." These are characterized by a regular alternation of places of highest density (nodes) and highest rarefaction (antinodes or loops) between which the density of the air decreases from the maximum to the minimum. At the place of maximum density the amplitude of the vibrating particles of air is at a minimum, and vice versa. The whole phenomenon can conveniently be described by graphs similar to that used for a vibrating string, if the point of highest

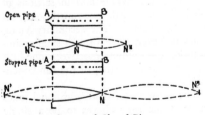

Open and Closed Pipes

amplitude is interpreted as the loop, the stationary point as the node. In an open pipe, a loop develops at each end, with a node in the middle; in a *stopped pipe, a node develops at the closed end, a loop at the open end. From the accompany-

ing drawing it appears that an open pipe generates a sound the wave length of which is double the length of the pipe (N'N'' = 2 AB), while a stopped pipe generates a sound the wave length of which is four times the length of the pipe (N'N'' = 4 AB) and which, therefore, is an octave lower than that produced by an open pipe of the same length. An open pipe sounding C measures approximately eight feet [see *Foot (2)].

Like a vibrating string, an air column vibrates not only as a whole but also in parts ($\frac{1}{2}$, $\frac{1}{3}$, $\frac{1}{4}$, $\frac{1}{5}$, etc., of its length), thus producing harmonics. While an open pipe produces all the harmonics (as does a string), a stopped pipe segments so as to give out only the odd-numbered harmonics, 1,3,5, etc. The reason is that an even harmonic (e.g., 2) would call for a loop (or a node) at both ends of the pipe, while in a stopped pipe there is always a loop at the open end, a node at the closed end [see *Wind instruments III; *Organ IX].

VI. *Interference.* This is the technical term (not a very fortunate one) for the numerous phenomena resulting from the

A
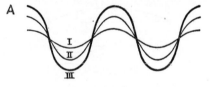

B
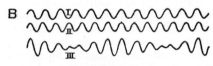

INTERFERENCE

Ex. A: Vibrations of the Same Frequency. *Ex. B:* Vibrations of Different Frequencies: I, of 12 cycles; II, of 14 cycles; III, resulting vibration showing 2(=14−12) maximum vibrations per second (beats).

superposition of two or more air vibrations. The general principles of the very complex phenomenon can be grasped from the drawing [Ex. A], showing two original vibrations (I, II) of the same frequency as well as the result of their superposition (III = I + II). More important is the interference of vibrations of different frequencies, e.g., of 2 and 3 cycles per second, or of 12 and 14 cycles per second [Ex. B]. The example illustrates the manner in which *beats are produced, in the present case 2 (14–12) per second. For a more complicated phenomenon of interference, see *Combination tones.

Related articles: Architectural acoustics; Beats; Bel; Cents; Combination tones; Comma; Consonance and Dissonance; Intervals, Calculation of; Just intonation; Pitch; Pythagorean scale; Resonance; Savart; Temperament; Timbre.

Lit.: W. T. Bartholomew, *Acoustics of Music* (1942; bibl.); P. C. Buck, *Acoustics for Musicians* (1918); J. Broadhouse, *Musical Acoustics* (1926); E. G. Richardson, *The Acoustics of Orchestral Instruments and of the Organ* (1929); J. Jeans, *Science and Music* (1937); D. C. Miller, *Science of Musical Sounds* (1916); J. Redfield, *Music: a Science and an Art* (1928); Stevens and Davis, *Hearing* (1938); A. H. Davis, *Modern Acoustics* (1934); N. W. McLachlan, *The New Acoustics* (1936); Olson and Massa, *Applied Acoustics* (1934). See also under *Architectural acoustics; *Electronic musical instruments. Additional bibliography in D. H. Daugherty, *A Bibliography of Periodical Literature in Musicology* . . . (1940), pp. 117ff.

Action. (1) Any kind of mechanism used in instruments as a means of transmitting the action of the fingers to the sound-producing parts; in other words, a sort of artificial prolongation of the fingers (or feet). On keyboard instruments, the action forms an essential, even the characteristic, part of the instrument [see *Pianoforte I; *Organ II]. The term is also applied to the key-mechanism of wood-wind instruments which enables the player to control holes which are out of reach of the hand (e.g., the *Boehm-action of the flute). The action of the harp is the mechanism controlled by the player's feet upon the pedals by which a transposition of a semitone or a whole tone can be effected [see *Harp].

(2) In modern French usage the word *action* sometimes is used for an opera, e.g., in Vincent d'Indy's *Fervaal* (1897).

Act tune. See *Entr'acte. between acts of plays - piece

Adagietto [It.]. (1) A tempo somewhat faster than adagio. — (2) A short adagio.

Adagio [It., comfortable, easy]. (1) Slow tempo, slower than andante and faster than largo. — (2) A movement written in slow tempo, especially the second (slow) movement of sonatas, symphonies, etc. See *Tempo marks.

Adagissimo. Extremely slow.

Adaptation. *Arrangement.

Added sixth. The sixth added to a triad, or the entire chord thus obtained e.g., c – e – g – a. In classical harmony, the chord of the added sixth occurs preferably on the fourth degree, i.e., with a subdominant function (f – a – c′ – d′ in C major; also f – ab – c′ – d′). It is usually explained as the first inversion of the seventh-chord on the second degree (d – f – a – c′). Although according to strict rules the chord must be resolved into the dominant or the tonic, it is used in more recent works [*Impressionism] as a color-modification of the triad which does not call for resolution. Jazz writers have abundantly availed themselves of this over-sweet effect, especially for the final chord of a piece.

Additional accompaniment. Designation for 19th-century revisions or enlargements of earlier orchestral scores, especially those of the 18th century (Handel, Bach). With the ever-increasing size of the 19th-century orchestra and concert hall, men felt the need of expanding the instrumentation; but with the ever-diminishing understanding of true Baroque style, many stylistic incongruities were allowed to enter. Thus, not only were admissible and sometimes necessary changes made (replacement of obsolete instruments by newer ones, doubling of certain parts, etc.), but also the voice leading was changed, the writing was "improved," new parts were added, and in many instances the original intention of the composer was thoroughly misunderstood or disregarded. The composers whose works were most frequently subjected to arrangement were Handel and Bach. The *Messiah* of Handel has been particularly unfortunate in this regard. Mozart was among the first to make a more modern arrangement of it; subsequently various other musicians made further arrangements of Mozart's arrangement. Many other works of Handel have fared similarly, e.g., under the hands of Mendelssohn, who later expressed regret for having published his arrangements. Bach's cantatas suffered mistreatment from Robert Franz. Wagner made arrangements of Beethoven's Ninth, of Gluck's *Iphigénie en Aulide*, etc. Recent times have witnessed a growing understanding of the Baroque style and a consequent demand for authentic, unarranged, performances. See *Aufführungspraxis. Cf. N. Kilburn, "Additional Arrangements to Handel's *Acis*" (*SIM* iii).

Addolcendo [It.]. Becoming dolce.

Addolorato [It.]. Sadly.

A deux [F.]. See *A due.

Adirato [It.]. Angered, infuriated.

Ad libitum [L., at will]. An indication which gives the performer the liberty: (1) to vary from strict tempo (contrast *a *battuta*); (2) to include or omit the part of some voice or instrument (contrast *obbligato); (3) to include a *cadenza according to his own invention.

A due [It.]. Direction in orchestral parts indicating that two instruments notated on one staff (e.g., Flute 1 and 2) are to sound in unison [see *All'unisono*]. However, the term is also used in the almost opposite meaning, synonymous with *divisi. The same ambiguity exists with the French term *à deux*. *A due corde*, see *Due corde. *A due

mani, for two hands. *A due voci* (*cori, stromenti*, etc.), for two voices (choirs, instruments, etc.).

Aengstlich [G.]. Anxiously.

Aeolian, aeolian mode. See *Church modes; *Modality.

Aeolian harp [Gr. Aeolos, the God of the Winds]. An instrument comprising a long narrow box, with six or more gut strings stretched inside over two bridges. The strings are tuned in unison, but vary in thickness and, therefore, tension. If the box is placed in a free current of air (preferably in an open window), the strings, according to their different tension, vibrate differently and thus produce a great variety of harmonics over the same fundamental (cf. the "singing" of the telephone wires). The sound varies considerably with the changing force of the wind and produces a highly romantic, mysterious effect. The instrument was known in ancient China and India, and in Europe during the Middle Ages. It enjoyed special popularity in the Romantic period around 1800. The intimate charm of this instrument is most beautifully set forth in Eduard Moerike's poem *Die Aeolsharfe* and in its musical settings by Brahms and (especially) Hugo Wolf.

Various attempts have been made to harness this elusive sound to a keyboard, with an artificial jet of wind provided by footbellows (Schnell's *Anémochord* or *Aero-clavichord*, 1789; H. Herz's *Piano Éolien*, 1851). Cf. *SaRM*, 16.

Aeoline. Old name for *mouth-harmonica. Also an early type of *harmonium (*aeolodicon*).

Aeolopantalon. An instrument invented in 1825 by Dlugosz, Warsaw; it was a combination of a harmonium-like instrument (*Aeolomelodikon*, with brass tubes affixed to the reeds) and a pianoforte, so that both instruments could be used in alternation. Its only claim to remembrance lies in the fact that the young Chopin played on it in various recitals.

Aequalstimmen [G.]. (1) The eight-foot pipes of the organ. — (2) *Equal voices.

Aerophones. See *Instruments III.

Aerophor (aerophon). A device invented by B. Samuels in 1912 by which the player of a wind instrument is provided with additional air from small bellows operated with the foot. The air is pressed, through a tube with mouthpiece, into the mouth of the player whenever his breath does not suffice, e.g., for long-held tones or long melodies in full legato. R. Strauss has written passages requiring the use of the aerophon (Alpine Symphony and Festal Prelude).

Aesthetics of music. I. Aesthetics is generally defined as the philosophy or study of the beautiful. Musical aesthetics, therefore, should be the study of the beautiful in music, the ultimate goal of such a study being the establishment of criteria which would allow us to say whether or why one particular composition is beautiful while another is not. The main objection to such a point of view is that beauty is by no means the only (and probably not even the foremost) criterion of what may be roughly described as "quality" or "artistic value." At least the possibility must be admitted that music, like other works of art, may be "valuable" without necessarily being "beautiful" — unless the term beauty is interpreted so broadly as to include features which may well be much closer to its opposite. Therefore, a definition such as the following provides a much better basis for the study in question: *Musical aesthetics is the study of the relationship of music to the human senses and intellect.* This definition corresponds exactly to the original meaning of the Greek word *aisthesis,* i.e., feeling, sensation. The following words by R. Schumann (*Gesammelte Schriften über Musik und Musiker,* i, 44) adequately describe the peculiar problem of musical aesthetics [translation by the writer]:

"In no other field is the proof of the fundamentals as difficult as it is in music. Science argues with mathematics and logic; poetry possesses the decisive, golden word; other arts have chosen nature as their arbiter, borrowing their forms from her. Music, however, is a poor orphan whose father and mother nobody can name. But, perhaps, it is precisely this mystery of her origin which accounts for the charm of her beauty."

II. For more than 2000 years philosophers have tried to solve the mystery of music. Among them we find Pythagoras (550 B.C.), who explains music as the expression of that universal harmony which is also realized in arithmetic and in astronomy; Plato (400 B.C.), for whom music is the most appropriate means of social and political education [also Confucius; see *Chinese music I]; Plotinus (d. 270), who interprets music as a mystic and occult power; Boethius (d. 524), who divides music into three fields, *musica mundana* (the Pythagorean harmony of the universe), *musica humana* (the harmony of the human soul and body), and *musica instrumentalis* (music as actual sound), a classification which prevailed in musical theory for more than 1000 years; J. Kepler (*Harmonices mundi libri* v, 1619), who in a great structure of thought correlates the musical tones and intervals with the movements of the planets and their astrological functions; W. Leibniz (1646–1716), who paves the way for the psychological method of musical aesthetics by interpreting music as the "unconscious exercise in arithmetic"; A. Schopenhauer (*Die Welt als Wille und Vorstellung,* 1819), who considers music the purest incarnation of the "absolute will" and as the expression of human feelings (love, joy, horror) in their abstract interpretation as metaphysical ideas; then G. T. Fechner (1801–87), who insists that music is the expression of "general mood" rather than specific "feelings"; and finally C. Stumpf (*Tonpsychologie,* 1883–90), who inaugurated the scientific study of musical psychology on the basis of experiments and statistics, especially with regard to the problem of *consonance and dissonance. Stumpf's procedure has been the point of departure for many investigations along similar lines, especially in America, e.g., C. E. Seashore, *The Psychology of Music* (1938); M. Schoen, *The Effects of Music* (1927), and others [see *Tests]. For a criticism of these methods, cf. C. C. Pratt, *The Meaning of Music* (1931), 131ff.

It will be seen that not until the advent of the 19th century did these theories of music begin to accord with the present-day interpretation of musical aesthetics as defined above, a statement which should not be construed as a depreciation of the much broader and, in a sense, "greater" views — cosmic, political, or theological — held by the philosophers of antiquity and of the Middle Ages. While in those periods music found its proper place and justification in the universe, in the state, or in God, for us it has lost these transcendental affiliations, but has instead gained a secure place in everyday life.

III. With the foregoing survey of the theories and views held by philosophers and psychologists as a general background, we may now turn to a study of the contributions to our problem made by the musicians themselves. As might be expected, these contributions aim at a more detailed penetration into the questions of musical aesthetics and are usually concerned with the study of individual composers or works rather than with music in the abstract. The various theories can be conveniently divided into two groups, according to whether they consider music (a) as a heteronomous art, i.e., as the expression of extramusical elements, or (b) as an autonomous art, i.e., as the realization of intrinsic principles and ideas (F. Gatz).

(a) In the former class we find the *Affektenlehre* of the 18th century and its 16th-century predecessors, the *Musica reservata* and the *Maniera*. In the 17th century, music was frequently interpreted as an oratorical art, by relating its structural and stylistic elements (such as *figura, repetitio, fuga, climax*) to corresponding principles of speech [cf. A. Schering, in *KJ*, 1908]. In the late Romantic period the interpretation of musical compositions was largely based upon programmatic and allegorical concepts. Music was understood as a sort of psychological drama and explained in terms such as "desperate struggle," "the knocking of Fate," "threatening fortissimo," "gloomy minor," etc. An early exponent of this school of thought is A. B. Marx, in his *L. van Beethoven* (1875). A more intelligent use of this approach was attempted by H. Kretzschmar, the inventor of *musikalische Hermeneutik* [see *Hermeneutics]. He considers music not as a substitute for the pictorial arts or for objects of nature, but rather for poetry, i.e., as a *Sprachkunst* of lesser clarity, but of finer shades and deeper effects, than the ordinary language. He goes back to the "affects" of the 18th century which, according to him, must be based upon the study of the musical detail (themes, intervals, rhythm, etc.). He also relates the music to the life of the composer (Beethoven's "period of happiness," etc.). The latter point was emphasized by H. Riemann, who maintains that the written composition as well as the actual performance is nothing but a means of transferring a psychological situation (*Erlebnis*) from the fancy of the composer to that of the listener. Kretzschmar's method has been elaborated by Schering [see under *Hermeneutics]. A recent American publication, E. Sorantin, *The Problem of Musical Expression* (1932), may be mentioned as an example of 20th-century *Affektenlehre* (expression of joy, grief, longing, etc.).

(b) In strong contrast to all these contributions is the more recent school of thought, which rejects the allegorical, emotional, programmatic, poetical foundation of musical aesthetics, and explains music as a purely musical phenomenon, as an autochthonous and autonomous creation which can be understood only in its own terms. The founder of this school was E. Hanslick who, in his *Vom musikalisch Schönen* (1854), formulated the sentence: "Musik ist tönend bewegte Form" — music is form moving in sounds (the term *form, naturally, must be taken in its widest sense, including all structural and stylistic elements of music). He admits the use of designations such as "powerful," "graceful," "tender," "passionate," but only in order to illustrate the musical character of the passage, not to suggest a definite feeling on the part of composer or listener. Still farther in this direction went August Halm (*Von zwei Kulturen der Musik*, 1913), who must be considered the most outstanding representative of musical aesthetics of the present day. The following quotation from the Talmud, given at the beginning of his book, is an adequate expression of the central thought of musical autonomy: "If you want to understand the invisible, look carefully at the visible." Halm, as well as his successors, E. Kurth, H. Hermann, F. Joede, and others, advocated the separation of the musical work from the emotional world of both the composer and the listener, and the emancipation of the musical thought from "sensuous intoxication and hallucination."

See also *Affektenlehre; *Hermeneutics; *Musica reservata; *Maniera.

Lit.: F. M. Gatz, *Musik-Aesthetik in ihren Hauptrichtungen* (1929); H. H. Briton, *Philosophy of Music* (1911); H. Riemann, *Catechism of Musical Aesthetics* (1895); R. Schaefke, *Geschichte der Musik-aesthetik* (1934); H. Besseler, "Grundfragen der Musik-aesthetik" (*JMP* xxxiii). For a bibliography of recent psychological studies, cf. D. H. Daugherty, *A Bibliography of Periodical Literature in Musicology* . . . (1940), pp. 108ff. Cf. also *MoML*, 538f.

Aevia. An artificial word, consisting of the vowels of *alleluia (u = v). It is occasionally used as an abbreviation in manuscripts of Gregorian chant. See *Euouae.

Affabile [It.]. In a pleasing manner.

Affaiblissant [F.]. Weakening, diminuendo.

Affanato [It.]. "Panting," i.e., as in distress.

Affannoso [It.]. Sadly.

Affektenlehre [G.; doctrine of affections]. The aesthetic theory of the *empfindsamer Stil (sensitive style) of the later 18th century, formulated by J. Quantz and Ph. Em. Bach, according to which the chief aim of music is to portray certain typical emotions, such as the tender, the languid, the passionate, etc. This theory, which is realized in the works of Ph. Em. Bach, marks an important advance over the superficiality of the Italian "stile galante" (*gallant style) and, in spite of its rationalistic nature and schematic methods, paves the way for the free expressiveness of the Beethoven style. See *Aesthetics III (a); *Musica reservata.

Lit.: W. Serauky, *Die musikalische Nachahmungsaesthetik im Zeitraum 1700–1850* (1929); M. Kramer, *Beiträge zu einer Aesthetik der Affectenlehre in der Musik von 1550–1700* (Diss. Halle 1924); H. Goldschmidt, *Die Musikaesthetik des 18. Jahrhunderts* (1915); G. Frotscher, *Bach's Themen-bildung unter dem Einfluss der Affektenlehre* (1926); R. Schaefke, "Quantz als Aesthetiker" (*AMW* vi); H. Abert, in *AMW* v; H. Kretzschmar, in *JMP* xviii, xix; F. Stege, in *ZMW* x; A. Schering, in *JMP* xlv.

Affetti [It.]. The term appears as a title of various publications around 1600 [*Dolci Affetti* (1595); S. Bonini, *Affetti spirituali in istile di Firenze or recitativo* · · · (1615); B. Marini, *Affetti musicali*, op. 1 (1617)], probably in order to emphasize the emotional character of the music. It is also used in early violin sonatas to designate a certain type of ornamentation, either tremolo or arpeggio [cf. *SchGMB*, no. 183; *RiHM* ii. 2, 120].

Affettuoso [It.]. Affectionate, with warmth.

Affrettando [It.]. Hurrying.

African music. See *Primitive music; *Arabian music; *Ethiopian Church music; *Coptic Church music.

Afternoon of a Faun, The. See *Symphonic poem IV.

Agende [L. *agenda*, that which has to be done]. The Protestant counterpart of the Catholic liturgy or of the Anglican rites, i.e., the entire ritual of the service of the German Protestant Church. Cf. H. Kretzschmar, *Die musikalische Agende* (1894); R. v. Liliencron, *Musikalisch-liturgische Geschichte des evangelischen Gottesdienstes 1523–1700* (1892).

Agevole [It.]. Lightly and easily.

Aggradevole [It.]. Agreeably.

Agilmente; con agilità [It.]. Lively, speedily.

Agitato [It.]. Agitated, excited.

Agnus Dei. The last item (except for the *Ite missa est) of the Ordinary of the Mass [see *Mass A and B III]; therefore, the final movement in Mass compositions. It consists of three invocations: "Agnus Dei, qui tollis peccata mundi: miserere nobis. Agnus Dei, . . . miserere nobis. Agnus Dei, . . . dona nobis pacem." The musical structure of the chant is usually A A A (sometimes with a different beginning for the middle A), or A B A. See *Gregorian chant IV.

Agogic. An accent is said to be agogic if it is effected, not by dynamic stress or by higher pitch, but by longer duration of the note [see *Accent]. In German writings the term *Agogik* is used to denote all the subtleties of performance achieved by modification of tempo, as distinct from *Dynamik*, i.e., gradations which involve variety of intensity. Thus, the use of rallentando and accelerando, of tempo rubato, the dwelling on certain notes, also rests, breathing signs, fermatas, etc., all fall under *Agogik*. The term was introduced by H. Riemann (*Musikalische Dynamik und Agogik*, 1884) particularly in order to describe those deviations from strict tempo and rhythm which are necessary for an intelligible rendering of the musical phrase.

Agréments. The ornaments introduced in French music of the 17th century, which were finally adopted into all European music and were generally indicated by stenographic signs or as notes in small type. The *agréments* are characterized by a definitely stereotyped melodic contour, a close relationship with a single note of the melody to be ornamented, and a small melodic range. See *Ornamentation II.   P. A.

Aida. Grand opera by Giuseppe Verdi (1813–1901), libretto by A. Ghislanzoni; commissioned by the Khedive of Egypt for the new Opera House at Cairo and produced there in 1871. The plot has an ancient Egyptian background and centers around the love of the Egyptian warrior *Radames* (Tenor) for the captive Ethiopian princess *Aida* (Soprano), and the jealousy of *Amneris* (Mezzo-soprano), daughter of the king of Egypt *Amonasro* (Bass). Amneris, repudiated by Radames, discovers a treacherous plot of the two lovers designed to aid Ethiopia, and both die.

Although reputedly making use of a few Egyptian musical themes, the general style of the opera is that of the Italian grand opera. Striking features are the brief atmospheric prelude (in place of a conventional operatic overture) and the use of a few *leitmotifs (e.g., Amneris' jealousy).

Aigu [F.]. High, shrill.

Air [F.]. (1) French 18th-century term for song in general [see under *Chanson]. — (2) In French opera and ballet of the 17th–18th centuries, an instrumental or vocal piece designed to accompany dancing, but not cast in one of the standard dance patterns such as the minuet, gavotte, etc. Sometimes (e.g., Rameau) it is qualified as *air tendre, air gracieux*, etc. — (3) In the *suites around and after 1700, a movement, found in the optional group, of a melodic rather than dance-like character — in a way, a "song without words" [cf. Bach's Partitas nos. IV and VI]. As yet, no clear connection between these airs and those described under (2) has been discerned, probable as it is that such a connection existed. —

(4) See *Ayre. For *air de charactère,* etc., see *Aria.

Air de cour [F., court song]. Short strophic songs, sometimes with a refrain, for one or more voices with lute accompaniment, which were cultivated in France in the late 16th and in the 17th century. They are in simple syllabic style and in binary form. The texts are chiefly love-poems in affected *précieux* language, some of them in *vers mesuré.* The repetition of each of the two sections was frequently ornamented at will by the singer. Principal composers are Pierre Guédron (*c.* 1565–1625); Antoine Boësset (*c.* 1585–1646); Jean de Cambefort (d. 1661); Michel Lambert (1610–96). Cf. Th. Gérold, *L'Art du chant en France au XVIIe siècle* (1921); L. de la Laurencie, †*Chansons au luth et airs de cour au XVIe siècle* (1931); A. Arnheim, in *SIM* x.   D. J. G.

Ais, aisis [G.]. See *Pitch names.

Akademie [G.]. *Academy. See also under *Académie.

Akkord [G.]. Chord.

Akoluthia [Gr.]. The order of the service of the Byzantine Church, particularly that of the office, thus usually not including the Mass, which was called *leiturgeia* (liturgy). Cf. E. Wellesz, *Byzantinische Musik* (1927), p. 23.

Akzent [G.]. Accent. *Akzentneumen,* accent neumes [see *Neumes II].

Alalá. A type of Galician folk song expressing passion and longing. Older examples use syllables such as *la-la* or *ai-le-lo-la* and are interesting because of the preservation of plainsong-like elements. Cf. F. Pedrell, †*Cancionero musical popular español* (1918–22), ii, 217ff.

A la mi re, alamire. See *Hexachord III.

Alba, albe, aube [F., dawn]. In the repertoire of the Provençal *troubadours, a poem dealing with the departure of the lover in the early morning. It usually is a dialogue between the lover and a guardian friend who warns him of some approaching danger [cf. *GéHM,* 301; *ReMMA,* 215]. The German Minnesinger counterpart of the alba is the *Tagelied* (day-song) or *Wächterlied* (guardian-song) which Wagner revived in the second act of his *Tristan* (Brangäne's warning call). Many examples of *Tagelied,* however, are of a more devotional nature, serving as a sort of morning prayer [cf. F. Runge, †*Die Sangesweisen der Colmarer Liederhandschrift,* p. 173]. See also *Alborada; *Aubade.

Alberti bass. Stereotyped figures of accompaniment for the left hand of the piano player, consisting of broken chords [see also *Murky bass]. They are named after Domenico Alberti (1710–40?) who used them extensively in his harpsichord

sonatas. An early example occurs in the fourth variation of the G minor aria in Pachelbel's *Hexachordum Apollinis* of 1698 [cf. *DTB* 2.i; *TaAM* ix, 64]. They are still frequent in the works of Haydn, Mozart, and the early Beethoven.

Albisiphone. See *Flute I (d).

Alborada [Sp., dawn song]. A type of Spanish (particularly, Galician) music, played on the *dulzaina* (rustic oboe) and *tamboril* (small drum), originally a morning serenade [cf. G. Chase, *The Music of Spain* (1941), p. 237]. Ravel's *Alborada del Gracioso* (1912) derives certain features from the Spanish alborada. See also *Alba; *Aubade.

Albumblatt [G.], album leaf. A fancy name for short pieces of 19th-century salon music such as might have served as a contribution to an autograph album.

Alcuna licenza, Con [It.]. With a little license, specifically regarding the tempo.

Al fine [It.]. To the end (for repetition of a piece from the beginning).

Aliquot strings, aliquot scaling. *Sympathetic strings added by some pianoforte makers (Blüthner) above the strings of the upper register in order to produce a fuller sound by resonance.

Alla breve [It.]. A tempo mark (¢) indicating quick duple time, i.e., with the half-note rather than the quarter-note as the beat; in other words, 2/2 instead of 4/4. Both the name and the sign are a vestige of *mensural notation and of the *proportions (*tempus imperfectum diminutum*). Originally and properly *alla breve* means that the unit of musical time (**tactus*) is represented by the *brevis* (corresponding to our double whole note), not as normally by the *semibrevis* (corresponding to our whole note). Today it means that the half-note should be regarded as the unit of time, not as normally the quarter-note. See also *Time signatures.

Allargando [It.]. Slowing down, usually accompanied by a crescendo; used chiefly towards the end of a piece.

Allegramente [It.]. Brightly, gaily.

Allegretto [It.]. (1) A tempo between allegro and andante; see *Tempo marks. — (2) A small allegro movement.

Allegro [It., cheerful]. Originally a designation for the joyful character of a piece; today employed to indicate quick tempo, regardless of the character and expression [see *Tempo marks]. Also used as a title for pieces in quick tempo, especially the first and last movements of a sonata.

Alleluia [Latinization of Hebrew *hallelujah*, praise ye the Lord]. An expression of joy and praise of God which occurs frequently in Gregorian chant. During Eastertide, the word alleluia is added to all antiphons, and to various other chants. It also occurs at the end of chants for Christmas, Corpus Christi, and other festivals. Alleluiatic antiphons are antiphons which consist of the word alleluia repeated three times [see, e.g., *LU*, 19]. More specifically, the term al-leluia denotes the third item of the Proper of the *Mass. It was introduced by Pope Damasus (368–384), first for Easter only. Pope Gregory (590–604) extended its use over the entire year except for Lent, for which season the original *tract was preserved. The alleluia of the Mass consists of the word *Alleluia* followed by a brief sentence referring to the occasion, the so-called vers (*versus alleluiaticus*, abbr. ℣), e.g.: *Alleluia. ℣. Surrexit Dominus de sepulcro* [cf. *GR*, 228; *LU*, 790; also *HAM*, no. 13; *EiBM*, no. 4; *ReMMA*, 180]. The music for the word alleluia closes with a long vocalization to the final vowel: (*Al-lelui*)*a*———, the so-called *neuma or *jubilus. See also *Gregorian chant III; *Psalmody II; *Sequence.

Allemande [F., German, *sc.* a dance]. A dance in moderate duple time which first appeared around 1550. Early examples occur in T. Susato's *Musyck Boexken* (1551); in P. Attaingnant's *Troisième livre de danseries* (1556); in B. Schmid, *Zwey Bücher einer neuen kunstlichen Tabulatur* (1577) [cf. W. Merian, *Der Tanz in den deutschen Tabulaturbüchern* (1927), p. 111]; in the *Fitzwilliam Virginal Book* (c. 1620), where the name Alman, Almayne is used. Arbeau, in his *Orchésographie* (1588), considers the dance already outmoded. The music of the 16th-century allemande in no way differs from that of the *passamezzo; the dance steps were simple, as appears from the following description by Th. Morley [*A Plaine and Easie Introduction . . .* (1597), p. 181]: "The Alman is a more heavie daunce then this [i.e., the galliarde] (fitlie representing the nature of the people, whose name it carieth) so that no extraordinarie motions are used in dauncing of it." Like the pavane and passamezzo, the allemande was frequently followed by a jumping dance in triple meter, called *tripla, *proportz, or, in the 17th century, by the courante. In the 17th century the allemande ceased to be actually danced and became a stylized dance type which was regularly used as the first

movement of the *suite. These allemandes are in very moderate 4/4-time,
with a short upbeat, and frequently make

use of short running figures which are
passed through the various voices of a
pseudo-contrapuntal fabric. Our three
examples (1. Ammerbach, 1571; 2. Purcell, c. 1660; 3. J. K. F. Fischer, c. 1690)
illustrate the stylistic development of the
dance.

In the late 18th century the name allemande was used in South Germany as
an equivalent for Deutscher Tanz, a
quick waltz-like dance in 3/4- or 3/8-
time. Cf. Beethoven's "A l'allemande"
in his Bagatellen, op. 119, and his *12
Deutsche Tänze für Orchester* (1795).
See *Dance music III.

Lit.: E. Mohr, *Die Allemande in der
deutschen Klaviersuite* (1932).

Allentando [It.]. Slowing.

Alliteration. A characteristic feature
of ancient Germanic poetry (e.g., Beo-
wulf, Edda), consisting of the use of

words with the same initial letter. This
principle was adopted by R. Wagner in
his *Ring des Nibelungs*, e.g., "Nach Wel-
ten-Wonne mein Wunsch verlangte aus
wild webendem Bangen."

Allmählich [G.]. Gradually.

Allonger [F.]. To slacken in speed.

All'ottava [It.]. See *Ottava.

All'unisono [It.]. In orchestral scores
this term indicates that two instruments
for which the same staff is employed
(e.g., two flutes) play in unison, i.e., the
same notes. See *A due.

Alman, almayne. Sixteenth-century
English corruption of *allemande.

Alpensinfonie, Eine (An Alpine
Symphony). See *Symphonic poem III.

Alphabet (in music). See *Pitch
names; *Letter notation; *Tablature.

Alphorn, alpine horn. A primitive
wind instrument, still used by the herdsmen in the Alps for signaling over great
distance and for simple melodies. It is
made of wooden staves bound with strips
of birch bark, is 5 to 10 feet long, and
appears in various shapes, straight or
bent. The tones produced are the harmonics [see *Acoustics IV], somewhat
modified by the material and by the irregular width of the inner tube. In particular, the fourth (11th harmonic) is
halfway between F and F-sharp (Alp-
horn-fa) [see *Ranz de vaches]. Similar
instruments are to be found in Scandinavia, Poland, and Rumania, and among
the South American Indians. Cf. SaRM,
7; Szandrowsky, in *Jahrbuch des Schweizer Alpenclubs* iv; K. Nef, in *De Muziek* v.

Al solito [It.]. As usual.

Alt. (1) In English usage the term is
sometimes applied to the tones of the
octave above the treble staff (g″ to f‴),
which are said to be "in alt." The tones
of the next higher octave are called "in
altissimo." — (2) In German, the lower
of the two female voices, i.e., the con-

tralto [see *Alto]. In connection with instruments (*Altklarinette*, *Altsaxophon*), the term denotes the second highest member of the family (alto clarinet, alto saxophone). See the various instruments. *Altgeige* is the viola alta [see *Violin family (d)], rarely the ordinary viola.

Alteration. (1) See *Mensural notation. — (2) The raising or lowering of a note by means of a sharp or flat; also called chromatic alteration. See *Accidentals; *Chromaticism; *Altered chord.

Altered chord. See *Harmonic analysis V.

Alternativo [It.], **alternativement** [F.]. In the suites of the Bach period, an indication found with a pair of dances (e.g., Bourrée I, alternativement — Bourrée II), calling for repetition of the first dance after the second, thus leading to the ternary arrangement A B A [cf. Bach's English Suite no. 2]. This structure persists in the Minuet (Scherzo) with Trio of the classical sonata [see *Trio].

Altgeige [G.]. See under *Alt (2).

Althorn. See *Brass instruments III (f).

Altistin [G.]. A contralto singer.

Alto [It., high]. (1) A female voice of low range, also called contralto. See *Voices, Range of. — (2) Originally the alto was a high male voice (hence the name) which by use of the *falsetto nearly reached the height of the female voice (contralto). This type of voice, also known as *counter-tenor, was especially cultivated in England, where the church music of the 16th and 17th centuries definitely implies its use. For the explanation of the term, see *Contratenor. — (3) The second-highest part of the normal four-part chorus; L. *altus.* — (4) In French and Italian, the secondhighest instrument of the violin family, i.e., the viola. — (5) In connection with clarinet, flute, saxophone, etc., the term refers to the third- or fourth-highest member of the family.

Lit.: G. E. Stubbs, *The Adult Male Alto or Countertenor* (1908); A. H. D. Prendergast, "The Man's Alto in English Music" (*ZIM* i); J. Hough, "The Historical Significance of the Countertenor" (*PMA* lxiv).

Alto clef. See *Clefs.

Altra volta [It.]. Encore.

Altschlüssel [G.]. Alto·clef.

Altus [L.]. See *Alto (3).

Alzati [It.]. "Raised," indication to take off the mutes.

Amabile [It.]. Lovable.

Amarevole [It.]. With bitterness, sadly.

Ambitus [L., compass, range]. The range of the melodies of Gregorian chant. It varies from a fourth (in the psalm tones) to an octave or ninth in the more melismatic chants (graduals, alleluias) [see also *Gregorian chant V (b)]. In the theory of the church modes, the ambitus is the chief mark of distinction between an authentic and a plagal mode. See *Church modes. Cf. Krasucki, "Ueber den Ambitus der gregorianischen Messgesänge" (*Veröffentlichungen der Gregorianischen Akademie zu Freiburg, Schweiz, 1. Heft*).

Ambo. In early Christian churches a special platform on the steps of which the gradual was sung.

Amboss [G.]. *Anvil.

Ambrosian chant. The liturgical chant, established by St. Ambrose, bishop of Milan (333–397), and still in use today in the cathedral of that city; therefore also called Milanese chant. It is one of the four "dialects" of Christian chant [see *Chant], and probably is closer to its original form than *Gregorian (Roman) chant. The Ambrosian melodies are usually more ornamented than the corresponding Gregorian melodies [cf. the comparative examples in *HAM*, no. 10; SchGMB, no. 2; BeMMR, 58; LavE i.1, 561; O. Ursprung, *Katholische Kir-*

chenmusik, 20; H. Gastoué, *Cours du chant grégorien*, 67, 128, 149]. Vocalizations including up to 200 notes are not rare. On the other hand, the Ambrosian psalm tones are simpler and lack the methodical arrangement to be found with the Gregorian psalm tones [cf. *GD* v, 267]. The Ambrosian rite occasionally differs from the Gregorian, for instance, in the names given to the chants: *ingressa* for introitus, *psalmellus* for gradual, *transitorium* for communion, etc. The use of the term "Ambrosian modes" for the four authentic church modes (in distinction from the "Gregorian," i.e., plagal, modes) is without any historical justification. For more details see *Church modes II. The earliest sources of Ambrosian chant (11th century) contain chants in the plagal as well as in the authentic modes.

Lit.: P. Wagner, *Einführung in die Gregorianischen Melodien* (1911–21), vols. i and iii; G. Bas, *Manuale di canto Ambrosiano* (Torino, 1929; bibl.); †*Antiphonale Ambrosianum* [see *Editions, XXIII, A, 5/6]; K. Ott, "Le Ingresse (Il Psalmellus) della liturgia ambrosiana" (*Rassegna Gregoriana* viii).

Ambrosian hymns. The hymns of the Roman and Ambrosian rites written and possibly composed by St. Ambrose.

I. *Text.* Formerly all the hymns (*c.* 120) of the Antiphonarium were ascribed to Ambrose, under the generic name of *hymni Ambrosiani*. Actually the number of true Ambrosian hymns is much smaller, about 20 [see Lit., Dreves]. With four of them Ambrose's authorship is placed beyond doubt by the testimony of St. Augustine (*De Musica*); these are: *Aeterne rerum conditor*; *Deus creator omnium*; *Jam surgit hora tertia*; *Veni redemptor gentium*. All the Ambrosian hymns are written in the simple scheme of eight stanzas; each consisting of four lines in iambic tetrameters, e.g.:

> Vení redémptor géntiúm
> Osténde pártum vírginís
> Mirétur ómne séculúm
> Talís decét partús deúm.

Regarding the early history, see *Hymn I, II.

II. *Music.* About a dozen melodies of Ambrosian hymns are preserved in sources none of which is earlier than the 12th century (an exception is the melody for the *Aeterne Christi munera*, given in *Daseian notation in the *Musica enchiriadis, c.* 850; cf. *GS* i, 154 and *RiHM* i.2, 17). Under these circumstances the question as to whether these melodies are compositions of Ambrose or — as has been surmised — "early Christian folk songs," or products of a later period, remains entirely open, the more so since in a number of cases different melodies are given for the same hymn. The melodies are syllabic, with occasional groups of two or three notes; the latter are usually omitted in modern transcriptions which try to give the melodies in what is believed to be their "original form." No less problematic is the question as to the true rhythm of these hymns, i.e., whether they are to be interpreted in duple or in triple time. The answer probably depends upon whether they are considered as melodies of the Ambrosian era or of the late Middle Ages (11th, 12th centuries). According to St. Augustine, the iambic feet of the Ambrosian hymns were "tria temporum" (in three beats). The accompanying example shows a hymn (a) in its 9th-century form and (b) in its hypothetical original state [cf. also *HAM*, no. 9].

Ae-ter-ne Christi munera et mar-ty-rum victo-ri-as

The term "Ambrosian hymn" [G. *Ambrosianischer Lobgesang*] is erroneously used for the *Te Deum.

Lit.: Biraghi, *Inni sinceri di S. Ambrogio* (1862); G. M. Dreves, "Aurelius Ambrosius . . ." (*Stimmen aus Maria Laach, Ergänzungsheft* 58, 1893); G. Bas, in *Musica Divina* xvii; J. Jeannin, in *TG* xxvi, 115.

Ame [F., soul]. Sound post.

✓ **Amen.** A Hebrew word, meaning "so be it," which is widely used in the Christian rites. It is usually spoken by the congregation (or recited by the choir) as a confirming answer to the lection or the prayer of the priest [cf. *AR*, 35*]. Especially important is its occurrence at the end of the minor *doxology, in the connection ". . . seculorum. Amen" [see *Evovae] and, in the Mass, at the end of the Gloria (". . . in gloria dei patris. Amen") as well as of the Credo (". . . et vitam venturi saeculi. Amen"). In the polyphonic Masses of the 17th and 18th centuries the confirming character of the Amen led to the writing of extensive finales in fugal style, called Amen-fugue or Amen-chorus, in which the word is repeated over and over again. This practice occurred first with Antonio Bertali (1605–69; cf. *AdHM* i, 516), and continued throughout the periods of Handel (famous Amen-chorus), Bach, Mozart, Beethoven, etc. In Cherubini's D minor Mass at the end of the Credo, the soprano alone repeats the word 107 times. For Amen-cadence see *Plagal cadence.

Amener [F.]. A 17th-century dance in moderate triple time with phrases of six measures (three plus three or four plus two) as a characteristic feature. It occurs in the suites of Heinrich Biber, J. K. F. Fischer, Alessandro Poglietti, in the instrumental suites edited by Écorcheville (1906), etc. The derivation of the amener from the *basse dance, given in most reference books, is very questionable. More likely, it is one of the numerous species of the *branle, a *branle à mener*, i.e., a branle in which one pair was leading while the others followed. See also *Minuet.

American Guild of Organists. See *Societies, Musical I, 1.

American Indian music. Although the collection and scientific study of tribal songs of the American Indians did not commence until the latter 19th century, there are numerous references to the music of the Indians from the early 17th century, shortly after the coming of English colonists. In William Wood's account of

his visit to Plymouth and Massachusetts Bay (London, 1634), he wrote of the Indians' singing: "To hear one of these Indian's unseene, a good eare might easily mistake their untaught voyce for the warbling of a well tuned instrument. Such command have they of their voices." Travelers and explorers occasionally reported that the Indians were musical, among them the Frenchman F. G. Sagard in his *Le grand Voyage du Pays des Hurons* (1632).

In the 18th century F. W. Marpurg, the German music historian, published *Remarks on Three Songs of the Iroquois* (Berlin, 1760), and William Beresford printed an Indian melody in his *A Voyage around the world; but more particularly to the northwest coast of America* (London, 1789). One of the early attempts at adaptation of an actual Indian melody was first published in London in 1784, and was called *Alknomook* (*Alkmoonok*), "The death song of the Cherokee Indians, an Original Air, brought from America by a gentleman long conversant with the Indian tribes, and particularly with the Nation of the Cherokees. The Words adapted to the Air by a Lady." The identity of the "Gentleman" is unknown, but the "Lady" was identified by Frank Kidson as Anne Hone Hunter, who was Haydn's hostess during his London visit. In America, James Hewitt included *Alkmoonok* in the score he arranged and composed for the ballad-opera *Tammany* (1794), and in 1800 Gilfert in New York and von Hagen in Boston published sheet-music editions of the song. Both American and English editions presented the melody in thoroughly conventional form.

The first serious study of Indian music by a musician was undertaken by Theodore Baker, a German-American who in 1880 was a student at the University of Leipzig. As a subject for his doctor's thesis he chose the music of the North American Indians, and visited the Seneca Reservation in New York State and the Indian school at Carlisle, Pennsylvania. In 1882 the thesis was published at Leipzig: *Über die Musik der Nordamerikanischen Wil-*

den. It analyzed some sixty melodies according to their poetry, vocalization, scales, melodic progressions, rhythm, notations, and instruments for performance.

Baker's studies were soon followed by those of Alice C. Fletcher, who visited the Omaha tribe, where she was assisted by John C. Fillmore of Harvard, who provided piano accompaniments for the melodies Miss Fletcher transcribed. Her findings were published at intervals from 1883 to 1911 by the Peabody Museum of American Archaeology and Ethnology and by the Bureau of American Ethnology in Washington.

B. J. Gilman and J. W. Fewkes were pioneers in applying scientific methods to analysis of Indian melodies. Gilman accompanied the Hemenway Southwestern Expedition among the Zuñi, Pueblo, and Hopi Indians, and measured the interval structure of their melodies by a mechanical device. Fewkes was one of the first to use the phonograph to record Indian singing (1890), and in 1891 Gilman published a study based on these records of Zuñi songs. Further studies of Zuñi, Pueblo, and Hopi songs were made by Natalie C. Burlin, while music of the Ojibways in Minnesota and Wisconsin was taken down and annotated by Frederick R. Burton.

The United States Government first undertook the perpetuation of Indian tribal melodies in 1911, by appointing trained investigators to collect the melodies with the aid of the phonograph and place them on record, with annotations, in the Smithsonian Institution. Reports on the research have been issued by the Bureau of American Ethnology. The most prominent worker under these auspices has been Frances Densmore, who has studied the music and customs of the Chippewas, Teton Sioux, Northern Ute, Mandan, Hidatsa, and others.

The question as to whether the music of the Indians is to be considered American folk music is open to debate. Certainly, if Western culture is considered predominant among the inhabitants of the nation, American Indian music is exotic and far different in conception from that which has been influenced by the parent nations of the white settlers and their descendants. When Indian melodies are reduced to the diatonic scale, and harmonized according to Western practice, the character of most of them is lost in the process. It is also inaccurate to refer to American Indian music as a unified body of folk-material. Originally there were more than fifty basic linguistic stocks, each of them divided into separate tribes. The government Office of Indian Affairs, even at the present time when the Indians seem to be approaching tribal extinction, deals with three hundred and forty-two tribes, a number which does not include the sub-tribal divisions. Each of these tribes had its own customs, religion, and characteristic music.

There are, however, a number of traits which are common to the music of various tribes. Music is rarely performed by the Indians for its own sake; generally songs belong to some tribal custom, and are sung only for the performance of that custom. A visitor to one of the tribes could not persuade the Indians to sing a hunting song for him because they were not actually hunting at the time. There are songs for treating the sick, war songs designed to bring success in battle, religious ceremonial songs, game songs, many of them for gambling, dream and vision songs, children's songs, and love songs for courtship. Among most of the tribes, three classes of songs exist. First, the old, traditional songs, which have been handed down from generation to generation. Second, the old ceremonial and medicine songs which are rarely performed because they belonged to men now dead, but which can still be sung by those who remember their owners' singing of them. Third, there are the comparatively modern songs, which show the influence of civilization. The property idea regarding songs is common to many tribes, and the individual owner of a song was often known to sell it to another member of the tribe. It could then be sung only by the purchaser.

Many of the Indian songs, like those of primitive races generally, are characterized by a descending melodic line. The descent may be interrupted, but it continues to the end. According to a tabulation of 820 songs by Frances Densmore, 67 per cent begin with a downward progression, and in 87 per cent the last tone is the lowest of the entire melody. Although many of the melodies cannot be accurately represented in diatonic notation, many of them approximate the pentatonic major or minor modes. Densmore found also that 67 per cent of 340 Chippewa songs end on tones which provide the ear with satisfactory keynotes. Rhythmically, Indian music is complex and irregular. The Indian is capable of performing involved polyrhythms, although Burton believed that the performers are unaware that their songs and the accompanying drum beats are cast in conflicting rhythms. See the examples under *Primitive music.

The musical instruments of the various tribes are flutes, whistles, rattles, and drums. Although flutes are commonly pictured as aiding in courtship, they are as frequently used for warning against the approach of an enemy. Whistles are part of the medicine man's equipment for treating the sick. Rattles are often regarded as sacred articles, for use in worship. Some of them are merely notched sticks, rubbed over a second stick, while others are receptacles holding loose objects. The drums are essential to Indian music, some tribes cannot sing without them. They are made in various sizes, from hand drums to immense kegs partly filled with water.

The effect of Indian music on the art music of the United States has been extensive, but limited. Edward MacDowell used Indian melodies in his Second Orchestral ("Indian") Suite of 1890; C. S. Skilton in his *Indian Dances* and *Suite Primeval*; C. W. Cadman in *Thunderbird Suite* and other works; Frederick Jacobi in his *Indian Dances*; C. T. Griffes in *Two Sketches for String Quartet*; Victor Herbert in the opera, *Natoma*; while H. W. Loomis, Arthur Farwell, Thurlow Lieurance, Carlos Troÿer, Henry F. Gilbert, and others have made many settings of tribal material. Among non-American

composers, Dvořák, with his symphony "From the New World," and Busoni, with his *Indianisches Tagebuch*, may be mentioned.

Lit.: F. R. Burton, *American Primitive Music* (1909); Natalie Curtis, *The Indian's Book* (1907); Frances Densmore, *Chippewa Music*, Nos. 1 and 2 (1910 and 1913), *Mandan and Hidatsa Music* (1923), *Northern Ute Music* (1922), *Teton Sioux Music* (1918); A. C. Fletcher, *Indian Story and Song from North America* (1900); F. Densmore, "The Study of Indian Music" (*MQ* i); *id.*, in *MQ* xvii, xx; F. W. Galpin, "Aztec Influence on American Indian Instruments" (*SIM* iv); M. Barbeau, "Asiatic Survivals in Indian Songs" (*MQ* xx); J. Tiersot, "La musique chez les peuples indigènes de l'Amérique du nord. . . ." (*SIM* xi; bibl.). An extensive bibliography is found in G. Herzog, *Research in Primitive and Folk Music in the United States* (1936).

J. T. H.

American music. This term is generally accepted as applying to music which is composed or has its origin in the United States. Similarly, an American composer is one who is either a native of the United States or has adopted the nation prior to his or her mature production. For other musical cultures of the American hemisphere see *American Indian music; *Latin American music; *Negro music; *Canadian music.

I. *17th and 18th Centuries.* The history of American music begins in the early 17th century, with the arrival of the first white settlers and colonists: Jamestown, Virginia, in 1607, and Plymouth, Massachusetts, in 1620. Little is known about the musical habits of the Virginia settlers, but a number of records exist to show the part music played in the lives of the New England colonists: the Pilgrims at Plymouth and the English Puritans who came to Massachusetts Bay (Boston), starting in 1630. Until the close of the century, musical activity was confined almost exclusively to psalm-singing. The only printed music used was contained in the psalters the Puritans brought with them (Sternhold & Hopkins, Ains-worth, Ravenscroft, etc.), for the *Bay Psalm Book (Cambridge, 1640) contained no music until a few tunes were added to a later edition at the end of the century.

Two factors were chiefly responsible for the small amount of music before 1700: one of them was the lack of opportunity in pioneer surroundings, and the other, the Puritan attitude towards music. The latter phase of early New England life has been the subject of considerable contro-versy in recent years. Percy Scholes, in his book The Puritans and Music (1934), claims that the Puritans in England, and those who came to America, were not hos-tile to music and that the tradition that they did not tolerate musical activity in the American colonies is fallacious. How-ever, the available evidence shows that while musical activity did become more general at the beginning of the 18th cen-tury, it was almost negligible in the 17th; and that while there are references in con-temporary records to a few musical instru-ments, the Puritan colonists viewed with suspicion and distrust secular amusements and pleasures, which they considered un-godly and sinful.

At the beginning of the 18th century, psalm-singing in the churches had become a haphazard practice. The lack of printed tunes had forced the worshipers to sing from memory, led by a deacon or elder. There was so little standardization of the few tunes in use that when several con-gregations met together the musical re-sults were bedlam. This condition led to reforms as well as to controversy. Several instruction books for singing appeared: John Tufts's A very plain and easy intro-duction to the whole Art of Singing Psalm Tunes, in 1720, and Thomas Walter's Grounds and Rules of Music Explained, in 1721, which at first met strong opposi-tion. Gradually the opposition was over-come, and singing schools were estab-lished to teach the rudiments of singing from note. Toward the latter part of the century there was considerable publication of tune and instruction books. Among the early ones were an American edition of William Tans'ur's A Complete Melody

in Three Parts (1755); James Lyon's Urania (1761, containing six original works by Lyon); and Josiah Flagg's A Collection of the Best Psalm Tunes (1764). In 1770 appeared the first of six books by William Billings (1746–1800), entitled The New England Psalm Singer. Billings is important in American music history because he was something of a radical. A number of his anthems, which he called "fuguing pieces" [see *Fugue-tune], were attempts at imitative coun-terpoint, and while he was largely un-tutored musically, his work had a rugged vitality which reflected vividly the back-ground of pioneer surroundings.

The controversies over music that troubled the Puritan denominations did not disturb the Anglican churches. Or-gans were used in the Episcopal services from an early date (the first was installed in King's Chapel, Boston, shortly after 1713), and such men as William Selby, who came to Boston from London about 1771 and became organist of King's Chapel, and William Tuckey, who came to New York from Bristol Cathedral in 1753 to become organist and choirmaster at Trinity Church, not only devoted their skill and energies to their church duties but were also active as composers and pro-moters and conductors of choral concerts. Tuckey directed the first American per-formance of excerpts from Handel's Mes-siah in 1770.

Some of the settlements to the south of New England were from their beginnings more musically inclined. In 1694 a group of German pietists founded a colony be-side the Wissahickon River, near Phila-delphia. These people had musical in-struments, and acquired a reputation for their singing. The Swedish Gloria Dei church, also near Philadelphia, had an organ as early as 1703, possibly earlier, and its pastor, Julius Falckner, was the author of several hymns.

The first known composer on American soil, according to present knowledge, was Conrad Beissel (1690–1768), a German mystic and founder of the "Seventh Day Dunkers." He was successively a baker, a violinist, and a theologian, and in 1720 he was banished for holding pietistic views. He emigrated to America and settled first in Germantown, Pennsylvania, where he founded the Dunker sect, and in 1735 established the "Order of the Solitary" and a communistic settlement at Ephrata, Pennsylvania, which became known as the Ephrata Cloister. Here the worshipers sang hymns and chorals in 4, 5, 6, and 7 parts, and it is said that Beissel composed over 1000 of them. Benjamin Franklin published an Ephrata Hymn Collection in 1730.

At Bethlehem, Pennsylvania, a Moravian colony was established in 1741. These people were intense music lovers. They brought instruments with them, and their orchestra, chamber music groups, and choruses performed the best music from Europe — works by Haydn, Mozart, etc. A number of composers among the Moravians wrote for various chamber music combinations. When George Washington visited Bethlehem in 1782 he was serenaded by the trombone choir.

Concert life in the American colonial cities commenced in the 18th century. According to newspaper announcements, the first concert of record was held in Boston in 1731; the second in Charleston, South Carolina, in 1732; the third in New York, 1736; and the fourth in Philadelphia, 1757. From these dates on, each of these cities enjoyed an increasing number of concerts, at which the programs were similar in content to those abroad, particularly in London, from which city the latest published music was sent regularly to America [see *Concert].

Philadelphia has the credit for producing the first native-born American composer of music, according to known records, in the person of Francis Hopkinson (1737–1791), a signer of the Declaration of Independence, Judge of the Admiralty from Pennsylvania, and a talented amateur musician. Hopkinson composed a number of songs in the current English style of Arnold, Shield, Storace, and others. The manuscript of the first of them, "My Days Have Been So Wondrous Free," bears the date 1759. Hop-

kinson's songs, and his musical activities, were characteristic of the taste and the customs of the period. He was one of a group of musical amateurs who met regularly in each other's homes to play together, and who joined with the professional musicians who were beginning to emigrate from abroad in giving public concerts.

The War of the Revolution interrupted musical activities for a number of years, but at its conclusion they began again, and more intensively. In the last fifteen years of the century the nation experienced a wholesale immigration from Europe, bringing musicians from England, and, after the French Revolution, from France. These men were generally well trained, and they accordingly took over the musical life of the new nation and became its principal concert-artists and teachers. The names of the few native composers who had been active up to this time (Hopkinson, James Lyon, Billings, etc.) disappeared almost completely from the concert programs which were printed in the newspapers, and were replaced by those of the newcomers — Benjamin Carr, Alexander Reinagle, James Hewitt, Raynor Taylor, Gottlieb Graupner, and dozens of others. American music doubtless benefited from the infiltration of better-trained musicians, but its growth as a native expression was arrested.

II. *19th Century.* By the early years of the 19th century these foreigners had become Americans, and gradually native-born composers began once more to come into prominence. The most widely known of them was Lowell Mason (1792–1872), a composer of hymn-tunes and a pioneer in music education. Mason succeeded in persuading the Boston school board to make the study of music a regular part of the curriculum (1836) and he established "musical conventions" in various parts of the country where teachers could have training. Another native composer was Oliver Shaw (1779–1848), who, although blind from early manhood, was active as a teacher and organist in Providence, Rhode Island. He was a composer of anthems, songs, and a number of instrumental pieces which were widely used.

By the middle of the century another type of foreigner had gained a foothold in America, the visiting virtuoso who dazzled large audiences with his reputation as well as his skill, and was rewarded with huge monetary returns. Ole Bull paid his first visit to America in 1843, and followed this visit with many others. Jenny Lind came in 1850, and under the management of P. T. Barnum enjoyed triumphs in every American city. One of the virtuosi, the pianist-composer Louis Moreau Gottschalk (1829–1869), was actually a native of New Orleans, but his Parisian training and reputation lent him a foreign atmosphere which helped materially towards his success. He made his American debut in New York in 1853, and from that year until he left the United States for the last time in 1865 (he died in Rio de Janeiro), his recitals in large cities and on tours all the way to California drew large and admiring crowds. As a composer he had a flair for a lightly sentimental type of piece which became enormously popular. His works were marked by a French elegance and a certain American flavor which resulted from his use of Creole melodies. His "Banjo" is based on a Negro-like tune which is closely akin to the spiritual, "Roll, Jordan, Roll." The glamor of such virtuosi led to the idol-worship which has been characteristic of American musical life from the 19th century to the present day, and which has often made it difficult for resident musicians who have not had the benefit of European reputations to secure the place to which the abilities of some entitled them.

Even before 1800 musical societies were founded, and after 1800 several were established which have continued to the present: the Handel & Haydn Society of Boston (1815); the Musical Fund Society of Philadelphia (1820); and the Philharmonic Society of New York (1842). In the mid-century another foreign immigration began which had a profound effect on musical life in America. The Central Europe revolutions of 1848 sent thousands of Germans, many of them musicians, to seek a new home in the United States. As in the closing years of the 18th century, these newcomers were better trained than the native musicians, for they had enjoyed wider advantages in Continental Europe. They settled not only in the seaboard cities, but went inland to settle also in Milwaukee, St. Louis, Cincinnati, and other interior towns, and hundreds of them became the principal orchestral musicians, teachers, and composers of the nation. Thus, for a full half-century, if not longer, the roster of the principal American organizations, orchestras, chamber music groups, and often choral societies, contained a high percentage of names of German origin. Carl Bergmann, Otto Dresel, Carl Zerrahn, the Mollenhauer brothers, and others of like origin were the leaders of American musical life. Even Theodore Thomas, who became the leading musical missionary of the nation by taking his orchestra all over the country, was born in Germany.

This influx of Germans saturated the entire American viewpoint with German ideas and idioms, so that the German composers became the principal models upon which music was composed in the United States. Native students studied at home with teachers of German origin, and to complete their studies, journeyed to Europe to work with German masters. The result was the stultifying of native character and spirit, and the postponement of anything approaching an American expression. The prevalence of the German influence did, however, result in the awakening of a national consciousness on the part of a few Americans who felt keenly that they and their works were neglected.

One of the first of these was a Bohemian by birth, Anthony (Anton) Philip Heinrich (1781–1861), who first came to America shortly before 1820, and after a few months in Philadelphia migrated to Kentucky, where he lived for a while in the comparative wilderness of Bardstown. It was there that he composed his collection of instrumental pieces and works, "The Dawning of Music in Kentucky," to which he appended a statement that he would be proud indeed to be called an "American musician." He died leaving a whole trunkful of manuscripts — grandiose orchestral works — dealing programmatically with American subjects, including the American Indian and such scenic marvels as Niagara Falls. A number of his smaller pieces were published, but he and his admirers felt that he was never accorded the place to which he was entitled.

Another to protest violently against alleged discrimination in favor of foreigners was William Henry Fry (1813–64), a music critic and composer who lived first in Philadelphia and later in New York. Fry composed the first American grand opera to be produced, *Leonora* (Philadelphia, 1845, and New York, 1858), and a second opera, *Notre Dame de Paris* (1864), as well as a Santa Claus symphony and numerous other works. He was militant in his struggle for recognition of American talent and declared that "until the American public shall learn to support American artists, Art will not become indigenous to this country" (1852). One of Fry's companions in arms was George F. Bristow (1825–98), also the composer of an opera (*Rip van Winkle*, 1855 and revived in 1870), and a number of orchestral works. He was also a violinist and a member of the New York Philharmonic, who resigned temporarily from that organization in protest against its neglect of American works.

Concurrent with this early and somewhat premature awakening of a national consciousness in the realm of art music was another movement which was largely overlooked by serious musicians. This was the development of a lighter type of entertainment which was typically American: the minstrel show which caricatured the humor and sentiment of the American Negro. The songs which the minstrel shows produced were not Negro songs nor were they connected primarily with the Negro's own folk music, but they did embody a carefree attitude, and a nostalgic sentiment which had their basis in the Negro character. The most lasting prod-

ucts of this field were the songs of Stephen Foster (1826–64), whose "Old Folks at Home," "Oh! Susanna," and dozens of others have become literally American folk songs. In Foster's time, however, these songs were regarded as nothing more than popular songs of the day, even though they embodied a far more typically American expression than the ambitious efforts of other composers to write symphonies in the manner of the German Romanticists.

In the latter 19th century an increasing number of native-born composers of art music appeared, and their works began to be included on the programs of major concert organizations. The first to come into lasting prominence was John Knowles Paine (1839–1906) whose first symphony was performed by the Theodore Thomas Orchestra in 1876, and who by 1899 had seen eighteen performances of his compositions by the Boston Symphony Orchestra alone. Paine studied at home, and in Germany with Haupt, and his works bear the German stamp and a solid, academic workmanship which may have lacked individuality, but which rendered them technically far in advance of anything that had been composed in America earlier. His major published works included two symphonies, two symphonic poems, and an opera. Of equal importance to his work as a composer, was Paine's influence as a teacher. In 1862 he was appointed instructor of music at Harvard and in 1873 was made a full professor, a chair he held for thirty years. His pupils included men who took their place among America's leading composers: Arthur Foote (1853–1937), Frederick S. Converse (1871–1940), John Alden Carpenter (b. 1876), Daniel Gregory Mason (b. 1873), and many others. In addition to launching his own pupils on successful careers, Paine was the artistic parent of a coterie of composers which became known as the "Boston," or "New England Group," so called because its members either derived from New England by birth or residence, or because they had the same ideals in common. They were academic in the German tradition.

but all of them had solid training and something definite to say musically. Besides Foote, the group included George W. Chadwick (1854–1931), Horatio Parker (1863–1919), Arthur Whiting (1861–1936), Mrs. H. H. A. Beach (1867–1944), Edgar Stillman Kelley (1857–1944), and others. Chadwick and Parker were perhaps the most distinguished of the set. Chadwick's work was marked by expert craftsmanship and had also a Yankee humor which gave it something of an American flavor. Musically, Parker's opera *Mona*, produced at the Metropolitan in New York in 1912, was the most effective of any American opera to date, and his oratorio, *Hora Novissima*, became standard in the repertoire of choral societies in America and in England.

Contemporary with the Boston group, but set apart from them because of his striking individuality, was Edward MacDowell (1861–1908), who, with the possible exception of Gottschalk, was the first American composer to achieve a foreign reputation. In spite of his Germanic training under Raff, MacDowell had a style that was distinctly his own, a Celtic boldness which derived, perhaps, from his Scotch ancestry. Like Grieg, he had his individual melodic and harmonic idiom, which imposed its own limitations when it became a mannerism. Although he is heard today chiefly through his piano pieces, his larger works are still performed, particularly the second Piano Concerto and the Second, "Indian," Suite for orchestra. MacDowell is still regarded by many as the outstanding American composer, because of his marked individuality and because of the vogue his music has enjoyed. The national consciousness, which had its origin in the middle of the last century, received an added impetus from the extended visit of the Bohemian Antonín Dvořák, who taught at the National Conservatory in New York from 1892 to 1895. Dvořák was deeply impressed by the native folk-material he heard in America, and urged his pupils to make use of it. He incorporated the spirit of Negro and Indian songs, if not actual melodies, into several works of his own, notably the "New World" Symphony and the American Quartet. It is true that Dvořák did not achieve an American expression in these works, he was too much of a Bohemian for that, but he did succeed in firing the imagination of American composers, and by his example persuaded many of them to look to their own soil for a national expression.

III. *20th Century*. The 20th century has witnessed a marked change in American music. Where there were dozens of composers in the latter 19th century, there are hundreds now. American composers have also had increasing opportunity for performance and publication of their major works, owing to considerable propaganda urging program-makers to promote native music and the public to demand it. It is, of course, not only the propaganda that has led to this change; it is also the tremendously increasing quantity and vastly improved quality of American compositions. Not only are there thousands of available compositions where a half, or even a quarter, of a century ago there were merely hundreds; the music itself is composed with craftsmanship and polished technique, and in countless cases it has something to say which has not already been said by older composers from abroad.

It is difficult to classify American composers into groups, for many of them have attempted work in a number of fields, and their styles and idioms have changed as they themselves have developed and progressed. There are composers who have remained conservative, and some who are looked upon by the radicals as conservative but who have nevertheless shown contemporary tendencies and seem modernistic to the layman who is accustomed only to traditional music. Among those who have never departed appreciably from 19th-century idioms are the late Henry Hadley (1871–1937), who composed prolifically and successfully in all forms and whose works were marked by a facility that was felicitous and stimulating; Deems Taylor (b. 1885), probably the best known of all American composers to the layman, whose operas, *The King's Henchman* and *Peter Ibbetson*, enjoyed a large number of performances for several seasons at the Metropolitan in New York; Charles Wakefield Cadman (b. 1881) who has written ballad-songs which have ranked with Broadway hits in popularity, and has also been active in the larger forms: several operas (including *Shanewis*), and a considerable list of orchestral works; the late Rubin Goldmark (1872–1936), a teacher of composers as well as a composer himself; and Walter Damrosch (b. 1862), who is more important as a conductor and musical missionary.

A number of composers have adopted contemporary methods in part, but have not departed far enough from accepted idioms to encounter resistance from the public. Among them are Carpenter, D. G. Mason, and Converse (already mentioned as pupils of J. K. Paine), Edward Burlingame Hill (b. 1872), Howard Hanson (b. 1896), director of the Eastman School of Music at Rochester, David Stanley Smith (b. 1877), Douglas Moore (b. 1893), and Randall Thompson (b. 1899).

Slightly further to the left, in that they have written in styles which have been a little more advanced than the average audience was ready to accept, are the late Charles Martin Loeffler (1861–1935), an Alsatian-born violinist-composer whose "Pagan Poem" is one of the most striking works composed in this country; Charles T. Griffes (1884–1920); Roy Harris (b. 1898), an Oklahoman by birth whose works represent an altogether national expression in seeming to derive from the vast spaces of the Southwest; Aaron Copland (b. 1900), more sophisticated and practical than Harris but inherently a valid American product; Roger Sessions (b. 1896) and Walter Piston (b. 1894), both champions of the "international" school of thought [see *Nationalism]; Quincy Porter (b. 1897); the Holland-born Bernard Wagenaar (b. 1894) and the German-born Werner Josten (b. 1888); Arthur Shepherd (b. 1880); Otto

Luening (b. 1900); and Ernst Bacon (b. 1898).

America has also its share of experimentalists. Among them are Charles Ives (b. 1876), for many years unrecognized by all but a few, and recently come into prominence through the performance of his Concord Sonata for piano. Ives delights in polytonal combinations and in complex rhythms, and has also experimented in quarter-tones. Henry Cowell (b. 1897) has sought a scientific basis in overtones for "tone-clusters." Adolph Weiss (b. 1891) and Wallingford Riegger (b. 1885) are avowed atonalists. Less radical, perhaps, than the others is Carl Ruggles (b. 1876), but the quality in his music that Lawrence Gilman characterized as "torrential and disturbing" places him in the experimental group.

Recent additions to the list of American composers include younger men of considerable talent and individuality, notably Samuel Barber (b. 1910), Leonard Bernstein (b. 1918), Paul Bowles (b. 1911), Paul Creston (b. 1906), David Diamond (b. 1915), Bernard Herrmann (b. 1911), Gail T. Kubik (b. 1914), Gian-Carlo Menotti (b. 1911), Paul Nordoff (b. 1909), Gardner Read (b. 1913), and William Schumann (b. 1910).

IV. *National Elements.* The movement toward using folk music which Dvořák instigated at the turn of the century had its inevitable reaction. Composers, and the public, found that a conscious and wholesale adoption of folk material did not in itself bring a national expression, particularly when the composers themselves were not of the same race as those who produced the folk songs originally. There have, however, been many excellent works based on native material, and a number of composers have been closely identified with its use. Charles Sanford Skilton (1868–1941) composed some strikingly effective Indian dances based on tribal melodies; John Powell's (b. 1882) Rhapsodie Nègre not only uses actual Negro melodies but reflects certain phases of the Negro's temperament. Powell has also used Anglo-Saxon material from the Appalachians. Percy Grainger

(Australia, b. 1882) has not only made exquisite settings of British folk songs, but has turned to American material since making his home in this country. Lamar Stringfield (b. 1897), a native of North Carolina, has made distinctive use of Southern material, from the Negroes and from the white mountaineers.

There are also many Negro composers who have been eloquent interpreters of their race. Among the older ones are Harry T. Burleigh (b. 1866) who was one of the first to make effective concert-settings of Negro spirituals, R. Nathaniel Dett (1882–1943), and Clarence C. White (b. 1880). Somewhat younger than these men are William Levi Dawson (b. 1895), and William Grant Still (b. 1895). See *Negro music.

Americans are now coming to realize that their less pretentious music, the so-called popular songs and dance music, has distinctive qualities which have given it a vogue throughout the world; in its best phases this music represents a typically national expression. From an earlier century the songs of Stephen Foster typified several features of American life — its humor, its sentiment, and the flavor of its Southern plantations. The marches of John Philip Sousa (1854–1932) had a verve and sparkle which set them apart from the common run of such pieces, while the quasi-Viennese melodies of the Victor Herbert (1859–1924) operettas possessed at least a cosmopolitanism which was characteristic of American urban life.

More important than these is the body of popular music which has for its basis the peculiar type of syncopation that has been borrowed from the Negro — the early ragtime of the 1890's and the later "jazz" and the still more recent improvised "swing" music. These have not only developed highly ingenious and complex rhythmic patterns, but have also evolved instrumentations which are often used by concert orchestras as well as by dance bands. The effect of this jazz vogue has been twofold. First, it has offered serious composers of art music a field for experimentation which has often been produc-

tive of excellent results. Carpenter, Copland, Louis Gruenberg (b. 1884), and dozens of others have found it a rewarding field, even though they have come to turn away from it because of its rather rigid limitations. In Europe, too, a number of composers have tried their hand at American jazz: Stravinsky, Křenek, Milhaud, Hindemith, Honegger, and many others [see *Jazz VI].

The other result of jazz has been that a number of composers who started their careers as composers of dance music and musical comedy scores have extended their efforts to the concert and grand-opera field. The outstanding member of this group is the late George Gershwin (1898–1937), who first became a most successful composer for Broadway shows and then drew the attention of critics and the music public with his Rhapsody in Blue, for piano and orchestra. This was followed by a Piano Concerto and a tone-poem, An American in Paris, and finally by the opera, Porgy and Bess. A number of our serious composers have derived from the popular field by acting as orchestrators of musical comedy and motion picture scores — Robert Russell Bennett (b. 1894), William Grant Still, and Otto Cesana (b. 1899). Morton Gould (b. 1913) has been associated with Broadway and the radio as a conductor, and has produced a long list of major works, which, like his Chorale and Fugue in Jazz, apply musical training to popular materials.

The result of this union of music-hall and dance music with art music has been extremely healthy. It has done much to rid the concert field of its self-conscious complacency and intolerance, and it has without doubt raised the standards of popular music, even though it has made some of it over-sophisticated and a bit self-conscious. It has, moreover, done much to make American music a native product, independent of Europe, and it provides American composers with a vehicle which represents a number of the highly intricate and varied phases of the American temperament. It is not, of course, the only type of music which is inherently American, nor does it cover all of the manifold facets of American life. Nevertheless, the adoption of popular elements which are in some ways a folk-spirit which characterizes Americans everywhere, rather than a single race or group, is a highly significant step in the evolution of a distinctively American music.

Lit.: J. T. Howard, *Our American Music* (1931); *id.*, *Our Contemporary Composers* (1941); Henry Cowell, *American Composers on American Music* (1933); Clare Reis, *Composers in America* (1938); W. T. Upton, *Art-Song in America* (1930–1938); W. Saunders, "The American Opera" (*ML* xiii, no. 2); O. G. Sonneck, "Early American Operas" (*SIM* vi); C. Lindstrom, "Wm. Billings and His Time" (*MQ* xxv); O. G. Sonneck, "Francis Hopkinson" (*SIM* v). See also under *Jazz, *Negro music.

J. T. H.

American Musicological Society. See *Societies, I, 2.

American organ. See *Harmonium.

Amorevole, amoroso [It.]. Loving.

Amorschall. See *Horn II.

Amphibrach [Gr.]. See *Poetic meter I.

Amplitude. See *Acoustics I.

Anabole [Gr., beginning]. *Humanistic (16th-century) name for *prelude.

Anacrusis. Upbeat.

Analysis. With reference to music, the study of a composition with regard to form, structure, thematic material, harmony, melody, phrasing, orchestration, style, technique, etc. Analysis of composition plays a predominant part in musical instruction (as a practical application of technical studies in harmony, counterpoint, orchestration) and in writings on music. Analysis is of little value if it is mere enumeration of statistics; such methods, frequently encountered in modern writings, overlook the synthetic element and the functional significance of the musical detail. Another drawback of cur-

rent methods is the one-sided application of only one point of view, for instance, that of form (D. F. Tovey, *Beethoven's Pianoforte Sonatas*) or of phrasing (H. Riemann, *Analyse von Beethoven's Klaviersonaten*). In present-day education special emphasis is placed on analysis of harmony [see *Harmonic analysis] and of form [see *Form]; melodic analysis, however, perhaps the most important and most informative of all, is usually neglected [see *Melody].

Lit.: A. J. Goodrich, *Complete Musical Analysis* (1887); K. Westphal, in *DM* xxiv, 5.

Anapaest. See *Poetic meter I.

Anche [F.], **Ancia** [It.]. *Reed. *Anche battante*, beating reed; *anche double*, double reed; *anche libre*, free reed.

Ancora [It.]. Once more (repeat). *Ancora più forte*, still more forte.

Ancus. See *Neumes I.

Andamento [It., from *andare*, to go] means, in 18th-century writings: (1) *Sequence. — (2) A special type of fugal subject [see *Soggetto]. — (3) In more recent writings the term is used preferably to denote fugal episodes.

Andante [It., from *andare*, to go]. Tempo mark indicating very moderate speed, between allegretto and adagio [see *Tempo marks]. To the present day there is no agreement among musicians as to whether andante belongs to the quick or to the slow tempo. While this question as such would seem to be rather irrelevant, it becomes important in the case of terms such as più andante, meno andante, molto andante, andantino. According to the former interpretation, which is supported by the literal meaning of the word, più andante and molto andante indicate a tempo quicker than the normal andante, while meno andante indicates a slower speed. Brahms was undoubtedly aware of this meaning of the term when, at the end of his andante from the pianoforte sonata op. 5, he wrote "andante molto"; the tempo of this closing section is, of course, quicker, not slower, than that of the preceding andante espressivo. Other composers however (perhaps the majority) use molto andante to mean a tempo still slower than andante. See *Andantino.

Andantino. Diminutive of andante, used mainly to characterize a short piece of andante tempo or character. If used as a tempo mark, it means a slight modification of andante the direction of which is, unfortunately, a matter of divergent opinion [see *Andante]. Beethoven was puzzled by the question whether andantino was to be understood as meaning faster or slower than andante, as appears from a letter he wrote to George Thomson [cf. A. W. Thayer, *The Life of Beethoven*, ed. by Krehbiel, 1921, ii, 246]. Most modern musicians apparently use the term as indicating quicker tempo than andante.

Andauernd [G.]. "Lasting," continuously.

Anemochord. See under *Aeolian harp; *Sostenente pianoforte.

Anenaiki. The term refers to an abusive treatment of Russian (*Znamenny) chant, practiced chiefly in the 16th and 17th centuries, in which long coloraturas in bad taste were sung to meaningless syllables such as a-ne-na. This method was known as *chomonie*. A similar method used in the Byzantine chant of the same period is known as *teretism*, owing to the use of such syllables as te-re-rem for the same purpose. The Russian syllables are probably related to the early Byzantine enechamata [see *Echos]. They appear in a manuscript as early as the 12th century [cf. the reference in *ReMMA*, 99]. See also *Noeane.

Anfang [G.]. Beginning; *Vom Anfang*, da capo.

Angelica. See *Lute III.

Angklung. See *Javanese music I.

Anglaise [Fr., English dance]. One of the numerous dance types used in the

French ballets of the late 17th century, whence it was introduced into the optional group of the suite [cf. J. K. F. Fischer, *Musikalischer Parnassus* (*c.* 1690); J. S. Bach, French Suite no. 3]. It is in quick duple time, without upbeat. The name was also used for other dances of English origin or character, e.g., for the (syncopated) *hornpipe and, around 1800, for the *country dance and the *écossaise. See *Dance music III.

Anglican chant. The method employed in the Anglican Church for the singing of the psalms, canticles, and other unmetrical texts. It is based on the recitation principle of the *psalm tones of the Roman Catholic Church but differs from these — aside from the English text — in the use of four-part harmony and of a more strictly metrical rhythm.

The practice of using harmonized versions of the psalm tones, known as *falsobordone*, was quite common in the 16th century (Josquin des Pres, Vittoria, and many others). The first English composers to harmonize the psalm tones were Tallis, Byrd, Morley, and Gibbons, who were followed by many others. Naturally, within the course of its 400 years of living existence, the chant has undergone many changes which, generally speaking, have not improved its quality. The earliest settings, although sacrificing the primal simplicity of the monophonic chant, did not impair its validity as a rhythmically free agent for the conveyance of the text because they did not alter the free oratoric rhythm of the plainsong.

It was in the late 17th century that rhythm, in the categorical sense, began to condition the free and expressive delivery of the words in chanting. Bar-lines emphasized the metrical quality of the rendition and the generally mechanical nature of the practice was not helped in later times by the adoption of specially composed chants often accompanied by harmonizations of mediocre quality. It is these metrical chants which are called Anglican and which supply the needs of many modern Protestant congregations. Ideally treated, Anglican chanting may be impressive to a certain degree, but it contains four defects which render it definitely inferior to its plainsong analogue. First, it is written with bar-lines enclosing measures of theoretically equal length; thus one measure may suffice for the singing of four or five words and the next may have to accommodate twelve or fifteen, so that the inevitable tendency is to rush the verbally crowded measures to make their length conform to the others. However much this tendency may be resisted, the tyranny of the bar-line cannot be wholly ignored. Secondly it has been customary to employ a system of "pointing" in the text whereby certain syllables or words over which appeared the sign (') served as a momentary point of stress or rest. While this device may have fulfilled the practical purpose of producing occasional unity amid verbal confusion, it tended to make the congregation hurry over the preceding words to dwell to an unnatural degree on the pointed word or syllable. Later hymnals have abandoned pointing in an effort to restore as nearly as possible the flexibility of the Plainsong Chant. Third, many Anglican chants contain equal notes of smaller value, and these, sung in strict time, further distort the flow of the text. And fourth, the invariable ending of the chant on a strong beat often leads to downright misaccentuation.

Anglican chant represents a relatively unsuccessful effort to carry over into a workable congregational method the ideal conditions belonging to plainsong; and in spite of devoted and skillful efforts at improvement, the two systems remain fundamentally irreconcilable because the Anglican represents a practice in which the accents of the prose are dictated by an arbitrary metrical scheme, while in plainsong the rhythmic sweep of the music is governed by the normal speech delivery of the text. At its best, Anglican chanting is a compromise; at its worst, it suggests the recitativo secco of 18th-century opera which provided for the disposal of large quantities of words in as short a space of time as possible. Contrasting examples of Anglican (1) and

Plainchant (2) drawn from *The New Hymnal* appear below.

Lit.: W. Douglas, *Church Music in History and Practice* (1937); P. Scholes, *The Oxford Companion to Music* (1938), article "Anglican Chant"; A. Ramsbotham, in *ML* i, no. 3; R. Bridges, in *MA* ii, iii; W. Barclay-Squire, in *SIM* viii; Ch. W. Pearce, "The Futility of Anglican Chant" (*MQ* vi).   A. T. D.

Anglican church music. See Anglican chant; Anthem; Cathedral music; Hymn IV; Litany; Psalter; Response; Service. Cf. *The Church Service Book*, ed. by G. Edward Stubbs (1906).

Angosciamente; con angore [It.]. With anxiety.

Anhalten [G.]. To hold on.

Anhang [G.]. *Coda.

Anhemitonic [Gr., without semitones]. An anhemitonic scale (also called tonal scale) is one which possesses no semitones, e.g., the *pentatonic scale c-d-f-g-a-c', or the *whole-tone scale.

Animato [It.], **animé** [F.]. Animated.

Anmutig [G.]. Gracefully.

Anonymous [Gr., without name]. Of unknown authorship. The Latin word

Anonymus (abbreviated *Anon.*) is applied to unknown writers of medieval treatises in the collections of Gerbert and Coussemaker [see *Scriptores], in which they are referred to as Anon. I, Anon. II, etc. It should be noticed, however, that the same numbering occurs in several volumes of Coussemaker and Gerbert. Therefore, the famous treatise known as Coussemaker's *Anon. IV* should more accurately be referred to as *Anon. IV* of Coussemaker i (*CS* i).

Anreissen [G.]. Forceful *pizzicato*.

Ansatz [G.]. (1) In singing, the proper adjustment of the vocal apparatus. — (2) In the playing of wind instruments, the proper adjustment of the lips [see *Embouchure (2)]. — (3) *Crook or shank of brass instruments. — (4) In violin playing, *attack.

Anschlag [G.]. (1) In piano playing, touch. — (2) Of a pianoforte, action (heavy or light). — (3) An ornament explained by K. P. E. Bach [see *Appoggiatura, Double III].

Anschwellend [G.]. Crescendo.

Anstrich [G.]. Up-bow.

Answer. In fugal writing the answer is the second (and fourth) statement of the subject, so called because of its relationship to the first (and third) statement. Therefore, the succession of statements is subject-answer-subject-answer. See *Fugue; *Tonal and real; *Antecedent and consequent.

Antecedent and consequent. The terms are usually applied to melodic phrases which stand in the relationship of question and answer or statement and confirmation, as in the accompanying example (Beethoven, String Quartet op. 18,

no. 2). Here, as in other examples, the dialogue character of the melody is emphasized by its distribution between two instruments [see *Durchbrochene Ar-*

beit]. The terms are also used as synonymous with subject and answer in fugues [see *Answer].

Anthem [from Gr. *antiphona*; Romanic *antefena*; Old English *antefn, antempne*]. An English choral composition written to English words from the Scriptures or to another sacred text and performed in the worship of the Anglican Church, where it holds a position similar to that of the *motet in the Roman rites. An anthem usually is with accompaniment, preferably by the organ. If it includes parts for solo singers it is called verse anthem; otherwise, full anthem.

The history of the anthem begins with the Reformation and the consequent establishment of English as the liturgical language. Although the anthem developed from the Latin motet, the first anthems, written by Tye and Tallis (*c.* 1560), show a marked difference in style from the previous and contemporary motets. They are rhythmically square, more harmonically conceived, more syllabic and in shorter phrases, features all of which result from the greater consideration given to matters of text and pronunciation. Towards the end of the 16th century a new form, the *verse anthem*, was introduced by Byrd (regarding an isolated earlier example, by Richard Farrant, cf. G. E. P. Arkwright, in *MA* i, p. 65 note) and developed by Orlando Gibbons [cf. *HAM*, nos. 151, 169, 171]. This form, in which sections for full chorus alternate with sections for one or more solo voices, was preferred throughout the 17th century, with the full anthem coming into prominence again in the subsequent period. While in the Elizabethan anthem the vocal part (or parts) of the verse-sections are contrapuntally conceived (i.e., as parts of a contrapuntal fabric the other voices of which are played on the organ), a new declamatory arioso-style of Italian origin [see *Monody] was introduced for the verse-sections around 1630, in the anthems of Monteverdi's pupil Walter Porter (*c.* 1595–1659; cf. Arkwright, in *MA* iv, 247) and, particularly, of William Child (1606–97; cf. the list of his anthems in *GD* i, 623; example in *OH* iii, 206). The Restoration anthem is represented by Henry Aldrich (1647–1710), Pelham Humphrey (1647–74), Michael Wise (1648–87), John Blow (1649–1708; cf. *GD* i, 396), Henry Purcell (1659–95), and Jeremiah Clarke (1659–1707). Blow and Purcell introduced instruments into the anthem, an innovation by which the multi-sectional anthem came to resemble a cantata. Another characteristic feature of the Restoration anthem, adopted in numerous later works, is a concluding hallelujah chorus in fugal style. The use of two choruses, called *Dec(ani)* and *Can(toris)* prevails in the anthem as well as in the Service music [see *Polychoral].

The Baroque anthem reached its highpoint in the grandiose anthems of Handel, nearly all of which were written for special festive occasions where an unusual display of means was possible and proper (Chandos Anthems, 1716–18; Coronation Anthems, 1727; Dettingen Anthem, 1743). Other composers of this period are William Croft (1678–1727), John Weldon (1676–1736), and Maurice Greene (1695–1755). Their anthems, as well as those of William Boyce (1710–79; cf. *GD* i, 441), are modeled after the somewhat simpler style of Purcell. The outstanding figure of the 19th century was S. S. Wesley (1810–76) whose two volumes of anthems, published in 1853, contain such standard works as "Blessed be the God and Father" and "The Wilderness." Among the more recent composers Ch. V. Stanford (1852–1924), B. Harwood (b. 1859), and Martin Shaw (b. 1875) must be mentioned.

Lit.: W. Davies, †*The Church Anthem Book* (1933); M. B. Foster, *Anthem and Anthem Composers* (1901); H. W. Shaw, "John Blow's Anthems" (*ML* xix. no. 4).

Anticipation. See *Nonharmonic tones I; also *Nachschlag.

Antienne [F.]. (1) *Antiphon. — (2) *Anthem.

Antiphon. A term denoting various categories of Gregorian chant, all of which are remnants of the early method of an-

tiphonal psalmody [see below, *History*].

(1) Short texts from the Scriptures or elsewhere, set to music in a simple, syllabic style, and sung before and after a psalm cr canticle. On greater feasts the antiphon is sung entire both before and after the psalm; at other times the first word or two only (*Incipit) are sung before, and the whole after. For more details, see under *Psalm tones. The present repertory of Gregorian chant includes more than 1000 such antiphons. The melodies are not all different, and can be classified in about 40 groups of closely allied chants [cf. F. A. Gévaert, *La Mélopée antique dans le chant de l'église latine* (1895)]. Aside from the antiphons for the psalms, there are similar enframing melodies for the *canticles, particularly the *Magnificat and the Benedictus Deus Dominus. These are somewhat more elaborate textually as well as musically [cf., e.g., *AR*, 541ff].

(2) The name antiphon is also used for two other types of chants which are not strictly antiphons, since they do not, as a rule, embrace a psalm or canticle but are independent songs of considerable length and elaboration. The first of these types includes the antiphons which at certain feasts (e.g., Palm Sunday) are sung preparatory to the Mass (Mass antiphon). They are usually of a narrative character, containing reports from the New Testament referring to the occasion, e.g.: "Cum appropinquaret Dominus Jerosolymam..." for Palm Sunday [cf. *GR*, 159ff]. The second class of pseudo-antiphons is the four antiphons B.M.V. (Beatae Mariae Virginis) or B.V.M. (Blessed Virgin Mary), namely: *Alma redemptoris mater*; *Ave regina coelorum*; *Regina coeli laetare*; *Salve regina* [cf. *AR*, 65–69]. These are more in the style of early hymns in free meter. They are sung during four different seasons of the year, at the offices of Lauds and Compline, by alternating choirs [see *Salve regina]. In the 15th and 16th centuries they were frequently composed polyphonically, for voices or for organ [cf. *HAM*, nos. 65, 100, 139].

(3) While the chants mentioned above are the only ones called antiphons in the liturgical books of the present day, the

name is also applied in historical studies to certain chants of the Mass itself, namely, the *Introit (introit antiphon, *antiphona ad introitum*), the *Offertory (*antiphona ad offerendum*), and the *Communion (communion antiphon, *antiphona ad communionem*). The justification for this terminology lies in the fact that these chants originally sprang from the same method of antiphonal psalmody which also survives, in a different form, in the antiphons embracing a psalm or a canticle [see *Psalmody].

History. In Greek theory, *antiphonia* (literally counter-sound) means the octave, in contradistinction to *symphonia*, the unison, and *paraphonia*, the fifth. In the early Christian rites, antiphonia came to denote the singing of the successive verses of a psalm by alternating choruses. This meaning of the term probably originated in the fact that the second chorus originally consisted of women or boys who repeated the melody at the higher octave. Very early antiphonal psalm-singing was enriched by the addition of a short sentence sung by the whole choir and repeated after each verse or pair of verses as a refrain. It was this additional text and melody which finally came to adopt and retain the name antiphon. For a survey of the various forms which sprang from the antiphonal psalmody, see *Psalmody III; also *Gregorian chant IV(c).

Antiphonal singing. Singing (or playing) in alternating choruses. The term, which originally belongs to the parlance of plainsong [see *Antiphon, history], is also used with reference to polyphonic music composed in two choruses. See *polychoral style. Regarding the use of antiphonal singing in Gregorian chant see *Responsorial.

Antiphonal, antiphoner, antiphonary [L. *Antiphonale, Antiphonarium*]. See *Liturgical books. The name *Antiphonarium Mediceum* is erroneously applied to the MS Florence, Bibl. Laur. *plut.* 29, *1* which actually is not a book of plainsong, but the most extensive collection of the polyphonic repertory of the School of

*Notre Dame (*c.* 1200). See *Magnus liber organi*.

Antiphonia. In Greek theory, the octave. See *Antiphon, history.

Antwort [G.]. Answer, in fugues.

Anvil. Small steel bars, struck with a hard wooden or metal beater, which have sometimes been used as a percussion instrument in operas, usually as a stage property (Auber, *Le Maçon*, 1825; Verdi, *Il Trovatore*; Wagner, *Rheingold*).

Anwachsend [G.]. Crescendo.

A piacere [It.]. Same as *a bene placito.

Apollo Club. A name given to American male singing organizations, generally amateur, corresponding to the French *Orphéon and the German *Männergesangverein. Remarkable for their higher ambitions are the Apollo Clubs of Boston (founded in 1871), of Brooklyn (1878), of Chicago (1872), of Cincinnati (1882), and of St. Louis (1893). Some of the clubs were expanded into a mixed chorus.

Apollonicon. See *Mechanical instruments III.

Apostropha. See *Neumes I.

Apotome. See *Pythagorean scale.

Appassionata, or **Sonata appassionata** [It., impassioned]. The name customarily given to Beethoven's Piano Sonata op. 57, in F minor. The title was not his, but was added by some publisher. The original title is "Grande Sonate pour Piano" (1806).

Appena [It.]. Hardly, scarcely.

Applicatur. Eighteenth-century German term for fingering.

Appoggiando [It.]. "Leaning," i.e., emphasized, also full legato.

Appoggiatura [from It. *appoggiare*, to lean on]. (1) In modern parlance, an important type of nonharmonic tones [see *Nonharmonic tones II].

(2) Originally, appoggiatura [F. *port de voix*; E. forefall, backfall, half-fall; G. *Vorschlag*] is an ornamental note, usually a second, that is melodically connected with the main note that follows it (i.e., the appoggiatura is sung in the same breath or played with the same stroke of the bow or articulation of the tongue or, in the case of keyboard instruments, slurred to that following note). It is indicated by means of a small note or special sign, but was also frequently introduced extemporaneously in performance. The interpretation of the appoggiatura has varied considerably since the 17th century, when it first became a conventionalized ornament.

I. In the Baroque period the appoggiatura was exceedingly flexible as regards both notation and rhythmic execution. In Ex. 1, A shows the various ways of indi-

cating the appoggiatura, and B the methods of performance that were prevalent around 1700. The choice between these interpretations was left to the discretion of the performer — a "discretion," however, which was not haphazard but was governed by rules (based upon the conduct of the melody and other parts, the tempo and phrasing of the passage in question, and the expression of the accompanying text) that were formulated in textbooks (e.g., Bacilly: *Remarques curieuses sur l'art de bien chanter*, 1668) and taught to every student of performance. With the exception of (a) and (b), which are exclusively French, these interpretations were taken over by musicians of all nationalities. They are valid for the performance of

music by J. S. Bach, Handel, Purcell, D. Scarlatti, etc. Ex. 2 illustrates the application of these principles to the music of J. S. Bach (a: Kleine zweistimmige Fuge c-moll; b: Goldberg Variations, aria; c: St. Matthew Passion, Bass aria no. 66; d: Sinfonia no. 3). See also *Appuy; *Port de voix.

II. After 1750 the performance of the appoggiatura was systematized by the German teachers and writers, K. P. E. Bach, Leopold Mozart, Marpurg, and Türk. The ornament is now divided into two types: the long, or variable appoggiatura (*veränderlicher Vorschlag*), and the short appoggiatura (*kurtzer Vorschlag*), both of which are to be performed upon the beat. The duration of the long appoggiatura is proportionate to that of the main note with which it is connected, according to the following rules: (a) If the main note can be divided into two equal parts the appoggiatura takes half its value; (b) an appoggiatura to a dotted note takes two thirds of its value; (c) in $\frac{6}{8}$ or $\frac{6}{4}$-meter an appoggiatura to a dotted note that is tied to another note takes the whole value of the dotted

note; (d) if the main note is followed by a rest, the appoggiatura takes the whole value of the main note, the latter is played in the time of the rest, and the rest ceases to exist. In Ex. 3 these four rules are illustrated by quotations from the works of

Mozart and Beethoven (a: Mozart, Piano Sonata K.V. 311; Beethoven, Piano Sonata op. 2, no. 1, Menuetto; b: Mozart, Piano Sonata K.V. 332; c: Mozart, Piano Sonata K.V. 332; d: Beethoven, Adelaide).

The short appoggiatura should be performed as a short note, regardless of the duration of the main note. It is to be used only in the following circumstances: (a) when the main note is itself an appoggiatura (i.e., a non-harmonic note occurring on the beat); (b) when the main note accompanies a suspension or syncopation; (c) when the appoggiatura fills up the intervals in a series of descending thirds; (d) when the main note is a short note that is followed by more notes of the same value; (e) when the main note is one of a series of reiterated notes [see Ex. 4 (a: C. P. E. Bach; Beethoven, Piano Sonata op. 2, no. 3; b: C. P. E. Bach; c: Mozart, Piano Sonata K.V. 279; d: Beethoven, Piano Sonata op. 22, Menuetto; e: Mozart, Piano Sonata K.V. 627)].

The notation of the appoggiatura, in this period, has no definite relationship to its performance. A few composers wrote the long appoggiatura as a small note of the exact value in which it should be performed, and distinguished the short appoggiatura from it by means of a single stroke across the stem (for a 16th-note) or a double stroke (for a 32nd-note), but this practice was by no means consistently carried out. In music by C. P. E. Bach, Gluck, Haydn, Mozart, Beethoven, the rules given above constitute a far surer guide to performance than does the physical appearance of the ornament, even in the most reliable editions. For an 18th-century practice of improvised appoggiatura, see *Ornamentation I.

III. The 19th century brings still further changes in the treatment of the appoggiatura. The long appoggiatura becomes absorbed in the ordinary notation. The short appoggiatura is now invariably indicated by a small note with a single stroke across its stem, called a *grace note* or (erroneously) an *acciaccatura*. The question now arises whether this grace note should be performed on the beat or in anticipation

of the beat. The latter possibility had already been admitted by some of the late 18th-century authorities (who referred to it as a *durchgehender Vorschlag*, distinct from both the *langer* and the *kurtzer Vorschlag*) for certain exceptional circumstances. After 1800 this execution becomes decidedly more popular; it seems to be indicated for most of the grace notes in the works of Chopin, Schumann, Brahms, etc. (Schumann often prescribes it, by placing the grace note before the bar-line), but lack of material evidence leaves the matter open to controversy in many cases. In modern music it is customary to snap the grace note sharply onto the following note, so that it slightly anticipates the beat and imparts a decided accent to the main note. See *Ornamentation; *Ornaments.

P. A.

Appoggiatura, Double. The term double appoggiatura has been applied to each of the three distinct ways in which two appoggiaturas can be used: I. two appoggiaturas performed simultaneously, at the interval of a third or sixth; II. two con-

junct appoggiaturas approaching the main note from the interval of a third above or below it; III. two disjunct appoggiaturas, one being placed below the main note, the other above it.

I. Little need be said of the simultaneous double appoggiatura save that each of its components is performed as though the other were not present, as in Ex. 1 (Bach, French Suite in Eb, Sarabande).

II. The conjunct double appoggiatura, or *slide*, was a common *agrément in the 17th and 18th centuries. The 17th-century English lutenists and viol players referred to the ascending slide as an *elevation* or *whole fall* and called the descending slide a *double backfall*. The signs and execution of these ornaments are illustrated in Examples 2 and 3. Their German equivalent is the *Schleifer*, which is indicated, in

the music of the Baroque period, either by a *custos* (*direct) or two grace notes [Ex. 4]. It should always be played on the beat.

The *punctierter Schleifer*, or dotted slide, is a complicated ornament very popular with the Rococo composers, between 1750 and 1780. Its performance is shown in Ex. 5 (by C. P. E. Bach). Another special form of slide, peculiar to keyboard music, is that in which the first note is held throughout. Introduced by the French clavecinistes, who called it *coulé sur une tierce*, this agrément is indicated and performed as shown in Ex. 6. It was adopted by Purcell and other English composers, who used the same notation but called it a *slur*. In Romantic and modern music this execution of the slide is indicated with a tie, as in Ex. 7 (Schubert, Moments musicaux op. 94, no. 3). The performance of the slide, in general, has changed very little since the 18th century; it is still begun on the beat, as in Ex. 8 (Beethoven, Bagatellen op. 119, no. 5).

III. The disjunct double appoggiatura was written in ordinary notes until the last half of the 18th century, when C. P. E. Bach gave it the name *Anschlag* and introduced the two tiny grace notes which have since been used to represent it [Ex. 9]. The first of the two notes which make up the Anschlag may be at any distance from the main note, but the second is only one degree removed from it. The ornament should always begin on the beat, as in Ex. 10 (Chopin, Rondo op. 16) and Ex. 11 (Chopin, Polonaise op. 44).   P. A.

Appreciation of music. This term has come to be accepted as a name for a type of musical training designed to develop in the seriously interested amateur an ability to listen intelligently to the music which he is likely to encounter in concert performances and in broadcast reproductions and thus to enhance the pleasure and satisfaction he may derive from listening to music. This type of musical education, which is very common in the United States and in Britain (but practically unknown in Germany), has frequently been criticized as leading to superficiality and presumption, without providing that thorough training which the professional considers indispensable. Such criticism is not justified, however, except in special cases of incapacity and abuse which, one must admit, have not been rare. As a principle, the idea of providing a special type of training for the average music lover is sound and more deserving of constructive coöperation than of adverse criticism on the part of professional musicians.

Lit.: M. Bernstein, *An Introduction to Music* (1937); M. D. Calvocoressi, *Musical Taste and How to Form It* (1925); A. Copland, *What to Listen for in Music* (1938); E. Dickinson, *The Spirit of Music* (1925); D. S. Moore, *Listening to Music* (1932); D. Welch, *The Appreciation of Music* (1927); A. H. Fox-Strangways, in ML viii, 395.

Appuy [F.]. French 18th-century term for a note having the quality of an *appoggiatura. Usually refers to the appoggiatura which constitutes the first note of the *tremblement* or *cadence* [see *Trill].
                              P. A.

Appuyé [F.]. See *Appoggiando.

Après-midi d'un faune, L' (*The Afternoon of a Faun*). See *Symphonic poem IV.

Apsidenchöre [G., from L. *apsis*, apse]. Same as *cori spezzati.

Apt, Codex. See *Sources, no. 19.

Arabesque [F., properly an ornamentation in Arabic architecture]. A fanciful title used by R. Schumann and others for *characteristic pieces of a more or less casual type. The term is also used in the sense of figuration, ornamentation of a melody.

Arabian music. The music of the Islamic nations and tribes in Arabia, North Africa, and Persia.

I. *History.* As is the case with all the Oriental nations, our knowledge of the history of Arabian music is restricted largely to the theoretical field. A considerable number of early treatises exist, e.g., Al-Kindi (9th century); Al-Farabi (*c.* 900–950); Avicenna (11th century); Safi-ud Din (13th century); Abd-el Kadr (15th century). The most important information to be gained from these manuscripts concerns the scale, as given by the frets of the two main instruments of Arabian mu-

sic, the '*ud* (a short lute), and the *tanbur* (a long lute; see below). Prior to Al-Farabi's time, the strings of the tanbur were divided into forty equal parts the first five of which were indicated by frets and used in playing. The result of this procedure is a small series of (unequal) quarter-tones. Al-Farabi, influenced by ancient Greek theory, introduced a new scale based on the interval of the fourth. The '*ud* as well as the tanbur were tuned in fourths (e.g., a-d'-g'-c'') and were provided with frets which gave a number of middle tones between the open string and its upper fourth's. Al-Farabi himself interpolated three such tones, namely, two successive (Pythagorean) whole-tones ($\%_8 = 204$ *cents) above the fundamental (open string) and one whole-tone below the fourth. Thus the tetrachord c-f included five tones which are almost identical with the tones c-d-eb-e-f of the modern scale (0–204–294–408–498, instead of 0–200–300–400–500 cents). Later on, the second whole-tone below the fourth was added, a tone which is very near to the modern db (294–204 = 90 cents; see *Limma). The addition of a similar tetrachord f-bb and of an extra tone b above it resulted in a scale of twelve tones which differs very little from the modern well-tempered scale, except for the slightly low db and gb. In the 13th century this scale was extended by the addition of five tones, each a quarter-tone (24 cents) below each diatonic whole-tone, i.e., below d,e,g,a,c', so that a 17-tone scale resulted. This scale

    90 90 24 90 90 90 24 90 90 90 24 90 90 24 90 90 90 24
Arabian 17-tone Scale

has been wrongly interpreted by Villoteau (*c.* 1820) and by Kiesewetter [*Die Musik der Araber* (1842)] as a scale of equal third-tones. Besides this division of the tetrachord, many others were in use, e.g., one named after the Bagdad lutenist Zal-zal (8th century) which used the tones 0–168–355–408–498 cents.

A special point of Arabic theory which has attracted much attention is that of consonance and dissonance. It has been claimed that, as early as the 10th century (Al-Farabi), the Arabs considered the third a consonance while in Western Europe it was not recognized as such until about 1300. The fact is that Arabian theory does not make any distinction between consonance and dissonance, but knows only decreasing degrees of consonance, namely those which are expressed by the following series of fractions: $\frac{2}{1}, \frac{3}{2}, \frac{4}{3}, \frac{5}{4}, \frac{6}{5}, \frac{7}{6}, \frac{8}{7}$. Here the major and minor third ($\frac{5}{4}, \frac{6}{5}$) range after the octave, the fifth, and the fourth, but are followed in turn by the intervals, $\frac{7}{6}$ (fifth below the seventh harmonic) and $\frac{8}{7}$ (inversion of the seventh harmonic), neither of which exists in Western theory, so that they must certainly be regarded as strong dissonances [see *Messel].

Much attention has also been given to the question of the influence of Arabian music, as practiced on the Spanish peninsula, on Western music (troubadours). The sweeping claims which have been made by various scholars (particularly by H. G. Farmer) have been greatly reduced by more recent investigations [see Lit., Ursprung]. It would appear that European music is indebted to the Arabs in the field of instruments (lute, drum), of theoretical acoustics (measuring of consonant lengths of a string — a study which, however, in turn goes back to the ancient Greeks), and of certain poetic forms [see *Zajal], but not for such phenomena as troubadour music, modal rhythm, organum, etc.

II. *Present-Day Status.* It goes without saying that the above-described scales with twelve or more tones represent what the chromatic scale represents in, say, the classical period of our music, i.e., the theoretical tonal material from which selections were made for the purpose of practical performance. In musical practice, Arabian music uses a seven-tone scale which includes four fixed tones, c,f,g,c′, and two more or less variable tones within each fourth. Especially frequent is the tetrachord c-db-e-f; however, the interval db-e of this progression is smaller than it is in our scale, the intervals of the tetrachord being approximately $\frac{3}{4}$, $1\frac{1}{4}$, and

$\frac{1}{2}$ of a whole-tone [cf. Zalzal's tuning] as against $\frac{1}{2}$, $1\frac{1}{2}$, and $\frac{1}{2}$ of a whole-tone in our system.

An important concept of Arabian music is the *maqam*. These were formerly (Kiesewetter) considered the Oriental counterpart of the Western *church modes. Actually, a maqam is characterized not only by features such as center tone and range, but especially by the preference of characteristic progressions, melodic formulae, rhythmic patterns, ornamentations, etc. A maqam, therefore, is a *melody-type, and a composition in a given maqam is written not only "in a given key," but also "in a given style or tradition." Some of these maqam go back to local traditions and may be compared to what we would call, for example, *à l'hongroise.* Others were originally melodies of famous composers which were imitated by other composers. For the Arabian musician such a maqam establishes a tradition similar to what we express by the term "Beethoven-style." Even today each piece of Arabian music is written in one of the maqam [see the *ragas* of *Hindu music]. However, the relationship of a composition to its maqam is difficult for the non-Oriental listener to discover. In many cases it appears to exist chiefly in the instrumental prelude which usually opens an Arabian composition. Evidently, by referring to the maqam in the prelude, the musician pays tribute to tradition and subsequently feels free to play as he pleases.

The more elaborate examples of Arabian music (chiefly instrumental) consist of a prelude in free rhapsodic style which serves to establish the maqam in the mind

Arabian Music

of the listener and which is followed by a series of pieces in strict rhythm but of freer invention in the same maqam. Thus the form is strongly reminiscent of that of a suite, with all the dances being in the same key.

The rhythm of Arabic melodies is similar to that of Hindu music. Typical is an $\frac{8}{8}$ meter with the rhythm of the measure alternating between the "European" arrangement 2+2+2+2 and the "Oriental" arrangement 2+3+3. The drums frequently provide a rhythmical counterpoint [see Ex. on p. 46].

The main instruments of Arabian music are the short-necked lute with four or five strings, tuned in fourths and called *'ud*, from which the European lute derived both its form and its name (*al 'ud*, *lud*, lute), and the long-necked lute called *tanbur* (originally *pan-tur*; Sumerian "bow-small," Greek *pandura), usually with two strings, tuned in minor seconds [see *Lute II]. The family of the bowed instruments is represented by the *rebab* and the *kemantche*, consisting of a long stick extending through a coconut [see *Violin II]. A frequently used wind instrument is the *arghool*, a double shawm with two pipes, one for the melody, the other for bourdon accompaniment. For an example cf. *HAM*, no. 3.

Lit.: F. S. Daniel, *The Music and the Musical Instruments of the Arabs* (1915; bibl.); H. G. Farmer, *A History of Arabian Music to the xiiith Century* (1929; bibl.); Ph. Thornton, *The Voice of Atlas* (1936); D. Salvador, *The Music of the Arabs* (1915); R. von Erlanger, *La Musique arabe* (1930); *LavE* i.5, 2676; A. Berner, *Studien zur Arabischen Musik . . .* (1937); E. A. Beichert, *Die Wissenschaft der Musik bei Al Farabi* (Diss. Berlin 1936); Hefny, *Ibn Sina's Musiklehre* (Diss. Berlin 1931); English translation of *Al Farabi* (Farmer); D. Stoll, "Music in Mediaeval Bagdad" (*MR* i); A. Z. Idelsohn, "Die Maqamen der arabischen Musik" (*SIM* xv); R. Lachmann, in *Wolf Festschrift* (1929) and in *AMW* v; H. G. Farmer, in *PMA* lii; O. Ursprung, in *ZMW* xvi; B. Bartok, in *ZMW* ii; J. Rouanet, in *RM* v, viii; R. P. Thibault, in *BSIM* vii (1911).

Arcata [It.]. See *Bowing (a); *arcato*, bowed.

Archet [F.], **archetto** [It.]. *Bow (of the violin).

Architectural acoustics. The study of the acoustic properties of a room (particularly, of concert halls, radio-studios) as to *resonance, reflection, echo, etc. Recent investigations have raised this field of study from the former stage of experimentation to an important branch of science.

Lit.: H. Bagenal, *Planning for Good Acoustics* (1931); A. H. Davis, *The Acoustics of Buildings* (1927); P. R. Heyl, *Architectural Acoustics* (1930); V. O. Knudsen, *Architectural Acoustics* (1932); P. E. Sabine, *Acoustics and Architecture*, (1932); F. R. Watson, *Acoustics of Buildings* (1930); H. H. Statham, in *PMA* xxxviii; A. Elson, in *MQ* vii.

Archives des Maîtres de l'Orgue. See *Editions, Historical, I.

Archlute, arciliuto [It.]. A lute with two pegboxes, one for the fingered strings, the other for the bass courses (theorboe, chitarrone). See *Lute III.

Arcicembalo, arciorgano. A quarter-tone harpsichord of the 16th century, described by N. Vicentino in his *L'antica musica* (1555) and *Descrizione dell'arciorgano* (1561). Each octave had 31 keys which were arranged in 6 manuals and which gave all the tones of the diatonic, chromatic, and enharmonic genera of ancient Greek theory. A simplified instrument of greater practical importance was built by the Belgian Charles Luython (1556–1620); it had 18 keys in each octave, namely — in addition to the diatonic tones — c♯ and db, d♯ and eb, f♯ and g♭, g♯ and ab, bb, e♯, and b♯. This instrument, called *Universal-clavicymbel* (M. Praetorius, in his *Syntagma musicum*, 1624, praises it as "instrumentum perfectum si non perfectissimum"), permitted enharmonic change and modulation in all the keys, without the compromise of equal temperament. Compositions such as John Bull's Fantasia on the Hexachord (*Fitzwilliam Virginal Book* I, 183) [see *Hexachord IV] are evidently written for this instrument.

Lit.: A. Koczirz, in *SIM* ix; Shohé Tanaka, in *VMW* vi; W. Dupont, *Geschichte der musikalischen Temperatur* (1935), 51ff.

Arco [It.]. Bow (of violins, etc.). See *Coll' arco.

Arditamente [It.]. Boldly.

A re, Are. See *Hexachord III.

Argentina. The beginnings of musical life in Argentina, as in other parts of Latin America, are associated with the efforts of the early missionaries to teach the arts and crafts of Europe to the native population. In the La Plata region, especially, important missions were established, with music playing a prominent role in their organization. The most gifted and zealous of these missionaries as regards the teaching of music was the Jesuit Father Luis Berger (1588–1641), under whose guidance the Indians became adept at playing many kinds of European musical instruments. His activities extended throughout the provinces, and even into Chile.

It is not until the period of Independence that we find other names which need claim our attention. First of all may be mentioned the composer of the Argentine National Hymn (1813), Blas Parera, a rather obscure teacher of piano and violin, of whose life little is known. In 1817 he was in Spain, where he died. His Hymn, officially adopted by government decree, has firmly entrenched itself in the affection of the Argentine people. The outstanding composers of the 19th century were amateurs who cultivated music in the midst of various kinds of public activity. They were Amancio Alcorta (1805–62), Juan Pedro Esnaola (1808–78), and Juan Bautista Alberdi (1810–84). All three were of Basque descent. Their music shows scarcely any local influence, being largely dominated by Italian tendencies. All the works composed by Alcorta from 1822 to 1830 — his most prolific period — have been lost. From 1832 he lived in Buenos Aires and continued to compose while holding various official positions. The works dating from this period were published by his family at Paris in two volumes (1869, '83), comprising chamber music, piano pieces, and songs.

Esnaola, a native of Buenos Aires, studied at the conservatories of Paris and Madrid and became an accomplished pianist. Upon returning to Buenos Aires in 1822 he founded there the Academia de Música. He composed orchestral works, church music, songs, and piano pieces, mostly unpublished. Alberti, born in Tucumán, had a distinguished career as a man of letters and composed music simply as a pastime. Most of his compositions have been lost, but some were published in a periodical called *La Moda*, founded by Alberdi himself (1837–38). His works are mostly for piano, and in 1832 he published a piano method for amateurs.

The dean of contemporary Argentine composers is Alberto Williams (b. Buenos Aires, 1862), grandson of Amancio Alcorta, of English descent on his father's side. After initial studies in Buenos Aires he attended the Paris Conservatory, studying piano and composition. In 1893 he founded the Conservatory of Buenos Aires, which now has many branches throughout the country, and of which he was still director in 1940. A prolific composer, he has written nine symphonies and several symphonic poems, concert overtures and suites for orchestra, many piano pieces, songs (to his own texts), choral works, chamber music, and technical treatises. Although his technique is entirely European and academic, he has essayed a national style in his Argentine Suites for strings, his *Aires de la Pampa* for piano, etc.

The contemporary Argentine school is vigorous and varied. Juan José Castro (b. 1895), pupil of d'Indy at the Schola Cantorum in Paris, is active as conductor and as composer (*Sinfonía Argentina, Sinfonía Bíblica*, etc.). In 1941 he appeared as guest conductor of the NBC Orchestra in New York. His brother, José María Castro (b. 1892), is a member of the "Grupo Renovación," which includes also Honorio Siccardi (b. 1897), Luis Gianneo (b.

1897), and Jacobo Ficher (b. Odessa, 1896). The radical Juan Carlos Paz (b. 1897) is an exponent of the twelve-tone system. Among the younger composers are Carlos Suffern, Isabel Aretz-Thiele, Roberto García Morillo, Julio Perceval, and Alberto Ginastera (who is exceptionally talented).

In Latin American countries native opera is rather rare, but the Argentine composers have been very active in this field. Their activity has no doubt been stimulated by the presence of the famous Teatro Colón in Buenos Aires, where both native and foreign operas are produced under excellent conditions. Prominent as opera composers are Pascual de Rogatis (*La Novia del Hereje*), Raul Espoile (*La Ciudad Roja*), Enrique Casella (*La Tapera*), and especially Felipe Boero, who scored a marked success with his folk opera *El Matrero,* dealing with life on the Argentine pampas. On the whole, Italian influence predominates in Argentine opera.

Other contemporary composers are Juan A. García Estrada (b. 1895), Gilardo Gilardi (b. 1889), Athos Palma (b. 1891), Arturo Luzzati (b. Turin, 1875), and Carlos López Buchardo. Musicians who have devoted themselves primarily to collecting, arranging, and performing folk music are Andrés Beltrame, Andrés Chazarreta, Vicente Forte, and Carlos Vega. The composer and pedagogue Josué T. Wilkes has also done interesting work in this field, notably with his arrangement of *Doce Canciones Coloniales.*

The folk songs and dances of Argentina are largely of Spanish (or at least European) origin, with only a slight Indian influence in certain songs such as the *vidala* (or *vidalita*) and the *triste,* which, as its name implies, is a rather sad love song. See also *Milonga; *Tango.

Lit.: J. Alvarez, *Orígenes de la música argentina* (1908); A. Schianca, *Historia de la música argentina* (1933); C. Vega, *Danzas y canciones argentinas* (1933); A. Williams, †*Antología de compositores argentinos. Cuaderno I: Los precursores* (1941); C. Vega, *La música popular argentina* (1941).   G. C.

Arghool, arghul. See *Arabian music II.

Aria. I. An elaborate solo song (occasionally for two solo voices; see *Duet) with instrumental accompaniment. The aria figures prominently in the cantatas and oratorios of the 17th and 18th centuries and in opera of all periods except the Wagnerian type. It is distinguished from the air, song, or Lied by (a) generally greater length; (b) non-strophic form (*through-composed); and (c) an accent on purely musical design and expression, often at the expense of the text. In fact the small regard which many aria composers have shown for the text has evoked serious criticism of the form and, in some instances, it has led writers of operas to banish the aria from the stage; Gluck, for instance, replaced it by the simpler Lied, and Wagner substituted his dramatic recitative. By and large such criticism cannot be justified. Although at certain periods (especially *c.* 1750 with Piccinni and *c.* 1850 with Meyerbeer) the aria style has been characterized by conventionalism and exaggeration, the great majority of arias represent a treasure of great musical value. Moreover, in opera the aria has a definite and important function, in representing lyric episodes which temporarily relieve the dramatic tension of the action.

II. The term aria occurs first as a title of wordless canzones ("Arie di canzon francese") in the second book of madrigals by Ingegneri (1579). Its first use to indicate a monodic song occurs in Caccini's *Nuove Musiche* (1602). Here, however, contrary to its later meaning, it is used to denote shorter, strophic songs [cf. *HAM,* no. 183; *SchGMB,* no. 191], while the longer, through-composed pieces which are more allied to the later aria are still called madrigals. The Caccini sense of the word aria was adopted by German composers such as Johann Staden (1581–1634; cf. *DTB* 7.i and 8.i); Heinrich Albert (1604–51; cf. *DdT* 12/13; *HAM,* no. 205; *SchGMB,* no. 193), Adam Krieger (1634–66; cf. *DdT* 19; *HAM,* no. 228; *SchGMB,* no. 209), and Joh. Philipp Krieger (1649–1725; cf. *DdT* 53/54). Those of Adam Krieger [see *Ritornell (2)] especially are important forerunners of the German strophic Lied of the 18th and 19th centuries [cf. *RiHM* ii.2, 331ff].

III. The early development of the aria proper took place in Italy during the 17th century. The first stage of this develop-

to the ternary scheme A B A. Early examples of this form occur in Monteverdi's *Orfeo* and *Poppea* [cf. *RiHM* ii.2, 197, 205, 238]. The form is more fully developed with Luigi Rossi (1598–1653; cf. *RiHM* ii.2, 374), Giacomo Carissimi (1605–74), Francesco Gavalli (1602–76), Marcantonio Cesti (1623–69), and others [cf. the operas of Cavalli and Cesti; also

	A				B				A		
a′	a″	a	----------		b	--------		(a′	a″)	a	---------
T		T	D	T	R	D_R	R		T	T	D	T

Scheme of the Da-capo Aria
T = tonic; D = dominant; R = relative key

ment (*c.* 1600–50) is characterized by the emergence of various formal schemes, including (a) an amorphous, continuous type of *monodic melody, midway between recitative and song, sometimes called *arioso; (b) a canzona-like type, consisting of contrasting sections, alternating in tempo, meter, etc.; (c) the basso-ostinato aria in which the melody is formed above a repeated ground. Arias of these types occur in: J. Peri, *Varie musiche* (1609); Alessandro Grandi, *Cantade et arie a voce sola* (1620; cf. *RiHM* ii.2, 38); Steffano Landi, *Arie a una voce* (1620; cf. *RiHM* ii.2, 50); Benedetto Ferrari, *Musiche varie* (1633–41; cf. *RiHM* ii.2, 55). While in the ostinato-aria of Peri, Grande, and Landi the repeated bass is a well-rounded musical sentence of considerable length, so that the resulting form might well be considered a strophic aria with a varied melody [see *Strophic bass], Ferrari was one of the first to use short, characteristic motives of the ostinato-type proper. This form, actually a "vocal passacaglia" [see *Chaconne and passacaglia], was frequently used by Italian, English, and French composers of the second half of the 17th century (Carissimi, Purcell, Couperin; cf. the Crucifixus of Bach's *B minor Mass*).

IV. The second stage (*c.* 1650–1750) is characterized by the establishment of the *da-capo aria* as the typical form. In this form the first section (A) is repeated *in toto* after the second (B), thus leading

Lit., Landshoff, Riemann]. It attained great artistic perfection in the hands of such men as A. Scarlatti, J. S. Bach, and Handel. A special feature, introduced by Scarlatti and largely adopted by Bach, was the opening announcement of the initial theme twice, first by the instruments (a′), then by the voice (a″), before the main statement in the voice (a). German writers call this announcement *Devise* (device), hence the name *Devisen-arie* (Riemann). Each of the three sections employs a three-part modulating scheme, B usually in the relative key (R). The material of B is generally different from that of A, but not of a highly contrasting character.

V. During the 18th century the da-capo aria became the vehicle of great virtuoso display and of a conventionalism which led to a codification and classification in various types prescribed by typical operatic situations, such as *aria cantabile, di bravura, parlante, di carattere* (*air de caractère*), *di mezzo carattere*, etc. [cf. *GD* i, 110]. The desire on the part of the great singers to show their ability in various musical styles led, about 1750, to a form consisting of two separate arias of contrasting character, usually the first dramatic, the second lyrical. Most of the operatic arias by Mozart are of this type, e.g., the famous "Register"-aria of Leporello in *Don Giovanni* (1st Act). In the operas of the later Neapolitan School (Leo, Porpora, Vinci, Jommelli) the use of the aria was so extended that the whole opera consisted of nothing but arias. This abuse was the main point of attack of Gluck's reform.

The aria remained in the favor of operatic composers throughout the first half of the 19th century (Beethoven, Auber, Rossini). While Wagner discarded it more or less completely in his first operas (*Rienzi*, 1840; *Der fliegende Holländer*, 1841), Verdi continued to use it except in his last two operas (*Otello*, 1886; *Falstaff*, 1893).

Lit.: B. Flögel, *Die Arientechnik in den Opern Händels* (Diss. Halle 1929); H. Riemann, †*Kantatenfrühling*, 4 vols.; L. Landshoff, †*Alte Meister des Belcanto*, 5 vols.; J. Godefroy, "Some Aspects of the Aria" (*ML* xvii); H. Goldschmidt, in *MfM* xxxiii. See also under *Opera; *Cantata.

Arietta [It.], **ariette** [F.]. (1) A small aria, usually in binary form and lacking the musical elaboration of the *aria; thus rather, a song or a *cavatina. — (2) In French operas before 1750, an aria to Italian words, usually in brilliant coloratura style. — (3) In the opéra-comique of the second half of the 18th century, a solo song (aria) in French, preceded and followed by spoken dialogue, the work being known as a "comédie mêlée d'ariettes."

Lit.: P. M. Mason, *L'Opéra de Rameau* (1930); G. Cucuel, *Les Créateurs de l'opéra-comique français* (1914). D. J. G.

Arioso [It., like an aria]. A style which is midway between that of an aria and a recitativo. A good example showing the difference between these three styles is a cantata by Cesti (*c*. 1650), reproduced in *AdHM*, 439ff. Bach uses the arioso repeatedly for the concluding section of a recitative when he wishes to bestow upon it a particular expression of assurance or confidence [see *Cavata]. Two examples, in the style of the *recitativo accompagnato, occur in the cantata *Ein feste Burg* illustrated. Beethoven, in the final movement of his Piano Sonata op. 110, uses the term for an accompanied recitative played on the pianoforte.

Arioso from *Ein feste Burg*

Arithmetic division. In 16th-century musical theory, the division of a string into sections of equal length, e.g., those indicated by the fractions $\frac{1}{6}, \frac{2}{6}, \frac{3}{6}, \frac{4}{6}, \frac{5}{6}, \frac{6}{6}$ as opposed to the harmonic (or geometric) division in which the denominator changes: $\frac{1}{6}, \frac{1}{5}, \frac{1}{4}, \frac{1}{3}, \frac{1}{2}, 1$. The theoretical interest of these two divisions (if applied to the string of a monochord) lies in the fact that, while the latter leads to the harmonics and, in particular, to the major triad, the former gives the tones of a minor triad:

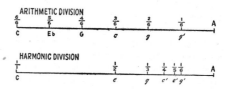

The right end of the string, A, is fixed, the other is altered by means of a fret.

These two divisions form the basis of Zarlino's "dual theory" [see *Dualism] in which minor mode is called *divisio arithmetica*; major, *divisio harmonica* [*Istituzioni harmoniche* (1558)].

Arlésienne, L'. Incidental music by Georges Bizet (1838–75) to Alphonse

Daudet's play *L'Arlésienne* ("The Woman of Arles"). It is usually played in the form of two orchestral suites [see *Suite V], arranged by Bizet in 1872.

Armenian music. Since Armenia was the first country officially to adopt the Christian faith (A.D. 303), the history of Armenian sacred literature and music has attracted much attention. The Armenian liturgy, like that of Byzantium, consists chiefly of hymns. The most ancient of these hymns were in prose. Later versified hymns became prominent, especially through the activity of the great poet Nerses Schnorhali (11th century). The official book of hymns, called *sharakan*, contains 1166 songs. The earliest preserved liturgical manuscripts containing musical signs date from the 14th century. The notation is a highly developed system of neumes (Armenian neumes) which certainly was the result of a long evolution [examples in *LavE* i.1, 552; Thibaut, *Notation neumatique de l'église latine* (1907), plate 4], but the lack of treatises explaining this notation renders the Armenian neumes undecipherable. In the early 19th century a new system of musical notation, similar to that of the present-day Greek church music, was introduced and is still in use. Whether the present-day melodies are identical with or similar to those of the early books cannot be ascertained, but the fact that the modern chants are grouped according to an *oktoechos based on melodic formulae suggests an ancient origin of the melodies. The continuity of tradition is more doubtful so far as the rhythmic interpretation of Armenian chant is concerned. The melodies of the present liturgy are based upon strict time, with the temporal unit (*kèt*, i.e., beat) divided into an elaborate system of rhythmic formations of smaller values, including 32d and 64th notes. Whereas scholars such as R. P. Dechevrens and J. C. Jeannin have considered this rhythm of great antiquity and have used it as an argument in favor of strictly rhythmical interpretation of Gregorian chant, P. Aubry considers it as a fairly recent innovation due to Turkish influ-

ence (15th century). The purest source of Armenian church music is undoubtedly the music in use at Edjmiadzin, which is also used at Tiflis and Eriwan. The collections issued by European and American communities differ widely from the traditional forms, chiefly owing to the use of cheap modern harmonizations.

Lit.: P. Bianchini, *Les Chants liturgiques de l'église arménienne* (1877); M. Ekmalian, *Les Chants de la sainte liturgie* (1896); A. Abgar, *Melodies of the Holy Apostolic Church of Armenia* (Calcutta, 1897); Nerses Ter-Mikaelian, *Das armenische Hymnarium* (1905); P. Aubry, *Le Rhythme tonique* (1903); A. Gastoué, in *LavE* i.1, 541; P. Aubry, in *TG* vii, viii, ix; E. Wellesz, in *AdHM* i, 139 and in *JPM* xxvii; K. Keworkian, in *SIM* i; A. Gastoué, in *RdM*, no. 31; *GD*, Suppl. Vol., 176.

Secular music: K. Keworkian, *Musique populaire arménienne* (1931); R. P. Komitas, *Musique populaire arménienne* (1925 and later); F. Macler, *La Musique en Arménie* (1917); F. H. Paelian, *The Music of Armenia* (1939; bibl.); R. Pesce, *La Musica armena* (1935); S. Poladian, *Armenian Folk Songs* (1942).

Armonioso [It.]. Harmoniously.

Armure [F.]. Key-signature.

Arpa [It.]. Harp. See also under *Psaltery.

Arpeggio [It., from *arpeggiare*, to play upon a harp; F. *arpègement* or *harpègement*; E. battery; G. *Brechung*]. A term applied to the notes of a chord when they are played one after another instead of simultaneously. In modern music the arpeggio is indicated by one of the signs given in Ex. 1. Its execution always starts with the lowest note, and as a rule it should begin at the moment when the chord is due (i.e., on the beat) whether indicated by sign or by tiny notes [Ex. 2, Mozart, Sonata E major; Ex. 3, Chopin, Nocturne op. 62, no. 1]. There are cases, however, in which the melody carried by the top note of the arpeggio will not bear the delay caused by this execution, so that the last note of the arpeggio must then be made to coincide with the beat [Ex. 4, Mendelssohn]. The latter performance is

generally to be recommended, in pianoforte music, whenever the arpeggio occurs in the left hand alone, as in Ex. 5 (Chopin, Mazurka op. 7, no. 3). A distinction should be made between an arpeggio played simultaneously with both hands [Ex. 6] and a long arpeggio in which the right hand succeeds the left [Ex. 7]. The latter is (or should be) indicated by a long arpeggio sign, joining the two staves. For the violin arpeggio, see *Bowing (i).

In the music of the 17th and 18th centuries the execution of the arpeggio varied considerably (often at the discretion of the individual performer) in respect to direction and number of notes. The French clavecinistes used the signs shown in Ex. 8 to indicate the *arpègement en montant* (ascending arpeggio) and those in Ex. 9 for the *arpègement en descendant* (descending arpeggio). Other special signs were used to indicate various kinds

of *arpègements figurés*, or arpeggios in which unwritten notes are introduced [see Ex. 10, 11 and 12]. It will be observed that in performance of these *arpègements figurés* all the notes are held except those that are foreign to the chord,

which are immediately released [see *acciaccatura]. An appoggiatura to an arpeggio chord is incorporated in the arpeggio, occasioning a delay of the particular note to which it belongs, as in Ex. 13. A combination of *arpègements figurés* and an appoggiatura is shown in Ex. 14, from Bach's Partita in E minor.

In music of the time of Bach and Handel the word "arpeggio" is sometimes found written at the beginning of a sequence of chords. The player, in this case, is at liberty to break the chords up and down several times, to extend them, and to interpolate foreign notes as he sees fit [cf. Handel's own notation of the last four bars of the Prelude to his keyboard Suite in D minor]. The note-values, and even the tempo of such passages, are entirely at the player's discretion. These chords (e.g., those in Bach's Chromatic Fantasia) are written in measured time only to facilitate reading, the style of performance being derived from the unmeasured preludes of the lutenists and early French clavecinistes (Louis Couperin, d'Anglebert, etc.; see *Prelude II). P. A.

Arpeggione, also called guitar violoncello, guitarre d'amour. A stringed instrument of the size of a violoncello, but with a guitar-like body, and with six strings tuned in E, A, d, g, b, e′, invented in 1823 by G. Staufer. It is played with a bow. Franz Schubert wrote the only existing composition for it, a sonata for the arpeggione and piano (1824; see the collected edition [B. and H.], Series viii).

Arpicordo. Italian 16th-century name for a harpsichord which differed in some unknown detail from the clavicembalo [see *Harpsichord II]. Cf. the title of a publication from 1551: *Intabulatura nova di varie sorte di balli da sonare per Arpichordi, Clavicembali, Spinette e Monachordi*; also G. Picchi, *Intabolatura di balli d'arpicordo* (1620) [see *Editions III, 2]. Cf. the article in *SaRM*.

Arraché [F.]. Forceful pizzicato.

Arrangement. The adaptation of a composition for instruments other than those for which it was originally written (thus, in a way, the musical counterpart of a literary translation). One may distinguish between arrangements which are made chiefly for study purposes and others which are for public performance. In the former class we find all the customary piano arrangements of operas, symphonies, quartets, etc. Here, strict adherence to the original text is rightly considered the foremost duty of the editor, who is permitted only to detract from, not to add to, the original. In the second category, which involves the creative participation of the arranger, various procedures have been followed at different periods, ranging from simple transcriptions in which the musical substance remains the same but is transferred to a new medium, to the complete reworking of a piece with additions and modifications. Noteworthy examples of this category are: the *Intabulierung* of the 15th and 16th centuries; Bach's arrangements of violin-concertos

by Vivaldi and others for the harpsichord and the organ, or of the fugue from his solo-violin sonata in G minor (no. 1) for the organ (D minor; *B.-G.* xv, 148); Haydn's *Die Sieben Worte am Kreuz* which appeared as an orchestral composition, as a string quartet, and as choral music [cf. A. Sandberger, in *JMP* x]; Liszt's concert arrangements of Schubert's songs and of scenes from Wagnerian operas; Brahms's arrangement for two pianofortes of his orchestral variations on a theme by Haydn (op. 56), etc.

In the last score of years there has been an extraordinary activity in transcribing Bach's organ works for the piano and the orchestra. Although this must be welcomed as a token of the ever growing interest in the work of the great master, yet the development has taken on forms which have recently led to a sharp reaction against the "business of arrangement." This opposition, however, is justifiable only with regard to certain methods of transcription. Several transcribers (e.g., Respighi), instigated by the display of modern orchestration or pianoforte-technique, have tried — and certainly with success — to bestow upon Bach's organ pieces an impressionistic lushness or a Romantic emotionalism which is inconsistent with the intrinsic clarity of his style.

Lt.: K. Grunsky, *Die Technik des Klavierauszugs* (1911); E. Friedländer, *Wagner-Liszt und die Kunst der Klavierbearbeitung* (1922); E. Howard-Jones in *ML* xvi, no. 4.

Arrescu [Sp.]. See *Aurrescu.

Ars antiqua [L., the ancient art]. I. The term *Ars antiqua* (*Ars veterum*) was used by writers of the early 14th century (e.g., *Speculum Musicae*, c. 1325; cf. *CS* ii, 429) to distinguish the late 13th-century school (Franco, c. 1260; Petrus de Cruce, c. 1290) from that of their own day which was called *Ars nova* (or *Ars modernorum*). Today, both terms are usually employed in a wider sense, denoting music of the 13th and 14th centuries respectively. The Ars antiqua, then, includes the School of Notre Dame with its two masters, Leoninus (second half of the

12th century) and Perotinus (*c.* 1160–1220), and the ensuing period, which, for want of other names, may be divided into the school of Franco (middle 13th century) and that of Petrus de Cruce (late 13th century). The School of Notre Dame was preceded by the School of *St. Martial (*c.* 1100–50).

Leoninus, called "optimus organista" by the English Anon. IV [*CS* i, 342] (i.e., greatest composer of *organa, not — as some modern writers believe — "very able organist"), was the creator of the *Magnus liber organi de gradali et de antiphonario* (great book of organa for the Mass and for the Office), which represents a complete cycle of two-part organa (organa dupla) for the ecclesiastical year, about 90 in all [see *Magnus liber].

Perotinus, "optimus discantor" (i.e., greatest composer of *discantus), partly rewrote this repertory in a more "crystallized" style which is characterized by the consistent use of modal meter [see *Modes, rhythmic] and by the increase of the number of parts from two to three and, occasionally, four (organum triplum and organum quadruplum; cf. *AdHM* i, 226, 228–232). He and his collaborators also added a large number of short compositions, mostly in two parts, the so-called *clausulae, which were designed to be used as substitutes for corresponding sections in Leonin's organa. These clausulae constitute the link with the following period, as they were frequently transformed into *motets. The motet is the representative form of the middle and second half of the 13th century, during which it was cultivated almost to the exclusion of any other type of music. The propensity of the 13th-century musicians (practically all anonymous) for this form would be difficult to understand were it not for the fact that the motet, which originally was a strictly liturgical form (a clausula provided with a full text in the upper part), soon underwent secular influence, partly from the tradition of the trouvères, which brought with it fresh impulses and even many heterogeneous elements (mixture of Latin and French, of liturgical tenors and love lyrics). The

repertory of the School of Notre Dame also includes a large number of *conductus, i.e., Latin songs in one to four parts, mostly to devotional texts, but without plainsong cantus firmus, such as occurs with all the organa, clausulae, and motets.

II. The 13th-century technique of composition may be described as "successive counterpoint." The composer starts out with one complete voice, the tenor, which is either a pre-existent plainsong melody (this is the case with organa, clausulae, and practically all motets) or written by the composer himself (this is the case with conductus). To this fundamental part the others are added successively, first the duplum (called *motetus* in a motet), then the triplum. Regarding the principles of consonance and dissonance, see *Harmony.

The most important contribution of the Ars antiqua lies in the field of rhythm. While the organa of the School of St. Martial employ for their upper part melismas in free, unmeasured rhythm, the period around 1150 marks the establishment of strict rhythm, based on the rhythmic modes [see *Rhythm III (b) (c)]. This new rhythm presents itself clearly in the clausula-sections of Leonin's organa, while the organal sections are written in a transitional style the rhythmic interpretation of which is still a matter of controversy [see *Organum]. With Perotinus, modal rhythm (usually corresponding to our ⁶⁄₈-meter) was universally adopted for the entire organa and their derivatives.

The most important sources of 13th-century music are, aside from those mentioned under *Magnus liber organi*, the codices Montpellier, Bamberg, and Huelgas [see *Sources]. For complete lists cf. F. Ludwig, in *AMW* v (also *ApNPM*, 201f, Sections II, III).

Related articles: Cantigas; Clausula; Conductus; Discant; Estampie; Hocket; Lauda; Minnesinger; Modes, Rhythmic; Motet I; Square notation; Sumer is icumen in; Theory II; Troubadours; Trouvères.

Lit.: *OH* i (preferably the edition of 1901; the transcriptions of organa are based on wrong principles); *ReMMA*, 272–330 (bibl. pp. 445–456); *AdHM* i, 214–265 (bibl. p. 294); *BeMMR*, 113–135 (bibl. p. 180); *ApNPM*, 215–337; †*HAM*, nos. 28–42; †*SchGMB*, nos. 16–20; H. Gleason, †*Examples of Music before 1400* (1942), pp. 36–75; R. Ficker, †*Perotinus, Sederunt principes* (1930); H. Schmidt, †*Drei Benedicamus Domino Organa* (1933); R. Ficker, "Polyphonic Music of the Gothic Period" (*MQ* xv). See also under *Motet and other related articles.

Arsis and thesis [Gr.]. *Arsis* means "lifting" [G. *Hebung*], *thesis* means "lowering" [G. *Senkung*]. In Greek poetry, these terms were used in a sense derived from bodily movement, such as the lifting and lowering of the foot (as in dancing) or of the hand (as in conducting). Consequently, *arsis* meant weak accent or lack of accent or weak beat, while *thesis* meant strong accent, strong beat:

```
 a   t   a   t   a   t
 .   |   .   |   .   |
```

Unfortunately, Roman and medieval writers reversed the meaning of the terms, by interpreting them as referring to the raising and lowering not of the foot, but of the voice. Since with a pair of tones the higher one is usually accented more than the lower one, the term arsis (high) was identified with accent, and thesis (low), with lack of accent:

```
 a   t   a   t   a   t
 |   .   |   .   |   .
```

It is in this sense that the terms are usually applied in French writings on meter and metrical music. The usage also persists in German terminology, in which *Hebung* (arsis) means strong beat, *Senkung* (thesis), weak beat [see *Vierhebigkeit*]. Recent English writers have returned to the original and proper meaning of arsis and thesis [see Webster, *Collegiate Dictionary*]. This usage is observed in the present book. See *Poetic meter.

A fugue "per arsin et thesin" is one in which the answer of the subject is made by contrary motion (e.g., Bach, *The Art of Fugue*, no. 5).

Ars nova. [L., the new art]. I. *General*. Generic name for the music of the 14th century, in contradistinction to *Ars antiqua, i.e., music of the 13th century. Properly, the name should be restricted, as it originally was, to the music of the first half of the 14th century (represented in France by Philippe de Vitry, in Italy by Giovanni da Cascia, Jacopo da Bologna). Indeed, compositions of the late 14th century, especially the French, show features of intellectual refinement, of formalism, and even decadence which are scarcely compatible with the term "New Art." In the early 14th century, however, the Ars nova began as a novel movement the chief champion of which was Philippe de Vitry (*c.* 1290–1361). About 1325, he introduced the term *Ars nova* as the title of a treatise which, unfortunately, deals primarily with the notational rather than the musical innovations of the period [*CS* iii, 13; transl. by P. Bohn, in *MfM* xx]. More illuminating from a general point of view are the discussions in the *Speculum musicae*, whose author (Jacobus of Liège; see *Theory II) gives extremely interesting information regarding the stylistic contrast between the Ars antiqua and the Ars nova, although he speaks from a decidedly anti-modern point of view [book vii, chapters 43–46: "Collatio veteris artis ad novam"; cf. *CS* ii, 384; 427–433]. On the other hand, Johannes de Muris, who was formerly thought to have written the *Speculum musicae*, actually was another leader of the new movement, as was the contemporary Italian writer Marchettus de Padua who, in his *Pomerium de musica mensurata* (*c.* 1320), contrasts the Italian and the French notation of the 14th century, and decides in favor of the latter. In the field of musical composition the 14th century saw continued activity in France and the rise of a new school of polyphonic music in Italy. There also are a limited number of English compositions of the 14th century; their main interest lies in their early use of sixth-chord style [cf. *ReMMA*, 399; see *Fauxbourdon].

II. *French Ars Nova*. From the point of view of the Ars antiqua, the achievements of the early French Ars nova lie in the direction of secularization, refinement, expressiveness, and, one might even say, Romanticism. In striking contrast to the rigidity of the Ars antiqua, the music of G. de Machaut (1300–77) shows free contrapuntal texture, supple rhythm, curved lines, and generally bears the stamp of high refinement, delicacy, individuality, and creative imagination. Whereas in his motets Machaut continued the tradition of the past [see *Isorhythmic], he established a completely new style in his secular works, the polyphonic *ballades, *rondeaux, and *virelais, by abandoning cantus-firmus treatment as well as "successive counterpoint" [see *Ars antiqua], and by creating the musical style known as "melody with accompaniment." Machaut is practically the only French composer of his time known to us, although a few motets of Philippe de Vitry survive [cf. H. Besseler in *AMW* viii, 245ff]. The ensuing period of French music, that is, the period between Machaut and Dufay, is, at present, the least explored period in the entire history of polyphonic music. This is chiefly due to the great difficulties presented by the notation of compositions from the end of the 14th century [cf. the chapter "Mannered Notation" in *ApNPM*, 403ff]. Very few compositions of this period have as yet been transcribed. A general judgment on the merits and demerits of composers such as Johannes Césaris, Baude Cordier, Cunelier, Grimace, Solage, Suzoy, must be postponed until further studies are available [see Lit., Dannemann]. To some extent the gap between Machaut and Dufay is filled in by the recent publication of the *Manuscript d'Apt* [see *Sources, no. 19] and of some pieces in Ch. van den Borren, *Polyphonia sacra* [*Sources, no. 24].

The harmonic style of the Ars nova shows some advance over that of the Ars antiqua, in so far as thirds are admitted more frequently. More interesting is the extremely bold treatment of dissonances, which frequently reminds one of the dissonant counterpoint of modern composers (e.g., Hindemith). The polyphonic texture stands, as it were, under the influ-

ence of "points of magnetic attraction" at which the parts start and converge in perfect consonances, mainly octaves, fourths, and fifths, while in between the lines move with a remarkable degree of individuality and independence from harmonic considerations.

The rhythmic treatment also is remarkably advanced and "modern," owing particularly to the introduction and bold use of *syncopation which results in frequent displacements of the beat or, in other words, in a free change of measures (mixture of $\frac{6}{8}$, $\frac{3}{4}$, $\frac{1}{4}$, $\frac{4}{8}$, etc.). In the late 14th century, especially, the rhythmic structure adopts a complexity which is unparalleled in the entire history of European music [cf. *ApNPM*, 403ff].

III. *Italian Ars Nova.* In the tradition of Italian 14th-century music two schools can be distinguished, the earlier of which is represented chiefly by Jacopo da Bologna and Giovanni da Cascia (c. 1300–50), the later by Francesco Landini (1325–97), Paolo Tenorista, Ghirardello da Firenze, and others. Musical as well as notational features indicate that Italian polyphonic music branched off from the French tradition of the late 13th century, particularly from the style of Petrus de Cruce. However, in the half-century from 1275 till 1325 it developed special traits which led to a style of a decidedly national character. The forms of the earlier school are the *madrigal and the *caccia, while in the later school the *ballata (the French *virelai) prevails. The style of the earlier compositions may best be described as an "ornamented conductus style." The voices, usually two, move simultaneously from measure to measure, but the upper part makes ample use of quick figures (frequently in sequential patterns) leading from one main note to the next. With Landini, a good deal of the elaborate polyrhythmic style of the French (Machaut) appears in Italian music. He adds to the French polyphonic texture an Italian charm of melody which makes him the outstanding master of the Trecento and one who foreshadows the transparent beauty of Dunstable and

Dufay. For lists of 14th-century sources see under *Sources.

Related articles: Ballata; Ballade; Caccia; Estampie; Isorhythmic; Madrigal (1); Rondeau (1); Syncopation; Virelai.

Lit.: *ReMMA* (bibl.); *AdHM* i, 265–294 (bibl.); *BeMMR*, 136–180 (bibl. p. 180); *ApNPM*, 337–435; M. Schneider, *Die Ars Nova in Frankreich und Italien* (1930); E. Dannemann, *Die Spätgotische Musiktradition in Frankreich und Burgund vor dem Auftreten Dufays* (1936); W. Korte, *Studie zur Geschichte der Musik in Italien* (1933); F. Ellinwood, †*The Works of Francesco Landini* (1939); F. Ludwig, †*Guillaume de Machaut, Musikalische Werke*, 3 vols. (1926–29); G. de Van, †*Les Monuments de l'ars nova* i (1939); †*HAM*, nos. 43–55; †*SchGMB*, nos. 22–28; †*WoGM* iii, nos. 13–62; F. Ludwig, "Die mehrstimmige Musik des 14. Jahrhunderts" (*SIM* iv); H. Besseler, "Studien zur Musik des Mittelalters" (*AMW* vii, viii); J. Wolf, "Italian Trecento Music" (*PMA* lviii); L. Ellinwood, "Origins of the Italian Ars Nova" (*PAMS*, 1937). See also under *Ballade, *Caccia, etc.

Art ballad. See *Ballade* [G.].

Arte Musicale in Italia, L'. See *Editions II.

Articulation. In singing, the clear and distinct rendering of the tones, especially in coloraturas without full text. See also *Phrasing.

Art of Fugue, The. *Die Kunst der Fuge,* the last work of J. S. Bach, written in 1749 and published posthumously, in a rather careless manner, by his sons in 1752. It contains some 20 fugues and canons, called "contrapuncti," all based on the same theme [Ex. 1], in which the various devices of imitative counterpoint such as inversion, stretto, augmentation, diminution, canon, double fugue, triple fugue, etc., are exploited in the most elaborate and ingenious manner. The number of pieces varies in the different editions, some of which combine two related pieces under one number. Until re-cently the *Art of Fugue* was considered chiefly a magnificent manual of advanced counterpoint, but during the last two decades it has become universally recognized as one of the greatest creations of musical

Art of Fugue

art. The turning point was the first public performance, promoted by W. Graeser (1906–28), in Leipzig in 1927. This event was the beginning of a sensational revival which has since spread over the entire musical world.

The inaccuracy of the first printed edition has given rise to a controversy of nearly one hundred years concerning the proper order of the contrapuncti, a controversy in which historical, paleographic, and artistic arguments as well as metaphysical speculations and mathematical abstractions have been advanced without leading to a final answer [see Lit., Hauptmann, Rust, Graeser, David, Tovey, Apel]. A special problem is presented by the last (unfinished) fugue, which has frequently been considered extraneous to the work, since none of its three subjects (the last of which is *B-A-C-H) is the principal subject of the *Art of Fugue* [cf. A. Schweitzer, *Bach*, I, 424]. H. Nottebohm (1817–82), however, showed that this subject can be contrapuntally combined with those of the last fugue [Ex. 2; cf. W. Apel, in *DM* xxii.4, 274]. This is sufficient reason for assuming that the unfinished "triple fugue" was planned as a gigantic quadruple fugue, a fitting climax of the whole work. The chorale *Wenn wir in höchsten Nöten sein* which was added by the editors "as a recompense for the incomplete fugue" does not belong to the work; yet, if played after the abrupt breaking off of the preceding fugue, it takes on a symbolic significance which may outweigh historical scruples. According to Mizler (1754), Bach planned to write still another quadruple fugue which could be reversed (crab motion) in all its parts [cf. *GD*, Suppl. Vol., p. 10].

Another problem of the *Art of Fugue* is that of medium and performance — the question as to whether it is keyboard, orchestral, or chamber music. The lack of any instrumental specifications in either the autograph or the first edition, together with the use of the scholarly name "Contrapunctus" as a designation for the various pieces, characterizes the *Art of Fugue* as a work which is not dependent upon specified medium or sound, a work which is rooted in the contrapuntal tradition of the Flemish School rather than in the ideas of the Baroque period. Therefore any kind of performance must be considered justifiable which is in conformity with the austere spirit of the composition. On the other hand, the fact should not be overlooked that all the pieces, with the exception of the mirror-fugues (nos. XII and XIII of the Peters ed.), are within the reach of the hands of a keyboard player. Evidently, in composing the work, Bach was thinking constantly of keyboard performance, if only for instructive purposes. F. Busoni, in his *Fantasia contrappuntistica* (1910), has offered a congenial modern version, fantastically expanded, of Bach's last fugue.

Lit.: †*B.-G.* xxv; other editions by Czerny, W. Graeser, H. Th. David, D. F. Tovey (with completion of the unfinished fugue); Roy Harris (for string quartet); E. Schwebsch (for 2 pianos); M. Hauptmann, *Erläuterungen zu Bach's Kunst der Fuge* (1841, '61); D. F. Tovey, *A Companion to the Art of Fugue* (1931); Roy Harris, in *MQ* xxi; C. S. Terry, in *MQ* xix; H. David, in *JMP* xxxiv; W.

Apel, in *DM* xxii.4; H. Husmann, in *BJ* xxxv.

As, asas [G.]. See *Notes.

Aspiratamente [It.]. Aspiringly.

Aspiration [F.]. See under *Nachschlag.

Aspramente [It.]. Harshly.

Assai [It.]. Very; e.g., *allegro assai,* very quick.

Assez [F.]. Fairly; e.g., *assez vite,* fairly quick.

Assieme [It.]. Together.

Assyrian music. See *Babylonian music.

Atem [G.]. Breath. *Atempause* (breathing pause) is a very short rest used in instrumental performance for the sake of articulation or phrasing. It is sometimes indicated by an apostrophe: '.

A tempo [I.]. Indicates return to normal tempo after deviations such as ritenuto, più lento, ad libitum, etc.

Atonality, atonal music. Atonality, literally "absence of tonality," is a term which is frequently but loosely and confusingly applied to compositions of the 20th century [see *New music], and one upon which writers and composers have voiced the most contradictory opinions. Obviously, it is impossible to clarify the meaning of atonality without a previous agreement regarding the term *tonality. In fact, the chief trouble seems to lie with the latter term rather than with its opposite. If, as is frequently the case, the word tonality is interpreted in its more orthodox sense, as indicating the regular vocabulary of 19th-century harmony, then any music which deliberately discards the fundamental principles of this system must be considered atonal, more or less (e.g., Busoni, and, still more so, Stravinsky, or Hindemith). It is in this sense that the word atonality is frequently used, especially by amateurs who upon hearing a composition of Hindemith or Stravinsky describe it as atonal because the familiar features of traditional harmony are lacking. However, these composers as well as many others of the same progressive group have repeatedly resented being referred to as atonal and have emphasized the existence of tonal centers in their style. If, in accordance with these views, the word tonality is understood in its widest sense, that is, as including any music in which tonal centers are still recognizable, then atonality would indicate — as it actually should — a still more radical break with the orthodox system, that is, the complete rejection of any tonal relationships. Taking this definition as a point of departure, the question arises as to the very existence of atonal music. In fact, it has been repeatedly maintained that atonal music is a contradiction in terms; in other words, that music, consisting of tones, necessarily must show relationship between these tones and hence cannot be completely "atonal." Such an argument is, perhaps, too mathematically correct to be artistically true. Tonal relationships, in the musical sense, are not a matter of demonstrable facts, but are a matter of intentions on the part of the composer. It is entirely possible to write music with a complete disregard of tonal relationships, although it is not possible to avoid all tonal relationship in writing music. No doubt, the music of Schönberg and of some of his followers is written with a conscious rejection of tonal relationships and hence must be considered atonal music. The protests launched repeatedly by "atonal" composers against their being labeled thus should not be taken too seriously (Schönberg also "hates to be called a revolutionist" — cf. his letter in N. Slonimsky, *Music Since 1900* (1937), p. 575), as they seem to originate largely in the understandable desire to avoid a denomination which, unfortunately but wholly without justification, has frequently been identified with "amusical."

To vindicate atonality from any such stigma and to accept the term as a proper denomination for an important current in New Music, does not, of course, imply any statement regarding the artistic merits and possibilities of this idiom. The

answer to this question still lies in the future. Certainly, the first ventures in atonality, Schönberg's *Drei Klavierstücke*, op. 11 (1908) [see Ex.] and *Sechs*

kleine Klavierstücke op. 19 (1911), were radical negations rather than constructive contributions. Around 1915, Schönberg began to feel that atonality needed a positive principle and a technique of its own. Obviously this had to be of a non-harmonic, hence, of a contrapuntal character. His *Twelve-tone technique was the answer to this problem. To the present day, it remains the only one that has been given.

Lit.: D. Milhaud, "Polytonalité et atonalité" (*RM* iv); A. Machabey, "Dissonance, polytonalité, atonalité" (*RM* xxi). See also *Twelve-tone system; *New Music.

Attacca, attacca subito [It.] indicates, at the end of a movement, that the next movement should follow without break.

Attacco. See under *Soggetto.

Attack [F. *attaque*]. Promptness and decision in beginning a phrase, especially in forte passages. In orchestral parlance, attack means precise entry of the instruments. In French orchestras, the concertmaster is called *chef d'attaque*.

Aubade [F., Sp. *alborada*, from L. *alba*, dawn]. Morning music, in contradistinction to *serenade, evening music. In the 17th and 18th centuries aubades were played in honor of royal or princely personages, at the levee. The term has been used by various composers (e.g., Bizet, Rimsky-Korsakov), to denote a sort of idyllic overture. The beginning of Beethoven's Pastoral Symphony and Wagner's Siegfried-idyll may be considered as idealized aubades. See *Alba.

Audition [F.]. (1) Faculty of hearing. — (2) Rehearsal; performance (particularly by students).

Aufführungspraxis [G., practice of performance]. This term has been widely adopted by German and non-German writers to refer to the manner in which early music was performed and should be performed. In particular, it refers to the many problems connected with the attempts at restoring, in so far as possible, the original sound of compositions from the early Middle Ages to Bach. The problems of Aufführungspraxis vary, of course, according to the period in question. In music prior to 1550, the foremost question is that of vocal or instrumental performance and participation, a question which arises from the fact that instruments are never specified in the sources, that the text is often carelessly underlaid, or, that long passages or even entire voices of an apparently vocal character are found without text [see *Vocalization]. Another serious difficulty results from the fact that the instruments of these periods, such as the psaltery, rotta, vielle, rebec of the 14th century, the viols, cornettos, theorboes of the 15th and 16th centuries, are all obsolete. It is only by long and patient experiments with modern reproductions of these instruments that one may hope to gain a clearer idea of the intended sound of ancient music and to solve some of the problems indicated above. Generally speaking, it must be borne in mind that the lack of clear and unequivocal indications of instruments, accidentals, etc., is not mere negligence on the part of the composer or carelessness on that of the scribe, but is an adequate expression — in fact, the necessary concomitant — of the intrinsically anti-rational viewpoint of the Middle Ages and the Renaissance. The idea of writing music for a specific instrument was just as foreign to the 15th-century musician as the idea of using one "correct" spelling for a word was foreign to a writer of this period. In both cases, the only thing that mattered was the idea, which remained the same, regardless of how it was realized.

In the 16th and 17th centuries the problems are relatively simpler. Important points are the correct execution of *thorough-bass, the performance of *ornamentations, either improvised or abbreviated, the size of the orchestra, the specifications of tempo and dynamics. Most of these questions have been rather satisfactorily clarified by musicologists [see, e.g., under *Dotted notes II]. The main obstacle to be overcome is the reluctance of modern interpreters, particularly orchestral conductors, to accept the historical facts, many of which, to be sure, are somewhat contrary to the aesthetic standards and principles of 19th-century music, particularly of Romantic music. According to the principles of Aufführungspraxis a work such as Bach's *St. Matthew Passion* should be performed by an orchestra of about 20 players (flutes, oboes, strings, organ, harpsichord) and a chorus of about the same number of singers; it should be played at a moderate speed, ranging from allegro to adagio, and with a clear distinction of forte and piano rather than with constant crescendos and decrescendos. In the period after Bach the problems of Aufführungspraxis practically disappear, owing to the greater care on the part of the composer to indicate clearly his intentions. See also *Ensemble (3).

Lit.: R. Haas, *Die musikalische Aufführungspraxis* (in *BüHM*); A. Schering, *Aufführungspraxis alter Musik* (1931); H. Leichtentritt, "Zur Vortragspraxis des 17. Jahrhunderts" (*KIM*, 1909, p. 147); A. Pirro, "Remarques sur l'exécution musicale . . ." (*c.* 1400; *KIM*, 1930, p. 55); G. Pietzsch, in *AM* iv, no. 2; H. Mersmann, "Beiträge zur Aufführungspraxis der vorklassischen Kammermusik" (*AMW* ii); cf. BeMMR, 319 (bibl.).

Aufgeregt [G.]. Excited.

Auflösung [G.]. Resolution (of a dissonance); cancellation (of an accidental). *Auflösungszeichen*, the natural sign, ♮.

Aufsatz [G.]. Tube of an organ reed pipe.

Aufschnitt [G.]. The mouth of an organ pipe.

Aufstrich [G.]. Up-bow.

Auftakt [G.]. Up-beat. For *Auftaktigkeit* see under *Phrasing.

Auftritt [G.]. Scene of an opera.

Aufzug [G.]. Act of an opera.

Augmentation and diminution. The presentation of a subject in doubled (augmentation) and in halved (diminution) values, e.g., with the quarter-note replaced by a half-note or an eighth-note respectively. These devices are an important element of variety in fugal writing. They are usually introduced towards the end of the fugue; thus used, diminution bestows a character of stretto; augmentation, one of grandeur. Examples are: Bach, *Wt. Cl.* i, no. 8 (augmentation), *Wt. Cl.* ii, no. 9 (diminution), *Art of Fugue, nos. 6 and 7 (simultaneous appearance of the normal form, diminution, augmentation, and double augmentation); Beethoven, Piano Sonata op. 110, last movement (similar combinations; see Ex.). Augmentation and diminution

are also used frequently in the development sections of symphonies, particularly those by Brahms and Bruckner.

Diminution (or augmentation) occurs first in a number of two-voiced *clausulae of the Perotinus period [see *Ars antiqua] in which a plainsong melody is used twice in succession, first in duplex longae (dotted half-notes in modern transcription), then in plain longae

(dotted quarter-notes) [cf. *ApNPM*, 253]. In the 14th century, diminution is explained in detail by theoretical writers (Joh. de Muris, Prosdocimus de Beldemandis) and is used almost regularly in the motets of G. de Machaut, the tenor having the cantus firmus twice, the second time in halved values [see *Isorhythmic]. With the beginning of the 15th century, augmentation and diminution become notational devices, since the change of note values is no longer indicated by longer or shorter notes, but by proportional signs [see *Proportions] or by verbal instructions, such as *per augmentationem,* or often by enigmatic inscriptions [see *Canon II]. A last example of this method appears in Bach's *Musical Offering.* Many of the *ricercars of the 16th century use augmentation or diminution, e.g., A. Gabrieli's *Ricercare del primo tono* [repr. in *Editions II, 7] in which each voice states the subject once in quadruple augmentation — exactly as in the Contrapunctus 7 of Bach's *Art of Fugue.*

Augmented intervals. See *Intervals; the augmented fourth is the *tritone. Augmented sixth chord [see *Sixth chord]. Augmented triad [see *Triad]. See also *Harmonic analysis V.

Aulos. The most important wind instrument of the ancient Greek. It is not a flute (as has frequently been stated) but rather an oboe, with double reed and a number of holes varying from four in the oldest instruments to fifteen in the later specimens. The numerous pictures of aulos players show that the aulos always consisted of two pipes; probably the larger pipe provided a few tones which were missing on the other. Many pictures show the player wearing a leather band which passes over the mouth and ties at the back of his head. This probably served to increase the resistance of the cheeks, which acted as bellows, and enabled the player to build up a considerable air pressure, thus producing a sound which occasionally must have been just as shrill as that of a modern bagpipe.

The aulos originally was an Oriental

instrument. According to legend, it was introduced into Greece, about 900 B.C., by Olympos, who was later glorified as the "inventor of music." Throughout the history of Greek music the aulos has retained its Asiatic character. It was adopted for the orgiastic music symbolized by Dionysos, whereas the *kithara represented the restrained character of autochthonous Greek music, symbolized by Apollo. The aulos music was rapid, rhythmic, exciting. The slight modifications of pitch which could be obtained by half-covering the holes of the aulos probably led to the enharmonic genus of Greek music. See also *Chroai.

Lit.: K. Schlesinger, *The Greek Aulos* (1939); *SaHMI*, 138ff; A. Howard, "The Aulos or Tibia," *Harvard Studies in Classical Philology*, iv and x.

Aurrescu, arrescu [Sp.]. An ancient ceremonial dance still popular in the Basque countries (northern Spain), executed with a great variety of violent steps and gestures symbolizing wooing ceremonies or other old usages. Cf. V. Alford, in *MQ* xviii; F. Gascue, in *BSIM* viii; *LavE* i.4, 2355ff.

Ausdruck [G.]. Expression, feeling.

Ausdrucksvoll [G.]. Expressively.

Ausgelassen [G.]. Exuberant, boisterous.

Aushalten [G.]. To sustain a note.

Auslösung [G.]. The repeating mechanism (escapement) of the pianoforte.

Aussprache [G.]. Diction, pronunciation.

Australian music. See *Primitive music. See also Addenda, p. 825.

Austrian music. See *German music.

Ausweichung [G.]. Modulation, especially passing modulation.

Auszug [G.]. Arrangement.

Authentic modes. See *Church modes.

Auto [Sp., act]. Spanish and Portuguese dramatic plays of religious or contemplative character, frequently with incidental music [see *Liturgical drama]. Such plays were written by Juan del'Encina (*c.* 1500), Gil Vicente (1492–1557), Lope de Vega (1562–1635), Calderon (1600–81), and others. Cf. G. Chase, in *MQ* xxv; A. Salazar, in *PAMS*, 1938.

Autoharp. A *zither on which simple chords such as are used in accompanying popular melodies are provided by special buttons which, upon being depressed, damp all the strings except those required for the chord.

Automelon and idiomelon. In Byzantine church music a chant is called *automelon* (other melody) if it is sung to a standard melody provided originally for another chant; *idiomelon* (own melody) if it has a specific melody of its own. The terms are also used with reference to other fields, e.g., the antiphons of Gregorian chant, most of which are automela [see the classification of Gevaert, mentioned under *antiphon (1)] while others are idiomela, e.g., the antiphons of the Mass or the antiphons B.M.V.

Auxiliary tone. See *Nonharmonic tones I.

Ave Maria. A prayer used in the Roman Catholic Church; see text and plainsong in *AR*, 123. The text has been repeatedly set to music by 19th-century composers. The same title also occurs with a rather lachrymose piece by Schubert, and a very lamentable piece by Gounod in which Bach's first prelude of the *Well-tempered Clavier* is misused as a harmonic background for a highly sentimental melody.

Ave maris stella. A hymn of Gregorian chant to which there exist various melodies in different modes (cf. *AR*, pp. [117]–[127]). These have been frequently used as tenors of motets and of organ-hymns, e.g., by Cabezon.

Ave regina coelorum. One of the four *antiphons B.V.M., sung as a Vesper hymn from Purification until Easter (text and plainsong in *AR*, 66). The melody is interesting because of its well-defined C major tonality (except for the plagal B-flat of the beginning).

Ayre. (1) A late-16th-century type of English song, similar to the Italian *canzonet or *balletto. The ayre is a strophic song in simple homophonic style, the melody being supported either by voices or by instruments or by both. For the early publications and their modern reprints see *Editions X, XI. Later publications are· *Select Ayres and Dialogues* (1652) and *New Ayres and Dialogues* (1678); these include songs with the accompaniment of lute, theorboe, bass viol, by H. Lawes, W. Webb, John Blow, Purcell, and others. Cf. A. Dolmetsch, *English Songs and Dialogues of the XVI and XVII Centuries* (1912); P. Warlock, *The English Ayre* (1926).   W. A.

(2) English writers of the 17th century use the term ayre (aire) in the meaning of key or mode, e.g., Th. Morley: "these aires which the antiquity termed *Modi*" (*Plaine and Easy Introduction*, p. 147); or Th. Mace: "every shake is to be made in the *Aire*" (*Musick's Monument*, p. 104); also Butler, *The Principles of Music* (1636), pp. 72, 80, 82; Locke, *Melothesia* (1673), Rule 6; Simpson, *A Compendium to Practical Musick* (5th ed., 1714), p. 36. See also under *Fancy.   H. J. S.

B

B. See *Pitch names; *Letter notation; *Hexachord; also *Accidentals (history), In *part-books of the 16th century, B stands for *bassus* (bass).

Baborak. A Bohemian national dance, including alternating sections in duple and in triple time.

Babylonian (Sumerian, Assyrian) music. Our knowledge of the musical culture of the ancient inhabitants of Mesopotamia is restricted chiefly to information about their musical instruments gained from pictorial and architectural illustrations. This material, however, is full enough to permit the reconstruction of a fairly adequate picture of the general trends in the musical evolution which took place there from about 3500 to 500 B.C. The chief instrument of the Sumerian period (*c*. 3500–2000) was the harp, usually without fore-pillar [see *Harp III]. It existed in a great variety of shapes and sizes. During the Babylonian rule (2000–1000) we find lutes, flutes, oboes, and drums, instruments which point to a greater refinement of musical culture. During the Assyrian rule (1000–500) music gradually lost its ancient cosmological character and strictly liturgical position and became more and more hedonistic and voluptuous, particularly through the incorporation of elements of contemporary Egyptian music. The attempt made by C. Sachs [*AMW* vii] to interpret certain signs on a Babylonian clay tablet dating from about 800 B.C. as harp notation, and his consequent reconstruction of a Babylonian hymn, have been withdrawn by him in an article [*MQ* xxvi] in which he also refutes another interpretation given by F. W. Galpin.

Lit.: F. W. Galpin, *The Music of the Sumerians . . .* , *Babylonians and Assyrians* (1937); *LavE* i.1, 35ff; C. Sachs, *Musik des Altertums* (1924); *id.*, in *AMW* vii and *MQ* xxvi, xxvii; *ReMMA*, 4ff (bibl. p. 426); *GD*, Suppl. Vol., p. 14 (ill.); *SaHMI*, 67ff.

Bacchetta [It.]. *Drumstick (— *di legno*, wooden; — *di spugna*, spongeheaded).

B-A-C-H. The letters which form Bach's name have, in German, a musical significance, namely: bb-a-c-b [see *Pitch names]. This interesting musical motive was first used by Bach himself in the last (unfinished) fugue of his *Art of Fugue.*

Another fugue on the same subject frequently ascribed to him [see ed. Peters, xxv] is definitely spurious. Various later composers have used the famous motive in fugues or fantasias, e.g., Albrechtsberger [cf. *DTOe* 16.ii]; Schumann (*6 Fugen über Bach,* op. 60); Liszt (*Fantasia and Fugue on B.A.C.H.,* for pianoforte and for organ); M. Reger (op. 46); W. Piston (*Chromatic Fantasy on Bach*). It also plays an important part in Busoni's *Fantasia contrappuntistica* (1910).

Bach-Gesellschaft. See *Societies II, 2.
Here follows a conspectus of the contents of the edition of the Bach-Gesellschaft, arranged according to subject matter.

   I. *Sacred Cantatas.* 1–10: vol. 1. — 11–20: vol. 2. — 21–30: vol. 5.i. — 31–40: vol. 7. — 41–50: vol. 10. — 51–60: vol. 12.ii. — 61–70: vol. 16. — 71–80: vol. 18. — 81–90: vol. 20.i. — 91–100: vol. 22. — 101–110: vol. 23. — 111–120: vol. 24. — 121–130: vol. 26. — 131–140: vol. 28. — 141–150: vol. 30. — 151–160: vol. 32. — 161–170: vol. 33. — 171–180: vol. 35. — 181–190: vol. 37. — 191–193: vol. 41. — 194: vol. 29. — 195–197 (Wedding Cantatas): vol. 13.i. — 198 (Trauer Ode): vol. 13.iii. — Unnumbered (doubtful or unfinished): vol. 41. [For the numbering of the cantatas 191ff cf. C. S. Terry, *Bach's Cantata Texts* (1926), 642.]
   II. *Secular Cantatas.* 201–205: vol. 11.ii. — 206–207: vol. 20.ii (also 34). — 208–212: vol. 29. — 213: vol. 34. — Unnumbered: vols. 34, 20.ii.
   III. *Oratorios.* Weihnachts-Oratorium: 5.ii. — Oster-Oratorium: 21.iii. — Himmelfahrts-Oratorium: 2 (= Cantata 11).
   IV. *Passion Music.* Mattheus: 4 (variant of Schluss-choral in 41). — Johannes: 12.i. — Lucas: 45.ii.
   V. *Masses and Parts of Masses.* B minor: 6. — F, A, G minor, G: 8. — 4 Sanctus: 11.i. — Sanctus, Kyrie, and Christe: 41.
   VI. *Magnificat.* 11.i.
   VII. *Motets.* Six and two doubtful: 39.
   VIII. *Chorales.* 1–185 (Collection of C. P. E. Bach): 39. — 3 Choräle zu Trau-

ungen: 13.i. (For a complete collection of Bach's Chorales cf. C. S. Terry, *Bach's Four-Part Chorals.*)
   IX. *Songs.* 39.
   X. *Orchestral Works* (cl. = clavier; vl. = violin; cont. = continuo). Four Overtures, 1 Sinfonia: 31.i. — Ouverture C moll: 45.i. — 6 Brandenburg concertos: 19. — Triple concerto for flute, cl. and vl.: 17. — 7 Concertos for one cl.: 17. — 3 Concertos for 2 cl.: 21.ii. — 2 Concertos for 3 cl.: 31.iii. — Concerto for 4 cl.: 43.i. — 2 Concertos for vl.: 21.i (also 45.i). — Sinfonia for vl.: 21.i. — Concerto for 2 vl.: 21.i.
   XI. *Chamber Music.* Sonata for flute, vl. and cont.: 9. — Trio, Canon for flute, vl. and cont. (from the Musical Offering): 31.ii. — Instrumentalsatz für vl., Hoboe und Cont.: 29. — 7 Sonatas for cl. and vl. (one doubtful): 9. — Suite for cl. and vl.: 9. — Sonata, Fugue for vl. and cont.: 43.i. — Sonata for two vl. and cont.: 9. — 4 Inventions for vl. and cl.: 45.i. — Sonata in G for vl. and cont.: Neue B.-G. 30, Lf. i. — 3 Sonatas, 3 Partitas for vl. solo: 27.i. — 6 Suites for cello solo: 27.i. — 3 Sonatas for gamba and cl.: 9. — 3 Sonatas for cl. and flute: 9. — 3 Sonatas for flute and cont.: 43.i.
   XII. *Clavier Music.* Six English Suites: 13.ii (new ed. in 45.i). — 6 French Suites: 13.ii (new ed. in 45.i; fragments in 36). — 6 Partitas: 3. — French Overture: 3. — Miscellaneous suites (fragments): 36, 42, 45.i. — Overture: 36. — Inventions, 2- and 3-part: 3. — Well-tempered Clavier: 14 (Variants: 36; Autograph: 45.i). — 7 Toccatas: 3 and 36. — Sonatas: 36, 42, 45.i. — Italian Concerto: 3. — 16 Concertos (Vivaldi): 42. — Goldberg Variations: 3. — Aria variata: 36. — 2 Capriccios: 36. — Chromatic Fantasia: 36. — Preludes (Fantasia) and fugues, Preludes, Fantasias, Fugues: 36. — 4 Duets: 3. — Clavier Uebung i,ii,iii: 3. —Notenbuch der Anna Magdalena Bach (1722, '25): 43.ii. — Clavierbüchlein für W. F. Bach (1720): 45.i.
   XIII. *Organ Music.* Seventy Chorale preludes (46 Orgelbüchlein; 18 Choräle; 6 Schübler): 25.ii. — 21 Chorale preludes (from Clavierübung iii): 3. — 65 Chorale

preludes (24 Kirnberger; 28 others; 13 doubtful): 40. — [10 Chorale preludes not included in B.-G. are reprinted in Ed. Peters, vol. 9]. — 6 Sonatas: 15. — 4 Concertos (after Vivaldi): 38 (variant in 42). — [2 other Concertos in Ed. Peters, 9]. — 18 Preludes and fugues: 15. — 3 Preludes and fugues: 38. — 3 Toccatas: 15. — Passacaglia: 15. — 8 Kleine Praeludien und Fugen: 38. — 6 Fantasias, 3 Preludes, 6 Fugues, Canzona, Allabreve, Pastorale, 2 Trios: 38. — [2 other Trios in Ed. Peters, 9].

XIV. *Art of Fugue.* 25.i (original form: 47). — Musical Offering: 31.ii, — Canons: 45.i.

Bach trumpet. See under *Clarin trumpet.

Backfall. English 17th-century name for the *appoggiatura. See also *Appoggiatura, Double II.

Badinage, badinerie [F., playfulness, banter]. A dance-like piece of jocose character which occurs as a movement in the optional group of the 18th-century suites, e.g., in Bach's Suite in B minor.

Bagatelle [F., a trifle]. A short piece, usually for the pianoforte. The name was used by François Couperin ("Les Bagatelles," see his *Pièces de Clavecin,* new ed. Augener, ii, ordre 10) and, in particular, by Beethoven, whose *Bagatellen* (op. 33, op. 119, op. 126) mark the beginning of the extensive literature of 19th-century *character pieces.

Bagpipe [F. *musette*; G. *Dudelsack, Sackpfeife*; It. *piva, zampogna*]. Generic name for a number of instruments which have one or (usually) several reed-pipes attached to a windbag from which the air is blown into the pipes; also, specifically, the name for the Irish and Scottish varieties of this family. [See the illustration on p. 152 (Clarinets).] One or two of the pipes, called chanter (chaunter), are provided with soundholes and are used for melodies, while the other, larger ones, called drones, produce one tone each and are used for the accompaniment. In the

earlier, Eastern specimens, both chanter and drones are clarinets (i.e., have single reeds) while in the modern types either they are both oboes (i.e., with double reeds), as in Italy and some parts of France, or the drones are clarinets while the chanter is an oboe, as in Scotland, Ireland, Brittany. Two categories of bagpipes may be distinguished, according to whether the wind in the bag is provided from the mouth through an additional blowing-pipe, or by a small pair of bellows placed under and operated by the arm. To the former type belong the *Old Irish bagpipe,* the *Highland bagpipe* (Scotland), the *biniou* (Bretagne), the *cornemuse* (France), the *Dudelsack* or *Sackpfeife* (Germany), the *zampogna* and *piva* (Italy); to the latter: the *Northumbrian bagpipe* (England), the modern *Irish bagpipe,* the *gaita* (Galicia), the *musette* (France). A more primitive instrument was the *bladder pipe,* a single or double clarinet with a bladder used as a bag [illustrated in *GD,* pl. LX].

The bagpipe was not known to the Babylonians, Jews, and Greeks, but was used in Rome (*tibia utricularis*). Nero is reported to have played on it. In the Middle Ages it is frequently mentioned under different names (*musa, chorus, symphonia, chevrette*). The famous illuminations of the 13th-century Spanish MS *Escorial j b 2* [see *Cantiga] show players of bagpipes [cf. *GD* iv, 184; *ReMMA,* 222]. In the British Isles the bagpipes have played, for many centuries, a prominent role in folk music and in military music. Their continental history is less interesting, except for a late 17th-century movement in France which, for a short time, raised the instrument to a standing in society and in art music [see *Musette]. See also *Pibroch.

Lit.: Wm. H. Grattan-Flood, *The Story of the Bagpipe* (1907); W. L. Manson, *The Highland Bagpipe* (1901); G. Askew, *A Bibliography of the Bagpipe* (1932).

Baguette [F., stick]. Drumstick (— *de bois,* wooden drumstick; — *d'éponge,* sponge-headed drumstick). Also the baton of the conductor and the stick of the violin bow.

Bajazzo, Der [G.]. See *Pagliacci, Gli.

Balalaika. A popular Russian instrument of the guitar family, characterized by a triangular body, a long fretted neck, and (usually) three gut strings tuned in fourths. It is played with a plectrum and is made in six sizes which constitute a balalaika band. [Illustration on p. 314.] The forerunner of the balalaika was the *domra [cf. SaRM]. Cf. A. S. Rose, in PMA xxvii.1; W. v. Kwetzinsky, in DM xxii.12.

Balancement [F.]. Eighteenth-century name for the *tremolo. Sometimes used synonymously with *Bebung.

Balg [G.]. Bellows of an organ.

Balinese music. See *Javanese music. Cf. C. McPhee, in BAMS vi.

Ballabile. A name given occasionally to dance-like pieces (ballets) in 19th-century operas.

Ballad [from L. *ballare*, to dance]. The term derives from medieval words such as *chanson balladé, *ballade [F.], *ballata, all of which originally denoted dancing songs but lost their dance connotation as early as the 13th century and became stylized forms of solo song. In England this process of change went still farther, and eventually (16th century) "ballad" came to mean a simple tale told in simple verse. There may have been a transitional period during which the recitation of the poems was still accompanied by some sort of dancing. Most ballads are narrative, and many deal with fabulous, miraculous, or gruesome deeds. Ballad singers made a living by singing their newest productions in the streets and at country fairs and by selling the printed sheets to the people. In its more recent (19th-century) meaning, a ballad is a popular song usually combining narrative and romantic elements, frequently with an admixture of the gruesome. These ballads are mostly written in common meter (4.3.4.3). Today the term "ballad" is loosely applied to any kind

of cheap modern song. For art ballad, see *Ballade [G.].

The word ballad is also used as an Anglicized form of *ballade* [F.], *ballata* [It.], or *Ballade* [G.]. Such usage, however, is misleading in view of the fact that these terms denote entirely different things.

Lit.: S. Foster Damon, †*Series of Old American Songs* (1936); C. Sandburg, †*The American Songbag* (1927); Cecil J. Sharp, *English Folk Songs from the Southern Appalachians*, 2 vols. (1932); John A. Lomax, *Our Singing Country* (1941); R. Smith, *South Carolina Ballads* (1928); A. K. Davis, *Traditional Ballads of Virginia* (1929); M. O. Eddy, *Ballads and Songs from Ohio* (1939); M. E. Henry, *A Bibliography for the Study of American Folksongs* (1937); J. W. Hendren, *A Study of Ballad Rhythm* (1936); C. A. Smith, "Ballads Surviving in the U. S." (MQ ii).

Ballade [F.]. A form of trouvère poetry and music. The poem usually has three stanzas, each of seven or eight lines, the last one or two of which are identical in all the stanzas, thus forming a *refrain. The musical form of the stanza is: a b a b c d E or a b a b c d E F [capital letters indicate the refrain], a scheme which, as far as the music is concerned, can be simplified as follows: A A B (A = ab; B = the remaining lines). This form is identical with that of the Provençal (troubadour) *canzo and of the German (Minnesinger) Bar [see *Barform], which, however, lack the refrain. Sometimes the form is enlarged to A A B B, usually in connection with enlarged stanzas of 12 or more lines.

The songs of the trouvères include a considerable number of monophonic ballades [see Lit., Gennrich i, nos. 356, 357, 362, 366, etc.]. In the 14th century, G. de Machaut revived the ballade as a polyphonic composition of great refinement and subtlety [cf. F. Ludwig's edition of his works; also AdHM i, 270]. His example was followed by the French musicians of the late 14th century (Soulage, Trébor, Cuvelier, etc.; see *Ars nova) with whom the polyphonic ballade became the principal form of music, treated with the highest degree of elaboration and occasionally with affectation [examples in *WoGM* ii, iii, nos. 55, 56, etc.; *ApNPM*, 419, 421, 423]. The form was also cultivated by Dufay and, occasionally, even by Josquin [cf. *Odhecaton A*, no. 10]. Several scholars use the term ballade also for the Italian 14th-century *ballata — a procedure which is bound to lead to errors, since the ballata is an entirely different form. E.g., the piece by Enrique reproduced in *RiMB*, no. 12, is a ballata (or *villancico), not a ballade. Examples in *HAM*, nos. 19a, 45, 47; *SchGMB*, nos. 26, 40; *ApNPM*, 352, 355, etc.; *RiMB*, nos. 4, 8.

Lit.: F. Gennrich, †*Rondeaux, Virelais und Balladen*, 2 vols. (1921); F. Brosch, *Die Balladen im Kodex von Turin* (Diss. Vienna 1931).

Ballade [G.]. In German usage the word *Ballade* denotes poems derived from the English ballads, but of greater artistic elaboration and poetic refinement. They usually deal with medieval matters, either historical or fancied (e.g., Goethe's "Ballade vom vertriebenen und zurückkehrenden Grafen"), or with romantic tales (e.g., Goethe's "Erlkönig"). Such Balladen were frequently set to music, usually as through-composed songs of great length. Probably the earliest examples of true Balladen-style are the interesting settings of Gellert's moralizing and dry *Fabeln* by Valentin Herbing (1759; *DdT* 42), written in a continuous recitative with a highly dramatic accompaniment. Later examples are written in the form of cantatas, i.e., in various movements of contrasting character [Joh. André, 1741–99; Joh. Zumsteeg, 1760–1802]. A Fantasie op. 109 by Beethoven's pupil Ferdinand Ries (1784–1838) for piano alone, written to Schiller's poem "Resignation," is an interesting example of what might be called a "Ballade ohne Worte" [repr. in *TaAM* xiv]. The classical master of the vocal Ballade (sometimes referred to as "art ballad") is Carl Loewe (1796–1869) whose fifteen volumes of *Balladen*

[complete ed. by M. Runze] include a number of truly great songs ("Archibald Douglas," "Erlkönig," "Der Pilgrim von St. Just," etc.). Loewe's form is a free combination of the strophic and the through-composed type. Schubert's songs include a number of Balladen, e.g., "Erlkönig." In the late 19th century Balladen were composed for solo or chorus with orchestral accompaniment, e.g., H. Wolf's "Feuerreiter." Chopin and Brahms used the term for piano pieces written in the ternary form A B A of the 19th-century *character piece. Here the highly dramatic character of A and the lyrical character of B seem to portray heroic deeds and knightly love, thus justifying the title *Ballade*.

Lit.: A. B. Bach, *The Art Ballad* (1891); Ph. Spitta, "Ballade" (*Musikgeschichtliche Aufsätze*, 1894); H. J. Moser, †*Die Ballade* (Martens, †*Musikalische Formen in historischen Reihen* iii, 1930); R. Batka, *Martin Plüddemann und seine Balladen* (1895); A. König, *Die Ballade in der Musik* (1904).

Ballad opera. A popular type of 18th-century stage entertainment, consisting of spoken dialogue and musical numbers not newly composed, but taken from folk songs or from famous tunes of contemporary composers. The ballad opera flourished in London from 1725 (A. Ramsay's *The Gentle Shepherd*) throughout the end of the century [cf. the list in *GD* i, 207, also in Tufts]. *The Beggar's Opera* (1728) by John Gay with music arranged by Joh. Pepusch (1667–1752) was the most successful of all. Two plays by Charles Coffey, *The Devil to Pay* (1728) and *The Merry Cobbler* (1735), played a decisive role in the development of the German *Singspiel. The music of the ballad operas included songs and arias from Locke, Purcell, Handel, Geminiani, Corelli, Scarlatti, and others; Playford's *Dancing Master* (numerous editions from 1650 to 1728) and similar collections were the chief source for the popular tunes employed in these operas. The style of the ballad opera has been imitated in Vaughan Williams' *Hugh the Drover* (1924) and in Kurt Weill's *Dreigroschen Oper* (1928), a highly successful imitation of John Gay's *Beggar's Opera.*

Lit.: E. M. Gagey, *Ballad Opera* (1937); F. Kidson, *The Beggar's Opera* (1922); W. E. Schultz, *Gay's Beggars Opera* (1923); W. Barclay-Squire, "An Index of Tunes in the Ballad-Operas" (*MA* ii); G. Tufts, "Ballad Operas" (*MA* iv); W. J. Lawrence, "Early Irish Ballad Opera . . ." (*MQ* ii).

Ballata [It.]. One of the chief forms of Italian 14th-century poetry and music [see *Ars nova III]. It is not derived from the French *ballade*, but from the *virelai*, which was also called *chanson balladé.* As a poem the ballata consists of various (usually three) stanzas (S) of six lines, each of which is preceded and followed by a refrain (R) of two lines, so that the following *rondeau-like scheme results: R S_1 R S_2 R S_3 R. Music is composed only for the first four lines and repeated for the others as follows:

R	S	R
1	2 3 4	5 . . .
A	b b a	A . . .

(the figures 1 to 5 represent double-lines, i.e., 10 single lines). 1 (and 5) are called *ripresa* (refrain); 2 and 3, *piedi;* 4, *volta.* Like the virelai, the ballata originally was a song accompanying round dances, and was performed alternately by the whole group (*ripresa*) and a solo singer (*piedi* and *volta*). However, none of the surviving examples shows evidence of dance-like rhythm or style. Monophonic examples of the ballata structure are to be found in the religious *laude of the 13th century. In the 14th century the form was treated polyphonically, especially by Francesco Landini of whom 87 two-voiced and 49 three-voiced ballatas are preserved (mostly with only one stanza; no. 148 of Ellinwood's collection has three stanzas). An example is reproduced (under the erroneous title "madrigal" and with incorrect underlaying of the text) in J. Wolf's †*Sing- und Spielmusik aus älterer Zeit* [for the correct version see Ellinwood]. The form of the bal-

lata (or virelai) persists in the songs of the *Cancionero musical* [see *Villancico] and, in a simplified form, in the *frottole of the early 16th century. Examples in L. Ellinwood, †*Francesco Landini* (1939); *HAM*, nos. 51, 53; *SchGMB*, 16 (text incomplete); *EiBM* 11; *WoGM* ii, iii, nos. 46, 51–53; *ApNPM*, 151, 408.

Ballet(t). Sixteenth-century English version of *balletto.

Ballet. I. Ballet is theatrical performance of a dancing group with costumes and scenery, to the accompaniment of music, but without singing or spoken word. The history of the modern ballet goes back to the 15th century, when dance performances were introduced at the French and Burgundian courts for the celebration of marriages, for the reception of foreign sovereigns, and for similar festive occasions. One of the most sumptuous of these entertainments was the "Ballet Comique de la Royne" (marriage of Margaret of Lorraine to the Duke of Joyeuse, Versailles, 1581). It is the earliest for which the music is preserved, and is especially remarkable on account of its inclusion of two monodic songs (new ed., see *Editions IV; cf. also *AdHM* ii, 642 and L. Celler, *Les Origines de l'opéra et le ballet de la Royne*, 1868). The culmination point of the ballet was reached under Louis XIV (1643–1715), who himself was a great dancer and who liked to appear in ballet performances. With the ballet-master Beauchamp and the musicians Cambefort (1605–61) and Lully (1632–87), the French ballet attained the highest cultural importance as well as great musical significance. It became the origin of a great number of new courtly dance types, such as the gavotte, the passepied, the bourrée, the rigaudon, which were later introduced into the optional group of the *suite. Of particular importance among these was the *minuet. Lully's activity in the ballet of the French court (*ballet de cour*) began in 1653 ("Ballet de la Nuit") and came to a climax in 1664 when he and Molière joined forces to produce a unification of play and ballet, the *comédie-ballet.* "Le

Bourgeois Gentilhomme" (1670) is the most famous example of this type [see *Entr'acte]. Lully also introduced the ballet into his operas, as did also his successors Campra and Rameau. Rameau's ballets are particularly interesting on account of their exotic background, Mexican, Persian, Chinese, etc. [see also *Ballet in opera]. A special type of ballet was cultivated in England, under the name of *masque. In the second half of the 17th century Vienna was a center of ballet presentations (Johann Heinrich Schmelzer and others; cf. *DTOe* 28.ii).

II. From 1700 till the end of the 19th century the history of the ballet includes a galaxy of famous dancers, such as Camargo (1710–70), Noverre (1727–1810), Vestris (1729–1808), Taglioni (1804–84), Fanny Elssler (1810–51), and others. Unfortunately, little of the music used in their presentations has come down to us. Noverre, the great reformer of the ballet, found musical collaborators in Stuttgart (Florian Deller, 1729–73; Johann J. Rudolph, 1730–1812; cf. *DdT* 43/44) as well as in Vienna (Ignaz Holzbauer, 1711–83; Christoph W. Gluck, 1714–87; Josef Starzer, 1726–87; Gluck's "Don Juan" in *DTOe* 30.ii). This list is completed by Beethoven's "Prometheus," produced in 1801 at the Burg Theater of Vienna.

III. Ballet music took a new start with Délibes' "Coppelia" (1870) and Tchaikovsky's three ballets "The Swan Lake" (1876), "The Sleeping Beauty" (1889), and "Casse-Noisette" ("The Nutcracker," 1892). The great period of modern ballet music, however, did not start until the early 20th century, when the Russian ballet of Diaghileff and Fokine began its triumphal career and attracted the interest of many prominent composers, e.g., Stravinsky, with "Firebird" (1910), "Petrouchka" (1912), "Le Sacre du Printemps" (1913), "Les Noces" (completed 1923), "Apollo Musagetes" (1927), "Card Party" (1936), and others; Ravel with "Daphnis and Chloë" (1906, 1912); Manuel de Falla with "The Three-Cornered Hat" (1919); Darius Milhaud with "Le Train bleu" (1924) and "La Création du

monde" (1923); Francis Poulenc with "Les Biches" (1923); Béla Bartók with "The Wooden Prince" (1922); Hindemith with "The Demon" (1924); Bax with "The Truth about the Russian Dancers" (1920), and others. In America, the vogue of the ballet has produced such works as John A. Carpenter's "Krazy-Kat" (1921) and "Skyscrapers" (1926); Copland's "Grogh" (1932) and "Hear ye, hear ye" (1934); Marc Blitzstein's "Checkmate" (1937); Walter Piston's "The Incredible Flutist" (1938), etc.

Lit.: W. Beaumont, *Complete Book of Ballets* (1937; sup. 1942); G. Goode, *The Book of Ballets* (1939); V. Arvey, *Choreographic Music* (1941); H. Prunières, *Le Ballet de cour en France* (1914); *DTOe* 28.ii ("Wiener Tanzmusik," *c.* 1650–1700); *DTOe* 43/44 ("Ausgewählte Ballette Stuttgarter Meister," *c.* 1750–1800); H. Prunières, "Le Ballet sous Louis XIII" (*BSIM* x); "Le Ballet au XIXᵉ siècle" (*RM* ii, special number); D. L. Murray, "The Future of the Ballet" (*ML* vii, no. 1); R. Lach, in *ZMW* iii (Beethoven's "Prometheus").

Ballet in opera. Ballets appear in opera usually as interludes unessential to the plot, although connected with it by some more or less specious pretext. Their function is thus to offer a diversion from the purely vocal and dramatic portions, and they frequently involve large choral groups and spectacular stage effects as well as dancing. They are therefore most appropriate in large-scale, serious, formal opera, and historically they are found chiefly in operas of the French school or works written under the influence of French taste. Ballets in comic opera are simpler and less formal than those in serious works, as for example the dances in the finale of the first act of Mozart's *Don Giovanni*.

Although Lully is commonly credited with having introduced the ballet into opera, it was not unknown in operas before his time. Without reckoning the choral dances of Greek tragedy, the general dances which frequently took place at the end of the medieval *mystery-plays, or the ballet portions of the 16th-century *intermezzi, we find closing dances in Peri's and Caccini's *Euridice* (both 1600), a "Ballo" at the end of Gagliano's *Dafne* (1608), and a "Moresca" danced by the shepherds in the finale of Monteverdi's *Orfeo* (1607). There are likewise ballets, though on a relatively small scale, in operas of the Roman school (e.g., Landi's *San Alessio*, 1632; M. Rossi's *Erminia sul Giordano*, 1637). The Venetian opera, along with its fondness for spectacular stage effects, made some use of the ballet, especially in works designed for festival occasions, like Cesti's *Pomo d'oro* (Vienna, 1667), which has several ballets in each act and a grand triple ballet in the finale.

The importance of the ballet in French opera is due to the long previous tradition of the Ballet de Cour in France and to the fact that Lully, in establishing the national operatic form, practically incorporated the entire apparatus of the ballet in the new type of entertainment. The designation of the opera company as "Académie royale de musique et de danse" in itself shows the intimate connection which was felt to exist between opera and ballet, a connection which has been maintained throughout the entire subsequent history of French opera. So strong was the French fondness for ballet that before the end of the 17th century a new form, the "opéra-ballet," was created (Campra, *L'Europe galante*, 1697), in which the dramatic content was reduced to a minimum in order to make room for practically continuous dancing, choral, and scenic elements (Rameau, *Les Indes galantes*, 1735). The dances of Lully's and Rameau's operas and opera-ballets furnish some of the finest examples of French instrumental music of their period.

English opera likewise introduced ballet, partly from the native tradition of the *masque and partly under French influence. There are ballets in Blow's *Venus and Adonis* (*c.* 1685) and Purcell's *Dido and Aeneas* (*c.* 1689), as well as in Purcell's other dramatic music (e.g., the Chaconne in *King Arthur*, 1691).

In Germany ballet in opera was intro-duced by foreign composers (C. Pallavicino's *Gerusalemme liberata*, Dresden, 1687), and, under French influence, by native composers as well (Joh. Sigismund Kusser's *Erindo*, Hamburg, 1693). The ballets in the original version of Keiser's *Croesus* (1711) were omitted in the revival of 1730.

In early 18th-century Neapolitan opera the ballet was of minor importance, with rare exceptions in festival works such as Fux's *Costanza e fortezza* (Prague, 1723). Toward the middle of the century, however, with the first movements toward reform of the Neapolitan model, ballet scenes began to be revived. This is especially evident in the works of Jomelli, written at Stuttgart in 1753–69, where the celebrated ballet master Jean-Georges Noverre was also in residence; and in the operas of Traëtta at Parma (1758–65) and St. Petersburg (1768–74), which show the influence of Rameau. Gluck's "reform" operas are filled with ballet scenes, quite on the model of their French prototypes, and the ballet remained a constant and important feature in the works of Gluck's disciples, as well as in the "grand opera" of the 19th century (Auber's *Muette de Portici*, 1829; Rossini's *Guillaume Tell*, 1829; Meyerbeer's *Robert le Diable*, 1831; Halévy's *La Juive*, 1835; Wagner's *Rienzi*, 1842; Berlioz's *Les Troyens*, 1856–58; Gounod's *Faust*, 1859/69). It will be noted that all the above-named works except *Rienzi* were first performed (or intended to be performed) at Paris, where a ballet was still considered to be an indispensable part of any large serious operatic work. Wagner's addition of the "Bacchanal" music for the Paris performance of *Tannhäuser* (1861) is a striking evidence of the power of this French tradition. Wagner in his later works occasionally had recourse to the ballet (*Die Meistersinger, Parsifal*), as did Verdi in *Aida* (1871). There are also important ballet scenes in Borodin's *Prince Igor* (performed 1890), but on the whole the decline of "grand opera" has led to a diminution of the importance of ballet in opera since the middle of the 19th century, and this has been accompanied by a steady rise of interest in ballet as a separate form [see *Ballet]. Incidental dance scenes, closely connected with the action, are to be found in some modern opera scores, e.g., R. Strauss's *Salome* (1905), Berg's *Wozzek* (perf. 1926), Hindemith's *Neues vom Tage* (1929), and others. The ballets in Milhaud's *Christophe Colomb* (1930) are on a grand scale, but this work can hardly be regarded as typical of modern practice in this respect.   D. J. G.

Balletto [It.], **ballett.** (1) Vocal composition of *c.* 1600, dance-like in character, written in a simplified madrigal style and frequently provided with a *fa-la-burden which was probably danced. The first publication in this field was Giov. Gastoldi's *Balletti a cinque voci . . . di cantare, sonare e ballare* (1591). It was imitated by Th. Morley in his *The First Book of Ballets to 5 voices* (1598), and similar publications until *c.* 1620. — (2) Instrumental compositions of a similar type and style. These appear frequently in the German *suites of the early 17th century, e.g., Joh. Hermann Schein, *Banchetto musicale* (1617; complete ed. by A. Prüfer, vol. ii), Paul Peurl, Melchior Franck, Valentin Haussmann, etc. Frescobaldi wrote ballettos for keyboard [cf. *TaAM* v].

Ballo, Tempo di [It.]. In dance-like character.

Bamberg, Codex. See *Sources, no. 5.

Band [F. *bande*; It. *banda*]. An orchestral group composed principally of wind instruments. Different types are: *brass band (brass only), wind band (winds only), military band (chiefly brass), jazz band (various combinations; see *Jazz), symphonic band (predominantly wood wind, with the addition of cello or double-bass). Other types are the balalaika-band, marimba band, etc. In modern Italian orchestra the group of brass and percussion is called *banda*. In earlier periods the name was applied to orchestral groups of highest distinction, e.g., to the "24 violons du roy" under Lully (La grande bande),

or to the 24 fiddlers of Charles II (The King's Private Band). See *Brass band; *Military band.

Bandola, bandolon. Same as *Bandurria.

Bandoneon. See *Accordion.

Bandora. See *Pandora.

Bandurria. See *Guitar family.

Banjo. A stringed instrument with a long neck and a body in the form of an open drum, spanned with parchment as a resonator. It usually has six strings, the highest of which, called the thumb-string, is placed next to the lowest, in the following arrangement: g'' g d' g' b' d''. The banjo is the typical instrument of the American Negroes and has been frequently used in jazz. It was imported by the slaves from western Africa (Senegambia), where it existed under the name "bania." In all probability it is not an aboriginal African instrument, but a modification of the Arabian or European guitar [see *Guitar family].

Bar. (1) In English, bar-line or, more usually, measure (included between two bar-lines). — (2) In German, see *Barform.

Barber of Seville, The. See *Barbiere di Siviglia, Il.

Barbershop harmony. Colloquial term for a type of highly chromatic, oversweet harmony used in popular American

part-singing. Diminished seventh chords, augmented sixths, and similar combinations prevail. Cf. S. Spaeth, *Barber Shop Ballads* (1940); also *Jazz II.

Barbiere di Siviglia, Il ("The Barber of Seville"). Opera buffa by Gioachino Rossini (1792–1868), based on Beaumarchais' comedy *Le Barbier de Seville* (1775), first performance in Rome, 1816 (New York, 1819). The scene is 17th-century Seville where *Count Almaviva* (Tenor) and *Dr. Bartolo* (Bass) are rivals for the love of *Rosina* (Soprano), with the former winning out by the aid of the resourceful barber *Figaro* (Baritone). Mozart's *Le Nozze di Figaro* centers around a later adventure of the amorous Count.

The *Barbiere* is one of the last examples of the 18th-century type of Italian opera and, in particular, the last to use the *recitativo secco*. Figaro's aria "Largo al factotum" is one of the most outstanding examples of *buffo* aria in rapid declamation [see *Parlando; *Patter song].

Barbitos. An ancient Greek instrument of the *lyre type.

Barcarole [from It. *barca*, boat]. A boat-song of the Venetian gondolieri, or an instrumental or vocal composition written in imitation thereof. Well-known examples for the piano are to be found in Mendelssohn's "Songs without Words" [op. 19, no. 6; op. 30, no. 6; op. 62, no. 5]; others were written by Chopin (op. 60) and Fauré. Vocal barcaroles occur in various operas with Italian settings, e.g., in Hérold's *Zampa* (1831), in Auber's *Fra Diavolo* (1830), in Offenbach's *Tales of Hoffmann* (1831); cf. also Schubert's song "Auf dem Wasser zu singen." Barcaroles are always in moderate 6/8 or 12/8 time and use a monotonous accompaniment suggestive of the uniform movement of the waves and the boat.

Bard. The hereditary poet-musicians (minstrels) of the Celtic nations, especially the Irish and the Welsh. In the early Middle Ages they exercised great political power, serving as historians, heralds, ambassadors, and, in brief, constituting the highest intellectual class. Their existence is documented as far back as the pre-Christian era by Greek writers such as Diodorus Siculus (1st century B.C.), who makes reference to the traditional instrument of the bards, i.e., the *crwth. The privileges of the Welsh

bards were fixed by King Howel Dha, in 940, and revised by Gruffyd ap Conan, in 1040. The first persecution (on political grounds) occurred after the conquest of Wales by Edward I, in 1284. The bards continued to exist, though far below their former standard and reputation, in Ireland till 1690 (battle of the Boyne), in Scotland till 1748. The congregations of the Welsh bards, called *Eisteddfod*, were revived in the early 19th century, after an interruption of about 150 years. Their standard, which was extremely low, has recently been considerably raised. See *Penillion.

The music of the Welsh bards has been the subject of much discussion and controversy. Many exaggerated claims have been made, chiefly on the basis of certain music manuscripts, one of which, called *Musica neu Beroriaeth* (Penllyn MS; Brit. Mus. Add. 14905; facsimile ed. by Cardiff University, 1936), bears the inscription, made by an 18th-century owner: "The music of Britain, as settled by the congress of chief musicians, by order of Gruffydd ap Cynan, about A.D. 1040, with some of the most ancient pieces of the Britons, supposed to have been handed down to us from the British Druids." Actually, this manuscript dates from the 17th century and shows nothing to substantiate any such claims or similar ones voiced by modern supporters of the "Mediaeval Bardic music" movement (e.g., A. Dolmetsch). The notation is but a modification of the German organ tablature of the late 16th century [see *WoHN* ii, 294]. The transcriptions given by Dolmetsch (who succeeded in clarifying certain peculiarities of this notation) still further discredit the fantastic legends so frequently told. It is probably permissible to interpret the style of these pieces as the result of "debasement through seepage," a process which can frequently be noticed in instrumental folk practice [see *Folk song II]. Such opinion is, of course, in the strongest possible opposition to the statement that "from internal evidence such music could not have been made later than the sixth century, and was probably much earlier" (A. Dolmetsch, in *The Consort*, no. 4, p. 14). The accompanying example, transcribed from

WoHN ii, 298, shows written-out figurations in the style of the 17th-century *arpègement figuré* [see *Arpeggio]. Only the beginning and the end of the piece are given here, but the intermediate measures can easily be found from the formula: 1111000010101110000110011, given in the original, which indicates the scheme of alternation for the two chords used in this piece, each being indicated by the figure 1 or 0, a method commonly used in 17th-century guitar tablatures [cf. *WoHN* ii, 171ff].

Lit.: Joseph Cooper Walker, *Historical Memoirs of the Irish Bards* (1786); Edward Jones, *Musical and Poetical Relicks of the Welsh Bards* (4th ed., 1825); Ch. de la Borde, *Essai sur les Bardes*, 3 vols. (1840); G. Borrow, *Celtic Bards, Chiefs and Kings* (1928); W. Evans, *The Bards of the Isles of Britain* (1930); A. Dolmetsch, †*Translations from the Pennlynn Manuscript of Ancient Harp Music* (1937); *id.*, in *The Consort* (1930ff); P. Crossley-Holland, "Secular Homophonic Music in Wales in the Middle-Ages" (*ML* xxiii, no. 2).

Barform [G.]. I. A term which is used frequently in modern German studies to denote one of the oldest and most important musical forms, that is, the form with the basic scheme a a b. The name is derived from the medieval German term for this form, namely *Bar*. This consisted of two *Stollen* (section a) and the *Abgesang* (section b) [cf. the imaginative description in R. Wagner's *Meistersinger*, Act I, 3, where Kothner says: "Ein jedes Meistergesanges Bar" . . . consists of . . . "unterschiedlichen Gesätzen" (sundry

stanzas); "ein Gesätz" . . . consists of . . . "zweenen (two) Stollen" . . . and . . . "Abgesang"; also Act III, 2, Hans Sachs]. The Bar is by far the most frequent form of the Minnesinger and Meistersinger [Ex. in *EiBM*, nos. 8, 9; *HAM*, nos. 20, 24; *SchGMB*, nos. 12, 21; *RiHM* i.2, pp. 268ff]. However, the Barform itself is of still earlier origin and of a much wider occurrence. It is adumbrated in the ancient Greek ode which consisted of *strophe* (a), *antistrophe* (a), and *epode* (b). The examples 13 and 42 in *BeMMR* illustrate its occurrence in the early medieval music of the Eastern churches. With the *canzo of the troubadours and the *ballade of the trouvères it established itself in European music. The German Bar is an imitation of these French forms. Although in France their further development lay in the direction of stylistic perfection (particularly in the polyphonic ballade of the 14th century), the Germans, restricting themselves to the monophonic type, exploited its formal aspect. A frequent feature, already found in the canzo [cf. *BeMMR*, 107], is the use of identical endings for the Stollen and the Abgesang so that the form: ‖: a + x : b + x re-‖ sults, as, e.g., in Walther v. d. Vogelweide's "Palestine Song" [see Ex. 1], in Hans Sachs's "Silberweise" [*SchGMB*, no. 78], and in many chorales of the 16th century,

e.g., "Wachet auf, ruft uns die Stimme" [cf. Bach's chorale prelude and the first movement of the cantata]. Another type is the "duplicated" bar: ‖: a :‖: b :‖ c, which forms a connecting link with the *sequence (*leich), and the "superimposed" bar, in which the Stollen itself is a complete Bar [Ex. in F. L. Saran, †Die Jenaer Liederhandschrift (1902) ii, 53 and 57].

II. Of particular importance is that type of Bar in which the Stollen is repeated in toto at the end of the Abgesang, thus leading to the scheme a a b a or ‖: a :‖ b a. A very early example of this form is the liturgical melody to a hymn, Ales diei nuntius, by Prudentius (d. c. 450), which probably is one of the oldest Christian melodies preserved [Ex. 2; cf. AR, 109; BeMMR, 52]. Minnesinger songs showing the same structure are quite numerous [cf. DTOe 37.i, p. 31; Saran ii, 29; HAM, no. 20c; ReMMA, 235]. The modern term for this is Reprisenbar or Rundkanzone (rounded chanson). Still another modification of a more recent date is the Reprisenbar with repetition of both sections: ‖: a :‖: b + a :‖. This occurs in numerous pieces of the 18th century as a modification of binary form, appropriately designated as cyclic binary form [see *Binary and ternary form II]. It is this form which must be considered as the precursor of *sonata-form, the exposition, development, and recapitulation of which correspond to the Stollen, Abgesang, and repeated Stollen of the Reprisenbar. Although there is, of course, no historical relationship between the medieval Bar and the classical sonata, the similarity is noteworthy, all the more as the Abgesang of the early songs frequently shows certain elementary development features, such as higher range, *Fortspinnung, and greater intensity in general, as appears, e.g., in the "Palestine Song" and in Hans Sachs's "Morgenweise" [EiBM, no. 9]. It may be noted that in pieces such as the first movement of Bach's cantata mentioned above the Barform of the chorale ("Wachet auf") leads to a structure which is quite similar to that of sonata-form. See also *Binary and ternary form.

A. Lorenz has tried to show (with questionable success) that the Barform is the leading principle of structure in R. Wag-

ner's operas, the recitative of which he interpreted as "superimposed" Bars (Kleinbar, Mittelbar, Grossbar).

Lit.: A. Lorenz, Das Geheimnis der Form bei R. Wagner, 4 vols. (1924–33); id., "Das Relativitätsprinzip in den musikalischen Formen" (Adler Festschrift, 1930); id., "Homophone Grossrhythmik in Bach's Polyphonik" (DM xxii.4); H. A. Grunsky, in ZMW xvi.

Bariolage [F., variety of colors]. A special effect of violin playing, obtained by quickly shifting back and forth from open strings to stopped strings. This technique is used for broken-chord passages [Ex. 1,

Bach, Solo Sonata in E major], or for a "coloristic" tremolo [Ex. 2, Brahms, Symphony no. 4, last movement].

Baritone or (rarely) **barytone** [from Gr. barys, heavy, low]. (1) The male voice intermediate between the bass and the tenor; see *Voices, Range of. — (2) In connection with instruments (oboe, horn, saxophone) the word indicates sizes above the bass size. — (3) Short for baritone horn [see *Brass instruments III(c)].

Baritone clef. See *Clefs.

Baritone horn. See *Brass instruments III(c).

Bar-line [Fr. barre; G. Taktstrich]. The vertical line used to indicate the beginning and the end of a measure. The consistent use of the bar-line is of relatively recent date. Original bar-lines appear first in the German organ tablatures of the 15th century (Ileborgh, 1448; Paumann, 1452). In the 16th century they were almost universally employed for the writing down of keyboard and lute music. Their use frequently differed considerably from that of the present day, however, as appears from the accompanying Example 1 (Pisador, Libro de musica de vihuela, 1552: "Pavana myllana"), in which the original barring is given on the staff, the modern barring below the staff. [For a similar example cf. *ApMZ* ii, 21; cf. also *ApNPM*, 65ff.] In ensemble (vocal) mu-

1: Pisador; 2: Josquin

sic the bar-line was not introduced until toward the end of the 16th century, when the notation in single parts gave way to notation in score arrangement. The arias of the 17th century frequently show the anomalous use of the bar-line referred to above, i.e., the disregard of upbeat or of triple time; in other words, the employ-ment of the bar-line as a means of simple orientation rather than as an indication of accent [cf. the explanations and examples in *RiHM* ii.2, 12, etc.].

Modern editors of polyphonic music of the 15th and 16th centuries have increas-ingly resented the "tyranny of the bar-line" and have tried to make this indis-pensable device of modern notation less conspicuous by replacing it by apostro-phes: ', by punctuated lines: ⦂, or by the *Mensurstrich*, i.e., a line drawn between, not through, the staves [Ex. 2, from Jos-quin, *Ave Christe, immolate*]. Unfortu-nately, the Mensurstrich is impracticable if different meters (mensurations) are used in different parts, e.g., $\frac{2}{4}$ against $\frac{3}{4}$, a practice which is not infrequent in the period of Obrecht and Josquin, and still more frequent in the compositions of the late *Ars nova*.

Lit.: W. H. Cummings, "Bar-lines" (*Musical Times*, 1904, p. 574); Th.Wieh-mayer, in *ZMW* vii; H. Keller, in *ZMW* vii; *WoHN* i, 427; *ApNPM, passim.*

Baroque music. The music of the pe-riod *c.* 1600–1750, following upon that of the *Renaissance. It is also frequently re-ferred to as the "thorough-bass period."

The term *baroque* (probably from Port. *barrocco*, a pearl of irregular form) was used formerly, and still is today, in a de-cidedly depreciatory sense, as meaning "grotesque," "in corrupt taste" [cf. Web-ster], "overladen with scroll-work," etc. Its application to the Fine Arts was based on the opinion (Jacob Burckhardt) that 17th-century style in architecture and paintings was a debased Renaissance style. This opinion, however, was thoroughly revised about 1900 by Heinrich Wölfflin, who was the first to point out the positive contributions and the great artistic quali-ties of Baroque art, and to vindicate the term Baroque from any implication of in-feriority. More recently, musical historians have followed suit and have adopted the term alongside others such as *Renais-sance, *Gothic, *Rococo [see *History of Music]. In view of this situation, the re-sistance which the term "Baroque music" is still encountering in some circles is hardly justified. If understood properly, this term has the advantage of placing an important and well-defined period of mu-sic history within the general frame of cul-tural development, and of avoiding the emphasis on a special feature of somewhat secondary importance which is implied in the term "thorough-bass period" — a term which, by the way, does not prop-erly include one of the most important branches of 17th-century music, namely, that for organ and harpsichord.

Both the beginning and the end of the Baroque period in music are rather clearly defined, much more so than those of most other periods, particularly the Renais-sance. Baroque music starts about 1600, with the rise of monody, opera, oratorio, cantata, recitative, and closes 150 years later, with the death of Bach and Handel. Preparatory phenomena are, on the one hand, the *ballettos and *villanellas with their reaction against the Flemish po-lyphony, and on the other hand, the style of the *Venetian School (G. Gabrieli), the pomp and splendor of which exceed the limitations of true Renaissance art and foreshadow the aesthetic basis of Baroque style. It may be noticed that throughout the 17th century the tradition of Renaissance music persisted to some extent in the *Roman School, and that, on the other hand, a new period, the *Rococo, had already begun when Bach and Handel were writing their greatest masterpieces, the true culmination points of Baroque music.

Generally speaking, the Baroque period is an era of ecstasy and exuberance, of dynamic tensions and of sweeping gestures, an era of longing and of self-denial, much in contrast to the assuredness and self-reliance of the Renaissance. It is the period in which men liked to consider this life as the "vale of tears," in which the statues of the Saints look rapturously toward heaven, in which the clouds and the infinite landscape were discovered. Much of this attitude is reflected in the expressive melodies of the 17th century, in its long coloraturas, in its pathetic recitative, its frequent use of chromaticism, its capricious rhythms. Particularly the early Baroque music (prior to 1650) shows, in its *canzonas and *toccatas, striking traits of capriciousness, exuberance, and irregularity, while later composers such as Carissimi and Corelli brought about a trend towards greater restraint and regularity of style. On the other hand, the structural, or, as one might call it, the architectural element in Baroque music must not be overlooked. More than any other period, the 17th century has contributed toward the development and establishment of clearly defined types and forms, such as the ostinato-forms, the variations, the suite, the sonata, the da-capo aria, the rondo, the concerto, the opera, the oratorio, the cantata.

From the point of view of style, Baroque music is characterized chiefly by the thorough-bass technique, leading to a texture of two principal contours, melody and bass, with the intervening space being filled in by improvised harmony. In Germany, however, the contrasting style of true polyphony not only persisted but reached, in Bach, its very acme of perfection and greatness. A third principle of Baroque style is the *stile concertante*, that is, contrasting effects, a principle which expressed itself in the abrupt changes of

the early *canzona as well as in the solo-tutti alternation of the *concerto grosso and in the *echo-effects of vocal and of organ music. Other basic conceptions of Baroque music are *improvisation and *ornamentation. Lastly, mention must be made of the final establishment of tonic and dominant as the principal chords of harmony and, about 1650 (Carissimi), of four-measure phrases [see *Vierhebigkeit].

At the beginning of the 17th century we find three great figures still rooted in the tradition of the Renaissance but inaugurating the novel trends of Baroque music, namely, Monteverdi, G. Gabrieli, and Sweelinck. They may be considered as the sources of three main streams running through Baroque music, that is, vocal, instrumental, and organ music, to which, in turn, the three styles mentioned above can be roughly coördinated, namely, accompanied melody, concerto style, and contrapuntal style.

The first of these streams, starting in Florence (Caccini, Peri, later Monteverdi), produces the *monodic style with the *recitative and *aria, and with the composite forms of the *cantata, *opera, and *oratorio (*passion). The second, "Venetian," stream finds its realization in the instrumental *canzona, the violin *sonata, the trio-sonata in its two varieties, *sonata da chiesa and *sonata da camera, and in the orchestral forms of the *concerto grosso [see also *Concerto III], the French *overture, and the *sinfonia. The last stream, starting with Sweelinck and Frescobaldi, but continuing chiefly in Germany (Scheidt, Froberger, Buxtehude, Pachelbel, Kuhnau, Muffat, Fischer, Bach), leads to the *fugue, *organ chorale (choral prelude), *toccata, and *suite (the latter also in France).

Lit.: R. Haas, *Die Musik des Barock* (*BüHM*, 1928); *LaMWC, passim*; *AdHM* i, 411–700; *RiHM* ii.3; W. Flemming, *Oper und Oratorium im Barock* (1933); P. Nettl, *Musikbarock in Böhmen und Mähren* (1927); E. Wellesz, *Die Anfänge des musikalischen Barock . . . in Wien* (1922); W. D. Allen, "Baroque Histories of Music" (*MQ* xxv); E. Schenck, "Ueber

Begriff und Wesen des musikalischen Barock" (*ZMW* xvii); E. Wellesz, "Renaissance und Barock" (*ZIM* xi); Th. Kroyer, "Zwischen Renaissance und Barock" (*JMP* xxxiv); C. Sachs, in *JMP* xxvi; A. della Corte, in *LRM* vi; *id.,* in *Editions XXIV B, 3/4.

Barpyknon. See *Pyknon.

Barre [F.]. Bar-line. See also *Barrer.

Barrel organ. See *Mechanical instruments II.

Barrer [F.]. Term of lute and guitar playing, calling for the simultaneous shortening of the vibratory length of several or all strings by putting the forefinger across them. An artificial substitute is the *capotasto [F. *barre*].

✓ **Bartered Bride, The** (*Prodaná Nevěsta*). Comic opera by Bedric Smetana (1824–84), text by Karel Sabina, composed in 1866. It has been widely sung outside of Czechoslovakia in the German translation, as *Die verkaufte Braut.* It describes an episode from 19th-century Bohemian peasant life, centering around the love of *Yenyik* (*Hans,* Tenor) and *Marhenka* (*Maria,* Soprano). The former agrees to give up his right to Marhenka's hand for a sum of money, under the condition that she marry "the son of Micha" whom everybody believes to be the stuttering *Vazhek* (*Wenzel,* Tenor). In the last scene, however, Yenyik is revealed as Micha's eldest son, so the "sales-contract" is fulfilled to everyone's satisfaction.

The Bartered Bride is one of the first and also one of the most successful examples of national opera. It is unparalleled in its display of gay spirit and rustic humor and in times of political oppression has contributed immensely to stimulate Czech patriotism.

Baryton. (1) See *Viol IV, 5.— (2) In French and German usage, *baritone (voice); also used in connection with instruments, e.g., Barytonhorn (euphonium), Barytonoboe, etc. — (3) In German usage, short for *Barytonhorn,* i.e., *euphonium.

Base viol. Same as bass viol. See *Viol II.

Basis. Fifteenth- and 16th-century humanistic name for bass.

Bass [Gr. *basis,* foundation]. (1) The lowest of men's voices [see *Voices, range of].— (2) German name (abbreviation of *Kontrabass*) for the double-bass. — (3) In connection with instruments, the term indicates the lowest and, consequently, largest type of the family, e.g., bass clarinet.— (4) In musical composition, the lowest of the parts. In the styles of the 18th and 19th centuries the bass adopts special significance as the determining factor of the harmonic structure [see *Harmonic analysis]. The special role of the bass is particularly conspicuous in the practice and theory of *thorough-bass. For the origin of the bass, see *Contratenor.

Bassa [It., low]. *Ottava bassa* (abbreviated *8va bassa*) means the lower octave of the written notes. *Con 8va bassa* means doubling of the written notes in the lower octave.

Bassadanza [It.]. See *Basse danse.

Bass-bar. In violins, etc., a strip of wood glued inside the table, about 11 in. long and diminishing at either end. Its function is to support the left foot of the bridge and to spread over the table the vibrations of the bridge produced by those of the strings.

Bass clef. See *Clefs.

Bass-course. See *Course.

Basse [F.]. *Basse chiffré,* or *continue,* means thorough-bass; *basse contrainte,* ground (basso ostinato); *basse profonde, chantante, taille,* see *Voices, Range of; *basse fondamentale,* *Fundamental bass; *basse-à-piston,* *Euphonium.

Basse danse. A French dance of the period 1450–1550 in which it plays a prominent role as the ceremonial court dance of the Burgundian culture [see *Burgundian School]. The name (*bas,* low) probably refers to the gliding or walking movement of the feet, in contrast to the jumping movements in dances such as the gaillarde (*danse haute, danse sautée*). Various sources from *c.* 1480 to 1580, theoretical, choreographic, and musical, together with many paintings of the 15th century [cf., e.g., *BeMMR*, 179, 195], provide information about this dance. Of particular interest are two choreographic sources, the MS Brussels *9085* [see Lit., Closson] and a book *L'Art et instruction de bien dancer* printed before 1496. These

contain illustrations such as are reproduced here [Ex. 1], the notes of which probably represent a melodic skeleton, giving only the chief note for each measure (to be played on a trombone?), with the real melody provided (extemporized?) by a melodic instrument, viol or recorder [for an example of such a "tenor-dance" see W. Merian, *Der Tanz in den deutschen Tabulaturbüchern des 16. Jahrhunderts* (1927), p. 44]. The letters underneath the notes indicate dancing steps. Nineteen (*sic*) basse danses for lute are preserved in P. Attaingnant's publication: *Dixhuit basses danses garnies de recoupes et tordions* (1529); others for keyboard in his *Quatorze gaillards, ... et deux basse danses* (1530); and for ensemble in his *Neuf basse danses, deux branles. . . en musique en quatre parties* (1530). Frequently the basse danse is followed by a *recoupe* and a *tordion*, thus forming an early type of suite. The basse danse is in moderate tempo, usually in duple time [Ex. 2], although there also exist a number of examples in slow triple time [Ex. 3; regarding a controversy on the meter of the basse danse cf. *ApNMP*, 67]. The latter variety would seem to have been favored in Italy since several dances in slow triple meter called *bassa danza* are

preserved in the lute books of Petrucci (1507/9). Some of the dances in Kotter's tablature of 1515 evidently belong to the same class, e.g., his "Spanieler" [see Merian's *Der Tanz . . .*]. Certain of the

basse danses in Attaingnant's book for ensemble are "à double employ," i.e., they are so written that they can be played in (slow) duple time as well as in (quicker) triple time, thus serving both as dance and "after-dance" [see *Nachtanz]. Around 1525 the chief vogue of the French basse danse was succeeded by that of the Spanish *pavane. See *Dance music II.

Lit.: E. Closson, *Le Manuscrit dit "Des Basses danses"* . . . (1912; facsimile ed.); *L'Art et Instruction de Bien Dancer* (facs. ed. by the Royal College of Physicians of London, 1936); F. Blume, *Studien zur Vorgeschichte der Orchester-Suite* (1925); E. Closson, in *SIM* xiv; O. Gombosi, "About Dance and Dance Music in the Late Middle-Ages" (*MQ* xxvii); E. Hertzmann, in *ZMW* xi; C. Sachs, in *AM* iii, no. 3. Examples in *HAM*, nos. 102, 104; *SchGMB* no 90; *ApMZ* ii.

Basse d'harmonie [F.]. *Ophicleide.

Basset horn. See *Clarinet family III.

Bassetto, bassett, bassettl. Eighteenth-century name for the violoncello.

Bassflöte [G.]. (1) Bass-flute. — (2) Eighteenth-century name for bassoon.

Bass horn. See under *Cornett.

Bassist [G.], **bassista** [It.]. A bass singer.

Bass lute, Basslaute [G.]. The *chitarrone, or the *theorbe.

Basso [It.]. Bass. *Basso continuo,* i.e., thorough-bass; *basso seguente* is an instrumental bass (organ, etc.), which merely duplicates the lowest vocal part [cf. *RiHM* ii.2, 75f]; *basso profondo, cantante,* see *Voices, range of.

Basson [F.]. Bassoon. *Basson quinte* is a smaller bassoon, also called tenoroon. *Basson russe,* *Russian bassoon.

Bassoon. See *Oboe family I, C.

Basso ostinato. See *Ground. Also under *Ostinato.

Basso ripieno [It.]. In 18th-century orchestral works, a bass part for the tutti-(*ripieno-) passages only, i.e., not for the solo sections.

Bassschlüssel [G.]. The F-clef.

Bass viol. Properly (17th century) the viola da gamba [see *Viol II]. Today, name for the double bass, a descendant of the old double-bass viol [see *Viol IV, 1].

Bathyphone. *See Clarinet family III.

Baton. The stick used by the conductor of an orchestra to beat time. The modern baton is made of tapered wood or some other light material, such as aluminum, celluloid, or lucite. The length varies from 15 to 28 inches. See *Conducting.

Battaglia [It., battle]. Name for programmatic pieces (battle pieces) in which the fanfares, drum rolls, cries, and general commotion of a battle are imitated. This was a favored subject of *program music from the 16th through the 18th centuries, the earliest example being Jannequin's vocal chanson *La Guerre* (1529), which was suggested by the famous battle of Marignano, 1515 [repr. in *Editions XVI (7); see also *GD* iii, 462]. This battle and that of Pavia (1525) were the subject of numerous *battaglias* of the 16th century, e.g., by Hans Neusidler [1535; cf. *DTOe* 18.ii] and by William Byrd [cf. *My Ladye-Nevells Booke,* ed. by H. Andrews]. In the 17th century similar pieces were written by Adriano Banchieri [cf. *ApMZ* i], by Johann Kaspar Kerll [*DTB* 2.ii], and others. Although these pieces

are of a rather limited artistic value, the quality is even lower in the numerous battle pieces (mostly English) of the 18th century, some of which actually prescribed the firing of guns at certain moments. Franz Kotzwara's *Battle of Prague* (1788) is still known today. Beethoven made a contribution to this repertory in his "Battle Symphony," *Wellington's Sieg oder die Schlacht bei Vittoria* (op. 91, 1813, publ. 1816). Cf. R. Gläsel, *Zur Geschichte der Battaglia* (Diss. Leipzig 1931); E. Bienenfeld, in *ZIM* viii; K. G. Fellerer, in *DM* xxxii.7.

Battement [F.]. French 17th-century term for any ornament consisting of an alternation of two adjacent tones, e.g., mordent, trill, vibrato.

Batterie [F.]. (1) The percussion group of the orchestra. — (2) A drum roll. — (3) Eighteenth-century name for arpeggio, broken-chord figures, *Alberti-basses, etc. — (4) A way of playing the guitar by striking the strings.

Battery. See *Batterie (3).

Battle pieces. See *Battaglia.

Battuta [It.]. Beat. *A battuta* indicates a return to strict time after some deviation (*ad libitum, a piacere,* etc.). In particular, *battuta* means the strong beat at the beginning of a measure; hence *ritmo di tre* (*quattro*) *battute* indicates that three (four) measures are to be grouped together in a phrase (cf. the Scherzo of Beethoven's Ninth Symphony).

Bay Psalm Book. A book of psalms, published in Cambridge, Massachusetts, in 1640 (the second book printed in North America). It had numerous later editions for over one hundred years. In 1690 music (in two parts) was added for twelve tunes. See *Psalter; *American music I. Example in *HAM,* no. 283.

Bayreuther Festspiele. See *Festivals III; *Bühne (Bühnenweihfestspiel).

BB♭ bass. See *Tuba (2).

B.C. Short for *basso continuo.

Be [G.]. The sign ♭.

Beak flute. *Recorder.

Bearbeitung [G.]. Arrangement.

Beat [F. *temps*; G. *Zählzeit, Schlag*; It. *battuta*]. (1) The temporal unit of a composition, as is indicated by the (real or imaginary) up-and-down movements of a conductor's hand. In modern practice, the duration of such a beat varies from M.M. 50 to M.M. 140, with M.M. 80 being a middle speed. In moderate tempo, the ¼ measure includes four beats, beat one and beat three being strong, the others weak, while the ¾ measure has three beats, only the first of which is strong. In quick tempo, there will be only two or even only one beat to the measure. In music prior to 1600, the beat was of much less variable duration [see *Tactus, *Tempus].

(2) A 17th-century English ornament which may be performed in two ways, depending on whether it is a *plain beat* (indicated by an ascending oblique line placed before or over the written note) or a *shaked beat* (indicated by a wavy line resembling the French sign for the trill). The plain beat is an inferior appoggiatura performed on the beat and of flexible duration. The shaked beat consists of several rapid repetitions of the appoggiatura and its resolution, beginning with the former, so that it resembles an inverted trill. In the 18th century the name beat is often applied to the ornament commonly known as the *mordent. P. A.

(3) See *Beats.

Beats [F. *battements*; G. *Schwebungen*]. An acoustical phenomenon, resulting from the interference [see *Acoustics VI] of two sound-waves of slightly differing frequencies. It is heard as minute, yet clearly audible, intensifications of the sound at regular intervals. The number per second of these intensifications, or beats, is equal to the difference of frequency of the two tones. Thus, a tone of 440 cycles will make four beats per second with a tone of 444; three, with a tone of 443; two, with 442; one, with 441; and the beats will disappear if the two strings are in perfect unison [see the illustration Interference, p. 14]. This phenomenon is, therefore, of fundamental importance in *tuning. Slow beats such as two to four to the second are not unpleasant to the ear. In certain organ stops (Voix céleste and Unda maris; see *Vox coelestis) beats are deliberately introduced by using two pipes slightly out of tune, in order to give the combined tone an undulating quality. Beats of 5 or 6 per second produce a distinctly less pleasant result, and the disagreeableness of the effect increases until the number of beats is *c.* 30. From there on the unpleasantness diminishes because the beats rapidly become too quick to be distinguished. This phenomenon is the basis of Helmholtz' theory of *consonance and dissonance. See also *Combination tones.

Bebization. See *Solmization.

Bebung [from G. *beben*, to tremble; F. *balancement*]. A *vibrato effect peculiar to the *clavichord, the action of which allows for a repeated pressure motion of the finger without releasing the key, a motion which causes the tangent momentarily to increase the tension of the string and which thus leads to slight variations of pitch. C. P. E. Bach, in his *Versuch über die wahre Art das Clavier zu spielen* (1753), considers the Bebung as a great advantage of the clavichord over the harpsichord and the pianoforte, both of which lack this effect. It is indicated by the sign shown in Example 1. [Cf. C. P. E.

Bach's *Probestücke*, published as *Sechs Sonaten* by E. Doflein, Ed. Schott, no. 2353]. The Bebung is mentioned in the theoretical writings of Printz (1668), Mattheson (1735), Marpurg (1750), C. P. E. Bach, and many later authors. The sign, however, does not occur in the literature for the clavichord before Bach.

The reference in many musical books to certain passages in Beethoven and Chopin as Bebung is misleading. An effect such as illustrated in Example 2 (Beethoven, Piano Sonatas opp. 106 and 110; also op. 69, op. 59, no. 2, op. 133 for violin) is a (slow) *tremolo (ondulé), not a vibrato. See *Tie.

Bec [F.]. The mouthpiece of the clarinet or recorder [see *Mouthpiece (b), (d)].

Bécarre [F.]. See *Accidentals.

Becken [G.]. *Cymbals.

Bedächtig [G.]. Thoughtfully, with moderation.

Bedeutend [G.]. With importance.

Bedrohlich [G.]. Menacingly.

Be fa, Befa. See *Hexachord III.

Beggar's Opera, The. See under *Ballad opera.

Begleitung [G.]. Accompaniment.

Behaglich [G.]. Comfortably, agreeably.

Behend [G.]. Nimbly, quickly.

Beherzt [G.]. "With heart," courageously.

Beisser [G., "biter"]. Eighteenth-century name for the *mordent [from L. *mordere*, to bite].

Bel [from Alexander Graham Bell]. A scientific unit for the measurement of loudness, i.e., the subjective reaction to intensity of sound. Loudness varies with the logarithm of intensity; this means that 20 violins playing with equal individual intensities are only 1.3 times louder than 10, and 100 violins only twice as loud as 10 (log 20 = 1.301; log 100 = 2). One-tenth of a bel is called a decibel (db); this represents the smallest change in loudness that the ear can detect. The sounds used in practical music vary from *c.* 25 db (softest violin tone) to 100 db (fortissimo of the full orchestra). Cf. John Mills, *A Fugue in Cycles and Bels* (1935); Stevens and Davis, *Hearing* (1938), pp. 450ff.

Bel canto [It., beautiful singing]. The term denotes the Italian vocal technique of the 18th century with its emphasis on beauty of sound and brilliancy of performance, rather than dramatic expression or Romantic emotion. In spite of the repeated reactions against the *bel canto* (Gluck, Wagner) and in spite of the frequent exaggeration of its virtuoso element (coloraturas), it must be considered as a highly artistic technique and as the only proper one for Italian opera and for Mozart. Its early development is closely bound up with that of the Neapolitan opera (Al. Scarlatti, Porpora, Jommelli, Hasse, Piccinni). See *Singing I.

Lit.: G. B. Lamperti, *Technics of Bel Canto* (New York); H. Klein, *The Bel Canto* (1923); H. Goldschmidt, *Die Italienische Gesangsmethode des 17. Jahrhunderts* (1892); B. Ulrich, *Die altitalienische Gesangsmethode* (1933); G. Silva, "The Beginnings of the Art of Bel Canto" (*MQ* viii).

Belebend [G.]. Becoming animated.

Belebt [G.]. Animated.

Belgian music. The present article deals with the musical history of the Catholic (southern, Flemish) part of the Low Countries, as distinguished from that of the Protestant (northern, Dutch) part, the Netherlands. The highly important role which Belgium played in the earlier history of music is greatly obscured by the name "Netherlands School" which is widely used for a school of 15th- and 16th-century composers nearly all of whom came from Belgium [see *Flemish School]. This great period during which Belgian musicians held leading positions everywhere in Europe was followed, after 1600, by a long period of low ebb. Only in the field of organ music did Belgium produce composers of some historical significance, e.g., Charles Luython (*c.* 1550–1620), Pieter Cornet (fl. 1600–25), Giovanni de Macque (d. 1614; see *Neapolitan School II), Charles Guillet (d. 1654), Abraham Kerckhoven (*c.* 1627 — after 1673), Jean-Baptiste Loeillet (1680–1730), and Joseph-Hector Fiocco (1703–41) [see *Editions XVII]. While the latter two followed the trends of the French Rococo (F. Couperin), the next Belgian composer to be mentioned, François Gossec (1734–1829) belongs to the *Mannheim group, and the slightly younger André Grétry (1741–1813) plays an important role in the history of the French opera (*Richard Coeur de Lion*, 1784; see *Leitmotif). It should be noted that Belgium has a certain claim to one of the greatest composers, namely Beethoven, whose ancestors lived near Antwerp and Mecheln [cf. P. Bergmans, *Les Origines belges de Beethoven* (1927); E. Closson, *L'Elément flamand dans Beethoven* (1928)].

In the 19th-century music of Belgium, César Franck (1822–90) is by far the most important personality. Like Tchaikovsky, he adhered to the conception of music as an international language, while Pierre Benoit (1834–1901) played a role comparable to that of Moussorgsky, namely, that of the initiator of national music, freed from German as well as French influence. He is particularly important in the field of the oratorio and of the cantata. Among his successors Jan Blockx (1851–1912) and Edgar Tinel (1854–1912) must be mentioned especially. Paul Gilson (b. 1865) adopted some elements of Russian music and is particularly known for his symphonic poem *La Mer* (1892). A composer who in a very short life wrote several works of great promise was Guillaume Lekeu (1870–94). Joseph Jongen (b. 1873) was active mainly in the field of symphonic and of chamber music. The novel trends of 20th-century music have found little response in Belgium. Paul de Maleingreau (b. 1887) is the main representative of neo-classical tendencies based on Bach.

Belgium has produced a number of outstanding music historians, notably François Fétis (1784–1871), Charles Coussemaker (1805–76; see *Scriptores), Pierre van Maldeghem (1810–93; published *La Trésor musicale*), Edmund van der Straeten (1826–95; *La Musique aux Pays-Bas*, 1867–88), and Charles van den Borren (b. 1874).

Lit.: Fl. van der Mueren, *Vlaamsche Muziek en Componisten* (1931); LavE i.3, 1815ff; Ch. van den Borren, "The General Trends in Contemporary Belgian Music" (*MQ* vii); id., "Belgian Music and French Music" (*MQ* ix); AdHM ii, 1074–77.

Bell. (1) A percussion instrument of metal sounded by a clapper usually placed inside the bell. The best alloy for bells is 76 per cent pure copper and 24 per cent pure tin. Sometimes small amounts of zinc or lead are added. The tone of a well tuned bell is characterized by a great number of overtones which, in old bells (chiefly those of the Continent), are slightly out of tune; owing to the efforts of English bell-founders (especially, Taylor of Loughborough), modern English bells have five overtones (including the minor, not the major, third) tuned with absolute accuracy. The pitch of a bell varies inversely with the cubic root of its weight. Therefore, if a bell weighing 100 pounds sounds c''' (the actual tone is nearer b''), a bell of 800 pounds ($\sqrt[3]{8} = 2$) will be needed for the tone of the half frequency, c'', one of 6,400 for c', of 51,200 pounds for c, and of 409,600 pounds for C. The largest bell ever founded was the Tsar Kolokol of the Kremlin of Moscow (1734, destroyed by fire in 1737) which, after the best estimation, weighed c. 500,000 pounds, and measured over 20 feet in diameter. The largest bell in existence is the Trotzkoi, also in Moscow, weighing c. 350,000 pounds. Old bells in France and in Germany weigh from 20,000 to 40,000 pounds. Large modern bells usually weigh from 5,000 to 15,000 pounds. The use of bells in churches can be traced back to the 6th century (Gregory of Tours, c. 560); the earliest record of large bells in England dates from the 10th century (Turketyl, Abbot of Croyland); the earliest preserved bells are to be found in Italy and in Germany (11th century).

Three ways of sounding church bells are distinguished: (a) chiming, in which the rope moves the bell just sufficiently for the clapper to strike it; (b) ringing, in which the bell is swung round full circle, thus giving a more vigorous sound; (c) clocking, in which the clapper is moved instead of, as usual, the bell — a method which should not be used since it is likely to cause the bell to crack. Whereas in continental Europe church bells are sounded in such a way as to produce a confused musical noise, the English bells are rung in succession according to certain elaborate systems so that a "melody" is produced. This method is known as *change ringing. See also *Carillon; *Campana.

The bell effect has been frequently required in orchestral works, the earliest known example being the two bells (probably an organ stop) in Bach's solo-cantata *Schlage doch gewünschte Stunde*. In the modern orchestra real bells are not used (because of their lack of definiteness in pitch), but are replaced by the "tubular bells" (*chimes; see also *Bells), i.e., a number (7 to 10) of cylindric metal tubes of different lengths, hung in a frame and struck with a hammer. Debussy's "La Cathédrale engloutie" and Busoni's "Sonatina in Diem Nativitatis Christi" contain bell effects produced on the pianoforte. See also *Campanella.

Lit.: G. S. Tyack, *A Book about Bells* (1898); J. J. Raven, *The Bells of England* (1906); S. N. Coleman, *The Book of Bells* (1938; bibl.); G. Morrison, *Bells — Their History and Romance* (1932); W. W. Starmer, "Bells and Bell Tones" (*PMA* xxvii); H. Bewerunge, "On the Tuning of Bells" (*ZIM* vii); J. Biehle, "Die Analyse des Glockenklangs" (*AMW* i).

(2) The bell-shaped opening of wind instruments such as the horn or the trumpet.

Bell harp. A sort of psaltery invented c. 1700 by John Simcock. It took its name from the bell-shaped form of its frame. Cf. *SaRM*, 44.

Bell-lyra. See under *Glockenspiel.

Bells. Recent name for the orchestral glockenspiel [see *Percussion instruments A, 2].

Belly. The upper plate of the resonant box in violins, lutes, etc. Also the *soundboard of the piano.

Be mi, Bemi. See *Hexachord III.

Bémol [F.], **bemolle** [It.]. Flat. See *Pitch names; *Accidentals.

Benedicamus Domino. A salutation of the Roman liturgy, with the response Deo gratias. It is used occasionally at the end of *Mass [cf. *GR*, 18*, 55*, etc.], and at the end of all Offices. For the latter purpose various melodies (*toni*) are provided [cf. *AR*, 58*]. The Benedicamus Domino plays a most important role in the history of early polyphony (Schools of St. Martial and Notre Dame; see *Ars antiqua; *Organum) since its melodies, especially the first one given in the Antiphonarium, have been very frequently used as the tenor of organa in two or three parts. In fact, the entire history of early polyphony could easily and, no doubt, quite instructively, be demonstrated by means of the numerous pieces written on this tenor [cf. *HAM*, nos. 28a–i]. Cf. also H. Schmidt, †*Drei Benedicamus Organa* (1933); *AdHM*, 179; *ReMMA*, 266; *BeMMR*, 97; *ApNPM*, *passim*.

Benediction. An extra-liturgical popular service of the Roman Catholic Church, usually following Vespers and including the blessing of the congregation with the Host. "Tantum ergo" and "O salutaris hostia" are the most important hymns of Benediction [cf. *AR*, 88*].

Benedictus Dominus Israel. The canticle [see *Canticum] of Zacharias. (Note that Benedictus alone will nearly always refer to *Benedictus qui venit.)

Benedictus (qui venit). Second part of the Sanctus of the Mass. In Mass compositions it is usually treated as a separate movement [see *Mass III].

Bequadro [It.]. Natural, the natural sign. See *Accidentals.

Berceuse [F.]. Lullaby. Usually the name refers to instrumental pieces (piano, orchestra) in moderate 6/8 time, and with an accompaniment reminiscent of the rocking of a cradle. The most famous example is Chopin's op. 57.

Bergamasca. (1) In the 16th and 17th centuries a popular tune from the district of Bergamo in northern Italy whose peasant inhabitants were proverbial for their clumsiness and backwardness. Frescobaldi (*Fiori musicali,* 1635) used this melody as a theme of one of his most elaborate canzonas, adding the remark: "Chi questa Bergamasca sonarà, non pocho imparerà" (He who plays this Bergamasca will learn a good deal). Jean-Baptiste Besard [cf. O. Chilesotti, in *RMC* i, 145] and Samuel Scheidt [cf. G. Harms, *Scheidt's Werke,* vol. 5] used its scheme of harmonies for continuous variations similar to a chaconne, except for the duple

Bergamasca

time. The same melody occurs, with slight modifications, in Salomone Rossi's "Varie Sonate . . ." (1623) and in Marco Uccellini's "Sonate, sinfonie, . . ." (1642). Two simple settings for the guitar are reproduced in *WoHN* ii, 166 and 188. Whether the somewhat similar melody "Kraut und Rüben haben mich vertrieben," which Bach uses in the final quodlibet of his Goldberg Variations [see Ex. under *Quodlibet] goes back to the old Italian melody, as has been frequently claimed, is uncertain. Cf. P. Nettl, in *ZMW* v; R. Lach, in *Museion,* 1920.

(2) The 19th-century bergamasca is a quick dance in 6/8 time, much like the *tarantella. Alfredo Piatti (1822–1901), a native of Bergamo, wrote a Bergamasca for cello solo. Debussy's "Suite Bergamasque" is a free composition based upon impressions from the peasant life of Bergamo.

Bergerette [F., from *berger,* shepherd]. (1) An 18th-century type of French lyric poetry with a pastoral or amorous subject. Cf. J.-B. Weckerlin, *Bergerettes* (Engl. ed. 1913). — (2) In the 15th century, bergerette denotes a

fixed form of French poetry, similar in construction to the *virelai, but with one stanza only. Such bergerettes occur in the Kopenhagen Chasonnier [ed. by K. Jeppesen] and in the *Odhecaton. Cf. H. Hewitt, *Harmonice Musices Odhecaton A* (1942), pp. 49f. — (3) In the 16th century the name occurs as a title for instrumental dances in quick triple time, similar to the saltarello. Cf. *RiML,* 155.

Berg(k)reyen [old German for *Bergreigen,* dance of a mountainous country]. Name of various 16th-century collections of songs from German mountainous countries (Silesia, Thuringia), composed in two or more parts, in simple note-against-note style (E. Rotenbucher, 1551; Melchior Franck, 1602). Therefore, "in Bergreyenweis" ("in the manner of a B.") is a 16th-century expression — slightly pejorative — for simple chordal style (*familiar style).

Bergomaska. See *Bergamasca.

Berkshire Festivals. See *Festivals.

Berlin School. Collective designation for a group of composers, also known as *Norddeutsche Schule,* who worked in Berlin during the second half of the 18th century. Most of them were connected with the court of Frederick the Great (1712–86) who, through his numerous flute sonatas and other compositions, contributed actively to the musical life of his residence. The most important members of the group were: J. J. Quantz (1697–1773; flute sonatas, etc.); Johann Gottlieb Graun (1702–71; symphonies, trio sonatas); Karl Heinrich Graun (1703–59; opera *Montezuma,* text by Frederick the Great [*DdT* 15] and oratorio *Der Tod Jesu*); Franz Benda (1706–86; violin sonatas, concertos); C. P. E. Bach (1714–88); Christoph Nichelmann (1717–62; songs, harpsichord sonatas); Friedrich Wilhelm Marpurg (1718–95; songs; editor of *Berlinische Oden und Lieder,* 1756; numerous theoretical books); Johann Kirnberger (1721–83; songs, harpsichord pieces, theoretical books); and Johann Fr. Agricola (1720–74; songs).

While in the field of instrumental music these men, particularly C. P. E. Bach, made significant contributions, their activity in the field of the *Lied (*Berliner Liederschule*) was largely frustrated by the spirit of rationalism and the Enlightenment to which Frederick the Great, a close friend of Voltaire, had given ready admittance. The situation changed when a younger generation, known as *Zweite Berliner Liederschule*, turned from the dry moralism of Gellert to the inspiring poems of Klopstock and the young Goethe. Johann P. A. Schulz (1747–1800), Johann F. Reichardt (1752–1814), and Karl F. Zelter (1758–1832) are the most important members of this group. See *Lied IV; also *Singspiel. The name *Berliner Schule* is sometimes restricted to this group.

Lit.: *AdHM*, 699ff; M. Friedländer, *Das deutsche Lied im 18. Jahrhundert*, 2 vols. (1902); Flueler, *Die norddeutsche Sinfonie* (Diss. Berlin 1910); H. Hoffmann, *Die norddeutsche Triosonate* . . . (Diss. Kiel 1924); E. Stiltz, *Die Berliner Klaviersonate zur Zeit Friedrichs des Grossen* (Diss. Berlin 1930); A. Mayer-Reinach, "K. H. Graun als Opernkomponist" (*SIM* i).

Bersag horn. See *Brass instruments IV.

Beruhigend [G.]. Calming down.

Bes [G.]. B-double flat.

Beschleunigt [G.]. Accelerando.

Beseelt [G.]. Soulfully.

Bestimmt [G.]. With decision.

Betont [G.]. Stressed, accented.

Beweglich [G.]. In an agile manner.

Bezifferter Bass [G.; *Ziffer*, figure]. Figured bass. i.e., *thorough-bass.

B fa. See *Hexachord III.

B.-G. Abbreviation for *Bach-Gesellschaft* [see *Societies II, 2].

B.-H. Abbreviation for Breitkopf und Härtel, publishers of numerous complete editions.

Bible regal [G. *Bibelregal*]. See *Regal.

Biblioteca di Rarità Musicali. See *Editions III.

Bicinium [L. *bis*, twice, and *canere*, to sing]. A 16th-century name chiefly used in German for vocal compositions in two parts. The Greek synonym *diphona* occurs also. The bicinia, which form a delightful contrast to the rich texture of the late-16th-century motet, madrigal, etc., represent a little-known treasure of great artistic value and educational significance. The most important publications are: G. Rhaw, *Bicinia Gallica, Latina et Germanica* (1545; partly republished by K. Ameln, Bärenreiter-Verlag; by Reichenbach, Verlag Kallmeyer); Kaspar Othmayr, *Bicinia Sacra* (1547; partly republ. by Lipphardt, Bär. V.); Erasmus Rotenbucher, *Diphona amoena et florida* (1549); Seth Calvisius, *Biciniorum libri duo* (1599, 1612); E. Bodenschatz, *Bicinia XC selectissima* . . . (1615; cf. *SchGMB*, no. 163). Outstanding examples are found among the works of Ludwig Senfl, Orlando di Lasso (complete works, vol. i), and Michael Praetorius (cpl. works, vol. ix, and *passim*; cf. *HAM*, no. 167b). An Italian publication of bicinia is Pietro Vinci, *Il primo libro della musica a due voci* (1560). Throughout the 17th century numerous two-part pieces were written in Italy, under the name *ricercare [see also *Invention]. S. Scheidt, in his *Tabulatura nova* (1624), uses the term Bicinium for organ verses and variations in two voice-parts. See *Tricinium.

Bina. Same as vina [see *Hindu music II].

Biniou. See under *Bagpipe.

Binary and ternary form. I. The terms signify two basic musical forms, consisting of two or of three main sections respectively. The binary form follows the scheme A B, with each section repeated; the ternary form (also called: *song form) follows the scheme A B A. Examples of the former category abound in the allemandes, gavottes, etc., of Bach's suites, while the latter occurs frequently in the slow movements of sonatas (e.g., Beethoven, Piano Sonata op. 7; op. 10, no. 3), in the Scherzo with Trio, and in practically all the *character pieces of the Romantic composers, such as Schumann's Novellettes, Chopin's Nocturnes, Brahms's Fantasias, etc.

It should be noticed that binary and ternary forms are not so similar in character as the nomenclature might suggest. In fact, to consider them as analogous forms is quite misleading. The binary form is essentially a stylistic and structural entity, a unified whole which, like many phrases in music, falls into two halves, the second of which forms the logical and necessary completion of the first. The ternary form, on the other hand, is usually the sum of three single units each of which is complete in itself. This difference is clearly reflected in the harmonic scheme normally found with these forms: in the binary form each section is harmonically "open," the first leading from T to D, the second back from D to T; in the ternary form each section is harmonically "closed," beginning and ending in the same key, but with a different key (dominant, relative key, parallel key) often used for the middle section. Stylistic considerations also corroborate this fundamental difference: the binary form uses the same or similar material throughout, whereas the ternary form uses different, frequently contrasting, material for the middle section. Briefly stated, the binary form is a continuous form, the ternary, a sectional form. The minuet (scherzo) with trio of the sonata shows both forms combined, since the whole movement is in ternary form, each section in binary form.

II. The historical development of the binary form is of particular interest since it includes one of the most important developments of music history, namely, that leading to the sonata-form of the classical sonata, symphony, etc. Owing to the fact that this form includes three main sections, the exposition, the development, and the recapitulation (= exposition), it is frequently considered a ternary form. Such an interpretation, although admissible from the point of view of program-notes, is too much of a "listener's simplification" to be accepted in serious studies. The main objection against it lies in the fact that it does not take into account the repetition of the exposition which is almost invariably prescribed in the works of the Viennese classics, including Brahms — an oversight for which the blame must be put on our conductors and pianists who consistently disregard in their performances a feature whose aesthetic importance was clearly recognized by the great masters of the sonata. Another objection is that in the sonata-form the middle section (development) is based on the thematic material of the first section (exposition), while in true ternary form it has different and contrasting material. Finally, the historical development of sonata-form clearly shows its derivation from binary schemes, such as were used in the dance movements of the suite [see *Sonata-form II]. Three such schemes can be distinguished: (1) the *symmetrical binary form*, in which both sections are of equal length; (2) the *asymmetrical*

binary form, the second section of which is longer than the first, owing to a "bulging-out" process at its beginning; (3) the *rounded binary form*, which has repetition (*in toto* or partially) of the first section at the end of the second [see Ex. 1–3]. The latter is structurally identical with the earlier type of sonata-form (Haydn, Mozart) in which both sections are repeated. The same scheme exists in many dance movements and other pieces of Bach (e.g., in the Anglaise from his French Suite no. 3 and in the Prelude in D of *Wt. Cl.* ii) as well as in practically all the minuets (scherzos) and trios of the classical period. In fact, any of these pieces may well serve as an example of sonata-form, showing its main sections in a condensed shape. Regarding a medieval type of binary form in which the first section only is repeated (as in the later examples of sonata-form), see *Barform.

III. The principle of ternary structure appeared first in the French chansons of the 16th century (Jannequin; cf. *RiHM* ii.1, 367). The idea of a contrasting middle section is quite clearly expressed in the shepherd's solo of Monteverdi's *Orfeo*, 1607 [cf. also his famous duet "Purti miro" from *L'Incoronazione*, 1642; *SchGMB*, no. 178]. Ternary form became clearly established in the *da-capo aria, c. 1700. Another realization of the ternary construction exists in the alternative use of two dances, the 'first being repeated after the second [see *Alternativo]. In 19th-century music, the ternary form was frequently broadened into a five-part scheme: A B A B A or A B A C A, particularly in slow movements of symphonies [cf., e.g., that of Bruckner's Symphony no. 7]. See *Forms, Musical; also *Rondo. Cf. E. J. Dent, "Binary and Ternary Forms" (*ML* xvii, no. 4).

Bind. Same as *tie.

Bird song. The song of the birds, being practically the only case of "music in nature," has been the subject of innumerable studies. Interesting facts are that only small birds sing, that the best singers (nightingale, lark, thrush, blackbird) are unobtrusively colored, that they prefer to sing in solitude rather than in flocks, that only male birds have loud musical voices, and that good singers are found only in moderate climates.

Much attention has been given to the question as to the relationship between bird song and our music. Certainly no biological relationship exists, as most animals do not sing. Whether or not our music developed in imitation of bird song, as has been frequently maintained, is a matter of mere speculation. Although it is true that bird song has many features in common with primitive folk song (irregularity, wavering of pitch, microtonic deviations from our scale, improvisation), it should be noticed that this type of folk song exists chiefly in the exotic countries (Africa, Asia) where there are no singing birds.

Lit.: S. P. Cheney, *Wood Notes Wild* (1891); F. Schuyler Mathews, *Fieldbook of Wild Birds and Their Music* (1904); W. Garstang, *Songs of the Birds* (1922); A. R. Brand, *Songs of Wild Birds* (1936; with records); E. M. Nicholson, *Songs of Wild Birds* (1936; with records); A. A. Saunders, *A Guide to Bird Songs of North-eastern United States* (1935), W. B. Olds, in *MQ* viii. Cf. also William Gardiner, *The Music of Nature* (1832), chapter XII.

Bis [F., twice]. (1) Same as *encore. — (2) Indication that notes or passages should be repeated.

Biscroma [It.]. See *Notes.

Bisdiapason [L.]. The interval or range of two octaves.

Bistropha. See *Neumes I (table).

Bitonality. See *Polytonality.

Bivirga. See *Neumes I (table).

Biwa. The Japanese lute. See *P'ip'a.

Bkl. Short for G. *Bassklarinette*, i.e., bass clarinet.

Black-bottom. See *Jazz III.

Blackening. Same as *coloration [see *Mensural notation V].

Bladder pipe [G. *Platerspiel*]. See under *Bagpipe.

Blanche [F.]. See *Notes.

Blasinstrument [G.]. *Wind instrument *Blasmusik*, music for wind instruments.

Blasquinte [G., "blown fifth"]. A term introduced by E. von Hornbostel for a fifth of 678 cents, i.e., ⅛ of a whole-tone lower than the Pythagorean (pure) or the tempered fifth of 702 or 700 cents respectively. This interval results if a stopped pipe (bamboo) is overblown. Hornbostel derived from this interval a circle of Blasquinten (*Blasquintenzirkel*) similar to that of the ordinary *circle of fifth and based on the absolute pitch of the Chinese *huang chung* [see *Chinese music I]. He was able to show that the tones resulting from this procedure recur in many musical cultures of the Far East and of South America, most clearly in the Javanese scale *pelog* [see *Javanese music II]. Recent studies by M. Bukofzer have shown, however, that the blown fifth is without physical foundation, and the theory of the circle of blown fifths has been contested.
Lit.: E. M. v. Hornbostel, "Die Massnorm als kulturgeschichtliches Forschungsmittel" (in *Festschrift für P. W. Schmidt*, 1928); *id.*, "Musikalische Tonsysteme" (in H. Geiger, *Handbuch der Physik*, viii, 1928); R. Lachmann, *Musik des Orients* (1929); M. Bukofzer, in *Zeitschrift für Physik*, 99 (1936) and in *Anthropos*, 32 (1937).

Blatt [G.]. Reed.

Blattspiel ("playing from the sheet"). Sight-reading.

Blechinstrument [G.]. Brass instrument; also called simply *Blech*.

Blechmusik. Music for brass bands.

Blockflöte [G.]. Blockflute, i.e., *recorder. See also under *Whistle.

Blue notes. In jazz music, name for certain degrees of the scale, mainly the third and the seventh, which are used both natural and flatted (E and E♭, B and B♭), and frequently with a deliberately "wrong" intonation in between. The resulting formations (blues scale) are a characteristic of the *blues.

Blues. See *Jazz II; *Negro music III; *Blue notes. Cf. W. C. Handy, *The Blues* (1925).

Blumen [G.]. Name for the coloraturas of the *Meistersinger.

B.M.V. See *Antiphon (2).

B mi. See *Hexachord III.

B moll [G.]. B-flat minor.

Bobisation. See *Solmization III.

Bocal [F.]. Mouthpiece of a brass instrument.

Bocca chiusa [It.]. Same as *bouche fermé. *Bocca ridente* (laughing mouth) indicates in singing a smiling position of the lips.

Bocedisation. See *Solmization III.

Bockstriller [G., from *Bock*, he-goat]. See *Tremolo (3).

Boehm clarinet (flute). See *Boehm system; *Clarinet (*Flute).

Boehm system. A system of keying a wood-wind instrument which allows the holes to be cut in the proper acoustical position and size, and yet to be within the spread of the average hand. It was invented around 1830 by the flutist Theobald Boehm of Munich (1794–1881) to supersede earlier methods of keying in which the holes were not placed exactly from the acoustical point of view, but in a sort of compromise-position, with greater regard to the hand than to the ear. In spite of its complicated mechanism and the fact that it detracts slightly from the tonal quality of the instrument, it has been universally adopted in the manufacture of flutes, and the benefits of the system have been applied also to oboes, clarinets, and (to a lesser extent) to bassoons. Duplicate fingerings are introduced which facilitate passages previously impossible, and the system has the advantage of keeping different keys more or less on the same level as regards difficulty. The pre-Boehm types of flutes and oboes are now obsolete, but clarinets with the older system are still used. Cf. H. C. Wysham, *The Evolution of the Boehm Flute* (1898). W. D. D.

Boethian notation. See *Letter notation.

Bogen [G.]. (1) The bow of a violin, etc. — (2) The tie. *Bogenform*, see *Forms, Musical (after A, I). *Bogenführung*, i.e., bowing. *Bogenklavier*, *Bogenflügel*, see *Sostenente pianoforte.

Bohème, La. Grand opera by Giacomo Puccini (1858–1924), based on Henri Murger's *La Vie de Bohème*, composed in 1896. The setting is Paris in the 1840's, and the opera gives a touching though somewhat sentimental description of the Bohemian life of young artists, centering around the love between the poet *Rodolfo* (Tenor) and *Mimi* (Soprano) who, in the last act, dies of consumption. The lighter side of Bohemian life and love is represented by another couple, *Marcel* (Baritone) and *Musetta* (Soprano).

The opera, one of the best-known examples of *Verismo, approximates, in its light texture, clarity of orchestration, and lyric style, the French rather than the typically Italian (Verdi) opera. Interesting are the *parallel chords in the opening to the second act. R. Leoncavallo wrote an unsuccessful opera on the same subject in 1897, without knowledge of Puccini's score.

Bohemian music. See *Czech music.

Bois [F., wood]. *Les bois*, the wood winds.

Boite de musique [F.]. Musical box. See *Mechanical instruments III.

Bolero. A Spanish dance said to have been invented by Sebastián Cerezo, a celebrated dancer of Cádiz, around 1780. It is a solo or couple dance including many brilliant and difficult steps, quick movements, such as the *entrechat* of the classical ballet, as well as a sudden stop in a characteristic position with one arm held arched over the head (*bien parado*). The music is in moderate triple time, with ac-

companiment of the castanets and rhythms such as:

$$\left| {}^3_4 \; \rightthreetimes \; \overline{} \; \overline{} \; \right| \; {}^3_4 \; \overline{} \; \overline{} \; \overline{} \; \right|$$

Probably the earliest extant example is a "Bolero a solo" by Beethoven [cf. W. Hess, in *DM* xxx.12]. Operatic boleros occur in Auber's *La Muette de Portici* and *Le Domino noir*, and in Weber's *Preziosa*. Particularly famous are Chopin's Bolero op. 19 for pianoforte, and Ravel's Boléro for orchestra (1928). The Cuban bolero is in 2/4-meter.

Bologna School. A term applied to a 17th-century group of instrumental composers who were active in Bologna. Included among its members are Maurizio Cazzati (1620–77), Giov. Battista Vitali (1644?–92), Pietro degli Antonii (1648–1720), Giov. Battista Bassani (1657–1716), Domenico Gabrielli (1658–90), Giov. Battista Borri (?), Giuseppe Torelli (d. 1708), Tommaso Antonio Vitali (1665–1747), and Giuseppe Aldrovandini (1665 or 1673–1707). See *History of music V.

The Bologna School was important in the formal development of the *trio sonata (Cazzati, Bassani, G. B. Vitali), solo violin sonata (degli Antonii, Aldrovandini), solo cello sonata (Gabrielli), *concerto grosso (Torelli, Gabrielli), and violin concerto (Torelli). The stylistic contributions of these men were in the direction of a disciplined formalism, an elegance of expression, and a pervasive lyricism. These characteristics, combined with their deliberate avoidance of virtuosity, were in reaction to the technical exuberance of the string composers of the early Baroque, Biagio Marini, Carlo Farina, Marco Uccellini (and their German successors Rosenmüller, Walther, Biber), who early developed such extreme features of violin playing as *col legno, scordatura, sul ponticello*, use of double and triple stops, and of higher positions (5th and 6th). The Bologna School thus constitutes a lyrical interlude between the virtuoso experimentation of the early Baroque and the bravura style of the later Baroque (Vivaldi, Tartini, Handel).

The most illustrious proponent of the Bologna style, although not a member proper of the school, was Arcangelo Corelli (1653–1713), who studied and worked at Bologna from 1666 till 1671, becoming a member of the famous Accademia Filarmonica of Bologna [see *Accademia] in 1670. His identification with the Bologna School is evident from the restrained classicism of his style as well as from the title "detto il bolognese" which appears in his op. 1 (1681), op. 2 (1685), and op. 3 (1689).

Much of the activity of the Bologna School centered around the chapel of San Petronio, which was organized by Cazzati in 1657. The reorganization of this institution, in 1701, in conformity with the new Neapolitan taste, probably marked the end of the Bologna School.

Lit.: G. Gaspari, *La Musica in San Petronio* (1868/70); *id.*, *Musicisti bolognesi* (1875/80); F. Vatielli, *Arte e vita musicale a Bologna* (1927); *id.*, †*Antichi maestri Bolognesi*, vol. ii; L. Frati, in *RMI* xxi, xxiv, xxvi, xxxii. Musical examples in †*SchGMB*, nos. 228, 241, 257; *HAM*, nos. 219, 244–246; Torchi, †*L'Arte musicale in Italia*, vol. vii; J. W. Wasielewski, *Die Violine im 17. Jahrhundert* (*Instrumentalsätze*, 1905). H. G. Mishkin, "The Solo Violin Sonata of the Bologna School" (*MQ* xxix, Jan.). H. G. M.

Bombarde, bombarda. (1) French (Italian) name for the *shawm, particularly the bass size of this instrument. In Germany, the perverted names Bomhart, Pomhart, Pumhart, Pommer, occur. See *Oboe family III. — (2). Same as *bombardon.

Bombardon. See *Brass instruments III(e).

Bombo [It.]. See *Tremolo (1).

Bomhart [G.]. See *Bombarde (1).

Bonang. See *Javanese music I.

Boogie-woogie. See *Jazz IV; *Divisions; *Ostinato.

Bordun [G.], **bordone** [It.]. See *Bourdon.

Boris Godunov. Opera by Modest Moussorgsky (1839–81), produced in 1874; orchestral revision by N. Rimsky-Korsakov, 1896. The setting is Moscow of *c.* 1600, where *Boris Godunov* (Bass), after having murdered Dmitri, the rightful heir to the throne, rules over Russia, but, suffering from a sense of guilt (in the Prologue he is in a convent in order to gain expiation), and frightened by the appearance of a "false Dmitri" (the young monk *Gregory*, Tenor), finally prays for forgiveness of his sin and, bequeathing the crown to his young son *Feodor* (Mezzo-soprano), falls dead.

Boris Godunov is the outstanding masterpiece of Russian national opera. Its musical style is remarkably advanced for the time it was written, and although its unconventional boldness aroused great resentment in professional circles, many innovations of a more recent date have been traced back to this work, e.g., the use of *parallel chords, of *modality, and other unorthodox devices. Particularly striking is the prominence of the chorus, representing the Russian people who, it has been said, are the real protagonist of the opera, rather than Boris himself.

Borre, borry, borea [It.]. See *Bourrée.

Boston, valse Boston. An American ballroom dance which was in vogue around 1915. It is in the character of a slow waltz, with a more subtle rhythm and a more sophisticated accompaniment than the ordinary waltz. In post-war Germany it acquired a prominent position as an "American importation" and was imbued with jazz-like elements. Numerous composers used the type, e.g. Hindemith (1st String Quartet; *Suite 1922*); Erwin Schulhoff (*Esquisses de Jazz*, 1927; *Partita*, 1925); Louis Gruenberg (*Jazzberries*, 1925); Conrad Beck (*Zwei Tanzstücke*).

Bouché [F.]. See Horn I.

Bouche fermée [F.], **bocca chiusa** [It.]. Singing without words and with closed mouth or, at least, closed teeth. This is occasionally used as a special effect of vocal accompaniment, e.g., in Verdi's *Rigoletto*, last act.

Bouffons [F., comedians]. (1) In the 15th and 16th centuries bouffons were costumed dancers probably similar to those who performed the *morisca and the *matasin. — (2) In 1752 the *Guerre des bouffons* (War of the Comedians) was a quarrel between two parties of Parisian musicians and opera-enthusiasts — those favoring the national French serious opera (Lully, Rameau, Destouches) and those preferring the Italian opera buffa (Pergolesi). Pergolesi's famous opera buffa *La Serva padrona* (The Servant as Mistress), which was composed in 1733, had been given in Paris for the first time in 1752, without arousing more than moderate interest. The second performance, however, given by a troupe of Italian comedians (*buffi*), led to a quarrel which divided Paris into two halves and became famous in the history of opera. The national party consisted largely of the aristocracy (including the King and Madame de Pompadour) and the plutocracy, while the Italian party numbered among its adherents the intelligentsia and the musical connoisseurs (including the Queen and such outstanding men as Rousseau, d'Alembert, Diderot). The latter considered the Italian opera superior because it had more melody, expression, and naturalness, and had shaken off completely the "useless fetters of counterpoint." Briefly speaking, the *guerre des bouffons* was a fight of the rising *Rococo against the dying *Baroque. [For a similar movement in Spain, see *Zarzuela.] Rousseau's famous *Lettre sur la musique française* (1753) was one of the hundreds of pamphlets issued in this controversy. The efforts of French musicians to compete with the popularity of the opera buffa resulted in a new kind of French comic opera known as *Comédie mêlée d'ariettes* [see *Comic opera II(c)].

Lit.: G. Cucuel, *Les Créateurs de l'opéra-comique français* (1914); L. Reichenberg, *Contribution à l'historie de la "Que-*

relle de Bouffons" (1937); E. Hirschberg, *Die Encyclopädisten und die französische Oper* (1903); L. de la Laurencie, "La grande saison italienne de 1752" (*SIM* viii).

Bourdon. The general connotation of this term is that of a low tone of long duration, that is, a *drone or *pedal point. The term was also applied to instrumental devices producing such tones, e.g., to the low-pitched bass-courses of the *viella and the *hurdy-gurdy which could be sounded continuously against a melody played on the higher strings [cf. Petrus Picardus, *CS* i, 153], to the large pipes of the organ, or to the drones of the bagpipe. In French 17th-century music, the name bourdon is given to pieces in which there is a uniform bass-accompaniment similar to that of the drones of a bagpipe, e.g., C-g-c-g C-g-c-g . . . [cf. F. Couperin's Air des viéleux in his harpsichord suite (*ordre) "Les Fastes de la grande Ménestrandise," ed. Augener ii, 209; also the musette in Bach's English Suite, no. 3].

Bourrée [English borry, borre, etc.]. A French 17th-century dance, probably from the Auvergne, usually in quick duple meter with a single upbeat [Ex. from

Bach's French Suite, no. 6]. The dance is mentioned by M. Praetorius (*Syntagma musicum*, 1615), but does not appear in musical composition prior to Lully's operas and ballets (*c.* 1670), whence it was transferred to the suites of the late 17th and early 18th centuries (Pachelbel, J. K. F. Fischer, J. S. Bach). See *Dance music III.

Bout d'archet [F.]. Point of the bow.

Boutade [F.]. A dance or ballet in a capricious style. The name is also used for 18th-century instrumental pieces of a similar character.

✓Bow [F. *archet*; G. *Bogen*; It. *archetto*]. This implement of violin playing takes its name (in all languages) from the fact that it had originally the form of a bow similar to that used in archery. Chinese and Arabian fiddles are still played with bows of such shape, as were stringed instruments in Europe until about the 15th century. During the 16th and 17th centuries various shapes of bows were used, some of which are reproduced here. Fig. 3 shows

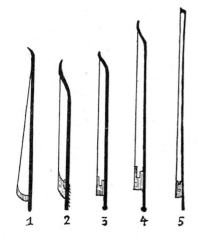

1 2 3 4 5

Corelli's bow which was short and of hard, unelastic wood, while Tartini's bow (Fig. 4) was longer and more elastic. In Germany a bow of a slightly curved shape (much less curved, however, than the early bows) was used, which facilitated the playing of polyphonic violin music such as was particularly cultivated in Germany (Biber, Bach). On these bows it was also possible to vary slightly the tension of the hair by a gentle pressure of the thumb.

The nut (frog) originally was a small piece of wood fastened to the stick, around which the hair was wrapped tightly. The horn-shaped nut shown on Fig. 1 is still reminiscent of this early shape. Fig. 2 shows a device which was used temporarily before 1700 in order to allow for an adjustment of the tension of the bow, namely a wire loop that could hook into a series of teeth (dentated bow). About 1700 this device was replaced by a screw mechanism such as is still used today [Figs. 3–5].

The bow received its classical and final form at the hands of François Tourte (1747–1833). The most important characteristics of his bow [Fig. 5] are the long, tapering, and slightly inward curving stick, the use of metal or ivory plates for the tip, of Pernambuco wood for the stick, the exact measurements for perfect balance, probably also the metal ferrule of the frog through which the hair passes evenly spread (this latter invention is also credited to Tourte's contemporary John Dodd).

The bows used for the viola, cello, and double-bass are of the same design as the violin bow, but successively heavier and, with the two last-named instruments, shorter.

Lit.: H. Saint-George, *The Bow* (3d ed., 1922); H. Dräger, *Die Entwicklung des Streichbogens* (1937); *LavE* ii.3, 1744.

Bowed harp. Modern name for the *crwth and similar instruments of Northern Europe. Cf. O. Andersson, *The Bowed Harp* (1930).

Bowing. The technique of using the bow on stringed instruments (violins, etc.). The mastery of the bow includes a considerable number of different manners of bowing, the most important of which are briefly described here. It should be noted that these terms, except for the most common ones like *détaché, sautillé, spiccato, staccato*, are not much used by players, and that the various effects are frequently not indicated exactly with their proper notation, although they are clearly suggested to the player by the character of the music.

(a) *Plain Bowing* (*legato*). This consists of two basic strokes: *Down-bow* [F. *tiré*; G. *Abstrich, Herabstrich, Herstrich, Herunterstrich, Niederstrich*; It. *arcata in giù*] and *Up-bow* [F. *poussé*; G. *Aufstrich, Heraufstrich, Hinstrich*; It. *arcata in su*]. In down-bow, indicated by the sign (1), the arm is moved away from the body, while in up-bow (sign 2) the arm moves towards the body. The slur (3) indicates the number of notes to be taken in a single stroke.

(b) *Détaché*. A broad vigorous stroke in which the notes of equal time value are bowed singly with a slight articulation

due to the rapid change of bow. This stroke is much used for loud passages of not too great speed. Sometimes it is indicated by lines under (or above) the notes, as in (4). When an exceptionally long stroke is used it is called *le grand détaché*.

(c) *Martelé* [It. *martellato*]. Literally a "hammered" stroke, this is played with very short bows at the point. The hammered effect is obtained by releasing each stroke forcefully and suddenly. It cannot be executed rapidly, and is indicated by an arrowhead, as in (5). It is generally found in loud passages.

(d) *Sautillé* [It. *spiccato*; G. *Springbogen*]. A short stroke played in rapid tempo in the middle of the bow in such a way that the bow bounces slightly from the string. This stroke requires good control on the part of the performer in order to keep it steady. It is a most brilliant effect and can be done from very soft to quite loud. It is indicated by dots, as in (6). Variants of this stroke are known as *piqué, picchettato*.

(e) *Jeté* (also known as *ricochet*). This is done by "throwing" the bow on the string in the upper third of the bow so that it will bounce a series of rapid notes on the down-bow. Notation as under (7). Usually from two to six notes are taken in one stroke, although a skillful player can do more than this number.

(f) *Louré*. A stroke useful in slow tempo to separate slightly each of several notes taken in a slur. It is indicated as

under (8). It can be played in a highly expressive manner and is capable of notable emotional intensity.

(g) *Staccato*. This is a solo effect and theoretically consists of a number of *martelé* notes taken in the same stroke. It can be executed with dazzling brilliance either up-bow or down-bow, but the latter is more difficult. When the bow is allowed to spring slightly from the string it is known as *Staccato volante* (flying staccato). Notation as under (9).

(h) *Viotti-stroke*. This is attributed to Giov. Battista Viotti (1753–1824), and consists of two detached and strongly marked notes, the first of which is unaccented and given very little bow, while the second comes on the accent and takes much more bow. It is done at the point, and is highly effective, especially at a fairly quick tempo. Notation as under (10).

(i) *Arpeggio* or *arpeggiando*. A bouncing stroke played on broken chords so that each bounce is on a different string, as in (11).

(j) *Tremolo*. This is primarily an orchestral effect and is produced by moving the bow back and forth in short and extremely rapid strokes, on the same note (12). See *Tremolo.

(k) *Sul ponticello* [F. *au chevalet*; G. *am Steg*]. A nasal, glassy effect produced by bowing very close to the bridge. Its use is confined almost entirely to chamber music.

(l) *Flautando, flautato* (also It. *sul tastiera*; F. *sur la touche*; G. *am Griffbrett*). A flute-like effect produced by bowing very slightly over the finger board. This stroke is generally confined to sustained passages or slow notes.

(m) *Col legno*. This is done by striking the string with the stick instead of the hair. A purely orchestral effect.

(n) *Flatter la corde*. A soft, expressive stroke in which the string is literally "caressed."

(o) *Ondulé* [It. *ondeggiando*]. An obsolete form of tremolo ("undulating tremolo") in which several notes are taken in the same bow [see *Tremolo (1)].　　　　　　H. N.

Brabanconne. See *National anthems.

Braccio [It., arm]. In the Baroque period, the term *braccio* was used to signify the members of the violin family (*viola da braccio*) which were held at arm level, as distinguished from the viols (simply *viola*) which were held downwards resting on the knees, or from the larger *viola da gamba* [*gamba*, leg] which was held resting between the legs of the player. Later, after the name violin had established itself, only the second-smallest size of the family retained the name *viola da braccio*, a name the first half of which survives in the English term viola, the second, in the German term *Bratsche*.

Brace [F. *accolade*; G. *Klammer*]. The perpendicular line combined with a bracket that joins the different staves in piano music or in scores. Hence, the entirety of the (two or more) staves to be read simultaneously.

Braille music notation. The method of writing music according to the principles of the Braille system for the blind. In this system, as is well known, raised dots are used in various configurations all of which are derived from an elementary configuration of six dots: ⁚⁚. Following are the signs for the C major scale and a few other symbols.

The rhythmic value of the note signs is an eighth note, unless a dot is added underneath to the right or to the left side.

Example of Braille Notation

In the former case, the value is ¼ or ¹⁄₆₄; in the latter, ½ or ¹⁄₃₂. If both dots are added, the value is ¹⁄₁ or ¹⁄₁₆. See the accompanying example. The octave position is indicated by special signs which normally appear at the beginning of each measure. Other signs indicate rests, time signatures, etc. For more details, cf. A. Reuss, *Development and Problems of Musical Notation for the Blind* (1932); WoHN i, 449ff; LavE ii.6, 3836.

Brandenburg Concertos. Six concertos written by Bach in 1721 and dedicated to Christian Ludwig, Margrave of Brandenburg. They represent the artistic acme of the *concerto grosso, although the traditional contrast between a group of solo instruments (*concertino*) and the ensemble (*ripieno*) is clearly manifest only in the second, fourth, and fifth concertos.

Brando [It.], **brangill** [Old E.]. *Branle.

Branle, bransle [F., from *branler*, to fling, to sway; It. *brando*]. A very popular group dance of the 16th century. It was executed in a great number of local varieties (Arbeau's *Orchésographie enumerates 26 species) many of which were of the "follow-the-leader" type, similar to the *farandole and the *cotillon. It was accompanied by singing and apparently included some "swaying" movements of the body or of the hands. The *branle simple* was in duple meter, the *branle gay* in triple meter. The *branle à mener* survived in the *amener of the 17th century and, very likely, in the *minuet. In England the dance was known under the name "brangill" or "brawl" [cf. Shakespeare, *Love's Labour's Lost* iii, 1]. A 17th-century Italian name is "brando" [cf. Carlo Farina, *Pavane, gagliarde, brandi* ... (1626–28)]. See *Dance music II.

Brass band. A small military band, ordinarily consisting of three or more cornets in B-flat, three E-flat alto Saxhorns, one or more baritones or euphoniums, basses, and drums, as well as, on occasion, trumpets, bugles, and kettledrums. It has not the variety of color possessed by the full military band, but on account of the relative ease with which instruments of the Saxhorn family are learned, a brass band is easier to establish and maintain. The brass band movement is particularly popular in the United States and in England, where such bands are frequently found attached to high schools and colleges, religious groups (Salvation Army), factories, etc. See *Brass instruments III; *Military band.   W. D. D.

Brassed. See *Horn I.

√Brass instruments [F. *instruments de cuivre*; G. *Blechinstrumente*; It. *stromenti d'ottone*].

I. *General.* That section of the orchestra which includes the instruments made of brass or other metal, such as trumpets, horns, trombones, tubas, as distinguished from those made of wood [see *Wood winds; also *Orchestra]. This feature, however, is of a merely external significance, since the material from which a wind instrument is made has a practically negligible effect upon its tone quality and its other properties [see *Wind instruments I]. Moreover, various instruments of the "brass family" were formerly made of wood [see V] and, on the other hand, the "wood-wind family" includes instruments made of metal, e.g., the flute and the saxophone. A more characteristic feature of the family in question is the mouthpiece, which nearly always has the shape of a cup, hence the name "cupped-mouthpiece family" which can be accepted for all practical purposes as a basis of classification. If even this definition is rejected — on the ground that in certain obsolete or Oriental instruments the mouthpiece can hardly be said to have the shape of a cup — the instruments in question must be defined as "lip-vibrated aerophones," i.e., wind instruments with which the lips of the player serve as a reed [see *Reed].

The "brass instruments" — as we may call them with due reservation — form an extremely large group, including not only numerous ancient instruments but also many of a more recent date which were invented in the 18th and 19th centuries for military purposes, for bands, and as improvements of older orchestral types. The subsequent grouping is intended to place the various instruments in certain general categories which show their historical or other position, a grouping which, needless to say, admits of some

overlapping. For the general acoustical properties of the brass instruments, see under *Wind instruments.

II. *Orchestral Instruments.* The brass section of the modern orchestra consists mainly of the *horn, the *trumpet, the *trombone, and the *tuba. The tuba is related to the horn, both having a pipe the diameter of which increases throughout the greater part of its length (conical pipe), while in the trumpet and the trombone the pipe is to a great extent (about two-thirds) cylindrical and widens only at the end into a relatively small bell. The mouthpieces also show a difference, being more cup-shaped than with the two latter instruments than with the former. For more details on these instruments, see the separate entries. Other instruments which have occasionally been used in the modern orchestra are the Wagner tubas [see *Tuba], the cornet, and several other types mentioned under III.

III. *Band Instruments.* Under this category we group all those brass instruments which are used chiefly in the brass band and in other bands, primarily for open-air performance of marches and of other popular music. Some of them, however, have occasionally been used in the orchestral scores of composers, mainly the cornet. Most of these instruments can be considered as hybrids between the horn and the trumpet in that they combine features of the horn (e.g., conical bore) with other features of the trumpet (e.g., cup-shaped mouthpiece). A methodical survey of these instruments is extremely difficult, owing to the large variety of types and sizes as well as, particularly, to the utterly confusing terminology. The subsequent survey of the most important types follows in principle the description given in N. Bessaraboff, *Ancient European Musical Instruments* (1941), pp. 150ff, which may be consulted for more details.

(a) Cornet [F. *cornet-à-pistons*; G. *Kornett*; It. *cornetta*]. An instrument similar in shape to the trumpet, but shorter and with a relatively longer conical part. It is pitched in Bb (sometimes in A), and has a written range from f♯ to c''', sounding a whole-tone (or three semitones)

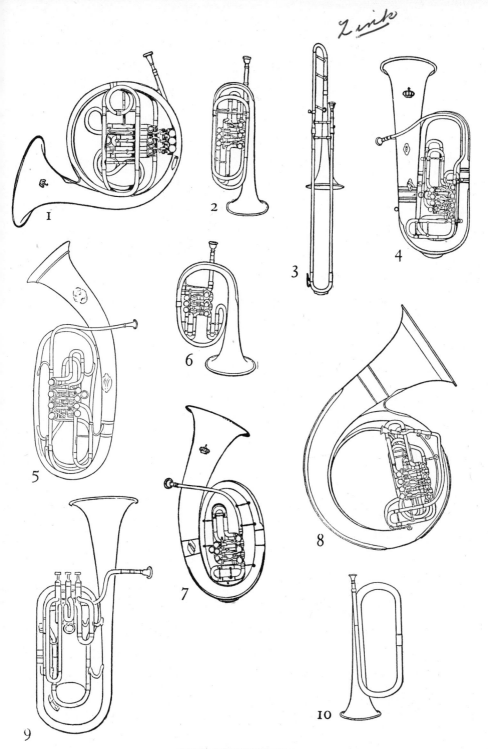

Zink

BRASS INSTRUMENTS I

1. French Horn. 2. Trumpet. 3. Trombone. 4. Tuba. 5. Wagner Tuba. 6. Cornet.
7. Euphonium. 8. Helicon. 9. Saxhorn. 10. Bugle.

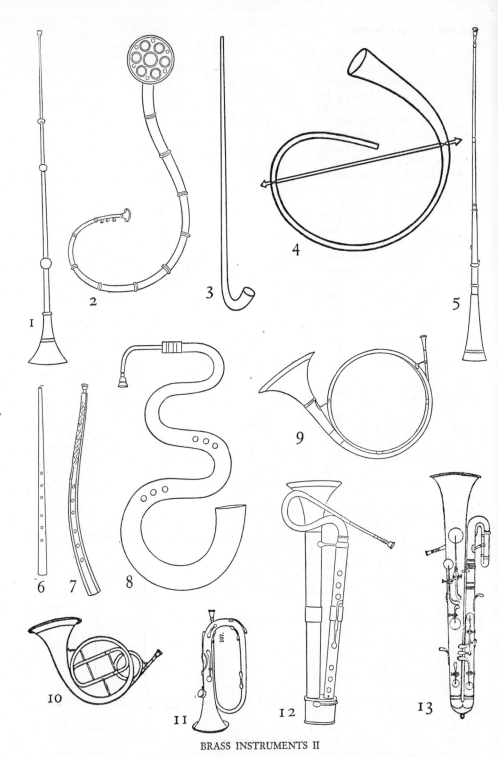

BRASS INSTRUMENTS II

1. Chinese Lapa. 2. Lur. 3. Lituus. 4. Buccina. 5. Buysine. 6. Straight Cornett. 7. Tenor Cornett.
8. Serpent. 9. Natural Horn. 10. Hand Horn. 11. Key Bugle. 12. Bass Horn. 13. Ophicleide.

lower. The cornet possesses a timbre similar to that of the trumpet. Owing to its shorter tube it has a considerably greater agility and has, therefore, been used a good deal by French and Italian composers (Berlioz, Bizet, Rossini). Its tone has been described as coarse and vulgar, and has been compared unfavorably with the brilliant tone of the trumpet. This difference, however, is largely due to a bad style of playing and to the music commonly associated with the instrument.

(b) Flügelhorn [F. *bugle*; It. *flicorno*]. An instrument similar in design and size to the cornet, but with a wider bore. It is usually built in Bb, more rarely in C. Its sound is somewhat similar to that of the horn, but lacks the latter's mellowness. The instruments named subsequently are larger sizes constructed after the principles of the Flügelhorn. They might be considered as forming a family for which the generic name "bugles" is often used. The largest members of the family are the *tubas and these are the only ones used in the orchestra. See also below, under (f).

(c) Baritone [F. *bugle ténor*; G. *Tenorhorn*; It. *flicorno tenore*]. This is a larger instrument pitched C or Bb, and built in two shapes, either in the usual shape of the trumpets with the bell pointing upwards, or oval with the bell facing backwards. The range is from E to b'b.

(d) Euphonium [F. *basse à pistons*; G. *Baryton*; It. *Eufonio*]. Its shape, pitch, and range are the same as those of the baritone. A larger bore, however, gives it a broader, mellower timbre and favors the lower notes. French and other composers have used it in place of the tuba, e.g., Stravinsky in *Petrouchka*.

(e) Helicon. These are bass and contrabass tubas in a circular form (similar to the shape of the horn) instead of the upright form of the tubas. The circle is wide enough to allow the player to carry the instrument over the shoulder. An American variety, characterized by a specially designed bell, is the *sousaphone* (named after John Philip Sousa who suggested it). In Germany similar instruments are called *Bombardon*.

(f) Saxhorn. This is an entire family of instruments invented by Adolphe Sax and designed on a uniform model. Their bore is somewhat narrower than that of the above-described instruments, resulting in a more brilliant timbre. They are all upright, with the pipe starting horizontally from the mouthpiece (as in the tubas, etc.), and the pistons stand on top of the upper horizontal part of the tube. It should be noticed that the Saxhorns made today frequently differ in details (width of bore, etc.) from Sax's original design and therefore approach the class of the Flügelhorns. Most authorities maintain that it is practically impossible to make a clear distinction between the Saxhorns and the Flügelhorns. Usually, the latter term is restricted to the one size described under (b). All agree that there is an inextricable confusion of nomenclature in this group. The most important types of Saxhorns are: (1) in Eb or F (Sopranino Saxhorn, Soprano Saxhorn, Soprano Flügelhorn, etc.); (2) in Bb or C (Soprano Saxhorn, Alto Saxhorn, Alto Flügelhorn); in low Eb or F (Alto Saxhorn, simply Saxhorn, Althorn, Tenor Saxhorn, etc.); in low Bb or C (Baritone Saxhorn, Althorn, Tenor horn, etc.). See *Saxtromba.

IV. *Military Instruments.* Under this heading brief mention may be made of instruments used for the purpose of signaling. They are all natural instruments, restricted to the tones 2 to 6 of the harmonic series, e.g., g-d'-g'-b'-d'' for an instrument built in G. The most common of these is the *bugle* [F. *clairon*; G. *Signalhorn*; It. *cornetta segnale*] built in G or Bb and occasionally in F. Bugles have been furnished with a single valve lowering the pitch a fourth, and these are known under the name *Bersag horn.*

V. *History.* (a) Trumpets and horns, though existing in many ancient cultures, were very late in acquiring those properties which made them useful as musical instruments in the proper sense of the word. Only a few tones of the harmonic series were available on the primitive instruments, a fact which restricted their use to the purpose of signaling, either in religious ceremonies or in military service. Moreover, the trumpets and horns of the Jews, Greeks, Romans, etc., possessed a sound which was far from agreeable but rather terrifying, as are to the present day the trumpets of China, Tibet, India. Plutarch likens the sound of the Egyptian trumpet to the bray of an ass, and the Jewish ceremonial horn, *shofar, even today fills the congregation with awe and fright. The Jews also had a long straight trumpet made of silver, the hasosra [see *Jewish music]. The Greek straight trumpet, called salpinx, was taken over from the Orient. The same shape occurs with the Roman tuba, a straight instrument made of bronze, about four feet in length. The Romans also had a trumpet which curved upwards at the end in the shape of a J, called lituus, while the buccina or cornu was entirely curved in the shape of a G and was provided with a wooden crossbar, forming the diameter, by which it was carried over the shoulder. Among the most interesting examples of ancient trumpets are the Nordic *lurer which, although of pre-historic age, show a high degree of perfection in bronze founding.

Horns were originally made from animals' horns as, e.g., the shofar, which is made from a ram's horn, or Babylonian ox-horns which, we are informed, were covered with gold and studded with precious stones. Metal horns, S-shaped and widening as the animal's horn, are much rarer in ancient cultures than the more cylindrical trumpets (whether straight or curved, as the cornu, which, in spite of its name, must be classified as a trumpet), probably owing to the greater difficulty of founding. They are also relatively rare among the Oriental nations.

(b) In Europe, also, trumpets appear much earlier than horns. With the Roman armies their various trumpets spread over Europe. After A.D. 1000 the straight tuba acquired the shape of a long and slim pipe with a rather large funnel-shaped bell. This instrument was called buisine (from Lat. buccina, which, however, was circular), while smaller sizes were called trombetta. From the early part of the 15th century we have the first evidence of a folded trumpet. The same principle was also applied to the larger buisine, which by the 15th century had acquired the distinguishing feature of the modern trombone, i.e., the slides [see *Trombone II]. In the 15th and 16th centuries trumpets became associated with heraldry [see *Trumpet II], while the wooden *cornett [G. Zink] acquired a prominent place in the chamber music of the 16th century. Its bass size was built in a clumsy serpentine shape and, therefore, called serpent. All these instruments had side-holes covered by the fingers [see *Wind instruments IV(d)]. Later a few keys were added in order to facilitate playing, particularly with the large serpent which, in an improved form, doubled up on itself like the bassoon, became known under the name of bass horn or Russian bassoon [see *Cornett].

(c) About 1650 begins the development of the modern horn and trumpet which is briefly described under *Horn II and *Trumpet II. Here it will suffice to mention a group of instruments which developed about 1800 and are characterized by the use of side-holes (as in the much older cornetts), operated by keys. This principle was applied, not only to horns and trumpets, but also to bugles [see IV] with which it proved more successful (Joseph Halliday, 1810). The key bugle or Kent bugle (Kent horn), as it was named in honor of the Duke of Kent [F. bugle à clés; G. Klappenhorn], remained in use until the second half of the 19th century. Later a larger size was constructed under the name ophicleide, which had the doubled-up shape of the Russian bassoon. Spontini prescribed it in his opera Olympia (1819), and Mendelssohn in his overture to A Midsummer-Night's Dream (1826). Although soon replaced by the tuba in the orchestra, the ophicleide was used in Italian, French, Spanish, and South American bands up to this century.

Lit.: A. Carse, "Brass Instruments in the Orchestra" (ML iii); J. M. Barbour, "The Use of Brass Instruments in Early Scores" (BAMS iv). See also under *Wind instruments; *Turmsonaten.

Bratsche [G., from It. *viola da *brac-cio*]. The German name for the viola. *Bratschist,* viola player.

Brautlied [G.]. Bridal song.

Bravoure [F.], bravura [It., literally "courage"], denotes greatest ease in conquering technical difficulties. Hence, the term *aria di bravura* [G. *Bravur-arie*] for an aria in a brilliant, virtuoso-like style.

Brawl. Old English perversion for **branle.*

Brazil. The first music school in Brazil, the Conservatorio da Fazenda Nacional de Santa Cruz, was founded by the Jesuits, who were the first to educate the natives of this country in European ways. Associated with this school was the greatest Brazilian composer of the Colonial period, José Mauricio Nunes Garcia (1767–1830), a priest who wrote mostly religious music, including an admirable Requiem in D minor, showing the influence of Mozart and Haydn. He was followed by Francisco Manoel (1795–1865), composer of the Brazilian National Anthem, and founder, in 1841, of the Conservatory in Rio de Janeiro which later became the Escola Nacional de Música. The prestige of Brazilian music was greatly enhanced abroad by the success of Carlos Gomes (1836–96), the most famous opera-composer produced by Latin America. He was trained in Italy, and several of his operas, including *Il Guarany* (1870), were received with acclaim at La Scala of Milan. The overture to *Il Guarany* is doubtless the best-known orchestral composition to come out of South America. Other operas by Gomes include *Fosca, Maria Tudor, Lo Schiavo,* and *Condor.* A pioneer symphonic composer was Leopoldo Miguez (1850–1902), who wrote the first symphonic poems composed in Brazil; he also wrote an opera of Wagnerian tendencies, *Saldunes,* and a notable Sonata for violin and piano. The Romantic tradition was represented by Henrique Oswald (1852–1931), noteworthy especially for his chamber music, and by Alexandre Lévy (1864–92), a brilliant pianist, author

of a Brazilian Rhapsody for piano and orchestra. Alberto Nepomuceno (1864–1920) was the precursor of the modern National school through his utilization of Brazilian elements in such works as his orchestral "Brazilian Suite" and prelude to *Garatuja.* He also composed many songs which laid the basis for the modern Brazilian *lied.* Another pioneer of nationalism in music was Brasilio Itiberé (1846–1913), whose orchestral fantasia, "Sertaneja," is based on Brazilian folk themes. In the popular field, the most noteworthy composer was Ernesto Nazareth (1863–1934), creator of the Brazilian tango and author of nearly 500 pieces in popular style.

Dean of contemporary Brazilian composers is Francisco Braga (b. 1868), who has also distinguished himself as a conductor. He has written symphonic and dramatic works, chamber music, etc. The Brazilian art song has been carried to a high degree of perfection by Oscar Lorenzo Fernândez (b. 1897), who is also the composer of a successful opera, *Malazarte* (Rio, 1941), and of several symphonic works imbued with Brazilian color, such as "Reisado do Pastoreio," "Imbapára," and "Batuque." In his chamber-music output, a trio for piano, violin, and cello is notable. An exact contemporary of Fernândez is Francisco Mignone, professor of conducting at the Escola Nacional de Música and composer of numerous orchestral works of brilliant coloring, among them three Brazilian Fantasias for piano and orchestra, and "Maracatú do Chico Rei." Other contemporaries who should be mentioned are Barrozo Netto (1881–1941), Fructuoso Vianna, and, among the younger men, Radamés Gnattali, Luiz Cosme, and especially Camargo Guarnieri, composer of a splendid Concerto for piano and orchestra and other works revealing a powerful creative temperament.

A place apart must be reserved for the greatest of contemporary Brazilian composers — and probably the most outstanding composer of all Latin America — Heitor Villa-Lobos (b. 1881), amazingly prolific and original creator of some 1400 works, including many characteristic piano pieces that mark a new style of writing for the instrument. Among his larger works, especially notable are the Chôros No. 8 for orchestra, Chôros No. 10 for orchestra and chorus, the symphonic poem "Amazonas," "Dansas Africanas" for orchestra, and "Momo Precoce" for piano and orchestra. Among his most recent works are 5 suites, for various instrumental combinations, entitled "Bachianas Brasileiras," being compositions in which the spirit of Brazilian folk music is fused with that of J. S. Bach. Although Villa-Lobos' production is uneven in quality, and though he lacks a finished technique and a sense of organic form, at his best he creates works which are entirely *sui generis* and which, more than any others, seem to represent the music of the New World. Villa-Lobos has been very active in promoting musical education in Brazil and at present he is director of public school music in Rio de Janeiro.

Most of the modern Brazilian composers have drawn freely upon the rich and colorful folk music of Brazil, which is composed of Portuguese (some Spanish), African, and Indian elements. Of these the African element is perhaps the most potent. A pioneer in the study and collecting of Brazilian folk music was Luciano Gallet, whose work in this field has been continued by such notable folklorists as Mario de Andrade and Luiz Heitor Correa de Azevedo, the latter professor of national folk music at the Escola Nacional de Música. Many Brazilian composers have written *modinhas*, the characteristic love song of Brazil, of Portuguese origin, usually of a rather melancholy and sentimental nature. Popular dances are the *Maxixe* and the *samba*.

Lit.: G. Pereira de Mello, *A Música no Brasil* (Bahia, 1908); R. Almeida, *Historia da Música Brasileira* (Rio de Janeiro, 1926); M. de Andrade, *Ensaio sobre Música Brasileira* (São Paulo, 1928); L. Gallet, *Estudos do Folclore* (Rio de Janeiro, 1934);† *Musique Brésilienne Moderne*, preface by Andrade Muricy (Rio de Janeiro, 1937); A. T. Luper, *The Music of Brazil* (1943).   G. C.

Breit [G.]. Broad. *Breit gestrichen*, broadly bowed.

Breve, Brevis. An old note value, written ◫ or ◪, and equal to two whole-notes. See *Notes; *Mensural notation. Also *Alla breve.

Breviary, Breviarium. See *Liturgical books I (b).

Bridge [F. *chevalet*, G. *Steg*, It. *ponticello*]. (1) In stringed instruments, the wooden support atop the table across which the strings are stretched. Its shape and size differ in the various instruments. The bridge of the double-bass has "legs." In spite of its symmetrical appearance, the two halves of the bridge serve somewhat different purposes. The right (treble) foot rests firmly upon the table, very nearly above the sound post, while the other, having no such support, transmits the vibrations of the string to the body of the instrument. The present-day shape of the violin bridge was developed in the time of Antonio and Gerolamo Amati (*c.* 1550–1630)

(2) Short for *bridge passage.

Bridge passage. In musical compositions a passage of subordinate importance serving as a connection between two themes. It consists of figurations, sequences, or other subsidiary material. Frequently it effects the modulation of key, e.g., from the first to the second theme in *sonata-form.

Brillenbass [G., from *Brille*, spectacle]. Derogatory nickname for stereotyped accompanying figures in the manner of the *Alberti bass the abbreviated writing of which [see *Abbreviations, Ex. 4, 5] suggests a pair of spectacles.

Brindisi [It.]. Drinking song, such as occurs in operas, e.g., in Verdi's *Traviata* ("Libiamo"), Mascagni's *Cavalleria rusticana* ("Viva il vino").

Brio, Con [It.]. With vigor and spirit.

Brisé [F.]. French 18th-century name for the *turn. In modern terminology, indication for arpeggio playing, or for detached bowing.

Broadcasting. See *Radio broadcasting of music.

Broderie [F.]. (1) French term for coloratura; also found in German writings, not so much for "virtuoso passages," but for carefully designed "embroideries," such as occur in the polyphonic music of the 15th century [Ockeghem; cf., e.g., SchGMB, no. 52].—(2) Same as auxiliary tone [see *Nonharmonic tones I, 5].

Broken chord. The tones of a chord played in succession, instead of simultaneously, either in the form of an *arpeggio, or in the form of quick passages. See also *Alberti bass.

Broken consort. See *Consort.

Broken octave. See under *Short octave.

Browning. A type of 16th- and 17th-century English instrumental music, similar to the *Innomine, but with the cantus firmus taken from a secular song: "The leaves be greene, the nuts be browne" or, perhaps, from other popular melodies. Examples by Byrd, Bevin, Woodcock, Stoninge, Coperario (?), and Jenkins (?) are preserved. Cf. E. H. Meyer, Die mehrstimmige Spielmusik des 17. Jahrhunderts (1934), pp. 13f.

Bruitisme [F.]. See *Futurism.

Brumeux [F.]. "Misty," veiled.

Brummeisen [G.]. *Jew's harp.

Brummscheit [G.]. Perverted from Trumscheit [see *Tromba marina].

Brummstimmen [G.]. Humming voices [see *Bouche fermée].

Brunette [F.]. A 17th- and 18th-century type of French popular song, with or without accompaniment, on idyllic, pastoral, or amorous subjects. They replaced the earlier *bergerettes and *vaudevilles. The name is probably derived from one famous example "Le Berger Tirsis," with the refrain "Ah petite brunette, ah tu me fais mourir." Ballard published three collections of Brunettes ou petits tendre airs

in 1703, 1704, and 1709. Some of these songs occur in the harpsichord pieces by Chambonnière and d'Anglebert, e.g., the Sarabande de Jeunes Zéphirs, and the Gavotte Où estes vous allez. Others were adopted later into the comic opera. Cf. P. M. Masson, in SIM xii.

Bruscamente [It.]. Brusquely.

Bruststimme [G.]. Chest voice.

Brustwerk, Brustpositiv [G.]. A special group of smaller organ pipes placed in the middle of the front of the organ, between the large pedal pipes. It is of softer intonation than the Hauptwerk (great organ) and is usually played on the second manual.

Buccina [L.]. An ancient Roman brass instrument [see *Brass instruments V (a)]. The name reappears in the medieval *buisine, in the German word Posaune (i.e., trombone), and in the French buccin. The last was a pseudo-antique variety of the trombone used during the French revolution for festive occasions, with the bell shaped into a dragon's head. Cf. LavE ii.3, 1449.

Buchstabenschrift. *Letter notation.

Buckwheat notation. See under *Fasola.

Bügelhorn [G.]. German term for the entire family sometimes referred to as *bugles. Cf. SaRM, 62.

Bühne [G.]. Stage. Bühnenfestspiel (stage festival play) and Bühnenweihfestspiel (stage-consecrating festival play) are names by Wagner, the former for his *Ring, the latter for his *Parsifal which was written for the dedication of the Bayreuth opera house, in 1882. Bühnenmusik means *incidental music for plays, or, in operas, music played on the stage itself, as for instance in the final scene of Mozart's Don Giovanni.

Buffet [F.]. Organ case.

Buffo [It., comic]. A comic character in Italian 18th-century operas, usually a basso buffo (e.g., Leporello in Mozart's

Don Giovanni). Hence, a singer for comic parts. See *Comic opera. *Buffonistenstreit*, see *Bouffons (2).

Bugle. A military instrument [see *Brass instruments IV]. The term is also used as generic name for the entire group of brass instruments described under *Brass instruments III (b)–(e). For the key bugle (Kent bugle) see *Brass instruments V (c).

Buisine. See *Buysine.

Bulgarian music. The history of Bulgarian music is closely linked with that of Russia. The folk song as well as the liturgical music of the Bulgarians has been much less exposed to Western influence than, e.g., that of the Czechs. The Bulgarians possess a large repertory of traditional songs, mostly heroic, which they consider one of their greatest treasures. Most of their folk music is dance-like, though irregular meters are frequent. A few examples of very early folk music in rhapsodic rhythm, uncertain intervals, microtonic ornaments (glissando), etc., still survive in some provinces. The chief instruments are the *gaida*, a bagpipe, and the *gusla*, a primitive bowed instrument with one string. The liturgical music of the Bulgarian Church was largely that of the Russian Church, until the adoption of the Greek rites, in the 19th century.

The activity in art music did not begin until 1900. Pancho Vladigerov (b. 1899) is the leading composer of the present.

Lit.: P. Panoff, *Die altslavische Volks- und Kirchenmusik* (Bücken's *Handbuch*, 1930); *id.*, "Die Volksmusik der Bulgaren" (*Melos* iv, H. 1); Ch. Obreschkoff, *Das bulgarische Volkslied* (1937); *AdHM*, 1169f; cf. *MoML*, 104.

Bund [G.; pl. *Bünde*]. Fret. *Bundfrei*, see *Clavichord.

Burden [from F. *bourdon*]. A refrain, particularly one consisting of syllables without meaning, as, e.g., "Hey troly lo," or "Fa la la." Such burdens are common in the *ballettos of the 16th/17th centuries [see also *Fa-la].

Burgundian cadence. See under *Landini cadence.

Burgundian School. The leading music school of the early 15th century, represented chiefly by Guillaume Dufay (*c.* 1400–74) and Gilles Binchois (*c.* 1400–67). It forms the link between the *Ars nova (14th century) and the *Flemish Schools (1450–1600) [see *History of music]. In older writings, the Burgundian School is called First Netherlands School [see *Netherlands Schools]. Today, the term Burgundian School is preferred because the musical activity of this period centered in the cultural sphere of the kingdom of Burgundy which, under Philip the Good (1419–67) and Charles the Bold (1467–77), included the whole of eastern France as well as Belgium and the Netherlands. Its court at Dijon was the leading center of culture for all Europe, a culture which manifested itself in the paintings of the brothers Van Eyck as well as in the fantastic fashion of peaked shoes, long cone-shaped hats, and extravagant colors which still survives in the "once-upon-a-time" setting of our fairy tales.

The music of the Burgundian School represents a reaction against the complexity and mannerism of the late Ars nova. Strongly influenced by the English Dunstable, Dufay and Binchois developed a musical language whose beauty and tender sweetness is just as lively today as it was 500 years ago. Perhaps their most important contribution was the establishment of the third as a principal interval of melodic design. Many melodies of Dufay and Binchois (particularly those from their later period) are "ornamented triads" [see Ex.; Dufay, *Craindre*

vous vueil]. No less striking is the extensive use of *fauxbourdon and of the *Burgundian cadence, which, with its two leading-tones, contributes largely to the transcendental sensuousness of Burgundian music, as do also the high range of the men's voices (high tenors, *falsetto), and the simultaneous use of strongly dissimilar instruments such as recorders, shawms, viols, and trombones (together with voices) which, in spite of their "earthly" incongruity merge into what may be called a "celestial symphony."

The Burgundian composers can be tentatively grouped in three generations, as follows [the single dates indicate years of their activity, at the Papal Choir, at the court of Dijon, etc., the only known records of their life]: (1) born *c*. 1375: Reginald Liebert, Pierre Fontaine (1420), Nicolaus Grenon (1421, '27), Johannes Brassart (1431); (2) born *c*. 1400: Guillaume Dufay (1400–74), Gilles Binchois (1400–67), Hugo de Lantins, Heyne von Gizeghem (1453, '68); (3) born *c*. 1425: Antoine Busnois (d. 1492), Johannes Regis (1463, '74), Philippe Caron. The last-named composers already show the influence of the early Flemish masters (Ockeghem, Obrecht) and form the transition to Josquin. Dufay and also various other Burgundian composers spent parts of their lives at Cambrai; hence, the name School of Cambrai, which would seem to apply chiefly to the latest members of the Burgundian School. Examples in *HAM*, nos. 65–72.

Lit.: W. Ambros, *Geschichte der Musik* iii (1891); E. Dannemann, *Die spätgotische Musiktradition in Frankreich und Burgund vor dem Auftreten Dufay's* (1936); J. Wolf, "Dufay und seine Zeit" (*StM* i); Ch. van den Borren, †*Polyphonia sacra* (1932); J. F. R. and C. Stainer, †*Dufay and his Contemporaries* (1898); K. Dèzes, †*Messen- und Motettensätze des 15. Jahrhunderts* (1927); W. Gurlitt, †*Gilles Binchois, 16 weltliche Lieder* (1927); H. Besseler, †*Guillaume Dufay, 12 geistliche und weltliche Werke* (1932); J. Marix, †*Les Musiciens de la cour de Bourgogne au XVe siècle, 1420–67* (1937). See also *Chansonnier.

Burla, burlesca, burletta [It., jest]. A composition in a jesting mood. Bach's A minor Partita has a Burlesca; Schumann's *Albumblätter* include a Burla.

Busine. See *Buysine.

Busspsalmen [G.]. *Penitential psalms.

Buxheim Organ Book [G. *Buxheimer Orgelbuch*]. A MS collection of organ music, written about 1470 and containing a large number of *Intabulierungen of *Burgundian chansons, some 30 *preludes and a copy of Conrad Paumann's *Fundamentum organisandi*. Cf. *MfM* 1888, Beilage; L. Schrade, *Die ältesten Denkmäler der Orgelmusik* (1927). Cf. also H. Schnoor, in *ZMW* iv.

Buysine, buzine, busine, buisine, buzanne [see *Buccina]. A medieval straight trumpet. See *Brass instruments V; also *Trombone II.

B.V.M. See *Antiphon (3).

Byzantine chant. I. The ecclesiastical chant of the Byzantine empire (founded A.D. 328 by Constantine the Great; destroyed in 1453, with the fall of Constantinople) With the exception of a few ceremonial songs, the *acclamations, no music other than the liturgical chants has been preserved. Although the language of the Byzantine Church was Greek, it has become more and more apparent that the Byzantine music — as well as the whole of Byzantine culture — was not a continuation of that of the ancient Greeks (as has long been assumed) but constituted a new tradition based to some extent on Oriental (Jewish) models [see Tillyard, Wellesz]. The Byzantine system of modes (*echoi), for example, differs sharply from that of the so-called Greek modes (*tonoi*) but is quite similar to that of the Western Church [see *Church modes].

II. The Byzantine chant has many features in common with Gregorian chant, being monophonic, unaccompanied, chiefly diatonic, and devoid of strict meter. A fundamental difference between the two bodies of chant, however, is that of their textual basis. While the Western tradition adopted the Jewish psalms as the basis of their texts, the liturgical texts of the Eastern Church are all free poetry (occasionally modeled after psalms), i.e., hymns. The earliest of these hymns, the *troparia* (4th, 5th centuries), were intercalations (*tropes) sung between the reading of the psalms, but the latter dropped out during the ensuing development. The 6th century marks the beginning of a new era, that of the *kontakion*, with Romanus (*c.* 500) and Sergios (*c.* 600) as the leading figures. A kontakion is an ode consisting of a short *prooemium* (introduction) and a great number (20–30) of stanzas of uniform structure which end with a refrain (either a single word such as ". . . time," or a complete line) and which, by their initial letters, form an acrostic. The most famous example of this species is the *acathistos*. Troparia and kontakia were superseded around 700 by' the *kanon* (Andrew of Crete, *c.* 650–720; John of Damascus; and Kosmas of Jerusalem, *c.* 750). The kanons are extremely long poems consisting of a succession of nine parts (called hymns, odes), each of which was supposed to contain allusions to one of the nine *canticles (as a rule, the second ode was omitted, on account of the somber nature of the second canticle; the others are all chants of praise and joy). The poetic activity came to an end in the 11th century, owing to the codification of the hymns and their final reception into the liturgy.

III. The earliest Byzantine sources containing musical signs date from the 9th century, and are written in *ekphonetic notation. According to recent interpretation [cf. C. Höeg, *La Notation ekphonétique* (1935)] these signs, which always occur in pairs (one at the beginning, the other at the end of a sentence), represent certain stereotyped formulae, which were used for phrases of frequent occurrence, such as: "And Jesus said." Beginning with the 10th century, sources show a more fully developed type of musical notation, indicating a continuous melody. As is the case in the notation of Gregorian chant, the early Byzantine "neumes" (*c.* 950–1200) cannot be deciphered. Only a few melodies from some of the latest MSS of this period, written in the so-called *Coislin system*, have been transcribed with the help of parallel versions existing in later sources, the notation of

which is that of a later stage, known as *middle* (or *round*) *notation*. The latter system, which was in use from *c.* 1100–1450, has been deciphered in all essential details, including the rhythmic significance of the neumatic signs, on the basis of information contained in certain theoretical manuals called *papadike*. The principal feature of this notation is that its signs do not indicate pitches (as do, more or less exactly, the Western neumes), but intervals to be taken from the tone reached previously. The starting note was indicated by a special sign (the *martyrion*), which signified the echos of the melody. Thus, in Byzantine notation, the melody d e g g a f g d would be notated as a succession of intervals according to the following scheme: (d) s t u s t_ s f_ (s = second, u = unison, t = third, f = fourth; descending intervals with a minus-sign) [example in *GD* i, 520].

IV. After 1400 the traditional chant, which was largely syllabic, was enriched by the introduction of coloraturas which, owing to abuse and individual license, soon led to a complete decadence of Byzantine chant. Kukuzeles, who flourished about 1300, seems to have been the first to introduce new signs for stereotyped melismas. These signs were generally adopted after 1400 (late Byzantine or

First Ode of a Canon for Saturday
in Holy Week

Kukuzelian notation; see also *Teretism). In the 18th century, Turkish and Arabian elements were introduced into the chant (Lampadarios, *c.* 1730–70), thus leading to a complete destruction of the tradition. At the beginning of the 19th century the Greek archimandrite Chrysanthos developed a notation which utilizes the principles and some of the details of the Byzantine notation and which is still used today for the chants of the Greek Church.

From our present-day state of knowledge, the MSS of the 12th and 13th centuries represent the classical tradition of Byzantine chant. The example on p. 106 [cf. *MQ* xxiii, 208] illustrates the style which prevails in the chants of this period [cf. also *HAM*, no. 8].

In 1935 C. Hoeg, H. J. W. Tillyard, and E. Wellesz started a complete edition of medieval Byzantine Musical MSS, under the title *Monumenta Musicae Byzantinae* [see *Editions XVIII]. This publication was taken over in 1942 by the Byzantine Institute (American Branch, Boston). See *Acathistus; *Acclamation; *Akoluthia; *Automela; *Echos; *Sticheron.

Lit.: H. J. W. Tillyard, *Byzantine Music and Hymnography* (1923); E. Wellesz, *Byzantinische Musik* (1927); O. Tiby, *La Musica bizantina* (1938); L. Tardo, *L'antica melurgia bizantina* (1938); ReMMA, 75ff; AdHM i, 126ff; GD i, 514ff; H. J. W. Tillyard, in MQ xxiii and in ML iv; E. Wellesz, in PMA i; O. Strunk, "The Tonal System of Byzantine Music" (*MQ* xxxviii); O. Gombosi, in *AM* x, xi, xii. For additional bibliography, cf ReMMA, 432ff and O. Tiby, in RMI xli, xlii.

C

C. (1) See *Letter notation; *Pitch names; *Hexachord. — (2) *C*, as an abbreviation, may stand for: *con* (*colla, coll'*), i.e., with [see *C.a.; *C.b.; *C.o.; *C.s.]; *cantus* [see *C.f.]; *capo* [see *D.c.]. In modern part songs *C* means *contralto*; in 16th-century part books, *cantus*.

C.a. Abbreviation for [It.] *coll' arco*, i.e., with the bow.

Cabaletta [It., possibly from *cobola, cobla*, i.e., couplet; the derivation from *caballo*, horse, is very doubtful]. A short operatic song characterized by popular style and natural simplicity, with a rather uniform rhythm in the vocal line and in the accompaniment. They are frequent in the operas of Rossini. One of the earliest examples is "La bella imagine" in Gluck's *Paride e Elena* (1770). In the later Italian opera (Verdi) the term was applied to the final stretto close of arias or duets in which elaborate treatment usually gives way to quick, uniform rhythm.

Caccia [It., chase, hunt]. An important form of 14th-century Italian poetry and music which was chiefly used in the first half of that century (Giovanni da Cascia, Jacopo da Bologna; see *Ars nova). The text deals with hunting and fishing scenes (*pescia*) or with similar subjects of a strongly marked naturalistic character (fire, cries of street vendors, etc.). The musical form is a strict canon in two parts at the distance of eight or more measures. These "chasing" voices are usually supported by a free tenor in longer note values. The form originated in France around 1300 (*chace*; cf. BeMMR, 131), but developed in Italy. For a Spanish 14th-century example, cf. O. Ursprung, in ZMW iv, 151.

Lit.: G. Carducci, *Caccie in rime* (1896; only texts); W. Th. Marrocco, †*The 14th-Century Italian Caccia* (1942; complete collection of all the caccias); †WoGM ii, iii, nos. 42, 56; HAM, no. 52; J. Wolf, †*Sing- und Spielmusik aus älterer Zeit*, no. 7.

Cachucha. An Andalusian dance similar to the *bolero. It was introduced to the opera by Fanny Elssler in the ballet of *Le Diable boiteux* (1836).

Cacophony [from Gr. *kakos*, bad]. Bad sound, discord. Richard Strauss's tone-poems were decried as cacophony at the time of their first performance.

Cadence [from L. *cadere*, to fall; G. *Kadenz*; It. *cadenza*]. I. A melodic or harmonic formula which occurs at the end of a composition, a section, or a phrase, conveying the impression of a momentary or permanent conclusion. In each period of music there exist a rather limited number of such formulae or, at least, a limited number of types of which all closing passages are but variations or modifications. Those which were in current use during the 18th and 19th centuries have been studied in great detail. Unfortunately, the classification and terminology in this field are greatly lacking in uniformity and frequently also in clarity. The following presentation is made with a view, not to completeness of the enumeration of terms, but to clarification of the essential points [cf. the chapter on "Cadences" in W. Piston, *Harmony* (1941)].

A cadence is called *perfect* (*final, full*) if it can be satisfactorily and normally used as the close of a composition. According to the standards of classical har-

penultimate chord, there is a choice between the dominant (V) and the subdominant (IV), both in root position. The combination V–I is called *authentic* cadence [Ex. 1], the progression IV–I, *plagal* cadence [Ex. 2]. The authentic cadence occurs usually in the fuller form IV–V–I (II⁶–V–I) [Ex. 3] or, still more complete, IV–I_4^6–V–I (II⁶–I_4^6–V–I) [Ex. 4]. All four of these last are sometimes called *mixed* cadences.

The remaining cadences fall into two classes, *imperfect*, and *deceptive* (or *interrupted*) cadences. The imperfect cadences are the same as the two elementary perfect cadences, except that they have the tonic chord in another arrangement, e.g., with the third or fifth in the soprano [Ex. 5]; or have the penultimate chord in inversion [Ex. 6] — these are called *inverted* or *medial* cadence, as opposed to a *radical* [L. *radix*, root] cadence; or occur in transposition to the dominant or (more rarely, the subdominant) [Ex. 7–10]. These "transposed" cadences occur almost regularly at the end of the first half of a musical phrase and are therefore termed *half-cadence* (authentic or plagal).

The deceptive cadence [F. *cadence rompue* or *évitée*; G. *Trugschluss*; It. *inganno*] is an authentic (or, sometimes, plagal) cadence the tonic chord of which (I) is — deceptively — replaced by some other chord, most frequently by VI [Ex. 11]. Some other possibilities are indicated in Ex. 12–14. See also *Masculine, feminine cadence.

II. The cadences of early music differ sharply from those described above, particularly prior to 1500 when progressions such as V–I and IV–I were very little used [see *Harmony]. The history of these cadences is interesting since the various formulae are characteristic of their period and may well serve as identifying marks. Prior to 1450, practically all cadences are based on the progression II–I in the lowest part (tenor). This cadence appears in various modifications [Ex. 15–19], among which that with two "leading-tones," one before the octave, the other before the fifth, is particularly frequent before and after 1400 [Ex. 16–18; see *Landini

mony this requires that the last chord be the tonic triad (I) and that it have the tonic note in the soprano. Regarding the

cadence]. After 1400 another modification of the II–I cadence appears in which the contra-tenor jumps up an octave from the lower fifth to the higher fifth [Ex. 20].

This cadence is interesting because it foreshadows the authentic cadence with its V–I movement in the lowest part [Ex. 21]. This as well as the plagal cadence was introduced around 1450, as a result of the addition of a true bass to musical texture (Ockeghem, Obrecht; see *Flemish Schools). The earlier type (II–I) survived only in the so-called *Phrygian* cadence [Ex. 22]. It should be noticed that, until 1500, the third is practically always omitted in the final chord of the authentic as well as of the plagal cadence [still in Purcell!; see *Picardy third]. In the 16th century the "suspension"-formula [Ex. 21] was universally accepted, while in the 17th century the "anticipation"-formula [Ex. 23] is very common. Composers of the 17th century frequently use both formulae simultaneously in two parts (violins) in a strikingly dissonant combination known as *Corelli-clash* [Ex. 24; for an early instance, in Stefano Landi's *San Alessio* (1634), cf. H. Gold-

schmidt, *Studien zur Geschichte der italienischen Oper* (1901), i, 212].

III. The cadences of the classical and romantic periods offer little historical interest since they usually conform with the standard types outlined in I. Toward the end of the 19th century, however, the amplification of the harmonic vocabulary brought with it numerous novelties in the writing of cadences, such as the use of modal cadences [Ex. 25; Moussorgsky, *Boris Godunov*, 1869], the use of a dissonant final chord [Ex. 26; Ravel, *Les grands vents*], of polytonal formations [Ex. 27; Busoni, *Sonatina Seconda*, 1912] and, more recently, the return to a "contrapuntal" type of cadence reminiscent of medieval cadences in the stepwise motion of the bass and in their "plagal" feeling [Ex. 28; Hindemith, *Sonate für Klavier*, 1936].

Lit.: A. Casella, *The Evolution of Music, through the History of the Perfect Cadence* (1924); E. M. Lee, "Cadences and Closes" (*PMA* xxxi); H. J. Moser, "Das Schicksal der Penultima" (*JMP* xli); H. J. Moser, "Die harmonischen Funktionen in der tonalen Kadenz" (*ZMW* i); C. Artom, "Cadenze e pseudocadenze" (*RMI* xxxiv); R. Tenschert, "Die Kadenzbehandlung bei Richard Strauss" (*ZMW* vii).

Cadence [F.]. French 17th-century name for the trill.

Cadent. See under *Nachschlag.

Cadenza. An extended section in free, improvisatory style inserted usually near the end of a composition where it serves as a retarding element, giving the player or singer a welcome chance to exhibit his technical brilliance shortly before the piece closes. Its traditional place is in the concerto, between the six-four chord (marked with a *fermata*) and the dominant chord of the final cadence [see Ex.]. Such cadenzas make ample use of highly virtuoso passage work, but also draw from the thematic substance of the movement, presenting its subjects in artfully devised modifications or combinations. They usually close with an extended trill on the dominant chord.

In the earlier concertos (Haydn; Mozart; Beethoven, Piano concertos nos. 1–4) the cadenzas are not included in

the composition, since they were supposed to be provided by the performer. In the 19th century cadenzas to the famous concertos were written by the outstanding virtuosos (Hummel, Thalberg, Moscheles, Reinecke, Joachim), frequently without proper regard to matters of style, so that it is not unusual to hear a Mozart concerto winding up with a cadenza full of the lush harmonies and heavy texture of the late Romanticism. Beethoven was the first to write his own cadenzas as an integral part of the work, in his last Piano Concerto, op. 76 (Emperor Concerto). His precedent was followed by most of his successors (Schumann, Brahms), who wanted to guard their works against the poor taste and the stylistic incongruities of the "pianist-composers." There exist authentic cadenzas (written by the composers themselves) for all the Beethoven concertos and for a number of the Mozart concertos. Although not entirely satisfactory, they should be consulted by anyone confronted with the necessity of choosing (or writing) a cadenza. Judicious artists will probably find them preferable to any of those in current use, with the sole exception of the excellent cadenzas to Mozart's piano concertos written by Busoni. In the piano compositions of Chopin and Liszt ample use is made of another type of cadenza, consisting of relatively short passages of glittering passage work, written in small notes, and inserted where a momentary retardation or a display of pianistic brilliancy was desired.

Cadenzas in the form of running passages following (rather than preceding)

the final chord of a cadence occur in the lute and keyboard music of the 16th century (Don Luis Milan, 1535; Girolamo Cavazzoni, 1542). Early examples of the modern cadenza, on I_4^6 are found in Corelli and Vivaldi (c. 1700). Throughout the 18th century improvised cadenzas of a highly virtuoso type were an established feature of the solo arias in the Neapolitan operas, whence they were adopted in the concerto (Mozart).

Lit.: R. Stockhausen. *Die Kadenzen zu den Klavierkonzerten der Wiener Klassiker* (Diss. Vienna 1936); H. Knödt, "Zur Entwicklungsgeschichte der Kadenzen im Instrumentalkonzert" (*SIM* xv); A. Schering, "Die freie Kadenz im Instrumentalkonzert des 18. Jahrhunderts" (*KIM*, 1906, p. 204).

Cadenzato [It.]. With determination (as in a cadence).

Caecilianismus [G.]. See *Cecilian movement.

Caisse [F.]. Drum. See *Percussion instruments B, 1–3.

Calando [It.]. Diminuendo, usually with rallentando.

Calascione. Same as *colascione.

Calata. Italian lute dance of the early 16th century, notated in $\frac{2}{4} - (\frac{4}{4} -)$ time, but actually in $\frac{3}{2} - (3 \times \frac{2}{4})$ meter, and therefore similar to the *bassa danza. Petrucci's *Intavolatura de lauto* iv (1508) contains 13 calatas, one for two lutes. Cf. J. W. Wasielewski, *Geschichte der Instrumentalmusik im 16. Jahrhundert* (1878), Beilage.

Calcando [It.]. "Trampling," i.e., accelerando.

Calino casturame. This title of a piece in the *Fitzwilliam Virginal Book* is probably a perversion of Irish "Cailinog a stuir me," "Young girl, my treasure."

Calithump. See *Charivari.

Calliope. Originally the name of the Greek Muse of Eloquence, the term was adopted for an instrument which its un-known inventor probably expected to have divine powers of persuasion, as it consisted of a number of steam-blown whistles (played from a keyboard) which could be heard over a distance of ten miles. It was used at American fairs to attract people from far and wide.

Calmato [It.]. Calmed.

Calore, Con [It.]. With warmth.

Cambiata [It., from *cambiare*, to change]. See *Nonharmonic tones I.

Camera [It., chamber]. In Baroque music (1600–1750) *da camera* indicates music for use outside of the church, as distinguished from *da chiesa*, i.e., music to be performed in the church [see *Chiesa]. This dichotomy was applied to sonatas, cantatas, duettos, etc. Especially in the first case it entailed a distinct difference of form which is discussed under *Sonata B, II. In modern Italian usage, *musica da camera* means chamber music.

✓**Camerata** [It., from *camera*, chamber, salon]. Name for a group of distin-guished literary men, artists and musi-cians who, shortly before 1600, used to gather in the palace of the Count Bardi at Florence to discuss the possibilities of a new musical style in imitation of the music of the ancient Greek drama [see *Nuove Musiche; *Opera]. Members of this "charmed circle" were the poet Ot-tavio Rinuccini and the musicians Vin-cenzo Galilei, Giulio Caccini, and Jacopo Peri.
Lit.: H. Martin, "La 'Camerata' du Comte Bardi et la musique florentine du xvie siècle" (*RdM*, nos. 42–44, 46, 47); G. Gilli, *Una Corte alla fine del '500* (1928).

Camminando [It.]. Proceeding, push-ing on.

Campana [It.]. *Bell. Campanology is the art of bell-founding and bell-ringing. *Campanella* (little bell) is the *glocken-spiel; also the title of a violin piece by Paganini and of an etude by F. Liszt (a

piano adaptation of the former) in which the sound of small bells is imitated.

Can. In English Service music, abbrevi-ation for *cantoris*. See *Polychoral style.

Canadian music. Cf. M. Barbeau and Edw. Sapir, *Folk Songs of French Canada* (1925); J. M. Gibbon, *Canadian Folk Songs* (1927); Soeurs de Sainte-Anne, *Dictionnaire biographique des musiciens Canadiens* (1935); E. Gagnon, *Chansons populaires du Canada* (7th ed., 1940); M. Barbeau, in *ML* xiii, no. 2.

Canarie, canario. A French dance of the 17th century, designed as an imitation of the "sauvages des îles Canaries," the natives of the Canary Islands who repre-sented the "exotic" element in the Euro-pean culture of the 16th and 17th centu-ries. It is in quick $\frac{3}{8}$ or $\frac{6}{8}$-time, with a dotted note on each strong beat, almost identical in rhythm with that of the gigue. The earliest examples are to be found in the harpsichord suites of Champion de Chambonnières (1602–72) and of Louis Couperin (*c.* 1626–61). Others occur in the operas of Lully, Purcell (*Diocletian*, 1690), in Johann K. F. Fischer's *Musikal-isches Blumenbüschlein* (1696), in Georg Muffat's *Florilegium primum* (1690), etc. Examples in *ApMZ* ii; *TaAM* vii, 43. Cf. P. Nettl, in *StM* viii. See *Dance music III.

Cancan. A popular dance of the late 19th century which developed from the quadrille and which became world-known for its vulgarity and indecorous-ness. J. Offenbach introduced it into his *Orphée aux enfers* (1874).

Cancel. Same as natural (sign).

Cancion [Sp.]. Song.

Cancionero [Sp.]. Collection of songs, particularly folk songs. Important pub-lications of this type have been issued by F. Pedrell and by E. M. Torner. For an important 15th-century MS, known as *Cancionero musical del palacio*, see *Sources, no. 27; *Spanish Music I.

Cancrizans [from L. *cancer*, crab]. In crab-wise motion; see *Retrograde.

Canntaireachd. See under *Pibroch.

Canon [Gr., law, rule]. (1) A polyphonic composition in which all the parts have the same melody throughout, although starting at different points. The canon is the strictest species of imitation. Accompanying is an example by Schubert

(Piano Trio op. 100, Scherzo). It appears that in a canon the normal contrapuntal texture of horizontal (melodic) and vertical (harmonic) relationships is "reinforced" by diagonal threads which consistently connect the places of imitation [see *Texture]. It is this added dimension which accounts for the special artistic charm of the canon. Any phrase, heard now in the leading voice (*dux, antecedent*), will soon be heard in the following voice or voices (*comes, consequent*); in the meantime, however, the *dux* has proceeded to another motive which thus sounds against the first and which, in turn, will soon occur in its *comes*.

I. *Types*. The following types of canon are commonly distinguished. (a) According to the temporal distance between the parts: canon of one, two, etc., measures; in earlier terminology: *canon ad minimam, ad semibrevem, ad brevem* (or *ad tempus*), i.e., in the distance of a minim, etc. (b) According to the interval of imitation: canon in unison, of the fifth, fourth, etc.; earlier terms are: *canon ad unisonum, ad hypodiapente* (the *comes* begins at the lower fifth), *ad hyperdiates-*

saron (the *comes* begins at the higher fourth), etc. According to special devices: (c) canon by *augmentation or diminution (the *comes* has the melody in doubled or in halved values); (d) canon by *inversion (the *comes* has the inverted melody; also called *per motu contrario*); (e) retrograde canon or crab canon or *canon cancrizans* (the *comes* imitates the *dux* in retrograde motion; see *Retrograde); (f) canon *al contrario riverso* (the *comes* is the retrograde inversion of the dux; such a canon can be executed by reading the melody with the page turned upside down; see *Retrograde, Ex. 2); (g) group canon (the *dux* and, consequently, the *comes* consist of two — or more — parts each; a famous example of this type is Byrd's motet "Diliges Dominum"; most of the many-voiced canons of the 17th century — for 12, 16, or even 48 voices — belong to this group); (h) *circle canon* or perpetual canon (i.e., one which leads back to the beginning and which, therefore, may be repeated several times; most of the popular canons, called *rounds, belong to this type); (i) *spiral canon* or *canon per tonos* (here the melody ends one tone higher than it started; thus the canon must be played six times, first in C, then in D, in E, in F-sharp, etc.; an example is found in Bach's *Musical Offering* under the title: "Ascendente modulatione ascendet gloria regis," i.e., "May the glory of the king rise as the modulation ascends"). A canon is called *mixed* if parts are added (usually in the bass) which do not participate in the imitation (e.g., the canons in Bach's *Goldberg Variations*).

II. *History*. In early music, the present-day type of canon occurs under names such as *rota or *rondellus (*round, e.g., the well-known *Sumer is icumen in* of circa 1310), *caccia (14th century), and *fuga (16th century), while the term canon has a much wider significance, namely, that of any kind of inscription ("rule") giving a clue as to the intended execution of a composition which is purposely notated in an incomplete or obscure manner (riddle canon). Such canons appear first in the works of Guillaume de Machaut, among which there is a motet "Trop plus est belle" [cf. F. Ludwig, *G. de Machaut, Musikalische Werke* ii, 71; J. Wolf, *Musikalische Schrift-tafeln* (1930), p. 23], the tenor of which is to be sung "ad modum rondelli" (rondellus means here, not round, but *rondeau), i.e., as follows: a b a a b a b, although only a b is notated. Examples of much greater complexity occur in the French MSS of the late *Ars nova [cf., e.g., the "Canon balade" in *WoHN* i, 375]. In the Flemish era (*c.* 1450–1550) the canonic inscriptions grow more and more enigmatic so that Tinctoris, in his *Diffinitorium* (*c.* 1500) aptly defines the canon as "a rule which shows the intention of the composer in an obscure way" [*CS* iv, 179]. Among the simpler examples of riddle canon are the various inscriptions indicating retrograde motion [see *Retrograde]. More complicated is the inscription given with the Agnus Dei of Dufay's *Missa L'homme armé*: "Cancer eat plenis et redeat medius" (The crab proceed full and return half). This means that the tenor should be read first backwards (a crab "proceeds" backwards) in the full note-values, then forward from the beginning, but in halved note-values. Even more oracular are inscriptions such as "Ne recorderis" (literally "Don't remember") which must be read "Ne re corderis," i.e., "Don't remember *re*," "Don't sing *re*," "Omit all the notes *re*," i.e., "*D*." Riddle canons of particular complication occur in the English 15th-century *Missa O quam suavis* [new ed. by H. B. Collins (1927)]. For more details see *WoHN* i, 427; *GD* ii, 713 ("Inscriptions"); *RiHM* ii.1, 83–95; *ApNPM*, 179.

Less obscure, hence of greater practical importance, are the so-called *mensuration canons* of the 15th and 16th centuries. Here, a single written part has to be read simultaneously in different *mensurations or *proportions. These canons, sometimes called *fuga, start simultaneously at the intervals of tonic and dominant, but proceed differently, owing to the different value of the longer notes (*longa, brevis*) under the various signs of men-

suration. Accompanying is a "Fuga trium vocum" by Josquin [cf. *ApNPM*, 180]. An interesting example of a "group-

canon" for two lutes occurs in Vincenzo Galilei's *Fronimo* (1563; see *Editions XIV, 4) under the name "Fuga."

In the 17th century, canons were frequently devised in such a way as to admit of a number of solutions. A well-known example is a "Non nobis domine" (attributed, probably wrongly, to W. Byrd), which admits 6 or 7 solutions differing according to number of parts, to the intervals, and to the distance of the imitating parts [cf. *GD* iii, 642f]. Pier Francesco Valentini (d. 1654) wrote a canon which boasts of more than 2000 solutions. At the same time, the English provided a great number of popular canons in their *catches. It was chiefly through Bach's genius that the canon again obtained an important position in musical art, a position which it has maintained to the present day. Particularly noteworthy are Bach's *Kanonische Variationen über das Weihnachtslied* and the canons in his *Goldberg Variations*. Haydn, Mozart, Beethoven, contributed many charming examples to the popular repertory, but also used canon technique in their sonatas (mostly in the menuets) and variations. A well-known example of a more recent date is the last movement of César Franck's Violin Sonata (1886) which, however, employs a rather facile technique, while Brahms made a more ingenious use of the canon, e.g., in his *13 Canons* (for women's voices), op. 113.

Lit.: S. Jadassohn, *Canon and Fugue* (1899); C. H. Kitson, *Invertible Counterpoint and Canon* (1927); E. Prout, *Double Counterpoint and Canon*; B.

Ziehn, *Canonical Studies* (1912); L. Feininger, *Die Frühgeschichte des Kanons bis Josquin* (1937); F. Jöde, †*Der Kanon* (1926); P. Mies, "Der Kanon im mehrsätzigen klassischen Werk" (*ZMW* viii); O. E. Deutsch, "Haydn's Kanons" (*ZMW* xv).

(2) In ancient Greek music, canon is the name of the monochord which served to demonstrate the "laws" of acoustics. See *Kanûn.

(3) In Byzantine chant, a special type of poetry, more correctly spelled kanon; see Byzantine chant II.

(4) In the Roman liturgy, canon is the central and most solemn part of the *Mass, said by the officiating priest after the Sanctus. It begins with the words *Te igitur* [cf. *LU*, 4].

Canonical hours. See *Office hours.

Canonic treatment, style. The term refers to short passages written as a more or less free canon and forming a part of a larger composition such as a sonata (frequently in the development section).

Canso. See *Canzo.

Cantabile [It.]. Singable, singing.

/**Cantata** [from It. *cantare*, to sing]. I. A composite vocal form of the Baroque period, consisting usually of a number of movements such as arias, recitatives, duets, choruses which are based upon a continuous narrative text, lyrical, dramatic, or religious. Owing to the activity of J. S. Bach, the church cantata (*cantata da chiesa*), i.e., a cantata of devotional subject matter, is particularly well known and clearly defined. However, the secular cantata (*cantata da camera*), was not only the earlier, but also the more frequent type throughout the 17th century, especially in Italy. The cantata appeared shortly after 1600 as the third offspring of the *monodic style [see *Opera, *Oratorio], replacing the 16th-century madrigal. In its early, experimental, stage (till 1630) it occurred under different names and in a great variety of forms and styles. Certain pieces in Caccini's *Nuove musiche* (1602) and in Peri's *Varie musiche*

(1609), written in the form of strophic arias with the same bass used for every stanza, but with different melodies for the voice [see *Strophic bass], may be considered as the point of departure. As a matter of fact, Alessandro Grandi's "cantade" (*Cantade et arie a voce sola*, 1620; first appearance of the name) follow the same scheme of the "strophic-bass cantata," as do also the majority of cantatas written before 1650 [cf. *RiHM* ii.2, 20, 31; *AdHM* i, 437]. On the other hand, a piece such as Peri's "Se tu parti" more clearly foreshadows the later cantata, since its three stanzas (written to the same bass) contain contrasting sections, arioso, and recitativo, separated by instrumental ritornellos, and thus anticipate to some extent the composite structure of the developed cantata. This structure becomes more clearly evident in the cantatas of Francesco Rasi (*Dialoghi rappresentativi*, 1620; cf. *RiHM*, 299), Gio. Pietro Berti (*Cantate ed arie*, 1624), G. F. Sances (*Cantade*, 4 vols., 1633–40), and Benedetto Ferrari (*Musiche varie*, 1637). The free composite cantata — in a way, the vocal counterpart of the contemporary *canzona da sonare — reached a peak in Luigi Rossi (1598–1653; cf. *RiHM*, 371ff), Giacomo Carissimi (1605–74; cf. *RiHM*, 383f), and Marc'Antonio Cesti (1623–69; cf. *AdHM* ii, 439). This form was taken over by the masters of the Neapolitan School (Provenzale, Stradella, Al. Scarlatti) who, however, standardized its structure into a form consisting of two arias of contrasting character, each introduced by a recitative. It is interesting to notice that an almost identical process of standardization took place simultaneously in the instrumental field, leading from the canzona to the sonata da chiesa and da camera. Stradella wrote more than 190, Al. Scarlatti more than 600 cantatas, mostly of the type described above, which was almost exclusively adopted in the 18th century as a convenient and conventionalized scheme for virtuoso display and sentimentality (Leonardo Leo, Leonardo Vinci, Niccolò Jommelli, Johann Hasse).

II. In France the first cantatas were

written by Antoine Charpentier (1634–1704), a pupil of Carissimi. It was, however, not until after his death that the Italian cantata became popular among French composers. A great number of cantatas, mostly to French texts, appeared between 1705 and 1730, written by André Campra (1660–1744), Nicolas Bernier (1664–1734), Michel Montéclair (1666–1737), Jean-Bapt. Morin (1677–1745), Nicolas Clérambault (1678–1749), J. J. Mouret (1682–1738), and Jean-Philippe Rameau (1683–1764). The latter's cantatas (complete ed., vol. iii) are all secular, mostly for one voice, and consist usually of three recitatives, each followed by an aria. Cf. *LavE* i.3, 1557ff.

III. The development of the cantata in Germany, although strongly influenced by the Italians, presents an entirely different picture, chiefly on account of the emphasis on the church cantata (Kaspar Kittel's *Arien und Kantaten* of 1638 are practically the only secular cantatas of the 17th century; cf. *RiHM*, 349). Schütz's *Symphoniae sacrae* (1629) contain several compositions which, although based on Latin texts, must be regarded as cantatas, being similar in form and style to those of Grandi or Rossi. However, the cantatas of Tunder (1614–67), Weckmann (1621–74; DdT 6), Rudolf Ahle (1625–73; DdT 5), Buxtehude (1637–1707; DdT 14), and J. S. Bach's uncle Johann Christoph Bach (1642–1703) already show a distinctly German character, being more serious, more genuinely dramatic, and more elaborate musically than the contemporary Italian cantata, owing chiefly to the inclusion of orchestral and choral participation. A specially interesting type is the *chorale cantata which was cultivated by Tunder, Johann Ph. Krieger (*DdT* 53/54), Kuhnau (*DdT* 58/59), and others, while Buxtehude's numerous cantatas are all based on free poetic texts and are, in a way, more "Italian" than those of the other German composers. The tendency from the chorale to free texts (and, as a consequence, from cantus-firmus pieces to entirely free composition) found a strong nourishment about 1700 when the pastor E. Neu-

meister began publishing annual sets of cantata texts from his own pen, mostly poetic paraphrases of scriptural passages proper for the various feasts of the church year. Some of these sets were written expressly for certain composers, e.g., for Krieger (Set i, 1704), for Philipp Erlebach (Set ii, 1708), and Georg Philipp Telemann (Sets iii, iv, 1711, 1714). However, many other musicians also were eager to seize upon these extremely timely and popular texts, above all J. S. Bach who, by the artistic greatness and religious dignity of his music, sanctioned Neumeister's "theatrical" poetry as well as the "operatic" form of the da-capo aria.

Bach's cantatas (195 are preserved out of a total number of probably close to 300) usually open with a chorus in fugal style which sometimes assumes great proportions, continue with a number of recitatives and arias, one for each of the two or three soloists, and close with a harmonized chorale. See *Chorale cantata.

After Bach, the cantata merged with the oratorio of which it represents the diminutive and more casual type. Most of these cantatas were written for special occasions, e.g., Haydn's *Birthday Cantata* for Prince Nikolaus Eszterházy (1763), or Mozart's cantata *Die Maurerfreude* (*The Joy of the Masons*, 1785), or Beethoven's *Der glorreiche Augenblick* (op. 136, 1814). Numerous later composers (Schubert, Spohr, Weber, Schumann, Mendelssohn, Liszt, Brahms, d'Indy, Saint-Saëns, Bennett, Stanford, Parry, Sullivan, Vaughan Williams) have made contributions to the repertory, but none of lasting importance. American composers of cantatas were John K. Paine and Dudley Buck (*The Voyage of Columbus*).

Lit.: E. Schmitz, *Geschichte der weltlichen Solokantate* (1914); M. Lange, *Die Anfänge der Kantate* (Diss. Leipzig 1938); K. F. Rieber, *Entwicklung der geistlichen Solokantate im 17. Jahrhundert* (Diss. Freiburg 1925); W. S. Hannam, *Notes on the Church Cantatas of J. S. Bach* (1928); W. G. Whittacker, *Fugitive Notes on Church Cantatas and Motets of J. S. Bach* (1923); E. J. Dent, "Italian Chamber Cantatas" (*MA* ii);

H. Prunières, "The Italian Cantata of the 17th Century" (*ML* vii, no. 1); E. Schmitz, "Zur Geschichte des italienischen Kammerduets im 17. Jahrhunderts" (*JMP* xxiii); E. B. Helm, in *BAMS* vi; H. Goldschmidt, in *ZMW* ii; H. Riemann, in *SIM* xiii; A. Heuss, in *ZIM* x; F. Treiber, in *AMF* ii.

Musical publications: *DdT* 3 (Tunder); *DdT* 6 (Bernhard, Weckmann); *DdT* 14 (Buxtehude); *DdT* 21/22 (Zachow); *DdT* 51/52 (Graupner); *DdT* 53/54 (Krieger); *DdT* 58/59 (Kuhnau, Schelle); *DTB* 6.i (Nürnberg masters); cantatas by Buxtehude (ed. by W. Gurlitt), Georg Böhm (ed. by J. Wolgast), Nikolaus Bruhns (ed. by F. Stein); H. Riemann, *Kantatenfrühling*, 4 vols.; *SchGMB*, nos. 212, 213, 260, 284; *HAM*, nos. 214, 227, 235, 258, 279.

Cante flamenco, cante hondo. See *Flamenco.

Canti carnascialeschi [It., carnival songs]. Early-16th-century part songs in the styles of the *frottola, the *villanella, the *canzonetta, the *balletto, etc., designed for the elaborate carnival festivities which took place at the court of the Medicis and of other Italian sovereigns. Heinrich Isaac wrote a number of such songs during his stay at the court of Lorenzo de Medici, c. 1480. Unfortunately these are lost. Numerous anonymous examples exist in several Italian MSS of the 16th century. Example in *HAM*, no. 123.

Lit.: F. Ghisi, *I canti carnascialeschi* (1937); *id.*, "Carnival Songs" (*MQ* xxv); P. M. Masson, †*Chants de Carnaval florentins* (1913); *Editions V, 43.

Canticum [E. canticle; F. *cantique*]. In the Catholic liturgy, biblical songs similar to a psalm but occurring elsewhere in the Scriptures than in the Psalter of David. They are classified as: (a) *cantica minora* (lesser canticles), i.e., those which occur in the Old Testament, and (b) *cantica majora* (major canticles, Gospel canticles), i.e., those from the New Testament. To the former class belong: "Audite caeli quae loquor" (*canticum Moysis II*), "Cantemus Domino" (*can-*

ticum Moysis I), "Audite verbum" (*canticum Jeremiae*), "Benedicite omnia opera Domini" (*canticum puerorum*); to the latter: "Magnificat anima mea" (*canticum Mariae* or *canticum B.V.M.*; see *Magnificat), "Benedictus Dominus Deus Israel" (*canticum Zachariae*), "Nunc dimittis" (*canticum Simeonis*). The chants of the latter class form the climax of Vespers, Lauds, and Compline respectively. *Canticum canticorum* is the Song of Solomon, selections from which have been frequently composed as motets (e.g., "Quam pulchra es," by Dunstable; cf. *SchGMB*, no. 34), most completely by Palestrina (29 motets; cf. compl. ed. vol. iv). See *Service; *Byzantine chant (*kanon*).

Cantiga. Spanish monophonic songs of the 13th century, mostly in honor of the Virgin Mary (C. de Santa Maria), which are preserved in great number (over 400) in four MSS of the Bibl. Nazionale and the Bibl. Escoriale, in Madrid. They were collected for the king Alfonso el Sabio ("the Wise," 1252–84) who was a great lover of poetry and music and who probably himself contributed a good part of the contents. The pictorial reproductions of instruments and players contained in the MSS are of the highest importance [cf. *GD* ii, 482; iii, 260; iv, 184]. The chief form of the cantigas is that of the *virelai. Regarding their textual as well as musical form the cantigas are very similar to the Italian *laudas of about the same period. However, the strict virelai form is more frequently used in the Spanish pieces. Examples in *HAM*, no. 22; *ReMMA*, 274; *OH* ii, 297; *BeMMR*, 166. The cantigas have been the subject of studies by various scholars the first of whom, J. Ribera, made sensational claims as to the Arabic origin of the songs and gave transcriptions in what he believed to be "Arabic rhythms," providing some of the songs with a 19th-century dance accompaniment. Actually, the cantigas are an outgrowth of the Provençal troubadour movement and must, therefore, be rendered, as these, in modal rhythm, less strictly applied, however, than in the case of the trouvère songs.

Lit.. H. Anglès, *Las Cantigas* (1927); G. Chase, *History of Spanish Music* (1942); *ReMMA*, 245 (bibl. p. 450); P. Aubry, *Iter Hispanicum* (1908), 37ff (facsimiles).

Cantilena. (1) A vocal melody of a lyrical rather than a dramatic or virtuoso character; also an instrumental passage of the same nature. — (2) In medieval writings the term is loosely used to denote secular vocal compositions, homophonic as well as polyphonic (ballades, rondeaux, etc.) [cf. *ReMMA*, 294, 322]. *Cantilena romana* is the Roman (i.e., Gregorian) chant.

Cantillation. Chanting in plainsong style, especially that of the Jewish service.

Cantino [It., F. *chanterelle*]. The highest string of lutes, viols, etc. A 16th-century German term is *Sangsaite.*

Cantio sacra. Latin name for the motet. Many collections of motets bear the title: *Cantiones Sacrae* (Tallis, Byrd, G. Gabrieli, Schütz). An Italian synonym is *Canzoni spirituali.*

Canto [It.]. Song; soprano; melody; subject. *Canto fermo,* *cantus firmus. Canto piano,* plainsong.

Cantor. In the Catholic service the leaders, two to six, of the chorus (the *schola*), who sing the solo portions of the chants (incipits and verses). In the Anglican service, see under *Polychoral style. In the Protestant church, the director of music (e.g., Bach in Leipzig). In the Jewish service, the solo singer, also called *chazzan.*

Cantus [L.]. Medieval and Renaissance term for melody; especially for the upper part (soprano) of polyphonic compositions (abbreviated C). Also for entire vocal compositions, chiefly secular, as, e.g., in the three volumes of the *Odhecaton which are designated: Canti A, Canti B, Canti C. *Cantus figuratus (figuralis), cantus fractus,* and *cantus mensuratus* all refer to the use of exactly measured (*mensuratus*) note-values (*figurae*) of different lengths such as result from

the breaking up (*fractus*) of a long note value into smaller parts. Hence, they designate polyphonic music, as opposed to plainsong (*cantus choralis, cantus planus*) with its notes of (supposedly) equal duration.

Cantus firmus [L., fixed melody]. A pre-existent melody which is made the basis of a polyphonic composition by the addition of contrapuntal voices. As regards their origin, the *cantus* (or *canti*) *firmi* usually belong to one of the four following groups: (a) plainsong melodies; (b) Protestant chorales; (c) secular melodies; (d) abstract subjects. To group (a), which is by far the most numerous, belong all the *organa and *clausulae, practically all the motets of the 13th and 14th centuries, a number of masses of the 15th and 16th centuries [see *Mass B, II (b)] as well as the numerous organ verses (*verset), organ hymns, etc., of the 16th century (Schlick, Cabezon, Redford, Titelouze). The latter pave the way to group (b) which includes the *organ chorales (*chorale preludes) of Buxtehude, Pachelbel, Bach, Brahms, etc., as well as the chorale choruses in cantatas, passions (for instance, the first chorus of Bach's St. Matthew Passion). Group (c)

Ave maris stella (1) by Cabezon; (2) by Dufay

includes some motets of the 13th century, and numerous masses of the 15th century, e.g., Missa *l'homme armé, Missa basse danse. To the last group belong the various compositions based on the hexachord (e.g., Sweelinck, Fantasia super ut, re, mi, fa, sol, la) or those based on a *soggetto cavato.

The cantus firmus appears most frequently in the *tenor, usually in long notes (*Pfundnoten) which form a strong contrast to florid design of the other parts [Ex. 1; Cabezon, Ave maris stella]. In many cases, however, the c.f. was subjected to considerable ornamentation and melodic elaboration, a process by which the original melody became more or less completely disguised [cf. the analyses in DTOe 19.i; also BeMMR, 202]. Particularly complex examples of this type exist in certain masses in which the discant is a free elaboration of the c.f. [see *Discant mass]. Less "scholarly" than these methods is the treatment encountered in hymns of Dunstable, Dufay, and Ockeghem in which the c.f. is used in the soprano, skillfully changed from a plainsong into a graceful melody in triple meter, and supported by two or three lower parts [Ex. 2: Dufay, Ave maris stella; cf. *Editions V, 49]. Examples in HAM, nos. 28–32, 44, 65, 67, etc. See *In seculum; *L'homme armé; *Felix namque; *Innomine.

Lit.: P. Aubry, Recherches sur les ténors français (latins) dans les motets du xiiie siècle (1907); id., in TG xiii; F. H. Sawyer, "The Use . . . of Cantus Firmus by the Netherland Schools" (PMA lxiii).

Cantus lateralis [L., song written side by side]. Fifteenth- and 16th-century term for the large *choir books in which the parts of a polyphonic composition were written "side by side" on the double page, in distinction from the *part books.

Cantus planus [L.]. Plainsong, Gregorian chant. The term was not used until the 13th century, earlier names being cantus choralis, cantilena Romana, etc. The word planus (even, level) is usually explained as referring to the fact that, in this period, the original tradition of Gregorian rhythm was lost and the chant began to be interpreted in uniform values of rather long duration (a brevis each), an interpretation which was probably a

concomitant of its adoption as a *cantus firmus for polyphonic compositions.

Cantus prius factus [L., song made in advance]. Same as *cantus firmus.

Cantus visibilis [L., visible song]. A misleading translation given by John Hothby (d. 1487) of the English term "sight," which was used in the 14th century in connection with improvised "English discant"; see Fauxbourdon (2).

Canun. See *Kanûn.

Canzo, canso [Provençal for chanson]. A form of troubadour music and poetry, also referred to in modern writing as canzone, Kanzone, chanson. It consisted of various stanzas of 6 to 7 lines each with music provided according to the following scheme:

$$\underbrace{1 \ 2}_{a} \quad \underbrace{3 \ 4}_{a} \quad \underbrace{5 \ 6 \ (7)}_{b}$$

This is the Provençal (troubadour) counterpart of the northern French (trouvère) *ballade and of the German (Minnesinger) Bar [see *Barform]. Examples in HAM, nos. 18b, c; ReMMA, 214f; BeMMA, 107; RiHM i.2, 251f.

Canzona or **canzone** (pl. canzone or canzoni). (1) In Italian poetry of the 13th through the 17th centuries, name for serious lyrical poems, usually in four or five stanzas of eight lines each. — (2) In 18th- and 19th-century music, name for lyrical songs (e.g., the canzone "Voi che sapete" in Mozart's Figaro) or for instrumental pieces of a similar character (e.g., the slow movement of Tchaikovsky's Symphony no. 4, designated "in modo di canzone"). — (3) See *canzo.

(4) A designation of 16th-century Italian secular vocal music, including: (a) certain members of the early *frottola family, set to free poems (called "canzoni") of Petrarch and others, which were important predecessors of the early madrigal (Examples in Canzoni, Sonetti, Strambotti et Frottole, 1517, reprinted 1941 by A. Einstein); (b) later popular forms of the villanella type [see *Villanella] also variously known as "Canzoni

Villanesche" (Nola, 1541; Cimello, 1545) and "Canzoni alla Napolitana" (Ferretti, 1573; Conversi, 1572). In the latter decades of the century, the *canzonetta became popular (Horazio Vecchi, 1580 and later years; Hassler, 1590). Cf. E. Helm, *The Early Italian Madrigal* (unpubl. diss. Harvard 1939); E. Hertzmann, *Adrian Willaert in der weltlichen Vokalmusik seiner Zeit* (1931).

(5) An important instrumental form of the 16th and 17th centuries. It developed from the Franco-Flemish chansons of Jannequin, Crecquillon, Clemens non Papa, and others [see *Chanson (3)] which were reprinted in Italy in great numbers, under the name "Canzon francese." The immense popularity of these pieces led to numerous arrangements for lute (Francesco da Milano, 1536, 1546, etc., and others) and for keyboard (Marc' Antonio da Bologna, 1523; Attaingnant, 1530, 1531; A. Gabrieli, *Canzoni alla francese per l'organo*, 1571). Composers furthermore wrote, in the style and form of certain vocal chansons, original instrumental pieces which were known as "Canzoni alla francese" or "Canzoni da sonare." It is this procedure which became the point of departure of a long and interesting development which in the instrumental field eventually led to the sonata of the 17th century [see *Sonata B, I], while in the field of keyboard music it paved the way for the *fugue. As early as the 16th century, canzones were designated either for keyboard (primarily organ) or for instrumental ensemble. They were characterized, like their chanson models, by clarity and balance of form (typical schemes are A B A, A B B, A A B C, etc.) and by variety of texture (free alternation of imitative, dialogue, and homophonic styles with the former in predominance). In contrast to the contemporary ricercar, they possessed a

Canzona Theme

lighter, less "learned" style and a more lively rhythm, moving in quarter- instead of half-notes and marked by the frequent appearance of repeated notes at the beginning of the subjects [see Ex.]. At first there were relatively few differences between keyboard and ensemble canzonas (those of Claudio Merulo, for example, appear to have been performed by both media). During the 17th century, however, the keyboard canzona became gradually more concentrated in its form, leading to the fugue, while that for ensembles became more sectional and finally identified itself with the sonata.

I. *Keyboard Canzona*. The first steps in the development of independent canzonas were taken by Girolamo Cavazzoni (*Intavolatura cioè ricercari, canzoni, ...*, 1542) in pieces such as his "Canzone sopra Falt d'argent" which uses the thematic material of Josquin's famous chanson "Fault d'argens," but differs from this in the contrapuntal elaboration of the themes [cf. *HAM*, nos. 91 and 118]. While Andrea Gabrieli's canzonas are mostly ornamented arrangements [see *Intabulierung] of vocal chansons, original organ canzonas were published by Merulo (1592, 1606, 1611), Pellegrini (1599), Mayone (1603, 1609), Cima (1606), Trabaci (1603, 1615), Cifra (1619), and others. These pieces are important as forerunners of the fugue; in fact, the name *Fuge* was used in Germany as synonymous with canzona (B. Schmid, 1607: "Fugen, oder wie es die Italiener nennen, canzoni alla francese"; Murschhauser, 1707: "canzona sive fuga"). Frescobaldi (1615, 1628, 1635, and 1645) established the *variation-canzona* consisting of various fugal sections, each based on a free rhythmic variation of one and the same theme, and frequently interspersed with free transitional passages. His example was followed by Froberger, Kerll, Poglietti, and many other German composers, including Bach (*B.-G.* vol. 38, no. 20).

II. *Canzonas for Instrumental Ensembles* were first composed in the 1570's [see *Editions XIV, vol. 2, for description and reprints of these works]. Flourishing chiefly in Lombardy and Venetia, such canzonas were published by Maschera

(1584); G. Gabrieli (1597, 1615); Canale (1600); Mortaro (1600, 1610); Rognioni (1605); Soderino (1608); Banchieri (1596, 1603, etc.); and many others. They fall into three types. Some works, generally in four parts and closely modeled on the chanson in style and form, were primarily contrapuntal in character (they always began with an imitative exposition) and had little stylistic contrast among their various sections. Canzonas of this rather conservative type continued to be written throughout the early 17th century. Another type, allied in principle to the ricercar, occasionally manifested tendencies toward thematic unity (Canale) of the sort found in the variation canzonas for keyboard written by Frescobaldi [cf. above]. A third type, represented by the brilliant polychoric canzonas of Giovanni Gabrieli and his followers (1597, Raverii Collection 1608, 1615), was freer in structure, consisting of an alternation between sections in lively imitation and four-four time, and homophonic sections in triple time. Occasionally these sections were very short and fragmentary in character [see *Flick-kanzone].

The free, multi-sectional type of canzona reached a climax in the ensemble works of Frescobaldi (four editions, 1623–34). These canzonas, marked in the later editions by systematic changes of tempo ("allegro" for the imitative sections in canzona style, "adagio" for the homophonic sections in slower rhythms), may well be considered a turning-point leading to the *sonata da chiesa*. Henceforth, the canzona identifies itself more and more with the sonata. Its individual sections, tending gradually to be reduced in number, are also more highly developed, and stylistically more sharply contrasted to one another. At the same time, vestiges of the old canzona, such as the A B A structure typical of the original chanson and the long introductory fugal section, remain for a long time. These characteristics may be observed in certain canzonas of Marini (1626), Buonamente (1636), Merula (1615, 1637, 1639, and 1651), Neri (1644, 1651), and Cazzati (1642, 1648, and later years). By *c.* 1650, the

terms "canzone" and "sonata" have become synonymous and the former is in general replaced by the latter (Legrenzi, Vitali). At the same time, the older term continues to be used by some composers. Long associated by theorists and composers with the "Allegro" style and also with the fugal style of writing, the word "canzona" (or "canzone") is sometimes found as the designation of the principal fugal movement of the sonata (Young, 1653; Purcell, 1683, 1697; Baldacini [1699], 1720; see also Brossard, 1706). It also occasionally enters the operatic *overture (e.g., in S. Landi's *S. Alessio*, 1634). See *Sonata B, I.

Lit.: J. M. Knapp, *The Canzone Francese and its Vocal Models* (unpubl. master's thesis, Columbia 1941); E. Crocker, *An Introductory Study of the Italian Canzona for Instrumental Ensembles* (unpubl. diss., Radcliffe 1943); A. Schlossberg, *Die italienische Sonate für mehrere Instrumente im 17. Jahrhundert* (1935); *RiHM* ii.2, *passim*. Examples in *HAM*, nos. 88, 118, 136, 175, 191, 194, 209, 210.   E. C.

Canzona francese. See *Canzona (5).

Canzonet, canzonetta. Diminutive of *canzona; denotes in the late 16th century short vocal pieces in a light vein, much in the character of a dance song [see *Balletto]. The term was used by Quagliati (1588), Vecchi (various publications between 1580 and 1600), Monteverdi (1584), H. L. Hassler [cf. *DTB* 5], and several of the English madrigalists [see *Editions X, vols. 1, 3, 20, 26, 28].

Caoine [pronounced Keen]. An Irish dirge of ancient tradition. Cf. the article in *GD.* See also *Coronach.

Capelle, Capellmeister [G.]. Old spelling for *Kapelle, Kapellmeister.

Capotasto [It., master fret; perverted forms are: *capodastro, capotaster, Kapodaster*; F. *barre*]. A mechanical contrivance used with guitars, lutes, etc., to shorten the vibrating length of all the strings simultaneously. It consists of a small piece made from hard wood or metal which can be fixed across the finger board.

By setting the capotasto across, e.g., the first fret, a piece in C-sharp can be played with the same fingering as if it were in C. See *Barrer.

Cappella [It.]. Chapel. See *A cappella.

Capriccio. [It.; F. *caprice*; from L. *capra*, goat]. (1) A term used by various 19th-century composers, for instance Mendelssohn and Brahms, for short piano pieces of a humorous or capricious character. They are usually in ternary form. It also appears as a title of *potpourris or fantasias [cf. Saint-Saëns, "Caprice sur les airs de ballet d'Alceste de Gluck"]. — (2) In the 17th century, capriccio is one of the four important prefugal forms [see *Ricercare, *Canzona (5), *Fantasia]. The capriccio, as the name suggests, is less restrained than the others and frequently involves certain peculiarities, such as the use of special themes. This is especially true in the case of Frescobaldi (Capriccio sopra il cucu; Capriccio sopra ut re mi fa sol la; Capriccio sopra la Bergamasca). Froberger's 18 capriccios are scarcely different from his canzonas, both being based upon the principle of Frescobaldi's variation-canzona [cf. *AdHM* i, 543]. Earlier examples of fugal capriccios for instruments (I) or for keyboard (K) are found in the publications of Lodovico Balbi (1586; I), Francesco Stivori (1594; I), Giovanni Maria Trabaci (1603; K), Biagio Marini (1626; I), etc. Later pieces, such as Johann Kaspar Kerll's *Capriccio sopra il Cucco* (c. 1680) and Bach's *Capriccio sopra la lontananza sel suo fratello dilettissimo* (c. 1705), are of the nature of free fantasias, the latter being a piece of program music picturing "the departure of his beloved brother."

Carcelera [Sp.]. A type of *cante hondo*, describing prison scenes.

Caricature. See *Satire in music.

Carillon [F., from L. *quadrilio*, a set of four]. A set of bells (originally four) hung in a tower of a church and played by means of a keyboard or by a clockwork mechanism. As early as the 13th century

sets of bells were operated mechanically. The use of a keyboard in connection with bells can be traced back to the early 16th century (Audenarde, 1510). Carillons became extremely popular and achieved high perfection in the Netherlands, Belgium, and Northern France from the 15th through the 18th centuries. In the 19th century they spread to England and, more recently, to America. A modern carillon consists of 30 to 50 bells with a clapper inside, tuned chromatically from C or G through three or four octaves. The clappers are connected by wires to long wooden keys, arranged like those of a manual and a pedal of an organ. The manual keys are struck with the closed hand which is protected by a glove. The largest carillons are those at the University of Chicago Chapel and at the Riverside Church of New York. The Curtis Institute, Philadelphia, offers instruction in carillon playing. Modern carillon players make ample use of tremolos, full chords, rapid passages, and other effective devices. There is, however, in certain circles, a tendency towards a more reserved style of playing which is certainly worthy of support.

Early composers of carillon music were Matthias van der Gheyn (1721–85), and Potthoff (b. 1726). Pieces by the former were published in 1862 by X. van Elewyck (ed. Schott). Old organ pieces called "Carillon" are found in O. Chilesotti, *Musica del passato*, and in Louis Couperin, *Oeuvres complètes* (ed. P. Brunold, 1936). Probably these were played by means of an organ glockenspiel such as is used also in Bach's cantata "Schlage doch, gewünschte Stunde." For a lute piece "Carillon d'Anvers" cf. *DTOe* xxvi.2, 64; also *Editions III, 8. Recent composers of pieces for carillons are Josef Denijn (b. 1862) and J. A. F. Wagenaar.

Lit.: J. Blavignac, *La Cloche* (1877); X. van Elewijk, †*Anciens Clavecinistes flamandes* (1877; contains two pieces by van der Gheyn); W. G. Rice, *Carillon Music* (1926); F. P. Price, *The Carillon* (1933); L. Rizzardi, *Les Carillons de Belgique* (1938); G. W. Rice, in *MQ* i; J. St. Archer, in *ML* xviii, no. 2; W. W. Starmer, in *PMA* xxxi; *id.*, in *ZIM* vi;

E. Buhle, "Das Glockenspiel in den Mi-niaturen des frühen Mittelalters" (*Fest-schrift für Liliencron*, 1910).

Carmagnole. A song of the French Revolution (1792), of unknown author-ship. It was sung to a rather vigorous dance of the same name.

Carmen [L., pl. *carmina*; song]. (1) A 14th- and 15th-century name, chiefly used by theorists, for the upper part (*cantus) of accompanied songs. — (2) Around 1500, name for instrumental polyphonic pieces in imitative style, usually (always?) without cantus firmus. They are fore-runners of the *ricercare. Examples exist in the *Glogauer Liederbuch* [see *Lieder-buch], in Isaac (*DTOe* xiv.1), in Hof-haimer (H. J. Moser, *91 gesammelte Ton-sätze Paul Hofhaimer's*, 1929), in Senfl, in Kotter's tablature of 1513, etc. Cf. H. J. Moser and Piersig, †*Carmina* (*Nagel's Musik-Archiv*).

Carmen. Opera in four acts by Georges Bizet (1838–75), composed in 1875 (li-bretto by Meilhac and Halévy, after a story by Mérimée). The central figure is the passionate gypsy *Carmen* (Soprano) who fascinates the sergeant *Don José* (Tenor), leads him to mutiny, lures him to join a band of smugglers, abandons him in favor of the toreador (bull fighter) *Escamillo* (Bass), and is finally stabbed to the heart by Don José in the moment when the victorious Escamillo emerges from the bull fight.

To this concise and exciting plot Bizet has written a music which, although in a "popular" vein, rises to greater heights of artistic perfection than hundreds of more ambitious and more "serious" operas. Al-though the music has been attacked as being "pseudo-Spanish" (which, in a way, it is), Carmen stands before the musical world as the inimitable incorporation of what the Spanish call *flamenco. It is in-teresting to note that the opera was far from being a success at its first perform-ances, and that its most fascinating piece, the Habanera, is not by Bizet [see *Ha-banera; also *Polo; *Seguidilla].

Carmina Burana. See *Goliard songs.

Carnaval. A piano composition by Ro-bert Schumann (op. 9, 1834) consisting of 20 short pieces which describe various scenes and characters of a masked ball. The subtitle: "Scènes mignonnes sur qua-tre notes" (Tiny Scenes Based on Four Notes), refers to the use of the word Asch (a Bohemian town where a lady friend of Schumann's lived) as a musical motive, the "translation" into notes being A-S-(i.e., Es, German for E-flat) C-H (Ger-man for B). These four notes, A-Eb-C-B, occur in the initial subjects of most of the pieces. Another interpretation of the same word is As-(German for A-flat) C-H (Ab-C-B) which is used in the pieces 10 to 18.

Carnival of Venice. An Italian pop-ular melody of the 19th century which has been chosen by a number of composers (Paganini, Schulhoff, Herz, Benedict) as a theme for variations. It also occurs as the main theme (followed by variations) of Liszt's Rhapsody no. 9, called "Carnival of Pesth."

Carnival songs. See *Canti carnascia-leschi.

Carol [F. *noël*; G. *Weihnachtslied*]. A traditional song for the celebration of Christmas; occasionally the term is used also for other devotional songs of a joyful character (Easter carol; May carol). The name is evidently derived from the medi-eval French word *carole for a round dance, the assumption being that this term was associated in English with the early pagan dance-songs performed in celebra-tion of the winter solstice, a ritual which later merged with that of Christmas. The earliest preserved examples, in two or three parts, date from the first half of the 15th century [*SchGMB*, no. 32 a, b]. Nu-merous carols of the 16th-18th centuries have been published in collections which also include French and German Christ-mas songs. See *Noël.

Lit.: P. Dearmer, †*The Oxford Book of Carols* (1928); id., *The Story of the Carol* (1911); E. B. Reed, *Christmas Carols printed in the 16th century* (1932); Ful-ler-Maitland, *English Carols of the 15th*

Century (1891); H.J.Massé, "Old Carols" (ML ii, no. 1).

Carole. Medieval French name for round dances, danced in a closed circle. The name is derived from L. *chorea*, dance, which was transformed into *choreola*, *carola*, *carole* [cf. the explanation: "chorea, gallice charole" given in the 13th-century *Dictionarius Johannes de Garlandia*; cf. *Collection des documents inédits sur l'histoire de France*, i. 603]. No specific music for such dances has survived. Possibly the *virelai in its original monophonic form was sung in connection with the carole. See *Dance Music II. Cf. T. Lacroix-Novaro, "La Carole" (*RdM*, no. 53).

Carrée [F.]. The double whole note, or breve.

Carrure [F.]. The symmetrical construction of musical phrases in measures of 2, 4, 8, etc., as occurs particularly in dances. See *Vierhebigkeit.

Cassa [It.]. Drum. See *Percussion instruments B 2, 3.

Cassation [probably from It. *cassare*, to say farewell; or from new Latin *gassatim*, street-like]. An instrumental form of the 18th century, designed for outdoor performance, which includes elements of the symphony as well as of the suite; hence, practically identical with the *divertimento and the *serenade. Mozart wrote three cassations (K.V. nos. 62, 63, 99).

Casse-Noisette. Original title of Tchaikovsky's ballet *The Nutcracker*. See *Nutcracker Suite.

Castanets [F. *castagnettes*; G. *Kastagnetten*]. Clappers consisting of two pieces of hard wood in the shape of a shell, hinged together by a string which passes over the thumb and first finger of the player. They are used by Spanish dancers as an accompaniment for the bolero, fandango, etc., usually in pairs (one in each hand). Similar instruments were used in ancient Rome and appear on pictorial representations contained in medieval manuscripts [see under *Cantigas*]. The castanets of the modern orchestra (e.g., in Bizet's *Carmen*) are provided with contrivances such as springs or handles which greatly facilitate the playing, but take away much from the fascination of true castanet playing.

Castrato. The castration of singing boys was frequently practiced in Italy from the 16th through the 18th centuries, in order to preserve the boyish character of the voice. The singing apparatus of the castrato (also called *evirato*) combines the larynx of a youth with the chest and lungs of an adult. Hence, it combines an unusually wide range with a sound of great power and of a special timbre which exercised great fascination upon the hearers. Famous castrati were F. Senesino (1680–c. 1750), G. Caffarelli (1703–83), and Carlo Farinelli (properly Carlo Broschi, 1705–82).

Lit.: F. Haböck, *Die Kastraten und ihre Gesangskunst* (1927); *id.*, *Carlo Broschi* (1923); G. Monaldi, *Cantati evirati celebri* (1921); *id.*, in *RMI* xxvi; F. Rogers, in *MQ* v; *AdHM*, 1221.

Catalectic [Gr., incomplete]. In poetry, a line is called catalectic if a syllable is missing in the last foot, for instance, in iambic meter ∪ ′ ∪ ′ ∪ ′ ′ or ∪ ′ ∪ ′ ∪ ′ ∪ instead of: ∪ ′ ∪ ′ ∪ ′ ∪ ′.

Catch. English *rounds of the 17th and 18th centuries. The first publication, the *Pammelia* (1609), was followed by a long series of collections, among which Hilton's *Catch That Catch Can* (1652–58) is the most famous. Catches were most in vogue in the reign of Charles II, and it was mainly in this period that the catches acquired that peculiarity which has relegated them to the "poison chest" of musical literature, namely, the indecent character of their texts. Numerous catches of the Restoration, including some of Purcell's, are so clearly obscene that their texts had to be altered or completely replaced in modern editions. A number of catches are so constructed that, owing to the presence of lengthy rests in their melody, a *hocket-like effect of alternation is produced by the voices singing in canon, as is

CATHEDRAL MUSIC

illustrated by our example (from *Pammelia*). Occasionally this device was used to bring about a special meaning, indecent or comical, resulting from the interlacing

arrangement of the words or phrases (catches *à double entente*; cf. *HAM*, no. 325). A complete list of the publications containing catches is given in *GD*. Modern publications (with revised texts) are: E. F. Rimbault, *The Rounds, Catches and Canons of England* (1864); H. Purcell, *Complete Works*, vol. 22.

Cathedral music. Music written for the choirs of the English cathedrals, consisting chiefly of *Services*and *anthems. Important early collections are: J. Barnard, *The First Book of Selected Church Music* (1641; contents cf. *GD* i, 226); W. Boyce and J. Kent, *Cathedral Music* (3 vols., 1760–78; new ed. by Novello; contents cf. *GD* i, 441); Samuel Arnold, *Cathedral Music* (4 vols., 1790; reprinted by Rimbault in 1847; contents cf. *GD* i, 117). The present-day cathedral choirs still draw on the repertory of these books which include among their authors practically every English composer from Tye and Tallis to Samuel Arnold and his contemporaries. However, numerous new compositions have been added by more recent composers, such as S. S. Wesley (1810–76), Th. A. Walmisley (1814–56), F. A. Ouseley (1825–89), John Stainer (1840–1901), Ch. V. Stanford (1852–1904), and many others. See also *Service.
Lit.: J. S. Bumpus, *A History of English Cathedral Music, 1549–1889* (2 vols., 1908); E. H. Fellowes and C. H. Stewart, *A Repertoire of Cathedral Music* (1922).

Catholic church music. See *Church music; *Gregorian chant; *Mass; *Psalm tones; *Psalmody.

CAUDA

Catholica. A name given by Glareanus [*Dodekachordon*, 1552] to contrapuntal pieces which are so designed that they may be sung in various church modes. The most famous example is Ockeghem's *Missa cujusvis toni* (Mass in Any Mode). Just which modes are admissible and which accidentals will have to be used in each single mode is a problem to which perhaps too much attention has been given by numerous scholars. At any rate, it is most unfortunate that this piece should have been reprinted in practically all the books on music history, thus perpetuating the popular misconception regarding Ockeghem and early Flemish music. See *Flemish School. Cf. J. S. Levitan, in *MQ* xxiii; also *RiHM* i.2, 233.

Cat's fugue. Popular name of a piece in fugal style by Domenico Scarlatti, so called because the subject consists of some irregular wide steps in ascending motion such as might have been produced by a cat stepping over the keyboard.

Cauda [L., tail]. (1) In mensural notation, the vertical dash attached to certain notes (*maxima, longa, minima*, etc.) or to ligatures.

With *ligatures, the presence or absence of the cauda determines the *proprietas*, i.e., the value of the initial note. In the early 14th century numerous note forms, called *semibreves caudatae* (or *signatae*), were derived from the *semibrevis* by upward and downward dashes, with or without flags, etc. They form the basis of the Italian notation of the 14th century [cf. *ApNPM*, 370ff].
(2) In 13th-century composition, a vocalizing cadenza at the end of a piece or a section thereof. Particularly *conductus were provided with such cadenzas (*conductus habens caudam*) and if so, were considered superior to the — probably earlier — *conductus non habens caudam* [Ex. in *ApNPM*, 239; *HAM*, nos. 38, 39]. Cadenzas in free rhythm are also frequent in the organa of the 13th century [cf. *ApNPM*, 240]. Short cadential passages

in downward scalar motion were called *copula.

Cavalleria Rusticana ("Rustic Chivalry"). Opera in one act by Pietro Mascagni (b. 1863), composed in 1890. The setting is a Sicilian village on Easter morning. The young farmer *Turiddu* (Tenor), lover of *Santuzza* (Soprano), is turning to his former love *Lola* (Mezzo-Soprano), now married to *Alfio* (Baritone). A trifle (Turiddu's entrance into the church at Lola's side) suffices to constitute a "break of the honor code," resulting in a duel between Alfio and Turiddu in which the latter is killed..

This opera, which was Mascagni's only success, owes its appeal to the concise and dramatic plot as well as to the realistic musical approach. Widely welcomed as a relief from the numerous imitations of Wagner, it inaugurated the musical movement known as *verismo and was responsible for a mushroom crop of one-act operas.

Cavata [from L. *cavare*, to hollow out, to engrave]. An inscription or an epigrammatic sentence in which an important thought is concisely expressed. In 18th-century music the term is used occasionally for short epigrammatic ariosos to be found at the end of a lengthy recitative (*recitativo con cavata*). Many examples of this method occur in Bach's choral works, e.g., in the recitativo no. 3 of his cantata "Ein feste Burg" [see *Arioso]. The cavatas in Traëtta's operas [cf. *DTB* 14.i] approach the *cavatina. See also *Soggetto cavato.

Cavatina [It., dimin. of *cavata*]. In 18th- and 19th-century operas and oratorios, a short solo song simpler in style than the aria and without repetition of words or phrases. The proper form for the *cavatina* would seem to be in one section without repetition (except for a short instrumental anticipation of the beginning of the song), in other words, just a "sentence" set to music [see *Cavata]. Examples of this type are the two cavatinas in Haydn's *The Seasons* as well as "Porgi amor" and "L'ho perduta" from Mozart's

Figaro, while the "Se vuol ballare" from the same opera shows an unusually developed type similar to an aria. Other examples occur in Rossini's *Barber of Seville* (1816), in Weber's *Freischütz* (1821), in Gounod's *Faust* (1859). The name has also been applied to instrumental pieces of a song-like character [e.g., Beethoven, Quartet op. 130].

C.B. Abbreviation for *col basso* or for *contrabasso*.

C.d. Abbreviation for [It.] *colla destra*, i.e., with the right hand.

Cebell. Old English name for the gavotte, used by H. Purcell and others.

Cecilian movement. A 19th-century movement for the reform of the Roman Catholic church music, initiated by K. Proske, Ratisbon choirmaster (1794–1861), and named after St. Cecilia, the patron saint of music. The movement aimed at the reinstallment of Palestrina's *a cappella* music instead of the pompous and rather worldly church music for choir and instruments that had come into use during the 18th century (e.g., Haydn's and Mozart's masses). It led, in 1867, to the foundation of the *Allgemeiner Deutscher Caecilienverein* (F. X. Witte, 1834–88), which was sanctioned by the Holy See in 1870. The term Cecilianism is used to denote the puristic and generally rather reactionary tendencies of this society.

Cefaut, ce fa ut. See *Hexachord III.

Celere [It.]. Quick.

Celesta. See *Percussion instruments A, 4.

Cello. Contraction of *violoncello.

Cellone. See *Violin family (i).

Cembal d'amour. *Clavecin d'amour.

Cembalo [It., abbr. of *clavicembalo*]. The Italian and German name for the *harpsichord. According to C. Sachs (*SaRM*, 75) the word is not derived from Gr. *kymbalon* (hollow vessel, bell; see *cymbal), but from *tympanon* (same root as tip, zip, G. *zupfen*, to pluck). There-fore the name does not point to a simi-larity of the sound of the instrument to that of bells, but to the plucking of the strings.

Centitone. See under *Intervals, Cal-culation of, V.

Cento [L.], **centone** [It., a patchwork quilt]. The term and its derivatives "cen-tonization," "to centonize" are used with reference to literary and musical works formed by selections from other works. The liturgical book compiled by St. Greg-ory (*c*. 670) was as early as the 9th century called "antiphonarius cento," on account of the theory (probably erroneous) that it was a combination of three earlier books written by Pope Gelasius [cf. P. Wagner, *Einführung in die Gregorianischen Me-lodien*, i, 199–214; O. Ursprung, *Katho-lische Kirchenmusik*, 21]. In poetry, cento denotes a poem consisting only of refrains [see *Refrain]. The term also applies to musical melodies pieced together from pre-existent fragments (a procedure not infrequent in Gregorian chant and in Oriental music) as well as to operas of the 18th century put together by several com-posers. See *Ballad opera and, in par-ticular, *Pasticcio; also *Quod libet.

Central America. Lit.: J. Castillo, "Autochthonic Music" [of Guatemala] (*Bull. of the Pan American Union*, vol. 62, no. 4); F. Densmore, *Music of the Tule Indians of Panama* (1926); N. Garay, *Tradiciones y Cantares de Panamá* (Brus-sels, 1930); R. González Sol, *Datos histó-ricos sobre el arte de la música en El Salva-dor* (San Salvador, 1940); N. Slonimsky, "Viewing a Terra Incognita of Music" (*Musical America*, 1941). See also gen-eral bibliography under Latin American music. G. C.

Cents. The unit of a scientific and exact method of measuring musical intervals which was introduced by A. J. Ellis (1814–90) and which has been widely adopted in acoustics as well as in *comparative musicology. The cent is one one-hun-dredth of the semitone of the well-tem-pered scale; thus, the semitone equals 100 cents, and the octave contains 1200 cents. The various tones of the chromatic scale are represented by the multiples of 100, as follows:

0 100 200 300 400 500 600
c c♯ d d♯ e f f♯

700 800 900 1000 1100 1200
g g♯ a a♯ b c

This scale can be conveniently used for diagrams showing the exact position of other intervals, e.g., those of the Pythag-orean scale, of just intonation, of exotic scales, etc. [see *Javanese music]. For readers familiar with the elements of arithmetic it may be remarked that cents are a logarithmic measurement; see *In-tervals, Calculation of, IV.

Cephalicus. See *Neumes.

Cercar la nota [It., to seek the note] indicates in vocal technique a slight anticipation of the following note, e.g., d--(c)-c. It may also occur in the form of a passing note, e.g., e--(d)-c.

Ces, ceses [G.]. See *Pitch names.

Cesolfa(ut), ce sol fa (ut). See *Hexachord III.

Cetera, cetra [It.]. (1) *Zither.— (2) Cittern [see *Guitar family].

C.f. Abbreviation for *cantus firmus.

Chace [F.]. See under *Caccia.

Chaconne and passacaglia. Two closely related forms of Baroque music, each in the character of a continuous vari-ation [see *Variation I] in moderately slow triple meter. An additional feature is a slow *harmonic rhythm, changing generally with the measure. The terms are interesting not only on account of the many futile attempts that have been made to explain their derivation and original meaning, but also on account of the at-tempts, equally numerous and futile, to make a clear distinction between them. As is shown subsequently, Baroque com-posers used the terms indiscriminately. This does not necessarily mean that they could not be put to better use in modern terminology. Unfortunately, modern writers have been entirely unsuccessful in this matter, and the music histories as well as reference books are full of contradictory and frequently arbitrary statements as to the distinction between a chaconne and a passacaglia. The only distinction which can and should be made is that between continuous variations with or without a *basso ostinato* (*ground). In order to conform with the titles of the two most famous examples, those composed by Bach, the former type will have to be called passacaglia, the latter chaconne. A passacaglia, then, is a continuous variation based on a clearly distinguishable ostinato which normally appears in the bass (ground) but which may also be transferred occasionally to an upper voice, as is the case in Bach's passacaglia. A chaconne is a continuous variation in which the "theme" is only a succession of chords which serves as a harmonic basis for each variation. The difference between these two types may be illustrated by the accompanying examples, the first two of which

[Ex. 1, 2] show a very frequent ground, the descending tetrachord in its diatonic form and in its chromatic modification, while Ex. 3 shows the use of a (related) scheme of harmonies, without ground. For a 16th-century adumbration of passacaglia, see under *Ostinato (Dump and Hornepype).

As has been mentioned previously, no clear distinction between passacaglia and chaconne exists in the praxis of Baroque composers. To the class of passacaglia (as

defined above) belong the "Passacaglia" of Bach (for organ) and that of Louis Couperin (for harpsichord) as well as "chaconnes" of Buxtehude, J. K. Kerll [*TaAM* vii, 104] (both for organ), and Pachelbel (for harpsichord; *TaAM* ix, 59). To the same class belong numerous vocal compositions contained in 17th-century operas and cantatas, e.g., Monteverdi's famous duet *Pur ti miro* [*SchGMB*, no. 178; see also *Aria III]. To the class of chaconne belong Frescobaldi's "Cento partite sopra il passacaglio" [*TaAM* v, 11] and Georg Muffat's "Passacaglia" [cf. *HAM*, no. 240] as well as Bach's "Chaconne." The interpretation, frequently given, of Bach's chaconne as an ostinato composition is erroneous. Although, with a reiterated scheme of harmonies, it is always possible to reconstruct to some extent a ground bass from the bass notes of these harmonies [cf. *RiML*, 295], such a procedure leads, in the case of Bach's chaconne, to a decidedly poor melody, such as Bach would never have chosen as a point of departure. Well-known 19th-century examples of chaconne are Beethoven's C minor Variations (1807), and the closing movement of Brahms's Symphony no. 4. More recent examples occur in F. Busoni's *Toccata: Preludio, Fantasia, Ciaccona* (1921) and in E. Krenek's *Toccata und Chaconne*, op. 13.

Finally it should be noticed that French Baroque composers usually applied the terms chaconne and passecaille to pieces in an entirely different form, i.e., that of the rondeau with reiterated refrain and several couplets [see *Rondeau (2)]. Examples are a Chaconne by Chambonnières [*HAM*, no. 212], a Chaconne-rondeau by d'Anglebert [*TaAM* vii, 135; *HAM*, no. 232], and a Passecaille by Fr. Couperin [*Pièces de clavecin* ii].

There is reason to believe that the chaconne originally was a wild and sensual Mexican dance which was imported into Spain during the 16th century. In 1599 we read about "an invitation to go to Tampico in Mexico and there dance the chacona." Queveda calls it the "chacona mulata," and Cervantes the "Indiana amulatada" [cf. C. Sachs, *A World His-*

tory of the Dance (1941)]. Once imported into Europe it lost its unbridled character entirely, as did also the *sarabande and, 300 years later, the *tango. The passacaglia (possibly from Sp. *pasacalle*, street song) also was originally a dance.

Chaleureux [F.]. With warmth.

Chalumeau [F., from L. *calamellus*, pipe]. (1) Seventeenth-century name for (a) an early oboe (shawm), (b) an early clarinet. The chalumeau in Gluck's *Orpheus* is probably a real clarinet (with keys).— (2) The lowest register of the modern clarinet.

Chamber music. I. *General*. Instrumental ensemble music performed by one player to the part, as opposed to orchestral music in which there are several players to the part. According to the number of players (or parts), chamber music is classified as follows: *trio (three players), *quartet (four), *quintet (five), *sextet (six), *septet (seven), *octet (eight). String trios (quartets, etc.) are for stringed instruments only [see *String quartet]; if one of the strings is replaced by another instrument, names such as pianoforte trio (pianoforte and two strings) or horn quintet (horn and four strings) are used. The violin (violoncello) sonata, for violin (violoncello) and pianoforte, is sometimes not considered as chamber music, on account of the markedly solistic character of the parts. In true chamber music, emphasis lies on the ensemble, not on the single player.

The present-day repertoire of chamber music begins with the late string-quartets (written after 1780) of Haydn and Mozart. In these works the basic principles of form and style were established to which practically all composers of chamber music have adhered: the form is that of the *sonata in four movements; the style is characterized by individual treatment of the parts and exclusion of virtuoso-like elements. Naturally, there exist examples in which these principles are not observed, a notable exception being Beethoven's string quartet in C-sharp minor, op. 131 with its extremely free form. Yet

the fact remains that in chamber music composers have shown a greater respect for tradition than in other fields, the obvious reason being that the relatively limited and fixed resources of, e.g., a string quartet prohibited the introduction of novel features comparable to those of contemporary orchestral or piano music.

The chamber music works (chiefly string quartets) of Haydn, Mozart, Beethoven (opus numbers below 100), and Schubert represent the classical period of chamber music. In his late quartets (op. 127, 130–133, 135, written between 1824 and 1827) Beethoven has created an entirely singular type of chamber music, a type which is too personal to be called classic, and yet too transcendental to be considered as Romantic. The Romantic period of chamber music embraces Schumann, Brahms, Dvořák, and Franck (to name only the most important composers), with Brahms ranking first among them. While Debussy, Ravel, and others (e.g., Schönberg, String Sextet Verklärte Nacht, op. 4) tried to exploit the impressionistic and coloristic resources of chamber music, there has been more recently a return to a purer and more appropriate style, as the result of the contemporary revival of the contrapuntal approach to musical composition, and of the adoption of a more objective and sober type of expression than prevailed in the late Romantic and in the Impressionistic schools [see *Neo-classicism]. For more details, see the entries for the different species of chamber music, particularly *string quartet.

II. *History.* Chamber music, in the widest sense of the word, already existed in the late Middle Ages. Instrumental ensemble pieces such as occur in the Glogauer Liederbuch (*c.* 1470; see *Liederbuch) or the *carmina of Obrecht, Isaac, Hofhaimer bear all the characteristic marks of true chamber music. So do the 16th-century ensemble ricercares [see *Ricercar I (a)] by Adrian Willaert, Buus, Padovano, as well as the instrumental canzonas [see *Canzona (5), I] from the end of this century. (Regarding the claim that a canzona by Allegri was the "first string quartet," see under *String quartet II.) Naturally, all these pieces were not written for, nor restricted to, specific instruments, but were performed on whatever instruments were available, viols, recorders, cornettos, or mixed ensembles. The chief type of Baroque chamber music is the *trio sonata in its two varieties, the sonata da chiesa and the sonata da camera. It developed in Italy and spread, around 1675, to France, Germany, and England where it replaced the earlier *fancy. Around 1750 there emerged a new type of chamber music, the string quartet, with its associates, the string quintet (Boccherini), and the string trio (Haydn); see *String quartet II.

An extended list of chamber music associations is found in Pierre Key's Music Year Book.

Lit.: W. W. Cobbett, Cyclopedic Survey of Chamber Music (2 vols., 1929); id., in PMA xxxviii; T. F. Dunhill, Chamber Music (1913); N. Kilburn, Chamber Music (1932); G. Stratton and A. Frank, The Playing of Chamber Music (1935); H. S. Drinker, The Chamber Music of Brahms (1932); W. Altmann, Kammermusik-Literaturverzeichnis seit 1841 (2d ed. 1931); N. Ruet, Musique de chambre (1930); LavE ii.5, 3144 (repertoire and bibliography); S. Laciar, "The Chamber Music of Schubert" (MQ xiv); H. Mersmann, "Beiträge zur Aufführungspraxis der vorklassischen Kammermusik in Deutschland" (AMW ii); L. de la Laurencie, "Les Débuts de la musique de chambre en France" (RdM, nos. 49–52).

Chamber opera. An opera of small dimensions, of an intimate character, and for small orchestra (chamber orchestra). The reaction against the great Wagnerian opera led to works such as R. Strauss's Ariadne auf Naxos (second version, 1924), Hindemith's Cardillac (1926), C. Douglas Moore's White Wings (1935).

Chamber orchestra. A small orchestra of about 25 players. Prior to 1800 orchestras usually were of this size, and recent composers have again written for such groups (chamber symphony).

Chamber pitch [G. Kammerton]. See *Pitch.

Change ringing. The ringing of a set (peal) of church bells by individual men and in a methodical order, the turn of the men being prescribed not by a musical melody, but by certain schemes of arithmetic permutation. For instance, a set of five bells: 1, 2, 3, 4, 5 may be played in the order: 4 5 2 3 1 or 3 5 1 4 2, etc. In actual performance, usually a limited selection of such permutations is played in succession, the main principle being the exchange of two numbers. For instance, in a peal of five bells, the first "change" would be 1 2 3 4 5, the second: 2 1 3 4 5, the third: 2 3 1 4 5, etc. Certain standard selections are known under traditional names such as "Grandsire Triple," "Treble Bob," etc. The history of change ringing goes back to the 16th century. An important landmark was the publication of Tintinnalogia by F. Stedman (1688). Change ringing is still widely practiced in England. In fact, it is a typically English sport in which healthy exercise is combined with a small but gratifying amount of mental effort.

Lit.: E. Morris, The History and Art of Change Ringing (1931); J. Stainer, in PMA xlvi [cf. the article in GD i, 602].

Changing note. See *Nonharmonic tones III.

Chanson [F.]. (1) The French term for song, hence, the counterpart of the German *lied. However, while in the German lied emphasis lies on the artistic production, the chanson is usually of a more popular nature. Throughout the last two centuries there has been an enormous output of popular chansons, short strophic songs mostly of an amorous character, which are frequently written, set to music, sung on the streets, and sold by one and the same man. It was not until the end of the 19th century that the chanson was cultivated as an artistic form [see *Song III].

The virtual non-existence of French art-songs in the 18th and 19th centuries is in striking contrast to the picture presented in earlier periods. In fact, the early history of the chanson (i.e., of songs with French text) is more ancient, fertile, and musically important than that of any other nation's song literature. The earliest preserved example, a Provençal song "Hora vos dic vera raizun" [cf. P. Aubry, *Les plus ancients monuments de la musique Française* (1905), pl. I], dates from the 11th century. The 12th and 13th centuries are the era of the *troubadours and *trouvères whose melodies, usually cast in one of the *formes fixes* (*ballade, *rondeau, *virelai), constitute an unparalleled treasure of early secular song. The 14th century sees the rise of accompanied songs, in the same forms, under G. de Machaut and his successors [see *Ars nova]. As an antithesis to the rhythmic and contrapuntal complexity of the late 14th century there developed, in the *Burgundian School of the 15th century (Dufay, Binchois, also Ockeghem, Obrecht), a new style of unsurpassed charm and beauty, perhaps the artistic high-point in the entire history of the French song. [For modern editions of 15th-century chansons see under *Burgundian School and *Chansonnier (2).] A limited number of popular melodies of the 15th century, especially the famous *L'homme armé*, survive in masses and motets for which they served as a cantus firmus. Around 1500 we have the beginning of another important era, that of the so-called polyphonic chanson, characterized by the abandoning of the formes fixes in favor of free composition, and by the adoption of the imitative counterpoint as the basic principle of style (Isaac, Josquin, Jannequin). It is this type to which the name chanson or *French chanson* usually refers in historical writings [see below under (3)]. With the early 17th century and the rise of the monodic style, the polyphonic chanson disappeared and, strangely enough, the creative activity in the field of art-song ceased abruptly. The interest turned to *vauxdevilles, *pastourelles, *bergerettes, and *brunettes, i.e., to the more popular types which dominated throughout the 18th and 19th centuries [see also *Air de court]. Extensive collections of such chansons

were published by Ballard, e.g., *Airs sérieux et à boire* (16 vols., 1627–54).

(2) In trouvère music, *chanson* is the equivalent of the Provençal (troubadour) *vers* (not of the *canzo), i.e., a through-composed song, in contradistinction to the repetition- and refrain-types (*formes fixes*): ballade, virelais, rondeau.

(3) The chanson of the 16th century, frequently called polyphonic or French chanson, is written in the imitative style of the contemporary motet, but with such modifications as were required by the different nature of purpose and text, i.e., quicker and more pungent rhythm, a leaning towards homophonic texture, sectional construction in relatively short phrases ending simultaneously in all the parts, and frequently repetition of a section for another line of the poem. A characteristic feature of the chanson (as well as of its derivative, the instrumental *canzona) is the use of repeated notes in the initial subject, as is illustrated in the accompanying example (Jacotin, *Je suis déshéritée*; cf. *SchGMB*, no. 117).

The earlier polyphonic chansons (Ockeghem, Obrecht, Isaac, Josquin, La Rue) show an elaboration of style and dignity of expression which are still in the best Flemish tradition [cf., e.g., Ockeghem's "Ma bouce rit" in *HAM*, no. 75, or the chansons of Josquin; see *Editions V, no. 3; see also *Odhecaton]. With Clément Jannequin (d. c. 1560 ?), Claude de Sermisy (c. 1490–1562), Pierro Certon (d. 1572), and numerous followers, the chanson changed its character from the Flemish into the typically French, from reserved intimacy into nimble elegance and frivolity. Jannequin's chansons are remarkable for their frequent use of *ternary form: A B A. A type of some special interest, though of very mediocre artistic value, is the program chanson of Jannequin [see *Program music]. The popularity of the new chanson found its proper expression in a vast number of contemporary publications as well as in the many hundreds of *Intabulierungen of French chansons which fill the German and Italian lute tablatures and keyboard books of the 16th century. Pierre Attaingnant alone printed 35 books of chansons between 1535 and 1549 [cf. *RiML, 298]; simultaneously Jacques Moderne published the ten books of his *Parangon des chansons* (1538–43). See also *Sonata B, I.

Lit.: *LaMWC*, 215; *AdHM*, 373; L. Laloy, "La Chanson française au xvie siècle" (*RMC* i), J. Tiersot, "Ronsard et la musique de son temps" (*SIM* iv), D. v. Bartha, "Probleme der Chansongeschichte im 16. Jahrhundert" (*ZMW* xiii). For publications of music see *Editions XVI and XIX; M. Cauchie, †*Quinze chansons français du XVIe siècle* (1931); L. de la Laurencie, †*Chansons au luth et airs de cour du xvie siècle* (1931). Examples in *HAM*, nos. 91 (118), 107, 145; *SchGMB*, nos. 116–118.

Chanson de geste [F., song of deeds]. The French epic poems of the Middle Ages, such as the Roman de Roland (11th century). They were of great extension (over 10,000 lines of nearly equal meter), and fell in sections of various lengths (20 or 50 lines) called *laisse*, each of which contained one continuous "thought" of the poem. They were probably sung to a short melodic formula which was repeated for every line of a laisse, with the exception of the last, for which a new melody with a more definite close was chosen (a a a a . . . . . . b). Only one such melody survives, in a late quotation inserted in Adam de la Halle's play *Le Jeu de Robin et Marion* [cf. *ReMMA*, 204]. See *Rotrouenge; *Chanson de toile.

Lit.: F. Gennrich, *Der musikalische Vortrag der altfranzösischen Chansons de geste* (1923); Raoul de Cambrai,

Chansons de geste du XIIe siècle (1932); *GéHM*, 258ff.

Chanson de toile [F., spinning song]. The "female counterpart" of the *chanson de geste. The chief character is always a woman, an ill-mated wife or a love-sick girl. The musical recitation was probably similar to that of the chanson de geste.

Chanson mass. See *Mass B, II (b).

Chanson mesurée. See *Vers mesuré.

Chansonnier. (1) Medieval (13th-century) manuscripts containing the songs of the troubadours and trouvères. Most of these have been published in facsimile editions, some of them with transcriptions [see *Trouvères; *AdHM*, 192; *ReMMA*, 448].—(2) Fifteenth-century manuscripts containing polyphonic chansons, e.g., the *Chansonnier cordiforme* (the pages have the form of a heart), or the *Copenhagen chansonnier* (publ. by K. Jeppesen, 1927).

Lit.: G. Raynaud, *Bibliographie des chansonniers français du xiiie au xive siècle* (1884); K. Jeppesen, †*Der Kopenhagener Chansonnier* (1927); E. Droz, †*Trois Chansonniers français du xve siècle* (1927); G. Thibault, "Le Chansonnier . . . de Copenhague" (*RdM* 1927); M. F. Bukofzer, "An Unknown Chansonnier of the 15th Century" (*MQ* xxviii).

Chant. General denomination for liturgical music in the character of plainsong, i.e., monophonic, unaccompanied, and in free rhythm. Music of this type exists in many Oriental and exotic cultures. In particular, the term applies to the liturgical melodies of the Christian Churches, e.g., *Byzantine chant, Russian chant, and the four branches of Western chant, namely, *Ambrosian (Milanese), *Gallican, *Mozarabic, and Roman chant, the last being usually known as *Gregorian chant or *plainsong. More specifically, the term refers to the traditional method of singing the psalms [see *Chanting]. In the *Anglican chant the monophonic recitations of the Gregorian psalmody are replaced by settings in four-part harmony.

Chantant [F.]. In a singing style.

Chanter. See *Bagpipe.

Chanterelle [F.]. See *Cantino.

Chantey. See *Shanty.

Chanting. The ecclesiastical singing of the psalms and canticles in the daily offices of the Roman Catholic and, in particular, of the Anglican Church. It is character- ized by the use of a melody, called psalm tone, which is repeated with every verse of the psalm but which can be adapted to the different lengths of the verses by the iteration of the same tone, the recitation tone. The psalm tones of the Latin, Gre- gorian, rite are monophonic and in free rhythm. The "Anglican" chants are har- monized and in strict meter. The Angli- can Church, however, makes frequent use of the Gregorian chant also. See *Psalm tones; *Anglican chant.

Chanty. See *Shanty.

Chapel [F. *chapelle*; G. *Kapelle*; It. *cappella*]. The term, which is derived from It. *cappella*, i.e., cape or cloak, orig- inally denoted a building in which re- vered cloaks or other relics of saints were housed. It was later extended to denote private churches of sovereigns, popes, bishops, as well as the entire staff attached to these churches and, in particular, the musicians and singers employed there. The connotation of "private body of mu- sicians" survives in the Chapel Royal of the English kings, an institution which played a valuable part in the development and cultivation of the English music [cf. *GD* i, 606; W. H. Gratton Flood, in *ML* v]. See also *Kapelle.

Characteristic note. Leading note.

Character piece [G. *Charterstück*]. A term rarely used, yet much to be recom- mended, to cover an important branch of 19th-century music (chiefly for the piano- forte) which includes a large repertoire of short pieces published under many dif- ferent fancy names, such as Bagatelle,

Impromptu, Moment musical, Capriccio, Fantasia, etc., aside from special titles of a more or less programmatic nature, such as: Albumblatt, Der Dichter spricht (Schumann), Jeux d'eau (Ravel), The Maiden's Prayer, etc. The last title has been deliberately included here in order to hint at the vast production of third- class literature which, of course, deserves no further mention here. However, all the great composers of the 19th century have made contributions in this field, first of all Beethoven, who opens the repertoire with his Bagatelles. Schubert followed with his Impromptus and Moments mu- sicaux (musical moments), Mendelssohn with his Songs Without Words and Kin- derstücke (Children's Pieces), Chopin with his Nocturnes, Préludes, Études, Im- promptus, etc. While these composers usu- ally included a number of pieces under one collective title, R. Schumann went a good deal further toward individualiza- tion and programmatic thought by choos- ing separate names for each piece, for in- stance, in his Kinderszenen op. 15 or in his Fantasiestücke op. 12. New collective names introduced by him are: Novelletten, Nachtstücke (Night Pieces), Bunte Blät- ter (Colored Leaves), Albumblätter (Al- bum Leaves). Brahms followed with Bal- laden, Rhapsodien, Capriccios, Inter- mezzi. Briefly, the character piece is the favored and characteristic form of Ro- mantic piano music, where it serves as the vehicle of expression for every con- ceivable mood, thought, vision, or emo- tion.

Naturally, no general statements can be made with regard to so diversified and so markedly personal a repertory. How- ever, the great majority of these pieces are written in the ternary form A B A, a form which proved especially suitable for the expression of two contrasting moods, the first dramatic (A), the other lyrical (B), or vice versa.

Interesting precursors of the 19th-cen- tury character piece are found in the harp- sichord suites by Couperin who would seem to be the inventor of an important technique of this genre, i.e., the use of a certain "pianistic figure" as the basic motive of the entire piece (cf., e.g., "Les Barricades mystérieuses" from the Sixième Ordre). Many pieces by Rameau and Domenico Scarlatti fall under the same category. Cf. W. Kahl, "Das lyrische Klavierstück Schuberts . . ." (*AMW* iii).

Charivari [Am. Shivaree]. A French term, of unknown origin, which signifies a deliberately distorted and noisy performance, as is given in provincial towns before the homes of unpopular or objectionable people, or as a mock serenade for a newly married couple. A German word is *Katzenmusik* (cat music), an Italian, *scampata*. There exists — believe it or not — a book on the history of the charivari from its origins to the 4th century (!): G. Peignot, *Histoire morale, civile, politique et literaire du charivari, depuis son origine vers le IVe siècle* (1833).

Charleston. See *Jazz III.

Chasse, La [F., the hunt]. (1) Nickname for Haydn's Symphony in D, no. 73, referring to the last movement; also for his Quartet in Bb, no. 2. — (2) Name of instrumental pieces (sonatas, etc.) of the 18th and 19th centuries, written in imitation of hunting scenes.

Chaunter. See *Bagpipe.

Check. A part of the action of the *pianoforte.

Chefs d'Oeuvre Classiques de l'Opéra. See *Editions IV.

Chef d'orchestre [F.]. Conductor. *Chef d'attaque*, concertmaster.

Cheironomic. See *Chironomic.

Chekker. See *Echiquier.

Chelys [Gr., turtle]. (1) Greek name for the *lyre, the body of which was frequently made from the shell of a turtle. —(2) Sixteenth-century humanistic name for the lute. See *Testudo.

Cheng. (1) A Chinese string instrument, similar to the *Ch'in. — (2) Incorrect spelling for the Chinese mouth organ *sheng.

Chest of viols. A set of six or more viols, usually including two trebles, two tenors, and two basses, which, in the 17th century, were kept in a chest with several partitions. Cf. Th. Mace's *Musick's Monument* (1676), 245. See *Consort.

Chest voice. The lowest register of a voice [see *Register (2)].

Cheute [F.]. French name for ornamental tones in the character of a passing tone (such as occur in the *arpègement figuré*; see *Arpeggio) or of an anticipation (*Nachschlag).

Chevalet [F.]. Bridge of violins, etc. See *Bowing (k).

Chevé system. A system of musical notation, invented by the French doctor E. Chevé (1804–64), and much used in France for teaching purposes. It combines the principle of the Movable Do with the old idea of indicating notes by figures (Spanish keyboard tablature of Cabezon, 1572 [see *Tablature II]; Jean Jacques Rousseau, 1742; Pierre Galin, 1817). The figures 1 to 7 represent the tones of the scale (in any given key); lower or higher octaves are indicated by a dot under or above the figures. A rest is indicated by o. Cf. E. Chevé, *Méthode elementaire de la musique vocale* (1846); *WoHN* ii, 403.

Cheville [F.]. Peg of stringed instruments. *Cheviller*, peg-box.

Chevrotement [F., from *chèvre*, goat]. Unsteadiness in singing, like the bleating of a goat. See also under *Tremolo (3) and *Vibrato (2).

Chiamata [It., call; F. *chamade*]. In Venetian operas of the 17th century, pieces written in imitation of the "call" after the finish of the hunt. See H. Kretzschmar, in *VMW* viii.

Chiaramente [It.]. Clearly, distinctly.

Chiarenzana. A rare 16th-century lute dance in quick triple meter. Examples occur in Marcantonio de Pifaro, *Intabulatura de lauto* (1546).

Chiave [It.]. Clef.

Chiavette, chiave trasportata [It.]. A late-16th-century system of writing vocal music with all the clefs moved up or down from their normal position, usually a third (e.g. the F-clef on the third or the fifth line). The chiavette might be considered the vocal analogon to the transposing instrument of the orchestra. Ex. 1 meant to the singer: c–e–g; how-

Chiavette

ever, the conductor gave the pitch a third lower (a, or ab), so that the actual sound was: A–c♯–e, or Ab–c–eb. (It will easily be noted that *absolute pitch would have been a severe handicap to the a-cappella singers of the Palestrina period.) The just mentioned notation is called "high chiavette," because the notation is higher than the actual sound. An example of the "low chiavette" (which is much more rarely used) would be as illustrated under Ex. 2 (actual sound: e–g♯–b). The transcription into modern notation of pieces written in chiavette is very simple; the notes remain in the same position on the staff, the clef is moved to its normal position, and the proper signature (A or A-flat for high chiavette; E or E-flat for low chiavette) is added [see Ex. 3].

Examples of pieces notated in the chiavette (i.e., with all the clefs moved down or moved up) are frequent between 1550 and 1600 (Palestrina, *Missa Papae Marcelli*; Tavernor-Tye, motet *O splendor*; Josquin, *De profundis*, cf. *RiHM* ii.1, 258). According to the above interpretation such pieces would actually be in the key of A or of A-flat. It should be noted, however, that recent scholars (Ehrmann) have denied the transposing effect of the chiavette, contending that the clefs were moved down only in order to avoid the use of ledger lines. According to this interpretation, the chiavette notation would

simply mean a change of clef [see Ex. 4]. Others (Kroyer) have insisted upon the transposing interpretation (i.e., change of pitch), at least as a possibility. In a way the whole question is futile since it depends entirely upon the absolute pitch of the 16th century about which nothing is known, and which, for that matter, probably did not exist. At any rate, the importance of the chiavette has been greatly exaggerated in scholarly studies as well as in books for instruction.

Lit.: Th. Kroyer, *Der vollkommene Partiturspieler* (1931); *id.*, in *Adler-Festschrift* (1930); *id.*, in *ZMW* xiii; A. Schering, in *ZMW* xiii; E. Ehrmann, in *StM* ix.

Chiesa [It., church]. In Baroque music, *da chiesa* indicates instrumental pieces (sonatas) or vocal pieces with instrumental accompaniment (cantatas) which are designed for use in the church, in contradistinction to similar pieces for domestic use, designated *da *camera*. See *Sonata B, II.

Chifonie [F.]. Medieval (12th–15th centuries) corruption of *symphonia, i.e., *hurdy-gurdy.

Chilean music. During the colonial period music in Chile was cultivated less as an art than as an adjunct of social, civil, and religious functions. There was no outstanding musical figure during this period. In the era of Independence, the first composer worthy of note was Manuel Robles (1780–1837), who composed the original national anthem of Chile, the so-called *Canción Nacional* (1820). Though this song enjoyed wide popularity, it was displaced as the official national anthem by the *Himno Patriótico* (1828), written by the celebrated Spanish composer Ramón Carnicer at the request of the Chilean ambassador in London, where Carnicer was then living as a political exile. This *Himno Patriótico* remains the official anthem of Chile. The best-known Chilean composer of the 19th century was José Zapiola (1804–85), clarinetist and bandmaster, who in 1839 composed a highly popular patriotic song,

Himno de Yunguay. In 1842 he founded a symphony orchestra in Santiago and in 1864 was appointed choirmaster of the cathedral there. Other important musical pioneers were Federico Guzmán (1837–85), pianist and composer of over 200 works in Romantic style; Guillermo Frick (1813–96), amateur composer and founder of the Club Musical of Valdivia; and Francisco Oliva, from 1860 director of the National Conservatory (founded in 1850).

Chile occupies a prominent place in the contemporary musical scene of South America, thanks to a notable group of composers born in the 1880's and '90's. Most of these composers, while not neglecting "pure" or abstract music, have imbued their works with national traits derived largely from Chilean folk music. The dean of this nationalist school is Humberto Allende (b. 1885), who studied at the National Conservatory in Santiago and has been active as a teacher of violin and composition. Among his major compositions are the symphonic poems *Escenas Campesinas Chilenas* and *La Voz de las Calles*, and *Tres Tonadas* for soli, chorus, and orchestra. Among his piano works, the *Tonadas de carácter popular chileno* have been widely played. He has also written a violin concerto, chamber music (incl. a String Quartet, 1926), songs, etc. His younger brother, Adolfo Allende (b. 1892), is also esteemed as a composer. Carlos Isamitt (b. 1885), who is both painter and composer, has written a notable orchestral work entitled *Friso Araucano* (the Araucanian Indians were the indigenous inhabitants of Chile), some chamber music (incl. 3 string quartets), *Childhood Scenes* for piano, etc. Samuel Negrete (b. 1893), Hector Melo (b. 1899), Prospero Bisquerrt (b. 1881), Alfonso Leng (b. 1884), Carlos Lavín (b. 1883), and Enrique Soro (b. 1884) are other notable composers. Most promising of the younger composers are Jorge Urrutia (b. 1905), René Amengual (b. 1911), and Alfonso Letelier (b. 1912).

Domingo Santa Cruz Wilson (b. 1899) is the leader of organized musical activity in Chile as well as an outstanding composer in the modern vein. A pupil of Soro in Chile and of Del Campo in Spain, he founded the Bach Society of Chile and in 1933 became dean of the faculty of fine arts of the University of Chile. He is also professor of composition and musicology at the National Conservatory, and since 1940 president of the newly-created Institute of Musical Extension, which centralizes and controls virtually the whole of Chile's concert activity (orchestra, chorus, chamber music, and ballet). As a composer Santa Cruz has written a Suite for Strings, a string quartet, choruses, *Cinco Poemas Trágicos* for piano, songs, etc. His music has depth and distinction, with polytonal tendencies.

Chile's principal conductor is Armando Carvajal (b. 1893), director of the National Symphony Orchestra. Claudio Arrau (b. 1904) is the best-known Chilean pianist, while the younger pianist Arnaldo Tapia-Caballero has gained favorable recognition.

There is no indigenous influence in the popular music of Chile, since the descendants of the aboriginal inhabitants have remained in isolation, preserving their own arts and customs instead of mixing with the Spanish population.

Chilean dances are the *cueca and the *esquinazo.

Lit.: E. Pereira Salas, *Los orígenes del arte musical en Chile* (Santiago, 1941); H. Allende, "Chilean Folk Music" (*Bull. of the Pan American Union*, vol. 65, no. 9); N. Slonimsky, "Chilean Composers" (*Musical America*, vol. 63, no. 10); C. S. Smith, "The Composers of Chile" (*MM* xix, no. 1).   G. C.

Chimes. See *Percussion instruments A, 5. The term is also loosely used for a set of bells (gongs, etc.) and for the orchestral *glockenspiel. Cf. W. W. Starmer, in *PMA* xxxiv, xxxvi.

Chiming. See under *Bell.

Ch'in. An important traditional instrument of the Chinese and of the Japanese, who call it *koto*. It is frequently referred to as "Chinese lute," although actually it is a long zither, consisting of a lengthy and slightly convex board over which seven silken strings are stretched. They are tuned: c d f g a c′ d′. Underneath the lowest string 13 places for stopping are marked by inlaid studs in a very peculiar arrangement, that is, symmetrically disposed from the center to the right and to the left in the following distances: ½, ⅓, ¼, ⅕, ⅖, ⅙, and ⅛ to one side, hence: ⅔, ¾, ⅗, ⅘, ⅚, ⅞ to the other. The resulting tones are as follows:

peror, Huang-Ti, around 2700 B.C. One of the most remarkable characteristics of the Chinese system is the existence of a principal tone of absolute pitch, the so-called *huang chung* (yellow bell; see *Blasquinte), which was considered a cosmologic and sacred element of music as well as the very foundation of the state and the people. During several centuries, the extinction of a dynasty was invariably ascribed to their failure to secure the true

Vibratory Length:	1	$\frac{7}{8}$	$\frac{5}{6}$	$\frac{4}{5}$	$\frac{3}{4}$	$\frac{2}{3}$	$\frac{3}{5}$	$\frac{1}{2}$	$\frac{2}{5}$	$\frac{1}{3}$	$\frac{1}{4}$	$\frac{1}{5}$	$\frac{1}{6}$	$\frac{1}{8}$
Frequency:	1	$\frac{8}{7}$	$\frac{6}{5}$	$\frac{5}{4}$	$\frac{4}{3}$	$\frac{3}{2}$	$\frac{5}{3}$	2	$\frac{5}{2}$	3	4	5	6	8
Pitch:	c	d*	e♭	e	f	g	a	c′	e′	g′	c″	e″	g″	c‴

(The d* is higher than that of our scale.)

Actually, the high notes of this series are not sounded, since the places to the right side of the above scheme are used only for the production of *harmonics, similar to those of the violin. Since, with this sort of touch, stopping at ⅕ produces the same pitch as ordinary stopping at ⅘, the tones of the right half actually duplicate those of the left half, but with a different timbre. The playing of the ch'in is a highly complicated technique, involving many peculiarities such as glissando, vibrato, pulling of the strings toward the player or away from him, tapping, etc. The koto is a similar instrument, usually with 13 strings. [Illustration on p. 823.] Cf. R. H. von Gulick, "The Lore of the Chinese Lute" (*Monumenta Nipponica*, i, ii, iii, 1938–40); *SaHMI*, 187f.

Chinese crescent. See *Crescent.

Chinese music. I. History. The music of China presents the singular picture of a traceable history of about 4000 years. Considering the — no less singular — traditionalism and conservatism of Chinese culture in general, there is no reason to distrust reports according to which it reaches back into the third millennium B.C., although modern research has placed doubt on the legend that the system of Chinese music was established by Ling-Lun, at the time of the Yellow Em-

huang chung; therefore, to new rulers it was a matter of prime concern to regain the exact measurement of the bamboo pipe of absolute pitch. The political and social importance of music was emphasized particularly by Confucius (551–478 B.C.) whose teaching anticipates in a striking manner the Platonic theory regarding the relationship between music and social order [see *Aesthetics of music II]. Numerical symbolism (e.g., the sacred number four, or the number twelve; see below) played a prominent part in Chinese musical theory, as in Chinese culture in general. In the centuries after Confucius the occupation with music, poetry, and other arts became so prevalent that the Emperor Shi Huang-ti, in 246 B.C., ordered all music books and instruments to be destroyed, in order to prevent a general neglect of practical affairs, agricultural, social, political, etc. This order caused the complete loss of innumerable priceless manuscripts as well as a severe setback of musical activity and development. Fortunately, the Emperors of the Han Dynasty (206 B.C.–A.D. 220) again favored music, which reached its classical period under the T'ang Dynasty (618–907) and the Sung Dynasty (960–1279). It is in this period that huge orchestras, numbering 300 or more instruments, were used for ritual and courtly music. The gamelang of present-day *Javanese music may well be a modest remainder and reminder of such performances. Very little information regarding the recent development of Chinese music is available. One of the few data is the theoretical establishment of well-tempered tuning by the Prince Tsai-yu, in 1596 [see *Temperament III]. In general, however, musical development would seem to have been declining or stagnating during the past three centuries, sinking from its former level as a great spiritual and political factor to a cheap and somewhat noisy entertainment for the masses [see below, III].

II. *Tonal System.* From the principal tone huang chung, represented subsequently by f (the actual pitch was, according to recent studies, between D and Eb), others are derived by means of bamboo tubes, called *lü*, the length of which is alternately in the relation of 2:4 and 4:3 to that of the preceding tube. Since 2:3 gives the higher fifth, 4:3 the lower fourth, the following series of tones (also called *lü*) results [see also under *Panpipes (p'sai hsiao)]:

The result is a cycle of fifths, identical with that of the Pythagorean system. The first five lü's, f–c′–g–d′–a, are the basis of Chinese music from the earliest eras to the present day. They lead to an anhemitonic penta-scale, f g a c′ d′, which was later (possibly as early as 1550 B.C.) broadened by the admission into actual music of the next two tones which form half-tones, called *pien*:

kung	shang	chiao	pien-chih
f	g	a	(b)
chi	yü	pien-kung	kung
c′	d′	(e′)	f′

Already in the earliest known writing on music, by Lü Pu Wei (*c.* 320 B.C.), the fifths are interpreted as pure fifths (3:2), possibly under Greek influence (Pythagoras). In the first century A.D. the Pythagorean comma was discovered, and the series of consecutive fifths was con-

tinued up to 60 and even 360 lü's until finally it became clear that this series never returns to its initial point. In theory, a very close approximation to the well-tempered 12-tone scale was established as early as the 5th century.

In Chinese music (especially of the sacred and traditional type) the principle of transposition is of prime importance. Melodies are played in one or the other lü (i.e., key) according to the month and the hour, each numbering twelve (the Chinese hour is a double-hour). Moreover, each melody belongs to one of five "modes," according to its center tone which may be any of the five fundamental tones.

III. *Musical Practice.* For a general survey, Chinese music may be divided into four classes: sacred music, chamber music, folk music, and operatic music. Music of the first type shows many features of an age-old tradition. A number of ancient hymns are preserved, all of which proceed in long-held tones of equal duration, usually in large intervals of the pentatonic scale [Ex. 2; cf. *AdHM*, 13].

Formerly, possibly already in the pre-Christian era, these hymns were accompanied by a large orchestral body (120 harps, 180 lutes, 200 mouth organs [see *sheng], 20 oboes, drums, bells, and chimes are mentioned in a description referring to the Tang Dynasty, A.D. 618–907), probably with the employment of parallel fourths and fifths, as in the medieval organum, and with the percussion-instruments supplying a monotonous rhythmic background [*LavE* 1.1, p. 124]. Rhythm, measures, and phrases almost invariably are arranged in groups of four. The Chinese chamber music, performed on the traditional instruments *ch'in* (a zither) and *p'ip'a* (a lute) is the most highly developed type of Chinese music [see Ex. 3]. The traditional opera, which goes back to the 14th century, is serious and restrained [see Lit., Kwan-chi Wang]. Today it is largely replaced by a popular type of opera which originated about 1850 and which is rather vulgar and noisy. Aside from this, music lives in China mainly as folk song and as cere-

monial music for weddings, funerals, etc. Example in *HAM*, 1.

IV. *Instruments*. Chinese musical instruments are traditionally classified into eight groups according to the material from which they are made: gourd (mouth organ, *sheng); bamboo (panpipe, *t'sai hsiao); wood (*chu, a wooden percussion instrument in the form of a trough); silk (zither, *ch'in and shê, both provided with strings from silk); clay (globular flutes, hsüan); metal (bell, chung; bell chimes, pien chung); stone (sonorous stone, ch'ing; stone chimes, pien ch'ing); and skin (drums, po fu). Particularly characteristic of the ancient and ritual music are the chimes made from stones (frequently in the shape of an L) or from bells of identical shape but differing in thickness. Such a chime usually consists of 16 stones or bells suspended in two horizontal rows from a rectangular stand. The upper row is tuned to the male, the lower to the female series of tones [see the explanation under *panpipes].

V. Finally it may be mentioned that the Chinese language belongs to the category of "tone-languages," i.e., a language which depends on certain inflections of

pitch for the conveying of the proper meaning of its words or syllables. The four basic inflections are a level, a rising, a falling, and a rising plus falling tone, and one and the same syllable has entirely different meanings according to whether one or the other of the above inflections is used for its pronunciation [cf. G. Herzog, in *MQ* xx].

Lit.: Sophia Chen Zen, *Symposium on Chinese Culture* (1931; article "Music" by Y. R. Chao); J. H. Lewis, *Foundations of Chinese Musical Art* (1936); J. A. van Aalst, *Chinese Music* (1884, 1933); Père Amiot, *Mémoires . . . sur la musique chinoise* (Peking, 1780); L. Laloy, *La Musique chinoise* (1914); G. Soulie, *La Musique en Chine* (1911); E. Fischer, *Beiträge zur Erforschung der Chinesischen Musik* (1910; also in *SIM* xii); Kwan-chi Wang, *Ueber die chinesische klassische Oper* (Diss. Bern 1934); Liu T'ien Hua, †*Selections from the Repertoire . . . of Mei Lan-fang* (1929); Chung Sik Keh, *Koreanische Musik* (Diss. Basle 1934); *AdHM*, 13ff; *LavE* i.1, 77; A. Dechevrens, "Etude sur le système musical chinois" (*SIM* ii); J. Yasser, "Rhythmical Structure of Chinese Tunes" (*Musical Courier* 88, 1924); A. Tcherenine, "Music in Modern China" (*MQ* xxi); E. M. v. Hornbostel, "Ch'ao-t'ien-tze, eine chinesische Notation" (*AMW* i); R. W. Marks, "The Music and Musical Instruments of Ancient China" (*MQ* xviii).

Chinese pavilion. See *Crescent.

Chironomic [from G. *cheir*, hand]. A term used with reference to neumes lacking clear indication of pitch, the inference being that such signs were interpreted to the choir by hand signs of the conductor [see *Neumes II]. See also *Conducting III.

Chitarra. Italian name for guitar. *Chitarrina* is a smaller type, used in Naples.

Chitarrone [It., great *chitarra]. See *Lute III.

Chiuso [It., closed]. In horn playing, same as stopped; see *Horn I. In 14th-century music, see *Ouvert and clos.

Choir. A body of church singers, as opposed to the secular chorus. The name is also used with reference to instrumental groups of the orchestra, e.g., the brass choir, the string choir, the wood-wind choir.

Choir-book [G. *Chorbuch*]. The large-sized manuscripts of 15th- and 16th-century polyphonic music which were placed on a stand and from which the whole choir (about 15 singers) sang. See the pictures in *BeMMR*, 234, 248. For choir-book arrangement [G. *Chorbuch-anord-nung*] see under *Score II. See also *Cantus lateralis.

Choir-organ. Originally a small organ such as is suitable for the acompaniment of the choir. Today the name is usually applied to the third manual of the normal organ which is provided with stops useful for accompanying purposes. See *Organ III.

Choir pitch. See *Pitch 2.

Chomonie. See *Anenaiki.

Chor [G.]. A chorus or a choir.

Choral, chorale. In view of the different meanings and of the confusing usage of these terms a few general explanations are needed. According to Webster, the word choral has two meanings, depending upon its accentuation: cho′ral (adj.) means: pertaining to a chorus or a choir: choral′ (noun) means a hymn tune, a sacred tune. For the latter meaning, the spelling chorale is given as second choice. Although, as a rule, this dictionary follows the first choice of Webster, the spelling chorale is adopted here because it makes possible a written distinction between the two meanings. Thus, a choral fantasia is a fantasia employing a chorus, whereas a chorale fantasia is a fantasia which is based on a hymn tune. Unfortunately, the situation is further complicated by the fact that the word chorale usually refers to the hymn tunes of the German Protestant Church which in German are called *Choral* (accent on the last syllable), while, on the other hand, the

equivalent of the English adjective choral is the German noun *Chor-* (united to the noun which it precedes). Thus, we have the following equivalents: E. choral fantasia — G. *Chorfantasie*; E. chorale fantasia — G. *Choralfantasie*. Similarly: choral cantata — *Chorkantate*; chorale cantata — *Choralkantate*.

Choral [G.]. (1) The plainsong of the Catholic Church, usually called *Gregorianischer Choral* [see *Gregorian chant]. Derivatives are: *Choralnotation* (*plainsong notation), *Choralnote* (plainsong note), and *Choralrhythmus* (plainsong rhythm). — (2) The hymn tunes of the German Protestant Church [see *Chorale]. Derivatives are: *Choralbearbeitung* (this term may also apply to the Gregorian *Choral*), *Choralfantasie* (chorale fantasia), *Choralkantate* (chorale cantata), *Choralpartita* (chorale partita), *Choralvorspiel* (chorale prelude).

Choralbearbeitung [G., chorale treatment, chorale composition]. Generic term for any composition based upon a *Choral* (chorale). The term chiefly refers to the various methods of composition applied to the Protestant chorales in the period from 1600 to 1750 [see *Chorale cantata, *Chorale fantasia, *Chorale prelude, *Chorale partita, *Organ chorale]; however, it also includes the 15th- and 16th-century settings of Catholic hymns (vocal settings by Dunstable, Dufay, Adam von Fulda, Heinrich Finck; organ settings by Schlick, Cavazzoni, Cabezon, M. Praetorius, Titelouze).

Choral cantata [G. *Chorkantate*]. A cantata which employs a chorus (as most cantatas by Bach do), in contradistinction to a solo cantata (the usual type of the 17th-century Italian cantata). For the German term *Choralkantate* see *Chorale cantata.

Chorale [G. *Choral*]. The hymn tunes of the German Protestant Church. The term *Choral* is also used to denote the Gregorian chant (Gregorianischer Choral), but this meaning is not generally accepted into English usage. The importance of the Protestant chorale lies in the central position it holds in the German music of the Baroque, as the basis of numerous cantatas and the whole tradition of the organ chorale.

The evolution of the Protestant chorale started with Martin Luther (1483–1546), the founder of the Protestant Church (1519). Luther, a rather accomplished musician himself, considered the chorale as one of the most important pillars of his reform movement and played a very active part in the building of a repertory of texts and melodies suitable for his purpose. In conformity with his principle of congregational participation, he favored vernacular texts and simple, tuneful melodies. In his search for suitable texts Luther chiefly resorted to the Catholic hymns, many of which he (or his collaborators) translated into German, e.g.: "Nun komm der Heiden Heiland" ("Veni redemptor gentium"); "Herr Gott Dich loben wir" ("*Te deum laudamus"); "Der Tag der ist so freudenreich" ("Dies est laetitiae"); "Wir glauben all an einen Gott" ("Credo in unum deum patrem omnipotentem"), etc. The chief sources for his melodies were secular folk songs which he or his collaborators provided with new (sacred) texts ["geistliche Contrafactur"; see *Parody]. Examples of chorale melodies borrowed from folk songs are: "Durch Adams Fall ist ganz verderbt" (from the Pavia song: "Freut euch, freut euch in dieser Zeit"); "Von Gott will ich nicht lassen" (from a love song: "Einmal tat ich spazieren"); "Was mein Gott will, das g'scheh' allzeit" (from the chanson: "Il me suffit de tous mes maulx," published by Attaingnant, 1529); "Auf meinen lieben Gott" (from Regnart's "Venus du und dein Kind").

The earliest sources of Protestant chorales are three publications of Luther's friend and collaborator Johann Walther (1496–1570), all from 1524: the so-called "Achtliederbuch" (containing 8 poems to four melodies; original title: *Etlich christlich lider Lobgesang ... in der Kirchen zu singen*) and two volumes *Enchiridion oder eyn Handbüchlein ...* with 25 poems to 15 melodies. In these books as well as in those published by Klug (Wittenberg, 1529, 1535, 1543), Blum (Leipzig, 1530), Schumann (Leipzig, 1530), and Babst (Leipzig, 1545, 1553), only melodies are given and these were sung by the congregation in unison. Many of the most beautiful chorales still sung today are found in these early books. It should be noted, however, that their original form shows a much less conventionalized and, for that matter, a much more impressive rhythmic form than that of the present day. Especially interesting is the irregularity of phrasing and meter [example in *AdHM* i, 448].

The year 1524 also marks the beginning of musical composition based upon the Protestant chorales. Joh. Walther's *Geystliches Gesangk Büchleyn* [see *Editions XXVI, 7] contains 38 polyphonic settings (three to six voices) of such melodies in the style of the Flemish motet, i.e., with the melody in the tenor and with occasional imitation in the contrapuntal voices [expl. in *HAM*, no. 111; *AdHM* i, 449]. Similar publications are: G. Rhaw, *Newe deudsche geistliche Gesenge* ... (1544; *DdT* 34) and Spangenberg, *Kirchengesenge Deudtsch* ... (1545). The involved polyphonic texture of these pieces naturally excludes the possibility of congregational performance or even participation. A decisive step toward fuller realization of Luther's ideal was made by Lukas Osiander (1543–1604) in his *Funffzig geistliche Lieder und Psalmen* (1586). Here the melody was placed in the discant and a simple homophonic style was adopted for the accompanying parts. His example was followed by Sethus Calvisius [*Harmonia cantionum ecclesiasticarum* ... (1597)], Hans Leo Hassler [*Kirchengesänge, Psalmen und geistliche Lieder ... simpliciter gesetzt* (1608)], and Samuel Scheidt [*Tabulaturbuch hundert geistlicher Lieder* (1650)].

The 17th century shows continued activity in the creation of chorale melodies (monophonic as well as polyphonic or with *figured bass), although generally with inferior results. The tunes do not possess the originality and forcefulness of the earlier ones, becoming more sentimental and conventionalized. Nonetheless, the tradition of the chorale was sufficiently strong to prevent it from becoming subdued by the superficialities of the operatic maelstrom, and composers such as Johannes Crüger (1598–1662), Johannes Schop (d. 1664), Johann Georg Ebeling (1637–76), Jakob Hintze (1662–1702), Johann Rudolph Ahle (1625–73), contributed many fine tunes to the texts of Paul Gerhardt, Johann Rist, and others. From the artistic point of view, however, the activity in the field of *Choralbearbeitung attracts the chief interest. The cantatas, oratorios, and passions of the late 17th and early 18th centuries (especially those of Bach) contain numerous examples of vocal chorale composition in a simple homophonic style as well as in elaborate contrapuntal texture. Simultaneously, there developed the no less impressive repertoire of the *organ chorale, or, as it is usually called, chorale prelude.

To the present-day musician the chorales are best known in their harmonization by Bach. It is interesting to compare Bach's settings with, e.g., those of Samuel Scheidt, his predecessor of 100 years (b. 1587). The accompanying example (*Jesus Christus unser Heiland*; a. Scheidt, b.

Bach) shows that all the elements of Bach's method are already present in Scheidt. See *Organ chorale. Examples in *HAM*, nos. 111, 167 b, 190.

Lit.: J. Zahn, *Die Melodien der evangelischen Kirchenlieder* (6 vols., 1889); Johann Westphal, *Das evangelische Kirchenlied in geschichtlicher Entwicklung* (1911); C. Böhm, *Das deutsche evange-*

lische Kirchenlied (1927); see also the books on Bach by Spitta, Schweitzer, and C. S. Terry; G. R. Woodward, "German Hymnody . . ." (*PMA* xxxii); additional bibliography in *MoML*, 396.

Chorale cantata [G. *Choralkantate*]. A term used, usually with reference to Bach's cantatas, to denote those in which chorale texts (and, as a rule, chorale melodies also) are used for movements other than the final one which is nearly always a harmonized chorale. The following types may be distinguished [cf. W. G. Whittaker, *Fugitive Notes on Church Cantatas and Motets of J. S. Bach* (1923)]: (a) those in which chorale texts are used for all the movements; (b) those in which some of the chorale verses are recast in free poetry in order to allow for aria-like treatment; (c) those in which chorale texts are used in some movements whilst the others are free recitatives or arias. The only example of (a) is his early cantata: "Christ lag in Todesbanden"; an example of (b) is: "Ach Gott vom Himmel"; of (c), "Wachet auf," "Ein feste Burg." C. S. Terry's book, *J. S. Bach, Cantata Texts* (1925), affords an excellent insight into this question since the chorale texts are distinguished from the free texts by being printed in italics. Bach's predecessors in the use of chorale texts and melodies for cantatas were: Franz Tunder (1614–?; *DdT* 3); Johann Kindermann (1616–55; *DTB* 13); Johann Rosenmüller (1620–84; *DTB* 6); Wolfgang Briegel (1626–1712); Johann Ph. Krieger (1649–1725; *DdT* 53/54); Johann Pachelbel (1653–1706; *DTB* 6), and Johann Kuhnau (1660–1722; *DdT* 58/59).

Chorale fantasia. An organ composition in which a chorale melody is treated in the free manner of a fantasia or even an improvisation. Samuel Scheidt's *Fantasia super Ich ruf zu Dir, Herr Jesus Christ* [*DdT* 1; also in K. Straube, *Alte Orgel-Meister* (1904)], his greatest organ composition, is actually a *chorale motet. True chorale fantasias occur in the works of Buxtehude, e.g., "Nun freut euch lieben Christen g'mein," and in some early compositions of Bach ("Christ lag in Todes-

banden"; "Ein feste Burg") which show
the influence of Georg Böhm (1661–
1733), particularly in the peculiar fragmentary treatment of the chorale melody
[cf. Georg Böhm, *Sämtliche Werke*, ed.
by J. Wolgast (1927), 132, "Vater unser
im Himmelreich"]. See *Organ chorale
II.

Chorale fugue. See under *Chorale
motet.

Chorale motet. A composition in which
a chorale melody is treated in motet
style [see *Motet II], i.e., as a succession
of fugal sections, each based on one of the
successive lines of the chorale. Examples
abound in vocal music (first movements
of Bach's Cantatas nos. 16, 27, 58, 60, 73,
95, etc.) as well as in organ music where
the chorale motet forms one of the principal types of organ chorale. Compositions
of the described kind are often referred to
as "chorale fugue" [G. *Choralfuge*].
Since, however, the basic structure is that
of the 16th-century motet rather than that
of the Baroque fugue, the former term
would seem to be more appropriate. Examples of true chorale fugues based on
one theme only (usually the opening motive of the chorale) occur among Bach's
organ chorales (e.g., "Gottes Sohn ist
kommen"). On account of their shortness
they are also called fughettas. See *Organ
chorale II.

Chorale partita. Variations [see *Par-
tita] for organ on a chorale melody.
Bach wrote several such sets which are
among the most remarkable compositions
of his pre-Leipzig period. In fact, their
style is sufficiently mature to raise doubts
as to whether they belong to his period of
"früheste Jugendzeit," as Spitta and
Schweitzer have contended. Many examples of the same type occur in the organ
works of Buxtehude, Pachelbel, Georg
Böhm (1661–1733), Johann Gottfried
Walther (1684–1748), and others [cf.
their complete works; also K. Straube,
Choralvorspiele alter Meister]. The number of variations is usually that of the
number of stanzas of the chorale; sometimes the character of a variation expresses

the textual meaning of the corresponding
stanza. A recent example of chorale partita is E. Krenek's variations on "Ja ich
glaub an Jesum Christum" (*Toccata und
Chaconne*, op. 13) in which the chorale is
treated as an Allemande, Sarabande, Gavotte, Walzer, Fugue, and Foxtrot (*sic!*).
The impression of sacrilege conveyed by
this procedure may be somewhat lessened
by the reference to what may have been
Krenek's model, namely, Buxtehude's
variations on "Auf meinen lieben Gott,"
which consist of an Allemande, Sarabande,
Courante, and Gigue, thus forming one
of the numerous examples of the 17th-
century fusion of variation and suite [see
*Variations IV(b)].

Chorale prelude [G. *Choralvorspiel*].
An organ composition based on a Protestant chorale and designed to be played
before the chorale is sung by the congregation. Because of the close historical connection between the Protestant chorale
prelude and the earlier organ hymns of
the Catholic service — which cannot be
considered as "preludes" — the whole
matter is treated under the heading *organ chorale.

Chorale variation. See *Chorale partita.

Choralfuge, Choralmotette [G.].
See *Chorale motet.

Choralis Constantinus. A cycle of
liturgical compositions for the entire ecclesiastical year, written by H. Isaac (*c.*
1450–1517) for the Cathedral of Constanz
(Switzerland). The first part [*DTOe* 5.i]
contains compositions of the Proper of the
Mass [see *Mass B, I], the second [*DTOe*
16.i], compositions for the Office of the
main feasts and of special saints. Cf. A.
zur Nedden, in *ZMW* xii; P. Blaschke, in
KJ, 1931.

Choralrhythmus [G.]. The rhythmic
interpretation of the "Gregorian chorale,"
i.e., of Gregorian chant [see *Gregorian
chant VI].

Choral Symphony. Popular name for
Beethoven's Ninth Symphony in D mi-

nor, op. 125, composed in 1823/24. The name refers to the use of a chorus for the last movement which begins with an instrumental introduction leading through a recitative: "O Freunde, nicht diese Töne" to a gigantic composition for chorus and orchestra of Schiller's poem: Freude, schöner Götterfunken. The original title is: Sinfonie mit Schlusschor über Schiller's Ode: "An die Freude," für grosses Orchester, 4 Solo- und 4 Chorstimmen.

Chorbuch [G.]. See *Choir-book.

Chord. The simultaneous occurrence of several tones, usually three or more. The chords can be divided into two main classes, consonant and dissonant chords. To the former belong the major and minor *triad and their *inversions, i.e., the *sixth-chord and the *six-four-chord; to the latter all the others, e.g., the *seventh-chord, the *ninth-chord, the augmented sixth-chord, and the numerous strongly dissonant formations of recent music, many of which are derived from the *fourth-chord [see also *Mystic chord]. The study of the chords, their relationships and functions, forms an important field of music theory called *harmonic analysis. See also *Consonance and dissonance II.

Chordal style. A style in which chords play a prominent role; see *Texture. In strict chordal style there is a given number of parts, usually four (e.g., a hymn tune); in free chordal style there is no such restriction (e.g., Chopin's Prélude no. 20). See also *Familiar style; *Homophonic.

Chorea [Gr., dance]. In medieval writings, a dancing song [Joh. de Grocheo, c. 1300; Robert de Handlo, 1326, cf. CS i, 402]. In the late 16th century, *chorea* is a generic term for dance; it is used for the *allemande [cf. Besardus, *Thesaurus Harmonicus* (1603): "Choreae quas Allemande vocant germanico"], for the *pavane [B. de Drusina, 1556], and other dances.

Chorister. A boy singer of an English choir. Cf. *GD* i, 641.

Chorlied [G.]. Choral song, particularly without accompaniment (Schumann, Mendelssohn, and others).

Chororgel [G.]. Choir organ.

Chorton [G.]. See *Pitch (2).

Chorus. (1) A large body of singers, not connected with a church [see *Choir]. Also music for such a body. — (2) Medieval Latin name for the *crwth or for the *bagpipe [cf. *SaRM*, 80].

Chorwerk, Das. See *Editions, Historical, V.

Christmas Oratorio [G. *Weihnachtsoratorium*]. Bach's Christmas Oratorio, composed in 1734, consists of 6 church cantatas, not intended to be performed in immediate succession, but on six different days, from Christmas Day to Epiphany. Most famous is the Pastoral Symphony from the second day and the aria "Schlafe mein Liebster" following upon it. A number of the pieces contained in the oratorio are borrowed from earlier cantatas. An important forerunner of Bach's work is H. Schütz's Christmas Oratorio, entitled: *Historia der freuden- und gnadenreichen Geburt Gottes und Mariens Sohn Jesu Christi* (1664). The edition by Spitta in vol. i of Schütz's complete works was completed (on the basis of newly discovered material) by A. Schering who also edited a score for practical use.

Chroai [Gr., colors]. In ancient Greek theory, the microtonic modifications of the two movable tones of the tetrachord. Aristoxenos mentions, in addition to the enharmonic tetrachord which divides the three whole tones of the fourth (a to e downwards) into the steps $2 + \frac{1}{4} + \frac{1}{4}$, divisions such as $1\frac{1}{4} + \frac{3}{4} + \frac{1}{2}$ (variant of the diatonic tetrachord $1 + 1 + \frac{1}{2}$) and $1\frac{5}{6} + \frac{1}{3} + \frac{1}{3}$ or $1\frac{3}{4} + \frac{3}{8} + \frac{3}{8}$ (variants of the chromatic tetrachord $1\frac{1}{2} + \frac{1}{2} + \frac{1}{2}$). These schemes probably represent attempts on the part of theorists to rationalize microtones such as occur in Oriental melodies, or in the playing of the *aulos. Cf. *RiHM* i.1, 218; Th. Reinach, *La Musique grecque* (1926), p. 20 ("Nuances").

Chromatic. The adjective is used in the following connections: (1) chromatic scale [see *Chromaticism]. — (2) Chromatic tetrachord or genus [see *Greek music II(b)]. — (3) Chromatic instruments are instruments capable of producing all (or nearly all) the tones of the chromatic scale. Thus, chromatic horn is the name of the valve horn, as distinct from the natural horn. For chromatic harp see *Harp. — (4) In the 16th century the word *cromatico* refers occasionally, not to the use of semitones, but to the employment of the black notes, *minima*, *semiminima*, *fusa* (or *croma*), *semifusa* (or *semicroma*), i.e., of the smallest values, corresponding to our 8th, 16th notes, etc. The term *madrigale cromatico* therefore simply means: madrigal in quicker movement (quicker than the earlier type, written in motet-like style). Occasionally, the term refers to the use of blackened notes instead of the normally white shapes (*brevis, semibrevis*; see *Coloration). This manner of writing was but an affectation meant to portray in "eye-music" such words as "night," "dark." Cf. A. Einstein, in *ZIM* xiv.

Chromaticism (from Gr. *chroma*, color]. The use of tones extraneous to the diatonic scale, e.g., in C major: c–d–d♯–e or c–d♯–e, instead of the *diatonic progression: c–d–e. The chromatic or diatonic character of a tone is frequently conditioned by harmonic considerations. For instance in the progression: c–e–f♯–g the tone f♯ is chromatic if the harmony stays on C, diatonic if it modulates to G. The

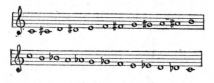

Chromatic Scale

introduction of all the chromatic tones leads to the chromatic scale [see Ex.], with twelve tones to the octave.

History. Chromaticism appeared first in Greek music (chromatic tetrachord, a–f♯–f–e; see *Greek music II(b)) prob-

ably as the result of Oriental influence [see *Aulos, *Choroi]. It is practically absent in European music prior to 1550. This statement is not contradicted by the fact that such tones as b♭, e♭, f♯ already occur in the 8th century *Musica Enchiriadis* [cf. *WoHN* i, 33], or that in the early part of the 14th century the full chromatic scale was not only discussed by theorists (Marchettus de Padua), but also found on organs (at least in the middle octave); actually, all these "chromatic" tones were not used for chromaticism but for "transposed diatonicism." True chromaticism was introduced by Adrian Willaert (*c.* 1480–1562) and his pupil Cypriano de Rore (1516–65), who, in his madrigal *Calami sonum ferentes* (1561), starts out with a chromatic subject (b–c–c♯–d–d♯–e–f♯–g) [cf. *RiHM* ii.1, 414]. Luca de Marenzio (*c.* 1560–99) and particularly Gesualdo (*c.* 1560–1614) exploited the new material harmonically (succession of chords such as A minor followed by F-sharp major, cf. *HAM*, no. 161; *SchGMB*, nos. 165, 167), experiments which had only temporary importance. In the Baroque period chromaticism is usually melodic, chromatic progressions being used mainly for two purposes: (a) for fugal subjects (Sweelinck, Frescobaldi, Kerll, and others; *SchGMB*, no. 158), particularly for counter-subjects (frequent in Bach: *Wt. Cl.* ii, no. 18; Harpsichord Fugue in A minor; the theme *B–A–C–H of the *Art of Fugue); (b) for programmatic and pictorial purposes to indicate grief or lament (very frequent in cantatas, operas, oratorios, and in instrumental program pieces; cf. *SchGMB*, nos. 177, 190, 197, 213, etc.).

In the classical period of Haydn, Mozart, and the early Beethoven chromaticism is comparatively rare, aside from the use of rapid chromatic scales in coloraturas, cadenzas, etc. It is not until Beethoven's latest works (e.g., the short slow movement of his Piano Sonata in A major, op. 101) that we find passages reminiscent of those from Bach's *Chromatic Fantasia* [see also *Harmony, Ex. 8, 9]. After Beethoven, however, a new era of chromaticism began, characterized by the exploitation of chromatically altered harmony. To describe this phase of chromaticism would be tantamount to writing a study on Romantic harmony. The examples given under *Harmony will suffice to show to what an extent chromaticism changed the appearance of music in the period from 1850 to 1900. After 1900 chromaticism lost its former connotation as a "color-modification" of diatonicism, and established itself as a tonal province in its own right, based on the equivalence of the twelve tones of the chromatic scale. This idea is clearly apparent in Debussy's *whole-tone scale. A. Schönberg, through his *twelve-tone technique, attempted a more radical solution by denying any pre-established relationship between the twelve tones or, in other words, by admitting any chordal or melodic combination of these tones as building material.

Around 1920, there began a reaction against the excessive chromaticism, whether romantic, impressionistic, or atonal (expressionistic). It found its most conspicuous manifestation in the *pandiatonicism of composers such as Stravinsky, Poulenc, and others who were influenced by Satie, the whimsical antipode of Debussy [see *Six, les].

Chromatic scale. See *Chromaticism.

Chronos, or **chronos protos** [Gr., time, "first" time]. The temporal or rhythmic unit of ancient Greek music, comparable in a way to our beat, but differing from this in the fact that it cannot be divided into smaller values and therefore constitutes a "first" or smallest unit. While the modern beat is a unit of multiplication as well as division, admitting of multiples as well as fractions of almost any note value, the *chronos* is a unit of

Cretic Meter

multiplication only, or, more properly, of addition, since irregular groupings in varying numbers are possible and typical, particularly in the Cretic meter.

The *chronos protos,* or, as it is called by French scholars, "premier temps," is also the basis of rhythm in many Oriental cultures, particularly of the Near East (Arabia, India; see *Rhythm II(b)). It also plays a fundamental part in the discussions of the rhythm of Gregorian chant [see *Gregorian chant VI).

Chrotta. See under *Crwth.

Church modes. I. The Church modes (ecclesiastical modes, or, simply, modes) are the tonal basis of the *Gregorian chant and of early music (till about 1600) in general. A church mode is an octave-segment of the diatonic (C major) scale, with one of its tones playing the role of a center tone (comparable to the tone C of the C major scale). The range of the octave is called *ambitus,* the center tone, *finalis.* In the complete system of modes there are six finales: d, e, f, g, a, c'. To each of these finales belong two modes, one whose ambitus starts with the finalis and ends at the higher octave, and another whose ambitus starts with the fourth below the finalis and extends to the fifth

above it. The former group of six modes is called *authentic,* the latter *plagal.* In the former group, the single names are: *Dorian* (finalis d; ambitus d–d'); *Phrygian* (e; e–e'); *Lydian* (f; f–f'); *Mixolydian* (g; g–g'); *Aeolian* (a; a–a'); *Ionian* (c; c–c''); in the latter the prefix hypo- is added: *Hypodorian* (d; A–a); *Hypophrygian* (e; B–b); *Hypolydian* (f; c–c′); *Hypomixolydian* (g; d–d′); *Hypoaeolian* (a; e–e′); *Hypoionian* (c; g–g′). It must be remembered that all these octaves are diatonic, that is, make use of only the white keys of the keyboard. The accompanying Ex. 1 serves as an illustration of Dorian and Hypodorian. The bracketed notes of this example designate an additional tone which was frequently admitted, the so-called *subfinalis* or *subtonium modi*. The fermatas indicate secondary center tones, called *dominant*. As a rule, the dominant is a fifth above the finalis in the authentic modes, a third above it in the plagal modes. However, the tone b which was not used as a finalis [see below, III] was also avoided as a dominant, and was replaced by c′ in the Phrygian and in the Hypomixolydian. Another exception occurs in the Hypophrygian the dominant of which is a (instead of g). Other so-called "characteristics" of the modes, such as *mediant, participant, modulation,* are of subordinate and even questionable importance [cf. *GD* i, 482]. Ex. 2 illustrates the main characteristics of the twelve modes.

II. In the various periods of the modal system different designations were used. These are shown below in a table; the

ment of the theoretical system preceded the actual writing of melodies, is in contradiction to the fundamental principles of musical development. Very likely the system of the modes did not originate until the 8th century, as an attempt to codify the large repertory of chants which had accumulated during the preceding centuries, and there is reason to believe that numerous chants were modified to conform with the theoretical system.

III. The above system of twelve modes appeared first in Glarean's *Dodekachordon* (1552). In modern writings it is sometimes enlarged by two more modes, the *Locrian* and *Hypolocrian*, based on the tone b as the finalis. However, these modes are entirely fictitious since they would involve a diminished fifth (b–f′) above the finalis. On the other hand, it is important to notice that prior to Glarean, that is, throughout the main period of the modal system (*c.* 800–1500) only the first eight of the above modes were known (cf. the terminology in the third column of our table). In fact, for the study of Gregorian chant — the most important exemplification of the church modes — only these eight modes are needed [see *Gregorian chant V*]. The eight-mode system

			Fin.	Amb.	Dom.
Dorian	Primus tonus	Protus auth.	d	d – d′	a
Hypodorian	Secundus t.	" plag.	d	A – a	f
Phrygian	Tertius t.	Deuterus auth.	e	e – e′	c′
Hypophrygian	Quartus t.	" plag.	e	B – b	a
Lydian	Quintus t.	Tritus auth.	f	f – f′	c′
Hypolydian	Sextus t.	" plag.	f	c – c′	a
Mixolydian	Septimus t.	Tetrardus auth.	g	g – g′	d′
Hypomixolydian	Octavus t.	" plag.	g	d – d′	c′
Aeolian	Nonus t.		a	a – a′	e′
Hypoaeolian	Decimus t.		a	e – e′	c′
Ionian	Undecimus t.		c′	c′ – c″	g′
Hypoionian	Duodecimus t.		c′	g – g′	e′

nomenclature of the third column is the earliest (8th–13th centuries). The designation of the authentic modes as "Ambrosian" and of the plagal modes as "Gregorian" is entirely without historical foundation. Particularly discreditable is the frequently repeated story that Ambrose "invented" the authentic modes and that Gregory "added" the plagal modes. Its inference, that the establish-

is particularly evident in the various recitation tones (*psalm tones, tones for the *Magnificat, etc.), for which eight different formulae, one in each mode, are provided. It is interesting to note that, e.g., the psalm tones do not in every respect conform with the scheme of the modes, since the finalis frequently differs from the theory; only ambitus and dominant (or, as it is called here, *repercussio, reci-*

tation-tone, tenor, tuba) are strictly observed. In fact, there is reason to believe that in the early days of plainsong (*c.* 500–900) the dominant, which is frequently touched in the melodies, was more decisive than the finalis. In order to accommodate certain melodies of Gregorian chant which were found to exceed the ambitus proper of the basic schemes, the *mixed mode* (*tonus mixtus*) was introduced, i.e., a mode which has the same finalis and dominant as the authentic mode, but the combined ambitus of the authentic and the plagal (e.g., mixed Dorian has the ambitus from A to d').

In the 17th century, French musicians adopted a new terminology for the 12 modes, applying thet erms Dorian, Phrygian, etc., to the scale degrees beginning not with D, but with C. This practice is fully explained in Ch. Guillet, *24 Fantaisies . . . disposé selon l'ordre des douze modes* (1610; new ed. in *Monumenta Musicae Belgicae* IV, 1938). It is also observed in Denis Gaultier's *La Rhétorique des Dieux* (new ed. by A. Tessier; see also O. Fleischer, in *VMW* 1886). [For other modifications of passing importance (Zarlino) cf. *RiML*, 889.]

IV. It has become customary in modern studies to treat the church modes together with the "Greek modes," considering the former as the derivatives of the latter. Such a procedure is not to be recommended. What are usually called "Greek modes" represent a phenomenon of such a complexity and one involving so many historical changes (many of which are still obscure) that summary statements are likely to be misleading rather than clarifying [see *Greek music II(c),(d)]. The most striking (though by no means the essential) difference between the Greek and the medieval systems is that in the former the names Dorian, Phrygian, Lydian, and Mixolydian (D,P,L,M) are associated with a descending series of tones, namely, e, d, c, b, while in the latter they occur in an ascending order (d, e, f, g). A (somewhat simplified) explanation of this change is that the Greek octave-segments had all one and the same "tonic," i.e., the tone *a* (*mese*) and that, by

transposing the descending segments into one and the same octave (e.g., a–a'), these "tonics" appear in an ascending order, as is shown below:

For a fuller discussion of this problem cf. *ReMMA*, 153ff.

V. As regards the use of the modes as the tonal basis of polyphonic composition, there is no evidence of methodical treatment prior to the later part of the 15th century when the *Flemish School brought about a renewed interest in the Gregorian tradition and in sacred music. Particularly the compositions of the 14th century are remarkably free in their tonality, as already appears from their liberal use of accidentals [see *Music ficta IV]. In this

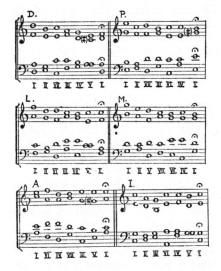

respect it is interesting to note that not until after 1500 did composers begin to write polyphonic settings of, e.g., the Magnificat in the various modes (*Magnificat primi toni*, etc.), and that designations such as *Toccata primi toni* do not occur prior to 1550 (Andrea Gabrieli). No less interesting is the fact that Glareanus, in his brilliant analyses of the compositions of Josquin and others (*Dodekachordon*) never investigates the mode of a polyphonic composition as such, but only those of the different voice parts [cf. W. Apel, *Accidentien und Tonalität* . . . (1937), p. 63, footnote]. The table on p. 147 illustrates characteristic harmonic progressions of the six authentic modes. For the role of the church modes in modern music, see *Modality (also *Mode). See also the special explanations of *Dorian, *Lydian, *Mixolydian, and *Phrygian.

Lit.: A. M. Richardson, *The Medieval Modes* (1933); books on Harmony, etc.; list of special studies in *ReMMA*, 442f. O. Ursprung, "Die antiken Transpositions-skalen und die Kirchentöne" (*AMF* v); H. E. Wooldridge, "Studies in the Technique of 16th-Century Music" (*MA* iii, iv); O. Gombosi, "Studien zur Tonartenlehre des frühen Mittelalters" (*AM* xi, xii).

Church music. The music of the Christian Churches consisted originally of *Chant. In the Eastern Churches (Byzantine, Armenian, Coptic, Syrian) it did not essentially develop beyond a stage reached in the Middle Ages, about 1000. In striking contrast to this conservatism, which eventually resulted in deterioration, is the development of music in the Roman Catholic Church which, as early as the 9th century, began to embrace polyphonic treatment, thus laying the foundation for the entire development of Western music. Following is a brief conspectus of the evolution of music of the Roman Catholic, the Anglican, and the German Protestant Church.

I. The music of the Catholic Church is rooted in the tradition of the Jewish liturgy, as already appears from the fact that the oldest portions of the Catholic service were the *psalms and the *canticles. A certain influence of Greek tradition appears in the hymns of St. Ambrose [see *Ambrosian hymns] which differ from the psalms and canticles by the strictly metrical structure of the text and by the syllabic rather than melismatic

style of the music. During the ensuing centuries a vast repertory of chants accumulated which, around 600, was standardized and made authoritative by St. Gregory [see *Gregorian chant]. Around 800, we find the first attempts to enlarge the Gregorian repertory by newly invented texts and melodies, an activity which is generally known as troping. This led to the monophonic *sequences, *tropes, and *liturgical dramas as well as, around 900, to the "polyphonic tropes," the *organa and their derivatives, the *clausulae and *motets of the 13th century. In the later part of the 13th century the motet, though still retaining its Gregorian ancestry in the cantus-firmus melody of the tenor, adopted secular (French) texts and occasionally even secular melodies [see *motet enté] for the upper parts, thus showing a first influence of elements which, from the standpoint of the Church, had to be condemned. This and other abuses of a similar nature led to the decree of Pope John XXII, issued from Avignon in 1322, by which the use not only of the sacrilegious French motets, but of all kinds of polyphonic music was forbidden, with the exception of the archaic organum in parallel fourths or fifths. It would appear that this decree had far-reaching results which, although advantageous to the aims of the Church, were detrimental to music. Indeed, the almost complete absence of sacred compositions in the French and Italian sources of the *Ars Nova may well be explained by the restrictions resulting from the edict; even as late as 1408, polyphonic music (discant) was forbidden in the Cathedral of Notre Dame in Paris [see also *fauxbourdon (1)]. The edict also interrupted the development of another type of Church music, namely the polyphonic *mass, the earliest examples of which, the Mass of Tournai (*c.* 1300) and that of Machaut (*c.* 1325?), are separated by nearly 100 years from those following next.

II. A new era of Church music began around 1425. After an interruption of 100 years, the center of musical activity again shifted back to the Church. Masses and motets became the chief forms of composers such as the English Dunstable (d. 1453), the Burgundian Dufay (1400–74), and the long series of *Flemish masters from Ockeghem (1430–95) and Obrecht (1430–1505) to Lasso (1532–94). Around 1550, Italian (Andrea Gabrieli, 1510–86; Palestrina, 1525–94) and Spanish (Morales, *c.* 1500–53; Vittoria, 1540–1611) composers appeared in successful competition with the Flemish masters, thus leading to an unparalleled acme of Catholic church music. There also started, around 1500, a remarkable development of ecclesiastical organ music, designed to supplant the choral performance of hymns, psalm-verses [see *Verset], of the Ordinary of the Mass [see *Organ Mass] and of certain chants of special importance, particularly the *Magnificat and the *antiphons B.M.V. [see *Salve regina]. Composers such as Arnolt Schlick (*c.* 1450–1527), John Redford (*c.* 1480–?), Girolamo Cavazzoni (*c.* 1500–?), Antonio de Cabezon (1510–66), made outstanding contributions in this field.

III. At the same time, however, the universal authority of the Roman Church was broken by the Reformation which, by 1550, led to the establishment of new bodies of church music, chiefly in England [see *Anglican chant] and in Germany. While the English movement found a somewhat limited artistic expression in the *anthem and in the *Service (Tallis, 1505–85; Byrd, 1543–1623; Purcell, 1658–95; Handel, 1685–1759), the German Reformation (Luther, 1483–1546) proved to be an event of the greatest consequence in music, owing chiefly to the establishment of the Protestant *chorale as a source of musical creation and inspiration, similar in character and significance to the Gregorian chant. The chorale not only brought about the great wealth of *organ chorales (Scheidt, 1587–1654; Tunder, 1614–?; Buxtehude, 1637–1707; Pachelbel, 1653–1706; Bach, 1685–1750), but also won a lasting — though gradually decreasing — influence on the *cantata, the chief type of German church music in the Baroque period [see also

*Chorale cantata]. Alongside the cantata there grew the *oratorio and the *passion, represented by a number of composers from Schütz (1585–1672) to Bach.

IV. In 17th-century Italy the tradition of Palestrina was continued by the *Roman school. More important than the activity of this conservative group was the development of instrumental church music, particularly the *sonata da chiesa (Biagio Marini, 1597–1665; Legrenzi, 1626–90; Corelli, 1653–1713) which, around 1685, spread to England, Germany, and France. Bach's singular universality makes him the crowning highpoint of Protestant (cantata, passion, organ chorale) as well as Catholic (Mass, Magnificat) church music of the Baroque.

V. In the period after 1750 the production of great church music became more scarce, and the ensuing history is a somewhat thinly spread succession of isolated masterworks rather than a continuous development. The oratorio, which found one of its greatest masters in Handel, is perhaps the only type of religious music which can boast of an almost uninterrupted line of composers, English as well as German. More and more, however, it became music for the concert hall rather than for the church. As a completion of our survey, it suffices to mention such outstanding compositions as Pergolesi's *Stabat mater* (*c.* 1735), Mozart's *Requiem* (1791), Beethoven's *Missa solemnis* (1823), Rossini's *Stabat mater* (1832), Brahms's *Deutsches Requiem* (1868), its stylistic antipode, the *Requiem* by Verdi (1874), and Bruckner's Masses (1864–67) and *Te Deum* (1881). Cf. also the examples by Perez and Jommelli in *HAM*, nos. 301, 306.

Lit.: E. Dickinson, *Music in the History of the Western Church* (1902); O. Ursprung, *Die katholische Kirchenmusik* (*BüHM*, 1932); K. G. Fellerer, *Geschichte der katholischen Kirchenmusik* (1939); F. Blume, *Die evangelische Kirchenmusik* (*BüHM*, 1932); A. T. Davison, *Protestant Church Music in America* (1933); H. W. Davies and H. Grace, *Music and Christian Worship* (1934); G. Gardner and S. Nicholson,

Manual of English Church Music (1923); Dom A. Hughes, "16th-Century Service Music" (*ML* v, no. 2); A. Coeuroy, "Les formes actuelles de la musique religieuse" (*RM* vi); H. B. Collins, "Byrd's Latin Church Music for Practical Use in the Roman Liturgy" (*ML* iv, no. 3); K. G. Fellerer, "Die vokale Kirchenmusik des 17/18. Jahrhunderts . . ." (*ZMW* xi).

Chute [F.]. See *Cheute.

Ciacona [It.]. See *Chaconne.

Cialamello [It.]. *Shawm.

Cimbalom. A large *dulcimer used by the Hungarian gypsies and recently adopted by dance bands. Cf. A. Hartmann, in *MQ* ii.

Cinelli [It.]. *Cymbals.

Cinfonie. See *Hurdy-gurdy.

Cinque-pace [from F. *cinque pas*, five steps]. The name, which also occurs in the versions *Sink-a-pace, Sinqua-pace, Sincopas,* is used by writers of the Elizabethan period for the *galliard which had five steps. Cf. *GD* iv, 772; suppl. vol., 123.

Ciphering. In organ building, the continued sounding of a pipe, due to some defect of the mechanism.

Circle canon. See *Canon (1), I (h).

Circle of fifths [G. *Quintenzirkel*]. The term refers to the fact that a succes-

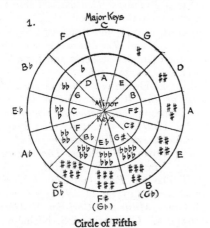

Circle of Fifths

sion of fifths (c–g–d' . . .) leads back after 12 steps to the initial tone, if octaves are disregarded. Thus, the fifths can be arranged in a circle which, simultaneously, shows the progression from one key to the next higher one, with one more

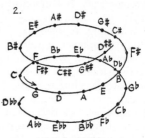

Spiral of Fifths

sharp in the signature. If the circle is passed through in the other direction (i.e., of descending fifths: c'–f–Bb . . .), the keys follow each other with one more flat in the signature. At one point of the circle the transition from the sharp keys to the flat keys must be made, for instance, at G-sharp = A-flat (*enharmonic change). The scheme of signatures might also serve for the minor keys, by starting from A, instead of from C. The series of fifths "closes" only in well-tempered tuning [Ex. 1]. If Pythagorean (pure) fifths are considered, the 12th of these fifths is higher by the *Pythagorean comma (about one-eighth of a tone) than the starting tone. Here, a "spiral of fifths" would give an adequate picture of the unending series of ascending and descending fifths [Ex. 2].

Circular canon. See *Canon (1), I (h).

Cis, cisis [G.]. See *Pitch names.

Cister, cistre, cither, citole, cittern. See under *Guitar family.

Civettando [It.]. Coquetting.

Cl. Short for *clarinet.

Clairon [F.]. Bugle [see *Brass instruments IV].

Claquebois [F.]. *Xylophone.

Clarinblasen [G.]. See *Clarin trumpet.

Clarinet family. The term is adopted here as a convenient collective designation for a large group of wind instruments characterized by the use of a single reed [see *Reed]. This group forms the contrast to the *oboe family which includes the wind instruments with a double reed.

I. *The Clarinet.* The clarinet, an orchestral wood-wind instrument, consists of an end-blown cylindrical pipe made of wood or ebonite (recently also of metal) with a characteristic mouthpiece (beak), which looks as if it were pinched to form a sharp edge at the top, and which has a single reed (made from a thin piece of cane) fixed to its back. The clarinet has the acoustical properties of a "stopped" pipe, thus overblowing at the twelfth, i.e., the second partial — the octave — and the even-numbered partials in general cannot be obtained by overblowing, a fact which also has a bearing on the *timbre of the clarinet. At a distance the clarinet is frequently confused with the similar-looking oboe from which, however, it is easily distinguished by the mouthpiece. While the oboe produces a "pastoral," slightly quaint and nasal sound of a rather unchanging quality, the clarinet is not only fuller and more "creamy" in timbre, but also shows a distinct variation of timbre in its various ranges (registers). It lends itself to the expression of love and passion as well as of fury and parody. On the whole, it is a much more "modern" (and, in fact, a much more recent) instrument than the oboe.

Owing to the fact that only the odd-numbered partials can be obtained by overblowing (e.g., c–g'–e''), a number of holes and, consequently, a complicated key mechanism are necessary to obtain the tones in between. The *Boehm system is popular in America, but has not been universally adopted. All clarinets have a written range as shown in Ex. 1, although the higher members of the family occasionally exceed this upwards, and the lower members become somewhat weak in their top octave. The least characteristic and most troublesome portion of their range is, to the average player, at the top of the first twelfth, i.e., as in Ex. 2,

the so-called "break" or throat register. The register below the break is termed *chalumeau,* that above it, *clarion* or *clarino.* All clarinets are notated as *transposing instruments.

II. *Present Forms.* The most common form is the *clarinet in Bb,* which sounds a whole tone lower than written. Next in importance is the *clarinet in A,* the part for which sounds a minor third lower than written. The former instrument is more brilliant than the latter without sacrificing any perceptible fullness. The clarinet in A is sometimes preferred for parts in the sharp keys which are, of course, easier to play on this instrument than on the other. The bass instrument of the clarinet family is the *bass clarinet in Bb,* the range of which is an octave lower than the clarinet in Bb, plus an additional semitone provided by a low Eb key, thus rendering possible the performance of music written for the now obsolete bass clarinet in A. To avoid a somewhat unwieldy length the lower end of the instrument is curved upward in a metal bell, while the upper end, likewise of metal, is curved downward, thus bringing the mouthpiece within reach of the player's mouth. The bass clarinet has less marked differences of register than the higher instruments and its top register is relatively weak. Its lower tones are of remarkable richness and have the advantage, as opposed to those of the bassoon, of a very wide dynamic range.

Additional types are the *clarinet in Eb,* a small instrument pitched a perfect fourth above the clarinet in Bb; the *alto clarinet in Eb,* pitched a fifth below the clarinet in Bb; and the *double-bass clarinet in Bb* (pedal clarinet, contrabass clarinet), pitched an octave below the bass clarinet. They are commonly found in

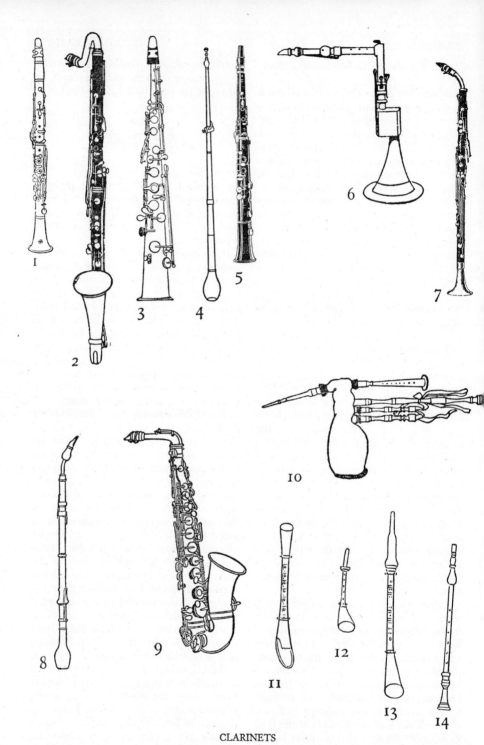

CLARINETS

1. Clarinet. 2. Bass Clarinet. 3. Heckel-clarina. 4. Holztrompete. 5. Tarogato. 6. Old Basset Horn.
7. Modern Basset Horn. 8. Clarinet d'amour. 9. Saxophone. 10. Bagpipe.
11. Pibgorn. 12. Hornpipe. 13. Stockhorn. 14. Chalumeau.

bands, but are occasionally demanded in orchestral scores. Parts for the E♭ clarinet are found in Strauss's *Ein Heldenleben*, in Stravinsky's *Sacre du Printemps*, and in Ravel's *Daphnis et Chloe*; for the double-bass clarinet in d'Indy's *Fervaal*, in Strauss's *Legend of Joseph*, and in Weingartner's *Orestes*. There are three obscure modern instruments, related to the clarinet only in that they possess a single reed, which have been invented for the sole purpose of playing the solo English horn part in Act III of *Tristan*. They are the **Heckel-clarina*, the *Holztrompete*, and the **Tarogato*. The music in question is generally played by the English horn.

III. *Obsolete Forms*. During the 19th century a great many other clarinets were built, e.g., the clarinet in C, the clarinet in D (called for in Liszt's "Mazeppa" and Strauss's "Eulenspiegel"; now replaced by the clarinet in E♭), the bass clarinet in C or A (Liszt, "Mazeppa"), the *bathyphone* (constructed by E. Skorra, 1839), etc. More interesting is the *basset horn*, an alto clarinet with a narrower bore, a thinner wall, and four semitones beyond the low E (which sounds A in the usual F pitch). Originally (*c.* 1770) it was crescent-shaped and in this form was used by Mozart singly or in pairs in *Clemenzo di Tito*, *Nozze di Figaro*, *Zauberflöte*, *Il Seraglio*, the *Requiem*, and in various instrumental works (e.g., K.V. 411). At about 1800 the crescent shape was replaced by a model which was sharply bent at nearly right angles and, somewhat later, it was given a straight form in which it is constructed nowadays. Beethoven used it only in *Prometheus*, and Mendelssohn wrote two concerted pieces for clarinet and basset-horn with piano (op. 113, 114). Rare modern examples, generally played on the alto clarinet in E♭, are to be found in *Salome* and *Electra* of Strauss, in Converse's *The Pipe of Desire*, and in the *Violin Concerto* of Roger Sessions. Finally, the *clarinetto d'amore* might be mentioned, a larger clarinet in G or A♭, with the pear-shaped bell of the oboe d'amore.

IV. *History and Repertory*. In early periods and in exotic cultures single-reed instruments are much rarer than double-reed instruments (oboes). Double clarinets (in pairs) were known in ancient Egypt, but scarcely at all in the Far East. To the present day a triple clarinet, called *launedda*, is used in Sardinia [cf. *SaHMI*, 91]. A primitive European instrument is the **pibgorn* (also called stockhorn, hornpipe), which was originally made of the shin bone of a sheep, with a part of a cow horn attached as a bell [cf. *GD* iv, 172; v, 141]. The forerunner proper of the clarinet is the *chalumeau* [the single-reed type; in addition there also existed a chalumeau with double reed, more properly called **shawm*], a small keyless cylindrical pipe. In the 17th century there existed a number of strangely shaped instruments of this type, especially for the bass size [cf. W. Heinitz, *Instrumentenkunde* (in *BüHM*), p. 57]. The change from the chalumeau to the clarinet took place between *c.* 1690 and 1720, owing to the activity of Johann Chr. Denner and his son Johann Denner who added finger keys and a speaker key [cf. *SaHMI*, 411f]. These early clarinets had the timbre of oboes rather than of the modern clarinet, owing chiefly to the use of small reeds. Thus, Johann Walther says in his *Lexicon* of 1732 (first mentioning of the name clarinet): "From a distance it sounds rather like a trumpet." This explains the name clarinet [cf. **Clarin trumpet; *Clairon*].

Chalumeaus, whether in their primitive or improved form, were used in Reinhard Keiser's operas *Croesus* (1711) and *Serenata* (1716), and are still prescribed in Gluck's *Orfeo* (1767). Rameau, J. W. Stamitz, and Gossec are the composers associated particularly with the early appearance of the real clarinet in the orchestra. Mozart used it in some of his later symphonies, notably that in E♭ (K.V. 543), in which prominent parts covering a wide range are given to the pair of clarinets. From that time, two clarinets are to be found in every normal orchestra. Berlioz was among the first to use various sizes of clarinets for their

particular tonal quality, a practice continued by Liszt, Strauss, and Mahler.
From the time of Wagner the number of
clarinets in the orchestra is often increased
— in *Salome* and *Electra* Strauss uses one
clarinet in Eb, two in Bb, two in A, one
bass clarinet, and two basset horns, practically the entire family. Composers since
Mozart have provided the instrument
with a repertory which in quality and
variety is equaled by that of no other wind
instrument. Outstanding compositions
are: clarinet concerto by Mozart, K.V.
622, Weber, op. 73, 74, Spohr, op. 26, 57,
and two in F and E minor; clarinet sonatas by Brahms, op. 120, nos. 1 and 2;
clarinet quintets by Mozart (K.V. 581),
Brahms, op. 115, Reger, op. 146; clarinet
trios by Beethoven, op. 11, Brahms, op.
114.

The clarinet family, as defined above,
also includes among its members the
saxophones. Since, however, these instruments deviate in important particulars
from the clarinet, they are usually treated
as a separate family. See *Saxophone.

Lit.: R. Dunbar, *Treatise on the Clarinet* (1939); *LavE* ii.3, 1436, 1545; O. W.
Street, in *PMA* xlii; F. G. Rendall, " . . .
the Clarinet in England . . ." (*PMA*
lxviii); P. Gradenwitz, "The Beginning
of Clarinet Literature" (*ML* xvii); L. de
la Laurencie, "Rameau et les clarinettes"
(*SIM* ix); G. Cucuel, "La Question des
clarinets dans l'instrumentation du xviiie
siècle" (*ZIM* xii). I to III by W. D. D.

Clarino. See *Clarin trumpet. The
name is also used for the high register of
the clarinet [see *Clarinet family I].

Clarin trumpet. The natural trumpet
of the 17th and 18th centuries, a low-pitch
and long-tube instrument, but played by
trumpeters trained specially and exclusively in the art of producing the highest
harmonics (*Clarino blasen*), i.e., from the
third octave onward, where they form a
continuous scale. It was this training that
enabled the trumpeters of the Bach epoch
to play (without valves!) those rapid passages in high position which have been
baffling the most outstanding trumpet
virtuosos of modern times [see Ex., from

Cantata 75, *B.-G.* xviii, 183]. The modern Bach trumpet (a short and straight
3-valve trumpet) which has been designed

for the rendering of such passages is only
a poor substitute, owing to its unsatisfactory tone quality.

Lit.: N. Bessaraboff, *Ancient European
Musical Instruments* (1941), 192ff and
413; W. F. H. Blandford, in *Monthly
Musical Record*, July, 1931 and March to
June, 1935; H. Eichborn, *Das alte Cla-
rino-Blasen* (1894); C. Sachs, in *AMW* ii;
R. Hofmann, in *BJ*, 1916.

Clarion. An ancient English trumpet
in round form [cf. *SaRM*].

Clarone [It.]. (1) Bass clarinet. —
(2) Older name for the *basset horn
(Mozart).

Clarsech, clairseach, clarseth. The
Irish harp [see *Harp III].

Classici della Musica Italiana, I.
See *Editions VI.

Classicism. In ordinary usage, the term
means [cf. Webster]: "of or relating to
the first class or rank; in particular, to the
ancient Greeks and Romans and their
culture." In music the word is used in
various connotations. Most commonly it
denotes an antithesis to Romanticism and
is, therefore, applied to periods prior to
the Romantic school, either to its immediate predecessors Haydn, Mozart, and
Beethoven (Viennese classics), or to what
the amateur considers to be "all music
before the Romanticism," i.e., from Palestrina to Beethoven. To others, the word
denotes music of established value and
fame, as distinguished from ephemeral
works which quickly disappear from the
programs. For still others, usually the
less educated people, it has the somewhat

deterrent meaning of "art-music" or high-brow music, in contradistinction to "popular music" or music for entertainment. The latter connotations are, of course, deteriorations which do not deserve serious consideration. The term should be used in one (or either) of the following meanings: (a) to denote only the "Viennese classics," that is, Haydn, Mozart, Beethoven, and, to some extent, Schubert; (b) in a more general way, to denote any period which gives the impression of greater stability, repose, clarity, balance, self-reliance, objectiveness, traditionalism, than those preceding and following it. If the latter meaning is adopted, the entire evolution of music might be understood as an incessant shift from the classical to the Romantic, with Romanticism adopting the meaning of unrest, exaggeration, experimentation, ostentation, diffusion, subjectivism, etc. Typically classical periods are those of the 13th century (Perotinus, Franco), the Flemish era (1450–1600), the period of Bach and Handel, and that of the Viennese classics, whereas the 14th century (Machaut and his successors) as well as the 17th (Frescobaldi, Froberger; see *Tombeau, *Courante) and the period of C. P. E. Bach show features more characteristic of Romanticism.

The period of the Viennese classics embraces the decades from 1770 to 1830 [see *German music V]. Its forms and style evolved in a very complex development which started around 1740 and to which various groups of composers in southwestern Germany (Mannheim), Vienna, Italy, and Bohemia contributed. See *Mannheim School; *Sonata; *Sonata form; *Symphony; *Quartet.

Clausula [L., close]. (1) Cadence, particularly the cadential formulae of 16th-century polyphonic music, usually provided with (improvised) ornamental notes. An elaborate system of classification and terminology, of little interest today, has been worked out by the 17th- and 18th-century theorists [cf. *GD* i, 527f; see also reference under *Glosa].

(2) In the repertory of the School of Notre Dame (c. 1200; see *Ars antiqua),

clausula is a polyphonic composition using as a cantus firmus a short melisma of a chant (gradual, alleluia), in contrast to the *organa which use the entire chant (i.e., the entire soloist section thereof). Accordingly, there is no complete text in the tenor of a clausula, but only one or two words, sometimes only a syllable [see *Incipit], which indicate from which chant the tenor is borrowed. For instance, the clausula GO (of which there exist a great number, with identical tenor, but different upper parts) is taken from the gradual *Benedicta es et venerabilis*, the verse of which begins with the words: *Vir- go Dei genetrix*. Accompanying is the beginning of this verse in plainsong [*GR* (99)] together with the beginning

of a clausula GO [cf. *ApNPM, passim*]. It goes without saying that all the parts of a clausula are sung in vocalization, in the present example to the vowel *o*.

A great number of such clausulae (well over 500; about a dozen in three parts, the others in two) are preserved in the sources of Notre Dame. They were written in the period of Perotinus of whom Anon. IV (*CS* i) says: "fecit clausulas sive puncta plurima meliora" (he wrote many beautiful clausulae or *puncta*). The clausulae were intended to serve as substitutes (*Ersatzklausel*, substitute clausula) for the corresponding sections (in the above case, the section GO) in the organa of Leoninus which form the *Magnus liber organi. These organa consist, in alternation, of "organal" sections in a relatively free rhythm, and of "discant" sections [see *Discant] in strictly measured counterpoint. It is the latter sections for which Perotinus and his collaborators provided substitutes, frequently shorter in length and more precise in rhythm [cf. *HAM*, nos. 28 and 30]. Occasionally, the original discant sections of the Leoninus organa are also spoken of as clausulae.

Although the clausulae were originally designed as alternative sections of the organa, they were also (possibly at a somewhat later period) used independently, though, of course, always in connection with plainsong. The following scheme for the Easter Alleluia [cf. *GR*, 223] illustrates such a method of performance which could well be revived by a modern choir [capital letters indicate clausulae (in two parts), ordinary letters plainsong]:

NOSTRUM
Alleluia, alleluia. (℣) Pascha NOSTRUM
LATUS
immo- LATUS est Christus.

[See also *Motet A, I.] It may be noticed that such a clausula-execution takes only a fraction of the time required for an organum-execution in which the entire vers would be sung polyphonically.

No less important than the backward reaching connection of the clausulae with organum and plainsong is another one, pointing towards the later development, that is, with the *motet. In fact, most of the early motets are directly derived from clausulae by retaining their music, but underlaying a full text to the melisma of the upper part. For the identification of a clausula (such as GO, *IN SECULUM, NOSTRUM, LATUS) the complete list given in F. Ludwig, *Repertorium organorum recentioris et motetorum vetustissimi stili* (1910), pp. 25–29 and, particularly, pp. 79–95, is indispensable. [For an explanation of Ludwig's somewhat cryptic terminology, cf. *ApNPM*, 238.] Cf. also *ReMMA*, 298ff; *AdHM* 218ff.

Clavecin, clavessin [F.]. *Harpsichord.

Clavecin d'amour, cembal d'amour, cembalo d'amore. A clavichord (not a cembalo, i.e., harpsichord), built by G.

Silbermann in 1721, in which the strings are double the normal length. They are plucked in the middle so that both sections sound the same tone, with a highly desirable result of increased volume of tone. Accordingly, this instrument had no damping-cloth woven between the strings such as are indispensable in the ordinary clavichord in order to dampen the shorter section of the string. In spite of its various advantages, the instrument did not gain popularity. It is described in Mattheson's *Critica musica* (1722–25), and in Adlung's *Musica mechanica* (1768), III, 123. Cf. E. van der Straeten, in *Musical Times*, Jan., 1924.

Clavicembalo [It.]. *Harpsichord.

Clavichord [G. *Klavichord*; It. *clavicordo*; earlier names are *manichord*, *manicordion*, *monachord*]. The earliest type of stringed keyboard instrument. It probably developed in the 12th century from the *monochord (or the *psalterium) by the addition of a keyboard. The clavichord consists of a wooden oblong box, varying in length from two to five feet, and resting on legs (earlier instruments were frequently without legs, being put on a table). The strings as well as the keyboard run parallel to the long side. The strings are put in vibration by small brass wedges, called tangents [from L. *tangere*, to touch], which are fastened to the rear of the lever. The tangents, by a sort of pressure-stroke from below, not only cause the string to vibrate, but also terminate their vibrating length, by dividing them in two parts the smaller of which is damped by a piece of cloth woven through the strings [see, however, *Clavecin d'amour]. The production of sound is therefore similar to that of a violinist merely "fingering" on a string. The tangent, in striking the string, also serves to terminate its vibrating length. This fact makes it possible to use one and the same string for several tangents and keys, though only for those which would never be used simultaneously, for instance, C and C-sharp. In fact, in all the clavichords prior to 1720 use is made of this possibility, the number of strings being considerably smaller than that of the keys. Such instruments are called *fretted* [G. *gebundenes Clavichord*]. The introduction of unfretted instruments [G. *bundfreies Clavichord*], i.e., clavichords in which there is a different string to each key, is ascribed to Daniel Tob. Faber (around 1720).

The tone of the clavichord is very soft and usually disappointing at first hearing. However, after becoming accustomed to the pianissimo-quality of the instrument, one is delighted with the subtleness and tenderness of its sound. Unlike the harpsichord, the clavichord admits dynamic modifications of intensity which are produced in a way similar to the technique of the pianoforte, by modifying the pressure of the fingers. A peculiar effect is the *Bebung, whose importance, however, is usually overrated.

History. Johannes de Muris, in his *Musica speculativa* (*c.* 1325), describes an instrument, called *monocordum*, which doubtless is a clavichord [cf. *SaHMI*, 331]. The earliest record of the name is found in a poem *Der Minne Regel* by Eberhard Cersne (1404), in which mention is made of *clavicimbalum, monocordium, clavichordium*, and *schachtbret*. In 1477 William Horwood taught the "clavychord" at Lincoln Cathedral. Other records from the late 15th century are mentioned in *GD* i, 661. The first clear description occurs in Virdung's *Musica getutscht* of 1511. The French name *manicordion* appears on the title of Attaingnant's publications: *Magnificat avec te deum et deux préludes, le tout mis en tabulature des orgues, espinettes et manicordions* ... (1530) or: *Dix-neuf chansons musicales reduictes en la tabulature des orgues espinettes manicordions et telz semblables instruments musicaux* . . . (1530). An Italian publication referring to the instrument is: *Intabulatura nova di varie sorte di balli, da sonare per arpichordi, clavicembali, spinette e manachordi* (1551). In the 17th century the clavichord fell into oblivion everywhere except in Germany, where it continued in use as a vehicle of expressiveness and sensitivity. The customary German name was *Cla-*

vier. To judge from the appearance of this name on title pages, quite a number of important keyboard publications of the century would appear to have been written expressly for the clavichord, e.g., Johann Kuhnau's *Neue Clavierübung* (1689, '95) or Bach's *Clavierübung*. Such a contention, however, is not borne out by the contents of these books [see the discussion of this question under *Klavier]. On the other hand, to classify the clavichord as a mere "practice instrument," as has been done by various writers, is equally wrong. It holds an important place in the musical life of the Baroque period as a domestic instrument of an intimate charm such as was foreign to the harpsichord as well as to the organ. A late revival of the clavichord took place in the period of the *Empfindsamkeit* [*see* *Empfindsamer Stil], owing chiefly to the strong interest which Ph. Em. Bach (1714–88) took in it. His *Versuch über die wahre Art das Clavier zu spielen* (1753; new ed. by W. Niemann, 1906, 1921) is an eloquent apotheosis as well as a most thorough study of the instrument and its technique. His *Probestücke zum Versuch* ... (1753; new ed. by E. Doflein, Ed. Schott) is perhaps the most idiomatic clavichord music ever written, and contains practically the only pieces in which the *Bebung is clearly indicated. Not without interest is the attempt made by F. W. Rust in a sonata from 1792 [see *Editions XII B (11)] to exploit still other resources of the clavichord. See also *Keyboard music.

Lit.: F. A. Goehlinger, *Geschichte des Klavichords* (Diss. Basle 1930); C. Auerbach, *Die deutsche Clavichordkunst des 18. Jahrhunderts* (1910); G. Le Cerf, "Notes sur le clavicorde et le dulce melos du ms. lat. 7295" (*RdM*, nos. 37, 38); E. Harich-Schneider, *Fray Tomás de Santa Maria, Anmut und Kunst beim Clavichordspiel* (1937; transl. from *L'Arte de tañer fantasia*, 1565); *id.*, in *AMF* ii; C. Parrish, in *BAMS* iii.

Clavicymbal. *Harpsichord.

Clavicytherium. A harpsichord with a vertical body (like the upright piano) [see *Harpsichord II]. It was in use during the 16th and 17th centuries. The earliest record is a reproduction contained in Virdung's *Musica getutscht* (1511). Cf. *SaRM*, 217; N. Bessaraboff, *Ancient European Musical Instruments* (1941), pp. 325f.

Clavier. (1) Pronounced klā'-vi-er, i.e., keyboard. — (2) Pron. kla-vēr', i.e., any stringed keyboard instrument, in modern times usually the pianoforte. — (3) For the German word, see *Klavier. — (4) The French word *clavier* has the meaning indicated under (1).

Clavier Hans. See *Keyboard III.

Clavierübung [G., Study for keyboard]. A title used by J. S. Bach for four publications of keyboard music. *Clavierübung* i (1731) contains the six *partitas; ii (1735), the Italian Concerto and the French Overture; iii (1739), a number of organ chorales preceded by the Prelude in Eb, and closed by the Fugue in Eb (*St. Anne's Fugue); iv (1742), the *Goldberg Variations. See remark under *Klavier. The title was adopted by Bach from former publications, such as Johann Kuhnau's *Clavierübung aus 14 Partien* . . . (1689), containing suites.

Clavilux. An instrument invented by Thomas Wilfrid, around 1920, for the performance of *color music [see *Color organ].

Clavis [L., pl. *claves*, key]. (1) A key of a keyboard [cf. the terms clavicembalo, clavier, Klaviatur, Klavier]. — (2) In medieval theory, *claves* are the pitch names a, b, c, . . . ; they were frequently written on the keys [cf. *CS* i, 214, 257]. — (3) In medieval theory, *claves signatae* are the clef signs (letters c, f, g).

Clef [from L. *clavis*, key; G. *Schlüssel*; It. *chiave*]. A sign written at the beginning of the staff in order to indicate the pitch of the notes. There are three such signs (see Example *a*).

These severally represent the tones g', c', and f, hence, the names G-clef, C-clef, and F-clef. The G-clef, also called violin clef, is used on the second line of the staff; it

indicates that the note on the second line is g'. The F-clef, also called bass clef, is used on the fourth line; it indicates that the note written on the fourth line is f. The C-clef is used in two positions, on the third line (alto clef or viola clef), or on the fourth line (tenor clef) (see *b*). The G-clef is used for the upper staff of pianoforte music and for all high instruments (violin, flute); the F-clef is used for the lower staff of pianoforte music and for all low instruments (cello, double bass). The alto clef is used for the viola and instruments of a similar range; the tenor clef for the high range of the cello, the bassoon, the tenor trombone, etc.

History. The above signs are evolutionary modifications of the letters they stand for. Example *c* shows early shapes, illustrating the gradual corruption of the letters c, f, and g. In music prior to 1750 each of these signs occurs in various positions. See Example *d* which also shows the position of middle C (c') in each clef.

CLEFS

a. The G-clef; three forms of the C-clef; the F-clef.
b. Position of the clefs on the staff.
c. Early forms of the clefs.
d. Positions of the clefs in music prior to 1750: (1) French violin clef; (2) Violin clef, G-clef, treble clef; (3) Soprano clef, descant clef; (4) Mezzo-soprano clef; (5) Alto clef, C-clef; (6) Tenor clef; (7) Bariton clef; (8) Bariton clef; (9) Bass clef, F-clef; (10) Sub-bass clef.

The great variety of clef-positions encountered in old music results from the desire to avoid ledger lines. Whenever the range of a voice exceeded the five-line staff, the position of the clef was changed or another clef was introduced. In modern musicological publications of 15th- and 16th-century music the old clefs are largely retained, a method which, although justifiable on historical and scholarly grounds, has definitely been detrimental to the furthering of studies and to the revival of early music. It is very gratifying to see that in some of the most recent publications only the F-clef and the G-clef are used, the latter also in a modification indicating transposition an octave below (see *e*).

As a matter of fact, this transposed clef is very well suited to replace the alto clef as well as the tenor clef since its range is practically the same as that of the other two (see *f*). For reforms of clefs cf. *WoHN* ii, 339. See *Chiavette.

Climacus. See *Neumes I (table).

Clivis. See *Neumes I (table).

Cloches [F.]. *Bells, especially those of the orchestra.

Clocking. See under *Bell.

Clock Symphony. Haydn's Symphony no. 101 (4) in D major, composed 1794 in London. The name refers to the ticking motive to be found in the Andante.

Clockwork instruments. See *Mechanical music instruments.

Clog box. A percussion instrument used in jazz bands and consisting of a block of wood, 7 or 8 inches long, with slots cut in it. It is struck with a drumstick.

Clos [F.]. See *Ouvert and clos.

Close. *Cadence.

Close harmony. Chords in close position, i.e., with all the four notes within an octave or a twelfth. See *Spacing.

Clubs, Musical. See *Societies.

Clutsam keyboard. See *Keyboard III.

C.o. [It.]. *Coll' ottava*, i.e., with the higher octave. *C.o.b*, *coll' ottava bassa*, i.e., with the lower octave.

Coda [It., tail]. A section of a composition which is added to the form proper as a conclusion. Practically all fugues close with a shorter or longer coda which is frequently based on a pedal point (e.g., Bach, *Wt. Cl.* i, C major). Bach's organ fugue in A minor closes with a coda in brilliant toccata style. Likewise in sonatas, symphonies, etc., a coda is found at the end of each movement. In slow movements it usually serves as an epilogue, whereas in fast movements it often leads to a final climax, frequently combined with quickening of tempo (*stretto). In movements in sonata form the coda frequently takes on considerable dimension, and occasionally becomes a second development section [cf. the first movement of Beethoven's Fifth Symphony]. A short coda is sometimes called codetta. However, this term commonly applies to the closing passage to be found at the end of sections, such as the exposition in sonata form or the first section (A) of a slow movement in ternary form (A B A). Beethoven's pianoforte Sonata op. 2, no. 3 may be recommended for a study of the coda in its various manifestations. Here even the Scherzo ends with a coda to be played after the repetition of the Scherzo ("Scherzo da capo e poi la coda").

Codetta. See *Coda.

Codex Bamberg, Burgos, etc. See *Sources. *Codex Calixtinus*, see also *St. Martial, School of.

Colascione, colachon. See *Lute II.

Colla, coll' [It.]. "With the." *Colla destra, sinistra,* with the right, left hand. *Colla parte, colla voce* (with the part) is an indication directing the player of the accompaniment to "follow along" with the main part, which is to be performed in free rhythm. *Coll' arco,* "with the bow," after a passage in pizzicato. *Colla punta d'arco,* "with the point of the bow."

Collect. In the Catholic rite, the prayer of the day at Mass and Offices, so called because it originally "collected" the prayers of the people. It is sung to special recitation tones, called *Toni Orationum* [cf. *AR*, 49*; *GR*, 109*; *LU*, 98].

Colleges. See *Music education IV, IX; *Profession I(c); *Degrees.

Collegium musicum. The term properly signifies musical associations connected with a university. A collegium musicum flourished at the university of Leipzig during the 17th and 18th centuries. For an American 18th-century institution, see T. M. Finney, in *PAMS*, 1937. The movement was revived by H. Riemann who established, around 1900, the first modern collegium musicum at the university of Leipzig. Today, every German university has its collegium musicum. At Harvard University a collegium musicum was established by this writer in 1938. These associations generally emphasize the amateur point of view and give preference to old or little played music. The performance is non-public or semi-public. An important step of the German movement was the introduction of old instruments, such as recorders, viols, gambas (W. Gurlitt, University of Freiburg, 1920). See M. Gondolatsch, in *ZMW* iii; M. Seiffert, in *SIM* ii.

Col legno [It., with the wood]. In violin playing, the striking of the strings with the bow-stick, instead of with the hair.

Coll' ottava [It.]. With the octave.

Colombia. The following were the outstanding musicians of Colombia during the 19th century: Enrique Price (1819–63), of English birth, who lived in New York for a time and then settled in Bogotá, where in 1846 he founded the Sociedad Filarmónica, out of which all subsequent musical organizations in Colombia developed. In 1847 he founded a School of Music in conjunction with the Philharmonic Society. Juan Crisóstomo Osorio y Ricaurte (1863–87) composed *zarzuelas (comic operas) and other light stageworks. Julio Quevedo Arvelo (1829–97) was primarily a composer of church music,

while José María Ponce de León (1846–82) has the distinction of having written the only two Colombian operas to have reached the stage, *Ester* and *Florinda*. Oreste Sindici (1837–1904) won fame above all as composer of the National Hymn. The patriarch of Colombian music is Jorge W. Price (b. 1853), who in 1882 founded the Academia Nacional de Música, now known as the National Conservatory of Music. Prominent as pedagogue and composer was Andrés Martínez Montoya (1869–1933), among whose works is a *Rapsodia Colombiana* for band. Santos Cifuentes (1870–1932) was a prolific composer of orchestral works, chamber music, operettas, etc. Among these may be mentioned the *Sinfonía sobre aires tropicales* and a Concerto for piano and orchestra. He was also the author of widely used theoretical works.

The most notable of contemporary Colombian composers, and one of the leading musical figures of Latin America, is Guillermo Uribe-Holguín (b. 1880). From 1910 to 1933 he was director of the National Conservatory at Bogotá; he was also founder and conductor of the Sociedad de Conciertos Sinfónicos del Conservatorio. Possessing a solid technical equipment, he has produced numerous works in many forms, including a quantity of chamber music. Among his orchestral works are a Symphony in F minor, *Sinfonía del Terruño*, and *Tres Danzas*. He has written a Requiem, a Te Deum, and other church music. From the viewpoint of musical nationalism, his most significant compositions are the 300 *Trozos en el sentimiento popular*, for piano. Other noteworthy contemporary composers are Jesús Bermúdez-Silva (b. 1884), Emilio Murillo (1880–1942), José Rozo Contreras (b. 1894), Carlos Posada Amador (b. 1908), Adolfo Mejía (b. 1909), and Guillermo Espinosa (b. 1905), conductor of the Orquesta Sinfónica Nacional, which he founded in 1936.

Lit.: J. I. Perdomo Escobar, "Historia de la música en Colombia" (*Boletín latinoamericano de música*, IV); F. C. Lange, "Guillermo Uribe-Holguín" (*op. cit.*).

G. C.

Colophane, colophony. See *Rosin.

Color [L.]. (1) In 13th-century theory the term *color* signified various special devices of composition and performance, such as the repetition of a melodic phrase, its imitation (in *Stimmtausch*), quotations from other sources [see *Refrain], or embellishments, especially the vocal *vibrato [cf. Joh. de Garlandia, *CS* i, 115/116]. The first meaning survived in the *color* of the *isorhythmic motet; the last, in the present-day term *coloratura. — (2) For *color temporis, color prolationis,* see *Mensural notation V.

Color and music. The physical and psychological relationships between the colors and the sounds have been the subject of numerous studies. From the physical point of view a fundamental analogy between the two phenomena exists in the fact that the various pitches of the musical scale as well as the colors of the optical spectrum are conditioned by waves and can be determined by frequencies of aerial and ethereal vibrations respectively. The frequencies of (audible) sound range from about 16 to 40,000 per second; those of (visible) light, from about 450 to 780 billions per second. Since the latter two figures are nearly in the relation of 1:2 it would seem reasonable to compare the visible spectrum from red to violet, not to the entire audible musical scale, but only to an octave or, more nearly, to a seventh, e.g., to the tones 450 to 780 (approximately a′ to g″). This analogy seems to be supported by the fact that the number of colors in the spectrum is the same as that of the diatonic tones, that is, seven. However, various incongruities of this analogy can easily be pointed out: (a) Newton's distinction of seven colors is arbitrary; in fact, his scheme was partly influenced by the preconceived analogy with the musical scale. (b) In reality, there are infinitely more colors in the spectrum than there are tones in the musical octave, since the former is a continuous, the latter, a discrete multitude. Only the violin portamento could be compared to the optical spectrum. (c) The most serious objection is that the spectrum lacks the phenomenon of the musical *octave, i.e., the identity or, at least, similarity, of its lower and upper end. (d) In general, the laws relating to colors (e.g., complementary colors, such as orange and blue, red and green) are of an entirely different nature from those governing the sounds (consonance and dissonance). The chief studies in the above field were made by I. Newton (1700), W. von Goethe (1810), and H. Helmholtz (numerous essays, 1860–80).

Among musicians the psychological or synaesthetic approach to the question of color and sound has been more popular than the physical. It seems that a number of musicians, particularly among Russians and Englishmen, possess a peculiar mental faculty which produces in their minds a coördination between sounds and colors. This faculty appears to be of a highly subjective nature, as the various schemes of coördination differ widely. For instance, Rimsky-Korsakov interpreted the keys of C, D, A, F and F-sharp (all major) as white, yellow, rosy, green, and grayish-green, respectively, while according to Scriabin they represent red, yellow, green, red, and bright blue.

Colors have also been associated with entire works — e.g., *Tannhäuser*: blue; *The Flying Dutchman*: green (the "blue cave" of Venus and the "green sea"?) — and even with composers (Mozart: blue; Chopin: green; Beethoven: black). An example of a composition based on color impressions is Arthur Bliss's *Colour Symphony* (1922) each movement of which represents the associations of a special color (e.g., purple: royalty, pageantry, and death). Oviously the whole matter of color-sound-synaesthesia is a largely subjective experience, comparable to personal likes and dislikes of smells and flavors.

More important are the synaesthetic analogies between the optical colors and the timbres (tone-"colors," G. *Klang-"farben"*) of instruments. The terms "orchestral colors" or "orchestral palette" are widely used to signify a musical technique reminiscent of, and largely derived from, methods used in modern painting [see *Impressionism]. However, it appears that these terms signify only the general technique of modern orchestration, without implying any specific analogy between special colors and special instruments. In fact, any such specific coordination is of a no less subjective nature than that of color-key relationship. It is doubtful how many musicians would subscribe to the statement, made by Bosanquet in 1876, that there exists a "remarkable agreement amongst musicians regarding the 'color of instruments,' that is, black for strings and voices(!), red for brass and drums, blue for wood." There is perhaps only one such association which is likely to meet with fairly general consent, that indicated by the expression: the silvery tone of the harpsichord. It is obvious, however, that in this expression reference is made, not to the "color silver," but to the "sound silver" (dropping of a silver coin). Color associations are frequent in Oriental musical cultures, China, India, Egypt, etc. Here they are part and parcel of a cosmologic symbolism which is far removed from the subjective and psychological approach of Western music [see Lit., Wellek]. See *Color organ.

Lit.: A. B. Klein, *Colour Music — the Art of Light* (1926; bibl.); O. Ortmann, *Theories of Synesthesia in the Light of a Case of Color-Hearing* (1933); A. W. Rimington, *Colour Music* (1912); T. F. Karwosli and H. S. Odbert, *Color-Music* (1938); F. Suarez de Mendoza, *L'Audition coloré* (1899; bibl.); G. Anschütz, *Kurze Einführung in die Farbe-Ton-Forschung* (1927); *WoHN* ii, 460; L. Sabaneew, in *ML* x, no. 3; E. Whomes, in *PMA* xiii; A. Wellek, in *ZMW* xi.

Coloration. See *Mensural notation V.

Coloratura [It.]. Rapid passages, runs, trills, and similar virtuoso-like material, particularly in vocal melodies of the 18th- and 19th-century operatic arias: *aria di coloratura, aria di bravura, Koloraturarie*. A famous example is the aria of the Queen of Night in Mozart's *Magic Flute*. Also used for the stereotyped ornamentation formulae of 16th-century keyboard and lute music [see *Colorists].

Colorists [G. *Koloristen*]. A name introduced by A. G. Ritter [see Lit.] and widely adopted to signify a group of German organ composers of the late 16th century, including Elias Nicolaus Ammerbach (1530–97), Bernhard Schmid the older (c. 1520–90), Jacob Paix (1556–1617), B. Schmid the younger (1548–?), and others. Although the name serves as a convenient designation, it is rather misleading in its literal interpretation as well as in its implied pejorative side meaning. It is true that the musicians of this group made abundant use of stereotyped and meaningless *coloraturas, particularly in their *Intabulierungen of motets and chansons. However, this method was internationally used by organists and lutenists throughout the 16th century; it occurs in the keyboard and lute books of Attaingnant (c. 1530) and in the lute books of Hans and Melchior Neusidler (1535, '75), as well as in A. Gabrieli's keyboard arrangements of French chansons (c. 1550) and in those of the *Fitzwilliam Virginal Book* (c. 1600). The harsh judgment imposed on the "colorists" by Ritter is all the more unjust since these composers actually made outstanding contributions in another field, i.e., dance music. It should also be noted that B. Schmid the older in his publication of 1577 expressly says that he would prefer to leave the "art of the composer unchanged," and that his "modest" coloraturas are added only for the benefit of the young and inexperienced players [cf. Frotscher i, 154]. To include Johannes Woltz (tablature of 1617) in this group, as Ritter does, is not correct, since Woltz renounces the addition of coloraturas altogether. Even more misleading is the inclusion of Arnolt Schlick [cf. *AdHM* i, 385] who is not only much too early but also much too great a composer to be grouped with the above.

Lit.: A. G. Ritter, *Zur Geschichte des Orgelspiels* (1884); G. Frotscher, *Geschichte des Orgelspiels und der Orgelcomposition* (1935); W. Apel, "Early German Keyboard Music" [*MQ* xxiii, 231]; W. Merian, †*Der Tanz in den deutschen Tabulaturbüchern* (1927; transcriptions).

Color organ. The keyboard of the organ, harpsichord, pianoforte, has been frequently used as a medium of coördinating sound and color [see *Color and music*]. In 1720 a Jesuit priest, L. B. Castel (1688–1757), constructed a "Clavecin oculaire" in which the keys were mechanically connected with colored tapes; similar contrivances were devised frequently during the 18th and 19th centuries. While these apparatus were based upon the idea of an exact correspondence between a single sound and a single color, thus producing what might be called an "optical translation of a composition," a more liberal attitude has been taken recently. Literal translation has been replaced by "general coördination" between musical and optical impressions. Examples are the color organ of Mrs. M. H. Greenwalt (exhibited in New York, 1921) and the *Musichrome* of G. L. Hall (Boston, 1930), which was designed "to create a color accompaniment which coördinates with the music and helps to enhance the mood and spirit of the composition." Still farther away from the idea of strict sound-color analogy is the *Clavilux* of Th. Wilfrid, which was exhibited in New York in 1922 and which, so far, has proved the most successful color organ, probably owing to the fact that it altogether renounces the coördination of sound and light, and merely bestows upon optical phenomena the essential musical factors of time, rhythm, and changing combinations. It has no sound-producing apparatus and is designed only as a medium for a new art of color, in which optical phenomena (colored circles, squares, spirals, etc., projected on a screen) move rhythmically in "crescendo," "decrescendo," "acceleran-do," "ritardando," etc. Mr. Wilfrid has created a number of "compositions," e.g., a "Triangular Etude." Performances of this type are occasionally shown in motion pictures, to the accompaniment of music.

Among composers, Scriabin was the most outspoken protagonist of color music. In his *Prometheus* (op. 60, 1910) he undertook to demonstrate the affinity, scientific and spiritual, that he believed to exist between tone and color. He prescribed a special instrument for it, a "clavier à lumière" invented by Rimington. The only recorded performance of the composition with color accompaniment took place in Carnegie Hall, in 1914. For literature, see under *Color and music*.

Colpo d'arco [It.]. Stroke of the bow (of violins, etc.).

Combination pedal, . . . stops. See *Organ IV*.

Combination tone [resultant tone; G. *Kombinationston*]. In musical acoustics, a tone of different pitch which is heard when two loud tones are sounded simultaneously. Its frequency is the difference (*differential tones*) or the sum (*summation tones*) of the frequencies of the two primary tones or of their multiples. For instance, if the two primary tones have the frequencies 1200 and 700, the following differential tones (D) and summation tones (S) can be heard: D_1: $1200 - 700 = 500$; D_2: $2 \times 1200 - 700 = 1700$; D_3: $2 \times 700 - 1200 = 200$; S_1: $1200 + 700 = 1900$; S_2: $2 \times 1200 + 700 = 3100$; S_3: $2 \times 700 + 1200 = 2600$, etc. The combination tones are frequently referred to as an acoustical phenomenon. Actually, however, they are a physiological phenomenon. If the vibrations 1200 and 700 are produced, none of the vibrations 500, 1700, etc., actually exist in the air; it is the inner ear (*cochlea*) which, owing to its "non-linear" organization, produces the aural sensations corresponding to the additive or subtractive frequencies. The term "non-linear," roughly explained, means that the combination of two sounds with the intensities a and b is not determined by the "linear" formula $a + b$, but by more complicated formulae, involving squares, etc. The "linear" formula is valid only for small intensities; as a matter of fact, combination tones are heard only if the original tones are sufficiently loud.

The differential tones (which are more easily recognized than the summation tones) were discovered by G. Tartini in

1714, and described in his *Trattato dei principii dell' armonia musicale* of 1754 (an earlier description appeared in a book of G. A. Sorge: *Vorgemach der musikalischen Composition*, 1745). The tone frequently referred to as "Tartini's tone" [It. *terzo suono*, "third tone"] is the first of the above combination tones, determined by the difference of the original frequencies. The accompanying table shows this tone for various intervals (c' arbitrarily = 300).

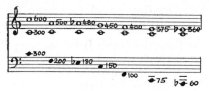

Combination Tone

Tartini's tone can easily be heard on the harmonium, the organ, and the violin. On the violin, it was recommended by Tartini and other violinists (Leop. Mozart) as a means of controlling the correct intonation of double-stops, since a slight inaccuracy results in a more easily noticeable change of the low-pitched differential tone. The name "beat-tones" formerly applied to the differential tones is misleading. It is derived from the theory advanced by Th. Young (1773–1823) according to which the differential tones are quick *beats (more than 40 per second). This theory was refuted by Helmholtz who discovered the summation tones by calculations based upon the principle of "non-linear superposition," thus paving the way for the modern theory. Recent research has brought about the startling result that certain well-established musical sounds, e.g., that of the G-string of the violin, are physically non-existent, being produced only aurally as the differential tones of their upper partials [see *Timbre].

Practical application of the first differential tone is made in the *acoustical bass of organs. For literature, see the books listed under *Acoustics.

Come [It.]. "As," "like." *Come prima, come sopra*, as at first, as previously; *come*

stà, as it stands, i.e., without improvised additions.

Comédie. A name occasionally used for operas in a light and slightly comical vein. For comédie-ballet, see under *Ballet, also *Entr'acte.

Comes [L.]. See *Fugue; *Canon (1).

Comic opera. I. *Definition.* General name for an opera or other dramatic work with a large admixture of music, on a light or sentimental subject, with a happy ending, and in which the comic element plays a certain part. The term thus comprises a number of types, such as the *operetta, *vaudeville, opéra-bouffe, musical comedy, etc., the distinctions between which are not always clearly marked. Until the middle of the 19th century comic operas (except for the Italian *opera buffa*) usually contained spoken dialogue; in more recent times this feature has tended to disappear, so that now the distinction on this basis is no longer generally valid. Incidentally, it should be noted that not all operas with spoken dialogue are "comic," though in France the name "opéra-comique" is traditionally applied to such works, even when they are serious or tragic in character, e.g., Bizet's *Carmen*. The music of comic opera is always more "popular" in style than that of serious opera, generally easier both to perform and to comprehend, and appealing to less sophisticated audiences. Its function is relatively less important than in serious opera, and in some forms (e.g., musical comedy) it is confined to a series of "hit" songs or other musical specialties. The scenes and personages of comic opera are apt to be taken from everyday life; or if fantasy is present it is treated in a sentimental or amusing fashion. Frequently there is satire of manners, allusion to current topics, or parody of the serious opera style.

II. *History.* a. Comic scenes early made their way into serious opera, and the juxtaposition of serious and comic episodes is a general feature of the 17th-century librettos. Examples may be found in Landi's *Morte d'Orfeo* (1619) and *San Alessio* (1632), in Mazzochi's *Catena d'Adone* (1626), and Cornachioli's *Diana schernita* (1629), all of the Roman school. L. Rossi's *Orfeo* (Paris, 1647) is another instance. The same practice may be observed in Venetian opera, e.g., in Monteverdi's *Incoronazione di Poppea* (1642), Cavalli's *Giasone* (1649), Cesti's *Pomo d'oro* (1667), and to an even greater degree in later Venetian works. The earliest independent comic operas are Mazzochi's and Marazzoli's *Che soffre speri* (1639) and Abbatini's and Marazzoli's *Dal male il bene* (1654), both to librettos by Giulio Ruspigliosi (later Pope Clement IX). The last-mentioned work is notable for its use of parlando-recitative and for its ensemble finales, both of which features are prominent in the later comic opera style. Another early example is Melani's *La Tancia* (Florence, 1657), which contains a parody of the famous "Incantation scene" of Cavalli's *Giasone*. In the second half of the 17th century Venice was the center of a considerable school of comic opera which has not yet been fully studied [cf. H. C. Wolf, "Die venezianische Oper," in *ZMW* xvi].

b. With the abolition of comic episodes in the "reformed" opera librettos of Zeno and Metastasio, the comic opera as a separate genre took on renewed importance. Comic opera in the 18th century shows well-defined national types. The Italian *opera buffa* began early in the century to evolve out of *intermezzi performed between the acts of serious operas. The fully developed independent form, of which the most famous early example is Pergolesi's *Serva padrona* (1733), retained traces of its origin in the designation "intermezzo" and in the customary division into two acts (as opposed to the three-act arrangement of the *opera seria*). The Italian buffo operas are remarkable for the liveliness and humor of their action, for the high development of comic characterization in their music, and for the use of ensemble finales. The leading composers were Logroscino, Galuppi, Pergolesi, Anfossi, Guglielmi, Piccini, Paisiello, Cimarosa, and Mozart. Toward the end of the century the Italian comic opera (like that of all other countries) tended to combine

with the earlier farcical intrigue type of plot some elements of the semi-serious, sentimental drama; at the same time the character of its music changed accordingly, becoming on occasion more expressive, lyric, and dignified. Examples of this later type are Piccini's *Buona figliola* (1760, libretto by Goldoni), Paisiello's *Nina* (1789), Mozart's *Nozze di Figaro* (1786), and Cimarosa's *Matrimonio segreto* (1792).

c. The French *opéra-comique*, beginning before 1715 with popular farces and satires mingling spoken dialogue with songs to familiar airs ("vaudevilles"), was given a new direction by the example of the Italian buffo opera [see Guerre des *Bouffons] and developed a type known as "Comédie mêlée d'ariettes," i.e., a "spoken comedy mingled with [originally-composed] songs," of which the chief composers were J. J. Rousseau (*Le Devin du village*, 1752), Gluck (*La Rencontre imprévue*, Vienna, 1764), Philidor (*Tom Jones*, 1765), Monsigny (*Le Déserteur*, 1769), and Grétry (*Zemire et Azor*, 1771; *Richard Coeur-de-Lion*, 1784). The romantic quality of the libretto of many of these works, and the frequent touching upon political and social problems, show the influence of Rousseau and the Encyclopedists.

d. The typical English 18th-century form was the *Ballad opera, which was succeeded by similar works using original music by such composers as Dr. Thomas Arne (*Love in a Village*, 1762), Charles Dibdin (*The Waterman*, 1774), William Shield (*Rosina*, 1783), and Stephen Storace (*The Haunted Tower*, 1789). With respect to subject matter and treatment the course of English comic opera in this period is parallel to that of the French opéra-comique.

The corresponding form for this period in Spain is the *Tonadilla [see also *Zarzuela; *Sainete].

e. In Germany the *Singspiel was cultivated at Leipzig by Joh. Adam Hiller, using for the most part plays adapted from French opéras-comiques by Chr. F. Weisse (*Die Jagd*, 1770, from Monsigny's *Roi et le fermier*). Other North German composers were Georg Benda (*Der Jahrmarkt*, 1775; in *DdT* 64), Chr. Neefe, and J. André. In Vienna a different type of Singspiel, strongly influenced by the Italian buffo style, developed. The chief composers were Umlauf (*Die Bergknappen*, 1778; in *DTOe* 18.i), Mozart (*Die Entführung aus dem Serail*, 1782), Dittersdorf (*Doktor und Apotheker*, 1786), and Joh. Schenk (*Der Dorfbarbier*, 1796; in *DTOe* 34).

f. In the 19th century the comic opera lost some of its earlier distinctive character, approaching on the one hand the style, form, and subject matter of serious opera or on the other hand tending toward the light, purely "entertainment" type such as the *vaudeville, *operetta, *zarzuela, etc. In Italy the *opera buffa* is continued by Simon Mayr, F. Paër, Rossini, and Donizetti. The French opéracomique is represented by Boïeldieu (*La Dame blanche*, 1825), Auber (*Fra Diavolo*, 1830), Hérold (*Le Pré aux clercs*, 1832), Adam (*Le Postillon de Longjumeau*, 1836), and Victor Massé (*Les Noces de Jeanette*, 1853). English comic operas were composed by Sir Henry R. Bishop (works 1804–40), but the best English works in the comic vein are Sullivan's operettas (*H.M.S. Pinafore*, 1878; *The Pirates of Penzance*, 1880; *The Mikado*, 1885). The best-known German comic operas of this period (known as *Spieloper*) are K. Kreutzer's *Nachtlager von Granada* (1834), Lortzing's *Zar und Zimmermann* (1839) and *Der Wildschütz* (1842), O. Nicolai's *Lustigen Weiber von Windsor* (1847), Flotow's *Martha* (1847), and P. Cornelius' *Barbier von Bagdad* (1858). One of the most popular comic operas of the 19th century was Smetana's *Bartered Bride* (1866).

Since the middle of the century, comic opera of various sorts has been cultivated in all countries, chiefly by composers not distinguished in any other field. These works are very numerous, but for the most part ephemeral. A few comic operas of lasting merit and on a large scale have been produced, of which four may be particularly mentioned: Wagner's *Meistersinger von Nürnberg* (perf. 1868), Verdi's *Falstaff* (1893), R. Strauss's *Rosenkavalier* (1911), and Hindemith's *Neues vom Tage* (1929). See also *Operetta.

Lit.: A. della Corte, *L'Opera comica italiana nel '700* (1923); M. Scherillo, *Storia letteraria dell' opera buffa napolitana* (1918); G. Cucuel, *Les Créateurs de l'opéra-comique français* (1913); D. J. Grout, *The Origins of the Comic Opera* (unpubl. diss. Harvard 1939); K. Lüthge, *Die deutsche Spieloper* (1924); R. Vené, "The Origin of Opera Buffa" (*MQ* xxi); M. Cauchie, "The High-Lights of French Opéra Comique" (*MQ* xxv); N. D'Arienzo, "Origini dell' opera comica" (*RMI* ii, iv, vi, vii); G. E. Bonnet, "André Philidor et la naissance de l'opéra-comique" (*RM* ii); Special Number, *RM* xiv; L. Holzer, "Die komischen Opern Glucks" (*StM* xiii); H. Abert, "Paisiello's Buffokunst und ihre Beziehung zu Mozart" (*AMW* i).   D. J. G.

Comma. A scientific term for the minute differences which exist between the pitches of the same tone in different systems of tuning or calculation. The two most important ones are: (a) the *Pythagorean comma.* This indicates the inaccuracy of the so-called *circle of fifths which, if based on pure fifths, actually is a "spiral of fifths." Starting from c = 1, the frequency of the 12th fifth, i.e., of b♯, is $\left(\dfrac{3}{2}\right)^{12} \times \left(\dfrac{1}{2}\right)^{7} = \dfrac{531441}{524288}$ (the first power indicates the number of ascending fifths; the second reduces this extremely high tone into the normal octave), a tone which is slightly higher than the tone c (frequency 1). The difference, of 24 cents, is the Pythagorean comma. (b) The *Didymic* (Didymos, Greek theorist, b. 63 B.C.) or *syntonic comma* which indicates the difference between E as the fourth tone of the circle of fifth (Pythagorean system): $\left(\dfrac{3}{2}\right)^{4} \times \left(\dfrac{1}{2}\right)^{2} = \dfrac{81}{64}$ and the E of *just intonation (fifth harmonic): $\dfrac{5}{4}$. The value of this comma is: $\dfrac{81}{64} \times \dfrac{4}{5} = \dfrac{81}{80} = 22$ cents. It shows that the final tone of the series c–g–d′–a′–e″ (pure fifths) is slightly higher than that of the series c–c′–g′–c″–e″ (partials). The third of equal temperament lies almost midway between these two other thirds, thus forming a comma with each: E (pyth.) = 408 cents; E (equ. temp.) = 400 cents; E (just inton.) = 386 cents. The Didymic comma also indicates the difference between the two whole-tones of just intonation, $\frac{9}{8}$ and

$$\frac{10}{9} : \frac{9}{8} \times \frac{9}{10} = \frac{81}{80}.$$

Yet another comma is the *schisma*, i.e., the difference between c and the (pure) third of the eighth Pythagorean fifth, i.e., the third above g♯. Its value is $\left(\frac{3}{2}\right)^8 \times \left(\frac{5}{4}\right) \times \left(\frac{1}{2}\right)^5$ (the last power reduces the accumulated intervals into the original octave) $= \frac{32805}{32768} = 2$ cents ($\frac{1}{100}$ of a whole-tone). This is one of the smallest intervals encountered in mathematical acoustics and is entirely negligible for all practical purposes. A simple calculation shows that the schisma also indicates the difference between the Pythagorean and the syntonic comma:

$$\frac{3^{12}}{2^{19}} \times \frac{5 \times 2^4}{3^4} = \frac{3^8 \times 5}{2^{15}}.$$

It very nearly equals the difference between the Pythagorean fifth $\frac{3}{2}$ and the fifth of equal temperament: $(\sqrt[12]{2})^7$. This comma (1.629 cents) is therefore also called schisma.

An idea of the practical importance of these micro-intervals might be obtained from the fact that the interval of 6 cents or, approximately, $\frac{1}{4}$ of the syntonic comma can still be recognized by very sensitive ears.

Commodo [It.]. Convenient, moderate.

Common chord. An older name for the major triad.

Common meter. See Poetic meter II.

Common of the Mass. See *Ordinary and Proper.

Common time. Name for 4/4-meter.

Commune Sanctorum. See under *Gregorian chant I.

Communion [L. *communio*]. In the Roman Catholic service, the last of the five items of the Proper of the *Mass, sung after (originally during) the distribution of the Host. Originally it was an antiphon with the psalm verse *Gustate et videte* (*Taste ye and see*) from Ps. 33 or with other psalm verses [see *Antiphon (3)]. However, these verses disappeared soon so that only an antiphon (*antiphona ad communionem*) remained. The communion antiphons are moderately melismatic melodies, sung chorally with a solistic *incipit.

Comparative musicology. The term which is a translation of G. *Vergleichende Musikwissenschaft* denotes a special field of musicological research, that is, the study of *exotic music. Early studies in this field were made by P. du Halde (Chinese music, 1736), by P. Amiot (Chinese music, 1779), by Andres (Arabian music, 1787), and by R. G. Kiesewetter (Arabian music, 1842). However, the systematic exploration of the field and the establishment of an organized activity along scientific lines is of a much more recent date (after 1900). Perhaps the most momentous step was the introduction of the phonograph as the only reliable means for the recording of exotic melodies which, regarding pitch as well as rhythm, usually defy the writing down in the European system of notation. Ellis' method of measuring intervals in *cents provided the scientific basis for the exact determination of exotic scales. See *Musicology.

Lit.: W. V. Bingham, *Five Years of Progress in Comparative Musicology Science* (1914; bibl.); C. Sachs, *Vergleichende Musikwissenschaft* (1930); C. Stumpf, *Die Anfänge der Musik* (1911); various articles in *Sammelbände für vergleichende Musikwissenschaft* (1922) and in *Zeitschrift für vergleichende Musikwissenschaft* i, ii (1933/35). E. v. Hornbostel, "Die Probleme der vergleichenden

Musikwissenschaft" [*ZIM* vii]; G. Schünemann, "Ueber die Beziehungen der vergleichenden Musikwissenschaft zur Musikgeschichte" [*AMW* ii]; E. Haraszti, "Fétis fondateur de la musicologie comparée" [*AM* iv, no. 3]. See also under *Musicology; *Primitive music.

Compass. The range of notes obtainable from an instrument or voice.

Competitions. For a list see Pierre Key's *Music Year Book*.

Compiacevole [It.]. Pleasing.

Complement. The difference between the octave and any interval, therefore identical with inverted interval [see *Inversion (1)]. For instance, the complement of the fifth is the fourth, that of the sixth is the third.

Compline. See *Office hours.

Composition. I. This article will not recommend methods or studies by which one may learn to compose. Neither will it number and discuss the various so-called elements of composition, harmony, rhythm, melody, counterpoint, etc. For composition means "putting together" and not "taking apart"; and while these elements may be studied separately, as various branches of theory, they should be studied as a whole when the subject is composition. Finally, the present article will say little about "inspiration" and its place in composition. The subject has already been be-labored, without anything very definite having ever been said. This article is concerned almost exclusively with the teaching (consequently, the learning) of composition, with the relation of theory to composition, and with certain other problems arising from such an inquiry.

In a sense, anyone who writes a piece of music is a composer, regardless of the length, originality, or artistic achievement of the piece. In the same way, anyone who daubs oil on a canvas may call himself a painter. But the world, fortunately, does not admit of such a lax view. The composer (as well as the painter) is

expected to show some skill in handling his materials (technique) and some degree of originality. The first of these requirements, technique, may be learned and acquired, provided that the student has a basic minimum of musical ability. This branch of music is called *Theory* and includes harmony, counterpoint, orchestration, etc. The second, the requirement of originality, can scarcely be learned, though it may be developed and cultivated.

Technique is usually developed through the imitation of existing models, the student striving to make his works as perfect as those he imitates. Paradoxically enough, such imitation may also be a means of stimulating originality; for the student may rearrange the given materials, or may add something that is distinctly his own; and he may well pass from imitation to originality. Perhaps when imitation ceases, composition may be said to begin. This is not to say that the composer must write something entirely *new*. The originality may lie in the way he employs older procedures and older idioms. Only there must be enough of himself in the result — regardless of how this originality manifests itself — to give his work the conviction and strength which purely imitative works cannot convey. An apt parallel may be drawn from the field of painting. The least highly regarded canvases are those which are the closest to photography, those which merely imitate; the most highly prized paintings display originality of treatment, even when portraying the most ordinary subject.

Musical theory is not greatly concerned with aesthetic problems of originality or even of beauty (an elusive word, which in music might be translated "strength"). It is concerned with correctness, with the manner of procedure, with the means and the materials of composition, without too much regard to the effect. In composition the reverse is true. The means is unimportant; correctness means nothing in itself; the effect is everything. Considered from this standpoint, musical theory and composition present no contradictions, since they belong in different spheres. Since composition is concerned exclusively with effect, the task of the composition teacher is to suggest ways in which the student may improve the effect — i.e., make the piece more beautiful. And as few can agree on what is beautiful in contemporary art, the teacher's position is often difficult. Yet there are certain qualities which, all musicians would agree, are fundamental to a successful composition: a sense of movement or flow; a balanced formal structure; a balance of unity and variety; a homogeneity of style. It is for the teacher to sense any deficiencies in these larger categories and to suggest remedies suitable to the piece in question.

II. The composer of recent times stands in a peculiar position in regard to the music of the past. By reprinting a great quantity of old music, musicology has given the composer ready access to compositions from all periods of music. As a result, many modern composers have received inspiration from the music of remote times, creating in old forms and employing archaic idioms (e.g., Malipiero, Holst, Vaughan Williams, Ernst Bloch, Debussy, Ravel, Hindemith; see *Modality; *Neo-classicism; *New Music). Many teachers of composition refer their students to old music for models; Palestrina, Bach, Mozart, and Beethoven are used with particular frequency. An extreme instance is to be seen in d'Indy's book Cours de Composition, in which the student is taken successively through the various stages of music history. It may be rightly questioned whether such backward-looking preoccupation with the past is a healthy phenomenon in the realm of creative music. In previous ages, the composer was concerned chiefly with the music of his own time and that of his immediate predecessors, upon which he built or against which he revolted. It may be that modern dependence on, and borrowing from, the past may betray weakness and creative impotence of the present.

III. Various books exist which purport to teach the art of composition. Some of

these are puerile and of little value; others are comparatively sound and contain information which is valid and useful to the student. The best books of the latter sort, however, fall rather in the sphere of theory — harmony, counterpoint, form, and analysis — and their best pages are concerned with these theoretical subjects. As such, they tell little about composition, which is the combination of these various elements. A real book on composition would have to be sub-titled: How to combine melody, harmony, rhythm, counterpoint, and form into a satisfactory whole. It is doubtful whether such a book can ever be written. Possibly the most useful books are those which treat chiefly of form (not of *forms*) in the sense of dynamic growth. How to develop a motive, construct and combine musical phrases, modulate effectively, balance musical masses and sections: these are matters which touch very closely upon composition.

The difficulty of writing about composition is strikingly evident in the variety of material contained in books bearing the word in their title. Some (e.g., the little book called *Composition* by Sir John Stainer) are little more than musical primers, treating of elementary harmonization and giving a few notions about melody, rhythm, accompaniments, etc. Some are even designed as textbooks, having questions and drills for the student (e.g., Hamilton: *Composition for Beginners*). Others discuss various aspects of music in an empirical way, treating of Rhythm, Melodies, Form, Color, etc. (e.g., Stanford: *Musical Composition*). Still others are concerned chiefly with the forms in which music is written (e.g., Kitson: *The Elements of Musical Composition*). Various books exist which deal with composition in a limited sphere (e.g., Newton: *How to Compose a Song*; Evans: *How to Compose within the Lyric Form*). An interesting study of melody is contained in Patterson's *How to Write a Good Tune*. Certain books on "composition" are primarily harmony texts (e.g., Weber: *Composition*; Goetschius: *The Materials Used in Musical Composi-*

tion). The book by d'Indy has been mentioned; it is in many respects unique, both in its approach and in its treatment of some of the fundamental problems of composition. Riemann's *Handbuch der Kompositionslehre* is a provocative book of individual stamp, which touches on many vital points of composition, including dynamic form, development, variation, etc., as well as treating certain specific forms. Prout's *Applied Form* should also be mentioned in this regard. Perhaps wisely, the author did not use the word composition in the title to his book. Nevertheless it is much more a book on composition than many in whose titles the word appears.   E. B. H.

Composition pedals (stops). See *Organ IV.

Compound binary form. Name for *sonata form. It expresses the fact that sonata form is originally and historically a binary form, but of great dimensions and of a composite structure. See also *Binary and ternary form.

Compound interval. See under *Interval.

Compound meter, time. See under *Meter.

Compound stop. Same as *Mixture stop.

Con [It.]. "With"; for instance, *con brio*, with vigor; *con moto*, with motion; *con ottava* (*con 8va*), with the higher octave, etc.

Concentus. See *Accentus, concentus.

√**Concert.** I. The public performance of music for a large audience. Those given by soloists are called recitals. Concerts in the above sense are a fairly recent institution. Through the end of the 17th century, musical performances took place in the churches, in the homes of princes or wealthy people who could afford a private orchestra [see *Chapel], or in closed circles, such as *academies or *collegia musica. Actually, the church was the only place where the common people could

hear well-prepared performances of good music. The first step toward public performance was made in opera, by the foundation of the *Teatro San Cassiano* in Venice, 1637 [see *Opera]. The first concerts (non-operatic) open to the public for admission were organized by John Banister, a London violinist, in 1672. They continued for six years, with a program daily in the afternoon. They were followed, in 1678, by a long series of concerts arranged by the London coal merchant Th. Britton which took place in a loft over his coal-house, continuing weekly for thirty-six years. Later followed: the *Concerts of Ancient Music* (1776–1848), which were largely devoted to the works of Handel; the *Salomon Concerts* (1791–95), for which Haydn wrote his famous twelve symphonies (*London Symphonies); the *Crystal Palace Concerts* (1855–1901), conducted by August Manns every Saturday afternoon.

II. In France concert activity started with the foundation, by Philidor, of the *Concerts spirituels*, which continued from 1725 to the beginning of the French Revolution (1791). They took place only around Easter time, and were largely devoted to sacred music. They became the model of similar institutions in Leipzig, Berlin, Vienna, Stockholm. Although revived in 1805, the Concerts spirituels lost their importance with the establishment of the *Concerts du Conservatoire* which were started by Habeneck in 1828 and which still continue. These concerts greatly enhanced the 19th-century development of orchestral music and contributed much to the growing interest in the music of Beethoven, Berlioz, Schubert, etc. A more popular enterprise, but of international fame, are the *Concerts populaires*, conducted by Pasdeloup from 1861 till 1884, and revived, under the name *Concerts Pasdeloup*, in 1920, by Rhené-Baton and Caplet.

III. The earliest German concert institutions are the *Gewandhaus Concerte* of Leipzig which started in 1781, under J. A. Hiller, as a continuation of his *Liebhaberkonzerte* (1763–78), and other enterprises of passing importance. Until

1884 they took place in the *Alte Gewand-haus* (Old Cloth Hall) which was replaced in that year by a new concert hall, the *Neue Gewandhaus*. Famous conductors were Mendelssohn (1835–47), under whom the concerts first attained international recognition, Nikisch, Furtwängler, and Bruno Walter.

For the development of concert life in America, see under *American music. For the various concert institutions, see *Orchestras.

Lit.: K. Meyer, *Das Konzert* (1926); G. Pinthus, *Die Entwicklung des Konzertwesens in Deutschland bis zum Beginn des 19. Jahrhunderts* (1932); E. Hanslick, *Geschichte des Konzertwesens in Wien* (2 vols., 1869/70); A. Dörffel, *Geschichte der Gewandhauskonzerte* (1881); Dandelot, *Les Concerts du Conservatoire* (1897); M. Brenet, *Les Concerts en France sous l'ancien régime* (1900).

Concertant [F.], **Concertato** [It.]. Eighteenth-century name for symphonies (*Symphonie concertante*) with participation of several solistic instruments, after the model of the earlier *concerto grosso*, but in the style and form of the Mannheim School. Such works were written by Cannabich, Karl Stamitz, Haydn, and Mozart. In 17th-century vocal works, *coro concertato* denotes a small body of solo-singers, in contrast to the large chorus, the *coro ripieno* or the *cappella* [see *Concertino* (1)]. Terms such as *Sonate concertate* (Merula, 1637) refer to the "rivaling" use of several instruments [see *Concerto grosso*].

Concertgebouw. See *Orchestras II.

Concert grand. The largest size of the pianoforte, built for concert performance. See *Pianoforte.

Concert halls. For a list of the most important concert halls see *Orchestras. For the acoustical properties of concert halls, see *Architectural acoustics. Cf. also *LavE* ii.6, 3860.

Concertina. See under *Accordion.

Concertino. (1) In Baroque music, the soloist group of the *concerto grosso. — (2) Nineteenth-century compositions in the style of a concerto but in free form, usually in one single movement with sections of varying speed and character. A German name for the same type is *Konzertstück*. Examples are: Weber, *Concertino for Clarinet*, op. 26; Schumann, *Introduction and Allegro appassionato*, op. 92 (piano and orchestra). Others are by Rubinstein (piano, op. 113), Bruch (violin, op. 84), Carpenter (piano), Dohnanyi (violoncello, op. 12).

Concertmaster [F. *chef d'attaque*; G. *Konzertmeister*; It. *violino primo*]. The first violinist of an orchestra. He is entrusted with violin solo passages, but also represents the orchestra in negotiations with the management and the conductor, assists the latter in rehearsing, and occasionally replaces him in conducting.

Concerto [F. *concert*; G. *Konzert*; It. *concerto*]. I. *General*. A composition for a solo player and an orchestra teamed, not in a master-servant relationship (as in the case of *accompaniment), but in one of rivalry on an equal basis (the term comes from L. *concertare*, i.e., "to fight side by side," "to compete as brothers-in-arms"). The development of the classical and modern concerto, i.e., from Mozart to the present day, generally follows that of the *sonata from which it borrowed its chief features of form and style. There are, however, the following differences: (a) the concerto practically always has three movements only, the scherzo being omitted (Brahms's Piano Concerto op. 83 is one of the few exceptions); (b) the first movement is written in a modified sonata form in which the exposition, instead of being repeated in full, is written out twice, for the first time in a preliminary and abbreviated form with the tonic as the main key throughout and for the orchestra only, then in its full form for the soloist and orchestra and with the proper modulation into the dominant, a form which is known as *concerto-sonata form*; (c) the last movement is usually in

[171]

*rondo form, a form the light character
of which lends itself well to the display
of brilliance and to the expression of a
"happy ending"; (d) a peculiarity of the
concerto is the soloist *cadenza which appears regularly in the first movement,
near the end of the recapitulation but may
occur also, less elaborately, in the other
movements. The solo part of a concerto
is always written in a highly virtuoso style
designed to show the equality, if not superiority, of the single player over the entire orchestra. According to the solo instrument, concertos are classified as piano,
violin, cello concertos. Concertos in a free
one-movement form are called *concertino or Konzertstück.

II. The Present Repertory. The present-day repertory of the piano concerto
opens with the latest concertos by Mozart,
composed between 1785 and 1791 (K.V.
466 in D minor; K.V. 467 in C major;
K.V. 482 in E-flat major; K.V. 488 in A
major; K.V. 491 in C minor; K.V. 503 in
C major; K.V. 537 in D major (Coronation Concerto); K.V. 595 in B-flat major).
In these compositions Mozart established
the classical form and style of the concerto. Beethoven's five piano concertos,
especially the last two, in G major (op. 58,
1805) and in E-flat major (Emperor Concerto, op. 73, 1809), represent the artistic
high-point of the entire literature. There
followed Weber (op. 11, 1810; op. 32,
1912; Konzertstück op. 79, 1821), Mendelssohn (op. 25, 1831; op. 40, 1837),
Chopin (op. 11, op. 21, both c. 1830), and
Schumann with his beautiful and effective Concerto in A minor, op. 54 (1841).
Chopin's concertos suffer from an inferior treatment of the orchestra and from
a lack of musical substance in the solo
part. Liszt's two concertos, in E-flat
(1849) and A (1849–57), show a tendency
towards technical display for its own sake
which continues particularly in the concertos of the Russian composers such as
Rubinstein (five concertos, notably op. 70,
in D minor and op. 94 in E-flat), Tchaikovsky (B-flat minor, op. 23, 1875; G
major, op. 44, 1880; E-flat major, op. 75,
1893), Rimsky-Korsakov (1882), and
many others. A conspicuous feature of

the Russian concertos is the prevalence of
octave-playing over the other aspects of
piano technique. Grieg contributed an
effective and very popular concerto in A
minor (1868). A new peak of artistic
perfection was reached by Brahms, in his
piano concertos in D minor, op. 15 (1854)
and B-flat major (1887). There followed
concertos by Franck (Variations symphoniques, 1885); MacDowell (D minor,
op. 23, 1890); Scriabin (op. 20, 1897);
Rachmaninov (op. 1, 1890; op. 18, 1901;
op. 30, 1909; op. 40, 1927, revised 1938);
Reger (op. 114); Prokofiev (op. 10, 1911;
op. 16, 1913; op. 26, 1917; op. 53, for the
left hand alone, 1931; op. 55, 1932);
Ravel (one for piano, one for the left hand
alone, both 1930–31); Stravinsky (for
piano and wind instruments, 1924);
Hindemith (op. 36, one for piano and
twelve solo instruments); Gershwin
(1925); Copland (1926); and Vaughan
Williams (1933). Some of the more recent works approach the idiom of the
Baroque *concerto grosso, in conformity
with the general trend towards *neo-
classicism [see below, Concerto for or-
chestra].

The repertory of the violin concerto is
somewhat smaller and, on the whole, less
significant. It includes works by Haydn
(9), Viotti (29), Mozart (7), Kreutzer
(19; 2 for two violins), Beethoven (1),
Rode (13), Paganini (2), Spohr (11),
Mendelssohn (1), Vieuxtemps (6), Gade
(1), Raff (2), Reinecke (1), Goldmark
(2), Joachim (2), Bruch (3), Svendsen
(1), Lalo (4), Brahms (1), Tchaikovsky
(1), Dvořák (1), Saint-Saëns (3), Sinding (2), Elgar (1), R. Strauss (1), Sibelius (1), Schillings (1), Pfitzner (1),
Reger (1), Holst (1 for two violins),
Scott (1), Casella (1), Krenek (1), Respighi (2), Szymanowski (2), Stravinsky
(1), Schönberg (1), Hindemith (1),
Piston (1), Bartók (1).

Several modern composers have written
compositions under the seemingly self-
contradictory title: Concerto for orchestra,
i.e., without a soloist instrument. This
trend occurred in connection with the
*neo-classical tendencies of the '20's, as a
revival of the *concerto grosso of the

Baroque in which the soloist aspect is much less pronounced than in the modern concerto. These concerti approach the old form in the use of a chamber orchestra, in their emphasis on "motoric" rather than emotional impulse, and on linear design rather than massed sound or orchestral effects (Stravinsky, *Concerto en mi* ♭, 1937/38). Some of them introduce the Baroque *concertino*, i.e., a group of three or two solo instruments alternating with the full ensemble, e.g., Kaminski, *Concerto grosso* (1923), E. Krenek, *Concerto grosso* I, II (1921, 1925), P. Hindemith, *Konzert für Orchester*, op. 34 (1925), W. Piston, *Concerto for Orchestra* (1933).

III. *History.* The term "concerto" was first used for vocal compositions supported by an instrumental (or organ) accompaniment, in order to distinguish such pieces from the then current style of unaccompanied *a-cappella* music. To this category belong the *Concerti ecclesiastici* (church concertos) by Andrea and Giov. Gabrieli (1587; cf. *HAM*, no. 157), Adriano Banchieri (1595), both for double-chorus, as well as those by Ludovico Viadana (1602; cf. *HAM*, no 185; *SchGMB*, no. 168) and Hortensio Naldi (1607; cf. *RiHM* ii.2, 313f), both for solo parts in the then novel monodic style. The use of the name concerto for accompanied vocal music persisted throughout the Baroque period, e.g., in Schütz's *Kleine Geistliche Concerten* of 1636, and in several cantatas by Bach which he calls "Concerto."

In the field of purely instrumental music the term adopted a more characteristic significance, viz., that of contrasting performing bodies playing in alternation. This style which some writers of the 17th century called *stile moderno* is one of the most typical traits of Baroque music. On the basis of the above definition, the history of the concerto prior to Mozart may conveniently be divided into three main periods, one from 1620 to 1670, the second from 1670 to 1750, the third from 1750 to 1780. It should be noticed that, particularly in the first period, the presence or absence of the name *concerto*, *concertante*, is not decisive, as various names, such as *canzona*, *sonata*, *sinfonia*, were used without clear distinction for a variety of styles and types.

(a). 1620–70. While Viadana's *Sinfonie musicali a otto voci* (1610) show the instrumental application of Giov. Gabrieli's double-chorus style, the *Sonate concertate in stilo moderno* by Dorio Castello (1621, '29) mark the beginning of an important literature, namely of *canzonas* (i.e., one-movement pieces written in a number of short sections in contrasting characters) with solistic passages, mostly for the violin. (For a slightly earlier example, by Usper, see A. Einstein, in *Kretzschmar Festschrift*, 1918.) This type, the *concerto canzona*, as it might be called, was further cultivated by Steffano Bernardi (*Sonate in sinfonia*, 1623), Gio. Batt. Fontana (d. 1630), Tarquinio Merula (*Canzoni, overe Sonate concertate per chiesa*, 1637; also *Canzoni da sonare*, 1651), Massimiliano Neri (*Sonate et canzoni*, 1644; *Sonate*, 1651; cf. *RiHM* ii.2, 150ff; also Wasielewski, *Instrumentalsätze*), Vincenzo Albrici (*Sinfonia à 6*, 1654), Antonio Bertali (MS sonatas, 1663).

(b). 1670–1750. In this period the Baroque concerto arrived at its peak. The main advance over the previous period is the replacement of the sectional canzona structure by a form in three or four different movements, and the adoption of a fuller, more homophonic style, with increasing melodic emphasis on the upper parts. Within the large literature of this period three types can be distinguished (according to A. Schering): the *concerto-sinfonia*, the *concerto grosso*, and the *solo concerto*. The first category, which is of only passing importance, uses contrasting technique (sections in tutti-character and others in a more brilliant style) rather than contrasting instrumental bodies and, therefore, deserves mention here only because it preceded the other two types and because it contributed to the development of a virtuoso violin style. It was cultivated first by the members of the *Bologna School, e.g., Cazzati, Bononcini, Aldrovandini, Torelli, later by Albicastro (*12 Concerti, c.* 1703), dall'Abaco (*Concerti da chiesa, c.* 1712), and others.

Of greater importance is the *concerto grosso*, which must be considered the classical type of the Baroque concerto, and which is characterized by the use of a small group of solo players (*concertino*) in contrast to the full orchestra (*concerto*) [see *Concerto grosso].

The solo concerto, i.e., the concerto for a single soloist, is the latest of the three types. Although solo-technique was extensively used in the concerto-canzonas, the first examples showing this style applied to the form of the Baroque sonata are contained in the *Sinfonie e concerti . . .* op. 2 (1700?) by Tomaso Albinoni. His concerti (also in his opp. 5, 7, 9) are usually in three movements and contain short solo passages, mostly in the character of figurative transitions. An important progress was made by the great master Giuseppe Torelli (d. 1708) who holds a central position in the development of all the various types of Baroque concerto. In his op. 6 (*Concerti musicali a 4*, 1698) and still more in his op. 8 (*Concerti grossi . . . ,* 1709; cf. *HAM,* no. 246; *SchGMB,* no. 257) the solo violin obtains equal importance with the orchestra. Torelli's idea was continued by Alessandro Scarlatti (1659–1725; cf. *HAM,* no. 260) and particularly by Antonio Vivaldi (*c.* 1680–1743) whose numerous violin concertos (*Estro armonico* op. 3, op. 4, op. 6, op. 7) became quickly famous owing to the solistic exploitation of the instrument and to a new style of rhythmic precision which pervades his compositions. Practically all his concertos are in three movements, quick, slow, quick, a scheme which became the standard form of the concerto to the present day. His style soon became the model of concerto style. Bach (together with J. G. Walther) transcribed a number of Vivaldi's concertos for the organ (or harpsichord) alone, and Bach also made, in his famous *Italian Concerto* (1735), an original contribution to the somewhat self-contradictory type of the concerto for a single player only who, in turns, represents the orchestra

and the soloist. It should be noted that pieces such as the introduction to his English Suites nos. 3 and 5 are also "Italian concertos," at least, first movements thereof.

Bach also wrote the first concertos for harpsichord and orchestra, starting with transcriptions of violin concertos (by himself, Vivaldi, and others). Among his 18 concertos for one to four harpsichords (with orchestra) only the one in C major for two harpsichords and the two for three harpsichords are original compositions. Handel's 18 organ concertos (publ. 1738, '40, '60) belong to the last examples of the Baroque solo concerto. Here, as also in his harpsichord suites, he mixes sonata movements with others of a dance character (minuet, musette, siciliano). In Italy the violin concerto remained the favored type, and violinists such as Francesco Maria Veracini (*c.* 1685–1750?), Carlo Tessarini (b. 1690), Pietro Locatelli (1693–1764), and Giuseppe Tartini (1692–1770) gradually worked away from the true Baroque style of the Vivaldi concerto and towards a new type characterized by more melodious, though frequently sentimental, themes, by a clearly homophonic structure, and by forms foreshadowing that of the classical concerto.

(c). 1750–80. In this period of transition from the Baroque concerto to the classical concerto the initiative falls to German composers, mainly to the three sons of J. S. Bach. Ph. Em. Bach's concertos follow in their first movements a scheme which clearly shows the trisection exposition — development — recapitulation, with the exposition played twice, first by the orchestra, then by the soloist, and with the recapitulation being shortened. While his exposition still lacks a second theme, this is usually found in the concertos by Johann Christian Bach (1735–82) which, more than any other, are the true predecessors of Mozart's piano concertos. Haydn's numerous concertos (20 for piano, 9 for violin, 6 for cellos, and others) seldom rise above the average level, and lack the inspiration which pervades his quartets and symphonies. Only one piano concerto and one or two cello concertos are ever heard today.

Lit.: A. Veinus, *The Concerto* (New York, 1944); A. Schering, *Geschichte des Instrumentalkonzerts* (1905, 1927); H. Daffner, *Die Entwicklung des Klavierkonzerts bis Mozart* (1906); F. Bauer, *Das vorklassische deutsche Violinkonzert* (Diss. Giessen); Hans Weber, *Das Violoncell-konzerts des 18. . . . Jahrhunderts* (Diss. Tübingen 1932); E. Rapp, *Beiträge zur Frühgeschichte des Violoncell-konzerts* (Diss. Würzburg 1934); G. Piccioli, *Il Concerto per pianoforte e orchestra da Mozart a Grieg* (1936); R. Erlebach, "Style in Pianoforte Concerto Writing" (*ML* xvii, no. 2); H. Mishkin, "The Italian Concerto before 1700" (*BAMS* vii); H. Uldall, "Beiträge zur Frühgeschichte des Klavier Konzerts" (*ZMW* x); H. Kretzschmar, "Die Konzertkompositionen grossen Stils" (*JMP* iii). See also *Concerto grosso.

Concerto grosso. The most important type of the Baroque concerto [see *Concerto III (b)], characterized by the use of a small group of solo instruments, called *concertino* or *principale*, against the full orchestra, called *concerto, tutti*, or *ripieni*. The concertino usually consists of two violins and a thorough-bass (violoncello plus harpsichord), i.e., the same ensemble which constitutes the *trio-sonata of the Baroque. The ripieni are a small string orchestra, later occasionally with the addition of wind instruments (trumpets, oboes, flutes, horns).

The earliest known examples of the concerto grosso principle occur in two "Sinfonie a più instrumenti" by Alessandro Stradella (*c.* 1645–82). Some concerti grossi by Corelli (1653–1713), although published much later, would seem to be of a date close to that of Stradella's, because they show the patchwork structure of the earlier canzona, with quick changes of a considerable number of short "movements" (nos. 1, 2, 5, 7 of the 12 *Concerti grossi*, op. 6, 1712). Georg Muffat's (1645–1704) 6 concerti grossi, published 1701 [*DTOe* 11.ii], probably belong also to the period around

1680. They contain suite-like movements (e.g., Sonata–Corrente–Grave–Gavotta–Rondeau) and show relatively little contrast between the concertino and the concerto. In Torelli's (1650–1708) concerti grossi (publ. 1709, written *c.* 1690) the two violins of the concertino are treated much more individually, so that the style approaches that of a concerto for two solo violins. These concertos, together with the later concertos of Corelli's op. 6, represent a high-point of classical balance and dignity. Francesco Geminiani (1687–1762; op. 2, 1732; op. 3, 1733) carried on the tradition of Corelli, adopting the four-movement scheme of the sonata da chiesa as the standard form (Corelli's concertos usually have five or more movements).

A new trend in concerto grosso style was inaugurated by the Venetian Antonio Vivaldi (*c.* 1675–1743) who established the three-movement scheme Allegro — Adagio — Allegro and who largely discarded the contrapuntal treatment of the earlier masters in favor of a novel style of rhythmic animation and precision, using stereotyped figures as the basis for a more dynamic manner of writing. He also established what might be called the classical form of the quick movements, i.e., a rondo-like alternation of a tutti-ritornello with varying episodes for the concertino. The concerti grossi of Pietro Locatelli (1693–1764) are direct imitations of Vivaldi's, as are also, on a much higher artistic level, Bach's *Brandenburg Concertos of 1721. Handel, in his Grand Concertos op. 6 (1740), although incorporating elements of Vivaldi's style, retained the larger number of movements, as found in Corelli.

The neo-classical movement of the 20th century has brought about a remarkable revival of the concerto grosso, chiefly as a reaction against the virtuoso-like solo concerto of the 19th century. See *Concerto I.

Lit.: A. Schering, *Geschichte des Instrumentalkonzerts* (1905), pp. 38ff; *LavE* ii.4, 2446ff; W. Krüger, *Das Concerto grosso in Deutschland* (Diss. Berlin 1932); A. Bonaccorsi, "Contributo alla storia del concerto grosso" (*RMI* xxxix). See also *Concerto.

Concert pitch. See *Pitch (2).

Concitato. See under *Stile.

Concord. A combination of sounds which is satisfactory to the ear (triads, seventh-chords, and other "agreeably sounding" chords), as distinguished from deliberately harsh and unpleasant combinations, called discord. The terms are used as aesthetic rather than technical categories.

Conducteur [F.]. In French usage, not a conductor, but an abridged orchestral score, as distinct from the *grande partition*, i.e., full score.

Conducting. I. Conducting, in the simplest sense, means the direction of a number of performers in a unified musical effort, by means of manual and bodily motions, facial expressions, etc. Its most elementary manifestation is time-beating, the motions of which are now embodied in a common practice. It is commonly assumed that a clear and decisive downstroke will fall on the first beat of each measure, and that the last beat is an upstroke, while a secondary accent of the measure is indicated by a stroke outward to the right. With the right hand the conductor indicates the beat, the tempo, strong accents, entrances of instruments or voices, while on the left hand falls the indication of subtler nuances of dynamics and agogics. It is true, of course, that within a general understanding, conductors, especially those in charge of virtuoso organizations, deal idiomatically and often freely with this matter. Modern orchestras are obliged to adapt themselves to the particular methods of visiting conductors, but however elastic these may be, certain elementary principles are taken for granted. (Diagrams of the commonly accepted time-beating gestures may be found in the books of Boult, Stoessel, and others; see Lit.)

Not all conductors elect to use a baton. Some feel more free in direction when they are unhampered by what is bound

to be a somewhat rigid factor. It is certainly true that the many possible positions of the hand may be more evocative than the motions of a stick; and choral conductors, especially, find this to be true. Choral singing is largely carried on by amateur groups which depend on the conductor for much more than the indications common in the leading of an orchestra. Directions must be more graphic, and to this end the hand, open or closed, with palm upwards or downwards, with the index finger rigid or all five fingers outspread, suggests much more to the singers regarding technique and text interpretation than a baton may do. Perhaps it is because the chorus is not so dependent as the orchestra on a traditional method of time-beating that choral conductors have often been wont to cultivate expressive but undisciplined motions which are neither musicianly nor specific in their implications. Such methods, plus the fact that the training of a chorus appears to require so much less of the conductor than does the training of an orchestra, have led to the popular acceptance of choral conducting as a stepsister of the more taxing and certainly more glamorous branch of the art. There is, however, a choral technique quite as detailed as that of the orchestra. The choral conductor whose ambitions lead him beyond the attainment of mere "mass" tone and conversational pronunciation, may produce a result as evocative and technically refined as that which is possible for the orchestra.

II. Brief mention may be made of certain recent methods which indicate a rather radical departure from the accepted standards of conducting. Attempts have been made by orchestras to operate on a conductorless basis. In Russia, where for obvious political reasons such an experiment would find favor, these attempts have aroused much interest. Aside from the fact that the field of music open to such a venture is necessarily limited, the basic difficulty lies in the distribution of responsibility for interpretation. Where each member of the group has a voice in interpretative matters, the dissenters, even with the best will in the world, will be unable to achieve unity of intention. Another attempt at innovation has been made by conductors who are also keyboard virtuosos and who have tried to revive an 18th-century practice by uniting the functions of player (in concertos) and conductor. This procedure is not, on the whole, commendable, as either the playing of a concerto or the directing of the accompaniment is important enough to command a concentration not possible when one individual serves in two capacities. Furthermore, the modern audience is likely to be distracted by the spectacle of the pianist sometimes standing, sometimes sitting, suddenly abandoning the conductor's gestures, and perhaps resuming his seat barely in time to take up the soloist's part. The demands of much of the purely orchestral music of the 18th century could doubtless well be met by combining the offices of performer and conductor; today the opportunity for such a procedure would seem to exist only in the case of 18th-century music, such as Bach's Concerti, performed by a small ensemble.

History. III. A review of the history of conducting must take into account not only the difference in size between the small groups of earlier times and the giant orchestras of the present day, but, first of all, the different principles of rhythm embodied in the various phases of music history. As is explained under *rhythm, three radically different concepts of rhythm might be distinguished: free rhythm, metrical rhythm, and measured rhythm. It is with the third type that the modern conductor is mainly concerned, although the rhythmic complexities of much contemporary music result in a degree of accentual irregularity which makes necessary a time-beating procedure much more elastic than that which applies, for instance, to the music of the 18th and 19th centuries. The first type is represented by Gregorian chant, and for its conducting a method called cheironomy has been traditionally employed. This consists of motions of the conductor's hand intended to guide the singer's performance, and, in the days when music was orally transmitted (by the so-called cheironomic

*neumes), to remind him of the direction of the melody. For all music which does not conform to any categorical method of direction, cheironomy is the logical usage as it ideally conveys the various inflections and the rhythmic freedom of the vocal line (e.g., in some modern Russian liturgical music, where the bar-lines are widely separated and the "measure" consists of from nine to thirteen beats). The second type embraces the rhythmically strict, but enormously complex music (choral as well as instrumental) of the 14th and 15th centuries, with its extensive use of complicated *cross rhythms, *syncopations, displaced measures, *proportions, etc., and its absence in general of regularly recurrent accents. Here the only possible method of conducting is what might be called "metronomic conducting," i.e., an up-and-down movement of the hand indicating the normal pulse [see *Tactus] without any attempt to convey accents or phrases, all of which must be left to the players or singers of the individual parts. In the case of choral music of the late 16th century (Palestrina, Byrd) the rhythm is generally less complex, but the absence of regular accent remains to present a problem to the modern conductor. Due to the fact that most modern editions resort to arbitrary barring in equal measures, or at best employ the expedient of unequal measures, the essential independence of each voice is often destroyed; and as the proper accent may conceivably fall on successive beats in the separate parts, false accentuation and phrasing is bound to take place. Some modern editions of 16th-century choral music are irregularly barred so that the inevitable after-bar accent in singing is made to coincide with the word or syllable which, according to good sense, should be stressed. Sir Donald Tovey's *Kirkhope Choir Magazine* and editions like the Polymetric are based on this idea, and Tovey's own method when conducting this music was to indicate each important pulse by a slight downward motion of the hand or finger. Obviously such a procedure puts a burden upon both conductor and chorus, but it is eminently justified by the results.

IV. Where the music was characterized by a strongly rhythmic character, where no refinements of tempo or interpretation were implied, as in folk singing, a general stamping of feet or clapping of hands served to attain that unity. Such a method was known to the Greeks, who used wooden shoes for this purpose, or even a sort of clapper hinged to the heel of the shoe. There are classic references, also, to thumb-snapping as a rhythmic device. How early in the history of conducting the baton was adopted it is impossible to say, but it was certainly in use in the sixteenth century. A roll of paper, the violin bow, and the cane have likewise served as implements of direction; and the last mentioned, in particular, was effective in marking the beat by sharp strokes on the floor. It is evident, in fact, that for a surprisingly long period in the history of conducting the performer was not expected to depend solely on his eye. Even after the adoption of the baton, conductors continued to make the beat audible; and this irritating method was doubtless finally abandoned because of popular protests against it which arose certainly as early as the 17th century.

During that period in which the harpsichord was an important member of the orchestra, small instrumental groups could doubtless depend on its incisive tone for whatever unifying direction was necessary; and it was, indeed, recognized as valuable in preserving a steady beat. The conductor could carry out his direction from the harpsichord or the organ, sometimes removing his hands from the keys for this purpose.

V. By the 18th century the first violin had acquired so much authority that the responsibility for direction shifted from the keyboard to the violin. During Haydn's visits to London in 1791 and 1794 control of the orchestra was divided between Haydn at the piano and Salomon with his violin. In 1787 Deldevez wrote a textbook with details about the practice of the violin-conductor, a type of which Habeneck (1781–1849) was the last representative. In England the concert-master is still referred to as the "leader,"

and he enjoys prerogatives and acknowledgments only second to the conductor himself. It is not surprising, then, that in England, as elsewhere in the 19th century, the relinquishment of the bow or the keyboard for the baton in the hand of a single authority was not accomplished without opposition. Spohr created an alarm in London when he first used a baton there, in 1820. By 1850, however, the baton had won universal acceptance. The only modern survival of primitive time-beating was that employed by American college glee club leaders of the previous generation who maintained an almost consistent and mechanical head-nodding throughout the performance. A single hand gesture would have been considered in bad taste; but as the leader was also often the best singer, his vocal contribution was inevitably slight, due to the persistent bobbing up and down of his head.

With the establishment by the *Mannheim orchestra in the 18th century of refinements which had hitherto been unknown, the career of the conductor as an individual is prophesied. In the 19th century, equipped with baton and with autocratic powers of control, he ceases to be an important participant and becomes the dominating figure. Upon him the spotlight of modern musical attention is now fixed. He has become the personification of virtuosity, surrrounded by adulators to whom all other conductors are inferior. His "readings" are authoritative and many a concert goer, it must be feared, is more interested in the attitudes and interpretations of his favorite than in the music itself. Not since the days of the celebrated "song birds" of the 18th century has such partisanship over the relative merits of performance been rife. Obviously, the temptation to the spectacular, to the occasional sacrifice of musical truth, is not to be invariably resisted. But to one who listens objectively, discounting over-praise and occasional lapses from good taste, and who bears in mind the slow physical development of the orchestra as a flexible and a sensitive instrument, and the long submergence of the conductor as the unique controlling force, the modern orchestra and the command of its resources by more than one living conductor must appear as one of the artistic miracles of our time. See also *Concert; *Orchestras and Concert halls.

Lit.: B. Grosbayne, *A Bibliography of Works and Articles on Conductors . . .* (1934); R. Wagner, *On Conducting* (transl., 1919); F. Weingartner, *On Conducting* (transl., 1925); A. Carse, *Orchestral Conducting, A Textbook* (1929); V. Bakaleinikoff, *Elementary Rules of Conducting*; C. Schroeder, *Handbook of Conducting* (191–?); A. Stoessel, *The Technique of the Baton* (1920, '28); H. Scherchen, *Handbook of Conducting* (1933); A. Boult, *A Handbook on the Technique of Conducting* (1932); A. T. Davison, *Choral Conducting* (1941); G. Schünemann, *Geschichte des Dirigierens* (1913); *AdHM* i, 1208ff; B. Grosbayne, "A Perspective on the Literature of Conducting" (*PMA* lxvii); G. Schünemann, "Zur Frage des Taktschlagens . . . in der Mensuralmusik" (*SIM* x); A. Chybinski, in *SIM* x; E. Vogel, in *JMP* v; R. Schwartz, in *JMP* xiv.   A. T. D.

Conductor's part. An abbreviated score of orchestral works. It usually includes the leading part (chiefly first violin) with the other important instruments cued in.

Conductus. Latin songs of the 12th and 13th centuries, either monophonic or polyphonic. They probably developed from rhymed *tropes which accompanied the entrance of the priest (introitus tropes; L. *conducere* means: to lead, to escort). In fact, the name appears first in a Daniel Play [*c.* 1140; see *Liturgical drama] in connection with melodies which accompany the coming and going of personages [cf. H. Coussemaker, *Drames liturgiques . . .* (1860)]. Towards the end of the 12th century the word was used as a generic term for Latin poems of varied form and content (religious, contemplative, lyrical, political, satirical), a repertory which forms the Latin counterpart of the French poetry of the troubadours and trouvères.

A large collection of monophonic *conductus* are preserved in the codex Florence, *Laur. plut. 29, 1* [see *Magnus liber organi; examples in *HAM*, no. 17b; *AdHM* i, 185]. More interesting musically are the polyphonic conductus which represent one of the chief types of 13-century polyphony. As distinct from the other forms of the period [see *Ars antiqua], the *organa, *clausulae, and *motets, the conductus are not based on liturgical chants but on freely invented melodies, for instance, on those of the monophonic conductus. Above these tenor-melodies one, two, or (rarely) three parts are added in strict note-against-note style, a technique which forms a sharp contrast to the rhyth-

micially differentiated style of the organa, clausulae, and motets. A special type of conductus which was considered to be of superior value was the *conductus habens caudam*, i.e., a conductus with cadential extensions over the final vowels of the various lines of the poem [see *Cauda (2)]. There exist a number of conductus, presumably by Perotinus, which show a considerably more elaborate texture and which represent the culmination point of the development [cf. *OH* i, 293ff].

The rhythmic interpretation of the (simply syllabic) conductus is still controversial. Some scholars advocate interpretation in modal rhythm, e.g., $\frac{6}{4}$ | ♩ ♩ ♩ ♩ |, instead of ♩ ♩ ♩ ♩. Others prefer the latter rendition, admitting modal rhythm only for the caudae which are written in the ligature system of *modal notation [cf. *ApNPM*, 224ff]. Examples in *HAM*, nos. 38, 39; *SchGMB*, no. 16 (the "instrumental" opening and close is actually *vocalization).

The term "conductus style" has been

widely adopted by musicologists to denote note-against-note style [see *Familiar style], particularly with reference to early 14th-century Italian compositions (*madrigals), which are written in what may be called "ornamented conductus style."

Lit.: E. Gröninger, *Repertoire-Untersuchungen zum mehrstimmigen Notre-Dame Conductus* (1939); *OH* i, 245–318; *ReMMA*, 307ff; L. Ellinwood, in *MQ* xxvii; J. Handschin, in *KIM*, 1925 and *ZMW* vi.

Confinalis. In the theory of church modes, a secondary final, usually the upper fifth of the finalis (e.g., *a* in the Dorian mode); therefore, practically identical with the dominant of the mode [see *Church modes].

Conga. A modern dance which originated in Cuba where it is used during the Carnival festivities. It is characterized by the use of brief melodic phrases and of normal rhythmic accents alternating with measures in syncopation. The texts are frequently political or satirical.

Conjunct, disjunct. Notes are called conjunct if they are successive degrees of the scale — disjunct if they form intervals larger than a second [see *Motion; *Melody; *Primitive music II]. For conjunct, disjunct tetrachord, see *Greek music.

Conjunctura. See *Square notation; also *Currentes.

Consecutives. See *Parallel fifths and octaves.

Consequent. See *Antecedent and consequent.

Conservatory. See *Music education V, IX; also *Profession; *Degrees.

Console. The case which encloses the keyboard, stops, etc., of an organ. Formerly placed in front of the organ, it is now often detached, the sole connection being by electric cable.

Consonance, Dissonance. The terms are used to describe the agreeable effect produced by certain intervals (consonant intervals, e.g., octave, third) as against

the disagreeable effect produced by others (dissonant intervals, e.g., second, seventh), or similar effects produced by chords.

Consonance and dissonance are the very foundation of harmonic music, in which the former represents the element of normalcy and repose, the latter the no less important element of irregularity and disturbance.

In spite of numerous efforts no wholly satisfactory explanation and definition of consonance and dissonance has yet been found. The shortcoming of the explanation given in the initial sentence of this article lies not so much in the fact that it is based entirely upon subjective impressions, but chiefly in its failure to account for the consonant quality of the fourth and fifth. Indeed, from the point of view of musical composition of all eras, these two intervals must be regarded as consonances second only to the unison and octave; however, according to the above definition they would certainly range after the third and sixth, and might perhaps be termed dissonant (especially the fourth makes a decidedly unpleasant effect upon an unbiased observer). It is chiefly for this reason that the "pleasant-unpleasant-theory" cannot be considered satisfactory. Following are the most important theories of consonance and dissonance.

I. (a) According to the Pythagorean theory, intervals are the more consonant the smaller the numbers which express the ratio of their frequencies (or of the lengths of the corresponding strings). This theory leads to an order of the intervals which conforms rather well with musical practice:

unis.	8ve	5th	4th	6th	3d
c–c	c–c′	c–g	c–f	c–a	c–e
1:1	1:2	2:3	3:4	3:5	4:5

3d	6th	2d	7th	7th
c–eb	c–ab	c–d	c–b	c–bb
5:6	5:8	8:9	8:15	9:16

The chief objection raised against this theory is its failure to account for the fact that a minute modification of a consonant interval — too slight to be noticed by the ear — brings about highly complicated ratios of frequencies. For instance, the well-tempered fifth which cannot be distinguished by the ear from the Pythagorean (pure) fifth, is (approximately) characterized by the fraction $\frac{293}{439}$. See also under *Arabian music I.

(b) Helmholtz' theory of beats [cf. Helmholtz-Ellis, *Sensations of Tone* (1912), p. 186, etc.] explains intervals as consonant if no disturbing *beats are produced by the two tones or by their harmonics; otherwise, they are dissonant [beats are most disturbing if they number 33 per second, least disturbing if they are less than 6 per second, or more than 120 per second]. The chief disadvantage of this theory is that the dissonant or consonant character of an interval varies with the octave in which it lies, as appears from the following table:

c–e	33 beats	c–d	16 beats
c'–e'	66 "	c'–d'	32 "
c''–e''	132 "	c''–d''	64 "
		c'''–d'''	128 "

It appears that the third c–e would be as "dissonant" as the second c'–d', and that the second c'''–d''' would be as "consonant" as the third c''–e''.

(c) Helmholtz' theory of *Klangverwandtschaft* (relationship of sounds). Two tones are defined as consonant if their harmonics (excluding the 7th, 9th, etc.) have one or more tones in common. From the accompanying table it appears

that there exist two or more such common tones in the case of octave, fifth, and fourth, one in the case of the other consonances, none in the case of dissonances. This definition is more satisfactory and useful than any other, particularly since it establishes a clear line of demarcation between consonant and dissonant intervals, a result which, from the musical

point of view, is more desirable than the "gradual decline of consonance" resulting from the other theories. Its only blemish lies in the fact that the "dissonant" harmonics, e.g., the seventh, have to be artificially eliminated (otherwise D, with the seventh harmonic c, would be consonant to C). Thus the definition presupposes the term to be defined. One could, however, argue that the seventh harmonic of D is noticeably lower than C ($\frac{63}{64}$ as against 1).

(d) C. Stumpf's theory of *Tonverschmelzung* (amalgamation of sounds). This is a psychological explanation based on large-scale experimentation. The consonant nature of an interval is measured by the degree to which the sound produced by the two simultaneous tones evokes, in the mind of musically untrained listeners, the impression of one unified sound instead of two different tones. Thus, the percentage of listeners judging (wrongly) in favor of "one tone" (*Verschmelzung*) gives a measurement of the degree of consonance or dissonance. Following is the result of Stumpf's experiment:

octave	fifth	fourth	third	tritone	second
75%	50%	33%	25%	20%	10%

It should be noticed that in this series the fifth and the fourth appear as better consonances than the third. The chief shortcoming of this theory lies in the fact that consonance and dissonance are no longer contradictory or exclusive terms, but only gradations.

(e) After an examination of all these scientific theories, the practical musician will probably be satisfied with a very simple common-sense rule, in a way a practical condensation of Helmholtz' *Klangverwandtschaft*: *Every interval contained in the major (or minor) triad and its inversions is a consonance, the other intervals are dissonances.*

II. Chords can be classified as consonant or dissonant on the basis of the following definition: A consonant chord is one in which only consonant intervals (octave, perfect fifth, perfect fourth, third, sixth) are found; a dissonant chord is one which includes at least one dissonant interval (second, seventh, etc.). This places the triads and their inversions (except for the diminished and augmented triad) in the former category, all the other chords (seventh chords, ninth chords) in the latter, in full conformity with musical experience and practice.

III. The ideas as to which intervals are consonant, which dissonant, have changed considerably during the course of music history. Apparently the fourth was the first interval to be considered as a consonance, with the fifth replacing it at a somewhat later date [9th, 10th centuries; see *Organum (2), I]. The third would seem to have been used in England and in other northern countries long before it was admitted as a consonance into the musical practice of the Continent. The English theorist Walter Odington (c. 1290; see *Theory II) was the first to recognize the third as a consonant interval, and in the 14th century it was gradually admitted as such in actual composition [see *Fauxbourdon; *Gymel; *Third]. By this admission the picture of harmony changed so radically that the entire history of harmonic music might be divided into three main epochs: that of pre-tertian, of tertian, and of post-tertian harmony. The latter term, of course, refers to the modern practice (beginning c. 1900) in which, after an ever-increasing use of dissonances, the triad begins to lose its position as the cornerstone of harmony [see *Harmony II].

Lit.: K. Jeppesen, *The Style of Palestrina and the Dissonance* (1927); E. Hartmann, *Konsonanz und Dissonanz* (Diss. Marburg 1922); R. Lenzen, *Geschichte des Konsonanzbegriffs im 19. Jahrhundert* (Diss. Bonn 1931); S. Krehl, "Die Dissonanz als musikalisches Ausdrucksmittel" (*ZMW* i); A. Machabey, "Dissonance, polytonalité, atonalité" (*RM* xii).

Consort (erroneous spelling of *concert*). A 17th-century term for instrumental ensembles of chamber music and for compositions written for such ensembles. A group including only instruments of the same family was called "whole consort"

(consort of viols, of recorders; see *Chest of viols), whereas a group consisting of various types was called "broken consort." Morley's *Consort Lessons* of 1599, written for treble lute, pandora, cittern, bass viol, flute, and treble viol, afford a good example of the broken consort. Later publications are: Philipp Rossetor, *Lessons for Consort* (1609); John Cooper (Coprario), *Royal Consort of Viols* (1612?); William Lawes (d. 1645), *The Royal Consort and Great Consorte* (MS; cf. *GD* iii, 118); Matthew Locke, *Little Consort of Three Parts* (1656) and *Consort of Foure Parts* (MS; cf. *GD* iii, 224). The compositions contained in these collections vary from ricercar-like fantasias [see *Fancy] in the earliest works to suite-like pieces in the latest. Locke's consorts [new ed. by P. Warlocke (1932)] are suites consisting of a Fantasia, Courante, Ayre, and Sarabande [see *Suite III]; according to Roger North (*Memoirs of Musick*, 1728) these were "the last of the kind that hath been made."

Contes d'Hoffmann, Les ("The Tales of Hoffmann"). "Opéra fantastique" in 3 acts with prologue and epilogue, by Jacques Offenbach (1819–80), based on stories by E. T. A. Hoffmann (1776–1822), composed 1880. In the prologue *Hoffmann* (Tenor) is shown drinking with his friends in an inn and relating the tales of three love episodes of his life, each ending tragically owing to the magic influence of some evil spirit. These episodes are shown in the three acts (Act I: Olympia; Act II: Giulietta; Act III: Antonia; all Sopranos), while in the epilogue the scene is the same as at the end of the prologue, the friends applauding and leaving Hoffmann alone with his thoughts. In its musical style the opera approximates the operetta, which Offenbach had cultivated in all his earlier works. Within this class, however, it belongs to the most ambitious and successful examples.

Continuo [short for basso continuo; see *Thorough-bass]. In the scores of Baroque composers (Bach, Handel), the bass part which was performed by the harpsichord or organ, together with a viola da gamba or cello.

Contra [It., against]. (1) Short for *contratenor.— (2) In connection with other terms the word appears in two meanings: (a) "Against"; e.g., in *contrapunctus* [see *Counterpoint] or in *contratenor, from which other terms such as contr'alto, haut-contre, basse-contre are derived. (b) Denoting the lower octave; this meaning is probably derived from the 16th-century manner of indicating the tones below the great octave (C, D . . .) by a dash written underneath (C̠, D̠ . . .), i.e., in a position "contrary" to that used for the higher octaves (c̄, d̄ . . or, c′, d′. . .). This led to the term contra-octave for the octave below the great octave and, consequently, to terms such as *contrabasso* [G. *Kontra-bass*], contra-bassoon, contrabass-clarinet which denote instruments of the lowest range.

Contra(b)basso [It.]. Double-bass.

Contra-bassoon. See *Oboe family I, D.

Contradanza [It.]. See *Contredanse.

Contrafactum [L.; G. *Kontrafact, Kontrafactur*]. A vocal composition in which the original text is replaced by a new one, particularly, a secular text by a sacred one, and vice versa. This practice prevailed largely in the 13th century. Many trouvère songs are French contrafacta of liturgical chants, i.e., they use older liturgical melodies with a new French text. Still more frequent is the substitution of new texts in the motets of the 13th century [cf. *AdHM* i, 234]. The second important period of contrafactum is the 16th century. Probably the great majority of the earliest Protestant chorales used pre-existing melodies for their new texts, and many of the melodies used for the Calvinist psalmbooks were also borrowed from secular songs [see *Souterliedekens].

Other terms designating a "change of text" are *parody and *paraphrase. Both of these, however, have side-meanings and should properly be used only where such side-meaning takes place. Parody usually implies caricaturing (except in the case of the 16th-century *parody mass), while paraphrase means simply free elaboration or free translation of an original text. For instance, the replacement of an original psalm-text (or, of its literal translation) by a free rhymed version which expresses the same thought is a paraphrase (psalm-paraphrase); the use of the original or paraphrased text in connection with a melody originally written for an entirely different (e.g., secular) text is a contra-factum. Cf. K. Hennig, *Die geistliche Kontrafactur im Jahrhundert der Reformation* (Diss. Königsberg 1909). See also under *Parody.

Contralto [It.]. (1) Same as *alto voice (female). — (2) See *Violin family (c).

Contra-octave. See under *Pitch names.

Contrappunto [It.; L. *contrapunctus*]. *Counterpoint. *C. doppio,* double counterpoint. *C. alla mente,* extemporized counterpoint [see *Discantus supra librum].

Contrapuntal. In the style of *counterpoint. The term is usually employed interchangeably with *polyphonic, although it may imply a certain individuality — rhythmic as well as melodic — of the parts which is not necessarily implied by the term polyphonic.

Contrary motion. See *Motion.

Contratenor, abbr. **Contra.** In compositions of the 14th and early 15th centuries, name for the third voice, in addition to the tenor and discantus. It has about the same range as the tenor with which it frequently crosses, so that the lowest note may fall to the tenor as well as to the contra. Its contour is usually much less melodic than that of the other two parts, to which it was added for harmonic completeness. With the establishment around 1450 (Ockeghem, Obrecht) of four-part writing and with the consequent separation of ranges, the contratenor split in two parts: the *contratenor altus* (high *c.*) or, simply, *altus* (alto), and the *contratenor* *bassus* (low *c.*) or, simply, *bassus* (bass). This process explains the name *alto (high) for a part which, from the modern point of view, can hardly be considered a "high" part, as well as the use of the term counter-tenor for the male alto.

Contra-violin. See *Violin family (b).

Contrebasse [F.]. Double-bass. *Contrebasson*, double-bassoon.

Contredanse [F; *G. Contratanz*]. A dance which attained great popularity in France and elsewhere during the later part of the 18th century. As a dance, it is characterized by the placement of two couples facing each other and moving against each other in a great variety of steps and movements. The music consists of a long series of eight-measure phrases which may be repeated over and over again. It is now generally accepted that the contredanse developed and took its name from the English *Country dance which it resembles in various respects. In this connection it may be noted that as early as 1699 we find "Contredanses anglaises" in Ballard's *Suites de danses.* . . . The contredanse developed later into the *française and the *quadrille. Beethoven wrote 12 Contredanses for the orchestra, one of which he used in the final movement of the Eroica Symphony. See also *Cotillon.

Conzert [G.]. See *Konzert.

Coperto [It.]. Covered. *Timpani coperti* are kettledrums muted by being covered with a cloth.

Copla [Sp.]. Couplet or stanza of refrain songs such as the *cantigas or the *villancico. The name for the refrain is *estribillo*.

Coptic church music. The liturgical music of the Christians living in Egypt. Cf. *GD*, suppl. vol., 178f.

Copula [L.]. In 13th-century polyphony (organum, conductus), a short cadential passage in quick notes through the descending scale [for examples see under *Harmony, Ex. 3; also *AdHM* i, 224, pas-

sage marked (d)]. Walter Odington [*CS* i, 247] also describes a similar type of copula in two or three parts [for an example cf. *ApNPM*, facs. 48, passage (i)]. As a "species of organum" [Joh. de Garlandia, CS i, 114 and 175; Franco, *ibid.*, 133], copula designates a style midway between the free organal style and the strict discant style. See also *Cauda.

Copyright, Musical. I. The Constitution of the United States gives Congress the power to "promote the progress of science and useful arts by securing for limited times to authors and inventors the exclusive right to their respective writings and discoveries." [Art. I, Sec. 8.] In 1790 the first copyright act of the United States received the approval of the President. Several general revisions and numerous amendments were enacted within the next century. The Act of 1831 granted a musical copyright but only within narrow limits. The Act of 1897 granted for the first time the right of public performance. The present law is based on the third general revision of March 4, 1909, which went into effect on July 1, 1909. Some amendments followed, the last on September 25, 1941 [cf. Solberg, *Copyright Miscellany* (1939), nos. 5 and 15; and *United States Code Annotated*, Title 17, "Copyright" (1927), with *Cumulative Annual Pocket Part* of November, 1941].

II. This Copyright Act of 1909 prescribes the following formalities: (1) Publication with the prescribed notice of copyright (Copyright 19   by   ). Such notice shall be affixed to each copy published or offered for sale in the United States [Secs. 9 and 18], and in the case of a musical work the notice shall be applied either upon its title page or the first page of music [Sec. 19].

(2) Promptly thereafter two complete copies of the best edition shall be deposited in the Copyright Office (one copy in case the author is a citizen of a foreign country and the work has been published with proper notice of copyright in a foreign country), accompanied by an appropriate application and the statutory fee of $2.00.

(3) "No action or proceeding shall be

maintained for infringement of copyright in any work until the provisions of this Act with respect to the deposit of copies and registration of such work shall have been complied with." [Sec. 12.]

(4) Copyright may also be secured for unpublished musical and dramatic works by deposit of copies and registration under Sec. 11.

(5) All books, including the copies deposited at the Copyright Office, have to be printed from type set within the limits of U. S. A. [cf. Sec. 15 for details]. This requirement does not apply to books of foreign origin in a language or languages other than English. It does not apply to musical or dramatic works.

(6) These formalities prevent the adherence of U. S. A. to the Berne Convention, whose leading principles involve the enjoyment and exercise of the rights of the Convention without being subject to any formality [Art. 4, par. 2 of the revised text of Rome]. About a mitigation of the formal requirements in relation to the partners of the fourth Pan-American Convention, cf. Solberg, *Misc.*, No. 15, p. 26.

III. As soon as the formal requirements are fulfilled, the authorized person, including a foreigner under the conditions above described, secures, among other things, the exclusive right: (a) to print, reprint, publish, copy, and vend the copyrighted work; (b) to arrange or adapt it if it be a musical work; (c) to perform or represent the copyrighted work publicly if it be a dramatic work; (d) to perform the copyrighted work publicly for profit if it be a musical composition.

Before the enactment of the law of 1909 American courts had decided that composers did not enjoy any legal protection against the making of any form of record by means of which their compositions could be mechanically reproduced. The composers fought these decisions, while the record manufacturers wanted to maintain the status quo. The law of 1909 represents a compromise. The composer is protected against mechanical reproduction, but protection is granted only for those compositions which have been published and copyrighted after the act went

into effect on July 1, 1909. Foreign composers enjoy this right only in case of reciprocity [cf. *infra* III]. The right of the author undergoes a further restriction as soon as either the author himself has reproduced the composition mechanically or has licensed someone else to do so. In such case any other person may make similar use of the copyrighted work and reproduce it mechanically upon the payment of a royalty of two cents on each such part manufactured (so called "compulsory license provision"). The reproduction or rendition of a musical composition by or upon coin-operated machines is not regarded as a public performance for profit unless a fee is charged for admission to the place where such reproduction or rendition occurs. For details cf. Toiner and Evans in the second and third annual of *Nathan Burkan Memorial Competition*; also the general rule of the revised Berne Convention, Art. 13.

Recent developments in musical activity, particularly technical achievements of moving pictures and of broadcasting, led to some fundamental judicial decisions. The most important are: *Herbert* v. *Shanley Co.*, 1917, about performances in hotels, dining rooms, and restaurants, open to guests without a charge for admission; *Harms* v. *Cohen*, 1922, concerning performances in moving picture theaters; *Witmark & Sons* v. *L. Bamberger & Co.*, 1923, regarding radio broadcasting; *Jewell — La Salle Realty Co.*, 1931, dealing with a case where a radio receiving set had been made available to the guests of a hotel by installing a loudspeaker. In all these cases the courts decided that a public performance for profit had taken place and had infringed the right of the composer [cf. Emerson in third annual of *Nath. Burk. Mem. Comp.* and *United States Code* 17, Section 1, 125ff; cf. the general rule of the Berne Convention about broadcasting, Art. 11 bis].

A person who infringes a copyright is liable to an injunction restraining such infringement and to pay damages as well as profits. Where actual damages or profits cannot well be ascertained, the law allows: in the case of a dramatico-musical or a choral or orchestral composition, $100 for the first and $50 for every subsequent infringing performance; in the case of other musical compositions, $10 for every infringing performance [Sec. 25]; but in no case shall such damages be less than $250.

The copyright secured by the Act of March 4, 1909 shall endure for 28 years from the date of first publication, but usually within one year prior to the expiration of the original term the proprietor of the copyright, or the composer and his heirs, can apply for extension for a further 28 years [Sec. 23]. The revised Berne Convention Art. 7 suggests the legal protection of the author for his lifetime and 50 years further. The British Copyright Act of 1911, effective since July 1, 1912, follows this suggestion.

After the First World War an act was approved on December 18, 1919, in order to protect authors who in consequence of the war had not been able to secure copyright in U. S. A. Under similar conditions the recent amendment of September 25, 1941 [cf. *supra* I] authorizes the President to proclaim an extension of time for authors and proprietors of copyrightable works to comply with the conditions of the American Copyright Law in cases where they were unable to do so because of the disruption or suspension of facilities essential for such compliance.

The developments of the last decades, particularly the increase of musical performances by broadcasting and recordings, make it almost impossible for the single author or proprietor to adequately protect his rights in individual capacity. Consequently, collective musical organizations have been established in most countries. The leading American organization is the American Society of Composers, Authors and Publishers (ASCAP). See G. H. Thring, *"The Copyright of the Composer"* (*ML* i, no. 4).

IV. The need for legal protection of copyright passes national boundaries. Scarcely any branch of modern law is subject to international regulations in a like degree to copyright. Several international conferences and numerous international treaties are the signposts of this development.

(1) The first Convention of Berne creating an International Union for the protection of literary and artistic works went into operation September 9, 1886. Three conferences followed, one at Paris (1896), one at Berlin (1908), the third at Rome (1928). The revised text of the Rome conference was signed by delegates of 28 countries [cf. Solberg, *Miscellany*, No. 7]. The United States has not as yet joined this Copyright Union although many attempts in that direction have been made in recent years. (About recent bills of 1925, 1930, 1935, 1937 cf. Solberg, *Miscellany*, nos. 7 and 15.)

(2) A special series of agreements has been entered into by the United States and South- and Central-American countries, known under the designation of Pan-American Copyright Conventions. Only two of these Conventions were ratified by the United States, namely, the Second Convention, signed at Mexico City on January 27, 1902 (proclaimed in 1908), and the fourth Convention, signed at Buenos Aires on August 11, 1910 (proclaimed July 13, 1914). The latter practically supersedes the former, and is in effect between the United States and the following Latin-American countries: Brazil, Colombia, Costa Rica, Dominican Republic, Ecuador, Guatemala, Haiti, Honduras, Nicaragua, Panama, Paraguay, Peru, and Uruguay.

(3) International copyright can be secured by individual treaties between single states, such as the treaties between the United States and China (1903), Japan (1906, 1908), Hungary (1912), Siam (1920).

(4) The law of the United States provides that, even without a treaty, mutual protection of copyright (reciprocity) can be acknowledged by a proclamation of the President. The copyright secured by the Act of 1909 extends to the work of an author or proprietor who is a citizen or subject of a foreign state or nation, when the foreign state or nation grants to citizens of the United States the benefit of

copyright on substantially the same basis as to its own citizens or copyright protection substantially equal to American law. In this case the existence of reciprocal conditions is determined by a proclamation of the President of the United States [Sec. 8k].

Numerous proclamations of this kind have been issued: (a) Proclamations already issued before the last general revision of 1909. As a matter of course they could only consider the former legal status and the limited legal protection as existing before 1909. The law of 1909 introduced decisive reforms, particularly within the realm of musical copyright [cf. *supra* III]. Therefore supplementary proclamation had to be issued in order to guarantee the reciprocity under the new law (thus: Austria, Belgium, Chile, Cuba, Denmark, France, Germany, Great Britain and her possessions, Italy, Netherlands and possessions, Norway, Spain, Switzerland);

(b) Some countries asked for the guarantee of reciprocity only under the Act of 1909. The proclamations issued according to these requests included: Luxembourg, Tunis, New Zealand, Australia and the territories of Papua and Norfolk, Canada, Union of South Africa, Poland, Czechoslovakia, Rumania, Finland, Irish Free State, Greece, Palestine except Transjordania, Free City of Danzig, Argentine (about Sweden cf. Solberg, *Misc.*, No. 15, p. 32);

(c) Some states do not enjoy the reciprocity of the law of 1909: China, Japan, which are governed by prior treaty.

(Minute details about these international relations are to be found in the *United States Code*, Title 17, historical notes to 8 and *Annotated Pocket Part 1941*, p. 17, as well as in *Copyright Protection throughout the World* edited by the United States Department of Commerce, Bureau of Foreign and Domestic Commerce.)

Lit.: Herbert A. Howell, *The Copyright Law* (1942); R. C. deWolfe, *An Outline of Copyright Law* (1925); A. Shafter, *Musical Copyright* (1939); St. P. Ladas, *The International Protection of*

Literary and Artistic Property, 2 vols. (1938); R. C. deWolfe, "Copyright in Music" (*Music Library Association, Notes,* December, 1943).   H. A.

Cor [F.]. (French) horn. *Cor anglais,* English horn; *cor à pistons,* valve horn; *cor de basset,* basset horn; *cor de chasse,* hunting horn; *cor des alpes,* alphorn; *cor d'harmonie,* valve horn; *cor simple,* natural horn. For more details see under *Horn I, II.

Coranto [It.]. See under *Courante.

Corda [It.]; **corde** [F.]. String. In piano compositions, *una corda* (abbr. *u. c.*) calls for the use of the left pedal (soft pedal) by which the entire keyboard is moved a little to the right so that the hammers strike only one string, instead of two or three. This muting effect is canceled by *tutte le corde* (*t. c.*) or *tre corde.* In the slow movement of his Sonata op. 106 Beethoven demands the almost impossible finesse: *poco a poco due e poi tre corde* ("gradually two and three strings"). *Corde à vide, corde à jour, corda vuota* mean open string (of the violin).

Corelli clash. See under *Cadence II [Ex. 24].

Coriolanus Overture. Beethoven's op. 62 (1807), an orchestral composition written as an overture to a play by H. J. Collins.

Cori spezzati [It.]. The "separated" and alternating choruses of the Venetian *polychoral style.

Corista [It.]. Orchestral pitch; tuning fork. *C. di camera,* chamber pitch.

Cornamusa [It.]; **Cornemuse** [F.]. See *Bagpipe.

Cornet [F. *cornet-à-pistons*; G. *Kornett*; It. *cornetto*]. See *Brass instruments III. Not to be confused with the *cornett. See the illustrations on p. 97 and on p. 98.

Cornett [F. *cornet-à-bouquin*; G. *Zink*; It. *cornetto*]. A 15th/16th-century instrument in the form of a straight or slightly bent tube made of wood (or, occasionally, of ivory), with a surface octagonal in cross section, with six fingerholes, and provided with a cup-shaped mouthpiece. (Illustration on p. 98.) Although in many books this instrument is referred to under the name of *cornet, thus leading to confusion with a 19th-century instrument of an entirely different kind, the practice of using a different spelling for these two types is now becoming established. The cornett had a very gentle sound which blended well with strings and with the human voice. It was widely used in church music, e.g., in eleven of Bach's cantatas, as a support for the chorale melody. In addition to the normal cornett (*Zink, cornetto*), pitched in *a*, there existed a soprano size (*Kleiner Zink, cornettino*) pitched in *e'* and a tenor size (*Grosser Zink; cornone*) pitched in *d*. While the above-mentioned instruments had a separate cup-shaped mouthpiece, there existed also a cornett, usually in straight form, which had a small funnel-shaped opening carved out from the upper end of its tube. This was the *Gerader Zink* (*cornetto diritto*), or *Stiller Zink* (*cornetto muto*), as it was called on account of its softer sound. In the 16th century a bass size was added which, in order to bring the fingerholes within easy reach of the hands, was bent in a clumsy serpentine shape and, therefore, was called *serpent*. In spite of its appearance, which has been compared to a "draining pipe suffering from intestinal disorder," it was a highly artistic instrument which was held in great esteem throughout the 16th century. It was particularly favored in French church music, hence the strange name *serpent d'Eglise* — "church serpent." The serpent was still in favor with early 19th-century composers, such as Rossini (*Le Siège de Corinthe*), Mendelssohn (*Meeresstille und glückliche Fahrt; Paulus*), Wagner (*Rienzi*), and Verdi (*Les Vêpres siciliennes*, 1855). By this time, however, the instrument had changed its appearance into a shape similar to that of the tuba. By 1789 the serpentine tube had been replaced by one bent back on itself in the shape of a bassoon and in this form it became known as *Russian bassoon*. An improved variety of this instrument was the *basshorn*, invented about 1800, also called *English basshorn* [F. *basse-cor*]. All these instruments retained the six fingerholes of the ancient cornetts. The addition of more fingerholes operated by keys led to the *chromatic basshorn* and to the *ophicleide*. Illustrations on p. 98. Cf. G. Karstadt, in *AMF* ii.

Cornetta [It.]. *Cornet.

Cornetto [It.]. *Cornett or *Cornet.

Cornett-ton [G.]. See *Pitch (2).

Corno [It.]. Horn. *Corno a mano,* natural horn; *corno a macchina* (*a pistoni, cromatico, ventile*), valve horn; *corno inglese,* English horn; *corno di bassetto,* basset horn; *corno da caccia,* hunting horn. In Bach's scores *corno* usually means the old *cornett [G. *Zink*]. For his *corno da tirarsi* see under *Trumpet II (slide trumpet). See also *Horn I, II.

Cornopean. Older name for the cornet.

Coro [It.]. Choir, chorus. In organ music *gran coro* means full organ.

Corona [L., crown]. Older term for *pause.

Coronach, corronach. A funeral dirge of Scotland. It was chanted by the bard (Seannachie) on the death of a chief or of other prominent personages of the clan. The verses described the virtues and the deeds of the dead. The music was rather wild and rude, frequently interrupted by the cries of the bewailing women. Similar songs and customs prevailed in Ireland (*caoine).

Coronation Concerto [G. *Krönungskonzert*]. Mozart's Pianoforte Concerto in D, K.V. 537 (1788).

Coronation Mass [G. *Krönungsmesse*]. Mozart's Mass in C, K.V. 317 (1779).

Corrente [It.]. See under *Courante.

Correpetitor [G.]. In German opera houses, the coach of the solo-singers who assists them in studying their parts.

Corrido. A Mexican type of narrative folk ballad, accompanied by guitars, harps, etc. It is on the direct line from the Spanish *romance*. Cf. Vicente T. Mendoza, *Romance y Corrido* (1939).

Cortège [F., procession]. Compositions written in the manner of a solemn or triumphal procession, or march.

Cortholt, cortol. Same as *curtall.

Cotillon. A popular dance of the 19th century, used especially for the close of an entertainment. It includes a great variety of steps and figures which are executed by a leading couple and imitated by all the others. The cotillon has no particular music; any kind of dance music (waltz, polka, mazurka) can be played with it. See also *Farandole.

Coulé [F.]. French 18th-century *agrément* in the character of an appoggiatura. For *coulé sur un tierce*, see *Appoggiatura, Double II; *Nachschlag.

Coulisse [F.]. The slide of a trombone or a slide trumpet.

Council of Laodicea, held in 367, played an important part in the development of Byzantine Church music. It abolished the use of instruments and the participation of the congregation in the performance of the Chant, in order to prevent it from deteriorating.

Council of Trent, held in 1543–63, played a decisive part in the development of Catholic Church music. It abolished all the *tropes, and the *sequences with the exception of five. The determination of the cardinals to restore the dignity of the service, after the growing corruption and secularization of the previous centuries, became an acute danger for the continued development of polyphonic music when they considered the complete abolishing in the service of all music other than plainsong. There is, however, no truth to the frequently repeated story that

Palestrina "saved music" by composing his *Missa Papae Marcelli* which, we are told, so greatly impressed the cardinals that they desisted from their plan. Actually, Palestrina's role in the Council was rather inconspicuous, and much slighter than that of Jacobus de Kerlle and others. Cf. O. Ursprung, in the preface to *DTB* 26. See also *Mass B, II (d). Cf. H. Leichtentritt, in MQ xxx, no. 3.

Counter exposition. A name sometimes given to the second exposition of a fugue.

Counter fugue [G. *Gegenfuge*]. A fugue in which the answer (*comes*) is the inverted form of the subject (*dux*). Cf. nos. 5, 6, 7 of Bach's *Art of Fugue*; also a Canzonetta by Buxtehude (complete ed., p. 124). See *Inversion.

Counterpoint [L. *contrapunctus*; F. *contrepoint*; G. *Kontrapunkt*; It. *contrappunto*]. I. *Definition and Description.* The term — derived from L. *punctus contra punctum* (note against note or, properly interpreted, succession of notes against succession of notes, i.e., melody against melody) — means the combination into a single musical fabric of lines or parts which have distinctive melodic significance. In music where there are present more than a single unaccompanied melody [see *monophonic], a musical texture exists which can be regarded from two points of view, the horizontal and the vertical; such a musical fabric is not dissimilar to a textile material with its warp and woof. The study of the vertical or chordal aspect of such music is ordinarily the object of harmony, while counterpoint is the study of the horizontal strands of melody and the various combinations that can be made with them without their losing their individuality as melodies. The singing or playing of voices or instruments in unisons or octaves is not contrapuntal since only one melodic line is present; nor are compositions contrapuntal in which one voice assumes all the melodic interest and in which the accompanying voices or instruments have no distinctive melodies of their own, but merely serve as blocks of harmonic color to enhance the beauty of the predominating melody, and consequently are completely subordinated to it [see *Homophonic]. On the other hand, music which is made up of individual melodic strands woven together is *contrapuntal or *polyphonic. Contrasting examples of homophonic and contrapuntal style are given under *Texture.

There are infinite degrees of gradation between music which is predominantly homophonic and that which is predominantly polyphonic; pure homophony or pure polyphony cannot rightly be said to exist, since in any music which has a texture there are bound to be both horizontal and vertical aspects. If the vertical aspect is particularly emphasized at the expense of the horizontal, the music is said to be homophonic, while if most of the interest is centered in the horizontal lines of melody, it is said to be polyphonic.

A basic feature of true counterpoint, yet one the importance of which is not generally understood, is the rhythmic independence of the different parts. In fact, it is through their rhythmic life no less than through their melodic independence that the voices of a contrapuntal fabric acquire that character of individuality which is the very essence of counterpoint [see *Texture].

II. *History.* Counterpoint has had a history of about a thousand years. A study of this history shows that at no time has there been a complete disregard of the vertical aspect of view. There has been, however, a good deal of change in this aspect, so much, indeed, that the consideration of this point serves as a convenient means of evolutionary classification in the history of counterpoint. This does not mean to imply that the other points of view — evolution of the melodic lines and of their rhythmic coördination — are less important, but only that, owing to their more complex nature, they do not lend themselves to the purpose of short description and survey.

The earliest type of counterpoint was *organum in two parts, based on the fourth and fifth as the only consonant intervals in addition to unison and octave. It went through various stages of development, in the course of which the upper voice gained increasing independence from the cantus firmus. Around 1200 (*School of Notre Dame) the number of parts was increased to three and, occasionally, four.

The 13th-century *Ars Antiqua, with the motet as its principal representative, cultivated mostly music in three parts, although many two-part and a certain number of four-part motets were also written. In the majority of these works each of the voices is strikingly independent melodically and often rhythmically. Harmonically the only places where concern was shown for euphony was at the accented parts of the measure (used in the modern sense) where unisons, fifths, and octaves are usually found; between these rhythmic nodes clashes of all sorts might take place, and little concern was shown over frequent parallel fifths and octaves. Generally speaking, there was little cultivation during this period of the euphonious interval of the third between voices, and the use of the complete triad is not at all frequent, but seems almost accidental [see *Third; *Harmony].

The *Ars Nova of the 14th century displays no sudden change in technique of contrapuntal writing. Composers of the late 13th century, like Petrus de Cruce, had already begun to differentiate the rhythmic character of the different voices. The triplum in particular became more animated, almost in the character of a rapid *parlando, while the duplum remained rhythmically quieter, and the tenor, with the cantus firmus, became less important as a melody and more important as a bass. Among the French composers of the 14th century (Machaut) the two main developments in contrapuntal writing were greater richness and euphony in voice combination, which is shown by greater use of parallel thirds and triadic forms, and the incorporation of all the voices into one organism of great melodic subtlety and rhythmic flexibility.

The most important contribution of the

15th century is the establishment of imitation as a contrapuntal device. After Dufay imitation is increasingly used by Ockeghem, Obrecht, Josquin, and others; it is exploited and more regulated by the generation of Gombert and Willaert, and its full significance realized by the composers of the last half of the 16th century (Orlando di Lasso, Palestrina). In the first half of the 15th century the knowledge and use of *fauxbourdon resulted in the decline of haphazard parallel intervals among moving voices and led to an appreciation of the triad and its inversions; moreover, it tended to cause greater attention to solid cadences and to emphasize the significance of non-harmonic melodic tones, such as the suspension, passing tone, and so on.

Although the importance of the harmonic aspect of music was increasingly realized through the 15th and 16th centuries, the plasticity and melodic equality of the different lines were carried to unsurpassed heights in the second half of the 16th century, this period being referred to often as the Golden Age of counterpoint.

Great contrapuntists were active in the 17th century, particularly in the field of sacred music. During this period a profound change in point of view gradually took place, the seeds of which had been planted at least two centuries earlier: more attention came to be given to tonal organization in music. Tonal organization did not spell the doom of counterpoint as a method, but it did result in a fundamental change in the manner of its conception; now the harmonic flow of music was so organized that compositions were in major or minor keys — were tonal — and although a composition might consist wholly of distinct melodic lines of great individual beauty, these lines had to conform basically to the underlying harmonic skeleton of the composition. The importance of the architecture as a whole superseded that of beauty of detail, out of which compositions had grown in the days of modality. The new type is commonly known as harmonic or tonal counterpoint.

From this time on practically all composers continued as always to undergo contrapuntal instruction as part of their musical training. However, its problems throughout the 18th and 19th centuries were subsidiary to those in architectural construction and to the exploitation of the harmonic aspect of music. Indeed, with the exception of a handful of men like Beethoven and Brahms, composers of the 19th century cannot be said to have had any fundamental interest in counterpoint.

With the coming of the 20th century a distinct renaissance of counterpoint has taken place. Among the first composers to adopt it as the basis of new music was Schönberg [see *Twelve-tone technique], although it can be said that practically all forward-looking composers of today consider it in some of its manifold forms as basic.

III. *Teaching.* During the early centuries of polyphonic music, the art of writing counterpoint was taught by specifying the intervals which the other voices should make with the notes of the given cantus firmus. The theoretical writings of the 13th and 14th centuries [see *Theorists] usually included detailed explanations on this subject. An interesting landmark is Conrad Paumann's *Fundamentum organisandi* of 1452, because practical examples were given in the place of verbal instruction. By the 16th century imitation was being taught as a method [Buchner's *Fundamentum* of *c.* 1520], and the instruction gradually became more methodical. N. Vicentino, in his *L'antica musica ridotta alla moderna prattica* (1555), and Zarlino, in his *Istitutioni armoniche* (1558), gave detailed explanations of the various types of double counterpoint and of canon.

Little is known about the teaching of counterpoint during the 17th century. By the 18th century the different manners of writing to a cantus firmus were codified, notably by J. J. Fux [*Gradus ad Parnassum*, 1725], into the five "species." Each species was based on a ten-to-fifteen note cantus, above and below which other voices were added: the first species consisted of inventing a new melody each note of which should sound with the corresponding note of the cantus; the second species consisted of two notes against each one of the cantus; the third species was built of four notes against each one; the fourth species consisted of syncopation; and the fifth species, which was called florid or "free," consisted mostly of combinations of the first four [see the accompanying example]. The species as a train-

ing is definitely a harmonic type of counterpoint, although the emphasis is still on intervals as it was in the great polyphonic period.

A second method of teaching counterpoint originated in the 19th century, in which still more emphasis is placed on harmony. It is usually based on the contrapuntal methods of Bach (particularly those in his organ chorales), the student learning to ornament basic harmonic progressions, making each individual voice of the compositions as melodious as possible. This method has its greatest value as an introduction to fugue writing.

With the upsurge of interest in counterpoint as a method of composition in the 20th century, there have been attempts to go back beyond both the Bach type of harmonic counterpoint and the species and to base the study on the results of careful analysis of music of the great polyphonic era of the late 16th century [see *Palestrina style], or in some cases even earlier

[cf. Jeppesen, in *MQ* xxi]. See also *Fugue; *Canon; *Discantus; *Linear counterpoint; *Polyphony; *Texture.

Lit.: L. Cherubini, *Counterpoint and Fugue* (1854); P. Goetschius, *Elementary Counterpoint* (1910); *id.*, *Applied Counterpoint* (1902); K. Jeppesen, *Counterpoint* (1939); C. H. Kitson, *Art of Counterpoint* (1924), and other books; A. T. Merritt, *Sixteenth-Century Polyphony* (1939); E. Prout, *Counterpoint, Strict and Free* (1890–96), and other books; H. Riemann, *Simple and Double Counterpoint* (1904); W. R. Spalding, *Tonal Counterpoint* (1904); F. Wright, *The Essentials of Strict Counterpoint* (1935); Y. Rokseth, "Le Contrepoint double vers 1248" (in *Editions XXIV, B, 3/4); R. Wood, "Modern Counterpoint" (*ML* xiii, no. 3); Ch. L. Seeger, "On Dissonant Counterpoint" (*MM* vii, no. 4); K. Jeppesen, in *MQ* xxi.   A. T. M.

Countersubject. See *Fugue.

Counter-tenor. An old name for the (male) *alto, derived from *contratenor altus* [see *Contratenor].

Country dance. A generic term for English dances of folk-like origin of which there exist a great variety, differing in the arrangement of the dancers as well as in the steps and gestures, but all belonging to the type of group dances. The dancers are usually placed along the long sides of a rectangle, men and women facing each other and moving against each other in movements which change with every eight-measure phrase of the music. There is a definite similarity (if not interdependence) between these English dances, which flourished especially throughout the 17th and 18th centuries, and the French *bransles of the 16th century. The melodies written for these dances are all simple, gay tunes with a marked rhythm, and in symmetrical eight-measure phrases. The authoritative source for the country dances is Playford's *The English Dancing Master* (1651; reprint London, 1933) which contains over a hundred charming tunes each accompanied by dancing directions and figures for the performance. Enlarged editions of this book continued to appear until 1728. Throughout the 18th century and the early 19th century (till 1830) numerous publications of country dances — frequently in small booklets of a shape convenient for the dancing master's pocket — were issued. Recently there has been a considerable revival of country dances, in England as well as in the United States. See *Contredanse; *Dance music III.

Lit.: C. F. Sharp, †*The Country Dance Book* (6 parts); *id.*, †*Country Dance Tunes* (11 parts); F. Kidson, *Old English Country Dances* . . . (1890).

Coup d'archet [F.]. Bow stroke.

Coupler [G. *Koppel*]. See *Organ IV.

Couplet. See *Rondeau (2) and *Rondo.

Courante [from F. *courir*, to run; It. *corrente, coranto*]. A dance which originated in the 16th century and which, in the mid-17th century, became one of the standard movements of the suite. Arbeau, in his *Orchésographie* (1588), describes it as a dance with jumping movements and with a great variety of evolutions, according to the ability and fancy of the dancer. The earliest known musical example, a "Corante du roy" in B. Schmid's tablature of 1577 [cf. W. Merian, *Der Tanz in den deutschen Tabulaturbüchern* (1927), p. 112], does not show any features of distinction from the *saltarello. However, a number of "Corrantos" of the *Fitzwilliam Virginal Book* vaguely adumbrate the 17th-century courante by a generally lighter texture and by short "running" figures [cf. *ApMZ* ii]. In the 17th century the dance became stylized in two types, the Italian corrente and the French courante [for a similar case, see under *gigue (2)].

(a) The Italian *corrente* is in quick triple time (3/4, sometimes 3/8), and with continuous running figures in a melody-accompaniment-texture. It would appear to be the direct outgrowth of the late 16th-century type as it is exemplified in

the *Fitzwilliam Virginal Book*. It must be considered as the earlier of the two types, as it appears already clearly established in Schein's *Banchetto musicale* (1617), Frescobaldi's *Toccate e partite d'intavolatura di cembalo* (1614/15; cf. *TaAM* iv), and S. Scheidt's *Tabulatura nova* (1624). Later examples occur in M. Cazzati's *Corrente e balli* (1667; the distinction made here between *c. alla francese* and *c. alla italiana* is scarcely borne out by a difference in style), in the *Sonate da camera* by Corelli, in the keyboard suites of Zipoli (*c.* 1716), etc.

(b) The French *courante* is a much more refined type. It is in moderate 3/2- or 6/4-time, with a frequent shift from one of these meters to the other (i.e., from the accents 1 2 $\overline{3}$ 4 $\overline{5}$ 6 to the accents $\overline{1}$ 2 3 $\overline{4}$ 5 6; see *Coloration, *Hemiola). The resulting instability of rhythm is a typical feature of the courante. Equally subtle is the texture of the courante, a free contrapuntal fabric in which the melodic interest frequently shifts for a moment from the upper to one of the lower parts. More than any other type of Baroque music the courante gives the impression of "blurred contours" which is a typical feature of Romantic periods in music history [see *Romanticism]. Quite properly it has been compared to the quickly changing movements of a fish plunging in the water [Écorcheville]. Examples of this type abound in the works of Chambonnières, L. Couperin, Froberger, d'Anglebert, F. Couperin, and others. The two accompanying examples (1: Frescobaldi; 2: d'Anglebert) serve to illustrate the corrente and the courante.

The courantes of Bach's suites are usually of the French type. Especially remarkable for its rhythmic ambiguity is the courante of the English Suite no. 2; in others, the change from 3/2 to 6/4 occurs chiefly in the final measure of each section. The Italian type occurs in the French Suites nos. 2, 4, 5, 6 and in the Partitas nos. 1, 3, 5, 6. In the original edition of the Partitas [*Clavierübung* i, 1731] the distinction between courantes and correntes is carefully indicated by

Bach; unfortunately, later editors, including those of the B.-G., have substituted

1. Corrente
2. Courante

the name Courante for some or all of the correntes. See *Dance music III.

Course [F. *ordre*; G. *(Saiten)chor*]. In stringed instruments, chiefly those of the lute type, a number of strings which are tuned in unison or in the octave, and which are plucked simultaneously in order to obtain an increased volume of sound. Unison-courses, numbering two or three strings, are used for the higher ranges of the pianoforte and of the harp. On the 16th-century lutes double-courses were used for the lower strings, as follows: G–g c–c' f–f' a–a d'–d' g''. In order to facilitate the terminology, the single string g'' is also spoken of as a course, so that the 16th-century lute would have 11 strings in 6 courses. A bass-course is a string (single or duplicated) which runs alongside the fingerboard without crossing the frets; hence, it is invariable in pitch. See *Lute.

Courtaud, courtall. Same as *curtall.

Covered fifths, octaves. Same as hidden fifths, octaves. See under *Parallel fifths, octaves.

Cow bells [G. *Kuhglocken*]. Instruments similar in shape and sound to the bells worn by the cows of the Alps, but without clapper and struck with a drumstick. They were used by R. Strauss in his *Alpine Symphony* (1915) and are also found in dance bands.

Crab motion, crab canon [G. *Krebsgang, Krebskanon*]. See *Retrograde; *Canon (1), I (e).

Cracovienne. See *Krakowiak.

Crash cymbals. See *Cymbals.

Creation, The. Title of an *oratorio by J. Haydn, composed in 1798.

Crécelle [F.]. *Rattle.

Credo [L., I believe]. The third item of the Ordinary of the *Mass. In plainsong, the first phrase, *Credo in unum Deum*, is sung by the officiating priest, and the chorus picks up at *Patrem omnipotentem*. Early (15th-century) settings of the Credo therefore begin with the latter phrase, and are usually indexed under *Patrem* in modern musicological editions. The Credo was the last of the five chants of the Ordinary to be introduced into the Mass (shortly after 1000). Even today the Credo-melodies (four, and two more "ad libitum"; the oldest, no. 1 of the Gradual, dating from the 11th century) are grouped separately from the other items (*GR* 59*, 89*).

In polyphonic mass compositions the Credo is usually treated in a majestic and forceful style, designed to bring about the feeling of unshaking belief in the Creed of the Church. A contrasting expression, however, is given to the sections *Et incarnatus est* and *Crucifixus* [see *Mass III].

Crembalum [L.]. *Jew's harp.

Crescendo, decrescendo, abbr. cresc., decresc., or decr.; indicated by the signs

―◁ and ▷―. The usual terms and signs for increasing or decreasing of tone volume. For the latter, the word diminuendo (dim.) is also in use. For the history, see *Expression III.

Crescendo pedal. See *Organ VII.

Crescent [Chinese (Turkish) crescent or pavilion or hat; Jingling Johnny; F. *chapeau chinois*; G. *Schellenbaum*]. A fancy percussion instrument consisting of a long pole with several transverse brass plates of crescent form and frequently topped by a hat-like pavilion, all of which are hung with numerous little bells. The instrument was used in the Turkish *Janizary music whence it was introduced into the military bands of many nations.

Cretic meter. See under *Chronos.

Criticism. See *Music criticism.

Croche [F.]. See *Notes.

Croisez, croisement [F.]. Indication to cross the hands in piano playing.

Croma [It.]. See *Notes.

Cromatico [It.]. Chromatic. See under *Chromatic (4).

Cromorne. See *Oboe family III. Cf. C. Sachs, in *SIM* xi.

Crook or **Shank** [F. *corps de rechange*; G. *Stimmbogen*]. See *Wind instruments IV (b); *Horn II; *Trumpet II.

Crooning. See *Jazz III.

Cross fingering. In the playing of wind instruments with side holes, those fingerings in which open holes occur between closed holes, as against the "normal" fingering in which all the open holes are at the bottom of the pipe, the closed ones at the upper end. While the normal fingering produces most of the diatonic tones of the main octave, cross fingering is necessary for the semitones and the tones of the higher octave. On the modern instruments (flutes, clarinets, oboes) cross fingering is largely avoided owing to the elaborate system of keys (*Boehm action).

Cross-relation [F. *fausse relation*; G. *Querstand*]. Cross-relation (or false relation) denotes the appearance in different voices of two tones which, owing to their mutually contradictory character — e.g., major and minor third of the same triad — are best placed as a melodic progression in one voice. In other words, cross-relation means the use in "diagonal" position of what properly is a "horizontal" element of the musical texture [see *Texture]. The most important progression of this kind is the chromatic progression, e.g., Eb–E, which is so strikingly "horizontal" that the ear is disturbed if it hears the first tone in one voice, the second in another [Ex. 1]. In classical har-

mony and counterpoint such progressions are considered bad (false), and the rule prohibiting them serves for the student as a useful preventive against common faults. Nevertheless, there are numerous cases in which the disturbing effect is sufficiently mitigated to make cross-relation acceptable, e.g., if it occurs between inner voices [Ex. 2] and, particularly, if the "false" relation between one voice and the other is rectified by a strikingly "good" relation in each of these voices; that means, if there is enough melodic (contrapuntal) individuality in each voice to distract the attention of the listener from the diagonal clash [Ex. 3; from Mozart]. Another, considerably weaker, type of cross-relation is that involving the tritone (e.g., E–Bb); it is usually avoided between two outer voices [Ex. 4].

Considering the corrective power of strongly marked voice progressions, it is not surprising to find ample use of cross-relation in earlier, contrapuntal music. The compositions of Byrd, Gibbons, Frescobaldi contain many interesting examples [Ex. 5, 6], also of what might be called, somewhat antithetically, "vertical cross-relation," i.e., the simultaneous sounding of the two chromatic tones [Ex. 7; other examples under *Musica ficta]. In modern harmonic style cross-relations are, of course, very frequent, the impression of "falsity" diminishing with the growing disintegration of the harmonic system of the 19th century.

Cross rhythm. See *Polyrhythm.

Crot. See *Crwth.

Crotales [F.]. Castanets. See *Cymbals.

Crotalum [L.]. A rattle (castanets?) used in ancient Egypt, Greece, and Rome.

Crotchet. See *Notes.

Crouth, Crowd, Cruit. See *Crwth.

Crucifixus. A section of the *Credo of the *Mass. In mass compositions it frequently appears as a separate movement.

Crwth. A bowed stringed instrument of the ancient Celtic nations, conspicuous by its rectangular shape which is strongly reminiscent of the Greek *kithara. The oldest illustrations (11th century) show the instrument without a finger board, thus indicating that it originally was a harp (frame harp). Later, a finger board was added by which it became an early member of the violin family [see ill. on p. 823; also GD, pl. 31 and 87]. The instrument was still used in Wales in the early years of the 19th century. It is also known under the Anglicized form crowd and under the Irish names crot and cruit. A medieval Latin name, used in the 11th to the 14th centuries, is chorus [cf. SaRM, 80]. The medieval form, without finger board, is usually called rotta, rotte. The chrotta, mentioned by Venantius Fortunatus (6th century), was probably not a lyre but a harp [cf. SaHMI, 262]. Cf.

N. Bessaraboff, *Ancient European Musical Instruments* (1941), pp. 314ff.

C.s. Abbreviation for It. *colla sinistra,* i.e., with the left hand.

Csardas. See *Czardas.

C sol fa ut. See *Hexachord III.

Cuba. The island of Cuba is interesting as the breeding place for various dances of mixed Spanish and Negro origin, such as the *Bolero, *Conga, *Habanera, *Guarache, *Rumba.

Lit.: I. Castellanos, *Instrumentos musicales de los afrocubanos* (Havana, 1927); H. Cowell, "The 'sones' of Cuba" (*MM* viii); E. Grenet, *Música popular cubana* (Havana, 1939); J. Molina y Ramos, *La Historia y desenvolvimiento del arte musical en Cuba* (Havana, 1924); F. Ortiz, "Afro-Cuban Music" (*Quarterly Journal of Inter-American Relations* i); S. Ramírez, *La Habana Artística* (Havana, 1891); A. Salazar, "El Movimiento Africanista en la Música de arte Cubana" (*Estudios Afrocubanos* ii); E. Sánchez de Fuentes, *Consideraciones sobre la Música Cubana* (Havana, 1936). See also general bibliography under *Latin American music.

Cue. In orchestral parts including a long rest, a short passage taken from another leading instrument and printed in small characters, in order to warn the player of the entry of his part.

Cueca (or *Zamacueca*). The most popular dance of Chile. It is a couple dance symbolizing a hen and a cock, and all the dancing gestures as well as the animating words of the bystanders agree with this symbol. Cf. P. Garrido, *Biografía de la Cueca* (Santiago, 1943); H. Allende, "Chilean Folk Music" (*Bulletin of the Pan American Union* ix, 917ff).

Cuivre [F., copper]. *Instruments de cuivre* or, simply, *les cuivres* are the brass instruments of the orchestra. *Cuivré* calls for a forced, harsh tone in the playing, especially of the horn [see *Horn I].

Currende [from L. *currendo canere,* i.e., street singing]. In the 16th and 17th centuries, name for the chorus of Latin schools (*Gymnasium*) in Germany. Their members were usually boys lacking in financial means who, by singing on the streets and for special occasions such as funerals and marriages, provided towards their support. There has been a recent revival of this custom in various German towns. See *Quempas. Cf. G. Schüne-mann, *Geschichte der deutschen Schulmusik* (1928); W. Nicolai, in *Bach-Jahrbuch* (1914).

Currentes. Same as *conjunctura* or, at least, the quick diamond-shaped notes of the conjunctura [see *Square notation; *Elmuahim].

Curtain tune. Same as act tune [see *Entr'acte].

Curtal(1). See *Oboe family III.

Cursus. In Latin prose and, in particular, in Gregorian chant, *cursus* denotes an important principle of textual construction, observed in the closing words of a sentence or a section thereof. A great number of these chants close with the *cursus planus*, i.e., with five syllables showing the following scheme of accents: ⁄ ∪ ∪ ⁄ ∪, e.g.: . . . glóriăm túăm; . . . átriă éjŭs; . . . Dómĭnŏ déo; . . . ópĕră éiŭs; . . . déxtĕră túă [cf. *GR*, 350–353]. The plainsong melodies frequently (but not always) follow and emphasize this scheme by placing longer melismas on the two strong accents, shorter ones (or single notes) on the three weak syllables,

a-   bri- a e-   jus.

as in the accompanying example. Much less frequent is the *cursus tardus* with the scheme ⁄ ∪ ∪ ⁄ ∪ ∪ (e.g., Dómĭnĭ íbĭmŭs), the *cursus velox* with the scheme ⁄ ∪ ∪ ∪ ∪ ⁄ ∪ ∪ (e.g., glóriăm cŏngrĕgéntiŭm), and the *cursus trispondaicus* with the scheme ⁄ ∪ ∪ ∪ ⁄ ∪ (e.g., éssĕ vĭdĕátŭr). All these schemes are based on the *rhythmical* cursus which follows the speech accent of the words, in contradis-

tinction to the older *metrical* cursus which follows the laws of quantity [see *Poetic meter]. Cf. H. B. Briggs, in *PMA* xxiv, 74f; H. Bewerunge, in *ZIM* xii; *Paléographie musicale* iv [see *Editions XXIII].

Custos [L., watcher]. See *Direct.

Cyclic, cyclical. This term is used in two meanings: (1) Generally, to denote any musical form including several movements; thus, sonata, suite, toccata, cantata, etc., are termed cyclic forms. — (2) Specifically, to denote compositions — usually sonatas or symphonies — in which the same thematic material is used in all or in some of the movements. The use of the term in this meaning is more common recently and is, no doubt, preferable. An early example of cyclic treatment is Schubert's *Wanderer-Fantasie*, op. 15. Still more conspicuous is the use of identical material in Berlioz' *Symphonie Fantastique* [see *Idée fixe]. Cyclic treatment was adopted by Bruckner who in several of his symphonies restates the initial theme of the first movement in the closing climax of the last. It was more clearly established as a principle of composition by César Franck and his French followers, Vincent d'Indy, Saint-Saëns, Fauré, Dukas. Statements regarding the presence of cyclical treatment in Beethoven's sonatas, etc., should be accepted with great reserve. The idea as such was certainly foreign to him, except, of course, in those obvious cases where a movement shows the insertion (usually in the character of a reminiscence) of a short section from another movement, as, e.g., in the Fifth Symphony, the Piano Sonata op. 101, and the Ninth Symphony. Cyclic treatment is, however, clearly indicated in many masses of the 15th and 16th centuries all the movements of which are based on the same tenor or begin with identical opening measures [see *Mass B, II]. It also is present to some extent in the early Baroque sonata [see *Sonata B, I].

Cylinder. See *Valve.

Cymbalon. See *Cimbalom.

Cymbals. See *Percussion instruments B, 6. Various modifications are used in jazz bands, e.g., the Choke cymbal, the Sizzle cymbal. "Cymbales antiques" (Debussy) and "crotales" (Ravel) are smaller cymbals of thicker metal, more exactly tuned.

Cythringen [G.]. See *Guitar family.

Czardas. A Hungarian dance, usually consisting of a slow, pathetic introduction called *lassu*, and a rapid and wild dance called *friss* or *friska*. F. Liszt's Hungarian Rhapsody no. 2 is a well-known example, while Schubert's wonderful Divertissement à la Hongroise, op. 54 (for four hands) is entirely forgotten. See *Hungarian music II.

Czech music. Evidence of the use of Gregorian chant in the Czech countries (formerly Bohemia; capital Prague) goes back to the 10th century. In the 14th century a special type of chant, called *Rorate*, sung first to Latin, later to Czech words, was introduced for the service of Matins during Advent. At the same time there existed an important school of Czech musicians and writers on music, headed by Magister Zavise (d. 1410). The reforming activity of Johan Hus (burned 1415), directed against abuses in the Catholic Church, was of disastrous results for the cultivation of music, which was entirely banned from the service. During the 16th century the Moravian Brothers were active in the edition of song books in the Czech language. One of these, published in 1561, contains 744 melodies. As a result of these tendencies, the use of the Czech language in the service was authorized in 1601. The splendid court of Rudolph II (1575–1611) at Prague numbered among its members musicians such as Jacobus Handl (Gallus), Hans Leo Hassler, Philipp de Monte, Jacques Buus, and Charles Luython. In the 17th and 18th centuries a small number of Czech (Bohemian) composers participated in the development of German or Italian music, e.g., Andreas Hammerschmidt (1611–75), Bohuslav Czernohorski (1684–1740; Italian opera), Jo-

hann Stamitz (1717–57) and Anton Filz (c. 1730–60) — both members of the *Mannheim School — Georg Benda (1722–95; see *Singspiel, *Melodrama), Johann Dussek (1760–1812; piano sonatas), Anton Reicha (1770–1836; chamber music), and others. Most of these, however, were of German extraction, as their names show. The history of Czech music in a proper sense of the word may be said to begin with František Skroup (Skraup; 1801–62), who composed the first opera in Czech language (*Dratenik, The Thinker), and also the Czech national anthem. From 1827 to 1857 he was conductor of the State Opera in Prague, succeeding Carl Maria von Weber. The first great figure in Czech music is Bedrič (Frederic) Smetana (1824–84) who founded the national movement in Czech music with his operas, symphonic poems, and national dances. His younger brother-in-arms was Antonin Dvořák (1841–1904) who, however, followed largely the German tradition (Brahms), particularly in his chamber music. Less known than these two is Zdenko Fibich (1850–1900) who in his numerous operas and orchestral works shows himself strongly influenced by Schumann and Wagner, and who remained relatively apathetic toward national expression. A similar statement can be made with regard to J. B. Foerster (b. 1859) whose music represents what may be called a "subjective idealism."

The national trend is more clearly expressed in the works of Leos Janaček (1854–1928) who developed an interesting personal style of veristic and highly dynamic prosody, somewhat influenced by Moussorgsky's style (*Jenufa*, 1904). The most influential Czech composer — the father of present-day Czech music — is Vitezlav Novak (b. 1870) whose works show a great variety of expression and style, Romantic as well as impressionistic, lyrical as well as intellectual and ironic. Josef Suk (1874–1935) represents a lyrical Romanticism of French color. Gustav Mahler, although born in Bohemia (Kalischt, 1860–1911), stands entirely outside of the development of Czech

music and must be considered in connection with the history of German music.
Composers of a later generation, such as
Alois Hába (b. 1893), Erwin Schulhoff
(b. 1894), Bohuslav Martinu (b. 1890),
have largely given up the nationalistic
approach to music, and have ranked themselves among the champions of the more
cosmopolitan trends of *New music;
Hába in the field of *atonality and
*quarter-tones, Schulhoff particularly in
"idealized jazz," while Martinu is one of
the most successful proponents of a neo-
romantic style of a purely musical design.
A happy amalgamation of national elements and of a rather modern idiom is
found in Jaromir Weinberger's (b. 1896)
opera *Schwanda, the Bagpiper* (1927)
which was a remarkable world success.
Lit.: R. Newmarch, *The Music of*

Czechoslovakia (1942); L. Urban, *The
Music of Bohemia* (1919); V. E. Helfert,
*Geschichte der Musik in der Tschechi-
schen Republik* (1936; also in French);
R. Batka, *Die Musik in Böhmen* (1906);
id., Geschichte der Musik in Böhmen, i,
900–1333 (1906); P. Nettl, *Beiträge zur
böhmischen und mährischen Musikgeschichte* (1927); *LavE* i.5, 2597; ii.1, 33
(modern); ii.5, 2956 (folk song); *AdHM*
ii, 1156; P. Nettl, "The Czechs in 18th-
century Music" (*ML* xxi, no. 4); *id.,*
"Schubert's Czech Predecessors" (*ML*
xxiii, no. 1); Z. Nejedly, "Magister
Závise und seine Schule" (*SIM* vii); D.
Orel, "Stilarten der Mehrstimmigkeit des
15. und 16. Jahrhunderts in Böhmen"
(*Adler-Festschrift*, 1930).

Czimbalom. See *Cimbalom.

D

D. See *Pitch-names; *Letter notation;
*Hexachord. In 16th-century *part books
D stands for *discantus* (soprano). In har-
monic analysis D means dominant.

Da capo [It. *capo*, head], abbreviated
D.C. "From the beginning." The term
indicates repetition of the piece from the
beginning to the end or to a certain place
marked *fine* (*da capo al fine*). It is most
frequently found at the end of the trio
to a scherzo (or minuet), indicating that
the latter be repeated after the trio. *Da
capo senza repetizione* means that the
repetitions within the scherzo should be
omitted, as is usually done even where
this remark is lacking. *Da capo e poi la
coda*, see *Coda. See also *Dal segno.

Da-capo aria. See *Aria IV.

Dactyl, dactylic. See *Poetic meter I.

Dämpfer [G.]. (1) The *dampers of
the piano. — (2) The *mutes of the violin. The term *dämpfen* (to damp) is also
used with reference to the muting of the
horn and other instruments.

Daily hours. See under *Office hours.

Dal segno [It., from the sign], abbreviated *d.s.*, means repetition, not from the
beginning [see *Da capo], but from another place (frequently near the beginning) marked by the sign §.

Damenisation. See *Solmization III.

Damper [F. *étouffoir*; G. *Dämpfer*; It.
sordino]. In pianofortes and harpsichords
that part of the mechanism which termi-
nates the vibration of the string — hence,
the sound — in the moment when the key
is released. The dampers of the pianoforte are small pieces of wood, lying above
the strings, and covered underneath with
felt [see *Pianoforte I]. See also *Mute.

Damper pedal. See *Pianoforte I; also
under *Sordino (2).

Dance music. I. To the modern man,
dance is a bodily activity in which recre-
ational, spectacular, and erotic elements
are combined. This, however, is not the
original meaning of dance. In prehistoric

periods as well as in many primitive cultures of the present (Africa), dance has primarily a ritual character, frequently with the inclusion of erotic symbolism. It serves to exert magic, to propitiate gods, to induce hypnosis and fear, or to heal illness. It is danced by the medicine man or by a selected group of warriors. Women are frequently not allowed to dance, but only to beat the drums. In more refined cultures the dance takes on a symbolic significance. Strictly regulated and stylized movements express thoughts and perceptions relative to the adoration of deities. The dances of the ancient Egyptians and of the Chinese belong largely to this class. In Greece, for the first time, dance developed into an "art," i.e., an expression of beauty for its own sake, although still retaining its religious significance. In the last centuries of the pre-Christian era there appeared in Greece as well as in Rome a large influx of Oriental dances of a strongly erotic and frequently obscene nature. Dance became the occupation, not of the priests, but of the prostitutes. Little is known about dancing in the early Middle Ages. The Church strongly opposed dancing which it rightly considered as a heathenish and lascivious element.

II. A violent reaction against this long suppression of dancing occurred in the 14th century in which the convulsive dances of the flagellants served to express the fright and despair of a population tortured by pestilence, fire, wars, and religious scruples. Simultaneously the cultural refinement of the higher classes, in particular of the Italian and French courts, led to what must be considered the origin of the modern dance. Freed from religious bondage or symbolical significance, dance becomes the expression of joy of life and of love. For the first time in the history of dance, men and women joined their hands in the folklike round dances (*chorea, charola; see *Carole) and in the courtly pair dances (danse, danse royale) of the 13th and 14th centuries [see also *estampie]. The 15th century, with its return of Church authority [see under *Flemish Schools],

would seem to have again brought about a partial suppression of the dance. The Münchner and Glogauer Liederbuch of c. 1460 [see *Liederbuch] are practically the only sources of 15th-century dance composition. The latter contains four-part instrumental pieces with titles such as Der Ratten Schwantz (literally: The Rat's Tail, i.e., The Rat's Dance) and Der Pawir Schwantz (Pawir, i.e., Bauer, peasant). This period of suppression was followed by a renewed outburst of dance music in the 16th century, a period which may well be called "the century of the dance." As a matter of fact, while in the 15th century only one dance is known to us, the courtly *basse danse of the French-Burgundian culture, a large variety of dances occurs in the lute, keyboard, and instrumental music of the 16th century. They usually appear in the twin-arrangement of a main dance in slow duple meter followed by a quicker dance (*Nachtanz, *Tripla, *Proportz, Hupfauf) in triple meter, such as the Spanish *pavane-galliard (c. 1500–50) and the Italian *passamezzo–saltarello (c. 1550–1600), or else in suite-like combinations such as: basse danse–recoupe–tordion (Attaingnant, 1530) and pavana–saltarello–piva (Petrucci, 1508). A highly important source of information about the dances of the 16th century is the *Orchésographie of Jean Tabourot (1588; new ed. in English by C. W. Beaumont, 1925), a high church dignitary who, under the pseudonym Toinot Arbeau, gives a detailed and lively description of the above dances as well as of many others, particularly the various kinds of *branles.

III. While, in the last decades of the 16th century, the English virginalists (Byrd, Bull, Gibbons) brought the pavane and galliard to a high-point of artistic perfection, comparable to that reached in the allemandes and sarabandes in Bach's suites, new dances appeared in the ballrooms which were to play a prominent part in the art music of the 17th century, the (German) *allemande, the (French) *courante, the (Spanish) *sarabande, and the (English) *jigg or *gigue. Around 1650 these dances became the standard movements of the *suite which, theretofore, had employed earlier types, such as the *paduana, gagliarda, intrada, etc. At the same time a host of new dance types, considerably more refined in character, grew up under the favorable auspices of the French court of Versailles, where King Louis XIII patronized dance and ballet to an extent unparalleled in history. Most of these were originally peasant dances of French provinces, e.g., the *bourrée (from the Auvergne), the *gavotte (from the Dauphiné), the *passepied (from the Bretagne), the *rigaudon (from the Provence), the *loure (from the Normandie), and, most important of all, the *minuet (from the Poitou). Together with certain dances of foreign origin, such as the *anglaise, the *hornpipe, or the *polonaise, they played a prominent part in the ballets and operas of Lully, Purcell, Rameau, and became, around 1700, the constituents of the optional group of the suite. An important national type of the 17th century is the English *country dance. In this period there appeared also the first "exotic" dance in the ballrooms of Europe, the *canarie (from the Canary Islands).

IV. The 18th century cultivated particularly the minuet, without adding much to the repertory of dance music until the end of the century when Vienna became a new center of dance music and when the first modern types of dances appeared, the vigorous *ecossaise (Beethoven) and the soft swaying *Ländler (Schubert), which soon changed into the most famous dance of all times, the *waltz. The period from 1830 to 1850 brought about a number of dances which quickly superseded one another in the favor of the public, e.g., the Polish *mazurka (Chopin), the Bohemian *polka, the *quadrille, and the *galop (Offenbach), all of which were launched in Paris, confirming the fame of this city as the world center of amusement. The rise of the National Schools led to the discovery by composers of a wealth of national dances, among which the Spanish dances figure prominently in variety and individuality of character [see *Spanish

music III]. In the early part of the 20th century, America made its epochal contribution to dance music in *rag-time and in *jazz. See also *Ballet; *Suite.

Lit.: C. Sachs, A World History of the Dance (1937); E. B. Long and McKee, A Bibliography of Music for the Dance (1936); Paul D. Magriel, A Bibliography of Dancing (1936); C. W. Beaumont, A Bibliography of Dancing (1929); V. Junk, Handbuch des Tanzes (1930); C. J. Sharp, The Dance (1924); E. Sharp, Story of the Dance (1928); E. Porter, Music through the Dance (1937) — Historical: F. W. Böhme, Geschichte des Tanzes in Deutschland, 2 vols. (1886); LavE, ii.5, 3082ff; Arbeau, Orchésographie, 1589 (transl. by Beaumont, 1925); W. Merian, †Der Tanz in den deutschen Tabulaturbüchern des 16. Jahrhunderts (1927); E. Halbig, †Klaviertänze des 16. Jahrhunderts (Cotta); P. Aubry, †Estampies et danses royales (1907); Cl. Gervaise, †Danseries [see *Editions XVI. 5]; †Wiener Tanzmusik (c. 1650–1700; DTOe 28.ii); J. Wolf, "Die Tänze des Mittelalters" (AMW i); O. Gombosi, "About Dance and Dance Music in the Late Middle-Ages" (MQ xxvii); id., "Der Hoftanz" (AM vii, no. 2); J. Pulver, "The Ancient Dance Forms" (PMA xxxix, xl); R. Eitner, †"Tänze des 15. bis 17. Jahrhunderts" (MfM vii, Beilage); L. Schrade, "Tänze aus einer anonymen italienischen Tabulatur, 1551" (ZMW x); P. Nettl, "Die Wiener Tanzkompositionen des 17. Jahrhunderts" (StM viii). See also under *Suite.

Dance of death. Death as a dancer or as a gruesome fiddler of dance tunes was a favored subject of 15th- and 16th-century painters and drawers (Holbein, Dürer), who took their mental picture from medieval or contemporary dance customs incorporating dancers masked as skeletons. Augustus Nörmiger's tablature of 1593 contains a piece entitled *Mattasin oder Toden Tantz, the peculiar syncopated rhythm of which is quite an adequate expression of fear and trembling. In the 19th century two composers have used the *Dies irae as the basis of compositions portraying the idea of the dance of death, namely, Liszt (Todten-Tanz for pianoforte and orchestra, 1849) and Saint-Saëns (Danse Macabre for orchestra, 1874). For a 14th-century Spanish example cf. O. Ursprung, in *ZMW* iv, 141ff.

Danish music. While, prior to 1800, Danish music was but a reflection of Flemish, French, English, Italian, or German influences [for Danish pupils of G. Gabrieli, e.g., see *Editions V, 35], it adopted a significance of its own when a German composer J. A. P. Schulz (1747–1800), who was Court Musical Director at Copenhagen from 1787 to 1795, founded the "Danish opera" by writing *Singspiele in the Danish tongue (*Hostgildet, Peters Bryllop, Indtoget*). He was followed by three other composers of German extraction: F. L. Kunzen (1761–1817; grand operas *Holger Danske*, 1789, and *Erik Ejegod*, 1789); C. E. F. Weyse (1774–1842), who in his operas *Ludlams Höhle* (1808) and *Faruk* (1814) introduced Danish folk songs; and F. Kuhlau (1786–1832, the well-known writer of sonatinas), whose opera *Elverhöi* (1828) is still popular in Denmark.

With Niels V. Gade (1817–90) we meet the first important composer of Danish extraction and also the most representative figure of Danish 19th-century music. He is the Danish counterpart of Schumann and, perhaps even more, of Mendelssohn, whose romantic lyricism he tinged with a distinctive touch of Nordic color. He is as characteristic of Danish refinement and sensitiveness as is Grieg of Norwegian vigor and ruggedness. A lesser known contemporary of Gade was I. P. E. Hartmann (1805–1900) who wrote music for several ballets, while P. A. Heise (1830–79) composed a number of charming lyrical songs.

The most important among the more recent Danish composers is Carl Nielsen (1865–1931), who has been called the "Danish Sibelius." In fact, his six symphonies are somewhat similar to those of the Finnish composer in their expansive emotionalism, in the "archaic" quality of the melodies, and in their contrapuntal texture. Practically all the living Danish composers stand under his influence, combining it with impressionistic or neoclassical tendencies, e.g., J. L. Emborg (b. 1876), Peder Gram (b. 1881), Rud Langgaard (b. 1893), Jörgen Bentzon (b. 1897), and Finn Höffding (b. 1899).

Lit.: *AdHM* ii, 1106 (bibl. pp. 1112); *LavE* i.5, 2594.

Danse macabre [F.]. *Dance of death.

Dante Symphony. See *Symphonic poem I.

Danza tedesca [It., German dance]. The *Ländler or the early *waltz (c. 1800).

Daseian notation [G. *Dasia-notation*]. A notational system of the 9th and 10th centuries in which the tones of the scale are represented by signs supposedly derived from the *prosodia daseia*, i.e., a

prosodic accent [Ex. a] of ancient Greek poetry. The signs given in Ex. b indicate the tetrachord d e f g, while others (derived largely from these by changing their position from upright to horizontal, or from right to left) indicate one lower and two-and-one-half higher tetrachords which repeat the basic tetrachord in exact transpositions of the fifth. There results a curious scale which avoids diminished fifths but, as a consequence, includes augmented octaves, as follows: G A Bb C | d e f g | a b c′ d′ | e′ f♯ g′ a′ | b′ c″♯. This notation is used in 9th-century treatises (*Musica enchiriadis*; cf. *GS* i, 152–229; also *CS* ii, 81) for the writing down not only of monophonic melodies (psalmtones, etc.), but also of examples of *organum [cf. *ApNPM*, 204ff].

Lit.: E. J. Grutchfield, "Hucbald: A Millenary Commemoration" (*The Musical Times* lxxi, 507, 704); Ph. Spitta, "Die Musica Enchiriadis und ihr Zeitalter" (*VMW* v); *WoHN* i, 31.

Davidsbündler-Tänze. Robert Schumann's op. 6, a collection of 18 characteristic pieces named after an imaginary "Davidsbund" ("League of David") to which he frequently referred in his writings on music and which was destined to fight — like David — against the Philistines, that is, against the mediocre taste and the reactionary tendencies of the average composers, performers, and musical amateurs of his day. The letters E. and F. given at the end of each piece mean Eusebius and Florestan, imaginary names which were meant to portray the lyrical (introvert) and the heroic (extrovert) side of his own self.

Deaconing. English term for *lining.

Dead interval. An interval occurring between the last note of a melodic phrase and the first note of the next, often involving separation by a rest. The term was introduced into the teaching of counterpoint in order to justify the occurrence of intervals such as the chromatic semitone or the augmented fifth which, in strict theory, are not permitted within the course of a phrase, but may well occur as a dead interval.

Deagan marimbaphone, nabimba, etc. Xylophon-like instruments invented by the American Deagan (d. 1936); they are used in P. Grainger's Suite "In a Nutshell."

Death and the Maiden Quartet. Schubert's String Quartet in D minor (1826) the second movement of which consists of variations on his early song "Death and the Maiden" (Der Tod und das Mädchen, op. 1).

Death and Transfiguration. See *Symphonic poem III.

Debile [It.]. Weak.

Début [F.]. First public appearance, beginning of a career.

D.C. Short for *da capo.

Dec. In English Service music, abbreviation for *decani.* See *Polychoral style.

Déchant [F.]. *Discant. *Déchant sur de livre,* see *Discantus supra librum.

Deceptive cadence. See *Cadence I.

Decibel. See *Bel.

Declamation. See *Text and music.

Decoration. Same as *ornamentation, *coloratura, florid style.

Decrescendo, abbreviated *decr.* or *decresc.* See *Crescendo.

Degree. In harmonic analysis, see *Scale degrees.

Degrees and diplomas. The degrees most commonly awarded to music students are:

1. B.A. (with major in music); given for completion of a liberal arts course (normally 4 years), in which music is stressed, but in which non-musical studies predominate. Graduation "with honors" means that the student has done some special work during his senior year, generally a paper of some magnitude, and has maintained a high scholastic average.

2. B.Mus.; given for completion of a course of study (normally 4 years), in which musical studies predominate. A minimum of non-musical study is required — generally English, history, and one or more foreign languages. Concentration is required in a particular instrument, or in voice, or in composition.

3. M.A. (in music). This degree represents the logical continuation of the B.A. degree course of study. Residence requirements vary from one to two years. An approved course of study (usually totaling 30 semester hours) must be completed. Some schools require that no grade shall be less than B. Most schools require a thesis upon a given phase of music, demanding some amount of research on the part of the student. A general or comprehensive examination is usually given, covering various branches of musical knowledge. In some instances the student must demonstrate reasonable ability in piano playing, reading at sight, and similar musical skills.

4. M.Mus. As in the B.Mus. degree, the accent is less on the academic and more on the professional side. This de-

gree is given chiefly by conservatories and schools of music. A certain number of advanced courses in music must be satisfactorily completed; one to two years of residence as a full-time student are required (most schools require only one). M.Mus. degrees are given in various fields of concentration — applied music, theory, composition, history, aesthetics, etc. The special requirements vary greatly among the various schools. Most schools require a thesis or its equivalent, such as a composition in a larger form, or a public concert in the case of an applied music student. The policy of granting a master's degree for work done primarily in applied music has been questioned by some educators, who feel that the higher degrees should be reserved more specifically for advanced academic work in theory, history, or the like.

5. Ph.D. (in music). This is the highest degree which may be taken, and relatively few have been granted. At least two years of residence are required (in the United States) by most universities granting the degree. The candidate must submit, and the university accept, a thesis showing distinctly original work, bringing to light new source material or treating known material in an original way. He must then pass an oral examination covering all branches and fields of music. Generally, in addition, he must present a satisfactory musical composition of some sort; this may be a piece in a larger form, if he is gifted in composition, or a fugue, if he is not. Some few schools give Ph.D. degrees in musical composition, substituting a large orchestral work, or the like, for the doctoral thesis.

6. Mus.D. The Doctor of Music is a purely honorary degree in the United States. It is given in recognition of outstanding excellence and achievement in music, in much the same way as the LL.D. is given in other fields. In England the Mus.D. may be "earned"; in America the highest "earned" degree is the Ph.D. in music.

7. Other degrees. The above-given are the most usual degrees. Mention may be made also of the following:

a. B.S. (Bachelor of Science). More or less equivalent to the B.A., but with less stress on the humanities — Greek, Latin, etc. In general not recommended for those intending to do graduate work.

b. Education degrees: B.Mus.Ed.; B. Pub. School Mus.; M.M.Ed.; Ed.D. These degrees are generally given by state universities and schools of music to students preparing to teach in the public schools.

c. M.S.M. (Master of Sacred Music) is conferred by some schools.

8. Diplomas, certificates, etc. It is impossible to describe the various awards of this kind which are made throughout the country. State teaching certificates are required of public school music teachers, and requirements vary widely from state to state. The New York State requirements are generally considered to be among the highest and have become accepted nationally as a norm. Music schools in particular give out a variety of diplomas, certificates, and the like. Since each individual school sets the standard, the value of such awards depends directly upon the excellence of the school granting it. Moreover, the achievement represented by the diploma or certificate is anything but standardized. In one school the diploma may be given for a minimum amount of work; in another it may represent a high — even the highest — standard of excellence. In some schools the term "artist's diploma" is used to indicate that it is given for excellence in performance.

9. Foreign degrees: a. Great Britain. The British system of degrees is the closest to the American. Mus.B., Mus.M., and Mus.D. degrees are given, the requirements varying somewhat among the various universities. Certain residence requirements exist in nearly every instance, and various examinations are given to test the candidate's knowledge of theory, history, and practical music. The Mus.B. candidate is expected to have already received the B.A. degree, or to pass preliminary examinations of equivalent difficulty. In this respect, as well as

in the fact that the Mus.D. may be "earned" instead of being purely honorary, the British degrees have a different meaning from the American. The Mus.M. is rather infrequently given. All the British degrees in music are concerned primarily with the candidate's possession of a technique of composition, although, in a few universities, performance or musicological research may be substituted. Several universities give Litt.B., Litt.D., or Ph.D. degrees for work in musical research. A great number and variety of diplomas are granted by various music schools in Great Britain (see Scholes, 256–257). In general three grades are observed — Associateship, Licentiateship, and Fellowship. The latter, being the highest, is sometimes purely honorary. Cf. *GD*, Suppl. Vol., 153f.

b. Germany. The only degree given in Germany is the Ph.D. (Dr. phil). Since this is so, the German Ph.D. in many instances represents a lesser achievement than the Ph.D. from an American university. Indeed, some of the German dissertations are no larger, and contain little more information, than an American undergraduate's term paper. Others, on the other hand, are splendid contributions to musical research and often have the proportions of full-sized books. In addition to writing a dissertation, the candidate must pass various examinations, in music as well as in three "related" fields (e.g., Philosophy, Mathematics, Acoustics). Certain teachers' certificates and diplomas are awarded by German schools of music. These have little significance outside of Germany and are designed chiefly to maintain standards within the country.

c. Other European countries. The remaining countries of Europe do not lay so much stress on academic degrees. In France the Doctor of Letters (Dr. ès Lettres) may be awarded for musicological research. The Paris Conservatory, however, and other similar schools (Brussels, for example) have systems of recognizing achievement by means of first and second prizes, certificates, and diplomas of various sorts.   E. B. H.

Dehors, en dehors [F.]. "Outside," i.e., made to stand out, with emphasis.

Delasol(re), De la sol (re). See *Hexachord III.

Delirante [It.]. Frenzied.

Démancher. In violin playing, the shifting of the left hand from one position to another.

Demi- [F.]. Half. *Demi-jeu*, see *Plein-jeu*; *demi-pause, demi-soupir*, see *Notes; *demi-ton*, semitone; *demi-voix*, *mezza voce.

Demisemiquaver. See *Notes.

Demuthsvoll [G.]. Humble, devotional.

Denkmäler der Tonkunst, etc. See *Editions VII, VIII, IX.

De profundis. Psalm 129 (130 of the King James Version: "Out of the depths have I cried unto thee, O Lord"). See *Penitential psalms.

Des, deses [G.]. See *Pitch names.

Descant. (1) Older name for the highest voice in part music, i.e., the soprano [G. *Diskant*]. Hence, names such as *descant viol, descant recorder* for the highest pitched instruments. Unfortunately, there is no consistency in the use of the terms descant and *treble. As terms for the upper voice in part music, they are used synonymously; however, descant viol (recorder) is a higher (and smaller) instrument than the treble viol (recorder); on the other hand, descant clef is a "lower" clef than treble clef [see *Clefs].

(2) As a designation for early part-music, written out or improvised, see *Discant and *Discantus supra librum.

(3) In hymn singing, descant is a more or less florid melody sung by a few picked trebles as an addition to the normal melody and harmony of the hymn. The practice as well as the term go back to the 14th-century *discantus supra librum* which was a method of improvisation to a plainsong melody. While, one hundred years or more ago, there still

were singers in England who improvised a descant, the modern practice is to supply such melodies in the printed books of standard hymn-tunes. The same method of singing is also known by the entirely inappropriate name *fauxbourdon* or *faburden* [see *Fauxbourdon* (5)]. See also under *Division.

Descort [F.]. See *Lai.

Descriptive music. See *Program music; *Word-painting.

Desolre(ut), De sol re (ut). See *Hexachord III.

Dessus [F.]. Old term corresponding to *treble, while *par-dessus* corresponds to *descant. Thus, *dessus de viole*, treble viol; *par-dessus de viole*, descant viol.

Détaché [F.]. See *Bowing (b).

Detonieren [G.]. To sing in wrong or inaccurate pitch; to waver in pitch.

Deuteros [G.]. See *Church modes II.

Deutlich [G.]. Clear, distinct.

Development [F. *dévellopement*; G. *Durchführung*; It. *svolgimento*]. An important technique of recent composition (18th and 19th centuries) which consists in the "unfolding" of the thematic material (themes, subjects) by means such as segmentation into fragments, iteration of themes or fragments thereof in various keys (usually modulatory), modification (frequently rhythmic) of motives [see *Metamorphosis], inversion of motives, fugal treatment, combination of different material in a contrapuntal fashion, etc. These devices are used in a manner designed to bring about a feeling of evolution and growth, of increased intensity and higher "temperature," of dynamic stress and climax, of a battlefield where the musical forces come to grips. Indeed, from the composer's point of view, the writing of a development-section might be said to be an affair of strategic, rather than creative, capacity. The development technique is used particularly in the second section of movements written in

sonata-form, that is, in the so-called development-section, in which material presented in the exposition is "developed" [see *Sonata-form]. However, the same technique (although usually on a minor scale) is also used in the exposition itself of larger symphonies, or, still more frequently, in the recapitulation, and occasionally in the *coda. It also occurs in slow movements written in binary or ternary form, in the *scherzos and *rondos, and in free compositions (program music). In brief, it is one of the cornerstones of classical and modern music in which it occurs as the natural corollary of the 19th-century "dynamic style."

The idea of breaking up a subject into fragments already appears in the fugues of Bach who frequently uses portions of the fugal subject as material for the episodes. However, here as well as in the mosaic-like technique found in many sonatas of Domenico Scarlatti, the leading principle is one of coördination and juxtaposition rather than of evolution and growth. The technique of "dynamic development" appears first in the symphonies of the *Mannheim school (*c.* 1740) and was fully exploited by Haydn, Mozart, and Beethoven.

Devisen-arie [G. *Devise*, device, inscription]. Modern term (Riemann) for the da-capo aria with preliminary announcement of the initial subject. Our illustration shows an early example, from

Cesti's opera *L'Argia* of 1669 [cf. *SchGMB*, no. 203]. See Aria IV.

Dezime [G.]. The interval of the tenth.

Diabelli Variations. Beethoven's op. 120 (1823), consisting of a series of 33 variations on a waltz by Diabelli. They were written in response to a request, sent by Diabelli (Viennese publisher) to 51 composers, to contribute one variation each to a collective set which was meant to represent a cross section of the compositional activity in Austria of his day. The entire collection was published under the title *Vaterländischer Künstlerverein* (Society of Artists of the Fatherland) in two volumes, the first of which contained the variations of Beethoven, the second those of the 50 other composers (Schubert, Moscheles, Kalkbrenner, Liszt — who was then eleven years old! — and others). Cf. the complete list in *GD* v, 457.

Diabolus in musica [L., the devil in music]. Nickname for the *tritone, which was considered in the theory of the 15th to the 19th centuries as the "most dangerous" interval.

Dialogue [G. *Dialog*; It. *dialogo*]. Seventeenth-century vocal compositions the text of which is in the nature of question and answer, or contains such portions. They are usually written for two singers whose parts alternate. In a way, they represent the vocal counterpart of the *stile concertante* of 17th-century instrumental music. Aside from the frequent use of this form in operas there exist various collections of cantatas written in the style of dialogues, so-called "dialoghi fuor di scena" (dialogues without stage performance), e.g.: Orazio Vecchi, *Dialoghi* (1608); Marco Gagliano, *Dialogo di Ninfa e Pastore* (1611; expl. in *RiHM* ii.2, 33); Giov. Franc. Capello, *Motetti e Dialoghi* (1615; expl. in *SchGMB*, no. 180); Andreas Hammerschmidt, *Gespräche zwischen Gott und einer gläubigen Seele* (1645; new ed. *DTOe* 8.i; expl. in *HAM*, no. 213); Rudolph Ahle, *Geistliche Dialoge* (1648; new ed. in *DdT* v); Henry Lawes, *Ayres and Dialogues* (1653, '55, '58). The dialogue-technique was frequently applied to choruses and arias of oratorios, passions, etc. Famous examples are the initial chorus and the alto aria "Sehet, Jesus hat die Hand" from Bach's *St. Matthew Passion*, in which the chorus comes in with questions such as: "Wo?" "Wohin?"

Dialogue-tropes of the 12th century (i.e., tropes written in the form of a dialogue) are considered the origin of the

*liturgical drama. Dialogue-technique occurs in the *frottola ("a botte e risposte") around 1500, and in Willaert's madrigals. The dialogue-laude of the 16th century are among the forerunners of the opera.

Lit.: Th. Kroyer, "Dialog und Echo in der alten Chormusik" (*JMP* xvi); A. Dolmetsch: †*Select English Songs and Dialogues of the XVIth and XVIIth Centuries* (2 vols., 1912).

Diapason [from Gr. *dia pason chordon*, through all the strings]. (1) In medieval theory, the interval which includes "all the tones," i.e., the octave [see *Diapente; *Diatessaron; *Intervals]. — Derived meanings, chiefly used in French terminology, are: (2) range of a voice; (3) *diapason normal*, i.e., concert pitch, or the tuning fork (*diapason à branches*) which indicates that pitch; (4) the fluepipe work of the organ which forms the backbone of each manual.

Diapente [Gr. *pente*, five]. Ancient Greek and medieval name for the fifth. *Epidiapente*, fifth above; *subdiapente* or *hypodiapente*, fifth below. Hence, *canon in epidiapente*, canon in the fifth above.

Diaphonia, diaphony. (1) In Greek theory, dissonance, in contrast to *symphonia, consonance. This meaning survives in various medieval writings (Marchettus de Padua, Joh. de Moravia, Tinctoris; cf. *CS* iv, 182). — (2) More commonly, the term is used by theorists of the 9th to the 12th centuries as synonymous with (early) *organum in parallel or contrary motion (e.g., *Musica enchiriadis*; cf. *GS* i, 165). The term *discantus is probably the Latin translation of diaphonia. — (3) *Diaphonia basilica* means pedal point (cf. the long-held tones of the organa of the 13th century). The name is derived, not from Gr. *basileus*, king (cf. the customary mistranslation "royal counterpoint"), but from Gr. *basis*, base.

Diastematic. See *Neumes II.

Diatessaron [Gr. *tessaron*, four]. Greek and medieval name for the interval of the fourth. *Epidiatessaron*, fourth above; *subdiatessaron*, *hypodiatessaron*, fourth below. See also *Diapente.

Diatonic. The term denotes the natural scale consisting of five whole tones and two semitones, as it is produced on the white keys of the keyboard. There is, of course, a corresponding scale in each key. Music is called diatonic if it is confined to the notes of this scale, to the exclusion of chromatic tones. For instance, in C major, the melodic progression c–d–e and the chord d a c′ are diatonic, while c–d#–e and d ab c are chromatic. Diatonicism is a term used for music the tonality of which is predominantly diatonic, i.e., non-chromatic, such as the works of Haydn and Mozart. For a recent modification of diatonicism, see *Pandiatonicism. — A diatonic semitone is one which involves change of degree, e.g., e–f, c–db, g#–a, in contradistinction to the chromatic semitone which involves modification of the same degree, e.g., c–c#, ab–a. In *just intonation the former is $\dfrac{16}{15}$ = 112 *cents, the latter only $\dfrac{25}{24}$ = 71 cents, while in well-tempered tuning they are, of course, identical (100 cents). For the diatonic genus of Greek theory, see *Greek music II (b).

Dictionaries of music. These are of several types: (1) those which offer merely the pronunciation translation, and brief description of foreign musical terms (e.g., Th. Baker, *A Dictionary of Musical Terms*); (2) those which cover the entire field of music with emphasis upon separate entries and definitions (e.g., H. Riemann, *Musiklexikon*), or upon longer articles comprehending all aspects of the topics (e.g., Grove's *Dictionary*); (3) those which cover all periods and fields of composition but are restricted to (a) biographies only (e.g., Th. Baker, *Biographical Dictionary of Musicians*), or (b) to topics without biographical entries (e.g., M. Brenet, *Dictionnaire pratique et historique de la musique*); and (4) those

which are limited (a) to a particular period (e.g., A. Eaglefield Hull, *A Dictionary of Modern Music and Musicians*), or (b) to a particular country (e.g., E. Refardt, *Historisch-biographisches Musikerlexikon der Schweiz*), or (c) to a particular field (e.g., W. W. Cobbett, *Cyclopedic Survey of Chamber Music*.

The subsequent list groups the dictionaries under three headings: I. Standard Dictionaries (including the above types 1, 2, 3) published after 1890; II. Special Dictionaries (including type 4) published after 1890; III. Earlier Dictionaries.

I. *Standard Dictionaries after 1890.*

A. United States: Th. Baker, *A Dictionary of Musical Terms* (25th ed., 1939). — *id.*, *Biographical Dictionary of Musicians* (4th ed., 1940). — W. S. Pratt, *The New Encyclopedia of Music and Musicians* (1924, originally planned as an abridgment of Grove; rev. ed., 1929). — O. Thompson, *The International Cyclopedia of Music and Musicians* (1939; rev. ed. 1944).

B. England: G. Grove, *Dictionary of Music and Musicians* (4th ed. by H. C. Colles, 1940, 5 vols., with *American Supplement*, 1938, and with *Supplementary Volume*, 1940). — P. Scholes, *The Oxford Companion to Music* (1938; 2d ed., 1941). — English ed. of *Riemann* (by Shedlock, 1893ff).

C. France: M. Brenet, *Dictionnaire pratique et historique de la musique* (new ed., 1930). — R. Vannes, *Essai de terminologie musical. Dictionnaire universelle* . . . (1925). — The *Encyclopédie de la musique et dictionnaire du Conservatoire* (ed. A. Lavignac and L. de la Laurencie, 1913–1931; 5 vols. *Histoire* and 6 vols. *Technique*), although frequently listed among musical dictionaries and probably intended to include one, actually lies outside the category. A short alphabetical index, mainly to composers, was compiled by R. Bruce (Yale University, 1936).

D. Germany: R. Eitner, *Biographisch-bibliographisches Quellen-Lexikon* . . . *bis zur Mitte des 19. Jahrhunderts* (1900–04, 10 vols.; supplementary *Miscellanea bio-bibliographica*, ed. by H. Springer and others, 1912–16, 3 vols.). — H. Riemann, *Musiklexikon* (1882; 11th ed., by A. Einstein, 1929, 2 vols.). H. J. Moser, *Musiklexikon* (1935). — H. Abert, *Illustriertes Musiklexikon* (1927). E. Italy: A. della Corte and G. M. Gatti, *Dizionario di musica* (1925; 3d ed., 1930). — C. Schmidl, *Dizionario universale dei musicisti* (1926, 2 vols.; supp., 1938). F. Other Countries: A. Iljinski and G. Pachulski, *Biographien der Komponisten des iv. bis xx. Jahrhunderts* (Moscow, 1904). — G. Keller and P. Kruseman, *Geillustreerd Muzieklexicon* (s'Gravenhage, 1932). — T. Norlind, *Allmänt Musiklexikon* (Stockholm, 1916; 2d ed., 1927–28, 2 vols.). — H. Panum and others, *Illustreret Musikleksikon* (Copenhagen, 1924–26; new ed., 1940). — A. Torellas and J. Pahissa, *Diccionario de la musica illustrado* . . . (Barcelona, 1930, 2 vols.). — H. Viotta, *Lexicon der Toonkunst* (Amsterdam, 1889, 3 vols.).

II. *Special Dictionaries after 1890.*
A. United States and England: A. Eaglefield-Hull, *A Dictionary of Modern Music and Musicians* (i.e., since 1880; 1924). — Stainer and Barrett, *Dictionary of Musical Terms* (1898). — W. W. Cobbett, *Cyclopedic Survey of Chamber Music* (1929–30, 2 vols.). — D. Ewen, *Composers of Today* (1935; 2d ed., 1936). — D. Ewen, *Living Musicians* (i.e., performers; 1940). — Cl. Reis, *Composers in America* (from 1912 to 1937; '38). — N. Slonimsky, "Concise Biographical Dictionary of Twentieth-Century Musicians" in *Music Since 1900* (1937; 2d ed., 1938; contains important corrections of dates in the dictionaries of Grove, Hull, Riemann, and Moser). — *Who is Who in Music* (1941 edition). — J. Towers, *Dictionary-Catalog of Operas and Operettas* (1910). — J. Pulver, *Dictionary of Old English Music and Musical Instruments* (1923). — J. Pulver, *Biographical Dictionary of Old English Music* (1927). — John A. Julian, *Dictionary of Hymnology* (1892; 2d ed., 1907ff). — Anselm Hughes, *Dictionary of Liturgical Terms* (1941). — *Bio-bibliographical Index of Musicians in the United States Since Colonial Times*

(District of Columbia Historical Records Survey, 1941).
B. France: F. Clément and P. A. Larousse, *Dictionnaire des opéras* . . . (Paris, 1872; rev. ed. by A. Pougin, 1905)
C. Germany: W. Altmann, *Kurzgefasstes Tonkünstlerlexikon* (1926); H. Müller, *Deutsches Tonkünstlerlexikon* (1928). — C. Sachs, *Reallexikon der Musikinstrumente* . . . (1913). — W. L. Lütgendorff, *Geigen- und Lautenmacher vom Mittelalter bis zur Gegenwart* (4th ed., 1922, 2 vols.). — J. Zuth, *Handbuch der Laute und Gitarre* (1926–28). — U. Kornmüller, *Lexikon der kirchlichen Tonkunst* (2d ed., 1895). — S. Kümmerle, *Encyclopedie der evangelischen Kirchenmusik* (1888–95, 4 vols.). — A. Weissenbäck, *Sacra Musica: Lexikon der katholischen Kirchenmusik* (1937).
D. Italy: A. de Angelis, *L'Italia musicale d'oggi: Dizionario dei musicisti, compositori, direttori d'orchestra* . . (1918; 3d ed., 1928). — C. Dessori, *Opere e operisti, dizionario lirico* (1903)
E. Other Countries: José Ruiz de Lihory, *La Musica en Valencia, diccionario biografico e critico* (Valencia, 1903). — E. Vieira, *Diccionario biografico de musicos portuguezes* . . . Lisbon, 1900, 2 vols.). — W. Neumann, *Lexikon baltischer Tonkünstler* (Riga, 1909), A Vodarsky-Shireff, *Russian Composers and Musicians, A Biographical Dictionary* (New York, 1940); E. Refardt, *Historisch-biographisches Musikerlexikon der Schweiz* (Zürich, 1928). — G. Černušák and V. Helfert, *Pazdirkův hudební Slovník naučný* (Brno, 1938).
III. *Earlier Dictionaries.* The earliest musical dictionary is an 11th-century *Vocabularium musicum* (repr. in J. La Fage, *Essai de diphtérographie musicale*, 1864). Much more complete is Joh. Tinctoris' *Terminorum musicae diffinitorium* from c. 1474 (repr. in *CS* iv and, with German translation, in *JMW* i). This was followed, but only after more than two centuries, by the *Clavis ad thesaurum magnis artis musicae* (Prague, 1701) of the Bohemian organist, Janovka, and by the *Dictionnaire de musique* (Paris, 1703) of Sébastien Brossard. From the latter, who

was unfamiliar with Janovka's work, stems the line of French musical dictionaries continued most notably by: J. J. Rousseau, *Dictionnaire de musique* (Geneva, 1768); the *Dictionnaire de musique* (I, 1791; II, 1818) by Framery and Ginguené, contained in the *Encyclopédie méthodique*; the first French biographical dictionary of musicians, namely the *Dictionnaire historique des musiciens*, of Choron and Fayolle (Paris, 1810–11, 2 vols.); F. H. J. Castil-Blaze, *Dictionnaire de musique moderne* (Paris, 1821; 2d ed., 2 vols., 1825; revised 1828); F. J. Fétis' exclusively biographical *Biographie universelle des musiciens* (Paris, 1834–35, 8 vols.; 2d ed., 1860–65; 2-vol. supplement by A. Pougin, 1879–81); and the still useful compilation, *Dictionnaire de musique d'après les théoriciens, historiens, et critiques les plus célèbres*, edited by M. and L. Escudier (Paris, 1844; 5th ed., 1872).

The German musical dictionaries begin with J. G. Walther's topical and biographical [*Alte und neue musikalische Bibliothek oder*] *Musikalisches Lexikon* (1728; greatly enlarged, 1732), and are subsequently represented — in addition to biographical and other material found in J. Mattheson's writings, especially his *Grundlage einer Ehrenpforte* (1740; modern edition by M. Schneider, Berlin, 1910) — chiefly by: E. L. Gerber's purely biographical *Historisch-biographisches Lexikon der Tonkünstler* (1790–92, 2 vols.; 2d ed., 1812–14, 4 vols.); H. C. Koch, *Musikalisches Lexikon* (1802; rev., 1865); G. Schilling's comprehensive [*Encyclopädie der gesammten musikalischen Wissenschaften oder*] *Universallexikon der Tonkunst* (1835–38, 6 vols.; suppl., 1842); and H. Mendel, *Musikalisches Konversationslexikon* (1870–79, 11 vols.; suppl., 1883).

Following an unimportant volume entitled *A short explication of such foreign words as are made use of in musick books* (1724), English musical lexicography produces its first significant work in J. Grassineau's purely topical *Musical dictionary* . . . (London, 1740; 2d ed., 1769), an expansion of Brossard, and its first biographical dictionary of musicians

in the *Dictionary of Musicians* (1824, 2 vols.; 2d ed., 1827).

Italy's first dictionary of music was the *Dizionario di musica sacra e profana* of P. Gianelli (Venice, 1801; 2d ed., 1820), which was superseded by P. Lichtenthal, *Dizionario e bibliografia della musica* (1826, 4 vols.).

Of American dictionaries in this field the most important early work is J. W. Moore, *Complete encyclopedia of music* (Boston, 1854; appendix to 1875), which was followed by the author's shorter *Dictionary of musical information containing also a vocabulary of musical terms, and a list of modern musical works published in the United States from 1640 to 1875* (Boston, 1876). Later came, among others, the *Cyclopedia of music and musicians* [composers only] by J. D. Champlin, Jr., and W. F. Apthorp (New York, 1888–90, 3 vols.) and the *American history and encyclopedia of music*, edited by W. L. Hubbard and others (New York, 1910, 12 vols.).

Works in other languages are: B. Saldoni, *Diccionario biográfico-bibliográfico de efemérides de musico espanoles* (Madrid, 1868, 4 vols.); J. de Vasconcellos, *Os musicos portuguezes* (Porto, 1870, 2 vols.), A. Sowinski, *Les musiciens polonais et slaves anciens et modernes* (Paris, 1857); *id.*, *Slownik muzyków polskich* (Paris, 1874).

For completion of the above list, reference may be had to E. Magni-Dufflocq, "Dizionari di Musica" (*Bolletino bibliografico musicale* viii), to the article "Dictionaries" in *GD* and the articles "Lexika" in *RiML* and *MoML*. L. H.

Didymic comma. See *Comma.

Dièse [F.]. Sharp; see *Pitch names.

Dies irae (Day of wrath). A rhymed sequence [see *Sequence (2)], probably by Thomas a Celano (d. 1256), which is among the most impressive products of medieval poetry and music. It is one of the five sequences still surviving in the Roman liturgy, being sung at Requiem mass [*GR*, 97*]. Its plainsong melody which is a good example of *Dorius mix-*

tus [see *Church modes] shows the sequence-like structure aa bb cc — this scheme being repeated with three stanzas (in the third stanza, the second c is re-

Di-es i-rae di-es il-la,Sol-vet saec-lum

in fa-vil-la,Tes-te Da-vid cum Si-bil-la.

placed by an extended coda: *lacrimosa — Amen*). The Dies irae is usually included in polyphonic settings of the requiem. In the older settings it is either sung simply to the plainsong melody (Palestrina, Vittoria), or this melody is used as the tenor of polyphonic composition (Orazio Vecchi, Francesco Anerio; cf. *GD* ii, 65). More recent composers have usually retained only the text and have written to it free music of a highly dramatic character (Mozart, Cherubini, Verdi). However, the initial phrases of the old melody [see Ex.] are used as a subject in Berlioz' "Symphonie Fantastique" (1828), last movement, and in his "Grande Messe des Morts" (1837), as well as in Liszt's "Symphonie zu Dante's Divina Commedia" (Inferno) and in Saint Saëns's "Danse macabre" [see *Dance of Death]. See also *Requiem.

Diesis. (1) It. for sharp; see *Pitch names. — (2) In older Greek theory (Pythagoras), the diatonic semitone of the *Pythagorean scale, also called *limma*. — (3) In later Greek theory (Aristotle) *diesis* means the quarter-tone, also called *pyknon*, of the enharmonic genus. In this meaning the term reappears in the writings of Niccola Vicentino (1511–72), who tried to restore the Greek system. — (4) In modern writings on acoustics the term is occasionally used to designate certain theoretical intervals, about a quarter-tone in size. The difference between four minor thirds (of just intonation) and the octave is called *great diesis* ($\left(\dfrac{6}{5}\right)^{4}$ $:2 = \dfrac{648}{625} = 63$ *cents); that between the octave and three major thirds

is called *minor diesis* or *enharmonic diesis* ($2:\left(\dfrac{5}{4}\right)^{3} = \dfrac{128}{125} = 41$ cents); see *Enharmonic (2).

Dietro [It.]. After, following. Also used in the meaning of *retrograde.

Diferencia. Sixteenth-century Spanish name for variations. The diferencias contained in Luis de Narvaez' *Delphin de Musica* (1543; cf. *ApMZ* ii) are among the earliest preserved examples of variations [see *Variations VI]. Cabezon wrote outstanding diferencias for the organ [repr. in *Editions XIII, 3/4 and 7/8]. Examples in *HAM*, nos. 122, 134. See also *Glosa.

Difference tone, differential tone. See *Combination tones.

Differentiae, differences [G. *Differenzen*]. The various endings of a *psalm tone. An older name is *tropus*. See *E u o u a e.

Dilettant [G.]. Amateur.

Diluendo [It.]. "Dissolving," dying away.

Dimeter. See *Poetic Meter.

Diminished intervals. See *Intervals.

Diminished seventh chord. See *Seventh chord.

Diminished triad. See *Triad.

Diminuendo [It.], abbreviated *dim.* or *dimin.* Same as *decrescendo.

Diminution [L. *diminutio*]. (1) In counterpoint and in mensural notation, see *Augmentation and diminution. — (2) The breaking up of the notes of a melody into quick figures, as is frequently done in variations; hence, synonymous with figuration or ornamentation. See also *Ornamentation I.

Di nuovo [It.]. Anew, once more.

Diphona [Gr.]. See *Bicinium.

Diplomas. See *Degrees.

Direct. A mark, similar in shape to the *mordent, which in early manuscripts and publications is given at the end of each staff (or only of the page) to warn the player of the first note of the following staff (or page). The Latin name is *custos.*

Directaneus. See *Psalmody I.

Dirge [from L. *Dirige Domine,* an antiphon from the Office for the Dead; cf. *AR* (154)]. A vocal or instrumental composition designed to be performed at a funeral or at memorial rites.

Dirigent; dirigieren [G.]. Conductor; to conduct.

Dis, disis [G.]. See *Pitch names.

Discant [L. *discantus*]. Although Webster gives discant only as a second choice of *descant, musical authorities (e.g., Wooldridge, in *OH* i) prefer the spelling discant — which is closer to the original Latin word — for the early meaning of the word, explained below. The Anglicized spelling descant may be reserved for the later meanings [see *Descant]. *Discantus* is a 13th-century term, possibly a translation of Gr. *diaphonia,* and used preferably to denote polyphonic music in strict (modal) rhythm [cf. the explanation of Joh. de Garlandia, *CS* i, 106: "Discant is the concurrence of various parts according to the principles of modal meter and of the equivalence of note-values"]. It therefore denotes that style which prevails in the organa, clausulae, motets, and conductus of the 13th century [see *Clausula; also *Harmony, Ex. 4], as distinguished from the rhythmically free "organal style" of the organa dupla of the 12th century (St. Martial and, possibly, Leoninus) in which the upper voice (*duplum*) moves on in relatively free melismas above a few sustained notes of the tenor [see *Harmony, Ex. 3; also under *Organum]. The 13th- and 14th-century treatises on discant deal chiefly with the rules of consonances and of voice-leading in part-writing. Thus, discant becomes tantamount to "teaching of counterpoint" — a meaning which sur-

vives in the "descant" of English 17th- and 18th-century treatises. For English discant, see *Fauxbourdon (2). In a few treatises prior to the 13th century the term *discantus* is used in various connotations (e.g., that of contrary motion), some of which are not entirely clear [see Lit., Handschin].

Lit.: *OH* i, chapter on "Discant or Measured Music"; J. Handschin, in *ZMW* vii and viii.

Discant mass [G. *Diskantmesse*]. A recent musicological term for Masses of the 15th century in which the borrowed *cantus firmus* appears, not — as usual — in the tenor, but in the upper part, usually disguised in figurations [see *Mass B, II]. This method was in vogue in the early 15th century (Dunstable, Dufay, Binchois) [ex. in *BeMMR,* 199]. •Cf. R. v. Ficker, "Die Colorierungstechnik der Trienter Messen" (*StM* vii).

Discantus supra librum [F. *déchant sur le livre,* "discant from the book"]. A 14th-century term for methods of improvising polyphonic music, with only one part (tenor) written "in the book," i.e., in the books of Gregorian chant. The *organum of the 9th and 10th centuries, proceeding chiefly in parallel fourths and fifths, may be considered as an early type of *discantus supra librum,* since its rules enabled a singer to improvise a second voice (*vox organalis*) to the plainsong tenor (*vox principalis*). Specifically, the term refers to certain more elaborate methods of improvised harmonization employed in the 14th century. The method described by S. Tunstede (*CS* iii, 361; see *Theory II) looks like a "modernization" of the early organum of fifths. Four singers perform doubled parallel fifths, with florid passages interspersed in the two

highest parts, whereas a fifth singer (called "discantor") occasionally introduces thirds [see Ex.]. (The black notes indicate the "discantor"; the arrows suggest the possibility of improvised figuration [see *Ornamentation I]; the lowest part is the tenor "from the book.") A more progressive and more important type of discantus supra librum is that known as English discant [see *Fauxbourdon (2)]. It may be noted that, in English writings of the 16th to the 19th century, the term descant is frequently used in a meaning derived from discantus supra librum [see *Descant (3)]. Cf. E. Ferand, *Die Improvisation in der Musik* (1939) and paper in *Proceedings of the Music Teachers' National Association* (1940); M. Bukofzer, *Geschichte des Englischen Diskants* . . . (1936).

Discantus visibilis. See *Fauxbourdon (2).

Discord. See *Concord and Discord.

Disinvolto [It.]. "Self-possessed," i.e., assured, easy.

Disis [G.]. See *Pitch names.

Disjoint, disjunct. See *Conjoint.

Diskant [G.]. Soprano (descant). See also *Discant.

Disperato [It.]. Desperate.

Disposition. The arrangement of stops, manuals, pedals, couplers, etc., of an organ.

Disque [F.]. Record.

Dissonance. See *Consonance and dissonance.

Distinction. In Gregorian chant, the phrases of the melody, such as are indicated by the sections of the text, e.g.: Omnes qui habebant infirmos/ ducebant illos ad Jesum/ et sanabantur [*AR*, 394]. In the Vatican editions of the monks of Solesmes vertical dashes (called *divisio*) of various lengths and positions are used to indicate smaller or longer rests to be made after each distinction. Cf. *GR*, p. xiii.

Dital harp. See *Harp lute.

Dithyramb [Gr. *dithyrambos*]. A song

in honor of the Greek god Dionysus. It seems as though it originally was a strophic song sung by a chorus or the whole crowd attending the feast of the god. From the 6th to the 4th century it grew more elaborate by the inclusion of the *aulos, of soloists, and of dancing groups. Thus it became a compound form consisting of various "movements" which has been compared to our cantata. It also adopted a dramatic and emotional character, full of unbridled passion. Towards the end of the 4th century it degenerated into a sort of show-opera in which various characters were frequently presented by one single actor. — Modern composers have occasionally adopted the word as a title of compositions of a very free and passionate nature. Cf. *ReMMA*, 12ff; *RiHM* i.1, 129; *AdHM* i, 58; Th. Reinach, *La Musique Grecque* (1926), 149.

Ditonus [L.]. Medieval name for the major third, equal to two whole-tones.

Div. Abbreviation for *divisi.

Diva [It., goddess]. Same as *prima donna.

Divertimento [It.]. An instrumental form of the second half of the 18th century which combines features of the suite with those of the symphony. It consists of a varying number (four to ten) of relatively short movements some of which are in the form and style of the symphony (sonata), while others are suite-like dances (especially minuets) or variations. Divertimenti were written for strings, winds, or mixed groups, usually with one or two players to the part; thus they are chamber rather than orchestral music. They were particularly popular in Vienna. Haydn wrote 66 divertimenti, Mozart 21; others are by Dittersdorf (1739–99) and Ignaz Holzbauer (1711–83; cf. *DTB* 15). Beethoven's Septett op. 20 and Schubert's Octett op. 166 belong to the same category. Closely related types are the *cassation and the *serenade. See also *Divertissement (4).

Divertissement [F.]. (1) Fugal episode. — (2) A musical potpourri, frequently in the form of pieces extracted from an opera. — (3) In the French Baroque opera, the ballets, dances, entr'actes, etc., in short all those pieces which merely served to entertain without being essential to the plot of the action. — (4) Same as *divertimento.

Divided stop. See *Stop.

Divisi [It.]. The term, abbreviated *div.*, is used in orchestral scores to indicate that an instrumental body, e.g., the first violins, is to be divided into two groups for the rendering of passages which include full chords, doubling in thirds, etc. See reference under *A due.

Divisio [L.]. (1) In Gregorian chant, see under *Distinction. — (2) In 13th-century notation, *divisio modi* is a small vertical dash of indefinite length which is regularly placed at the end of an *ordo, i.e., of a melodic phrase in modal meter. It is equivalent to a rest. See *Modes, rhythmic. — (3) In 14th-century Italian notation, *divisiones* are metrical schemes comparable to our 4/8, 6/8, 9/8, 12/8, etc., meters, so called because they are arrived at by dividing a long note (*brevis*) into smaller values. Cf. *ApNPM*, 370ff.

Division. A 17th- and 18th-century term for *figuration, that is, for the breaking up of a melody into quick figures and passages [see also *Ornamentation I; *Coloratura]. In particular, the term refers to the prevailingly English practice of a harpsichordist playing a ground bass (with its thorough-bass chords), to which a viol- or flute-player, "having the said ground before his eye, plays such a variety of descant or division in concordance thereto as his skill and present invention do then suggest unto him" [Chr. Simpson, *The Division Violist* (1659)]. Such music, chiefly extemporized, was called divisions upon a ground. Important English publications other than that of Simpson are: John Playford, *The Division Violin* (1685); Henry Playford, *The Division Violin* (1688, '93); *The Division Flute* (anon., 1722). See *Improvisation III; *Partimento.

A modern counterpart of the 17th-century method of divisions exists in that recent type of jazz known as *boogie-woogie.

Division viol. See *Viol IV, 2.

Divoto [It.]. Devout.

D la sol (re). See *Hexachord III.

Do, doh. See *Solmization I; *Tonic Sol-fa.

Dodekachordon [from Gr. *dodeka,* twelve, and *chordos,* string, tone]. Title of an important theoretical book by H. Glareanus (1488–1563), published in 1547, in which the traditional system of eight *church modes is enlarged to a system of twelve. The book is also remarkable for its highly judicious and comprehensive analysis of the works of Josquin and other masters of the early 16th century. A German translation by P. Bohn appeared in 1899. Cf. A. Schering, "Die Notenbeispiele in Glarean's D." (*SIM* xiii).—The name was adopted by Claude Le Jeune (d. 1606) as a title for a cycle of motets based upon the twelve modes of Glarean [see *Editions XVI, 8].

Dogliosamente [It.]. Sorrowful.

Doigté [F.]. Fingering.

Dolce [It.]. Sweet and soft.

Dolcino, dolcian, dulcian. See *Oboe (history).

Dolcissimo [It.]. Very sweet and soft.

Dolente, doloroso [It.]. Doleful.

Domchor [G.]. The choir of a German cathedral (*Dom*), either Protestant or Catholic.

Domestic Symphony. See *Symphonic poem III.

Dominant. (1) The fifth degree of the major or minor scale, so called on account of its "dominating" position in harmony as well as in melody. Many melodies show the fifth as a tone second in importance only to the first degree, the *tonic [see *Scale degrees]. However, the fifth degree is even more important in harmony as a bass tone, i.e., the root of the dominant triad (g–b–d' in C major). In *harmonic analysis, this triad is indicated by the numeral V or the letter D. It is most frequently resolved into the tonic triad (I) [see *Cadence]. Other chords with dominant function are the dominant seventh chord [see *Seventh chord], the *diminished seventh chord, and the dominant ninth chord [see *Ninth chord]. Of particular importance in harmonic analysis are the so-called *secondary dominants*, i.e., the dominants of any degree of the scale other than the tonic. It is these chords which account for the majority of accidentals found in music which is essentially diatonic. The designation for such chords is: V of II (V/II), V of III (V/III), etc. [see Ex.]. See

*Harmonic analysis V. — (2) For the dominant of modes, see *Church modes I.

Dominant seventh chord. See *Seventh chord; *Dominant.

Dominica [L.]. Sunday [see under *Feria].

Domp(e). See *Dump.

Domra. A Russian long-necked lute [see *Lute II] of the 16th and 17th centuries, the forerunner of the *balalaika. Cf. A. S. Faminzin, *The Domra* (1891; Russian); *LavE* i.5, 2494f.

Don Giovanni ("Don Juan"). Opera (*dramma giocoso*) in two acts by W. A. Mozart (1756–91), text by Da Ponte, composed in 1787. The action takes place in Seville during the 17th century and centers around the libertine of legendary fame, Don Juan or *Don Giovanni* (Baritone), who is assisted in his numerous amorous adventures by his servant *Leporello* (Bass). Three women are involved

in the plot: *Donna Anna* (Soprano), whose father, the *Commendatore* (Bass), is killed by Don Giovanni in the first scene and who, together with her betrothed, *Don Ottavio* (Tenor), swears vengeance; *Donna Elvira* (Soprano), Don Giovanni's deserted wife who seeks to regain his love and, in the final scene, implores him — in vain — to mend his ways; and *Zerlina* (Soprano), a pretty peasant girl about to be married to *Masetto* (Bass). An especially dramatic touch is added to the action by the Statue of the dead Commendatore whom Don Giovanni mockingly invites to dine with him and who, in the final scene, comes to deliver the unrepentant sinner to the demons of hell.

Don Giovanni, one of the greatest, if not *the* greatest, operas of all time, needs no words of praise. Suffice it to point to the overture the slow beginning of which anticipates the music accompanying the appearance of the Commendatore in the final scene, to the "Catalogue aria" by Leporello in which he reads to Donna Elvira the list of Don Giovanni's "1003 loves," and to Don Giovanni's "Deh vieni alla fenestra" sung to the accompaniment of a mandolin.

Donnermaschine [G.]. *Thunder machine.

Don Quixote. See *Symphonic poem III.

Doppel- [G.]. Double. *Doppel-be*, double flat; *Doppelchor*, double chorus; *Doppelfuge*, double fugue; *Doppelgriff*, double stop; *Doppelkreuz*, double sharp; *Doppelpedal*, double pedal; *Doppelschlag*, turn; *Doppeltriller*, double trill; *Doppelzunge*, double-tonguing. In connection with instruments, the term usually denotes *duplex instruments [cf. *SaRM*, 114–117].

Doppio [It.]. Double. *Doppio bemolle*, double flat; *doppio diesis*, double sharp; *doppio movimento* (*tempo*), double speed; *doppio pedale*, double pedal.

Dorian. See *Greek music II (c); *Church modes I; *Modality. Dorian sixth is the major sixth used in a minor key (e.g., in C minor: c–e♭–f–g–a–g), so called because it appears in the Dorian church mode (d–f–g–a–b–a). Cf. Hipkins, "Dorian and Phrygian" (*SIM* iv).

Dot [F. *point*; G. *Punkt*; It. *punto*]. In musical notation a dot is used: (a) after a note, to indicate augmentation of its value by one-half [see *Dotted notes]; (b) above a note, to indicate *staccato or *portato. See also *Punctus.

Dotted notes. I. *Present Usage*. A dot placed after a note adds to it one-half of its value. Thus, a dotted half-note equals three quarter-notes [Ex. a]. Two dots after a note add to it one-half plus one-quarter of its value. Thus, a double-dotted half-note equals 4 + 2 + 1 = 7

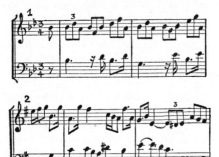

eighth-notes [Ex. b]. In modern practice, dotted notes are used only if their value does not extend over a bar-line; otherwise tied notes are used [Ex. c]. Brahms revived an older practice when he wrote dotted rhythm as shown in Ex. d.

II. *In Baroque Music*. In music prior to 1750 the dot is frequently used in a manner which differs from the modern practice and which has been the object of much investigation and controversy. The only proper answer to this question is that in the period under consideration the dot indicates a prolongation of undetermined value, depending upon various factors such as the character of the piece, the rhythm of the other parts, the tempo, the interpretation of the performer, etc. Statements to this effect are found in practically all theory books written between *c.* 1680 and 1750. In this connection it may be noted that Leopold Mozart in his *Versuch einer gründlichen Violinschule* (1756) would seem to have been the first to use the double dot, thus paving the way for a clearer indication of different degrees of prolongation. The following cases of the freely used dot are noteworthy:

(a) If dotted notes are used against triplets in another voice, the dotted rhythm may be modified (attenuated)

into a triplet rhythm [Ex. 1; Bach, Partita no. 1]. According to contemporary writers this modification was, however, not obligatory, but was left to the discretion of the performer. In this respect the gavotte from Bach's Partita no. 6 [Ex. 2] is informative since here neither the "exact" nor the "attenuated" rhythm can be consistently maintained, since the same dotted figure appears in conjunction with triplet-groups as well as with groups of four notes. Consistency in this matter (as in many others) concerned Bach much less than it does the student of today.

(b) According to French writers of the early 18th century, compositions written in "French style" (i.e., the style of the slow section in Lully's French *overture) call for a more pronounced rhythm than is indicated in writing, so that a dotted note should be performed almost as a double-dotted value as in Ex. a. This rendition, if used with taste and modera-

tion, helps to bring out the pompous quality of the French overture style and should be applied, though without ostentatious exaggeration, to pieces such as the prelude to Bach's Partita no. 6 and the prelude in E-flat minor from his *Wt. Cl.* i, a composition the true character of which is far removed from the gentle and somewhat boring lyricism in which it is usually interpreted. On the other hand, it cannot be denied that some modern writers and performers have gone too far in recommending strict double-dotted execution for all sorts of pieces which show a remote resemblance to the style of the French overture (e.g., the D-major Fugue of *Wt. Cl.* i).

(c) Another free usage of the dot, but less likely to lead to confusion, is illustrated by Ex. b (used as early as Kotter's tablature, c. 1515; cf. *ApNPM*, 30).

(d) Around 1700 dotted rhythm became a sort of fashionable folly. Certain French or French-minded composers introduced reiterated dotting for running passages, as in Ex. c, or even Ex. d [cf. Georg Muffat, *Florilegium* (1695/96); *DTOe* 2.ii, p. 48], and players applied this rhythm to running figures written in plain eighth- or sixteenth-notes. This method of playing was known as *inégales*. Some modern writers have done ill service to the cause of *Aufführungspraxis by advocating this passing mannerism as the true style of late Baroque music in general. Cf. E. Borrel, in *TG* viii, 267ff, and in *RdM*, no. 40; G. Horn, in *RdM*, no. 53; G. Scheck, and E. Schenck, in *DM* xxi.8 and 11.

III. *Inverted Dotting.* The rhythm which is the reverse of the ordinary dotted rhythm; in other words a dotted note which is preceded, not followed, by its complementary short value (e.g., ♪♩.). This rhythm is generally known under the name *Scotch snap*, because it is a typical feature of the *strathspey and of other Scottish folk tunes. Its occurrence, however, far exceeds the province of Scotch music. It is a typical feature of American Negro music and of jazz, and it has been maintained that the syncopated effects of jazz have their origin in the Scotch snap [see reference under *Jig]. On the other hand, it should be noted that inverted dotting is also very frequent in Oriental and in primitive music [see *Primitive music IV], where the normal dotted rhythm is rather rare. In this connection it is interesting to note that the author of the *Speculum musicae* (c. 1320), in defending the *Ars antiqua against the refinements of the *Ars nova, maintains that the iambic rhythm ♪♩ is

preferable to the trochaic rhythm ♩♪, because it is "a rhythm full of strength and harmonizing with nature which is always stronger at the end than at the beginning" [cf. *ApNPM*, 339].

In art music, the inverted dotting appears first in French songs of the late 16th century, as a means of correct pronunciation [cf. *ApNPM*, 129]. It is extremely frequent in Italian music of the early 17th century and, in fact, represents one of the most typical embodiments of the somewhat exaggerated expressiveness of early Baroque music [examples in Caccini, *Nuove Musiche* (1602); toccatas of Trabaci and Mayone, 1603, cf. W. Apel in *MQ* xxiv, 436; Frescobaldi, e.g., his Toccata per l'elevazione; Cazzati, Cantata of 1649, cf. H. Riemann. *Kantaten-Frühling* ii, 14; Alessandro Scarlatti, cf. *TaAM* ix, 112]. Italian terms for the inverted dotted rhythm are *alla zoppa* or *Lombardic style*. This rhythm also figures prominently in the English music of the 17th century (John Blow, Henry Purcell), in which it is used effectively in order to bring out the short, but accented, first syllables which occur in so many English dissyllabics.

Double. (1) The French word *double* is an 18th-century term for a simple type of variation, consisting chiefly in the addition of embellishments. It occurs preferably with certain dances of a suite (cf. Bach, 1st English Suite: courante with two "doubles"; 6th English Suite: sarabande with "double"). — (2) The English word double, if used in connection with instruments, indicates either instruments of lower pitch or a combination of two instruments in one. The former meaning, which is derived from the double octave, occurs with the *double-bass, the double-bass clarinet, the double-bass trombone, the double bassoon, etc., while the latter occurs with the double horn, the double trumpet, and the double flageolet. See *Duplex instruments.

Doublé [F.]. Term of the French clavecinists for the *turn.

Double-bass, also called *bass viol* or *contrabass* [F. *contrebasse*; G. *Kontrabass*; It. *contrabasso*]. The largest member of the *violin family, serving in the orchestra somewhat in the capacity of a 16-foot organ stop and frequently doubling the celli in the lower octave. The modern instrument has four strings tuned $E_1 A_1 D G$, notated an octave higher (E A d g). Some instruments have a fifth string, tuned C_1. The upper limit for orchestral parts is a (notated a') although virtuosos extend the range of the instrument considerably by the use of harmonics. Famous double-bass players were Dragonetti (1763–1846), Bottesini (1822–89), and Koussevitzky (b. 1874).

More than any other instrument of the violin family the double-bass has been subjected to modification and experimentation, regarding shape, size, number and tuning of the strings, etc. As a matter of fact, the principles of violin building have never been fully applied to this instrument which, to the present day, retains various features of the viol family, e.g., the sloping shoulders, the flat back, the tuning of the strings in fourths rather than in fifths, etc. This ancestry appears also in the current names bass viol and double-bass, both of which are abbreviated versions of the full and proper name double-bass viol [see *Viol family IV, 1]. In the 19th century, instruments with three strings, tuned $A_1 D G$ or $G_1 D A$, were in great favor. What these lose in compass, they gain in brightness of tone on account of the smaller pressure upon the table. Even today there are players (particularly in Europe) who hold the bow in the manner of viol playing, i.e., with the hand underneath the stick.

Double-bass clarinet, trombone. See *Clarinet family II; *Trombone.

Double C (D, etc.). See *Pitch names II.

Double cadence [F.]. A compound ornament, frequently introduced at cadences in music of the 17th and 18th centuries and consisting of a *cadence*, or trill,

upon each of two successive notes. The interpretation of the double cadence was quite flexible, its details being left to the discretion of the performer, but the following sequence of notes, in which the first trill is reduced to a five-note turn, is typical:

In this example *a* shows how the double cadence is indicated in 17th-century music (Chambonnières, d'Anglebert, etc.), while *b* represents the 18th-century notation (Bach, Handel, François Couperin, Rameau) of the same ornament. The name double cadence (or its abbreviation, *doublé*) was often applied to the turn alone.   P. A.

Double chorus. The term refers to the use of two choruses in alternation. See *Polychoral style.

Double concerto. A concerto for two solo instruments and orchestra, such as Mozart's Concerto for violin and viola, K.V. 364.

Double corde [F.]. Double-stop.

Double counterpoint. See *Invertible counterpoint.

Double croche [F.]. See *Notes.

Double-flat. See *Accidentals.

Double fugue. A fugue with two subjects. The term is applied to two different types of fugue with two subjects. (a) A genuine double fugue consists of three distinct sections, each complete in itself: a fugue on the first subject (I), a fugue on the second subject (II), and a fugue on both subjects in contrapuntal combination (I + II). Examples are Bach's great harpsichord fugue in A minor and his organ fugue in E-flat major (the so-called St. Anne's Fugue). His fugue in C-sharp minor from *Wt. Cl.* i represents a somewhat simplified scheme, including the sections I and I + II. His *Art of Fugue* contains not only double fugues (nos. 9, 10) but also triple fugues of a similar scheme (nos. 8, 11) and an (unfinished) quadruple fugue [see *Art of Fugue].— (b) Usually, the term is applied to a much simpler type of fugue, i.e., an ordinary fugue in which the counter-subject has an individual character and is consistently used throughout the piece, combined with the main subject; in other words, fugues represented by the last section only of the above scheme. Examples of this type are quite frequent, but usually treat the secondary theme more freely than is the case in the double-fugue proper. For an example cf. *Wt. Cl.* i, no. 14 (F-sharp minor).

Double pedal. In organ playing, the use of both feet, not, as usual, in alternation, but simultaneously, for the rendering of intervals or of two parts. This technique is documented as far back as 1448 [cf. W. Apel, "Die Tabulatur des Adam Ileborgh" (*ZMW* xvi)]. It was fully developed by the North-German organ masters of the 17th century (Tunder, Buxtehude) and by their successor J. S. Bach, whose organ chorales on "Wenn wir in höchsten Nöten sein" and "An Wasserflüssen Babylons" have a complete part for each foot. In modern organ pieces octave-doubling is very frequent. It is also used by organists as a means of exploiting the limited resources of smaller organs.

Double-sharp. See *Accidentals.

Double stop [F. *double corde*; G. *Doppelgriff*]. The execution of two or more simultaneous tones on the violin and similar instruments (intervals, chords, passages in two or more parts). The curved position of the strings — conditioned by the curved shape of the bridge — frequently compels the player to resort to an arpeggio-like rendering, particularly in the case of chords of three or four tones in piano. Double-stop technique is already used to a remarkable degree in Ganassi's "ricercares" for viola da gamba (1552; cf. *HAM*, no. 119) and in the earliest violin sonatas [Biagio Marini (1626); cf. *SchGMB*, no. 183]. It reaches the climax of artistic perfection in Bach's

sonatas for violin solo, that of brilliant virtuosity in the compositions of Paganini.

Double-tonguing. See *Tonguing.

Double touch. A modern principle of organ construction, devised by Hope-Jones, which allows the keys of the organ to be depressed in two successive degrees, so that different registrations become available simultaneously on the same manual, e.g., a small group of accompaniment stops on the first touch, and a solo stop on the second. Its application is practically confined to theater organs. See also *Harmonium II.

Double trill. The simultaneous trill on two different notes, usually in the distance of a third. Its perfect and rapid execution is one of the most difficult technical feats on the piano as well as on the violin. For the latter instrument it appears as early as the middle 17th century [J. Schop; cf. A. Moser in *Kretzschmar Festschrift* (1918)]. For the piano, the long double trills in Beethoven's Piano Concerto in G major, op. 58, are among the earliest examples.

Douloureux [F.]. Dolorous, mournful.

Doxology [Gr. *doxa*, glory, and *logos*, word]. In the Roman liturgy, the name of two important texts, known as (a) the *Lesser Doxology*: "Gloria patri (et filio et spiritui sancto, sicut erat in principio, et nunc et semper et in saeculum saeculorum. Amen)"; and (b) the *Greater Doxology*: "Gloria in excelsis deo (et in terra pax hominibus bonae voluntatis," etc.). The greater doxology is the *Gloria of the Mass. The lesser doxology (D) is a part of all the introitus, which follow the scheme A V D A [see *Psalmody III]. It also is added as a final verse to all psalms and nearly all the canticles, its last six syllables being indicated by their vowels only, thus: *E u o u a e [see also *Psalm tones]. It is also used elsewhere, e.g., in connection with the *Deus in adjutorium* [*GR*, i*].

Drängend [G.]. Urging forward.

Drag. See *Percussion instruments B, 1.

Dragma [Gr., spike, ear]. A note-form of the late 14th century which occurs, with a variety of meanings, in the theoretical and practical sources of the period. Cf. *ApNPM, passim.*

Dramatic music. The term, aside from its obvious meaning, is used to denote music written for a drama or play (*incidental music), particularly the incidental music written by Henry Purcell, in order to distinguish it from his only complete opera, *Dido and Aeneas.* Cf. E. D. Rendall, in *ML* i; W. Barclay Squire, in *SIM* v.

Drame lyrique [F.]; **dramma lirico** [It.]. Modern terms for opera, not necessarily of a lyrical character. The English term "lyrical drama" is used in the same meaning.

Dramma per musica [It.]. The earliest name for Italian operas (17th century), particularly those of a serious character (the later *opera seria*). Bach used the term for secular cantatas in dialogue-form which were designed for a modest stage performance (*Der Streit zwischen Phöbus and Pan, Kaffeekantate,* etc.).

Dreher [G. *drehen,* to twirl]. An Austrian dance, similar to the *Ländler.

Drehleier [G.]. *Hurdy-gurdy.

Drehorgel [G.]. *Street organ.

Dreiklang [G.]. Triad.

Dreinfahren [G.]. To play roughly, without consideration.

Dreitaktig [G.]. In phrases of three measures.

Dringend [G.]. Urgent, pressing on.

Drohend [G.]. Menacing, threatening.

Drone. (1) The low pipes of the *bagpipe. — (2) A primitive bagpipe, capable of playing only a few low tones and used to accompany other instruments or voices. — (3) In musical composition, long sustained notes, usually in the lowest part

(drone bass) [see *Pedal point; *Bourdon].

Drum. I. Generic name for instruments the sound-producing agent of which is a skin stretched on a frame or vessel and struck with the hands or a stick. Drums are, therefore, practically identical with the category "membranophones" of the scientific classification [see *Instruments II]. There exist, however, in some of the most primitive cultures, drums which have no membrane, consisting of a tree trunk which is hollowed out from a narrow longitudinal slit (slit-drum; cf. *SaHMI,* 29f). These are, in scientific classification, "idiophones."

II. The membranophonous drums are by far the most ancient and most widespread of all instruments. They are found in all exotic cultures, with the most primitive African or South American tribes as well as in China, India, Arabia, etc. [see *Exotic music]. A gigantic bass drum of man's size is depicted on a Sumerian vase of the third millennium B.C. [cf. *SaHMI,* pl. IV]. Egyptian drums from about 1800 B.C. are preserved, and drums are mentioned in one of the earliest Chinese poems, dating from 1135 B.C. Drums existed and still exist in a large variety of sizes and shapes, in the form of a barrel, a cylinder, an hourglass, a goblet, etc.

From the Orient the drum was introduced into the Western world, into Greece — where the use of the "tympanon" was restricted to the orgiastic cult of Dionysus and Cybele — as well as into medieval Europe where the earliest evidence is an English 12th-century miniature showing a juggler disguised as a bear and striking with his hands a barrel drum suspended from his neck. One of the famous Spanish miniatures of the 13th century shows the player of an hourglass drum, which he carries on his shoulder [cf. *GD* iii, opp. p. 734]. Such exotic forms were probably imported from the Orient during the crusades. Of greater importance was the introduction, around 1300, of the Arabian *nagarah* (naqqarah), small kettledrums used in pairs and called *nacaires* in France, *nakers* in England, *naccheroni* in Italy.

The cylindrical drum appeared at about the same time under the name *tabor* or, later, *tambourin*. In the 15th century the drums, kettledrums as well as side drums, were adopted by the armies as an indispensable part of the military equipment. They remained restricted to this sphere until the end of the 17th century when the kettledrums were first used in the orchestra. See *Percussion instruments A,1; B,1-4.

Drum Roll Symphony. Haydn's Symphony in E flat, 1795 (Salomon Symphonies no. 8), so called on account of the drum roll in the opening measure.

Drum Stroke Symphony. Same as *Surprise Symphony.

D.S. *Dal segno.

Dualism, dualistic theory. A theory according to which the tonalities of major and minor are not in the relationship of something "primary" and "secondary," but are phenomena of equal right of birth, one being the inversion of the other. The theory is based upon the fact that by reckoning downwards the intervals of the major triad the tones of the minor triad are arrived at; e.g., c'-e'-g' becomes, by strict inversion, c'-ab-f. This explanation of major and minor was already given by Zarlino (1588; see also *Arithmetic division) and was revived by Rameau (1737), Vallotti (1778), and M. Hauptmann (1853). A. v. Oettingen [*Harmoniesystem in dualer Entwicklung* (1866); *Das Duale Harmoniesystem* (1913)] and H. Riemann [*Das Problem des harmonischen Dualismus* (1905) and his other books on harmony] developed this principle to the fullest extent and made it the basis of har-

monic analysis. The accompanying example serves as an illustration. It will be noted

that the "minor dominant" corresponds to the "major subdominant," and vice versa. The greatest shortcoming of the theory lies in the fact that in a minor mode the triad is determined, not by its lowest, but by its highest tone, i.e., the fifth. Hence, the first chord on the lower staff must not be read: c (fundamental)-eb (minor third)-g (fifth), but downwards: g (fundamental)-eb (major third)-c (fifth). This forced explanation is in contradiction to the most elementary facts of acoustics and of musical experience. The theory has not gained much ground except within the school of Riemann.

Lit.: A. v. Oettingen, *The Dual Harmonic System* (1913); S. Karg-Elert, *Polaristische Klang- und Tonalitätslehre* (1931); H. Westerby, in *PMA* xxix; O. Ortmann, "The Fallacy of Harmonic Dualism" (*MQ* x).

Ductia. An instrumental form of the Middle Ages (13th century) which, according to Johannes de Grocheo, is a *stantipes* [see *Estampie] of smaller extension, i.e., with three to four *puncti*, instead of five or more. The term does not occur in actual musical sources. However, examples of the above type exist in the "Dansse Real" of the *Chansonnier du roy* [cf. P. Aubry, *Estampies et danses royales* (1906)], in several two-part instrumental pieces from the MS Brit. Mus. *Harleian 978* [cf. *ApNPM*, 246f], and in the melodies "Chose Tassin" and "Chose Loiset" which occur as tenors of motets in the *Bamberg Codex* [see *Sources, no. 5]. Examples in *HAM*, nos. 41, 42.

Dudelsack [G.]. *Bagpipe.

Due [It.]. Two. *Due corde,* i.e., two strings, indicates in violin music that the same tone should be sounded on two strings, for greater volume of sound; in piano music, see *Una corda. See also *A due.

Duet [F. *duo*; G. *Duett* or *Duo*; It. *duetto*]. A composition for two performers of equal importance, with or without accompaniment. The most important types are: (a) the vocal duet, i.e., songs or arias for two voices with accompaniment [G. *Duett*]. These play a prominent part in operas, particularly as "love-duets" (practically the whole second act of Wagner's *Tristan* is a "love-duet"). Non-operatic duets occur among the songs of Schubert, Schumann, Brahms, and many others. An early type of unaccompanied vocal duet is the **bicinium* of the 16th century. In the 17th century the chamber-duet (chamber cantata for two singers, with accompaniment) was a much cultivated type. Cf. L. Landshoff, †*Kammerduette des 17. Jahrhunderts* (1927); E. Schmitz, in *JMP* xxiii; also *RiHM*, ii.2 and ii.3. A famous operatic duet of early date is the finale of Monteverdi's *L'Incoronazione di Poppea* (1642; see *SchGMB*, no. 178).— (b) The instrumental duet, for instance for two violins with or without pianoforte accompaniment [G. *Duo*]. Only a few composers (Rode, Spohr, Romberg) have written such pieces, in which the pianoforte part is usually mere chord filling. For works in which this part has individual significance as, for instance, in the sonatas by Bach, the term **trio sonata* is used. — (c) The pianoforte duet, i.e., music for two pianoforte players (four hands), either on the same or on two instruments [see **Piano duet*].

Dugazon. See under **Soubrette*.

Dulce melos. See under **Echiquier*.

Dulcimer [F. *tympanon*; G. *Hackbrett*; It. *salterio tedesco*]. A variety of the **psaltery*, almost identical in shape, but played by small hammers held in the hand (the psaltery is plucked). Thus dulcimer and psaltery stand in a similar relationship as their ultimate descendants, the pianoforte and the harpsichord. The dulcimer originated in the Middle Orient (Assyria, Persia) whence it migrated in three directions: (1) to Spain and western Europe where it appeared as early as the 12th century as is shown by the reliefs of the Cathedral Santiago de Compostela (1184); (2) to Turkey and hence to Hungary where it still is used by the gypsies under the name **cimbalom*; (3) to China where it appeared around 1800 and was

called *yang ch'in*, i.e., "foreign zither" [see **Chinese music*, Ex. 2]. In the early 18th century Pantaleon Hebenstreit revived the instrument in a greatly enlarged and improved form, the so-called **pantalon*. See **Instruments* IV, A, 1 (b).

In current usage the name dulcimer designates home-made zithers plucked with the fingers.

Dulcitone. A variety of the celesta, with tuning forks instead of steel plates.

Dulzian [G.]. Same as **dolcino* [see **Oboe family* III].

Dumka [pl. dumky]. A type of Slavic (originally Russian) folk song, of a narrative character and with sudden changes from melancholy to exuberance. The term has become familiar to musicians through Dvořák whose Dumky-Trio op. 90 consists of six movements each in the character of a dumka. He also wrote a Dumka op. 35 and a Furiant with Dumka op. 12, both for pianoforte.

Dump, domp. An early type of English or Irish song, lamenting and sorrowful in character. A dance for harpsichord entitled "My Lady Careys Dompe" from the early 16th-century MS Brit. Mus. *Roy. App. 58* probably belongs to this class [cf. *HAM*, no. 103; J. Stafford Smith, *Musica Antiqua* (1812), p. 42; see **Ostinato*]. A piece called "The Irish Dumpe" is contained in the *Fitzwilliam Virginal Book* [new ed. ii, 236]. Shakespeare, in *Romeo and Juliet*, IV, 4, mentions "doleful dumps" and "merry dumps." For an example of a more recent date which has been arranged by Beethoven [*Irische Gesänge*, no. 171], cf. *GD* i, 109.

Duo [F., G.]. **Duet*.

Duodecuple scale. The chromatic scale in its modern interpretation as a series of twelve tones of equal rights. See **Twelve-tone technique*.

Duodezime [G.]. The interval of the twelfth.

Duplet [F. *duolet*; G. *Duole*]. A group of two notes to be played in the time of three. See **Triplet*.

Duplex instruments. Instruments, usually of the brass family, which are a combination of two instruments. The two most important members of the class are: (a) The *double euphonium* which has a wide euphonium bell and a narrow Sax-tromba bell either of which may be used by manipulating a controlling valve which directs the wind-stream through one or the other of the bells; thus two different tone qualities are available on one instrument. (b) The *double horn* in F and B-flat which combines two instruments of the same timbre, but of different pitches. The change is effected by an additional valve. Numerous other constructions, mostly of an experimental nature and of ephemeric importance, are mentioned in *SaRM*, 123 (also 115–117). Cf. also *LavE* ii.3, 1461.

Duplex longa. Thirteenth-century name for the *maxima.

Duplum. In the organa and clausulae of the School of Notre Dame [see *Ars antiqua], the part above the tenor. In the 13th-century motets this part was called *motetus* because here the duplum was provided with "mots" [F., words, i.e., text]. *Triplum, quadruplum* are other parts above the tenor, frequently of the same range as the duplum. See *Organum (2).

Duramente [It.]. With harshness.

Dur and **Moll** [from L. *durus,* hard; *mollis,* soft]. The German terms for major and minor. For instance: *C-dur,* C major; *A-moll,* A minor; *Dur- (Moll-) tonart,* major (minor) tonality; *Dur- (Moll-) akkord, Dur- (Moll-) dreiklang,* major (minor) triad. Originally, the names *Dur* and *Moll* have nothing to do with a feeling of "hardness" or "softness" conveyed by one tonality or the other, but stem from two different forms of the letter b, the *b durum* (so called on account of its angular shape) and the *b molle* (round shape). See *B; *Hexachord.

Durchbrochene Arbeit [G.]. A technique of writing in which fragments of a melody are given to different instruments

taking turns [see Ex.; Haydn]. This technique, which is frequently used in symphonies, quartets, etc., appeared first

in the works of Haydn and Mozart [cf. *RiHM* ii.3, 178]. A medieval type of this technique is the *hocket. See also *Antecedent and consequent.

Durchdringend [G.]. Penetrating.

Durchführung [G., "through-leading"]. The term is used in two different and almost opposite meanings according to whether it occurs with reference to sonata-form or to the fugue. In the former case it means development; in the latter, exposition. Thus, the sonata-form follows the scheme: *Themenaufstellung* (exposition), *Durchführung* (development), *Reprise* (recapitulation); the scheme of the fugue is: *Durchführung* (exposition), *Zwischenspiel* (episode), *Durchführung, Zwischenspiel,* etc.

Durchgangsnote [G.]. *Passing-tone.

Durchimitieren [G.]. The term refers to a style in which imitation is applied equally to all the parts. It is particularly used with reference to the fully developed imitative polyphony of the Flemish period, as distinguished from those pieces of the same (or earlier) period in which the tenor has a *cantus firmus.*

Durchkomponiert [G.]. *Through-composed.

Durezza [It., hardness]. In modern music, *con durezza* means: to play with an expression of harshness and determination. In the 17th century, *durezza* means dissonance. Hence, *toccata di durezza e ligature* (Frescobaldi) means: toccata with dissonances and with tied notes; in a way, a composition study in appoggiaturas. The earliest examples occur in the works of Gio. Macque (d. 1614; see *Editions XVII, 4) and his pupil Gio. Trabaci [see W. Apel, in *MQ* xxiv], both members of the early *Neapolitan School of organ music.

Dusk of the Gods, The. See *Ring des Nibelungen, Der.

Dux [L.]. See *Fugue; *Canon (1).

Dynamic marks. The whole of words, abbreviations, and signs which indicate degrees of sound-volume. The commonest are: pianissimo (pp); piano (p); mezzopiano (mp); mezzoforte (mf); forte (f); and fortissimo (ff); crescendo (cresc., ⊏⊐⊏⊐) and decrescendo or diminuendo (decr., dim., ⊐⊏) ; sforzato (sf); and forte-piano (fp). See the various heads. For the use of dynamic marks in music prior to 1750, see *Expression III.

E

E. See *Letter notation; *Pitch names; *Hexachord.

Ear-training. The important field of elementary instruction [see *Solfège] designed to develop in the student sensitiveness to musical phenomena, particularly with regard to intervals and rhythm. The usual method is to play intervals, rhythms, etc., and have the student recognize and record them.

Lit.: W. Earhart, *Music to the Listening Ear* (1932); O. Ortmann, *Problems in the Elements of Ear-diction* (1934); G. A. Wedge, *Advanced Ear-training and Sight-singing* (1922).

Ecclesiastical modes. See *Church modes.

Echappée. See *Nonharmonic tones I.

Échappement [F.]. Escapement (of the pianoforte).

Échelette [F.]. *Xylophone.

Échelle [F.]. Scale.

Echiquier [*eschiquier eschequier, eschaquier, escacherium, exaquir*]. An early stringed keyboard instrument which is mentioned in various literary sources of the 14th and 15th centuries. In a letter written by the Spanish king, John I of Aragon, who tried to obtain such an instrument from Duke Philip the Bold of Burgundy (1387), it is described as an "instrument semblant d'orguens, qui sona ab cordes" (similar to the organ, but sounding with strings). The same instrument is probably meant by the English *chekker* and by the German *Schachtbret* (i.e., Schaftbret, quillboard, not chessboard as has frequently been surmised) which is mentioned in a poem *Der Minne Regeln* by Eberhard Cersne (1404). Both the etymology of the name and the nature of the instrument are obscure. According to C. Sachs it was an upright harpsichord [cf. *SaHMI*, 336f], while F. W. Galpin identifies it with a 15th-century instrument called *dulce melos*, for which he readopts the theory already advanced by Bottée de Toulmin [*Dissertation sur les instruments de la musique* (1840)] that it was a clavichord with a hammer action anticipating that of the pianoforte [cf. *GD*, Suppl. Vol., 118]. In the original description, however, no hammers, only a checking device, are mentioned. Cf. W. H. Grattan Flood, in *ML* vi, no. 2; G. Le Cerf, in *RdM*, nos. 37, 38.

Echo. (1) Acoustically: see *Architectural acoustics.— (2) Musically: echo-like effects occur frequently in the polyphonic works of Josquin and his followers, as the result of a special technique of imitation; see the accompanying example from Kotter's tablatur (c. 1515); also *Imitation, Ex. 2. However, it was not until the end of the 16th century that the echo was exploited as a source of sound-variety and of realistic effects. Lassus, in a piece from his *Libro de villanelle* (1581; cf. complete ed. x, 140), exploits the humorous effect of a constantly repeated echo in a most skillful manner. Echo-like repetitions of short motives, first in f, then in p, are among the most typical devices of the

organ style of Sweelinck, Scheidt, Nivers, Gigault, etc. Of greater artistic value and interest are the echo-effects in 17th-century vocal pieces (operatic arias, cantatas) in which the personified Echo answers the laments of the deserted lover, of the distressed fugitive, etc. A most beautiful example is found in Carissimi's oratorio *Jephtha* [cf. *SchGMB*, no. 198; also *RiHM* ii.2, 35]. A charming instrumental echo-piece by J. K. F. Fischer is reproduced in *DdT* x, 84. For an echo-effect in Bach, see the last movement (Echo) of his French Ouverture (1735). Mozart wrote a very ingenious Notturno en Écho (1777) in which four groups of players produce a quadruple echo. Nineteenth-century operatic composers have frequently used the echo-repetition of military signals, hunting-calls, etc. (Beethoven, *Fidelio*; Wagner, *Tristan*). Cf. Th. Kroyer, "Dialog und Echo . . ." (*JMP* xvi).

Echo attachment. A special valve attached to brass instruments (horns, trumpets, cornets) by which a bell of smaller opening is brought into operation. The tones thus produced sound as if they were played at a great distance.

Echo organ [G. *Echowerk*]. See *Organ III.

Echos [pl. *echoi*]. In the ancient Syrian and Byzantine chant, a system of tonal classification which corresponds to the system of modes [see *Church modes] of the Roman chant. The echoi existed in the same number — eight — as the Western church modes and were collectively referred to as *octoechos* (eight echoi). They differed, however, from the modes

in that they were not abstract scale formations but melodic formulae which included the characteristic features (tonic, cadential endings, typical progressions) of all the melodies written in one echos. Thus they belong to the category of *melody types.

The earliest mention of the *octoechos* is found in a Syrian source of about 515 [see *Syrian chant], 300 years before the earliest account of the eight church modes which were probably derived from the Syrian (or Byzantine) echoi, possibly by amalgamating them with the ancient Greek system of octave species (*tonoi*; see *Greek music II (d)). Various other Eastern churches, e.g., the *Armenian, *Russian, *Serbian, utilize to the present day a classification based on echoi, i.e., melodic formulae, rather than on modes, i.e., scales [cf. *ReMMA*, 102; *GD*, Suppl. Vol., 175, 181].

It is believed that some traces of the early echoi are preserved in the *enechemata* of 12th- and 13th-century Byzantine MSS, which were sung as an intonation to the chant proper much in the same way as a pianist sometimes strikes a few chords in order to "establish the key." Each enechema was sung to certain syllables the meaning of which is obscure; e.g., the enechema of the first plagal mode was g–g–a–g–f–g, and was sung to the "word" *Aneanes* [cf. *ReMMA*, 87; see also *Ane naiki; *Noeane; *Solmization].

Lit.: *ReMMA*, *passim* (bibl. 432f); O. Strunk, in *MQ* xxviii, xxxi, no. 3; P. J. Thibaut, in *RMC* i.

Éclatant [F.]. Brilliant; or piercing.

Eclogue. An idyllic poem in which shepherds are introduced conversing (after the model of Vergil's ten *Bucolic Eclogues*). In the 16th century such poems were frequently written in the form of dramatic plays and were performed on the stage, particularly in Spain. These presentations, which probably involved music, are believed to be among the various precursors of opera. Cf. A. Salazar, in *PAMS*, 1938, p. 98. — Modern composers have used the term Eclogue (Eglogue) as a title for compositions of an idyllic, pastoral character.

Eco [It.]. Echo.

École d'Arcueil. A group of 20th-century French musicians (Henri Sauguet, Roger Désormière, Maxime Jacob, Henri Cliqué-Pleyel) who convened at Arcueil in the home of Erik Satie, whom they considered as their leader. The group was founded in 1923 [cf. N. Slonimsky, *Music Since 1900* (1937), p. 236]. See also *Six, Les.

Écossaise [F., Scotch, i.e., dance]. A dance which, in spite of its name, has nothing in common with genuine Scotch dance music [see *Reel, *Strathspey], but which belongs to the English *country dances. It appeared around 1780 in England and in France and had a great vogue in the early 19th century. Beethoven as well as Schubert wrote collections of Écossaises, all in quick 2/4 time. See *Dance music IV.

Editio Medicea; Ratisbonensis; Vaticana. See under *Liturgical books.

Editions, Historical. Under this heading (which corresponds to the German term *Denkmäler*) there follows a list of the important serial publications of early music (I, Instrumental; K, Keyboard; L, Lute; Op, Opera; Or, Oratorio; S, Song; V, Vocal). Italics indicate original titles.

I. *Archives des maîtres de l'orgue* (10 vols., ed. by A. Guilmant, 1898–1910). 1: J. Titelouze, Oeuvres complètes. — 2: A. Raison, *Livre d'orgue.* — 3: T. Roberday, Fugues et caprices; L. Marchand, Pièces choisies; L. N. Clérambault, *Livre d'orgue*; Du Mage, *Livre d'orgue*; L. C. Daquin, *Livre de noëls.* — 4: N. Gigault, *Livre de musique.* — 5: N. de Grigny, *Livre d'orgue*; F. Couperin (de Crouilly), Pièces d'orgue; L. Marchand, Pièces d'orgue. — 6: J. Boyvin, Oeuvres complètes. — 7: F. Dandrieu, *Livre d'orgue*; Guilain, *Pièces d'orgue pour le Magnificat.* — 8: S. A. Scherer, Oeuvres. — 9: N. le Bègue, Oeuvres. — 10: *Liber fra-*

trum Cruciferorum Leodensium (pieces by A. Gabrieli, Sweelinck, Merulo, and others).

II. *L'Arte musicale in Italia* (7 vols., ed. by L. Torchi, 1897). 1: Motets, madrigals, frottole, *c.* 1520–80. — 2: Motets, madrigals, *c.* 1580–1625. — 3: Organ compositions, 16th and 17th centuries. — 4: Madrigals, Madrigal comedies, *c.* 1600. — 5: St. Landi, *San Alessio* (Op); Anon., *Daniel* (Or); solo cantatas, 17th cent. — 6: Peri, *Euridice* (Op); Monteverdi, *Combattimento* (V); *id.*, *Ballo delle ingrate.* — 7: Instrumental music, 17th century.

III. *Biblioteca di rarità musicali* (9 vols., ed. by O. Chilesotti, *c.* 1885–1915). 1: Danze del secolo xvi (Caroso, Negri; L). — 2: *Balli d'arpicordo* (Picchi, 1621; K). — 3: *Affetti amorosi* (G. Steffani, 1621; S). — 4: *Arianna* (B. Marcello, 1727; Op). — 5: Arie, canzonette e balli (H. Vecchi, 1590; V). — 6: Partite . . . (Frescobaldi, 1614; K). — 7: Airs de court (J. B. Besard; L). — 8: Musica del passato (1536–*c.* 1750; L). — 9: Madrigali, villanelle ed arie di danza (J. B. Besard; L).

IV. *Chefs d'oeuvre de l'opéra français* (various editors, *c.* 1880; piano reductions of Baroque operas). Beaujoyeux, *Le Ballet-comique de la Reine.* — Cambert, *Pomone*; *Les Peines et les plaisirs d'amour.* — Campra, *L'Europe galante*; *Les Fêtes vénitiennes*; *Tancrède.* — Catel, *Les Bayadères.* — Collasse, *Les Saisons*; *Thétis et Pélée.* — Destouches, *Issé*; *Omphale.* — Grétry, *La Caravane, Céphale et Procis.* — Lalande et Destouches, *Les Éléments.* — Lesueur, *Ossian ou les Bardes.* — Lully, *Alceste*; *Armide*; *Atys*; *Bellérophon*; *Cadmus et Hermione*, *Isis, Persée*; *Phaeton*; *Proserpine*; *Psyché*; *Thésée.* — Philidor, *Ernélinde.* — Piccinni, *Didon*; *Roland.* — Rameau, *Castor et Pollux*; *Dardanus*; *Les Fêtes d'Hébé*; *Hyppolite et Aricie*; *Les Indes galantes*; *Platée*; *Zoroastre.* — Sacchini, *Chimène ou le Cid*; *Renaud.* — Salieri, *Les Danaides*; *Tarare.*

V. *Chorwerk, Das* (49 vols. of 15th-17th-century vocal music, ed. by F. Blume, 1930–). Alphabetical list of composers; collective volumes at the end. 32: Adam von Fulda, Hymnen. — 31: Aulen, Missa. — 22: G. Binchois, Sechzehn weltliche Lieder. — 25: A. Caldara, Ein Madrigal und 18 Kanons.—27;36;39: Chr. Demantius, Deutsche Johannes Passion; Der 116. Psalm; Motetten. — 28: G. Dressler, Fünf Motetten. — 19;49: G. Dufay, Zwölf geistliche und weltliche Werke; Sämtliche Hymnen. — 9;21;32: H. Finck, Acht Hymnen; Missa in summis; Hymnen. — 24;38: M. Franck, Fünf Motetten; Musikalische Bergkreyen. — 10: G. Gabrieli, Drei Motetten. — 40: A. Grandi, Drei konzertierende Motetten. — 44: J. Hähnel, Ostermesse. — 47: B. Harzer, Johannespassion. — 7: H. Isaac, Missa carminum. — 1;3;18;20;23;30;33;42: Josquin, Missa Pange lingua; Weltliche Lieder; Vier Motetten; Missa Da pacem; Drei Evangelien-Motetten; Acht Lied- und Choralmotetten; Drei Psalmen; Missa De beata virgine. — 13;34;37;41;48: O. di Lasso, Madrigale und Chansons; Busstränen des heiligen Petrus i, ii, iii; Prophetiae Sibyllarum. — 15: J. Lupi, Zehn weltliche Lieder. — 46: J. Martini, Drei geistliche Gesänge. — 4: J. Ockeghem, Missa mi-mi. — 17: H. Purcell, Fünf geistliche Chöre. — 11: P. de la Rue, Requiem und eine Motette. — 12;36: H. Schein, Sechs deutsche Motetten; Der 116. Psalm. — 29: P. Schöffer, Fünfzehn deutsche Lieder. — 26: Th. Selle, Johannes-Passion. — 6: Th. Stoltzer, Der 37. Psalm.— 16: J. Theile and Chr. Bernhard, Zwei Kurzmessen. — 2: J. Vaet, Sechs Motetten. — 5;8: A. Willaert, Italienische Madrigale; Volkstümliche italienische Lieder.

Collective Volumes: 14: Sieben chromatische Motetten. — 32: Zwölf Hymnen. — 35: Nordische Gabrieli-Schüler. — 43: Karnevalslieder der Renaissance. — 45: Deutsche Lieder des 15. Jahrhunderts.

VI. *Classici della musica italiana, 1* (Raccolta Nazionale diritta da Gabriele d'Annunzio; 36 vols.; the titles do not always correctly indicate the contents). 1: A. Banchieri, Musiche corali (V). — 2: G. B. Bassani, Canzoni (S). — 3: L. Boccherini, Sonate (I). — 4: G. Caccini, Arie

(S). — 5: G. Carissimi, Oratorii. — 6: G. Cavazzoni, Composizioni (K). — 7: L. Cherubini, Arie (contains 3 operatic overtures). — 8: M. Clementi, Sonate (K). — 9: A. Corelli, Sonate (I). — 10: E. del Cavalieri, *Rappresentazione di anima e di corpo* (Or). — 11: F. Durante, Sonate . . . (K). — 12: G. Frescobaldi, Sonate (K). — 13: B. Galuppi, *Il Filosofo di Campagna* (Op). — 14: Gesualdo da Venosa, Madrigali. — 15: N. Jommelli, *La Passione di Gesu' Cristo* (Or). — 16: P. Locatelli and F. G. Bertoni, Composizioni (I). — 17: B. Marcello, Cantate (S). — 18: G. B. Martini, Sonate (K). — 19: C. Monteverdi, *Il Combattimento* ... (V) — 20: G. Paisiello, *La Pazza per amore* (Op). — 21: P. L. da Palestrina, Canzonette e madrigali (V). — 22: P. D. Paradisi, Sonate (K). — 23: G. B. Pergolesi, Opere (Op, V). — 24: J. Peri, *L'Euridice* (Op). — 25: N. A. Porpora, Sonate (I). — 26: M. Rossi, Composizioni (K). — 27: G. Rutini, Sonate (K). — 28: G. B. Sammartini, Sonate (I). — 29: P. G. Sandoni e Serini, Sonate (K). — 30: A. Scarlatti, Cantate (S). — 31: D. Scarlatti, Composizioni (K). — 32: G. Tartini, Sonate (I). — 33: F. Turrini, Sonate (K). — 34: F. M. Veracini, Sonate (I). — 35: A. Vivaldi, *Le Stagioni* (I). — 36: D. Zipoli, Composizioni (K).

VII. *Denkmäler der Tonkunst in Oesterreich,* (*DTOe,* 83 volumes, 1894 to date; in annual issues (Jahrgänge): i.1; i.2; ii.1; ii.2, etc., reproduced here as follows: 1.i; 1.ii; 2.i; 2.ii, etc.). Alphabetical list of composers; collective volumes at the end.

16.ii: J. G. Albrechtsberger, Instrumentalwerke (I).

38.i: Bl. Amon, Kirchen-Werke (V).

10.i: O. Benevoli, Festmesse und Hymnus (V).

36.i: St. Bernardi, Kirchenwerke (V).

5.ii; 12.ii: H. F. Biber, Violinsonaten (I).

25.i: H. F. Biber, Messen (V).

30.i: H. F. Biber, Requiem (V).

13.i: A. Caldara, Kirchenwerke (V).

39: A. Caldara, Kammermusik für Gesang (S).

3.ii; 4.ii: M. A. Cesti, *Il Pomo d'oro* (Op).

43.ii: K. Dittersdorf, Instrumentalwerke (I).
23.i: A. Draghi, Kirchenwerke (V).
28.i: J. E. Eberlin, *Der blutschwitzende Jesus* (Or).
4.i; 6.ii; 10.ii: J. J Froberger, Orgel- und Klavierwerke (K).
35.i: E. A. Förster, Kammermusik (I).
1.i: J. J. Fux, Messen (V).
2.i: J. J. Fux, Motetten (V).
9.ii: J. J. Fux, Instrumentalwerke (I).
23.ii: J. J. Fux, *Concentus musico-instrumentalis* (I).
17: J. J. Fux, *Costanza e fortezza* (Op).
21: Fl. Gassmann, *La Contessina* (Op).
45: Fl. Gassmann, Kirchen-Musik (V).
21: W. Gluck, *Orfeo ed Euridice* (Op).
30.ii: W. Gluck, *Don Juan* (Ballet).
44: W. Gluck, *L Innocenza giustificata* (Op).
8.i: A. Hammerschmidt, *Dialogi* (V).
6.i; 12.i; 15.i; 20.1; 24; 26: J. Handl, *Opus musicum* (V).
42.i: J. Handl, Messen (V).
14.ii: M. Haydn, Instrumentalwerke (I).
22: M. Haydn, Drei Messen (V).
32.i: M. Haydn, Kirchenwerke (V).
5.i; 16.i: H. Isaac, *Choralis Constantinus* (V).
14.i; 16.i: H. Isaac, Weltliche Werke (V, I).
25.i: J. K. Kerll, Messe (V).
30.i: J. K. Kerll, Requiem (V).
33.ii: J. Lanner, Ländler und Walzer (I).
29.i: Cl. Monteverdi, *Il Ritorno d'Ulisse* (Op).
1.ii; 2.ii: Georg Muffat, *Florilegium* (I).
11.ii: Georg Muffat, *Auserlesene...Instrumentalmusik; Armonico tributo* (I).
3.iii: Gottl. Muffat, *Componimenti musicali* (K).
29.ii: Gottl. Muffat, 12 Toccaten und 72 Versetl (K).
37.i: Neithart v. Reuenthal, Lieder (S).
8.ii: J. Pachelbel, 94 Kompositionen, zumeist über das Magnificat (K).
36.ii: P. Peuerl, *Neue Paduanen ...* (I, V).
13.ii: A. Poglietti, Klavier- und Orgelwerke (K).
36.ii: I. Posch, *Musikalische Tafelfreud* (I, V).
13.ii: G. Reutter, Klavier- und Orgelwerke (K).

13.ii: F. T Richter, Klavier- und Orgelwerke (K).
34. J. Schenk, *Der Dorfbarbier* (Op).
25.i: H. Schmelzer, Messe (V).
28.ii: H. Schmeltzer, Ballette (I).
3.i: J. Stadlmayer, *Hymnen* (V).
30.i: Chr Straus, Requiem (V).
35.ii: J Strauss, Vater, Walzer (I).
32.ii: J. Strauss, Sohn, Walzer (I).
38 ii: Jos. Strauss, Walzer (I).
18.i: I. Umlauf, *Die Bergknappen* (Op).
9.i. O. von Wolkenstein, Geistliche und weltliche Lieder (S, V).
Collective Volumes:
20.ii: Gesänge von Frauenlob, Reinmar von Zweter und Alexander (S).
37.ii: Gesellschaftslied, Das deutsche, 1480–1550 (V).
41: Italienische Musiker 1567–1625 (V).
18.ii, 25.ii: Oesterreichische Lautenmusik im xvi. Jahrhundert; zwischen 1650 und 1720 (L).
33.i: Deutsche Komödienarien, 1754–58 (S).
43.i: Salzburger Kirchenkomponisten (Biber, Biechteler, Eberlin, Adlgasser; V).
7; 11.i; 19.i; 27.i; 31; 40: Sechs (Sieben) Trienter Codices (V) [see *Trent Codices].
15.ii; 19.ii: Wiener Instrumentalmusik vor und um 1750.
13.ii: Wiener Klavier- und Orgelwerke (c. 1650–1700).
27.ii; 42.ii. Wiener Lied, Das (1778–91, 1792–1815; S).
28.ii: Wiener Tanzmusik (c. 1650–1700; I).

VIII. *Denkmäler der Tonkunst in Bayern* (DTB, published as Denkmäler deutscher Tonkunst, *Zweite Folge*; 36 volumes, 1900–13, see remark under VII).

1; 9.i: E. F. dall'Abaco, Augewählte Werke (I).
10.i: G. Aichinger, Ausgewählte Werke (V).
4.ii: Chr. Erbach, Ausgewählte Werke (K).
14.ii: W. Gluck, *Le Nozze d'Ercole e d'Ebe* (Op).
10.ii: A. Gumpelzhaimer, Ausgewählte Werke (V).

4.ii: H. L. Hassler, Werke für Orgel und Klavier (K).

5.ii: H. L. Hassler, *Canzonette*; *Neue Teutsche Gesang* (V).

11.i: H. L. Hassler, Madrigale (V).

26: J. de Kerle, *Preces speciales* (V).

2.ii: J. K. Kerll, Ausgewählte Werke (K, V).

13;21–24: J. E. Kindermann, Ausgewählte Werke (V, S, K).

18: J. and J. Ph. Krieger, Gesammelte Werke für Klavier und Orgel (K).

9.ii: L. Mozart, Ausgewählte Werke (K, I, S).

18: F. X. Murschhauser, Gesammelte Werke für Klavier und Orgel (K).

2.i; 4.i: J. and W. H. Pachelbel, Klavierwerke, Orgelkompositionen (K).

27/28: J. Chr. Pez, Ausgewählte Werke (I, Op).

29/30: A. Raselius, *Cantiones sacrae* (V).

12.i: A. Rosetti, Ausgewählte Sinfonien (I).

25: A. Rosetti, Orchester- und Kammermusik (I).

3.ii: L. Senfl, Werke: Motetten und Magnificat (V).

7.i; 8.i: J. Staden, Ausgewählte Werke (V, S, I).

6.ii: A. Steffani, Ausgewählte Werke (S, V).

11.ii: A. Steffani, *Alarico* (Op).

12.ii: A. Steffani, Ausgewählte Werke (selections from operas).

19/20: P. Torri, Ausgewählte Werke (selections from operas).

14.i; 17: T. Traetta, Ausgewählte Werke (selections from operas).

Collective Volumes:

3.i; 7.ii; 8.ii: Sinfonien der Pfalzbayerischen (Mannheimer) Schule (J. Stamitz, F. X. Richter, A. Filtz, I. Holzbauer, J. Toeschi, Chr. Cannabich, C. Stamitz, F. Beck, E. Eichner; I).

6.i: Nürnberger Meister der zweiten Hälfte des 17. Jahrhunderts. Geistliche Konzerte und Kirchenkantaten (P. Hainlein, H. Schwemmer, G. K. Wecker, J. Pachelbel, J. P. Krieger, J. Krieger; V).

15; 16: Mannheimer Kammermusik . . . (F. X. Richter, I. Holzbauer, J. B. Wendling, J. Toeschi, Chr. Cannabich, E. Eichner, K. Stamitz, Abt G. J.

Vogler, A. Stamitz, F. Danzl, J. Stamitz, A. Filtz, F. X. Sterkel, W. Cramer, J. F. Edelmann; I).

IX. *Denkmäler deutscher Tonkunst* (*DdT*; 65 volumes, 1892–1931; see remark under VII).

12/13: H. Albert, Arien (S).

5: J. R. Ahle, Ausgewählte Gesangswerke (S).

56: J.Christoph Friedrich Bach, *Die Kindheit Jesu*; *Lazarus* (Or).

42: J. Ernst Bach, *Sammlung auserlesener Fabeln* (S).

48: J. Ernst Bach, *Passionsoratorium*.

64: G. Benda, *Der Jahrmarkt* (Op).

6: Chr. Bernhard, Solokantaten und Chorwerke (V).

45: G. Böhm, Heinrich Elmenhorsts Geistliche Lieder (S).

11: D. Buxtehude, Instrumentalwerke.

14: D. Buxtehude, Abendmusiken und Kirchenkantaten (V).

43/44: Fr. Deller, *Orpheus und Eurydice* (Ballett).

31, 41: Ph. Dulichius, *Centuria* (V).

46/47: Ph. Erlebach, *Harmonische Freude* (S).

10: J. K. F. Fischer, *Journal de Printemps* (I).

45: J. W. Franck, Heinrich Elmenhorsts Geistliche Lieder (S).

16: M. Franck, Ausgewählte Instrumentalwerke.

57: J. V. Görner, *Sammlung neuer Oden und Lieder* (S).

15: C. H. Graun, *Montezuma* (Op).

51/52: Chr. Graupner, Ausgewählte Kantaten (V).

40: A. Hammerschmidt, Ausgewählte Werke (V).

20: J. Hasse, *La Conversione di S. Agostino* (Or).

2: H. L. Hassler, *Cantiones sacrae* (V).

7: H. L. Hassler, Messen (V).

24/25: H. L. Hassler, *Sacri concentus* (V).

16: V. Haussmann, Ausgewählte Instrumentalwerke.

42: V. Herbing, *Musikalischer Versuch* (S).

8, 9: J. Holzbauer, *Günther von Schwarzburg* (Op).

32/33: N. Jommelli, *Fetonte* (Op).

37/38: R. Keiser, *Croesus*; *L'Inganno Fedele* (Op).
58/59: S. Knüpfer, Ausgewählte Kirchenkantaten (V).
19: Ad. Krieger, Arien (S).
53/54: Joh. Ph. Krieger, Ausgewählte Kirchenkompositionen (V).
4: J. Kuhnau, Klavierwerke (K).
58/59: J. Kuhnau, Ausgewählte Kirchenkantaten (V).
60: A. Lotti, Messen (V).
55: C. Pallavicino, *La Gerusalemme liberata* (Op).
63: J. Pezel, Turmmusiken und Suiten (I).
23: H. Praetorius, Ausgewählte Werke (V).
18: J. Rosenmüller, *Sonate da camera* (I).
43/44: J. J. Rudolph, Ballette (I).
1: S. Scheidt, *Tabulatura nova* (K).
58/59: J. Schelle, Ausgewählte Kirchenkantaten (V).
10: D. A. Schmicorer, *Zodiacus* (I).
39: J. Schobert, Ausgewählte Werke (I).
17: J. Sebastiani, Passionsmusik (Or).
35/36: Sperontes, *Singende Muse* (S).
65: Th. Stoltzer, Hymnen und Psalmen (V).
28: G. Ph. Telemann, *Der Tag des Gerichts*; *Ino* (Or).
57: G. Ph. Telemann, 24 Oden (S).
61/62: G. Ph. Telemann, *Tafelmusik* (I).
17: J. Theile, Passionsmusik (Or).
3: F. Tunder, Gesangswerke (V).
26/27: J. G. Walther, Gesammelte Werke für Orgel (K).
6: M. Weckmann, Solokantaten und Chorwerke (S, V).
45: P. L. Wockenfuss, Heinrich Elmenhorsts Geistliche Lieder (S).
21/22: F. W. Zachow, Gesammelte Werke (V, I, K).
Collective Volumes:
29/30: Instrumentalkonzerte deutscher Meister (Pisendel, Hasse, C. P. E. Bach, Telemann, Graupner, Stölzel, Hurlebusch).
34: *Newe deudsche geistliche Gesenge*, ed. by Georg Rhau, 1544 (numerous composers).
49/50: Thüringische Motetten der ersten Hälfte des 18. Jahrhunderts (Topff,

Niedt, Arnoldi, Flender, Erlebach, J. M. Bach, Liebhold, Kellner, Telemann).

X. *The English Madrigal School* (36 vols., ed. by E. H. Fellowes, 1913–24; p = parts; v = voices). 1: Th. Morley, *Canzonets to 2, 3 v* (1593, '95). — 2: Th. Morley, *Madr. to 4 v* (1594). — 3: Th. Morley, *Canzonets to 5 and 6 v* (1597) — 4: Th. Morley, *Ballets to 5 v* (1600) — 5: O. Gibbons, *Madr. and motets of 5 p* (1612). — 6: J. Wilbye, *First set of madr.* (1598). — 7: J. Wilbye, *Second set of madr.* (1609). — 8: J. Farmer, *Madr. to 4 v* (1599). — 9: Th. Weelkes, *Madr. to 3, 4, 5 and 6 v* (1597). — 10: Th. Weelkes, *Ballets and madr. to 5 v* (1598). — 11: Th. Weelkes, *Madr. of 5 p* (1600). — 12: Th. Weelkes, *Madr. of 6 p* (1600). — 13: Th. Weelkes, *Airs or Fantastic Spirites* (1608). — 14: W. Byrd, *Psalms, Sonnets and Songs for 5 v* (1588). — 15: W. Byrd, *Songs of sundry natures* (1589). — 16: W. Byrd, *Psalms, Songs and Sonnets* (1611). — 17: H. Lichfield, *Madr. of 5 p* (1613). — 18: Th. Tomkins, *Songs of 3, 4, 5 p* (1622). — 19: J. Ward, *Madr. to 3, 4, 5 p* (1613). — 20: G. Farnaby, *Canzonets to 4 v* (1598). — 21: Th. Bateson, *First set of madr.* (1604). — 22: Th. Bateson, *Second set of madr.* (1618). — 23: J. Bennett, *Madr. to 4 v* (1601). — 24: G. Kirbye, *Madr. to 4, 5, 6 v* (1597). — 25: F. Pilkington, *First set of madr.* (1613). — 26: F. Pilkington, *Second set of madr.* (1624). — 27: R. Carlton, *Madr. to 5 v* (1601). — 28: H. Youll, *Canzonets to 3 v* (1608). — 29: M. East, *First set of madr.* (1604). — 30: M. East, *Second set of madr.* (1606). — 31: M. East, *The madr. in his third and fourth books* (1610, '18). — 32: Th. Morley, *The Triumphes of Oriana* (1601) — 33: R. Allison, *An hour's recreation in Music* (1606). — 34: Th. Vautor, *Songs of divers airs and natures* (1619). — 35.1: R. Jones, *Madr. of 3, 4, 5, 6, 7 and 8 p* (1607). — 35.2: J. Mundy, *The madr. in his Songs and Psalms . . .* (1594). — 36. Madrigal writings of Michael Cavendish (1598); Thomas Greaves (1604); William Holborne (1597), etc.

XI. *The English School of Lutenist Song-writers* (2 series of 16 vols. each, ed.

by E. H. Fellowes, 1920–32). *First Series:* J. Dowland, *First (Second, Third) Booke of Songs and Ayres* (1597; 1600; '03); *A Pilgrim's Solace* (1612; vol. 2 includes three songs from Robert Dowland's *A Musicall Banquet*, 1610). — Th. Ford, *Songs in Musicke of Sundrie Kindes* (1607). — F. Pilkington, *First Booke of Songs or Ayres* (1605). — Ph. Rosseter and Th. Campian, *A Booke of Ayres* (1601). — Th. Morley, *Little Short Songs to the Lute.*

Second Series: Th. Campian, *First (Second, Third, Fourth) Booke of Ayres* (undated). — R. Jones, *First (Second, Third, Fourth, Fifth) Booke of Songs and Ayres* (1600–10). — J. Attey, *First Booke of Ayres* (1622). — J. Bartlett, *A Booke of Ayres* (1606). — M. Cavendish, *Airs* (1598). — W. Corkine, *Ayres* (1610); *Second Booke of Ayres* (1612). — J. Danyel, *Songs* (1606). — A. Ferrabosco (the younger), *Ayres* (1609). — Th. Greaves, The Songs in *Songes of Sundrie Kindes* (1604). — T. Hume, The Songs in *Musicall Humors* (1608); *Poeticall Musicke* (1607).

XII. *Das Erbe deutscher Musik* (present continuation of the former *Denkmäler*, various editors, 1935 to date. Two series: *Reichsdenkmale*, i.e., documents of general importance; *Landschaftsdenkmale*, i.e., documents of chiefly local importance).

A. *Reichsdenkmale.* 1: Alt-Bachisches Archiv, Motetten (M. Schneider). — 2: Alt-Bachisches Archiv, Kantaten (M. Schneider). — 3: Joh. Christian Bach, Quintette op. 11 (R. Steglich; I). — 4: Das Glogauer Liederbuch i (H. Ringmann; V, I). — 5: L. Senfl, Sieben Motetten (A. Loehrer). — 6: G. Ph. Telemann, *Pimpinone* (Th. W. Werner; Op). — 7: Trompeterfanfaren . . . (G. Schünemann; I). — 8: Das Glogauer Liederbuch ii (H. Ringmann; I, V). — 9: Orgelchoräle um J. S. Bach (G. Frotscher; K). — 10: L. Senfl, Deutsche Lieder i (A. Geering; S). — 11: Gruppenkonzerte der Bachzeit (K. M. Komma; I). — 12: Lautenmusik des 17/18. Jahrhunderts (H. Neemann; L). — 13: L. Senfl, Motetten . . . Messen ii (W. Gerstenberg; V).

B. *Landschaftsdenkmale* (numbering not original). (1) N. Bruhns, Kirchenkantaten i (F. Stein). — (2) N. Bruhns, Kirchenkantaten ii, Orgelwerke (F. Stein). — (3) Chr. Demantius, *Neue teutsche weltliche Lieder* (K. Stangl; S). — (4) J. W. Franck, *Die drey Töchter Cecrops'* (1679; G. F. Schmidt; Op). — (5) J. H. Herbst, Drei mehrchörige Festkonzerte (G. Ferber; V). — (6) Hochzeitsarien und Kantaten Stettiner Meister nach 1700 (H. Engel; S). — (7) J. S. Kusser, Arien . . . aus *Erindo* (H. Osthoff; Op). — (8) R. J. Mayr, Ausgewählte Kirchenmusik (K. G. Fellerer; V). — (9) Moritz Landgraf von Hessen, Ausgewählte Werke (K. Dane; I). — (10) Preussische Festlieder (J. Müller-Blattau; V). — (11) F. W. Rust, Werke für Klavier und Streichinstrumente (R. Czach; K, I). — (12) J. Schultz, *Musikalischer Lüstgarte* (1622; H. Zenck; V, I).

XIII. *Hispaniae Schola Musica Sacra* (ed. F. Pedrell, 1895–98). 1: Chr. Morales, Composiciones (V). — 2: F. Guerrero, Composiciones (V). — 3;4: A. de Cabezon, Composiciones . . . (K). — 5: J. G. Perez, Composiciones (V). — 6: Fray Tomas de Santa Maria, F. Guerrero, T. L. de Victoria, Cenallos, uncertain author, Psalm compositions (V). — 7;8: A. de Cabezon, Composiciones (K).

XIV. *Istituzioni e monumenti dell' arte musicale italiana* (6 vols., 1931 to date). 1: Musiche strumentali . . . sino al 1590 (I, V). — 2: Canzoni e sonate . . . di G. Gabrieli (I). — 3: Le Cappelle musicale di Novara (G. Battistini, 1665–1719; V). — 4: Vincenzo Galilei (V, L). — 5: Schola musicale di Napoli (Montella, Trabaci, Gesualdo; V). — 6: La Musica in Cremona (Ingegneri, Monteverdi; V).

XV. *Lira sacro-hispanica* (10 vols., ed. by M. H. Eslava, 1869; Spanish sacred music, chiefly motets; detailed list of contents in *GD* ii, 177). Two vols. "16th Century" (Fevin, Morales, Guerrero, Victoria, and others). — Two vols. "17th Century" (Comes, Lobo, Heredia, Salazar, and others). — Two vols. "18th Century" (Bravo, Muelas, Soler, Ripa, and others). — Four vols. "19th Century" (Garcia, Secanilla, Ledesma, Eslava, and others).

XVI. *Les Maîtres musiciens de la renaissance française* (23 vols., ed. by H. Expert, 1894–1908; French vocal music of the 16th century). Alphabetical list of composers; numbering not original. (1) P. Attaingnant, *Trente et une chansons musicales* (1529). — (2) A. Brumel, P. de la Rue, *Missa.* . . . — (3) E. du Caurroy, *Mélanges.* — (4) G. Costeley, *Musique* i,ii,iii. — (5) Cl. Gervaise, E. du Tertre, *Danceries* (1). — (6) Cl. Goudimel, *Les 150 psaumes* i,ii,iii. — (7) Cl. Jannequin, *Chansons.* — O. de Lassus, *Les Meslanges.* — (8) Cl. Le Jeune, *Dodecacorde* i. — (9) Cl. Le Jeune, *Le Printemps* i,ii,iii. — (10) Cl. Le Jeune, *Mélanges.* — (11) Cl. Le Jeune, *Psaumes en vers mesurez* i,ii,iii. — (12) J. Mauduit, *Chansonettes mesurées.* — (13) J. Mouton, Fevin, *Missa.* . . . — (14) F. Regnard, *Poésies de P. de Ronsard.*

XVII. *Monumenta Musicae Belgicae* (ed. by J. Watelet, 1932–38). 1: J. B. Loeillet, Werken voor Clavecimbel. — 2: A. Kerckhoven, Werken voor Orgel. — 3: J. H. Fiocco, Werken voor Clavecimbel. — 4: Ch Guillet, Giov. de Macque, C. Luython (K).

XVIII. *Monumenta Musicae Byzantinae* (ed. by C. Hoeg, H. J. W. Tillyard, and E. Wellesz; 1935–). A. Facsimiles. 1: Sticherarium. — 2: Hirmologium Athoum. B. Subsidia. 1.i: H. J. W. Tillyard, Handbook of the Middle Byzantine Musical Notation. — 1.ii: C. Hoeg, La Notation ekphonétique. — 1.iii: E. Wellesz, Byzantine Elements in Gregorian Chant. C. Transcriptions. 1: E. Wellesz, Die Hymnen des Sticherarium für September. — 2: H. J. W. Tillyard, The Hymns of the Sticherarium for November.

XIX. *Monuments de la musique française au temps de la renaissance* (10 vols., ed. by H. Expert, 1924–29, as a continuation of the *Maîtres Musiciens*). 1: Cl. Le Jeune, *Octonaires de la vanité* i. — 2: P. Certon, *Messes à 4 voix.* — 3: D. Le Blanc,

Airs de plusieurs musiciens. — 4–7: A. de Bertrand, *Amours de Pierre de Ronsard,* i–iii. — 8: Cl. Le Jeune, *Octonaires* . . . ii. — 9: Cl. Goudimel, *Messes à 4 voix.* — 10: P. de l'Estocart, *Octonaires de la vanité* i.

XX. *Musica Divina* (10 vols., ed. by C. Proske and J. Schrems, 1853–63; contains selections of 16th-century vocal sacred music). *Annus primus.* 1: Liber missarum. — 2: Liber motettorum. — 3: Psalmodia, Magnificat, Hymnodiam, Antiphonas B.M.V. complectens. — 4: Liber vespertinus. — *Annus secundus.* 5–8 (same titles as 1–4). — 9,10: Selectus novus missarum.

XXI. *Musica Sacra* (26 vols., ed. by F. Commer, 1839ff; contains selections of sacred music, mostly of the 16th and 17th centuries). 1: Sammlung . . . für die Orgel (new ed. by F. Redlich under the title *Meister des Orgelbarock*). — 2,3: Choral music (Carnazzi, Cordans, Durante, Caldara, Gabrieli, and others). — 4: Solo songs with piano accompaniment (Durante, Hasse, Jommelli, and others). — 5–12: Lasso. — 13,14: Hasler. — 17, 18: Mahu, etc.

Beginning with vol. 5 there appeared under the same name a parallel publication by A. H. Neithardt and others (vols. 5–16), containing also 19th-century German church music by Bortnianski, Grell, Homilius, and others. Still another publication of the same title has been published by Dörffel (ed. Peters).

XXII. *Old English Edition* (25 vols., ed. by G. E. P. Arkwright, 1889–1902). 1: Th. Campion, *Masque for Lord Hayes's Marriage* (1607). — 2: Th. Arne, Six Songs — 3–5: G. Kirbye, Madrigals (1597). — 6–9: W. Byrd, *Songs of Sundry Natures* (1589). — 10: Ch. Tye, *Mass Euge bone.* — 11–12: Ferrabosco, Madrigals. — 13–15: Th. Weelkes, Madrigals and Ballets (1598). — 16–17: Weelkes, *Ayres or Phantastick Spirites* (1608). — 18–20: F. Pilkington, *Songs or Airs* (1605).—21: White, Kirbye, Wilbye, and Daman, Anthems, Motets, etc. — 22: J. Milton, Six Anthems. — 23: J. Blow, Six Songs. — 24: H. Purcell, Six Songs from

"Orpheus Britannicus." — 25: J. Blow, *Venus and Adonis.*

XXIII. *Paléographie musicale* (17 vols., ed. by the Benedictines of *Solesmes, 1889 to date; containing facsimiles and studies of plainsong MSS).
A. First Series. 1: Le Codex 339 de Saint-Gall. — 2,3: Le répons-graduel Justus ut palma. — 4: Le Codex 121 d'Einsiedeln. — 5,6: Antiphonarium Ambrosianum (Cod. Add. 34209 . . . Brit. Mus.). — 7,8: Antiphonarium tonale missarum (Cod. H. 159 . . . Montpellier). — 9: Antiphonarium monasticum (Cod. 601 . . . , Luque). — 10: Antiphonale (Codex 239 . . . de Laon). — 11: Antiphonale (Codex 47 . . . de Chartres). — 12: Antiphonaire monastique (Codex f. 160 . . . de Worcester). — 13: Le Codex latin. 903 . . . de Paris (Graduel de St. Yrieux). — 14: Le Codex 10673, Bibl. Vaticane (Graduel Bénéventain). — 15: Le Codex VI.34, Bénévent.
B. Second Series. 1: Antiphonale, Codex Hartker . . . de Saint-Gall. — 2: Cantatorium (Codex 359 . . . de Saint Gall).

XXIV. *Publications de la société française de musicologie* (various editors, 1925 to date). A. Monuments: 1. Deux livres d'orgues parus chez Pierre Attaingnant (Y. Rokseth; K). — 2. Oeuvres inédites de Beethoven (G. de Saint-Foix). — 3,4 (falsely designated 4,5): Chansons au luth et airs de cour (L. de la Laurencie; S). — 5: Treize Motets . . . pour orgue (Y. Rokseth; K). — 6,7: *La Rhétorique des dieux* . . . de Denis Gaultier (A. Tessier; L). — 8: J. H. d'Anglebert, *Pièces de Clavecin* (M. Roesgen-Champion; K). — 9: J.-C. de Mondonville, *Pièces de Clavecin avec accompagnement de violon* (*c.* 1730; M. Pincherle; I). — 10: Le Manuscrit . . . d'Apt (14th/15th cent.; A. Gastoué; V).
B. Documents: 1,2: Inventaire du fonds Blancheton de la Bibliothèque du Conservatoire de Musique de Paris (de la Laurencie). — 3,4: Mélanges offerts à M. L. de la Laurencie. — 5,6: Documents inédites relatifs à l'orgue français (Dufourcq). — 7: Catalogue des livres de musique de la Bibliothèque de l'Arsenal à Paris (de la Laurencie, Gastoué). — 8: Bibliographie des poésies de P. de Ronsard mises en musique au 16e siècle (Thibault, Perceau).

XXV. *Publikationen älterer Musik* (various editors, 1926 to date). 1.i; 3.i; 4.ii: Guillaume de Machaut, Musikalische Werke (Ludwig; V). — 1.ii: Johannes Ockeghem, Sämtliche Werke i (Plamenac; V). — 2: Luys Milan, *Libro de musica* (Schrade; L). — 3.ii: Sixtus Dietrich, Ein Beitrag . . . zur Musikanschauung . . . (Zenck). — 4.i; 6: Luca Marenzio, Madrigals (Einstein; V). — 5; 7: Das Graduale der St. Thomaskirche . . . (P. Wagner). — 8: Ottaviano Petrucci, *Frottole* (Schwartz; V). — 9: Adrian Willaert, Sämtliche Werke i (Zenck; V).

XXVI. *Publikationen älterer praktischer und theoretischer Musikwerke* (33 vols., ed. by Eitner, 1869–1905). Alphabetical list of composers (our numbering is according to volumes; an optional numbering according to annual sets [see, e.g., *MoML* 157] is added in parentheses). 20(24): M. Agricola, *Musica instrumentalis deutsch* (1528). — 22(26): J. a Burgk, Geistliche Lieder und Passion (V). — 10(9): G. Caccini, *Euridice* (Op). — 12(11): F. Cavalli, *Giasone* (Op). — 12(11): M. A. Cesti, *La Dori* (Op). — 23(27): 60 Chansons des 16. Jahrhunderts (Attaingnant; V). — 24(28): G. Dressler, Motetten (V). — 21(25): J. Eccard, *Neue geistliche und weltliche Lieder* (1589; V). — 8(7): H. Finck, Lieder und Motetten (V). — 29(33): G. Forster, *Frische teutsche Liedlein* (V). — 10(9): M. da Gagliano, *Dafne* (Op). — 16(16): Glarean, *Dodekachordon.* — 15(15): H. L. Hassler, *Lustgarten* (V). — 6(5): Josquin, Ausgewählte Kompositionen (V). — 18(21/22): R. Keiser, *Prinz Jodelet* (Op). — 25(29): Gr. Lange, Motetten (V). — 27(31): J.-M. Leclair, Zwölf Sonaten für Violine und Generalbass (1732; I). — 14(13): J. B. Lully, *Armide* (Op). — 10(9): Cl. Monteverdi, *Orfeo* (Op). — 9(8): E. Oeglin, Liederbuch (1512; V).

— 1–4(1–4): J. Ott, Liederbuch (1544; V). — 13(12): M. Praetorius, *Syntagma Musicum* ii. — 19(23): J. Regnart, Villanellen (V). — 14(14): A. Scarlatti, *La Rosaura* (Op). — 5(4): A. Schubiger, *Musikalische Spicilegien.* — 17(19/20): G. C. Schürmann, *Ludwig der Fromme* (Op). — 26(30): O. Vecchio, *L'Amfiparnasso* (Op). — 11(10): S. Virdung, *Musica getutscht* (1511). — 7(6): J. Walter, *Wittembergisch geistlich Gesangbuch* (1524; V). — 28(32): M. Zeuner, 82 geistliche Kirchenlieder (1616; V).

Raccolta nazionale. See VI.

XXVII. *Trésor musicale* (58 vols., ed. by R. J. van Maldeghem, 1865–93; contains sacred and secular vocal music of the 16th century; each year two volumes, one "Musique religieuse," one "Musique profane," were published; detailed index in *GD* v, 377ff).

XXVIII. *Tudor Church Music* (10 vols., 1923–29; contains 16th- and 17th-century English Church music). 1: Taverner (Masses). — 2: W. Byrd (English Services, etc.). — 3: J. Taverner (Magnificats, hymns, motets). — 4: O. Gibbons (Services and anthems). — 5: R. White (Motets, anthems). — 6: Th. Tallis (Motets, hymns). — 7: W. Byrd, *Gradualia* I, II. — 8: Th. Tomkins (Services). — 9: W. Byrd (Masses, motets). — 10: H. Aston, J. Marbeck, O. Parsley.

XXIX. *Vereeniging voor Noord-Nederlands Muziekgeschiedenis* (c. 40 vols., the most important of which are listed below, excluding the complete publication of Sweelinck [by M. Seiffert] and of Obrecht [by J. Wolf]). 22: C. Boskoop, 50 Psalmen Davids (V). — 30: Driestemmige Oud-Nederlandsche Liederen (c. 1500; V). — 26: Een duytsch Musyck-Boeck (1572; V). — 41: P. Hellendaal, Vier Sonates voor Violoncel (c. 1750; I). — 32: C. D. Hurlebusch, *Compositioni musicali per il Cembalo* (c. 1750; K). — 25,27: Nederlandsche Dansen der 16de eeuw (Susato, Phalesius; I, arranged for piano). — 19: A. van Noort, *Tabulatuur-Boeck* (1659; K). — 34: Orkestcomposities . . . (early 17th cent.; I). — 37: Oud-Nederlandsche Klaviermuziek (mu-

sic book of Anna Maria van Eijl, 1671; K). — 13: A. Reinken, *Hortus musicus* (1687; I). — 14: A. Reinken, *Partite diverse . . .* (K). — 28: J. Schenk, *Scherzi musicali* (c. 1700; I). — 5: C. Schuyt, Drie Madrigalen (c. 1600; V). — 29: T. Susato, *Het ierste Musyck-boexken* (1551; V). — 24: J. Tollius, Zesstemmige Madrigalen (after 1600; V). — 42: J. van den Vondel, *Kruisbergh* (1640; V). — 8: J. Wanning, Bloemlezing uit die 52 *Sententiae* (c. 1600; V). — 35: A. Willaert, *Missa super Benedicta* (c. 1550; V).

Education. See *Music education.

Effleurer [F.]. To touch very lightly.

Eglogue. Same as *Eclogue.

Eguale. See *Equale.

Egualmente [It.]. Equally, evenly.

Egyptian music. Pictorial representations of instruments show that there existed a musical culture in Egypt as early as the 4th millennium B.C. The instruments of the Old Kingdom (prior to the 18th century B.C.) were chiefly small harps and flutes. The music was quiet and reserved, probably similar in character to that of the ancient Chinese. Investigations made on two preserved flutes of the early second millennium suggest that the melodies moved in relatively large intervals, e.g., d–f–a–b [cf. C. Sachs, in *AMW* ii]. With the beginning of the New Kingdom (16th century B.C.) a complete change took place, owing to the infiltration of Asiatic instruments and music. We now find a greatly enlarged orchestra, including large harps, oboes, lutes, and many percussion instruments, such as the sistrum and the drum. Careful measurements of the numerous instruments preserved from this era have shown that small intervals are now preferred. All evidence points to the rise of music of an entirely different character, full of ecstasy and passion. As later in Greece, the "Apollinian" element was superseded by the "Dionysian" [see *Greek music]. The trend towards individual and unrestrained expression and the consequent dissoluteness of civilization led, around 600 B.C., to a reaction and to the re-establishment of the old sacred rites. It is to this rather artificial state of affairs that Herodotus, Strabo, Plato, and other Greek writers refer in their reports telling about the high ethical standard of Egyptian culture and the restrained character of the music. It is very likely that Egyptian music and theory exercised a great influence upon those of Greece. In the early Christian era, Alexandria was an important center of Christian worship and of psalm-singing.

Lit.: A. Hemsi, *La Musique orientale en Egypte* (1930); J. Pulver, "The Music of Ancient Egypt" (*PMA* xlviii); C. Sachs,"Die Tonkunst der alten Aegypter" (*AMW* ii); *id.*, "Die Namen der altägyptischen Musikinstrumente" (*ZMW* i); *ReMMA*, 6ff (bibl. p. 426).

Eight-foot. See *Foot (2).

Eilend [G.]. Hurrying.

Eingestrichen [G.]. One-line (octave, C, etc.).

Einklang [G.]. Unison.

Einleitung [G.]. Introduction.

Einlenken [G.]. To lead back.

Einsatz [G.]. (1) Attack. — (2) The entrance of an orchestral part.

Einstimmig [G., one-voiced]. Monophonic.

Eintritt [G.]. Entrance, particularly of a fugal subject [see *Einsatz].

Eis [G.]. See *Pitch names.

Eisteddfod. See *Bards; *Penillion.

Eklogen. See *Eclogue.

Ekphonetic notation [from Gr. *ekphonesis*, lecture, pronunciation]. The term denotes certain primitive systems of musical notation, consisting only of a limited number of conventional signs designed for the solemn reading of a liturgical text. Originally, they were nothing but accents indicating a raising or lower-

ing of pitch, or signs calling for special inflections used to bring out grammatical peculiarities, such as questions, exclamations, affirmations, etc. Later, they developed into somewhat more elaborate formulae the exact nature of which is obscure. Ekphonetic signs occur in Byzantine, Armenian, Syrian, Coptic, manuscripts of the later Middle Ages (*c.* 600–1500). In Jewish chant a system of ekphonetic signs, called ta'amim, is used to the present day [see *Jewish music]. Especially important are the Byzantine signs, e.g. / ~ \ +, the deciphering of which has been greatly furthered in recent studies of C. Hoeg [cf. the reproduction in *BeMMR*, 32]. The ekphonetic signs are distinguished from the neumes by the fact that they indicate, not a freely invented melody, but a succession of fixed melodic formulae. Moreover, they usually occur only at certain places in the text (most frequently the beginning and end of a phrase), without giving a continuous melody. They probably represent a type of singing similar to that used in the psalm-tones of Gregorian chant. See *Notation II; *Byzantine chant II.

Lit.: J. B. Thibaut, *Monuments de la notation ekphonétique et neumatique de l'église latine* (1912); C. Hoeg, *La Notation ekphonétique* (1935); *WoHN* i, 61; E. Wellesz, "Die byzantinischen Lectionszeichen" (*ZMW* xi).

E la (mi); elami. See *Hexachord II.

Elargissant [F.]. Broadening.

Electronic musical instruments. Prior to the latter part of the 19th century all musical instruments were based on mechanico-acoustical or pneumatico-acoustical principles of sound production. A string, a reed, a piece of metal, a stretched membrane, or the air enclosed in a tube was set into vibration by energy supplied by the player, thus generating waves in the surrounding air. These methods of producing musical sound were all in use as far back as history can trace, and for thousands of years no new ones were discovered. Not until the 19th century, when electrical science began to take an interest in the subject, was a fundamentally new method of making music devised; and not until the three-element vacuum tube was developed, in the second decade of the present century, did this new method become really practical. Today there are musical instruments which, without the aid of soundboards or other acoustical amplifiers, achieve any desired volume of sound by means of electrical circuits and appliances such as are used in radio receivers; and there are others whose vibrations originate not as motions of solid bodies or particles of air but as electrical impulses.

Perhaps the earliest of these instruments was the *Telharmonium*, invented towards the close of the 19th century by Thaddeus Cahill (b. Iowa, 1867). This was a kind of organ which, instead of generating sound waves in the air by means of pipes, employed rotary generators to create electrical impulses at frequencies corresponding to the rates of vibration of musical pitches, and telephone receivers to convert the electrical impulses into sound. Designed to distribute music over telephone lines, it proved commercially impractical because it interfered with telephone service. Moreover, it was enormously complex and bulky, comprising no less than thirty carloads of machinery. It is hardly surprising that electronic music made little headway until science evolved, in the form of vacuum tubes no larger than ordinary electric light bulbs, a substitute for the tons of steel and copper used in Cahill's generators. Since 1920, progress has been rapid and many kinds of electronic instruments have been developed. In 1939 an orchestra composed exclusively of such instruments was organized by T. A. Cracraft and introduced to the public in broadcasts over the network of the National Broadcasting Company. The principal electronic instruments in current use are briefly described below. For more detailed information consult the sources listed at the end of this article.

I. *Keyboard Instruments*. Various types of electronic piano are available. These instruments retain all of the essential piano mechanism except the soundboard, whose function (i.e., reinforcement or "amplification" of sound waves generated by the vibration of the strings) is performed electrically. There are several methods of converting string vibrations into electrical impulses without the aid of a microphone. These are commonly called "pickup" systems. The types most widely used are the electromagnetic and electrostatic systems. In the former, a tiny coil with a magnetic core is mounted near the string, but far enough from it to prevent contact as the string vibrates. When the string is set in motion its vibrations generate alternating current in the coil. The electrical impulses thus produced are conducted by wires through amplifiers which increase their strength, and finally to a loudspeaker which converts them into sound waves. In the electrostatic system the coil and magnet are replaced by a simple conductor, and the string itself is charged. As the string vibrates, variation of the distance between it and the conductor generates alternating current which is amplified and converted into sound waves in the manner described above. Such a method of amplification makes it possible not only to obtain great volume from a small instrument but also to control the characteristics of its tone. Harmonics may be altered in intensity, or omitted altogether, thus changing the timbre of the original sound, and the dynamic envelope of the tone may be controlled to vary the apparent manner of generation and decay — e.g., the percussive impact of the piano hammer may be eliminated so that the tone builds up gradually. By such means the piano may be made to produce sonorities resembling those of stringed or wind instruments. The power amplifier and loudspeaker are usually built into the piano cabinet but may be separately housed and connected by cable to the pickup system. To this class of instruments belong the *Neo-Bechstein* (invented by W. Nerust) and the *Elektrochord* (invented by H. Vierling).

Numerous electronic organs have been developed. Some are similar in operation to the pianos described above, converting mechanically generated sound frequencies which are amplified and then converted back into sound; others omit the first step in that process and begin with electrically generated frequencies. Representative of the former type are the wind-blown reed organs of R. H. Ranger and B. F. Miessner and the now widely known Everett *Orgatron*. The Ranger instrument utilizes a photoelectric pickup system, light reflected from the vibrating reeds being translated into electrical energy by means of a photoelectric cell [see VII]. Miessner employs an electrostatic pickup system which makes it possible to obtain more than one timbre from a single reed. The Orgatron also has electrostatic pickup and is available in models with two manuals, pedal board, swell pedal, and tablet-form controls similar to the stops of a modern pipe organ.

Among keyboard instruments utilizing electrical sound generation the best known are the *Hammond Organ* and the *Novachord*. The former resembles the spinet in size and shape but has two five-octave manuals. A series of small, motor-driven rotary generators produces alternating current at frequencies corresponding to those of the tempered scale, and harmonic controls provide a very large number of timbres, some of which are pre-set. These are controlled by means of keys located at the left-hand end of each of the two manuals. Sliding bars located above the upper manual enable the player to select other timbres. Pedal board and swell pedal are provided, and the amplifier and loud-speaker are contained in a separate cabinet.

The *Novachord*, a six-octave, single-manual instrument which also resembles the spinet in form, employs a purely electronic tone-generating system. Twelve vacuum tube oscillators (i.e., circuits capable of producing alternating current at given frequencies) operate at the frequencies of the highest octave of the instrument. There is a separate oscillator for each note of the chromatic scale, and associated with each oscillator are five divider tubes, each of which operates at one-half the frequency of the preceding tube. Thus one oscillator and the five dividers associated with it supply the six octaves of one

note of the scale. Controls mounted on one end of the panel above the keyboard provide different tone colors by varying the harmonic components of the tone, and similar controls on the other end operate another set of vacuum tubes which varies the tonal envelope to produce either percussive effects, similar to those of the piano, or sustained tones, similar to those of stringed or wind instruments. The power amplifier and loudspeaker are built into the console.

The principles utilized in the Novachord have recently been adapted, with some modifications, to produce the *Solovox*, an instrument designed to add a sustained melodic voice to the conventional piano. A miniature keyboard of three octaves, which is mounted just below the right-hand end of the piano keyboard, controls a master oscillator and five divider tubes. When a key is depressed it tunes the master oscillator to the pitch associated with that key in the highest octave of the instrument, and selects the proper divider to produce the tone in the desired octave. As there is only one master oscillator, only one fundamental pitch can be produced at one time, but harmonic controls afford a considerable variety of tone color. The performer plays the principal melodic part on the Solovox with the right hand and accompanies it on the piano keyboard with the left hand.

II. *Bowed Instruments*. Electronic violins, violas, violoncellos, and basses usually consist of skeleton frameworks just sufficient to support the finger board, bridge, and strings (and to afford some guidance to the player's hand), with non-microphonic (usually electrostatic) pickups attached to the bridge. Amplifiers and loudspeakers are contained in separate cabinets connected by cable to the pickups. Certain variations of tone quality are available in some models.

III. *Fretted Stringed Instruments*. Electronic amplification has been applied to guitars of all types, banjos, and mandolins. Of these instruments the most successful is the so-called *steel guitar*, now widely used in popular dance orchestras. In appearance it bears little resemblance to any traditional form of guitar, its body consisting of a small box-like structure which affords no acoustical amplification. The pickup system is similar to that used for bowed instruments and the amplifying equipment is separately housed. Its advantages include widely variable amplification, greater sustaining power, and control of tone quality.

IV. *Wind Instruments.* Electronic wind instruments apparently have not passed the experimental stage. This is probably due chiefly to the fact that their inherent volume is usually sufficient for all purposes. Miessner has adapted pickup systems to reed instruments such as the clarinet and saxophone, chiefly for the purpose of providing them with variable tone quality, but they do not appear to have emerged from the laboratory. Electronic brass instruments seem to be non-existent.

V. *Percussion Instruments.* Electronic methods make it possible to obtain from small and inexpensive devices sounds resembling those produced by bells weighing many tons. One form of electronic carillon consists of a set of coiled steel reeds similar to those used in clocks. Equipped with a keyboard controlling electrically operated strikers, it is played in the same manner as is the piano, and its amplifying system increases its volume to any degree desired. Another form utilizes loosely suspended lengths of piano wire. The latter method has proved especially successful in reproducing the inharmonic partials characteristic of bells.

Radio listeners may be interested to know that the familiar chimes heard between programs on the NBC network are produced by a mechanism (invented by Capt. Richard H. Ranger) which resembles the old-fashioned music box. Steel reeds, plucked by pins set in a revolving barrel, produce vibrations which are converted into electrical frequencies, amplified, and finally broadcast. A more recent chime device, similar in purpose but different in principle, has been developed by J. L. Hathaway, an NBC engineer. This employs a system of oscillators to produce frequencies which are converted by a loudspeaker into tones of bell-like quality. It

is used to give time signals in public places such as Rockefeller Plaza in New York.

A very practical percussion instrument is a chromatic kettledrum invented by Miessner. It consists of thirteen short bass viol strings which are stretched over a rectangular frame and tuned in semitones. When the strings are struck with ordinary kettledrum sticks their vibrations, picked up electrostatically and amplified through a suitable loudspeaker, produce sounds closely resembling those of conventional kettledrums. The obvious advantage of this electronic instrument is that it provides in a compact and easily portable form the equivalent of thirteen actual drums, since all of its pitches are available simultaneously.

VI. *Space-controlled Instruments.* One of the first electronic instruments to attract public attention was the *Theremin*, invented about 1924 by the Russian scientist whose name it bears. This instrument uses a radio-frequency beat system of tone generation based on the dissonance between two oscillators. One oscillator operates at a fixed frequency and the other at varying frequencies determined by the proximity of the player's hand to a short rod antenna which is charged with alternating current from the second oscillator. The difference between the frequencies of the two oscillators produces a "beat" — i.e., a third frequency, which is the audio frequency that operates the loudspeaker. The volume of sound is controlled in a similar manner by the player's other hand. A serious defect of this instrument in its earliest form was its inability to change from one pitch to another without an intervening glissando, but that defect has been remedied to some extent in later models by means of an improved volume control. In recent years Theremin has developed other types of instrument, including an electronic cello that has neither strings nor bow but utilizes the cellist's conventional left-hand technique for pitch determination. Volume is controlled by means of a variable resistance operated by a lever which is manipulated by the player's right hand. Another instrument of this type is the *Trautonium*, invented by the German Friedrich Trautwein. Originally it was operated by the hands in the same manner as the Theremin, but later a metal string was placed over a metal rail having marks to indicate where the string should be pressed on the rail for the correct pitches of the tempered scale.

VII. *Photoelectric Instruments.* The sound track of a modern motion picture film is recorded by photoelectric methods. In one system, sound vibrations are converted into varying intensities of a beam of light which produces on the film a permanent pattern of variable density corresponding to the variations in pitch and volume of the sounds recorded. Another system uses an oscillating beam to trace a pattern of variable area.

Radio Engineers, 1936); L. Stokowski, "New Horizons in Music" (*Jour. Acoustical Soc. of America*, 1932); *id.*, "New Vistas in Music" (*Atlantic Monthly*, Jan., 1935); E. G. Richardson, "The Production and Analysis of Tone by Electrical Means" (*PMA* lxvi); J. Schillinger, "Electricity, a Musical Liberator" (*MM* viii, no. 3); A. N. Goldsmith, "Electricity becomes Music" (*MM* xv, no. 1); J. M. Barbour, "Music and Electricity" (*PAMS*, 1937).   E. P.

Elegy [G. *Elegie*]. A plaintive poem; hence, a musical composition of a sad or mournful character.

Elektrochord. See *Electronic musical instruments I.

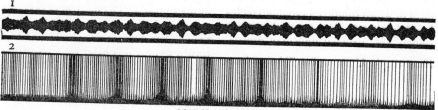

1

2

SOUND TRACKS
1. Variable area sound track. 2. Variable density sound track

When the film is exhibited the process is reversed. A beam of light passing through the sound track falls on a photoelectric cell which converts the varying intensities or areas of light into audio-frequency current, and this current, after amplification, operates a loudspeaker which reproduces the original sounds. Various musical instruments have been designed to operate on this principle of tone generation but none has come into general use. Information concerning experiments in this field will be found in B. F. Miessner's article on "Electronic Music and Instruments" [see Lit.].

Lit.: C. Chavez, *Toward a New Music* (1937); Th. Cahill, "The Cahill Telharmonium" (*Electric World*, 1906); B. F. Miessner, "The Electronic Piano" (*Proceedings, Music Teachers' Nat. Assn.*, 1937); *id.*, "The Application of Electronics to the Piano" (*Proceedings, Radio Club of America*, 1934); *id.*, "Electronic Music and Instruments" (*Proceedings, Inst. of*

Elevation [L. *elevatio*; It. *elevazione*]. (1) The music played during the Elevation of the Host. It consists either of a motet or of an organ piece. A "Toccata per l'elevazione" and other similar pieces are contained in Frescobaldi's *Fiori musicali* (1635). See *Offertorium. — (2) See *Appoggiatura, Double II.

Eleventh. See *Intervals. Eleventh chord, see under *Ninth chord.

Elmuahim, elmuarifa. Terms used by 13th-century theorists [cf. *CS* i, 339; 341] to denote the *semibrevis* which has the shape of a rhomb. They come from Arabian *al ma'luma* and *al ma' rufa*, i.e., "the known thing," terms used in Arabian translations of Euclid for the rhomb. Cf. J. Handschin, in *ZMW* xiv, 321; H. G. Farmer, in *Journal of the Royal Asiatic Society*, 1925, p. 76.

Embellishment. (1) Same as *ornamentation.—(2) Same as *auxiliary tone.

Embouchure. (1) The *mouthpiece of wind instruments, especially of the brass and the flute. — (2) In the playing of these instruments, the proper disposition of the lips, the tongue, etc. Also called "lip," "lipping."

Emmeles [Gr., within the melos]. Early medieval term for the *subfinalis*, i.e., the tone below the final of a church mode, e.g., c in Dorian. See *Church modes I.

Emperor Concerto. Colloquial name for Beethoven's Piano Concerto in E-flat, op. 73 (1809), evidently suggested by the grandeur of the work.

Emperor Quartet [G. *Kaiserquartett*]. Colloquial name for Haydn's String Quartet in C, op. 76, no. 4, the slow movement of which comprises variations on his Emperor's hymn: "Gott erhalte Franz den Kaiser," the *national anthem of Austria.

Emperor's Hymn. See *National anthems.

Empfindsamer Stil [G., sensitive style]. Denomination for the North-German style of the second half of the 18th century represented by W. F. Bach, C. P. E. Bach, Quantz, G. Benda, Reichardt, and others who, in the period from *c.* 1750 to 1780, tried to arrive at an expression of "true and natural" feelings, anticipating to some extent the Romanticism of the 19th century. Unfortunately, a somewhat narrow and rationalistic point of view toward musical expression, which hampered rather than freed the imagination, prevented the movement from becoming more than a Romantic variety of *Rococo style. These views appear particularly in the *Affectenlehre of this period. Aside from the works of W. F. Bach and C. P. E. Bach, the *volkstümliche Lied and the *Singspiel are among the foremost results of this movement. See *Gallant style.

Empfindung, Mit [G.]. With feeling, emotion.

Emporté [F.]. "Carried away," excited.

Empressé [F.]. Eager.

Ému [F.]. With emotion, affectation.

Enchaînement [F.]. Voice-leading, proper connection of chords.

Enchainez [F.]. Same as *segue.

Enchiriadis, Enchiridion [Gr., from *cheir*, hand]. Medieval term for handbook, manual. *Musica Enchiriadis is the title of an important treatise of the 9th century, formerly ascribed to Hucbald [*GS* i, 152]; *Enchiridion* is the title of several early publications of Protestant *chorales.

Enclume [F.]. Anvil.

Encore [F., again]. In public performance, the repetition of a piece, or an extra piece played in response to the applause of the audience. The practice of encoring started in the 17th century with the rise of the operatic virtuoso-singers. Haydn had turned against this habit by 1799, at the occasion of the first performance of his *Creation*; in a note printed on the program he begged the audience not to insist upon the repetition of any number.

Endings. See *Differentiae.

Enechema. See *Echos.

Engführung [G.]. Stretto of fugues.

English flute. Eighteenth-century name for the end-blown flutes (*recorder or *flageolet), in contradistinction to the side-blown type (cross-flute) which was known as German flute.

English discant. See under *Fauxbourdon (2).

English horn. See *Oboe family I, B.

English Madrigal School. See *Editions, Historical, X.

English music. I. The history of English music, considered as a whole, presents a picture with many peculiar traits such as are not encountered in the musical history of the Continental nations. Most striking is the fact that the evolution of English music, instead of moving in extended and organic curves of growth and decline, follows a rather irregular and somewhat eruptive line of evolution, involving short periods of extraordinary flowering between centuries of low ebb and almost complete stagnation. The high points of English music history are marked by a limited number of great personalities: Dunstable around 1400; Tallis, Byrd, and Gibbons before and after 1600; Purcell and Handel before and after 1700. Between these culmination points there lie periods of eclipse, the most obscure being that which separates Purcell and Handel from contemporary composers such as Vaughan Williams and Holst, who signify the beginning of a nobler creative period of English music.

II. Evidence of musical culture in England begins with the report that Gregorian chant was introduced there during Gregory's lifetime (c. 600) by St. Augustine of Kent, the first Archbishop of Canterbury. Later (10th century) special rites (Uses) developed in Salisbury (*Sarum Use), Hereford, and at other great cathedrals. In the 10th century we hear of a remarkable activity in organ building, particularly in Winchester where, around 950, a giant organ having 26 bellows and 400 pipes was built, as is reported by a monk Wulstan (d. 963) [see *Organ XII].
Musical and theoretical sources of the 11th century (*Winchester Troper,* new ed. by W. H. Frere, 1884), treatise by John Cotton (c. 1100; cf. *GS* ii, 230) show England participating actively in the development of "free organum" [see *Organum]. The spread of French polyphony to England is also demonstrated by the fact that the earliest of the four preserved MSS containing the repertoire of the *School of Notre Dame (before and after 1200) was written in Scotland (St. Andrews, now Wolfenbüttel 677; see *Magnus liber organi). Although the bulk of its contents is French music, it contains in a separate fascicle a great number of short pieces which show certain peculiar traits and which are therefore believed to be of "insular origin" (Handschin).
An English contribution of great importance is the singing in parallel thirds, usually known under the 14th-century

name *gymel, and its more developed variety in parallel thirds and sixths, commonly known as *fauxbourdon. Writers of the 14th century praise this type of music as "merry to the singer and to the hearer." This characterization is interesting because it indicates a typically English penchant for harmonic euphony which possibly accounts for the striking changes from artistic greatness to mediocrity encountered in English music history. A very noteworthy, though somewhat overpraised example of English music is the canon *Sumer is icumen in (c. 1310). Important 13th-century theorists, studying and working in France, are Johannes de Garlandia (born c. 1195), Anonymus IV [*CS* i; see *Anonymous], and Walter Odington (born c. 1250).

III. During the 14th century English music (known to us chiefly through some fragmentary MSS from Worcester) employed a simple *conductus style which is strikingly backward in comparison with the highly developed melodic and rhythmic resources of contemporary French and Italian music [see *Ars nova], but which is historically important owing to the extended use of progressions in sixth chords, called English discant [see *Fauxbourdon (2); examples in *HAM*, no. 57 a, b]. A great number of early 15th-century English composers are known to us from various MSS, partly of English origin (Old Hall MS; see *Sources, no. 25), partly of Continental (*Trent codices; Bologna, see *Sources, nos. 20, 22). Since the composers (as well as the musical style) represented by the latter differ strikingly from the former, they are believed to belong to two schools, an insular school of strictly conservative trends (Cooke, Damett, Sturgeon, Typp, and others), and a Continental school of progressive tendencies (Dunstable, Leonel Power, Bedingham, Benet, and others; examples in *HAM*, nos. 60–64). Among these, John Dunstable (c. 1370–1435) stands out as a composer of the highest artistic significance. His invigorating influence on the French music of the 15th century (*Burgundian School) is attested in a poem "Le Champion des dames" (c.

1440) saying that Dufay and Binchois "ont prins de contenance Angloise et ensuy Dunstable" [cf. *ReMMA*, 412]. The most striking trait of this "English countenance" is a most beautiful type of melody based on the degrees of the triad [see *Third]. Unfortunately, Dunstable had no English successors worthy of his rank.

IV. A new trend in English music, leading from the sacred to the secular, becomes discernible in the compositions of Robert Fayrfax (d. 1521), William Cornyshe (c. 1465–1523), and their royal patron, King Henry VIII. They wrote secular part-songs to English or French texts, frequently of a humorous or even satirical character [examples in *HAM*, nos. 85, 86]. Fayrfax is also noteworthy for his activity in the field of the motet (little cultivated by his predecessors), which he was followed by the T-triad of early Tudor composers, John Taverner (1495–1545), Christopher Tye (1500–72), and Thomas Tallis (1505–85) [see *Editions XXVIII]. Tye and Tallis were the first to make contributions to the church music of the Reformation, in their *anthems and *Services. Only brief mention need be made here of the numerous composers who contributed to the glory of the Elizabethan era, notably Tallis' pupil William Byrd (1543–1623), and the numerous English madrigalists [see the list of *The English Madrigal School*, under *Editions X]. The 16th century also sees the rise of English keyboard music. After the strikingly advanced *Hornepype of Hugh Aston (c. 1480?–1522?) there follows a large repertory of liturgical organ music (organ verses, organ hymns, *Felix namque, by John Redford, 1485–1545 [cf. C. Pfatteicher, *John Redford*] and many others [cf. H. Miller, in *MQ* xxvi]), a repertory which, in turn, is followed by that of the *Virginalistic School. English Renaissance music, vocal as well as instrumental, reached an expression of fin-de-siècle refinement in Orlando Gibbons (1583–1625) and in the lutenist and songwriter John Dowland (1563–1626) who is the most outstanding among numerous others active in the field of lute songs [see the list no. XI under *Editions]. The late

16th century also saw the rise of English chamber music, mainly for viols [see *Fancy; *Innomine; *Consort].

V. Practically all the composers of the Elizabethan period died around 1625. In an almost tragic manner the development of English vocal and keyboard music came to an end, and only in the field of chamber music was the tradition carried on, though in a somewhat conservative manner, by composers such as John Jenkins (1592–1678), Henry Lawes (1595–1662), William Young (d. 1672), and Matthew Locke (1630–67). Roger North, in his interesting account of English musical life during the 17th century (*Memoires of Musick*, 1728), tells us that Locke's consorts were "the last of the kind that hath been made." As a matter of fact, around 1670 the character of English music changed completely, owing to the intrusion of French (Lully) and, somewhat later, Italian (Cazzati, Vitali) elements. This change is apparent in John Blow (1648–1708), whose numerous anthems and Services, influenced by the Italian aria style, show facility rather than creative imagination and whose main importance lies in the fact that he established the basis upon which his pupil Henry Purcell (c. 1658–95) created a number of truly great works, anthems, secular songs, and *dramatic music, particularly his only full opera, *Dido and Aeneas* (c. 1689). English Baroque music reached its peak in Handel (1685–1759), Bach's contemporary and compatriot, who spent practically all his creative career in England and whose late oratorios and organ concertos are the most perfect embodiment of the spirit of English music, while his operas incline more towards the Italian tradition. See also *Browning; *Catch; *Ground; *Masque.

VI. Typically English productions of the 18th century are the *ballad opera, the *glee, and the *voluntary. Among the more important composers of this period are Thomas Arne (1710–78; numerous operas, glees), William Boyce (1710–79; anthems, publication of *Cathedral Music*), Benjamin Cooke (1734–93; odes, glees, catches), and Samuel Webbe (1740–

1816; glees, catches). There followed Samuel Wesley (1766–1837), famous for his organ improvisation and well known for his initiative on behalf of Bach's music, composer of anthems and Services as well as of Masses, motets (he joined the Roman Catholic Church in 1784) and of organ music (organ concertos, voluntaries). His son Samuel Sebastian Wesley (1810–76), influenced by Mendelssohn and Schumann, contributed much towards raising the low standard of English church music, in his anthems and Services. The musical Romanticism is more clearly represented by John Field (1782–1837; *nocturnes) and William Sterndale Bennett (1816–75; piano and orchestral music). Around 1880 the English opera found its greatest national representative since Purcell in Arthur S. Sullivan (1842–1900).

VII. At about the same time English music in general took a start to a new period of artistic production. The development from 1880 till 1940 may be conveniently divided into three periods: that of German influence, that of national and impressionistic tendencies, and that which stands under the influence of *New music.

To the first period belong Ch. H. Parry (1848–1918), Charles Stanford, and Edward Elgar (1857–1934). The first two of these were influenced by Schumann, Wagner, and Brahms, although individual traits are by no means missing, particularly in some works of Stanford in which elements of his native Ireland are prominent. Elgar wrote in a rich and strongly emotional style which sometimes tends to ostentatiousness and even vulgarity. The second group includes "nationalistic" composers such as Frederick Delius (1862–1934), Ralph Vaughan Williams (b. 1872), Percy Grainger (b. 1882), Arnold Bax (b. 1883), and the "impressionist" Cyril Scott (b. 1879). Vaughan Williams took an active part in the revival of old English folk song and embodied its archaic idiom into his compositions. Grainger, now living in America, combined English folk elements with a certain open-air frankness which is probably derived from his native Australian background. Bax's leaning towards a roman-

tically colored mysticism and wistfulness, a spiritual heritage of his partly Irish blood, has earned him the title of "Yeats in music." In the third group we find Gustav Holst (1874–1934) and Arthur Bliss (b. 1891) who, in their later works, show the neo-classical influence of Stravinsky. The most hopeful among the youngest English composers is William T. Walton (b. 1902), whose Concerto for Viola (1929) and Symphony (1935) have raised high expectations among music-lovers and critics. Alan Bush (b. 1900) takes a particular interest in "socialistic" music, Constant Lambert (b. 1905) works in jazz idioms, and Benjamin Britten (b. 1913) can, at the age of thirty, look back at an astonishingly copious number of works written with an easy and yet technically reliable hand, and embracing pieces for film, stage, radio, as well as for the concert hall.

See also reference to other articles under *Anglican Church music.

Lit.: H. Davey, *History of English Music* (1921); E. Walker, *A History of Music in England* (1924); Wm. H. Hadow, *English Music* (1931); W. Nagel, *Geschichte der Musik in England* (1894/97); J. Pulver, *A Dictionary of Old English Music and Musical Instruments* (1923); id., *A Biographical Dictionary of Old English Music* (1927); H. O. Anderton, *Early English Music* (1920); Wm. H. G. Flood, *Early Tudor Composers* (1925); E. H. Meyer, *Die mehrstimmige Spielmusik des 17. Jahrhunderts . . .* (1934); H. Davey, *English Music, 1604–1904* (1906); J. A. F. Maitland, *English Music in the 19th Century* (1902); W. A. Barrett, *English Church Composers* (1926); G. Cecil, *The History of Opera in England* (1930); C. Forsyth, *Music and Nationalism, a Study of English Opera* (1911); F. Kidson and M. Neal, *English Folk Song and Dance* (1915); C. J. Sharp, *Folksongs of England*, 5 vols. (1908); F. W. Galpin, *Old English Instruments* (1932); H. Hughes, †*Early English Harmony* (1913); Dom Anselm Hughes, †*Worcester Mediaeval Harmony* (1928). D. Attwater, "English Folk Song" (*ML* ix, no. 2); M. Bukofzer, "The First Motet with English

Words" (*ML* xvii); *id.*, "The First English Chanson on the Continent" (*ML* xix); A. H. Fox Strangways, "English Folksongs" (*ML* v, no. 4); A. Hughes, "Old English Harmony" (*ML* vi, no. 2); J. Mark, "Dryden and the Beginnings of Opera in England" (*ML* v, no. 3); J. Pulver, "Music in England during the Commonwealth" (*AM* vi, no. 4); H. Reichenbach, "The Tonality of English and Gaelic Folksong" (*ML* xix, no. 3); J. B. Trend, "The First English Songs" (*ML* ix, no. 2); S. T. Warner, "An Aspect of Tudor Counterpoint" (*ML* ii, no. 1).

English School of Lutenist Songwriters, The. See *Editions XI.

English violet. See *Viol IV 4.

Enharmonic. (1) In Greek music, the term enharmonic denotes a tonality (scale, tetrachord, genus) which includes quarter-tones [see *Greek music II (b); cf. H. Husmann, in *JMP* xliv; C. del Grande, in *RMI* xxxvi].

(2) In modern theory, the term is used for tones which are actually one and the same degree of the chromatic scale, but are named and written differently, e.g.: g# and ab, c# and db, etc., according to the key in which they occur. Enharmonic intervals are intervals consisting of the same tones, but "spelt" differently, e.g.:

A well-known example of "enharmonic equivalents" is the *diminished seventh chord which can be written in four or more different ways. Enharmonic change is the change of meaning of a tone or a chord (frequently a diminished seventh chord) from sharp to flat, or vice versa, as is frequently the case in modulations, e.g. (to quote one of the earlier instances, from Handel's *Samson*):

The statement regarding the identity in pitch of enharmonic tones is correct only in our modern system of well-tempered tuning, but not in other systems of either theoretical or historical significance (*Pythagorean system, *just intonation, mean-tone systems; see *Temperament). In just intonation, e.g., c# (upper third of a) is $\frac{25}{24}$ while db (lower third of f) is $\frac{16}{15}$; the difference between these tones is the enharmonic *diesis, $\frac{128}{125} = 41$ *cents (very near one-fifth of a whole-tone). While piano-players naturally have fully adopted the view that enharmonic tones are identical in pitch, violinists and singers frequently insist that they differ and that this difference should be brought out in performance. Thus, in the example (a) given

below, the db would sound nearly a quarter-tone lower than the preceding c#. The main objection against this procedure is that it arbitrarily introduces a dash of just intonation into a performance which in all other respects is based upon equal temperament, e.g., in the intonation of the triad. Moreover, in an example like (b), the recommended distinction is obviously impossible since the "changeable" tone is tied over. Finally, it should be noticed that the enharmonic change is by no means restricted to chromatic tones such as c# and db, but that it may occur also on any of the diatonic degrees of the scale. For instance, example (a) in exact transposition a major third upwards becomes example (c). However, even the most sensitive violinist would probably not think of playing this passage as it should be played in enharmonically correct intonation, that is, as indicated under (d).

(3) Enharmonic instruments are keyboard instruments which provide separate keys and strings (pipes, etc.) for the different enharmonic tones. The most complete instrument of this type was Bosan-

quet's 53-tone clavier of 1851. For a 16th-century construction see *Arcicembalo. Cf. also W. Dupont, *Geschichte der musikalischen Temperatur* (1935).

Enigmatic canon. See under *Canon II. Enigmatic scale, see *Scala enigmatica.

Enigma Variations. Theme with variations, for orchestra, by Edward Elgar (op. 36, 1899), so called because each variation is addressed to one of his friends, the dedication being indicated enigmatically by their initials.

Ensalada [Sp., medley, potpourri]. Spanish 16th-century songs of a humorous character. An early example contained in the *Cancionero musical* (*c.* 1500) is a *quodlibet [cf. *RiHM* ii.1, 203]. Whether the ensaladas by Matea Flecha (1581) were also quodlibets cannot be ascertained since the bass part only is preserved. It would seem that the name refers here only to the choice of humorous texts, dealing with scenes from the life of soldiers, students, muleteers, etc. Cf. *LavE* i.4, 2011ff.

Ensemble [F., the whole]. The term generally denotes the coöperation of several performers. Thus, one speaks (1) of a "good ensemble" or a "bad ensemble" with reference to the degree of balance and unification attained in the performance of a string quartet, etc. — (2) In operas, ensemble is a piece for more than two singers (duet) or for the soloists together with the chorus. Such pieces usually occur at the end of an act (finale).

(3) In the study of early music (prior to 1600), a distinction between ensemble music (i.e., music performed by more than one participant) and soloist music (i.e., music for a single performer) is of fundamental importance, since it explains many features of style and clarifies various problems of *Aufführungspraxis, e.g., the question of improvised coloraturas, which are possible only in soloist music, either monophonic (e.g., the soloist portions of Gregorian chant) or polyphonic (i.e., keyboard and lute music). Similarly, *Freistimmigkeit is restricted to (polyphonic) soloist music as was also free variability of

tempo [see *Expression III]. It may be noticed, however, that the "soloist-versus-ensemble" point of view can also be successfully applied to the question as to how ensemble music is performed. In fact, motets or chansons may be reproduced either in "ensemble performance," i.e., with more than one singer to each part, or in "soloist performance," i.e., with only one singer to the part. While ensemble performance calls for strict adherence to the music as written, soloist performance leaves the singer free to insert improvised coloraturas, particularly in the highest part. There is ample evidence to show that, toward the end of the 16th century, ensemble performance of motets was frequently superseded by soloist performance (including improvised coloraturas), a procedure which evidently foreshadows the *monodic style of the 17th century.

The distinction between ensemble music and soloist music plays a basic role in the study of the notation of polyphonic music [see *Notation V]. It also may be recommended to supplant the customary, but unsatisfactory, classification of early polyphonic music as "vocal music" and "instrumental music." The following defects of this classification may be noticed: (a) Prior to 1550 (i.e., prior to the period of strict *a-cappella music) instrumental participation was frequently called for, or admitted, in the performance of "vocal" music; this admixture is particularly conspicuous in the accompanied songs (ballades, etc.) of the 14th century, and in the frottole of the early 16th century. (b) Several publications of the 16th century [e.g., Willaert, *Ricercari* ... (1559)] bear the remark: "da cantare e suonare d'ogni sorte di stromenti," showing that such textless pieces could be sung (in *vocalization) as well as played on any type of melody instruments (viols, recorders, cornettos). Evidently such pieces cannot be classified as either instrumental or vocal music; however, they are definitely "ensemble music." (c) The field of "instrumental music" includes such strongly heterogeneous styles as that of a keyboard toccata and a lute prelude on one side, and a ricercar by Willaert or Padovano [see (b)] on the other side. This contrast of style is easily explained if it is recalled that the former types are soloist music, the latter ensemble music. Parenthetically it may be mentioned that ensemble music may well be changed into soloist music, a method which was generally known in the 16th century as *Intabulierung. This practice, however, does not invalidate the basic distinction between genuine ensemble music and genuine soloist music, as little as the existence of 19th-century arrangements (e.g., of a Beethoven string quartet) invalidates the distinction between chamber music and piano music. Cf. *ApNPM*, xxi f; L. Hibberd, *The Early Keyboard Prelude* . . . (unpubl. diss. Harvard 1941); *id*. in *MQ* xxii, no. 2.

Enté [F., grafted]. *Motet enté* is a special type of 13th-century motet, the texted upper part being constructed in a manner suggestive of "grafting" a fresh twig upon an old tree, that is, by inserting a new text (and melody) between portions of a pre-existing text (and melody). The "old material" is usually one of the numerous popular *refrains taken from the ballades, rondeaux, etc., of the trouvères and split into two or more portions between which new words are interpolated. For instance, the refrain *"E ai! Ke ferai! Je mur d'amouretes, comant garirai?"* of a trouvère ballade [cf. F. Gennrich, *Balladen, Rondeaux und Virelais* (1921) i, 148] leads to the following triplum of a motet: *"He, ha, que ferais?* Belle, je vous ai Tant amée . . . Et nuit et jour je chant: *Je muir d'amouretes!* Se vostre amour n'ai . . . ou je languirai, *Et coument en garrai?"* [cf. Y. Rokseth, *Polyphonies du xiiie siècle* (1936) iii, 52]. For another example (*"Hé amours . . . avoir merci"*) cf. *AdHM* i, 242. Obviously this method of textual amplification is derived from the identical procedure used in the liturgical *tropes. See *Refrain III; *Farce.

Entführung aus dem Serail ("The Abduction from the Seraglio"). Comic opera (*Singspiel) in three acts by W. A. Mozart, text by G. Stephanie, first performed in 1782. The action takes place at a Turkish castle where *Belmont* (Ten-

or) and his servant *Pedrillo* (Tenor) seek *Constanze* (Soprano) and her maid *Blondchen* (Soprano), who are held captive in the seraglio of the pasha *Selim* (speaking part), guarded by the terrible Moor *Osmin* (Bass). Pedrillo's success in making Osmin drunk gives the two couples a chance to reunite and to flee. They are, however, trapped and brought before Selim who, to the delight of Osmin, condemns them to die and then, touched by their love and grief, pardons them.

The *Entführung* is Mozart's first real opera in the German language and actually the first German opera of significance. It was written as a sort of wedding gift for his wife, Constanze Weber, whom he married one month after its production, and it truly reflects the happiness of this period in its long array of arias and scenes of irresistible charm and overflowing humor. See *Janizary music.

Entr'acte. A piece (usually instrumental) performed between the acts of a play or opera, e.g., Beethoven's compositions for Goethe's play *Egmont*, or Bizet's entr'actes for his opera *Carmen*. The music of Lully's *comédie-ballets* is mostly in the form of entr'actes (intermedes) for Molière's plays, e.g., *Le Bourgeois gentilhomme* [see *Ballet]. Purcell's instrumental entr'actes are known as act-tunes or curtain tunes. The term *intermezzo is sometimes used for entr'acte.

Entrada, entrata [It., Sp.]. See *Intrada; *Entrée.

Entrée. In Lully's operas and in similar works, pieces of a march-like character which are played during the entry of dancing groups or of important personages. The term also occurs in connection with non-operatic compositions of a similar character, e.g., in Bach's Suite in A for violin and harpsichord [see *Intrada]. In the French ballet of the 17th–18th centuries an entrée is a subdivision of an act, roughly corresponding to a "scene" in opera [see *Quadrille (2)]. It also occurs as equivalent to "act," e.g., in Rameau's *Les Indes galantes*; in these works, each entrée has its own plot, unconnected with that of any other entrée.   D. J. G.

Entremes [Sp.]. The Spanish variety of the operatic *intermezzo.

Entremet [F.]. In the French and Burgundian courts of the 14th and 15th centuries, a short entertainment performed between the courses of a banquet, often including dancing to vocal or instrumental accompaniment.

Entrückt [G.]. As if "removed" from earth.

Entry. The "entering" of the theme in the different parts of a fugue, at the beginning as well as in the later expositions, particularly if preceded by a rest, as is frequently the case.

Entschieden [G.]. Determined.

Entschlossen [G.]. Resolute, determined.

Enunciation. A term occasionally used as a synonym for "exposition" in sonata form.

Epechema. Same as *enechema.

Epidiapente, epidiatessaron. See *Diapente, *Diatessaron.

Epilogue. Synonym for *coda (in sonatas, etc.).

Épinette [F.]. Spinet, harpsichord.

Epiphonus. See *Neumes I.

Episema [Gr., superior sign]. In neumatic MSS of the 9th and 10th centuries, written in chironomic neumes, *episema* is a subsidiary sign in the form of a vertical dash attached to a neume. It occurs most frequently in connection with the *clivis*, as illustrated here. It plays a promi-

nent part in the present-day studies of Gregorian rhythm [see *Gregorian chant VI]. The name is also used for other subsidiary signs, e.g., those which have been believed to indicate quarter-tones [cf. *WoHN* i, 45].

Episode. Secondary sections of a composition, chiefly fugue and rondo, in which the principal subjects are missing, being replaced by subordinate subjects (as in the rondo) or by motives derived from the principal subjects (as frequently in the fugue). Episodical form is another name for *rondo form.

Epistle. In the Catholic liturgy, a passage from the Scriptures, usually from the Epistles of St. Paul, which is monotoned, or chanted with simple inflections (*tonus epistolae*; cf. *GR*, 114*) at *Mass after the Collect.

Epistle sonata. A 17th- and 18th-century instrumental piece designed to be played in the church before the reading of the *epistle. Mozart composed several for organ and violin, etc.

Epithalamium [It. *epitalamio*; from Gr. *thalamos*, bed]. In Greek poetry (Sappho) poems designed to be sung by a chorus at wedding ceremonies. Hence, organ pieces intended for use at weddings. J. J. Kuhnau's program composition "Jacob's Heyrat" (*Biblische Historien*, 1700) contains an *epitalamio*.

Epitrita. Greek term, used by some 16th-century theorists, for *proportio sesquitertia* [see *Proportions].

Equale [Aequale, Eguale]. A composition for *equal voices, i.e., all male or all female, or for equal instruments. In particular, a composition for four trombones, written for solemn occasions. Beethoven composed three such pieces (1812) which, arranged for male chorus, were performed at his funeral.

Equal temperament. See *Temperament.

Equal voices. The term is used to designate compositions for male voices only, or for women's voices only, in contradistinction to mixed voices. Less frequently, it is used in the meaning of: for soprano voices (or others) only. See *Equale.

Erbe deutscher Musik, Das. See *Editions XII.

Ergriffen [G.]. Deeply moved.

Erhaben [G.]. Sublime.

Erhöhungszeichen; Erniederungs-zeichen [G.]. Sharp; Flat.

Erlöschend [G.]. "Extinguishing," dying away.

Ermattend [G.]. Tiring, weakening.

Ernst [G.]. Serious.

Eroica [It., heroic]. Beethoven's Third Symphony, in E-flat, op. 55, composed in 1803. It was written in homage to Napoleon whom Beethoven admired as a hero of democracy. However, upon Napoleon's assuming the role of a dictator and the title of an emperor, Beethoven, greatly infuriated, withdrew the planned dedication and changed the title from: "Sinfonia grande; Buonaparte" to: "Sinfonia eroica, per festeggiar il sovvenire d'un gran uomo" (. . . to celebrate the memory of a great man). See remark under *Contredanse.

Eroticon. A love song, or an instrumental piece portraying passionate love.

Ersatzklausel [G.]. See *Clausula.

Erschüttert [G.]. "Shaken," deeply moved.

Ersterbend [G.]. Dying away.

Erstickt [G.]. Suffocated.

Erzähler [G.]. *Narrator.

Erzlaute [G.]. *Archlute.

Es, eses [G.]. See *Pitch names.

Esaltato [It.]. "Exalted," excited.

Escapement. See under *Pianoforte.

Eschequier. See *Echiquier.

Eserzicio [It.]. Exercise, *Etude.

Eskimo music. Lit.: H. L. Thuren, *The Eskimo Music* (1912); E. Vogeler, *Lieder der Eskimos* (1930); W. Thalbitzer, *Legendes et chants esquimaux du Greenland* (1929); D. Jenness, in *MQ*

viii; H. J. Thuren, in *ZIM* xii; *id.*, in *BSIM* vii.

Espringale. Medieval name for a jumping dance as distinguished from *carole, a round dance.

Esquinazo [from *esquina*, corner]. A Chilean type of serenade, in 3/4- or 6/8-meter, with dotted rhythms. It is also sung as a Christmas carol.

Esquisse [F.]. Sketch.

Estampie, estampida, istanpitta [probably from old F. *estampir*, to resound]. The most important instrumental form of the 13th and 14th centuries. Similar to the (vocal) sequence [see *Sequence (2)] from which it was evidently derived, it consists of several sections (four to seven), called *puncti*, each of which is repeated: a a; b b; c c; . . . Different endings, called *ouvert* and *clos* [It. *aperto* and *chiusso*], are provided for the first and second statement of each punctus, as in the modern *prima* and *seconda volta*. In some cases the same two endings are used for all the puncta, so that the following scheme results: a–x, a–y; b–x, b–y; c–x, c–y; . . . The earliest known example of this form is the troubadour song "Kalenda maya" (The Month of May; cf. *HAM*, no. 18d; *AdHM* i, 190) the text of which, according to a pretty story, was written by the troubadour Raimbaut de Vaqueiras (fl. 1180–1207) to the melody of an "estampida" played by two "joglar de Fransa" (French jongleurs) on their *vielles [cf. *AdHM* i, 190]. All the other existing examples are purely instrumental monophonic pieces. Eight estampies are contained in the 13th-century *Chansonnier Roy* [see Lit., Aubry; cf. *HAM*, no. 41c], while the 14th-century MS Brit. Mus. *Add. 29987* [see *Sources, no. 12] contains eight "istanpittas," with subtitles such as "Belicha," "Palamento," "Isabella," "Tre fontane" [Ex. in *HAM*, no. 58; *SchGMB*, no. 28]. These charming pieces are in the character of idealized dances, thus suggesting the theory that the estampie originally was a true dance. Among the earliest preserved pieces for organ is an estampie called "Petrone" [*HAM*, no. 58].

Owing to the similarity of name and structure, the estampie is usually identified with the *stantipes*, a form described by Johannes de Grocheo (*c.* 1300; see *Theory II) as consisting of from five to seven "puncta." This theory, however, has not remained unchallenged (C. Sachs). Grocheo distinguishes the stantipes from the *ductia*, characterizing the latter as having four (or fewer) puncta. It may be noticed, however, that the "estampida" Kalenda maya has only three puncta. The problem is further complicated by the fact that two 14th-century treatises on poetry describe a "vocal" estampie which apparently lacked the puncta but possessed a refrain. See also *Ductia; *Dance music II.

Lit.: P. Aubry, †*Estampies et danses royales* (1906); C. Sachs, *A World History of the Dance* (1937), pp. 292f; L. Hibberd, "Estampie and Stantipes" (*Speculum*, 1944); J. Wolf, "Die Tänze des Mittelalters" (*AMW* i); J. Handschin, "Über Estampie und Sequenz" (*ZMW* xii); H. J. Moser, "Stantipes und Ductia" (*ZMW* ii).

Estey organ. See *Harmonium.

Estinguendo [It.]. "Extinguishing," dying away.

Estinto [It.]. "Extinct," i.e., *ppp.*

Estompé [F.]. Toned down.

Estribillo [Sp.]. See under *Copla.

Éteint [F.]. "Extinct," i.e., *ppp.*

Ethiopian church music. Lit.: *GD*, Suppl. Vol., 179ff; *AdHM* i, 138; J. M. Harden, *The Anaphora of the Ethiopic Liturgy* (1929); M. Cohen, *Chants éthiopiques* (1931); E. Wellesz, in *Oriens Christianus* (1920).

Ethos. In ancient Greek music ethos designated the "ethical" character of the various modes (harmoniai). The (Greek) Dorian (similar to our Phrygian) was considered manly and strong, representing the ancient tradition; the

Phrygian, ecstatic and passionate; the Lydian, feminine and lascivious; the Mixolydian, sad and mournful. Similar characterizations, doubtless influenced by the Greek ideas, occur in the 16th-century discussions of the church modes. For instance, Diruta, in *Il Transilvano II* (1609), describes the *primo tono* as "grave e modesta," the *secondo tono* as "mesta e calamitosa," . . . the *settimo tono* as "allegro e suave," the *undecimo tono* (practically our C major) as "vivo e pieno di allegrezza." Cf. also the ragas of *Hindu music.

Lit.: *ReMMA*, 42; L. Harap, in *MQ* xxiv; E. M. von Hornbostel, in *Festschrift für Johannes Wolf* (1929).

Et in terra pax. See *Gloria.

Étouffé [F.]. Damped, muted (kettledrums, violins). *Étouffoir* is the French name for the damper of the pianoforte.

Etude. A piece designed to aid the student of an instrument in the development of his mechanical and technical ability. An etude is usually devoted entirely to one of the special problems of instrumental technique, such as scales, arpeggios, octaves, double stops, trills, etc. While etudes are written in the form of a complete piece, finger-exercises are short formulae which have to be repeated many times, either on the same pitch, or moving through the degrees of the scale. Many modern teachers prefer the finger-exercises because they are more efficient than etudes.

Finger-exercises were already known in the early 16th century. The tablature of Oswald Holtzach (1515, Univ. Bibl. Basle) contains sequential passages in 16th-notes, entitled: "Lauffwerck, mit beiden Händen zu bruchen" ("running passages, to be used with both hands"). A similar piece is contained in Leonard Kleber's tablature (*c.* 1520, St. Bibl. Berlin). Towards the end of the 17th century the Italian *toccata became a sort of etude, owing to the large use of stereotyped passage work and to the deterioration of the musical quality [Al. Scarlatti,

Pasquini; cf. F. Boghen, *Antichi maestri Italiani: Toccate*]. A publication by F. Durante (1684–1755), *6 Sonate per cembalo, divise in studii e divertimenti*, contains 6 "sonatas," each consisting of a "studio" and "divertimento," the former being somewhat serious and difficult to play, the latter in the lighter vein of the "gallant style" [see *Editions VI, 11]. The originator of the modern etude is Muzio Clementi (1752–1832), whose *Préludes et Exercises* (1790) and *Gradus ad Parnassum* (1817) mark the beginning of the enormous literature of the 19th-century etude. Outstanding collections of etudes for the pianoforte were written by Cramer, Czerny, Moscheles, Bertini; for the violin by Kreutzer, Rode, Paganini, d'Alard, Bériot. Chopin, in his 27 Etudes (op. 10, op. 25, and three single pieces), created the concert etude which is designed not only for study purposes but also for public performance and which combines technical difficulty with high artistic quality. His example was followed by F. Liszt (*Études d'exécution transcendante*, and others), Scriabin (op. 8, op. 42, op. 65), and Debussy (twelve *Études*, dedicated to the memory of Chopin, 1915).

Lit.: E. Gork, *Die Entwicklung der Klavier-Etude von Mozart bis Liszt* (Diss. Vienna 1930).

Eunuch flute. See *Mirliton.

E u o u a e. In the liturgical books of the Roman rites, the usual abbreviation for "seculorum. Amen" [cf. the vowels of these two words], the closing words of the *Gloria Patri* [see *Doxology]. It is given at the end of the Introitus and of the Antiphons in order to indicate the proper ending (*differentia) which leads back to the final repetition of the Introitus or of the Antiphon. For more details, see *Psalm tones. The spelling *Evovae*, frequently found in older books, has been confused by some writers with the ancient Greek word *Evoe*, causing wonderment and indignation over the use in the Catholic service of a bacchanalic exclamation of joy.

Euphonium. See *Brass instruments III (d).

Evangelium [G.]. *Gospel.

Evangelist. In passions, the *narrator who recites the text of the Gospel.

Éveillé [F.]. Awakened.

Evensong. Same as *vespers.

Evirato [It.]. Same as *castrato.

Evovae. See *E u o u a e.

Exalté [F.]. Excited.

Exequiae [L.]. Exequies, i.e., music for funeral rites.

Exotic music. The musical cultures outside the European tradition. The term is frequently used in a rather thoughtless manner, as if "exotic" were synonymous with "barbaric" or "primitive." Actually, however, the field of exotic music includes phenomena of widely different degrees of cultural evolution, for instance, the Chinese music which as far back as 3000 years ago reached a stage of "classicism," the Javanese music with its highly developed orchestral technique, the Japanese music with its lyrical songs and traditional opera, the Hindu music with its ancient theory of scales and modes, — all these side by side with really primitive cultures which show no evidence of methodical training and historical development. The latter receive treatment in this book under the head *Primitive music, while the others are treated separately: see *Arabic music; *Chinese music; *Hindu music; *Japanese music; *Javanese music. See also the articles on *Comparative musicology; *Oriental music.

Exposition. The initial section of musical forms (sonata, fugue) which contains the statement of the chief subject. The German term for the exposition of a sonata is *Themenaufstellung*; for that of a fugue, *Durchführung*. See *Sonata-form; *Fugue.

Expression. Expression may be said to represent that part of music which cannot be indicated by notes or, in its highest manifestation, by any symbol or sign whatsoever. It includes all the nuances of tempo, dynamics, phrasing, accent, touch, bowing, etc., by which the mere combination and succession of pitch-time-values is transformed into a living organism. Although, as far as the written notes are concerned, the performer is strictly bound to the composer's work, he enjoys a considerable amount of freedom in the field of expression, which may be said to represent the creative contribution of the performer. In early music, i.e., prior to 1600, the line of demarcation between "composition" and "expression," i.e., between written pitch-time-values and nuances of performance, is very clear, since composers never provided anything but the bare notes, leaving the matter of expression entirely to the performer [see below, III]. With the gradual rise of more specific and detailed manners of expression, composers more and more felt the necessity of providing at least some basic indications, in order to clarify their intentions and to prevent mistakes or arbitrariness on the part of the performer. This trend led to the gradual introduction of *tempo-marks, *dynamic marks, signs for touch, bowing, phrasing, and, in the 19th century, of the numerous terms such as "dolce," "amarevole," "passionato," which are meant to describe the general character of the composition or a passage thereof. It goes without saying that, however detailed and subtle these indications may be, they give only the general outline and still leave ample room for what has been termed above the "creative contribution of the performer." In the following explanation separate treatment is given to (I) the composer's and (II) the performer's share in expression; a third paragraph (III) deals with the question of expression in early music.

I. *Expression in musical composition* is one of the many important innovations of the *Mannheim School (c. 1750). This does not mean that earlier music lacks in expression, but only that its nuances are so limited in scope and follow so closely the design and structure of the composi-

tion that they do not appear as an extra element of independent importance. It was in the symphonies of the Mannheim School that devices of expression for its own sake, such as sudden *ff* and *pp*, long crescendos and decrescendos, were for the first time exploited. While in these works the details of expression are not always justified by the music itself, but frequently appear as a somewhat extraneous admixture, a complete amalgamation of "expression" and "composition" is reached in the classical works of Haydn, Mozart, Beethoven, and Schubert. Here we find expression in complete harmony with the musical substance which has become expressive in itself. In the Romantic movement, the possibilities of expression were exploited to the fullest extent. An immense array in shades of subtlety appeared, and composers spent a good deal of their ingenuity in the invention of new nuances as well as of words or signs to indicate them. Although this tendency has greatly enriched the musical palette, it has not always been to the advantage of creative progress. There can be no doubt that the late 19th-century over-indulgence in "expressiveness" and in expression signs or words [cf. the works of Scriabin, Reger, R. Strauss, Debussy, Fl. Schmitt] has been the cause (or the result?) of a marked deterioration of the musical invention. The anti-Romantic movement of the 20th century [see *New Music] brought with it a marked reversal of attitude. Erik Satie was probably the first to write intentionally unexpressive (dry) music, and to ridicule the Romantic tendencies by ironic expression marks, such as: "corpulentus," "caeremoniosus," "devenez pâle," etc. Recent composers such as Poulenc, Stravinsky, Hindemith, frequently write in an intentionally unexpressive style, use expression signs very sparingly, and sometimes indicate their intentions by remarks such as "sans expression," "Mit wenig Ausdruck."

II. *Expression in performance.* The ideal performer is the one who succeeds in bestowing upon the composition a personal and original expression within the stylistic frame of the work and in full compliance with the intentions shown by the composer's indications. Unfortunately, the second part of this postulate is seldom realized. The arbitrariness of so many virtuosos is partly responsible for the excess of expression marks to be found in the works of composers who thus hoped to forestall distortion and misinterpretation. Yet, complete control over the performer is not only impossible but also undesirable. The only remedy is to improve the education of performers in matters of musical style and taste. The most common fault is the application of a Romantic, i.e., a highly expressive, treatment to non-Romantic music, such as the works of Bach, Mozart, Beethoven. The deplorable result is an overdoing of all nuances: the use of prestissimo instead of allegro, of larghissimo instead of adagio, of *fff* and *ppp* instead of *f* and *p*, of frequent crescendi and decrescendi instead of an even level of sonority, of numerous rubatos, ritardandos, and accelerandos instead of strictly kept tempo, etc. In view of all these tendencies nothing seems to be more important for the student than to learn to play without expression. Only the pianist who has learned to play Bach's *Chromatic Fantasia* or Beethoven's *Appassionata* in the most rigid way will be able to add that amount of nuances and shades which these works properly require.

III. *Expression in early music.* The absence or extreme scarcity of expression marks in music prior to 1750 does not mean that the compositions of the Middle Ages, the Renaissance, and the Baroque period were always played without any gradation of intensity or of tempo. Although no gradation of intensity was possible on the organ and the harpsichord, it would be foolish to assume that singers or players of stringed instruments performed the expressive lines of a 14th-century ballade or the dramatic curves of a Bach cantata in an intentionally uniform tone. However, no special signs were needed since these gradations remained within modest and natural limits, following closely the rise and fall of the melody. It was not until the advent of the 17th century with its characteristic technique of con-

trasting bodies of sound [see *Stile concertato; *Echo] that the necessity of introducing indications for *forte* and *piano* was felt. The earliest pieces provided with such indications (*forte, piano*) are Gio. Gabrieli's *Sonata pian'e forte* [*SchGMB*, no. 148] and several organ pieces by Adriano Banchieri [*ApMZ* i], all dating from about 1600. Shortly after this, abbreviating letters must have been used, because Domenico Mazzochi, in the Preface to his *Partitura de Madrigali* . . . of 1638, says that "the . . . letters F. P. E. t for Forte, Piano, Echo, and trill are already common affairs known to all." In Th. Mace's *Musick's Monument* (1676) dynamic contrast is indicated by *Lo:* (loud) and *So:* (soft) [cf. *WoHN* ii, 226].

Prior to the middle of the 18th century crescendo and decrescendo were used chiefly for the vocal performance of single sustained tones [see *messa di voce]. Mazzocchi seems to have been the first to indicate these effects by signs, a *V* for a crescendo (called by him *messa di voce*), and a *C* for a crescendo followed by a diminuendo (the *messa di voce* proper) [see Harding, p. 91]. The modern signs for crescendo and diminuendo were much later to appear, the earliest known instance being in Geminiani's *Prime Sonate* of 1739. Crescendos and diminuendos extending over lengthy musical phrases were also known throughout the 17th century, but were always indicated by prescriptions such as: "forte, piano, pianissimo" (Mazzocchi), or "Lowd, Soft, Softer" (M. Locke), or "lowder by degrees" (M. Locke, Curtain Tune in *The Tempest*, 1675). The members of the *Mannheim School were the first to cultivate all the dynamic effects in the modern way, for the purpose of orchestral coloring and of climactic or anticlimactic effects.

As regards the history of tempo marks, it must be noted in the first place that in music prior to 1600 indications such as allegro, adagio, etc., were unnecessary since the tempo of a piece or a section thereof was clearly expressed in the notation itself [see *Tactus]. It is significant that the earliest instances of free tempo variability occur in soloist music [see *Ensemble

(3)], namely, in the lute book *El Maestro* (1535) of Luys de Milan who prescribes for certain passages of his fantasias "a priesa" (quick), for others, "a espacio" (slow). Particularly interesting is the detailed information regarding free tempo (rubato) which Frescobaldi gives in the preface to his *Fiori musicali* (1635; cf. *TaAM* iv, p. x).

The monodic style of the early Baroque made musicians conscious of the importance of subtly shaded expressions. Caccini, in the preface of his *Nuove musiche* (1601), illustrated the new style of singing by sample pieces provided with remarks such as: "Esclamazione spiritosa," "senza misura quasi favellando," etc. [cf. *GD* v, 20]. Pieces by Banchieri (*c.* 1600) are among the earliest to show the use of tempo indications such as: "Allegro," "Adasio," "Presto" [cf. *ApMZ* i]. About 100 years later François Couperin made consistent use of captions such as: "gravement sans lenteur," "gayement," "gracieusement et légèrement," etc. [cf. his *Pièces de Clavecin*, 4 vols. (1713–30)].

Expression marks in Bach are practically limited to a handful of pieces in which different degrees of sonority are indicated by *f*, *p*, and *pp*. In view of the excessive amount of expression marks found in modern editions of Bach it may be stated that the entire manuscript of the *Well-tempered Clavier* contains nothing but the notes and signs of ornamentation.

Lit.: R. E. M. Harding, *Origins of Musical Time and Expression* (1938); G. Langley, in *PMA* xxxviii; A. Heuss, "Die Dynamik der Mannheimer Schule" (*ZMW* ii); M. Brenet, "Sur l'origine du crescendo" (*BSIM*, 1910); G. Cucuel, in *BSIM*, 1911; C. Mennicke, *Hasse und die Brüder Graun als Sinfoniker*, p. 317 (Diss. Leipzig 1906); *RiHM* ii.2, 146.

Expressionism. A term which was widely used in the second decade of the present century to denote certain radical trends of modern music [see *New music], particularly Austrian and German. It was taken over from the Fine Arts in which it designated a school of the early years of the century (Picasso, Kandinsky,

Feininger, Klee) who represented a reaction against the "impressionistic" school (Degas, Renoir, Monet, Manet). The provocative replacement of the prefix "im" by "ex" was meant to indicate a complete reversal of thought, i.e., the change from "impressions gained from the outer world" to "expression of the inner self," more properly, of the "subconscious self," in the psycho-analytical sense of the word. Technically this meant the replacement of a highly refined naturalism and color technique by abstract and strangely distorted forms combined in utter disregard of the traditional principles of "beauty," "symmetry," etc. In music, a roughly parallel change took place around 1910, leading from the sensuous program music and the coloristic effects of Debussy to an avowedly abstract type of music in which, likewise, distorted melodies, discordant harmonies and disintegrated lines were used in utter disregard of all traditional principles of musical art. Since the painter's term "impressionism" had already been adopted in the musical vocabulary as a designation for Debussy's school, the champions of the new movement pointedly designated themselves as expressionists, in order to emphasize their sympathy with the new ideas of their colleagues in the Fine Arts, and to demonstrate their antagonism against the musical impressionism and romanticism. Unfortunately, in music such a designation was bound to lead to a misunderstanding, that is, to confusion with the term "expression" (which, it may be noted, hardly exists in the Fine Arts). Actually, expressionistic music is no more "expressive" than impressionistic or Romantic music. In a way, one might say that "expressive" and "expressionistic" music stand in the same relation as "emotion" to "psycho-analytical complex."

The main representatives of the expressionistic school are Arnold Schönberg and his followers Anton von Webern, Alban Berg, and Ernst Krenek [see *Atonality; *Twelve-tone technique; *Quarter-tones]. The earlier works of Hindemith (between 1920 and 1925) also seem to fall under the classification of expressionism.

The new and more constructive tendencies which appeared after 1925 (*Neoclassicism) mark the end of expressionism.

Expressive organ [F. *orgue expressif*]. *Harmonium.

Extemporization. See *Improvisation.

Extended phrase. A phrase which, by some sort of modification, is extended to include one or several measures more than in its original form. A famous example is the third statement of the initial motive of Wagner's *Tristan*.

Extravaganza. A term applied to music of a caricaturing character [see *Satire in music]. Gilbert and Sullivan used it as a title for *Trial by Jury*.

F

F. (1) See *Pitch names; *Letter notation; *Hexachord. — (2) Abbreviation for *forte; ff (fff), abbreviation for fortissimo. F-clef, see *Clefs. F-holes, see *Sound-holes.

Fa. See *Pitch names; *Solmization; *Hexachord. *Fa fictum* means, in Guido's system of hexachord and mutation, the *fa* (fourth degree) of the *hexachordum molle* (beginning with f), i.e., B-flat; or, the same degree of the transposed hexachord starting on B-flat, i.e., E-flat. Both tones belong to the *musica ficta, hence the name.

Fabordone, faburden. See *Fauxbourdon (4).

Facilmente [It.]. Easily, without strain.

Fackeltanz [G., torch dance]. A traditional dance of the Prussian court-ceremonial of the 19th century, for weddings and similar celebrations, in the manner of a slow procession with torches. Spontini, Flotow, and Meyerbeer have written music for such occasions.

Fado (also Fadinho). The popular music par excellence of the cities of Portugal, frequently heard in the cafés and on the streets. It consists of song and dance to the accompaniment of the guitar. Cf. G. Chase, *The Music of Spain* (1941), p. 241; R. Gallop, in *MQ* xix, xx and in *ML* xiv, nos. 3 and 4.

Fa fictum. See *Fa.

Fagott [G.], **fagotto** [It.]. Bassoon. *Fagottino* is the tenor oboe (tenoroon), *fagottone* the contrabassoon. *Fagottgeige* is a large viol of the 18th century, the strings of which were overspun with silk and therefore produced a buzzing sound reminiscent of that of the Fagott. *Fagottzug* is a stop-mechanism of old pianofortes (around 1800) which produced a buzzing effect by means of a paper strip coming in contact with the strings.

Fa-la, fa-la-la. A special type of 16th-century songs in which the syllables "fa la la" or similar ones are used as a refrain, e.g.: "Now in the month of maying, When merry lads are playing, Fa la la la la, fa la la la la" (Th. Morley). An early example, with the refrain "san san san sarir . . . ," occurs in Baldassare Donati's *Villanesche alla Napoletana* (1550?), numerous others in the works of Gastoldi, Lasso, Vecchi, and others. Through Gastoldi's *Balletti di cantare sonare e ballare* (1591) the fa-la's became known in England (Morley; Weelkes; Hilton) and in Germany (Hans Leo Hassler; Widman; Staden; Friderici). Expls. in *HAM*, nos. 158, 159.

Falsa musica. See *Musica ficta.

False. *False cadence*, same as deceptive *cadence. *False fifth* (*triad*), old term for the diminished fifth (triad). *False modulation*, see *Modulation. *False relation*, see *Cross relation.

Falsetto [It.]. An artificial method of singing used by male singers, particularly tenors, to obtain notes above the ordinary range of their voice. Since such tones are somewhat nasal in timbre and rather weak when compared with the normal tones of a voice, falsetto is usually considered as of inferior quality. In early music, however, falsetto singing was highly esteemed, and was much used for the higher parts of polyphonic masses and motets, when boys were not available. In England, particularly, falsetto singing was widely practiced [see *Alto]. In fact, a well-trained falsetto voice, though lacking the powerful volume and the dramatic expressiveness of a tenor, has its own charm of a veiled and undynamic transparence; it stands in the same relationship to the normal tenor voice as the recorder to the flute, the viol to the violin.

Falsobordone. See *Fauxbourdon (4).

Falstaff. Opera in three acts by Giuseppe Verdi (1813–1901), libretto by A. Boito, after Shakespeare's *The Merry Wives of Windsor*, composed in 1893. The libretto relates, with slight alterations, the well-known episodes from Shakespeare's play, with the "merry wives" Mistress *Ford* (Ford's wife, called *Alice* in the libretto; Soprano), Mistress *Page* (Soprano), and Mistress *Quickly* (Contralto) plotting against the lecherous *Sir John Falstaff* (Baritone) and, at the same time, succeeding in marrying Ford's daughter *Anne* (called *Nanetta*; Soprano) to the young *Fenton* (Tenor), instead of to Ford's protégé, Dr. *Caius* (Tenor).

It will always remain one of the miracles of creative genius that a man 79 years of age could write an opera which, for its brilliance and bustling humor, might well be the work of a youthful composer; were it not for the fact that in every measure it displays a consummate skill (final fugue "Tutto nel mondo"), a lucid plasticity, such as only lifelong experience can produce. *Falstaff*, together with the earlier *Otello* (1886), represents the climax of Verdi's operatic work. Influenced by Wagner's music drama, Verdi largely abandoned here the "number style" of his earlier works [see *Number opera] and adopted something like Wagner's unending recitative. In view of this influence it is interesting to note that he remained completely untouched by the harmonic innovations of Wagner whose chromatic harmonies (*Tristan*, 1865) are conspicuously absent in *Falstaff*.

Familiar style [translation of It. *stile famigliare*]. A term used to denote vocal music in which the voices (usually four) move uniformly regarding note-values as well as syllables of the text, as in a church hymn. From the point of view of musical texture, familiar style is co-terminous with "strict *chordal style," the only difference being that the latter term is not restricted to vocal music and, hence, carries no implication as to textual treatment. See *Texture.

The term *stile famigliare* probably originated in the 16th century. Baini, in his *Memorie . . . di Palestrina* (1828) ii, 415, speaks of "lo stilo semplice di nota e sillaba che fu denominato familiare," and mentions Josquin's Mass *Dung aultre amer* as the first model. Actually, the history of familiar style goes back to the earliest periods of part music. Prior to 1100 *organum is essentially in note-against-note texture with syllabic treatment. Likewise, most of the conductus of the 13th century move in chordal blocks (two to four parts), one each to the syllable; hence the name "conductus style" as another synonym for familiar style, used preferably with reference to the 13th and 14th centuries. In the works of the *Burgundian School frequent use is made of three-voice chordal sections in *fauxbourdon chords. For an interesting example of three-voice harmony around 1425, cf. *HAM*, no. 56. Longish sections in four-voice harmony appear in the works of Obrecht who therefore has been considered the inaugurator of familiar style, a statement which overlooks or dismisses the previous development outlined above [regarding the transition from three-part to four-part harmony, see *Flemish School]. In the motets of Josquin and his successors the prevailingly polyphonic (more properly, *polyrhythmic) texture is usually balanced by sections in familiar style. This style became increasingly prominent in the later course of the 16th century, particularly in the more popular forms [chanson, frottola, canzone, villanella; see also *Fauxbourdon (4)]. After 1600 it persisted chiefly in the harmonized hymns and chorales. Cf. H. Bush, *The Development of Chordal Style* (Diss. Cornell 1939).

Fancy (Fantasy). A 17th-century term for instrumental ensemble music of English origin. Though fancies occur in the virginal and organ books of the period [see *Fantasia (5)], they were more commonly performed by the consort of viols. The fancy stems from the Italian *fantasia of the 16th century. Throughout the first half of the 17th century the contrapuntal style of the fantasia-ricercare was rather strictly kept by the English musicians, but towards the end of the development (c. 1680) the influence of the new Italian melodic style (Carissimi, Italian opera) was strongly felt. It goes without saying that the fancy does not include any elements of "free fantasia" such as characterize the fantasia of Bach, Mozart, Beethoven, etc. However, from the 17th century point of view, the name was wholly appropriate, being indicative of a greater freedom and variety of style, form, structure, etc., than was admitted in the ricercare [see *Fantasia (5)]. The earliest type of fancy is described by Morley [*A Plaine and Easie Introduction* ... (1597), p. 181] as follows: ... "when a musician taketh a point at his pleasure, and wresteth and turneth it as he list, making either much or little of it according as shall seeme best in his own conceit. In this may more art be showne then in any other musicke. ... And this kind will beare any allowances whatsoever tolerable in other musick, except changing the ayre & leaving the key, which in fantasie may never bee suffered." [For the meaning of the term "ayre," see *Ayre (2).] In the 17th century a more sectional treatment, similar to that of the contemporary *canzona, and a more instrumental type of melody were introduced. Towards the middle of the

century this form adopted suite-like features by combining with dance type movements, such as the pavan, galliard, allemand, saraband, etc., to make longer works. Example for the older ricercare type: Byrd, in *The English Madrigal School*, xvi, 71; for the canzona-type: Byrd, *ibid.*, 166; for the suite type: Locke, in Ed. Warlock and Mangeot, *Six String Quartets*.

The most important composers of fancies were William Byrd (1543–1623), Thomas Morley (1557–1603), John Coperario (1570–1627), Alfonso Ferrabosco (1578–1628), Richard Deering (d. c. 1630), Orlando Gibbons (1583–1625), Thomas Lupo (?), Thomas Tomkins (d. 1656), William Lawes (d. 1645), John Jenkins (1592–1678), and Henry Purcell (1658–95). Their works constitute a treasure of early chamber music which Roger North, in his *Musicall Grammarion* (c. 1725) aptly characterized in the words: "If ye musick was not so Ayery, it was sound and good."

Lit.: E. H. Meyer, *Die mehrstimmige Spielmusik des 17. Jahrhunderts . . .* (1934); E. H. Walker, "An Oxford Book of Fancies" (*MA* iii); R. Erlebach, "William Lawes and his String Music" (*PMA*, 1932–33); C. W. Hughes, "Richard Deering's Fancies for Viols" (*MQ* xxvii); H. J. Sleeper, "John Jenkins and the English Fantasia–Suite" (*BAMS* iv); E. Fellowes, †*O. Gibbons. Nine Fantasias* ... (1924); E. Warlock and E. Mangeot, †*Locke. Six String Quartets* (1932); id., †*Purcell. Three, Four and Five-Part Fantasias for Strings* (1927); E. Meyer, †*Englische Fantasien* ... (1934); E. Mangeot, †*Three Fancies for String Quartet* (1936); †*Nine Fantasias in Four Parts* (New York Public Library).   H. J. S.

Fandango. A Spanish dance in moderate to quick triple time with rhythms such as Ex. 1, danced by a single pair to the accompaniment of guitar and castanets, in alternation with sung couplets. The fandango appeared in Spain in the early 18th century. A popular melody [Ex. 2] was used by Gluck in his ballet *Don Juan* (1761), as well as by Mozart in his *Figaro* (1786; finale of the third act, section in ¾ time). More recently, Rimsky-Korsakov (*Caprice Espagnol*, 1887) and E. Granados (*Goyescas*, 1912) have

written fandangos. Local varieties of the dance are the *Malagueña (from Malaga), the *Granadina* (from Granada), the *Murciana* (from Murcia), the *Rondeña* (from Ronda), etc.

Fanfare. (1) A short tune for trumpets, used as a signal for ceremonial, military, or hunting purposes. Since they are intended for natural instruments, they include the tones of the triad only. The various nations possess a large repertory of such melodies. — Fanfare-like motives have been frequently used in art-music. They already occur in the *caccias of the 14th century [cf. also the virelai in *BeMMR*, 141], in Josquin's *Fanfares royales* [*SchGMB*, no. 62], in Jannequin's program-chanson *La Guerre* (*c.* 1525), and in other *battle pieces [cf. *ApMZ*, Banchieri], in the introductory "Toccata" of Monteverdi's *Orfeo* (1607), and in Bach's *Capriccio sopra la lontananza dello suo fratello dilettissimo*. Various operatic composers have made a highly effective use of the fanfare, e.g., Beethoven in his *Fidelio* (Act II, arrival of the governor; see also his Leonore Overture), and Wagner in the horn-call scene of his *Tristan* (introduction to the first scene of Act II).

Lit.: G. Schünemann, "Sonaten und Feldstücke der Hoftrompeter" (*ZMW* xvii); G. Schünemann, †*Trompeterfanfaren, Sonaten und Feldstücke* (1936) [see *Editions XII A (7)]; K. Taut, *Beiträge zur Geschichte der Jagdmusik* (Diss. 1926).

(2) French term for a brass band, either military or civilian.

Fantasia [F. *fantaisie*; G. *Fantasie, Phantasie*]. Generally speaking, a composition in which the "free flight of fancy" prevails over contemporary conventions of form, style, etc. Naturally, the term covers a great variety of types which may be tentatively classified into five groups. (1) Pieces of a markedly improvisatory character; written records, as it were, of the improvisation-technique of the various masters. Examples are Bach's Chromatic Fantasia and his (lesser known) Fantasia in A minor for harpsichord (ed. Peters, vol. xviii), Mozart's Fantasia in D minor for pianoforte and Beethoven's Fantasia op. 77. The numerous "Fantasien" by C. P. E. Bach also belong to this category. — (2) *Character pieces of the Romantic era. Here, fantasia is one of the various titles used to indicate dream-like mood, or some other whim of fancy. Examples are Brahms's Fantasien op. 116. — (3) Sonatas in freer form, or of a special character; for instance, Beethoven's op. 27, nos. 1, 2, the latter being known as Moonlight Sonata, both of which deviate in various respects from the normal form and style of the sonata; Schubert's Wanderer-Fantasie in which a song of his ("Der Wanderer") is used as the main subject for all the movements [see *Cyclic]; Schumann's Fantasie op. 17, which is a Romantic hybrid of sonata form. — (4) Operatic potpourris of a free and somewhat improvisatory treatment, as if written in remembrance of a performance; e.g., F. Liszt's Don Juan Fantaisie (1841).

(5) In the 16th and 17th centuries the name fantasia occurs frequently with instrumental pieces which are written in a more or less strict contrapuntal style, apparently lacking any features of "free flight of fancy." Although the use of the name fantasia for such pieces seems strange from the modern point of view, it is entirely reasonable from that of the 16th-century musician, to whom the fantasia was a free variety of the strictly contrapuntal and learned *ricercare. In this meaning, the term was adopted first by the lutenists who, although anxious to include in their repertoire the motet-like technique of the ricercare, found themselves handicapped by the technical limitations of their instrument, but succeeded in developing a free instrumental adaptation of the motet, the fantasia. A large

literature of lute fantasias exists in the publications of Marco d'Aquila (1536; *SchGMB*, no. 94), Luis de Milan (1536), Francesco da Milano (1547; *SchGMB*, no. 115), etc.

In the field of keyboard music the "lessening of rigidity" which characterizes the fantasia may have originated in the 16th-century practice of improvising ricercares, a practice which existed particularly in connection with competitions for the position of an organist [Lit., Deffner]. At any rate, it is important to notice that the name fantasia seldom occurs in the keyboard literature prior to about 1580, a piece in Kotter's tablature of 1515 (actually a "Prelude and Fugue"; cf. W. Merian, *Der Tanz in den deutschen Tabulaturbüchern*, 1927, p. 58) and A. Gabrieli's "Fantasia allegra" (see *Editions II (3), p. 67) being practically the only examples. The latter composition, with its free mixture of imitation and figuration, foreshadows the English fantasia of the late 16th and early 17th centuries, which, under the hands of W. Byrd (4), John Bull (2), Giles Farnaby (10), John Munday (2), Peter Philips (2), and others, became a somewhat more clearly defined type of keyboard music (the numbers in parentheses indicate the number of fantasias contained in the *Fitzwilliam Virginal Book*). Nonetheless, the name fantasia covers here a wide range of forms and styles, such as free ricercares, program pieces, and intabulated chansons. In the 17th century, also, the name was applied, as may be expected, to compositions of widely different types of keyboard music, as a comparison of the fantasias by Sweelinck with those of Frescobaldi and Froberger readily shows.

The instrumental (more properly *ensemble) fantasia is represented chiefly by the English *fancy of the 17th century. The meaning of the term in publications such as A. Willaert, *Fantasie et Ricercari* ... (1549; also 1559) and G. Tiburtino, *Fantasie e Recercari a 3 voci* (1549) is not clear, since the contents of these books do not show any differentiation such as might be expected from the title [see *Ricercare I (a)]. H. Expert edited 6 vols. of *Fanta-

sies pour 3 et 4 instruments by Claude Lejeune and Eustache Caurroy (around 1600).

Lit.: O. Deffner, *Über die Entwicklung der Fantasie für Tasteninstrumente bis Sweelinck* (1927); E. H. Meyer, *Die mehrstimmige Spielmusik des 17. Jahrhunderts* (1934); P. Hamburger, "Die Fantasien in Emanuel Adriansen's Pratum Musicum, 1600" (*ZMW* xii). See also under *Fancy.

Fantasia section. Same as development section in *sonata-form.

Fantasiestück [G.]. See *Fantasia (2).

Fantastic Symphony. See *Symphonie phantastique.

Fantasy. (1) See *Fantasia; *Fancy. — (2) The development section (fantasy section) in *sonata-form.

Farandole. A Provençal dance which is performed in a long chain of men and women, holding each other by the hands and following the leader through a great variety of evolutions, to music played on the *pipe and tabor. The dance seems to be of very ancient origin (symbolic celebration of Theseus' escape from the labyrinth ?) and is still danced today, usually under the name of polonaise. For similar dances see *Branle and *Cotillon. The music of the farandole is usually in moderate ⁶/₈ meter. The dance has been introduced into opera by Bizet (*L'Arlesienne*) and by Gounod (*Mireille*). Cf. G. Beaucaire, in *RMC* v.

Farbenklavier [G.]. *Color organ.

Farce, farse [It. *farza*; from L. *farsa, farcitura*, stuffing, filling]. (1) Originally designation for interpolations, chiefly the liturgical tropes which appear as insertions between two words of the authentic text, for instance, the farced Kyrie: Kyrie — fons bonitatis — eleison [see *Trope (4)]. For another example of farcing see *Enté. — (2) In plays and operas, chiefly of the 18th century, farcing means the introduction of alien elements, usually of a humorous, comical, or even lascivious nature [see *Intermezzo]. This meaning persists in present-day usage in which farce is a light comedy, sometimes vulgar, frequently a travesty of a serious model. Around 1800, Italian comic operas in one act were called *farza*, e.g., Rossini's *La Cambiale di matrimonio* (1810).

Farewell Symphony [G. *Abschieds-symphonie*]. Haydn's Symphony in F-sharp minor, composed in 1772 (no. 45 of the B.u.H. edition; cf. *GD* ii, 586). The name refers to the last movement, the close of which is so designed that the players can leave one by one, the last measures being played by only two violinists. The charming jest was meant to convey to the Prince of Esterhazy, whom Haydn served as a conductor, the desire of the orchestra to leave for Vienna.

Fasola. A system of *solmization, much used in England and in America during the 17th and 18th centuries, in which only four of the six Guidonian syllables are used, the syllables fa sol la being applied to c–d–e as well as to the identical pro-

gression f–g–a, and the mi being used for the seventh degree, b. Prior to 1800 the fasola method was used in certain American song books, the letters F, S, L, F, S, L, M being placed on a staff (e.g., in *The Psalms and Hymns . . .* , 1737). In 1802 William Little (*The Easy Instructor*) introduced four different shapes of notes for each of the syllables, a method which was known as "buckwheat" or "four-shape" or "shape" note [see Ex.], and which proved very successful in the rural districts of the South.

Lit.: G. P. Jackson, "Buckwheat Notes" (*MQ* xix); Ch. Seeger, "Contrapuntal Style in the Three-voice Shape-note Hymns" (*MQ* xxvi); K. P. Fuller, in *Etude* lvii, 501; *WoHN* ii, 369.

Fassung, Mit [G.]. Calm, resigned.

Fastoso [It.]. Pompous.

Fausse relation [F.]. *False relation [see *Cross relation].

Fauxbourdon [F.; Middle English, *faburden*; It. *falso bordone*; Sp. *fabordone*]. (1) A 15th-century term which has been adopted into modern usage as a general denomination for harmonic progressions based on parallel sixth chords. [In scholarly writings a designation such as "sixth-chord style" would seem to be preferable, with the term fauxbourdon being restricted to its original and proper meaning; see (2).]

Such progressions occur in Bach, Mozart, Beethoven (Piano Sonata op. 2, no. 3, last movement), Brahms, and others [see Ex. 1, from Bach's Cantata *Ach wie*

flüchtig]. Sixth-chord style plays, however, a much more important role in the music of the late Middle Ages (*c.* 1300–1450). All evidence points to an English origin of this style. In fact, the earliest instances are found in English MSS of *c.* 1300, that is, of the period when French music was based chiefly on the principle of contrary motion in the "perfect" consonances (octave, fifth, fourth). For examples cf. *ReMMA*, 399; *HAM*, no. 57; A. Hughes, †*Worcester Mediaeval Harmony* (1928). Short progressions in sixth chords are quite frequent in the works of Landini [cf., e.g., *RiHM* i.2, 330], especially for cadences [see *Landini cadence]. The sixth-chord style reached its high-point in the compositions of Dufay and Binchois [see *Burgundian School] which frequently include long phrases and even entire sections in sixth-chord harmonies [Ex. 2; cf. *HAM*, nos. 65ff; *SchGMB*, nos. 39, 40; *AdHM* i, 299].

The introduction of sixth-chord style constitutes an important landmark in the evolution of harmony, since it is the first step towards the emergence of the third and the full triad as the basic element of harmony [see *Harmony]. Sixth-chord style proper dropped out largely around 1475 when Ockeghem and Obrecht established four-part writing [see *Flemish School]. Traces, however, survived under the name *falso bordone* throughout the 16th and 17th centuries [see (4)]. It will be noticed that the above description clearly refutes the theory advanced by H. E. Wooldridge (*OH* ii, 89ff) and adopted in numerous books, according to which "fauxbourdon" originated as a result of a decree of Pope John XXII, issued from Avignon in 1322, by which the use in the service of elaborate polyphonic music was forbidden. See also *Gymel.

(2) Historically and properly, fauxbourdon is the designation for a French (Burgundian) 15th-century technique of composition in which a soprano part (usually a plainsong hymn transposed to the higher octave) is notated together with a lower part (contra) moving along in the lower sixth or octave, while the middle part is extemporized by a singer doubling the melody in the lower fourth throughout [see Ex. 3, from Dufay's *Juvenis qui*

3

Càntus Fàulxbourdon.   Contratenor.

Quia ipsa coniunx

puellam; cf. *WoGM* ii, 57ff and iii, 87; in the similar section *Quamvis benedixeritis* (ii, 59) the tenor part is erroneously omitted in Wolf]. The term fauxbourdon (i.e., false bass) is explained by the use in the lowest part of a "false," i.e., a derivative melody, instead of the cantus firmus itself, as was the earlier tradition. The first mention of the term occurs in Burgundian-Italian sources from *c.* 1430.

This French method should not be confused with an English method described as *discant* in various 15th-century treatises (Lionel Power, *c.* 1425, Pseudo-Chilston,

c. 1450) and referred to in modern writings (Bukofzer) as *English discant,* in order to distinguish it from the (French) 13th-century discant in contrary motion and perfect consonances [see *Discant]. Here only one part, the tenor, is notated, and the other two singers improvise melodies resulting in sixth chords with occasional open triads (1–5–8). The principle may be explained as follows: the tenor sings the plainsong as written, e.g.: d–e–f–g–f–e–d; the other singers derive from this a slightly modified melody, by replacing each tone, except the first and the last, by its lower third, as follows: d–c–d–e–d–c–d; this modified melody is sung by the highest voice (treble) an octave higher, by the middle voice (*meane) a fifth higher. The result is sixth-chord harmony with the cantus firmus in the lowest part [Ex. 4]. This method was known under

4

such names as *discantus supra librum,* *sight* (referring to the two different "sights" — i.e., ways of looking at, or renditions — of the plainsong, one performed by the singer of the meane ["meane-sight"], the other, of the treble ["treble-sight"]), or Latin equivalents such as *discantus visibilis* (visible discant), *fictus visus* (feigned sight), and *perfectio ocularis* (ocular completion). For an occasional practice of five-voice discant see under *Treble.

English discant, i.e., sixth-chord style with the cantus firmus in the tenor (not, as in fauxbourdon, in the soprano), was used in English compositions as early as *c.* 1300 [see under (1)]. As a result of this long-standing method of composition there grew up, probably towards the end of the 14th century, the above-described practice of improvised discant.

(3) The (French) connotation of fauxbourdon persists in English 16th-century organ books (period of John Redford, *c.* 1550) in which "verses on the faburden of the plainsong" denote polyphonic elaborations, not of the original plainsong, but of a derivative melody which is a third above

the plainsong (with occasional unisons). According to the explanations given under (2) these faburdens must be properly explained as being in the lower sixth above the octave-transposed plainsong (with occasional lower octaves). Cf. H. Miller, in *MQ* xxvi.

(4) Fauxbourdon harmonization was frequently applied to the monotonic recitations of psalm tones. One of the early examples is a *Magnificat* by Binchois [cf. J. Marix, †*Les Musiciens de la court de Bourgogne* (1937), p. 196]. After the change from three-voice to four-voice harmony, the name was retained for harmonizations of psalm-tones, Magnificats, etc., in accordance with the fact that four-voice harmonies are frequently fauxbourdon (sixth chords) with a bass tone added below. Four-voice harmonizations of recitation chants, called *falso bordone* [It.] or *fabordone* [Sp.], were particularly frequent in Italy and Spain during the 16th

century [see *Editions XIII]. Cabezon wrote similar settings for the organ [Ex. 5; cf. *ApMZ* ii]. Such harmonized organ verses were used in alternative performance with the plainsong verses [see *Magnificat]. In 16th-century English usage simple harmonizations of metrical psalm tunes were called *faburden*, and Heinrich Schütz, in the preface to his *Historie von der . . . Auferstehung* (1623), speaks of the instrumental accompaniment to the Evangelist's recitations as "falsobordone." The use of falso bordone compositions (particularly Palestrina's *Lamentations) in alternation with Gregorian chant was authorized for special occasions by Pius X in his *Motu proprio* (1903).

(5) In present-day English usage fauxbourdon denotes "a means of giving interest to hymn-singing by supplying the choir sopranos with a freely written part, which often soars above the hymn-tune as sung by the congregation" [cf. P. A.

Scholes, *The Oxford Companion to Music* (1938), p. 305]. This would seem to be one of the various more recent meanings of the term which are the result of a misunderstanding of its proper connotation. A more appropriate name for this method of singing is descant [see *Descant (3)].

Lit.: M. Bukofzer, *Geschichte des englischen Diskants und des Fauxbourdon...* (1936); Th. Georgiades, *Englische Diskanttraktate aus der 1. Hälfte des 15. Jahrhunderts* (1937); *OH* ii, 89ff; M. Bukofzer, in *MQ* xxvi; S. S. Meech, "Three Musical Treatises in English from a 15th-century Manuscript" (*Speculum*, July, 1935).

Feeders. In organ building, small bellows employed to supply the large bellows with wind. See *Organ I.

Fe fa ut, Fefaut. See *Hexachord II.

Feierlich [G.]. In a holy, solemn mood.

Feldtrompeter [G., field trumpeter]. In the 17th century, the military trumpeters as distinguished from the *Kammertrompeter* (chamber trumpeter), who were members of the orchestras [cf. *SaHMI*, 328]. The pieces of the *Feldtrompeter* were called *Feldstücke, Feldsonaten, Feldpartitas*. They usually consisted of fanfares in four-part harmonies. See Lit. under *Fanfare.

Felix namque. Title of 16th-century cantus-firmus compositions for the organ, chiefly English [Redford, Tallis; cf. C. F. Pfatteicher, *John Redford* (1934) and *Fitzwilliam Virginal Book*]. The cantus firmus (a–c'–c'–d'–c'–b–a ...) is not that of the offertorium *Felix namque es* of the Roman ritual (*GR* [95]). See *Innomine.

Fellowships. See *Scholarships, Fellowships, and Prizes.

Feminine cadence. See *Masculine and feminine cadence.

Feria, ferial. Any weekday in the calendar of the Catholic Church on which no feast occurs is called *feria*. This meaning is the reverse of the original meaning of L. *feria*, that is, a festival day. The reversal came about by extending the use of the word from Sunday to the other days, Sunday being named *feria prima*, the others *feria secunda*, *tertia*, etc. Later, Sunday was called *Dominica*, whereas for Saturday the Hebrew name of *Sabbato* was kept. — It should be noted that the adjective ferial (days, rites) is used in a meaning closer to the original, that is, including Sunday, provided there occurs no special feast. The opposite is festal (days, rites), which refers to feasts on weekdays or Sundays.

Fermamente, con fermezza [It.]. Firmly.

Fermata [G., It.]. Pause.

Fernwerk [G.]. Echo organ.

Feroce [It.]. Ferocious.

Fervore, Con [It.]. With fervor.

Fes [G.]. See Pitch names.

Festal. See *Feria, Ferial.

Festivals. I. *England.* The earliest instances of musical festivals are the French *puys* which originated with the troubadours of the 13th century and continued until the 16th century. The *Sängerkriege* of the German *Minnesinger, of which Wagner gives a lively picture in his *Tannhäuser oder der Sängerkrieg auf der Wartburg*, were an imitation. Of similar age are the Eisteddfod of the Welsh *bards. A new development started in England in the 17th century with the *Festival of the Sons of the Clergy* which was founded in 1655 and which still continues, in the form of a musical service on grand lines. There followed, in 1724, the *Three Choirs Festivals* which combine the choral forces of Gloucester, Worcester, and Hereford and which last for several days. Others are the *Birmingham Festival* (1768–1912), the *Norwich Festival* (1770 to date, since 1824 triennially), and the *Leeds Festival* (1858, from 1874 triennially), all of which are held for the benefit of local charitable institutions. The *Handel Festivals* in the Crystal Palace began in 1857 and are now held triennially.

II. *America.* The earliest American festivals on record are those of the Handel and Haydn Society of Boston (1857) and at Worcester (1858). In 1869 P. S. Gilmore organized his monster festival *Peace Jubilee* as a celebration of the conclusion of the Civil War, employing an orchestra of 1000 and a chorus of 10,000. In his *World's Peace Jubilee* of 1872 he doubled these forces and added electrically fired cannons, chimes, and powerful organs. The *Worcester Festivals* (present conductor Arthur Stoessel) became an established annual institution in 1869, and Cincinnati followed with its biennial *May Music Festival* in 1871 (founded by Th. Thomas; present conductor Eugene Goossens). The *Ann Arbor May Festivals* of the University of Michigan were founded in 1879 (Dr. Stanley till 1921, succeeded by Earl V. Moore). At Bethlehem College in Lindsborg, Kansas, annual performances of *The Messiah* were begun in 1882 and have developed into a festival week. The *Bethlehem Bach Choir* of Bethlehem, Pa. (preceded by the *Bethlehem Choral Union*, 1882) was founded in 1900 and has given numerous festivals, each including a performance of Bach's B Minor Mass. There followed festivals in Portland, Me. (1897), Bangor, Me. (1897), Springfield, Mass. (1903), and Norfolk, Conn. (1906). At Northwestern University festivals were established in 1909 and, after a lapse in 1932, were revived in 1937 as the *Evanston Music Festivals* (Edwin S. Mills). In the same year (1909) began the *Spring Festivals of Cornell University*, founded by Hollis Dann, now held at irregular intervals (Paul J. Weaver). Next in chronological order are the festivals of Peterboro, N. H. (1910), Lockport, N. Y. (1916). Outstanding among the more recent developments are: the *Berkshire Festivals of Chambermusic* at Pittsfield, Mass. (established 1918 by Mrs. Elizabeth Sprague Coolidge, held irregularly after 1924; numerous first presentations of chamber music works); the *Westchester Music Festival* (1925, now held at White Plains, N. Y., under Hugh Ross); the *Coolidge Festivals* (established 1925 at the Library of Congress by Mrs.

Elizabeth Sprague Coolidge; eight festivals to the present day); the *Rochester Festival of American Music* (1931, directed by Howard Hanson); the *Westminster Festival* at Princeton, N. J. (1936; programs of American music); the *Berkshire Symphonic Festivals* at Stockbridge, Mass. (founded by Henry K. Hadley in 1934, since 1936 in connection with the Boston Symphony Orchestra under S. Koussevitzky, now held in a permanent structure at Tanglewood); and the *Silvermine Guild of Artists Festival* at Silvermine, Conn. (1937).

For detailed information on these and other festivals see Pierre Key's *Music Year Book*.

III. *Other Countries.* Outside of the United States and England music festivals are found mainly in Germany and Austria. Among these the *Niederrheinische Musikfeste* (founded 1817; held alternately in Cologne, Düsseldorf, and Aachen) come closest in character to the American or English choral festivals. More important from the artistic point of view were the *Tonkünstlerfeste* of the *Allgemeiner deutscher Musikverein*, founded by F. Liszt in 1861, and held annually in different cities, the last (1932) in Zurich. Celebrations of great German composers are frequently held in their native cities, e.g., the *Beethovenfeste* in Bonn, the *Bachfeste* in Eisenach, the *Mozartfeste* in Salzburg, Austria. Most famous among these are the *Bayreuther Festspiele*, dedicated to the cause of Wagner's operas. The *Kammermusikfeste* at Donaueschingen, founded 1923, have been very important in the development of modern music [see *Gebrauchsmusik*]. Similar in purpose are the festivals of the *International Society for Contemporary Music* (president, Edwin Evans) dating from 1923 which have been held in successive years at Salzburg, Prague, Venice, Zurich, Frankfurt a.M., Siena, Geneva, Liège, Oxford, Vienna, Amsterdam, Florence, Prague, Barcelona, Paris, London, Warsaw (1939), New York (1941), and San Francisco (1942). Complete programs of these festivals (from 1923 to 1937) are given in Slonimsky's *Music Since 1900* (1937).

Festschrift [G.]. Name of German publications designed as a present for outstanding musicologists (60th birthday, etc.). They contain contributions from pupils and colleagues. Cf. *MoML*, 218.

Festspiel [G.]. See *Festival III; also *Bühnenfestspiel.

Feurig [G.]. Fiery.

Ff. Abbreviation for fortissimo.

F fa ut. See *Hexachord II.

F-holes. See *Sound-holes.

Fiato [It.]. Breath. *Stromenti da fiato,* wind instruments.

Fiddle. Colloquial for violin and the like, particularly the American homemade varieties. Also used to designate the primitive ancestors of the violin, as found in many Oriental cultures. See *Violin (history).

Fidelio (or *Die Eheliche Liebe,* "Conjugal Love"). Opera by Beethoven (1770–1827), text by J. Sonnleithner and G. F. Treitschke, produced 1805 (revised 1806 under the name *Leonore*; final revision 1814). The scene is 18th-century Spain in a prison near Sevilla where the nobleman *Florestan* (Tenor) is held captive by the tyrannic *Pizarro* (Baritone). Florestan's wife *Leonore* (Soprano), disguised as a boy and under the name of *Fidelio,* enters the service of the jailer *Rocco* (Bass) and, in the second act, helps him to dig a grave for Florestan whom Pizarro is determined to kill. In the last moment trumpet calls are heard heralding the arrival of the minister *Don Fernando* (Bass), who frees Florestan and arrests Pizarro.

In spite of moments of great emotional tension (grave-digging scene, trumpet calls) the opera lacks, on the whole, that dramatic flow which Beethoven, more than any other composer, commanded in his symphonies and other instrumental works. His note to Treitschke: "The whole business of opera is the most distressing thing in the world" very likely reflects his inner relation to opera-writing as well as the adverse circumstances which accompanied the production of Fidelio. Nevertheless, the music shows Beethoven's hand in many scenes, and the opera, though not "Beethoven at his best," certainly belongs to the classical operatic repertoire. Regarding the various overtures, see *Leonora Overtures. See also reference under *Melodrama.

Fidicen [L., from *fides*, stringed instrument]. Humanistic (16th-century) name for a string player.

Fiedel [G.]. (1) Colloquial for violin and the like. — (2) Generic term for medieval violin-instruments (*vielle*, *fidula*) and modern imitations thereof.

Fiero [It.]. Proud.

Fife. A small flute with six to eight finger-holes and usually no key, used chiefly in military bands. It has been replaced in the Drum Corps by the piccolo.

Fifteenth. Name for organ stops sounding two octaves (fifteen notes) above normal. Hence, 2-foot stops.

Fifth. The fifth degree of the diatonic scale, or the interval formed by a tone and the fifth tone above it. See *Intervals; *Consonance; *Circle of fifths; *Triad; *Parallel motion; *Organum; *Blasquinte.

Fifre [F.]. *Fife.

Figaro's Marriage. See *Nozze di Figaro, Le.

Figura [L.]. In medieval theory, generic name for the notational signs. Franco (*CS* i, 119) distinguishes the *figurae simplices*, i.e., the single notes (*longa*, *brevis*, *semibrevis*), from the *figurae compositae*, i.e., the ligatures. *Figura obliqua* means the oblique form of *ligatures.

Figural, figurate, figured [G. *figuriert*]. The terms are rather indiscriminately used in two different, though related, meanings. (1) As a translation of L. *musica figurata*, a 15th- and 16th-century term for any polyphonic music, in contradistinction to *musica plana*, i.e., plainsong. In particular, the term figural

music or style [G. *Figuralmusik*, *figurierter Stil*] is used with reference to the highly florid polyphonic style of the early Flemish composers such as Ockeghem and Obrecht, as distinguished from the less complex style of Josquin and his successors [see *Musica reservata]. — (2) With reference to 17th- and 18th-century music the terms denote the use of stereotyped figures or *motives, particularly in variations or in the accompanying parts of organ chorales [see *Figuration; *Figured chorale]. The ambiguous and inconsistent use of these terms is to be deplored, particularly since the term "figured" is used with still another meaning in the designation: *figured bass. Tentatively the following distinctions may be recommended: Figurate = florid [see Webster]; figural = using musical figures [see under *Motive]; figured = provided with numerals. Hence: figurate melody; figural variation or chorale; figured bass. See the subsequent articles.

Figuration. The use of stereotyped figures, particularly in variations of a theme. See *Figural (2); *Variations III [Ex. var. 1].

Figure. See under *Motive.

Figured bass. A bass-part provided with figures (numerals) to indicate harmonies [see *Thorough-bass].

Figured chorale [G. *Figurierter Choral*]. A species of *organ chorale (chorale prelude) in which a certain *figure — i.e., a short and characteristic group of notes — is used consistently in one or several of the contrapuntal parts, against the plain notes of the chorale which usually occurs in the soprano. Most of the chorales in Bach's *Orgelbüchlein* belong to this class (e.g., nos. 2, 10, 12, 13, 17, 20, 24, 25, etc.). No. 24 (Ich ruf zu Dir) is an especially good example. A more appropriate denomination would be "figural chorale" [see *Figural, figurate, figured].

Figured melody. Same as ornamented or florid melody. A more appropriate denomination would be "figurate melody" [see *Figural, figurate, figured].

Filar il tuono [It.], **filer le son** [F., "to spin the tone"]. An 18th-century term, properly synonymous with *messa di voce*. Modern writers and singers frequently use it in a different meaning, i.e., as calling for sustained notes without the crescendo and decrescendo implied by *messa di voce*.

Film music. The interested reader is referred to the description (and criticism) in A. Copland, *Our New Music* (1941). Cf. also C. Austin, in *ML* v, no. 2; E. Irving, in *ML* xxiv, no. 4.

Final, finalis. See *Church modes I.

Finale [It.]. (1) The last movement of a sonata or any of the cognate forms, symphony, quartet, etc. In the classical sonata it is usually a quick movement either in *rondo-form or in *sonata-form; occasionally it is written as a slow theme with variations (Beethoven, Piano Sonata op. 111; Brahms, Clarinet Quintet op. 115). While Haydn and Mozart planned their finale as a "happy end," Beethoven frequently bestowed upon it a character of final triumph and apotheosis. In this respect, Bruckner followed and even surpassed him. — (2) The last piece of an operatic act. The operatic finales are usually of greater length and elaboration than the other pieces (arias), since a good deal of the dramatic action is likely to take place at the end of an act. They frequently include various sections of contrasting character [cf. the finales in Mozart's *Figaro*]. Alessandro Scarlatti is considered the originator of the dramatic finale. Nicola Piccinni (1728–1800) introduced the sectional construction, including change of tempo, of key, etc.

Lit.: M. Fuchs, *Die Entwicklung des Finales in der opera buffa vor Mozart* (Diss. Vienna 1932); A. O. Lorenz, "Das Finale in Mozart's Meisteropern" (*DM* xix.9); E. J. Dent, "Ensembles and Finales in 18th-Century Italian Opera" (*StM* xi, xii).

Fin' al segno [It.]. "As far as the sign," indicating repetition from the beginning to the sign §.

Fine [It.]. End, close.

Finger board. In stringed instruments a long strip of hard wood (black ebony) fixed to the neck, over which the strings are stretched. The finger boards of older instruments such as the lute, guitar, viola da gamba, lyra, etc., were provided with *frets.

Fingerfertigkeit [G.]. Agility of the fingers, virtuosity.

Fingering [F. *doigté*; G. *Fingersatz, Applicatur* (obs.)]. The methodical use of the fingers in the playing of instruments. More than any other instrument, the pianoforte has what might be called a "natural system of fingering," owing to the natural conformity which exists between the arrangement of the fingers and that of the keys. Three chief types of fingering may be distinguished: (1) Normal fingering. This applies to passages involving no more than five keys, e.g., $\frac{c\ e\ g\ d\ f\ e\ c}{1\ 3\ 5\ 2\ 4\ 3\ 1}$; (2) contracted or expanded fingering, e.g., $\frac{g'\ g\ a\ b\ c'\ a\ f\ g\ c}{5\ 1\ 3\ 4\ 5\ 4\ 2\ 3\ 1}$. This fingering usually leads to a "shift of position," that is, the thumb does not return to its original key. It is very frequent in extended passages of "zigzag" design (bent figures) which have no more than five tones in either direction (e.g., in the first etude of Chopin); (3) passing fingering, i.e., the thumb passes under a finger (second, third, fourth) or any of these fingers pass over the thumb. This fingering must be used whenever there are more than five tones in the same direction, hence, particularly in scales.

The modern principles of fingering are of a rather recent date, their definite establishment by Clementi (1752–1832) being practically simultaneous with the replacement of the harpsichord and clavichord by the pianoforte. The earlier fingering is distinguished from the modern method chiefly by the very sparing use of the thumb and of the fifth finger in scale passages. Throughout the 16th and 17th centuries, scales were played with a fingering such as: $\begin{smallmatrix} c\ d\ e\ f\ g\ a\ b\ a\ g\ f\ e\ d\ c \\ 2\ 3\ 2\ 3\ 2\ 3\ 4\ 3\ 2\ 3\ 2\ 3\ 2 \end{smallmatrix}$ [see Ex.; also the article in *GD* ii, 236 and

Weitzmann-Seifert, *Geschichte der Klaviermusik* (1899), pp. 11, 13, 70, 82, 84, 160, etc.]. This method of passing one finger over the other, which from the modern point of view appears the extreme of clumsiness, was considerably less awkward on the old instruments whose keys had a smaller "fall" than those of the pianoforte and required much less force of touch. Particularly on the clavichord, passages sound more even if played without the thumb. The normal position of the hand was with the middle fingers lying almost flat on the keys, and with the thumb hanging down in front of the keyboard. On the other hand, it is entirely possible that great virtuosos such as John Bull, Sweelinck, and Scheidt used a more advanced method of fingering which they kept secret. The modern fingering for the descending scale (54321321) occurs in the keyboard works of Al. Scarlatti with each finger represented by a special symbol, *, /, etc. (cf. the modern edition by Shedlock). J. S. Bach was one of the first to make systematic use of the thumb and to develop more considered methods of fingering [cf. his *Klavierbüchlein für Friedemann Bach*, new ed. by H. Keller (1927), pp. 15 and 23]. He played with curved fingers and brought the thumb to the surface of the keyboard. An interesting document is Johann Kirnberger's *Klavierübungen nach der Bach'schen Applikatur* (1762–64). Another step towards modern fingering was made by Bach's son C. P. E. Bach [cf. his *Versuch über die wahre Art das Klavier zu spielen*, new ed. by Niemann (1906)]. The next in line was Clementi.

Until recently, English musicians used an older method of numbering the fingers, known as English fingering: x 1 2 3 4, i.e., with a cross for the thumb and with 1 for the index finger (as in violin playing). This is now almost completely abandoned for the "German fingering" 1 2 3 4 5. It is curious to note that the "English system" was widely used in Germany as well as in other countries during the 18th century and that, on the other hand, the first record of the "German fingering" occurs in English virginal books (*c.* 1600). Purcell used the English fingering, but in reversed order for the left hand, i.e., with the x for the fifth finger. For the system of fingering utilized for stringed instruments, see *Positions. Cf. H. Gleason, "Organ Instruction before Bach" (*BAMS* iv).

Finlandia. See *Symphonic poem II.

Finnish music. Finland possesses a large wealth of folk songs, ancient and modern. The earliest, called *joiku*, are recitative-like in character. Next follow the *runos* (sung to the traditional poems of epic character, called "runes"), which are melodic and rhythmically vigorous, frequently employing a characteristic $\frac{5}{4}$-measure. The most famous of these epic poems is the *Kalevala* which has been used by numerous Finnish composers as a basis for songs or for symphonic poems (Sibelius). The latest manifestation of Finnish folk music consists of modern folk songs which, in spite of their relatively recent origin, have retained certain ancient features, particularly in their use of modal progressions. The traditional Finnish folk instrument is the *kantele*, a *psaltery in the form of the wing of a bird, originally with 5, today with 20 to 30 strings.

The development of Finnish art music started around 1850 with the activity of German musicians, e.g., Friedrich Pacius (1809–91; born in Hamburg; professor of music at Helsingfors University from 1834; composer of the opera *Kung Karls jakt*, 1852, and of the Finnish *national anthem *Maamme*) and Richard Faltin (1835–1918; professor at Helsingfors Conservatory, 1871–96; compiler of a collection of Finnish folk songs). The first native-born composer was Martin Wegelius

(1846–1906), who became director of the new Helsingfors Conservatory in 1882 and who wrote a number of theoretical books (in Swedish). Robert Kajanus (1856–1933) cultivated Finnish folk music in his symphonic poems *Aino* and *Kullervo*, but it was Jean Sibelius (b. 1865) who established the national Finnish style and who made Finnish music an important factor of international musical life. His symphonic poems (*Finlandia*, 1899; *Pohjola's Daughter*, 1906; *Tapiola*, 1925, etc.; see Symphonic poem IV) and his seven symphonies have become standard works of the orchestras, particularly in America and in England. Modern composers of lesser importance and fame are: A. Järnevelt (b. 1869; symphonic poems *Korsholma*, *Luvattu Maa*; choral works *Laula vuoksella*, *Suomen synty*, etc.); Erkki Melartin (1875–1937; opera *Aino*; symphonies, symphonic poems, etc.); Selim Palmgren (b. 1878; opera *Daniel Hjort*; piano concertos "The River" and "Metamorphoses"; numerous lyrical piano pieces); Leevi Madetoja (b. 1887; symphonies, numerous symphonic poems; opera *Pohjalaisia*); Armas Launis (b. 1884; operas, orchestral and piano music; also scholar and writer; see Lit.). Representatives of the youngest generation, somewhat influenced by the trends of *New music, are Yrjö Kilpinen (b. 1892; songs), Aarre Merikanto (b. 1893; much symphonic and chamber music), and Väinö Raitio (b. 1891; ten symphonic poems, two operas, some chamber music).

Lit.: A. Launis, *Ueber Art, Entstehung und Verbreitung der estnisch-finnischen Runenmelodien* (1910); I. Krohn, *Geistliche Volksmelodien in Finland* (1899); *AdHM* ii, 1122ff; *LavE* i.5, 2586ff; K. Flodin, "Entwicklung der Musik in Finland" (*DM*, 1903/04); F. Bose, "Typen der Volksmusik in Karelien" (*AMF* iii); J. H. Kruisinga, "La Mélodie populaire des Finnois" (*Revue Musicale Belge* xv); H. Pudor, in *SIM* ii.

Fioritura [It., from *fiore*, flower]. Embellishment, either written out or improvised. See *Ornamentation.

Fipple flute. Same as *Whistle flute.

Firebird, The (L'Oiseau de Feu). See *Ballet III.

Fireworks. See *Symphonic poem IV.

First-movement form. Same as *sonata-form. The term is unfortunately chosen, since the same form also occurs frequently in the slow and in the final movement of a sonata.

Fis, fisis [G.]. See *Pitch names.

Fistelstimme [G.]. *Falsetto.

Fistula [L.]. Medieval name for flute, organ pipe (*fistula organica*). *Fistula punis*, *panpipe.

Fitzwilliam Virginal Book. See *Virginal book.

Five, The. Designation for a group of five Russian composers who, around 1875, united their efforts toward the creation of a truly national school of Russian music. The group included: Cesar A. Cui (1835–1918), Alexander P. Borodin (1833–87), Mily A. Balakirev (1837–1910), Modest P. Moussorgsky (1839–81), and Nicolas A. Rimsky-Korsakov (1844–1908). See *Russian music II.

Five-three chord. The common *triad, so called because, in figured bass, it is indicated by the figures $\frac{5}{3}$ (third and fifth) above the root.

Fixed-do(h). See under *Movable-do(h).

Flagellant songs. See *Geisslerlieder.

Flageolet. See under *Whistle flutes. Flageolet tones, see *Flageolett-töne.

Flageolett-töne. German term for the *harmonics of stringed instruments. The English term flageolet tones is rarely used.

Flam. See under *Percussion instruments B, 1 (Side drum).

Flamenco. The "gypsy" style of Spanish dance and dance music. It is this style, characterized by fanciful and colored costumes, alluring and pointedly erotic movements, stamping of the feet (*zapateado*), and clapping of the hands (*palmada*), which is commonly thought to be "typically Spanish." Truly Spanish dancing, however, is of an entirely different character, darkly glowing rather than brilliant, silent rather than noisy, introvert rather than extrovert in its expression of passion and love. The gypsy style is supposed to have originated in the early 19th century from the *cante hondo* or *jondo* ("deep song") of Andalusia, a highly emotional and tragic type of song, probably influenced by the Sephardic Jews and cultivated particularly among prisoners (*carcelera*), many of whom were gypsies. In the middle of the century it was taken up by the educated people, as was the case with jazz. The meaning of the name "flamenco" (Flemish? flamingo-colored?) is obscure. Cf. *LavE* i.4, 2391; D. Duff, in *MM* xvii, no. 4; M. de Falla, in *LRM* xi.

Flat [F. *bémol*; G. *Be*; It. *bemolle*]. The sign ♭ which indicates the lowering of the pitch of a note by a half-step. See *Accidentals; *Pitch names. The term is also used to indicate incorrect intonation on the under side.

Flatté, flattement. In French 17th-century viol music an agrément equivalent to the pincé of the clavecinistes [see *Mordent]. After the middle of the 18th century the term is occasionally applied to the *Schleifer* [see *Appoggiatura, double], probably due to a mistaken translation.

Flatterzunge [G.]. Flutter tonguing [see *Tonguing].

Flautando, flautato. See *Bowing (1).

Flautino [It.]. A small flute, either the flageolet or the descant flute.

Flauto [It.]. Flute. *Flauto a becco, flauto diritto, flauto dolce, *recorder; flauto d'amore*, see *Flute II (b); *flautone*, alto flute or bass flute; *flauto piccolo*, piccolo (flute). Until the middle of the 18th century, e.g., in Bach, *flauto* always means the recorder, the flute being called *flauto*

traverso [see *Flute III]. In the same period, *flauto piccolo* means, not the transverse piccolo, but a small recorder [see *Recorder].

Flaviol. A small Spanish one-handed flute, used for dance music. See *Pipe and tabor.

Flebile [It.]. Mournful.

Flehend [G.]. Imploring.

Flemish School. I. The leading school (or schools) of the *Renaissance, c. 1450–1600, following the *Burgundian School. The name Flemish, which has by now been fairly universally adopted instead of the earlier name Netherlandish [regarding the ramifications of these names, see *Netherlands Schools], expresses the fact that practically all the numerous members of this school came from Flanders, i.e., the southern part of the present Belgium (Antwerp, Brussels), and the adjoining section of northern France (Cambrai, Arras, Lille). Nonetheless, the Flemish School is not a national school in the narrower sense of the word — as was, for instance, the French or the Italian *Ars nova — but an international movement of great dimensions. This characteristic trait is due to the fact that the Flemish composers seldom stayed in their home country, but emigrated to other countries where they held high positions in church choirs and in the chapels of princes. In the first half of the 16th century their stimulating influence brought about the rise of national talents in France, Germany, Italy, England, and Spain. The second half of the 16th century presents a unique picture of artistic rivalry and co-operation between the Flemish teachers and their "foreign" pupils.

II. The origin of the Flemish School is still veiled in obscurity. Early musicians of Flemish extraction such as Willem Malbeke (fl. *c.* 1430) and Heyne van Gizeghem (fl. *c.* 1450) would seem to belong to the late Burgundian School. The obvious surmise that the Flemish music developed from the Burgundian School has little weight, considering the sharp cleavage between the style of Dufay and that of Ockeghem and Obrecht [see below]. More likely there was a line of development leading from Dunstable (via Reginald Liebert ?) to the early Flemish.

Following is a list of the most important Flemish composers, arranged according to generations:

1425: Johannes Ockeghem (1430–95); Jacob Obrecht (1430–1505).
1450: Gaspar van Werbecke (c. 1440–after 1514); Hendrik Isaac (1450–1517); Josquin des Près (1450–1521); Pierre de la Rue (c. 1460–1518).
1475: Jean Mouton (1470–1522); Adriaen Willaert (c. 1485–1562); Nikolaus Gombert (?–c. 1560).
1500: Jachet de Mantua; Jachet Berchem; Jachet (Jacques) Buus; Jacob (Jachet) Arcadelt (c. 1505–after 1557); Clemens non Papa (c. 1510–after 1557); Thomas Craquillon (?–after 1557). (The chronology and, consequently, the arrangement in this generation and in the preceding one are open to doubt.)
1525: Cypriano de Rore (1516–65); Philipp de Monte (1521–1603); Jacobus Kerle (1531–91); Orlando di Lasso (1532–94); Jacques Wert (1536–96).
1550: Jacobus Regnart (1540–99); Charles Luython (1556–1620); Gio. de Macque (c. 1550–).

The great contribution of the Flemish masters is the establishment of a new polyphonic style characterized by the (ideal) equivalence of all the parts and, beginning with Josquin, the consistent use of imitation as the chief means to achieve this equivalence. This tendency appears even in those compositions in which a cantus firmus stands apart from and in balance to the contrapuntal web of the other voices (tenor masses and motets of the 15th century). Masses and motets are the backbone of the vast repertory of Flemish composers; to these were gradually added the various "national" types of secular music, the (French) *chanson, the (Italian) *madrigal, the (German) *Lied, and finally the many popular forms of *villa-

nella, the *canzonetto, the *balletto, etc., which indicate the approaching decadence.

III. Following is a brief account of the development within this general frame: The contrast between the Burgundian School (Dufay) and the first Flemish masters (Ockeghem, Obrecht) can be briefly characterized as the change from three-part writing to four-part writing; from a relatively high range to a considerably lower range (first appearance of the bass); from a medieval timbre (*Sound-ideal) of "instrumental transparence" to a full vocal sonority, probably a-cappella; from *fauxbourdon to the full triad; from a (decorated) chordal style, frequently of the melody-accompaniment type, to a truly polyphonic style with highly embroidered lines in all the parts; from aristocratic subtleness and refinement to pious devotion and mystic expression.

Although Ockeghem and Obrecht are usually named in one breath (as "musical twins," like the "two Gabrieli," or "Schubert and Schumann"), the difference between their styles is considerable. Of the two, Ockeghem is by far more purely Flemish and presents a much stronger contrast to Dufay than Obrecht, who frequently introduces chordal passages, full cadences, and sectional treatment. In fact, these two streams can be traced throughout the entire development of Flemish music: the former (strictly polyphonic, continuous, non-cadential, uniform sonority) being represented by the names Ockeghem, Isaac, La Rue (?), Gombert, de Monte, Palestrina; the latter (partly chordal, sectional, cadential, using contrasting sonorities) by Obrecht, Josquin, Willaert, G. Gabrieli [regarding the appearance of chordal style in Flemish music, see *Familiar style]. Although the Flemish composers occasionally made use in their Masses of proportional complications and of canonic riddles [see *Proportions; *Canon], an entirely misleading impression has been created by numerous writers who have made this feature the main point of their characterization. Up to the present day, books have been published in which Ockeghem is represented only by his 36-voiced canon or his *Missa* *cujusvis toni* [see *Catholica], and Josquin by his early canonic *Missa l'homme armé*. In this connection it may be noted that English composers of the mid-15th century far surpassed their Flemish colleagues in the devising of canonic enigmas [see *English music III] and that the proportional complications in the works of Ockeghem, Isaac, Josquin, are only a modest remainder of those encountered in the French music between Machaut and Dufay [cf. *ApNPM*, "Mannered Notation"]. See also *Imitation; *Mass; *Motet; *Musica reservata.

Lit.: P. Lang, "The So-called Netherland Schools" (*MQ* xxv); H. Besseler, "Von Dufay bis Josquin" (*ZMW* xi); see also *Belgian music.

Flexa. (1) See *Psalm tones. — (2) Same as *clivis (also *flexus*).

Flick-kanzone [G., "patchwork"-canzona]. A term introduced by H. Riemann for a special type of canzona [see *Canzona (5), II] which shows a particularly quick change of extremely short sections in contrasting characters and styles. An example of this relatively rare type is a canzona by Hermann Schein [cf. the complete ed. by Prüfer, vol. i, 41]. For another example, by G. B. Grillo (1608), cf. *RiHM* ii.2, 127.

Flicorno [It.]. An Italian make of *Flügelhorn.

Fliegende Holländer, Der ("The Flying Dutchman"). Opera by Richard Wagner to his own libretto, produced at Dresden in 1843. The opera centers around the legendary *Flying Dutchman* (Baritone) who is condemned to range the seas eternally unless he can be redeemed by the love of a woman. The destined woman is *Senta* (Soprano), daughter of the Norwegian sea-captain *Daland* (Bass). She deserts the young huntsman *Erik* (Tenor) and follows the Flying Dutchman into death — and final salvation.

The *Fliegende Holländer*, one of Wagner's earliest works, approximates with its supernatural touch the Romantic opera of Weber (*Freischütz*) and Marschner.

The musical style also descends from these precursors, both in the broad melodic style and in the rich and colorful orchestral accompaniment, while typically Wagnerian features, such as the use of *leitmotifs, continuous melody, and symphonic treatment of the orchestra, are not yet developed.

Fliessend [G.]. Flowing.

Flöte [G.]. Flute.

Flötenuhr [G.]. See *Mechanical instruments III.

Florid. The adjective is used as synonymous with ornamented, embroidered, decorated, *figurate, etc., chiefly with reference to contrapuntal music in which the lines move largely in relatively quick notes from one beat to the next. Thus, the works of the early Flemish masters (Ockeghem, Obrecht, Isaac) are said to be in florid style [cf. *HAM*, no. 73; *SchGMB*, nos. 52, 55]. Florid counterpoint specifically denotes the use of ornamented lines in the teaching of counterpoint [see *Counterpoint].

Flos [L., flower]. A 13th-century term for embellishments, somewhat like the trill, mordent, or vibrato. Johannes de Moravia (*CS* i, 92) likens the *flos harmonicus* to the rippled surface of a water moved by a gentle wind.

Flott [G.]. Quick, without hesitation.

Flottant [F.]. Floating.

Flourish. (1) A trumpet call or fanfare. — (2) A decorative passage of a somewhat showy character, frequently one added by the performer.

Flue pipes (stops, work). See *Organ VIII, IX.

Flüchtig [G.]. Fleet, agile.

Flügel [G., wing]. The grand pianoforte, so called because of its wing-shaped form.

Flügelhorn. See *Brass instruments III (b).

Flüssig [G.]. "Fluid," flowing.

Flute. For the general characteristics of the flutes, see under *Wind instruments. I. *Present Forms*. (a) Flute [F. *flûte*; G. *Flöte*; It. *flauto*]. The modern flute is a cylindrical tube with a stopped parabolic head at the upper end. In the head is a side hole (embouchure) across which the player blows, thus setting in vibration the column of air inside the tube. The lowest octave of the fundamental scale is overblown by increased wind pressure, thus providing the second octave of the compass. The remaining part of its three-octave range is produced by further overblowing and by cross fingering. The modern flute was largely developed by Th. Boehm [see *Boehm system] who devised the instrument as described above. It is generally made of silver, though older instruments were of wood, and gold is occasionally used. The timbre varies considerably at different levels, the lowest tones being thick and breathy, the lighter

ones becoming more bright and penetrating. The flute is extremely agile. Most trills and tremolos are possible, and rapid reiterations of a pitch are easy of execution by means of *tonguing. Its range is as shown in Fig. 1, although it appears that some instruments had the low B♭, and the high C♯ and D are occasionally written. (b) The Piccolo [F. *petite flûte*; G. *Kleine Flöte, Pickelflöte*; It. *flauto piccolo* or *ottavino*]. A small flute, pitched an octave above the flute. Its written range is as shown in Fig. 2, sounding an octave higher. It is one of the brightest and most penetrating instruments of the orchestra, and its upper register must be used with care. (c) The Alto Flute [F. *flûte alto*; G. *Altflöte*; It. *flautone*], sometimes called bass flute. An instrument built in G, i.e., a perfect fourth lower than the normal flute, with a range from g to c'''. It is notated as a transposing instrument, a fourth above its actual sound (c' to f'''). (d) The Bass Flute, sometimes

called contrabass flute. An instrument built an octave below the regular flute. A recent construction is the *Albisiphone* (invented by A. Albisi, 1910). The body of this instrument is held vertically, the extension being shortened by means of a double U-tube between the embouchure and the tuning slide. The mouth part is bent horizontally to form the top of a T. The fingering is that of the regular Boehm system. The compass is from B to f''♯. (e) Flutes and piccolos in D are occasionally encountered. These are treated as transposing instruments, having the written range of the regular flute. See also *Giorgi flute.

II. *Obsolete Forms*. (a) The Third flute [G. *Terzflöte*]. So called from being built in E♭, a minor third higher than the standard instrument. (b) Flûte d'amour [It. *Flauto d'amore*; G. *Liebesflöte*]. A flute built a third lower than the regular flute. The alto flute [see I (c)] is sometimes called by this name.

III. *History*. Flutes are among the most ancient and widespread of all instruments. They existed in Sumer, Egypt, and Israel, as well as in Mexico and in South America, where they were frequently made from clay. In Europe, the first evidence of the transverse flute is a miniature in the *Hortus Deliciarum*, an encyclopedia from the end of the 12th century where it is called *swegel* [see *Schwegel]. Throughout the Middle Ages, the Renaissance, and the early Baroque periods the cross flute was mainly a military instrument (fife), associated particularly with Germany, hence the name German flute under which it was generally known. For artistic purposes, the end-blown flute, the *recorder, was preferred. Around 1650 the instrument, which formerly had a cylindrical bore, was provided with a conical bore, a change which procured a much smoother tone. Before 1750 the *flûte traversière* became, for the first time, an important solistic instrument, as is shown by the appearance of Quantz's epochal treatise: *Versuch einer Anweisung die Flöte traversière zu spielen* (1752). It may be noticed that in Bach and Handel the plain name *flauto* still

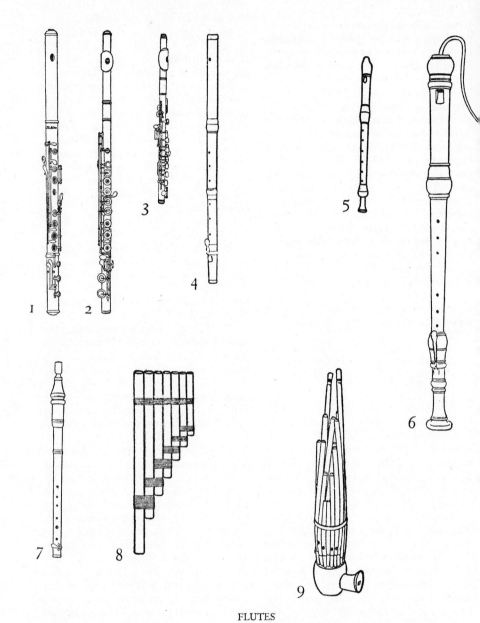

FLUTES

1. Boehm flute, wood. 2. Boehm flute, metal. 3. Boehm flute, piccolo. 4. Flute, 18th century.
5. Recorder. 6. Bass Recorder. 7. Flageolet. 8. Panpipes. 9. Sheng (not a flute).

invariably means the recorder, the cross flute being called *flauto traverso* or *traverso*. Lully was probably the first composer to use the flute in the orchestra, but not until the time of Haydn did the flute become a permanent member thereof. Beginning with *c.* 1800 attempts at improvement were made, caused chiefly by the incorrect position of the side holes which were cut to conform with the reach of the fingers rather than with the laws of acoustics. The final step in this development was the system of Boehm, who also changed the bore back to its former cylindrical shape. This change made the pitch more accurate, but destroyed the sweet timbre of the conical flute. It made the flute a most useful member of the orchestra, but practically useless as a solo instrument.

Lit.: D. C. Miller, *The Flute and Flute Playing* (1922); D. Ehrlich, *The History of the Flute from Ancient Times to Boehm's Invention* (1921); H. M. Fitzgibbon, *Story of the Flute* (1914); C. Welch, *History of the Boehm Flute* (1896); E. Prill, *Führer durch die Flötenliteratur* (1899); L. Fleury, "The Flute and its Powers of Expression" (*ML* iii); T. L. Southgate, "The Evolution of the Flute" (*PMA* xxxiv); *id.*, "Flute Music" (*PMA* xxxvi); D. C. Miller, "Modern Alto, Tenor and Bassflutes" (*PAMS*, 1938); J. Wynn, in *MQ* xv.

Flûte [F.]. Flute. *Flûte traversière, allemande*, cross flute, i.e., flute. *Flûte à bec, flûte douce*, *recorder. *Flûte d'amour*, see *Flute II (b).

Flutter-tonguing. See *Tonguing.

Flying Dutchman, The. See *Fliegende Holländer, Der.

Focoso [It.]. Fiery.

Folia, follia, folies d'Espagne. A famous melody of the 17th century which has been used as a theme for continuous variations [see *Variations II] — similar in form and style to the *chaconne or passacaglia — by a great number of composers, e.g., Michael Farinelli (for violin, 1649;

hence the name "Farinelli's Ground" under which this piece appeared in Playford's *The Division Violin*, 1685); D'Anglebert (for harpsichord, 1689; cf. *TaAM*, vii, 122); Pasquini (for harpsichord; cf. *TaAM* viii, 117 and 125); Alessandro (Domenico?) Scarlatti (for harpsichord; cf. *TaAM* ix, 112); Marin Marais (for viola da gamba; *Pièces de viol* ... 1681); Corelli (for violin; op. 5 no. 12, 1700); F. Liszt (*Rhapsodie Espagnole*, 1863); Rachmaninov (*Variations on a theme by Corelli*, op. 42, 1932). The beginning of d'Angelbert's set is reproduced here.

The tune itself, without variations, already appears in Carlo Milanuzzi's *Scherzi delle ariose vaghezze* (for guitar, 1623), in Caliginoso's *Intavolatura di Chitarra Spagnola* (1629; cf. *WoHN* ii, 183), and elsewhere. It was furthermore quoted frequently in operas, e.g., in J. P. Förtsch's *Die grossmütige Thalestris* (1692), in R. Keiser's *Der lächerliche Prinz Jodelet* (1726, Overture), in Bach's *Peasant Cantata* (1742), in Gretry's *L'Amant Jaloux* (1778), in Cherubini's *L'Hotellerie Portugaise* (1798), etc. Frescobaldi's *Partite sopra la Folia* (1615; cf. *TaAM* iv) are based on a different tune. On the other hand, the famous folia melody is clearly adumbrated in certain early Spanish "pavanas" for lute [Valderravano, *Silva de Sirenas* (1547); Diego Pisador, *Libro de cifra* (1552); see the Ex. under *Barline; also F. Pedrell, *Cancionero popular* ... (1890), iii, 138].

Lit.: P. Nettl, in *ZMW* i; A. Moser, in *AMW* i; H. Riemann, in *DM* x.24; O. Gombosi, in *AM* viii.

Folk song. I. Folk song may be defined as the musical repertory and tradition of communities, as opposed to art music which is the artistic expression of musically trained individuals. It develops anonymously, usually among the "lower classes," together with artless poems dealing with the various phases of daily life: working songs, love songs, cradle songs, drinking songs, patriotic songs, dancing

Barney, I havn't a moment, So don't you hinder me now, For

I'm in haste to the meadow I'm going to milk the cow.

T'aje fat-ta la gon-nel-la An-to-ni-a

a. Te l'a-je fat-ta col-la cre-den-za

Im Krug zum grue-nen Kranze, da kehrt ich

durstig ein, Da sass ein Wan-drer drin nen

Ack, Vär-me land, du skö-ne, du här-li-ga

land du kro-na bland Sve-a-ri-kes lä n-der.

songs, mourning songs, narrative and epic songs, etc. Songs of this kind exist among practically every nation, race, or tribe, and they form, considered as a whole, an

immense wealth of material which is of great interest and importance, particularly from the ethnological point of view. Folk songs of the different nations have certain characteristic features which, although difficult to describe, are clearly felt to represent the general national traits of the people. Our example, showing an American (1), an Italian (2), a German (3), a Swedish (4), and a Hungarian (5) folk song, will be sufficient to demonstrate this point. On the other hand, there exist numerous examples of melodies found among different and widely separated nations which show a striking similarity of melodic or rhythmic design. Certain Hungarian folk songs, for example, have been found to be almost identical with melodies sung in Anatolia, Scotch folk tunes have been said to be similar in some respects to those of Arabia, and Russian gypsy songs are surprisingly close in character to Brazilian melodies. While in many cases such similarity may be merely incidental, it often points to a common origin of such melodies and, in such cases, gives a clue as to the presumable age of the songs, which obviously must be anterior to the period in which the two people migrated into different places. By such methods (which would be applicable in the case of Hungary and Anatolia, but certainly not in the case of Scotland and Arabia or Russia and Brazil) it has been possible to establish scientifically the age of certain folk songs. To mention this point is all the more important since nowhere in musical studies have pure fancy and wishful thinking been given free rein to such a degree as in the study of folk music, where millenniums are treated with unparalleled generosity, and melodies are "believed to date back to pre-Christian eras" which show unmistakable traces of having been invented in the 17th or 18th century [see under *Bards]. Actually, most of the folk melodies of the "civilized" nations are of a relatively recent origin. For instance, practically all the folk songs which are in current use in Germany date from the period around 1800. Those of Italy are still more recent, while the English ones frequently show traits of an earlier origin (16th, 17th centuries).

II. The great majority of folk songs as they exist today belong to what might be termed "civilized folk song," i.e., folk songs which show the influence of art music. That most of our folk songs belong to this class becomes immediately clear if any of them is compared with a truly "aboriginal folk song," such as are found in primitive cultures [see *Primitive music], and occasionally still in secluded regions of the Balkan peninsula, of Finland, of Scotland, etc. Strict meter and measure, clear and regular phrases, well-defined tonality (sometimes with traces of modality), definite form, triadic intervals, etc., are features which have their origin in the rationalized vocabulary of art music and which have, in the course of one or two centuries, sunk down to the lower classes in a characteristic process of seepage [G. *abgesunkenes Kulturgut*]. (An interesting example illustrating the "city influence" on Spanish folk song is given by H. Angles in *AMF* iii, 350.) The discovery of this influence "from above to below" is, of course, in diametrical opposition to the still largely current opinion according to which folk song is the "foundation" of all music, an opinion which is reflected in many books on the history of music in which the traceable history is preceded by an introductory chapter on "Folk song." Such a procedure would have some justification if examples of really primitive folk music were discussed, instead of folk songs which evidently belong to the 17th and 18th centuries.

It is important and interesting to note that the process of seepage has exercised a much more penetrating effect on the texts than on the melodies of folk songs. Numerous texts of folk songs have been shown to be but modified, frequently distorted, versions of art poems. Similar examples are rare, however, as far as the melodies are concerned. Here the influence "from above" is of a more general character, establishing the general framework of style and design only, but admitting original creation within this frame. This observation is important because it shows that music is much closer to the "heart" of the masses than literature or poetry.

Needless to say, in the question of authorship, also, modern scholars take a much more sober view than earlier writers who surrounded the folk song with an aureole of "divine origin," of mystic "self-conception," or of "collective creation." Each folk song is, of course, the product of an individual, and the "collective" point of view is justifiable only in so far as the "original" song has, in the course of decades, centuries, or millenniums, been modified by others.

III. Perhaps the earliest true folk songs traceable in written form are Icelandic songs and the Polish war song *Bogarodicza*, which are preserved in 13th-century MSS [see *Icelandic music; *Polish music]. A famous 15th-century example is *L'homme armé*, and numerous German songs from the same century are preserved [see *Liederbuch]. One of the most beautiful German folk songs of the present day, *Innsbruck ich muss dich lassen*, is a composition by Heinrich Isaac (1450–1517). Particularly interesting is a Hungarian melody preserved in a *Cronica* of 1544 because it is the earliest folk song showing unmistakable "national" traits [cf. *LavE* i.5, 2615f]. A number of charming English folk tunes (*Goe from my window, John come kiss me now*) are preserved in the *Fitzwilliam Virginal Book* (c. 1600) where they are used as themes for variations. Most of the English folk melodies date from the 17th century while those of Germany originated mostly around and after 1800. Many of the most popular folk songs are of traceable authorship, e.g., the *Lorelei* (German; text by Heine, music by F. Silcher, 1789–1860), *Dixie* (Daniel D. Emmett, 1859), or *Estrellita* (Mexico; Manuel Ponce). As regards the folk songs of the United States, a clear line of distinction must, of course, be drawn between the aboriginal melodies of the Indians and the civilized folk songs of the white settlers and the Negroes. For the former, see *American Indian music; for the latter, *Ballad; *Shanty; *Negro music.

Lit. (selection of books and collections of a general character): W. Danckert, *Das europäische Volkslied* (1939); *LavE* ii.5, 2866–3014 (bibl.); M. E. Sears, *Song Index* (1926; Suppl. Vol. 1934); A. M. Buchanan, *American Folkmusic* (Index, Bibliography; National Federation of Music Clubs, 1939); F. Howes, "Recent Work in Folk-Music" (*PMA* lxiv); H. Mersmann, "Grundlagen einer musikalischen Volksliedforschung" (*AMW* iv). Collections. (a) *International:* F. H. Botsford, *Folk Songs of Many Peoples*, 3 vols. (1921); G. R. Bantock, *One hundred Folksongs of All Nations* (1911); H. Möller, *Das Lied der Völker*, 3 vols. — (b) *National:* C. J. Sharp, *Folksongs of England*, 5 vols. (1908–12); Ilmari Krohn, *Suomen kansan sävelmiä* (Finnish), 4 vols. (1893–1912); J. Tiersot, *60 Folksongs of France* (1915); Erk-Böhme, *Deutscher Liederhort* (German), 3 vols. (1893–94); L. Chr. Erk, *Deutscher Liederschatz* (German), 3 vols. (1859–72); B. Bartók, *Hungarian Folk Music* (1931); W. A. Fisher, *Sixty Irish Songs* (1915); D. de Lange and others, *Nederlandsche Volksliederenboek* (1900); E. Grieg, *Norges Melodier* (Norway); N. A. Rimsky-Korsakov, *100 Chants nationaux russes* (1925); A. Moffat, *The Minstrelsy of Scotland*; K. Schindler, *Folk Music and Poetry of Spain and Portugal* (1941); G. Hagg, *Songs of Sweden*. For American folk song see under *Ballad; *Negro music; *American Indian music. Add. bibl. in *MoML*, 922ff.

Follia. See *Folia.

Fonds d'orgue [F.]. Foundation stops of the organ.

Foot. (1) In versification, see *Poetic Meter. — (2) In organ building, terms such as eight-foot (written 8-ft. or 8′), four-foot (4′), sixteen-foot (16′), etc., are used to differentiate stops which sound at the pitch indicated by the corresponding key from others sounding higher or lower octaves or even other intervals. If, e.g., the key C is touched, an 8′-stop sounds C, while a 4′-stop sounds c, and a 16′-stop sounds C_1. The terminology is derived

from the fact that, in a normally pitched flue-stop, such as 8′-principal, the length of the pipe sounding C measures about 8 feet (the other pipes of the same stop being, of course, correspondingly longer or shorter), whereas, in a stop of the 4′-class, the pipe sounded by the same key is only half as long, etc. [see *Organ V]. In mutation stops, i.e., those stops which are designed to reinforce the harmonics of the unison stops [see *Organ VI, IX(e)], still other foot-measurements occur. For instance, $2\frac{2'}{3}$ is a pipe of one-third $\left(2\frac{2}{3} = \frac{8}{3}\right)$ the length of the normal pipes; it therefore produces the third partial, i.e., the twelfth (g for the key C); $5\frac{1'}{3}\left(= \frac{16}{3}\right)$ sounds the lower octave of this, G, and $1\frac{1'}{3}\left(= \frac{4}{3}\right)$ the higher one, g′ Similarly, $1\frac{3'}{5}\left(= \frac{8}{5}\right)$ gives the fifth partial, i.e., the third two octaves above the fundamental, e′, while multiples of this fraction, such as $3\frac{1'}{5}\left(= \frac{16}{5}\right)$ and $6\frac{2'}{5}\left(= \frac{32}{5}\right)$ give lower thirds, e, E, and $\frac{4'}{5}, \frac{2'}{5}$ still higher ones, e″ e‴. The seventh partial appears in stops such as $1\frac{1'}{7}\left(= \frac{8}{7}\right)$, etc.

This terminology has been borrowed for similar distinctions in other fields, e.g., for the designation of octaves (8-ft. octave, 4-ft. octave) or of instruments, e.g., in the term 4-ft. instrument for the piccolo flute, etc.

Forefall. English 17th-century term for *Appoggiatura.

Forlana, furlana. A dance from northern Italy (Frioul). In dance collections of the 16th century [Phalèse, *Danseries* (1583)] it has a character similar to that of the *passamezzo* (even meter), whereas, in Baroque music, it is a gay dance in triple meter (6/4, 6/8) with dotted rhythm, similar to the gigue. It appears frequently in the ballets of Campra [*L'Europe galante* (1697), *Les Festes Vénitiens* (1710)]. Bach's orchestral suite in C major includes a forlana. In 1914 attempts were made (ostensibly under the auspices of the Pope) to revive the forlana in place of the "offensive" tango. Cf. J. Écorcheville, in *BSIM* x; P. Nettl, in *RM* xiv.

Form. A term which has different meanings depending on whether it occurs in the connection: "form *in* music" or: "form(s) *of* music." In the former combination it has a very general and loose significance, simply expressing the basic fact that music, like all art, is not a chaotic conglomeration of sounds, but that it consists of sounds arranged in orderly manner according to numerous obvious principles as well as to a still greater number of subtle and hidden relationships which evade formulation. In this meaning, form is so essential to music that it is difficult to imagine a procedure by which it could be avoided. Perhaps a wild portato up and down the violin mingled with some scratching and knocking of the bow would come pretty near to this. Even the simplest melody shows relationships of pitch (intervals), of time values (rhythm), of grouping (phrases), etc., in other words, has "form." In speaking of "forms *of* music," however, something quite different and much more specific is meant, namely the existence of certain schemes which govern the structure-at-large of a composition and which were traditionally used in the various epochs of music history, e.g., the fugue or the sonata.

As may well be expected, the ambiguity of the term — an ambiguity which has by no means been made sufficiently clear in numerous writings — has been the source of numerous misunderstandings and somewhat futile argumentation. Much of this could be avoided if, in speaking of a specific composition, a clear distinction were made between the "form *in* this composition" and the "form *of* this composition." The much-discussed problem of "form and contents" offers an example. Considering, e.g., a typical statement such as: "In the last analysis form and content cannot be wholly independent of each other," it appears that this is entirely correct if form here means: "form *in* a composition." In fact, in this case the somewhat cautious and defensive wording of the phrase may be replaced by the frank statement: "the form *in* a composition is entirely dependent on its contents." If, however, form were meant here to denote "form *of* a composition," the almost opposite statement would be correct, namely: "the form *of* a composition (if it has a 'form') is essentially independent of its contents." If we conceive of the sound-material as a somewhat amorphous substance comparable to the flesh and cells of a body, then form might be said to represent the support by which this substance is held and shaped, this support being of two kinds: one forming a highly complicated inner structure comparable to the bones and muscles (form *in* a composition); the other determining its outer contour, somewhat like the skin (form *of* a composition).

Regarding the details of "form *in* music," it suffices to say that practically all the theoretical and compositional principles of music fall under this category, e.g., tones, intervals, scales, tonality, consonance and dissonance, meter, rhythm, phrase, theme, motive, repetition, variation, modification (metamorphosis, transformation), transposition, modulation, sequence, inversion, and all the higher devices of counterpoint. Most of these categories receive treatment under their own heading. For "forms *of* music" see *Forms, Musical.

Formant. See under *Timbre (1).

Forms, Musical. This means — or at least is understood here to mean — the general principles and schemes which govern the structure-at-large of a composition [see remarks under *Form]. In other words, a musical form is the plan of construction — comparable to an architect's ground plan — which exists in the mind of the composer when he sets out to write, say, a fugue or a sonata. History shows that in almost every period of European music (much less so in Oriental music) certain formal schemes became traditionally established and were used by the composers as molds, setting the general frame for their creative imagination. The most important — at least, the most clearly defined — forms may be classified as follows:

I. Single Forms
  A. Repetition Forms
    (1) a a′ a″ . . . *Variation form
    (2) a b (properly ‖: a :‖: b :‖) *Binary form
    (3) ‖: a :‖: b a :‖ Rounded binary form
    (4) ‖: a :‖ b a *Sonata-form
    (5) a b a Ternary form
    (6) a b a c a Five-part form (also called *Rondo form)
    (7) a b a c a b a *Rondo form (Rondo-sonata form)
    (8) a b a c a d . . . a Rondeau [see *Rondeau (2)]
    (9) Medieval forms, see *Ballade; *Rondeau (1); *Virelai (*Ballata)
  For the forms (2) to (5) see *Binary and ternary, also *Barform. The forms (3) to (7) have a structure similar to an arch ("arch form" or "bow form"; G. *Bogenform*), while (1) and the *sequence resemble the structure of a chain ("chain form"; G. *Kettenform, Reihenform*). Forms such as (8) combine both structures.
  B. Continuation forms
    (1) Cantus-firmus forms: *organum; 13th-century *motet; chorale compositions
    (2) Imitative forms: 16th-century *motet; *ricercar; *fugue
II. Compound Forms (consisting of various "movements")
  A. Instrumental: *sonata; *concerto; *suite; *toccata
  B. Vocal: *cantata; *mass; *passion; *oratorio; *opera

Naturally this list is not complete or without serious defects, and should be considered only as a general outline illustrating the subject under discussion. There exist, of course, a large number of "hybrids" which do not fit into the above classification or which represent borderline cases. For instance the fugue which is classified above as a continuation form might also be considered in a way a repetition form, owing to the characteristic alternation of expositions and episodes.

In other cases — in fact, in most of them — the evolutionary element has to be taken into account. For instance, the toccata which, in the period of Bach, is a compound form consisting usually of five distinct movements, starts out, around 1550, as a single continuation form (A. Gabrieli), and gradually acquires sectional character (Merulo, c. 1600) which finally leads to the breaking up into movements. Particularly interesting and important are the changes of sonata-form which, by a complicated process, lead from a clearly binary scheme via the sonata-form proper to a ternary scheme [see *Sonata-form].

The above interpretation of "forms of music" as a composer's ground plan does not, of course, claim to represent a generally accepted definition. In fact, it would be impossible to find a definition which would be likely to meet with the universal approval of musicians and scholars. It may be noticed that many writers use the term in a wider sense, including in it what might be more properly termed "stylistic types," e.g., the chaconne and the passacaglia (which are stylistic types of variation form), or the allemande, courante, etc. (which are stylistic types of binary form). Others prefer to use it in a narrower sense, by restricting its application to those schemes which are based upon the principle of repetition [see category I, A of the above classification]. Such restricted usage has a certain advantage. No doubt, the repetition forms are not only more clearly defined than the continuation forms, but also conform more fully to the general notion of form as a "pre-existing mold." For the continuation-types the name "procedure" has been suggested and, indeed, would appear to be appropriate. Thus in the case of a fugue, one would speak of "fugal procedure" rather than of "fugal form."

Although with the fugue one might argue whether it is a form or a procedure (or both combined), the appropriateness of the latter term is clearly indicated in many types of vocal music, namely those in which the text provides the sole "ground plan" of the composer, as in the recitativo, the through-composed song, in Wagner's "unending melody," etc. A similar situation exists with regard to the "compound vocal forms" [II, B] and to the symphonic poem in which the composer "proceeds" on the basis of the programmatical idea.

There exists a widespread tendency among modern composers and writers to deny, or at least to minimize, the importance of musical forms, the view being that each composition creates not only its own inner form (form *within* the composition; see under *Form) but also its outer structure (form *of* the composition). As far as the repertory of classical music and the greater part of early music are concerned, such a statement is obviously wrong. It finds its justification mainly in the numerous examples of 19th- and 20th-century program music, and in the attempts of recent composers to modify, particularly in their symphonies, the traditional scheme of the sonata. Nonetheless, it should be noticed that even such compositions as the symphonies of Sibelius and Shostakovitch, or the piano sonatas of Hindemith, clearly show that the composers, in writing them, were thinking in terms of the traditional principles of sonata writing. Although in the history of music there have repeatedly been periods in which there was an emphasis on "free procedure" rather than on "established form," such periods have always been of relatively short duration and of limited importance. One is probably justified in extending this observation to the present epoch.

Lit.: E. Prout, *Musical Form and Applied Forms* (1893/95); D. F. Tovey, articles "Contrapuntal Forms" and "Sonata Forms" in *Encycl. Brit.*; P. Goetschius, *Lessons in Music Form* (1904); St. Macpherson, *Form in Music* (1908); M. H. Glyn, *Analysis of the Evolution of Musical Form*; H. Leichtentritt, *Musikalische Formenlehre* (1927); R. Stöhr, *Musikalische Formenlehre* (1933); W. H. Hadow, "Form and Formalism in Music" (*PMA* xxiv); E. J. Dent, "Binary and Ternary Forms" (*ML* xvii); A. Lourié, "The Crisis in Form" (*MM* viii,

no. 4); R. von Ficker, "Formprobleme der mittelalterlichen Musik" (*ZMW* vii); M. Bauer, "Formprobleme des späten Beethoven" (*ZMW* ix); H. Mersmann, "Zur Geschichte des Formbegriffs" (*JMP* xxxvii). See also under *Sonata, *Fugue, and the bibliography in *MoML*, 231.

Forte [It.], abbr. *f*, loud; *fortissimo*, abbr. *ff* (*fff*), very loud; *più forte*, louder; *forte-piano*, abbr. *fp*, loud followed by soft; *mezzoforte*, abbr. *mf*, medium loud. See *Dynamic marks.

Fortepiano [It.]. (1) See *Forte.— (2) Older name for the pianoforte.

Fortfahren [G.]. To continue (e.g., with the same speed).

Fortspinnung [G., spinning forth]. In melodic construction, the process of continuation, development, or working out of material, as opposed to repetition in a symmetrical arrangement. In modern writings on melodic analysis (W. Fischer) a distinction is frequently made between *Fortspinnungstypus* and *Liedtypus*, terms which may be translated: continuation-type and repetition-type. A melody of the latter type is symmetrical in design and structure, whereas one of the former proceeds differently, frequently from longer phrases to shorter ones. An illustration is afforded by the accompanying two themes [(a) last movement of

Mozart's Symphony in G minor; (b) scherzo of Beethoven's Fifth] which are usually cited as an example of "identical material" (even of plagiarism!), but which are more interesting as an example of "contrasting treatment of the same material," the former being treated in repetition, the latter in continuation. Other terms for the same two types are "static" and "dynamic" melody (E. Kurth). Cf. W. Fischer, in *StM* iii.

Forty-eight, The. Popular name for the 48 preludes and fugues of Bach's *Well-tempered Clavier* i and ii (24 in each).

Forzando, forzato [It.]. Forcing, forced.

Fougeux [F.]. Impetuous.

Foundation stops. Designation for all organ pipes except the mutation stops [see *Organ VI].

Fountains of Rome. See *Symphonic poem IV.

Fourniture [F.]. Mixture-stops of the organ. See also *Organ IX (f).

Four-shape note. See *Fasola.

Fourth. The fourth degree (note) of the diatonic scale, or the interval formed by a tone and the fourth tone above. While in classical harmony the fourth occurs only as the inversion of the fifth [see *Sixth-chord; *Six-four chord], it is of basic importance in ancient Greek music [see *Tetrachord] and in early medieval polyphony [see *Organum], and it has once more acquired independent importance in modern harmony. Scriabin introduced chords consisting of successive fourths, e.g., C–F♯–B♭–e–a–d′ [see *Mystic chord], and contemporary composers (Stravinsky, Hindemith) make extensive use of similar combinations (fourth-chords). See *Harmony II, 9; *Quartal harmony. Cf. O. Beer, in *DM* xxii.2.

Fox-trot. A species of ragtime which dates from 1912. The term has become a generic designation for all jazz in duple time, except the foreign importations such as the rhumba, tango, etc. Thus the "Blues" is spoken of as a slow fox-trot, and "Swing" can be considered as a fast fox-trot with improvised performance.

Fp. Short for *forte-piano* [see *Forte].

Frais, fraîche [F.]. Fresh.

Frappant [F.]. "Striking," marking.

Frauenchor [G.]. Women's chorus.

Freddamente [It.]. Coldly, indifferently.

Fredon [F.]. A rather indefinite term applied by 17th-century French musicians to a trill or a short *roulade. In the 18th century it is generally used in a derogatory sense for excessive ornamentation.

Freemason songs. Cf. P. Nettl, in *MQ* xvi; also in *Drei Ringe*, 1927.

Freischütz, Der ("The Freeshooter"). Opera in three acts by Carl Maria von Weber (1786–1826), libretto by F. Kind, produced at Berlin in 1821. The plot is based on the story of "magic bullets" which never miss their mark and which can be obtained through a pact with the spirits of hell. The hunter *Max* (Tenor), on the advice of his sinister companion *Caspar* (Bass), resorts to this scheme (nightly scene in the wolf's glen) in order to win *Agathe* (Soprano), who is to be given as a prize to the winner in the marksmen's prize shooting. Six of the seven bullets reach their goal, but the seventh (Max does not know this) is under the control of the hellish spirit *Samiel* (speaking part), who directs it against Agathe. She is, however, protected by the *Hermit* (Bass) and by her bridal wreath, and Samiel, failing in his scheme, seizes Caspar who dies with a curse on his lips.

The *Freischütz* marks the beginning as well as the peak of the German Romantic opera. Folklore, nature, and legendary superstition are the roots out of which grows a music which is admirable both for the charm of its folk-like melodies and dance tunes, and for its touches of dramatic tension and Romantic excitement. Particularly remarkable is the bold use of the wind instruments: the horns which capture the atmosphere of the "German forest"; the trombones which accompany the hermit; the clarinet which characterizes Agathe; and the low regis-

ter of the flute which portrays Samiel.
See reference under *Melodrama.

Freistimmig [G., from *frei*, free;
Stimme, part]. Modern German term for
a "pseudo-contrapuntal" style in which
there is no strict adherence to a given
number of parts, that is, in which voices
are allowed freely to enter or drop out,
and in which also chordal elements occur.
The natural idiom for such a style is the
keyboard or the lute. Indeed, it makes its
first appearance in the 15th- and 16th-
century preludes for these instruments.
It is frequently found in the works of
Frescobaldi [see Ex.; cf. *ApMZ* i, no. 19]

and forms a characteristic trait of the
style of Froberger. Naturally, the contrapuntal treatment in 19th-century compositions, such as Beethoven's sonatas, is always more or less freistimmig. See also
*Texture; *Ensemble (3).

French chanson. See *Chanson (3).

French harp. Older name for the
*mouth-organ.

French horn. The *horn, in contradistinction to the English horn, which is a
member of the *oboe family.

French music. From a bird's-eye point
of view, the history of French music
shows three climactic periods: an early
one embracing three centuries (1150–
1450), during which France was the un-
disputed leader in musical development;
another of about 100 years, during the
Baroque era (Chambonnières, Lully,
Couperin, Rameau), and a third one, that
of modern French music, beginning with
Berlioz.

I. During the 5th and 6th centuries
there existed in France a special branch of
Christian worship, the Gallican Rite,
which had its special music, known as
*Gallican chant. After the establishment
of the Roman Rite (by Pipin, 752–768)
the cathedral of Metz became the leading
French center of Gregorian chant, well
known particularly for its neumatic
manuscripts written in a special type of
neumes, the Messine neumes [see
*Neumes I]. In the 9th century the
monastery of St. Martial in Limoges
played a leading part in the early development of the *sequence, a development
which reached its high-point in Adam de
St. Victor (d. 1192). From the period of
Charlemagne (768–814), a number of
songs in the Latin language are preserved
which, of course, can be claimed with
equal right as "French" or "German"
(e.g., the *Planctus Karoli*; cf. *GD* v, 1;
AdHM i, 160). The oldest song in the
French (Provençale) language is a *Hora
vos dic dera raizun* of the 10th century
[cf. P. Aubry, *Les plus ancients monuments de la musique française* (1903),
pl. I]. Of slightly later date is the Spon-
sus-play with a mixed Latin and Provençal text, and the northern French
Daniel play, from Beauvais [see *Liturgical drama].

II. The great period of medieval
French music begins around 1150 in two
parallel lines of epochal importance: that
of monophonic secular music, represented
by the *troubadours and *trouvères; and
that of polyphonic music, represented by
the anonymous composers of the School
of *St. Martial (*c.* 1150), by the School of
*Notre Dame with Leoninus and Pero-
tinus (before and after 1200), by the *Ars
antiqua of the 13th century, and the *Ars
nova of the 14th century (Philippe de
Vitry, *c.* 1290–1361; Guillaume de Machaut, 1300–77), which, after a transitional period (Césaris, Tapissier, Solage,
and many others), led to the last period
of medieval French music, the *Burgundian School, with Dufay (*c.* 1400–
74), and Binchois (*c.* 1400–67). Late
Burgundian musicians such as Antoine
Busnois (d. 1492) and Loyset Compère
(d. 1518), both pupils of Ockeghem, form
a group sometimes referred to as the
School of Cambrai (Dufay lived in Cam-

brai from 1450 till his death) which already shows the influence of the Flemish style (figurate counterpoint with imitation; cf., e.g., *BeMMR* 212, 213). In the works of other French composers such as Josquin des Prés (1450–1521), Pierre de la Rue (*c.* 1460–1518), and Antoine Brumel (fl. around 1500), the Flemish influence is so dominating that they are usually classified as *Flemish composers.

The Flemish style took on a typically French tinge with Clément Jannequin (1485–1560), the founder of the French *chanson, that witty and frivolous type of music which established France's leadership in the field of amorous and hedonistic music, but also marked the end of its artistic eminence. Alongside this, there goes an academic strain through the French music of the 16th century, characterized chiefly by the cultivation of the *vers mesuré (Claudin, Costeley). A large repertoire of French 16th-century lute music (mostly dances and arrangements of chansons) exists in the lute books of Attaingnant (1530), Morlaye (*c.* 1550), Adrian Le Roy (*c.* 1550), and others [see *Lute music], while only a few remnants of 16th-century French organ music have been preserved in the organ books published by Attaingnant around 1530, and in the works of the great organ composer Jean Titelouze (1563–1633), the "French Sweelinck," as he might be called.

III. In the 17th century, French music was entirely under the patronage of the court of Versailles (Louis XIII, 1610–43; Louis XIV, 1643–1715), the pomp and splendor of which was enhanced by the *ballet (Cambefort, 1605–61; Lully, 1632–87; Campra, 1660–1744), and by the opera (Cambert, 1628–77; Lully; Campra; Rameau, 1683–1764) [see *Opera IV]. Here originated the *minuet, the *gavotte, the *bourrée, and numerous other dances which were later adopted into the *suite. Of great artistic significance is the French lute music of the 17th century, represented chiefly by Denis Gaultier (*c.* 1600–72), and the harpsichord music which leads from the reserved dignity of Chambonnières

(1602–72) and Louis Couperin (*c.* 1626–61) over the Baroque peak of Henry d'Anglebert (1635–91) to the Rococo hedonism of François Couperin (1668–1733), coming to its close in the masterworks of Jean-Philippe Rameau (1683–1764), with their almost Beethovenian traits of ingenious characterization and dramatic surprise. The French organ music of the Baroque (Gigault, 1625–1707; Le Begue, 1630–1702; Dandrieu, 1684–1740) is notable for its ventures in registration rather than for truly artistic achievements. The French song literature of this period includes the *air de cour, the *bergerette, and the *brunette [see *Chanson].

The invasion of the Italian opera buffa (1752; *guerre des *bouffons) marked the end of the French Baroque opera and the beginning of the less significant *opéra comique. For an entire century, from 1750 to 1850, the history of French music was practically restricted to the efforts to build up a new "great opera," efforts in which the German Gluck (1714–87), the Italians Cherubini (1760–1842) and Rossini (1792–1868), the German Meyerbeer (1791–1864) participated side by side with French composers such as Grétry (1742–1813), Méhul (1763–1817), Boieldieu (1775–1834), Auber (1782–1871), and Halévy (1799–1862).

IV. Much more important than the mediocrities of these operas is the symphonic work of Hector Berlioz (1803–69), the heir to the tradition of Beethoven and perhaps the greatest figure in the French music of the 19th century. With all their "flaws" his compositions show an originality, passion, and vigor which is rarely encountered in the more academic works of his successors, César Franck (1822–90), Charles Saint-Saëns (1835–1921), Gabriel Fauré (1845–1924), and Vincent d'Indy (1851–1931). These four form what might be called the classical school of French music. They amalgamated the classical forms of the symphony, quartet, variations, etc., with a romantic vocabulary of harmonies and with a thorough study of counterpoint. Their academic and somewhat dogmatic leanings became patent in the *Schola cantorum (founded by d'Indy and others in 1894) which continued the tradition of César Franck, combining it with the study of Gregorian chant and of 16th-century counterpoint (Palestrina). The tendency towards a greater subjectivism, a more lyrical expressiveness, a richer orchestral palette, and a typically French exquisiteness of taste appears in the works of Henri Duparc (1848–1933), the creator of the modern French song [see *Chanson], Ernest Chausson (1855–99), and Paul Dukas (1865–1935). Unfortunately, each of them produced only a few works of importance. To the foregoing may be added Florent Schmitt (b. 1870) who, more than any other French composer, was influenced by the emotional exuberance of German Romanticism. Modern French music found its most characteristic expression in the *impressionism which was prepared by Édouard Lalo (1823–92) and Emmanuel Chabrier (1841–94), and brought to full realization by Claude Debussy (1862–1918) and Maurice Ravel (1875–1937).

The revolutionary tendencies of the after-war period brought a strong reaction against the refinement of impressionistic style, a reaction which found its clearest formulation in the words of Cocteau: "After the music with the silk-brush, the music with the ax." In this movement Erik Satie (1866–1925) played a role comparable to that of Arnold Schönberg in Germany. He founded the school known as Les Six [see *Six] which includes the most prominent among the contemporary French composers, notably Darius Milhaud (b. 1892), Arthur Honegger (b. 1892), Francis Poulenc (b. 1899), and George Auric (b. 1899). While the first two of these show the influence of Schönberg's *atonality, the last two embrace a facile and popularizing hedonism which has also been adopted by some of the youngest French composers, e.g., Jean Françaix (b. 1912). A separate place must be reserved for Albert Roussel (1869–1937) who, though influenced successively by d'Indy, Debussy, and Stravinsky, has nonetheless developed a highly personal style of a basically contrapuntal construction, but varying greatly from one composition to the next.

The repertoire of the modern French opera is characterized by Gounod's *Faust* (1859), Bizet's *Carmen* (1875), Saint-Saëns's *Samson et Dalila* (1877), Massenet's *Manon* (1884), Lalo's *Le Roi d'Ys* (1878), Chabrier's *Gwendoline* (1886), d'Indy's *Fervaal* (1897), Charpentier's *Louise* (1900), Debussy's *Pelléas et Melisande* (1900), Dukas' *Ariane et Barbe-bleue* (1907), Ravel's *Heure Espagnole* (1911), and Fauré's *Pénélope* (1913). After the first World War French composers became interested chiefly in the ballet [see *Ballet III.]

Lit.: *LavE* i.3, 1176 (till 1814), ii.1, 56 (modern); P. Lasserre, *The Spirit of French Music* (1917); M. Hargrave, *The Earlier French Musicians, 1632–1834* (1917); A. Hervey, *French Music of the 19th Century* (1903); A. W. Locke, *Music and the Romantic Movement in France* (1920); E. B. Hill, *Modern French Music* (1924); A. Coeuroy, *La Musique française moderne* (1922); G. Jean-Aubry, *French Music of Today* (1919); H. Grace, *French Organ Music, Past and Present* (1919); A. Cortot, *French Piano Music* (1932); A. Koechlin, "Sur l'évolution de la musique française avant et après Debussy" (*RM* xvi). See *Editions XVI, XIX, XXIV.

French overture. See *Overture I, II.

French sixth. See *Sixth chord.

Frenetico [It.]. Frenzied.

Frequency. See under *Acoustics I.

Fresco [It.]. Fresh.

Fret [F. *touche*; G. *Bund*, pl. *Bünde*; It. *tasto*]. Frets are raised lines across the finger board of certain instruments (lute, guitar, viols, balalaika, banjo, and various Indian and Arabic instruments) which mark the position for the stopping of the strings. Formerly they were made from pieces of catgut which were tied tightly around the neck. In more recent instruments they are narrow strips of wood or metal fixed on the finger board. On European instruments the frets are always so arranged as to give a succession of semitones [see *Tablature III].

Frettevole [It.]. Hurried.

Friss, friszka. See *Czardas.

Fröhlich [G.]. Happy, joyful.

Frog. Colloquial term adopted from the G. *Frosch, for the *nut of the violin bow.

Frog Quartet [G. *Froschquartett*]. Popular name for Haydn's Quartet in D (no. 50, or op. 50, no. 6), so called on account of the character of the main theme of the last movement.

Froidement [F.]. Coldly, indifferently.

From the New World. See *Symphonic poem I.

Frosch [G., frog]. The *nut (*frog) of the violin bow.

Frottola [It. dimin. of *frutto*, fruit?]. A type of late 15th- and early 16th-century North-Italian poetry and music. As a poetic form, the frottola consists of various stanzas of three (or four) double-lines each, with a refrain (called *ripresa*) of two double-lines before and after each stanza, a form similar to the 14th-century *ballata, and the contemporary Spanish *villancico. The music always consists of several short sections which are arranged and repeated in various schemes, the following one being frequent:

Text: r r s s s r r

Music: a b a a b a b

(r stands for two lines of the refrain, s for two lines of the stanza).

The style of the frottola is essentially chordal in three or four parts, with the upper part standing out as a melody. They were probably performed as accompanied songs, the lower parts being played on instruments. There is, however, no foundation for the theory, advanced by H. Riemann and repeated by others, that the textless sections which frequently occur at the end of a frottola were "instrumental afterludes" [compare the mis-

leading renditions in *SchGMB*, nos. 69, 70, with the correct (vocalizing) interpretation in *BeMMR*, 220]. The most important source for these songs are the eleven books, *Frottole*, published by Petrucci in 1504–14. In these books, as well as in present-day usage, the term frottole is also employed as a generic designation for Italian secular songs of the period around 1500, including, in addition to the frottola proper, other poetic-musical types such as the *canzona (4), the *ode and the *strambotto.

The frottola grew up in the social atmosphere of the courts at Verona, Padua, Venice, and particularly Mantua, where the most fertile composers of frottole lived, Marco Cara and Bartolommeo Tromboncino. H. Isaac and Josquin des Près also wrote in this form, which became a forerunner of the *villanella as well as of the *madrigal. Expls. in Ambros, *Geschichte der Musik* v; *Editions II, vol. 1; *HAM*, no. 95.

Lit.: R. Schwartz, cf. *Editions XXV, vol. 8; A. Einstein, †*Canzoni, Sonetti, Strambotti e Frottole . . .* (1941); W. H. Rubsamen, *Literary Sources of Secular Music in Italy* (1943); E. B. Helm, in *MQ* xxvii; E. T. Ferand, in *MQ* xxvii; E. Gizzarelli, in *BAMS* i; R. Schwartz, in *VMW* ii; *id.*, in *JMP* xxxi; *id.*, in *Festschrift für Th. Kroyer*; A. Einstein, in *ZMW* x; E. Ferand, in *AM* x; K. Jeppesen, in *AM* xi; A. Pirro, in *RdM*, 1922; F. Vatielli, in *RMI* xxviii.

Frühlingslied [G.]. Spring song.

Füllstimme [G.]. A mere "filling" voice, lacking in independent importance.

Fuga [It.; L.]. (1) Italian for *fugue. — (2) The original meaning of the (Latin) term is not fugue, but canon, particularly the canon in which the different voices sing the same melody — as in the modern canon or in the mensuration canon — as distinguished from the enigmatic canons [see *Canon II]. In this meaning the term is already used by Oswald v. Wolkenstein, 1377–1445 [cf. H. J. Moser, *Geschichte der Deutschen Musik* (1930),

p. 196], later by J. Ockeghem [Ambros V, p. 18], Johannes Buchner [c. 1525; see *Fundamentum], Hans Gerle [Musica Teusch (1532)], A. de Cabezon [see *Editions XIII], and Vincenzo Galilei [see *Editions XIV, vol. 4, p. 12]. Around 1600 the word fuga adopted the present meaning as a generic term for pieces in the fugal style, either canzonas [cf. B. Schmid, Tabulaturbuch (1607): "Fugen oder, wie es die Italiäner nennen, Canzoni alla Francese"], extended ricercares [S. Scheidt, Tabulatura nova (1624); cf. DdT i, 99], or any of the precursors of the fugue proper.

Fugato. A passage in fugal style which forms part of a primarily non-fugal composition. Such passages occur frequently in the development sections of symphonies, sonatas, quartets.

Fughetta. A short fugue.

Fugue [from L. fuga, flight; F. fugue; G. Fuge]. The latest and most mature form of imitative counterpoint, developed during the 17th century and brought to its highest perfection by J. S. Bach.
I. Structure. The main features of a fugue are as follows: (a) A fugue is always written in contrapuntal style, i.e., in a texture consisting of a certain number of individual voices, usually three or four [see *Counterpoint; *Texture]. — (b) It is based on a short melody, called "subject" or "theme," which is stated at the beginning of the fugue in one voice alone, being taken up ("imitated") by the other voices in close succession and reappearing throughout the entire piece repeatedly in all the voices at different places according to principles to be explained subsequently. — (c) In each voice the horizontal space between one statement and the next of the subject is filled out by a freely invented counterpoint which, however, is usually rendered homogeneous by the consistent use of small motives of a unified melodic and rhythmic pattern. These motives are derived either from the subject itself, or, more frequently, from its continuation which forms the counterpoint to the first

imitation (second statement) of the subject, near the beginning of the fugue. Frequently, but not always, this continuation takes on a rather definite form, somewhat comparable in distinctiveness and importance to the subject. In this case it is called "countersubject," and will then be found reappearing throughout the fugue in a similar manner to the main subject, though less rigidly. — (d) A section during which the theme appears at least once in each voice is called exposition. Frequently an exposition includes one more statement than the number of parts, e.g., four in a three-voiced fugue, the subject appearing once more in the part in which it appeared for the first time. However, this does not usually happen in the first exposition which, in other respects also, is the most normal and strictest of all the expositions. Sometimes the term exposition is restricted to the first exposition, without any special name being applied to the later sections of similar construction. — (e) A section of the fugue which does not include a statement of the subject is called an episode. The episodes are based chiefly on short motives derived from the subject or its continuation (countersubject). They frequently show sequential treatment [see *Sequence (1)]. The accompanying example (J. K. F. Fischer, Ariadne Musica,

c. 1700) illustrates the beginning of a fugue. — (f) The structure-at-large of a fugue is an alternation of expositions and episodes. The episodes, although still in strict counterpoint, are somewhat "lighter in weight" and stand to the preceding expositions in the relationship of relaxation to tension. A fugue may have three, four, or more expositions, separated from one another by episodes. The middle expositions usually involve modulations into other keys, such as the relative minor, the dominant, or the subdominant, with return to the main key in the last exposition. — (g) While in the first exposition the statements of the subject follow in rather close succession, they usually occur more widely spaced in the later expositions, separated by what might be called "secondary episodes." In the accompanying schematic graph of the first fugue from Bach's *Wt. Cl.* ii these are designated

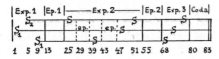

by the symbol ep., in contradistinction to the "primary episodes," designated Ep. (The figures given underneath the graph indicate the measures.) The three subjects of the initial exposition are designated S_1 and S_2, in order to indicate that they appear in two different keys, namely, tonic (S_1) and dominant (S_2) [see *Imitation]. With respect to this tonal relationship they are referred to as "subject and answer," or "antecedent and consequent," or "dux (leader) and comes" (follower). Usually the answer is not an exact transposition, but one involving the modification of certain steps, e.g., the replacement of a fifth (c–g) by a fourth (g–c', instead of g–d') [see *Tonal and real answer].

It must be noticed that the above scheme of a fugue represents what is called a "student's fugue," as distinguished from a "composer's fugue," such as those by Bach, few of which agree with the theoretical description in every detail. It is interesting to observe that Bach treated the fugue much more freely than Mozart, Haydn, and Beethoven the sonata. The question may well be raised whether there really exists such a thing as the "form of the fugue," and whether it would not be more proper to speak of "fugal procedure" rather than "fugal form" [see *Forms, Musical]. At any rate, the statement repeated in numerous books that "a fugue is a three-part form" is rather misleading.

While the above explanations indicate the basic principles of the fugue, fugal style includes many special devices of lesser or greater complexity, somewhat learned in character, but artistically justified as elements not only of additional interest and variety but also of increased intensity. Most of these are found under separate entries [see *Augmentation and diminution; *Inversion; *Stretto; *Double Fugue; see also *Art of Fugue].

II. *History.* The principle of imitative counterpoint, which is the basis of the fugue, was established by the early *Flemish masters (Ockeghem, Obrecht) and was consistently applied first in the *motets of Josquin, around 1500. The style and form of Josquin's motet, characterized by a great number of relatively short "expositions" (points), each based on a different subject, and following one another in a dovetailing fashion, were imitated in the organ *ricercare (Cavazzoni, 1540), not however without certain modifications already foreshadowing the future tendencies, i.e., reduction of the number of points (i.e., themes), and expansion of each point into a well-defined section including a greater number (up to 15 and more) of statements of the subject. Besides these "polythematic" ricercares, which are of considerable extension, there occur also examples of the shorter "monothematic" ricercar (e.g., by Luzzascho Luzzaschi; cf. *TaAM* ii, 27). Another important forerunner of the fugue is the organ *canzona which is similar in form to the polythematic ricercar, but more lively in character, less scholarly in treatment. The ricercare style persists in slow fugues, such as nos. 4 and 22 of *Wt. Cl.* i, while the canzona type leads to the more flexible and individual subjects such as occur in the quicker fugues [see *Soggetto].

The details of the development leading from the ricercar and canzona of the 1600-period to the fugue of Bach have never been thoroughly investigated and clearly outlined. The problem is very difficult indeed owing to the enormous wealth of material and the variety of trends and schools. In restricting ourselves to the organ fugue (i.e., omitting the no less important development of fugal style in instrumental and vocal music) it can be said that this development takes place chiefly in Germany ["fugues" by Frescobaldi, which have been frequently reprinted in modern collections (e.g., L. Oesterle, *Early Keyboard Music* (1932) i, p. 59) are definitely spurious] and that in a slow process of gradual changes the typical features of the Bach-fugue appear, such as individual design of subject and countersubject, restriction to one subject, and loosening up of the uniformly heavy contrapuntal texture by the use of episodes. The interested student will find this process illustrated by the following examples, contained in A. Ritter, *Zur Geschichte des Orgelspiels*, vol. ii (1884): Wolfgang Carl Briegel, 1626–1710 (p. 206); Georg Caspar Wecker, 1632–95 (p. 120); Johann Christoph Bach, 1643–1703 (p. 172); cf. also *HAM*, nos. 215, 234, 236. The fugues in Johann Krieger's *Anmutige Clavier-Uebung* (1699; new ed. in *DTB* 18) contain practically all the elements of fugal style which enabled Bach to lead the form to its high-point of artistic perfection.

The excellence of Bach's fugues over those of his predecessors results from various factors: greater contrapuntal skill, clarification of the formal structure, more advanced methods of harmonic treatment, and others. While all these traits can be, and must be, understood as representing progress by degrees, there is one which puts Bach's fugues entirely into a class of their own, namely, the incomparable artistic quality of their themes [see *Melody]. The great master of the fugue after Bach is Beethoven who, in various movements of his latest piano sonatas (opp. 106, 110), quartets, and other works has shown that the potentialities of this form were by no means exhausted by the Baroque masters. After Beethoven composers seldom used the fugue as a serious art form. Recently, however, the *neo-classical tendencies of present-day music have stimulated a new creative interest in this form (Hindemith and others).

Lit.: A. *Instructive:* C. H. Kitson, *The*

Elements of Fugal Construction (1929); E. Prout, *Fugue* (1891); *id., Fugal Analysis* (1892); J. Knorr, *Lehrbuch der Fugenkomposition* (1911); A. Gédalge, *Traité de la fugue* (1901); W. Apel, *Die Fuge* (5 lectures, 1932); S. Levarie, "Fugue and Form" (*BAMS* vii).

B. *Historical:* J. Müller-Blattau, *Grundzüge einer Geschichte der Fuge* (1924, 2d ed. 1931); W. Wesely, *Die Entwicklung der Fuge bis Bach* (Diss. Prague 1928); E. P. Schwartz, *Die Fugenbeantwortung vor Bach* (Diss. Vienna 1932); J. S. Shedlock, "The Evolution of Fugue" (*PMA* xxiv); F. Deutsch, "Die Fugenarbeit in the Werken Beethoven's" (*StM* xiv); M. Zulauf, "Zur Frage der Quintbeantwortung bei J. S. Bach" (*ZMW* vi).

Fugue-tune, fuguing piece. Early American hymns which make some use of imitation. A number of such pieces were written by William Billings (1746–1800) who declared them to be "more than twenty times as powerful as the old slow tunes." Example in *HAM*, no. 324. Cf. Cl. Dickinson, †*Billings . . . Three Fuguing Tunes* (1942); E. H. Pierce, in *MQ* xvi. See also *American music I; *Hymns, English.

Functional harmony [G. *Funktionslehre*]. A relatively recent system of *harmonic analysis, developed chiefly by H. Riemann, and aiming not only at a simplification of the traditional methods but particularly at a clearer insight into the essentials of harmonic progressions. Its basis is the idea that, in a given key, there exist only three "functionally" different chords, namely, tonic (I), dominant (V), and subdominant (IV), and that all other chordal combinations, even the most complex and chromatic, are but variants of one of these three chords, in other words, that they have either tonic-function, dominant-function, or subdominant-function. The chief substitute for each of the three principal triads is its relative minor; thus VI stands for I; III for V; II for IV. However, the "upper relative" may also serve as a substitute: III for I; VII for V; VI for IV. The resulting ambiguity in meaning of, e.g., III (which may appear in tonic-function or in dominant-function) is an essential feature of the system in which a chord is determined, not as an isolated phenomenon by its degree (as is largely the case in the current system of harmonic analysis), but by its function within a series of progressions. Particularly the *subdominant occurs in a great number of substitutes; among these is the *Neapolitan sixth which, in functional harmony, is simply a (doubly altered) S, while in the orthodox system it is the "first inversion of the lowered submediant." Another example of functional interpretation is the six-four chord of the first degree (I_4^6) which functionally is nearly always a plain dominant (V) involving a double appoggiatura.

Riemann's system has not gained a foothold outside of Germany. Although one might argue about the advisability of its full acceptance, it certainly deserves more recognition as a corrective of the traditional system with its somewhat dogmatic method of labeling which is not always conducive to an understanding of harmonic life. The accompanying example

(Schumann) illustrates the traditional and the "functional" methods.

Lit.: H. Riemann, *Vereinfachte Harmonielehre* (1893); E. Kirsch, *Wesen und Aufbau der Lehre von den harmonischen Funktionen* (1928); H. Moser, in *ZMW* i.

Fundamental, Fundamental tone. The lowest tone, i.e., the bass note of a chord. Also, the first *harmonic.

Fundamental bass [F. *basse fondamentale*]. In J. Ph. Rameau's theory [see *Theory II (d)] *basse fondamentale* is a

fictitious bass line which consists of the roots of the chords occurring in a succession of harmonies. Only if a chord is in root position does the basse fondamentale coincide with the real bass. Rameau used the basse fondamentale in order to demonstrate his then novel theory of the inverted chords.

Fundament-instrument [G.]. In the *thorough-bass period, all instruments used for the playing of the bass part, either the written part only (violone, viola da gamba, violoncello, bassoon, etc.), or with accompanying chords (organ, harpsichord, chitarrone, theorbo, etc.).

Fundamentum organisandi. A title used by the 15th-century German composer Conrad Paumann (*c.* 1410–73) for a collection of organ pieces designed mainly to serve as an instruction in composition [for the meaning of the term *organisandi*, see *Organum (2)]. Aside from the MS of 1542 which contains also the Lochamer *Liederbuch* [facs. ed. by K. Ameln, 1925; transcr. in *JMW* ii], two slightly enlarged collections are preserved in the *Buxheim Organ Book. — The title was also used by Joh. Buchner (1483–1538) for a collection of similar purpose, compiled *c.* 1520, though much larger in scope and more advanced in technique (including fugal style) [cf. K. Päsler, in *VMW* v].

Funktionslehre. See *Functional harmony.

Furiant. A rapid and fiery Bohemian dance, in ¾ time, with frequently shifting accents. It has been used repeatedly by Dvořák [op. 12, *Dumka and Furiant*; op. 42, *Two Furiants*; also in his chamber music] and by Smetana [*The Bartered Bride*; *Czech Dances*]. A piece called "Furie" in Türk's *Klavierschule* (1789) is an early example of this dance type.

Furlana. See *Forlana.

Furniture stop. Same as mixture stop.

Fusa [Old G. *Fusela, Fusel*]. See *Mensural notation I.

Futurism. The term *futurismo* was introduced by the Italian writer Marinetti in 1909 in order to denote the extreme radicalism in literature and in all the arts. His ideas were transferred to music by Francesco Pratella, at least theoretically, in his *Musica Futurista* (1912), which contains the following characteristic sentences: "Dare l'anima musicale delle folle (of the masses), dei grandi cantieri industriali (industrial ship yards), dei treni (railways), dei transatlantici (steamboats), delle corazzate (battleships), degli automobili e degli aeroplani. Aggiungere ai grandi motivi centrali del poema musicale il dominio della Macchina ed il regno vittoroso della Elettricità" [cf. the full text in N. Slonimsky, *Music Since 1900* (1937)]. Pratella also gives a detailed description of a composition for an "or-chestra" consisting of machine guns, sirens, steam-whistles, etc. His music, however, is not more than a mild Debussyism, mingled with Puccinian idioms. Real futuristic music was composed by Luigi Russolo (b. 1885), who constructed a number of noise instruments. Although his few performances of futurist music remained entirely without success, it is interesting to note that the program of futurism (a similar French movement was called *bruitisme*, noise-music) was partly realized by the "machine-music" of Bartók, Milhaud, Stravinsky (*c.* 1920–30). See *New music. Cf. J. Écorcheville, in *BSIM* ix; N. C. Gatty, in *MQ* ii.

Fz. Abbreviation of *forzando, forzato*, same as *sforzando (sf, sfz).

G

G. See *Pitch names; *Letter notation; *Hexachord; *Clefs.

Gabelgriff [G.]. *Cross fingering.

Gagliard, gaillarde. See *Galliard.

Gai [F.], **Gaio** [It.]. Gay.

Gaïta. See *Bagpipe.

Galanterien [G.]. Eighteenth-century name for short entertaining pieces in homophonic, i.e., non-fugal style, such as airs, variations, dances. In particular, denomination for the more recent dances in the optional group of the suite, such as the bourrée, passepied, gavotte, etc., which are composed in a lighter style than the traditional allemand, courant, sarabande, and gigue. Cf. the title of the first part of Bach's *Clavierübung*: ". . . Sarabanden, Giquen, Menuetten und anderen Galanterien." See *Gallant style.

Gallant style [F. *style galant*; G. *galanter Stil*; It. *stile sueto*]. In the 18th century, the light and elegant style of the *Rococo, as opposed to the serious and elaborate style of the *Baroque era (*strenger Stil, gearbeiteter Stil, stile osservato*). The appearance of this new style indicated the change from the church to the "salon" as the cultural center, from fugal treatment to accompanied melody, from architectural greatness to playful pettiness, from cantatas and masses to amorous songs. This transition is already noticeable in the harpsichord compositions of F. Couperin and his German imitators (such as J. K. F. Fischer, F. X. Murschhauser, Th. Muffat) — as well as in the optional dances (menuets, bourrées, gavots, etc.; see *Galanterien) in the suites of Bach [cf. also the (spurious?) dances — menuets, marches, polonaises — in the *Notenbüchlein der Anna Magdalena Bach*]. The whole-hearted adoption of this style led, around 1750, to an unusually low ebb of musical production, particularly in the works of Italian composers such as Rutini, Paganelli, Pescetti [cf. *TaAM* xii], and in England. In Germany it produced more important results under the hands of Telemann, Mattheson, Theophil Muffat. In the second half of the 18th century Bach's sons Wilhelm Friedemann and Philipp

Emanuel endowed the new style with an expressiveness [see *Empfindsamer Stil] for which the somewhat derogatory word "gallant" is hardly an adequate denomination, just as little as in the case of Mozart's works which are directly derived from the gallant style of the Italians (including Johann Christian Bach). See *Rococo; *Haffner collection.

Lit.: W. Dahms, "The 'Gallant' Style of Music" (*MQ* xi); P. Gradenwitz, "Mid-18th Century Transformations of Style" (*ML*, xviii, no. 3); E. Bücken, "Der galante Stil" (*ZMW* vi); see also under *Rococo.

Galliard [F. *gaillarde*; It. *gagliarda*, i.e., gay, rollicking]. A 16th-century dance in moderately quick triple time, with or without upbeat. It was executed with exaggerated leaps which, toward the end of the 16th century, took on features of gross obscenity. The earliest examples are preserved in Attaingnant's *Quatorze gaillardes, neuf pavanes, sept branles et deux basses dances* (1530) [cf. *ApMZ* ii, 21, 22]. A great number of *gagliardas*, each named after a muse or another lady, occur in Vincenzi Galilei's *Intavolatura di liuto* of 1584 [see *Editions XIV, 4, p. 101]. After 1550 the galliard usually appears as an after-dance to the *pavane. See *Cinque-pace; *Dance music II.

Gallican chant. The French (Provençal) branch or "dialect" of the plainsong tradition of the medieval Western Church [see *Chant]. It was in use in France until the introduction of the Roman chant and rite under Pipin [see *French music I]. A small number of melodies survive in manuscripts of the 11th century. Certain portions of the Gallican chant were incorporated into the Roman liturgy, e.g., the *Improperia and the hymn *Crux Fidelis* (*GR*, 204).

Lit.: A. Gastoué, *Histoire du chant à Paris* (1904); *id.*, *Le Chant gallican* (1939; also published in *Revue du Chant Grégorien*, 1937–39). For additional bibl. cf. *ReMMA*, 436.

Galop. A quick round-dance of the mid-19th century (*c.* 1825–75) with rhythms such as those shown in the illustration. It was executed with many changes of steps

and with hopping movements. Offenbach used it parodistically in his *Orpheus in the Underworld* (1858). F. Liszt wrote a *Grand Galop Chromatique* (1838) and a *Galop de Bal* (*c.* 1840). See *Dance music IV.

Galoubet. See *Pipe and Tabor.

Gamba, Gambe [G.]. See *Viola da gamba.

Gambang. A Javanese xylophone, consisting of a number of wooden or metal bars, resting on a boat-shaped resonating box. It occurs in a great variety of sizes and timbres.

Gambenwerk. See under *Sostenente pianoforte.

Gamelan. The Javanese orchestra [see *Javanese Music]. Cf. G. Knosp, "Le Gamelan" (*RMI* xxxi, xxxiii).

Gamma [Greek name of the letter g]. In medieval theory the lowest tone of the scale, the G of the modern scale. In the Guidonian terminology it received the compound name *gamma-ut* [see *Hexachord II]. Later, the term was metaphorically used to denote "all the tones from Gamma," i.e., the entire scale. This meaning persists in the French word *gamme* for scale, and in the English *gamut* for scale or range.

Gamme [F.]. Scale. See under *Gamma.

Gamut. See under *Gamma.

Ganze Note, ganze Pause [G.]. See *Notes.

Ganzton [G.]. Whole tone. *Ganztonleiter*, whole-tone scale.

Ganzschluss [G.]. Full cadence.

Gapped scale. A scale which is derived from a more complete system of tones by the omission of some of these. Thus, the pentatonic scale is a gapped scale of the diatonic system, and this, in turn, can be considered as a gapped scale of the chromatic scale. Another selection, made from the chromatic system, leads to the chromatic scale of the ancient Greek theory. Most of the scales of Oriental music are gapped scales, as the tones used in actual music are only a small selection from a more complete system which is designed only for theoretical demonstration [cf., e.g., the 22 sruti and the 7-tone scales, sa-grama and ma-grama, of *Hindu music].

Garbatamente [It.]. Gracefully.

Gassenhauer [G., from *Gasse*, alley]. In present German usage a vulgar street song. In publications of the 16th century, e.g., in Egenolff's *Gassenhauerlin und Reutterliedlein* (1535; facs. ed. by H. J. Moser, 1927), the term simply denotes popular songs, without the implication of vulgarity. In fact, these collections include some of the most beautiful lyric songs of Isaac, Hofhaimer, and Senfl.

Gathering note. In hymn singing, a note sounded by the organist as a signal to the congregation, to give them the correct pitch of the hymn.

Gaukler [G.]. See *Minstrels.

Gavotte. A French dance of the 17th century the name of which is said to be derived from the "gavots," i.e., the in-

habitants of the Pays de Gap in Dauphiné. The dance is in moderate 4/4-time, with an upbeat of two quarter-notes, and with the phrases usually ending and beginning

in the middle of a measure. Earlier examples, however, are frequently notated without upbeat [see Ex.]. The dance is already mentioned in Arbeau's *Orchesographie* (1588) as a "recueil de branles," but apparently did not come in vogue until the middle of the 17th century when Lully introduced it into his ballets and operas. From here it found its way into the *ordres* of d'Anglebert and Fr. Couperin, and into the German suites of Pachelbel and J. K. F. Fischer. Bach used it frequently as one of the optional dances of his instrumental and keyboard suites. See *Dance music III.

Gebrauchsmusik [G.]. This recent term, for which "utility music" or "workaday music" is occasionally used as a translation, denotes music which is designed for "practical use" by amateurs, in the homes or at informal gatherings, as opposed to music written "for its own sake" (*l'art pour l'art*) and designed chiefly to be used in concert performance by professionals or virtuosos. Characteristic traits of Gebrauchsmusik are: forms of moderate length; simplicity and clarity of style; small ensembles; avoidance of technical difficulties; parts of equal interest and so designed that they can be played on whatever instruments are available; soberness and moderation of expression; emphasis on "good workmanship." The rise of Gebrauchsmusik is one of the most characteristic features of *New Music in which it characterizes the reaction against the exaggerated individualism and the *fin-de-siècle* refinement of the late Romanticism and of the impressionism. The movement which started under Hindemith and others in the festivals of Donaueschingen [see *Festivals III] gained support from two sides: from the socialistic tendencies of the German post-war era, and from the revival of early music, particularly of Bach. In fact, Bach's cantatas were frequently cited as the earliest examples of Gebrauchsmusik in the sense of "music written for immediate consumption or on commission" (Bach had to write a cantata for every Sunday). While 19th-century composers would have considered such a demand as an infringement upon the free creative inspiration of the artist, musicians such as Hindemith and Krenek have taken a pride in adopting the less ostentatious attitude which was natural to the masters of earlier periods. Hindemith's introductory notes to his *Plöner Musiktag* (1932) and to *Wir bauen eine Stadt* (1931) contain many pertinent remarks on Gebrauchsmusik. Cf. *DM* xxi.6 and xxiv.3; H. Closson, "The Case against Gebrauchsmusik" (*MM* vii).

Gebrochener Akkord [G.]. Broken chord.

Gebunden [G.]. Legato.

Gebundener Stil [G. *gebunden*, tied, restricted]. The strict contrapuntal style of the 17th and early 18th centuries (fugues), as opposed to *freier Stil* (free style), i.e., either accompanied melody or *Freistimmigkeit. The Italian synonym is *stile osservato* [see *Stile].

Gedackt [Old G.], **gedeckt** [G.]. *Stopped. The former term is used for an organ register consisting of stopped pipes, the latter for modern "stopped" instruments such as the clarinet.

Gedämpft [G.]. Muted, muffled.

Gedehnt [G.]. "Stretched out," sustained.

Gefährte [G., companion]. The answer of a fugal subject.

Gefällig [G.]. Agreeable, pleasing.

Gefühlvoll [G.]. Full of feeling.

Gegenbewegung [G.]. Usually contrary motion (between two voices); sometimes used in the meaning of inversion (of a subject).

Gegenfuge [G.]. Counter-fugue.

Gegensatz [G.]. Contrast. In older writings the term is used to denote a countersubject or second theme.

Gegenthema [G.]. Countersubject (of a fugue) or second theme (of a sonata movement).

Gehalten [G.]. Sustained.

Gehaucht [G.]. Whispered.

Geheimnisvoll [G.]. Mysterious.

Gehend [G.]. "Going," i.e., andante.

Geige [G.]. Violin; see under *Gigue (1). *Geigenwerk*, see under *Sostenente pianoforte.

Geisslerlieder [G.]. German 14th-century songs which were sung during the penitential processions of the flagellants. Cf. P. Runge, *Die Lieder und Melodien der Geissler des Jahres 1349* (1900); *ReMMA*, 239.

Geistertrio [G. *Geist*, spirit, ghost]. Popular name for Beethoven's Pianoforte Trio in D, op. 70, with reference to the ghost-like character of the slow movement.

Geistlich [G.]. Sacred, religious, spiritual. *Geistliche Konzerte* (Schütz) are concerted pieces (vocal and instrumental) for the use in the church; see *Concerto III.

Gekkin. A Japanese guitar; see *Guitar family.

Gekoppelt [G.]. Coupled.

Geläufigkeit [G.]. Technical fluency.

Gelassen [G.]. Quiet, calm.

Gemächlich [G.]. Comfortable.

Gemässigt [G.]. Moderate.

Gemeindelied [G.]. Congregational hymn, chorale.

Gemendo [It.]. Moaning.

Gemessen [G.]. "Measured," restrained.

Gemischte Stimmen [G.]. Mixed voices.

Genau [G.]. Exact.

Gendèr. A Javanese metallophone, consisting of thin bronze slabs over resonating bamboo tubes [see *Javanese Music I].

Genera. Plural of L. *genus.*

Generalbass [G.]. *Thorough-bass.

Generalpause [G., abbreviated *G.P.*]. In orchestral works, a rest for the entire orchestra, coming in unexpectedly after a climaxing passage. This effect was one of the startling innovations of the *Mannheim School.

Generalprobe [G.]. The dress rehearsal of symphonic concerts, usually open to the public.

Gentilmente [It.]. Gently, delicately.

Genus. See *Greek music II (b).

Gequält [G.]. Painful.

German flute. Eighteenth-century name for the transverse (cross) flute, as distinguished from the English flute, i.e., the recorder.

German music. The development of German music, if compared with that in France, England, Italy, started strikingly late. In the field of polyphonic music in particular, it was not until the middle of the 15th century — that is, at the time when the great period of *French music came to its close — that Germany came to the fore. From then on, however, German music progressed in a continuous line which, even aside from its many outstanding summits, has maintained an exceptionally high level up to the present day, thus making Germany the leading nation in the more recent era of music history.

I. *Prehistory and Middle Ages.* The *lures, beautiful long trumpets of the Nordic bronze age, are remarkable as evidence of a high standard of bronze founding rather than of "prehistoric German music," as has occasionally been claimed. Late Roman and early medieval writers have frequently made unfavorable comments upon the musical ability of the ancient Germans, particularly in regard to their singing [see Lit., Moser, p. 47]. In the 9th century the monastery of St. Gall (founded by Irish monks) became one of the most important centers of cul-

tivation of Gregorian chant, particularly remarkable for its contribution to the development of the *sequence (Notker Balbulus, *c.* 840–912; Tuotilo, d. 915; Wipo, 11th century) and of musical theory (Notker Labeo, d. 1022; Hermannus Contractus, 1013–54). In the 12th century the Provençal troubadour movement spread to Germany, leading to a first flowering of German secular song among the *Minnesinger, with Neithart von Reuenthal (d. after 1245) as the outstanding musical personality. Toward the end of the 14th century their tradition deteriorated, but was continued by the *Meistersinger, with Hans Sachs (1494–1576) as the main representative.

Meanwhile, polyphonic music had made a late and slow start in the strikingly primitive pieces (written in the style of 11th-century *organum) of the 14th-century codex Engelberg 314 [cf. F. Ludwig, in *KJ* xxi, 48–61, and in *AMW* v, 305ff], and in the slightly less archaic pieces of the Münch of Salzburg (fl. around 1375; cf. Moser, p. 184ff) and of Oswald von Wolkenstein (1377–1445; cf. *BeMMR*, 180; *SchGMB*, no. 46; complete works in *DTOe* 9.i). Attractive examples of unpretentious domestic chamber music exist in the *Lochamer Liederbuch* and in the *Glogauer Liederbuch* (both *c.* 1460; see *Liederbuch). Closely related to the Lochamer MS, which is also an important source of German 15th-century folk song, is the *Fundamentum organisandi* (1452) of Conrad Paumann (1410–73), an important source of German organ music, preceded by the tablature of Adam Ileborgh (1448; cf. W. Apel, in *ZMW* xvi) and followed by the *Buxheim Organ Book* of *c.* 1470.

II. *Renaissance.* The late 15th century saw the rise of the first important school of German polyphonic music, represented by Adam von Fulda (*c.* 1440–1506; cf. W. Niemann, in *KJ*, 1902), Heinrich Finck (1445–1527), and Alexander Agricola (1446–1506) [see *Editions V, nos. 9, 21, 32]. The Flemish master Heinrich Isaac (1450–1517) played a leading role in this development, particularly in the field of the German part-song ("Innsbruck ich muss dich lassen"), to which Paulus Hofhaimer (1459–1537), court-organist to Maximilian II, Thomas Stoltzer (c. 1480–1526), and Ludwig Senfl (c. 1490–c. 1550), a Swiss, also contributed many examples of great beauty [cf. H. J. Moser, *Paulus Hofhaimer* (1929); *DTOe* 37.ii; *DdT* 34; *HAM*, nos. 93, 108–111; *SchGMB*, nos. 76, 84–87; *BeMMR*, 265ff]. Senfl's *quodlibets are an interesting source for the reconstruction of the early German folk song. Around the middle of the 16th century this autochthonous development was interrupted to a certain extent by the great influx of Flemish composers who held the key-position in all the musical centers (de Monte in Prague; Le Maistre and Scandellus in Dresden; Lasso in Munich), until their German pupils such as Jacobus Gallus (Handl, 1550–91), Leonard Lechner (1553–1606), and Hans Leo Hassler (1564–1612) were ready to continue their tradition. Gallus and Hassler, together with Heinrich Praetorius (1560–1629) and Michael Praetorius (1571–1621), contributed also to the dissemination of the *Venetian polychoral style. Towards the end of the century a number of musicians known as *colorists were active in the field of keyboard music.

III. *Baroque.* The 17th century found German composers active in practically all the fields of vocal and instrumental music, and soon leading particularly in the various forms of church music, the *cantata, *passion, and organ composition. Here the Lutheran *chorale provided a basis of tradition as well as of progress, which largely accounts for the spiritual integrity and, as a result, for the high artistic quality of German Baroque music. An idea of the scope of German Baroque music can be gained by glancing through the list of the German *Denkmäler* [see *Editions VII, VIII, IX]. The most outstanding figures are (arranged in contemporary groups):

Schütz, Schein, Scheidt (b. c. 1585, 100 years before Bach)
Tunder, Froberger, Rosenmüller (b. c. 1615)
Buxtehude, Georg Muffat, Biber (b. c. 1640)

Johann Ph. Krieger, Fischer, Pachelbel (b. c. 1650)
Böhm, Bruhns, Kuhnau (b. c. 1660)
Telemann, Walther, J. S. Bach (b.c. 1685).

At the outset of the 17th century we find an interesting activity in the field of the instrumental dance and *suite, represented by Johann Hermann Schein (1586–1630), Valentin Haussmann, Isaak Posch, and Paul Peuerl. Simultaneously Heinrich Schütz (1585–1672) brought the vocal church music (*passion, *oratorio) to an artistic height comparable to that of Bach, and Samuel Scheidt (1586–1654) laid the foundation for the development of German organ music [see *Organ music II (a); *Organ chorale, etc.]. The next generation saw the rise of harpsichord music under Johann Jacob Froberger (1616–67) [see *Suite III], and around 1650 the church cantata emerged as an exclusively German product [see *Cantata III]. Lute music reached an artistic climax in the works of Esaias Reusner (1636–79) and Silvius Weiss (1686–1750) [see *Lute music], while violin music was cultivated by Johann Schop (d. 1665), Nicolaus Adam Strungk (1640–1700), and Heinrich Biber (1644–1704), masters whose virtuosity paved the way for Bach's pieces for violin solo. In the field of orchestral music Johann Rosenmüller (1620–84) stands out as an early master of original significance, while later composers such as Georg Muffat (1645–1704), and Philipp Erlebach (1657–1714), incorporated elements of the Italian and French orchestral styles. The German Baroque *lied* found an outstanding master in Adam Krieger (1634–66) [see *Lied III], and only in the field of the opera have German musicians failed to compete successfully with their foreign models [see *Opera VII]. In all these fields, except the two last-mentioned, the development is climaxed by J. S. Bach (1685–1750).

IV. *Rococo.* Contemporaries of Bach, such as Georg Philipp Telemann (1681–1767), Valentin Rathgeber (1682–1750), and Gottlieb Muffat (1690–1770), were quick to embrace the novel and facile style of the *Rococo, and "progressive" writers such as Johann Mattheson (1681–1764) helped to throw overboard the last vestiges of a tradition which, from their point of view, they were justified in considering old-fashioned and useless. After a comparatively short period of low ebb, German music took a new start in two directions: one towards a novel type of expressiveness, the *empfindsamer Stil*; the other towards the exploitation of modern orchestral resources and the formal development of the classical sonata, symphony, and string quartet. In the former field Bach's sons, Wilhelm Friedemann Bach (1710–84) and Carl Philipp Emanuel Bach (1714–88), are outstanding; in the latter, the numerous musicians collectively known as the *Mannheim School*. Concomitant with this development is the rise of the *Singspiel, and of the *volkstümliches Lied [see also *Berlin School].

V. *Classicism, Romanticism, and Modernism.* The man who molded the formal and stylistic elements of the late Rococo into a new work of art, thus laying the foundation for the musical period known as *classicism, was Franz Joseph Haydn (1732–1809). From 1770 on, his symphonies and string quartets, as well as those of Mozart (1756–91), show more and more clearly that full mastery and maturity which has led to the designation "classical." No less immortal than these works are Haydn's oratorios and Mozart's operas. Beethoven (1770–1827) brought this development to its acme and, in his latest works, prepared the musical *Romanticism, side by side with Franz Schubert (1797–1828), the great master of the German lied. The Romantic spirit is more clearly patent in the operas and piano works of Carl Maria v. Weber (1786–1826), and was whole-heartedly embraced by Robert Schumann (1810–56), who more than any other composer represents the Romanticism with all its novel wonders and with all its inherent defects.

The story of German music from 1830 to 1940 may be told here in the form of a short account based on a chronological list of the important compositions produced in this period.

1830–40: The Romantic decade *par excellence*, including practically all the important works of Schumann and Mendelssohn.

1840–50: Schumann's last works (Piano Concerto), and Wagner's (1813–83) first operas: *Holländer, Tannhäuser, Lohengrin.*

1850–60: Wagner's *Rheingold, Walküre, Tristan.* F. Liszt (1811–86) establishes the *symphonic poem (*Faust, Dante, Mazeppa*), and writes his *Études transcendentales* and most of the Hungarian Rhapsodies. Brahms (1833–97) appears with his Piano Sonatas (opp. 1, 2, 5) and D minor Concerto, op. 15.

1860–70: Wagner and Brahms still dominate the scene, the former with *Siegfried* and *Meistersinger,* the latter with opp. 18–50, including the Handel Variations, the Magelone Songs, and the *Deutsches Requiem.*

1870–80: Wagner's *Götterdämmerung,* the last opera of the *Ring des Nibelungen.* Brahms writes his first two symphonies and chamber music (up to op. 86). Bruckner (1824–96) appears with his symphonies nos. 2–6.

1880–90: Wagner climaxes the opera with his *Parsifal*; Bruckner and Brahms, the symphony with their symphonies nos. 7–9 and 3–4. Brahms writes his last chamber works and the Piano Concerto in B-flat. Richard Strauss (b. 1864) brings new life to the symphonic poem in his *Don Juan* and *Tod und Verklärung.* Hugo Wolf (1860–1903) writes most of his songs.

1890–1900: The last works of Brahms (opp. 114–121). High-point of Strauss's symphonic poem: *Till Eulenspiegel, Don Quixote, Zarathustra.* Gustav Mahler's (1860–1911) symphonies nos. 2–4. Heinrich Pfitzner's (b. 1869) Romantic opera *Der arme Heinrich.*

1900–1910: The Romantic movement comes to its close in Mahler's Symphonies nos. 5–9, in Strauss's operas *Salome* and *Electra,* and in the chamber music of Max Reger (1873–1916). Arnold Schönberg (b. 1874), after the impressionistic *Pelleas und Melisande,* writes the atonal *Drei Klavierstücke* (1909), the first examples of the radical break leading to the *New music.

1910–20: Last vestiges of the Romantic tradition in Strauss's *Rosenkavalier* and *Alpensinfonie*, in Pfitzner's opera *Palestrina*, and in Schreker's (1878–1934) operas *Der ferne Klang* and *Der Schatzgräber*. Schönberg's *Pierrot Lunaire* and the completely atonal *Sechs kleine Klavierstücke*. Ferruccio Busoni (1866–1924) writes the first *neoclassic pieces (Sonatinas and *Fantasia contrappuntistica*).

1920–30: The heterogeneous after-war decade with its experiments in twelve-tone technique, jazz idiom, primitive rhythms, neo-classic forms, etc., brings to the fore a group of young composers, notably Paul Hindemith (b. 1895) with stage works such as *Cardillac*, sonatas, string quartets, *Das Marienleben*; Ernst Krenek (b. 1900) with *Johnny spielt auf* and piano and chamber works; Ernst Toch (b. 1887) with chamber and piano music; Kurt Weill (b. 1900) with the highly successful *Dreigroschenoper*.

1930–40: The most outstanding productions are Hindemith's *Mathis der Maler* and Piano Sonatas, conspicuous for their return to more conservative methods.

The most recent development of German music deserves a few additional remarks. While Hindemith, in compositions such as the sonatas for pianoforte (3; 1936), organ (2; 1937), violin (1935), flute (1937), oboe (1938), arrives at a happy synthesis of progressive and conservative elements, Krenek has wholeheartedly embraced the radical methods of Schönberg's *twelve-tone technique of which he is at present the main champion. Practically the whole group of composers now working in Germany stands under the influence of the "back-to-Bach" idea. Heinrich Kaminski (b. 1886) has written a number of works of great artistic perfection in what might be called "neo-Gothic" style, pieces in which a polyphonic texture and a rich vocabulary of chromatic harmonies are used for the expression of a deeply religious ecstasy and mys-

ticism. Hugo Herrmann (b. 1896) uses a linear style frequently approaching atonality. Johann Nepomuk David (b. 1895) reverts to the Flemish polyphony of the 15th and 16th centuries in works such as *Ricercare* (1928), organ hymns (1928), *Fantasia super L'homme armé* (1930). Wilhelm Maler (b. 1902), Heinrich Spitta (b. 1902), Kurt Thomas (b. 1904), Wolfgang Fortner (b. 1907), Hugo Distler (b. 1908), and others, work along the same line, trying to put archaic idioms to new use. Several of them have devoted themselves to the revival of church music in a-cappella style.

Lit.: H. J. Moser, *Geschichte der deutschen Musik*, 3 vols. (1920–24); *LavE* i.2, 971–1175; H. v. d. Pfordten, *Deutsche Musik* (1920); Arnold Schering, *Deutsche Musikgeschichte im Umriss* (1917); R. Malsch, *Geschichte der deutschen Musik* (1926); J. A. Fuller-Maitland, *Masters of German Music* (1894); J. Müller-Blattau, *Das deutsche Volkslied* (1932); L. Schiedermaier, *Die deutsche Oper* (1930); *AdHM* ii, 1002–1038 ("Die Moderne"; bibl.).

German Requiem. A work for solo voices, chorus, and orchestra by Johannes Brahms, op. 45, composed 1857–68, as a memorial for his mother. It consists of seven movements based on German texts freely selected from Scriptures, instead of the authoritative Latin text of the liturgical Requiem Mass [see *Requiem]. Its first performance in the United States was at the Cincinnati Festival of 1884.

German sixth. See *Sixth chord.

Gerührt [G.]. Moved, touched.

Ges, geses [G.]. See *Pitch names.

Gesamtausgabe [G.]. Complete edition. Most of the German *Gesamtausgaben* have been published by Breitkopf and Härtel, Leipzig. Cf. *MoML*, 262.

Gesang [G.]. Song.

Gesangbuch [G.]. Hymn-book, either of the Catholic or of the Protestant Church. For the earliest publication of Protestant hymn-books see *Chorale; cf. also *MoML*, 268, 396.

Gesangvoll [G.]. Cantabile.

Geschleift [G.]. Slurred.

Geschwind [G.]. Quick.

Gesellschaftslied [G.]. Recent musicological term for songs which socially belong to the bourgeois class, as opposed to *Hoflied* (court-song) or *Volkslied* (folk song). The term is used particularly with reference to the German 16th-century polyphonic songs of Hofhaimer, Senfl, and others, but it may also be used to include the Italian madrigal, the French chanson, etc.

Ge sol re ut, gesolreut. See *Hexachord II.

Gesprochen [G.]. Spoken, or "as if spoken."

Gesteigert [G.]. Increased.

Gestopft [G.]. The stopped notes of the horn. See *Horn I.

Gestossen [G.]. Detached, staccato.

Geteilt [G.]. Divided. See *Divisi.

Getragen [G.]. Sustained, slow.

Gewandhaus [G.]. See *Orchestras II.

Gewichtig [G.]. "Weighty," with importance.

Gezogen [G.]. "Drawn out," sustained.

Ghironda [It.]. *Hurdy-gurdy.

Gigelira [It.]. Xylophone.

Gigue. (1) Medieval name for string instruments, perhaps particularly the *rebec, the pear-shaped form of which is reminiscent of a ham [F. *gigot*, ham]. In the late 13th century a French poem mentions the "gigueours de l'Alle-maigne," i.e., the gigue-players of Germany [cf. *GéHM*, 400]. Probably the German word *Geige* (Old German *gíge*) for violin is derived from the French term gigue.
(2) In the suites of the 1650–1750 period the gigue [It. *giga*] is one of the four constituent dance movements, usually the

final one [see *Suite; *Dance music III]. Its chief characteristics are: compound triple time (⁶⁄₈, ⁶⁄₄), dotted rhythm, wide intervals (sixths, sevenths, octaves), and fugal writing, usually with the inverted subject [see *Inversion (2)] used for the second section. See the accompanying example from Bach, French

Suite, no. 4. The gigue developed from the 16th-century Irish or English *jig which, on the Continent, was subjected to two different processes of idealization, in France and in Italy. The French type (Gaultier, Chambonnières) is that described above, while the less frequent Italian type, the *giga*, is much quicker (presto gigue), non-fugal, with quick running passages over a harmonic basis [for a similar case, see *courante and corrente]. This type occurs in the works of Vitali [*Balletti, Corrente, Gighe, Allemande, e Sarabande* (1688)], Corelli, Zipoli [cf. *Editions VI, 36]. It survives in the ⁶⁄₈-presto pieces of the 18th century [cf. a gigue by C. H. Graun, 1701–59, in W. Niemann, †*Alte Meister des Klaviers*] which, in turn, are the model of such movements as the presto-finale of Beethoven's Piano Sonata op. 2, no. 1. The gigues in the suites of Froberger, Handel, Bach, etc., are usually of the French type. Notable exceptions are the gigues of Bach's Partita no. 1 and of his English Suite no. 2.
Lit.: W. Danckert, *Geschichte der Gigue* (1924).

Gigue-fugue. Popular name for Bach's Organ Fugue in G major [ed. Peters ix, no. 4], so called on account of the gigue-like character of the theme.

Gimel. See *Gymel.

Giocoso [It.]. Playful.

Gioioso [It.]. Joyful.

Giorgi flute. A flute invented by Giorgi (1888) which has finger-holes for each chromatic tone, thus making cross-fingering unnecessary. Cf. *SaRM*, 158; H. Standish, in *PMA* xxiv.

Gipsy music. See *Gypsy music.

Giraffe piano [G. *Giraffenklavier*]. An early 19th-century variety of the pianoforte, somewhat like the grand piano, but with the wing-shaped part of the case put upright, thus vaguely resembling the neck of a giraffe.

Giro [It.]. *Turn.

Gis, gisis [G.]. See *Pitch names.

Gitano [Sp.]. *Gypsy.

Gittern. Same as *cittern.

Giulivamente [It.]. Joyously.

Giustamente [It.]. With exactitude.

Giustiniane. Same as *Justiniane. See under *Villanella.

Glänzend [G.]. Brilliant.

Glasharmonika. See *Harmonica.

Glatt [G.]. Smooth, even.

Glee. An 18th-century type of choral music, unaccompanied, in three or more parts, for solo men's voices (including a male alto), comparatively brief and sectionally constructed. In the course of its development its texture often became less polyphonic and more in the harmonic style of the part song. The glee is one of two 18th-century forms (the other being the *ballad opera) which are English through and through, demonstrating the native English virtues of sincerity and forthrightness as no choral music after the madrigal has done. In the latter part of the century societies both of amateur and professional musicians devoted themselves to the composition and performance of the glee. Among these were the Noblemen's and Gentlemen's Catch Club, the Anacreontic Society, the Glee Club, and the Concentores Sodales. During the

first half of the 19th century glee singing was much in vogue, but those qualities of the part song which it has assumed finally became merged with the part song itself and the glee's artistic virtues were reduced to a shadow in the hands of Victorian composers of the shorter choral forms. Among the most celebrated glee writers were Dr. Benjamin Cooke (1734–93); Samuel Webbe (1740–1816), perhaps the most typical of glee composers, who wrote over three hundred glees and whose "Glorious Apollo" invariably opened the programs of the Glee Clubs; Stephen Paxton (1735–87); and John Callcott (1766–1821). Representative glees are to be found in Novello's *Standard Glee Book*.

"Glee" is derived from the Anglo-Saxon word "gligg" which is usually translated simply "music"; but it has also been taken to include entertainment in general, especially such entertainment as was connected with minstrelsy — playing, singing, dancing, and perhaps even acrobatic feats. Up to fairly recent times it was in the spirit of this latter definition that American College Glee Clubs, with rare exceptions, interpreted the word glee. About 1918, after a few years in which their programs were made up of a mixture of college and classical music, the Harvard Glee Club began to devote itself to the latter exclusively, at the same time severing its connection with the Instrumental Clubs made up of banjos and mandolins. This step initiated a wave of interest in the singing of serious music by college choral organizations and has had no little effect upon the quality of the music sung by secondary school glee clubs. Lit.: Wm. A. Barrett, *English Glees and Part-songs* (1886); D. Baptie, *Sketches of English Glee Composers* (1896); J. Spencer-Curwen, "Regarding the English Glee" (*ZIM* vi).   A. T. D.

Gleemen. See *Minstrels.

Gleichmässig [G.]. Equal, even.

Glissando [F. *glisser*, to slide]. The execution of rapid scales by a sliding movement. In piano-playing, the nail of the thumb or that of the third finger is drawn rapidly over the white keys. The same technique can also be applied to the black keys. A much more difficult feat is the glissando in parallel thirds, sixths, or octaves which is performed by a sliding movement of the hand with two fingers held in a strongly fixed position. It is surprising to note that Mozart already has a glissando in parallel sixths in the cadenza of his piano variations "Lison dormait." It should be noted, however, that the glissando was much easier to perform on the old instruments with their light Viennese action. This fact also explains the octave-glissandi in the last movement of Beethoven's Waldstein-Sonata which are almost impossible to perform on modern instruments. The first record of a glissando occurs in a publication by Moyreau, *Premier livre de pièces de clavecin* (1722). — Glissando is much used in the playing of the *harp. — On the violin the glissando is a difficult virtuoso effect produced by a rapid succession of minute distinct movements of the hand. This effect should not be confused with the *portamento, which is easily produced by a continuous movement of the hand. The so-called glissando of the trombones practically always is a portamento.

Glocke [G.]. Bell.

Glockenspiel. See *Percussion instruments A, 2. The portable glockenspiel of the military bands consists of steel bars fixed on a frame in the shape of the ancient Greek lyre, hence the name belllyra [G. *Lyra*]. In German terminology the word *Glockenspiel* is also used to denote what it properly means, namely a set of bells [*Glocke*, i.e., bell], i.e., a *carillon. In the late 18th century there existed Glockenspiels to be played from a keyboard, similar to the modern *celesta. This is probably the instrument called for in Mozart's *Zauberflöte* under the name *strumento d'acciaio* (steel instrument).

Glogauer Liederbuch. See *Liederbuch.

Gloria in excelsis. The second item of the Ordinary of the Mass, also known as greater *doxology. See *Mass A; B III. In plainsong the first phrase, *Gloria in excelsis Deo*, is sung by the officiating priest, and the chorus picks up at *Et in terra pax*. Early (15th-century) polyphonic settings of the Gloria therefore begin with the latter phrase, and are usually indexed under *Et in terra* in modern editions.

Gloria patri. See *Doxology.

Glosa [Sp.]. Spanish 16th-century name for diminutions [see *Ornamentation I]. Diego Ortiz' *Tratado de glosas sobre clausulas* . . . (1553; reprint by M. Schneider, 1913, 1936) contains a great number of instructive examples, illustrating the methods of ornamenting a cadential formula (*clausula*). Cabezon [*Obras de musica* (1578)] uses the term for simple figurative variations of harmonized psalm tones (*fabordone y glosas*; cf. *ApMZ* ii, 18), while more elaborate variations are called *diferencias.

G.O. In French organ music, abbreviation for *grand orgue*.

Götterdämmerung. See *Ring des Nibelungen, Der.

Goldberg Variations. A series of 30 variations by J. S. Bach, commissioned by the Russian Count Kayserling, and named after Bach's pupil Johann Theophilus Goldberg (*c.* 1720–60), who was in the count's service as a pianist. Bach published them in the fourth part of the *Clavierübung* (1742). The work, which is among the greatest in the field of variations, is written according to a special plan: two variations in free style (frequently of a highly virtuoso character) are always followed by a canonic variation (nos. 3, 6, 9, etc.). The latter are unsurpassed masterpieces of canonic technique, being canons at different intervals within the same harmonic frame. The final variation is a *quodlibet.

Golden sequence. Popular name for the *sequence *Veni Sancte Spiritus*.

Goliard songs. Latin poems of the 10th to the 13th century, written by goliards, i.e., wandering students or young ecclesiastics who played an important part in the cultural life of that period. The most famous collection is the *Carmina Burana* (named after the monastery of Benedict-Beuren in southwest Germany, where the manuscript was preserved). Some of these poems are provided with staffless neumes which cannot be deciphered. The only decipherable melody of a Goliard song is that to the 10th-century poem *O admirabile Veneris ydolum* [BeMMR, 72]. Cf. ReMMA, 200; H. Spanke, in ZMW xiii.

Gondola song, Gondellied [G.], **Gondoliera** [It.]. See *Barcarole.

Gong. See *Percussion instruments, B, 7. See also *Chinese, *Javanese music.

Gopak. A lively dance of Little Russia, in duple time. A well-known example is contained in Moussorgsky's unfinished opera *Sorotchinskoe Fair.*

Gorgia [It., throat], **gorgheggio.** Generic term for the late 16th-century method of improvised coloraturas such as were used in the performance of motets, masses, madrigals, etc. [see *Ornamentation I; cf. F. Chrysander, in VMW vii, ix, x (Zacconi)]. *Gorgheggio* is also a modern term for vocal passages in rapid speed.

Gospel [L. *Evangelium*]. In the Catholic rites, a passage from one of the four Gospels, chanted at *Mass in monotone or with inflections (*Tonus Evangelii*; cf. GR, 115*). — Gospel canticles are the three major *canticles. — For Gospel hymn, see *Hymn, English. — Texts from the Gospels have been very frequently composed, in motets (Gospel motet, *Evangelienmotette*), passions, oratorios, and cantatas. Cf. H. J. Moser, *Die mehrstimmige Vertonung des Evangeliums* (1931).

Gothic music. A term used by various modern writers to denote music coeval with, or culturally related to, the Gothic era in architecture, sculpture, and painting. It is usually understood to embrace the period from 1200 (Perotinus) to 1450 (Dufay), that is, prior to the beginning of the *Renaissance [see *History of music]. The term also carries a certain geographical implication, referring to the Nordic cultures (northern France, England, Netherlands, Germany) rather than to those of the south. In fact, the music of the Italian *Ars nova is perhaps too "earthly" and "lively" (too much: "protorenaissance") to be termed Gothic. Of the two contemporary early Flemish masters, Ockeghem and Obrecht, the former may be considered as representing the end of Gothic, the latter, the beginning of Renaissance music [see *Flemish School III]. Cf. LaMWC, passim.

Metaphorically, the word Gothic is also applied to later works showing traits suggestive of Gothic spirituality and irrealism, for instance, to the "transcendental" organ toccatas of Buxtehude or Bach. Modern works showing a similar attitude have been called neo-Gothic (Hindemith, Kaminsky) [see *Neo-classicism].

G.P. In German orchestral scores, abbreviation for *Generalpause. In French organ music, abbreviation for *grand positif*, i.e., great and choir organ coupled.

G.R. In French organ music, abbreviation for *grand récitatif*, i.e., great and swell organ coupled.

Grace. Term applied by early English musicians to any kind of musical ornament, whether written out in notes, indicated by sign, or improvised by the performer. In lute and viol playing a distinction was made between *smooth graces*, produced by sliding the finger along the finger board (appoggiaturas, slides, and Nachschläge), and *shaked graces*, in the performance of which the finger shakes, producing several repercussions of the same tone (trills, relishes, and beats). Another distinction is that between *open graces*, i.e., those involving a whole fret (semitone), and *closed graces*, i.e., those involving a smaller interval (vibrato).

P. A.

Grace note. A note printed in small type to indicate that its time value is not counted in the rhythm of the bar and must be subtracted from that of an adjacent note. Large groups of grace notes sometimes make an exception to this rule in that together they fill up the time value of a single note that has been omitted from the score (as in the so-called "cadenzas" by Chopin and other Romantic composers), in which case the rhythm of the grace notes is flexible and not subjected to a strict beat. Most grace notes are used to represent *graces, or musical ornaments.   P. A.

Gracieux [F.]. Graceful.

Gradatamente [It.]. Gradually.

Gradevole, gradito [It.]. Pleasing.

Gradual [L. *Graduale*, from *gradus,* step]. (1) The second item of the Proper of the *Mass. It belongs to the class of responsorial chants. The original name was *responsorium graduale* (i.e., the *responsorium* sung from the steps of the altar or ambo), in contrast to other *responsoria. The graduals are highly florid melodies, in their choral as well as in their soloist sections (verse). For the form of the graduals, see *Psalmody II. For polyphonic compositions of the graduals, see *Mass B, I. — (2) See *Liturgical books.

Gradus ad Parnassum [L., steps to Parnassus, the abode of the Muses]. Title of two publications designed to lead up to the highest perfection in their fields: a treatise on counterpoint by J. J. Fux (1725), and a collection of piano etudes by M. Clementi (1817).

Grail. English name for *Gradual, used in the Anglican Church.

Gramophone [G. *Grammophon*]. See *Phonograph.

Gran cassa, gran tamburo [It.]. Bass drum.

Grand [F.]. *Grand jeu, grand orgue,* full organ; *grand opéra,* i.e., opera (usually serious) with fully composed text, as distinct from *opéra comique.*

Grandezza, Con [It.]. With grandeur.

Grandisonante [It.]. Sonorous.

Grandsire. See *Change ringing.

Gran gusto, Con [It.]. See *Gusto.

Grasshopper. See *Pianoforte I.

Grave [It.]. Slow, solemn.

Gravicembalo. Italian 17th-century name for the harpsichord, possibly for a large variety used especially for orchestral accompaniment. The name may be a corruption of *clavicembalo, or may refer to the presence of a "grave" 16-foot stop.

Graziös [G.], **grazioso** [It.]. Graceful.

Greater perfect system. See *Greek music II (a).

Greek music. In the entire history of music there is no field so embarrassing to the student as that of ancient Greek music. There are two main reasons for this: first, the perplexing incongruity that exists between the considerable quantity of available theoretical information and the small number of preserved musical documents, that is, five or six complete compositions and as many fragments; secondly, the fact that the theoretical information is largely of a highly speculative and scholastic character, frequently incomplete, obscure, and contradictory. Stimulated rather than discouraged by this situation, modern scholars have spent — not to say wasted — an incredible amount of time, labor, and ingenuity trying to clarify the many perplexing incongruities and hairsplittings of Greek theory. The essay on Greek music contained in Lavignac's *Encyclopédie* (*LavE* i.1, 377–537) is the *ne plus ultra* of dry and useless scholasticism, an effusion compared with which medieval treatises read like a detective story. It is to be regretted that even in the most recent books the intricacies of Greek theory are treated with a thoroughness which can only be explained as the (unconscious) desire on the part of the author to make his readers suffer for what he has suffered himself in preparing and writing his study. The article by C. Sachs in Bücken's *Handbuch der Musikwissenschaft* is a noteworthy exception, which has served as a model for the subsequent description.

I. *History*. The fact established by modern philologists [Ed. Meyer] that Greek culture was not entirely autochthonous and aboriginal, but developed under the strong influence of Egyptian, Phoenician, and Asiatic cultures (Mycenaean period, *c.* 2000–1500 B.C.; cf. O. Gombosi, in *BAMS* vi) suggests the theory that Greek music, too, owed its origin to that of other nations of a more ancient cultural life. Indeed, even the most typically Greek instrument, the *kithara, has an Oriental ancestry, to say nothing about the purely Oriental *aulos. There developed, however, in the Homeric era a national Greek culture which was looked upon by later generations as the Golden Age of music also. The chief instrument of the Homeric poems is the *phorminx*, a lyre, with which the *aioidos* (singer, bard) accompanied his recitations of heroic deeds. For this he used certain traditional standard melodies, called *nomos*, which may have been but short phrases repeated over and over again (similar to the *chanson de geste of the Middle Ages?; see also *Melody types). While Olympos, said to have "invented" music, remains legendary, Terpander of Lesbos (*c.* 675 B.C.) is the earliest definite figure of Greek music. By his time the *nomos* must have been a much more elaborate composition, since he increased the number of its "sections" to seven. While Terpander appears to us as the climaxing figure of the Greek "ars antiqua" (to use a term of medieval music history), a younger contemporary, Archilochos, introduced novel features, such as triple rhythm, quicker tempo, and possibly folklike elements. The lyrical poetry of Sappho, Alkaios, Anakreon, was, no doubt, a musical as well as a literary art, probably created simultaneously by the poet-musician. The 6th century sees the rise of the Greek drama in which music, chiefly choral, played an important part. Occasionally scenes were accompanied by

the Dionysian *aulos, while the *kithara, the instrument of Apollo, remained restricted to the field of religious and hymnic music. Around 500 began a new period of Greek music which has been compared to the Baroque era of our musical history. Its chief characteristics are subjective expression, free forms, more elaborate melody and rhythm, the introduction of chromaticism, and even quarter-tones, the emergence of the professional musician and of the virtuoso. Phrynis of Mythilene (*c.* 450), Euripides (d. *c.* 406), and Timotheos of Milet (*c.* 400) appear as the main representatives of this new movement. Practically no details are known regarding the development — or rather decline — of music in the remaining period of Greek history.

II. *Theory*. a. *Tetrachord and Scale*. The point of departure of Greek musical theory is the tetrachord, i.e., a succession of four descending tones forming the intervals T T S (T = whole tone; S = semitone), e.g., a–g–f–e. A complete two-octave scale (descending, like all Greek scales) was arrived at as a succession of four tetrachords plus an added lowest tone, as follows:

Nete hyperbolaion	a'	I. Tetr.
Paranete hyperbolaion	g'	hyperbolaion
Trite hyperbolaion	f'	
Nete diezeugmenon	e'	
Paranete diezeugmenon	d'	II. Tetr.
Trite diezeugmenon	c'	diezeugmenon
Paramese	b	
Mese	a	
Lichanos meson	g	III. Tetr.
Parhypate meson	f	meson
Hypate meson	e	
Lichanos hypaton	d	IV. Tetr.
Parhypate hypaton	c	hypaton
Hypate hypaton	B	
Proslambanomenos	A	

Judging from the names of the tetrachords, III was the nucleus of the system; the name of II ("disjunct") refers to the fact that its lowest tone lies above the highest of the other, while I and IV are added in a "conjunct" fashion, i.e., with one note in common. The name "hypaton" (highest) for IV is probably explained by the fact that the kithara players tilted their instrument in such a way that the lowest strings were in the highest position [an analogous phenomenon exists in the 16th-century Italian lute tablatures; see under *Tablature III]. The names for the single tones also show that the whole system developed from the playing of the kithara: *nete* (*chorde*) means lowest strings (actually the highest in pitch); *paranete*, next to the lowest; *trite*, the third, etc.

The entire two-octave scale was called *systema teleion* (usually translated: Greater Perfect System; henceforth referred to as disdiapason). There also existed a Lesser Perfect System which consisted of the lowest octave (A to a) plus a tetrachord added conjunctly above a (therefore called *synemmenon*, i.e., "hooked"), thus providing the tones (a), bb, c′, and d′.

b. *Genera*. The fundamental tetrachord was capable of certain chromatic modifications which, however, affected only the pitch of its two middle notes (*kinoumenoi*, "movable"), never that of the two outer tones (*hestotes*, "fixed"). The alterations were made in such a way that the highest of the three intervals of the tetrachord was widened from a whole tone (a–g) into an interval of three semitones (a–gb) or, of four (a–f). The remaining interval (gb–e, or f–e) was halved, a procedure which, in the latter case, involved the introduction of quarter-tones. These three types of tetrachords were distinguished as diatonic, chromatic, and enharmonic. By a procedure identical with that described under (a) two modified disdiapasons were obtained, the chromatic (a′–gb′–f–e–db′–c′–b′–a . . .) and the enharmonic (a′–f′–x–e′–c′–y–b–a . . .). For still other microtonic experiments, see *Chroai. See also *Pyknon.

c. *Octave Species* (*Harmoniai*). In a similar manner as in the medieval *Church modes, segments each comprising an octave were cut out of the disdiapason and named as follows:

a′–a: Hypodorian (Hyperphrygian, Aeolian, Lokrian)
g′–g: Hypophrygian (Hyperlydian, Ionian, Iastian)
f′–f: Hypolydian
e′–e: Dorian
d′–d: Phrygian
c′–c: Lydian
b′–B: Mixolydian (Hyperdorian).

(The alternative names given in parentheses are later usage; some of them properly refer to lower or higher octaves, e.g., Hyperphrygian — i.e., a fifth above Phrygian, hence a′–a; Hypodorian — i.e., a fifth below Dorian, hence a–A.) These octave-species (*harmoniai*) have been — and still are — frequently referred to as "Greek modes." Although there exists a certain similarity between the two systems, it must be noted that the Greek octave-species differ from the medieval modes not only in the somewhat external matter of denomination (the octave e–e′, for instance, is Dorian in Greek, Phrygian in medieval theory; see the explanation under *Church modes) but chiefly in the question of the tonic or center tone. In the medieval system, this is (considering the authentic modes only) the lowest tone of the octave; in Greek theory, however, the center tone was probably always the *mese*, a. Thus, a medieval and a Greek octave of the same ambitus, e.g., f–f′, have different tonics, the medieval a well-characterized f, the Greek, a much less clearly defined a or, possibly, no prescribed tonic at all.

d. *Transposed Scales* (*Tonoi*). For practical reasons, such as the normal range of a singer and, particularly, the limited range of the kithara, the above octave-species were always used in transposition into the e′–e octave of the Dorian and, in this transposition, were called *tonoi* (modern denomination: transposition-scales). They can be conveniently indicated in modern notation by the addition of proper key-signatures to the standard scale on E [see Ex. 1]. Some modern writers in-

1
D. P. L. M. H-D. H-P. H-L

sist that the tonoi existed before the harmoniai. This may be true to some extent since the former are more closely allied to musical practice (kithara playing) than the latter. The theoretical explanation in this reversed order, however, involves considerable intellectual complications which might well be avoided. Needless to say, the principle of transposition was also applied to the chromatic and enharmonic scales; thus, the "chromatic mixolydian tonos" is: e′–d′–cb′–bb–a–gb–f–e.

Recent investigations have shown how the tonoi were obtained on the *kithara. A kithara with six strings tuned pentatonically: e′ d′ b a g e was probably the original type. On this instrument, the missing tones of, e.g., the Dorian, namely c′ and f, were obtained by stopping (between two firmly pressed fingers) the strings b and e so that they sounded a semitone higher. For students familiar with 16th-century Italian lute *tablature the accompanying scheme [Ex. 2] will

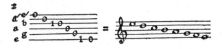

prove clarifying. Around 500 and later the kithara and consequently the tonoi were frequently used in the compass f′–f, a semitone higher than the earlier one. Thus, two kinds of Dorian, etc., tonoi were distinguished, "low Dorian" and "high Dorian." Finally, the method of transposition was extended to the entire disdiapason with the result that the characteristic distinctions of the octave-species disappeared and that only a two-octave minor scale in the 14 different chromatic transpositions from F to g (each in three genera, hence the number total of 52) remained. It is this stage of the theory which is represented by the compendious tables of Alypios (c. 360 B.C.; cf. GD ii, 444ff), the main interest of which lies in the accompanying notational signs. For the Greek notation cf., e.g., WoHN i; also C. Sachs, in ZMW vi, vii.

III. The Musical Documents. The most important (because relatively complete) documents are two Delphic Hymns to Apollo, dating from about 130 B.C., two brief Hymns to the Muse, a Hymn to Nemesis (probably by Mesomedes, c. B.C. 130), and the *Seikilos Song, dated variously from 200 B.C. to A.D. 100. Their late date renders them rather useless as

evidence of the musical practice of Greek antiquity. Needless to say, they are all monophonic. We know, however, that Greek musicians made use of a primitive type of "polyphony," described by Plato as *heterophony. The melodies are not unimpressive in their somewhat puristic simplicity and reservedness, but, on the whole, would seem to confirm the impression that the great artistic contributions of the ancient Greeks lie in the fields of architecture and sculpture rather than in those of painting and music. See also: Chroai; Dithyram; Ethos; Hydraulis; Hyporchema; Kithara; Lyre; Magadis, Pyknon; Pythagorean scale.

Lit.: C. Sachs, The Rise of Music (1943), pp. 198ff; id., Musik des Altertums (1924); id., "Antike Musik" (in BüHM); The. Reinach, La Musique grecque (1926; contains all the pieces in transcription); ReMMA, 11–53; LavE i.1, 377–537; R. P. Winnington-Ingram, in ML x, no. 4; Ph. Barry, in MQ v. Additional bibliography in ReMMA 427ff.

The modern development of Greek music started around 1850 under the influence of the Italian opera (Spiridion Xyndas, 1812–96, and others). Particularly successful was Spiro Samara (1861–1917), a pupil of Delibes, with the opera Flora Mirabilis (1886). A national movement started with the songs of George Lambelet (b. 1875), and found a more definite expression in the works of Manuel Kalomiris (b. 1883) whose opera Protomastoras (1916) has been compared to Glinka's A Life for the Czar. The compositions of Petro Petridis (b. 1891) show neo-classical influence. Other living composers are George Poniridis (b. 1892) and Mario Varvoglis (b. 1885).

For Greek church music see *Byzantine chant.

Greghesca, pl. **greghesche.** See under *Villanella.

Gregorian chant. The liturgical chant of the Roman Catholic Church. It is named after Pope Gregory I (590–604) under whom it received its final arrangement and codification [see VII]. The term Gregorian chant has the disadvantage of excluding, strictly speaking, the early development leading up to the Gregorian period, as well as the (comparatively minor) changes introduced afterwards. Another common name is plainsong [F. *plain-chant*; L. *cantus planus*]; this, however, is frequently used in a wider and more technical meaning [see *Plainsong]. The most appropriate term would be Roman chant, because it properly describes the repertory in question as one of the four "local dialects" of the music of the Western Church, the others being Milanese (*Ambrosian), *Gallican, and *Mozarabic (Visigothic) chant. In fact, the earliest name used for Gregorian chant was *Cantilena Romana* (9th, 10th centuries), while *cantus planus* (*musica plana*) came into use during the 13th century, as a distinguishing term from *musica mensurata*, i.e., measured polyphonic music.

Whereas formerly musicians looked disdainfully on Gregorian chant, particularly because it "lacks" harmony, it is now becoming more and more fully recognized as an unsurpassed treasure of purely melodic music. In particular, its freely flowing rhythm, far from being chaotic, shows subtleties of structure and organization which are doubtless superior to the comparatively platitudinous devices of rhythm in harmonized music, with its meter, measures, beats, regular phrases, etc. The present-day repertory of Gregorian chant consists of nearly 3000 melodies, all monophonic (unisonous), rhythmically free, and sung partly choral (by the *schola, i.e., choir) and partly solo (by the *cantor). These will be considered subsequently according to: I. Liturgical categories; II. Text; III. Style; IV. Forms; V. Tonality; VI. Rhythmic interpretation; VII. Historical development.

I. *Liturgical Categories.* The days of the liturgical year fall into four classes: (a) *Ordinarium* (*Divini Officii*), i.e., those Sundays and weekdays on which there is not a special feast; (b) *Proprium de tempore*, i.e., the feasts of Our Lord, and of the Holy Trinity (this category includes all the great feasts, Christmas, Easter, etc.); (c) *Proprium Sanctorum*, i.e., the feasts of individual Saints, such as the Blessed Virgin Mary, St. Stephen, St. Peter; (d) *Commune Sanctorum*, i.e., the feasts of Saints grouped under classes, such as Apostles, Martyrs, Confessors, Virgins, etc. On each day [see *Feria] service is held at certain hours, the so-called *Office hours. The whole repertory of chants falls into two main classes, those for the *Mass, and those for the *Office, i.e., for all the other services of the day. The former are contained in the *Graduale Romanum* (*GR*), the latter in *Antiphonale Romanum* (*AR*; see *Liturgical books; also the "List of Abbreviations," p. viii). The Antiphonale falls into four main sections, one each for the above-mentioned categories: (a) pp. 1–209; (b) pp. 210–577; (c) pp. 578–930; (d) pp. [1]–[103]. To these are added the *Toni Communes*, i.e., the recitation tones for the psalms, benedictions, orations, etc. (pp. 1*–65*), and an Appendix containing chiefly the chants for the (extra-liturgical) *Benediction. The Graduale opens with three sections, each containing the variable items of the Mass (*proprium missae*; see *Mass) for the days of the second, third, and fourth of the above-mentioned categories: (b) pp. 1–366; (c) pp. 367–606; (d) pp. [1]–[132]. There follows a section: *Ordinarium Missae*, pp. 1*–94*, containing the invariable chants of the Mass (Kyrie, Gloria, etc.), one containing the *Missa pro defunctis* (*Requiem Mass, pp. 95*–108*), one containing recitation tones for the Mass (Lection, Epistle, etc.), and chants for several special occasions. The Graduale also contains the chants for special services introductory to Mass, e.g., the *antiphons (Mass antiphon) and *responsoria for Ash Wednesday (pp. 73–76), Palm Sunday (pp. 155–166), Maundy Thursday (pp. 186–191), and Purification (pp. 405–410). It may be noticed that the usual form of Antiphonale printed now is the *Antiphonale pro diurnis horis* (A. for the day hours; see *Office hours), the service for *Matins (*matutinum*), which contains chants of great beauty and special interest, being omitted because this service is celebrated today in monastic churches only. These chants are, however, included to some extent in the *Liber Usualis* (*LU*), a modern edition which contains the chants both for the Office and the Mass more clearly arranged in the way they follow one another during the service of the day. The reader may compare the service for Christmas (*Nativitas Domini*) as given in *LU*, pp. 364–414 (beginning with Vespers, i.e., the evening service of the preceding day), with the corresponding sections in *AR*, pp. 259–273 and *GR*, pp. 27–35; pp. 368–392 of *LU* contain the service for Matins, which is not given in the two other books.

II. *Text.* By far the greater part of the chants are based on prose texts, and of these the great majority are taken from the *psalms. Entire psalms sung to a *psalm tone form a regular part of the Office; single psalm verses prevail in the "verses" (℣) of the Introits, Graduals, Alleluias, Tracts, as well as in the opening Antiphons and Responses of these chants and in the Communions and Offertories [see *Psalmody]. Non-psalmodic Scriptural texts occur in the *canticles and in a number of Introits, Graduals, etc., particularly in those which belong to a feast of a Saint [e.g., the Gradual of St. John's Feast: "Fuit homo missus a Deo, cui nomen Joannes erat: hic venit. ℣. Ut testimonium perhiberet de lumine, et parare Domino plebem perfectam" (*GR*, 504ᵛ); cf. St. John, 6, 7]. In the liturgical books, *Ps.* (in the Introits) always denotes a verse from the Psalms, while ℣. indicates a verse either from the Psalms or from other Scriptural texts. The most outstanding non-Scriptural prose texts are those of the Ordinary of the Mass (Kyrie, Gloria, Sanctus, Credo, Agnus Dei). The chants based on poetic texts (medieval) are the *hymns and the *sequences. A semi-poetic type of text occurs in the four *Antiphons B.M.V., particularly in the *Ave regina*. However, the musical setting of these Antiphons is different from that of the hymns and sequences [see the following chapter].

III. *Style.* Three melodic styles of the prose chants are usually distinguished by modern writers: (a) syllabic style; (b) neumatic or group style; and (c) melis-

matic style. (a) Chants composed in *syllabic style* have one note to each syllable of the text; occasionally a group of two or three notes will be found to one syllable. To this type belong the various recitation-tones of the Office (psalm tones, lection tones, *toni orationum*; *AR*, 1*–57*) and of the Mass (*toni orationum, epistolae, evangelii, praefationum*, of the *Gloria Patri*, etc.; *GR*, 109*–125*) as well as the numerous Antiphons of the Office (throughout the *Antiphonarium*), the hymns and the various melodies for the *Credo* [*GR*, 59*–69*]. The recitation-tones are "inflected *monotones," whereas the other chants have fully developed melodies in ascending and descending lines. — (b) The chants in *group-style* show a more frequent use of groups of two to four or more notes to one syllable. The most important chants of this class are the Introitus and Communions (throughout the *Graduale*), and the Responsoria of Matins; other examples are the Kyries, Sanctus, and Agnus Dei of the Ordinary of the Mass [*GR*, 1*–59*], while the melodies for the Gloria belong more to the melismatic type. — (c) To the *melismatic type*, involving extended coloraturas, belong the chants of the Proper of the Mass other than the first (Introitus) and the last (Communion), that is, the Graduals, Alleluias, Tracts, and Offertories. In the first three of these classes, which belong to the category of responsorial chants, the melismatic style is usually still more clearly marked than in the Offertories (and Glorias). See the accompanying Ex. 1.

Credo in unum Deum, Patrem omni-potentem

Pu-er na-tus est no-bis

Al-le-lu - ia

The rather strict adherence to a given style in any of the liturgical items is one of the most remarkable traits of Gregorian chant. According to a carefully-laid-out plan, each type of chant receives that treatment which conforms with its liturgical position and significance. In this respect it is interesting to note that one and the same text is composed in totally different styles according to whether it is used as an Antiphon, a Gradual, or for any other purpose. A famous example is the psalm-verse *Justus ut palma* for which there exist more than 20 different melodies, ranging from the simplest to the most ornate [cf. *Editions XXIII A, 2/3].

The musical style of the hymns and sequences is mainly syllabic, but differs radically from that of the prose chants with regard to rhythm [see VI]. The hymn melodies, which generally are much later in date than the prose chants [see, however, *Ambrosian hymns] are syllabic tunes with regularly recurrent accents conforming with those of the text (usually iambic dimeters). They are thus more closely allied to measured music than any other type of plainsong.

IV. *Forms.* From the point of view of formal structure, the chants fall roughly into the following categories: (a) *Through-composed chants.* Under this rubric fall: the Glorias, Sanctus, and Credos of the Ordinary of the Mass, and the Graduals, Offertories, and Communions of the Proper of the Mass [for the last three, see *Psalmody II, III]. Naturally, the classification of these chants as through-composed does not preclude the occasional repetition of motives or more extended phrases [cf., e.g., the passages "Benedicamus te," "Adoramus te," "Glorificamus te" in the *Gloria X*; GR, 36*; similarly in many tracts, e.g., *Commovisti*; GR, 67]; such reiterations are a peculiarity of the individual chants, not of the category to which they belong.— (b) *Strophic chants.* Practically all the hymns belong to this class [e.g., the *Aeterne rerum conditor, AR*, 6]. Partly strophic are the *sequences. The *Kyries and *Agnus Dei may also be classified under this category. A chant of particularly complicated structure is the *Te deum laudamus.— (c) *Cyclic chants.* This term is used here to denote several types of chants the structure of which involves repetition of certain sections. They

are all reductions — more or less drastic — of the rondo-like structure of early psalmody, responsorial or antiphonal. This species, which is the most characteristic and most interesting in Gregorian chant, receives separate treatment under the heading *Psalmody.

V. *Tonality.* The melodies of Gregorian chant are based upon the system of the eight *Church modes. With each chant, its mode is indicated at the beginning, e.g., *Intr. 6.*, i.e., Introitus in the sixth mode. The indexes of the *Graduale* and the *Antiphonarium*, in which the modes are given preceding the title (e.g., under Introitus: 6. Cantate Domino) make it easy to investigate the relative frequency of any mode in the entire repertory, or in a special rubric. Naturally, a closer study of the chants reveals many deviations from the strictly modal scheme. Scholars are now generally agreed upon the fact that most of the melodies existed long before the theoretical scheme of the eight modes came into being, and that, after the adoption of this theory (9th, 10th centuries), the repertory of the chants was subjected to a process of adaptation which, however, was not carried out completely, thus leaving (fortunately enough) various discrepancies between theory and practice. Among these one finds: (a) The use of B-flat, chiefly in order to avoid the tritone [see, e.g., the tract *Beatus vir*; for a melody in the "first" mode with a B-flat throughout, and without the *subtonium (therefore actually in D minor) see the introitus *Da pacem*]. It has been maintained that the "classical" tradition of Gregorian chant utilized also other chromatic alterations (F-sharp, E-flat), but that these were eliminated later (Cistercian reform of the 12th century) by transposing the chants or sections thereof [cf. U. Bomm, *Der Wechsel in der Modalitätsbestimmung in der Tradition der Messgesänge im XI. bis XIII. Jahrhundert* (1929)]. — (b) Excessive ambitus of the melodies. These amplifications of the theoretical range of the modes — which, by the way, are rather infrequent — were accounted for in theory by the introduction of the "mixed modes," combining the range of the authentic (e.g., d–d′) with that of the plagal (A–a). However, the passage from the Gradual *Omnes gentes* quoted in Ex. 2

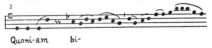

Quoni-am bi-

[*GR*, 2**] shows that the ambitus was occasionally exceeded in a manner not included in the broadened system of the modes (range from d to f′). — (c) Much attention has been given in recent studies to the "pentatonic background" of the Gregorian melodies. Although the sweeping contention that all these melodies are essentially "pentatonic melodies with ornamental *pien-tones*" [cf. the reference in *ReMMA*, 160] is without foundation, the fact remains that a considerable number of chants are clearly pentatonic [see Ex. 3, from the Communion *In splendo-*

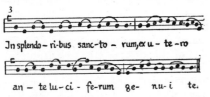

In splendo- ri-bus sanc-to - rum,ex u - te -ro

an – te lu-ci - fe-rum ge- nu-i te.

ribus; *GR*, 30]. Such examples do not actually constitute a deviation from the modal system, but deserve mention here because they are indicative of a stage of evolution previous to that of the establishment of the full scalar modes. A similar statement can be made with respect to the use of fixed melodic patterns in the chants belonging to one mode, a procedure which occurs also in various other bodies of liturgical or Oriental music [see *Melody types*].

VI. *Rhythmic Interpretation.* This constitutes the most vexed and disputed problem of Gregorian chant, a problem which, in spite of the efforts of numerous scholars, is still far from being solved. It arises from the fact that the notation of the chants [see *Neumes*; also *Plainsong notation*] contains no clear and obvious indication of temporal values and that, as early as the 13th century, the oral tradition of the rhythmic performance of the melodies was lost. Unsuccessful attempts at

reconstruction were made in the 19th century when the re-editors of the *Editio Medicea* [see *Liturgical books*] made the mistake of interpreting the neumatic signs of plainsong as mensural notes and ligatures (longa, brevis, semibrevis, etc.; see *Notation; also *Square notation). The result is illustrated by Ex. 4. Still more

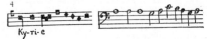

Ky-ri- e

distorting is the interpretation of H. Riemann who applied his principle of *Vierhebigkeit to the Gregorian melodies [cf. *RiHM* i.2, 39]. Today, all scholars are agreed that Gregorian rhythm belongs to the category termed "measured rhythm" in our article on rhythm, in particular to the "chronos-protos" variety thereof [see *Rhythm II (b)]. There exists, however, a sharp cleavage between two main schools, one of which maintains that in Gregorian rhythm there exists practically only one time-value, say, the eighth-note, while the other admits the existence of two time-values, the above and its double (quarter-note), possibly also of its triple (dotted quarter-note).

To the former school belong the *accentualists* (Dom Pothier), who consider the textual accent as the organizing factor within the succession of uniform time-values (a theory which would be difficult of application in the case of extended textless melismas), and their successors, the monks of *Solesmes (Dom Mocquereau and others) who, on the contrary, completely discard the textual accent as a basis of musical accentuation. Instead, they divide the melody into elementary groups of two or three notes, groups which in turn are combined into larger rhythmic divisions: incises, members, phrases, and periods. The beginning of each binary or ternary group is marked by an *ictus. Only at the end of a phrase are notes of longer value admitted. In addition to these principles the monks of Solesmes have worked out a special manner of performing Gregorian chant which is characterized, among others, by the almost complete absence of contrasts of intensity (piano, forte), the voices moving along, quite impressively, in a subtly shaded mezzopiano.

Among the adherents of the second school (sometimes called *mensuralists*), the admission of two time-values naturally leads to a considerable disagreement as to which notes of the chants are long, which short. Here the various scholars (Dechevrens, Peter Wagner, Dom Jeannin, Bonvin, Jammers) differ mainly in the question as to the correct interpretation and relative importance of early theorists as well as of certain special signs found in the early neumatic manuscripts, such as the *episema, the *Romanian letters, the virga and punctum [see *Neumes], etc.

Ex. 5 serves to illustrate the various methods (a: Riemann; b: Bernouilli-

5

Spe- ci-e   tu- a

Houdard; c: Wagner; d: Jeannin; e: Solesmes). Only the last three are still deserving of consideration. Cf. also *ReMMA*, 148.

Without attempting an evaluation of the above methods, it can be said that the mensuralists "have an impressive amount of historical evidence on their side" [*ReMMA*, 146], and that the Solesmes interpretation would seem to derive its main justification from the results embodied in their actual performances and recordings which, so far, have not been challenged by similar attempts on the part of any of the mensuralists. As regards the historical truthfulness of the Solesmes interpretation, it has been said that it "prob-

ably stands in the same relation to its medieval counterpart as a Romanesque church of 1880 to its 11th-century model" [*BeMMR*, 15]. Finally, since the history of Gregorian chant embraces at least six centuries (600–1300) and numerous localities, there can be no single "correct answer." It would be foolish to assume that the chant was performed in the same manner at the time of St. Gregory, as it was in the 9th or 12th century. Even the current designation of the 9th and 10th centuries as the "Golden Age" of Gregorian chant is rather arbitrary, not to mention the possibility of local differences within this era (Metz, St. Gall, etc.).

VII. *History.* There has been an extended controversy regarding the origin and roots of Gregorian chant. Opinion was, and still is, divided among those who maintain the Greek lineage and those who point to the tradition of the Jewish Synagogue. An interesting evidence in favor of the former opinion was found in the striking resemblance between one of the few remaining Greek melodies, the Seikilos song [see *Greek music III] and the Gregorian antiphon *Hosanna David* [cf. *ReMMA*, 115]. However, such a single instance weighs little if the dissimilarity in general between Greek music (strict meter, syllabic style, poetic texts) and Gregorian chant (oratoric rhythm, melismatic style, recitation tones, prose texts) is considered. Already the fact that practically all the early texts of the Roman Church are taken from the psalms points to a strong Jewish influence. Also the general character of Gregorian music is "Oriental" rather than "Greek." This point of view has gained considerable support by the recent investigations of Idelsohn [cf. *ZMW* iv], who has shown that melodies still sung today by Jewish tribes living in isolated spots (South Arabia, Persia) are strikingly similar to lection tones of the Roman Church.

During the early centuries of the Christian era there accrued a large repertory of chants from various sources, pagan (neoPlatonists), heretic (Gnostics, Therapeuts; see *Hymns), East-Christian (Syria, Alexandria), etc. Pope Gregory (590-604) collected the chants and standardized their use in the service, a task which was continued to some extent by later popes (8th century). Already in the earliest preserved MSS of Gregorian chant, dating from the 9th century, the arrangement is largely the same as in all the later sources. The post-Gregorian development of the chant comprises chiefly the *tropes and *sequences which flourished from the 9th through the 13th century, but were mostly abolished by the *Council of Trent. From the 14th through the 19th century the history of plainsong is one of increasing deterioration, first with regard to the rhythmic interpretation, later also with regard to the melodies themselves [*Editio Medicea, Ratisbonensis*; see under *Liturgical books; see also *Machicotage; *Plainchant musicale]. Simultaneously, the monophonic chants were increasingly replaced by polyphonic settings, first by the 13th-century *organa, *clausulae, and *motets (portions of the Proper of the Mass), later by compositions of the Ordinary of the Mass (14th and subsequent centuries), of the hymns (15th century, Dunstable, Dufay, and successors), and of the psalm tones (16th century; see *Fauxbourdon (4); *Verset). The return to the medieval tradition of unaccompanied chant is largely the work of the monks of *Solesmes [see *Liturgical books II].

See also (main articles are italicized): Alleluia; Antiphon; Benedicamus; Benediction; Benedictus; Canticum; *Cantus planus*; Cecilian movement; Chant; Communion; Cursus; Dies irae; Doxology; Euouae; Gradual; Hymn; Ictus; Improperia; Incipit; Introitus; Jubilus; Lamentations; Litany; *Liturgical books*; Machicotage; Magnificat; *Mass*; Miserere; Missa; Motu proprio; Neuma; *Neumes*; Offertorium; *Office hours*; Ordinary; Plainchant musical; Psalm; *Psalmody*; *Psalm tones*; Requiem; Responsorium; Salve Regina; Sarum use; Sequence (2); Solesmes; Te Deum; Tenebrae; Tract; Trishagion; Trope.

Lit.: *Practical:* Dom Johner, *A New School of Gregorian Chant* (1925); A. Robertson, *The Interpretation of Plain-*

chant (1937); J. Schrembs, *The Gregorian Chant Manual* . . . (1935); G. Sunyol, *Text Book of Gregorian Chant* (1930). Books on the objectionable practice of plainsong accompaniment are not listed.

Historical: P. Wagner, *Einführung in die gregorianischen Melodien,* 3 vols. (1901–21); vol. i appeared in English as *Introduction to the Gregorian Melodies, Part I* . . . (1907); Dom A. Mocquereau, *Le Nombre musical grégorien* . . . , 2 vols. (1908, '27); Dom Gajard, *Notions sur le rhythme grégorien* (in *Monographies Grégoriennes,* 1935); Dom Jeannin, *Etudes sur le rhythme grégorien* (1926); E. Jammers, *Der gregorianische Rhythmus* (1937); H. B. Briggs, "The Structure of Plainsong" (*PMA* xxiv); C. H. Phillips, "The Aesthetics of Plainsong" (*ML* xv, no. 2); E. Wellesz, "Some Exotic Elements of Plainsong" (*ML* iv, no. 3); P. Wagner, "Zur Rhythmik der Neumen" (*JMP* xvii); L. Bouvin, "The 'Measure' in Gregorian Music" (*MQ* xv); J. Jeannin, "Il mensuralismo Gregoriano" (*RMI* xxviii, xxix, xxx). See also *Editions XXIII; *Neumes. Comprehensive bibliography in *ReMMA,* 437ff.

Gregorian modes. See under *Church modes II.

Gregorian tones. Same as *psalm tones.

Gr. Fl. Short for *Grosse Flöte* [G.], i.e., the ordinary flute.

Griffbrett [G.]. Finger board (of violins, etc.). See *Bowing (1).

Griffloch [G.]. Finger-hole (of flutes, etc.).

Griffschrift [G.]. A general name for systems of notation the signs of which refer directly to the position of the fingers on the instrument, rather than to the result of these positions, the tones. While the latter method is the normal one, the former has been used repeatedly in the evolution of musical notation, particularly in the lute tablatures of the 16th century. A modern instance is the notation for the guitar or *ukulele in popular music. See *Tablatures; cf. also *ApNPM,* 54.

Grimmig [G.]. Grim, furious.

Groppo [It.]. See *Gruppo.

Gross, grosse [G., great]. *Grosse Flöte*, the ordinary flute. *Grosses Orchester*, full orchestra. *Grosse Trommel*, bass drum. *Grosse Sext* (*Terz*), major sixth (third); *Grosse Quinte* (*Quarte*), perfect fifth (fourth). *Grosse Oktave*, great octave.

Grosse caisse [F.]. Bass drum.

Ground, ground bass. A short melodic phrase (normally from four to eight measures) which is repeated over and over again as a bass line, with varying superstructures (melodies, harmonies) added each time in the upper parts. The resulting composition is also called "ground." It is the contrast between the fixed framework of the bass and the free display of imagination in the upper part or parts that constitutes the peculiar charm of this form. The ground bass or *basso ostinato* [It.] may vary in elaborateness from such simple formations as the descending tetrachord: a–g–f–e (one note to the measure; see Ex. under *Chaconne) to full-length melodies, as in the accompanying example (Purcell). The ground

is a characteristic form of *Baroque music and was cultivated especially in England [cf. *HAM*, no. 257], frequently with improvisation of the upper parts [see *Division].

The ground belongs to the general category of "continuous variations" [see *Variations I] within which it properly applies to those examples which have a clearly distinguishable bass motive. Thus, many passacaglias and chaconnes [see *Chaconne and passacaglia] are grounds, and there would be little objection in extending this denomination to those passacaglias which — as, e.g., Bach's Organ

Passacaglia — have the motive occasionally transferred to an inner or an upper voice. To say, however, that passacaglias (and/or chaconnes) as a species belong to the general category of grounds is a misleading statement, since many passacaglias (and chaconnes) lack the main characteristic of the ground, i.e., the reiterated bass motive. For a somewhat different type of reiterated bass see *Strophic bass.

The statement, found in several books, that "the ground had its origin in the church music of the polyphonic era, in the frequent reiteration of the cantus firmus by the tenor" is wholly erroneous. The use of the same extended cantus-firmus melody (e.g., *L'homme armé) for each movement of a Mass is something essentially different — technically as well as ideally — from the immediate reiteration of a concise melodic phrase within a single composition. The origin of the ground must be looked for in variations, probably in variations of a dance-like character. See under *Ostinato.

Lit.: R. Litterscheid, *Zur Geschichte des basso ostinato* (Diss. Marburg 1928); L. Walter, *Die konstructive und thematische Ostinatotechnik des 17. und 18. Jahrhunderts* (Diss. Munich 1940); L. Nowak, *Grundzüge einer Geschichte des basso ostinato* . . . (1932); H. Riemann, "Basso ostinato und basso quasi ostinato" (*Liliencron Festschrift*, 1910); *id.*, in *SIM* xiii; H. Shaw, "John Blow's Use of the Ground" (*MQ* xxiv); O. Gombosi, "Italia: Patria del basso ostinato" (*LRM* vii).

Grund- [G., basis, foundation]. *Grundlage*, root position. *Grundstimmen*, the 8-foot registers of the organ. *Grundton*, root of a chord. *Grundtonart*, main key.

Gruppetto, gruppo, groppo. Italian 16th-century name for an ornamentation in the character of a *trill. See *Ornamentation I.

G.S. or **GS.** Short for Gerbert's *Scriptores*. See *Scriptores.

G sol re ut (**G solreut**). See *Hexachord II.

Gsp. Short for *Glockenspiel.

Guajira, guaracha. Spanish-Cuban dances with a characteristic shift from ⁶⁄₈ meter to ¾ or to ²⁄₄ meter (the eighth-notes remaining unchanged in length). A charming example is the guarache in the ballet of Auber's *La Muette de Portici* (1828), Act I.

Guerre des bouffons. See *Bouffons (2).

Guida [It., leader]. (1) Subject (dux) of a fugue. — (2) *Direct. — (3) An abbreviated orchestral score [see *Conducteur].

Guidon [F.]. *Direct.

Guidonian hand. The term refers to the use by Guido of Arezzo (born *c.* 995) of the human hand as an aid in memorizing the scale and its solmization syllables. Although it is nothing but a sketch of a hand with the names of tones inscribed in its various parts, it attained an almost supernatural significance as the symbol of the complete mastery of the medieval system of *hexachord and *mutation, as the epitome indeed of the entire system of the church modes. Thus, for instance, chromaticism was strongly objected to as late as the 16th century, because it was not contained "in the hand" ("non est in manu"). In the accompanying sketch the

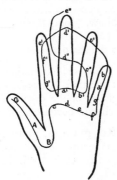

tones are indicated by the modern pitch names, instead of the composite solmization-names (Gamma ut, A re, B mi, etc.; see *Hexachord II) which are regularly used in the early treatises. For Guidonian letters, see *Letter notation.

Guimbarde [F.]. *Jew's harp.

Guiro. See *Percussion instruments B, 8.

Guitar [G. *Guitarre*; It. *chitarra*]. A plucked stringed instrument, similar to the lute, but distinguished by its body which has a flat back and inward curving sides, somewhat like that of the violin. The modern guitar has six strings which are tuned: E A d g b e′. The music is notated one octave higher than it sounds. Today the guitar is chiefly a popular instrument used to provide a simple chordal accompaniment to a dance or a song, the chords being indicated in a manner similar to the principles of the 16th-century lute tablatures [see *Tablatures VI]. Most of the great guitar virtuosos were Spanish: Dionisio Aguado (1784–1849), who established the principles of modern guitar playing in a method written in 1825 and still used today; Fernando Sor (1784–1839), who aroused the admiration of Méhul, Cherubini, and Fétis, and who wrote numerous brilliant compositions for the guitar; Francesco Tarrega (1852–1909), the greatest of all guitar players, who initiated the present-day renascence of the instrument; and his pupil Andres Segovia (b. 1896), who has made known the instrument all over the world and who has contributed much to a revival of old (16th-century) guitar (*vihuela) music. Modern composers for the guitar include Manuel de Falla, Joaquin Turina, Rodolfo Halffter, Albert Roussel, Alexander Tansman, and others. Percy Grainger has used it in several compositions [see C. Forsyth, *Orchestration* (1926), p. 480].

The earliest compositions for the guitar are contained in Miguel Fuenllana's *Orphenica lyra* (1554); they are, however, written for a four-stringed guitar tuned c–f–a–d′ [cf. *WoHN* ii, 161]. While these pieces are entirely in the "pseudo-polyphonic" style of 16th-century lute music, a new style, consisting of chordal accompaniment only, was inaugurated by G. Montesardo who, in his *Nuova Inventione per sonare li balletti sopra la Chitarra Spagniuola* (1606), invented a new notation (stenographic indication of the chords) which was broadened by other guitarists, such as Caliginoso (1629) and Lucas Ruiz de Ribayaz (1677).

In the 17th century, when lute music under Denis Gaultier, Esaias Rausner, and others reached its high-point of artistic perfection, the guitar rose to prominence as an instrument of much lesser ambition and, consequently, greater popular appeal. In the late 17th century the instrument became fashionable in the French court-circles, and painters à la mode, like Watteau and Boucher, depicted it in the hands of beautiful ladies and of comedians. Boccherini used the guitar in some of his chamber music works, as did also other composers of the 18th century. Schubert's so-called Guitar Quartet, however, is only an adaptation of a guitar trio of a Bohemian Matiegka, published in 1807. See also *Guitar family; *Electronic musical instruments III.

Lit.: D. Prat Marsal, *Diccionario ... de guitarras ...* (1934); B. Terzi, *Dizionario del chitarristi e liutai Italiani* (1937); J. Zuth, *Handbuch der Laute und der Gitarre* (1926); *LavE* ii.3, 1997–2035; *WoHN* ii, 157–218; A. Koczirz, "Die Fantasien des Melchior de Barberis ..." (*ZMW* iv); *id.,* "Die Gitarrenkompositionen in Miguel de Fuenllana's Orphenica lyra" (*AMW* iv); W. Tappert, "Zur Geschichte der Guitarre" (*MfM* xiv); E. Schmitz, "Guitarrentabulaturen" (*MfM* xxxv); O. Chilesotti, "La Chitarra francese" (*RMI* xiv); M. R. Brondi, "Il Liuto e la chitarra" (*RMI* xxxii, xxxiii).

Guitar family. This category is understood here to include the instruments which have the general characteristics of the lute family, except for the flat body as found with the guitar. Like the lute, the guitar is of Oriental origin. It appears in various shapes in the famous miniatures of the 13th-century Cantigas MS of the Escorial [cf. *GD* ii, 482]. Various such instruments existed in the 16th and 17th centuries under different names which make exact identification difficult. The most important among these was the *cittern* (also *gittern, cister, cither, cithara, cetera, cistola, citole*) which had an oval belly and back, similar to that of the lute,

and wire strings [cf. *AdHM* i, 604]. The *"Cythringen"* (*Cithrinchen*) on which the miller Veit Bach, J. S. Bach's great-great-grandfather, is reported to have entertained himself while grinding the flour, was a smaller instrument of this type. In the 18th century the cittern was much used in England under the name *English guitar* [cf. *GD* ii, pl. XXXI]. A direct derivative of the cittern is the *bandurria* and its larger variety, the *bandolon* [cf. *SaRM*]. The name of these instruments (probably also that of the modern *banjo) comes from the 16th-century *pandora*, a guitar with a peculiar doubly scalloped body, thus forming three lobes, somewhat like an oak leaf. The name *quinterne* (probably from *guitterne*) was also used for instruments of the guitar family, as well as for certain members of the lute family, e.g., the mandola. A Portuguese guitar, much used in the Azores, is the *machete*, which is the ancestor of the modern *ukulele. Of the various guitar instruments of Russia only the *balalaika survives today. A circular guitar with a short neck is used in China under the name *yüeh ch'in* and in Japan under the name *gekkin* [cf. *SaHMI*, 216–218]. The Japanese *samisen* has a nearly square body with rounded sides. It is covered with skin, has a long neck, and three silk strings tuned in fourths or fifths. It is a popular instrument used by street singers and for the dance of the geisha girls. See also *Vihuela.

Gusla, gusle. The chief instrument of Bulgarian folk music. It is a primitive violin, with a round wooden back, a belly made from skin, and only one string made from horsehair. The player of the instrument is called *guslar.* Ill. in *SaRMI*, 170. The gusla should not be confused with the Russian *gusli* (*guslee*), a large zither which is used in balalaika bands [see *Psaltery]. Cf. W. Wunsch, *Die Geigentechnik der Guslaren* (Diss. Prague 1937?).

Gusto, Con [It.]. "With taste," i.e., in fitting character and speed.

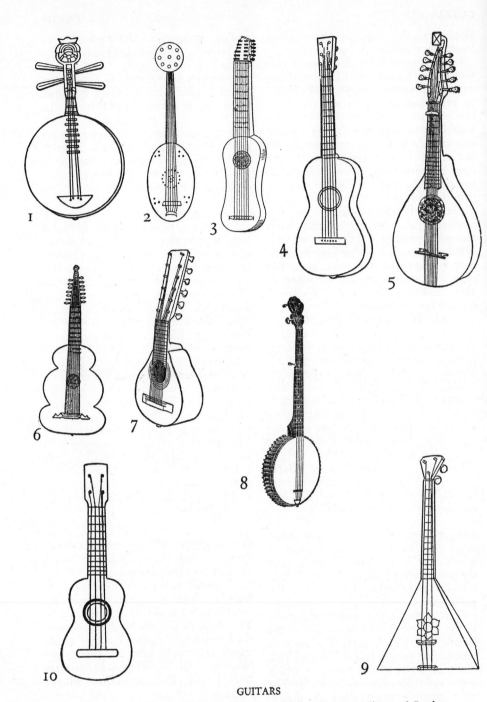

GUITARS

1. Yüeh-ch'ing. 2. Moorish Guitar. 3. Vihuela. 4. Modern Guitar. 5. Cittern. 6. Pandora.
7. Bandurria. 8. Banjo. 9. Balalaika. 10. Ukulele.

Gymel, gimel [from L. *cantus gemellus*, twin song]. A late medieval term for two-part polyphony based chiefly on parallel thirds. Guilelmus Monachus (15th century) describes it together with *fauxbourdon, declaring both methods to be of English origin [cf. *SchGMB*, no. 33]. This claim is supported by the style of 13th-century English compositions (two-part hymns, etc.) which show a much more extended use of thirds than Continental (French) sources of the same period. Of particular interest is a two-part hymn in praise of St. Magnus, the patron of the Orkneys, which proceeds almost entirely in parallel thirds [cf. *AdHM* i, 167; *HAM*, no. 25d]. Gymel, then, would seem to represent a typically English type of parallel *organum, as against the French organum in parallel fourths and fifths. However, it would be wrong to assume that parallel thirds were unknown in France [cf. J. Handschin, in *Festschrift für Guido Adler*, 1930, p. 57]. Cf. M. Bukofzer, "Gymel, the Earliest Form of English Polyphony" (*ML* xvi, no. 2); *ReMMA*, 388.

Gypsy music. Whether the gypsies ever possessed an aboriginal musical tradition is a matter of doubt. Their chief activity was probably one of communication, a task for which their wandering habits and their assimilative character predestined them. The so-called gypsy-scale, c–db–e–f–g–ab–b–c [see *Scale I], with two augmented seconds, is probably of Indian origin, and was introduced by the gypsies into eastern Europe, particularly into Hungary, where it became a pseudo-nationalistic feature [see *Hungarian music]. It also is frequent in modern Turkish and Jewish music as well as in Greek church music. The gypsies have also played a certain role in the cultural and musical life of Spain [see *Flamenco]. Cf. *LavE* i.5, 2646ff; W. Starkie, "The Gipsy in Andalusian Folk-music" (*PMA* lxii).

H

H. See *Pitch names; *Letter notation. Abbreviation for Horn (in orchestral scores). *H dur* (*moll*), German for B major (minor).

Habanera. A dance from Cuba (Havana), in slow to moderate duple time and with a variety of characteristic rhythms somewhat similar to those of the *tango.

The usual assumption that it was introduced into Cuba from Africa by the Negroes is entirely without foundation. All evidence points to a Hispanic background for this dance as well as for the tango. It acquired, however, a certain exotic tinge which contributed much to making it famous and popular when, around 1850, it was reimported to Spain. Sebastian Yradier (1809–69), who lived in Cuba for some time, wrote the two most famous habaneras, the popular song *La Paloma*, and another, *El Arreglito*, which became world famous as a composition of Bizet in his *Carmen*, first act [cf. R. Laparra, *Bizet et l'Espagne*, p. 18]. Other well-known habaneras are by Chabrier (1885) and by Ravel (*Rhapsodie Espagnole*, 1907).

Hackbrett [G.]. See *Dulcimer.

Haffner Collection. An important collection of early pianoforte (harpsichord) sonatas, published by Haffner around 1760–70. The complete publication, which was issued in three parts under the titles: *Oeuvres mêlées*, *Raccolta musicale*, and *Collection récréative*, contains 114 sonatas in *gallant style by Ph. Em. Bach, Wagenseil, Schobert, Marpurg, Bertoni, Galuppi, Paganelli, Rutini, and others. Eighteen sonatas from the *Raccolta mu-*

sicale have been republished by G. Benvenuti under the title: *Cembalisti Italiani del Settecento* (G. Ricordi). See *Sonata B III (a) and (b).

Haffner Serenade. Mozart's Serenade in D [K.V. 250] composed in 1776 for a wedding in the family of Sigmund Haffner, burgomaster of Salzburg. His Haffner Symphony in D [K.V. 385] was composed in 1782 for a similar purpose.

Hakenneumen [G.]. Hook neumes; see *Neumes II.

Halb, halbe [G., half]. *Halbe Note* (*Pause*), half-note (-rest). *Halbinstrument*, half-tube instrument. *Halbschluss*, half-cadence. *Halbsopran*, mezzosoprano. *Halbton*, semitone.

Half. Half-close, imperfect cadence. Half-fall, see *Appoggiatura. Half-shift, the first shift on the violin. Half-step, i.e., semitone. Half-tube instruments, see *Wind instruments II.

Hallelujah [from Hebrew *hallel*, praise, and *Jah*, Jehovah]. A Biblical word, expressing joyful praise of God. For its use in Gregorian chant, see *Alleluia. In choral compositions of the 17th and 18th centuries the word Hallelujah frequently serves as the text for an extended final movement in fugal style. Famous examples are the Hallelujah-choruses in Bach's cantata *Christ lag in Todesbanden* and in Handel's *Messiah* (close of Part II).

Halling. A Norwegian folk dance, which is executed with a great variety of movements, varying from the intentionally awkward to the really violent [cf. the description in *GD* ii, 499]. Grieg has used the dance in several of his *Lyric Pieces*.

Hammerklavier [G.]. Early 19th-century name for the pianoforte. Beethoven used it for his sonatas op. 101 and 106 [the latter frequently known as Hammerklavier-sonata], probably for no other reason than to avoid the Italian word.

Hammond organ. See *Electronic musical instruments I.

Hand horn. See *Horn II.

Hand organ. The term is used for two mechanical instruments similar in construction but different in purpose: the English *barrel organ, used formerly in small churches; or the street organ of the Italian organ grinders.

Handstück [G.]. Late 18th-century term for instructive piano pieces.

Handtrommel [G.]. *Tambourine.

Harfe [G.]. *Harp.

Harmoniai. See *Greek music, II (c).

Harmonic. See *Acoustics, IV.

Harmonica. (1) The Glass Harmonica. An instrument invented by Benjamin Franklin in 1763, in which a series of glass basins of graded sizes are fixed on a horizontal spindle which is made to revolve by a treadle operated by the foot of the player. The spindle is fitted into a trough filled with water so that the glasses are kept wet. The sound is produced by a delicate friction of the fingers [ill. in *GD* ii, 522]. The instrument had an extraordinary vogue, particularly in Germany and Austria where, together with the *aeolian harp, the *nail violin, and other "ethereal" instruments, it became a characteristic vehicle of *Empfindsamkeit. Among various compositions for the harmonica, Mozart's Adagio in C major (K.V. 356) and Quintet (K.V. 617, for harmonica, flute, oboe, viola, and cello), both composed in 1791, are the most interesting [cf. the compl. ed., x]. Beethoven used the harmonica in a melodrama, *Leonora Prohaska*, composed in 1814 [Supplementary volume of the B. and H. edition]. Other composers who wrote for the instrument were J. G. Naumann, Padre Martini, Hasse, Galuppi, and Jomelli. Cf. C. F. Pohl, *Cursory Notices on the Origin and History of the Glass Harmonica* (1862).

(2) The Mouth Harmonica or Mouth Organ. This instrument, widely used for popular music making, consists of a small, flat box with a number of channels on the oblong side, each of which leads to a metal reed inside the box. The instrument is placed against the lips and moved in one

direction or the other, according to the notes desired. Alternating notes of the scale can be obtained by blowing or by suction. A great number of harmonica bands exist in the United States and elsewhere, and a remarkable degree of virtuosity has been achieved by players to be heard on the stage. The instrument was probably invented by F. Buschmann in 1821 [cf. *SaHMI*, 406]. Other reference books mention Sir Charles Wheatstone as the inventor (*Aeolina*, 1829).

(3) In French and German the name is also used for a variety of instruments of the xylophone type, i.e., consisting of tuned strips of wood (*harmonica de bois*, *Holzharmonika*), steel (*harmonica à lames d'acier, Stahlharmonika*, i.e., *Glockenspiel*), stone (*harmonica à lames de pierre*, e.g., the Chinese *pien ch'ing*; see *Chinese music IV), etc. *Ziehharmonika* [G.] is the accordion.

Harmonic analysis. I. *General.* In the more restricted sense harmonic analysis is for the purpose of determining the structure of each chord in a piece of music; in the larger and truer sense its objective is to determine how a piece of music is constructed from the chordal point of view. The latter includes the former as a matter of course, but no particular end is served if account is not taken of how progressions of chords are organized to form logical units which make musical sense. Such musical units, which are called *phrases, are comparable to literary phrases. Just as a sentence is constructed of single words, so is a phrase of music constructed of single chords, and we must know not only how these chords are spelled and how they sound individually, but how they are organized into musical units. The classical system of tonal harmony, that current in the 18th century and continued fundamentally, but enlarged considerably, in the 19th, forms the basis of harmonic analysis at the present time. Such analysis will show that composers — any of them from Bach to Fauré — have had certain common habits in forming sequences of chords. If the music of Bach and that of Fauré do not sound alike, it is not because their basic chordal progressions differ essentially; they differ only superficially in that the individual chords of the latter may be more complicated and colored, the rhythm with which the music moves may have a different gait, the phrases may be differently conceived in terms of length, and the non-essential connections between the chordal pillars, the ornamentations, may be handled differently. But as any building, regardless of its appearance, must obey the laws of gravity, so must tonal music obey the fundamental laws of harmony.

II. *Triads.* The basis of classical harmony, hence of harmonic analysis, is the *triad. There are three different kinds of triads among those erected on the seven degrees [see *Scale degrees] of the major scale: I, IV, and V, the tonal degrees, have major triads; II, III, and VI, the modal degrees, have minor triads; and VII, which is indeterminate, has a diminished triad. I, V, and IV are the roots of the basic chords in the major key, and ordinarily in pieces in such a key these chords are used preponderantly over the chords whose roots are the modal degrees. The following illustration shows the triads on each degree of the major scale and its tonic (parallel) minor and the relations among them [Ex. 1].

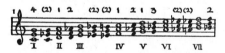

(Chords written in white notes are used in the major key; those in black notes are used in the minor key; those marked 1 are common to both modes; those marked 2 are often borrowed from the minor mode to be used in the major; that marked 3 is used only under certain circumstances even in the minor; that marked 4 is sometimes used as a final chord in pieces in the minor, in which case the chord is said to have a Picardy third; and those marked (2), which can be borrowed from the minor for use in the major, are mostly so used in the 19th century, the tonic minor having such usage mostly as a melodic device in popular American music of the "blues" type.)

Besides the practice of exchange of chords from one mode to the other, which in itself makes the two modes practically identical, certain other alterations have come into practical usage which further color, and therefore confuse, the two modes; it is hardly going too far to say that in the late 19th century practically any note of any chord could be sharped or flatted, and that if this were done judiciously the feeling of a central tonality could still be preserved, although it might not be possible to determine whether the resulting tonality was major or minor.

III. *Seventh and Ninth Chords.* Besides the triads illustrated above, music of the 18th and 19th centuries makes great use of *seventh chords.* These chords are triads with another diatonic third superposed. Each degree of the scale is capable of having a seventh chord erected upon it. *Ninth chords,* used more in the 19th century than before, are seventh chords with still another diatonic third superposed. Seventh chords and ninth chords are designated by adding the figure 7 or 9 to the Roman numeral indicating the root, thus: I^7, I^9. The symbol I^9_{7b} means a ninth chord with the seventh degree flatted [see Ex. 2]. For more details see *Seventh chord; *Ninth chord.

IV. *Root Position and Inversion.* When any chord built of superposed thirds stands in its original position it is said to be in root position, since the note on which the structure is built, the *root, lies in the bass or lowest part. Thus a chord built on C, whether it be a triad, a seventh, or a ninth chord, or even greater, is in root position, so long as C remains in the bass, no matter what arrangement the other notes take above it or how many notes there are in the chord. All the chords of Ex. 1 and 2 are in root position.

If the third of the chord, E in the examples above, lies in the bass the chord is in first inversion; if the fifth, G in the above examples, is in the bass the chord is in second inversion; and if the seventh is in the bass it is in third inversion. The Arabic figuring of these chords indicates the characteristic intervals which lie be-

tween the lowest note (bass note, not the root) and those above it. Thus, the designation for the first inversion, known as *sixth chord,* is I^6 (properly I^6_3), for the second inversion, known as *six-four chord,* I^6_4 and similar symbols are used for the inversion of the seventh chord [Ex. 3].

See *Inversion; *Sixth chord; *Six-four chord; *Seventh chord.

V. *Altered Chords.* These are chords in which one or several notes are chromatically altered, i.e., by accidentals foreign to the key. The minor subdominant in a major key (e.g., f–ab–c' in C major) is usually not considered an altered chord. The commonest among the altered chords are illustrated in Ex. 4: (a) diminished seventh chord; (b) Neapolitan sixth; (c) augmented fifth; (d) diminished fifth, while (e) represents the more complex type frequently found in modern music. Closely related to the diminished seventh

chords are the augmented sixth chords. See *Seventh chord; *Sixth chord.

The secondary dominants are a particularly important type of altered chords [see *Dominant].

VI. *Modulation.* Modulation, one of the most valuable devices in tonal music, is accomplished by means of pivot chords. The C major triad, for instance, is not only I in the key of C major, but also IV in G, V in F, III in A minor, VI in E minor, the Neapolitan II in B, and VII in D minor; treated as a secondary dominant its functions are still extended, since it can be considered as V of III in D minor, V of III in D-flat, V of V in B-flat, and so on. The diminished seventh chord and the augmented sixth chords are also valuable as pivots since the same chord is to be found in a variety of keys. These pivot chords serve as connections between different keys in much the same manner as doors serve to connect different rooms, and it is by means of them that modulation is effected. See *Modulation.

VII. *Non-Harmonic Tones.* These are tones dissonant to the harmonies with or after which they are sounded, and they serve the purpose usually of melodic smoothness of flow and ornamental embellishment. They are of two main types, accented and unaccented. The unaccented non-harmonic tones are (1) passing tones, (2) auxiliary tones, (3) anticipations, (4) échappées, and (5) cambiatas, while the accented ones are (6) appoggiaturas and (7) suspensions, although the last has no rhythmic accent on the note itself at the moment when it causes dissonance. All the non-harmonic tones may be found either ascending or descending, and in any voice part. See *Nonharmonic tones.

VIII. *Harmonic Rhythm.* An important aspect of harmonic analysis is harmonic rhythm, the rate of speed with which harmonies change in the course of a phrase or series of phrases. It is essential to notice that some phrases experience a greater number of harmonies than others in the same length of time, and that certain parts of single phrases likewise have faster-moving harmonies than other parts. The tendency in single phrases is to have faster harmonic change in the latter part than in the first, but this will depend on the structural idea which the composer has in mind for the piece as a whole and the psychological effect he wishes to convey. See *Harmonic rhythm.

See also *Harmony; *Functional harmony; *Texture; *Dualism.

Lit. (attempt at a selection out of hundreds of text books): W. Piston, *Harmony* (1940); *id., Principles of Harmonic Analysis* (1933); P. Hindemith, *Traditional Harmony* (1943); C. H. Kitson, *Elementary Harmony* (1920); *id., Evolution of Harmony* (1914); N. Rimsky-Korsakov, *Practical Manual of Harmony* (1930); E. Prout, *Harmony* (16th ed., 1901); A. P. Scholes, *The Beginners Guide to Harmony* (1922ff). H. A. Miller, *New Harmonic Devices* (1930); R. Lenormand, *Study of Modern Harmony* (1915); A. F. Barnes, *Practice in Modern*

Harmony (1937). For historical studies, see under *Harmony.   A. T. M.

Harmonic division. See *Arithmetic and harmonic division.

Harmonic inversion. See *Inversion (1).

Harmonic minor (scale). See *Major and minor.

Harmonic rhythm. The rhythmic life contributed to music by means of the underlying changes of harmony. The pattern of the harmonic rhythm of a given piece of music, derived by noting the root changes as they occur, reveals important and distinctive features affecting the style and texture. Chief of these are the frequency of harmonic change, and the rhythmic quality of that change. There may be no change of harmony over several measures of music, as for example in the opening of Beethoven's Ninth Symphony. A contrast to this is the rapid succession of root changes, a different chord appearing with each note of the melody, as in Ex. 1 (Chopin, Mazurka op. 59, no.

2). Between these extremes all variations can be found. In general it may be said that music of a contrapuntal character employs fewer chord changes than do other types.

The pattern of the harmonic rhythm is made up of strong and weak rhythmic quantities. Certain root progressions, such as II to V, are regarded as strong progressions, that is, having the rhythmic effect of weak to strong. Others, like III to V, are weak, with strong to weak, or even static rhythm [Ex. 2]. Usually, however, the pattern contains several root progressions, so that a judgment of their comparative rhythmic values involves consideration of other factors. The most

II V III V II V I

V7 I   V7 I

important influence on the rhythmic stress is the element of time. Long time values are generally accepted as being heavy, or strong, in comparison with shorter values [Ex. 3]. A dissonant chord with its resolution may constitute either a weak or a strong progression [Ex. 4]. Dynamic indications usually underline the natural rhythm of the music but are sometimes used by composers in a contrary sense, to give an accent where one would not normally occur.

The strong beats of the harmonic rhythm are commonly in agreement with the first beats of the measures, thus coinciding with what one feels to be the pulse of the music, although this is by no means always the case. The pattern of the harmonic rhythm is capable of considerable independence of the meter and of the various melodic rhythms to which it serves as background. Ex. 5 (Beethoven, Sonata op. 31, no. 3) serves as an illustration. It should be noted in this example that the pattern of the harmonic rhythm, while it is the product of the combination of the melodic lines, is unlike any one of the melodic rhythm patterns, and does not agree with the regularity of the meter.

The resource of harmonic rhythm is largely abandoned by some composers of the twentieth century who seek to write a purely contrapuntal music as opposed to harmonic music. This accounts for a certain static quality often noticed in mod-

ern music. Increased melodic and contrapuntal rhythmic complexity and the use of irregular and changing meters are in

E b:I ———— II—I ———— IV V

I VI II V I

some instances a compensation for the loss in rhythmic interest and vitality due to the absence of harmonic rhythm. See *Harmonic analysis VII.   W. P.

Harmonics. The term is used in two different, though related meanings: (a) to denote a general acoustical phenomenon, (b) its application to the violin. For the former, see *Acoustics IV.

The harmonics of the violin (and cello), sometimes called flageolet tones [G. *Flageolet-töne*], are high tones of a flute-like timbre which are produced by lightly touching the string, instead of pressing it down, as is done in ordinary stopping. By doing so, the string is allowed to vibrate in its entire length, but the formation of a node is enforced at the point touched. Our sketch, Ex. 1, shows the vibration of (a) an open string,

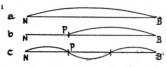

(b) a stopped string, (c) a lightly touched string. If the open string sounds g, the stopping at P (in our example at one-third of the entire length) produces the fifth d' (vibrating length 2/3), while light touch will produce the harmonic d" (vibrating length is 1/3). The formula for the determination of the harmonics is $\dfrac{1}{h} = 1 - \dfrac{1}{t}$, h and t being the relative frequencies of the harmonic and the normal tone produced at the same point. For instance, in determining the harmonic obtained by lightly touching "the c" of the g-string, t is $\dfrac{4}{3}$ (relative frequency of the fourth; see *Intervals, Calculation of), therefore: $\dfrac{1}{h} = 1 - \dfrac{3}{4} = \dfrac{1}{4}$, or h = 4, i.e., the frequency of the second octave; hence, the harmonic is g″. In the accompanying Ex. 2 the lozenges indicate,

as usual, the point of touch, the black notes the pitch of the resulting harmonic.

Stopping and light touch can be used simultaneously. The tones thus obtained are called "artificial harmonics," the others, "natural harmonics." In compositions for violin (or cello), the latter are indicated by a small circle placed above the desired tone, while for the artificial harmonics the method exemplified under Ex. 3 is used in which the position of the fingers as well as the resultant tones is indicated.

The introduction of the harmonics is variously ascribed to Domenico Ferrari (1722–80), a pupil of Tartini, and to Jean de Mondonville (1711–72). The latter seems to have made the first practical application of the harmonics in his six sonatas *Les Sons harmoniques*, op. 4 (1735). See also *Ch'in; *Tromba marina.

Harmonic (minor) scale. See *Major and minor; *Scales.

Harmonic series. The series of the acoustical harmonics [see *Acoustics IV].

Harmonie [F., G.]. Harmony. In French usage the term also denotes the wind section of the orchestra, or special wind bands. *Cor d'harmonie* is the French horn.

Harmonika [G.]. Either the *Mundharmonika*, mouth-harmonica [see *Harmonica (2)], or the *Ziehharmonika*, i.e., *accordion. B. Franklin's harmonica is called *Glasharmonika*. See also *Harmonica (3).

Harmonious Blacksmith. Air with variations from Handel's Harpsichord Suite no. 5, in E (1720). No plausible explanation for the name has been given.

Harmonium. I. A keyboard instrument the tones of which are produced by thin tongues of metal set in vibration by a steady current of air which is provided by a pair of bellows operated by the feet of the player. The metal tongues act as free reeds [see *Reed]. The harmonium is usually considered as a popular substitute for the organ with which it has various features in common, e.g., the wind supply, the keyboard, the ad libitum sustained tones, and stops which provide for variety of timbre. If properly used, however, the modern harmonium is an instrument in its own right. In particular, it is capable of producing gradations of sound which make it a more "expressive" instrument than the organ (by means of the expression stop which puts the pressure in the bellows under direct control of the feet operating the bellows). Needless to say, it is bad taste to use this device for the rendering of Bach's organ works. However, it lends itself well to many organ compositions of the 19th century (Mendelssohn, Schumann, Liszt, Reger), or for the pieces written directly for the instrument (Karg-Elert, Dvořák, Reger, César Franck).

II. The harmonium developed in the 19th century, from Grenié's *orgue expressif* (1810, influenced by the Chinese *Sheng) over a great number of more or less experimental instruments (Organo-violin, 1814; Aeoline, 1816; Aeolodicon. Physharmonica, 1818; Aerophone, 1829; Séraphine, 1833; Mélophone, 1837; and many others) to the first real harmonium

(A. Debain, 1840) which combined the useful devices found separately in the earlier constructions. Important improvements made afterward are: the *percussion* (small hammers like those of the pianoforte, acting upon the tongues and causing a quicker and more precise "start" of the sound); the *prolongement*, by which single tones can be automatically prolonged (pedal-points); the *melody-attachment*, which puts the highest notes in relief over the others; the *pedal-substitute*, by which, contrariwise, the lowest note of a chord can be made to stand out; the *double touch* (1855), which permits a certain gradation of sound by a slighter or greater depression of the key; and finally the *expression* (invented by Mustel, 1854), by which the volume of sound is controlled directly by the feet of the players — a delicate device which, however, calls for more practice than most harmonium players are willing to give to it.

III. An important variety of the harmonium is the *American organ*, in which the wind is not forced outward through the reeds by compression, but drawn inwards by evacuation of the air in the bellows. In addition, the tongues of this instrument are smaller and more sharply twisted than those of the harmonium. All these devices render the tone softer and more organ-like, but lacking the expressive quality of the harmonium. Modern instruments have electric wind-supply, leaving the feet of the player free to operate a pedal-keyboard like that of the organ. The principle of the American organ was invented about 1835 by a workman in the harmonium-factory of Alexandre, Paris, who subsequently emigrated to America. Here his ideas were put into reality by Estey, Brattleboro (*Estey organ*, 1856) and by Mason and Hamlin, Boston (1861). In France and England the *Mustel organ* is very popular. For a 16th-century type of harmonium, see *Regal.

Lit.: A. Mustel, *L'orgue expressif, ou l'harmonium* (1903); *LavE* ii.3, 1374; L. Hartmann, *Das Harmonium* (1913; bibl.); C. Sachs, in *Zeitschrift für Instrumentenbau* xxii (1924).

Harmony. In general, any simultaneous combination of sounds, hence synonymous with *chord. The narrower use of the term in the meaning of "agreeable chord" conforms to some extent with the earlier practice, but has been rendered pointless by the recent development of music. There is, however, a difference between chord and harmony in that the former term applies to the single formations, the latter to successions of chords and to the relationships between them. Thus, harmony denotes the chordal (or vertical) structure of a musical composition, in contrast to counterpoint, i.e., its melodic (or horizontal) structure [see *Texture]. The principles of the "classical system" of harmony (18th, 19th centuries) are explained under *harmonic analysis. In the present article the subject is treated from the historical point of view.

I. Harmony, the vertical aspect of music, came to be appreciated considerably later than counterpoint, the horizontal aspect. Although even in the early day of counterpoint (9th–12th centuries; see *Organum) it was apparent that certain intervals were better sounded simultaneously than others and although the ensuing progress of counterpoint necessarily entailed an increased consideration of the harmonic point of view, it was not until the mid-16th century that musicians began to think of harmonies as a primary building material of music. In fact, it was not until the early 18th century that Rameau (1722), Fux (1725), and others formally recognized them as structural and compositional elements. This late recognition is all the more striking in view of the extended use of plain chordal progressions in various periods of early music history [see *Familiar style] and, particularly, in view of the 17th-century practice of *thorough-bass which is essentially harmonic in nature. Actually, the recognition of the harmonies as building elements depended upon another concept which did not evolve until after 1650, namely, *tonality, which superseded polyphonic modality and which made possible an over-all conception of a piece of music from the harmonic point of view.

Only when tonality was firmly established could the relative importance of chords built on the different degrees of the scale be determined in relation to a key center or tonic; only when this was accomplished could a logical departure from this tonic into other keys and return from those keys to it — modulation — be consummated.

When chords came to be conceived as entities it became possible to enlarge the small chords such as the triad with its inversions to bigger ones with three or more thirds (seventh chords; ninth chords). For the sake of color, moreover, it was possible to raise or lower the various notes of these chords without allowing them to lose their identity and their relationship with the central tonic. From the beginning of the 18th century onward the beauty of melodic lines depended largely on the effectiveness of arrangement of the pillars of harmony on which they were draped; no more did they unite to form these pillars.

But the very conception of tonality contained the seeds of its own eventual weakening, for with the passage of time and with the increasing boldness of composers in modulating to ever more distant keys, and in coloring, or altering, the notes of their chords more and more, the strength of the single tonal center became diluted. Added to this, the gradually growing tendency of 19th-century composers to fuse the major and minor modes, using chords typical of one mode in the other (Schubert), and to avoid strong tonal cadences and to substitute for them all kinds of deceptive cadences which in turn veiled contours of phrases (Liszt and Wagner) gave to their music a far less well-defined feeling of tonality than the compositions of the 18th century possessed. Another practice which acted adversely on the strength of classical tonality was the use by certain nationalist composers towards the end of the century of a preponderance of modal degrees of the scale in the harmonization of the folk or folk-like melodies which they often used as the basis of their compositions (Dvořák and Moussorgsky). This, with its logical complement of writing consecutively a

number of chords on adjacent scale degrees (*parallel chords; Debussy), led harmony back in many respects to the paths which it had followed in the period of modality. During the 20th century certain composers have abandoned tonality altogether and once again depend on the conjunction of melodic lines to form their harmonies (*atonality; Schönberg), while others retain only the triad as the basic chord with which phrases must begin and end, and allow any combinations of notes to form the harmonies in the course of the phrases, so long as they are arranged logically in regard to increasing and decreasing dissonance as the phrase proceeds, an arrangement called "harmonic fluctuation" (Hindemith).

II. Considering the triad as the most important harmony, the millennium of harmonic music may be divided into three main periods: a central period in which the triad is sovereign (period of tertian harmony, c. 1450–1900); a previous period in which the potentialities of the triad are not yet exploited (period of pre-tertian harmony, c. 900–1450); and a period in which, after the exhaustion of the triad, new combinations are sought after (period of post-tertian harmony, c. 1900–?). The following brief survey is based on this classification:

(A) *Pre-Tertian Harmony* (900–1450)

(1) 900–1050: Parallel fourths or fifths in two parts [Ex. 1, *Musica enchiriadis*]; see *organum.

(2) 1050–1200: Octaves, fifths, and fourths as chief consonances of two-part writing in parallel and in contrary motion; thirds, sixths occur, but are treated and considered as dissonances; seconds and sevenths are frequent in appoggiaturas and passing tones [Ex. 2a, Treatise of Milan; 2b, School of St. Martial; 3, clausula, c. 1200]. See also *Gymel.

(3) 1200–1350: Open triads (1–5–8) — including those with a diminished fifth — as the main consonance in three-part writing; full triads (1–3–5) occur occasionally in weak position; harsh dissonances (consecutive seconds, etc.) are freely admitted as passing notes and appoggiaturas [Ex. 4, motet c. 1250].

(4) 1350–1450: Open triads in conjunction with first inversions (3–5–8) in succession: *fauxbourdon [Ex. 5, Landini]. See also *Landini cadence.

(B) *Tertian Harmony* (1450–1900)

(5) 1450–1600: Full triads and first inversions in three, four or more parts; the roots of the triads move preferably in seconds or thirds (I–II; I–III; I–VI), in other words, in modal sequence [Ex. 6, *c.* 1450; Ex. 7, *c.* 1550]. Daring chromatic combinations around 1600 (Gesualdo).

(6) 1600–1750: Triads and seventh chords with all their inversions, in four parts or in free chordal style; increasing predominance of the first, fifth, and fourth degrees as the central chords (tonic, dominant, subdominant), leading to the establishment of the major and minor tonality in all the keys [*Well-tempered Clavier*, 1722] and to modest modulations; appearance of altered chords such as the diminished seventh and the Neapolitan sixth; occasionally extensive use of chromatic progressions; enharmonic change [Ex. 8, Weckmann, *c.* 1660; Ex. 9, J. S. Bach].

(7) 1750–1825: Reduction of the har-

monic vocabulary of the late Baroque [Ex. 9] to its bare "essentials," the tonic, dominant, and subdominant, which are used functionally as the carriers of extended melodies and as the vehicle of dynamic development (*Mannheim School; Viennese classics). Distant modulations, with or without pivot chords [Ex. 10, Schubert].

(8) 1825–1900: The period of Romantic harmony; fullest exploitation of the triadic system to the farthest consequences; extensive use of chromatic alterations, of unprepared and — towards the end of the century — of unresolved appoggiatura chords; free modulation into distant keys [see the description under I]. Gradual disintegration of the "system." [Ex. 11, Chopin; Ex. 12, Wagner.]

(C) *Post-Tertian Harmony* (1900–)

(9) 1900–present: Deliberate violation of the harmonic system by the use of *parallel chords (Debussy), of *fourth chords (Scriabin), etc., leading to the complete abandonment of harmonic restrictions, i.e., to *atonality (Schönberg;

c. 1910) and to a period of unlimited experimentation in the field of novel usages, frequently of a contrapuntal nature, most of which defy classification [see *New music]. Around 1925, gradual return to

less radical solutions [see *Neo-classicism; *Pandiatonicism]. For examples see the different special articles; also under *Cadence.

Lit.: Ch. Macpherson, *A Short History of Harmony* (1917); A. Casella, *The Evolution of Music through the History of the Perfect Cadence* (1919); G. Haydon, *The Evolution of the Six-four Chord* (1933); K. Jeppesen, *The Style of Palestrina and the Dissonance* (1927); H. Andrews, *Modern Harmony* (1934); R. Lenormand, *A Study of Modern Harmony* (1915); E. Kurth, *Romantische Harmonik* (1920); A. Schönberg, "Problems of Harmony" (*MM* xi, no. 4); Dom A. Hughes, "The Origins of Harmony" (*MQ* xxiv); H. Leichtentritt, "Harmonic Daring in the 16th Century" (*MM* v, no. 1); *id.*, "Handel's Harmonic Art" (*MQ* xxi); A. Liess, "L'harmonie dans les oeuvres de Debussy" (*RM* xii); A. Coeuroy,

"Debussy et l'harmonie romantique" (*RM* ii); G. Knosp, "Essai d'harmonie exotique" (*RMI* xxxviii, xxxix).

A. T. M. and W. A.

Harp [F. *harpe*; G. *Harfe*; It. *arpa*]. I. *The Double Action Harp.* The modern double action (or double pedal) harp was introduced about 1810 by Sébastien Érard. It has a range of six octaves and a fifth with seven strings to the octave, tuned normally in the key of Cb major, i.e., from C_1b to g''''b. At the foot of the instrument are seven pedals, one controlling all the C-strings, one all the D-strings, etc. Each pedal can be depressed to two notches — hence the name double action — and each time the corresponding strings are shortened to sound one semitone higher than normally. Thus, the C-pedal in high position gives the tone Cb, in the first notch the tone C, and in the second notch the tone C♯. With all the pedals in the first notch the tuning of the instrument is C major; with all in the second, C♯ major. Operation of single pedals makes all the major and minor keys available as well as altered chords so long as they do not involve "cross-relations," i.e., the simultaneous use of C♮ and C♯, or Eb and E♮. Special effects can be obtained by enharmonic substitutions. For instance, the following tuning: c d♯ eb f♯ gb a b♯ c makes it possible to produce the diminished seventh-chord c eb f♯ a in a rapid glissando over all the strings. Of special charm are the harmonics of the harp which are produced by putting the palm on the middle of the string. The resulting tone is, of course, the higher octave of the normal tone, but with a different, mysterious timbre. Still another timbre can be obtained by plucking the strings close to the sounding board.

II. *The Chromatic Harp.* This harp was introduced in 1897 by the Parisian firm of Pleyel. It abandons the pedal mechanism entirely, substituting a string for each semitone of the octave. Objections to its general adoption are: (a) the number of strings is nearly doubled; (b) a new finger technique is demanded of performers; (c) its tone is poorer than that of the double action harp; (d) it cannot play the diatonic or chordal glissandos written for the double action harp. For advantages, one may mention: (a) there are no pedals, thus the player is free to devote his entire attention to controlling the strings with his hands; (b) the instrument stays better in tune than the double action harp since the strings are not continually shortened and lengthened; (c) for the same reasons the strings last longer; (d) there is no restriction with regard to the simultaneous use of natural and chromatic degrees, and anything playable on the piano is playable on the chromatic harp. Its main exponents are composers of the modern French school, but its special literature is as yet small.

W. D. D.

III. *History.* In the scientific classification of instruments harp is the generic term for chordophones (practically always plucked) in which the plane of the strings is vertical to the soundboard (not parallel as, e.g., in the zither or the pianoforte); see *Instruments IV, D. Harps are among the oldest instruments. In Mesopotamia they are documented as far back as c. 3000 B.C., and a great variety of forms existed there as well as in Egypt [see *Babylonian, *Egyptian music]. In spite of the innumerable references to "King David playing the harp" it is not certain whether the Jews had a harp. King David's instrument, the *kinnor*, was not a harp but a lyre, similar perhaps to the Greek kithara [cf. SaHMI, 106]. In Greece there existed various types of harps, such as the *pektis* and the *magadis.*

In Europe, harps made their first appearance in Ireland, which still uses the harp (*clarsech*) as its heraldic symbol. Whether the instruments represented on the famous Irish crosses of the 8th/9th centuries were harps or lyres is still a matter of controversy among scholars [cf. SaHMI, 262; N. Bessaraboff, *Ancient European Musical Instruments* (1941), p. 215; also p. 418, footnotes 460 and 461]. On the other hand, the ancient English *rotta* probably was a harp. In Wales

harps (*telyn*) were known before A.D. 1000. Regarding the "ancient bardic harp music," see under *Bards. In the 12th century the harp spread over to the Continent and was held in high esteem by the troubadours, trouvères, and Minnesinger. Antonio de Cabezon's *Obras de musica* of 1572 bears the remark "para tecla, harpa y vihuela" thus showing that the same compositions were played on keyboard instruments, harps, and lutes. Harps of the late 17th century had hooklike gadgets by means of which the length of the strings could be shortened so that the sharped tone was produced. In 1720 Hochbrucker replaced these hooks by pedals each of which altered the tuning of a string and its octaves.

IV. *Repertory.* The harp was occasionally used in Italian opera of the early 17th century (Monteverdi, *Orfeo*, 1607; see *Orchestration II), and then almost disappeared from the orchestra. Handel and Gluck used it but a few times, the former in *Esther* (1720), the latter in *Orpheus* (1762). Mozart wrote a Concerto for flute and harp (K.V. 299) and Beethoven used the harp in his *Prometheus*. Berlioz, Liszt, Wagner, and most of the later composers included the harp in their orchestral scores, and composers such as Debussy and Ravel have used it prominently as a vehicle of impressionist coloring, often writing parts for two harps.

The solo literature for the harp is restricted in quantity as well as quality. The earliest extant compositions for the harp, by Joh. Bapt. Krumpholz (1745–90), are musically valuable, and Fétis thought highly of the harp compositions of Marie-Martin de Marin (1769–after 1861). Harp virtuosos of the early 19th century, such as Martin d'Alvimare (1772–1839), Robert Nicolas Bochsa (1789–1856), and Elias Parish-Alvars (1808–49), obligingly tendered to the demands of the harp-playing ladies in the salons of Paris and London. It was not until the end of the 19th century that music of artistic merit was written for the harp, mainly by French composers such as Saint-Saëns (Fantasia for violin and harp), Debussy (Sonata for flute, viola, and harp), Ravel (Septet for strings, flute, clarinet, and harp), Roussel (Serenade for flute, violin, viola, cello, and harp), Florent Schmitt (Quartet for strings and chromatic harp), and Inghelbrecht (Sonatina for flute and harp; Quintet for strings and harp). Other chamber music works calling for the harp are by D. G. Mason (Suite for flute, violin, viola, cello, and harp), Bax (Sextet for strings, harp, and horn; Sonata for viola and harp), and Carlos Salzedo.

Lit.: C. Salzedo, *Modern Study of the Harp* (1921); W. H. Grattan Flood, *The Story of the Harp* (1905); *LavE* ii.3, 1892–1971; R. B. Armstrong, *The Irish and the Highland Harps* (1904); H. J. Zingel, *Harfe und Harfenspiel . . . bis ins . . . 18. Jahrhundert* (Diss. Halle 1932); A. Kastner, "The Harp as a Solo Instrument and in the Orchestra" (*PMA* xxxv); *id.*, "The Use of the Modern Harp" (*ZIM* xiii); F. W. Galpin, "The Sumerian Harp of Ur, *c.* 3500 B.C." (*ML* x); *id.*, "The Origin of the Clarsech" (*KIM*, 1911, p. 317); H. Panum, "Harfe und Lyra im alten Nordeuropa" (*SIM* vii); H. J. Zingel, in *AM* vii, *AMF* ii, *ZMW* xvii.

Harp lute. An early 19th-century instrument combining features of the guitar (rather than the lute) with those of the harp. It may be described as a guitar which, instead of the neck, has a harplike structure attached on the top of the body, thus giving room for a greater number of strings. Similar constructions appeared under the names *Ditial Harp* and *Harp-lute Guitar*. Cf. the illustrations in *GD* ii, opp. p. 70 and p. 542.

Harp Quartet. Popular name for Beethoven's Quartet op. 74, in E-flat, so called on account of some pizzicato-arpeggios in the first movement.

Harpsichord [F. *clavecin*; G. *Cembalo* (*Clavicimbel, Kielflügel*); It. *clavicembalo*]. I. A keyboard instrument of the 16th to the 18th century, similar in shape to the modern grand piano, but differing from it chiefly in the production of sound, the string being plucked (mechanically)

by a plectrum instead of being struck by a hammer. If the pianoforte may be looked upon as a keyed *dulcimer, the harpsichord may be regarded as a keyed *psaltery. The characteristic part of its action is the jack, a long piece of wood

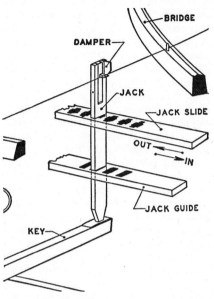

Action of the Harpsichord (from N. Bessaraboff, *Ancient European Musical Instruments*, 1941)

which at the upper end bears a plectrum made from crow quills or from leather. The jack rests on the rear end of the prolonged lever of the key which, on being depressed, causes it to jump up so that the quill plucks the string. To each key belong several jacks which produce a slightly different timbre, owing to the different material used for the plectrum. There are also several strings to each key which produce higher or lower octaves (4', 8', 16'). The harpsichord has two manuals and several stops by which the various jacks and strings can be brought into play, so that a modest degree of registration is possible, chiefly a change from pp to p and f.

From the modern viewpoint the greatest deficiency of the harpsichord is its inability to produce gradation of sound by lighter or stronger touch. Considering, however, the style of Baroque music, this objection loses much of its weight. Actually, the harpsichord is just as perfect a medium for the music of the Baroque period as is the pianoforte for that of the 19th century. In particular, it is definitely superior to the pianoforte as a medium for contrapuntal music, since the middle and lower parts of a composition stand out with an amazing clarity. A misleading statement, thoughtlessly repeated in numerous books, is that regarding the sustaining power of the sound of the harpsichord, which is said to be very slight in comparison with that of the pianoforte. Actually, the sustaining power of the two instruments is practically equal, if equal sonorities (piano, forte) are considered. Even the most tenacious adversaries of the harpsichord concede its excellence as an accompanying instrument for violins. In fact, the combination of a violin and a harpsichord in a sonata by Bach is acoustically much more satisfactory than that of a pianoforte and a violin in a sonata by Beethoven. Throughout the Baroque period the harpsichord was the chief instrument for the realization of *thorough-bass accompaniment, always in chamber music and often (in place of the organ) in church music.

II. *History.* The earliest records of what may possibly have been a harpsichord-like instrument date from the 14th century [see *Echiquier]. Around 1400 the name *clavicymbalum* occurs in various manuscripts. It points to the addition of a keyboard (claves) to an earlier instrument *cymbalum*; very likely this had nothing to do with the bell-like *cymbals, but was a *dulcimer, for which even today the name *cymbalom exists in Hungary [the original form of the word may have been *tympanon*, from Gr. *typtein*, "to beat" — the same root as in timpani; cf. *SaRM* 74/75]. The earliest accurate information about the instrument is preserved in S. Virdung's *Musica Getutscht*, of 1511. Around 1500, crow quills were introduced in addition to the earlier plectra which were made from leather. Between 1500 and 1800 there existed a variety of shapes and constructions under different names which cannot always be identified with a given type. We find instruments in the shape of a long wing (*harpsichord, clavicembalo, clavecin, virginal*), of a rectangular box (*virginal, spinet, spinetto*), of a pentagonal box (*spinetto*), of an upright box (*clavicytherium*), and of a short wing extending diagonally (spinet) [illustrations in *GD* i, 664; ii, 546; v, 552]. See *Arpicordo; *Clavicytherium; *Spinet; *Virginal; also under *Pedal piano.

In the late 18th century the harpsichord was gradually displaced by the pianoforte. It is interesting to note that the original editions of almost all the Beethoven sonatas up to op. 27 bear the inscription: "Pour le Clavecin ou Pianoforte." This does not mean that such essentially pianistic works as the Moonlight Sonata were composed for the harpsichord; but it shows that harpsichords were still widely in use around 1800 and that the publishers (who in all probability were chiefly responsible for such inscriptions) were anxious to accommodate the players and owners of the old instrument as well as those of the more modern one. Regarding the distinction between the repertory of the harpsichord and that of the clavichord, see *Keyboard music. See also *Pianoforte music; *Organ music.

Lit.: Ph. James, *Early Keyboard Instruments* . . . (1930); W. Landowska, *Music of the Past* (1926); E. Harich-Schneider, *Die Kunst des Cembalo-Spiels* (1930); A. Pirro, *Les Clavecinistes* (1926); *LavE* ii.3, 2036; C. V. Pilkington, in *PMA* lxii; F. Müller, "Vom Cembalo in J. S. Bach's Kirchenmusik" (*AM* x). See also under *Keyboard instruments; *Keyboard music.

Harp-way tuning. See *Viol IV (3) (Lyra-viol).

Hasosra. See *Jewish music; *Brass instruments V.

Hastig [G.]. Hasty, impetuous.

Haupt- [G., chief, principal]. *Hauptstimme*, principal part (usually soprano); *Haupttonart*, principal key, i.e., the original key after a modulation; *Hauptwerk*, great organ; *Hauptsatz*, first theme (or section) in sonata-form [see under *Satz].

Hausmusik [G.]. Music for domestic use, as opposed to music for public performance. See *Gebrauchsmusik.

Haut, haute [F., high]. *Haute-contre*, high tenor, male *alto, usually replaced by a female contralto. *Haut-dessus*, high treble, soprano. *Haute-taille*, see *Taille.

Hautbois, hautboy [F.]. *Oboe.

Haye, hay, hey. A dance or a dance figure of the Elizabethan period. The name is probably derived from F. *haie*, i.e., hedge, the point in comparison being the arrangement of the dancers in two hedge-like rows. Cf. *GD* ii, 625.

Hb. Short for *hautbois*, i.e., oboe.

Head-voice. See *Register (2); *Voice.

Hebrew music. See *Jewish music.

Hebrides, The, or **Fingal's Cave.** Concert Overture by Mendelssohn (B minor, op. 26, 1830). The composition was inspired by a visit to the famous cave in Scotland during his first tour through the British Isles.

Hebung [G.]. See under *Arsis.

Heckel-clarina [sometimes erroneously spelled *heckel-clarind*]. See *Clarinet family II.

Heckelphone. See *Oboe family II, E.

Heftig [G.]. Violent.

Heirmos. See *Hirmos.

Heldenleben, Ein. See *Symphonic poem III.

Heldentenor [G. *Held*, hero]. A tenor voice of great brilliancy and volume, suited for the parts of the "hero" of operas, e.g., Siegfried.

Helicon. See *Brass instruments III (e).

Hemidemisemiquaver. See *Notes.

Hemiola, hemiolia [Gr., one and one-half]. In early musical theory the term is used in two meanings, both of which imply the ratio of 3:2. (1) If applied to pitches, *hemiola* means the fifth, since the lengths of two strings sounding this interval are in the ratio of 3:2 [see *Acoustics III].

(2) In treatises on mensural notation (15th, 16th centuries) the term is applied to time-values which are in the relationship of 3:2, particularly to the use of blackened notes in *tempus perfectum* [see *Mensural notation V], or, in modern terms, of three half-notes instead of two dotted half-notes: $\frac{6}{4}|\,\d\cdot\d\cdot|\d\d\d|$ or $\frac{3}{4}|\d\cdot|\d\cdot|\d\d|\d\d|$. This change from 6/4 to 3/2 or vice versa is frequent in Baroque vocal music [cf. H. H. Wintersgill, "Handel's Two-length Bar" in *ML* xvii, no. 1] and forms a typical feature of the *courante. Among the modern composers Brahms is known for his frequent use of

this rhythmic device [see Ex., from Symphony no. 2]. See also *Sesquialtera; *Polo, *Courante.

Hemitonium [Gr.–L.]. Semitone.

Heptachord [Gr. *hepta*, seven]. The term is occasionally used to denote the modern concept of the octave (which consists of seven different tones) as against the earlier one of the *hexachord (which includes only six).

Herabstimmen [G.]. To tune down a string.

Herabstrich, Heraufstrich [G.]. See *Bowing (a).

Heraufstimmen [G.]. To tune up a string.

Hermeneutics [Gr. *hermeneuein*, to interpret]. The term, which properly applies to the interpretation of the Scriptures, has been introduced into musical aesthetics by H. Kretzschmar (*c.* 1900) as a designation for his method of "interpreting" musical motives as the expression of human emotions, feelings, etc. This method, which was also adopted by A. Heuss and A. Schering, is similar in principle to the *Affectenlehre of the 18th century, but is distinguished by a greater emphasis on scientific methods and on detailed, systematic investigation, based upon the study of intervals, motion, rhythm, rests, etc. See *Aesthetics of music III (a). Cf. H. Kretzschmar, in *JMP* ix, xii; A. Schering, in *Bericht des Berliner Kongresses für Aesthetik* (1913).

Herunterstimmen [G.]. To tune down a string.

Herunterstrich [G.]. See *Bowing (a).

Hervorgehoben, hervortretend [G.]. Emphasized, made to stand out.

Herzhaft [G.]. "With heart," courageous.

Heterophony [Gr. *heteros*, other; *phonos*, sound]. A term used by Plato [*Leges* vii, 812D] and adopted by modern musicologists to describe what may be considered a primitive type of polyphony, namely, the use of slightly modified versions of the same melody by two

(or more) performers, e.g., a singer and an instrumentalist adding a few extra tones (ornamentations) to the singer's melody. How far in Greek music the

accompanying part was allowed to wander from the main melody we do not know. However, a general idea of the possibilities of heterophonic treatment can be obtained from a study of *Chinese, *Japanese, *Javanese, African music, all of which make ample use of it. Particularly, the scores of Javanese orchestral music are largely based upon heterophonic technique. See also *Chinese music, Ex. 3; *Japanese music, Ex. 3.

Lit.: G. Adler, "Ueber Heterophonie" (*JMP* xv); Ph. Barry, "Greek Music" (*MQ* v); A. Dechevrens, "Sur le système musicale chinois" (*SIM* ii).

Hexachord [Gr. *hexa*, six; *chordos*, string, tone]. I. A group of six diatonic tones, with a semitone interval in the middle, e.g., c d e f g a. The hexachord is the basis of the medieval theory of Guido of Arezzo (b. 995). It stands in the middle between the Greek (and early medieval) system based on the *tetrachord and the modern system based on the octave (*heptachord) as the fundamental segment of the scale. In the diatonic (C major) scale there are two — and only two — hexachords, one beginning with c and another beginning with g. If, however, the b-flat (long in existence before Guido) is added, there is a third hexachord, starting on f. The hexachord on c was called *hexachordum naturale*, that on g, *hexachordum durum*, because it included the *b durum*, i.e., B-natural [see *B], that on f, *hexachordum molle*, because it included the *b molle*, i.e., B-flat (also called *Fa fictum). Since medieval theory did not consider tones of higher or lower octaves as "identical," there resulted seven hexachords in the scale from G to e':

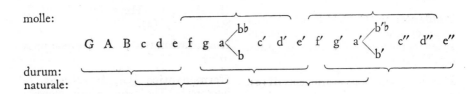

It appears that, in medieval teaching, the compass of tones was obtained, not by adjoining octaves, but by dovetailing hexachords. This method, although generally considered inferior to the modern procedure, is actually superior in at least one point, namely in that it produces the scale without establishing at the same time a preference regarding tonality. Indeed, in the modern system the initial tone C automatically becomes a tonal center (in other words, our diatonic scale is necessarily a "C major scale"), while in the system of the hexachord such a fixation is avoided in a very ingenious way.

II. As an aid in memorizing, Guido designated the six tones of the hexachord by the vocables [L. *voces, voces musicales*] ut, re, mi, fa, sol, la. These are the initial syllables of the first six lines of a then well-

```
gag e f gd |a g af ga a |gf d ce d
Sol- ve polluti|La-bi-i re-a- tum,|Sancte Johannes.
```

(That with relaxed (vocal) chords thy servants may be able to sing the wonders of thy deeds, remove the sin from their polluted lips, O holy John.) These syllables were used as a "movable solmization," being applied to each of the seven hexachords. Thus, the tone d was *sol* (fifth) in the hexachord on G, and *re* (second) in that on c.

III. In order to indicate the various "functions" of a given tone, compound names were formed which included its pitch-letter as well as all its syllables, e.g., D sol re (desolre), thus indicating that the tone d may appear either as a *sol* or a *re*. Following is a survey of the entire nomenclature (D. = durum; N. = naturale; M. = molle):

```
e''
d''
c''
b'
bb'
a'                              ┌ la
g'                              │ sol
f'                              │ fa
e'                       ┌ la   │ mi
d'            ┌ la       │ sol   │ re
c'            │ sol      │ fa   └ ut
b             │          │ mi   N.
bb            ┤ fa       │
a      ┌ la   │ mi       │ re
g      │ sol  │ re       └ ut
f      │ fa   └ ut       D.
e ┌ la │ mi   M.
d │ sol│ re
c │ fa └ ut
B │ mi  N.
A │ re
G └ ut
  D.
```

```
                 ┌ la    E la (Ela)
          ┌ la   │ sol   D la sol (Delasol)
          │ sol  │ fa    C sol fa (Cesolfa)
          │      ┤ mi    B mi (Bemi)
          ┤ fa   │       B fa (Befa)
          │ mi   │ re    A la mi re (Alamire)
          │ re   └ ut    G sol re ut (Gesolreut)
          └ ut    D.     F fa ut (Fefaut)
          M.             E la mi (Elami)
                         D la sol re (Delasolre)
                         C sol fa ut (Cesolfaut)
                         B mi (Bemi)
                         B fa (Befa)
                         A la mi re (Alamire)
                         G sol re ut (Gesolreut)
                         F fa ut (Fefaut)
                         E la mi (Elami)
                         D sol re (Desolre)
                         C fa ut (Cefaut)
                         B mi (Bemi)
                         A re (Are)
                         G ut (Gamma ut)
```

known hymn to St. John [cf. *AR*, 733], the melody of which has the peculiarity of beginning one tone higher with each successive line:

```
c  d  f  de d|d  d cd e e |
Ut queant la- xis | Re-sonare fibris |

efg e  d cd |f  ga gf d d |
Mi- ra gestorum | Fa-muli tu-orum |
```

To a certain degree the compound names served to differentiate octaves, e.g., C fa ut (c), C sol fa ut (c'), and C sol fa (c'').

IV. In order to accommodate melodic progressions which exceeded the compass of one hexachord, two (or more) hexachords were interlocked by a process of transition, called *mutation*. For instance, in order to interpret the melody: c e d g a b a, the tone g was considered as a pivot-tone, being *sol* in the lower hexachord c–a, and *ut* in the higher hexachord g–e′. Hence, the solmization of this melody would be: *ut mi re sol*(= *ut*) *re mi re*. If, however, the melody were: c e d g a bb a, the mutation would have to be made into the hexachord f–d′: *ut mi re sol*(= *re*) *mi fa mi* [for more details, cf. *GD* iv, 805].

The six tones of the hexachord have repeatedly been used as a cantus firmus

although theoretically not exactly of the same size, may, for all practical purposes, be considered as "quarter-tones" of 55 *cents each. They are, of course, never used in entirety (as they are in modern quarter-tone music), but form the tonal material from which, by selection [see *Gapped scales], practical scales of seven tones each are formed. The two oldest of these, already explained by Bharata, are called *sa-grama* and *ma-grama* (grama, "octave"). The intervals of *sa-grama* are:

Sa	Ri	Ga	Ma	Pa	Dha	Ni	Sa	(solmization-syllables)
0	4	7	9	13	17	20	22	(number of sruti)
0	204	386	498	702	906	1088	1200	(pitch in cents)

for vocal or instrumental compositions. Josquin, Brumel, Palestrina, and others wrote masses on Ut Re Mi Fa Sol La, or "supra voces musicales"; Bull, Sweelinck, Caurroy, Frescobaldi, used it as a subject for organ fantasias [cf. *SchGMB*, no. 86]. Bull's Fantasia [*Fitzwilliam Virginal Book*, i, 183] is especially interesting on account of its modulatory scheme, the hexachord (ascending and descending) being successively used in the keys of G,A,B,Db,Eb,F and Ab,Bb,C,D,E,F# [see reference under *Whole-tone scale; *Arcicembalo]. See also *Solmization; *Mi-fa.

Lit.: H. Riemann, *Geschichte der Musiktheorie* (1921); *RiHM* i.2, 173ff.

Hexameter. See *Poetic meter.

Hey. See *Hay.

Hichiriki. A Japanese oboe. See Japanese music V; *Oboe family III.

Hidden fifths, octaves. See under *Parallel fifths, octaves.

Hilfslinie [G.]. Ledger line.

Hinaufstrich [G.]. See *Bowing (a).

Hindu music. The music of India. I. *Theory.* The Hindu system of scales goes back to Bharata who lived about A.D. 500 [treatise *Natya Sastra*, French translation by Joanny Grosset, 1898]. It is based upon the division of the octave into 22 small intervals, called *sruti*. These intervals,

A comparison of the cent-values with those of our chromatic scale (0, 100, 200, 300, etc.) shows that this very closely approximates our C major scale: c d e f g a b c′. Ma-grama differs from sa-grama only with respect to the fourth tone which is 11 sruti, or 590 cents, therefore, practically f#. Naturally, the identification of sa-grama with our C major scale and of ma-grama with our G major scale is correct only with regard to the intervallic construction, not to tonal functions. Various tones of the Hindu scale may assume the significance of a tonic (particularly, the third tone, e), although these tonics are considerably less clearly defined than they are in our modes. In present-day practice the above two scales are of much lesser importance than variants in which some of the original tones are flatted, e.g.: c–db–e–f–g–ab–b–c, or c–db–eb–f#–g–ab–b–c.

A basic concept in Hindu music is the *raga*. The ragas have frequently been called the "modes" of Hindu music. However, such a comparison is rather misleading. Actually the ragas fall under the classification of *melody-types which play so important a role in Oriental music and which have even left scant traces in the tradition of Western plainsong. A raga is a much more specialized tonal frame than a mode; it prescribes more or less rigidly not only a scale and a center-tone (*amsa*), but also the avoidance of certain tones [in actual music, the seven-tone scales (hepta-scales) described above are usually reduced to six-tone scales (hexa-scales) or five-tone scales (penta-scales)]. It further prescribes the use of typical progressions, stereotyped melodic formulae, rhythmic patterns, and ornamentations. The theoretical system (there are, of course, many variants in the different local schools) knows 6 (main) ragas and 30 *raginis*, each of which are duplicated according to the sa-grama or the ma-grama scheme (perfect or augmented fourths), thus leading to a system of 72 "primary ragas." The speculative fancy of certain theorists has broadened this into a system of as many as 800 ragas, a figure which, however, appears less fantastic if it is realized that a Hindu musician with ordinary training is likely to be able to play and improvise in 50 or 60 ragas. Each raga (literally "color," "mood") has not only musical characteristics, but also a very definite "ethical" and "emotional" significance, and is furthermore associated with a special season or hour of the day. For instance, the raga *Bhairava* is based on the scale: c–db–e–f–g–ab–b, has the center-tone c, expresses reverence, and belongs to dawn. The accompanying Ex. 1

shows the raga *Megha-Mallbar*; the brackets indicate important formulae; the pauses, the two main tones. The most important ragas have also certain symbolistic pictorial associations which have been portrayed in many paintings [see Lit., Lachmann, p. 134].

II. *Style and Form.* Hindu music is essentially monophonic, except for a monotonous drone provided by the *tambura*, an unfretted lute, and for a rhythmic background provided by drums. The rhythm of Hindu music is based on the *tala*, i.e., a more or less elaborate rhythmic pattern which is repeated over and over again. Ex. 2 shows three frequently used tala's.

Cross rhythms between two drums or between the drum and the *vina* [see below] are very frequent. Essential characteristics of Hindu melody are the elaborate ornamentations (*gamaka*), vocal as well as instrumental. These form a basic part of instruction and practice, especially in the playing of the vina, the main melody instrument of Hindu music. This is a "stick zither" [see *Instruments IV], with seven strings, four of which run over a fretted finger board in the form of a long stick, while three others run alongside as open strings (bass courses). The stick is fastened to characteristic resonance chambers made of gourds, two of equal size in the Northern *bin*, or only one in the southern vina [see ill. under *Zithers]. Typical gamaka executed on the vina are a wild and rapidly increasing tremolo (often at the distance of a third or fourth), an abruptly ending portamento performed either by a slide of the left hand (as in violin playing) or by a lateral pull of the strings, etc.

The older tradition of Hindu music survives to some extent in the sacrificial *Sama* chants (Vedic chants), simple liturgical melodies which move chiefly within a tetrachord. The fact that they are not considered to be "in a raga" points to their early origin, certainly anterior to the introduction of the ragas (*c*. A.D. 600). It has been surmised that they show Greek influence (Lachmann, p. 107). The present-day music is, of course, of an entirely different character. A vocal piece usually begins with a drone accompaniment (tambura), followed by a vocalizing improvisation over the main outlines of the raga, followed in turn by the song, accompanied by the drums. A typical form of the south (Carnatic) is the *kirtanam* the construction of which has been compared to that of sonata-form, since it includes the following sections: *pallavi* (first subject), *anupallavi* (second subject), *caranam* (development), and *pallavi* (first subject). Each "subject" is a short melody (four or eight measures) which is repeated several times in free variations which preserve only the main outlines and the chief notes of the "theme,"

The first subject and its variations move around the "tonic" (*amsa*) of the raga, whereas the second subject emphasizes the "dominant," i.e., the fifth above. In the "development section" both subjects are "combined," that is, they appear in immediate succession. Such pieces usually are opened and closed by a short instrumental passage (four measures) in which all the tones and characteristic traits of the raga are given. An example reproduced in Lachmann, p. 118, has a slightly extended form. Another form, used chiefly in the north (Hindostan), is the *khyal*. This resembles our rondo, as it consists of a short ostinato-like motive which is repeated many times between free couplets [cf. Fox-Strangways, p. 287].

Lit.: A. H. Fox-Strangways, *Music of Hindostan* (1914); H. A. Popley, *The Music of India* (1921); C. R. Day, *Music and Musical Instruments of Southern India and the Deccan* (1891); A. B. Fyzee-Rahamin, *The Music of India* (1925); E. Clements, *Lectures on Indian Music* (1927, '30); E. Rosenthal, *The Story of Indian Music* (1929); A. Bake, "Researches in Indian Music ..." (*Indian Art and Letters*, New Ser. 7, 1933); Ph. Stern, "The Music of India and the Theory of the Raga" (*ibid.*); Th. Kornerup, *Indisches Tonsystem* (1931); R. Lachmann, *Musik des Orients* (1929); I. M. van der Hoogt, *The Vedic Chant* (1929); *LavE* i.1, 257; C. R. Day, "Notes on Indian Music" (*PMA* xx); Robindra Lal Roy, "Hindustani Ragas" (*MQ* xx); W. Sargeant, "A Study in East Indian Rhythm" (*MQ* xvii); A. F. Fox-Strangways, "The Hindu Scale" (*SIM* ix); P. Runge, "Die Notation des Somanatha" (*MfM* xxxvi); E. M. v. Hornbostel, "Phonographierte Indische Melodien" (*SIM* v); R. Lachmann and E. v. Hornbostel, "Das indische Tonsystem bei Bharata ..." (*Zeitschrift für vergleichende Musikwissenschaft* iv); H. Engel, in *AMF* iv; P. Stern, in *RM* iv, no. 7; G. F. Checacci, in *RMI* xv.

Hinsterbend [G.]. Dying away.

Hinstrich [G.]. See *Bowing (a).

Hirmos. In early *Byzantine music (9th–12th centuries) a melody composed for the first stanza of a hymn (the ode of a *kanon) and repeated with the following stanzas, in the manner of a strophic song. Naturally, the procedure was more flexible than with a modern strophic chant, admitting adjustments to the varying number of syllables in the different stanzas, similar to the method used with the psalm-tones. Most of the hirmoi (which were collected in books called *hirmologion*) were composed in the 7th and 8th centuries, and were later used for other hymns written after the model of the earlier music. See *Tract.

Lit.: H. Gaïsser, *Les Heirmoi de Pâques* (1905; also in *RMC* ii); A. Gastoué, *Les Origines du chant romain* (1907), p. 60. See also the general literature under *Byzantine chant.

Hirtenflöte [G.]. Shepherd's flute. *Hirtenlied*, shepherd's song.

His [G.]. See *Pitch names.

Hispaniae Schola Musica Sacra. See *Editions XIII.

History of music. This article is designed as a survey of epochs and schools, with reference to other articles from which additional information can be gathered.

I. *The Main Periods.* The history of European music falls very conveniently into a number of periods of strikingly equal duration — a fact which has been little noticed in general. Three times in musical history, at an interval of 300 years, the evolution led to changes which were so strikingly novel in character that contemporary writers adopted the term "new" as a characterization: the *Ars Nova* of 1300, the *Nuove Musiche* of 1600, and the *New Music* of 1900. It would be admissible to add to these "landmarks of innovation" the year 1000, as indicative of one of the most epochal inventions in music, i.e., the musical *staff (Guido and his predecessors). There exist other landmarks of no lesser importance which occur almost exactly at the middle of each of our 300-year periods.

Of these, the year 1750 (marked by the death of Joh. Seb. Bach is familiar to every music student. Around 1450 we find the rise of the *Flemish School, marking the end of medieval music, and the beginning of the Renaissance; around 1150, the first important school of polyphonic music, the School of St. Martial. Finally, the middle of the 9th century can be regarded as the "beginning of polyphony," judging from the date of the earliest preserved records. The periods of 150 years each resulting from the above consideration can be conveniently identified by terms long used in the Fine Arts and coming to be adopted more and more by musical scholars:

gorian chant). Around 850 (Romanesque period) there began a period of amplification of the traditional repertory, leading to the *tropes, *sequences, and finally to the *liturgical drama. More epochal than these "horizontal broadenings" is the simultaneous rise of polyphonic music which, in its early period, can be characterized as "vertical broadening" of the chant, i.e., as polyphonic settings of plainsong *cantus firmi. In the ensuing three centuries these settings, known as *organa, underwent slow but remarkable changes of style. Around 1150 the School of *St. Martial stands out as an important landmark in this evolution, being followed, around 1175, by the still more im-

350: Ambrosian Chant	} Patristic Period	
600: Gregorian Chant	} Early Middle Ages	
850: Beginning of Polyphony	} Early Romanesque ⎤	
1000: Invention of the Staff	} Late Romanesque ⎥	
1150: School of St. Martial	} Early *Gothic ⎬ Later Middle Ages	
1300: *Ars Nova	} Late Gothic ⎦	
1450: Rise of *Flemish School	} *Renaissance	
1600: *Nuove Musiche	} *Baroque	
1750: Death of Bach	} *Rococo, *Classicism, *Romanticism	
1900: *New Music	} *Modern (*New) Music	

It goes without saying that, in reality, the border lines between these periods are not as neatly marked off as the above table, taken literally, would suggest. However, it is only on the basis of a clearly-drawn sketch that the finer lines of historical evolution can be inserted at their proper place [cf. ML, p. 545 for other schemes of periods].

II. *Up to 1300.* For want of other pertinent information, the history of pre-Christian music in Europe is practically limited to that of *Greek music [see also under *Roman music]. The early Christian era sees the rise of the Christian Chant (plainsong) which would appear to be rooted chiefly in the tradition of the *Jewish synagogue. The most important of the various branches of Christian Chant [see *Chant], that of the Roman Church, reached its high-point ("Golden Age") around 900, after the codification of the repertory by St. Gregory (c. 600; see *Gre-

portant School of *Notre Dame with its two masters Leoninus and Perotinus, which is usually considered as the beginning of the *Ars antiqua (13th century). Secondary forms of this school are the non-liturgical *conductus, and the *clausulae — fragments, as it were, of organa which acquired particular importance as the starting point of the *motet, the most characteristic form of the Ars antiqua proper (Franco of Cologne, Petrus de Cruce). The early Gothic period also sees the rise of secular music in the Provençal *troubadours (c. 1100–1300), who are followed, half a century later, by the northern French *trouvères (c. 1150–1300) and the German *Minnesinger (c. 1150–1350). The latter tradition continued to live in the *Meistersinger (c. 1400–1600), the last representatives of monophonic music, aside from *folk song which, to be sure, is not restricted to any period of history. Monophonic music also had a relatively short period of flowering, chiefly during the 13th century, in Spain (*cantigas) and in Italy (*laude).

III. *1300–1450.* With the advent of the late Gothic period or, to speak in musical terms, of the *Ars nova, the picture of music underwent a striking change from the sacred to the secular, a change which brought about the appearance of an entirely new repertory of music, the polyphonic *ballades, *rondeaux, *virelais, in France (Machaut), and of *madrigals, *caccias, *ballatas, in Italy (Jacopo da Bologna, Francesco Landini). The motet continued to be cultivated in France, adopting large dimensions and peculiar features of structure [see *Isorhythmic]. Toward the end of the 14th century the Ars nova movement deteriorated into a somewhat mannered style of writing (Cunelier, Césaris). A glorious revival, however, bringing the musical Gothic to a fitting climax, was brought about by the English Dunstable, whose great genius left scant traces in his home-country [see *English music] but became all the more important as the inspiring force of the renovation of French music, leading to the *Burgundian School of Dufay and Binchois.

IV. *1450–1600.* The middle of the 15th century (*Renaissance) brought about a renewed emphasis on sacred music under the first masters of the *Flemish School (or Schools), Ockeghem and Obrecht. Although their masses and motets, particularly those of the former, are far removed from what the term Renaissance suggests, Renaissance-like features — the "sun of Italy," as it were — appeared in the secular compositions of Obrecht and still more so in those of his great successor Josquin. In the early 16th century — similar in this respect to the early 14th century — numerous secular forms arose: the Italian *frottola, the German polyphonic *Lied, the Spanish *villancico, the Italian *madrigal. The tradition of sacred music, however, continued in the numerous masses and motets, and reached its "Golden Age" under Palestrina, Lasso, Byrd, and Vittoria. The beginning of the Renaissance also marks the starting-point

of a continuous development of *instrumental music, for *ensemble as well as for the organ and, slightly later, the lute [see *Prelude; *Intabulierung; *Ricercare; *Canzona (4); *Fantasia; *Toccata; *Variations; *Dance music, the last-mentioned with interesting forerunners in the 13th and 14th centuries (*estampie)]. The Renaissance came to an impressive close in the pompous splendor of the Venetian *polychoral style of G. Gabrieli [see *Venetian School].

V. *1600–1750.* In spite of the attempts on the part of various scholars to show that "nothing new happened" around 1600 (Baroque), this year remains one of the most fundamental landmarks in music history [see *Nuove musiche; *Baroque], bringing about the rise of the *recitativo, the *monodic style, and the *thoroughbass, together with such novel forms as the *opera, the *oratorio, the *cantata, the *basso-ostinato forms, and leading quickly to a development of instrumental music equal in importance to that of contemporary vocal music. The fact that all these styles and forms can be traced back to earlier roots may be mentioned here as another caution against overlooking the necessarily flexible character of all border lines. Additional evidence of this fundamental truth is the continued influence of the Venetian as well as the *Roman School of the 16th century, or the fact that the two chief forms of Baroque instrumental music, the *suite and the *sonata are both rooted in 16th-century developments [see *Canzona (4)], while the contrast style of the *concerto is more exclusively an affair of the Baroque [see also *Bologna School]. In a way, the Baroque period is the most "international" period in music history, with Italy, Germany, and France competing on almost equal terms, and England being a "good second." No other period can boast of a similar variety of forms, nor of an equal number of great composers, nor of a summit comparable to that represented by the name of Bach.

VI. *1750–1900.* Although, in a way, the change taking place after Bach's death (1750) is more clearly present in the mind of most students of music his-

General Periods	Musical Periods	Monophonic Music	Part Music, Vocal
600	Early Middle Ages	↑ Gregorian Chant	
800		Sequences. Tropes	
900			Organum
1000	Romanesque	Liturgical Drama	
1100			
	St Martial (Early Gothic)	Troubadours Trouvères Minnesinger	Clausula
1200	Notre Dame	Laude Cantigas	Conductus Motet
	Ars Antiqua		
1300	Ars Nova (Late Gothic)		Rondeau Madrigal Mass / Virelai Caccia / Ballade Ballata
1400	Burgundian School		
		Prelude Meistersinger	Chanson Frottola
1500	Flemish School (Renaissance)	**Part Music, Instrumental**	Madrigal Chorale
	Venetian School	Toccata Variation / Canzona Fugue (Ricercare) / Suite	Anthem
1600	Nuove Musiche		Aria Opera
	Roman School		Cantata Oratorio Catch
	Bologna School (Baroque)	Sonata (Baroque) Concerto (Baroque)	
1700	Neapolitan School		
	Mannheim School (Rococo)	Sonata (modern) Symphony Concerto (modern) String Quartet	Lied Glee
	Berlin School		
1800	Viennese Classics	Character Piece Symphonic Poem	
	Romanticism (Modern)		English, French Song
	Nationalism		
1900	Impressionism		
	New Music		⦂ Indicates sporadic continuation

[337]

tory than any of the preceding ones, there actually is more (at least, just as much) "transition" here than elsewhere, namely, in the *Rococo movement which started in France (Couperin) around 1700 and continued, under the name *gallant style, chiefly in Italy and Germany. In the latter country, under the hands of W. F. and C. P. E. Bach, it took on, after 1750, a greater expressiveness [see *Empfindsamkeit; also *Berlin School] which heralds the achievements of the classical and even the Romantic period. At the same time the members of the *Mannheim School (and other composers also) laid the foundation for the formal development of the *sonata, the dominating form of the 19th century, with its orchestral and chamber music varieties, the *symphony and the *quartet. Vienna became the musical world center under the Viennese classics Haydn, Mozart, Beethoven, and Schubert [see *Classicism], the last of whom, the great master of the *lied, marks the transition to the *Romanticism of the 19th century. The early Romanticists (Schumann, Mendelssohn, Chopin) cultivated particularly the *character piece for pianoforte in which they achieved more perfect results than in the large forms of the classical period. The symphonic tradition was revived, however (c. 1870–90) by the symphonies of Bruckner, Brahms, Tchaikovsky, C. Franck, and came to a close with those of Mahler (c. 1890–1910). Around 1850 the *symphonic poem developed as a novel type of symphonic music, and the opera took a new start under Wagner, who added even more weight to the power of German music. Against the dominant position of German music there arose, around 1860, the *National Schools which brought the "peripheric" nations (Bohemia, Norway, Russia, Spain, England) into play, and, around 1900, the *Impressionism which carried France back into the spotlight.

VII. From 1900. The impressionism was the first indication of a quickly growing antithesis against the Romanticism and the musical tradition of the 19th century in general. The ensuing revolution-

ary tendencies, summed up under the term *New music, embrace a variety of attempts, experiments, and aspects for which there is no parallel in the entire history of music. It is not until recently (c. 1930) that this wild uproar has partly subsided and that a more steady course, known as *neo-classicism and represented chiefly by Stravinsky and Hindemith, becomes visible.

The accompanying table illustrates the development of the most important forms of music (straight lines indicate the main period of existence; dotted lines a more sporadic continuation).

Related articles (in approximately chronological order): Gregorian Chant; Byzantine Chant; Bards; Middle-Ages; Troubadours; Trouvères; Minnesinger; Gothic music; St. Martial; Ars antiqua; Ars nova; Burgundian School; Flemish School; Renaissance; Musica reservata; Humanism; Colorists; Virginalists; Venetian School; Roman School; Baroque; Nuove musiche; Bologna School; Neapolitan School; Rococo; Mannheim School; Berlin School; Classicism; Romanticism; Nationalism; Modern music. See also the articles on the various nations, listed on p. 2, and the article on Form.

Lit.: *Standard books:* Oxford History of Music (new ed., 7 vols., 1929–34; for the medieval history the vols. i, ii of the first edition, 1901, are preferable); A. W. Ambros, *Geschichte der Musik* (5 vols., 1862 and later); G. Adler, *Handbuch der Musikgeschichte* (2 vols., 1929); H. Riemann, *Handbuch der Musikgeschichte* (5 vols., 2d ed. 1921/22); J. Combarieu, *Histoire de la musique* (3 vols., 1913–20); A. Lavignac, *Encyclopédie de la musique* . . . (1912/20), part i (5 vols.).

Synoptic books: H. Prunières, *A New History of Music* (1943); K. Nef, *An Outline of the History of Music* (1935); Stanford and Forsyth, *History of Music* (1922); P. Láng, *Music in Western Civilization* (1941); H. Leichtentritt, *Music, History and Ideas* (1938); A. Einstein, *A Short History of Music* (1938); E. Dickinson, *The Study of the History of Music* (1908); D. N. Ferguson, *A History of Musical Thought* (1935); Th. M. Finney,

A History of Music (1935); W. S. Pratt, *History of Music* (1935); P. A. Scholes, *The Listener's History of Music* (1923 and later); A. Schering, *Tabellen zur Musikgeschichte* (1921).

Collections of Examples: A. T. Davison and W. Apel, †Historical Anthology of Music (*in preparation*); A. Schering, †*Geschichte der Musik in Beispielen* (1931); A. Einstein, †*Beispielsammlung zur Musikgeschichte* (1917); H. Riemann, †*Musikgeschichte in Beispielen* (1929); G. Kinsky, *History of Music in Pictures* (1930). For collections of records see under *Phonograph.

Articles: F. Malipiero, "The History of Music and the Music of History" (*MQ* ix); A. Mendel, "Spengler and Music History" (*MQ* xx); A. Lorenz, "Periodizität in der Musikgeschichte" (*DM* xxi.9); A. Schering, "Historische und nationale Klangstile" (*JMP*, 1927); H. Osthoff, "Die Anfänge der Musikgeschichtsschreibung in Deutschland" (*AM* v, no. 3); Ch. van den Borren, "Une Conception nouvelle de l'histoire de la musique" (*RM* ix).

Hoboe. Old spelling for *oboe.

Hoch Kammerton [G.]. See *Pitch.

Hocket [L. *hoketus*, *ochetus*; F. *hocquet*, *hoquet*; It. *ochetto*; the root of the word is possibly the same as in hiccough]. In medieval polyphony (13th, 14th centuries) the truncation of a melodic line

into fragments (frequently single notes) which are given to two parts in alternation. The accompanying examples [(1): motet *In Bethlehem*; (2): anonymous

*chace, cf. *BeMMR*, 131] serve as an illustration [cf. also *HAM*, no. 35]. Theorists of the 13th century mention *hoketus* not only as a technique to be applied within the course of a motet, etc., but also as an independent musical form. This probably refers to pieces in which hocket technique is used consistently between the two upper parts. A limited number of such pieces, mostly instrumental, are preserved [cf. P. Aubry, *Cent motets*, nos. 102, 103, 104, 106, 107, 108; Y. Rokseth, *Polyphonies du XIIIe siècle* ii, 160].

The hocket technique loses much of its seeming oddity if it is realized that a rather similar type of technique exists in the "*durchbrochene Arbeit" used in compositions by Haydn, Mozart, and Beethoven. Some of the 17th-century *catches likewise show a fragmentary alternation of voice-parts similar in principle to the hocket technique. Cf. Marius Schneider, in *ZMW* xi.

Hoflied [G.]. See under *Gesellschaftslied.

Ho-hoane. Corruption of Irish "ochone," that is, *lament. In the *Fitzwilliam Virginal Book* there is a piece labeled "The Irish Hohoane" [ed. Barclay-Squire, i, 87].

Hold. Same as *pause.

Holz- [G., wood]. *Holzblasinstrumente*, wood winds. *Holzbläser*, player of wood winds. *Holzharmonika*, *Holzstabspiel*, xylophone. *Holzschlegel*, wooden drumstick. *Holztrompete*, see *Clarinet family II; also *SaRM*, 181.

Homme armé, L'. See *L'homme armé.

Homophonic [from Gr. *homos*, same, similar]. Designation for music in which one voice leads melodically, being supported by an accompaniment in chordal or in a somewhat more elaborate style. Thus practically all music of the 19th century is homophonic. The term is the opposite of *polyphonic, i.e., music in which all parts contribute more or less equally to the musical fabric [see *Texture]. In

German terminology *Homophonie* (*homophon*) has a different meaning, namely of part-music in which all the voices move in the same rhythm (cf. the literal meaning of the Greek term). Hence, *Homophonie* is the equivalent for "strict chordal style" or *familiar style. Some American writers have adopted this meaning.

The French use the term *homophonie* in the meaning of (1) *monophonic music; (2) *enharmonic change [cf. M. Brenet, *Dictionnaire* . . . , p. 197].

Hook neumes. See *Neumes II.

Hopper. See *Pianoforte I.

Hoquet, hoquetus. See *Hocket.

Horizontal. See under *Texture.

Horn. I. The modern orchestral instrument, called French horn (in order to distinguish it from the *English horn, a member of the *oboe family), is a *brass instrument with a narrow conical bore, circular-wound, and with a large flaring bell and a funnel-shaped mouthpiece. It has three rotary valves, and is therefore also referred to as valve horn [F. *cor-à-pistons, cor chromatique*; G. *Ventilhorn*; It. *corno ventile, corno a macchina*], in contradistinction to the early valveless instruments [see II]. Illustration on p. 97. For the basic principles of tone production on the horn, see *Wind instruments.

Normally the horn is pitched in F, and the series of its natural tones is F_1 F c f a c' f' g' a', etc. Owing to the narrow bore, however, the lowest tone of this series (*pedal tone) is practically unobtainable, so that the series starts with F. By operating the valves a complete chromatic scale from B_1 to bb″ becomes available, the last five tones of which, however, are of little use. The horn is notated as a transposing instrument, written a fifth higher than it sounds. For the lowest notes the bass-clef is used, usually (in older scores always) with the notes written a fourth lower — instead of a fifth higher — than their actual sound [see Ex.]. In older scores key-signatures are avoided for the horn parts, the chromatic alterations being given with each single note; but there is now a strong tendency to write horn parts with a key-signature which, owing to the transposed notation, has one flat less or one sharp more than that of, e.g., the violins (E-flat for a composition in A-flat, etc.).

The horn has the reputation of possessing the most difficult technique of all the orchestral instruments. Horn playing involves several special methods of tone production which are not always clearly presented in writings on the topic. The foremost of these is the *stopping*, achieved by inserting the hand into the bell. Formerly, on the natural horn (which had no valves) the missing tones of the natural series were produced by inserting the flat hand into the bell and closing it 1/4, 1/2, or 3/4. This gave a continuous scale mostly of diatonic tones, which, however, was not very satisfactory as the stopping changed the timbre of the tone. Nowadays "stopping" [G. *gestopft*, F. *bouché*, It. *chiuso*] is used only to obtain a special effect. By blocking the bell with the hand the tube length is shortened and the tone rises approximately a semitone. Stopped tones are indicated thus: +. To a limited extent (mainly in the lower two octaves) stopping can also be used to lower the pitch to the extent of a semitone. The different methods of stopping depend largely upon the individuality of the player, and defy explanation in hard and fast rules.

The *mute* [F. *sourdine*; G. *Dämpfer*] is a pear-shaped addition made of metal, wood, or cardboard, which is inserted into the bell in order to obtain yet another timbre (muted horns) entirely different from that of the stopped horns. The modern mutes are non-transposing, while the older ones, smaller and of a slightly different shape, raised the pitch.

The word *cuivré* often encountered in French music [G. *schmetternd*] indicates that a "brassy" tone is desired. It is obtained through an increased tension of the lips and can be produced either open, stopped, or muted.

Horns are also built and occasionally demanded in other sizes, e.g., E, E♭, D, low C, low B♭, and also in high B♭, an octave above the largest size. A "double horn" has latterly come into use, a combination of the horns in F and B♭ *alto* [see *Duplex instruments*].

The solo and chamber music literature for the horn includes the following pieces: Handel: three *Concerti a due corni*; Haydn: three concertos for one horn, and one for two horns, also a trio for horn, violin, and violoncello; Mozart: four concertos, three divertimenti for two horns and strings, and a quintet for horn, violin, two violas, and cello; Beethoven: Sonata for piano and French horn, op. 17; Sextet for two horns and strings, op. 81b; various pieces for several wind instruments (op. 16, 20, 71, 103, 146); Spohr: Octet for two horns, clarinet, and strings; Weber: Concertino for horn; Schumann: Adagio und Allegro for horn and piano, op. 70, Concertstück for four horns and orchestra, op. 86; Brahms: Horn trio, op. 40; R. Strauss: Concerto for horn, op. 11; Hindemith: Chamber music for five winds, op. 24, no. 2.

II. *History*. The following explanation deals only with the most immediate predecessors of the modern horn, the other "members of the horn family" being treated under the general article on *brass instruments. The earliest type is the Hunting Horn, a plain pipe which was coiled in a circle large enough to permit carrying over the shoulder. It had a shallow mouthpiece of the trumpet pattern and as a consequence its tone was loud and brilliant. Towards the close of the 17th century the same instrument was built in a considerably smaller size, proper for use in the orchestra. These instruments were similar in most respects to the modern horn, except that they had no valves or crooks [see below] so that only the tones of one and the same harmonic series could be obtained. The details of the development leading from the hunting horn to the "natural horn" [F. *cor d'harmonie*; G. *Naturhorn, Waldhorn*;

It. *corno naturale*] are difficult to trace. Throughout the first half of the 18th century the orchestral horns had a trumpet-like sound and were frequently objected to as being coarse and vulgar. It was not until 1750 that the instrument took on those proportions which gave it its typical "mellowness" of timbre.

Around 1760 the horn-player Kölbel constructed an instrument called *Amorschall*, i.e., a horn with a modified bell and with lateral holes covered by keys, the first instance of the use of keyed brass instruments. Around 1770 the horn-player Hampl of Dresden discovered that the natural tones of the horn could be lowered to the extent of a semitone or a tone by inserting the open hand with the fingers close together into the bell. This technique made it possible for the first time to produce "artificial" horn tones, thus bridging to some extent the gaps between the natural tones. The natural horns thus played were called "hand horn" [It. *corno a mano*].

In the late 18th century horns were provided with *crooks, i.e., additional lengths of tubing by which the fundamental tuning of the instrument could be changed. Thus, a horn in F could be made into a horn in E or E♭, etc. At first these crooks were pieces inserted immediately underneath the mouthpiece. This method had the drawback of removing the instrument from the body of the player so that, if longer crooks or several crooks were used, the playing became quite inconvenient. The above-mentioned Hampl is credited with the invention of curved sliding crooks to be inserted into the body, and these became known as "inventions," hence the name *Inventionshorn* for this instrument. By the use of crooks together with stopped notes the horn became an almost completely chromatic instrument. However, the stopped notes differed in timbre from the natural notes and the change of crooks was a time-consuming process. The invention of *valves by Blümel in 1813 did away with these inconveniences and revolutionized the playing of the horn. The first part for the valve horn is in Halévy's *La*

Juive (1835). The hand horn, however, continued for some time to be used side by side with the modern type, owing to its more brilliant tone. See the illustrations on p. 98.

Lit.: F. Piersig, *Das Horn in der Kunstmusik bis Bach* (Diss. Halle 1927); E. Paul, *Das Horn in seiner Entwicklung vom Natur- zum Ventilinstrument* (Diss. Vienna 1932); D. J. Blaikley, "The French Horn" (*PMA* xxxv); H. Kling, "Le Cor de chasse" (*RMI* xviii); G. de St. Foix," Les Concertos pour cor de Mozart" (*RdM* x). See also *Brass instruments.

Horn fifths [G. *Hornquinten*]. See under *Parallel fifths.

Hornpipe. (1) An obsolete wind instrument, probably identical with the *pibgorn. — (2) A dance popular in England from the 16th through the 19th century [see *Dance music III] which, at least in its later development, was performed as a solo dance by sailors, with folded arms and many characteristic steps and gestures. The earliest preserved hornpipe ("hornepype") is a composition of Hugh Aston, dating from *c.* 1525 [repr. in John Stafford Smith, *Musica Antiqua* (1812), in J. Wolf, *Sing- und Spielmusik* . . . (1931), and (slightly abridged) in *ApMZ* ii]. It is one of the most remarkable compositions in the field of early keyboard music, noteworthy for its sheer inexhaustible flow of melodic inspiration above an extremely simple harmonic scheme, i.e., alternation of tonic and dominant [see *Ostinato]. The numerous hornpipes of the 17th and 18th centuries are usually in moderate 3/2-time, later in 4/4-time, with a characteristic "scotch-snap"-rhythm [see Ex.]. Examples exist in the dramatic works of Purcell, in Han-

del's Concerto Grosso no. 7, in Th. Muffat's *Componimenti Musicali* (1739), in a *Collection of Original Lancashire Hornpipes* (1705), and in the various books of *country dances. Cf. *GD* ii, 670; also

Stainer and Barrett, *Dictionary of Musical Terms*, 233.

Hornquinten, Hornsatz [G.]. *Horn fifths.

Hosanna, Osanna. A Hebrew word expressing triumph and glorification. In the connection *Hosanna in excelsis* it occurs in the Sanctus of the Ordinary of the Mass [see *Mass B, III]. In polyphonic masses it is always treated as a brilliant coda.

Hptw. [G.]. Short for *Hauptwerk (in organ music).

Hr. Short for Horn.

Huehuetl. See *Mexican music.

Hufnagelschrift [G.]. See *Nagelschrift.

Humanism, humanistic music. Music of the 16th century which shows the influence of the literary humanism, that is, of the revived study of the ancient Greek and Roman literature. These tendencies found their clearest musical expression in the composition of the Horatian *odes, in the *vers mesuré, in the revival of Greek theory, and in the resulting experiments in chromaticism and *enharmonic tones. In a wider sense, the term is used to denote the entire school of composers of the early 16th century (chiefly German and French) who had close contact with the leading representatives of the literary humanism (Erasmus of Rotterdam, Ulrich von Hutten, Johann Reuchlin, Ronsard, Baïf) and who became imbued with a humanistic feeling for culture, refined taste, balance, and repose (Hofhaimer, Senfl, Jannequin, Claudin). A significant trait of this period is the use of scholarly names, such as *prooemium* [L.] or *anabole* [Gr.] for prelude [cf. W. Merian, *Der Tanz in den deutschen Tabulaturbüchern* (1927), pp. 60, 62, 63]. Cf. *MoML*, 341. See *Renaissance.

Lit.: *LaMWC, passim*; H. J. Moser, *Geschichte der deutschen Musik* (1920ff) i, 397; *LavE* i.3, 1298; D. P. Walker in *MR* ii, iii; P. Masson, in *Le Mercure musical* ii.12.

Hummel, Hümmelchen [G.]. A primitive German bagpipe of the 16th and 17th centuries.

Humor in music. See *Satire.

Humoreske [G.]; **humoresque** [F.]. Nineteenth-century name for instrumental compositions of a humorous or, at least, good-humored character showing traits of capriciousness or whimsicality. R. Schumann (op. 20) used it for a long composition in which the expression frequently changes from one extreme to another.

Hungarian music. I. Around 1000, Christian monks brought the Gregorian chant into Hungary. From about the same time date the earliest reports of a tradition of national bards and minstrels reciting heroic poems to the sounds of the ancient Hungarian national instrument, the *koboz*, a short lute. In this connection the stay at the Hungarian court of the French troubadour Peire Vidal (d. 1215) may be mentioned. In the 13th and 14th centuries German minstrels known as *kokler* [from G. *Gaukler*] were frequent in Hungary and from the 14th century two Hungarian musicians are known by name, Stephanus Fiellator [see *vielle] and Nicolaus, dictus Kobzos (both c. 1350). Hungarian music came to a great flowering under King Mathias Corvinus (1458–90) to whose wife, Beatrix, Tinctoris dedicated his *Diffinitorium* [see *Dictionaries III]. Thomas Stoltzer and Adriaen Willaert stayed at the court of King Louis until 1562, the year of the battle of Mohàcs against the Turks which marked the end of Hungary's independence and the beginning of Turkish influence. Nonetheless, it was after this disastrous event that Hungarian composers emerged for the first time, particularly lute composers such as Sebastian Tinodi (1505?–56; cf. *RiML*, 1847), and Valentin Bakfark (1507–76; cf. *DTOe* 18.ii). The former was also an outstanding historian, and in his *Cronica* (1554) several Hungarian airs are given, among which the one memorizing the siege of Eger is most remarkable for its

truly national flavor [*LavE* i.5, 2615; see reference under *Folk song III]. Toward the end of the century Hungarian dances of an equally characteristic nature made their appearance in German books, e.g., a *Passamezzo ongaro* in Jobin's tablature of 1572 and, particularly, the *Ungarescha* in Paix's [see *Colorists] keyboard tablature of 1583 [cf. W. Apel, *Concord Classics for the Piano* (1938)]. At the same time many collections of secular and religious melodies (psalms) appeared, containing numerous songs which are conspicuous for their use of Hungarian rhythms, such as the "Scotch" snap. An interesting repertory of Hungarian harpsichord (virginal) music is preserved in four MSS of the 17th century, containing simple arrangements of folk melodies as well as dance pieces arranged in suites [cf. *RiML*, 1951].

II. In the 18th century there developed national Hungarian dances of a very picturesque character, e.g., the *verbunkoche* (or *verbunko*, from G. *Werbung*, draft) which was danced by soldiers in full uniform with swords and spurs. It is very wild in character and consists of two sections, a slow *lassu* and a quick *friss* (*friska*). A more civilized variety is the *palotache*, which is of a more regular design and shows the influence of the polonaise. This aboriginal music deteriorated after 1800 under the influence of Western idioms while, on the other hand, Western composers adopted Hungarian idioms in numerous compositions "All' ongarese," e.g., Haydn and Schubert, whose *Divertissement à la Hongroise* for four hands (op. 54) portrays, one might feel, the Hungarian spirit more purely than Liszt's famous rhapsodies. The *Czardas* (*Tschardache*) is said to be a 19th-century revival of the old verbunko and shows also the division into two sections, a slow and a quick one, sometimes with the addition of an ornamented middle section, the *czifra*. A typical feature of Hungarian dance music is the virtuoso treatment of the violin, chiefly in the hands of gypsies who added to the melodies their characteristic touch of rubato execution and of improvised cadenzas. Nonetheless, F. Liszt was in error when, in his *The Gipsies and their Music* (1859), he gave the gypsies a central place in the creation of Hungarian dance music. Actually, this place should be reserved for Hungarian composers such as Johann Bihari (1764–1827) and A. Czermak (1771–1822), while to the gypsies falls the role of performers and propagators. Typical features of this music are *alla zoppa*-rhythms, augmented seconds (Gypsy scale), ornamented cadential formulae, and the playing of the *cimbalom. There is also a genuine gypsy music amongst the rural gypsies, but this differs markedly from the "Hungarian gypsy music," as do also the aboriginal Hungarian peasant songs which have been collected in great number by Béla Bartók [cf. E. Haraszti, in *KIM*, 1930, p. 140].

III. The father of modern Hungarian music is Ferenc Erkel (1810–93), who wrote the first national operas *Bathory Maria* (1840) and *Hunyady Laszlo* (1844). The most famous Hungarian composer, Franz Liszt (1811–86), embraced the trends of German Romanticism in his symphonic poems and other works, while his Hungarian Rhapsodies represent a type which is rejected by modern Hungarian scholars as a "pseudo-national" falsification. Ödön Mihalovich (1842–1929) wrote a few operas in Wagnerian style. Much more important is Ernst von Dohnanyi (b. 1877) with his orchestral and chamber music modeled after Brahms; and in Béla Bartók (b. 1881) a composer of outstanding significance has appeared who, together with the Russian Stravinsky and the German Hindemith, is the leading representative of present-day music. The artistic significance of his compositions is paralleled by the scholarly importance of his research in the field of folk music. Other composers of renown are Zoltan Kodaly (b. 1882) and Paul Kadosa (b. 1903).

Lit.: G. Kaldy, *A History of Hungarian Music* (1903); E. Haraszti, *La Musique ongroise* (1933); *LavE* i.5, 2597ff; *AdHM*, 1170ff; B. Bartók, *Hungarian Folk Music* (1931); O. Gombosi, *La Vita musicale alla corte di Re Mattia* (1929); *id.*, *Die ältes-*

ten *Denkmäler ungarischer Vokalmusik* (1931); B. Bartók, "Hungarian Peasant Music" (*MQ* xix); E. Kilenyi, "The Theory of Hungarian Music" (*MQ* v); J. de Göry, "Hungarian Music" (*PMA* xxix); F. Korbay, "The Hungarian Folk-Songs" (*PMA* xxxv); B. Scabolski, "Probleme der altungarischen Musikgeschichte" (*ZMW* vii, viii); L. Fökövi, "Musik am Hofe des Matthias Corvinus" (*KJ*, 1900); A. Bartha, in *AMF* ii; E. Haraszti, in *KIM*, 1930, p. 140. For Hungarian literature cf. *RiML*, 1899ff. Cf. also *AdHM*, 1180.

Hunting horn. See *Horn II.

Hunting music [G. *Jagdmusik*]. Cf. K. Taut, *Beiträge zur Geschichte der Jagdmusik* (Diss. Leipzig 1927).

Hunt Quartet, Hunt Symphony. See *Chasse, La.

Hupfauf [G., jump-up]. See *Nachtanz.

Hurdy-gurdy [F. *vielle* (*de roue*); G. *Drehleier*; It. *ghironda*; Sp. *zanfonia*]. A medieval stringed instrument in the general shape of a lute or viol in which the strings are put in vibration, not by a bow, but by a rotating rosined wheel, operated by a handle at the lower end of the body and turned by the right hand. The instrument usually possessed three to four unfingered bass-strings which were allowed to sound continuously, thus producing a drone harmony (c–g–c') and two melody strings (tuned in unison) running over the finger board which were stopped by tangents connected with keys. The instrument was very popular in the 10th to the 14th century; later it became a beggar's instrument despised by serious musicians. Praetorius, in his *Syntagma Musicum* (1615), expressly declines to speak of the "Bauern- und umblaufenden Weiber-Leyer" (the lyre of the peasants and itinerant wenches). However, in the 18th century it became fashionable, together with the musette, in French society-circles [see *Musette]. Haydn wrote five concertos and seven *notturnos for two hurdy-gurdies. He calls the instrument *lyra* or *lira organizzata*, a name which has been erroneously interpreted as *lira da braccio. Some 18th-century specimens of the hurdy-gurdy have a small number of organ pipes attached in the body, and it is probably to these that the term "organizzata" refers. The name *lyra* as well as the use of a crank has also led to confusion with the street-organ [G. *Leierkasten*]. Schubert's well-known song "Der Leiermann" portrays the player of a hurdy-gurdy, not of a street-organ. See the illustration on p. 800.

The hurdy-gurdy was described by Odo of Cluny (d. 942) in his study entitled *Quomodo organistrum construatur*. Pictures from the 12th and 13th centuries show a much larger instrument than the later type, held and played by two men. The original name *organistrum* was replaced around 1300 by the names *armonie* and *symphonia*, the latter of which was perverted into *chifonie, cinfonie, zanfonja, zampugna, *sambuca*, etc. In the 15th century the instrument adopted the name *vielle*, after the old *vielle (a fiddle) had become obsolete. Cf. *SaHMI*, 271; *GD* ii, 685; E. de Bricqueville, in *BSIM*, 1909.

Hurtig [G.]. Nimble, quick.

Hydraulis [from Gr. *hydor*, water; *aulos*, pipe]. The organ of the ancient Greeks, invented by Ktesibius of Alexandria (*c*. 300–250 B.C.). The water did not, as older writers fancifully believed, run through the pipes, but was enclosed in separate containers and served as a means of communicating hydraulic pressure provided by hand pumps. A clay model found in the ruins of Carthage and portions of an actual instrument discovered in 1931 at Aquincum, near Budapest. have given full insight into the details of its construction [illustrations in *GD* ii, 690; also *GD*, Suppl. Vol., 289]. The hydraulis was used particularly in Rome in connection with the gladiatorial shows. Nero is reported to have performed on it [see *Roman music]. See *Magrepha; *Organ XII.

Lit.: H. G. Farmer, *The Organ of the Ancients from Eastern Sources* (1931); *SaHMI*, 143; Ch. Maclean, in *SIM* vi; J. W. Warman, in *PMA* xxx; Nagy Lajos,

Az Aquincumi orgona (1934; in Hungarian, with a summary in German); W. W. Hyde, in *Transactions and Proceedings of the American Philological Association*, Philadelphia, 69 (1938).

Hymn. A song of praise or adoration of God (originally, in honor of Apollo; two hymns to Apollo of *c*. 150 B.C. are among the most complete remnants of Greek music; cf. *HAM*, no. 6a, b). In the earliest Christian era, the term hymn was applied to all songs in praise of the Lord; later on it was restricted to newly written poems, as distinguished from the scriptural psalms and canticles [see *Gregorian chant II].

I. *Hymns of the Eastern Churches.* In the early Christian era Antioch (Syria) and Constantinople (Byzantine empire) were the centers of hymn writing (hymnody). The movement apparently started among the Gnostics, a sect which flourished in the 2d century. Bardesanes (d. 223) and his son Harmonius wrote a complete *Gnostic Psalter*, i.e., a collection of poetic paraphrases of the psalms. The great success of this popularizing enterprise (cf. the *psalters of the 16th century!) led to imitations among the Christians. The Syrian Saint Ephrem (306–373) is usually considered the father of Christian hymnody. The Eastern Churches (Syrian, Byzantine, Armenian) gave the hymns a much more prominent part in the service than they ever attained in the Western Church [see *Byzantine, *Armenian, *Syrian chant]. The earliest preserved hymn melody is that of the *Oxyrhynchos hymn of the 3d century. Cf. H. J. W. Tillyard, *Byzantine Music and Hymnography* (1923); *Editions XVIII.

II. *Latin Hymns.* St. Hilarius, Bishop of Poitiers (d. 366), is credited with having written the first Latin hymns, in imitation of the Syrian hymns which were, of course, in Greek (as are all those of the early Eastern Churches). His hymns being all lost (except one), St. Ambrose (d. 397) is actually the father of the hymnody of the Catholic Church [see *Ambrosian hymns], together with Aurelius Prudentius (d. after 405) and St. Augustin (354–430). Ambrosius' iambic dimeter (◡◡, ◡◡◡, e.g., *Vení creátor spíritús*) became the standard meter of the innumerable Latin hymns of which there are about 120 still in use, chiefly for the Office [cf. *AR*, 230*; a number of hymns of much later date, the so-called Rococo hymns, are listed separately, under *Varia*, p. 232*]. The more than fifty volumes of G. M. Dreves' and Cl. Blume's *Analecta Hymnica* are a practically complete collection of medieval hymn-texts; a useful index for quick reference is U. Chevalier's *Repertorium Hymnologicum*. The earliest sources of hymn melodies date from the 11th century. The great majority of these melodies introduce groups of two to four notes which fall just as frequently on the strong as on the weak syllable. Evidently, they do not admit a strictly metrical rendering [cf. P. Wagner, *Gregorianische Formenlehre*, p. 462]. The polyphonic composition of hymns started in the 13th century [cf. *SchGMB*, no. 10; *BeMMR*, 169; O. Ursprung, *Katholische Kirchenmusik*, p. 142]. Later composers were Dunstable, Dufay [cf. *DTOe* 27.i], A. v. Fulda, Thomas Stoltzer [*DdT* 65], Tallis, Vittoria, Byrd, and many others. In 1589 Palestrina published a collection, *Hymni totius anni*, i.e., hymns for the entire year. Organ hymns were written by A. Schlick, G. Cavazzoni [cf. *SchGMB*, no. 103: Inno], Cabezon, Titelouze, etc.; see *Organ chorale I.

III. *German Hymns*. For the German hymns of the Catholic rites, cf. *MoML*, 395 (*Kirchenlied*); for those of the Protestant Church, see *Chorale.

IV. *English Hymns*. See subsequent entry.

Hymn, English. I. Even before the 18th century it was evident that the limitations, psychological no less than artistic, which surrounded the *Psalter as a congregational musical form, were bound to produce a reaction in favor of the hymn. The Lutheran *Chorale, in particular, had demonstrated the power of the hymn form, and its failure of acceptance in other lands cannot be laid to any lack of musical

persuasiveness or of practicability, but simply to the persistence of the tradition of sacro-sanctity with which Biblical texts were surrounded to the detriment of the purely "man-made" hymn texts of German Reformation writers. The Germans must be credited with a greater catholicity of viewpoint than many of their neighbors, for editions of the French Psalter were at one time or another in use in Germany. England was not so receptive, for though Coverdale's *Goostly Psalms and Spiritualle Songs* (1539, '46) included thirty-six Chorales, these failed to make their way. The volume was, to be sure, banned by Henry the Eighth, but even royal disfavor can hardly account for what appears to have been a pretty complete rejection. Indeed, had the success of the hymn as a form in England depended solely upon the support of the crown, it would have come into its own during the reign of Elizabeth, for by decree she admitted it to a part in the English Service and permitted its inclusion in Day's Psalter. Again, about the end of the first quarter of the 17th century, James I gave to George Wither a patent allowing him to have his *Hymns and Songs of the Church* bound in the same volume with the Psalter. But the grip of the latter upon the English Service was so strong that it was not, perhaps, until a hundred years later that the hymn was fully established and hymn books began to appear.

Watts's first hymnal appeared in 1707 and was followed in 1737 by John Wesley's hymn book published in Georgia. After the Wesleys returned to England they continued the work undertaken in America; and as singing was an important feature of the Methodist movement, the contributions of the Wesleys were of inestimable value, the use of their hymns spreading, as well, into many of the other non-conformist branches of the Church. The 18th century was prolific in the production of hymns which as music do not in all cases warrant enthusiasm. The period should not be judged by the extraordinary *fuguing tunes in which one or another part dropped out momentarily, sometimes making, upon its re-entrance, unintentional rearrangements of the text which, while more innocent than those to be found in some *catches, are not less mirth-provoking. The period was, perhaps, near enough to the Psalter tradition to retain an essential musical dignity which, in the Psalter itself, must have been so all-pervading as to be occasionally oppressive. In any case the hymn book output of the 18th century is, with reservations, more to be commended than the bulk of 19th-century production. A notable exception, however, resulted from the rise of interest in Plainsong and the Chorale which occurred in England about the middle of the 19th century and which introduced into the hymnal an element of vitality and musical excellence long overdue. This was the real achievement of 19th-century English hymnody and helps us to forget a little the ensuing pallid reflections of romanticism that characterize the hymns of the Victorians. The 18th-century hymn may have been at times dull, but it has never been charged with musical feebleness or sentimentality.

II. In America, as in England, the 18th century saw an effort to extend the borders of congregational musical expression beyond the field of psalm singing. The first American hymns are credited to William Billings (1746–1800), who was followed by Lowell Mason (1792–1872). English standards of hymn composition were generally adopted in America in the late 19th century and although some hymnals included psalter and chorale material, the emphasis was strongly on the Victorian side. One phenomenon connected with American congregational song of the latter part of the 19th century was the *gospel hymn*. Many of its texts were closely connected with the doctrine of "salvation by grace" so that their content is often no more than an irritatingly priggish assumption of Christian superiority. Both as literature and as music they plumbed the depths of commonness, but, in spite of this, their influence extended beyond the confines of the revival meeting and into the regular services of the church.

Two evils, in particular, have beset the modern Protestant hymnal. First, the editorial obsession that the music must be familiar and that the traditional partnership between certain texts and tunes must be preserved. Devotion to this policy has resulted in the perpetuating from generation to generation of many texts and much music of inferior worth. The average quality of denominational hymnals is not high, but in recent years three books of outstanding merit have appeared, namely, *The English Hymnal* (2d ed. 1933), *The Oxford Hymn Book*, and *Songs of Praise*. Second, the publishing of the melodies in part arrangements has been detrimental to congregational singing. The best hymn tunes are generally within the range of the average voice, but many worshipers prefer to indulge in a modest tonal excursion which, they hope, and perhaps believe, is a rendition of the alto, tenor, or bass part. If congregations could be induced to unite on the melody and leave the harmony to the organ, the vigor and assured quality of hymn singing would miraculously increase.

Lit.: W. Douglas, *Church Music in History and Practice* (1937); J. T. Lightwood, *Hymn Tunes and Their Story* (1906); F. J. Metcalf, *Stories of Hymn Tunes* (1928); J. Moffat, *Handbook to the Church Hymnary* (1935); P. Scholes, *The Oxford Companion to Music* (1938), article "Hymn"; H. B. Marks, *The Rise and Growth of English Hymnody* (1937); G. Dearmer, "The Fall and Rise of the Hymn Tune" (*ML* vi, no. 1).   A. T. D.

Hypate [Gr.]. See *Greek music.

Hyper-, hypo- [Gr., above, below]. Prefixes denoting higher and lower pitches. *Hyper- (hypo-)diatessaron* is the upper (lower) fourth; *hyper- (hypo-)diapente*, the higher (lower) fifth. In Greek theory, terms such as *Hyperdorian* and *Hypodorian* signify modes (more properly, octave-species) which start a fifth above and below the initial tone of the original octave, e.g., *Dorian* on e, *Hyperdorian* on b, *Hypodorian* on A [see *Greek music II (c)]. In the medieval system of church modes the prefix *hypo-* denotes modes the range (ambitus) of which is a fourth below that of the corresponding primary (authentic) mode [see *Church modes II].

Hyporchema [Gr.]. An ancient Greek dancing song from Crete.

I

I. This letter was introduced by Kirnberger to denote the natural seventh, i.e., the seventh *harmonic, such as is produced on the natural horn. Its pitch ($7/4 = 969$ *cents) is noticeably lower than that of the well-tempered seventh (1000 cents) and that of the seventh in *first intonation (996 cents).

Iamb, Iambic. See *Poetic meter; also *Modes, Rhythmic.

Iastian. See *Greek music II (c).

Icelandic music. The inhabitants of Iceland possess a highly remarkable tradition of folk music which probably reaches farther back than any of the other folk-traditions of Europe [see *Folk song III]. A comparison of early manuscripts [*Arna-magnäan MS*, University Library of Copenhagen; cf. *WoHN* i, 119] with recent collections shows that music has been stationary in Iceland for at least 600 years. A characteristic feature of the *rimur* (dancing songs, ballades) is the frequent change of meter. Particularly interesting is the *twisöngur* (twin-song), i.e., two-part singing in parallel fifths, which is obviously a remnant of the parallel *organum of the 9th century, and which is still practiced today in certain remote parts of Iceland [cf. *GD* iv, 44; *ReMMA*, 271].

Lit.: B. Thorsteinsson, *Islenzk Thjód-lög* (1906–09); J. Leifs, *Isländische Volks-lieder* (1929); A. Hammerich, in *SIM* i; E. M. v. Hornbostel, "Phonographierte isländische Zwiegesänge" (*Deutsche Is-landforschung*, 1930); J. Leifs, in *ZMW* xi and *DM* xvi.1.

Ictus. In prosody, a stress or accent. The term has been introduced into music mainly by the monks of *Solesmes, as an integral part of their rhythmic interpretation and performance of Gregorian chant

[see *Gregorian chant VI]. It serves primarily to mark off those groups of two and three notes which form the basis of their rendering of the chant. The *ictus* has nothing to do with the speech accent (tonic accent); in numerous cases it falls on the weak syllable [see Ex.]. The monks

of Solesmes make it a point that, in actual performance, the ictus should not be rendered as a stress ("ictus nulla cum intensitate connectionem habet"), nor by lengthening of the tone (in the Solesmes rhythm all notes have the same duration). The question as to which communicable form it actually takes has therefore become a sort of mystery. Probably the mental perception of alternating points of elevation and repose (aided by cheironomic graphs and by analogies such as the waves of the sea or an elastic ball) enable the singer to produce a minimal degree of distinction. See the authoritative explanation in *LU*, p. xi. Also all the Solesmes books [Dom Mocquereau, *Le nombre musical*, etc.; particularly, Dom Gajard, *Notions sur le rhythme grégorien* (1935)].

Idée fixe. Berlioz' name for the principal subject of his Symphonie Phantastique in which it occurs in all the movements [see *Cyclic; *Metamorphosis], representing the artist in various stages of his life. It is considered an important forerunner of Wagner's *leitmotive.

Idiomatic style. A style which is proper to the instrument for which the music is written. To write idiomatically is a matter of prime concern for modern composers, particularly in orchestral scoring, since the quality of the score is judged largely by the degree to which the various parts exploit the technical and sonorous resources of the instruments without exceeding them. With regard to early music, however, including that of Bach, the question of idiomatic style has become somewhat of an issue, since examples abound in which the style of writing does not conform with the technical properties of the instrument or the voice. For instance, a piece such as the E major Fugue from *Wt. Cl.* ii is neither in harpsichord style nor in clavichord style, but rather in organ or even instrumental ensemble style (string quartet). Many examples of this type show that inattention to idiomatic writing cannot always be considered an argument against the quality of the music or the composer.

Idiomelon. See under *Automelon and Idiomelon.

Idiophones. See *Instruments (Classification).

Imbroglio [It., muddle]. Operatic scenes in which the idea of utter confusion is artfully carried out, by giving the singers and players parts which, although properly coördinated harmonically, are advisedly incongruous and contrasting as to rhythm and meter. The three orchestras in the ballroom scene of Mozart's *Don Giovanni* [end of Act I], and the street scene of Wagner's *Meistersinger* [end of Act II] are famous examples.

Imitation. The restatement in close succession of a melody (subject, motive) in different parts of a contrapuntal texture. This device is most consistently employed in the *canon, in which the full length of a voice-part is imitated in another (canonic imitation). Applied to subjects, it forms an essential feature of the *fugue (fugal imitation) as well as of the 16th-century motet and of the various pre-fugal forms, the *ricercare, *canzone, *fantasia, *capriccio. While in a fugue the imitation is normally restricted to one subject, there are usually a variety of such subjects in the earlier forms.

Following a preliminary exploitation in

the *organa of Perotinus (*c*. 1225; see Ex. 1) and in certain 13th-century motets [cf. Y. Rokseth, *Polyphonies du XIIIe siècle*, iv (1941)], imitation found its first defi-

nite realization in the *caccias (canons) of the 14th century. The works of Landini, Dunstable, Dufay and, particularly, Hugo de Lantins show a gradually increasing use of initial imitation [cf. *SchGMB*, nos. 29, 41, 53, 54, 55; *HAM*, nos. 60, 68, 72]. With Josquin (*c*. 1500) imitation was consistently applied to the successive motives of the motet [Ex. 2; see *Point (3)]. Throughout the 16th century and the Baroque period imitation remained the basis of contrapuntal style (*imitative counterpoint). It may be noticed that, prior to 1700, fugal imitation at the interval of the fourth (lower fifth) is much more frequent than that of the fifth. Bach would seem to have been one of the first to establish imitation at the interval of the fifth as a characteristic feature of fugal writing [Ex. 3].

The *Rococo period (*c.* 1700–1780) brought about a sharp reaction against the fugal style of the Baroque era [see *Gallant style]. However, imitation freely used made its come-back in the mature style of Haydn's and Mozart's later symphonies and quartets — and has since remained an important feature of composition-technique, particularly in the development section of symphonies, quartets, sonatas, etc. See also *Imitative counterpoint; *Repetition.

Lit.: G. Adler, "Die Wiederholung und Nachahmung in der Mehrstimmigkeit" (*VMW* ii). M. Schneider, "Zur Satztechnik der Notre-Dame Schule" (*ZMW* xiv). See also the literature under *Fugue, *Canon.

Imitative counterpoint. Contrapuntal music based upon *imitation, that is, the use of the same thematic material in all the parts. The three chief types are: *canon (imitation of an entire voice-part), *fugue (imitation throughout the piece of an initial subject), and *motet (imitation of several subjects, each one being used for one *point of imitation). The preludes in Bach's *Wt. Cl.* offer many interesting examples of "free imitative counterpoint" [e.g., vol. ii, no. 19].

Imperfect. See *Perfect, imperfect.

Imponierend [G.]. In an imposing, grand, style.

Impressionism. A musical school of the late 19th and early 20th centuries, represented chiefly by Claude Debussy (1862–1918) and Maurice Ravel (1875–1937). Foreshadowed in the works of Edouard Lalo and Alexis Chabrier [see *French music IV], it found its first full realization in Debussy's *Prélude à l'après-midi d'un faune* (1892) and still more so in his ensuing works, such as the three

Nocturnes for orchestra (1893–99), the orchestral suite *La Mer* (1903–05), the opera *Pelléas et Mélisande* (1902), or the collections for pianoforte *Images* (1905, '07), *Préludes* (1910–13), and *Études* (1915).

Impressionism, as most new movements, was rooted in antagonism. Debussy instinctively disliked the dramatic dynamism of Beethoven, the heated atmosphere and pathetic exhibitionism of Wagner, the introspective emotionalism of the Romantic composers in general. The paintings of the French impressionists, Monet, Manet, Renoir, and the refined poetry of Verlaine, Baudelaire, Mallarmé, suggested to him a new type of music, eminently French in character, a music which seems to hint rather than to state; in which successions of colors take the place of dynamic development, and "atmospheric" sensations supersede heroic pathos; a music which is vague and intangible as the changing lights of the day, the subtle noises of the wind and the rain. The realization of these ideas led to a complete abandonment of such typically "German" achievements as sonata, symphony, thematic material, development technique, and resulted in the introduction of various novel devices which are antithetic to the principal features of classical and romantic harmony. Prominent terms of the impressionistic vocabulary are: unresolved dissonances, mostly triads with added seconds, fourths, sixths, sevenths; the use of chords, consonant as well as dissonant, in parallel motion: *parallel chords (or gliding chords); the *whole-tone scale in melodic as well as chordal combinations; frequent use of the tritone; modality, particularly avoidance of the leading-tone; avoidance of "direction" in the melodic contour (preference of vague "zigzag" design); irregular and fragmentary construction of phrases.

Next to Debussy, Ravel is the main representative of impressionism, although his classical inclinations, his general feeling for form, his dance-like rhythms, his "verve" and elegance are traits hardly compatible with impressionism in its purest sense. In fact, except for its founder, impressionism has not found any full-fledged representative, although it has left its imprint upon the works of a great number of composers, for instance the French Dukas, Roussel, de Séverac; the English Delius, Bax, Cyril Scott; the German Gräner, Schreker, Niemann; the American Loeffler, Carpenter, Griffes; the Spanish Albeniz; the Italian Respighi; the Czech Novak; and many others.

After a relatively short time impressionism began to lose much of its original fascination. Its over-refinement and fin-de-siècle character were not conducive to active contribution and development. It is interesting to note that Frenchmen played an important part in what might be called "subversive activities" against impressionism. Debussy's friend Erik Satie contributed much to discrediting the rich impressionistic palette by his whimsical and barren sketches which look like a cynical caricature of the impressionistic technique [e.g., his *Embryons desséchés*]. It was the French novelist Cocteau who pronounced the death-sentence of impressionism in his aphorism: "After the music with the silk brush, the music with the axe." It is a somewhat tragic truth that Debussy's work stands before the eye of the present-day viewer not as what he intended: the negation of Romanticism — but as a part thereof, in fact, its very acme and conclusion. On the other hand, it should be noticed that some impressionistic devices have been taken over with characteristic modifications into the vocabulary of *New music, particularly the parallel chords, modified from a coloristic into a rhythmic effect [see *Parallel chords]. See also *Modern music.

Lit.: E. B. Hill, *Modern French Music* (1924); R. Lyr, *Les Musiciens impressionistes* (1938); H. G. Schulz, *Musikalischer Impressionismus* (Diss. Würzburg 1938); H. F. Kölsch, *Der Impressionismus bei Debussy* (1937); O. Wartisch, *Studien zur Harmonik des musikalischen Impressionismus* (Diss. Erlangen 1928); E. Evans, "French Music of Today" (*PMA* xxxvi); P. Landormy, "Le Declin de l'impressionisme" (*RM* ii); W. Danckert,

"Liszt als Vorläufer des Impressionismus" (*DM* xxi.5); A. Capri, "Le Origini dell' impressionismo musicale" (*LRM* xi).

Impromptu [F., improvised]. A name used as a fanciful designation for 19th-century *character pieces of the Romantic period. The best-known examples are Schubert's Impromptus op. 90 and op. 142 (probably their title is not Schubert's but that of his publisher, Haslinger; cf. *GD* ii, 700) and Chopin's Impromptus opp. 26, 36, 51, 66. The title does not refer to the presence of improvisatory elements in these pieces (all of which are in straight style and form), but is meant to characterize their somewhat casual origin in the mind of the composer.

Improperia [L., reproaches]. In the Catholic liturgy, chants proper to Good Friday morning. They consist of three passages from the prophets (Popule meus, quid feci tibi; Quia eduxisti per desertum; Quid ultra debui facere tibi) each of which is followed by the *Trisagion and a number of other short texts, sung in alternation with *Popule meus* [cf. *GR*, 198]. They were introduced (around 1200) from the *Gallican rites. Palestrina composed them in simple four-part note-against-note style [*falso bordone*; see *Fauxbourdon (4)]. It is with reference to these pieces, the artistic significance of which has been frequently overrated [see also *Miserere], that the word *improperia* is commonly used. They have been annually performed on Good Friday in the Sistine Chapel since 1560 [for more details, cf. *GD* ii, 700]. Vittoria and other masters of the 16th century composed the famous text in the same style as Palestrina.

Improvisation, extemporization. I. The art of performing music as an immediate reproduction of simultaneous mental processes, that is, without the aid of manuscript, sketches, or memory. In a more restricted sense, the art of introducing improvised details into written composition. The former type is a "soap-bubble" phenomenon the evanescent nature of which defies documentation and detailed description. This is true, at least, of the great days of improvisation in which masters such as Bach, Handel, Beethoven were just as famous for their art of improvising as for their written compositions. Today, the recording machine would afford an easy means of fixation; unfortunately, the great art of improvisation is lost, since it is no longer practiced by the composers and survives chiefly among organ virtuosos.

II. Early musicians famous for their improvisation were Francesco Landini [cf. G. Frotscher, *Geschichte des Orgelspiels* (1935) i, 68] and Paulus Hofhaimer [*ibid.*, 105]. In the 16th century the ability of improvising in fugal style was a common stipulation for the appointment to the position of organist [*ibid.*, 181, 247; see *Fantasia (5)]. Important information on this matter is contained in the *Arte de taner fantasia* of the Spanish theorist Tomas de Santa Maria [cf. O. Kinkeldey, *Orgel und Klavier im 16. Jahrhundert* (1912)]. In the 17th century the organ improvisations of Sweelinck, Frescobaldi, and Buxtehude attracted people from far-distant places. Bach is known to have improvised a prelude and a fugue, an organ-trio (i.e., a piece in three obbligato parts), a chorale prelude, and a final fugue, all on one and the same hymn-tune. In 1747, on visiting Frederick the Great in Potsdam, he extemporized a fugue on that "royal theme" which he subsequently worked out in his *Musical Offering*. John Hawkins is one of several who have given a vivid description of the effect of Handel's extemporization. Mozart frequently extemporized fugues or variations on a given theme. There exist a number of enthusiastic accounts about Beethoven's fascinating improvisation [cf. Thayer, *Life of Beethoven* ii, 347]. In the Romantic period, Moscheles, Liszt, Franck, and Bruckner were famous for their improvisations which frequently formed a part of their concert programs.

III. The second category of improvisation, i.e., the introduction of improvised details within a written composition, is a more tangible phenomenon. It probably played an important role in the emergence of the more ornate (melismatic) types of

Gregorian chant, particularly, the alleluias [see *Ornamentation]. More clearly discernible is its role as an improvised accompaniment to a cantus firmus in the fauxbourdon practice of the 14th and 15th centuries [see *Fauxbourdon (2)]. In the 16th century the improvised execution of ornaments and coloraturas (*diminution; *glosa) played an important part in musical instruction and practice [cf. Diego Ortiz, *Trattado de glosas* (1553); Agostino Agazzari, *Del suonare sopra il basso* (1608); see *Ornamentation II; also under *Ensemble (3)]. The "melodic improvisation" continued particularly in the English *divisions of the 17th century while a new and particularly important practice arose in the "harmonic improvisation" of the *thorough-bass [see also *Partimento]. In the 18th century the improvised coloraturas of vocal virtuosos led to the *cadenzas of the classical concerto. An interesting revival of improvisation technique exists in the swing music and jam sessions of contemporary *jazz. See also *Penillion.

Lit.: Th. C. Whitmer, *The Art of Improvisation* (1934); A. M. Richardson, *Extempore Playing* (1922); M. Dupré, *Traité d'improvisation à l'orgue* (1926); id., *Cours complet d'improvisation à l'orgue* (1937); G. F. Wehle, *Die Kunst der Improvisation* (3 vols., 1925–32); E. Ferand, *Die Improvisation in der Musik* (1938; historical); Martin Fischer, *Die Organistische Improvisation im 17. Jahrhundert* (1929); P. Rosenfeld, "A Plea for Improvisation" (*MM* xix, no. 1).

Incalcando [It.]. "Trampling," i.e., accelerando.

Incalzando [It.]. Pressing forward.

In campo aperto [L., in the open space]. See *Neumes II.

Incantation. Properly, a song designed to spell magic. In operas, the term refers to scenes in which spirits are conjured. Famous examples are the song of Medea in Cavalli's *Il Giasone* of 1649 [cf. *SchGMB*, no. 201] and a scene in Massenet's *Roy de Lahore* of 1877.

Incidental music. Instrumental music designed to be performed during a play. Properly speaking, the term does not include the music to be played before and between the acts [*overture, *entr'acte]. The Greek dramas and the *liturgical plays of the Middle Ages made ample use of incidental music [for the latter, cf. E. Coussemaker, *Drames liturgiques du moyen-âge* (1860)]. Shakespeare frequently prescribed incidental music, not only marches, dances, and songs, but also music as a background to monologues or dialogues [cf. the beginning of *Twelfth Night*]. Nearly all of Purcell's *dramatic music is incidental music for plays. More recent examples are Beethoven's music to Goethe's *Egmont* and to Kotzebue's *The Ruins of Athens*, Mendelssohn's music to *A Midsummer-Night's Dream*, Bizet's music to Daudet's *L'Arlésienne* (1872), and Grieg's music to Ibsen's *Peer Gynt* (1875).

Lit.: Norman O'Neill, "Music to Stage Plays" (*Musical Times*, 1914); *LavE* ii.5, 3373; Ad. Aber, *Die Musik im Schauspiel* (1926). See also under *Dramatic music.

Incipit [L., it begins]. (1) In Gregorian chant, the first words of a liturgical text (also called *intonation*) sung by the cantor before the chorus picks up at the place indicated by an asterisk; e.g., *Ad te levavi* *animam meam . . . [GR, 1].*—(2) In psalm tones, etc., same as *initium (inceptio).* — (3) In the cantus-firmus motets of the 13th and 14th centuries, a word or two given at the beginning of the tenor and serving as a reference to the chant from which the tenor is taken; for instance, *Manere*, referring to the melisma on the word "manere," which occurs in the introit Exiit sermo (inter fratres . . . moritur. Ỿ. Sed: sic eum volo *manere . . .*) [*GR*, 39]; see *Motet I. Cf. P. Aubry, *Recherches sur les "Tenors" latins* (1907).

Incominciando [It.]. Commencing, starting.

Indeciso [It.]. Undecided.

Indian music. See *American Indian music; *Hindu music.

Indicato [It.]. Assured, prominent.

Indirectum (properly: *in directum*). See *Psalmody I.

Indo-Chinese music. Cf. Gaston Knosp, "Notes sur la musique Indo-Chinese" (*RMI* xvi, 821) and "Über annamitische Musik" (*SIM* viii).

Inégales [F., unequal (notes)]. See *Dotted notes II (d).

Inflection, inflexion. See under *Monotone.

Inganno [It., deception]. Deceptive *cadence.

Ingressa. Name for introitus in *Ambrosian chant.

Initium. The two or three opening notes of a *psalm tone.

Innig [G.]. Heartfelt.

Inno [It.]. Hymn.

Innomine [L. *in nomine*, "in the name" (of God)]. Title of a large number of English instrumental pieces (for viols or keyboard) based on a cantus firmus: d f d d d c f g f g a. . . . This cantus firmus has nothing to do with the introit *In nomine Jesu* [*GR*, 48, 541], as is stated in a recent reference book, but is almost identical with the melody of the antiphon *Gloria tibi Trinitas* [*AR*, 518]. (An "In-

glo — ri-a ti-bi Tri-ni-tas ae-qua-lis

nomine" by John Bull [*Fitzwilliam Virginal Book*, i, 160] is correctly labeled: "Gloria tibi Trinitas.") Why these compositions should be named Innomine is not clear. The Innomine, together with the *Felix namque, was the most favored type of cantus firmus composition among English composers, comparable to the *L'homme armé of the Flemish masters. The earliest example (by Taverner) occurs in the Mulliner Book of *c.* 1560 [see *Virginal books]; others by Blitheman,

Parsons, John Bull, are found in the *Fitzwilliam Virginal Book*. Still larger than the number of keyboard compositions is that of the Innomines for viols [example, by Tomkins, in *HAM*, no. 176]. The main period of the Innomine is the second half of the 16th century. Purcell's Innomines represent a late attempt at revival. For an interesting description by Roger North (1728), see P. A. Scholes, *The Oxford Companion to Music* (1938), p. 465. Cf. E. H. Meyer, *Die mehrstimmige Spielmusik des 17. Jahrhunderts ...* (1934), pp. 133ff; *id.*, "The 'In Nomine' ..." (*ML* xvii, no. 1).

Inquieto [It.]. Restless, uneasy.

Inscription. In enigmatic *canons, the words which indicate, more or less clearly, the manner of its resolution [see *Canon (4)].

In seculum. One of the most popular tenors (cantus firmi) of the 13th-century clausulae and motets, taken from the Easter Gradual *Haec dies* [*GR*, 221] and beginning as follows: c c b c d e c b c c b [cf. *HAM*, nos. 30d, 32d]. This cantus firmus is particularly interesting because it also occurs in a number of "instrumental motets" contained in the Bamberg Codex [cf. P. Aubry, *Cent motets du XIIIe siècle* (1908), ii, nos. 104/8]. One of them, reproduced in *SchGMB*, no. 20, bears the inscription *In seculum viellatoris*, possibly with reference to a well-known *vielle-player who composed it [cf. *ReMMA*, 325]. Cf. H. Gleason, in *BAMS* vi.

Inständig [G.]. Imploring.

Instante [G.]. Urgent.

Instrument. In 16th–18th-century usage, specifically the harpsichord, occasionally also the clavichord; in the early 19th century, the pianoforte.

Instrumental music. Music performed on instruments, as opposed to music performed by voices (*vocal or choral music). Since in mixed participation the voices are usually treated as the more important body, compositions for voices and instruments (cantatas, operas) are usually classified as vocal music. Two main types of instrumental music might be distinguished: *ensemble (chamber, orchestral music) and soloist (piano, organ, lute, etc.). Following is a concise synopsis of the development of instrumental music, arranged in three periods in which instrumental music was (a) inferior, (b) equal, and (c) superior in importance to vocal music. [Regarding the dichotomy instrumental-vocal in early music, see *Ensemble (3).]

A. *Period of Inferior Importance:* 1250–1600. Thirteenth century: French *estampies; instrumental motets *In seculum (for the *vielle?). — 14th century: Italian estampies (estampida); *Intabulierungen of motets for the organ; *variations. — 15th century: German polyphonic dances [Glogauer and Münchner *Liederbuch, *c.* 1450]; *preludes and arrangements of chansons for the organ [Ileborgh, Paumann, Buxheimer Orgelbuch; see *Organ music]; *carmina and other instrumental pieces by Isaac [*DTOe* 14.i] and Josquin [*SchGMB*, no. 62]. — 16th century: numerous *dances for keyboard, lute [see *Lute music] and ensemble; *ricercare; *fantasia; *canzona; *prelude; *toccata; *variations.

B. *Period of Equal Importance:* 1600–1750. Chamber music: instrumental *canzona; *fancy; *sonata da chiesa; *sonata da camera; *trio sonata; *ground. — Orchestral music: operatic *overture and *sinfonia; orchestral *suite; *concerto grosso. — Keyboard music: *suite; *toccata; *fugue; *chaconne and passacaglia; *variations.

C. *Period of Superior Importance:* 1750–present. Chamber music: *String quartet and other types of modern *chamber music; *violin sonata. — Orchestral music: *Cassation; *divertimento; *symphony; *symphonic poem. — Piano music: *Sonata; *variations; *character pieces.

Lit.: To *A:* L. Schrade, *Die handschriftliche Ueberlieferung der ältesten Instrumentalmusik* (1932); J. Wolf, "Die Tänze des Mittelalters" (*AMW* i); J. v. Wasielewski, *Geschichte der Instrumentalmusik im 16. Jahrhundert* (1878). — To *B:* L.

Torchi, *La musica instrumentale nei secoli XVI–XVIII* (*RMI*, 1897ff; also as separate publication); K. Nef, *Zur Geschichte der deutschen Instrumentalmusik des 17. Jahrhunderts* (1902); E. H. Meyer, *Die mehrstimmige Spielmusik des 17. Jahrhunderts* (1934). See the literature under the various forms; also under *Organ music; *Piano music; *Violin music; *Lute music; *Dance music.

Instruments [from L. *instruere*; cf. instruction]. The generic name for all mechanisms producing musical sounds; hence for all musical media with the exception of the human voice (and, possibly, whistling).

Classification. While former studies in the field of musical instruments were restricted to those of European art-music, the scope of investigation has been widened considerably by the recent inclusion of the non-European (Oriental, African, etc.) instruments which outnumber many times those of European music. The European instruments were, and usually still are classified under three heads, namely: *stringed instruments, wind instruments,* and *percussion instruments.* In the scientific classification of all instruments the first group is called *chordophones* [Gr. *chordos,* string; *phonos,* sound]; the second, *aerophones* [Gr. *aeros,* air, wind]; the third group, which is extremely numerous in non-European music, is divided into two classes, *idiophones* [Gr. *idios,* self], i.e., instruments which simply consist of elastic material (metal, wood) capable of producing sound, and *membranophones* [L. *membranum,* skin], i.e., instruments in which a stretched skin is the sound-producing agent. To these four classes a fifth has been added recently, i.e., the *electrophones,* in which the acoustical vibrations are produced by electric contrivances. Within each of these categories further distinctions are made, as appears from the subsequent survey based on the classification established by C. Sachs and E. M. von Hornbostel [cf. *SaHMI,* 455ff]:

I. *Idiophones.*
    A. Struck: *triangle; *gong; *bell;

*chimes; *Glockenspiel; *cymbals; *xylophone; *celesta; *castanets [see *Percussion instruments]. Also numerous exotic instruments, e.g., the Javanese *gambang (xylophone) and the Chinese ch'ing (stone chimes; see *Chinese music IV).
    B. Shaken: *rattle, *sistrum; *crescent.
    C. Plucked: *Jew's harp; also the musical box.
    D. Rubbed: *glass harmonica; *nail violin.

II. *Membranophones.* Chiefly *drums. Classifications can be made according to shape (tubular drums, kettledrums, frame drums) or material (wood, metal, coconut, gourd, etc.), fastening of the skin, etc. The *mirliton may be mentioned as a membranophone which is not a drum.

III. *Aerophones.*
    A. Free aerophones. Instruments which act on the principle of the free (more properly, idiophonous) *reed: *harmonium; *accordion; *regal; *sheng; the reed section of the organ [see *Organ X].
    B. *Wind instruments, i.e., instruments in which the sound-generating medium is an enclosed column of air. According to the device which sets that air into vibration, the following classes are distinguished:

1. Trumpets and horns. The device is the compressed lips of the player: lip-vibrated aerophones, commonly called *brass instruments.
2. Flutes. The device is the sharp edge of a mouth-hole.
    a. Vertical flutes. The mouth-hole is formed by the upper aperture of the pipe (as in blowing on a hollow key). Found occasionally in Egypt and Arabia; *panpipes.
    b. Cross flute. The mouth-hole is cut in the side of the pipe. Flute proper; see *Flute family.
    c. Whistle flutes. The player blows from the upper end through a flue against the sharp edge cut in the side: *recorder; *flageolet; the flue section of the organ [see *Organ IX].
3. Reed pipes. The device is a (heterophonous) reed.

a. A single reed: clarinets. See *Clarinet family.

b. A double reed: oboes. See *Oboe family.

IV. *Chordophones.* Four categories can be distinguished:

A. Zithers. The strings are stretched between the two ends of a plain-shaped body, such as a board or a stick.

    1. Board zithers. The body has the form of a flat board.

        a. Psalteries. The strings are plucked: *psalterium; *zither; *kantele; *kanun. Keyboard psalteries: *harpsichord; *virginal; *spinet.

        b. Dulcimers. The strings are struck with a hammer: *dulcimer; *cimbalom; *pantalon. Keyboard dulcimer: *pianoforte.

        c. The strings are touched by tangents: *clavichord.

    2. Stick zithers. The body has the form of a stick: several exotic instruments, particularly the Hindu *vina.

    3. Long zithers. The body has the form of a long board with a slightly curved surface (originally made from the longitudinal segment of a bamboo pipe): the Chinese *ch'in (Japanese koto).

B. Lutes. Instruments having a body with a neck. The following families can be roughly distinguished:

    1. Plucked: *lute family (round back); *guitar family (flat back).

    2. Bowed: fiddles; *violin family; *viols; *vielle; *hurdy-gurdy; *tromba marina.

C. Lyres. Instruments having a yoke, that is, two projecting arms connected at their upper end by a crossbar: *kithara, *lyre, *crwth, *kinnor.

D. Harps. Instruments in which the plane of the strings is vertical, not parallel, to the soundboard. See *Harp.

V. *Electrophones.* See separate entry under *Electronic musical instruments.

History. Restricting ourselves to the consideration of the instruments in the field of European culture it will suffice to mention the various instruments of the Bible [see *Jewish music], the *kithara, *lyre, and *aulos of the Greeks, and the use of the *hydraulis, *tuba (salpinx), and *lituus in Rome (chiefly for gladiatory shows and for military purposes), in order to briefly characterize the pre-Christian history of instruments. The fact that, under the late Roman Empire, instruments were chiefly in the hands of the *mimus* (actors), the *joculares* (jongleurs), dancers, and other providers of amusement caused a general hostility against the practical use of instruments in the medieval Christian Church though they occur frequently in the writings of the Church Fathers as religious symbols. Nonetheless, there existed — outside the Church — a variety of instruments, as is shown in numerous pictorial representations ranging from the 6th to the 13th century. Particularly informative in this respect are the famous miniatures of the 13th-century Spanish codex of *Cantigas (numerous reproductions in *GD*). Among the medieval instruments are plucked instruments such as the *harp, the *lyre, the *psaltery, the *lute, the *chrotta; bowed instruments such as the *crwth, the *rebec, the *rubebe, the *vielle, the *hurdy-gurdy, the *tromba marina; various wind instruments (trumpets, horns, flutes, shawms, bagpipes); the *portative (organ), and the *equichier (clavichord or harpsichord); bells and bell chimes, drums (nacaire), and castanets. Most of these instruments came from the Orient, probably through the Arabs *via* Spain. Except for the organ and the vielle, these instruments were used chiefly for the improvised (or, at least, unrecorded) accompaniment of singers and dancers.

During the 15th and 16th centuries most of the above types continued to be used, and developed into more elegant forms. As regards the 15th century, our knowledge is in the main restricted to what has been recorded by the painters and drawers, particularly in their numerous representations of "celestial harmony" showing beautifully shaped and decorated instruments in the hands of angels (van Eijk, Memling; cf., e.g., *SaHMI*, 304). In the 16th century there developed an independent repertory of music for the organ, the harpsichord, and the lute [see *Instrumental music]. Many other instruments, however, were built and used, as is shown by the writings of Sebastian Virdung: *Musica getutscht* ("Music Germanized," 1511); Martin Agricola: *Musica instrumentalis deudsch* (1528); and Michael Praetorius: *Syntagma musicae* ii (1618). These books, together with other evidence such as, e.g., the preserved lists of instrumental collections, show that the 16th century placed a marked emphasis on the wind instruments. The collection of 381 instruments left by King Henry VIII of England, e.g., comprised 272 wind instruments (cross flutes, recorders, shawms, cromornes, horns, cornets, organs, bagpipes) as against 109 stringed instruments (virginals, lutes, viols, guitars, clavichords). An important feature of this period was the building of instruments in families; in fact, the playing of music in homogeneous groups, e.g., on four recorders, four viols, four trombones, replaced to a large extent the mixed ensembles of the 15th century which enjoyed the simultaneous sound of contrasting timbres [see *Sound ideal].

The 17th century (Baroque) brought about a marked trend toward the stringed instruments, the soft viol, the delicate lute, the "singing" violin. The lute, especially, existed in a great variety of sizes and types, the chitarrone, the theorbo, the cittern, the mandola, etc. [see *Lute and *Guitar]. Special types of viols are the viola d'amore, the baryton, and the viola pomposa [see *Viol family]. Among the wind instruments of the Baroque, the recorder and the oboe are prominent, with the trumpet and horn coming into use after 1700. For the ensuing history and the usual classification of the modern orchestral instruments, see *Orchestra and orchestration.

Lit.: C. Sachs, *The History of Musical Instruments* (1940); *id., Handbuch der Musikinstrumentenkunde* (2d ed. 1930); *id., Reallexikon der Musik-Instrumente* (1913); F. W. Galpin, *A Textbook of European Musical Instruments* (1937); N. Bessaraboff, *Ancient European Musical*

Instruments (1940); H. W. Schwartz, *The Story of Musical Instruments* (1938); A. J. Hipkins, *Musical Instruments, Historic, Rare and Unique* (1888; repr. 1921); K. Schlesinger, *A Bibliography of Musical Instruments and Archaeology* (1912); Karl Geiringer, *Musical Instruments, Their History . . .* (1943); W. Heinitz, *Instrumentenkunde* (*Bücken's Handbuch*, 1931). For special literature, see the bibliography in *SaHMI* and in Bessaraboff; see also under *Orchestra.

Inszenierung [G.]. Get-up (of an opera, play), *mis en scène.*

Intabulierung [G.; It. *intavolatura*]. In 16th-century music, the arrangement of vocal music (motets, chansons) for keyboard or the lute. The term is derived from *tabulatura*, i.e., *tablature, and refers to the change from the original notation in single parts (*mensural notation) into the score-like (vertical) notation used for the tablatures of the soloist instruments, the organ and lute. The Intabulierung of a motet or a chanson is the 16th-century counterpart of the piano arrangement of a modern symphony or quartet. The chief difference between the early and the modern procedure lies in the greater freedom of the former. Not only were original parts omitted or differently

distributed wherever their range was inconvenient for the reach of the hand, but also the texture was enriched by the addition of coloraturas, passing-notes, etc. [see Ex.]. The artistic importance of these arrangements, which appear in distressing quantity in the keyboard and lute books of the 16th century, is, of course, very slight. They have been drawn upon chiefly for the study of *musica ficta* [E. Frerichs, in *ZMW* vii; W. Apel, *Accidentien und Tonalität in den Musikdenkmälern des 15. und 16. Jahrhunderts* (1936)], and of ornamentation [A. Schering, *Studien zur Musikgeschichte der Frührenaissance* (1914); O. Kinkeldey, *Orgel und Klavier im 16. Jahrhundert* (1910)]. See *Arrangement. Examples in *HAM*, nos. 145, 160; *SchGMB*, nos. 35/36 and 62b/63.

Intavolatura [It.]. See *Intabulierung. In titles of Italian publications of keyboard music (16th/17th century) the designation "Toccate (Canzone, Capricci, etc.) d'intavolatura" indicates that the music is notated on two staves (piano-score), as distinguished from "di partitura" (or "spartiti"), that is, pieces notated on a different staff for each part, as in the open score.

Integer valor [L., integral value]. In mensural notation of the 15th and 16th centuries the normal value of a note (*brevis, semibrevis*), as distinguished from the reduced or enlarged values caused by the proportions. See *Proportions.

Interference. See *Acoustics VI.

Interlude. Any type of inserted music [see *Entr'acte; *Intermezzo]. Specifically, short organ pieces played between the various verses of a hymn or a psalm. These were usually improvised; hence, they are rarely found in printed books, except in those of the early 19th century when the art of improvisation had begun to decline. One of the few early books containing interludes is: Daniel Purcell, *The Psalms Set Full for the Organ or Harpsichord . . . as also with their Interludes of Great Variety* (*c.* 1680; cf. Nagel, in *MfM* xxx, 47). The low standard of the later interludes is illustrated by an example from Gresham, *Psalmody Improved . . .* (*c.* 1780), which is reproduced in P. A. Scholes, *The Oxford Companion to Music*, pl. 83 (opp. p. 466). In the German

Protestant service short interlude-like passages were inserted between the various lines of the chorale, rather than after a complete stanza. Certain organ chorales by Bach illustrate this procedure, e.g., his *In dulci jubilo* (B.-G. xl, 74).

Intermedium [L.], **intermède** [F.], **intermedio** [It.]. See *Intermezzo (1).

Intermezzo. (1) A theatrical entertainment of light character, introduced between the acts of a serious play or opera (interpolations consisting only of instrumental music are more properly termed *entr'actes). They are important because twice in music history they have led to new forms: the 16th-century *intermedii* of stage plays are among the forerunners of the opera [see *Opera II], and the 18th-century intermezzi of operas were the origin of the *opera buffa* [see *Comic opera II (b)]. A similar process took place in the 13th century when certain *tropes (in a way, intermezzi of Gregorian chant) developed into the medieval *liturgical drama.

The most famous of the 16th-century intermedii were those performed between the acts of Bardi's *L'Amico fido* during festivities attending the marriage of the Grand Duke of Tuscany at Florence in 1589, the music for which was composed by Marenzio, Cavalieri, Malvezzi, Bardi, Peri, and Caccini. They included solo madrigals, airs, madrigal choruses, and ballets with considerable instrumental accompaniment. These intermedii usually had no relation to the drama nor between themselves, each having its own character, e.g., "The Harmony of the Spheres," "The Infernal Regions," etc. [cf. *AdHM* i, 414; O. G. Sonneck, in *MA* iii].

In the later part of the 17th century most of the Italian operas performed at Paris were furnished with *intermèdes* (ballets and vocal music) by French composers, especially Lully [cf. H. Prunières, *L'Opéra italien en France* (1913)]. In Italy itself the intermezzi took on a particularly important development which can be traced back to 1623 when an opera *L'amorosa innocenza* was performed in Bologna with intermezzi which, although

inserted between different acts, formed a little continuous opera of its own, called *Coronazione di Apollo.* This was the beginning of a practice of "interwoven twin-operas" which continued throughout the 17th century, uniting a serious plot and a lighter one into a unique kind of entertainment. In the Neapolitan opera of the early 18th century the comic intermezzi appealed so much to the popular taste that they became a dangerous rival of the somewhat stereotyped plots of the main opera. The final stage of this development is represented by Pergolese's *La Serva padrona* which, originally performed as an intermezzo to the serious opera *Il Prigionero superbo* (1733), was so successful that it continued to exist independently, as the first *opera buffa* [see *Comic opera II]. See also *Masque.
Lit.: J. Pulver, "The Intermezzi of the Opera" (*PMA* xliii); O. G. Sonneck, ". . . Intermedi 'Psyche and Amor'; 1565" (*MA* iii).

(2) One of the numerous titles of 19th-century *character pieces, suggestive of a somewhat casual origin of the piece, as if it were composed between works of greater importance (Schumann, Brahms).

International Musical Society (*Internationale Musikgesellschaft*) and others, see *Societies III.

Interpretation. The personal and creative element in the performance of music which, similar in this respect to the dramatic play, depends upon a middleman forming the link between the composer and the audience. The player or conductor, while studying the composition, absorbs it and, consciously or unconsciously, models it according to his own general ideas and taste [see also *Expression]. His personal intepretation is the great privilege of the performer, granted him by the composer. A really fine performer will always be aware of the responsibility towards the work which this privilege imposes upon him.

In the case of early music, interpretation is primarily a matter of study of standards and styles entirely different from those of the current repertory. Already Bach presents many problems of interpretation which are not primarily questions of personal taste, but of historical facts. See *Aufführungspraxis.

Interrupted cadence. See *Cadence.

Interval. The difference in pitch between two tones. The names of the intervals indicate the number of the tones of the diatonic scale included therein. Following is a tabulation of the terminology in English, German, French, Italian, and Latin (medieval):

	c–c	c–d	c–e	c–f	c–g	c–a	c–b	c–c′
E:	unison (prime)	second	third	fourth	fifth	sixth	seventh	octave
G:	Prime	Sekunde	Terz	Quarte	Quinte	Sexte	Septime	Oktave
F:	uni(sson)	seconde	tierce	quarte	quinte	sixte	septième	octave
It:	prima	seconda	terza	quarta	quinta	sesta	settima	ottava
L:	unisonus	tonus	ditonus	diatessaron	diapente	tonus cum diapente	ditonus cum diapente	diapason

The intervals larger than an octave are called compound intervals. The first five of these also receive special names as follows, c–d′: ninth or compound second [F. *neuvième*; G. *None*]; c–e′: tenth or compound third [F. *dixième*; G. *Dezime*]; c–f′: eleventh or compound fourth [F. *onzième*; G. *Undezime*]; c–g′: twelfth or compound fifth [F. *douzième*; G. *Duodezime*]. The same intervals occur between any two notes, e.g., f–a is a third, g–d′ is a fifth, b–c′ is a second. Intervals leading down from a note are characterized by the adjective "lower"; e.g., the lower fifth of c is F, etc. See also *Complement; *Inversion (1).

Although, e.g., a third always includes three tones, there exist various kinds of thirds, according to whether the intervals between the tones are whole-tones or semitones, or, in other words, according to the number of chromatic steps contained in the interval. The following tabulation shows the classification and terminology (in English and German; the figures indicate the number of semitones in each interval):

third are $2n$, $\frac{3}{2}n$, and $\frac{5}{4}n$ respectively. In terms of intervals (initial tone $= 1$) this means that the octave is 2, the fifth $\frac{3}{2}$, the third $\frac{5}{4}$: O $= 2$; F $= \frac{3}{2}$; T $= \frac{5}{4}$.— (2) Intervals are added by multiplying their re-

	Diminished (verminderte)	Minor (kleine)	Major (grosse)	Augmented (übermässige)
Second	c♯–d♭ (0)	c–d♭ (1)	c–d (2)	c–d♯ (3)
Third	c♯–e♭ (2)	c–e♭ (3)	c–e (4)	c–e♯ (5)
Sixth	c♯–a♭ (7)	c–a♭ (8)	c–a (9)	c–a♯ (10)
Seventh	c♯–b♭ (9)	c–b♭ (10)	c–b (11)	c–b♯ (12)

		Perfect (reine)	
Fourth	c♯–f (4)	c–f (5)	c–f♯ (6)
Fifth	c♯–g (6)	c–g (7)	c–g♯ (8)
Octave	c♯–c′ (11)	c–c′ (12)	c–c♯′ (13)

Intervals, Calculation of. The following explanation presupposes a knowledge of elementary arithmetic, including powers, roots, and (optionally) logarithms.

I. The pitch of a tone is determined by its frequency, that is, by the number of vibrations per second produced by the tone [see *Acoustics I]. The interval between two tones is determined by the quotient (not the difference; see later) between the two frequencies. For instance, the interval between the tones 500 and 800 is $800 : 500 = 1.6$; that between the tones 512 and 1024 is $1024 : 512 = 2$ (the octave); the interval between 512 and 728 is the same as that between 384 and 546, i.e., 1.42. In the calculations of intervals the actual pitches are, of course, irrelevant. An arbitrary tone, usually c, is chosen as the point of departure and is designated by the frequency 1.

II. Practically all calculations of intervals are based upon three elementary intervals, namely, the octave (O), the fifth (F), and the major third (T). Experiments already conducted by Pythagoras (6th century B.C.) lead to the following laws: (1) If the frequency of a tone is n, those of the octave, fifth, and (major)

spective fractions. E.g., the interval of the twelfth (upper fifth) is: $F + O = \frac{3}{2} \times 2 = 3$; that of the major seventh is: $F + T = \frac{3}{2} \times \frac{5}{4} = \frac{15}{8}$, that of the third octave is: $O + O + O = 2 \times 2 \times 2 = 8$, etc. — (3) An interval is subtracted by multiplying with its inverted fractions: $-O = \frac{1}{2}$; $-F = \frac{2}{3}$; $-T = \frac{4}{5}$. E.g., the fourth is $O - F = 2 \times \frac{2}{3} = \frac{4}{3}$; the minor third is $F - T = \frac{3}{2} \times \frac{4}{5} = \frac{6}{5}$; the major sixth is $2 \times \frac{5}{6} = \frac{5}{3}$ (octave minus minor third), etc.

III. The calculation of the intervals, particularly of the more complicated ones, can be considerably simplified by disregarding the octave or, in other words, the factor 2. In doing so, the fifth becomes 3 (actually the twelfth), the third becomes 5 (actually the second higher third): $F = 3$; $T = 5$. Naturally, by using these figures, the results are not correct as regards their octave position; however, they can easily be corrected by multiplying them with such a power of 2 $(2,4,8,\frac{1}{2},\frac{1}{4},\frac{1}{8})$ that will cause the product to lie between 1 and 2. Examples: (1) Calculation of the major seventh, i.e., fifth plus third: $F + T =$ $5 \times 3 = 15$; to be divided by 8, hence: $\frac{15}{8}$. (2) Calculation of the fourth, i.e., lower fifth: $-F = \frac{1}{3}$; to be multiplied by 4, hence $\frac{4}{3}$. (3) Find the syntonic comma, that is, the difference between the tone e of the *Pythagorean system (fourth consecutive fifth) and the natural third: $4F - T =$ $3^4 : 5 = \frac{81}{5}$, to be multiplied with $\frac{1}{16}$, hence $\frac{81}{80}$. This method is especially convenient for the reversed calculations, i.e., the determination of the interval if the ratio is given. Examples: (4) Which interval is represented by $\frac{9}{8}$? In disregarding all powers of two $(8 = 2 \times 2 \times 2)$ we find that the interval is 3×3, i.e., $F + F = 2F$, hence the second consecutive fifth, d. (The fact that the original figure lies between 1 and 2 shows sufficiently that this is the d within the normal octave, hence, the second.) (5) Determine the interval $\frac{25}{18}$. Solution: $\frac{5 \times 5}{3 \times 3} = 2T - 2F$, hence two consecutive thirds minus two consecutive fifths, that is, F-sharp. (6) Determine the interval $\frac{45}{32}$. Solution (the denominator contains only powers of 2, $2^5 = 32$): $3 \times 3 \times 5 = 2F + T$, that is, F-sharp. Naturally, this F-sharp is not (exactly) the same as the one before; the difference between them is again the syntonic comma, as can easily be found by dividing the two figures (a quicker method is to subtract the two "symbols": $(2F + T) - (2T - 2F) = 2F + T - 2T + 2F = 4F - T$, a quantity which always indicates the syntonic comma).

IV. *Logarithmic Intervals.* Several

drawbacks of the above method are avoided if logarithms are used. According to the fundamental equation of logarithms: $\log a \times b = \log a + \log b$, the logarithm of a product is equal to the sum of the logarithms of the factors (e.g., $\log 15 = \log 3 + \log 5$). If, therefore, two intervals i_1 and i_2 are represented, not by their frequencies f_1 and f_2, but by the logarithms of these figures, $\log f_1$ and $\log f_2$, the compound interval $i_1 + i_2$ is represented, not as before by $f_1 \times f_2$, but by $\log (f_1 \times f_2) = \log f_1 + \log f_2$. It follows that, if logarithmic frequencies are used, "addition" or "subtraction" of intervals is done by actually adding and subtracting figures, instead of multiplying or dividing them. The chief advantage of the logarithmic frequencies is that equal musical intervals are represented by equal distances of a geometric scale. For instance, in the usual logarithmic scale of *cents, the various octaves are indicated by the equidistant figures 0, 1200, 2400, 3600 [Ex., b], while in ordinary frequencies they are indicated by the figures 1, 2, 4, 8... [Ex., a]:

Notice that in the ordinary measurement the fifth g $(1\frac{1}{2}, 3, 6)$ lies exactly in the middle of the octave, although properly this place should be occupied by the well-tempered f♯, as is actually the case in the logarithmic scale.

V. Logarithmic frequencies are particularly important — in fact, indispensable — in all calculations concerning tempered intervals or microtonic intervals (exotic scales). The well-tempered scale consists of twelve equal intervals (semitones) within one octave. If the interval of the semitone be i, the successive tones of the chromatic scale would have the frequencies: 1 (c), i (c♯), i^2 (d), i^3 (d♯), etc., until i^{12} (c'). Since, on the other hand, the octave has the frequency 2, we have the equation: $i^{12} = 2$; hence $i = \sqrt[12]{2} = 1.05946$. The successive powers of this figure gives the relative frequencies of the successive tones of the well-tempered scale (e.g., d would be $1.05946 \times 1.05946 = 1.12246$, etc.). In using logarithms, the intervals of the well-tempered scale are found much more simply as the multiples of $\log i = 0.0251$: $c = 0$; $c\sharp = 0.0251$; $d = 0.0502$; $d\sharp = 0.0753$; $\ldots c' = 12 \times 0.0251 = 0.3010 \ (= \log 2)$. The only flaw in this scale is that the important interval of the octave is represented by the rather cumbersome figure 0.3010. This defect, however, can easily be corrected by multiplying the scale with a convenient factor. Various such "enlarged logarithmic scales" are in use; the most widely adopted one is that suggested by Ellis, in which the enlarging factor is $\frac{1200}{\log 2}$, so that the octave becomes exactly 1200. The unit of this measurement is called *cent*; each chromatic semitone equals 100 cents [see *Cents]. The for-

mula for the conversion of interval ratios (i) into cents (c) is: $c = \frac{1200}{\log 2} \times \log i = 3986 \times \log i$. For nearly all purposes the factor 3986 can be replaced by 4000. E.g., the calculation of the fifth is as follows:

$$F = 4000 \times \log \frac{3}{2} = 0.1761 \times 4000 =$$

$704.4 \approx 704$ cents. If very accurate results are desired, the following correction should be made: Subtract from the result 0, 1, 2, 3, or 4, according to whether the interval lies next to c, eb, f♯, a, or c'. Therefore, the accurate figure for F is 702 cents. A similar calculation for T leads to

$$T = \log \frac{5}{4} \times 4000 = 0.0969 \times 4000 =$$

387 cents, corrected to 386. With these figures for F and T, all the other intervals of *just intonation and of the *Pythagorean system can easily be calculated. For instance, the major seventh $T + F$ is: $702 + 386 = 1088$. This result shows that the major seventh of just intonation is 12 cents lower than that of equal tempera-

	P		**E**		**J**
Semitone	$\frac{256}{243} =$	90	i $=$ 100		$\frac{16}{15} =$ 112 (C–Db); $\frac{135}{128} = 92$ (C–C♯)
Whole-tone	$\frac{9}{8} =$	204	$i^2 =$ 200		$\frac{9}{8} =$ 204 (C–D); $\frac{10}{9} = 182$ (D–E)
Minor Third	$\frac{32}{27} =$	294	$i^3 =$ 300		$\frac{6}{5} =$ 316
Major Third	$\frac{81}{64} =$	408	$i^4 =$ 400		$\frac{5}{4} =$ 386
Fourth	$\frac{4}{3} =$	498	$i^5 =$ 500		$\frac{4}{3} =$ 498
Augm. Fourth	$\frac{729}{512} =$	612	$i^6 =$ 600		$\frac{45}{32} =$ 590
Dim. Fifth	$\frac{1024}{729} =$	588	$i^6 =$ 600		$\frac{64}{45} =$ 610
Fifth	$\frac{3}{2} =$	702	$i^7 =$ 700		$\frac{3}{2} =$ 702
Minor Sixth	$\frac{128}{81} =$	792	$i^8 =$ 800		$\frac{8}{5} =$ 814
Major Sixth	$\frac{27}{16} =$	906	$i^9 =$ 900		$\frac{5}{3} =$ 884
Minor Seventh	$\frac{16}{9} =$	996	$i^{10} =$ 1000		$\frac{16}{9} =$ 996 (D–C); $\frac{9}{5} = 1018$ (E–D)
Major Seventh	$\frac{243}{128} =$ 1110		$i^{11} =$ 1100		$\frac{15}{8} =$ 1088 (C–B); $\frac{256}{135} = 1108$ (C–Cb)
Octave	2 $=$ 1200		$i^{12} =$ 1200		2 $=$ 1200

ment, 1100. An extensive tabulation of intervals is given in *RiML*, 1857–64 (here our letter F is replaced by Q, i.e., *Quinte*). The figures of the second column ("Basis 10") are the ordinary logarithms of the ratios. They can easily be converted into cents by multiplication with 4000 (plus the above-mentioned correction).

VI. Opposite is a tabulation of the most important intervals in relative frequencies and in cents. The letters E, J, and P indicate the tones of the systems of Equal Temperament (powers of i), of Just Intonation (factors 3, 5, and 2), and of Pythagoras (factors 3 and 2). For a graphic table see *Temperament III.

It must be understood that the systems P and J actually consist of an infinite number of tones within one octave (P one-dimensional, J two-dimensional); only the simplest of these are given above.

Unfortunately, the measurement based on cents is not the only one in use; various others are employed, all of them logarithmic, but differing in the number of units contained in the octave. Following is a survey of these other systems:

Savart (301 to the octave) = 1000 $\times$

$\log i \approx \frac{1}{4}$ cents (1 savart = approximately 4 cents)

Millioctave (1000 to the octave) $= \frac{1000}{\log 2} \times$

$\log i = \frac{5}{6}$ cents (1 millioctave $= \frac{6}{5}$ cents)

Centitone (600 to the octave) $= \frac{600}{\log 2} \times$

$\log i = \frac{1}{2}$ cents (1 centitone = 2 cents)

For instance, the well-tempered fifth is: 700 cents = 175.6 savarts = 583.3 millioctaves = 350 centitones.

See *Pythagorean scale; *Just intonation; *Temperament; *Comma.

Intime [F.], **Intimo** [It.]. Intimate.

Intonation. (1) In ensemble performance, intonation denotes the singing or playing in tune, either as good or bad. —

(2) In Gregorian chant, the same as *incipit (1). The opening notes of a psalm tone are more properly called *initium* or *inceptio* [cf. *AR*, 3*]. — (3) See *Just intonation.

Intonazione. Sixteenth-century Italian name for a prelude, designed chiefly for liturgical use. The best-known examples are those contained in: *Intonazioni d'organo di Andrea Gabrieli, et di Gio. suo nepote*, of 1593. They are usually ascribed to Giovanni Gabrieli [cf. *Editions II, 3, p. 131], although stylistically they would rather seem to be in the idiom of his uncle Andrea, to whom they are actually ascribed in B. Schmidt's *Tabulaturbuch* (1607). Cf. the correct ascription in *EiBM*, 35.

Intrada, entrada [It., entrance]. Sixteenth/17th-century name for opening pieces of a festive or march-like character, written in full homophonic style [see *Entrée]. A number of intradas for 5–6 instruments (the earliest ones in existence?) are contained in a publication by Alessandro Orologio, of 1593 [cf. *GD* iii, 772]. Intradas in duple or triple meter figure prominently among the dance-types of the German orchestral suites of the early 17th century, in which they usually, but not always, appear at the beginning [cf. the suites of M. Franck and V. Haussmann, in *DdT* 16; H. Schein, *Banchetto musicale* (1617), new ed. by Prüfer, vol. I; *EiBM*, no. 26; *SchGMB*, nos. 153, 154, 157; *RiHM* ii.2, 173]. Mozart (*Bastien and Bastienne*) and Beethoven (*Battle of Vittoria*) used the name for short overtures.

Intrepido [It.]. Bold.

Introduction. A slow opening section, frequently found at the beginning of symphonies, quartets, sonatas, etc. An introduction of unusual elaboration and extension is that of Beethoven's Seventh Symphony.

Introitus, introit. The initial chant of the (Proper of the) *Mass. It belongs to the antiphonal chants [see under *Antiphon (3)] and is usually in a moderately ornate style. For the form of the introit, see *Psalmody III. It was introduced by Pope Coelestine I (*c.* 400) as a chant accompanying the entrance of the priest to the altar [cf. the Ambrosian analogue *ingressa*] and consisted originally of an entire psalm sung antiphonally. The text, particularly that of its first section (antiphon), frequently refers to the occasion, e.g., the Christmas introit *Puer natus est nobis* [cf. *GR*, 33]. Several Sundays derive their name from the initial word of their introit, e.g., Laetare Sunday (fourth Sunday in Lent) from the text: *Laetare Jerusalem* [*GR*, 127].

Invention. A term of rare occurrence, but known to every musician from Bach's collection (1723) of 15 keyboard pieces in two parts, called "Inventiones," and 15 pieces in three parts, called "Sinfoniae." The usual denomination, "two-part and three-part inventions," is not authentic, but would seem to be justifiable on account of the similarity of style in both groups. Bach's reason for choosing his terms is entirely obscure. The word sinfonia was, of course, widely used in his day, but for an entirely different type of music [see *Sinfonia]. The term invention was used by Vitali as a title for pieces involving special tricks ("inventioni curiose," 1689; see *Editions II, 7) and by Antonio F. Bonporti as a synonym for suites (partitas) in a publication, *La Pace: "invenzioni o dieci partite a violino e continuo"* (1714). Four of Bonporti's "inventions" have been reprinted as works of Bach in vol. xlv, pp. 172–189 of the *B.-G.* [cf. W. Wolffheim, in *BJ*, 1911; Ch. Bouvet, in *RdM*, 1918]. No less obscure than the origin of the name is the development leading to the type represented by Bach's inventions and sinfonias which may be characterized best as "studies in double or triple counterpoint." Possibly an investigation of the numerous 17th-century Italian publications of two-part "ricercares" [see *Ricercar II (d); *inventio* = translation of ricercare?] would throw light upon the question whether Bach "invented the inventions." It may be noticed that the invention style is very

frequent in the preludes of Bach's *Wt. Cl.* (e.g., vol. i, nos. 3, 9, 11, 13, 15, 18, 19, 20), and that it occurs also in the preludes of the first three partitas [see *Suite I].

Inventionshorn. See *Horn II.

Inversion. The general meaning of the term is substitution of higher for lower tones and vice versa. There are two main types of inversion, harmonic inversion and melodic inversion. In harmonic inversion, a note is shifted to the lower (higher) position by means of octave-transposition; this device is applied to the simultaneous tones of intervals, chords, or entire parts. In melodic inversion, a note above an optional level is made to appear beneath it in the same distance. This device is used chiefly for the successive tones of a melody (hence the name).

(1) *Harmonic Inversion.* An interval is inverted by transferring its lower note into the higher octave, or its higher note into the lower octave. For instance, the inversion of d–a is a–d′ or A–d. By inversion, a fifth changes into a fourth, a third into a sixth, etc. (the numbers indicated in the names of the two intervals will always add up to nine, e.g., $5 + 4 = 9$; $3 + 6 = 9$). Both intervals together form an octave [see *Complement]. Major intervals become minor, augmented intervals become diminished, while a perfect interval produces another perfect interval. For verification, see the table given under *Intervals in which inverted intervals can easily be found by looking out for two figures adding up to twelve, the number of semitones in the octave, e.g., augmented second and diminished seventh: $3 + 9 = 12$ [Ex. 1a]. — A chord (triad, etc.) is inverted by applying the principle just explained to its lowest tone, e.g., by

changing g–b–d′ into b–d′–g′ [Ex. 1b]. For more details see *Harmonic analysis

IV. —In counterpoint, the principle of harmonic inversion leads to an exchange of higher and lower parts by means of octave-transposition [Ex. 1c]. For more details see *Invertible counterpoint. — The term inverted pedal(-point) denotes the occurrence of a sustained note (pedal), not in the bass, but in a higher part [see *Pedalpoint].

(2) *Melodic Inversion.* A melody (subject) is inverted by changing each ascending interval into the corresponding descending interval, and vice versa. By this process, an ascending fifth c–g changes into a descending fifth c–F, the ascending progression c–d′–e′ into the descending progression c–b–a. The result is a mirror-like exchange of upward and downward movements, comparable to the contours of a forest and its reflection in a lake [Ex. 2, from Bach's *Wt. Cl.* i]. Inversion is

2

said to be strict (or real) if the original and the inverted intervals agree exactly with regard to their semitonal distance. For instance, the strict inversion of c–d′–e′ is c–b♭–a♭. Since this procedure destroys the tonality, it is practically never used, except in Schönberg's *twelve-tone system in which tonality has no place. Normally, inversion is "tonal," i.e., it utilizes the degrees of the scale of the key. Inversion plays an important part in fugal writing [see *Counter-fugue], in the *gigues, and

3

in the development sections of sonatas and symphonies [Ex. 3, Bruckner, Symphony no. 7].

Inverted mordent. See *Schneller.

Invertible counterpoint. Counterpoint, i.e., a passage in contrapuntal texture, is called invertible if it is so designed that, by means of transposition — usually of an octave — the lower part may become the higher part, or the higher the lower [Ex. 1]. This is an application of the

principle of harmonic inversion [see *Inversion (1)]. The method, if applied to two parts, is called double counterpoint; if applied to three (four) parts, triple (quadruple) counterpoint.

Although instances of double counterpoint occur in 13th-century music [cf. Y. Rokseth, "Le contrepoint double vers 1248" in *Editions XXIV, B, 3/4], it was not until the mid-16th century that it became adopted as a standard technique of contrapuntal style. Ex. 2 (Beethoven, op. 10, no. 3) illustrates its use in more recent composition.

In the 16th and 17th centuries double counterpoint was occasionally treated in a more elaborate manner, involving transposition at intervals other than the octave.

For instance, in double counterpoint of the fifth (tenth, twelfth), one part is transposed to the higher fifth (tenth, twelfth), whereas the other appears at the same pitch or merely in octave-transposition. Several examples of this technique occur in Scheidt's *Tabulatura nova* of 1624 [Ex. 3, "Bicinium duplici contrapuncti"; cf. *DdT* i, 130]. Particularly remarkable is its application in Bach's *Fünf canonische Veränderungen über "Vom Himmel hoch da komm ich her"* [Ex. 4]. Other examples occur among the canons of his *Art of Fugue*. This technique is in general somewhat less "labored" than it is frequently thought to be. A comparison of the various intervals (unison, second, third, . . .) with their equivalents in, e.g., double counterpoint of the fifths (fifth, sixth, seventh, . . .) easily shows which intervals will make good consonances in the original as well as in the inverted position. These intervals, therefore, must be taken as the basis for the devising of the parts. Extensive studies of these and other devices of a still more learned character (usually combinations of the double counterpoint with canonic treatment) are to be found in most of the books on counterpoint [cf. also the article in *GD* ii, 722].

The term invertible counterpoint is occasionally applied to the melodic inversion of a subject, etc. [see *Inversion (2)]. Such a usage is unfortunate not only from the point of view of clearer terminology, but chiefly because melodic inversion, although frequently to be found in contrapuntal writing, does not in any way involve counterpoint, since it applies essentially to a single melody. For the exchange of parts without any transposition, see *Stimmtausch.

Invitatorium. In the Roman Catholic rites, the first psalm of *Matins, "Venite exsultemus Domino" (Ps. 94; Ps. 95 of the King James Version: "O come let us sing unto the Lord"). It is remarkable as one of the few remaining examples of the original method of antiphonal psalmody [see *Psalmody III], the antiphon being sung not only at the beginning and the end, as usual, but also between each pair of verses. It is sung with varying antiphons throughout the year. Being a chant

of Matins, it is not included in the usual *Antiphonarium*, except for the invitatorium of Requiem Mass (*AR*, [152]). The *Liber usualis*, however, has the invitatoria for Christmas, Easter, Whitsuntide, Corpus Christi, and Requiem Mass [*LU*, 368, 765, 863, 918, 1779]. The invitatorium was taken over, minus the antiphon, into the Anglican chant where it forms, under the name *Invitatory (Psalm)*, a part of the Morning Prayer; see *Service.

Ionian. See *Church modes; *Greek music II (c).

Iratamente [It.]. Irate, angry.

Irish music. The history of Irish music is interesting chiefly for its contribution to folk song and for its role in early medieval music. Irish monks were among the first propagators of Gregorian chant and founded in the 9th century the monastery of St. Gall in Switzerland which later became the leading center of plainsong in Germany. In the 9th century Johannes Scotus Erigena (*c.* 815–877) wrote his *De Divisione Naturae* which contains interesting remarks about music [cf. J. Handschin, in *ZMW* ix]. In the 12th century Giraldus Cambrensis repeatedly points out the achievements of Irish instrumentalists and their influence on Scottish and Welsh music [cf. *ReMMA*, 392]. The oldest pictorial evidences of Irish instruments (lyres? harps?; see *Harp III) are reliefs on stone crosses of the 8th and 9th centuries. Ever since, the harp has been considered the national instrument, the heraldic symbol of Ireland. Various claims to precedence and eminence of early Irish music, such as have been advanced by G. Flood and others, are not substantiated [see *Bards]. Prominent Irish composers are Th. Roseingrave (1690–1766), John Field (1782–1837), Michael W. Balfe (1808–70), composer of the opera *The Bohemian Girl*, Charles V. Stanford (1852–1924), Hamilton Harty (b. 1879), Arnold E. T. Bax (b. 1883, partly Irish).

Lit.: W. H. G. Flood, *A History of Irish Music* (1905; not always trustworthy); R. Henebry, *Handbook of Irish*

Music (1928); Ch. M. Fox, *Annals of the Irish Harpers* (1911); H. Hughes, †*Irish Country Songs*; id., †*Historical Songs and Ballads of Ireland*; A. W. Patterson, "The Folkmusic of Ireland" (*MQ* vi); W. L. Lawrence, "Early Irish Ballad Opera . . ." (*MQ* viii); J. Travis, "Irish National Music" (*MQ* xxiv); F. Lacy, in *PMA* xvi; A. W. Patterson, in *PMA* xxiii; J. S. Bumpus, "Irish Church Composers . . ." (*PMA* xxvi); W. H. G. Flood, "Irish Musical Bibliography . . ." (*SIM* xiii; also *KIM*, 1911, p. 359).

Isometric. The term is usually applied to compositions in which all the voices proceed approximately in the same rhythmic pattern, e.g., as synonymous with strict chordal style (*familiar style). See *Polymetric.

Isorhythmic [Gr., same rhythm]. A term introduced by F. Ludwig [*SIM*, 1902] to denote a constructive principle frequently used in the motets of the 14th century, particularly in their tenors. Its main feature is the employment of a re-iterated scheme of time-values for the presentation of a liturgical cantus firmus. The tenor of G. de Machaut's motet *Hé Mors — Fine Amour — Quare non sum mortuus* [cf. *OH* ii, 28; *WoGM* ii, iii, no. 14; F. Ludwig, *Guillaume de Machaut, Musikalische Werke* iii, 9] may serve as an example [Ex. 1]. The repeated scheme

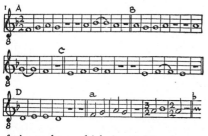

of time-values which is used in the sections A, B, C and (half of it) in D, is called *talea* in 14th-century treatises. Beginning with a, the entire liturgical melody, the so-called *color*, is repeated in halved values (diminution), — a procedure which is usual with Machaut [cf. *HAM*, no. 44.]

The isorhythmic principle, although usually thought of as a characteristic feature of the *Ars nova, is the logical development of the modal rhythm of the 13th century. Modal patterns such as:

[cf. *SchGMB*, no. 12] differ from the *taleae* of the 14th century only in length. Particularly interesting are examples in which the number of notes in *color* and *talea* (i.e., in the melodic and in the rhythmic pattern) are not in proportion, thus leading to the repetition of the melody (cantus firmus) in different rhythmic patterns. The tenor of an Alleluia by Perotinus [cf. *ReMMA*, 301] serves as an illustration [Ex. 2]. Since here the *color*

(*a*, *β*, *γ*, . . .) includes nine notes and the *talea* (A, B, C, . . .) five, the *color* would have to be repeated five times until both schemes would come to a simultaneous close. Actually, Perotinus stops after the fourth *color*, thus leaving the last *talea* incomplete.

In the 14th century the isorhythmic principle was not only the chief method for the rhythmic organization of the tenors, but was also applied — more freely — to the upper parts [for an example by Philippe de Vitry cf. *ReMMA*, 338]. Later composers, however, used it so rigidly that the motet falls into a number of "melody-variations" of the same rhythmic skeleton (Dunstable, Dufay, and various other composers of the Trent Codices, the Old Hall *MS*, etc.; cf. Dunstable's hymn "Veni creator," in *RiMB*, no. 7). Around 1400 one finds numerous examples in which the isorhythmic principle is applied to the upper parts only, the tenor being free [cf. Ch. v. d. Borren, *Polyphonia sacra* (1932), no. 25].

Israel in Egypt. Oratorio by G. F. Handel, composed in 1738. See *Oratorio III.

Istar Variations. See *Variations IV (d).

Istesso tempo [It.] indicates that, though the meter changes, the duration of the beat remains unaltered. For instance, if there is a change from 2/4 to 6/8, it means ♩ = ♩.; if the time changes from 2/4 to 3/4, it means ♩ = ♩. The situation is, of course, different if the tempo is so quick that the half note becomes the beat. In this case, a change from 2/4 to 3/4 would have to be interpreted according to the equation ♩ = ♩.; in any case, equations between note values are a much more secure indication than the somewhat ambiguous term *istesso tempo*.

Istituzioni e Monumenti dell' Arte Musicale Italiana. See *Editions, Historical, XIV.

Italian Concerto. A composition for harpsichord by Bach, so called because it is written in the form and style of the instrumental concerti of the early 18th century Italian school (Vivaldi); see *Concerto III (b).

Italian music. I. Among the leading musical nations Italy has the distinction of being that with the longest recorded history and, considered as a whole, with the most influential position. Foremost among the musical contributions of Italy is the development of Christian chant, which took place in Rome (*cantus romanus*, Roman chant) and which is usually referred to as *Gregorian chant, in recognition of the role which Pope Gregory I (590–604) played in its final codification. Even 200 years before Gregory, St. Ambrose (333–397) had established a rite which is used today only in Milan (*Ambrosian chant, Milanese chant), while his hymns [see *Ambrosian hymns] were incorporated into the Roman repertory. The contributions of Italy to the post-Gregorian development of the *sequences and *tropes seem to have been restricted to their latest period, the 13th

century, when Thomas a Celano wrote the Dies irae, Thomas Aquino the Veni sancte spiritus, and Jacopone the Stabat mater [see *Sequence (2)]. Guido of Arezzo (*c*. 980–1050) not only made (or established) the epochal invention of the *staff, but also discussed, in his *Micrologus*, the primitive polyphony of his day [see *Organum II], as did also the anonymous author of the important Milanese treatise *Ad organum faciendum* (*c*. 1100). Nonetheless, until the end of the 13th century, the development of polyphonic remained the privilege of France [see *French music II], and Italy's contribution to the music of the *Ars antiqua remained restricted to monophonic religious songs, the *laude. The 14th century sees the first flowering of Italian polyphonic music in the *caccie and *madrigals of Giovanni da Cascia (or de Florentia) and Jacopo da Bologna (fl. *c*. 1350), leading to one of the outstanding peaks of musical art in the blind Francesco Landini (1325–97), whose *ballatas owe their artistic perfection to an amalgamation of French polyphony with Italian melody [see *Ars Nova]. Other composers of the Landini period are Laurentius de Florentia and Paolo tenorista. The trends of Italian music around and after 1400 have not been wholly clarified. Composers, such as Matheus de Perusio, Antonellus and Filipoctus de Caserta, Bartolomeo de Bononia, Nicolaus Zacharias, wrote mainly secular pieces of French derivation (ballades, virelais, rondeaux, frequently with French texts) in a highly complex, even mannered, style [cf. *ApNPM*, 403ff]. Giovanni Ciconia, who appears as the central figure of this period, cultivated sacred music (motets, mass items) in a more dignified and "festive" style, similar to that of Dunstable, as did also his younger contemporary Antonius Romanus [cf. *SchGMB*, nos. 29, 30; for additional examples, cf. *WoGM* ii, iii, nos. 30ff]. Important theorists are Marchettus de Padua (*Pomerium*, *c*. 1325; not 1274, cf. *ApNPM*, 368ff), Theodoricus de Campo (*c*. 1350), and Prosdocimus de Beldemandis (*c*. 1400).

II. *Renaissance.* During the 15th century Italian music fell into an almost complete eclipse, at least as far as our knowledge goes. Northern composers, however, such as the Burgundian Dufay and the Flemish Obrecht Isaac, Josquin, traveled to the south, and features of harmony or balance found in their works have frequently, though with doubtful authenticity, been ascribed to the "Sun of Italy." While art music declined, folk song seems to have flourished [see *Villota], and it is from this sphere that, towards the end of the 15th century, Italian music came to new life, in the *frottola (Marco Cara, Tromboncino) and in the *canti carnascialeschi. Once more, Flemish masters took the lead in raising these unpretentious songs to the high standard of the *madrigal, but after 1550 we find Italian composers, such as Costanzo Festa, Andrea Gabrieli, Luca Marenzio, Gesualdo, in successful competition with the *oltramontani*. In the field of sacred music (*motet, *mass) Rome became the central place through Palestrina (1525–94) and his numerous successors [see *Roman School], while in Venice Giovanni Gabrieli (1557–1612), by uniting masses of choral and instrumental sounds, achieved an unparalleled peak of pomp and splendor [see *Venetian School]. Hardly less consequential were the contributions of 16th-century Italian organ composers (Cavazzoni; Andrea Gabrieli; Claudio Merulo), who created the *ricercare, the *canzona, and the *toccata.

III. *Baroque*. The epochal events which, around 1600, led to the inauguration of a new era of music history, the Baroque, are too well known to be repeated here. Suffice it to mention terms such as *camerata, *Nuove musiche, *monody, *thorough-bass (basso continuo), *opera, *oratorio, *cantata, — all of which are exclusively Italian affairs — and names such as Caccini, Peri, Cavalieri and, above all, Monteverdi. To the numerous masters of the vocal forms (opera: Monteverdi, Cesti, Cavalli, Al. Scarlatti, Pergolese; oratorio: Cavalieri, Carissimi, Caldara; cantata: Grandi, Carissimi, Stradella, Al. Scarlatti, Leonardo Leo, Jommelli) must be added others who worked in the field of instru-

mental music (*sonata, *concerto grosso: Rossi, Marini, Legrenzi, Buonamente, Vitali, Vivaldi, Corelli, Tartini, Veracini; see also *Bologna School) and of organ music (Trabaci, Mayone [see *Neapolitan School], Frescobaldi, Michelangelo Rossi, Pasquini, Zipoli, Domenico Scarlatti). Around 1750, when Italian vocal music declined in an overgrowth of empty virtuosity, composers such as Sammartini, Locatelli and Piatti worked towards the conquest of a new style in instrumental music, simultaneously with the *Mannheim School of Germany. The leadership, however, soon fell to Germany, and Italian music remained in the hands of academics such as Padre Martini or cheap entertainers such as Paradisi, Rutini, Paganelli [see *Rococo; *Gallant style]. A résumé of Italian Baroque music would be incomplete without mentioning such outstanding achievements in the field of musical reproduction as the *bel canto [see also *castrati] and the building of violins [see *Violin].

IV. *Opera 1760–Present*. Around 1760 the leadership in the field of instrumental music passed from Italy to Germany and for about 100 years Italian composers devoted their exclusive interest to the opera. Instead of building up a national opera, however, most of them were attracted by the operatic centers outside of Italy, mainly Paris. It was in Paris that Niccola Piccinni (1728–1800) became a dangerous rival of Gluck and that Antonio Sacchini (1734–86) competed with Piccinni. Antonio Salieri, the teacher of Beethoven and Schubert, worked in Vienna and Paris, and Maria Luigi Cherubini (1760–1842) became the central figure of French music during the Napoleonic era, while Gasparo Spontini (1774–1851) played a similar role at the court of Berlin. Gioachino Rossini (1792–1868) was the first to write again a great Italian opera in his *Barbiere di Siviglia* (1816). His *Guillaume Tell* (1829), written for Paris, marks the beginning of the "grand opéra" which was continued by Gaettano Donizetti (1797–1848) and Vincenzo Bellini (1801–35), whose early death terminated an artistic activity of great promise.

In marked contrast to the above-mentioned stands Giuseppe Verdi (1813–1901), who devoted his long life to the establishment of a national opera. From the early *Nabucco* (1842) to the late masterworks *Otello* (1886) and *Falstaff* (1893) his style shows a steady progress to great artistic heights, a progress which is all the more remarkable since he succeeded in escaping the all-pervading influence of Wagner. He was followed by three composers each of whom wrote only one successful opera: Arrigo Boito (1842–1918; *Mefistofele*, 1868), Pietro Mascagni (b. 1863; *Cavalleria Rusticana*, 1890), and Ruggiero Leoncavallo (1858–1924; *I Pagliacci*, 1892), the last two being known as the founders of the *Verismo. Italian opera took on a more lyrical and slightly sentimental tinge with Giacomo Puccini's (1858–1924) world successes *La Bohème* (1896) and *Madame Butterfly* (1904). Among the more recent operatic composers Italo Montemezzi (b. 1875; *L'Amore dei tre Re*, 1913) and Ildebrando Pizzetti (b. 1880; *Debora e Jaele*, 1921) are outstanding.

V. *Modern Instrumental Music.* It was not until the late 19th century that a renewed activity in instrumental music started in Italy. Giovanni Sgambati (1841–1914) wrote symphonies and chamber music in the style of Brahms, as did also Giuseppe Martucci (1856–1909). Neither these, however, nor their successors, such as Enrico Bossi (1861–1925) or Leone Sinigaglia (b. 1868), succeeded in breaking the all-powerful position of the opera, and not until 1910 did tendencies towards a more universal and cosmopolitan attitude become noticeable. The radicalism of the *Futurists remained a purely theoretical affair, but opened the door for really constructive work done by composers such as Ottorino Respighi (1879–1936; see *Symphonic poem), Francesco Malipiero (b. 1882), Alfredo Casella (b. 1883). While Respighi in his symphonic poems builds on the tradition of the late Romanticism, the other two, together with several younger composers, represent an essentially modern *neoclassicism.

Lit.: R. A. Streatfield, *Masters of Italian Music* (1895); *LavE* i.2, 611–910; ii.1, 146ff (*modern*); *AdHM* ii, 1087ff (*modern*). — *Middle Ages and Renaissance*: *ReMMA*, 360ff (bibl. p. 458ff; see also list of records, p. 476f); W. Korte, *Studie zur Geschichte der Musik in Italien im 1. Viertel des 15. Jahrhunderts* (1933); E. Dent, *Music of the Renaissance in Italy* (1934); see also *Laude; *Ars nova; *frottola; *madrigal; *Editions XIV. — *Baroque*: L. Torchi, *La Musica instrumentale italiana nei secoli XVI–XVIII* (1901; also in *RMI*, 1897–1901); F. Torrefranca, *Le Origini italiane del Romanticismo musicale* (1930); *Editions II.

Italian overture. See *Overture I.

Italian sixth. See *Sixth-chord.

Italian Symphony. Mendelssohn's Fourth Symphony, in A (1831), so called because of the Italian character of the themes (the last movement is a *tarantella).

Ite, missa est, Deo gratias [L., "Go, the congregation is dismissed; thanks to the Lord"]. The concluding salutation at *Mass. It forms a part of the Ordinary [cf. *GR*, 7*, 18*, etc.]. The word Mass [L. *missa*] is derived from this sentence.

J

Jack. See *Harpsichord I.

Jagd- [G., hunt]. *Jagdhorn*, hunting horn; *Jagdquartett, Jagdsymphony*, see La *Chasse.

Jaleo. A Spanish solo-dance in moderate triple time, accompanied by castanets.

Jalousieschweller [G.]. *Venetian swell.

Jam session. See *Jazz IV.

Janizary music [G. *Janitscharenmusik*]. Music of the Janizary, the military bodyguard of the Turkish sovereigns (*c.* 1400–1826) or pieces written in imitation thereof. The characteristic instruments of the Janizary were big drums, cymbals, triangles, and the Turkish *crescent. Around 1800, this type of music was extremely popular in Europe [see *Military band]. Mozart imitated it in his *Abduction from the Seraglio* and in the *Türkischer Marsch* of his Pianoforte Sonata in A (K.V. 331); Beethoven, in his *Ruins of Athens* (cf. also his Variations op. 76) and, most effectively, in the finale of his Ninth Symphony (tenor-solo: Froh wie Deine Sonnen fliegen). The harpsichords and pianofortes of the late 18th century were frequently provided with the *Janitscharenzug* (Janizary stop) which produced a rattling noise. Cf. N. Bessaraboff, *Ancient European Musical Instruments* (1941), pp. 20ff; P. Panoff, "Das musikalische Erbe der Janitscharen" (*Atlantis* x).

Janko keyboard. See *Keyboard III. Cf. R. Hausmann, in *ZIM* v.

Japanese music. Japan owes its music, as its culture in general, to the Chinese. Not only, however, have the Japanese actively developed this heritage, but they have also preserved many elements of older Chinese music which have been lost in its home country.

I. *Types of Music*. The music of the Japanese can be divided into two main categories which correspond to the sacred and secular fields of Western music. In the former category we find: (a) *Gagaku*. This is the ancient Chinese temple music which was introduced into Japan around A.D. 600 and which marks the beginning of Japanese musical history. It is orchestral music, performed by small shawms (*hichiriki*), flutes (*shakuhachi*), mouthorgans (*sho*), lutes (*biwa*), drums, and gongs. — (b) *Ka(n)gura*. This is the indigenous Japanese temple (Shinto) music which is used today for the most solemn worship. It originated in the 13th century (Heian period) when Japan became con-

scious of its aboriginal culture, and may well contain elements of a tradition prior to the Chinese influence. Today it is played on the *koto* and flutes. It is a recitative confined to a few tones [Ex. 1]. To

the same category belong the *Saibara* songs, autochthonous songs used at the Emperor's court and executed by a soloist, a small group of singers, together with *sho*, *hichiriki*, and *fuye* (flute). — (c) Halfway between sacred and secular is *Nogaku*, or *No*. This is a musical play which may be compared to the *liturgical drama of the Middle Ages with which it was coincidental in rise (*c.* 1000–1200). The performance of the *No* is strictly traditional, restrained, ceremonial, with idealized action and typified characters (the warrior, etc.). The music is a very ancient type of recitation (said to be of Buddhistic origin), moving in small intervals of somewhat uncertain intonation, including numerous Oriental ornamentations (portamento, tremolo, vibrato), dramatic and emotional, and quickly varying in speed and mood [Ex. 2]. The singer is sometimes accompanied by flutes and small drums [cf. Lachmann, p. 107].

The secular music as it exists today originated in the 16th to the 18th century (Edo period). It is fresh and lively, strongly rhythmical, and is played chiefly on the *samisen* and the *koto* [see V]. It includes operatic music, instrumental chamber music, and vocal music. Within the field of operatic music (*Katarimono*) the Japanese distinguish between a great number of types, according to subject-matter, social standards, etc. For instance, *Ithyu-busi* is an aristocratic type which, in a way, may be compared (socially) to the French opera of Lully; whereas *Gidayu* is "music for the merchant," i.e., a popular opera or operetta, rather noisy and full of cheap effects. The chamber music (frequently instrumental and vocal combined) is the most interesting field of Japanese music. A favored form, which dates back to the 18th century, is the *Jiuta*. It consists of an opening song (S), an instrumental piece (I), and a final song (S). Sometimes the scheme is broadened to a rondo-like arrangement: S I S I S. Another form of special interest is the *Danmono*. These are melodic variations on a theme of 7 or 8 measures, for the koto alone [cf. the example in *GD* ii, 76]. Another type of 18th-century chamber music is the *Sankyoku*, performed on the samisen, koto, and shakuhachi. *Kumi* are pieces for voice and koto.

II. *Scales*. The most frequent scale of Japanese music is a semitonic penta-scale [see *Pentatonic]: c db f g bb c' (descending: c' ab g f db c), called *zokugakusempô*. It exists in three modes: *hirajoshi*, *kumoi*, and *iwato*. Older scales of Chinese origin and of rarer occurrence (chiefly used in sacred music) are: c d f g a c' (*ritsusen*) and c d e g a c' (*ryosen*). (It must be noted that the information on the Japanese scales, as found in different sources, is extremely varied; the above details are therefore given with reservation.) All these scales have the absolute pitch of the *Chinese *huang chung* (c= f). Tritone progressions such as f–g–b–c are frequent in popular music.

III. *Rhythm*. Japanese music, like Chinese, is practically always in duple time. However, the phrases are frequently of irregular length (five or seven measures), in contrast to the more strictly "regular" scheme of Chinese music. The rhythms provided by the drums are in those peculiar arrangements also found in Hindu, Javanese, Arabic music which, for the European ear, obscure the fundamental time and beat, e.g.: $\frac{4}{4}$ | ♪ ♪ ♩. ♩. |

IV. *Counterpoint, Harmony*. Although Japanese music, as all Oriental music, is

essentially monophonic, it frequently includes certain "polyphonic" (*heterophonic) elements. The rhythm of the drums is markedly independent from — in fact, operating against — that of the singers or players of melodic instruments. The music for voice and koto shows *heterophonic treatment, frequently with a peculiar technique of anticipation, the

koto playing the chief notes of the vocal melody just one eighth-note before it appears in the voice or vice versa [cf. Lachmann, pp. 75, 115]. See Ex. 3. On the koto, "harmonies" such as g–d, g–db, g–b–c', etc., are used sparingly.

V. *Instruments*. The most important instrument of Japanese art-music is the *koto*, the Japanese variety of the Chinese *ch'in*. Other instruments directly taken over from China are the *sho* (Chinese *sheng), the *biwa* (Chinese *pip'a). More strictly indigenous instruments are the *samisen*, a guitar used by street singers and geishas [see *Guitar family]; the *hichiriki*, an oboe (not a flute) with a characteristic metal disk encircling the mouthpiece; the *kokyu*, similar in shape to the samisen, but bowed; and the *shakuhachi*, a long flute of ancient origin which calls for an especially difficult technique of blowing [cf. *SaHMI*, 213].

Lit.: F. T. Piggott, *The Music of the Japanese* (2d ed. 1909); D. Arima, *Japanische Musikgeschichte auf Grund der Quellenkunde* (Diss. Vienna 1933); Hisao Tanabe, *Japanische Musik* (1936); R. Lachmann, *Musik des Orients* (1929); Ch. Leroux, *La Musique classique japonaise* (1911); N. Peri, *Essai sur les gammes japonaises* (1935); *LavE* i.1, 242; F. T. Piggott, in *PMA* xviii; H. Werckmeister, in *MQ* xiii; O. Abraham and E. v. Hornbostel, in *SIM* iv (14 pp. of music); K. Takano, in *AMF* ii (bibl.); R. Lachmann, "Musik und Tonschrift des No" (*Kongressbericht der Deutschen*

Musikgesellschaft, 1926); K. Takano, in *LRM* xii. — †*Collection of Japanese Koto Music* (from Sh. Isawa, *Extracts from the Report . . . on Music . . .*, 1884); Sh. Isawa, †*Collection of Koto Music* (Tokyo, 1888 and 1913); †*Denkmäler der Japanischen Tonkunst*, ed. by Kanetune-Kiyoske and Syioti Tudi (Tokyo, 1930ff; cf. Hornbostel, in *ZMW* xiv, 235); Tōkyō Ongaku Gakkō (Tokyo Music School), *Sōkyokushū* (Songs accompanied by the Sō), 2 vols. (1914).

Jarabe. A 19th-century Mexican dance derived from the Spanish zapateado (shoe-tapping). The music is similar to the mazurka, and the dancing imitates a lover pursuing an evasive girl.

Javanese music. I. *Orchestra*. Javanese music is particularly noteworthy for its highly developed orchestral art which is cultivated at the various provincial courts and villages as a musical background for festivities and dances. The Javanese orchestra, called *gamelan* (*g*), includes chiefly various types of chimes, made from wood (*gambang*, a xylophone); from bronze slabs (*gender, saron, demoeng*); from bamboo pipes of different lengths (*angklung*); from metal disks, or vases (*bonang*; set of gongs); etc. While these, together with a two-stringed violin (*rebab*) played by the conductor, a psaltery (*tjempelung*), and flutes (*soeling*), represent the "melody-section" of the Javanese orchestra, single gongs and drums supply the punctuating percussion. The musical texture of the orchestral pieces is a *heterophonic web of great rhythmical variety. All the instruments follow one and the same melodic line in various degrees of rhythmic animation and melodic elaboration [see Ex.]. This music probably came from China [see *Chinese music I], but developed in Java into a flamboyant style of its own.

II. *Scales*. The scales of Javanese music

are of particular interest because they include intervals which differ more radically from those of our scale than the intervals of Chinese, Japanese, and Hindu music. The tones frequently lie just between our chromatic tones, thus approximating quarter-tones. Two different tone systems (wrongly called "modes") are distinguished, namely *slendro* and *pelog*. Each

of these is said to exist in three modes, which, however, are not clearly characterized. The Javanese describe slendro as consisting of wide intervals, pelog of narrow steps. In fact, slendro is a pentatonic scale consisting of five nearly equal intervals of 240 cents (a whole-tone plus a quarter-tone) each, as shown in the accompanying drawing. Pelog is more

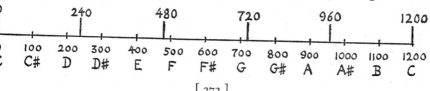

difficult of explanation, since there is a considerable variation in different instruments. Hornbostel's theory, according to which it originated as a succession of *Blasquinten*, has been questioned by recent scholars (M. F. Bukofzer, C. Sachs) who interpret it as consisting of two conjunct tetrachords each of which is divided (approximately) into a semitone and a major third, similar to the chromatic genus of ancient Greek music, as follows (descending):

$$\overbrace{e' \qquad c'\ b} \atop \underbrace{b \qquad g\ f\sharp} \quad e$$

The two thirds are filled in by two additional tones thus leading to a seven-tone scale from which, however, selections of five tones are made for practical purposes. Following is an example of the actual pitches of a pelog instrument (read descending):

1	2	3	4	5	6	7	8
e	f+	g	(a+)	b	c	(d−)	e
110	150	255	140	115	190	240	

According to Bukofzer, the slendro system originated in the 8th century A.D., when invading Buddhists selected from the older pelog scale the tones 1, 3, 4, 6, 7, 8. The result is a scale of almost equidistant pentatones, such as occur in slendro. The corresponding tones in pelog and slendro could be shown to be of the same pitch.

Pieces in slendro partake of the static character of Chinese music [cf. Lachmann, *Musik des Orients*, Beispiel 6, 7 (pp. 111, 113); *LavE* i.5, 3156], while pieces in pelog show more conjunct, even chromatic, motion, use quicker rhythms and ornamental figures, and are more dynamic and expressive [cf. Lachmann, *ibid.*, Beispiel 8 (p. 113); *id.*, "Ausser-Europäische Musik," p. 21]. Pelog probably represents an autochthonous musical style.

Lit.: J. Kunst, *De Toonkunst van Java* (1934); *id.*, *De Toonkunst van Bali* (1925); *id.*, *Hindoe-javaansche Muziekinstrumenten* (1927); R. Lachmann, *Musik des Orients* (1929); *id.*, "Ausser-Europäische Musik" (in *BüHM*); *LavE* i.5, 3147ff; McPhee, in *BAMS* vi; C.

Stumpf, "Tonsystem und Musik der Siamesen" (*Sammelbände für vergleichende Musikwissenschaft* i, 1922); E. v. Hornbostel, "Formanalysen an siamesischen Orchesterstücken" (*AMW* ii); M. F. Bukofzer, "The Evolution of Javanese Tone Systems" (*Intern. Congress of the AMS 1939* [1944]); Ch. Koechlin, in *BSIM*, 1910 (transcription for European instruments of a gamelang piece). Extensive list of special studies in J. Kunst, *De Toonkunst*, vol. ii.

Jazz. A generic name for 20th-century styles in the music usually associated with American popular dancing; more properly, that branch thereof which came (*c.* 1915) to be distinguished in some respects from its predecessors *Ragtime* (*c.* 1890–*c.* 1915) and *Blues* (*c.* 1910ff), as well as, by some enthusiasts, from the more recent *Swing* (*c.* 1935ff). Such distinctions as are valid between these types will best appear from the following chronological account, which is presented with due warning that the distinctions are not always present owing to cross influences between one style and another.

I. *Ragtime* makes its appearance at an indeterminable date toward the end of the 19th century, one of the first published rags being the "Harlem Rag" (1895) by the pianist T. M. Turpin, which was soon followed by W. Scott Joplin's "Maple Leaf Rag" (1899), and others. Ragtime descended from the early minstrel show tunes (cakewalk, buck-and-wing, jig) of the 1840's and later (an early example is "Old Zip Coon," better known as "Turkey in the Straw," 1834), as well as from the early marches ("Jagtime Johnson's Ragtime March," 1901). Like theirs, its harmony is conventional and is based largely on the common tonic, dominant, and subdominant triads of the major mode, with a regular phraseology. However, owing to its (often improvisatory) creation and performance primarily by pianists (who rejected, as in later Jazz, the subtler pedal effects in favor of a percussive tone), with or without a small unstandardized group of additional instruments, the melody of Ragtime becomes somewhat more instrumental in style (most of the rags had no text) through the persistent exploitation, as a fundamental characteristic, of Negroid rhythmic complications such as the use of melodic motives comprising groups of three or six notes in conflict with the 2/4- or 4/4-meter [see Ex. 1], which, by giving

different distributions of the notes with respect to the normal accentuation of the measure, produces a form of syncopation sometimes called "secondary rag" or "*polyrhythm." "Primary rag," on the other hand, is produced by other types of syncopation, such as: (1) the placing of a shorter note on what is normally a relatively accented and a longer note on what is normally a relatively unaccented portion of the measure, a procedure by no means unknown to European classical music (found notably in Schumann), and very frequently in Negro spirituals, as shown in Ex. 2 (this is a figure typical of the cakewalk and tango); (2) the suppression, by a rest or tie, of an accent proper to the normal rhythmic pulse already established by the same voice, or else in a counter-rhythm to the normal pulse simultaneously present in other parts [see, e.g., Ex. 3, 4]; (3) the anticipation or retardation of an accent, especially by having it appear on the fraction of a beat, e.g., Ex. 5 becomes as Ex. 6 or Ex. 7.

One of the earliest "bands" (in popular idiom any group of instruments combined for the purpose of playing marches or popular dance music) which played marches, etc., in the free improvisatory manner later characteristic of true Jazz was that of the Negro cornettist Buddy "King" Bolden (c. 1895ff) at New Or-

leans (the fount of so much Ragtime and Jazz), most of whose (5–7) musicians could not read music, and improvised collectively, often with surprising dissonant and contrapuntal effects. The introduction of Ragtime to the rest of the world is credited to the white pianist Ben Harney, who appeared at Tony Pastor's in New York in 1897 and published a piano method, his *Ragtime Instructor*, the same year, while the first New York stage appearance (Proctor's Theater) of an orchestra playing such music seems to have taken place in 1905 (Will Marion Cook's Memphis Students) from which time to about 1910 Ragtime reached its peak, thereafter to decline in favor of the Blues so that by 1915 it had all but disappeared (merging into Jazz) with the notable exception of the instruction books and pianistic *tours de force* of Zez Confrey ("Kitten on the Keys," 1921). Irving Berlin's "Alexander's Ragtime Band" (1911) has none of the rhythmic complexity of the true rag and belongs to the transition period to Jazz.

II. Despite evidence of earlier examples ("Mamie's Blues," c. 1900) the traceable history of the *Blues* (which influenced so much Ragtime and Jazz) begins with the "Memphis Blues," written by the Negro cornettist and band leader W. C. Handy, in 1909, though not published till 1912 (his "St. Louis Blues," 1914). The principal sources of the Blues appear to be the Negro work songs and spirituals [see *Negro music II, III]. The Blues were originally distinguished from Ragtime by several features: (1) in the early, and many later, examples groups of 12 measures are characteristic rather than those of 8, 16, and 32 found in Ragtime (and Jazz); (2) although, as in Ragtime, Jazz, and spirituals, the major mode predominates, there is, in the Blues, more frequent harmonization with seventh-chords of the dominant type, especially with those on the flat or subdominant side of the key (I^{b7}, IV^{b7}) — heretofore exceptional in American popular music — as well as with those in rapid successions producing so-called *barbershop harmonies [Ex. 8]; (3) the melody is in the tradition of the work songs and spirituals and differs from that of Ragtime owing to the fact that, unlike the latter, the Blues (whose greatest

exponent was the Negro singer Bessie Smith) began as vocal music and only later developed as a type for instruments alone (Ellington's "Blue Light"), and consequently the early Blues are more singable than Ragtime; (4) Blues usually possess special melodic features (also found in spirituals) such as (a) certain "blue" notes, that is, notes (in particular the III and VII degrees) whose intonation is unstable and lies between the normal major and minor pitches, (b) the use of portamento, and (c) cadential formulas which avoid the VII degree in favor of II or VI as penultimate tone of the melody; (5) the nature of many early texts bewailing the loss or absence of a lover influenced the general style toward the declamatory with a steady pulsating accompaniment, and invited a smoother, less percussive and less staccato rhythm as well as a slower tempo in the Blues of New Orleans and St. Louis (as contrasted with the fast Blues of Texas); (6) the Blues (e.g. "Memphis Blues") frequently use habanera or tango rhythms such as in Ex. 9; (7) and finally, the Blues introduced the "break," i.e., brief improvised instrumental cadenza (usually about two measures) characterized by many syncopations.

III. Waning Ragtime and waxing Blues together contributed (c. 1910ff) the earliest ingredients of *Jazz*, a word of uncertain origin, which first appears in print in 1916. An important figure in the transition is the Negro pianist-composer Ferdinand "Jelly Roll" Morton (1885–1941) whose compositions ("King Porter Stomp") and adaptations ("Tiger Rag" from a French quadrille) have formed the basis of much subsequent Jazz treatment. From about 1912 onward Jazz begins to spread beyond its source — the cheap saloons ("barrel houses") and brothels of New Orleans' red light district (Storyville) — through the activities of the Negro Jim Europe's syndicated dance orchestras of the Clef Club in New York (1912), as well as of the first white orchestra to play the Negro type of music, the Original Dixieland Jazz Band (1912ff; Chicago Boosters' Club, 1914; Reisenweber's in New York, 1917–18). From this time on there emerges a "refining" influence, largely the product of white musicians (Art Hickmann at the St. Francis Hotel, San Francisco, 1914ff). In its early stages Jazz inherited the various devices of syncopation and the regular 16- and 32-measure groupings of Ragtime, while from the early vocal Blues it inherited a more vocal type of melody — emphasized from about 1929 by a special soft, sliding, and sentimental style of singing known as *crooning* (Rudy Vallée, Bing Crosby) — and greater melodic ("blue" notes) and harmonic resources (borrowed dominant seventh-chords) along with a somewhat slower tempo and smoother rhythm as well as the use of "breaks." In the course of time (1920's), other and non-Negroid influences enter, among them the sentimental ballad-type of melody (often with a Viennese operetta flavor, as with Sigmund Romberg and Jerome Kern) along with harmonic devices derived from 19th-century Romanticism and 20th-century impressionism (added sixths, minor sevenths, and ninths to final and other triads, e.g.: c–e–g–a, c–e–g–bb, c–e–g–bb–d). As a consequence, Jazz becomes a heterogeneous body of popular pieces some of which, e.g., Whiting and Donaldson's ("My Blue Heaven," 1927) are devoid of any (written) syncopation or other inheritance from either Ragtime or Blues, and, as they stand, are Jazz only in the sense that they were performed by Jazz bands and served for dancing the fox trot, which had displaced (c. 1914) the earlier two-step and one-step and had become a generic term embracing such special steps as the Shimmy (c. 1918–23), the Charleston (c. 1922–26) with its characteristic rhythm [Ex. 10 or Ex. 11], the Black Bottom (1926), and their successors, though not including the definitely foreign importations (tango, rhumba, conga) or the perennial waltz.

$$10 \left| \overline{} \; \right. \quad 11 \left| \right|$$

These melodic and harmonic developments were accompanied by that toward a more or less standardized instrumental group. In Jazz the piano largely relinquishes the primacy it possessed in Ragtime; for although it is firmly entrenched for harmonic functions and as the backbone of the "rhythm" section (with banjo or guitar, stringed or wind bass, and drums with "traps," i.e., percussion instruments and other effects too numerous to mention), nevertheless the melodic element passes to other instruments. The latter are conventionally divided into "reeds" (clarinets, saxophones) and "brasses" (trumpets, cornets, trombones), with other instruments (violins, etc.) occasionally added, especially as, in the course of the 1920's, the orchestras grew larger and the style more pretentious ("Symphonic Jazz" of Paul Whiteman and others), often with emphasis laid upon showmanship (Waring's Pennsylvanians). With the increase in resources, jazz treatment spread from tunes written for such treatment to compositions from the standard concert literature (Paul Whiteman's version of Rimsky-Korsakov's "Song of India," 1924). Smooth professionalized performance, achieved after laborious and meticulous rehearsal, replaced the earlier spontaneous and impromptu rendition, and the arranger (notably Ferdie Grofé with Whiteman, 1919ff) emerges as at least as important as the composer. Under these conditions Jazz becomes, indeed, a highly sophisticated and standardized product — much of it ("production numbers") designed for revues and musical comedies on stage and screen — which was no longer the output of obscure performers but of certain specialists in this type of composition whose work is handled by a group of music publishing houses in New York (recently also with connections in Hollywood) known collectively since the turn of the century as

"Tin Pan Alley." Milestones in the history of this type of Jazz were the inclusion of popular tunes on the program of the serious concert singer Eva Gauthier in 1923, and Paul Whiteman's Aeolian Hall concert (1924) of Jazz and Blues, which included the first performance of the "Rhapsody in Blue" by George Gershwin (1898–1937). Gershwin's works from 1919 ("Swanee") onward, including numerous musical shows (Pulitzer prize winner, "Of Thee I Sing," 1931–32) as well as the folk opera *Porgy and Bess* (1935), represent the peak of this genre not excelled by his contemporaries and successors such as Cole Porter (from "An Old Fashioned Garden" in "Hitchy-Koo," 1919), Richard Rogers (from the show "A Connecticut Yankee," 1927), and Marc Blitzstein who has employed Jazz (and other styles) in his satirical "Play with music," "The Cradle Will Rock" (1937).

IV. While the white musicians (Whiteman, Ted Lewis, Guy Lombardo) were largely concerned in developing commercial Jazz of the type just described, the true tradition was continued by small groups (4–7 men), mainly Negroes, and produced an important figure in the Negro trumpet virtuoso and "scat" singer (i.e., interpolation of nonsense syllables and other peculiar vocal effects), Louis Armstrong. Largely under the influence of Armstrong there arose (c. 1925) the type known as "Hot Jazz" (Armstrong's Hot Five) as distinct from the conventional types thereafter known as "Sweet" or "Symphonic Jazz." Apart from Armstrong's influence on other cornettists (most notably the white musician "Bix" Beiderbecke, 1923–31), attempts were made to imitate his vibrato and his short expressive phrases on other instruments such as the clarinet, the saxophone, the trombone, and even the piano (by brief and light broken-octave tremolos). In addition to these and other innovations of timbre (e.g., a coarse or "dirty" tone) and technique (e.g., the contrapuntal and melodic liberation of the left hand on the piano, or the practice of beating on the drum all four quarters instead of only the

1st and 3d, or 2d and 4th), Hot Jazz is marked by a general freedom from restraint as well as a more subtle type of improvisation and a more personal style of playing with each performer. The informal conditions of performance under which Hot Jazz originated are similar to those which had produced early Ragtime, so that a fundamental resemblance between the two is to be expected. Unfortunately, however, the subtleties of performance, especially in the realm of improvisation, which are characteristic of both Hot Jazz and Ragtime (and may exist to some extent even in Sweet Jazz), are matters which defy notation and are lost to us in the case of Ragtime — whose reign antedated the phonographic recording of much music in this category — though they are preserved in the case of Hot Jazz, whose early records have become collectors' items among enthusiasts. *Jam sessions*, i.e., impromptu performances, with their emphasis on melodic interpolations (often lasting through several choruses) by various soloists collectively or in turn, led to: (1) in composition, a simplification of the harmony (fewer and less complicated chords and modulations) as compared to Sweet Jazz; (2) a more energetic rhythm, though not necessarily a faster tempo; (3) an avoidance of complete preparation of all details in rehearsal and of commercial "Tin Pan Alley" arrangements; (4) an abandonment of any deliberate attempt to preserve an easily singable melody — while certain passages (especially for the trumpet) approach a type of vocal declamation; (5) a return to the creative function of the performer (as improviser).

On the East Coast the pioneers in Hot Jazz numbered Fletcher Henderson (who developed [*c.* 1930ff] the modern technique of Jazz orchestration by giving his arrangements the effect of improvisations in characteristic Jazz idioms), the white drummer Ben Pollock and his orchestra, and, above all, the Negro band leader and composer ("Mood Indigo") "Duke" Ellington, whose arrangements (some in "jungle style" calling for the growling effect produced by "wa-wa" trumpet

mutes) provided for improvisation as an integral part of the composition. Passing over the somewhat lighter and less percussive "Kansas City style" of the early 1930's with its *riff* technique (short *osti-nato melodic figures by the band against which one of the instruments improvises), mention must be made of a special type of piano blues known as *Boogie-woogie*, which was heard at Negro "rent parties" in Chicago in the early 1920's (Jimmy Yancey, "Pine Top" Smith) long before it became famous in the world at large (*c.* 1936) with Albert Ammons and Meade "Lux" Lewis ("Honky Tonk Train Blues"). This type of playing is characterized by an ostinato bass figure, usually sharply rhythmic, against which the right hand rhapsodizes freely, the sections usually comprising 12 measures and the treatment often being contrapuntal (sometimes in only two widely-spaced parts), with repeated tones, broken-octave tremolos, and short figures reiterated in great rhythmic variety.

V. From about 1935 on, with the rise of the clarinettist Benny Goodman and the brothers Tommy and Jimmy Dorsey, the term *Swing* (a word which seems to be of largely subjective import referring to subtle and desirable rubato, and which is accompanied by a strange and wonderful jargon of technical terms, such as "licorice stick" for clarinet, etc.) comes into use to denote what appears to be a continuation of the Hot Jazz tradition. "Swinging" of the classics and even of folk music (e.g., the version of "Loch Lomond" by the Negro singer Maxine Sullivan) takes place, and with the increase in numbers (big bands) and varieties of instruments (vibra-harp, electric guitar, harpsichord), the cultivation of crispness of attack (especially in the "rhythm" section), as well as of precision in ensemble (Goodman), and of performance divorced from dancing (Swing concerts), Swing gives occasional indications of rounding out a cycle similar to that from Ragtime to Symphonic Jazz almost two decades earlier.

VI. Occasional claims to the contrary notwithstanding, Jazz shows no signs of becoming the American art music of the future, perhaps because, despite the interest and stimulation it affords, its appeal is too primitive and immediate. Nevertheless — quite apart from the essays in the traditional larger forms by Jazz composers themselves (Gershwin's "Concerto in F" for piano and orchestra, 1925; Morton Gould's "Chorale and Fugue in Jazz," 1936) — Jazz has contributed at least a variety of rhythmic and instrumental effects to music in general, and direct imitations as well as more subtle influences from this type of music are found in the work of more serious composers from the time of Debussy ("Golliwog's Cake Walk" from his *Children's Corner*, 1908), and especially during the decade or so after the visits to Europe of Will Marion Cook's Southern Syncopators (with the eminent Negro clarinettist Sidney Bechet) in 1917 and of Jim Europe in 1918 (Paris), as the following (necessarily incomplete) list of examples shows:

1915 John Alden Carpenter, *Concertino* for Piano and Orchestra (ragtime rhythms)

1917 Erik Satie's ballet (for Diaghileff) *Parade* ("Rag-Time du paquebot")

1918 Igor Stravinsky, *Histoire du soldat* (movement "Ragtime" for solo violin and other instruments)

1918 Igor Stravinsky, *Ragtime* for eleven instruments

1920 Darius Milhaud's ballet *Le Boeuf sur le Toit* (jazz rhythms)

1922 Paul Hindemith, *1922 Suite für Klavier* (movements "Shimmy" and "Ragtime")

1922 John Alden Carpenter's ballet (jazz pantomime) *Krazy Kat* ("Fox trot," "Blues")

1923 D. Milhaud's Ballet nègre *La Création du Monde* (jazz rhythms and instrumentation; blues intonations)

1924 Louis Gruenberg, *The Daniel Jazz* for small ensemble and solo voice, to text by Vachel Lindsay

1925 A. Honegger, *Concertino* for piano and orchestra (jazz rhythms)

1925–26 E. Krenek's opera *Jonny spielt auf* ("Shimmy," "Blues," "Spiritual")

1926 John Alden Carpenter's ballet *Sky-*

scrapers (fox trot rhythms, blues melodies)

1926 Aaron Copland, *Concerto* for piano and orchestra (Charleston and other jazz rhythms; special jazz mutes for trombone)

1927 Maurice Ravel, *Sonata* for violin and piano (second movement: "Blues")

1928 Constant Lambert, *Rio Grande* for voices and orchestra (jazz rhythms)

Lit.: W. Sargent, *Jazz Hot and Hybrid* (1938; bibl.); Ch. Delaunay, *Hot Discography* (1941); R. Goffin, *Aux frontières du jazz* (1932); B. Goodman and I. Kolodin, *The Kingdom of Swing* (1939); W. C. Handy, *Father of the Blues, an Autobiography* (1941); W. Hobson, *American Jazz Music* (1939); H. Panassié, *Hot Jazz* (1936); id., *The Real Jazz* (1942); F. Ramsay and C. E. Smith, *Jazzmen* (1939); P. E. Miller, *Down Beats Yearbook of Swing* (1939); Miller's *Yearbook of Popular Music* (1943); Ch. E. Smith and others, *The Jazz Record Book* (1942); M. R. Rogers, "Jazz Influence on French Music" (*MQ* xxi); C. Austin, in *ML* vi, no. 3; V. Thompson, in *MM* xiii, no. 4 and xiv, no. 3 (on Swing).   L. H.

Jeté [F.]. See *Bowing (e).

Jeu [F., play]. In organ music, *jeu* means stop; *jeu de fonds*, foundation stop; *jeu de mutation*, mutation stop; *jeu à bouche*, flue stop; *jeu d'anche*, reed stop. *Jeu de timbres*, *Glockenspiel. *Jeu-partie*, see *Tenso.

Jewish music. I. *The Original Tradition*. The frequent references in the Bible to musical instruments have been put together by modern scholars (Idelsohn) into a lively picture full of interesting traits. The music of the temple (the "High-Church" in Jerusalem, comparable to St. Peter's in Rome) was in the hands of professional musicians, the Levites. It would seem that instruments such as the *hasosra* (*chatzotzra*, a silver trumpet, used in numbers up to 120 in Solomon's time), the *magrepha* (a pipe organ of a very powerful sound), the *tziltzal* (cymbals), and others chiefly served for signaling purposes, i.e., to announce the entrance of the priests, to give the sign for the congregation to prostrate themselves, etc. Many instruments mentioned in the Scriptures have an Egyptian ancestry, e.g., the *nevel* (probably a large harp, played with the fingers), the *kinnor* (a lyre, played with a plectrum, similar to the Greek kithara; see *Harp III), the *halil* (probably a double-oboe and, like the Greek *aulos*, used for highly exciting and virtuoso-like music; it had to be banned from ritual use), etc. The only instrument to survive up to the present is the *shofar*, a ram's horn which also belonged (and still belongs) to the class of signaling instruments. [Cf. the detailed study of the Biblical instruments in *SaHMI*, 106–127.]

The instrumental music of the temple fell into oblivion after its destruction, in A.D. 70. The chanting, however, of the Bible (believed to have been established in the 5th century B.C.) survived in the various synagogues and to the present day, representing the oldest extant type of Jewish music [see section II]. Particular interest attaches to the singing of the psalms which is expressly indicated in inscriptions such as "To the chief Musician on Neginoth" [for a correct interpretation of these inscriptions, see *Psalms]. The singing was entrusted to professional musicians. A number of psalms, however, give evidence that the congregation occasionally participated in the performance by responding "hallelujah" or "amen" after each verse of a psalm [see *Responsorial]. Some early sources also make reference to choral singing in two answering groups, i.e., to the method known as *antiphonal singing.

Although no documents of early Jewish music exist, considerable light has been shed upon the state of music in the late pre-Christian era by the studies of Idelsohn who examined the musical tradition of Jewish tribes in Yemen (South Arabia), Babylonia, Persia, Syria, etc. A comparison revealed a startling similarity among the chants sung by these tribes which, living in strict isolation, could hardly have had any contacts with each other after their separation from their common home. The conclusion to be

drawn from these facts is that these melodies date back to a period anterior to the destruction of the temple and that they have been preserved for about 2000 years with only slight alterations. They may therefore be held to approximate very closely the Jewish chant of the pre-Christian era. No less interesting is the close resemblance between some of these melodies and certain melodies of Gregorian chant. For instance, a chant used by the Jews of Yemen for the recitation of the Pentateuch (as well as of certain psalms) shows a striking similarity to the Gregorian psalm tones [Ex. 1].

II. The Main Types of Jewish Chant. The oldest type of Jewish ritual music is the chant used for the reading of the prose books of the Bible, such as Pentateuch, Prophets, Ruth, etc. This chant, usually referred to as *cantillation*, consists of a succession of stereotyped melodic formulae each of which is represented stenographically by a sign written above or below the scriptural text. These signs, the *ta'amim* or *accents*, developed, no doubt, from an earlier system of grammatical accents designed to assist the reader in the proper emphasis and rendition of the important words of the text [see *Ekphonetic notation]. The oldest extant source for the ta'amim is a MS of the 9th century (London, Brit. Mus. *no. 4445I*; for 11th/12th-century MSS cf. A. Gastoué in *TG* xxii). For almost one thousand years the musical meaning of these signs was handed down orally among the Jewish singers and, therefore, has been exposed to extensive variation in the different periods and localities. Fortunately their late-medieval status has been re-

corded by Johannes Reuchlin (*De Accentibus*, 1518) and S. Münster (*Institutiones*

Hebraicae, 1524). The accompanying Ex. 2 shows one of these signs, the "t'lishá (talsá) gadolá" ("major drawing out") in four variants: (a) as recorded by Münster; (b) as sung today in Northern Europe; (c) from Morocco; (d) from Egypt and Syria.

It must be noticed that even within one and the same rite, e.g., that of the North-European (Ashkenasic) Jews, a given sign indicates different melodic formulae depending on which book of the Bible is chanted. Each of these books has its own mode, usually based on a tetrachordal scale (e.g., d–g, g–c'), and therefore the rendition of the ta'amim varies in pitch and other details from one book to another. Ex. 3 shows the same text sung

(a) in the ordinary Pentateuchal mode, (b) in the penitential Pentateuchal mode, and (c) in the Prophetal mode. Extensive tables of the ta'amim are given in *The Jewish Encyclopedia*, article "Cantillation" and in Idelsohn's *Jewish Music . . .*, p. 46; cf. also F. L. Cohen, in *PMA* xix; S. Rosowsky, in *PMA* lx. Example in *HAM*, no. 7.

Next in antiquity to the cantillation of the Bible is that of the prayers. This is not based on a set of stereotyped melodic formulae indicated by signs, but rather belongs to the general category of *melody types. For each service there exist certain traditional themes or motives, but the actual singing is a free vocal fantasia, frequently of a highly virtuoso character, which retains only the barest outline of the prayer-motive (mainly in the closing formula). These more or less freely created melodies are known as *hazzanut*, a word derived from *chazzan*, the name of the professional precentor to whom the singing of the prayers is entrusted. From

the Middle Ages through the end of the 19th century these chazzanim were the main carriers of Jewish ritual music. They were chosen mainly for the beauty of their voices and for their ability in improvising upon the prayer-motives. Even the most famous among them had, until the middle of the 19th century, no knowledge of music and were unable to read notes.

Finally there exist a number of melodically fixed chants. These represent the most recent development of ritual music, starting after the 9th century. Most of these melodies show evidence of contact with different strata of Gentile music. E.g., the famous Kol Nidre is partly borrowed from Gregorian chant; the beginning of Maoz Zur is taken from the Protestant chorale "Nun freut Euch Ihr frommen Christen," and one of the melodies for Adonai Melek is borrowed from Verdi's opera *La Traviata*.

III. *Semi-religious and Folk Song.* To the former category belong the *zmiroth*, i.e., the table chants used for the singing of grace in the home or, e.g., for the domestic recitation of the "Haggadah," the story of the redemption from Egypt. An important treasure of semi-religious songs exists in the hasidic melodies, created by the Hasidim, a pietist sect which originated in the early 18th century in Poland and Russia. Music played an important part in their creed as a means of ecstatic communication with God.

The Jews of East Europe possess a large repertory of domestic songs, including love songs, working songs, lullabies, wedding tunes, dance melodies, etc. Some 3000 such songs have been gathered under the auspices of the Petrograd Jewish Folk-Song Society, founded by pupils of Rimsky-Korsakov. Outstanding among the collectors of Jewish folk song was A. Z. Idelsohn whose *Thesaurus of Oriental Hebrew Melodies* (10 vols., 1914ff) includes the results of his research in Morocco, Yemen, Bocchara, Persia, Palestine, Poland, etc.

IV. *The European Development.* Shortly after 1600, Jews for the first time participated in the musical life outside of the ghetto. Abramo dall'Arpa Ebreo was a famous singer at the court of Mantua, from 1542 to 1566. Allegro Porto Ebreo published a book *Nuove musiche* in 1619 and two collections of madrigals in 1625. The most important of these Jewish composers was Salomone Rossi (d. 1628), who was one of the pioneers of violin music [see *Sonata B, I; *Romanesca; *Ruggiero] and who was the first to compose polyphonic music for the Jewish service, in his *Hashirim Asher Lishlomo* of 1622. Needless to say, these compositions, written for chorus and soloists, completely break away from the Jewish tradition. His procedure remained without immediate succession.

Around 1700 some of the wealthier German synagogues employed instrumental music for the Friday-evening service and had organs installed, and choirs were fairly generally employed. Since there was no traditional music available for such performances, the current repertoire of non-Jewish music was used, and the lack of tradition and authority in this matter easily accounts for the rapid intrusion of secular and even operatic elements, of dance-tunes and Rococo-arias. Ahron Beer (1738–1821), one of the first chazzans who possessed some musical knowledge, made an extensive collection of compositions for the service and of traditional Jewish songs, including two versions of the Kol Nidre, marked 1720 and 1783. A different line was followed by Israel Jacobson (1768–1828), who was an exponent of the reform movement and who, in the first Reform Temple (Seesen, Westphalia, 1810), not only used organ and bells, but also German chorales, provided with Hebrew texts [cf. Idelsohn, p. 237]. The natural reaction against Jacobson's complete Christianization of the Jewish service led to the moderate reform of Salomon Sulzer (1804–90), who declared that the "restoration should remain on historical grounds" and that "the old tunes should be improved, selected and adjusted to the rules of art" (*Denkschrift*, 1876). Although Sulzer succeeded in bestowing upon the musical service a fundamental character of dignity and ap-

propriateness, his compositions and versions of songs leave much to be desired, because they represent current European idioms rather than Jewish tradition. A similar statement is true with regard to Louis Lewandowski (1821–94) whose thorough training in musical theory, harmony, etc., enabled him to write choruses in the character of Mendelssohn's oratorio style. His complete service, *Kol Rinnah* (1871), has been widely adopted, on account of the facile and pleasing nature of its tunes. In America, synagogue music started by imitating the current European examples (Alois Kaiser of Baltimore; Max Spickler and William Sparger of New York; Edward Starck of San Francisco). Recently, however, there has been a remarkable movement towards independent development, represented by a number of choral compositions of a distinctly Hebraic character, mostly for the Sabbath Service. Among the contributors we find Ernest Bloch, Frederick Jacobi, Lazare Saminsky, and Isadore Freed.

Throughout the 19th and 20th centuries, Jews have played an active part in the development of European music, as composers (Giacomo Meyerbeer, 1791–1864; Jacques Halévy, 1799–1862; Felix Mendelssohn, 1809–47; Jacques Offenbach, 1819–80; Karl Goldmark, 1819–80; Gustav Mahler, 1860–1911; Arnold Schönberg, b. 1874; Ernest Bloch, b. 1880; Darius Milhaud, b. 1892; George Gershwin, 1898–1937; Aaron Copland, b. 1900, and many others), and even more prominently as performers and conductors (Joachim, Kreisler, Heifetz, Menuhin, Godovsky, Schnabel, Serkin, Myra Hess, Damrosch, Bruno Walter, Klemperer, to name only the most outstanding).

In the past twenty years there has been a movement to create what might be called a "Jewish national music," comparable to the national music of other countries and races. The leader of this movement is Ernest Bloch who, in his *Israel Symphony* (1915), *Symphonie Orientale*, and other works, has used distinctly Hebraic idioms.

Lit.: A. Z. Idelsohn, *Jewish Music in its Historical Development* (1929); *id.*,

†*Thesaurus of Hebrew Oriental Melodies*, 10 vols. (1914ff); S. B. Finesinger, *Music Instruments in the Old Testament* (1926); L. Saminsky, *Music of the Ghetto and the Bible* (1935); G. Salesky, *Famous Musicians of a Wandering Race* (1927); *LavE* i.1, 67; ii.4, 2287; Richard Wagner, *Judaism in Music* (1850; transl. 1910); P. Nettl, "Some Early Jewish Musicians" (*MQ* xvii); L. Sabaneev, "The Jewish National School in Music" (*MQ* xv); A. Z. Idelsohn, "Parallelen zwischen gregorianischen und hebräisch-orientalischen Gesangsweisen" (*ZMW* iv); *id.*, "Parallels between the Old French and the Jewish Song" (*AM* v, no. 4; vi, no. 1); *id.*, "Deutsche Elemente im alten Synagogengesang" (*ZMW* xv); *id.*, in *ZMW* viii; H. Loewenstein, in *ZMW* xii. Additional bibl. in *MoML*, 374.

Jew's harp or **trump** [F. *guimbarde*; G. *Maultrommel*]. A primitive instrument consisting of an elastic strip of metal fixed in a small iron frame in the shape of a horseshoe. The frame is held between the teeth (the name Jew's harp is probably a perversion of Jaw's harp), and the elastic strip is made to vibrate by a twang of the fingers. Although the instrument as such produces only one sound, the different partials can be made prominent by shaping the mouth in different ways. The instrument is very ancient and widespread. It is mentioned and depicted in a Chinese book of the 12th century, and specimens have been found in Japan, Borneo, Siberia, North-Germany (14th century), Norway, etc. In the early 19th century it was temporarily revived by virtuosos who used larger instruments with several vibrating reeds. Cf. *SaHMI*; bibl., p. 471; M. Heymann, "La Guimbarde" (*RM* iv).

Jig. An English popular dance of the 16th century which is especially important as the forerunner of the *gigue. Probably the name is not derived from the medieval *giga* [see *Gigue (1)], but is an old English word [L. *jocus*] denoting some sort of farcical ballad. Names such as Kemp's Jig, Slaggin's Jig, refer to fa-mous clowns of the English comedy. The "Nobody's Jigg" which appears in various sources is the jig of the clown R. Reynolds who played the role of "Nobody" in the popular comedy *Somebody and Nobody*. The English comedians who, in the early 17th century, invaded the Netherlands, Scandinavia, and Germany, introduced the jig into these countries. According to a recent theory, the jigs were also introduced into America where they were imitated by the Negroes and gradually transformed into the grotesque dances of the minstrel shows. In this respect, it is interesting to note the "jazz-like" rhythm [see *Dotted notes III] in our example [Mr. Slaggin's Jigg, from *The Dancing

Master (1686); cf. M. Danckert, *Zur Geschichte der Gigue* (1924), p. 17].

Jingling John. See *Crescent.

Jodel. See *Yodel.

Jongleur. See *Minstrel; *Troubadours. Also reference under *Estampie.

Joropo. The most characteristic dance of Venezuela. It is in quick ¾-meter with short melodic phrases and strongly accented accompaniment in simple rhythms, occasionally (particularly in the coastal regions) with some syncopation.

Jota [Sp.]. A dance of Aragon (northern Spain) in rapid triple time, performed by one or more couples and accompanied by castanets. One of the most popular melodies has been used by Liszt in his Spanish Rhapsody no. xvi (*Folies d'Espagne et Jota Aragonese*) and by Glinka in his orchestral overture *Jota Aragonesa*. Other examples occur in Falla's *The Three-cornered Hat* and in compositions of Saint-Saëns, Albeniz, etc. Statements regarding the medieval or Arabic origin of the Jota [cf. J. Ribera, *La Musica de lo Jota Aragonesa* (1928)] are, needless to say, entirely unfounded. Cf. G. B. Brown, in *BAMS* ii; Ex. in *LavE* i.4, 2373ff.

Jubilus. The long melismatic vocalization of the Alleluias, sung to the final vowel a- - - [e.g., *GR*, 5]. See *Alleluia; *Neuma; *Sequence.

Jupiter Symphony. Mozart's Symphony in C major, K.V. 551, composed in 1788. The name is unauthentic, but aptly expresses the "majestic" character of the symphony which offers a striking contrast to the G minor Symphony (K.V. 550) written in the same year.

Justiniane. See under *Villanella.

Just intonation [G. *Reine* or *natürliche Stimmung*]. A system of intonation and tuning in which all the intervals are derived from the natural (pure) fifth and the natural (pure) third [see *Acoustics III]. Therefore, all the intervals of just intonation are contained in the formula $m \times F + n \times T$ (F = fifth, T = third). The formula for the relative frequencies is therefore: $\left(\frac{3}{2}\right)^m \times \left(\frac{5}{4}\right)^n$. Their calculation is particularly easy if [as explained under *Intervals, Calculation of, III] the octaves, i.e., all the factors 2, are disregarded at first, so that the formula for the relative frequencies becomes: $3^m \times 5^n$, in which m and n designate the number of fifths and thirds contained in the interval in question. There result the following values for the C major scale:

c	d(= 2F)	e(= T)	f(= -T)	g(= F)	a(= T-F)	b(= T+F)
1	9	5	$\frac{1}{3}$	3	$\frac{5}{3}$	15

Reduced into the normal octave, they become:

	c	d	e	f	g	a	b	c'
t = 1:	1	$\frac{9}{8}$	$\frac{5}{4}$	$\frac{4}{3}$	$\frac{3}{2}$	$\frac{5}{3}$	$\frac{15}{8}$	2

t = 24: 24 27 30 32 36 40 45 48
Intervals: $\frac{9}{8}$ $\frac{10}{9}$ $\frac{16}{15}$ $\frac{9}{8}$ $\frac{10}{9}$ $\frac{9}{8}$ $\frac{16}{15}$

Owing to the presence of two constituents (F and T) the complete system of just intonation forms a two-dimensional infinite multitude of tones [G. *Tongewebe*; cf. C. Eitz, *Das mathematisch-reine Tonsystem*,

1891]. A selection of these tones is given under *Intervals, Calculation of, VI.

Just intonation has the advantage of giving the three fundamental triads: c–e–g, f–a–c', and g–b–d' as "natural triads" (characterized by the ratio 4:5:6; e.g.: 24:30:36 = 4:5:6), which are more "euphonious" than those in *Pythagorean or in *well-tempered tuning. However, its disadvantages are much more numerous and, in fact, so serious as to make it practically useless. The chief disadvantages are: (a) The tones of the C-major scale include one "dissonant" fifth, namely d–a, which is $\frac{40}{27}$ $\left(\frac{80}{54}\right)$ instead of $\frac{3}{2}$ $\left(\frac{81}{54}\right)$. (b) The C-major scale has two different whole tones, $\frac{9}{8}$ (major tone) and $\frac{10}{9}$ (minor tone); their difference is the syntonic *comma $\frac{81}{80}$. (c) Modulation is impossible; already the first three tones of the G-major scale: g–a–b have different intervals from those of the C-major scale: c–d–e. Hence, two different tones *a* would be necessary, one for the sixth of c, the other for the second of g. The difficulties would rapidly increase with the introduction of chromatic tones. (d) In chordal music, just intonation produces pure triads and has, therefore, been considered ideal for *a cappella* music in the style of Palestrina, etc. However, the principle of pure triads can be maintained only at the expense of a constant lowering in pitch. For instance, if the succession of chords indicated in our example were sung in pure triads, the

notes indicated by black heads would have the following frequencies: $c = 1$; $a = \frac{5}{3}$;

$d = \frac{5}{3} \times \frac{4}{3} = \frac{20}{9}$; $g = \frac{20}{9} \times \frac{2}{3} = \frac{40}{27}$;

$c = \frac{40}{27} \times \frac{2}{3} = \frac{80}{81}$, i.e., the syntonic comma ($\frac{81}{80}$) lower than the initial c. Since harmonies including the supertonic (this chord is responsible for the lowering of pitch) are particularly frequent in the Palestrina style, just intonation proves unsatisfactory for exactly that type of music for which it has frequently been recommended. The conclusion to be drawn from all these facts is that the interest of just intonation lies only in the theoretical field, and that its application to actual performance is limited to occasional chords (initial, final triads) in a capella music.

Lit.: J. M. Barbour, "Just Intonation Confuted" (*ML* xix); *id.*, in *BAMS* ii; L. S. Lloyd, "Just Temperament" (*ML* xx). See also under *Acoustics; *Temperament; *Intervals.

Just note and accent. These words occur in Milton's sonnet "To Mr. H. Lawes on his Airs." The first eight lines are as follows:

Harry whose tuneful and well measur'd Song
   First taught our English Music how to span
   Words with just note and accent, not to scan
   With *Midas* Ears, committing short and long;
Thy worth and skill exempts thee from the throng,
   With praise enough for envy to look wan;
   To after age thou shalt be writ the man
   That with smooth aire couldst humor best our
      tonge.

Whatever Milton may have had in mind — and his judgment certainly was not entirely objective, inasmuch as Henry Lawes set music to the poet's masque *Comus* — in the sense in which the phrase "just note and accent" is now generally taken, much more is implied than the mere coincidence of a normally accented word or syllable with a strong or secondary strong beat; indeed, all the subtleties of text setting are suggested: variations of meter within the bar which supply flexibility of declamation; the selection of a note in the melody which does not lay too much stress upon a relatively unimportant bit of text, and, in general, the whole character of the melody as it partners and interprets the words to which it is set. Both William and Henry Lawes followed the tradition of text treatment established in the earliest Italian operas, applying those principles to the English language. See *Text and Music. Cf. E. J. Dent, *Foundations of English Opera* (1928); H. C. Colles, *Voice and Verse* (1928).

A. T. D.

K

K. Sometimes used instead of *K.V.

Kadenz [G.]. (1) *Cadence; (2) *Cadenza.

Kaiserquartett [G.]. See *Emperor Quartet.

Kalevala. The Finnish national epic [see *Finnish music]. Sibelius has composed a number of *symphonic poems based on stories from this epic.

Kalt [G.]. Cold.

Kammer- [G., Chamber]. *Kammerton*, chamber pitch [see *Pitch (2)]. *Kammermusik*, chamber music. *Kammerkantate*, chamber cantata, etc.

Kanon. (1) German for *canon. — (2) A type of medieval Byzantine poetry [see *Byzantine chant II]. — (3) See *Kanûn.

Kantate [G.]. *Cantata.

Kantele. See under *Finnish music.

Kantorei [G.]. In the 15th and 16th centuries a singing group in the employ of a church or of a prince's court; subsequently groups of amateurs who provided music for the service of their communities. For literature cf. *MoML*, 384.

Kanûn. An Arabic *psaltery with 26 gut strings. The name, which is derived from the Greek word *canon*, i.e., monochord [see *Canon (2)] occurs as early as the

10th century in a story of *The Arabian Nights*. In the later Middle Ages (12th century?) the instrument was imported into Europe. See *Psaltery.

Kanzone [G.]. (1) *Canzona.— (2) *Canzo.

Kapelle [G.]. *Chapel, usually in the connotation of "private or small orchestra," e.g., *Hofkapelle* (court orchestra), *Militärkapelle* (military band). *Kapellmeister*, originally an honorable title (Bach served as a Kapellmeister to Prince Ernst of Cöthen, from 1717 to 1723), is now an old-fashioned provincialism for *Dirigent* (conductor). The term *Kapellmeistermusik* is a derogatory designation for compositions of a formally correct design, but lacking in imagination and originality — as the pieces of the Kapellmeister were.

Kapodaster [G.]. *Capotasto.

Katzenmusik [G.]. *Charivari.

Kazoo. See *Mirliton.

Keck [G.]. Audacious.

Kehraus [G.]. The last dance of a ball.

Kemantche. See *Arabian music II.

Kentbugle, Kenthorn. Same as key bugle; see *Brass instruments V (c).

Kerabe. Old German for *Kehraus. See *Nachtanz.

Kesselpauke, Kesseltrommel [G.]. Kettledrum. See also *Pauke.

Kettenform [G.]. See under *Forms, Musical (after A, I).

Kettledrum. See *Percussion instruments A, 1; also *Drums.

Key. (1) On pianos, organs, etc., the visible parts of the action [F. *touche*; G. *Taste*; It. *tasto*] which are depressed by the fingers of the player [see *Keyboard]. In wood winds the term applies to comparable devices, i.e., the levers covering the side-holes [F. *clef*; G. *Klappe*; It. *chiave*].

(2) By way of specialization the term adopts the meaning of "main key" to which other keys are tonally related, hence practically coterminous with *tonality [F. *tonalité*; G. *Tonart*; It. *tonalità*]. Some writers maintain that there is a subtle difference between key and tonality, but usually fail to make this distinction sufficiently clear [see *Tonality]. There is, however, a distinct difference between key and scale, the former term encompassing many melodic and harmonic formations which are not contained in the scale (e.g., the Neapolitan sixth f–ab–db' in C major).

According to the 12 tones of the chromatic scale, there are 12 keys, one on C, one on C-sharp, etc. (this number is increased to 14 or 15 by the notational distinction between *enharmonic keys, such as C-sharp and D-flat, G-sharp and A-flat). With any given key there is a choice of *modality, i.e., of certain variations in the tones which form the scale. E.g., in C we have the choice between major (mode): c d e f g a b c'; minor (mode): c d eb f g a(b) b c'; Lydian mode: c d e f# g a b c'; and others derived from the *Church modes. Of these, only the first two are usually considered, and are actually (though not quite logically) distinguished as different keys, thus leading to a total number of 24 keys, one major and one minor on each tone of the chromatic scale. See *Key-signature; *Key relationships. Cf. W. W. Roberts, "Key Quality" (*ML* xi, no. 1).

Keyboard. I. The whole set of keys, such as in pianofortes, organs, harpsichords, etc. (*Keyboard instruments). The modern keyboard usually includes

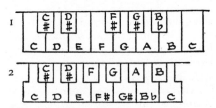

eighty-eight keys for seven full octaves, from C₁ to c'''', and a quarter octave added at the lower end of the compass.

In each octave there are seven white and five black keys, arranged as illustrated in Ex. 1. This arrangement is the natural result of the fact that the fundamental scale of European music consists of seven tones which are given to the white keys. Except for the steps e–f and b–c′ the intervals between these tones are wholetones each of which admits the introduction of a semitone in between, represented each by a black key. Although the introduction of equal temperament, by permitting unlimited transposition, seriously weakened the dominating position of the white keys, the old "C major keyboard" has proved fully capable of adapting itself to the new system and has, to the present day, successfully withstood all attempts at reform, e.g., the adoption of the truly "chromatic keyboard" [Ex. 2] in which the arrangement — and consequently the fingering — would be the same for all the scales.

II. *History.* The earliest keyed instrument was the organ. According to Galpin's reconstruction of the Greek *hydraulis, this instrument had 19 keys about 8 inches long and 2 inches wide. Organs of the 9th and 10th centuries A.D. had a number (8 to 10) of large keys, called *linguae* (tongues), which were pulled out and pushed in. The trustworthiness of reports that keys of organs were so large and heavy that they were played with the fist is rather doubtful. Around 1200, the keyboard covered nearly three octaves (from G to e″; see *Hexachord). From then on, its compass as well as the number of chromatic keys steadily increased. The early 14th-century organ pieces from the Robertsbridge Codex (Brit. Mus. *Add. 28550*) make use of all the chromatic tones in at least one octave. A normal device of all the old keyboards was the *short octave. The 16th-century experiments in the field of enharmonic music (Vicentino) led to the construction of keyboards with separate keys for C♯ and D♭, etc. [see *Arciorgano]. In the 17th century, keyboards had an average compass of four octaves, with all the chromatic notes, except for the lowest range. Bach's harpsichord had over five octaves. Broadwood,

in 1794, made the first keyboard (pianoforte) with six octaves, from C_1 to c″″; this was the compass of the Broadwood instrument used by Beethoven from 1817 on.

III. *Modern Reforms.* Within the past fifty years various unsuccessful attempts have been made to improve the keyboard. The *Janko keyboard* (patented 1882) had six rows of short keys arranged somewhat similarly to the keys of a typewriter. Each row included the keys for a wholetone scale, that beginning with C in the rows 1, 3, 5, and that beginning with C♯ in the rows 2, 4, 6. Thus, each octave had 36 keys, three for each tone of the chromatic scale. In spite of certain advantages and of initial success (Liszt and Rubinstein recommended it), the Janko keyboard failed to supersede the traditional one. Later modifications and simplifications (*Adam keyboard, Durand keyboard, Clavier Hans*) met with the same fate. *Mageot's keyboard*, called "piano a doubles claviers renversés" (1878), had two keyboards the lower of which, intended for the right hand, had the usual arrangement, whereas the higher one, for the left hand, had the reverse arrangement, i.e., with the keys for the high notes on the left side. The advantage claimed for this innovation was identical fingering of, e.g., the ascending scale, for both hands. The *Clutsam keyboard* (1909) arranged the keys in a slightly curved instead of a straight line, taking into account the fact that the arms of the player move in arcs. This arrangement has become widely adopted for organ pedals. Moor's *Duplex Coupler Grand Piano* imitates the two manuals of the harpsichord. The upper of the two keyboards, otherwise normal, gives the tones of the higher octave, and can be coupled with the lower. This keyboard greatly facilitates the execution of the usual virtuoso effects and permits the execution of many others not possible on the usual keyboard. Its failure to win acceptance might be ascribed to the decreasing interest in purely virtuoso playing. If invented 50 years earlier it would probably have been a great success. Another use of two keyboards is made in the *quarter-tone keyboards* (Haba, 1923;

Stoehr, 1924), in which the upper keyboard is a quarter-tone higher than the lower. At present, it would seem that attempts to enlarge the traditional keyboard are less likely to succeed than those leading in the opposite direction, by eliminating the highest and lowest tones which, being seldom used in domestic music, unnecessarily raise the size and the price of the instrument.

Keyboard instruments. Generic name for instruments having a keyboard, particularly with reference to the period prior to *c.* 1750 during which there was frequently no clear distinction between the repertoires of the organ, the harpsichord, the clavichord, etc. [see *Keyboard music].

Lit.: Ph. James, *Early Keyboard Instruments from Their Beginnings up to 1820* (1930); *id.,* in *PMA* lvii; V. G. Woodhouse, "Old Keyed Instruments and their Music" (*ML* i, no. 1); C. Krebs, "Die besaiteten Klavierinstrumente bis zum Anfang des 17. Jahrhunderts" (*VMW* viii); H. Brunner, *Das Klavierklangideal Mozarts und the Klaviere seiner Zeit* (1933); see also under *Keyboard music; *Pianoforte.

Keyboard music. The term is particularly used with reference to the periods prior to 1750 in which there was frequently no clear distinction between music for the organ, harpsichord, or clavichord. In modern German writings the term *Klaviermusik* is occasionally used in the same meaning. A 16th-century Spanish term is *tecla* [cf. A. de Cabezon's *Obras de musica para tecla, harpa y vihuela* (1574), "Musical works for keyboard, harp, and lute"]. Regarding the numerous attempts — not wholly successful — of modern scholars to draw clearer lines of distinction within the realm of early keyboard music, particularly between the repertories of the harpsichord and the clavichord, cf. N. Wilkinson, in *ML* iv, no. 2; L. A. Coon, in *PAMS*, 1936; K. Nef, in *JMP* x; E. Bodky, in *DM* xxiv, no. 2; R. Buchmayr, in *Bach Jahrbuch*, 1909; various authors in *Bach Jahrbuch*, 1910. See also *Clavichord; *Harpsi-

chord; *Instrument; *Klavier; *Pianoforte music; *Organ music.

Key bugle. See *Brass instruments V (c).

Keynote. Same as *tonic.

Key-relationship. A term used to indicate the degree of relationship or affinity between two keys. All keys are related, but in different degrees. The order of relationship generally follows that of the tones in the series from consonant to dissonant: fifth (dominant), fourth (subdominant), third (mediant), etc. In particular, the following species are distinguished: (a) Parallel key: major and minor key with the same tonic (C major and C minor). (b) Relative key: major and minor key with the same signature (C major and A minor; C minor and E-flat major). (c) Related keys: keys the signature of which differs by not more than one sharp or flat from that of the main key (in C major: A minor, G major, E minor, F major, D minor; in A minor: C major, E minor, G major, D minor, F major). Cf. W. H. Frere, "Key-relationship in Early Medieval Music" (*PMA* xxxvii; also in *KIM*, 1911, p. 114).

Key signature. The sharps or flats appearing at the beginning of each staff which indicate the *key of a composition.

A given signature indicates one of two keys, a major key or its relative minor key; these are designated in the accompanying table by a white or a black note. Memorizing of this scheme is facilitated if it is observed that in a sharp signature the keynote is immediately above the last sharp if the key is major; below, if it is minor; and that in a flat signature the keynote is that of the penultimate flat if the key is major, or a third below, if it is minor (e.g., three sharps, f#, c#, g#: A major or F-sharp minor; three flats, bb, eb, ab: E-flat major or C minor). Normally the number of key signatures is twelve, corresponding to the twelve chromatic tones of the octave. This number is increased, however, to 13, 14, or even 15 by the notational distinction between *enharmonic keys, e.g., C-sharp and D-flat. See also *Circle of fifths.

In early music the use of key signatures is very limited. Until the late 15th century the only signature of frequent occurrence is one flat (Dorian, Lydian); and this is used mostly in the lower voices only [see *Partial signatures]. In the 16th century the increased use of transposed modes led to signatures (usually partial) with two flats. Not until the middle of the 17th century were sharps generally adopted as signatures. Actually, the scope of keys in use was somewhat wider than is suggested by the variety of signatures, since the keys were usually written with fewer signs in the signature than they are today, and with more accidentals during the course of the composition. Thus, the flat minor keys (D minor, G minor, C minor) were usually notated with one flat less than in modern practice, the flat for the sixth being omitted. Likewise, the major keys (G major, D major, A major) are sometimes notated without a sharp for the leading tone in the signature. A well-known example is Handel's Harpsichord Suite in E (containing the *Harmonious Blacksmith) which has three sharps only in the original.

Key trumpet. See *Trumpet II.

Kielflügel [G.]. Old name for the harpsichord.

Kin. See *Ch'in.

Kindlich [G.]. Child-like.

Kinnor. See *Harp III; *Jewish music I.

Kirchen- [G., church]. *Kirchenjahr*, church year; *Kirchenkantate*, church cantata; *Kirchenmusik*, church music; *Kirchenschluss*, plagal cadence; *Kirchensonate*, sonata da chiesa; *Kirchenton*, church mode; *Kirchenlied*, church song, either the Protestant *chorales or the Catholic hymns written in German (in contradistinction to the older Latin *hymns).

Kit [F. *pochette*; G. *Taschengeige*]. A small, narrow fiddle to be carried in the pocket, and used by the dancing masters of the 18th and early 19th centuries. It existed in two different types, one a diminutive violin, the other a descendant of the medieval *rebec. Ill. on p. 800.

Kithara. The foremost instrument of ancient Greece, consisting of a wooden soundbox, two curved lateral arms, and a crossbar. A number of strings, varying from five (8th century B.C.) to seven (7th century) and finally eleven (5th century), was stretched between the soundbox and the crossbar. The tuning of the traditional type with five or six strings was anhemitonic: e g a b d' (e'). The tuning of the outer strings could be changed to f and f' [see *Greek music II (d)]; the additional strings of the later periods would seem to have been mainly octave-duplications of the original ones. Although there was no finger board on the kithara, a limited degree of stopping was possible by merely pressing a finger against the string near to its lower end. Thus, the pitch of a string could be raised a quarter-tone, a semitone or a whole-tone. It was this practice which led to the curious system of Greek instrumental notation, as has been convincingly shown by C. Sachs [cf. his *Musik des Altertums* (1924); also *AdHM* i, 45]. The kithara was the instrument of Apollo, and represented the Greek ideal of *kalokagathia* (harmonious moderation), as contrasted with the "emotional" *aulos, the attribute of Dionysos. Illustration under *Zithers. See *Lyra.

Kl. Short for Klarinette.

Klagend [G.]. Lamenting.

Klang [G.]. Sound, sonority. *Klangboden*, sounding board. *Klangfarbe*, tone color, timbre; *Klangfolge*, chord progression; *Klanggeschlecht*, mode (major or minor); *Klangideal*, see *Sound ideal.

Klappe [G.]. Key of wind instruments. *Klappenhorn, -trompete,* i.e., key bugle, key trumpet.

Klarinette [G.]. Clarinet.

Klausel [G.]. Cadence, particularly those of 16th-century polyphonic music.

Klaviatur [G.]. Keyboard.

Klavier [G.]. Pianoforte. *Klavierauszug*, piano-arrangement; *Klavierstück*, piano piece; *Klavierspiel*, piano playing. Sometimes the term is used in the meaning of manual (*Orgel mit 2, 3, "Klavieren"*). — Prior to the introduction of the pianoforte, that is, until about 1775, the term *Klavier* (usually spelled *Clavier*) was applied generically to denote either or both the harpsichord and the clavichord. Hen·e, titles such as *Clavierübung*, or *Wohltemperiertes Clavier* contain no evidence as to the intended instrument. With Ph. Em. Bach and his contemporaries Clavier preferably means the clavichord.

Kleine Oktave [G.]. The "small octave," from c to b. See *Pitch names.

Kl. Fl. [G.]. Short for *Kleine Flöte*, i.e., piccolo.

Klingend [G.]. Sounding, resonant.

Kl. Tr. [G.]. Short for *Kleine Trommel*, i.e., side drum.

Knarre [G.]. *Rattle.

Kniegeige [G., knee violin]. Viola da gamba.

Koechel-Verzeichnis. See *K.V.

Kollectivzug [G.]. Composition stop or combination stop of the organ.

Kolorieren [G.]. To introduce coloraturas, ornamentations, into a pre-existing composition, as was frequently done in the *intabulierungen* of the 16th century. See *Colorists.

Komponieren; Komponist [G.]. To compose; composer.

Kondakarion. In Russian church music, manuscripts of the 12th and 13th centuries which contain collections of short hymns of praise (*kondak*, from *Kontakion?*). They contain melodies written in an early type of notation, the so-called *kondakarny*-notation, which has not yet been deciphered. See *Russian music I. Cf. also *ReMMA*, 96; *WoHN* i, 90.

Kontakion. See *Byzantine chant II.

Kontra- [G.]. *-bass*, double-bass; *-factur*, *contrafact; *-fagott*, contra bassoon; *-bassklarinette*, double-bass clarinet; *-oktave*, contra octave [see *Pitch names]; *-punkt*, counterpoint; *-subject*, counter-subject.

Kontretanz [G.]. *Contredanse.

Konzert [G.]. Concert or concerto. *Konzertmeister*, concertmaster.

Konzertstück, see *Concertino (2).

Kopfstimme [G.]. Head voice.

Koppel [G.]. Coupler.

Korean music. The musical culture of Korea is largely based upon that of *China. Cf. A. Eckhardt, *Koreanische Musik* (1930); Chunk Sik Keh, *Die Koreanische Musik* (Diss. Basle 1934); J. L. Boots, *Korean Musical Instruments* (Seoul, 1940).

Kornett [G.]. See under *Cornet.

Kortholt. Same as *Curtall; see *Oboe III.

Koto. See *Ch'in; *Japanese music.

Krakowiak [G.] *Cracovienne.

Krebskanon [G.]. Crab canon; *krebsgängig*, in retrograde motion.

Kreisleriana. Title of Schumann's op. 16, a collection of eight "Fantasien" for the pianoforte, composed 1838. The name refers to the whimsical and capricious figure of the Kapellmeister Kreisler who plays a prominent role in several fantastic novels by the German novelist E. T. A. Hoffmann [see *Contes d'Hoffmann, Les].

Kreutzer Sonata. Beethoven's Violin Sonata op. 47, composed in 1803, originally composed for the Negro violinist

Bridgetower (1780–1860) whom Beethoven accompanied on the first performance. Beethoven, however, dedicated the composition to the violin-composer and virtuoso Rodolphe Kreutzer (1766–1831).

Kreuz [G.]. Sharp.

Kriuki (Krjuki). See *Russian music I; *Znamenny chant.

Krummhorn [G.]. *Cromorne; see *Oboe III.

Kuhreigen [G.]. *Ranz des vaches.

Kujawiak. A Polish dance from the province of Kujawy. It is a rapid variety of the mazurka. Chopin's mazurkas op. 6, no. 6; op. 30, no. 4; op. 41, no. 1 are kujawiaks.

Kunst der Fuge. See *Art of Fugue.

Kunstlied [G.]. A term — used in America rather than in Germany — for the "art songs" of German composers such as Schubert, Schumann, Brahms, in contrast to German folk songs. It is also applied to the 16th-century polyphonic songs with German text (Hofhaimer, Senfl).

Kurz [G.]. Short. *Kurz Oktave,* short octave. *Kurzer Vorschlag,* short appoggiatura.

K.V. Abbreviation for *Köchel-Verzeichnis,* that is, the chronological list of all the works of Mozart which was made by L. von Köchel (published in 1862, revised edition of Einstein in 1937; supplements in *MR* i, ii). Mozart's compositions are usually referred to by the numbers of this list, e.g., K.V. 357, or K. 357.

Kyriale. See *Liturgical books.

Kyrie [Gr. *Kyrie eleison,* Lord, have mercy]. The first item of the Ordinary of the *Mass. Its full text is: *Kyrie eleison; Christe eleison; Kyrie eleison.* Each of these three invocations is sung three times, usually with the melodies repeated according to the scheme: aaa bbb ccc [cf. *GR,* 18*], or aaa bbb ccc', the last reiteration being slightly extended [cf. *GR,* 8*]. Another frequent scheme, probably of later origin, is: aba cdc efe [cf. *GR,* 11*]. In the 10th and 11th centuries the Kyries were frequently troped (farced Kyrie) by the interspersion of attributes, e.g., Kyrie *lux et origo* eleison [see *Trope (4); *Farce]. Although these tropes have disappeared, the Kyries are still named after them, e.g., *Kyrie lux et origo.*

Kyrieleis [G.]. See *Leise.

L

L. Short for left or [G.] *links;* L.H., left hand; [G.] *linke Hand.*

La. See *Solmization; *Pitch names; *Hexachord.

Labial pipes [G. *Labialpfeifen*]. Same as *Flue stops.

Ländler. An Austrian dance in the character of a slow waltz. It was very popular in the early 19th century, before the *waltz came in vogue. Mozart (K.V. 606), Beethoven (11 *Mödlinger Tänze,* 1819), and Schubert (op. 171) wrote collections of Ländler. See *Dance music IV.

Lage [G.]. Position, either with reference to violin-playing (*erste, zweite, . . . Lage,* i.e., first, second . . . position) or to chords (*enge* or *weite Lage,* i.e., close or open position); or to ranges of voices and instruments (*hohe* or *tiefe Lage,* i.e., high or low range; *gute* or *schlechte Lage,* good or bad range).

Lagnoso [It.]. Doleful.

Lai, Lay [G. *Leich;* not to be confused with *Leis(e) or *Laisse]. A form of medieval French poetry and music characteristic of the *trouvères of the 13th century, adopted later by the German

Minnesinger (14th century). From the
standpoint of text the lais are poems (usually addressed to the Virgin or to a lady)
consisting of 60, 100, or more lines of
from 4 to 8 syllables each; the whole falling into irregular stanzas of from 6 to 16
or more lines each. Each stanza is based
on one or two rhyme-syllables, and there
is a great variety in the schemes of meter
and rhyme to be found in the various
stanzas, for instance: $a^4 a^4 b^7 a^4 a^4 b^7 a^4 a^4$
$b^7 b^7 b^7 b^7 b^7 b^7 b^7$ (the letters indicate
lines with the same rhyme; the figures
give the number of syllables in the line).

The musical structure of the lai is essentially that of the sequence [see *Sequence (2)] from which it evidently derived, but with certain additional traits
of elaboration or modification, such as
one may expect to find in the later stages
of a development. Instead of the double
versicles of the sequence, there are triple
versicles and quadruple versicles (a melody three or four times repeated), as well
as "single versicles," involving no repetition. Following is the scheme of one of
the shortest lais, Guillaume le Vinier's
"Espris d'ire et d'amour" [Jeanroy, no. 8;
cf. *HAM*, no. 19 e]:

I		II	III	
A	B	C	D	E
a a	$b_1 b_2 b_1 b_2$	c c	d d d	$e_1 e_2 e_1 e_2$
IV		V		
F	G	H		I
f f	g	h h h		i

(a, b, etc., are the versicle melodies; A, B,
etc., the musical sections; I, II, etc., the
poetic stanzas, according to Jeanroy; b_1,
b_2 denote different endings for the same
melody.) Another name for the lai is
descort ("disorder"), a term which has
been interpreted as referring to the extremely variable structure of the lai in
contrast to the "fixed forms," such as the
ballade, rondeau, etc., or to some other element of irregularity [cf. *ReMMA*, 225].

The German counterpart of the lai is
the 14th-century *Leich*. Here the double-
versicle structure of the sequence is, as a
rule, rigidly observed. For instance, Heinrich Frauenlob's "Unser Frauen Leich"
[cf. Runge, p. 1] consists of 44 stanzas
("lieder") sung to 22 melodies ("töne").

It is interesting to note that Machaut's lai,
the last example of the French repertory,
is written in a form which is still closer
to that of the sequence, in which the first
and the last melody usually were sung
only once. In fact, the scheme A BB CC
DD . . . PP Q is strictly observed by
Machaut, the only modification being that
A and Q are sung twice instead of once,
B–P four times, instead of twice.

Lit.: A. Jeanroy, L. Brandin and Pierre
Aubry, †*Lais et descorts français* (1901);
F. Wolf, *Ueber die Lais, Sequenzen und
Leiche* (1841); F. Gennrich, "Das Formproblem des Minnesangs" (*Deutsche Vierteljahrsschrift für Literaturgeschichte*, ix,
319). P. Runge, †*Die Sangesweisen der
Colmarer Handschrift* (1896); G. Hase,
Der Minneleich Meister Alexanders
(1921); Holz-Saran-Bernouilli, †*Die Jenaer Liederhandschrift* (1901); *DTOe*
20.ii (Frauenlob and others); H. Spanke,
in *ZMW* xiv; J. Handschin, in *ZMW* xii.
See also the general literature under
*Trouvères and *Minnesinger.

Laisse. See *Chanson de geste.

Lament. Scottish and Irish music for
bagpipes and, sometimes, song, used at
the funeral of members of the clan or at
other occasions of a mournful character.
Each clan had its traditional tune. Cf.
GD iii, 79; see also *Ho-hoane.

Lamentations. Music set to the Lamentations of Jeremiah. In the Roman
Catholic service the lamentations are
sung at the office of matins on Thursday,
Friday, and Saturday of Holy Week
(*tenebrae), in a simple recitation-tone
[*LU*, 626, 669, 715]. A characteristic
feature of the text, taken over from the
Bible, is the enumeration of the verses by
Hebrew letters: *Aleph*. Quo modo sedit
. . . *Beth*. Plorans ploravit . . . , etc. From
the mid-15th throughout the 17th century, many composers wrote polyphonic
settings of the famous text in order to enhance the dramatic character of tenebrae.
A simple chordal style similar to that of
the *passions was preferred. The earliest
example is by Ockeghem (1474). In
1506, Petrucci published two volumes,

Lamentationes Jeremie Prophete, which include settings by Johannes Tinctoris, de Orto, Tromboncino, and others. In 1532, a setting by Carpentras (real name Elzéar Genet, c. 1475–1548) was published which was used until 1587 at the Papal Chapel instead of the ancient plainsong. In 1557, Leroy and Ballard published a collection of settings (*Piissimae et sacratissimae lamentationes Jeremiae prophetae*) which, in addition to Carpentras' composition, included others by Pierre de la Rue, Févin, Arcadelt, Festa, and Claude le Jeune. In 1588, Palestrina published his *Lamentationum liber primus* [complete ed., vol. 25] which supplanted Carpentras' composition in the service of the Papal Chapel [for more details, cf. *GD* iii, 80]. Other settings are by Stephan Mahu, Gaspar Werbecke [*SchGMB*, no. 58], Cristobal Morales (1564), Tallis, Byrd, Handl (*DTOe* 15.i), Giov. Maria Nanini, and Gregorio Allegri. In 1640, the latter's composition was added to the (incomplete) setting of Palestrina. Even today, the Sistine Choir uses the settings of these two composers. For Palestrina's complete and original composition, cf. R. Casimiri, *Il Codice 59* (1919). A composition by F. Couperin illustrates the application of a highly expressive aria style to the text.

Lamento. Music of an elegiac, mournful character. A dance of the 14th century bears for an obscure reason the title: *Lamento di Tristan* [*SchGMB*, no. 28]. In 17th-century opera the Lamento is a scene expressing utter despair, usually placed shortly before the unexpected "turn to the happy end." This type was inaugurated by Monteverdi's famous *Lamento d'Arianna* of 1607 [*SchGMB*, no. 177]. Cf. A. Westrup, in *MR* i. See also *Tombeau.

Landini cadence. A cadence, named after Francesco Landini (1325–97), in

which the sixth degree (a, "Landini sixth") is inserted between the leading

tone (b) and the octave (c′). Frequently the altered fourth (f♯) appears in the middle part, as a leading tone to the dominant (g) [see Ex., a], a formation which properly belongs to the Lydian mode [Ex., b]. The use of this cadence is much more extended than is suggested by its name. It occurs in the works of G. de Machaut (1300–77; cf., e.g., *SchGMB*, no. 26, "loyaument"), is used frequently by Landini, and forms a characteristic feature of the music of the *Burgundian School, usually in the ornamented variety illustrated under c. There are cases, however, in which the "flatted" formula [Ex., d] would seem to be required [cf. *ApNPM*, 106]. See *Cadence II.

Langsam [G.]. Slow.

La Poule [F., The Hen]. Haydn's Symphony in G minor (no. 83, 1786), the second of the "Paris" Symphonies. The name seems to refer to the second subject of the first movement.

La Reine [F., The Queen]. Haydn's Symphony in B-flat (no. 85, 1786), the fourth of the "Paris" Symphonies. The name refers to Queen Marie Antoinette who was particularly fond of the symphony.

Larga [L.], **large**. In mensural notation, rare name for the largest values, either the maxima or even multiples of it [cf. *RiML*, 997].

Largando. Same as *Allargando.

Larghetto [It.]. The diminutive of *largo, therefore, less slow than this tempo. Also, title for pieces in such a tempo.

Largo [It., broad, large]. Very slow in tempo, usually combined with great expressiveness. See *Tempo marks.

Latin American music. See articles under *Argentina, *Brazil, *Chile, *Colombia, *Mexico, *Peru, and *Venezuela.

Lit.: *Bibliography of Latin American Folk Music*, compiled by G. Chase (Library of Congress, 1942); Ch. Seeger, *Music in Latin America* (1942); N. Slonimsky, "Music of Latin America" (in preparation); *Boletín Latino-Americano de Música*, ed. by F. C. Lange (5 vols. published, 1935, '36, '37, '38, '42, with musical supplements); G. Chase, *The Music of Spain* (1941; chapter on "Hispanic Music in the Americas," with bibliography and record list); G. Durán, *Recordings of Latin American Songs and Dances* (Music Division, Pan American Union, Washington, 1942); E. Hague, *Latin American Music* (1934); *Handbook of Latin American Studies*, an annual bibliographical guide published by Harvard University Press, includes a section on music; F. C. Lange, *Latin-American Art Music for the Piano* (1942); *Partial List of Latin American Music Obtainable in the United States* (Music Division, Pan American Union, Washington, 1942). K. G. Izikowitz, *Musical . . . Instruments of the South American Indians* (in *Göteborgs Kungliga Vetenskaps . . . Samhället*, vol. v, 1936). See also bibliographies under *Central America; *Cuba; *Libraries II. G. C.

Laube Sonata. See *Moonlight Sonata.

Lauda [It., pl. *laude*; praise; the less correct forms *laude* (sing.), *laudi* (pl.), are also used]. Hymns of praise and devotion in the Italian language which from the 13th century down to the middle of the 19th century played an important part in the religious life of the Italian people. Their origin and early development were closely connected with the activity of St. Francis of Assisi (1182–1226) as well as with that of the many penitential fraternities (flagellants; see *Geisslerlieder) of the 13th and 14th centuries. Later, numerous congregations, called *Companie de Laudesi*, or *Laudisti*, were founded who devoted much of their activity to the cultivation of devotional singing among the Italian people. The musical and dramatic representations which took place in their meeting-halls led, in the 16th century, to the *oratorio. Till the middle of the 19th century the laudesi continued to be centers of religious life.

The laude of the 13th century are monophonic songs which show a certain in-

fluence of the French troubadour music. Their textual structure is that of a refrain poem, consisting of several (from two to ten and more) stanzas (S) of four or six lines each, alternating with a refrain (*ritornello, R) of usually two lines: R S R S . . . S R. Music is provided for the refrain and the stanza, and that of the latter usually borrows some melodic member from the former, in a great variety of schemes, e.g.: A B a b a b, A B c d a b, A B c d e b, A B c c d b, A B c c a b (capital letters indicate the refrain). The last scheme, which may also be represented thus: A b b a (or, with repetition of the refrain, A b b a A) is that of the French *virelai (or of the Italian *ballata). This form, however, plays a much less prominent part in the laude than some scholars have maintained. Only about a dozen of the laude are cast in the form of the virelai, and most of these show considerable modifications in the repeated phrases, such as are not found in the virelai proper [cf. Sancto Lorenzo in *AdHM* i, 211]. One of the few examples of strict virelai form is given in *HAM*, no. 21b. The usual transcription in four-four meter [Liuzzi; *BeMMR*, 153f] is, to say the least, hypothetical [cf. Y. Rokseth, in *Romania* (Paris) lxv, no. 259; see also under *Vierhebigkeit]. The original MSS are in *plainsong notation.

There is a wide difference in time and in style between the 13th-century laude and the next ones preserved, contained in collections by Petrucci from the early years of the 16th century. These are polyphonic, in a simple chordal style borrowed from the *frottola [Ex. in *BeMMR*, 218]. In the second half of the 16th century Fra Serafino Razzi inaugurated a vast literature of laude in the popular styles of the villanella, canzonetta [Ex. in *SchGMB*, no. 120]. Frequently folk songs and dance melodies were used for the religious texts, a procedure which shows a striking similarity to the methods of the Salvation Army. The numerous publications of the 17th century are important sources of early Italian folk song [see reference under *Ruggiero].

Lit.: F. Liuzzi, †*La Lauda e i primordi*

della melodia italiana (2 vols., 1935); N.
Garzi, *Le Laudi di cod. Cortenese* (1936);
K. Jeppesen, *Die mehrstimmige italien-*
ische Lauda um 1500 (1935); D. Alaleone, "Le laudi . . . nei secoli XVI e XVII"
(*RMI* xvi); E. J. Dent, "The Laudi Spirituali . . ." (*PMA* xliii); K. Jeppesen, "Die
neuentdeckten Bücher der Lauden . . ."
(*ZMW* xii); J. Handschin, in *AM* x.

Laudes [L.]. (1) See *Office hours
(lauds). — (2) Name for Gloria tropes
[see *Trope (4)].

Lauf [G., run; pl. *Läufe*]. A rapid passage, particularly in scales. For *Laufwerk*
see *Mechanical instruments III.

Launedda. A Sardinian triple clarinet,
evidently of Oriental origin [see *Clarinet IV]. It consists of three pipes made
of cane, the two longer of which are tied
together. The two highest pipes have
four holes each, the lowest one is an unchangeable bourdon. The music played
on the launeddas is, therefore, in two parts
over a sustained pedal. Cf. G. Fara, in
RMI xx, xxi, xxv. For the peculiar technique of blowing, cf. *SaHMI*, 91; also
*Oboe family III.

Laute [G.]. Lute. *Lautentabulatur*,
lute tablature.

Lautenclavicymbel. A harpsichord
with gut strings, instead of the usual
metal strings. The tone was very much
like that produced by the gut strings of
the lute (the reference to "checking by a
damper of cloth" — *GD* iii, 115 — is evidently a confusion with the lute-stop of
the ordinary harpsichord). Such harpsichords are mentioned as early as 1511, by
Virdung. For the description of an instrument of 1718, cf. *SaRM*, 239. In 1740
Bach had such an instrument made for
his own use which, according to Adlung,
Musica mechanica ii, 139, produced a
sound like a theorbo or, if damped by the
lute-stop, like a lute. Cf. O. Fleischer, in
ZIM i.

Lavolta. See *Volta (1).

Lay. See *Lai.

Leader. (1) Conductor (in America)
or concertmaster (in England). — (2)
See *Fugue I (g).

Leading motive. See *Leitmotif.

Leading tone or **note** [F. *note sensible*; G. *Leitton*]. The seventh degree of
the scale, a semitone below the tonic; so
called because of its strong tendency to
"lead up" (resolve upwards) to the tonic.
This progression (b–c′) is the character-

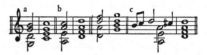

istic step of the regular cadence in major
as well as minor [see Ex., a] and is, therefore, extremely frequent in music of the
17th to the 19th century.

The consistent and compulsory use of
the leading tone is one of the chief features of modern major and minor, as
opposed to the modes, most of which
(Dorian, Phrygian, Mixolydian, Aeolian)
have a whole tone (*subtonium*) below the
tonic, not a semitone (*subsemitonium*)
[see Ex., b]. Although in modal music
the subsemitonium, i.e., the leading tone,
could be introduced by sharpening the
subtonium, this did not result in a complete suppression of the diatonic seventh
[see *Musica ficta]. Thus, earlier music
usually wavers between the natural and
the sharped varieties, as illustrated in our
example (c). In the 14th and early 15th
centuries the sharped degrees were more
frequent than they were during the ensuing period of Flemish music (1450–
1600) [see *Landini cadence]. Cf. L. H.
Skrbensky, *Leitton und Alteration in der
abendländischen Musik* (Diss. Prague
1938).

League of Composers. See *Societies,
Musical I, 4.

Lebendig, lebhaft [G.]. Lively.

Ledger lines. Short lines drawn
through the stem of notes which are too
high or too low to be represented on the
staff. They are usually avoided in early
music, by the introduction of lower or

higher clefs. The earliest source in which they are extensively used is Marcantonio da Bologna's organ book *Ricercare, motetti, canzoni* of 1523 [cf. *ApNPM*, 4].

Leere Saite [G.]. Open string.

Legato [It., bound]. To be performed without any perceptible interruption between the notes (a), as against *leggiero*

or non-legato (b), *portato* (c), and *staccato* (d). *Legatissimo* is either a more forceful indication of legato, or a sort of super-legato in which the preceding note is held for a short moment together with the following one (e). The first line in the illustration shows the notes as written; the second line shows the approximate effect.

Legende, légende [G., F.]. Romantic name for compositions based upon, or suggestive of, a devotional or legendary narration. For F. Liszt's *Die Legende von der heiligen Elisabeth*, see under *Oratorio IV.

Leger lines. See *Ledger lines.

Leggiero, con leggerezza, leggiadro. Light and graceful, with slight pressure of the key or of the bow, and with a touch of non-legato [see *legato].

Legno [It., wood]. *Col legno* means, in violin playing, tapping the strings with the stick of the bow, instead of bowing them. *Stromenti di legno*, wood-wind instruments.

Leich [G.]. See *Lai.

Leicht [G.]. Light.

Leidenschaftlich [G.]. Passionate.

Leier [G.]. Usually, the *lyre. In earlier usage, the *hurdy-gurdy (*Drehleier, Radleier, Bettlerleier*). Schubert's well-known song, *Der Leiermann*, portrays a

player of the hurdy-gurdy (not of the street organ; see *Leierkasten).

Leierkasten [G.]. Street organ.

Leise [G.]. Soft.

Leise [G.]. Medieval congregational hymns in the German tongue, so called because of their refrain: kyrie *eleis*(on) which was abbreviated into *kirleis* or *leis*. The oldest specimen, *Unsar trohtin*, dates from the 9th century. Several Protestant chorales belong to this category, e.g., *Nun bitten wir den heiligen Geist*, and *Christ ist erstanden* [cf. *AdHM*, 448]. There is frequent confusion of the terms Leise and *Leich [cf. *GD* i, 636].

Leiter [G.]. (1) Scale (Tonleiter).— (2) Leader of an orchestra.

Leitmotif [German spelling *Leitmotiv*, i.e., leading motive]. A term coined by R. Wagner's friend H. von Wolzogen (in "Motive in Wagner's Götterdämmerung," *Musikalisches Wochenblatt*, 1887; Wagner himself had used the term *Grundthema*, basic theme) to denote the funda-

mental method of composition in Wagner's later operas, that is, the representation of the acting personalities, of typical situations, and of recurrent ideas by musical motives. For instance, in the *Ring des Nibelungs* there are motives characterizing the Ring (Ex. 1), the Contract (Ex. 2), Valhalla (Ex. 3), the Sword (Ex. 4), etc. These leitmotifs are used, not as rigidly fixed melodies, but in a very flexible manner, frequently modifying their rhythm, intervals, according to the special requirement of the momentary situation [see *Metamorphosis]. It should be noticed that the extensive "Tables of Leitmotifs" usually found in the popular editions of Wagner's operas are not by him, nor are any of the names they bear.

Undoubtedly, enthusiastic writers and editors have gone too far in their search for leitmotifs and in their dogmatic tabulation which is obstructive rather than conducive to an understanding of the true meaning of this device.

Although Wagner was the first to make consistent use of the leitmotif, his method is adumbrated in various earlier compositions. In Grétry's *Richard Coeur de Lion* (1785) the theme "Une fièvre brûlante" [cf. *AdHM*, 747; Beethoven wrote variations on it] appears nine times. Mozart in his *Don Giovanni* uses the same motive for the two appearances of the dead Commendatore (Act II, Scenes iii and v). In Méhul's *Ariodante* (1799), a characteristic theme called "cri de fureur" is used repeatedly to express the vengeance of the deceived lover [cf. *AdHM*, 748]. A well-known example, though outside the field of opera, is the *idée fixe* of Berlioz' Symphony Fantastique. The recurrent use of thematic material in Carl Loewe's *Balladen* may also be mentioned. Many of the post-Wagnerian operatic composers (Richard Strauss, Pfitzner, d'Indy) have adopted Wagner's procedure, which also had an influence on symphonic music, particularly the symphonic poem.

Lit.: K.Wörner, *Beiträge zur Geschichte des Leitmotivs in der Oper* (Diss. Berlin 1931); id., *ZMW* xiv; M. Lamm, *Entwicklung des musikalischen Motivs in den Tondramen R. Wagners* (Diss. Vienna 1932); L. Sabanew, "Remarks on the Leitmotiv" (*ML* xiii, no. 2); G. E. H. Abraham, "The Leitmotiv since Wagner" (*ML* vi, no. 2); E. Haraszti, "Le Problème du leit-motif" (*RM* iv).

Leitton [G.]. Leading tone.

Lento [It.]. Slow. See *Tempo marks.

Leonora Overtures. The three overtures which Beethoven wrote for his opera *Fidelio*, prior to the final overture, known as Fidelio (or, somewhat incorrectly, Leonora no. 4) Overture. Leonora no. 2 was written for a performance in 1805, no. 3 for one in 1806, no. 1 for a performance planned at Prague, in 1807. The name refers to the original title of

the opera *Leonore*. The Fidelio Overture was written in 1814.

Lesson. Seventeenth- and 18th-century name for English instrumental pieces, particularly for the harpsichord or the organ. The term does not imply any special connotation of form or style, nor necessarily a pedagogical purpose; in fact, it would seem to be just as general and, therefore, meaningless, as the modern term "piece." In the 17th century the term is frequently used for a suite (Suite of Lessons), e.g., in Matthew Locke's *Melothesia, A Choice Collection of Lessons for the Harpsichord and the Organ* (1673). In the 18th century we find organ-verses as well as sonata-like compositions thus named.

Letter notation. The use of letters for the indication of tones is restricted today to theoretical and instructive purposes; see *Pitch names. In earlier periods they were also used for the writing down of music. This usage occurred first in ancient Greece [see *Notation II]. In the Middle Ages the letters a, b, c, . . . were used in different ways for the tones of the diatonic scale [cf. *ApNPM*, 27]. A system starting with the letter A for the tone c seems to have been employed chiefly in connection with certain instruments, such as the monochord, or sets of bells (*nolae, tintinnabulae*). Two other methods of a more advanced character are given below:

(1)		a	b	c	d	e	f	g	h	i
(2)	Γ	A	B	C	D	E	F	G	a	b
Modern:	G	A	B	c	d	e	f	g	a	b

(1)		k	l	m	n	o	p			
(2)		c	d	e	f	g	a⎬	b⎬	c⎬	
Modern:		c'	d'	e'	f'	g'	a'	b'	c"	

The method (1) which is frequently (but with doubtful justification) called *Boethian notation* is of interest because its letters were used in various books of Gregorian chant to clarify the pitch of the neumatic signs, e.g., in the Antiphonarium Montpellier, *H. 159* [cf. *Editions XXIII, A, 7,8; also *WoHN* i, opp. p. 44], as well as for the setting down of early two-part compositions [cf. *ApNPM*, 207f]. The system (2), usually known as *Guidonian letters*, already occurs in the treatise of

Oddo of Clugny [see *Theorists] and is therefore more properly termed *Oddonic* (*Odoistic*) *letters*. This system was universally adopted for theoretical and demonstrative purposes, for which it is used, with minor modifications, to the present day. In the 16th century, however, it attained practical significance in the German keyboard tablatures and in the French lute tablatures [see *Tablatures]. See also *Romanian letters.

Leuto. Old Italian spelling for *lauto*, lute.

Levalto. See *Volta (1).

Levare [It.]. To take off. *Si levano i sordini*, take off the mutes.

Levatio, levazione [It.]. *Elevation.

L.H. Left hand.

L'homme armé [F., "The armed man"]. A 15th-century French folk song [according to Pietro Aron's *Toscanello* (1523) by Busnois, who probably was the first to set it polyphonically] which rose to immortality because of its frequent use as a tenor of polyphonic Masses [see *Mass B, II (b) and (d)]. The tune, with

L'hom-me l'hom-me l'homme ar- me'

L'homme ar- mé doibt on dou- ter.

On a fait par tout cri-er Que chas-cun se vienque ar-

Da capo al ∩

mer D'un hau-bre-gon de fer.

its recently discovered text [cf. D. Plamenac, in *Rapport sur le congrès archéologique et historique* (Bruges, 1925)], is here reproduced. There exist more than thirty Masses based on this melody (*Missa l'homme armé*). Among the composers were Dufay [cf. *HAM*, no. 67], Busnois, Caron, Ockeghem [cf. *HAM*, no. 73], Obrecht, Tinctoris, Josquin, Brumel, de

la Rue [cf. *HAM*, no. 92], Pipelaere, Senfl, de Orto, Morales, Palestrina, and, in the 17th century, Carissimi. In 1930, Joh. N. David composed a "Fantasia super L'homme armé." Cf. O. Strunk, in *BAMS* ii; O. Gombosi, in *ZMW* x, xi, xii.

Libraries. The making known of the contents of music libraries on a comprehensive scale is one of the uncompleted tasks of musicology. A beginning was made by Robert Eitner in his *Biographisch-bibliographisches Quellen-Lexikon* (Leipzig, 1900–04, 10 vols.) and its supplement, *Miscellanea musicae bio-bibliographica* (Leipzig, 1912–16, 3 vols.), which together list and locate in libraries the principal MS and early printed sources for the period up to about 1800. The discovery of much new material and, in particular, the rapid development of United States collections since the turn of the century have made the *Q-L*, though still indispensable, inadequate for contemporary needs.

The compilation of a new "world-Eitner" would take account, as he did, of the necessary preliminary work of organizing and cataloguing collections of music and the publication of their catalogues. A "Catalogue of music catalogues," which might well be a first step in this program, has been in the course of compilation at the headquarters of the International Society for Musicology in Basle [cf. *AM* v, 141].

In the absence of a modern *Q-L*, the musicologist must rely on a knowledge of the principal general and special union lists now available, a practical working knowledge of the contents of the principal collections of musical material, familiarity with the existing published catalogues of these collections, and acquaintance with the principal literature on music library resources.

In the lists below an attempt is made to present this information systematically for the principal geographical regions. Mention is made, however, only of the few most outstanding collections of research materials in each country. For the others, the cited literature must be consulted. In the case of the United States, the information is preceded by an account of some general developments of library resources and services.

I. *United States.* At the time of the appointment of O. G. Sonneck as chief of the music division of the Library of Congress (1902), only a few libraries in the United States possessed notable research material in music [cf. Sonneck in *SIM* v, 329ff]. The development of these resources at the Library of Congress by Sonneck and his successors, Carl Engel, Oliver Strunk, and Harold Spivacke, has been the most notable of any single United States Library. Other public reference collections have grown substantially, however, and while libraries in the United States can never be expected, in the nature of the case, to equal the richness of European collections in primary sources, in some special fields they are equal or superior to European libraries, even in European material. Music has also shared in the development of general library services. Among these, the system of inter-library loans has been of great value in making library resources more generally available. (For the code under which this system operates, cf. American Library Association, *Bulletin* 34: 199–200, March, 1940, and, with revisions, *Library Journal* 65: 802–3, Oct. 1, 1940.) Intercontinental library loans, while made to a limited extent when conditions were favorable, may be expected to be virtually eliminated in the future by the development of inexpensive processes of photoduplication. These have, in fact, reduced the number of such loans made within single countries.

A. *Photoduplication.* A comparatively recent development that has greatly expanded the resources of libraries is the application of microphotography to the duplication of library materials. Many libraries have taken advantage of this inexpensive method of securing copies of rare material, and several coöperative projects among United States libraries have resulted in the copying of very large quantities of early material in history and literature. General projects in which mu-

sic is included are the filming by the Library of Congress of Americana in United States libraries, and the copying of irreplaceable material in English libraries which was begun in the summer of 1941 with the financial support of the Rockefeller Foundation. American musicologists have supplied lists of desiderata for both projects. In both, negatives will be deposited in the Library of Congress and copies made available to other libraries and to scholars.

A special project in music is the Music Microfilm Archive, Otto E. Albrecht, director, which is supplying subscribers, with 2500 frames a year. Material to be copied is selected from an as yet unpublished census of European music MSS in the United States, compiled by Dr. Albrecht. Material which has been filmed by the Archive is included in the *Union List of Microfilms*, cited below. Films sent to subscribers in 1941–42 include such items as holographs of Mozart's symphony K. 318 and of the first symphonies of Schumann and Brahms; three MSS of English virginal music; Spohr's unpublished opera, *Alruna*; and the Laborde and Mellon chansonniers.

Lit.: *Journal of Documentary Reproduction* (1938–; general and technical articles and bibliographies); R. C. Cibella, *Directory of Microfilm Sources* (1941); *Union List of Microfilms*, Philadelphia Bibliographical Center (1942); O. E. Albrecht, "Microfilms and musicology" [*PAMS*, 1938].

B. *Phonograph Records.* Nearly all United States music libraries with an organized music collection have added phonograph records to their materials in recent years. Usually equipment is provided for playing the records on the premises, but some libraries circulate records also. The Carnegie Corporation of New York has aided this development substantially through its College Music Set (catalogues 1933 and 1937). This contains a basic stock of books, music, and records, and has been presented to institutions to enable them to expand their music instruction. The phonograph record is also the medium for the collection and preservation of a vast folk song literature. The largest collection is in the Archive of American Folk Song, Division of Music, Library of Congress (cf. its *Check List of Recorded Songs in the English Language to July 1940*, Washington, 1942, 3 vols.), from which copies are available to libraries and scholars. The contents of other United States collections are summarized in George Herzog's *Research in Primitive and Folk Music in the United States*, Washington, 1936 (Bulletin no. 24 of the American Council of Learned Societies).

C. *Music Library Association.* This association, founded in 1931, aims to further the development of collections of music in the United States and Canada. It has contributed substantially to the solution of technical problems and has initiated important projects in cataloguing of music and phonograph records, bibliography, indexing of periodicals, microfilming, etc. Its publication, *Notes*, 1934–, issued four times yearly, should be consulted for numerous articles on Association projects and activities.

D. *Catalogues and Union Lists.* For information on general works that locate material in United States libraries, cf. C. M. Winchell, *Locating Books for Interlibrary Loan* (1930) and I. G. Mudge, *Guide to Reference Books* (6th ed., 1936, and supplements, 1939 and 1941). Some of those most important and useful for the musical material they contain are: the union catalogue at the Library of Congress (contains literature only, not music, with location of copies in United States libraries); S. de Ricci, *Census of Medieval and Renaissance Mss. in the United States and Canada* (1935–40, 3 vols.); M. B. Stillwell, *Incunabula in American Libraries* (1940); *Union List of Serials in Libraries of the United States and Canada* (1927, and 2 supplements, 1931–33; new edition in press, Summer, 1942); *Union List of Microfilm* (literature and music, with locations of originals and of film copies). Catalogues of this kind devoted especially to musical material are the Albrecht *Census* mentioned above and a revision (1934), in the Music Division of

the New York Public Library, of the Library of Congress' *Catalogue of Early Books on Music* as a union list of this material in United States libraries.

E. *General Literature on United States Music Collections.* Music Teachers' National Association, *Music Departments of Libraries* (1922; Bulletin, 1921, no. 33, of the U. S. Bureau of Education); "Libraries and Collections of Music . . . United States of America" (*GD* iii, 185 and Suppl. Vol., 360); O. Strunk, *State and Resources of Musicology in the United States* (1932; Bulletin no. 19 of the American Council of Learned Societies), supplemented by the Council's *Report on Publication and Research in Musicology* (1938); L. R. McColvin, *Music Libraries*, vol. 2 (1938, pp. 274–292); O. E. Albrecht, "Music Libraries in Philadelphia" (*Overtones*, Dec., 1939 and reprinted).

F. *Principal Public Reference Collections. Library of Congress, Division of Music.* In extent (*c.* 1,500,000 volumes and pieces) and richness of resources, one of the greatest music libraries of the world. To its virtually complete American material, secured through the provisions of the copyright act, have been added comprehensive collections of music and literature of all countries and periods. The Coolidge and Whittall foundations in the Division have made it a center for the advancement and performance of chamber music, and have also enriched its notable collection of holographs, most recently with those belonging to the late Jerome Stonborough of Vienna. The Archive of American Folk Song is a section of the Music Division. One copy of each of the Library's printed catalogue cards is contained in the Library of Congress depository catalogues, which are available in the larger public and university libraries throughout the country. This author catalogue is being lithoprinted and will be available in book form, covering holdings as of June 30, 1942. Like the depository catalogue it will contain an entry for every title for which cards have been printed, that is, for nearly all of the Library's books about music but almost none of its music. Special catalogues, all prepared by or under the direction of Sonneck, are: Dramatic music, full scores, 1908; Orchestral music, scores, 1912; Early books on music to 1800, 1913; Opera librettos printed before 1800, 1914, 2 vols. (the world's largest collection of this material).

Lit.: Reports of the chief of the music division are contained in the annual report of the Librarian of Congress, 1903–, and were also separately reprinted from 1928/29 to 1939/40. These are the best sources of information on the growth of the collection and the expansion of its services.

New York Public Library. The music division of the reference department has a collection of more than 110,000 volumes and pieces, including valuable early theoretical works, tablatures, and opera and orchestral scores. Special collections include United States music, songs, and portraits of musicians. The Division has published scores and parts of otherwise unavailable early music from its own and other collections, including *Early Psalmody in America*, Series I–III. Cf. *Catalogue of Music Available in Black Line Print*, 1935, and unpublished supplements. Cf. H. Botstiber, in *SIM* iv; O. Kinkeldey in *Library Journal* 40: 589–592 (Aug., 1915); and the annual *Report* of the Library, especially Kinkeldey in vol. 36 (1932) on the accessions at the Wolffheim sale.

Boston Public Library. An important general collection of more than 43,000 volumes, with several European and United States rarities and autographs. A catalogue of the reference collection, the gift of Allen A. Brown, was published in 1916, 3 vols. and supplement.

Newberry Library, Chicago. A well-developed collection of about 20,000 volumes with especially good collections of periodicals and American hymnology. A number of important rarities are described in the chapter on the music collection in the Library's *Handbook*, 1938.

Henry M. Huntington Library and Art Gallery, San Marino, California. Like the general collection, the music is chiefly English and American. In two fields it is probably the strongest in the United States: English music printed before 1640 and musical incunabula. *Catalogues: Printed Music, 1467–1800, in the Huntington library* (2500 items), compiled by Edythe N. Backus (to be published); *Early English Music, 1540–1640* (90 items), No. 7 of the Library's price lists of photostats. Cf. E. N. Backus in Music Library Association, *Notes*, no. 7, May, 1940, and no. 14, Aug., 1942.

Folger Shakespeare Library, Washington. Notable for its substantially complete collection of original editions of English music and musical theory of the period 1588–1623.

G. *Colleges and Universities.* A few of the larger university collections of music are equal in size and importance to some of the principal reference collections named above. The *Sibley Musical Library* of the Eastman School of Music, University of Rochester, contains more than 40,000 volumes, including an exceedingly well-developed general collection and much important source material. Cf. C. Engel, in *AM* v, no. 1 (a list of recent accessions), and the annual reports of the University library. The collections at Harvard and Yale are also outstanding among university libraries, the former especially for its *Isham Library* of organ and early keyboard music, containing photostatic copies of the principal MS and early printed works in the field. A special collection at Yale is the *Lowell Mason Collection* of church music.

In addition to Eastman, Harvard, and Yale, the best developed collections are at Columbia, Princeton, Smith, and Vassar, and also at California, Cornell, North Carolina, and Wellesley.

The principal conservatory libraries are those of the Curtis Institute of Music, Philadelphia; New England Conservatory of Music, Boston; Oberlin Conservatory of Music, Oberlin, Ohio; Juilliard School of Music and Institute of Musical Art, New York; and Peabody Conservatory of Music, Baltimore.

H. *Public Circulating Libraries.* The public libraries of a number of the larger cities have well-developed general music collections available for circulation. For the most part these libraries emphasize music in practical rather than historical editions, and musical literature in English. A collection of phonograph records is usually provided, and many of these are operated on a circulating basis. The largest collection of this kind, also notable for its collection of music of the 20th century, is the Music Library of the Circulation Department of the New York Public Library. Other well-developed music collections are in the public libraries of the following cities: Baltimore (Enoch Pratt Library); Boston (in addition to the reference collection described above); Chicago; Cleveland (including the White collection of folklore); Detroit; Los Angeles; Minneapolis; Northampton, Mass. (Forbes Library); Philadelphia (which also houses the unequaled Fleisher collection of orchestral scores and parts, Catalogue, 1933); Portland, Oregon; Providence, R. I.; St. Louis; and San Francisco.

II. *Latin America.* Although the musical contents of some of the archives and libraries in Latin America are unquestionably rich, little is known about them. For a preliminary survey, cf. C. S. Smith, "Music Libraries in South America" (Music Library Association, *Notes*, no. 11, Aug., 1941). Further information, when available, may be expected to appear in the music and libraries sections of the *Handbook of Latin American Studies* (1935–), the basic bibliography in this field, and in a guide to Latin American music being compiled by Gilbert Chase of the music division, Library of Congress.

III. *Europe.* The subsequent survey lists the most important of the European music libraries. Numerous others are described in *GD*.

Lit.: E. Vogel, "Die Musikbibliotheken nach ihrem wesentlichsten Bestande aufgeführt" (*JMP* i); "Libraries and Collections of Music . . . Europe" (*GD* iii, 150; Suppl. Vol., 350); G. Kinsky, in *Philobiblon* vi, 55–67 (1933); L. R. McColvin, *Music Libraries*, ii (1938), 213–274; C. S. Smith, in Thompson's *International Cyclopedia* (1939), pp. 1003–09.

A. *Belgium and Holland.* Lit.: J. G.

Prod'homme, "Les Institutions musicales . . . en Belgique et en Hollande" (*SIM* xv); C. van den Borren, "Inventaire des manuscrits de musique polyphonique . . . en Belgique" (*AM* v, nos. 2–4; vi, nos. 1–3).

Brussels. Bibliothèque Royale. A principal part of this library consists of the Fétis collection. Catalogue: Brussels, 1877. — *Conservatoire Royale de Musique.* Important 16th-century MSS, Italian opera librettos of the 17th–18th centuries, best collection of C. P. E. Bach. Catalogue by A. Wotquenne, 1898–1912, 4 vols. and supplement (librettos), 1901.

The Hague. The Scheuerleer Museum houses the greater part of the library and instrument collection of the late D. F. Scheuerleer (1855–1927). Catalogues 1893–1910, 3 vols., and 1923–25, 2 vols.

B. *France. Paris. Bibliothèque Nationale.* Unrivaled collection of French music, printed and MS, from the earliest times. Catalogue by J. Écorcheville, 1910–14, 8 vols. The books on music are contained in the Library's *Catalogue général des livres imprimés*, 1900– (158 vols., A to Rukser, to 1939). — *Conservatoire Nationale de Musique.* Important early and general material, with outstanding collection of holographs. Catalogues: of part of the early material, by J. B. T. Weckerlin, 1885; of the Fonds Blancheton (important for the early symphony), by L. de La Laurencie, 1930–31, 2 vols.; of the *Philidor MSS, by E. H. Fellowes in *ML* xii. Cf. J. G. Prod'homme, "Two Musical Libraries of Paris" (*MQ* xxiv); articles on the manuscripts of special composers and in special categories in *RdM*, 1926–32.

C. *Germany and Austria.* The *Deutscher Gesamtkatalog*, a union catalogue of printed books in sixteen German and Austrian libraries, has been in course of publication since 1931 (14 vols., A to Beeth, to 1939). It contains musical literature, including librettos.

Berlin. Preussische Staatsbibliothek. One of the largest and richest collections in the world, especially notable for its manuscripts of the German classic masters. Cf. W. Altmann in *ZMW* iii, 426ff, on the history and organization of the music department; in ii–ix, lists of the more important current acquisitions; J. Wolf in *AM* iii, 119 and 171 (acquisitions, 1928–31).

Breslau. The Stadtbibliothek contains the collection of 16th–17th-century works scored by Emil Bohn. Cf. his *Bibliographie der Musik-Druckwerke bis 1700* (1883), a catalogue of material in three Breslau libraries.

Dresden. Sächsische Landesbibliothek. Catalogue by Eitner and Kade, 1890 (Beilage to *MfM*). The original musical manuscripts are catalogued by A. Reicherts in vol. 4 of L. Schmidt's general catalogue of the Library's MS, 1923.

Leipzig. Musikbibliothek Peters. An exceedingly well-developed general collection, founded and maintained by the music publishing house of C. F. Peters. Catalogues: R. Schwartz, *Katalog I: Bücher und Schriften*; *id.*, "Bach Manuscripte" (1910) (*JMP* xxvi). Publication of a list of the library's holdings of material of the kind listed in Eitner was begun in *JMP* xlvi.

Munich. Staatsbibliothek. One of the world's great collections, particularly rich in MS and printed works of the 16th century. Catalogue of the manuscripts to 1700 by J. J. Maier, 1879.

Vienna. Nationalbibliothek. Besides a rich collection of early MS and printed material, this library houses the von Hoboken collection of photostats of manuscripts of the classic masters. Part of the Library's MSS, catalogued by J. Mantuani, are listed in vols. 9–10, 1897–99, of its general catalogue of manuscripts. The Este collection, now in the Nationalbibliothek, has been catalogued by R. Haas (Regensburg, 1927). Cf. R. Haas, in *ZMW* vi, viii, ix, xi (lists of important acquisitions) and in *JMP* xxxvii (history of the collection). — *Gesellschaft der Musikfreunde.* Exceedingly rich collection, including, among others, the libraries of Gerber, Köchel, and Brahms. Notable MSS of the Viennese classical composers. Cf. K. Geiringer in *Anbruch* xix (history of the collection).

D. *Great Britain.* Cf. W. H. Frere,

Biblioteca liturgica: a descriptive handlist of the Latin liturgical mss. of the Middle Ages preserved in the libraries of Great Britain and Ireland, 2 vols. (1901–32).

Cambridge. Fitzwilliam Museum. Important MSS are the *Fitzwilliam Virginal Book* and a large Handel collection. Catalogue by J. A. Fuller-Maitland (1893). — *University Library.* The musical resources of the University library have been augmented by the deposit on loan, since 1936, of the great private library of Paul Hirsch, formerly of Frankfurt. Catalogue, by Hirsch and Kathi Meyer, 3 vols. (1928–36) and a fourth in preparation.

London. British Museum. One of the world's great collections, with exceptional resources in MS and printed music and musical literature of all countries and periods. Catalogues: *Ms. Music,* by A. Hughes-Hughes, 3 vols. (1906–09); *Printed Music published between 1487 and 1800,* by W. Barclay Squire, 2 vols. (1912), including 1st supplement, 2d supplement, by Wm. C. Smith (1940). An accessions catalogue of modern printed music has been published since 1884. Printed books on music are contained in the Museum's catalogue of printed books, 1881–1900 and supplements to 1905; new edition, 1931– (32 vols., A to Carr, to 1941). The King's Music Library, on permanent deposit in the Museum, is best known for its unexcelled collection of Handel MSS. Catalogue, by W. Barclay Squire and Hilda Andrews, 3 vols. (1927–29). — *Royal College of Music.* An extensive collection, with much valuable printed and MS material. Catalogues, by W. Barclay Squire: Printed music (1909); MSS (more than 4000), unpublished typescript, with copies at British Museum, Bodleian (Oxford), and Cambridge University library.

Tenbury. St. Michael's College. Important MSS, including 350 volumes of the Toulouse-Philidor collection of 17th–18th-century French music [see *Philidor, Collection]. Catalogue by E. H. Fellowes (Paris, 1935); and, of the Philidor MSS, in *ML* xii, no. 2.

E. *Italy.* The *Associazione dei musicologi italiani* has been publishing since

1909 catalogues of early music and theoretical works, printed and MS, existing in Italian libraries and archives, public and private. In 1930–31 Albert Smijers began preparation of a card catalogue of MS compositions by Netherlands composers of the 15th and 16th centuries which are in Italian libraries. Copies are at the Netherlands Historical Institute in Rome and at the musicological institute of the University of Utrecht. Cf. H. Antcliffe in *Chesterian* xvii, 112–115 (March, 1936).

Bologna. Liceo Musicale. One of the principal collections of the world, comprising, among others, the library of Padre Martini. Catalogue, by G. Gaspari and others, 4 vols. (1890–1905).

Florence. Biblioteca Nazionale Centrale. Cf. *Mostra bibliografica di musica italiana* . . . (1937; catalogue of an exhibition of the principal musical treasures of the city's libraries). — The *Biblioteca Medviceo-Laurenziana* possesses two of the most precious medieval music manuscripts, *plut. 29, 1,* the most extensive source of the School of Notre Dame [see *Magnus liber organi] and *Pal. 87,* the Squarcialupi Codex [see *Sources, no. 13].

Rome. Vatican Library. Like the other collections of the city, especially notable for its liturgical MSS. Catalogue of the music archives of the Papal chapel by F. X. Haberl, 1888 (Beilage to *MfM*).

F. *Spain. Barcelona. Biblioteca Musical de la Diputació.* Important early printed and MS works, especially of Spain and Italy. Catalogue by F. Pedrell, 1908–09, 2 vols.

Madrid. Biblioteca Nacional. Valuable MS and printed works by composers of Spain, Italy, and the Netherlands.

R. S. A.

Librement [F.]. Freely.

Libretto [It., little book]. The text book of an opera, oratorio, etc. Famous writers of librettos (librettists) were: Rinuccini, fl. *c.* 1600 (for Peri, Caccini, Monteverdi); Philippe Quinault, 1635–88 (for Lully); Pietro Metastasio, 1698–1782 (for A. Scarlatti, Hasse, Handel, Mozart); Raniero de Calzabigi, 1714–95 (for Gluck);

Lorenzo da Ponte, 1749–1838 (for Mozart's *Figaro, Così fan tutte,* and *Don Giovanni*); Eugène Scribe, 1791–1861 (for Auber, Meyerbeer, Halévy, Boildieu); Arrigo Boito, 1842–1918 (for Verdi's *Otello* and *Falstaff*); Hugo v. Hofmannsthal (for R. Strauss); William Gilbert, 1836–1911 (for Sullivan). Richard Wagner set a new turn in the history of the libretto by writing his own texts, and by insisting upon a degree of unification between text and music theretofore unknown. His example was followed by Cornelius, Pfitzner, Schreker, and others.

Large collections of librettos of early operas (17th and 18th centuries) exist at the Library of Congress (Collection A. Schatz) and in various European libraries [cf. *RiML*, 1035].

Lit.: O. G. T. Sonneck, *Catalogue of Opera Librettos printed before 1800* (2 vols., 1914); E. Istel, *The Art of Writing Opera Librettos* (1922); E. de Bricqueville, *Le Livret d'opéra français de Lully à Gluck* (1888); M. Ehrenstein, *Die Operndichtung der deutschen Romantik* (1918); F. Vatielli, "Operisti-librettisti dès scoli XVII e XVIII" (*RMI* xliii); H. Prunières, "I Libretti dell' opera veneziana nel secolo XVII" (*LRM* iii); T. M. Baroni in *RMI* xii (Metastasio); M. Callegori in *RMI* xxvi, xxviii (Metastasio).

Licenza, con alcuna [It., with some liberty]. Indication of some license of performance, or of composition, e.g., *canone con alcuna licenza.*

Liceo [It.]. Name of various Italian conservatories, e.g.: Liceo Padre Martini (Bologna, also known simply as Liceo Musicale, famous for its library; see *Libraries III, E); Liceo Rossini (Pesaro); Liceo B. Marcello (Venice); Liceo Verdi (Torino); etc.

Lichanos [Gr.]. See *Greek music II (a).

Liebesfuss [G.]. The pear-shaped bell of the English horn and the oboe d'amore.

Liebesgeige; -oboe [G.]. Viola d'amore; oboe d'amore.

Lied [G.]. A song in the German vernacular. The history of the Lied can be divided into the following periods: I. Minnesinger and Meistersinger (*c.* 1250–1550); II. The polyphonic Lied (15th/16th century); III. The accompanied Lied ("Generalbass-lied") of the Baroque (1600–1750); IV. The "volkstümliches Lied" (1775–1825); V. The "German Lied" of the 19th century.

I. See *Minnesinger, *Meistersinger.

II. The 15th-century composers Oswald von Wolckenstein (1377–1445) and the Münch von Salzburg (fl. *c.* 1400) were the first to write polyphonic songs, rather primitive imitations of 14th-century French models or of still earlier styles [cf. O. Ursprung, in *AMW* iv, v; *DTOe* 9]. Important collections of 15th-century folk songs, some monophonic, some in polyphonic setting, are the *Glogauer*, the *Münchner*, and the *Lochamer Liederbuch* [see *Liederbuch]. The polyphonic songs of Adam v. Fulda and of Heinrich Finck (1445–1527) show remarkable progress of style (true polyphonic treatment, imitation), thus leading to the masterly compositions of Heinrich Isaac (1450–1517; cf. *DTOe* 14.i; *HAM*, no. 87), Paulus Hofhaimer (1459–1537; cf. H. J. Moser, *Paulus Hofhaimer*, 1929; *HAM*, no. 93), Stoltzer (1480–1526; *DdT* 65; *HAM*, no. 108), and Ludwig Senfl (1490–after 1540; cf. *DdT*, no. 34; *Editions XII A, 10; *HAM*, no. 110). Isaac's "Innsbruck ich muss dich lassen" became one of the oldest and most beautiful folk songs in the German language. Important sources of real German folk song are Senfl's *quodlibets in which many popular songs of his day are cited. Important collections of polyphonic songs are G. Forster's five books *Ein Ausszug guter alter und neuer teutscher Liedlein* (Nürnberg, 1539–56; the second book, *Frische teutsche Liedlein*, republished by Eitner; see *Editions XXVI, 29), and G. Ott's *115 guter neuer Liedlein* (1544, republished by Eitner; see *Editions XXVI, 1–4). In the second half of the 16th century Orlando di Lasso composed numerous German texts with his never-failing imagination and dexterity [*Newe Teutsche Liedlein mit fünff*

Stimmen, 3 vols., 1567, '72, '76; *Newe Teutsche Lieder . . . mit vier Stimmen*, 1583, etc.; cf. the complete ed., vol. xxi]. In the works of the foreigners, Mattheus Le Maistre (d. 1577), Antonio Scandello (1517–80), and Jacob Regnart (1540–99), the lighter vein of the Italian *canzonette and the "Bauernharmonie" (peasant harmony) of the *villanella superseded the polyphonic style of the earlier period [cf. *Editions XXVI, 19; *SchGMB*, no. 139]. The two great masters from the end of the 16th century, Leonhard Lechner (1553–1606; *Neue Teutsche Lieder*, 1582, new ed. by E. F. Schmid, 1926) and Hans Leo Hassler (1564–1612; *Canzonette and Neue teutsche Gesäng*, 1596, new ed. in *DTB* 5.ii; *Lustgarten*, 1601, new ed. cf. *Editions XXVI, 15) combine a *fin de siècle* refinement of technique with a typically German depth of feeling and expression [see *Madrigal IV]. The development of the polyphonic Lied came to an end with Johann Hermann Schein (1586–1630; *Venuskränzlein*, 1609; *Musica boscareccia*, 1621; cf. complete ed. by A. Prüfer, vols. i, ii; also *SchGMB*, nos. 187, 188).

III. The accompanied solo-Lied of the Baroque period ("Generalbass-lied," i.e., song with thorough-bass accompaniment) made its first appearance in Johann Nauwach's (*c.* 1595–?) *Erster Theil teutscher Villanellen mit 1, 2 und 3 Stimmen* (1627), in Johann Staden's (1581–1634) *Hertzenstrosts-Musica* (1630) and *Geistlicher Musik-Klang* (1633), in Thomas Selle's (1599–1663) *Deliciorum juvenilium decas* (1634), and *Monophonetica* (1636) [cf. H. J. Moser, †*Alte Meister des deutschen Liedes*, 1931]. With H. Albert's (1604–51) *Arien* (1638/50; *DdT* 12, 13; cf. also *HAM*, no. 205; *SchGMB*, no. 193) and Andreas Hammerschmidt's *Weltliche Oden* (1642/49; cf. Moser, *Alte Meister*; *SchGMB*, no. 194) it freed itself from the Italian model and became a truly German type of song, combining popular simplicity with artistic taste. This development reached its high-point in the inspired songs of Adam Krieger (1634–66; cf. *DdT* 19; H. Osthoff, *Adam Krieger*, 1929; *HAM*, no. 228; *SchGMB*, no. 209) who used the instrumental ritornello to be played at the end of each stanza. This "ritornello-Lied" was also cultivated by Johann Erasmus Kindermann (1616–55; cf. *DTB* 21/24), Johannes Theile (1646–1724; cf. *SchGMB*, no. 210), and Philipp Heinrich Erlebach (1657–1714; cf. *DdT* 46/47). Towards the end of the century the religious song found a master in Johann Wolfgang Franck (1641–*c*. 1700; *Geistliche Lieder*, 1681–1700; new ed. *DdT* 45). The arias of Bach and Handel deserve only passing mention here since they do not properly fall under the category Lied. In fact, during the first half of the 18th century the Lied practically ceased to exist, giving way to the elaborate treatment of the aria. On the other hand, a great number of Lieder occur, under the name aria, in the operas of Joh. Sigismund Cousser [*SchGMB*, no. 250], Reinhard Keiser [*SchGMB*, nos. 268, 269], Telemann, etc. Sperontes' *Singende Muse an der Pleisse*, 1742/45 [*DdT* 35, 36; cf. *SchGMB*, no. 289] gives a good cross section of the period of deterioration and disintegration of the Generalbass-lied. Cf. also *DdT* 57 for songs (*Oden*) by Telemann and Görner.

IV. Matters took a new turn after 1750 when Johan Adam Hiller (1728–1804), the founder of the *Singspiel, replaced the worn-out pathos of the late Baroque by an affected expression of naïveté in songs which he frequently addressed to children [*Lieder für Kinder* (1769); *Geistliche Lieder für Kinder* (1774); *Der Kinderfreund* (1782); cf. Moser, *Alte Meister*]. J. A. P. Schulz (1747–1800) found a more genuine expression of folk-like simplicity (*Volkston*; see *Volkstümliches Lied*), while other members of the second *Berlin School, such as J. F. Reichardt (1753–1814) and K. F. Zelter (1758–1832), introduced a new lyricism, particularly in their settings of Goethe's poems. In the songs of Haydn, Mozart ("Das Veilchen"), and the early Beethoven this movement found its conclusion and artistic climax. Cf. *DTOe* 27.ii and 42.ii for a survey of the Viennese Lied from 1778 to 1815.

V. At the beginning of the greatest period of the German Lied stands Franz Schubert (1797–1828) who, after a few preliminary songs in traditional style, opened a new era with his *Gretchen am Spinnrad* (Oct. 19, 1814, "the birthday of the German Lied"), a miracle of musical art as well as of psychological intuition, being the work of a seventeen-year-old. There followed quickly a flood tide of immortal masterworks, including the *Erlkönig, Wanderer's Nachtlied, Der Tod und das Mädchen, Der Wanderer* (1815/16), later the song cycles *Die Schöne Müllerin* (1823), *Winterreise* (1827), and *Schwanengesang* (1828). Measured by the artistic perfection of these songs, even the most beautiful Lieder of Schumann and Brahms seem to be somewhat slight in imagination, and only Hugo Wolf's compositions stand the proof of comparison. It will suffice to add to the just-mentioned names those of Mendelssohn, Liszt, Wagner, Robert Franz (1815–92), Peter Cornelius (1824–74), Gustav Mahler (1860–1911), Richard Strauss (b. 1864), Hans Pfitzner (b. 1869), and Max Reger (1873–1916), in order to outline the development of the Romantic Lied.

The revolutionary tendencies of the 20th century found their first clear expression in Schönberg's *George-Lieder* (op. 15, 1907 and later) which, in addition to their novel harmonic style, show a new type of vocal (or, rather, un-vocal) line, a sort of speech-like declamation in which the rise and fall of the speaking voice is reflected in wide "atonal" steps of augmented fifths, octaves, etc. Hindemith's masterly *Marienleben* (op. 27, 1924), inspired by the constructive ideals and the polyphonic style of Bach, is a landmark which may well indicate the road to a new future of the Lied.

Lit.: O. Bie, *Das deutsche Lied* (1926); H. Bischoff, *Das deutsche Lied* (1905); M. Friedländer, *Das deutsche Lied im 18. Jahrhundert* (3 vols., 1902); H. Kretzschmar, *Geschichte des neuen deutschen Liedes i: Von Albert bis Zelter* (1911); W. K. von Jolizza, *Das Lied . . . bis zum Ende des 18. Jahrhunderts* (1910); H. Moser, †*Alte Meister des deutschen Liedes* (2d ed. 1931); id., †*Corydon* (1933);

M. Breslauer, *Das deutsche Lied bis zum 18. Jahrhundert* (1908; bibl.); A. Prüfer, *J. H. Schein und das weltliche Lied*; R. Velten, *Das ältere deutsche Lied unter dem Einfluss der italienischen Musik* (1915); H. Rosenberg, *Untersuchungen über die deutschen Liedweisen im 15. Jahrhundert* (Diss. Berlin 1931); H. H. Rosenwald, *Das deutsche Lied zwischen Schubert und Schumann* (Diss. Heidelberg 1931).

Periodicals: 15th cent.: O. Ursprung, in *AMW* iv, v, vi (bibl.); R. Eitner, in *MfM* viii, ix, xii (Beilagen); H. Riemann, in *SIM* vii; W. Krabbe, in *AMW* iv; J. Müller-Blattau, in *ZMW* xvii; *id.*, in *AMF* iii; R. Molitor, in *SIM* xii. — 16th cent.: R. Eitner, in *MfM* xxvi, xxxvii; F. Spitta, in *Riemann Festschrift* (1909); A. Becker, in *ZMW* i; H. J. Moser, in *JMP* xxxv. — 17th cent.: F. Noack, in *ZMW* i; P. Epstein, in *ZMW* x; W. Vetter, in *ZMW* x. — 18th cent.: M. Seiffert, in *Liliencron Festschrift* (1910); B. Seyfert, in *VMW* x; H. J. Moser, in *JMP* xxxix; G. Frotscher, in *ZMW* vi. — 19th cent.: E. Hughes, in *MQ* iii (Liszt); R. Gerber, in *JMP* xxxix (Brahms). — 20th cent.: H. Nathan, in *MM* xiv, no. 3. See also under *Minnesinger; *Meistersinger.

Liederbuch [G.]. A term commonly applied to 15th/16th-century collections of German songs, mainly: (a) *Lochamer Liederbuch, c.* 1450 [facsimile ed. by K. Ameln, 1925; description with transcriptions in *JMW* ii (1867); improved transcription by K. Ameln and by Escher-Lott (1926); cf. C. Ursprung, in *AMW* iv, v, vi; H. Rosenberg, in *ZMW* xiv; F. Müller-Blattau in *AMF* iii; see also *Fundamentum organisandi]. — (b) *Glogauer* [formerly: *Berliner*] *Liederbuch, c.* 1460 (new ed., see *Editions XII A, 4 and 8; also in *MfM* vi, no. 5 and viii, Beilage). — (c) *Münchner* (also *Walther's* or *Schedel's*) *Liederbuch, c.* 1460 [*MfM* vi, no. 10, and xii, Beilage; selection by H. Rosenberg in Bärenreiter Verlag].

The *Lochamer Liederbuch* is the most important source of early German folk song (some monophonic, some in three-voice composition). The two other collections contain, in addition to vocal pieces, interesting instrumental dances [see *Dance music II] and canons. For literature see under *Lied (15th century); also *BeMMR*, 229.

Important 16th-century publications are *Oeglin's Liederbuch* of 1512 and *Ott's Liederbuch* of 1544, both containing 4-part arrangements of songs [new ed. see *Editions XXVI, 9 and 1–4].

Liedercyclus, Liederkreis [G.]. *Song cycle.

Lieder ohne Worte [G.]. Songs without Words, the title of several of F. Mendelssohn's collections of piano pieces, written in the style of a Lied, that is, with a singable melody and a pianistic accompaniment, frequently in broken-chord patterns.

Liedertafel [G., song table]. A male singing society, founded by Zelter in 1809, the members of which at first sat around a table with refreshments. Various similar societies sprang up during the 19th century. More recently the name has been superseded by *Männergesangverein*.

Liedform [G.]. *Song-form.

Lieto [It.]. Joyous.

Lievemente [It.]. Lightly.

Ligatura [It.]. (1) *Ligature. — (2) In the 17th century, a tied note; see under *Durezza.

Ligatures. I. Notational signs of the 13th to the 16th centuries which combine two or more notes in a single graph. They developed in the late 12th century as square-shaped modifications of the neumes [see illustration; see also *Notation]. From these they inherited certain graphic peculiarities which can only be

understood as the result of this evolution, e.g., the initial stroke of the "descending" forms (1 and 3) which is lacking in the "ascending" forms (2 and 4). Although in plainsong and in the related bodies of monophonic music these signs are but graphic modifications of the neumes [see *Plainsong notation], they adopted definite rhythmic meanings in polyphonic music. The first step in this direction occurred in the modal notation of the School of Notre Dame, in the early 13th century. Here, ligatures are the ordinary notational signs for all the parts, single notes being used only for special reasons (long notes of the tenor). Their rhythmic evaluation depends entirely upon their grouping, according to the different rhythmic *modes [see *Square notation]. The rise of the *motet (c. 1225) greatly diminished the use of ligatures in the upper parts, owing to the presence of a full text in these parts. (The notes of a ligature must always be sung to one syllable; the inference, frequently found in modern writings, that parts written entirely in ligatures — e.g., the tenors of motets — indicate instrumental performance is wholly unfounded; in practically all cases such parts were sung as *vocalizations.) The final step in the development of the ligatures was made around 1250 by Franco of Cologne who succeeded in assigning an unambiguous metrical significance (independent of the modes) to each of the various shapes. His rules remained unaltered throughout the ensuing period of mensural notation. The subsequent explanations refer mainly to the period of white mensural notation (after 1450).

II. According to the number of notes contained in a ligature a distinction is made between *ligatura binaria* (two), *ternaria* (three), *quaternaria* (four), etc. In each of these categories there exists a variety of shapes which are designated by the terms *proprietas* and *perfectio*. The former of these refers to the modifications concerning the initial notes, the latter to those of the final note. The various types of the ligatura binaria are illustrated in the accompanying table in which *c.c.* means: *cum* (with) *proprietate et cum perfectione*; *s.c.*, *sine* (without) *proprietate et cum perfectione*, etc., while *c.o.p.* designates a special type, known as *cum*

opposita proprietate (*B* = *brevis*; *L* = longa; *S* = *semibrevis*):

	Desc.	Asc.	Value	
c.c.	♭	⌐	B	L
s.c.	⌐	⌐	L	L
c.s.	⌐	⌐	B	B
s.s.	⌐	⌐	L	B
c.o.p.	⌐ ⌐	⌐ ⌐	S	S

These principles cover also the various types of *ternaria, quaternaria*, since the middle notes occurring in these ligatures are (normally) always *B*.

For practical purposes the following set of rules may be used [cf. *ApNPM*, 91f]:

A. Notes with stems.

  1. A note with a downward stem at the right is *L*.

  2. An ascending stem to the left of the initial note makes it and the following note *S* each.

  3. An initial with a downward stem at its left is *B*.

B. Other notes.

  4. All middle notes are *B*.

  5. An initial note in descending position (i.e., followed by a lower note) and a final note in descending position (i.e., preceded by a higher note) are *L*.

  6. An initial in ascending position and a final in ascending position are *B*.

  7. A final note in oblique form is *B*.

As a further illustration an instructive example of ligatures together with a ren-

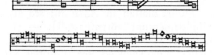

dering in single notes is given. It should be noticed that oblique writing has no rhythmical significance unless it occurs at the end of a ligature and that, even here, it affects only the last of the two notes comprised in its graph (rule 7).

Lit.: *ApNPM*, 87ff, 231ff, 312ff; O. Ursprung, in *AM* xi; H. Rietsch, in *ZMW* viii; see also under *Mensural notation.

Lilliburlero. A 17th-century political tune the melody of which appeared first under the name "Quickstep" in *The Delightful Companion* (1686). This melody [cf. *GD* iii, 198] was, in the following year, used to a political text, satirically directed against the Papists and the Irish Roman Catholics, which began as follows:

> Ho, broder Teague, dost hear de decree,
> Lilliburlero, bullen a la.

The melody has been used for various other texts of the same type. It also appears under the name "A New Irish Tune" in *Musick's Hand Maid* for the Virginal and Spinet (1689) with H. Purcell given as the composer, either of the tune or of the keyboard version. Purcell also used it as a ground bass in his play *The Gordian Knot Unty'd* (1691).

Limma[Gr.]. See *Pythagorean scale.

Linear counterpoint. A term introduced by E. Kurth (*Grundlagen des linearen Kontrapunkts,* 1917) in order to emphasize the "linear," i.e., horizontal aspect of counterpoint, as opposed to the harmonic (or vertical) point of view which prevailed at the time the book was published. Today the "linear" character of counterpoint is generally recognized. The term is also used as a designation for what the Germans call *rücksichtsloser* (reckless) *Kontrapunkt,* i.e., the modern type of counterpoint which pays little attention to harmonic combination and euphony (Hindemith, Stravinsky).

Lining. In American and English psalm and hymn singing, the practice of having each line read by the minister or some other person before it is sung by the congregation. This custom, which sprang up from the insufficient familiarity of the people with the texts, prevailed through the end of the 19th century. In England it was known as "deaconing." See *Psalter.

Linke Hand [G.]. Left hand.

Linz Symphony. Mozart's Symphony in C, no. 36, K.V. 425, believed to have been written at Linz in 1783.

Lip. See *Embouchure.

Lippenpfeife [G.]. Labial pipe.

Liquescent neumes. See *Neumes. Cf. H. Freisted, *Die liquescierenden Noten des Gregorianischen Chorals* (1928).

Lira. A 15th/16th-century type of violin, characterized by a heart-shaped neck with front pegs and by the presence of drone strings. The *lira da braccio* was held in the arm, the larger *lira da gamba* (*lirone*) between the knees. See illustration on p. 800. See also *Violin II.— For Haydn's *lira organizzata* see *Hurdy-gurdy.

L'istesso tempo [It.]. Same tempo.

Litany. In the Roman Catholic Church, solemn supplications addressed to God, to the Virgin (*Litaniae Lauretanae, AR,* 117*), or to the Saints (*AR,* 74*), etc. They open with the Kyrie eleison, continue with numerous exclamations such as "Mater Christi, ora pro nobis," sung responsively to a short inflected monotone, and close with the Agnus Dei. The most famous of these litanies, the Litaniae Lauretanae (named after Loreto in Italy), are frequently used at processions, at the exposition of the Blessed Sacrament at Benediction, and at many popular services where they are sung by the whole congregation (particularly in Italy). They have been frequently composed in a simple chordal style (*falso bordone*), for instance, by Palestrina [complete ed., vol. 26], by Lasso [see *Editions XX, 4], and others. Cf. *GD* iii, 217.

The Anglican Litany is a very extended prayer consisting of recitations by the minister, interspersed with short choral answers, such as "Spare us, good Lord," "Good Lord, deliver us," etc.

Liturgical books. I. Under this heading the most important books of the Roman Catholic service are briefly described. (a) The *Missale* (missal) contains the full service of the Mass; the smaller current editions contain the texts only; the larger editions as well as the early MSS include also the chant (chiefly recitation) for the celebrating priest, but not that for the choir (*schola*).— (b) The *Breviarium* (breviary) contains the service for the Office, in similar arrangements. — (c) The *Graduale Romanum* (*GR*) contains that part of the Mass which is sung by the choir, i.e., the Graduals, Introits, etc. [see *Mass]. — (d) The *Antiphonale Romanum* (*AR*) contains the choir-chants for the Office, i.e., the entire musical service other than the Mass. — (e) The *Liber Usualis* (*LU*) is a modern combination of the Graduale and the Antiphonale in which the items of the Office and of the Mass are given in their proper order of the day, together with the (changeable) lections, etc., from the Missale. It is more handy for the layman, and clearer particularly in the rendition of the psalm singing [see *Psalm tones]. It also includes the service of *Matins (for the great feasts) which, unfortunately, is omitted in the other two books because it is rarely held in ordinary Churches [see *Gregorian Chant I].— (f) The *Kyriale* is a reprint of the last section of the Graduale, and contains only the Ordinary of the Mass (beginning with Kyrie).— (g) *Tonarium* or *Tonale* is a medieval book in which the chants are arranged according to the eight modes.— (h) *Sacramentary* is an earlier form of the Missal, with the Epistles and Gospels omitted, as these were sung or read from other books (*Epistolarium, Evangelistarium*) by the assistant ministers.— (i) The *Pontificale* contains the services used in functions where a bishop or prelate officiates, e.g., the consecration of a church, or ordinations.— (j) The *Processionale* contains the chants for use in processions.— (k) *Troparium* (Troper) is a medieval book containing *tropes.— (l) *Vesperale* (Vesperal) is a book containing the service of *Vespers, usually also that of *Compline and parts of the Lesser Hours.

II. The first printed edition of plainsong was the so-called *Editio Medicea* of 1614 (prepared by Anerio and Soriano, not by Palestrina) which, however, contains the chants in a state of utter deterioration. When, in the middle of the 19th century, the interest in Gregorian chant

was revived [see *Cecilian movement] F. X. Haberl unfortunately reintroduced the Medicean versions in his *Editio Ratisbonensis* (Regensburg, 1871–81). Owing to the initiative of the monks of Solesmes this edition was replaced in 1908 by the *Editio Vaticana* which is based on the earliest available sources, from the 10th to the 12th century. See *Gregorian chant* VII; *Solesmes; *Motu proprio.

Liturgical drama or play.
Medieval plays (chiefly 12th and 13th centuries) representing Biblical stories with action and music. They never formed a part of the official liturgy, and therefore would be more properly called religious drama. They developed, during the 10th and 11th centuries, from *tropes to the Introits for Christmas and Easter which were written in the form of a *dialogue (so-called dialogue tropes), i.e., of question and answer. One of the earliest examples is the trope *Hodie cantandus est* (possibly by Tuotilo, d. 915) to the Christmas Introit *Puer natus est* [Schubiger, p. 39; abridged in *SchGMB*, no. 3; cf. *GR*, 33]. A more fully developed type, in fact a real play, is the 10th-century trope *Quem queritis* for the Mass of Easter [*SchGMB*, no. 8; cf. *ReMMA*, 194 for an account of how it was performed at Winchester, in the middle of the 10th century]. Later plays, mostly of French origin, deal with the story of Daniel, the Plaint of Rachel, the Massacre of the Innocents, the Foolish and the Wise Virgins (Sponsus Play), etc. [cf. *AdHM* i, 170]. A favored subject of later plays (14th century) was the miracles of Saints, particularly of St. Nicholas (miracle play).

In the 14th to the 16th century the "mysteries" [perversion of L. *ministerium*, service] were extremely popular. These were dramatic representations based on Biblical subjects, such as the Life of Christ, the Acts of the Apostles, the Creation, etc., elaborately staged and, in some instances, continued over a period of 20 or more days. They used music only incidentally, for processions, fanfares, some plainsong, popular songs, etc. In Italy they were known as *sacre rappresenta-*

zione, in Spain and Portugal as **auto*. It is chiefly from these plays that the European drama developed. See also **Opera II.

Lit.: A. Schubiger, *Die Sängerschule St. Gallens* (1858); *id.*, in **Editions XXVI, 5*; C. Coussemaker, †*Les Drames liturgiques du moyen âge* (1860); A. Gastoué, *Le Drame liturgique* (1906); J. Combarieu, *Histoire de la musique* (1913–20) i, 282–328; *GéHM*, 232ff; *ReMMA*, 193ff; J. Handschin, "Das Weihnachts-Mysterium von Rouen . . ." (*AM* vii); O. Ursprung, "Das Sponsus-Spiel" (*AMF* iii); J. B. Trend, "The Mystery of Elche" (*ML* i). For additional bibliography cf. *ReMMA*, 444f.

Liturgical hours. See **Office hours.

Liturgy. The officially authorized service of the Christian Churches, particularly of the Roman Catholic, as distinguished from extraliturgical services, such as processions, or the **benediction. See **Gregorian chant; **Mass; **Office hours; **Liturgical books; also **Liturgical drama.

Lituus. (1) A Roman trumpet; see **Brass instruments V (a). — (2) Seventeenth-century Latin name for the **cornetto, or for the **cromorne. The two *litui* in Bach's Cantata no. 119 are obviously tenor-trumpets in B-flat [cf. *SaRM*, 244].

Liuto [It.]. Lute.

Livret [F.]. Libretto.

Lo. Abbreviation for *loco* [It., place], used to indicate return to the normal octave, after **all' ottava* or similar designations.

Lochamer Liederbuch. See **Liederbuch.

Locrian, lokrian. See **Church modes; **Greek music II (c).

Lohengrin. Opera in three acts by Richard Wagner, to his own libretto, composed 1846–48. The scene is the court of King Henry I (10th century) where *Elsa* (Soprano) is accused by Count *Friedrich von Telramund* (Baritone) of having murdered her brother Gottfried, but is victoriously defended in an ordeal of combat by a strange knight arriving on a boat drawn by a swan — *Lohengrin* (Tenor) — who makes the condition that she shall never ask his name (Act I). Telramund and his wife, the heathen magician *Ortrud* (Mezzo-soprano), are deprived of their former status and plan revenge. The latter accuses Lohengrin, when about to enter the church with Elsa, of being a magician who conceals his identity for evil reasons. Elsa, however, assures Lohengrin of her confidence and the marriage takes place (Act II). Lohengrin and Elsa express their love for each other, but Elsa, influenced by Ortrud's accusations, cannot resist asking the fateful question. Lohengrin reveals his name and sorrowfully announces that he now must return to the Holy Grail, the castle of his father Parsifal. The swan reappears and, upon Lohengrin's prayer, takes on the form of Elsa's brother who had been transformed by Ortrud. A dove descends and leads Lohengrin away.

Lohengrin marks the transition from Wagner's early operas (*Rienzi, The Flying Dutchman, Tannhäuser*) to the late master works (*Ring, Tristan, Meistersinger, Parsifal*). Here Wagner for the first time made consistent use of his "continuous melody," as against the "number" style [see **Number opera] which still occurs in the *Tannhäuser*. There is also a modest use of **leitmotifs, to characterize the most important personages and emotions. On the whole, the style is lyrical and soft, a notable exception being the ominous scene between Friedrich and Ortrud which foreshadows the atmosphere of the *Ring*.

Lombardic style. See **Dotted notes III.

London Symphonies. (1) Haydn's last twelve symphonies, nos. 93–104, written in 1790–95 for the Salomon Concerts in London [see **Concerts I], are known as the London (or Salomon) Symphonies. Particularly, the seventh of these (no. 104), in D, is known as "The London Symphony." — (2) "A London Symphony" is the title of a composition by

Ralph Vaughan Williams, composed in 1914 which, although written largely in the form of a classical symphony, incorporates programmatic elements (Westminster chimes, London street cries).

Longa, long. See *Mensural notation.

Longeur [F.]. See *Vibrato (1).

Loop. See *Acoustics V.

Lourd [F.]. Heavy.

Loure [F.]. (1) French 16th-century name for the bagpipe [cf. SaRM, 245]. — (2) A French 17th-century dance (originally accompanied by the instrument loure?) in moderate 6/4 time and with dotted rhythms leaning heavily on the strong beats [see *Dance music III]. Early examples occur in Lully's opera *Alceste* of 1677; the loure in Bach's French Suite no. 5 is easily the most beautiful example of this dance type.

Louré [F.]. See *Bowing (f).

Lur [pl. lurer]. A prehistoric Nordic trumpet of bronze, preserved in numerous examples dating from the 12th to the 6th century B.C. They are in the shape of a long contorted S, with a flat ornamented disk attached to the end of the tube, and are usually found in pairs turned in opposite directions, suggestive of a pair of mammoth's tusks. These instruments, being almost the sole evidence of musical activity of the Nordic people of the pre-Christian era, have been the subject of much speculation and exaggerated claims ("three-voiced harmony, 3000 years ago" in K. Grunsky, *Kampf um die deutsche Musik*, 1933) which are generally considered untenable today. The tone of the lurer is variously described as "rough and blatant" [*GD* iii, 251] and as "sanft posaunenartig" [H. J. Moser, *Geschichte der Deutschen Musik* i, 32]. Illustration on p. 98.

Lit.: A. Hammerich, in *VMW*, x; H. Schmidt, in *Prähistorische Zeitschrift* vii (1915); O. Schrader, in *Reallexikon der Indogermanischen Altertumskunde* (1923).

Lusingando [It.]. Flattering, intimate.

Lustig. [G.]. Cheerful.

Lute [F. *luth*; G. *Laute*; It. *lauto, liuto, leuto*; L. *testudo* or *chelys*, i.e., "turtle," a humanistic misnomer referring to the tortoise-shell of the ancient Greek *lyra].

I. *General.* A plucked stringed instrument with a round body in the shape of a halved pear, a flat neck with 7 or more frets and a separate pegbox, bent back at an angle. The instruments of the 16th century had 11 strings in 6 *courses, tuned: G–c–f–a–d′–g′, with the two lowest courses doubled in the higher octave, and the three following ones doubled in unison. In the 17th century an increasing number of bass-courses (up to six) were added which ran alongside the fingerboard and, therefore, were unalterable in pitch. They were normally tuned: F E D C, etc. Around 1640 another system of tuning, introduced by the great lutenist and lute-composer Denis Gaultier (*c.* 1600–72), was generally adopted, under the name *nouveau ton:* A–d–f–a′–d′–f′, which persisted as long as the lute was used (end of the 18th century).

II. *History.* The history of the lute is unusually long and interesting. One must distinguish between two types of lute, the *long lute* with a neck much longer than the body, and the *short lute*, with a neck slightly shorter than the body. The long lute is by far the more ancient instrument. It appears in Mesopotamian figurines as early as about 2000 B.C. From Babylon it spread to Egypt (*c.* 1000 B.C.) and Greece, where it was called *pandura*. This lute had a small body covered with parchment through which the long handle was pierced [cf. SaHMI, 102]. The later development of the long lute took place in Persia where it was called *setār* ("two-strings"), *čartār* ("four-strings"), or *pančtār* ("five-strings"), according to the number of strings — and in Arabia where it was named *tanbur. For the peculiar tuning of the early Arabian long lutes (prior to Al-Farabi, *c.* A.D. 900), see *Arabian music. A European offshot of the Arabian long lute was the *colascione* of the 16th and 17th centuries [cf. *WoHN* ii, 125], and the Russian *domra (dombra).

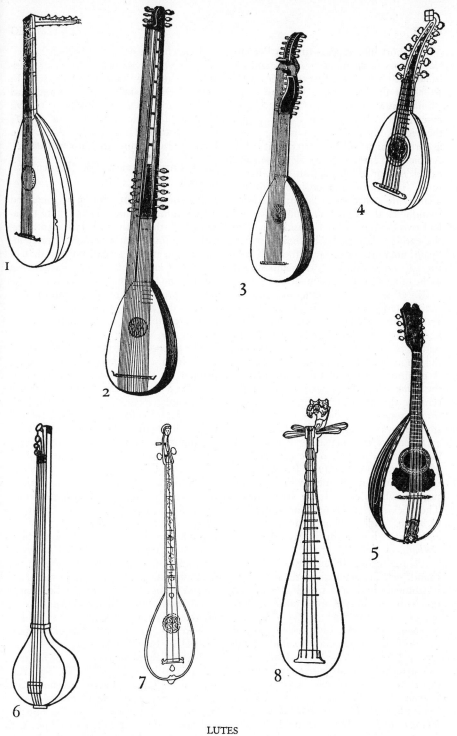

LUTES

1. Lute. 2. Chitarrone. 3. Theorboe. 4. Mandola. 5. Mandolin. 6. Tanburi. 7. Colascione. 8. P'ip'a.

The short lute appears first on Persian clay figures from about 800 B.C. and on Indian reliefs from the first centuries A.D. At about the latter time we find it in China, under the name *p'ip'a [Japanese: biwa]. In these early instruments the neck is formed by the tapering body, a form which still occurred with the Arabic short lute of the medieval periods, called 'ud (or al'ud, Spanish laud, hence lute). The transformation into an instrument with a distinct neck and a central soundhole, the European lute (the 'ud had two crescent-shaped soundholes, like the early viols), probably took place in Spain, not very long before the 15th century. From Spain, the instruments spread to the other European countries.

III. *Other Types.* Numerous varieties of the lute were used during the 16th and 17th centuries. The mandola or mandore had a long pegbox slightly curved and with a head-scroll reminiscent of that of the violin [cf. SaHMI, 245; GD iii, 252]. A diminutive form of this instrument is the *mandolin. The angelica was a 17th-century variety with 17 different strings for the tones of the diatonic scale, so that stopping was largely avoided. During the 17th century the increasing demand for bass instruments led to the construction of archlutes [G. Erzlaute; It. arciliuto], i.e., of double-neck lutes with a second pegbox which carried the bass-courses. There existed a "short" archlute, the theorboe, and a "long" archlute, the chitarrone. For a third type, the liuto tiorbato, cf. SaHMI, 372.

All the above instruments have the round back characteristic of the lute. The instruments with a flat back are treated under the heading *Guitar family. Only one of them, the Spanish *vihuela, may be mentioned here because its musical repertory is closely allied to that of the lute [see *Lute music; *Lute tablatures].

The term lute is also used as a scientific denomination for a large class of stringed instruments. See *Instruments IV, B.

Lit.: F. Zuth, Handbuch der Laute und Guitarre (1926); N. Bessaraboff, Ancient European Musical Instruments (1941), pp. 220ff; K. Geiringer, "Vorgeschichte und Geschichte der europäischen Laute" (ZMW x); M. Brenet, "Notes sur l'histoire du luth en France" (RMI v, vi); F. Behn, "Die Laute im Altertum und frühen Mittelalter" (ZMW i); M. Brondi, "Il Liuto e la chitarra" (RMI xxxii, xxxiii); G. Kinsky, "Alessandro Piccinnini und sein Arciliuto" (AM x).

Lute harpsichord. See *Lautenclavicymbel.

Lute music. Lute music, as preserved in the numerous lute books (*lute tablatures) of the 16th and 17th centuries, forms an important repertory of early instrumental music, second only to that of the organ and harpsichord. Particularly during the 16th century, the lute occupied a prominent place in musical culture, as the chief instrument of domestic music, comparable to the piano of the present day.

The preserved literature for the lute extends from 1507 (Intabolatura de lauto, printed by Petrucci) to about 1770. It includes a vast number of printed books and manuscripts of Italian, French, German, Spanish, and English origin [cf. the practically complete lists in WoHN ii, 27, 66, 95]. The sources of the 16th century contain dances (*bassadanzas, *pavanes, *gaillards, *passamezzos, *saltarellos, etc.), pseudo-contrapuntal *ricercares and *fantasias, *variations (mostly in the Spanish books), and free *preludes (called ricercares in the earliest Italian books), in addition to a disproportionately large quantity of *Intabulierungen of vocal music (motets and chansons). The most outstanding composers are (the figures indicate dates of publications): the *Spanish* Luis Milan (1536), Luis de Narvaez (1538), Enriquez de Valderrabano (1547), Diego Pisador (1552), Miguel de Fuenllana (1554); the *Italian* Dalza and Spinaccino (1507, '08), Francesco da Milano (1536, '46, '48, '63), Antonio Rotta (1546), Paolo Borrono (1546, '48, '49, '63), Giacomo Gorzanis (1561, '63, '64, '65, '79), Vincenzo Galilei (1563), Fabritio Caroso (1581), and Giov. Ant. Terzi (1593, '99); the *French* Attaingnant (publisher, 1529, '30), Adrian le

Roy (1551, '52, '62), Guillaume Morlaye (1552, '54), Albert de Rippe (1553, '54, '58), to whom the *Hungarian* Valentin Greff (pseud. Bacfarc, 1552, '64, '65, '68) may be added; the *German* Arnolt Schlick (1512), Hans Judenkunig (1523), Hans Gerle (1532, '33, '52), Hans Neusiedler (1536, '40, '44), Wolff Heckel (1556), Melchior Neusiedler (1574), Matthaeus Waisselius (1573, '91, '92), and Sixtus Kargel (1586); the *English* John Dowland (1597, 1600) and Thomas Morley (1597, 1600), who, in the early 17th century were followed by Francis Pilkington (1605), Thomas Campion (1606), and Robert Dowland (1610).

In the 17th century, lute music persisted chiefly in France and in Germany while Italy and Spain turned to the more popular guitar. The repertory consisted chiefly of preludes and of idealized dances (allemandes, courantes, sarabandes, etc.). While in the books of the early 17th century these dances are compiled separately (cf. Jean-Baptiste Besard, *Thesaurus harmonicus*, 1603, which falls into ten "books," one each for preludes, allemandes, courantes, etc.), they were later arranged according to keys in groups which resemble the *suites (e.g., Denis Gaultier's *La Rhétorique des dieux, c. 1650; new ed. by A. Tessier). After 1650 the center of artistic activity shifted to Germany. The suites by Esaias Reusner (1636–79) and the sonatas of Sivius Leopold Weiss (1686–1750) — the latter astonishingly Bach-like in style — represent the culmination-point of the entire literature. J. S. Bach wrote a number of pieces for the lute (ed. by Bruger).

Lit.: *A.* Collections of Music. O. Chilesotti, †*Lautenspieler des 16ten Jahrhunderts* (1891); G. Morphy, †*Les Luthistes espagnoles du xvie siècle* (1902; many errors in the transcriptions); H. D. Bruger, †*Pierre Attaingnant* (1927); *id.*, †*Alte Lautenkunst aus drei Jahrhunderten; id.*, †*Joh. Seb. Bach, Kompositionen für die Laute* (1921); H. Quittard, †*A. Francisque, Trésor d'Orphée,* 1600 (1907); *DTOe* 18.ii and 25.ii (German lute music); *Editions XI (English); XII A, 12 (German); XXIV A, 6/7

(French); XXV, 2 (Spanish); III, 1, 7, 8, 9 (Italian).

B. Bibliography. O. Körte, *Laute und Lautenmusik bis zur Mitte des 16. Jahrhunderts* (1901); E. Engel, *Die Instrumentalformen in der Lautenmusik des 16. Jahrhunderts* (1915); L. de la Laurencie, *Les Luthistes* (*Les Musiciens célèbres,* 1928); J. Zuth, *Handbuch der Laute und Guitarre* (1926/28); F. Dodge, "Lute Music of the XVIth and XVIIth Centuries" (*PMA* xxxiv); H. M. Fitzgibbons, "The Lute Books of Ballet and Dallis" (*ML* xi); J. Bal, "Fuenllana and the Transcriptions of Spanish Lute Music" (*AM* xi); R. Newton, "English Lute Music . . ." (*PMA* lxv); A. Koczirz, "Verschollene neudeutsche Lautenisten" (*AMW* iii); H. Neemann, "Die Lautenhandschriften von Silvius L. Weiss" (*AMW* x); F. Ecorcheville, "Le Luth et sa musique" (*BSIM,* 1908); F. Dodge, "Ornamentations as Indicated by Signs in Lute Tablature" (*SIM* ix); O. Chilesotti, "Note circa alcuni liutisti italiani . . ." (*RMI* ix); E. Haraszti, ". . . V. Bakfark" (*RdM* x); W. Apel, "Early Spanish Music for Lute and Keyboard" (*MQ* xx).

Lute tablature. (1) The notational systems used for the writing down of lute music during the 16th, 17th, and 18th centuries; see *Tablatures III, IV, V. — (2) The manuscripts and books in which this notation is employed; hence, practically all the lute books of the same period [see *Lute music].

Lutherie [F.]. The art of making lutes or stringed instruments in general. *Luthier* is the maker of such instruments, nowadays of violins, etc.

Luttuoso [It.]. Mournful.

Lydian. (1) See *Greek music II (c). — (2) The fifth *church mode, represented by the segment f–f' of the diatonic scale, with f as the tonic. From the modern point of view it assumes the character of a major mode (F major) with the augmented fourth (B-natural, Lydian fourth, i.e., tritone) instead of the perfect fourth

(B-flat). Owing to the presence of the tritone f–b in prominent position, examples of pure Lydian are rare, in monophonic music (Gregorian chant) as well as in polyphonic music. The *Alleluia Exaltabo* (*GR*, 50) is one of them [Ex. 1].

Usually, Lydian occurs in Gregorian chant as a "mixed" tonality, using the B-natural (preferably for descending motion) as well as the B-flat (for ascending motion). A similar situation exists in polyphonic music from *c.* 1200 to 1550. Ex. 2 shows a purely Lydian passage from a 13th-century motet [cf. *SchGMB*, no. 19], while Ex. 3 [c. 1470; cf. *ApMZ* i, 4] illustrates the more frequent occurrence of a tonality mixed of F major and Lydian idioms, melodic as well as harmonic. This mixed tonality, which is very characteristic of polyphonic music prior to 1550, should not be destroyed by editorial accidentals [see *Musica ficta (Ex. 8); *Partial signature]. A particular Lydian formation is the raised fourth of the Burgundian cadence [see *Landini cadence]. Beethoven revived the Lydian in the "Dankgesang" (slow movement) of his String Quartet op. 132. As a characteristic of Slavic folk song it appeared in Chopin's Mazurkas [see *Modality].

Lyra. (1) An ancient Greek instrument, similar to the *kithara but of much lighter construction, smaller in size, and usually with the soundbox made from the shell of a turtle. It was played with a plectrum [ill. under Zithers; the drawing in *GD* iii, 259 is a kithara]. The lyra persisted in the early Middle Ages, probably under the name *rotta, while the term lyre was adopted for several instruments which have only a remote relationship to the Greek lyra, namely: — (2) a medieval fiddle, similar to the *rebec (hence the name *lira for a 16th-century violin; see *Violin II); — (3) the *hurdy-gurdy, particularly in the connection *lyra rustica* (peasant's lyra) and *lyra mendicorum* (beggar's lyra). — (4) In modern German usage, the military *Glockenspiel, on account of the shape of the frame which is similar to that of the Greek lyra. The "Lyra" used in several compositions by Haydn is not the *lira da braccio* [cf. *GD* ii, 584], but the *hurdy-gurdy. See also *Lyre. Cf. H. Panum, "Lyra und Harfe im alten Nordeuropa" (*SIM* vii).

Lyraflügel. An early 19th-century variety of the upright piano, with a case shaped in the form of the Greek lyre.

Lyra viol. See *Viol IV, 3.

Lyra way. See under *Viol IV (3) (Lyra viol).

Lyre. As a specific instrument, see *Lyra. As a scientific term for a class of instruments, see *Instruments IV, C. Illustrations under Zithers.

M

M. In organ music, manual or manualiter. See also *Metronome.

Maatschappij. See *Societies II, 5.

Machete. See *Guitar family; *Ukulele.

Machicotage [F.; L. *macicotaticum*]. A French practice of ornamenting plainsong by the insertion of improvised grace notes or coloraturas between the authentic notes of Gregorian chant. The term comes from *machicot*, a designation for church officials of a rank superior to that of the ordinary singers. The practice of *machicotage* is documented as far back as 1391 [cf. Godefroy, *Dictionnaire de la langue française*] and continued throughout the 18th and early 19th centuries. Usually *machicotage* was used with the solo songs while the chants of the *schola* (choir) remained unadorned. The adoption of the Solesmes versions has made an end to this corruptive practice. See also *Plain-chant musical.

Madrashe. See *Syrian chant.

Madrigal. Name for two different types of Italian vocal music, one of the 14th, the other of the 16th century. Two derivations of the name are given, namely, "matricale," i.e., poem in the mother tongue, or "mandriale," from *mandra,* flock — hence, pastoral song. The latter interpretation would seem to be preferable since early writers connect the madrigal with the *pastourelle of the troubadours.

I. *The 14th-Century Madrigal.* As a poetic form, the madrigal consists of two or three strophes of three lines each which are followed by a final strophe of two lines, called *ritornello. In each strophe, two lines rhyme with one another. The lines are always iambic pentameters. Following is the beginning of a famous 11-line $(3 + 3 + 3 + 2)$ madrigal as well as its complete scheme of rhymes [cf. *HAM*, no. 49].

Nel mézzo a séi paón ne vídi un biánco
Con crésta d'óro e cón morbída pénna
Si bél che dólceménte il cór mi spénna

I	II
...bianco	...bellezza
...penna	...colore
...spenna	...amore
III	*Ritornello*
...guardando	...canto
...parte	...manto
...arte	

The contents of the madrigal is usually contemplative, idyllic, as in the above example: "In the midst of six peacocks I saw a white one; with a golden crown and languid feathers; so beautiful that my heart softly trembled."

These lyrical texts were composed usually in two, sometimes in three voice parts, and in a form which follows closely that of the poetry, the same music (a) being provided for the three strophes and different music (b) for the ritornello, so that the form a a a b for the 11-line madrigal, or a a b for the eight-line madrigal, results. The latter form is similar to — but probably not directly derived from — that of the French *ballade [see also *Barform]. Madrigals were composed chiefly by the members of the early Italian School, e.g., Jacopo da Bologna and Giov. da Cascia, while in the second half of the 14th century the madrigal was largely abandoned in favor of the *ballata. Landini, for instance, has only 12 madrigals as compared to 140 ballatas.

The style of the trecento madrigal may be best described as an "ornamented *conductus style," contrasting sharply with the genuinely polyrhythmic style of contemporary French music (G. de Machaut). Its impressively designed ornamenting lines foreshadow the Italian coloraturas of the 17th century. Nonetheless, A. Schering's interpretation of the madrigal as "coloriertes Orgelmadrigal" [*SIM* xiii] is historically untenable, both as to the implied method of "added coloraturas" and as to the organ as the proper idiom. It is interesting to note that Landini, in his nine two-voiced madrigals, rather strictly adheres to the just described type, but arrives at a freer treatment in his three-voiced examples. These are all through-composed, and show French influence in their polyrhythmic texture as well as — in one instance, the wonderful *Musica son* — simultaneous use of the different texts after the fashion of the motet, the three stanzas of the poem being sung at the same time, a unique experiment in the history of vocal music. Examples in: *WoGM* ii, iii, nos. 38–44, 47, 49, 50, 54, 55; L. Ellinwood, †*The Works of Francesco Landini* (1939), nos. 1–12; *HAM*, nos. 49, 50, 54; *SchGMB*, no. 22; *ReMMA*, 362; *AdHM* i, 278; *BeMMR*, 156. The "Madrigale" in J. Wolf, †*Sing- und Spielmusik aus älterer Zeit* (1931), no. 6, is a ballata.

Cf. J. Wolf, in *JMP* xlv; A. Schering, in *SIM* xiii.

II. *The 16th-Century Italian Madrigal.* As a literary type, the madrigal of the 16th century is a free imitation, without any strict form, of the 14th-century madrigal which Italian humanists (Cardinal Bembo and his followers) used as a point of departure in their endeavors to arrive at a poetry of a more refined quality than that of the previous period (*frottola, *strambotto). Although these antiquarian attempts were not very profitable from the point of view of poetry, the movement proved to be a great stimulus to musical activity. The musicians of the early 16th century, at first Netherlands composers working in Italy (Verdelot, Willaert, Arcadelt), coöperated with the poets in order to arrive at a new style of courtly refinement and of artistic expression. Naturally, they did not take their cue from 14th-century music which was entirely forgotten. In fact, it was only the literary bond which justified the use of the old name for the new compositions. As a musical composition the madrigal of the 16th century is an outgrowth of the *frottola. In fact, the style of the earliest madrigals, published in 1533 (including 8 pieces by Verdelot, 3 by Carlo, 2 by Festa, etc.), differs little from that of the late frottolas (1531; cf. *SchGMB*, nos. 72 and 98).

The development of the madrigal in Italy is usually divided into three phases: (a) *The Early Madrigal:* Philipp Verdelot (*c.* 1500–65), Costanzo Festa (d. 1545; the first Italian composer of madrigals), Jacob Arcadelt (*c.* 1505–*c.* 1557). The style is, in spite of considerable imitation, prevailingly homophonic; the writing is in three or four parts; the expression is quiet and restrained. — (b) *The Classic Madrigal:* Adriaen Willaert (properly intermediate between a and b), Cypriano de Rore, Andrea Gabrieli, Orl. Lasso, Philipp de Monte, Palestrina (publications between 1550 and 1580). Here the writing is in four to six (usually five) parts, the style is more genuinely polyphonic and imitative, approaching that of the contemporary motet, the expres-

sion is deepened and closely allied to the text regarding meaning as well as pronunciation. A collateral type of this period is the *madrigale spirituale*, designed for devotional use [e.g., by Palestrina; complete ed., vol. 29]. — (c) *The Late Madrigal:* Luca Marenzio, Gesualdo, Monteverdi (publications between 1580 and 1620). Here, the development leads to a highly elaborate type of music, even exaggerated and mannered, in which all the experimental tendencies of the *fin de siècle* found refuge: chromaticism, word-painting, coloristic effects, declamatory monody, virtuosity of the solo-singer, dramatic effects — all treated with the greatest superiority and ease. Particular importance attaches to the fact that, at this late date, the madrigal was malleable enough to drop its traditional polyphonic texture and to adapt itself to the novel methods of *stile concertante* and *stile rappresentativo* [see *Stile]. The transition is particularly apparent in the madrigals of Monteverdi whose *libro i, ii, iii,* and *iv* (1587, '90, '92, 1603) are purely polyphonic and a cappella, whereas in the following books (*v,* 1605; *vi,* 1614) the style becomes increasingly soloistic; book *vii,* called *Concerto* (1619), is entirely in *stile concertante* with basso continuo. Caccini's *Nuove musiche* of 1602 contains "madrigals" for solo voice which form the point of departure for the 17th-century *aria.

III. *The English Madrigal.* Outside of Italy, the madrigal was cultivated chiefly in England. A few isolated pieces such as Edwards' "In going to my naked bed" (composed not later than 1564) make it probable that the influence of the Italian madrigal was felt in England shortly after 1550. William Byrd (1543–1623) would appear to have been the first English composer to fully grasp the importance of the madrigal [see *Editions X, 14 and 15]. He, together with Th. Morley (1557–*c.* 1603), represents the earlier period of the English madrigal, the style of which corresponds to a certain extent to that of the second Italian school. Nonetheless, from its very outset the English madrigal became "naturalized," owing to the peculiarities of the English language as well as to the instillation of an unmistakable touch of English merriment or melancholy. The publication of the *Musica Transalpina* (a collection of Italian madrigals provided with English text, published by N. Yonge, 1588, a few months after the appearance of Byrd's first book) gave the movement new impetus and a different direction. The younger Englishmen, notably Thomas Weelkes and John Wilbye, tended more clearly towards Italy, and exploited the innovations of Marenzio and Gesualdo, though in a somewhat more conservative manner. The English madrigals appeared under a variety of names, such as Songs, Sonets, Canzonets, Ayres. See *Editions X.

IV. *Other Countries.* In Germany, the influence of the madrigal appears to some extent in the works of Le Maistre, Scandello, Regnart, Lassus [see *Lied II], all of whom were foreigners, a fact which may account for the failure of the movement to gain artistic significance comparable to that of Italy or England. Hans Leo Hassler [*DTB* 11.i] may be mentioned as the outstanding German representative, although many of his madrigals have Italian texts. Spanish madrigals were published by Pedro Vila (1561), Juan Brudieu (1585), and Pedro Ruimonte (1614) [cf. *LavE* i.4, 2015ff].

Lit. (other than that given in *GD* iii, 279, 282, 283; *GD, Suppl. Vol.*, 413; and *AdHM* i, 373): E. B. Helm, *The Beginnings of the Madrigal and the Works of Arcadelt* (unpubl. Diss. Harvard 1939); H. Heinrich, *John Wilbye in seinen Madrigalen* (1931); E. Dent, "The Musical Form of the Madrigal" (*ML* xi, no. 3); *id.*, "William Byrd and the Madrigal" (*Festschrift für J. Wolf*, 1929); A. Einstein, "Das Madrigal zum Doppelgebrauch" (*AM* vi, no. 3); *id.*, "Dante im Madrigal" (*AMW* iii); *id.*, "Narrative Rhythm in the Madrigal" (*MQ* xxix, 4); H. Engel, "Marenzios Madrigale . . ." (*ZMW* xvii; also in *AM* viii); *id.*, "Contributo alla storia del madrigale" (*LRM* iv); Ch. van den Borren, "Les Madrigaux de Jean Brudieu" (*RM* vi); J. Racek, "Les

Madrigaux à voix seule de Luzzascho Luzzaschi" (*RM* xiii); H. J. Moser, "Vestiva i Colli" (*AMF* iv).

Madrigal comedy. Modern designation for an alleged "pre-operatic" type of the late 16th century in which an entire play [It. *commedia*] was set to music in the form of madrigals and other types of contemporary polyphonic vocal music. Among the first and most famous examples is the *Amfiparnasso* by Orazio Vecchi (performed in Modena, 1594, printed 1597). According to current opinion the inner contradiction between the ensemble character of the music (which is in five parts throughout, without instruments) and the solistic demand of a theatrical performance was solved by a queer compromise: when the plot called for single characters, the singers of the other parts were made to sing behind a curtain. This surmise, however, is utterly unlikely, not only for practical considerations, but mainly because Vecchi states expressly in the preface that "this spectacle (*spettacolo*) appeals to the imagination (*mente*) through the ear (*orecchie*), not the eye (*occhi*)." The *Amfiparnasso*, therefore, is not a pre-operatic type, but an idealized presentation of a loosely knit dramatic plot, comparable in a way to the presentation of an oratorio. This plot is more clearly designed here than in other, similar works by Vecchi, the *Selva di varia ricreazione* (1590), the *Convito musicale* (1597), and the *Veglie di Siena* (1604), each of which, however, includes a number of dramatic "scenes." The *Amfiparnasso* is a mixture of comical and sentimental portions. Alessandro Striggio's *Il Cicalamento delle donne al bucato* (The Babbling of the Women on a Wash-day, 1567) may be considered as a predecessor of the former; Simone Balsamino's *Novellette* (after Tasso's *Aminta*, printed 1594), of the latter. Other models exist in the *Greghesche of Andrea Gabrieli and other Venetian composers. An imitator of Vecchi was, among others, Adriano Banchieri [cf. *RiML* i, 104; example in *HAM*, no. 186].

Lit.: E. J. Dent, in *SIM* xii; A. Heuss,

in *SIM* iv, 175, 404. Re-publication of the *Amfiparnasso* in *Editions II, 4 and XXVI, 26.   A. E.

Mächtig [G.]. Mighty, powerful.

Männergesangverein [G.]. Male choral societies, similar to the American *Apollo-clubs and the French *Orphéon.

Mässig [G.]. Moderate.

Maestro [It., master]. Honorary title for distinguished teachers, composers, conductors.

Magadis. An ancient Greek harp with twenty strings on which playing in octaves was possible. The strings were apparently arranged in ten courses, each of which gave the fundamental and its octave (as was customary with the lutes of the 16th century). The term "magadizing" is sometimes used to describe playing in octaves which is considered by some writers the "beginning of polyphony."

Maggiolata [It.]. Popular songs for the month of May. For 16th-century examples composed in the style of the *villanella, cf. A. Bonaventura, in *RMI* xxiv.

Maggiore [It.]. Major key.

Magic Flute, The. See *Zauberflöte, Die.

Magnificat. The *canticle of the Virgin, text ("Magnificat anima mea dominum," My soul doth magnify the Lord) from St. Luke 1: 46–55. It consists of twelve verses. In the Catholic rites it is sung at the Office of Vespers by alternating choruses to one of eight "toni," recitation chants similar to the psalm-tones [cf. *AR*, 8*; *LU*, 207ff]. In the polyphonic music of the 15th through the 18th century the composition of the Magnificat in eight different modes (corresponding to the eight tones of plainsong) has played a prominent role. Among the earliest composers of the Magnificat are Dunstable, Dufay, Binchois [cf. *SchGMB*, no. 43], and Obrecht. While Binchois' composition (other settings in J. Marix, *Les Musiciens de la cour de Bourgogne*, 1937) is

based on the entire text, Obrecht composed the even-numbered verses only, the odd-numbered being sung in plainsong — a practice which was widely adopted by the later composers. Numerous 16th-century composers (Senfl, Lasso, Palestrina, de Kerle, Le Maistre, Mahu, Morales) have provided compositions of the famous text. Later composers of the Magnificat are Schütz, Steffano Bernardi (*DTOe* 36.i), Rudolf Ahle (*DdT* 5), and, above all, J. S. Bach, who composed it as a cantata.

The alternatim-method of composition was also adopted by organ composers who provided organ settings for the even-numbered verses. Such Magnificat-*versets for the organ occur in Attaingnant's *Magnificat sur les huit tons . . .* (1531; new ed. by Y. Rokseth); in Cavazzoni's *Intavolatura . . .* (1543); in Cabezon's *Obras de Musica* (1578); in Titelouze's organ works [cf. E. Kaller, *Liber Organi* (1931)]; in E. Kindermann's *Harmonia organica* (1645; *DTB* 21, 23); in Joh. Caspar Kerll's *Modulatio organica* (1686); and in Pachelbel's *94 Magnificat Fugues* (*DTOe* 8.ii) the subjects of which occasionally still show a remote relationship to the plainsong melodies. See *Verset.

The Magnificat, in the English translation, was taken over into the Anglican *Service where it forms a part of the Evening Prayer.

Lit.: C. H. Illing, *Zur Technik der Magnificat-kompositionen des 16. Jahrhunderts* (Diss. Kiel 1934); Th. W. Werner, "Die Magnificat-compositionen Adam Rener's" (*AMW* ii); G. Frotscher, *Geschichte des Orgelspiels* (1935), *passim*.

Magnus Liber Organi [L., The Great Book of Organa]. According to Anon. IV (*CS* i, 342), the title of the collection of two-voice *organa for the entire ecclesiastical year which was composed by Leoninus and partly re-written by his successor Perotinus (around 1200; see *Ars Antiqua). The collection includes 34 pieces for the Office ("de antiphonario") and 59 pieces for the Mass ("de gradali"; see *Mass B, I) [for a 16th-century collection of similar scope see *Choralis Constantinus]. Three 13th-century MSS, from Florence (*Fl*) and Wolfenbüttel (*W₁*, *W₂*) contain the *Magnus liber organi* in a more or less complete form, together with numerous other pieces (clausulae, conductus, motets). A list of the collection in the Florentine Codex (Florence, Bibl. Laur. *plut. 29, 1*, also erroneously called *Antiphonarium Mediceum*; *plut.* stands for L. *pluteus*, book shelf, not *Plutarch*, as is suggested in *OHM* ii, p. xiii) is given in F. Ludwig, *Repertorium organorum . . . et motetorum . . .* (1910), pp. 65–75, where the letters O and M refer to the pieces for the Office and the Mass respectively [cf. *ApNPM*, 201, 238 (footnote)]. See *Ars antiqua; *Mass B, I; *Organum IV; *Square notation; *Sources, no. 3.

Magnus Opus Musicum. Title of a publication containing 516 compositions (motets) of O. di Lasso (1530–94), published in 1604 by his brothers, in six volumes.

Magrepha. The Hebrew name of the Greek water organ (*hydraulis). Various Talmudic treatises describe it and its use in the Temple. Cf. *SaHMI*, 124. See *Organ XII.

Magyar music. See *Hungarian music.

Main [F.]. Hand. *Main droite* (*gauche*), right (left) hand. *À deux* (*trois, quatre*) *mains,* for two (three, four) hands.

Maîtres Musiciens de la Renaissance Française. See *Editions, Historical, XVI.

Maîtrise [F.]. The choir school and the choir of a French church. These institutions, which go back to the 15th century, if not earlier, were under the direction of a "maître de chapelle," and provided board as well as education, general and musical. They resembled in organization and purpose the *conservatorii* of Italy. In the French Revolution (1791) they were suppressed and replaced by the *conservatoires.* Today the name denotes church-choirs, without any educational implication. Cf. *GD* iii, 296.

Majeur [F.]. Major.

Major, minor [F. *majeur, mineur*; G. *Dur, Moll*; It. *maggiore, minore*]. Opposed terms used (1) for the distinction of intervals, e.g., major second (c–d), and minor second (c–db) [see *Intervals].— (2) For two types of scales, triads, or keys, which are distinguished mainly by their third, this being a major third (c–e) in the major scale (key, etc.), a minor third (c–eb) in the minor scale (key, etc.). The major scale is the same ascending and descending [Ex. 1]. The minor scale, however, has descending a flatted seventh

(bb) and sixth (ab) in addition to the flatted third [Ex. 2]. The aesthetic justification for this lies in the fact that, without the flatted seventh and sixth, the descending minor scale would sound like a major scale until its sixth tone is reached. Since the minor scale just described is evolved from melodic considerations (upward and downward movement), it is called "melodic minor scale." There exists another minor scale which, ascending as well as descending, combines the flatted sixth with the unaltered seventh [Ex. 3]. This scale is termed "harmonic minor scale," because it is built out of the tones contained in the three main harmonies of the minor key [Ex. 5].

A key is called major or minor according to whether it is based upon the major or minor scale. In the major key, the three main triads, tonic (T), dominant (D), and subdominant (S; see *Scale degrees), are all major triads [Ex. 4]. In a minor key, T and S are minor, D is major [Ex. 5]. See also *Mode.

The establishment of major and minor as the tonal basis of music took place during the 17th century [see *Harmony II,

B (6)]. Prior to this, music was based on the church modes most of which have the minor third of the minor scale, but differ from this in some of the other degrees [see *Church modes]. Compositions approximating the major key are much more scarce in early music and, for this reason, have attracted the special attention of historians [see, e.g., *Sumer is icumen in]. The major mode has been claimed to be of "popular" origin or to be a characteristic attribute of the northern races. For an unbiased study of these claims cf. the article by C. Sachs.

Lit.: C. Sachs, "The Road to Major" (*MQ* xxix, no. 3); A. H. Fox-Strangways, "The Minor Chord" (*ML* iv, no. 1); Dom Jeannin, "Etude sur le mineur et le majeur" (*RMI* xxii); H. J. Moser, "Der Durgedanke als Rassenproblem" (*SIM* xv).

Malagueña [Sp.]. According to available information the term denotes three different types of southern Spanish folk music, all localized in the provinces of Malaga and Murcia: (1) Usually a local variety of the *fandango.— (2) A type of highly emotional song, in free style and rhythm [cf. *LavE*, 1.4, 2390].— (3) An older type of dance music, based upon the ostinato-like repetition of the harmonies VIII–VII–VI–V (in minor), played in parallel triads, and with an improvised melody on top [cf. *RiML*]; thus, a passacaglia on the descending tetrachord, as were written frequently during the 17th century [see *Chaconne and passacaglia, Ex. 2].

Malinconia [It., melancholy]. A composition in a melancholic mood. Beethoven thus called a short introductory movement before the finale of his Quartet op. 18, no. 6.

Malinconico [It.]. Melancholic.

Man. Short for *manual.

Mancante [It.]. Dying away.

Manche [F.]. Neck of the violin, etc.

Mandola, mandora. See *Lute III.

Mandolin. The most recent instrument of the lute family and the only one found in general use today, particularly in southern Italy. The Neapolitan mandolin has five double-courses (ten strings) tuned in fifths. It is played with a plectrum of tortoise shell or other flexible material. The tones are rendered as a sustained tremolo which is produced by a quick vibrating movement of the plectrum. An older type, the Milanese mandolin, forms the transition from the *mandola to the modern Neapolitan type. The mandolin has been occasionally used in art-music, e.g., in Handel's Oratorio *Alexander Balus* (1748), in Grétry's *L'Amant jaloux* (1778), in Paesiello's *Il Barbiero de Sevilla* (1780), in Mozart's *Don Giovanni* (1787), in Verdi's *Otello* (1887), and in Mahler's Seventh Symphony (1908). Five pieces by Beethoven for mandolin and piano are contained in the supplementary volume of the B.-H. edition [cf. also *BSIM* viii, no. 12, p. 24]. Illustration on p. 413.

Lit.: J. Zuth, "Die Mandolinhandschriften in der Bibliothek der Gesellschaft der Musikfreunde in Wien" (*ZMW* xiv); G. de Saint-Foix, "Un fonds inconnu de compositions pour mandoline" (*RdM*, no. 47).

Maneria [L.]. A term used by some early writers on plainsong to denote the *church modes in their authentic as well as plagal variety. Thus there are four maneriae: protus, deuterus, tritus, and tetrardus. Cf. *ReMMA*, 153.

Maneries [L.]. A thirteenth-century term for modus, i.e., rhythmic *mode, mentioned by Garlandia (*CS* i, 175), Pseudo-Aristotle (*CS* i, 279), and Anon. IV (*CS* i, 327).

Manica [It.]. Shift of position in violin playing.

Manico [It.]. Finger board of the violin, etc.

Manicordion, manichord. Sixteenth-century name for *clavichord.

Maniera [It., manner (of composition)]. A 16th-century term explained by numerous theorists and used to denote the aesthetic basis of contemporary musical composition. It was established shortly after the death of Josquin des Près, probably in Italy where it was maintained throughout the 16th century. The maniera constitutes an idealistic type of composition, in so far as the composer was guided by an imaginative ideal concerning musical style and culture, thus fixing a classical standard for his work. There was also a distinct perception of the evolutionary process in the history of human culture (Glarean, Zarlino, Vasari, Vincenzo Galilei, and others).

The theory of the maniera centered around the "concetto" (concept). This regulated the relationship between the work of musical art and the world of nature. Since, according to this theory, the work of art originated by way of imitating nature, imitation was the creative and formative quality that made it an "opus supranaturale." The imitation of nature worked two ways: either as deviation from nature — musically this produced an asymmetrical, "anti-natural," structure; or as exact copy — literal realism was then the result by which the musical work was supposed to compete with nature (Zuccari, Zarlino, Danti, Galilei, Lomazzo; in part also Zacconi).

Since music has no given objects in nature to imitate, except for the "numero sonoro" (sounding number, i.e., the numerical relationships between the intervals), it was the first task of the composer to establish such "objects." This he did in the "soggetto" (musical subject, theme) whose "modi" (modes, manifestations) were said to be infinite, from the "numero in musica" (sounding number) down to the "soggetto delle parole" (subject based on the text) and the "soggetto della cantilena" (cantus firmus, borrowed or invented, in full or in part). After having fixed the soggetto, the composer had to reveal its inner capacities, that is, the "verità del soggetto" (truth of the subject). This could only be done by way of imitation which always gave rise to the work of art.

The basic idea of the maniera, i.e., imi-

tation, was also applied to certain styles of the musical past. Thus, musicians of the 16th century grew fully aware of stylistic nuances in the works of earlier composers. On this ground, the striking turn made by Palestrina in the late 50's toward the old school of Ockeghem acquires a new significance. Cf. L. Schrade, in ZMW xvi, 3–20, 98–117, 152–170. L. S.

Manieren [G.]. An eighteenth-century German name for ornaments of restricted melodic range, approximately equivalent to *agrément. In modern German usage, the term *Manier* (*manieriert*) means "mannerism" ("mannered").

Mannheim School. An important German school of the mid-18th century, located at Mannheim and connected with the orchestra of Karl Theodor (1743–99), Elector of Pfalzbayern (hence also the name Pfalzbayrische Schule). Johann Stamitz (1717–57), who joined the orchestra in 1745 and soon became its conductor, inaugurated here an entirely novel style of orchestral music and of orchestral performance, thus laying the foundation for the symphonic style of the Viennese classics at the time when the tradition of Baroque music reached its culmination point in the late works of Bach and Handel. Conspicuous features of the new style are: melodic prominence of the violins in an essentially homophonic, non-contrapuntal texture; abandonment of imitation and fugal style; presto-character of the quick movements; use of dynamic devices such as extended crescendos, unexpected fortes and fortissimos; general rests (*Generalpause*); a novel type of subjects and figures which quickly rise over a wide range, usually in broken chords, the so-called "Raketen" (rockets, Roman candles); orchestral effects such as the tremolo and broken chords in quick notes; replacement of the thorough-bass accompaniment by written-out orchestral parts. Johann Stamitz' activity was continued by Ignaz Holzbauer (1711–83; came to Mannheim in 1753), F. X. Richter (1709–89; came to Mannheim in 1747), and by a younger generation including Anton Filtz (c. 1730–60), Franz Beck

(1730–1809), Christian Cannabich (1731–98), and Johann Stamitz' sons Karl Stamitz (1746–1801) and Anton Stamitz (1754–1809).

The importance of the Mannheim composers lies in their historical position as forerunners of the classical period rather than in the intrinsic value of their works. Contrary to the opinion voiced by H. Riemann, the symphonies of Johann Stamitz, typical products of a one-sided and fanatic innovator, are even less satisfactory from the artistic point of view than those of the later Mannheimers who turned from Stamitz' fragmentary and incoherent mosaique style (somewhat similar to that of Domenico Scarlatti; see *Sonata-form II) to a more continuous and melodic manner of writing which, however, is not free from the sentimentalities of the gallant style and which, needless to say, is inferior to that of their contemporaries Haydn and Mozart. Mozart's father referred to the extravagant novelties of this School as the "vermanirierte Mannheimer goût" (the mannered taste of the Mannheimer).

The importance of the Mannheim School as the founders of the modern symphony and chamber music was strongly emphasized by their discoverer, H. Riemann. More recently his claims to precedence and superiority have been challenged by other historians who have been pointing to similar tendencies in Vienna (Georg Monn, 1717–50; Georg Wagenseil, 1715–77; cf. G. Adler in preface to DTOe 15.ii), Italy [cf. F. Torrefranca, Le Origini italiane del romanticismo musicale, 1930], and Bohemia [cf. W. Helfert, in AMW vii]. No doubt, the novel ideas of style and form were "in the air" around 1740 and a great number of musicians, among whom Sammartini (1701–75) must be mentioned particularly, worked in the same direction, laying the foundation for the work of Haydn, Mozart, and Beethoven. Perhaps some of the contradictory claims can be settled if a clearer distinction is made between the various features which enter into the complex picture of the classical sonata or symphony. As is explained under *So-

nata-form, the Viennese composers were definitely much more advanced than the Mannheimers in the establishment of the formal principles of the sonata. On the other hand, the importance and the true meaning of the new principles of symphonic style [see the description above] were more clearly understood in Mannheim than elsewhere, probably owing to the favorable conditions existing at the Electoral orchestra. Examples in HAM, nos. 294, 310, 311, 320. See also *Sonata III; *Sonata-form; *Symphony II.

Lit.: F. Waldkirch, Die konzertante Sinfonie der Mannheimer (Diss. Heidelberg 1931); RiHM ii.3, 119ff; P. Gradenwitz, "The Symphonies of Johann Stamitz" (MR i); id., "Mid-18th-century Transformations of Style" (ML xviii, no. 3); W. Fischer, "Zur Entwicklungsgeschichte des Wiener klassischen Stils" (StM iii); A. Heuss, "Ueber die Dynamik der Mannheimer Schule" (Riemann Festschrift, 1909); id., in ZMW ii; id., "Zum Thema 'Mannheimer Vorhalt'" (ZIM ix); R. Sondheimer, "Die Sinfonien von Franz Beck" (ZIM iv); L. Kamienski, "Mannheim und Italien" (SIM x). Re-editions in DTB 3.i; 7.ii; 8.ii; 15/16; DdT 39; DTOe 15.ii; 19.ii [see *Editions VIII, IX].

Manual. On the organ, the keyboards provided for the hands, in contradistinction to the *pedal [see *Organ III]. In German organ pieces Man. I, II, III, and IV designate the Great manual, the Swell organ, the Choir organ, and the Solo organ respectively. The two keyboards of the harpsichord are also distinguished as first and second manual. *Manualiter* means playing with the hands only.

Manualkoppel [G.]. Manual coupler; see *Organ IV.

Manubrio. The knobs and handles of the organ stops.

Maqam. See *Arabian music II; *Melody-types.

Maracas. See *Percussion instruments B, 8.

Marcato [It.]. Marked, emphasized.

March. Music designed to promote orderly marching of a large group, especially soldiers. Marches are, of course, always in simple rhythm and regular phrases. The standard form, derived from the minuet-with-trio, is that of a march repeated after one or several trios of a more melodious character and frequently in softer orchestration: M T M, or M T M T M.

The earliest traces of the march as an art form are found in the numerous *battaglias of the 16th century. More definite examples are various virginal pieces contained in *My Lady Nevells Book* [see *Virginal books]: "The March before the Battle," "The March of the Horsemen," "The March of the Footemen," etc., pieces which would seem to indicate that the English musicians of the 16th century were more military-minded than their colleagues of other nationalities. Many examples of march music, usually dignified and ceremonial rather than military in character, are contained in the operas of Lully, Handel, etc. (Handel's *Scipio* contains a march which is to the present day the parade march of the British Grenadier Guards.) There are two charming little marches — probably not by Bach — in the *Notenbüchlein der Anna Magdalena Bach.* Similar pieces occur in the suites of J. Ph. Krieger, of J. K. F. Fischer, etc. Mozart exemplifies two different types of march music in his *Figaro* (Non più andrai) and in his *Magic Flute* (March of the Priests). The movement "Lebhaft, Marschmässig" in Beethoven's Sonata op. 101 represents the highest artistic transfiguration of the march. Schubert's *Marches Militaires* deserve mention for their admirable variety and ingenuity. The processional march of Wagner's *Die Meistersinger* may be mentioned (with distinction, to be sure) as one of the numerous marches in the 19th-century operas. A special type is the funeral march (marcia funebre), of which well-known examples exist in Beethoven's *Eroica* and in Wagner's *Götterdämmerung.* Among modern composers, Pro-

kofiev has frequently been noted for his propensity for march-like rhythm and structure.

Lit.: K. Strom, *Beiträge zur Entwicklungsgeschichte des Marsches* (Diss. Munich 1926).

Marche [F.]. *March. Marche harmonique, *sequence (1).

Marcia [It.]. *March. Marcia funebre, funeral march. Alla marcia, in the manner of a march.

Marien-antiphon [G.]. Name for the Antiphons B.M.V.; see *Antiphon (2).

Marimba. An African and South American *xylophone, consisting of a number of wooden plates of different size and thickness fixed in a frame and played with two drumsticks, sometimes by two players simultaneously. Underneath each plate there is a tuned resonator, made of gourds, of cedar boxes, or, more recently, of metal tubes. See *Percussion instruments A, 4.

Marimbaphone. An improved marimba, invented by the American Deagan. Percy Grainger used it in his suite *In a Nutshell.*

Marine trumpet. See *Tromba Marina.

Markiert [G.]. Marked, accented, emphasized.

Markig [G.]. Vigorous.

Marriage of Figaro, The. See *Nozze di Figaro, Le.

Marsch [G.]. Marche. Marschmässig, in the character of a march.

Marseillaise [F.]. The famous song of the French Revolution, "Allons enfants de la patrie," written and composed by Rouget de Lisle during the night of April 24, 1792. It acquired its present name when it was sung in Paris by Marseilles troops. Cf. the detailed article in *GD* iii, 329; additional bibliography in *RiML,* 1120, and in *MoML,* 710 (Rouget de Lisle); L. Fiaux, *La Marseillaise,* 1918 (bibl.).

Martelé [F., from *marteau*, hammer].
A special method of violin bowing; see
*Bowing (c). *Martellando, martellato*
[It.] designates either the *martelé* of the
violin, or a somewhat similar technique
of piano playing in which the hands act
like hammers, usually in rapidly alternating octaves.

Martellement [F.]. In the 17th century a *mordent performed on stringed
instruments. In the 18th century a mordent or a short trill preceded by a long
appoggiatura.

Martyrion. See *Byzantine Chant III.

Marziale [It.]. Marchlike.

Mascherata. See under *Villanella.

Masculine, feminine cadence. A
cadence or ending is called masculine if
the final chord occurs on the strong beat
[Ex. 1], feminine, if it is postponed to fall
on a weak beat [Ex. 2, 3]. The masculine

ending must be considered the normal
one, with the feminine preferred in more
"Romantic" styles. It is interesting to note
that feminine endings appear for the first
time around 1600, thus forming one of
the various novel features of the Baroque
era. One of the earliest examples known
to this writer is a "Sarabrande" by Gibbons [see the above Ex. 2; cf. M. H. Glyn,
*Orlando Gibbons, Complete Keyboard
Works*, vol. ii]. It may well be this novel
feature to which Shakespeare alludes in
his famous line: "That strain again, it
had a dying fall." Feminine endings are
frequent in Frescobaldi. Beethoven shows
a strongly marked preference for feminine endings in his late style. The feminine cadence is a typical feature of the
*polonaise.

Masque, mask. Sixteenth- and 17th-
century stage productions, designed for
the entertainment of the nobility and con-

sisting of a combination of poetry, vocal,
and instrumental music, dancing, acting,
etc., applied in the most lavish way to the
representation of mythological and allegorical subjects. The masques originated
in Italy and France where the members
of the court played an active part in their
preparation as well as performance. B.
de Beaujoyeulx' famous "Ballet comique
de la Royne" [see *Ballet I], performed
in the Louvre in 1581, was one of the first
plays in which there was a unified plot
going through all the scenes.

The masque was introduced into England during the 16th century and remained in great favor here during the
17th century. A famous writer of masques
was Ben Jonson who, from 1605 till 1631,
exercised a privilege to provide the court
with masques. A specialty of his plays
was the *antimasque*, i.e., intermediate
scenes of a grotesque character (similar
to the operatic *intermezzo). The earliest
known composers of music for masques
are Thomas Campion (1567–1620), Alfonso Ferrabosco II (1575–1628), Robert
Johnson (d. about 1634), and John Coprario (*c.* 1570–1627). While the music
of these masques consists of *ayres and
*ballettos, later composers, such as Nico-
las Lanière (1588–1666), Henry Lawes
(1595–1662), and William Lawes (d.
1645), introduced the "stile recitativo."
Henry Lawes wrote the music to Milton's
masque *Comus*, produced in 1634 [republ.
by the Mermaid Society, 1904; example
in *HAM*, 203]. After the Civil War
(around 1660) the opera gradually superseded the earlier plays which deteriorated
into mere fancy dress balls. One of the
latest masques was *Freyas Gift*, text by
J. Oxenford, music by G. A. Macfarren,
which was produced on the marriage of
Edward VII, in 1863. See *Opera VI.

Lit.: J. Mark, "The Jonsonian Masque"
(*ML* iii, no. 4); W. J. Lawrence, "Notes
on a Collection of Masque Music" (*ML*
iii, no. 1); Campion, *Masque in Honour
of the Marriage of Lord Hayes* (see *Editions XXII, 1); P. Reyher, *Les Masques
Anglais* (1909); W. W. Greg, *A List of
Masques . . .* (1902); A. H. D. Prendergast, in *PMA* xxiii.

Mass [L. *missa*; F. *messe*; G. *Messe*; It. *méssa*]. The most solemn service of the Roman Catholic rites, representing the commemoration and mystical repetition of the sacrifice of Christ on the Cross. The name is derived from the words "Ite, missa est (congregatio)," i.e., "Depart, the congregation is dismissed," sung at the end of the service [cf., e.g., *GR*, 28*]. The subsequent explanations refer to its full form known as High Mass [see *Missa solemnis].

A. *The Mass in Gregorian Chant.* The Mass has a complex structure, consisting of a number of items some of which vary from day to day (this is the Proper of the Mass, *proprium missae*), while others remain the same in every Mass (Ordinary of the Mass, *ordinarium missae*). Another classification can be made according to whether the item is (a) recited to a *monotone or in an elevated speech, or (b) sung to a distinct melody. The former category falls to the celebrant priest and his assistants, the latter to the choir (*schola*). The following table shows the normal structure of the Mass, with the items classified under four categories, Ia: Proper sung; Ib: Ordinary sung; IIa: Proper recited (or spoken); IIb: Ordinary spoken.

Sung		Recited or Spoken	
Ia Proprium	Ib Ordinarium	IIa Proprium	IIb Ordinarium
1. Introitus			
	2. Kyrie		
	3. Gloria		
		4. Oratio (prayers, collect)	
		5. Lectio (Epistle)	
6. Graduale			
7. Alleluia or Tractus (with Sequence)			
		8. Evangelium (Gospel)	
	9. Credo		
10. Offertorium			
		11. Secreta	
		12. Praefatio (Preface)	
13. Sanctus			
			14. Canon
	15. Agnus Dei		
16. Communio			
		17. Post-communio	
	18. Ite missa est or Benedicamus Domino		

Regarding the texts of the items Ib and IIb (and other texts not included above) the student is referred to the *Ordo Missae*, given on pp. 1–7 of *LU*. The variable texts (Oratio, Evangelium, etc.) are given with the different Masses, e.g., pp. 318ff of *LU*, while the recitation tones of the items 4, 5, 8 are found in *LU*, 98–111 or in *GR*, 109*–121*. The items Ia with their melodies are given with the different Masses, e.g., *LU*, 318ff (*GR*, 1ff), while those for Ib are found in *LU*, 11–94 (*GR*, 1*–94*).

Naturally, the items of the classes Ia, Ib are those interesting to the musician, and it is to these exclusively that reference is made in the studies of Gregorian chant, as well as in the following explanations. What is usually known to the music student as "Mass" are the items of the rubric Ib, the (sung) Ordinary of the Mass. The reason for this narrow and actually misleading conception is the fact that these alone (with the exception of the *Ite missa est*, however) were composed polyphonically after 1300 [see under B]. From the point of view of the plainsong, the Proper of the Mass (Ia) is much more important and musically interesting. These chants and their texts are also much older than those of the Ordinary as appears from the fact that they are all derived from the psalms [see *Psalmody]. Thus, the Introit originally was a *psalmus ad introitum*, the Communio a *psalmus ad communionem*, etc. Around 500, the Mass consisted only of the chants of the Proper, alternating with lections from the Epistles, etc. Gradually, the chants of the Ordinary were introduced, probably in the following chronological order: Sanctus, Kyrie, Gloria, Agnus Dei, Credo.

B. *The Polyphonic Mass.* I. 1200–1400. The earliest polyphonic settings of the Mass chants are those of the Proper. During the 12th and 13th centuries a great number of the chants of the Proper of the Mass were composed, as *organa. The "de gradali"-section of the *Magnus liber organi*, e.g., contains 59 such compositions, all Graduals or Alleluias. (For details regarding the composition, see *Organum, particularly the scheme for *Viderunt.) Under Perotinus (*c.* 1160–1225), the repertory of compositions for the Proper was considerably enlarged by the numerous *clausulae, many of which were later (after 1225) transformed into liturgical motets (e.g., all the motets with the tenor *Omnes* form a part of the Christmas Gradual Viderunt). Around 1300, the composition of the Proper practically died out [see, however, *Choralis Constantinus and Byrd's *Gradualia* of 1605/07], and the composition of the Ordinary began to attract exclusive interest. The reason for this change lies in the fact that, while the composition of, e.g., a Gradual could be heard only once a year, compositions of a Kyrie, Sanctus, etc., could be performed on many different occasions. The earliest examples of this category are two-part compositions (organa) of the *Benedicamus and of Kyrie-tropes [Ex. in *HAM*, nos. 26b and 37; *SchGMB*, no. 9]. Two-voice settings of Sanctus and Agnus tropes, probably of English origin, are contained in fasc. 11 of the Wolfenbüttel codex W_1 [cf. *ReMMA*, 394]. Two-part compositions of troped and plain Kyries as well as a three-voiced Et in terra occur in the Codex Huelgas from c. 1275 [cf. H. Anglès, *El Codex Musical de las Huelgas*, 3 vols., 1931]. The first example of a complete Mass (Ordinary) is the *Messe de Tournai* of c. 1300 which, however, is probably a compilation of individual compositions written at different periods [new ed. in E. Coussemaker, *Messe du XIIIe siècle*, 1861]. Machaut's Mass (said to have been composed for the coronation of Charles V in 1364, but probably of a considerably earlier date, judging from its Ars antiqua style) is the first example of a complete Mass by a single composer [cf. *WoGM* iii, nos. 17, 18]. Curiously enough, his example was not followed until nearly 100 years later. The MSS of the late 14th century (e.g., London, Brit. Mus. *Add. 29987* [cf. *WoGM* i, 268] and Codex Apt [cf. H. Besseler, in *AMW* vii, 203f; also *Editions XXIV, A, 10]) contain a number of Kyries, Glorias, etc., but no complete Mass. In England the practice of writing single Mass movements prevailed throughout the 15th century (Dunstable; numerous composers of the *Old Hall MS).

II. 1400–1600. The main period of Mass composition begins with Dufay (c.

1400–74) and comes to an end with Palestrina (1525–94). The writing of complete Masses in five movements (Kyrie, Gloria, Credo, Sanctus, Agnus Dei) or frequently in six (with a separate movement for the Benedictus) now becomes one of the main concerns of composers. The majority of these Masses show the following two peculiarities: (a) the use of borrowed material, monodic or polyphonic in nature, sacred or secular as to source; (b) cyclical treatment, i.e., the use of the same material in all the movements. The following main categories of Mass composition can be distinguished:

a. Plainsong Mass (*missa choralis*). This is a non-cyclical type of Mass, in which each movement draws its musical material from the corresponding item of a monophonic (Gregorian) Mass. This genre is found throughout the period, but to a far lesser degree than the cyclical Mass type. Examples are the Mass of Reginald Liebert [Trent Codices; cf. *DTOe* 27.i], Morales' *Missa de beata Virgine*, and Palestrina's *Missa pro defunctis*.

b. Cantus-firmus Mass. This term is commonly used to denote Masses in which all the movements are based on one and the same melody, usually in the tenor [see *Tenor Mass]. (It will be noticed that the terms "plainsong Mass" and "cantus-firmus Mass" are far from being correct and proper designations: the "plainsong" of the former category is usually a cantus firmus, and the "cantus firmus" of the latter category is frequently taken from plainsong.) This cyclical type is perhaps the most frequent of all. According to the source of the cantus firmus three species can be distinguished, i.e., Masses based on (a) a liturgical, (b) a secular, and (c) an invented cantus firmus. Among the liturgical cantus firmi the antiphons B.M.V. [see *Antiphon (2)] and hymns are most often used. Examples are Josquin's *Missa Pange lingua* and Palestrina's *Missa Salve regina*. This genre, although found throughout the period, is more characteristic of the 16th century than of the 15th, at which time secular cantus firmi were preferred.

Particularly popular were French chansons (chanson Mass), above all, the famous *L'homme armé. Other examples are Ockeghem's *Missa De plus en plus* and Obrecht's *Missa Fortuna desperata.* In England the tune *Western Wynde* was popular (Shepherd, Taverner, Tye). Isaac's *Missa carminum* is an example of the *quodlibet Mass in which several secular melodies are combined. Around 1500 the use of "invented" cantus firmi became popular, either of a *soggetto cavato, e.g., Josquin's *Missa Hercules Dux Ferrarie,* or of the *hexachord, e.g., Palestrina's *Missa Ut re mi fa sol la* (*Missa super voces musicales*).

c. Parody Mass. See separate entry.

d. The freely invented Mass. For freely invented Masses, which form a relatively small group, general designations such as *Missa quarti toni* (Vittoria), *Missa cuiusvis toni* (Ockeghem), *Missa sine nomine* (Obrecht; cf. *HAM*, no. 77), *Missa brevis* (Palestrina) were used. It must be noted, however, that the complete originality of any Mass written during the period is possibly open to question, and that a cantus firmus is often used where none is indicated in the title. This is especially true for Masses composed after the *Council of Trent at which the use of secular cantus firmi was forbidden. For instance, Palestrina's *Missa quarta* (1582) is based on *L'homme armé.*

Naturally, within each of these categories the treatment varies considerably according to the period of composition. The earliest type (though by no means restricted to the early period) is the use of the cantus firmus, without alterations, in long notes [*Pfundnoten] in the tenor. Later we find the cantus firmus shared among the other voices and also omitted altogether in certain sections, e.g., in the Christe eleison and in the Credo. Another modification is the use of a melodically and rhythmically altered cantus firmus, a sort of free variation of the borrowed melody which was used not only as a tenor but also as a soprano melody [see *Discant Mass]. By the end of the 15th century the techniques of variation upon a borrowed tune are extremely

highly developed; the cantus firmus may be completely absorbed throughout the polyphonic texture, so that a derivative Mass is indistinguishable in style from a freely composed one. A frequent device of cyclical treatment is the use of the same motive at the beginning of all the movements [cf. *HAM*, no. 77]. See also *Organ Mass.

III. 1600–present. After 1600 the composition of the Mass lost its former importance. In Italy [see *Roman School] the a-cappella tradition of Palestrina (*stile antico*) was continued by composers such as Steffano Bernardi (d. 1628; cf. *DTOe* 36.i), Antonio Draghi (1635–1700; cf. *DTOe* 23.i), and Antonio Lotti (1667–1740; cf. *DdT* 60), while others enlarged the vocal resources to gigantic choirs of 32 and 48 voice-parts (Orazio Benevoli, 1605–72; cf. *DTOe* 10.i). In Germany the development followed more progressive trends, by the inclusion of the orchestra and of the 17th-century styles of the concerto, aria, etc. (*stile moderno*). The Masses by Biber, Schmeltzer, and Kerll [cf. *DTOe* 23.i] may be mentioned as landmarks on the road leading to Bach's *B minor Mass* (1733–38). Concomitant with the tendency to a greater variety of styles was the division of the Mass into a greater number of movements, particularly within the Gloria and the Credo. Following is the structure of Bach's Mass:

Kyrie
   Kyrie eleison (Lord, have mercy)
   Christi eleison (Christ, have mercy)
   Kyrie eleison (Lord, have mercy)
Gloria
   Gloria in excelsis Deo (Glory be to God on high)
   Laudamus te (We praise Thee)
   Gratias agimus tibi (We give Thee thanks)
   Domine Deus (Lord God)
   Qui tollis peccata mundi (Who takest away the sins of the world)
   Qui sedes ad dexteram patris (Who sittest at the right hand of the Father)
   Quoniam tu solus sanctus (For Thou only art holy)
   Cum sancto spiritu (With the Holy Spirit)
Credo
   Credo in unum Deum (I believe in one God)
   Patrem omnipotentem (Father almighty)
   Et in unum Dominum (And in one Lord)
   Et incarnatus est (And was incarnate)

Crucifixus (Crucified)
Et resurrexit (And rose again)
Et in Spiritum Sanctum (And [I believe] in the Holy Spirit)
Confiteor unum baptisma (I confess one baptism)
Sanctus
   Sanctus (Holy)
   Hosanna in excelsis (Hosanna in the highest)
   Benedictus qui venit (Blessed is He that cometh)
Agnus
   Agnus Dei (Lamb of God)
   Dona nobis pacem (Give us peace)

The Masses by Francesco Durante (1684–1755), Johann Hasse (1699–1755), Haydn (1732–1809; see *Paukenmesse), and Mozart (1756–91) are indicative of the trend towards secularization of the music for the Mass, and it was not until Beethoven's *Missa solemnis* (op. 123, 1819–23) that a work was created which stands the proof of comparison with Bach's Mass. Beethoven treats the text in a more continuous manner than Bach but has, in the Credo, a separate movement for *Et homo* (after *Et incarnatus*) and *Et vitam* (after *Confiteor*), this being treated as an extended closing fugue.

Cherubini (1760–1842) wrote several Masses between 1809 (*Mass in F* for three voices and orchestra) and 1825 (*Coronation Mass*) which deserve more attention than is given them, as do also the six Masses by Schubert. Mass composition was continued by Carl-Maria von Weber (2), Franz Liszt (4, including the *Graner Mass*, 1855), César Franck (2), Charles Gounod (9), and culminated in the three Masses of Anton Bruckner, particularly his *F minor Mass* (1867), the only great Mass composition after Bach and Beethoven.

Lit. *Liturgical:* A. Cabrol, *The Mass, Its Doctrine and History* (1931); O'Brien, *History of the Mass* (1893); P. Parsch, *The Liturgy of the Mass* (1936); cf. *MoML*, 502. — *To A and B:* P. Wagner, *Geschichte der Messe* i (till 1600; 1913); O. Ursprung, *Die katholische Kirchenmusik* (*BüHM*, 1932). — *To B, I:* F. Ludwig, "Die mehrstimmige Messe des 14. Jahrhunderts" (*AMW* vii). — *To B, II:* R. Ficker, "Die frühen Messenkompositionen der Trienter Codices" (*StM* xi);

id., "Zur Kolorierungstechnik der Trienter Messen" (*StM* vii); H. B. Collins, "John Taverner's Masses" (*ML* v); F. X. Haberl, "Die Messen Adriaen Willaerts" (*MfM* iii); J. Schmidt, "Die Messen des Clemens non Papa" (*ZMW* ix); see also *Organ mass: *Parody mass. — *To B, III:* G. Adler, "Zur Geschichte der Wiener Messkomposition . . ." (*StM* iv); H. A. Sander, *Italienische Messkompositionen des 17. Jahrhunderts* (Diss. Breslau 1932). — *To B, IV:* A. Schnerich, *Messe und Requiem seit Haydn und Mozart* (1909); B. A. Wallner, "C. M. von Weber's Messen" (*ZMW* viii).

Mastersingers, The. See *Meistersinger, Die.

Matasin, matassin, mattachin. A 16th-century dance performed by costumed dancers, representing men in armor or in other disguises [see *Bouffons; *Dance of death; *Morisca]. An example called "Mattasin oder Toden Tantz" occurs in Nörmiger's tablature of 1593 [cf. W. Merian, *Der Tanz in den deutschen Tabulaturbüchern* (1927), 256]. A similar melody called "Matachina" is found in a French guitern tablature of 1570 [cf. W. Tappert, *Sang und Klang aus alter Zeit*, p. 39].

Matins [L. *Matutinum*]. See *Office hours.

Maultrommel [G.]. *Jew's harp.

Ma Vlast (My Fatherland). See *Symphonic poem II.

Maxima. See *Mensural notation I.

Maxixe. The oldest urban dance of Brazil. It originated in the late 19th century, and appeared in Europe around 1890, virtually opening the vogue of exotic dance music. It is in moderate duple meter, with simple syncopated rhythms. See *Samba.

Mazeppa. (1) A *symphonic poem by F. Liszt. — (2) An opera by Tchaikovsky (1883).

Mazurka, mazur. A Polish national dance, in triple meter and in moderate speed, frequently with strong accents on the second or, particularly, the third beat [see Ex.]. It is performed by four or eight

couples, with a great variety of steps, often improvised.

The mazurka appeared in Germany in the mid-18th century, spreading to France around 1800 and to England around 1830. Chopin was the first to introduce the dance into the realm of art music. His mazurkas are particularly interesting because of the occasional use of modal idioms, the earliest indication of the 19th-century use of *modality as a folkloristic device. Later composers of mazurkas are Glinka, Tchaikovsky, and Szymanowski. See Kujawiak; *Dance music IV.

M.d. Abbreviation of *main droite* [F.] or *mano destra* [It.], i.e., right hand.

Meane, mene. In 15th- to 17th-century English music, a middle part of a polyphonic composition. See, e.g., the following passage from a 15th-century MS [cf. G. Schad, *Musik und Musikausdrücke in der Mittelenglischen Literatur* (19–?), p. 13]: "Primus pastor: 'Let me syng the tenory.' Secundus pastor: 'And I the tryble so hye.' Tertius pastor: 'The meyne fallys to me.'" Organ compositions of the pre-Virginalistic period frequently show inscriptions such as "Salvator with a meane," possibly denoting a hidden cantus firmus. A long poem by Redford on the *mene*, which unfortunately contributes little towards a further clarification of the term, is reprinted in C. Pfatteicher, *John Redford* (1934), p. 64. Sometimes, but not always, such a middle part is written in black notes, as contrasted with white notes in the other parts [cf. *ApNPM*, 10ff].

Originally the term was used for the middle voice in the three-part fauxbourdon of the 14th century [see *Fauxbourdon (2); also under *Treble]. It was also applied to instruments (viols) playing the middle part as well as to the two middle strings (small meane, great meane) of the viol.

Mean-tone system. See *Temperament II.

Measure [F. *mesure*; G. *Takt*; It. *misura*]. A measure is a group of beats (units of musical time) the first of which bears an accent. Such groups, in numbers of two, three, four, or, occasionally, five each, recur consistently throughout the composition and are marked off from one another by bar-lines. The basic scheme of note-values within a measure is called *meter or time (duple, triple, 6/8-meter, etc.). Occasional deviations from the regularity of accent, e.g., *syncopation, emphasize rather than destroy the general scheme of measure and time.

As appears from these explanations, the concept of measure stands or falls with the principle of regular accent, a principle which is of primary importance in almost all music generally known today. By no means, however, has music always embodied this principle. Disregarding dance music which, for obvious reasons, is nearly always "measure-music," one may divide the history of European music into four periods alternating from "measure-free music" to "measure-music," namely: (a) 500–1200: no measure (plainsong, organum purum); (b) 1200–1450: measure based upon the rhythmic *modes, the *mensurations, or, in Italy, on the *divisiones; (c) 1450–1600: prevalence of measure-free (Flemish) polyphony; (d) 1600–1920: measure based upon the principles of harmony and regular melodic phrase. With respect to period (c), the reader must be warned not to confuse "measure-music" (as defined above) with "measured music" in the sense of *mensural music. The difference is that mensural music (which prevailed throughout the period in question), although embodying the principle of regular groups of beats (*tempus perfectum, imperfectum*, etc.), frequently lacks the most important characteristic of "measure-music," that is, the accent on the first beat of such a group. See also *Rhythm II (a).

Mechanical composition. Cf. H. Gerigk, "Würfelmusik" (*ZMW* xvi).

Mechanical instruments. I. Appliances designed to produce musical performance mechanically, i.e., without an actual performer. Prior to the end of the 19th century such apparatus were always based upon the principle of the barrel-and-pin mechanism. The hand, or a mechanical clockwork, turns a wooden cylinder bearing pins acting against levers or similar gadgets, which in turn operate upon the hammers of a keyboard instrument, the clappers of a set of bells, the mouthpieces of organ pipes, etc. As early as the 14th century, carillons were operated by such a mechanism. In the 16th century the same principle was applied to harpsichords and organs. In the collection of instruments left by Henry VIII at his death in 1547 was a "virginal that goethe with a whele without playing uppon." As a curiosity an instrument may be mentioned which was sent by Queen Elizabeth to the Sultan of Turkey in 1593, and which included an organ, a carillon, "trumpeters," "singing byrds," etc., and which had the particular distinction of going into action automatically every six hours. About the same time Hans Leo Hassler took an active interest in the fabrication and sale of musical clockworks. Of particular interest is a mechanical spinet which is preserved with six pieces from the early 18th century, probably the earliest examples of "phonographic" music [cf. P. Nettl, in *ZMW* ii, 523]. Mozart wrote three compositions for the mechanical organ (*Orgelwalze*), an Adagio and Allegro in F minor (K.V. 594), a Fantasia in F minor (K.V. 608), and an Andante in F major (K.V. 616).

II. The only instrument of the barrel-and-pin type which attained considerable practical importance was the English barrel-organ. This was a small organ connected with an arrangement of interchangeable barrels, each containing a number of the most popular psalm and hymn tunes. The great popularity which these automatons enjoyed in English churches during the 18th and 19th centuries was a principal cause of the deplorable state of organ music in England

up to recently. Mason, in his *Essays, Historical and Critical, on English Church Music* (1795), says that he prefers "the mechanical assistance of a Cylindrical or Barrel Organ to the fingers of the best parochial organists" — a statement which reflects on the skill of the parochial organists rather than on the barrel-organ. See also *Serinette; *Orgue de barbarie.

III. Towards the end of the 18th century various small instruments called *Flötenuhr* (flute-clock) were made (by P. Niemecz, librarian to Prince Esterhazy), which combined an ordinary clock with a set of small pipes and bellows operated by the clockwork. For these instruments (also called *Laufwerk*) Haydn wrote a number of charming pieces [cf. E. F. Schmidt, †*Werke für Laufwerk* (1931), and in *ZMW* xiv].

Passing reference may be made to the well-known "musical boxes" (*boîte à musique; tabatière de musique; Spieldose*) whose whimsically high and thin tones have frequently been imitated in piano pieces, e.g., by Liadov, Leschetitzky, and, ironically, by Stravinsky in his *Petrouchka* (Valse). A truly remarkable specimen was a "musical bustle" which was presented to Queen Victoria in 1887 and which was "so designed as to provide a performance of the National Anthem (God Save the Queen) whenever the wearer sat down."

In the early 19th century a number of instruments were built for the mechanical reproduction of entire orchestras, e.g., Maelzel's *Panharmonicon* (1804), for which Beethoven originally wrote the "Sieges-Symphonie" of his *Battle of Vittoria* (1813), the *Apollonicon* built by Flight and Robson (1817), the *Orchestrion* (Kaufmann, 1851), and numerous others the descendants of which are still found in taverns throughout Europe, taking the place of the American "juke box."

IV. An important advance over the barrel-and-pin mechanism was the perforated paper-roll of the late 19th century. A roll of cardboard is pierced with small openings corresponding in position and length to the pitch and duration of

the tones of the composition to be reproduced. This passes over a cylinder furnished with numerous small apertures
(similar to those of the mouth harmonica) which are connected by pipes with
the action of a pianoforte. As often as an
opening in the cardboard passes over the
cylinder, a stream of air is pushed (or
drawn) through the corresponding pipe,
thus setting the hammer in motion. This
principle has been applied with a considerable degree of perfection in instruments
such as the *Player-piano*, the *Welte-Mi-
gnon*, the *Pianola*, the *Phonola*, etc. The
player-rolls are usually reproductions of
performances by famous virtuosos. In
most of the instruments the rendition can
be modified according to the taste of the
player who can regulate to a certain degree the speed and the dynamic details.
Needless to say, the possibility of beating
the speed-record of world-famous pianists
has added considerably to the commercial value of these instruments. Some
modern composers (Hindemith, Toch)
have written original compositions for
such mechanical pianofortes, availing
themselves of the possibility of producing
sound effects which are not obtainable by
a pianist, e.g., chords consisting of thirty
and more notes, or the simultaneous use
of the lowest, the middle, and the highest
registers.

The extraordinary success of the *phonograph and the radio has put all these
attempts into eclipse.

Lit.: H. Leichtentritt, in *MQ* xx; *LavE*
ii.3, 2117; G. C. A. Jonson, in *PMA* xlii;
G. L. Jaccard, in *Hobbies* 43, nos. 8, 9.

Mechanik [G.]. The action of a pianoforte, etc.

Medesimo tempo [It.]. The same
tempo.

Medial cadence. See *Cadence I.

Mediant. See *Scale degrees.

Mediation [L. *mediatio*]. See *Psalm
tones.

Medicean edition [L. *Editio Medicea*]. See *Liturgical books II.

Medicinale. See *Psaltery.

Medieval music. See *Middle Ages.

Medium [L., half]. *Cantus per medium*
is, in 16th-century theory, singing in
"halved" values, i.e., in proportio dupla
[see *Proportions] or, in modern parlance, *alla breve*.

Medley. Same as *potpourri. The term
was already used by the virginalists.

Mehr- [G., more, several]. *Mehrchörig*,
polychoral. *Mehrstimmig*, in more than
one part, i.e., polyphonic. *Mehrstimmigkeit*, polyphony.

Meistersinger [G., mastersingers].
I. A literary and musical movement of
the 15th and 16th centuries which was
cultivated by the guilds of the German
craftsmen, and which represents the middle-class continuation of the activity of
the aristocratic *Minnesinger of the 12th
to the 14th century. The desire of the
Meistersinger to emphasize the aura of
such a lineage led to a store of naïve legends concerning the origin of their movement. A. Puschmann, e.g., in his *Gründ-
licher Bericht des deutschen Meistergesanges und der Tabulatur* (1574; new ed.
by R. Jonas, 1888), relates that the Meistergesang was founded, upon the initiative of the Roman Emperor, Otto I, at
Paris in 962 by twelve "first masters"
among whom were Walther v. d. Vogelweide and Heinrich Frauenlob — men
who actually flourished around 1200 and
1300 respectively! The statement that
Heinrich Frauenlob was the first Meistersinger is still frequently found in modern
writings, although the accuracy of this
tradition was already questioned by the
German professor J. Chr. Wagenseil,
in his *De civitate Norimbergi commen-
tatio*, 1697, the source book of Richard
Wagner's *Meistersinger* libretto. Actually it is not until the early 15th century
that names such as Muskatblüt, Harder,
Der Zwinger, suggest a greater participation of commoners. Even Michael Be-
haim (1416–74), who might be more
properly regarded as the first Meistersinger, falls outside the category proper,

since he conducted a traveling life — like the bards — whereas the Meistersinger were resident members of reputable city guilds, united in local schools. Real Meistersinger are: *Conrad Nachtigall*; *Hans Sachs* (1494–1576); *Hans Folz* (all in Nuremberg); *Sebastian Wilde* (in Augsburg); *Adam Puschmann* (1532–1600, in Breslau). In the 16th century the movement spread over almost all of Germany, but declined rapidly during the 17th century. Certain schools existed throughout the 18th century; that of Ulm was dissolved in 1839.

II. Characteristic features of the *Meistergesang* are the rigid and pedantic rules which regulated the procedure at their weekly meetings (Sunday, after church), the establishment of competitions and of prizes, the promotion of the members into various classes (*Schüler, Schulfreund, Singer, Dichter, Meiser*, i.e., pupil, friend, singer, poet, master), etc. The rules were set down in the so-called *Tabulatur* (tablature). The title Dichter was given for the invention of a new poem (called *Lied, Gesang*), the title Meister for a new melody (called *Ton, Weise*). Most of the numerous poems were sung to standard melodies the names of which referred to their composers (e.g., *Brant-weise*; *Der Wilde Ton*) or to other characteristics of a more or less obscure nature (e.g., *Rosenton, Grasmückenweise* — "warbler-melody"), while names such as *Schwartz-Dintenweis* ("black ink melody"), *Kurtze-Affenweis* ("short monkey melody"), show that the Meistersinger did not lack a sense of humor. The whole setup has been most vividly (and accurately!) described by Wagner in his *Die Meistersinger von Nürnberg* [particularly Act I, David and Kothner].

III. The musical repertory of the Meistersinger, as it is preserved, consists of a great number of monophonic melodies, written in *plainsong notation in a more or less free rhythm. Practically all of them are in the *Barform, the traditional form of the Minnesinger. Among the songs of Hans Sachs there are several attractive melodies [cf. *HAM*, no. 24;

EiBM, no. 9; *BeMMR*, 271; *SchGMB*, no. 78]. On the whole, however, the Meistersinger melodies are clumsy and barren, often overcrowded with meaningless coloraturas (*Blumen*).

Recent investigations have shown that the Meistersinger probably derived elements of their ceremonial not only from the Minnesinger, but also from the scholastic procedure of medieval doctor examinations, from pious fraternities, similar to the Italian *laudesi [cf. the prevailingly Biblical repertory of the Meistersinger], and possibly from the French *puys.

Lit.: H. J. Moser, *Geschichte der deutschen Musik* i (1930), 303–318; P. Runge, †*Die Kolmarer Liederhandschrift* (1896); G. Münzer, †*Das Liederbuch des Adolf Puschmann* (1907); R. Staiger, †*Die Liederhandschrift des Benedikt von Watt* (*BIM* II, 13); H. Thompson, *Wagner and Wagenseil* (1927); G. Münzer, "Hans Sachs als Musiker" (*DM* v.19); P. Runge (also G. Münzer, E. Bernouilli), "Ueber die Notation der Meistersinger" (*KIM*, 1906, p. 17; 1909, p. 84).

Meistersinger von Nürnberg, Die ("The Mastersingers of Nuremberg"). Opera in three acts by Richard Wagner (1813–83), to his own libretto, first performance, Munich, 1868. The plot, which is based on careful studies of original sources (Wagenseil, 1697), reveals a true and lively picture of the life and customs in the Mastersinger guilds of the 16th century [see *Meistersinger], with the cobbler-poet *Hans Sachs* (Baritone) as the central figure. The dramatic action is carried chiefly by the young knight *Walther von Stolzing* (Tenor) who, in the first scene (Church), falls in love with *Eva* (Soprano) and enters the guild in order to compete (victoriously, of course) at the contest where he wins the hand of Eva through his prize-song "Morgenlich leuchtend im rosigen Schein," in spite of the intrigues of his rival *Beckmesser* (Bass buffo).

The *Meistersinger* represents an artistic peak in Wagner's work comparable to that represented by the Waldstein

Sonata and the Emperor Concerto of Beethoven: the sovereign and assured maturity of his middle period. In its perfect balance of means, in its "C-major atmosphere," in its happy variety of scenes and expressions, the opera offers a striking contrast to the earlier *Tristan* (1865) with its exuberant chromaticism and over-passionate expression of tragic love-madness. The overture to the *Meistersinger*, frequently performed in concerts, is one of the greatest examples of 19th-century instrumental music and one which makes us regret that Wagner concentrated his interest exclusively on the opera. See *Opera X. Cf. H. Thompson, *Wagner und Wagenseil* (1927).

Melisma. (1) An expressive vocal passage sung to one syllable, in contradistinction to the virtuoso-like and frequently stereotyped *coloratura. The term is used particularly with reference to Gregorian chant, but may also be applied to expressive or characteristic passages in other vocal styles. The distinction between melismatic style and syllabic style is of fundamental importance in Gregorian chant [see *Gregorian chant III] as well as in 13th-century polyphonic music [cf. *ApNPM*, 212ff]. — (2) The term has occasionally been used (F. Ludwig) for the more common term *clausula, because the clausulae are polyphonic elaborations of plainsong melismas (vocalizing sections in the graduals and alleluias).

Melodrama. Music designed as an instrumental accompaniment to a spoken text [see, however, *Melodramma]. Experiments in melodramatic style have not been rare, but have scarcely met with lasting success, on account of the acoustic incongruity of the spoken word and of music. In the Greek drama, which made ample use of melodramatic performance, this contrast was considerably less noticeable, because of the more "musical" character of the Greek language, and the more "speech-like" nature of Greek music. Modern speech, with its monotonic pitch, and modern music, with its richness of harmonies, do not combine very well.

However, melodramatic accompaniment has been effectively used as an occasional contrast to song, e.g., in the grave-digging scene of Beethoven's *Fidelio*, in the incantation scene of Weber's *Der Freischütz*, in the final scene of Busoni's *Doctor Faust*, etc.

More specifically, the term melodrama (also monodrama, duodrama) applies to complete plays written in this style, as was repeatedly done in the 18th century: J. E. Eberlin (1706–62), *Sigismundus* [cf. *DTOe* 28.i]; J. J. Rousseau, *Pygmalion* (1762); Georg Benda, *Ariadne auf Naxos* (1775; new ed. by A. Einstein, 1920; cf. *AdHM*, 752) and *Medea* (1778). The latter's plays, especially, made quite a sensation, and caused Mozart to introduce two long melodramatic monologues in his *Zaïde* (1780). Around 1800, ballads were frequently recited to a pianoforte accompaniment; an interesting example, by F. Ries, Beethoven's pupil, is reproduced in *TaAM* xiv. Goethe wrote various plays for melodramatic performance, e.g., *Proserpina* (1776). Modern examples of melodrama are *Enoch Arden* by R. Strauss (op. 38, 1898), *The Dream of Jubal* by A. C. Mackenzie (1889), A. Schönberg's *Pierrot Lunaire* (uses a semimelodramatic "Sprechstimme" on definite pitches indicated in the score), passages in Honegger's *King David*, etc.

Lit.: J. F. Mason, *The Melodrama in France* (1912); *LaMWC*, 1056; E. Istel, *Die Entstehung des deutschen Melodramas* (1906); *id.*, in *DM*, v. 9–12; E. C. van Bellen, *Les Origines du mélodrame* (1927); R. Augsten, *Les premiers mélodrames français, composés aux modèles allemandes* (1912); M. Steinitzer, *Zur Entwicklungsgeschichte des Melodrams und Mimodrams* (1918); H. Martens, †*Das Melodrama* (1932).

Melodramma [It.]. Common Italian term for opera (not *melodrama).

Melody. I. In the most general sense, a succession of musical tones, as contrasted with *harmony, i.e., musical tones sounded simultaneously. Thus, melody and harmony represent the horizontal and the vertical elements of the musical *texture. By its very nature melody cannot be separated from rhythm. Each musical sound has two fundamental qualities, pitch and duration, and both of these enter into those successions of pitch-plus-duration values which we call melodies. To consider melody and rhythm as separate, or even as mutually exclusive phenomena — as is usually done — is misleading. If a distinction between the pitch quality ("high-low") and the time quality ("long-short") is needed, the proper terms are *motion and rhythm. Melody may thus be said to consist of motion plus rhythm, and every melody can be separated into a motion skeleton and a rhythm skeleton, as the accompanying example illustrates.

In musical composition, melody may occur either without any additional element of texture (*monophonic music), or in combination with one or more other melodies (*polyphonic music), or supported by harmonies (*homophonic music). These three categories roughly describe the entire development of music: the first embraces the period from its beginnings through the first millennium of the Christian era (Greek music, Gregorian chant; up to the present in *primitive and *Oriental music and in *folk song); the second, that from 1000 to about 1750 (Middle Ages, Renaissance, Baroque; see *History of music); the third, that from 1750 to the present day. In the last period, particularly during the 19th century, there has been an increasing tendency to make melody subservient to harmony or, at least, to consider it as the mere result of harmonic progressions. The current explanation of melody as the "surface of harmony" clearly illustrates this point of view. Writers have gone so far as to maintain that a melody which cannot be interpreted harmonically is simply incomprehensible. It should suffice to point to the great treasure of purely

melodic music in Gregorian chant in order to refute so utterly false a conception.

II. Although the present interest in polyphonic music has resulted in a revision of the greatest misconceptions, the real importance of melody is still far from being fully and generally recognized. It must be observed that among the various components of the musical composition, such as melody, harmony, rhythm, orchestration, the first-mentioned is, from the historical as well as from the creative point of view, far superior to all the others, so superior indeed that the others can hardly be considered as being on the same plane of importance. The 19th-century development of music, with its growing emphasis on the exploitation of novel harmonies, of orchestral colors, and of rhythm as an independent element, has temporarily obscured the fact that melody is the only element in common to music of all times and all races and that, moreover, it is the cornerstone and touchstone of artistic quality. Harmony, orchestration, and rhythm are subject to certain rational premises which make them capable of being learned systematically; many composers of mediocre artistic rank have been extremely adept at such studies and their practical application. Only the great artists, however, possess that power of imagination and creation which goes into the making of a great melody. It is significant, as well as deplorable, that in the past fifty years hundreds of books on harmony and on orchestration have been written and that courses on these subjects form an indispensable part of the curriculum of all the teaching institutions, while the study of melody is almost completely neglected.

III. It is encouraging, however, to see that in the past twenty years several writers have turned their attention to the study of melody, not as a mere ornamentation of a harmonic structure, but as an elementary principle in its own right. General characterizations such as "tuneful," "simple," "touching," "expressive," "dramatic," etc., are not entirely without significance, but are too vague to provide a basis for a thorough study. A more promising aspect — indeed the one most likely to prove successful — is that derived from what one might call the face value of a melody, i.e., from the fact that it consists of successive notes of varying pitch. This point of view leads to a consideration of a melody as a "geometrical" design including upward and downward steps, and, still more important, as a "physical" phenomenon reminiscent of a moving body which is subject to forces causing and regulating its motion. A very important concept of such a theory is that of "musical gravity," a term which describes the fact that the "natural" movement of a musical line is downward [see the scales of *Greek music] and that an ascending motion has always a character of tension and energy. Of course, a melody will practically always combine ascending and descending movements; but the greater emphasis on, or the precedence of, one or the other is a point of prime importance, as may readily be seen from a comparison of melodies by Bach and Beethoven with those of Mendelssohn, for example. The accompanying illustration (a: Bach; b: Mendelssohn) shows two opposite graphs of musical gravity, melodies which, the student will not fail to notice, differ markedly in their physical as well as artistic "weight."

IV. Another consideration of basic importance is that of the steps in which a melody moves, i.e., whether narrow (conjunct) or wide (disjunct). This distinction is of prime interest in the study of primitive and Oriental music. For instance, Japanese music is prevailingly conjunct — hence, emotional, expressive — while ancient Chinese music is disjunct — hence, static, reserved [see also the two scales, slendro and pelog, of *Javanese music, and remark under *Primitive music III]. In European folk song it has

frequently been noticed that the French and Italians prefer narrow steps and ranges, as distinguished from the northern races, English, German, etc.

In art music the above dichotomy becomes one between scalar and chordal progressions, i.e., progressions through the tones of the scale or of a chord (triad, seventh-chord). Influenced by the current preoccupation with the harmonic point of view, writers usually consider the latter the more important one and frequently consider scalar progressions as mere passing-notes between main notes forming a chordal progression. In order to refute this point of view, it suffices to point to the theme of Beethoven's first Piano Sonata [Ex. 1, a] which, with the "ornamental" notes suppressed [Ex. 1, b], loses its character entirely, while it is not fundamentally affected by a substitution of scalar, instead of chordal, motion for the initial notes [Ex. 1, c]. In fact, scalar

motion is not only much earlier and more frequent than chordal motion, but also more important from the musical and artistic point of view. Only the scale possesses that character of "logical continuation," of "variety and unity," which is the lifeblood of melody. In fact, in a progression such as c-b-a-g-a-b-c' each tone has its own significance and function, leading from one level to another, while a similar chordal progression, such as c'-g-e-c-e-g-c', is, in spite of its greater range, a mere reiteration of one element. Many melodies of the great composers begin with a chordal motion and continue with scalar motion, thus showing a progression from a "static" beginning to a "dynamic" continuation [see the accompanying examples 2–4, by Mozart (Piano Sonata, K.V. 309), Beethoven (Eroica), and Bruckner (Symphony no. 7)].

Although modern composers have frequently been indifferent to (or incapable of?) melodic creation, interesting themselves chiefly in tone color, harmony, or rhythm, a distinct emphasis on the me-

lodic point of view is noticeable in the works of at least one outstanding contemporary composer, Paul Hindemith.

Lit.: E. Toch, *Melodielehre* (1923); P. Goetschius, *Exercises in Melody Writing*; W. Danckert, *Ursymbole und melodische Gestaltung* (1932); A. Lourié, "An Inquiry into Melody" (*MM* vi); A. H. Fox-Strangways, "Tune" (*ML* iii, no. 1); H. J. Watt, "Melody" (*ML* v, no. 3); O. Bie, "Melody" (*MQ* II).

Melody-types. A term used in modern writings on exotic and on early European music to denote a practice of fundamental importance in the more primitive stages of music, that is, the existence of a traditional repertory of melodies, melodic formulae, stereotyped figures, tonal progressions, ornamentations, rhythmic patterns, etc., which serve as a model for the creation of new melodies. Evidently such a procedure forms the strongest possible contrast to the modern ideal of "free invention" and "originality." An imaginary school of musicians writing deliberately in "Beethoven-style" would be an approximately analogous case to what still is the normal procedure among Arabian and Indian musicians — a procedure which largely accounts for the absence of the evolutionary element in Oriental music. To the category of melody-types belong the ancient Greek *nomos*, the *echos* of Byzantine and Armenian church music, the Syrian *risqolo*, the Javanese *patet*, the Hindu *raga*, the Arabian *maqam* [see also *Psalms*], and, in Europe, the Russian *popievki* and the

Weisen or *Töne* of the Meistersinger [see the entries *Greek music, etc.*].

Former writers have usually considered the ragas, maqams, echoi, etc., as the "modes" of Hindu, Arabian, Byzantine, etc., music. Actually, they represent an earlier stage of development in which the "model" prescribes not only a scale with a given ambitus and center-tone — as does a mode — but also typical motives and tone-progressions. (For an example, see under *Hindu music; a Syrian example is given in *GD, Suppl. Vol.*, 175.) The medieval system of the eight churchmodes probably developed through a process of rationalization from an earlier system of melody-types, possibly from the Byzantine *echoi*. The traces of this descent are still distinctly noticeable in Gregorian chant, as has been shown by Gevaert (*La Mélopée antique dans le chant de l'église Latin*, 1895) who reduced the numerous (more than 1200) antiphons to 47 types. Another example is the frequent recurrence of a figure such as c'-c'-a in many graduals [cf., e.g., *GR*, 15, 25, 28, 34, 331, etc.]. An exhaustive study of melody-types (*timbres*) in the late sequences is contained in E. Misvet and P. Aubry, *Les Proses d'Adam de Saint-Victor* (1900). Cf. *AdHM* 19f.

Melophone. See *Harmonium.

Melopiano. See *Sostenente pianoforte.

Mendelssohn Scholarship. See under *Scholarships, Fellowships, and Prizes II.

Mene. See *Meane; also *Fauxbourdon (2).

Ménestrandise. Early French term for the guilds of professional musicians (*ménestrel*, i.e., minstrel). François Couperin pictured a procession of minstrels, jongleurs, beggars, and acrobats with their bears and monkeys in a piece called "Les Fastes de la grande et ancienne Mxnxstrxndxsx" [cf. his *Pièces de clavecin*, ed. by J. Brahms and F. Chrysander, ii, 208].

Meno [It.]. Less. *Meno mosso*, less quickly.

Mensur [G.]. (1) Measure, meter, mensuration. — (2) In organ building, same as *scale, scaling (2).

Mensural music (also mensurable, mensurate). Translation of L. *musica mensurata* (*cantus mensurabilis*) which, in early theory (13th–16th centuries), is used in contrast to *musica plana*, i.e., plainsong. It denotes polyphonic music in which every note has a strictly determined value, as distinct from Gregorian chant with its free rhythm. See *Mensural notation; also under *Measure.

Mensural notation. The system of musical notation which was established, around 1250, by Franco of Cologne and which remained in use until 1600. Actually, this period embraces a variety of systems differing from each other in many particulars [see under *Notation]. The following explanation refers to the final stage of the development (*c.* 1450–1600) which is called white mensural notation, with reference to the white shapes of the larger note-values used instead of the former black shapes. See remark under *Proportional notation.

I. *Notational Signs.* These fall into two classes: single notes and ligatures. The single notes are: *maxima* (*Mx*), *longa* (*L*), *brevis* (*B*), *semibrevis* (*S*), *minima* (*M*), *semiminima* (*Sm*), *fusa* (*F*), and *semifusa* (*Sf*). On the next column is a table of the single notes and the corresponding rests, together with the modern forms derived from them.

For the transcription into modern notation it is advisable not to use the exact equivalents ($S =$ whole-note, etc.),

	Mx	L	B	S	M	Sm	F	Sf
Notes:								
Rests:								
Modern:								

but smaller values which more properly conform with the actual temporal duration of the old signs. In the subsequent explanations a reduction 1:4 is used so that the S is rendered as a quarter-note. For the ligatures, see the special article.

II. *Mensuration.* Mensuration is the general term for the temporal relationships between the note-values, comparable to the different meters of the modern system. Special terms are: *modus* (relationship between L and B), *tempus* (B and S), and *prolatio* (S and M). While in modern notation a note (unless dotted) is invariably equal to two notes of the next-smaller value, in mensural notation the chief notes, namely L, B, and S, may equal either two or three. This dichotomy is indicated by the terms *imperfect* and *perfect*. Omitting the *modus* which is usually imperfect, there result four combinations of *tempus* and *prolatio* (e.g., *tempus perfectum cum prolatione imperfecta*) which constitute the four main mensurations of mensural notations and which are indicated by special signs. They are the exact equivalent of four basic meters of modern notation, as indicated below:

	Tempus	Prolatio	Sign	Value of B	S	Example
I.	Imperfect	Imperfect	C			
II.	Perfect	Imperfect	O			
III.	Imperfect	Perfect	C			
IV.	Perfect	Perfect	☉			

The subsequent explanations refer chiefly to the mensuration II. As a matter of fact, in I the metrical relationships between the various notes are the same as in modern notation; this mensuration, therefore, presents no problems, aside from the use of ligatures and of coloration [see V.]. The principles for the mensuration III can easily be derived from those for II, by replacing each note by the next-smaller note, e.g., the *B* by the *S*, the tempus by the prolatio, etc. The mensuration IV practically never occurs in the sources of white notation and is rare even in the 14th century.

III. *Imperfection and Alteration.* The normal values of the *B* and *S*, i.e., three and one *S* respectively, are frequently modified according to principles known as imperfection and alteration. By imperfection the *B* is reduced from three *S* to two *S*, and by alteration the value of the *S* is doubled. The following rules comprise the most frequent cases: If a *B* is followed by one or by more than three *S*, it is "imperfected." If a *B* is followed by two *S*, the second of these *S* is altered [Ex. 1]. The last of these exam-

ples shows that a *B* may also be "imperfected" by a preceding *S*, a process which is called *imperfectio a parte ante*, as contrasted with the more frequent *imperfectio a parte post*. Rests cannot be imperfected or altered, but may cause imperfection or alteration of a note [Ex. 2].

IV. *Punctus divisionis, punctus additionis.* In order to indicate deviating groupings and also in cases of ambiguity a dot, called *punctus divisionis*, is used. This is equivalent to the modern bar-line in 3/4 meter, as it always marks off

groups of three *S* (perfection). Other specifications, such as *punctus perfectionis, imperfectionis, alterationis,* are both superfluous and confusing. The dot is also used, however, in an entirely different meaning, that is, as a *punctus additionis* which is identical with the dot of modern notation. The distinction between the two meanings of the dot is facilitated by the observation that a dot which follows upon a perfect note is necessarily a punctus divisionis, and that, on the other hand, a punctus additionis must always be complemented — sooner or later — by a single note equal to the value of the dot, i.e., half of the value of the dotted note. In the accompanying example the first and fifth dots are puncti divisionis, the others are puncti additionis.

V. *Coloration.* Coloration is the use of blackened notes (*B, S, M*) instead of the normal white forms (originally, red ink was used for this purpose):

The general principle of coloration is that three blackened notes are equal to two white notes. The result is different according to whether the blackened notes replace two imperfect or two perfect notes. In the former case [Ex., a and b] triplets result while in the latter case [c and d] the effect is a change of rhythm similar to that encountered frequently in the courantes of the 17th century [see *Hemiola]:

A special case of coloration is the so-called *minor color,* that is, the combination *S-M* in blackened notes. Originally, this indicated triplet rhythm, as above under (c). Owing to the shortness of the notes, however, its meaning changed into a dotted rhythm, as illustrated under (e). It is frequently followed by a series of *Sm*, as under (f). In a combination like this it should be observed that, notwithstanding their identity in shape as well as rhythmic value, the first of the stemmed notes is a blackened *M*, while the others are "white" (i.e., normal) *Sm*.

The accompanying example serves to

Discantus

Tenor

Transcription

illustrate the principles explained above. It also includes passages in *proportion. For all other details of mensural notation reference must be made to special books on the subject. See also *Notation; *Score II.

Lit.: W. Apel, *The Notation of Polyphonic Music* (1942; 2d ed., 1944); A. Bellermann, *Mensuralnoten und Taktzeichen* (1858; 3d ed., 1930); E. Praetorius, *Die Mensuraltheorie des Franchinus Gafurius . . .* (1906); H. Birtner,

"Die Probleme der spätmittelalterlichen Mensuralnotation . . ." (*ZMW* xi); A. M. Michalitschke, "Zur Frage der longa in der Mensuraltheorie des 13. Jahrhunderts" (*ZMW* vii); *id.*, in *ZMW* xii. See also under Notation, Ligatures, etc.

Mensuration. See Mensural notation II.

Mensuration canon. See *Canon II.

Mensurstrich [G.]. See under *Barline.

Mente, Alla [It.]. Improvised.

Menuett [G.], **menuetto** [It.]. See *Minuet.

Mer, La. See *Symphonic poem IV.

Mescolanza [It.]. *Medley.

Mese. See *Greek music II (a).

Mesotonic. Same as *mean-tone (system).

Messa di voce [It., placing of the voice]. A special vocal technique of the 18th-century *bel canto, consisting of a gradual crescendo and decrescendo over a sustained tone; see *Expression III. Modern singers use it extensively for training, but sparingly in performance. The term should not be confused with *mezza voce. See also *Filar il tuono.

Messanza [It.]. *Quodlibet.

Messe [F., G.]. Mass. *Messe des morts,* requiem mass.

Messel [corrupted from Arab. *mithal*]. The unit of measurement in the Arabian theory of intervals. Intervals were indicated by lengths of strings, in such a manner that the shorter string (the one giving the higher tone) was considered the unit. For instance, with the fifth c-g, the string for g would be the *messel*, and the string for c would measure $1\frac{1}{2}(\frac{3}{2})$ messel; with the fourth c-f, the string for f would be the messel, and the string for C would measure $1\frac{1}{3}(\frac{4}{3})$ messel. Thus, in this theory, the figures for the various intervals are exactly the same as the modern figures, which indicate quotients of frequencies. The messel has nothing to do with an early recognition of the third and the sixth as consonances, as has been erroneously supposed [cf. *RiML*, 1165 and 2102; also *Arabian music I].

Messiah. See under *Oratorio III.

Messine (Messenian) neumes. See *Neumes I.

Mesto [It.]. Mournful.

Mesure [F.]. Measure or meter.

Metamorphosis. The modification of a musical subject or motive made with a view to "changing its personality." This is a 19th-century device which differs markedly from earlier, more "technical," methods of modification as, e.g., the augmentation and diminution of a fugal subject, or the ornamentation of a theme. A characteristic example of metamorphosis is found in the various appearances of the "idée fixe" in Berlioz' Symphonie

Fantastique. F. Liszt exploited the principles of "transformation des thèmes" in his symphonic poems, and Wagner applied it to the *Leitmotiv of his operas [see Ex. 1, from *Siegfried]. In Sibelius' symphonies the metamorphosis is of a more abstract character, as the examples under 2 (Symphony no. 5, first movement) show. It will be noticed that the versions b-e retain the characteristic rhythm of the main theme (1), while f

preserves its melodic contour with a different rhythm.

Meter [F. *mesure*; G. *Takt*; It. *misura*]. The basic scheme of note values and accents which remains unaltered throughout a composition or a section thereof and which serves as a skeleton for the rhythm [see *Rhythm II (a)]. For instance, 3/4-meter (or 3/4-time) means that the basic values are quarter-notes and that each third of these receives a strong accent. This grouping is indicated by bar-lines which mark off *measures.

According to whether there are two, three, or four units to the measure, one speaks of duple (2/2, 2/4, 2/8), triple (3/2, 3/4, 3/8), and quadruple (4/2, 4/4, 4/8) meter, 4/4 being also called common meter. All these are called simple meters. Compound meters are derived from the above by multiplication with three: compound duple (6/2, 6/4, 6/8), compound triple (9/4, 9/8), and compound quadruple (12/4, 12/8, 12/16). For 4/4, 2/2 the signs C, ¢ are used [see *Allabreve]. *Quintuple meter (5/4) is either 2/4 + 3/4, or 3/4 + 2/4, according to where the secondary accent lies. An example of septuple meter, written 3/4 + 4/4, occurs in Brahms's *Variations* op. 21, no. 2. See also *Poetic meter; *Time signature.

Metrical psalms. See *Psalter.

Metronome. An apparatus to indicate the exact tempo of a piece. The instrument in general use today was constructed by Mälzel in 1816, hence the name Mälzel Metronome (abbr. M.M., or simply, M.). It had been preceded by numerous earlier attempts which go back as far as the late 17th century [cf. the article in *GD*]. Mälzel's metronome is constructed upon the principle of the double pendulum, that is, of an oscillating rod which has a weight at both ends, the one at the upper end being movable along a scale. By adjusting this weight away from or towards the pivot, the oscillations can be made slower or quicker respectively. An indication such as M.M. 80 means that the pendulum makes 80 oscillations per minute. Hence in a piece marked M.M. $\quad\!\!\!=80$ the duration of the half note will be $\frac{60}{80}=\frac{3}{4}$ second.

Metronomic indications can be used to estimate the approximate duration of a piece. The formula is $\frac{n \times t}{M}$, where M is the metronome figure, t the number of measures of the piece, and n the number of notes — those to which the metronome figure refers — in a measure. For instance, a piece of 160 measures in $\frac{3}{4}$-time with the metronome mark M.M. $\!\!\!= 90$ will last $\frac{3 \times 160}{90} = 5\frac{1}{3}$ minutes, or 5 minutes and 20 seconds.

The first composer to use the metronome was Beethoven. In 1817 he published metronomic indications for all the movements of his (then) eight symphonies (*Allgemeine Musikalische Zeitung*, 1817, no. 51). Unfortunately, the tempi indicated in his Hammerklavier-sonata and Ninth Symphony are almost impossibly fast, as are those indicated in the works of Schumann. See *Tempo.

Lit.: R. E. M. Harding, *Origins of Musical Time and Expression* (1938); R. Kirkpatrick, "Eighteenth-century Metronomic Indications" (*PAMS*, 1938); E. Borrel, "Les indications métronomiques . . . du xiiie siècle" (*RdM*, no. 27); R. Kolisch, "Tempo and Character in Beethoven's Music" (*MQ* xxix, nos. 2 and 3).

Mette [G.]. *Matins.

Mettez [F.]. Draw (an organ stop).

Metzer Neumen [G.]. Messine (Messenian) neumes; see *Neumes I.

Mexico. Mexico in pre-Hispanic times was dominated by the Aztecs, a tribe which is said to have come from a legendary region in the north called Aztlan. They settled in the fertile valley of Anahuac toward the beginning of the 12th century and in A.D. 1325 founded the city of Tenochtitlan (Mexico), which became the capital of their powerful empire. The social, political, and religious life of the Aztecs was full of elaborate ritual and ceremony, in which music played an indispensable role. On public occasions many thousands participated in the ceremonial dances and chants, accompanied by numerous percussion and wind instruments. The former consisted of drums, rattles, and bells; the latter, of various kinds of flutes, whistles, shell-trumpets, and tubular trumpets made of wood, cane, or clay. The Aztecs had flutes with three, four, or five holes, made of bone or baked clay. Notched bones which were scraped with a stick were widely used as musical instruments, producing, in the words of a Spanish chronicler, "música muy triste" (very sad music). The ancient Mexicans had two principal types of drum. One of these was the *huehuetl*, a cylindrical drum about two feet in diameter and about five or six feet high, generally made out of a single piece of hollowed-out wood. It was placed vertically; authorities differ as to whether it was played with a stick or with the bare hands. The *teponaztli*, or slit-drum, was shorter, and was placed horizontally. It was beaten at the center instead of the end. It had a narrow slit on the top, in the form of a letter H, which formed two tongues facing each other. As they were of different thicknesses, each of these tongues produced a different tone when struck. The teponaztli, therefore, was really a sort of xylophone. As to the actual form and structure of ancient Aztec music, we can only rely on conjecture, supported by such evidence as may be supplied by musical instruments that have been preserved. Aztec music was monophonic and its melodic possibilities were very limited. It appears to have been based on a pentatonic scale without semitones, and Carlos Chávez affirms that it "was regulated in conformity with a well-established system." No actual vestiges of this music have remained.

With the coming of the Spaniards, music in Mexico inevitably underwent a profound transformation. The missionary zeal of the Spaniards entailed an inculcation of European musical methods, especially as related to the ritual of Christian worship. Only three years after the capture of Mexico City by Cortés (1521), the first European school of music was founded in Texcoco by Pedro de Gante, a Franciscan missionary. The Indians were taught the elements of plain-chant, and they not only learned to play various European instruments, but were also taught to construct them. While the friars were teaching the Indians to form choirs for the churches that were springing up throughout the land, secular forms of music also were cultivated, and as early as 1526 we hear of a certain Ortiz who played the guitar and taught dancing. In 1539 a printing press was established in Mexico City, and in 1556 there appeared the first book with music printed in America, an Ordinary of the Mass. The first choirmaster of the Cathedral of Mexico City was Juan Juárez, appointed in 1538.

Notable among composers of the Colonial period was Antonio de Salazar, choirmaster of the Cathedral from about 1685 to 1715. He was succeeded by Manuel de Sumaya, who wrote the first opera composed in Mexico. Other Colonial composers were José de Torres, José María Aldana, and Antonio Juanas.

During the 19th century Mexican music was largely dominated by Italian opera and by pseudo-romantic salon patterns. Among composers born during the first half of the century the most prominent were Aniceto Ortega, Cenobio Paniagua, Melesio Morales, and Julio Ituarte.

Toward the close of the 19th century the two most prominent composers were Gustavo E. Campa (1863–1934) and Ricardo Castro (1864–1907), both of whom were entirely under European influences. However, they broke away from the Italian influence that had so long dominated Mexican music, substituting instead that of France (in the case of Campa) and Germany (in the case of Castro). Castro was an excellent pianist and as such attained conspicuous success in Europe and the United States. In his compositions he repeated the formulae of German Romanticism, and at the same time he revealed a

much greater technical competency than had any of the Mexican composers of the previous generation. Two of his operas, *Atzimba* and *La Leyenda de Rudel*, were produced in Mexico City.

It was not until after the turn of the century that musical nationalism began to emerge in Mexico. The initiator of this movement was Manuel M. Ponce (b. 1886), whose *Canciones Mexicanas* for piano were written in 1905. Ponce made his reputation abroad with his stylizations of Mexican popular songs, of which *Estrellita* is the best-known example. He has also published many pieces for piano based on Mexican traditional themes and rhythms, such as his *Danzas Mexicanas*. His larger works include the symphonic poem *Chapultepec* (1929), a Concerto for piano and orchestra, and a Concerto for guitar and orchestra. He has been widely active as teacher, editor, conductor, and pianist. Contemporary with Ponce are José Rolón (b. 1883) and Candelario Huizar (b. 1888), who fluctuate between nationalistic and universal tendencies. Occupying a unique position is Julián Carrillo (b. 1875), champion and practitioner of a new system of musical composition which he calls "Sonido 13," based on fractional tones ($1/4$, $1/8$, and $1/16$).

Two composers born in the same year (1899) but differing widely in temperament and technique are Silvestre Revueltas and Carlos Chávez. The former, who died prematurely in 1940, identified himself spontaneously with the spirit of Mexico's popular music, producing works that are highly original and at the same time entirely unaffected. He became internationally known through his music for the film *Redes* (The Wave). He also composed the symphonic poems *Caminos, Cuanahuac, Esquinas,* and *Sensemaya* (with chorus); several ballets, chamber music, and piano pieces. Chávez, founder and conductor of the National Symphony Orchestra of Mexico (1928), is the leading modernist of Mexico and is also an ardent exponent of musical nationalism, seeking to incorporate indigenous elements and pre-Hispanic traditions into his art. He has appeared frequently as guest-conductor with leading orchestras in the United States. Among his best-known compositions are two symphonies, *Sinfonía India* and *Sinfonía de Antígona*; the ballets *H.P.* (Horsepower) and *Los Cuatro Soles*; *Energía* for small orchestra. A number of his smaller works have been published in the United States by the "New Music" edition.

Mexico has a group of outstanding young composers, comprising Luis Sandi (b. 1905), Daniel Ayala (b. 1908), Pablo Moncayo (b. 1912), Salvador Contreras (b. 1912), and Blas Galindo (b. 1911). Of these, the first three are most definitely nationalistic. Ayala is of pure Mayan (Indian) blood and seeks a direct racial expression in his music. Another young composer who holds a distinctive place is Miguel Bernal Jiménez (b. 1910), who was trained in Italy and represents the Catholic tradition in contemporary Mexican music. He has written much church music, also the opera *Tata Vasco* (Mexico, 1941), based on the life of the famous missionary Vasco de Quiroga.

Mexican dances are the *Corrido and the *Jarabe.

Lit.: M. Galindo, *Historia de la música mejicana*, tomo I (Colima, 1933); G. Saldívar, *Historia de la música en México* (Mexico, 1934); O. Mayer-Serra, *Panorama de la música mexicana* (Mexico, 1941); R. Lach, "Die . . . Altmexikanischen Tempelgesänge" (*Festschrift für Joh. Wolf*). G. C.

Mezzo, mezza [It.]. Half. *Mezzo forte* (abbr. *mf*), half-loud, moderately forte. *Mezza voce*, with "half voice," i.e., with restrained volume of tone [see, however, *Messa di voce*]. *Mezzo legato*, half legato. *Mezzo-soprano*, see *Voices, Range of.

Mf. Mezzo forte.

M.g. [F.]. *Main gauche*, i.e., left hand.

Mi. See *Solmization; *Pitch names; *Hexachord. Being the third degree of the hexachord, *mi* adopts in the Guidonian system the meaning of the leading-tone (e, b) [see *Mi-fa].

Micanon. See *Psaltery.

Mi contra fa. See *Mi-fa.

Micrologus. A treatise by Guido of Arezzo (d. 1050; see *Theory) which is an important source for the development of organum [see *Organum II]. Re-edition by A. Amelli (1904); German translation by R. Schlecht in *MfM* v.

Microtone. Any interval smaller than a semitone, e.g., the *chroai* of Greek music or the *sruti* of the *Hindu scale. During the last fifty years there has been much experimentation with microtones: quarter-tones, sixth-tones, eighth-tones, and even sixteenth-tones (Haba, Busoni, Juan Carillo). Only in the field of quarter-tone music have definite results been gained [see *Quarter-tone].

Middle Ages, Music of the. The music of the Christian era prior to the Renaissance, thus roughly comprising the millennium from 500 to 1500 (1450). In view of the extension of this period it is necessary to divide it into periods of lesser duration comparable to those of other periods of music, such as the Renaissance and the Baroque. See *History of music and the special articles *Gregorian chant; *Ars antiqua; *Ars nova; *Burgundian School. Also the initial chapters of *French music; *Italian music; *English music, etc.

Lit.: G. Reese, *Music in the Middle Ages* (1940); H. Gleason, †*Examples of Music before 1400* (1942); H. Besseler, *Musik des Mittelalters und der Renaissance* (1931–35); Th. Gérold, *Histoire de la musique des origines à la fin du XIVe siècle* (1936); R. von Ficker, *Die Musik des Mittelalters* (1930).

Middle C. The C near the middle of the keyboard, that is c' [see *Pitch names]. It is represented on the first ledger line below the violin staff, or on the first ledger line above the bass staff.

Mi-fa. In the medieval theory of *hexachords a general expression of cautioning the singer against special or dangerous intervallic progressions. From the fol-

[445]

lowing table, showing the *mi*'s and *fa*'s of the three hexachords, it appears that the combination mi-fa designates a semitone if the two syllables are taken from the same hexachord, a tritone, if from successive hexachords (see the diagonal lines):

	Mi	Fa
Hexachordum durum (on G):	B	c
Hexachordum naturale (on C):	e	f
Hexachordum molle (on F):	a	bb

It is particularly to the *tritone, the "diabolus in musica," that the warning term *mi contra fa* ("mi contra fa, diabolus in musica") refers.

Milanese chant. See *Ambrosian chant.

Military band. The rise of military bands and of military music is coeval with that of the development of organized armies, during the 15th and 16th centuries. The mercenary troops of the Austrian emperor Karl V and of the French king François I had large bands of trumpets and kettledrums, and when they met in the battles of Marignano (1515) and Pavia (1525) the clash of the instruments was as fierce and famous as that of the weapons [see *Battaglia]. The military trumpeters became organized in guilds (G. *Feldtrompeter*) and were endowed with many privileges which distinguished them from the *Kammertrompeter*, i.e., the members of the civilian orchestras. The kettledrummers were expected to use all sorts of extravagant and affected movements such as survive to the present day with the drum majors and majorettes [cf. *SaHMI*, 330]. The music of these groups was, of course, limited to signals, and it was not until the advent of the 18th century that the introduction of melody instruments, such as the oboe, the bassoon, the French horn, and the clarinet, led to a rise of a broader repertory of military music, including marches and similar pieces. The bands of Louis XIV (1643–1715), organized by Lully, consisted of oboes, bassoons, and drums, while those of Frederick II (1740–86) included oboes, clarinets, horns, and bassoons. Around 1800, the vogue of Turkish mu-

sic [see *Janizary music] resulted in the adoption of noise-making instruments such as cymbals, triangles, the military Glockenspiel, and the crescent. Infantry regiments under Napoleon had bands consisting of one piccolo, one high clarinet, and sixteen ordinary clarinets, four bassoons, two serpents, two trumpets, one bass trumpet, four horns, three trombones, two side-drums, one bass drum, one triangle, two pairs of cymbals, and two crescents. A landmark in the development of military music was a performance given in honor of the Russian emperor by Carl Wieprecht, the organizer of Prussian military music, in Berlin on May 12, 1838, at which he conducted the united bands of sixteen infantry and sixteen cavalry regiments, totaling 1000 wind instruments and 200 drummers. Around 1850, Adolphe Sax reorganized the French military bands by the introduction of his novel valve brass instruments.

In the history of American military music Patrick Sarsfield Gilmore (1829–92) and John Philip Sousa (1854–1932) are outstanding. The former was bandmaster in the United States Army during the Civil War and organized a brass band in New York (Twenty-second Regiment) which became widely known through its concert tours in America and Europe (1878: Liverpool, Dublin, London, Paris, etc.). Sousa was leader of a band of the United States Marine Corps from 1880 to 1892, when he resigned and organized his own world-famous band (first concert, 1892, in Plainfield, N. J.; world tour 1910/11).

The composition of a military band varies in different countries and even in different regiments. An American band of 28 musicians consists of 1 bass BBb (sousaphone), 1 bass Eb (sousaphone), 3 trombones, 3 horns, 1 baritone (or euphonium), 5 cornets (1 solo), 1 trumpet, 5 Bb clarinets, 1 Eb clarinet, 1 piccolo, 3 saxophones (alto, tenor, baritone), 1 snare drum, 1 bass drum, 1 cymbal.

Lit.: H. G. Farmer, *Military Music and its Story* (1912); M. Brenet, *La musique militaire* (1921); P. Panoff, *Militärmusik in Geschichte und Gegenwart* (1921); G. Dyson, "The Composer and the Military Band" (*ML* ii, no. 1); M. Brenet, "French Military Music in the Reign of Louis XIV" (*MQ* iii); H. E. Adkin, *Treatise on the Military Band*, 3 vols. (1931); St. Gallo, *The Modern Band* (1935); G. Parés, *Traité d'instrumentation . . . des musique militaires . . .*, 2 vols. (1898); War Department, Basic Field Manual, *The Band* (FM 28–5; 1941), V. F. Safranek, *Complete . . . Manual for Field Trumpeters and Drummers* (1942); R. B. Reynolds, *Drill and Evolution of the Band* (1943). For additional bibliography cf. B. Grosbayne, in *Musical America*, Oct., 1943.

Milonga. An Argentine dance of the late 19th century, originating in the suburbs and slums of Buenos Aires. Around 1900 it was absorbed into the tango, of which it represents a quicker variety.

Mimodrame. Older name for *panto-mime.

Minaccevole [It.]. Menacing.

Mineur [F.]. Minor.

Miniature score. Open scores of orchestral or chamber music in pocket size and of low price, designed chiefly for the student, or for the amateur who wants to read the music while listening to the performance. This important and successful publishing enterprise was started by A. Payne in Leipzig and was taken over in 1892 by E. Eulenburg, Leipzig, who developed it greatly. Recently publications have been issued which include a great number of scores in one volume (e.g., all the chamber music of Beethoven). These are the size of ordinary music but contain on each page four pages of miniature score.

Minim [L. *minima*]. (1) English name for the half-note. — (2) See *Mensural notation I.

Minnesinger, Minnesänger [from G. *Minne*, love]. Aristocratic German poet-musicians of the 12th to the 14th century who, inspired by the French

*troubadours (rather than the *trouvères), became the leading — in fact, practically the sole — representatives of German music during the Middle Ages. The start of the movement is usually traced to the marriage of Frederick Barbarossa to the French princess Beatrix of Burgundy, in 1156. The close relationship of the Minnesinger to the troubadours is demonstrated, among others, by a Provençal *vers of the troubadour Guyot de Provins which also exists with a German text by Friedrich von Husen who flourished in the 12th century [cf. *BeMMR*, 106, 108]. Following is a (tentatively chronological) list of the most important Minnesinger of whom melodies are preserved (1, 2, etc. = number of melodies; *J* = *Jenaer Handschrift*; *C* = *Colmarer Handschrift*):

Before 1200: Spervogel (1; *J*).
Early 13th century: Walther von der Vogelweide, d. 1230 (1 and fragments in a Münster MS); Neithart von Reuenthal, *c.* 1180–1240 (62; cf. *DTOe* 37.i); Bruder Wirner (6; *J*); Meister Alexander (5; *J*).
Middle 13th century: Tannhäuser (2; *C*); Konrad von Würzburg (7; *C*); Rumelant (10; *J*, *C*); Der Meissner (15; *J*).
Late 13th century: Heinrich von Meissen, called Frauenlob, d. 1318 (26; *C*, *J*); Wizlav von Rügen, d. 1325 (13; *J*); Hermann der Damen (5; *J*).
Fourteenth century: Heinrich von Müglin (4; *C*); Hermann Münch von Salzburg, *c.* 1350–1410 (10; *C*); Hugo von Montfort, 1357–1423.

The Münch von Salzburg also wrote the earliest extant German polyphonic pieces which, like those of Oswald von Wolkenstein (1367–1445), fall outside the repertory of Minnesinger music.

In spite of the French influence the music of the Minnesinger differs considerably from that of the troubadours and trouvères. The texts are narrative rather than amorous or idyllic (Neithart von Reuenthal being a notable exception) and usually of a devotional character, many of them being songs in praise of the

Virgin. The melodies are more markedly modal (church modes) than the French
ones and many of them are conspicuous
for their extensive use of the interval of
the third [for an example, see under
*Third]. Textual considerations as well
as a certain "Teutonic massiveness" of
the musical line forbid the application of
*modal interpretation (¾-meter) which
is generally accepted for the trouvère
songs. Finally, the French refrain forms,
the *virelai and the *rondeau, are absent
in the German repertory, which uses only
two forms: the *Barform, derived from
the French *ballade, and the *Leich, derived from the French *lai. Owing to the
large number of preserved songs and the
individual charm of his melodies, Neithart von Reuenthal stands out as the central figure of Minnesinger music, though
from the literary point of view he already
represents a decline from the refined
courtly lyricism (Walther von der Vogelweide) into a realistic, and occasionally
slightly vulgar, naturalism. Ex. in HAM,
no. 20.

Lit.: H. J. Moser, Geschichte der deutschen Musik i (1930); K. K. Müller,
Phototypische Facsimile-Ausgabe der
Jenaer Liederhandschrift (1893); F. L.
Saran, †Die Jenaer Liederhandschrift, 2
vols. (1902); H. Rietsch, †Gesänge von
Frauenlob, Reinmar von Zweter und Alexander (DTOe 20.ii, 1913); W. Schmie-
der, †Neidhart, Lieder (DTOe 37.i,
1930); P. Runge, †Die Sangesweisen der
Colmarer Handschrift und die Liederhandschrift Donaueschingen (1896); id.,
Die Lieder des Hugo von Montfort . . .
(1906); H. Rietsch, Die Mondsee-Wiener
Liederhandschrift (Acta Germanica iv,
1902); F. Ebert, Die Liedweisen der
Colmarer Liederhandschrift (Diss. Göt-
tingen 1932); F. Gennrich, Das Formproblem des Minnegesangs (1931); H. J.
Moser, in ZMW vii; id., in KIM, 1924;
E. Jammers, in ZMW vii; O. Ursprung,
in AMW v; R. F. Molitor, "Die Lieder
des Münsterer Fragments" (SIM xii); C.
Weinmann, P. Runge, "Der Minnesang
und sein Vortrag" (MfM xxxv, 51, 83).

Minor. See *Major and Minor.

Minstrels [from L. ministrellus, serv-
ant]. Originally and properly, the professional musicians (instrumentalists) of
the Middle Ages, especially those who
were employed in a feudal household.
Today the term is used as a generic denomination for the entire field of popular
music entertainment, from the mimes of
antiquity to the show-business of the
present day.

The earliest known representatives of
this field were the Roman mimes
(mimus), the actors of the late Roman
theater. After its decline, during the Mi-
grations, these mimes, who already in
Roman law were considered as outcasts
(infami), devoted themselves to various
activities — frequently of a dubious nature — among which was the playing of
instruments. The efforts of Church and
State authorities to suppress their influence are documented in numerous edicts.
Nevertheless, the mimes or, as they were
later called, joculatores [from L. jocus,
play; F. jongleur; E. juggler; G. Gau-
kler], survived and gradually became
more secure and reputable — at least
those among them who were willing to
abandon the dissolute and roving conduct
of life, and to become members of the social order. We may reasonably assume
that they were the bearers of a tradition
of folk music which occasionally crept
into art music. In the 11th/12th centuries the jongleurs were employed by
the troubadours and trouvères [see
*Troubadours]. In the 14th century the
name jongleur was replaced by ménes-
trier, probably in order to distinguish a
class of higher social standing and professional repute. They became organized
in guilds similar to those of the medieval
craftsmen and known as *ménestrandise.

In England, a class of acrobat-musi-
cians was known as gleemen, in Germany, as Gaukler. A vivid description of
their activities is given in a German report of the 12th century according to
which they were expected "to play the
drum, the cymbals, and the hurdy-gurdy;
to throw small apples and to catch knives;
to perform card-tricks and to jump
through four hoops; to play the citole and

mandora, the manichord, the guitar, and many other instruments." With the early 14th century the term *minstrel* appears. Guilds and fraternities were gradually formed the history of which can be traced, at least up to the beginning of the 17th century [see *Waits]. The German counterparts of these guild-musicians are the *Stadtpfeifer*. See also *Negro music I.

To include the *bards under the term minstrel is somewhat misleading since these always held a very high position in the social order of their countries, notably Wales and Ireland.

Lit.: E. Duncan, *The Story of Minstrelsy* (1907); J. J. Jusserand, *English Wayfaring Life in the Middle Ages* (1888 and later); W. Grossmann, *Frühmittelalterliche Zeugnisse über Minstrels* (Diss. Berlin 1906); P. Aubry, "La légende dorée des jongleurs" (*RMC* i); *id.*, "Un coin pittoresque . . ." (*RMC* iv); *id.*, in *TG* vi; J. Sittard, in *VMW* i; *ReMMA*, 241.

Minuet [F. *menuet*, from *menu*, i.e., small (steps); or, more likely, from *amener]. A French dance of rustic origin which was introduced at the court of Louis XIV about 1650. The king himself is said to have danced "the first" minuet, composed by Lully, in 1653. The minuet was soon adopted as the official court dance of the régime of the Roi Soleil, and it quickly spread all over Europe, superseding completely the older types (courantes, pavanes) and establishing a new period of dance and dance music. The fact that a number of early minuets (e.g., those contained in the Collection *Philidor) show phrases of three measures suggests a derivation of the minuet from the *branle à mener, or *amener [example in *HAM*, no. 229]. Lully introduced the minuet into his ballets and operas; Muffat, Pachelbel, J. K. Fischer, in their suites (around 1700). Many of these minuets already show the "alternativement" arrangement of two minuets: M_1–M_2–M_1 which is the origin of the minuet-and-trio movement of the sonata [see *Trio].

The minuet was the only one of the numerous dance types of the Baroque which did not become obsolete after the decline of the suite (*c.* 1750). The statement that Haydn was the first to introduce the minuet into the symphony is far from being correct. The operatic sinfonias of Alessandro Scarlatti (1659–1725) and others usually close with a minuet, as do also numerous independent symphonies and sonatas of the pre-Haydn period. The minuet with trio as the next-to-last movement is found in practically all the symphonies of the *Mannheimers [see *Sonata B, III (a)].

The minuet is in $\frac{3}{4}$-meter and, originally, in very moderate tempo. The accompanying example (Lully's minuet

"Dans nos bois," as given in d'Anglebert's *Pièces de clavecin* [see *Editions XXIV, A, 8]) shows the graceful dignity which characterizes the early minuet and which still lives in the famous minuet in Mozart's *Don Giovanni*. In the symphonies of Haydn and Mozart, however, the minuet took on greater speed and a more humorous or whimsical character, gradually leading into the *scherzo. See also *Dance music and (regarding the internal structure of the minuet) *Binary and ternary form II.

Minuta [It.]. See *Ornamentation III.

Miracle play. See *Liturgical drama.

Mirliton [F.]. An instrument in the form of a pipe closed at one end by a membrane, and with a side-hole into which one sings in one's natural voice, the tone issuing in a nasal and caricatural timbre. In the 17th century the instrument was known as *flûte-eunuque* (Eunuch flute) and was admired by men of such high standing as Mersenne for its "new charm" [cf. *GD* ii, 180]. Today it is only a musical toy (also known as *kazoo*). See *Instruments II.

Mirror fugue [G. *Spiegelfuge*]. The principle of mirror-reflection can be applied to a melody in two different ways: (a) with the mirror placed at the end of the melody, thus leading to a crab — or *retrograde version; or, (b) with the mirror placed underneath, in which case the inverted form (i.e., contrary motion) results. The latter method is the one indicated by the term mirror fugue which designates a fugue written in such a manner as to lead, by means of the method of vertical reflection, to another fugue which will also be satisfactory as to sound. In the reflected fugue, the position of the voices as well as each interval in every single voice is inverted. The only examples known to have been composed are two in Bach's *Art of Fugue* (Contrapunc-

tus XVI, in three parts, and Contrapunctus XVIII, in four parts). A passage from the latter is given here as an illustration. The fugue and its mirror version are, of course, meant to be played one after the other, not simultaneously. Contrapunctus XVI appears also in a four-part version for two harpsichords (Contrapunctus XVII), in which a free fourth voice is added.

Miserere. Psalm 50 (Vulgate): *Miserere mei Deus* ("Lord have mercy upon me"). In the Catholic rites it is sung at the end of the office of *tenebrae (also at Requiem Mass) to a psalm tone with antiphon. It is one of the *Penitential

Psalms and has been composed as such, but also independently, owing to the particular impressiveness of its text. The earliest example is a setting by Costanzo Festa (1517) for two choruses, one of four parts, the other of five, in familiar style (*falsobordone*). Various other compositions in the same style, usually retaining the "traditional" number of nine parts, were written, among them the celebrated composition by Gregorio Allegri (1582–1652) which has remained in use at the Papal Chapel to the present day, alongside Palestrina's *Improperiae and *Lamentations for the same service. A host of legends and stories — including that of the young Mozart copying it from hearing, against the express law of the Church — have been formed, all intended to extol this work into a sphere of superhuman beauty and importance. Actually it is a rather undistinguished work in a plain falsobordone style, the monotony of which is somewhat relieved by "abbellimenti" (probably 18th-century additions) at the end of each verse. The mediocrity of Allegri's Miserere does not, of course, prevent it from being very effective, if it is presented with all the solemnity characteristic of the Pontifical rites, and all the suavity of performance characteristic of the present-day Sistine choir. A much more beautiful and imaginative composition of the text is the Miserere by Josquin.

Missa [L.]. *Mass. — Missa pro defunctis*, Requiem Mass, *requiem. — Missa solemnis* (Solemn Mass, High Mass) is the Mass in its full form, with all the items (except for lections, etc.) sung, while in the *Missa lecta* (Read Mass, Low Mass) there is no music, except perhaps hymn singing. *Missa cantata* (Sung Mass) is, from the musical point of view, identical with the High Mass, but is celebrated in a less elaborate manner. From the above it appears that the title *Missa Solemnis* chosen by Beethoven for his Mass (op. 123) carries no connotation which would not also apply to a Mass by Palestrina or Bach.

Missal [L. *missale*; G. *Missel*]. See *Liturgical books I.

Mistic(h)anza [It.]. *Quodlibet.

Misura [It.]. Measure, beat. *Alla misura*, in strict time; *senza misura*, without strict time.

Mixed cadence. See *Cadence I.

Mixed mode. See *Church modes III.

Mixed voices. A combination of male and female voices [see *Equal voices].

Mixolydian. (1) See *Greek music. — (2) The seventh *church mode (*septimus tonus*; *tetrartus*), represented by the segment g–g′ of the diatonic scale, with g as the tonic. From the modern point of view it is a major mode with a minor seventh (F instead of F♯). See also *Modality.

Mixture stop. See *Organ VI, IX (f).

M.M. See *Metronome.

Modal. In the character of a mode, either of a church mode (e.g., in modal harmony, *modality), or of the rhythmic modes of the 13th century (modal notation, modal interpretation, modal rhythm). See *Mode.

Modality. The term is generally used with reference to harmonic and melodic formations based on the *church modes, in contradistinction to those based on the major and minor modes (*Tonality). In particular, it is used to denote the occurrence of modal idioms in the prevailingly tonal music of the 19th and 20th centuries. This phenomenon may be traced back to three different sources: (a) the desire to imitate the tonal language of 16th-century sacred music; (b) the influence of Slavic or other folk song which shows modal features; (c) the antagonism against the system of classical harmony. Examples of (a) are Beethoven's "Dankgesang an die Gottheit in der lydischen Tonart" (String Quartet in A minor, op. 132, 1825) — probably the earliest example of 19th-century modality — and the compositions of Vaughan Williams; examples of (b) occur in Chopin's mazurkas and in numerous compositions of Moussorgsky, Tchaikovsky, and other

"national" composers; the last-mentioned tendency is conspicuous in the works of Debussy [see *Impressionism] and of contemporary *neo-classical composers (Hindemith). The accompanying examples illustrate the use of modality. Ex. 1 (Chopin, Mazurka no. 15) is *Lydian

(B-natural instead of B-flat); Ex. 2 (Franck, Symphony) is transposed *Dorian (major sixth D-sharp instead of minor sixth D); Ex. 3 (Brahms, Symphony no. 4) combines *Phrygian (minor second F instead of F-sharp) with *Mixolydian (minor seventh D, instead of the leading-tone D-sharp); Ex. 4 (Sibelius, Symphony no. 2) is *Aeolian (minor sixth and seventh, F and G instead of F-sharp and G-sharp).

Modal notation. See *Square notation.

Modal rhythm. A rhythm based on the (rhythmic) *modes. See also *Rhythm III (b).

Modaltheorie [G.]. Modal interpretation. See under *Plainsong notation.

Mode. The term is used for two entirely different concepts, both rooted in medie-

val music, namely (1) one of scale formation, and (2) one of rhythm.

(1) Mode, in the widest sense of the
word, denotes the selection of tones, arranged in a scale, which form the basic
tonal substance of a composition. In any
given key (i.e., for any given center-tone
or tonic, e.g., E) a great number of modes
are possible, some of which are indicated
in our illustration: 1 is the "Dorian mode"
(transposed from D to E); 2 is the "Phrygian mode" (untransposed); 3 is the "major
mode" (usually called major key); 4 is the
"minor mode" (usually called minor key);
5 is a "pentatonic mode"; 6 is the "whole-
tone mode." See *Scale III. In a closer
sense of the word, the term mode refers
only to those scales which go back to the

Mode

medieval *church modes (modes 1 and 2
of the example). It is with reference to
these that the terms "modal," "modality,"
are commonly used. For the use of the
term mode with reference to Oriental
(Hindu, Arabian, etc.) music see *Melody
types.

(2) See *Modes, rhythmic. Also *Modus.

Moderato [It.]. In moderate speed,
i.e., between andante and allegro.

Modern music. A term which is somewhat loosely used to denote a period of
music with a clearly fixed ending — the
present day — while its beginning is
variously set by different writers at about
1830 [W. H. Hadow, *Studies in Modern
Music* (1923), which includes Berlioz,
Schumann, Wagner, Chopin, Dvořák,
Brahms], 1860, 1890, or 1910. This fact
renders the term rather difficult to use for
exact reference. Most people would probably agree that modern music started
around 1890, when composers such as
Elgar, R. Strauss, Sibelius (all born

around 1860), produced their first significant works. The half-century of modern
music comprises an extremely great variety of trends and styles so that further
classifications are indispensable. The
above-mentioned composers, together
with many others, form the school known
as *Neo-romanticism, since they built upon the tradition of the Romanticism. A
greater determination to break away from
the "German" Romanticism is patent in
the *Impressionism of Debussy and
Ravel, while the radical break occurred
around 1910, leading to a new period of
music history for which the term *New
music has been widely adopted.

See also: Atonality; Film music; Five,
The; Futurism; Gebrauchsmusik; Impressionism; Modality; Nationalism;
Neo-classicism; New music; Pandiatonicism; Parallel chords; Quarter-tones; Satire; Six, Les; Twelve-tone technique;
Verismo; Whole-tone scale.

Lit.: G. Abraham, *This Modern Stuff*
(1939); M. Bauer, *Twentieth Century
Music* (1933); G. Dyson, *Progress of
Music* (1932); D. Ewen, *The Book of
Modern Composers* (1942); C. Gray, *A
Survey of Contemporary Music* (1927);
E. B. Hill, *Modern French Music* (1924);
J. T. Howard, *This Modern Music*
(1942); A. Eaglefield-Hull, *Dictionary of
Modern Music and Musicians* (1924);
D. G. Mason, *Contemporary Composers*
(1918); G. Pannain, *Modern Composers*
(1933); N. Slonimsky, *Music Since 1900*
(1937; a chronological reference book);
E. Goossens, in *PMA* xlviii; A. Bliss, in
PMA xlix; G. Dyson, in *PMA* l; E.
Wellesz, in *MQ* x; R. D. Welch, in *MQ*
vii.

Modes, Rhythmic. A 13th-century
system of rhythm, characterized by the
consistent repetition of certain simple
rhythmic patterns in ternary meter. Usually six modes are distinguished, as shown
on the next page. The Greek names
conveniently serve to identify the modes;
their application is, however, of a relatively late date (W. Odington, c. 1290;
see *Theory II) and should not be construed to indicate a derivation of the

modes from the feet of ancient Greek poetry [see *Poetic meter].

As applied to musical compositions, the

First (trochaic): | ♩ ♩ | ♩ ...

Second (iambic): | ♩♩ | ♩ ...

Third (dactylic): | ♩. | ♩ ♩ | ♩. | ...

Fourth (anapaestic): | ♩♩ | ♩. | ♩♩ | ...

Fifth (spondaic): | ♩. | ♩. | ♩. | ...

Sixth (tribrachic): | ♩♩♩ | ♩ ...

above patterns were reiterated a number of times, depending on the length of the phrase or, in medieval terminology, on the *ordo*. The ordo indicated the number of times a pattern was repeated without interruption, e.g.:

First mode, third ordo: | ♩ ♩ | ♩ ♩ | ♩ ♩ | ♩ 𝄾 |

Third mode, second ordo: | ♩. | ♩♩ | ♩. | ♩♩ | ♩. | 𝄽 |

The modes form the rhythmic basis of the organa, the clausulae, and the motets of the 13th century, which are therefore said to be written in modal notation [see under *Square notation]. Usually the first, second, and sixth modes occur in the upper parts; the third and the fifth in the lower (the fourth mode is very rare). Naturally, in the practical application of the modes, certain modifications of the normal patterns were admitted, such as occasional omission of a weak beat (*extensio modi*) or breaking up of one note into two or three (*fractio modi*). See the example under *Square notation. See also remark under *Perfect, imperfect.

Lit.: *ApNPM*, 228ff; A. Michalitschke, *Die Theorie des Modus* (1923); H. Sowa, in *ZMW* xv.

Modinha. A type of song which originated in Portugal, but exists now mainly in Brazil where it was imported in the second half of the 19th century. The Brazilian modinha is an urban type of folk song. Its style is that of a sentimental romance, occasionally with light syncopations. It bears an unexpected and inexpli-

cable resemblance to Russian and gypsy songs. Cf. Mario de Andrade, *Modinhas imperiais* (S. Paulo, 1930).

Modulamen, modulatio, modulus. Humanistic (16th-century) misnomers for motet.

Modulator. See *Tonic Sol-fa.

Modulation. The change of key within a composition. Such changes are among the commonest devices of harmonic variety, and are found in practically every piece of some extension. In order to make an effective modulation the initial as well as the new key should be established by a cadence.

Modulations are accomplished by means of "pivot chords," i.e., a chord which is common to both the initial and

the new key. For instance, in Ex. 1, the third chord is the pivot chord, being I in the old key (C), and IV in the new key (G), hence the designation $\begin{smallmatrix} C: I \\ G: IV \end{smallmatrix}$. In Ex. 2, the same chord adopts the function of VII in D (properly, D minor), while, in Ex. 3, V of C is re-interpreted as III of E (properly, E minor).

Modulations are usually classified under three types, diatonic, chromatic, and enharmonic. A diatonic modulation is one made through a chord which is diatonic in both keys. The above three examples belong to this type. A chromatic modulation is one made through a chord which is chromatically altered in one or both keys, a very common example being the modulation through the Neapolitan sixth [Ex. 4]. The field of chromatic modulation is very large, and its exploitation has been one of the main achievements of 19th-century harmony. Enharmonic modulation is one which involves the enharmonic change of one or several notes. This is frequently achieved through the diminished seventh chord [Ex. 5].

If the new key is touched upon only momentarily, leading quickly into a third key, the modulation is said to be "false" or "passing." The former term is used if the third key is the initial key [Ex. 6], the latter, if it is still another key [Ex. 7]. The latter case occurs mainly in sequential progressions (sequential modulation). Naturally, the interpretation of a modulation as "real," "false," or "passing" depends largely on the impression of permanence (to the second key) and, therefore, frequently on subjective judgment.

Aside from the above-described "pivot-modulations," change of key is frequently effected in a more direct manner, by simply juxtaposing the old and the new key, a very effective device which, by some writers, is not held to fall under the category proper of "modulation." The example 10, by Schubert, given under *Harmony illustrates this method which usually involves a shift of a whole-tone or of a semitone. Even in these cases, however, an analysis according to the principles of pivot chords may be made in order to explain the harmonic relationships. See *Harmonic analysis VI.

Lit.: A. Foote, *Modulation and Related Harmonic Questions* (1919); C. Zöller, *The Art of Modulation* (1930); S. Ancis, *Scheme Modulations* (1929); Th. Otterstroem, *A Theory of Modulation* (1935);

M. Reger, *Supplement to the Theory of Modulation* (1904); H. Riemann, *Systematische Modulationslehre* (1887).

Modus [L.]. (1) *Church mode; in this meaning the term *tonus* is more commonly used in early music. — (2) *Mode, rhythmic. — (3) In *mensural notation, *modus major* (*modus maximarum*) denotes the relationship between the maxima and the longa; *modus minor* (*modus longarum*), or simply *modus*, that between the longa and the brevis. In English books Morley's translations "greater mood" and "lesser mood" are frequently used in this connotation. Both modi figure prominently in the theoretical explanations of mensural notation from the 14th to the 17th century, but are of little practical significance, on account of the long duration of the note values involved. For the relationship of the mensural modus to the modus (rhythmic mode) of the 13th century cf. *ApNPM*, 293f. See also under *Perfect, imperfect.

Modus lascivus. Medieval name for the tonality of C major, which was avoided in plainsong, but was frequently used in secular music.

Modusschrift [G.]. *Modal notation.

Möglichst [G.]. As much as possible.

Moll. German for minor key (*G moll*, G minor). See *Dur.

Molto [It.]. Very. *Molto allegro* (*adagio*), very quick (slow).

Moment Musical [F.]. A name, used first and chiefly by Schubert, for lyrical pieces in Romantic style. See *Character piece.

Monacordo [It.]. Sixteenth-century name for the clavichord.

Mondscheinsonate [G.]. *Moonlight Sonata.

Monochord [Gr. *monos*, one; *chorde*, string]. A contrivance consisting of a single string which is stretched over a lengthy wooden resonator to which a movable fret is attached so that the vibrating length of the string can be varied. The monochord is said to have been invented by Pythagoras (6th century B.C.). It was widely used in Antiquity and the Middle Ages for the investigation and demonstration of the laws of musical acoustics, a purpose for which it is still used in schools [see *Acoustics II]. In the later Middle Ages the number of strings was increased to two or three, so that intervals and chords could be made audible. Such monochords were the probable ancestors of the clavichord which as late as the 16th century was called *monacordo in Italy.

Lit.: S. Wantzloeben, *Das Monochord als Instrument und System* (1911); *GéHM*, 407.

Monocordo. In violin playing, the performance of a piece on a single string. This effect was used first by Paganini, in his Sonata "Napoleon" for the G string.

Monodrama. See *Melodrama.

Monody [Gr. *monos*, one; *ode*, song]. Literally, music for one singer. The term is occasionally used as synonymous with *monophonic music, or for accompanied solo song in general. More properly it denotes that particular type of accompanied solo song which developed around 1600 as the reaction against the polyphonic style of the 16th century, and which is characterized by the recitativo-

like design of the voice part and by the thorough-bass accompaniment. Accompanying is one of the earliest examples of

true monody, from Caccini's *Nuove musiche*, 1602 [for others, cf. *HAM*, nos. 182–185; *SchGMB*, nos. 169, 171–173, 176, etc.; see also *Nuove musiche; *Aria III; *Cantata; *Recitative].

Forerunners of the monodic style are the numerous 16th-century songs with lute accompaniment [Schlick, *Tabulaturen etlicher lobgesang und lidlein* (1512); Luis Milan, *El Maestro* (1535); Enriquez de Valderravano, *Libro de Musica de vihuela* (1547)] and polyphonic madrigals arranged for a solo singer and an accompanist for the lower parts [e.g., Luzzascho Luzzaschi; cf. *SchGMB*, no. 166]. Bottrigari, in his *Desiderio* (1594; new edition by K. Meyer, 1924), informs us about an extensive practice of solo song in the *laudi, the *intermedii, and in folk singing.

Lit.: A. Schering, "Zur Geschichte des begleiteten Sologesangs im 16. Jahrhundert" (*ZIM* xiii); E. Schmitz, "Zur Frühgeschichte der Monodie" (*JMP* xviii); W. Krabbe, "Zur Geschichte der Monodie im 16. Jahrhundert" (*Allgemeine Musikalische Zeitung*, Jan., 1922); P. Nettl, "Über ein handschriftliches Sammelwerk von Gesängen italienischer Frühmonodie" (*ZMW* ii); A. Einstein, "Firenze, prima della monodia" (*LRM* vii); L. Torchi, "Canzoni . . . ad una voce nel secolo XVII" (*RMI* i).

Monophony, monophonic [Gr. *monos*, one; *phonos*, sound]. Music comprising only a single melodic line without additional parts or accompaniment, as contrasted to *polyphonic, *homophonic, etc. [see *Texture]. Monophonic music is the purest realization of the melodic element [see *Melody]. It is the oldest type of music, being the only one employed in ancient Greek music, in the various branches of early church music (Gregorian chant, Byzantine chant), in the music of the troubadours, trouvères, Minnesinger and Meistersinger, in the Spanish cantigas, and the Italian laude of the 13th century, and universally in Oriental and primitive music as well as in European folk music. See remark under *Monody.

Monotone. The recitation of a liturgical text on an unchanged pitch, as in psalms, prayers, lessons, reading from the Scriptures, etc. Usually, the monotonic declamation is modified by *inflections, that is, a few ascending or descending tones at the beginning, middle, or end of the phrase of the text. See *Psalm tones. The name "inflected monotone" has also been applied to rather elaborate chants which have been interpreted as a highly ornamented type of monotone [cf. *GD* ii, 709; iv, 368].

Montpellier, Codex. The name usually refers to an important source of 13th-century polyphonic music, Montpellier, Fac. des Méd., *H 196* [see *Sources, no. 4; *Ars antiqua II], not to be confused with an equally important source of Gregorian chant, *H 159* [see *Editions XXIII, A, 7/8; also *Letter notation].

Monumenta, Monumenti, Monuments. See *Editions XIV; XVII; XVIII; XIX.

Mood. See *Modus (3).

Moonlight Sonata [G. *Mondscheinsonate*]. Popular but unauthentic name for Beethoven's *Sonata quasi una fantasia*, op. 27, no. 2. The name probably goes back to a review written by Heinrich Rellstab (1799–1860) in which the first movement was likened to a boat wandering by moonlight on Lake Lucerne. Another name is Laube Sonata, from German *Laube*, "bower," referring probably to a fancied place of its composition. Curiously, this name is entirely unknown in Germany. See remarks under *Mute and under *Sonata B, IV.

Moralities. Religious plays in which the virtues and vices are personified. Such plays were popular in the 17th century. See *Mysteries.

Morbido [It.]. Gentle, soft (not morbid).

Morceau [F.]. Piece, composition.

Mordent [G.; F. *pincé, pincement*; Old Engl. beat, open shake, sweetening; It.

mordente]. A musical ornament consisting of the alternation of the written note with the note immediately below it. It is indicated in the music by one of the signs given in Ex. 1 (the third sign occurs only

in music for bowed instruments). In performance the mordent always occupies part of the value of the written note and should not be introduced before it. The alternations of the written note and the auxiliary may be either single or double [Ex. 2]; there is a special sign for the latter [Ex. 3] but it is not often used and the choice between these executions is generally left to the discretion of the performer, who bases his decision chiefly upon the duration of the written note. If two mordents occur in close succession contemporary authorities recommend that one should be made single and the other double, as in Ex. 4 (Bach).

In the works of J. S. Bach the mordent often appears fully written out [Ex. 5, Adagio of the D minor Organ Toccata]. All of Bach's mordents, with the exception of those which occur in pieces with a particularly vigorous rhythm, should be performed comparatively slowly, as in Ex. 6 [a: Italian Concerto; b: Wt. Cl. ii, no. 1]. When a mordent and an appoggiatura occur on the same note the mordent must be delayed until the appoggiatura has been held its normal duration, as in Bach's Chorale Prelude, "Wenn wir in höchsten Nöten sein" [Ex. 7]. After 1750 all mordents were performed more rapidly than at the time of Bach. The ornament apparently became absorbed in the ordinary notation before the classical period, for it is not found in the works of Mozart and Beethoven.

The mordent occurs in the German organ tablatures of the 15th and 16th centuries, where it is indicated by the signs illustrated (a: Buxheim Organ Book, c. 1470; b: Kotter, Buchner, c. 1520). The execution was, however, somewhat different, since the main note was held, and only the lower auxiliary was quickly repeated [cf. WoHN ii, 22; ApNPM, 24]. For the so-called "inverted mordent" see under *Schneller.   P. A.

Morisca, Moresca [from Sp. morisco, Moor]. A pantomimic dance of the 15th and 16th centuries, which was executed in Moorish costumes and other disguises of a grotesque character, the dancers having their faces blackened and small bells attached to their legs. Arbeau, in his *Orchésographie (1588), reports having seen the morisca danced in his youthful days (around 1530) by "un garçonnet machuré et noircy, des grelottières aux jambes." The morisca, which was easily the most popular dance for the ballets and mummeries of the Renaissance, occurs in two types, as a solo dance and as a dance between two groups representing a sword-fight between Christians and Mohammedans. The latter type was known also as Danse des *bouffons [see also *Matasin]. Dances of this type are still known today in Spain, Corsica, and Guatemala. They have survived particularly in England under the name Morris

dance, partly in a continuous tradition, partly as the result of a revival made around 1900. The Morris was danced chiefly as a part of the May games. It included, in addition to six dancers in two opposing groups, certain solo characters, such as the "Mayde Maryan," represented by a boy disguised as a girl, or by a dancer with a hobbyhorse. Cf. GD iii, 521ff; also C. Sachs, A World History of the Dance (1940). See also under *Villanella.

Mormorando [It.]. Murmuring.

Morris dance. See *Morisca.

Motet [from Fr. mot, word]. The most important form of early polyphonic music, particularly during the Middle Ages and the Renaissance. On account of the great changes it underwent during the more than five hundred years of its existence (c. 1250–1750) it is almost impossible to give a general definition which would cover all the various phases of its development. As a rule, a motet is an unaccompanied choral composition, based on a Latin sacred text, and designed to be performed in the Catholic service, chiefly at Vespers. There are, however, lateral developments branching out into the secular field (13th-century French motet; 15th-century ceremonial motets), as well as motets for soloists (13th-century motet; also in the late 17th century) or with orchestral accompaniment and to texts in the vernacular (17th century, Germany; the English motets are called *anthems). The history of the motet may be divided into three periods: A, that of the medieval motet (c. 1225–1450); B, that of the Flemish motet (1450–1600), as it might be called after its inaugurators although it became international property after 1550; C, that of the Baroque motet (1600–1750).

A. The Medieval Motet. I. The medieval motet originated in the early 13th century, possibly as early as 1200, by the addition of a full text to the upper part (duplum) of the *clausulae of the Perotinus period, a procedure which is strikingly similar to that which, in the 9th century, led from the vocalized melismas of the alleluias to the fully texted *sequences. Owing to the addition of "mots," the texted *duplum* was called *motetus*, a name which was adopted for the entire composition. The tenor of a motet (as that of a clausula) is practically always a melismatic (vocalized) passage taken from a chant of the Gregorian repertory (usually a gradual, alleluia, or responsorium) and identified by the same word or syllable (**incipit*) with which it occurs in the original plainsong. The only change is that of rhythm, namely from the free oratoric rhythm of plainsong into a strict modal pattern [see *Modes, rhythmic]. The accompanying example shows the motet O Maria—

Nostrum [cf. *ApNPM*, 285] and the Easter Alleluia [cf. *GR*, 222] from which the tenor NOSTRUM is taken. It is important to realize that, at least originally, a motet is not an independent composition but—like the clausulae—a polyphonic interpolation (polyphonic *trope) of the chant to which it is allied by its tenor. The following scheme—a modification of that given under *clausula—shows two motets in their proper liturgical position (ordinary print indicates plainsong; capital letters the motets; italics the added text of the upper part):

>   *O Maria* . . .
> Alleluia, alleluia. ℣. Pascha NOSTRUM
> *Radix venie* . . .
> immo- LATUS   est Christus.

The liturgical background of the 13th-century motet is furthermore illustrated by the fact that, in the early and in the classical periods (*c.* 1225–75), the text of the motetus is always a paraphrase of the fundamental thought expressed in, or suggested by, the tenor and its plainchant. As a matter of fact, so great was the desire of the 13th-century ecclesiastical poet-musicians to give new and individual expression to the sacrosanct ideas of the Church that, when the number of parts was increased from two to three, still another textual paraphrase was chosen for the third part (triplum), e.g.:

> *In seculum, Artifex seculi* . . .
> *In seculum, supra mulieres* . . .
> IN SECULUM

[cf. *ReMMA*, 313; see *In seculum]. Examples in *HAM*, nos. 28, f-i and 32, c-d.

II. An early precursor of the 13th-century motet exists in a number of compositions dating from the early part of the 12th century (School of *St. Martial) in which the duplum of a Benedicamus-Domino organum is provided with a full text [cf. J. Handschin, "Der Ursprung der Motette" (*KIM*, 1924)]. There is reason to believe that the development of the 13th-century motet started, not with two-voice motets, but with a special type of three- (or four-) voice motets in which a conductus-like superstructure of two (or three) voices with identical rhythm and text is combined with a tenor having different text and generally slower rhythm ("conductus-motet"; cf. *ApNPM*, 227; *HAM*, no. 32c). The three-voice motet with two different Latin texts and with individual rhythm in each part must be considered the classical type of the 13th-century motet. In the later part of the 13th century, however, a new phase of evolution was inaugurated by the intrusion of secular texts in the French language. Since the tenor always retained its liturgical derivation, there resulted a musical type of startling incongruity, if not profanity, since the French texts usually dealt with amorous subjects, occasionally even lascivious. Unfortunately, in modern writings this type of motet, which, no doubt, represents a phenomenon of cultural extravagance, is emphasized over the liturgical motet which, far from being incongruous, is a perfect expression of the theological universalism of Thomas of Aquino and other medieval philosophers. Nonetheless, the amalgamation of sacred and secular things, the merging of the Gregorian tradition with the trouvère movement, the frequent exchanges and substitutions, musical as well as textual, are features which contribute towards making the final development of the motet a fascinating study [cf. *HAM*, nos. 28, 33–35]. Examples illustrating the extraordinarily manifold relationships within the repertory of the 13th-century motet are found in *AdHM* i, 237 and 240 (F. Ludwig). For an example showing the transition from a clausula to a (French) motet, cf. *ApNPM*, 260 and 272 (*Flos filius*); also *HAM*, no. 28d and h, also i.

III. The explanation, not infrequent in modern books, of the motet as a *quodlibet is quite misleading. Actually, only a limited number of motets can be shown to include combinations of different pre-existing melodies [see *Refrain; *Enté]. The rhythmic texture of the motets is invariably based on the rhythmic *modes, the upper parts frequently employing a quicker pattern (first, second, sixth mode) than the tenor (third, fifth mode), as illustrated (schematically) in our ex-

ample. Towards the end of the century the strict modal rhythm (Franco and predecessors) was modified by the introduction (Petrus de Cruce) of quick notes, four to seven in the place of one brevis (quarter-note) and sung syllabically in a quick parlando (Petronian motet; example in *HAM*, no. 34). See also *Ars antiqua.

IV. In the 14th century the motet lost its former dominant position [see *Ars nova] but, as a recompense, increased in elaboration, length, and rhythmic variety. A feature of special interest is the introduction of the *isorhythmic principle. Practically all the motets of Guillaume de Machaut (1300–77) are isorhythmic (example in *HAM*, no. 44), and a number of them have this principle applied not only to the tenor but also, with a certain amount of freedom, to the upper parts [cf. *ReMMA*, 354]. The isorhythmic principle continued to be used through the middle of the 15th century, in motets by Dunstable, Dufay, and others [see *Isorhythmic]. There exists a considerable repertory of English 14th-century motets [cf. *HAM*, no. 57a], some with English words [cf. M. Bukofzer, in *ML* xvii, no. 3].

Beginning with the 15th century, novel methods of composition were applied to motets. The two characteristics of the medieval motet, that is, polytextuality and cantus-firmus tenor, were abandoned in favor of free composition with the same text in all the parts. Occasionally motets of this period have a plainsong melody (or snatches thereof) in the soprano. The origin of these novel types of motet is found in similar methods of composition which, in the later part of the 14th century, were applied to hymns or to the antiphons B.M.V. Another type of this period is the solo-motet with instrumental accompaniment — evidently the result of an influence of 14th-century French secular song (*ballade). Cf. the examples by Dunstable and Power in *SchGMB*, nos. 34, 37. For a further study of the interesting but complex period of transition from *c.* 1400 to 1450, the reader is referred to the analysis of Dunstable's motets in *ReMMA*, 414.

B. *The Flemish Motet*. The return to sacred music, which characterizes the *Flemish School, brought the motet back into prominence as a musical form second in importance only to the Mass. The motet now becomes a choral composition of a Latin scriptural text, in four to six or more voice-parts. The cantus-firmus in long-held notes [see *Pfundnoten] is still found in many motets of the period 1450–1500 — one of the most famous examples

being Josquin's *Stabat mater* [cf. W. Ambros, *Geschichte der Musik*, v, 62] — but
was gradually superseded by a completely
free treatment. The first master of this
period, Jean Ockeghem (*c.* 1430–95),
usually contrasts the long cantus-firmus
notes with highly florid lines in the other
parts [cf. *SchGMB*, no. 52], while his
contemporary Obrecht (*c.* 1430–1505)
prefers a more equal treatment of the
parts, including imitation and passages in
chordal (*familiar) style [cf. *SchGMB*,
no. 54; *HAM*, no. 76]. While German
masters such as Adam von Fulda (*c.* 1440–
1506) and Heinrich Finck (1445–1527)
would seem to have followed the model
of Ockeghem, Obrecht's method became
the point of departure for the splendid
development represented by Josquin
(1450–1521), Heinrich Isaac (1450–
1517), Pierre de la Rue (*c.* 1460–1518),
Antoine Brumel (fl. *c.* 1500), and all the
later Flemish masters. With Josquin the
imitative treatment of successive portions
of the text, resulting in a succession of
*points, became the classical style of the
motet — a style which has been so fully
identified with this form that it is usually
referred to as "motet-style" [see *Imitative counterpoint; *Chorale motet].
Chordal style, however, also plays an important part in the works of this period,
and the classical motet frequently shows
a mixture of polyphonic and homophonic
treatment. Usually the motets of the 16th
century fall into two or three larger sections, called *Prima, Secunda, Tertia Pars.*
While Josquin's motets are mostly in
from four to six voice-parts, eight or more
voices are frequent in the later motets,
particularly in connection with *polychoral treatment. This novel style, which
already occurs in some motets of Gombert
(fl. 1520–40), led to a new type of motet,
the "Venetian motet," as it is called, in
contradistinction to the "Netherlands
motet."

Around 1530 the motet spread throughout Europe, and the Flemish masters
(Josquin, Gombert, de Monte, Lasso)
found disciples of equal rank in Italy (A.
Gabrieli, Palestrina, Giov. Gabrieli),
Spain (Morales, Vittoria), England (Tallis, Byrd), Germany (Senfl, Handl, Hassler), and France (Goudimel, Regnart).
In England the adoption, about 1560, of
texts in the vernacular led to a special type
of motet, the *anthem.

Important collections of 16th-century
motets are: *Motetti A, B, C* (Petrucci,
1502, '03, '04); *Motetti della corona* (4
books, Petrucci, 1514–19); *Motetti del
frutto* (Gardano, 1539); *Motetti del fiore*
(5 books, Moderne, 1532–42); *Novum et
insigne opus musicum* (2 vols., Ott, 1537,
'38; cf. *RiML*, 1284); *Thesaurus musicus*
(Montan and Neuber, 1564); *Novus
Thesaurus musicus* (ed. by Joanelli,
1568; cf. *RiML*, 1284); *Promptuarium
musicum* (ed. by Abr. Schade and Kaspar Vincent, 1611–17; cf. *RiML*, 1435);
Florilegium Portense (ed. by Bodenschatz, 1603, '18; cf. *RiML*, 519).

C. *The Baroque Motet.* After 1600 the
style of the motet changed considerably,
owing chiefly to the abandoning of the
pure a-cappella style and to the use of solo
voices as well as of instrumental accompaniment. This does not mean that the
16th-century style was completely abandoned. The traditional character of the
motet easily accounts for the fact that the
"stile antico" of Palestrina [see *Stile] as
well as the Venetian style with its massive
sound was continuously cultivated in the
motets of the Baroque, sometimes in almost unchanged manner as, e.g., in
numerous motets written by the members
of the *Roman School [cf. the motets by
Fux, *c.* 1700, in *DTOe* 2.i]. Usually,
however, the old methods were modified
according to the stylistic devices of the
17th century, such as instrumental participation, solo voices, aria style, recitativo,
etc.

The earliest examples of the new practice occur in Viadana's *Concerti ecclesiastici* (1602, '08) which contain motets for
one, two, three, and four voices with organ accompaniment. While organ accompaniment is already prescribed in the
Concerti ecclesiastici of A. and G. Gabrieli (1587) and of Banchieri (1595), Viadana's innovation is the use of solo voices
instead of choral performance, an innovation which is particularly conspicuous in

the pieces for one or two voices [cf. *SchGMB*, no. 168]. The solo-motet for two or three singers with organ accompaniment prevailed in Italy throughout the Baroque, side by side with the choral style of the Roman or Venetian tradition; not a few motets of this period make use of both styles, e.g., solistic treatment in the first part, choral treatment in the second (e.g., Carissimi). Antonio Caldara (1670–1732) seems to have been one of the first in Italy to use instruments in addition to the organ [*DTOe* 13.i].

More interesting is the development in Germany, the beginning and end of which is indicated by two composers of the highest rank, Schütz (1585–1672) and Bach (1685–1750). Schütz's *Symphoniae sacrae* (1629, '47, '50) contain an inexhaustible treasure of masterpieces written in a great variety of styles, incorporating instrumental participation, solo voices, expressive coloraturas, characteristic motives in rapid notes, echo-like alternation of two singers or instruments, realistic effects, trumpet calls, etc. Most of these pieces, particularly those from the later collections, are written to German texts, as are also the majority of motets written by the successors of Schütz. It goes without saying that this practice makes it even more difficult, if not impossible, to draw a line of distinction between the German motet and other types of church music, such as the cantata, the spiritual song, the "geistliche Konzert," and others. As a rule, the use of the chorus marks the German form, since in Germany (as distinguished from Italy) the motet remained a choral, frequently an a-cappella type. An idea of the German motet before Bach can be obtained from the selection contained in *DdT* 49/50 (Thüringer Motetten: Liebhold, Joh. Michael Bach, Topf). Continuing with Reinken, Buxtehude, Pachelbel, and others the German motet arrived at its peak in the six motets by Bach, four of which are written for unaccompanied double-chorus of eight voices, while one ("Jesu meine Freude") is for five voices and one ("Lobet den Herrn") for four voices with organ.

An important but little known development took place in France, beginning with Marc-Antoine Charpentier (*c.* 1634–1704) and continuing with Lully (1632–87), Michel Lalande (1657–1726), Campra (1660–1744; cf. *HAM*, no. 263), François Couperin (1668–1733; *HAM*, no. 266), and Rameau (1683–1764). While Lully's motets are still a-cappella for double chorus, those by Campra and Couperin are for solo voices with organ or instruments, and those of Rameau employ chorus, soloists (for the "airs"), organ, and orchestra.

For modern reprints see *Editions, particularly V, VII–IX, XV, XX, XXI, XXVII.

The rather unimportant development of the motet after Bach may be briefly characterized by the names of Hasse, Graun, C. P. E. Bach, Mozart (*Ave verum*), Mendelssohn, Schumann, and, particularly, Brahms (opp. 29, 74, 110). A somewhat more continuous development took place in France, under Gounod, Saint-Saëns, Théodore Dubois, Franck, Charles Borde, d'Indy, and other members of the *Schola cantorum.

Lit., *General:* H. Leichtentritt, *Geschichte der Motette* (1908).

To A. *13th century:* F. Ludwig, *Repertorium . . . motetorum vetustissimi stili* (1910); W. Meyer, *Der Ursprung des Motets* (1897); *OH* i, 176ff; *ReMMA*, passim; G. Kuhlmann, *Die 2-stimmigen französischen Motetten des Kodex Montpellier* (Diss. Frankfurt 1937); P. Aubry, †*Cent. motets du xiiie siècle*, 3 vols. (1908; Codex Bamberg); Y. Rokseth, †*Polyphonies du xiiie siècle*, 4 vols. (1936–39; Codex Montpellier); F. Ludwig, in *AMW* v; *id.*, in *SIM* vii; J. Handschin, in *KIM*, 1924; H. Besseler, in *AMW* vii; H. Husmann, in *AMF* ii. — *14th and 15th centuries:* F. Ludwig, †*G. de Machaut, Musikalische Werke*, vol. iii (1929); A. Hughes, †*Worcester Mediaeval Harmony* (1928); Ch. van den Borren, †*Polyphonia sacra* (1935; MS Oxford, *Canonici 213*); A. Ramsbotham, †*The Old Hall Manuscript*, 3 vols. (1933–38); †Trent Codices, in *DTOe* [see *Editions VII]; M. Bukofzer, in *ML* xvii, no. 3; H. Besseler, in *AMW* viii.

To B: W. Stephan, *Die burgundisch-niederländische Motette zur Zeit Ockeghems* (Diss. Heidelberg 1931); K. P. Kempers, *Die Motetten von Clemens non Papa* (Diss. Munich 1925); J. Neyses, *Studien zur Geschichte der deutschen Motette* (Diss. Bonn 1927); A. Orel, in *StM* vii (15th cent.); Th. W. Werner, in *ZMW* vii (Josquin).

Motet style. See *Motet B.

Motetus [L.]. (1) Latin for motet. — (2) In the medieval motet, the voice above the tenor; see *Motet A, I; *Duplum.

Mother Goose Suite. See *Symphonic poem IV.

Motion pictures. See under *Film music.

Motive, motif [G. *Motiv*]. The briefest intelligible and self-contained fragment of a musical theme or subject. As few as two notes may constitute a motive, if they are sufficiently characteristic, e.g., the descending fourth at the beginning of Beethoven's Piano Sonata A major, op. 2, no. 2; or the descending fifth at the opening of his Ninth Symphony [see the example under *Phrase]. The motives are the very bricks or germinating cells of the musical composition. It is through their highly developed use (repetition in the same or in other parts; transposition into other pitches; rhythmical modifications; contrapuntal combination with other motives) that Bach as well as Beethoven has bestowed upon his work a unique quality of logical coherence and well-motivated organization. In particular, the development-sections of the sonatas are entirely based upon the motives derived from the various subjects of the exposition. See also *Leitmotif.

The term "figure" is frequently used as synonymous with motive. A distinction could, however, and should be made, namely, that motives are derived from themes, while figures are not and, therefore, are of a more secondary importance, frequently serving as material for an ac-

companiment or counterpoint to a melody. The "motival" technique is therefore, generally speaking, much more recent than the "figural" technique. Early examples of the consistent use of figures occur frequently in the keyboard pieces of the late 16th and early 17th centuries (English virginalists, Sweelinck [e.g., *TaAM* iii, 3–5], Scheidt, and others). See *Figural chorale.

Motion. That element of a melody which is the result of the pitch quality ("high-low") of the musical sounds, as distinguished from rhythm which is the result of their duration quality ("long-short"). In fact, any melody can be separated into a motion-pattern and into a rhythm-pattern as is shown under *Melody. Motion may be ascending or descending, in the narrow steps of the scale (conjunct), or in the wider steps of a chord (disjunct). The study of these features is of prime importance in melodic analysis. See *Melody I, IV; also *Primitive music III.

The term is also used to describe the relative changes of pitch in two or more simultaneous voice-parts. Two such parts are said to be in *parallel motion*, if they stay in the distance of the same interval [Ex., a]; in *similar motion*, if they move

in the same direction, but change their distance [b]; in *contrary motion*, if they move in opposite directions [c]; in *oblique motion*, if one part remains stationary on the same pitch [d].

Moto, Con [It.]. With motion, quick.

Motu proprio [L., of his own motion]. Generally, a Papal decree, referring to the administration of the Church. Particularly, a decree issued by Pope Pius X in 1903 which contained a new regulation of the music in the Catholic service. The most important points of this decree were: (a) Abolishment of the theatrical and worldly style of church music which had spread during the 19th century, particularly in the Roman countries. (b) Return to Palestrina's music as the model of polyphonic church music. (c) Restoration of Gregorian chant according to the principles of the monks of *Solesmes; abolishment of the Editio Medicea and introduction of the Editio Vaticana [see *Liturgical books]. (d) Suppression of instrumental music — save for special occasions — and reduction of organ-playing to a modest role. (e) The admission of modern compositions (vocal, of course) provided their character was in agreement with the spirit of the service and the liturgical functions. For the complete text (English) cf. N. Slonimsky, *Music Since 1900* (1937), pp. 523ff.

Mouth harmonica, mouth organ. See *Harmonica (2).

Mouthpiece [G. *Mundstück*]. That portion of a wind instrument which is inserted into the player's mouth or applied to his lips. In a way, the mouthpiece is the most characteristic part of an instrument since it indicates to which family an instrument belongs. The following five types can be distinguished:

(a) Cupped mouthpiece, used for the *brass instruments. This is an enlargement of the bore to which the lips of the player are applied to form a kind of double reed. Cupped mouthpieces occur in a great variety of shapes, varying from the true "cup" of the trumpet to the "funnel" of the horn. Cf. the illustrations in *SaHMI*, 418.

(b) Single reed mouthpiece, used for the *clarinets. This mouthpiece [called F. *bec*, G. *Schnabel*] consists of a beak-shaped chamber with an opening on the under side to which a single reed is fixed.

(c) Double reed mouthpiece, used for the *oboes (usually not considered as a "mouthpiece," but included here for the sake of completeness and comparison). This consists of two reeds so shaped that they form at the top a narrow ( )-shaped slit. Older oboes had much larger reeds (approaching the size of the bassoon reeds) than the modern instrument. In

certain 16th-century types, e.g., the *cromornes*, the reed was covered by a wooden cap which acted as a windchest (similar to the reed pipes of the organ) [see *Reed].

(d) Fipple mouthpiece, used with the *recorders. This consists of a beak-shaped chamber which is stopped by a plug leaving only a narrow flue to lead the breath towards the sharp edge of a side hole. The principle is the same as in the flue pipes of the organ.

(e) Mouth hole, used in *flutes. This is a lateral orifice and the stream of air is directed against its lower edge. Because the mouth hole of a flute does not form a separate "piece" of the instrument, it is not spoken of as a "mouthpiece," but referred to as "embouchure," a term which is also applied to the class (a).

Mouvement [F.]. (1) Movement. — (2) Tempo.

Movable Do(h). Generally, any system of *solmization so designed that the syllables can be used in transposition for any key, as distinguished from Fixed Do(h) in which the syllables correspond to invariable pitches of notes. See also *Solfège.

Movement [F. *mouvement*; G. *Satz*; It. *tempo*]. The various complete and comparatively independent divisions which form the *sonata, *symphony, etc. One speaks of a "first, second, movement" or of a "fast, slow, movement." The *suite also consists of various movements, each in the character of a dance. See *Cyclic (1).

Movente [It.]. Moving.

Mozarabic chant. The chant of the medieval Christian Church of Spain [see *Chant]. The name refers to the Mozarabs, i.e., the Christians living in Spain (particularly in Aragon, Castile, Leon) under the Arab domination (711–1085). A coterminous name is *Visigothic chant*, referring to the Visigoths who conquered Spain in the 5th century. Neither name is wholly appropriate since the chant goes back at least to the fourth century (the

Visigoths, who brought with them an Arian Christianity, adopted the Catholic faith of Spain). St. Leander (d. 599), St. Isidore (*c.* 570–636), and St. Ildefonsus (d. 667) played an important role in the development of the chant which remained in use, untouched by the Gregorian reforms, until about the 11th century. See *Spanish music I.

Lit.: *ReMMA*, 110ff (bibl., 436); A. Gastoué, *Cours du chant grégorien* (1917), pp. 71, 79 (examples); P. Wagner, *Der Mozarabische Kirchengesang* . . . (1928); C. Rojo and G. Prado, *El Canto Mozarábe* (1929); P. Aubry, in *SIM* ix; M. Sablayrolles, in *SIM* xiii; G. Prado, in *Speculum* III, no. 2 (1928).

Mozarteum. An institution at Salzburg (Austria), headquarters of the *Mozart-Gemeinde*, and devoted to the memory of Mozart and to the study of his works.

Mp. Mezzo piano.

M.s. *Mano sinistra* [It.], left hand.

Muance [F.]. *Mutation (3).

Müde [G.]. Tired, languid.

Mühelos [G.]. Effortless.

Muineira, muneira. A dance of the Spanish province of Galicia in quick ⁶⁄₈-meter and evenly flowing motion. Cf. *LavE* i.4, 2368.

Multiple tonality. See *Polytonality.

Mundharmonika [G.]. Mouth organ. See *Harmonica (2).

Muneira. See *Muineira.

Murciana [from Murcia, a town in Southern Spain]. A local variety of the *fandango.

Murky. An 18th-century name of unknown origin, given to pieces with a bass accompaniment in broken octaves (Murky bass) [cf. *SchGMB*, 289, 2; *DdT* 35/36]. This unimaginative accompaniment was widely used in the second half of the 18th century (*Rococo). An early instance of broken octaves is found in François Couperin's "La Tri-

omphante" (*Pièces de Clavecin*, ordre X), where it serves a pictorial purpose. It may be compared with the highly dramatic "murky" in the first movement of Beethoven's Pathétique.

Murmelnd [G.]. Murmuring.

Musette. (1) The French *bagpipe of the 17th and 18th centuries. It had two chanters and a number of drones and bellows operated by the arm. The instrument became fashionable, together with the vielle [see *Hurdy-gurdy] in French society when, during the reigns of Louis XIV (1645–1715) and Louis XV (1715–74), the court circles indulged in a sophisticated crave for "Arcadia," disguising themselves as shepherds and peasants. The instruments of this period were splendidly decorated, the bags being covered with elaborate needlework, the pipes being inlaid with ivory and precious stones. A selection of pieces for musette and vielles is contained in H. Expert, *Amusements des musiciens français du XVIIIe siècle* (Sénart, Paris), which includes compositions by Jacques Aubert (1678–1753), Charles Bâton (d. 1758), and Nicolas Chédeville. Cf. also *GD*, articles Anet; Boismortier. — (2) Dance-like pieces of a pastoral character with a long-held drone, as could easily be played on the above instrument. Well-known examples are found in Bach's English Suites nos. 3 and 6. An amusing piece written in the same style occurs in Mozart's *Bastien et Bastienne* where it announces the arrival of the Sorcerer.

Lit.: E. Thoinau, *Les Hotteterre et les Chédeville* (1894); De Bricqueville, *Les Musettes* (1894).

Musica, the Latin word for music, occurs in early writings in the following connections: *musica divina* or *sacra*, church music; *musica vulgaris*, secular music; *musica mensuralis*, *mensural (measured, i.e., polyphonic) music; *musica plana*, *plainsong; *musica figurata*, *figural music; *musica ficta* or *falsa*, music involving chromatic tones. See also the classification by Boethius, under *Aesthetics.

Musica Divina. See *Editions, historical, XX.

Musica Enchiriadis [from Gr. *encheiridion*, handbook]. An important treatise of the 9th century (before 867, according to J. Handschin, in *Deutsche Vierteljahrsschrift für Literaturwissenschaft*, v), formerly attributed to the monk Hucbald (*c.* 840–930), but now believed to have been written by Hoger of Werden (d. 905) or by Otger of St. Pons (d. 940), repr. in *GS* i, 152–173. It is the earliest treatise dealing with polyphony and containing examples of parallel *organum. It also makes use of the *Daseian notation. A slightly later commentary is the *Scholia enchiriadis* (*GS* i, 173–212). See *Theory II.
  Lit.: H. Müller, *Hucbald's echte und unechte Schriften über Musik* (1884); Ph. Spitta, in *VMW* v; R. Schlecht, in *MfM* vi; A. H. Fox-Strangways, in *ML* xiii, no. 2; H. Sowa, in *ZMW* xvii; *ReMMA, passim.*

Musica ficta, musica falsa. I. In the music of the 10th to the 16th century, the theory of the chromatic tones, that is, of the tones other than those contained in the diatonic scale based on the *hexachord. At an early time the B-flat was admitted in practice (Gregorian chant) as well as in theory (Guido's hexachord) and was, therefore, frequently considered as not falling under musica ficta. The introduction of the chromatic tones became necessary for two reasons, namely, melodic modifications of the church modes or transposition of the church modes. For instance, a C-sharp may occur either as an artificial leading tone in (untransposed) Dorian, or as the normal third of Mixolydian, transposed a second above. The distinction between these two provinces is useful for the clarification of certain problems [cf. W. Apel, *Accidentien und Tonalitaet* (1938), p. 30], although it is not indicated in the medieval terminology, as has been maintained by R. v. Ficker, according to whom the former type was called *musica falsa*, the latter *musica ficta* [cf. his "Beiträge

zur Chromatik des 14. bis 16. Jahrhunderts," *StM*, 1914]. *Musica falsa* is simply the older term (13th century) which was supplanted by the other in the 14th century, probably because its implication of falseness became objectionable.
  II. The earliest reference to chromatic tones is found in the writings of Odo of Clugny (d. 943) who in an interesting table [*GS* i, 274; cf. H. Riemann, *Geschichte der Musiktheorie*, p. 63] considers transpositions of the fundamental gamut G–e″ to A (involving c♯ and f♯), to C (involving e♭), and to D (involving f♯). However, he emphasizes the speculative character of these tones, and explains them only in order to prevent their use by the singers. Nothing definite is known about the development of the altered tones in the following two centuries during which apparently the name *musica falsa* was introduced. As early as 1250 Pseudo-Aristotle (Magister Lambert) turned against this name, declaring that the system is "non falsa sed inusitata" — not false but little used [*CS* i, 258] or that "falsa musica quandoque necessaria est." The progress made in the ensuing period appears plainly from Philippe de Vitry's much more positive statement, made around 1325, that *musica falsa* is "non falsa, sed vera et necessaria" — not false but true and necessary [*CS* iii, 18]. Walter Odington (*c.* 1300) already knows the flatted E and B, as well as the sharped C and F. For more details concerning the treatises on *musica falsa*, cf. *WoGM* i, 109ff. In the 13th century the writers on *musica falsa* discuss the chromatic tones only with reference to the single line, emphasizing chiefly the *subsemitonium (leading tone) and the avoidance of the *tritone in progressions such as: g–f(♯)–g; c–e–f(♯)–g; f–a–b(♭)–a; etc. In the 14th century Joh. de Muris (*c.* 1325) approaches the problem from the point of view of simultaneous

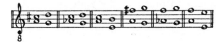

voice-leading, forbidding the tritone as a chordal formation [see *Tritone] and postulating that the third or sixth before a fifth or octave should be major if the upper voice ascends, minor, if it descends [see Ex.; cf. *WoGM* i, 116f].

III. In modern musicological writings, *musica ficta* denotes not so much the theory of early chromaticism, but the problems arising from the very scarce indication of chromatic tones in the musical sources prior to 1600, or, in other words, from the striking incongruity in this matter between the theoretical and the musical sources. Considering the fact that W. Odington already discusses most of the chromatic tones it is disconcerting, indeed, to find throughout the 16th century many long compositions completely lacking in any indication of accidentals. Beginning with H. Riemann, musicologists have shown a strong inclination to emend the original texts of this period by editorial accidentals which, in reliable editions of a scholarly character, are placed above the notes, in order to distinguish them from those given in the original sources. Although, generally speaking, the necessity of such emendations cannot be denied, matters have been carried decidedly too far in many editions published between 1900 and 1930. In fact, there has been a distinct tendency, frequently expressed in prefaces of scholarly publications, to approximate the tonal language of the Middle Ages and the Renaissance periods to the standards of the fully developed system of major and minor. Fortunately, the 20th-century ventures in dissonance and atonality have largely discredited the 19th-century bias against unfamiliar formations, and have thus paved the way for an unprejudiced examination of the whole problem.

IV. Aside from general prejudice, most studies in this field suffer from their failure to take the evolutionary point of view into account. It is, of course, futile to strive for an answer which would apply equally to music of the 13th and of the 16th century. With a problem of such subtleness and flexibility only special studies of periods, schools, and, perhaps, single manuscripts can be expected to prove successful. An unbiased examina-

tion will show that, prior to 1450, the musical sources are, as a rule, fully provided with all the necessary accidentals. In the 13th century the tonal resources of polyphonic music are so limited, the harmonies so clearly modal, that very seldom are accidentals needed aside from a B-flat which is frequently found as a signature in one of the lower parts [see *Partial signature, also *Tritone]. The manuscripts of the 14th century show a striking increase of notated accidentals, in conformity with the broadened system of harmonies and "keys." Signs for C-sharp, F-sharp, G-sharp, E-flat, are found in considerable quantity so that additional editorial accidentals will seldom be found to be really necessary. A most striking change, however, takes place with the rise of the Flemish School (*c.* 1450), in so far as now accidentals disappear almost completely from the sources, manuscript as well as printed. Whether this means only a clerical simplification or a real return to the church modes as the basis of polyphonic writing is a question which still remains to be decided. Without anticipating a decision, it may be noticed that a reversal to the sacred field is one of the most characteristic features of the early Flemish School [see this article] and that, as late as 1550, one of the most outstanding writers, Glareanus, discusses the tonality of numerous compositions by Isaac, Josquin, and others, without ever mentioning the possibility of the *subsemitonium* (raised seventh) in modes such as the Dorian, Phrygian, Mixolydian, Aeolian. It would not be impossible to assume that Glarean's *Dodekachordon* represents a last attempt to epitomize the modal character of the Flemish polyphony which was endangered by the rise of a novel tonality brought about by the secular music (chanson, madrigal) and by the music for organ and lute. In this connection it should be noticed that some compositions by Josquin and, possibly, other composers of his day strongly suggest an extended scheme of harmonic modulation, leading as far as A-flat [cf. Lowinsky]. Such cases serve to emphasize the importance of the general principle outlined at the beginning of this paragraph.

The foregoing explanations may be complemented by a number of examples showing unusual but entirely legitimate formations. See also *Leading tone.

Lit.: W. Apel, *Accidentien und Tonalität in den Musikdenkmälern des 15. und 16. Jahrhunderts* (1937); *ApNPM*, 104ff, 120; articles by Schwartz, Kroyer, Wolf, and Bernouilli in *KIM*, 1909, pp. 109ff; L. Hibberd, "Musica ficta and Instrumental Music" (*MQ* xxviii); Ch. W. Fox, "Accidentals in Vihuela Tablatures" (*BAMS* iv); E. E. Lowinsky, in *MQ* xxix, no. 1; E. St. Wilfort, in *ZIM* x; W. Apel, in *BAMS* ii; A. Einstein, in *SIM* viii (Merulo); E. Frerichs, in *ZMW* vii (organ tablatures); A. Cauchie, in *Kroyer Festschrift* (French vocal music).

Musical box. See *Mechanical instruments III.

Musical glasses. See *Harmonica (1).

Musical Offering. English for "Das Musikalische Opfer," one of the latest works of Bach, composed in 1747, and dedicated to King Frederick II of Prussia. It contains a number of contrapuntal pieces of a highly learned character all of which are based upon a theme of the king's invention, upon which Bach had extemporized during his visit to Potsdam in 1747. The dedication copy bears the inscription: "Regis Iussu Cantio Et Reliqua Canonica Arte Resoluta" (By command of the king, the theme and other things developed in canonical art), a sentence which, if read acrostically, spells RICERCAR, thus emphasizing the learned character of the work. In fact, together with the *Art of Fugue, the Musical Offering represents the summary and consummation of three centuries of contrapuntal art. Particularly interesting are the various enigmatical canons and the trio-sonata in the last movement of which the royal theme appears once in each part.

Lit.: Ph. Spitta, *Bach*, Engl. transl., iii, 191–197, 233, 292, 294; H. David, in *MQ* xxiii; A. Orel, in *DM* xxx, 2 and 3.

Musica reservata. A term used first by Adrian Coclico in his *Compendium musices* (1551) as a characterization of the music of Josquin and his followers in contradistinction to that of the preceding period (Ockeghem, Obrecht, Isaac). The literal meaning of the term has been much disputed, the word "reservata" having been explained as referring to the greater restriction of the more recent style in the use of figurations and ornamental design; or as pointing to some secrets of musical technique (improvisation, expression of the text by musical motives, chromaticism not indicated by accidentals); or as indicating the exclusive character of music written for classes of high cultural standing. At any rate, *musica reservata* denotes the Renaissance-like clarity, balance, and expressiveness, the full-blooded humanism, of the Josquin period, in contrast to the abstract and mysterious transcendentalism of the earlier masters, particularly Ockeghem and Isaac. In the late 16th century the term was more narrowly used in the meaning of "expressive interpretation of the text," as was natural in the period of the late madrigal and the approaching *nuove musiche. Thus, *musica reservata* constitutes a forerunner of the *Affectenlehre of the 18th century. See *Maniera.

Lit.: M. van Crevel, *A. P. Coclico* (1940); A. Coclicus, *Compendium musices* (1552); G. Zarlino, *Istituziones* (1558), cap. 63; Th. Kroyer, "Von der Musica Reservata" (*Festschrift für Heinrich Wölfflin*, Dresden, 1934); A. Sandberger, *Beiträge zur Geschichte der bayrischen Hofkapelle unter O. di Lasso* i, 51ff; K. Huber, *Ivo de Vento* (1918); H. Leichtentritt, in *BAMS* vi; E. Lowinsky, in *BAMS* vii.

Musica Sacra. See *Editions XXI.

Music box. See under *Mechanical instruments I.

Music criticism. I. Music criticism is generally understood today as the reviewing of public performances in a newspaper or periodical. Before entering into a description of this most important branch of critical activity it may, however, be well to point to the somewhat less conspicuous, but no less important criticism of musical compositions as found in a number of books. Long before the era of the newspaper, Glareanus, in his *Dodekachordon* (1547), offered profound critical analyses, still worth-while reading today, of the works of Josquin, Isaac, and other masters. About 200 years later we encounter a more aggressive type of criticism in Mattheson's *Critica musica* (1722), in Scheibe's *Der critische Musicus* (1737–40), and in Marpurg's *Der kritische Musicus an der Spree* (1749–50). The reviews of Robert Schumann are a highly important landmark in the development of music criticism. These, although published in a magazine, the *Neue Zeitschrift für Musik* (founded by Schumann and still issued today), may be mentioned here because they are concerned with the critical analysis of compositions rather than with an account of their performance. Other great composers who were also more or less active as critics are Weber, Berlioz, Liszt, Wagner, Hugo Wolf, Debussy. In general, however, creative artists of high rank, in spite of their superior knowledge of musical art, are not good critics, because their subjective point of view makes it very

hard, even impossible, for them to do justice to others. Schumann was a solitary exception, inasmuch as he had, in addition to his creative capacity, the faculty of understanding and appreciating other personalities. Indeed, he had an almost miraculous power of vision, as is shown by his numerous reviews, favorable or adverse, of an op. 1 or op. 2, e.g., those of Chopin, Berlioz, Brahms. Among the more recent writers of critical studies we should like to single out D. F. Tovey in England and A. Halm in Germany.

II. Turning now to musical journalism or, in other words, to the activity of the professional music critic, we enter quite a different phase of music criticism. While books are addressed mainly to the professional students or the musical amateur, the newspaper critic speaks to the general public. Up to the time of the French Revolution music had developed under the auspices of the Church or aristocratic societies. In the 19th century, however, the masses of the middle classes became the prime supporters and patrons of musical performance, and the consequence of this process of democratization was the demand to see the public concerts critically discussed in the daily papers. Thus came into existence a new profession, music criticism. Eduard Hanslick, who wrote from 1864 for the *Neue Freie Presse* (Vienna), may justly be called the father of musical journalism, if only for the reason that, in his one-sided attitude against Wagner and for Brahms, he introduced into music criticism an element of personal aggressiveness and prejudice which, unfortunately, was imitated by a number of later critics. Hanslick's successor as critic for the *Neue Freie Presse* was Julius Korngold who, until the rise of Hitlerism, exercised great power.

In the 20th century Berlin acquired the leadership in music criticism, in consequence of this city's rise as the world's center of musical activities. Here the leading critics were the Wagnerian Wilhelm Tappert; Leopold Schmidt at the *Berliner Tageblatt* and his successor Alfred Einstein; Adolf Weissmann, the champion of modernism; Hermann Springer at the

Deutsche Tageszeitung. In the widely read *Frankfurter Zeitung* Paul Bekker (d. in New York) and Karl Holl have acquired great authority. Among the contemporary English critics Ernest Newman is best known internationally, from his long activity on the *Manchester Guardian* and the *London Sunday Times.*

III. In the United States music criticism began with J. D. Dwight (1813–93), William H. Fry (1813–64), and John R. G. Hazzard, Fry's successor on the New York *Tribune.* Toward the turn of the century there appeared on the scene a galaxy of eminent critics who have done honor to the profession. Of the older generation J. G. Huneker (New York *Times,* New York *World*), H. E. Krehbiel (New York *Tribune*), W. J. Henderson (New York *Sun*), Lawrence Gilman (New York *Herald Tribune*), Philip Hale (Boston *Herald*), H. T. Parker (Boston *Evening Transcript*), R. Aldrich (New York *Times*), have acquired the greatest reputation. At present, Olin Downes (New York *Times*), Oscar Thompson (New York *Sun*), Virgil Thomson (*Herald Tribune*), Samuel Chotzinoff (New York *Post*), Francis Perkins (*Herald Tribune*), Leonard Liebling (New York *American*), with others, are the best known and most esteemed critics. An essential difference between music criticism in the United States and in Germany, for example, is the much greater emphasis in America on the journalistic side, which requires the critic to have his review in the paper the morning after the performance. In Berlin, reviews frequently appeared in the form of weekly reports, sometimes several weeks after the concert took place.

IV. It is generally agreed that music criticism, as practiced today, is, on the whole, unsatisfactory. It cannot be denied that the average music critic exercises an arbitrary and undeserved authority, not backed by sufficient ability, training, and experience in the field he represents. In many places music criticism is assigned to a reporter who has bare knowledge of music and who is really at home in an altogether different field. On the other hand, the reviews of famous critics, past as well as present, frequently bear the stamp of presumption and arbitrariness rather than of integrity and knowledge. Eduard Hanslick is only one of the many who have greatly misused the ascendency inherent in their position. Various efforts have been made by modern writers, e.g., Ernest Newman and M. D. Calvocoressi, to advance music criticism from the level of a hit-or-miss reaction of individuals to the rank of a real science; to establish certain general principles of approach and judgment which might serve as a common basis for all the members of the profession. Perhaps Calvocoressi has come closest to the establishment of a general method by outlining three main considerations which enter into the mental activity of the critic: (1) "predispositions," (2) "direct data," (3) "indirect data." The first of these is the critic himself, his personality, temperament, experience, biases, etc. The second is the composition as written and performed. The third category includes numerous accessory facts, such as knowledge previously acquired about the composer from other compositions or through outside information; about his position within the general development of music or within a particular school; about the relationship of the composition to others of the same composer, etc. To separate these considerations and, in particular, to avoid undue prevalence of the personal "predisposition" over the factual "data" is the foremost task of the critic.

Even more important, perhaps, than theories and methods of music criticism is the establishment of a living tradition inaugurated by men of outstanding qualities and perpetuated by others who try to emulate them. These qualities, not frequently combined in one individual, may be summed up as follows: Practical and theoretical knowledge of music in its various fields; literary talent; a wide spiritual horizon; a great feeling of responsibility; a character in which sensitiveness, benevolence, sincerity, and fearlessness are coupled with tact and some degree of diplomacy; finally, that scent for the new, valuable, and important which is the outstanding trait of the specific critical talent.

For a list of living critics see Pierre Key's *Music Year Book*.

Lit.: M. D. Calvocoressi, *The Principles and Methods of Music Criticism* (1923); S. Langford, *Musical Criticism* (1929); P. Rosenfeld, *Discoveries of a Music Critic* (1936); O. Thompson, *Practical Criticism* (1934); H. Andres, *Beiträge zur Geschichte der Musik-kritik* (Diss. Heidelberg 1938); Y. Bannard, "Composer-Critics" (*ML* v, no. 3); W. Wright Roberts, "Berlioz, the Critic" (*ML* vii, no. 1); J. D. Rorke, "The Personal Note in Musical Criticism" (*MQ* xiii); P. C. Buck, in *PMA* xxxii; A. H. Fox-Strangways, in *PMA* lxv; M. D. Calvocoressi, in *MQ* ix; A. Schering, "Aus der Geschichte der musikalischen Kritik in Deutschland" (*JMP* xxxv); F. Stege, "Die deutsche Musikkritik des 18. Jahrhunderts . . ." (*ZMW* x); A. Damerini, "Gli albore della critica musicale Italiana" (*LRM* vi); G. del Valle de Paz, "I primordi della critica musicale in Francia" (*RMI* xxxviii).   H. L.

Music drama. Designation for the Wagnerian type of opera. See *Opera X.

Music education in the United States. I. *Public and Private Schools.* The first music instruction in the schools of this country was offered in Boston in 1838. From a modest beginning an imposing system has developed until today music in some form is everywhere recognized as a feature of school education. That this system has not been more productive is due to the fact that the project has become almost as much a commercial as an educational one; that instruction has aimed not primarily at musicalness but rather at definitely measurable results — an objective similar to that sought in the teaching of essentially factual subjects; and that the quality of most of the music used in teaching has been unworthy of respect. Music supervisors and teachers have been trained to be methodologists first of all, and too often lack the prime essential of musicianship, namely, good

taste. Thus, provided children could read at sight effectively, the value of the music itself has been held to be of slight importance. Book companies have met these ideals by issuing volumes of inferior music, with the result that children, wearied by mechanical musical discipline and by an experience of songs that are to a great extent merely exercises, have not, in maturity, generally cared to cultivate music actively. This is shown, in part, by the comparatively small number of amateur choruses which exist in this country. Within the last years great emphasis has been laid on the orchestra and the band, and in certain school systems applied music is accorded diploma credit. Courses in appreciation and in the technical branches are also offered. At the moment there is evident a tardy disposition to improve the quality of all school music and to adopt a more enlightened pedagogy. This appears in the work of most private schools, in a few public school systems, and it is reflected in the output of one or two publishing companies. Recognition for much of the improvement should be given to the late Thomas W. Surette who for many years waged an almost single-handed fight against overemphasis on sight-reading, and who constantly advocated a higher standard of music.

II. *Children's Concerts.* In cities where there are symphony orchestras, a series of concerts for children is not uncommon. The opportunity of making young people acquainted with music which they can appreciate and understand, presented without the medium of transcription or mechanical devices, is most valuable. For various reasons these performances too often become an amusement enterprise in which humor, surprise, and mere entertainment predominate to the exclusion of any systematic plan of instruction. At the other extreme are performances of entire symphonies which require for their understanding and enjoyment a background of experience not possessed by children; and romantic and emotionally complex works with which the young can have no intelligent contact. The programs which have been most successful educationally are those which have been devoted, in the main, to music of a markedly melodic and rhythmic character cast in the simpler forms; the music of composers like Haydn, Mozart, and Bach. Not the least valuable in awakening the interest of children in music have been recitals of chamber music, particularly music of the classical period.

III. *The Phonograph and Radio.* The phonograph and the radio have assumed an important role in music education, and the former, in particular, has made available for classroom use a wide variety of material. Especially in locations where orchestras are not available and where the teacher's competence as a performer is not adequate, both the phonograph and the radio are indispensable adjuncts to music instruction. The total efficiency of the radio as a means of music education is, however, still debatable. The many physical impediments to a satisfactory reception of the music are but one difficulty. Another is certainly the fact that the radio (as well as the phonograph) belongs too much to the common currency of experience to stimulate and hold attention. The radio is at its best when it simply transmits music unaccompanied by speech. Present efforts are unfortunately marked by overemphasis on the personality of the radio instructor, and on amusing and sensational features rather than on sound and progressive teaching. It may be said that neither the phonograph nor the radio as mechanical intermediaries between the music and the listener can satisfactorily compensate for the absence of the teacher himself. His gestures and facial expressions are most important in conveying his ideas regarding the music, especially where children are concerned. Perhaps television will overcome at least some of these difficulties.

IV. *Colleges.* In colleges, music instruction is offered in theory (harmony, counterpoint, fugue, and analysis), composition, form, history, musicology, appreciation, and applied (practical) music. Musicology is the latest addition to the curriculum, and instruction in this branch of learning is not widespread as yet. The work of glee clubs, bands, and orchestras, for which degree credit is awarded in many universities, is extensively and often productively carried on. The tendency in college music teaching has been either to overemphasize the performing aspect of music at the expense of the other branches, or to stress the academic side, taking student competence in applied music for granted. The college course is not long enough to permit more than moderate achievement in either field, and the problem has been best solved by those colleges which have treated music from the point of view of the Liberal Arts curriculum, recognizing the necessity for some practical skill, encouraging students to strive for it, but leaving it, in the main, to the conservatory. Colleges so situated that students cannot avail themselves of applied teaching often wisely include teachers of practical music on their faculty.

In some colleges regular course work is supplemented by tutorial instruction intended to cover important aspects of the subject not dealt with in classes. At the end of the senior year general examinations are held which test the student's knowledge of the whole field, especially those parts of it which he has worked under the supervision of his tutor.

V. *Conservatories.* The standard of instruction in conservatories, together with diploma requirements, has greatly improved during the last twenty years, with the result that professional music training in some institutions has drawn up level with that traditionally maintained in European conservatories. Those severe disciplines which are inevitable in the production of sound musicianship and technical accomplishment are now required, and the distinction of American trained composers, orchestral players, and solo performers is generally recognized. As the musicianship of any executant, however, may justly be assumed to include more than brilliance in technique, many conservatories, without attempting to compete with the colleges, pay not a little attention to the study of the history of music and of musical styles.

VI. *Settlement Schools of Music.* One

of the most praiseworthy and rewarding features of American music education is the settlement school. Those who are unable to pay for instruction in regular conservatories may receive there, for a comparatively small fee, a training in music which is often of a high grade of excellence. These schools sometimes serve as an animating center for the whole musical life of the community, creating a social bond which would otherwise be lacking, and at the same time they offer to the ordinary as well as to the talented individual an opportunity for the development of musical skill according to his capacity.

VII. *Adult Education.* For those whose formal education is ended, but who wish in after-life to make an acquaintance of music denied them by previous indifference or the deficiencies of early school training, opportunity for study and participation is offered by numbers of adult centers. In some cities, too, laymen's courses in listening to music are given. But as not a few of these courses seem to be predicated on the assumption that it is the function of the professional to make music, and the part of the amateur to listen passively, the fundamental value of this type of teaching may be doubted. The most successful results have been obtained where instruction has concerned itself first with an active experience of music gained by membership in choruses and orchestras maintained as part of the musical organization of the adult center.

VIII. *Conclusion.* In many fields, music education in the United States is steadily improving. At the moment, however, it is more notable for the extent of its cultivation than for its adherence to any considered philosophy. The tendency is to view each step in music training as a separate issue having its own aims unrelated to those which precede or follow. The lack of any generally adopted or integrated plan, the use of so much inferior music, and preoccupation with the more mechanical aspects of instruction have resulted in a lethargic attitude toward music on the part of the average adult which will be remedied only when really valu-

able and permanent objectives are set up. Of all branches of music education, that connected with public schools is the most static and reactionary, and in that quarter enlightened progress is painfully slow. On the whole, the faults of the American system are those which are characteristic of any country in its youth; as, for example, our present tendency to revere degrees and diplomas more than the knowledge they represent. But the American is no less innately musical than members of other races. He needs only wise and skillful educational guidance to convert his native musicalness into an active, enthusiastic, and intelligent interest.

It follows, therefore, that the greatest need is a teaching body that is better educated musically; one that is thoroughly trained at least in those branches of the art which are pertinent to school music instruction. The most serious demand, however, is for teachers whose knowledge and experience of music is wide enough to guarantee a sound musical taste. Only when there is intelligent revolt against much educational material that now passes for music, will there be hope for a productive music education in this country.　　　　　　　　　　　　A. T. D.

IX. It has not been considered advisable to include in the present book information on the single institutions of higher musical education, whether conservatories or music departments of colleges. To include them all would be impossible as well as undesirable. To include part of them — assumedly the better part — would involve a process of grading which the author wants to avoid for obvious reasons. The author's decision has been greatly facilitated by the fact that accurate and complete information on all these institutions is easily available in Pierre Key's *Music Year Book* [see also R. Thompson, *College Music*, and numerous separate entries in O. Thompson, *The International Cyclopedia of Music and Musicians* (1939)]. For the English institutions see A. Eaglefield-Hull, *Dictionary of Modern Music* (1924), article "Academies"; for the German, see *RL* article "Konservatorium"; for the French see *LavE* ii.6, 3451ff. See also *Degrees and diplomas; *Profession; *Scholarships.

Lit.: E. B. Birge, *History of Public School Music in the United States* (1928); A. T. Davison, *Music Education in America* (1926); W. Earhart, *The Meaning and Teaching of Music* (1935); J. D. Schenck, *Music, Youth and Opportunity* (1926); O. S. Stokowski, *The Layman's Music Book* (1935); T. W. Surette, *Music and Life* (1917); R. Thompson, *College Music* (1935); A. D. Zanzig, *Music in American Life* (1932); *id., Music and Men* (1941); T. L. Mursell, *Music in American Schools* (1943).

Musicology. A term recently adopted from French *musicologie* into the English usage to denote the scientific study of music. It is the equivalent of the German term *Musikwissenschaft* (science of music) which was introduced by F. Chrysander in the preface to his *Jahrbücher für musikalische Wissenschaft* (1863) in order to emphasize the idea that musical studies, particularly those in the field of history, should be raised to the same level of seriousness and accuracy which had long been adopted in the other fields of knowledge, natural sciences as well as humanities. Guido Adler, in the first volume of the *Vierteljahrsschrift für Musikwissenschaft* (1885), wrote an article "Umfang, Methode und Ziel der Musikwissenschaft" (Scope, Method and Aim of Musical Science) in which he drew up an extensive and all-inclusive table of the entire province of music study. This table included, side by side with paleography (musical notation), esthetics, acoustics, history, such subjects as harmony, rhythm, melody, teaching of counterpoint, etc., as well as a final category "Musikforschung" (musical research). Similar programs have been laid down by other writers, e.g., by Waldo S. Pratt in his article "On Behalf of Musicology" (*MQ* i). The current interpretation of musicology may be illustrated by the following quotations: "Musicology must include every conceivable discussion of musical topics" (Pratt, in *MQ* i); "the whole body of systematized knowledge

about music, which results from the application of a scientific method of investigation or research, or of philosophical speculation and rational systematization to the facts, the processes and the development of musical art, and to the relation of man in general (or even animals) to that art" (Kinkeldey, article "Musicology" in O. Thompson, *International Cyclopedia of Music and Musicians*, 1939); "Musicology unites in its domain all the sciences which deal with the production, appearance and application of the physical phenomenon called sound" (H. Láng; cf. L. Harap, "On the Nature of Musicology," *MQ* xxiii).

Although these definitions differ to some extent, they all indicate the tendency to interpret musicology as a broad category of "musical science," including everything that is not clearly "practical" music (composition and performance). Thus, traditional fields of study such as harmony, counterpoint, music history would fall under the term musicology. One might argue whether this tendency is desirable and commendable. The unfavorable reception which, on the whole, musicology has encountered since its introduction in this country some 30 years ago may well be due largely to the somewhat boastful manner in which its champions have laid claim upon fields which had an old standing of their own. Another undesirable aspect of the present situation is the fact that, owing to the very broad interpretation of the term, people have been able to call themselves "musicologists" who are not good in any musical field at all.

The main fault of the interpretation of musicology as the "science of music" or the "scientific approach to music" is that it comes half a century *post festum*. The situation of the 1860's, which caused Chrysander to insist upon "musikwissenschaftliche Methoden," no longer exists. The general standards of scientific treatment, such as seriousness, accuracy, correctness with regard to material and sources, have been so generally adopted in recent musical studies that scientific procedure can be taken for granted, in a book (or course) on harmony, as well as in one on the life of Wagner, etc. If, then, the scientific approach is taken for granted in all studies of musical theory, history, etc., there remains one category of Adler's table which stands apart as something different, namely the last-mentioned, *Musikforschung*, i.e., musical research. If we interpret musicology as research-work in music, then it denotes that activity — in any of the fields mentioned previously — which is bent upon the discovery of unknown or obscure matters, an activity which is comparable to that of the research-chemist, as opposed to the "commercial chemist" who makes the discoveries of his colleague available to the public for consumption. The musicologist, then, is the pioneer of music study, the explorer who is equipped with the same zeal which spurs and guides every discoverer, whether he sets out to find the North Pole, a new chemical element, or a new mathematical truth. If the result of his research is valid and important, it will, sooner or later, be accepted into general usage, in other words, it will change from the field of musicology into the domain of the theorist, the essayist, the biographer, the performer, and perhaps even the creative artist. An example illustrating the situation and the process just outlined is the case of Bach. Around 1850, his work was largely forgotten, most of his compositions being scattered around in obscure manuscripts. The men who undertook to "discover Bach" (Chrysander was one of them) were musicologists in the true sense of the word. When their work was done, when Bach's compositions were available for every student, the work of the musicologist was finished. A student who now examines, say, a partita by Bach, is not a musicologist, any more than is the performer who plays it, or the creative artist who derives from it new inspiration. This does not mean that musicological study in connection with Bach was finished after the publication of the B.-G. There were — and still are — many aspects connected with his works to be investigated, an example in point being

Spitta's studies of their historical background, or Ernst Kurth's work on Bach's counterpoint, or Terry's thorough investigation of the details of his life.

Perhaps the difference between the program just outlined and that given by Adler and others is not so much a difference of scope (Adler's being much wider), but one of emphasis. It goes without saying that most, if not all, the categories of Adler's program are more or less directly connected with musicology, either as preparatory or as peripheric categories. The important point, however, is that the category Musical Research (Musikforschung) must be given the central position in the plan, with theory, music history, etc., forming the foundation, while aesthetics, acoustics, etc., represent adjunct fields of study.

Viewed from this angle, it appears only natural that the efforts of musicology are directed mainly towards the history of music in which there are still so many facts to be discovered or clarified. As a matter of fact, the progress in the fields of harmony, composition, etc., is made, not by theoretical investigation (efforts of this type, as, e.g., novel theories of quarter-tones, have usually remained without practical results), but as the result of the natural development of the musical art. There is, however, another field of musical research which has attracted the attention of many recent investigators, that of primitive and Oriental music which, because of the special methods involved, is classified separately as *comparative musicology. Important progress has also been made in the fields of musical acoustics, particularly in the recent studies of pitch and on timbre (theory of formant). As a rule, however, such studies involve methods of physics, physiology, and psychology rather than of musical research.

Although the above interpretation of musicology as the "research laboratory" of music is not the one generally accepted, it might seem worth while to stress it, only in order to secure for musicology that place in the American institutions of higher learning to which it is, no doubt entitled and from which it is, equally doubtless, still far removed. The leaders of such institutions are likely to take "rigorous technique" and "scientific treatment" as matters of course in any of their departments, but may be willing to give some thought to the necessity of providing in the field of music a type of instruction similar to that which is the very basis of progress in all the other fields of higher learning.

Lit.: G. Haydon, *Introduction to Musicology* (1941); L. Schiedermaier, *Einführung in das Studium der musikgeschichte* (1930); H. Riemann, *Grundriss der Musikwissenschaft* (1908); Ch. Seeger, in *AM* xi; L. Harap, in *MQ* xxiii; P. Láng, "Musicology for Music" (*MM* xix, no. 2); R. Sessions, "Musicology and the Composer" (*BAMS* v); various authors, in *PAMS*, 1936; A. Machabey, in *RdM*, nos. 38, 39. Add. bibl. in *MoML*, 551. See also *Periodicals VII.

Musikalisches Opfer [G.]. *Musical Offering.

Musikwissenschaft [G.]. See under *Musicology.

Mustel organ. See *Harmonium.

Muta [It., change] indicates change of tuning in the orchestral parts for kettledrums and, in earlier score, change of crooks for horns and natural trumpets. For instance, "muta in G/d" means that the two kettledrums shall be tuned in G and in d.

Mutanza [It.]. Old (16th-century) term for variation.

Mutation. (1) The change from soprano or alto to tenor or bass which takes place in a boy's voice during adolescence, usually between the ages of 14 and 16. — (2) The term is occasionally used to denote the *shift in violin playing. — (3) See *Hexachord IV.

Mutation stops. See *Organ VI. Also Foot (2).

Mute. A device for softening or muffling the tone of a musical instrument. In violins, etc., the mute is a three-pronged clamp which is placed on the bridge and which renders the tone veiled and somewhat nasal. It is usually called for by the remark *con sordini*. This effect has been frequently used for the purpose of creating a mysterious or uncanny atmosphere, one of the earliest examples being in a sleeping scene of Lully's *Armida* (1686). Beethoven used muted violins in the prison scene of his *Fidelio*, and Berlioz for the "Valse des Sylphes" of his *La Damnation de Faust*, to mention only a few of the earlier instances. The mutes are very effective on the violin and the viola, but not on the cello, where a much heavier device would be necessary to produce a comparable result. — Brass instruments, particularly horns, are muted by inserting a pear-shaped piece of wood or metal into the bell. — Kettledrums were formerly muted by placing a cloth over the parchment; today sponge-headed drumsticks are generally used. — In pianofortes, the sound is muted by the left pedal (soft pedal) which causes the whole keyboard with the hammers to shift a little to the right side (hence the German name *Verschiebung*, shift) so that the hammers strike only one string, instead of two or three (hence the Italian name *una corde*, one string); see *Pianoforte I. In upright pianos a similar effect is achieved by reducing the ambit of the hammer.

The term mute is frequently identified or confused with *dampers. Properly, a damper serves an entirely different purpose, namely to deaden a sound. The difference between mute and damper is particularly clear on the piano where the left pedal is a mute, while the right pedal is connected with the dampers, setting them out of action upon being depressed. Unfortunately, Webster encourages and perhaps justifies the looseness of terminology when, under "to mute," he says: "to muffle or deaden the sound." The same ambiguity of terminology exists with the Italian word *sordino* which is applied to the muting of the violins (*sordini alzati* or *levati*, remove the mutes) as well as to the dampers of the piano, while the muting of the piano is called *una corda*. The confusion has been brought to its climax by modern (German and English) editors who, reading the indication "senza sordini" in the first movement of Beethoven's Moonlight Sonata, considered this an error and changed it into "con sordini" or "una corda." Actually, Beethoven's *sordini* are the dampers of the piano and his indication "senza sordini" means "without dampers," i.e., "with the right-hand pedal," — not "with the left-hand pedal." See *una corda.

Mutig [G.]. Bold.

M.v. *Mezza voce.

Mystery. See *Liturgical drama.

Mystic chord. A chord invented by Scriabin, consisting of a series of six fourths: C–f#–bb–e'–a'–d". It forms the harmonic basis of his *Prometheus* (1910) and the Seventh Piano Sonata, op. 64. Scriabin, in other compositions, used similar chord formations, e.g., c–f#–b–e' (op. 57), and A–d#–g–c'#–(f')–b'–e" (Eighth Piano Sonata, op. 66). Cf. A. Eaglefield-Hull, in *PMA* xliii. See *Fourth.

N

Nabla, nablum. A stringed instrument mentioned by Greek writers, probably the *nevel* of the old Hebrews [see *Jewish music I].

Nacaire. See *Drum II.

Nachahmung [G.]. Imitation.

Nachdrücklich, mit Nachdruck [G.]. With emphasis.

Nachlassend [G.]. Slackening.

Nachschlag [G.]. (1) In modern German terminology, the two terminating notes which are usually played at the end of a trill [see *Trill IV].
(2) In 17th/18th-century music, an ornament consisting of one or several short notes attached to the preceding main note. The ornamenting notes constitute a melodic movement away from the preceding note, and are to be performed as a part of this, i.e., *before* the next main note. Thus the Nachschlag is the exact opposite of the *appoggiatura, which is a melodic movement towards, and forms a part of, the following note. The accompanying illustration shows the simplest method of

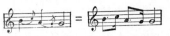

notating the Nachschlag, together with the correct rendition.
In French music of the 17th and 18th

centuries the most common form of Nachschlag is the agrément variously called *accent, aspiration,* or *plainte,* which consists of a raising of the pitch a half tone or whole tone at the end of a sustained note. The *accent* was indicated by several different signs: an inverted V, a short vertical stroke, or a tiny grace note. All these signs are invariably suppressed in modern editions. Ex. 1, from Rameau's opera *Hyppolyte et Aricie,* shows the notation and the approximate effect of the *accent.* The 17th-century English equivalent of the accent is called the *springer.* It was used chiefly in music for the lute or viol, and was performed by lightly touching the string at a higher fret (without plucking it again) at the end of a sustained note. The sign for the springer is an ascending oblique stroke placed slightly to the right of the written note (or letter, in the case of tablatures) as in Ex. 2.
The Nachschläge described above were rarely used in Germany, but a similar ornament occurs in German music of the Baroque period. It always appears between a series of descending thirds and is indicated by a curved hook extending to the right of the main note, as in the accompanying example by J. S. Bach [Ex. 3]. This ornament had no sign in the contemporary French music. Its use was taken for granted, however, by French musicians, and it should be in-

serted, in performance, in all passages where thirds descend in notes of equal value. This practice was known as "couler les tierces."

A special type of Nachschlag is that which anticipates the following note, i.e., the "anticipation" of modern composition [see *Nonharmonic tones]. The descending anticipation was very common as an ornament in the 17th century, when it was known in France as a *cheute*, in England as a *cadent*. Its sign is the same in the music of both countries — a descending oblique line to the right of the written note. The proper execution is given in Ex. 4. In the 18th century the most common use of this type of Nachschlag is as an anticipation of the final note of a phrase [Ex. 5]. The Nachschlag, in this position, is usually written as an ordinary note or else left to the discretion of the performer. Particularly frequent is the Nachschlag as the closing note (or notes) of a *trill. In modern German usage the term Nachschlag usually refers to this practice [see (1)].

Romantic composers returned to some extent to the earlier custom of writing Nachschläge as grace notes. Since they generally do not trouble to slur the grace note to the preceding note there is some danger of confusing it with an appoggiatura, unless the composer is careful (as Schumann always was) to place the Nachschlag before the bar-line [Example 6, *Warum*]. There is no strict rule which will eliminate this confusion entirely, but it may at least be assumed that whenever the grace note is identical with the following note (as in the Ex. 7, from Chopin's Nocturne op. 32, no. 2) the ornament is a Nachschlag. P. A.

Nachspiel [G.]. Postlude.

Nachtanz [G., after-dance]. In the dance music of the 16th century a quick dance in triple meter which follows upon a slower dance in duple meter [see *Dance music II]. Other names for such after-dances were: *Der Sprungk* (jump, jumping dance), *Hupfauf* ("hopping up"), *Proportz* or *Tripla* (from *proportio tripla*, with reference to the triple meter), or *Kerabe* (*Kehrab*, lit. "sweep-off," i.e., closing dance). Especially frequent combinations of dance and after-dance were: pavane-gaillarde (c. 1500–1600); passamezzo-saltarello (c. 1550–1620); allemande-courante (c. 1600–50); the last-named combination was taken over into the *suite. Frequently the *Nachtanz* is a rhythmic variation of the main dance. This practice, which already occurs in the early 14th century (cf. *SchGMB*, no. 28), is regularly observed in the *Proportz. Examples in *HAM*, nos. 83, 102, 105, 137, 154a, 179.

Nachtmusik [G.]. *Serenade.

Nachtstück [G., night piece]. *Nocturne. However, the pieces by Schumann and Hindemith (*Suite 1922*) bearing this title are much more suggestive of nightly visions and dreams than are Chopin's nocturnes.

Nagarah. See *Drum II.

Nagelgeige [G.]. *Nail violin.

Nagelschrift, Hufnagelschrift [G.]. A German variety of *neumes used during the 14th and 15th centuries, and so named on account of the similarity of its characters to the nails used with

[477]

horseshoes. Another name is Gothic neumes.

Nail violin, nail harmonica. An instrument — if it may be called thus — consisting of a semicircular sounding-board in which nails or U-shaped iron pins of various lengths are driven around the edge. The nails are made to vibrate by a violin bow. The nail violin (invented by J. Wilde, *c.* 1740) belongs to the same period of *Empfindsamkeit* (late 18th and early 19th century) which also produced the *Aeolian harp, as a result of its general penchant for the ethereal and bodyless. Illustrations in *SaHMI*, 403 and *AdHM*, 632. There exists a quartet by F. W. Rust for nail violin, two violins, and cello [see *Editions XII, B(11)].

Naked fifth. Same as *open fifth.

Nakeres, nakers. See *Drum II.

Napoletana. See under *Villanella.

Narrante [It.]. In a declamatory manner.

National anthems. The songs adopted by the various nations to be played on official occasions and to represent them in international gatherings. The most important among the older ones are given here in a chronological order: Netherlands: *Wilhelmus van Nassouwe* (1570, music first in 1626). — England: *God Save the King* (comp. by H. Carey, 1744; its melody is used in the American song *My Country 'tis of Thee*, as well as in the German pre-war anthem *Heil Dir im Siegerkranz* and in the anthems of several other nations). — Denmark: *Kong Kristian* (J. Ewald – J. E. Hartmann, 1768?). — France: *La *Marseillaise* (comp. by Rouget de Lisle, 1792). — Poland: *Jeszce Polska* (Wybicki–Oginsky, 1795). — Austria: *Gott erhalte Franz den Kaiser* (comp. by Haydn, 1797, now sung to the text *Sei gesegnet ohne Ende*; Haydn's melody is used also with the German anthem *Deutschland, Deutschland über alles*, text by Fallersleben, 1841). — Hungary: *Rakoczy March* (J.

Bihari, 1809). — Argentine: *Oid, mortales* (V. Lopez – J. Blas Parera, 1813). — United States of America: *The *Star-spangled Banner* (1814). — Belgium: *La Brabançonne* (Jenneval – Campenhout, *c.* 1830). — Finland: *Maamme* (comp. by F. Pacius, 1848).

The political changes following after the first World War have found an expression in three new anthems: Italy: *La Giovinezza* (M. Manni – Giuseppe Blanc, 1909). — Germany: *Horst Wessel Lied* (text by H. Wessel, *c.* 1925). — Russia: *Hymn of the Soviet Union* (music by A. V. Alexandrov), adopted officially by March 15, 1944 instead of the *Internationale* (E. Pottier, 1871 – P. Degeyter, 1888).

Lit.: S. Rousseau and Montorgueil, *Les Chants nationaux de tous les pays* (1901); E. Bohn, *Die Nationalhymnen der europäischen Völker* (1908): E. Murillo, *National Anthems of the Countries of North, Central and South America* (1935); *id., Le Livre des chants nationaux* (1917); D. R. Wakeling and G. de Frame, "National Anthems" (*MR* iii; complete list); H. Abert, "Eine National-hymnen-sammlung" (*ZIM* ii).

Nationalism. A movement of the later part of the 19th century and still continuing today, which is characterized by a strong emphasis on the national elements and resources of music. It is based upon the idea that the composer must make his work the expression of national and racial traits, chiefly by drawing upon the folk melodies and dance rhythms of his country as an inspiring factor, and by choosing scenes from national history or life as subjects for operas and symphonic poems. Nationalism, therefore, represents an antagonism to what was theretofore considered one of the greatest prerogatives of music, namely the universal or international character of its language, which made the works of the great masters appeal equally to audiences everywhere in the world.

In order to defend their cause, champions of the national movement have taken the stand that music always has been, and will be, national. They have been pointing out that the music of Bach, Beethoven, Schumann, and Wagner is thoroughly German, and that that of Scarlatti, Rossini, and Verdi is just as unmistakably Italian as that of Byrd or Sullivan is English. There is, no doubt, a good deal of truth in such statements. Although it is not easy, and perhaps impossible, to point out in detail what is German, Italian, or French in musical style and expression, it would be admissible to make some broad characterizations, such as "idealistic" for German music, "corporeal" for Italian, "spirited" for French, the limitations of such tags being readily conceded. Such characterizations, however, whether summed up in words or merely felt, have nothing to do with nationalism in the proper sense of the word. Nationalism — in music and, perhaps, in general also — is not a matter of fact but a matter of intention. No composer can help belonging to some nation and inheriting from it, together with his language, certain general traits of feeling and of character. The question is whether he takes these matters for granted or whether he emphasizes them. Briefly, the difference between an "international" and a "national" composer of Italian extraction is the difference between one who cannot help speaking Italian and one who wants to speak Italian. It is only the latter that belongs to the Nationalistic movement in music. It is quite misleading to stamp Schumann as a Nationalistic composer simply because he "expressed the German spirit" (which, after all, Schütz, Bach, and Beethoven also did); or Chopin because he is "typically Polish" and composed mazurkas; or Wagner because he favored Teutonic subjects in his operas. In all these composers there is nothing to indicate that breaking away from the idea of music as a universal language and that emphasis on "my country's language" which characterizes the Nationalistic composer.

The National movement started, and must be understood, as a reaction against the supremacy of German music. With-

out being unfair, it is permissible to characterize it as a movement of despair, started by talented musicians who found themselves faced with the necessity of competing with men like Beethoven, Wagner, Brahms, and who, in their national treasure of melodies, dances, etc., found a weapon with which they could hope successfully to wage the combat. This consideration explains the fact that the Nationalistic movement is practically non-existent in Germany. Neither is there such a movement worth mentioning in France. Debussy, who comes immediately to mind, showed enough ingenuity to combat the Germans by purely musical means which, though very "French," are in no way nationally inspired. The absence of a definite Nationalistic movement in Italy has been explained as the result of the fact that Italy has no folk song tradition. Probably the reason is that Italy, like Germany and France, had an old musical tradition to draw upon and did not need to resort to the somewhat extraneous resources of the Nationalistic movement.

Nationalism, therefore, was actually an affair of the "peripheral" nations, for which it proved, in most cases, the first opportunity to advance into the center of the musical scene. After some preliminary attempts of a somewhat indecisive nature, it found its first realization in Glinka's opera A Life for the Czar (1836). Around 1860 the movement gained fresh impulse in Bohemia, Norway, and Russia, with Smetana's Bartered Bride (1866), Grieg's first book of Lyric Pieces (op. 12; e.g., Folk Song, Norwegian Melody), and Borodin's Prince Igor (1867). In Russia, the group known as *The Five formed a strong bulwark of Nationalism against the internationally inclined Tchaikovsky and Rubinstein. Particularly Moussorgsky's Boris Godunov (1872) is a landmark in the history of the Nationalistic movement. In Bohemia, Smetana's work was carried on to some extent by Dvořák (1841–1904), more whole-heartedly however by Leos Janáček (opera Jenufa, 1904). Toward the end of the 19th century the movement spread to Spain where it found ample nourishment in the immense wealth of Spanish dance rhythms and dance melodies. Albéniz (1860–1909), Granados (1867–1916), and Falla (b. 1876) are the most outstanding representatives. In Finland, Sibelius (b. 1865) must be mentioned as a composer who in his first period ardently supported Nationalism but later turned to "absolute" music which, nonetheless, remained largely Finnish in character. The main representative of the English national school was Edward Elgar (1857–1934). Outstanding Nationalistic composers of Latin America are Heitor Villa-Lobos (b. 1881, Brazil) and Carlos Chavez (1899, Mexico).

In the United States the Nationalistic movement started with H. F. Gilbert (1868–1928) whose compositions are marked by a racy flavor derived largely from Negro music (*Negro Rhapsody*, 1913). Frederick Converse (1871–1939) drew inspiration from the American landscape (*California*; *American Sketches*). Among the living composers Roy Harris (b. 1898) is the most prominent champion of Nationalism in America.

While in most of the European countries the Nationalistic movement has already lost most of its impetus, it still continues in the United States, not so much as an active force represented by a considerable number of prominent composers, but as a hotly debated issue. There are those who ardently maintain that the American composer must cease to imitate German, French, or other foreign models, must cease to write in the international vocabulary of "abstract" music, but must turn whole-heartedly to his own country, its landscape, its national traits, its folk tunes, its treasure of aboriginal (Indian) music, and its singular musical possession, jazz, as his main resource of inspiration. There are others who consider such demands as somewhat immature and as too easy a solution of the task of building up a great American school of composers (MacDowell, Roger Sessions, Walter Piston). They feel that Europe with its old musical tradition still has the

lead and that American composers, for the time being, can use their talents best if they follow the general trend of international music, contributing their share to make music continue what it has been for a thousand years: the universal language of mankind, understood by everybody, though sometimes spoken with a noticeable dialect.

Lit.: C. Forsyth, *Music and Nationalism* (1911); R. Vaughan Williams, *National Music* (1934); *LaMWC*, 938ff; D. Hussey, "Nationalism and Opera" (*ML* vii, no. 1); F. Toye, "A Case for Musical Nationalism" (*MQ* iv).

Natural. (1) A note that is neither sharped nor flatted, e.g., G-natural in contradistinction to G-sharp or G-flat. — (2) The sign ♮ which indicates the natural note in cases in which otherwise the note would be altered, either according to the signature or to a previous accidental. See *B; *Accidentals.

Natural horn, trumpet. Horns or trumpets consisting only of a pipe without side-holes operated by keys or extra tubing operated by valves. Such instruments can produce only the *natural tones, aside from certain artificial chromatic alterations produced by stopping (stopped notes). They were used until the end of the 18th century when the first keyed instruments were invented (key trumpets, key bugle). See *Horn II; *Trumpet II.

Natural tones. See *Wind instruments II.

Naturhorn, Naturtrompete [G.]. Natural horn, natural trumpet.

Neannoe. See *Noeane.

Neapolitan School. I. An operatic school of the late 17th and the 18th centuries which was domiciled in Naples. It included a great many composers of greater or lesser significance, e.g., Francesco Provenzale (d. 1704), Alessandro Scarlatti (1659–1725), Francesco Feo (1685–c. 1745), Niccolo Porpora (1686–1766), Leonardo Vinci (1690–1730),

Leonardo Leo (1694–1744), Nicola Logroscino (1698–1765), Giovanni Batista Pergolesi (1710–36), Gaetano Latilla (1711–91), Davide Perez (1711–after 1780), Domenico Terradellas (1711–51), Niccolo Jommelli (1714–74), Pasquale Anfossi (1727–97), Tommaso Traetta (1727–79), Pietro Guglielmi (1728–1804), Niccolo Piccinni (1728–1800), Giacomo Tritto (1733–1824), Antonio Sacchini (1730–86), Giovanni Paisiello (1740–1816), and Domenico Cimarosa (1749–1801). Scarlatti's German pupil Johann Adolf Hasse (1699–1783) also belongs to this group.

Most of these composers were born at or near Naples and had their musical education in one of the famous *conservatorii* of this city. Their activity, however, spread to many other places all over Europe, to Rome (Anfossi, Piccinni), Lisbon (Perez), Paris (Piccinni, Sacchini), St. Petersburg (Paisiello), Stuttgart (Jommelli), Vienna (Cimarosa), etc. They established a type of opera which was rather rigidly fixed in matters of the plot, the cast, of musical form and style, all these elements being classified under definite categories, such as: opera seria, opera buffa, opera serioridicola, comedia per musica, pastorale; *prima (seconda) donna, primo (secondo) uomo; aria cantabile, aria di mezzo charattere, aria di bravura, etc. As regards the formal structure, the opera consisted mainly of recitatives and arias, choruses being almost never used. The form of the aria is the da-capo aria. It was in the Neapolitan opera that the style known as *bel canto was developed and carried to an unparalleled degree of vocal virtuosity. The famous *castrati of the period played a leading part in this development. See *Opera VIII; also *Overture (Italian). For literature, cf. *RiML*, 1252 and *MoML*, 1001; also S. di Giacomo, in *RMI* xxii, xxiii.

II. Around 1600 there existed in Naples a school of harpsichord composers who were important links of transition from the keyboard style of the 16th century (A. Gabrieli, Cabezon) to that of the early Baroque (Frescobaldi). This school

seems to have been inaugurated by the Belgian Giovanni Macque (d. 1614) who came to Naples in 1586. Antonio Valente, Giovanni Trabaci, and Ascanio Mayone, his collaborators or successors, published collections of keyboard music between 1580 and 1615. See *Editions XVII (4); cf. W. Apel, in *MQ* xxiv.

Neapolitan sixth. See *Sixth; also *Harmonic analysis V.

Nebel, neble. See *Jewish music I (*nevel*).

Neben- [G., at the side of, auxiliary, accessory]. *Nebenthema, Nebensatz*, second theme (of a sonata). *Nebendreiklang*, any triad other than I, IV, and V. *Nebennote*, a note other than those conditioned by the harmony, i.e., auxiliary notes, passing notes, appoggiaturas, etc. *Nebentonart*, a key other than the main key of a composition, for instance, the dominant and subdominant, the relative keys, etc. *Nebenstimme*, subordinate or accompanying part.

Neck. The projecting portion of a violin, lute, guitar, etc., which carries the finger board.

Negligente [It.]. With insouciance, with indifference.

Negro music. I. The songs of the American Negro form one of the choicest bodies of folk music originating on the North American continent. The term "Negro Music" is generally applied to music composed by the Negro himself, either as a folk-group creation or by individual authors, and is not to be confused with the Negro-dialect songs which have been composed largely by white men: the "plantation songs" of Stephen Foster, the "coon songs" of the late 19th century, and the recent imitations of "blues" songs which are produced by a highly commercialized "Tin-Pan Alley." In the last-named field, however, there are so many Negro composers engaged in the "jazz" and "swing" industry that it is often impossible to distinguish between genuine Negro music and its imitation by white men.

References to Negro music date back to the 18th century. Thomas Jefferson wrote of the musical talents of the Negro in his *Notes on Virginia* (1784); Aird's *Selection of Scotch, Irish, and Foreign Airs* (Glasgow, 1782) contained a "Negro Jig," J. Carr of Baltimore published in 1801 a "Negro Song," composed or arranged by Benjamin Carr, an English musician who made his home in America from 1793; and Gottlieb Graupner provided one of the forerunners of the minstrel show by singing in costume "A Gay Negro Boy" between the acts of a play in Boston, 1799. Thus, white men's descriptions and imitations of the Negro's singing came into vogue long before his own music was collected and preserved. The minstrel shows received their impetus directly from the Negro, however. According to tradition, which is partially confirmed by known fact, this type of entertainment was popularized by Thomas Rice, who dressed in clothes borrowed from a Negro and imitated the Negro's manner of singing a song called "Jim Crow." This occurred somewhere around 1830, and from that time the movement was contagious and dozens of minstrel troupes came into prominence. Most of the songs written for the minstrels were composed by white composers, among them Stephen Foster, and for decades these Negro-dialect songs constituted the chief source of information that many Americans, particularly Northerners, possessed regarding the musical talents of the Negro.

It was not until after the Civil War that native Negro singing, and songs, became known to the country at large, and this knowledge came from the traveling groups of Negro singers from the industrial schools, Fisk University, Hampton, and Tuskegee Institutes, which were established after the War to educate emancipated slaves. Fisk University was established at Nashville, Tennessee, in 1866, and in its early years had difficulty in raising sufficient funds for maintenance. In 1871 George L. White, in charge of singing at the school, embarked on a concert tour with thirteen students, singing native Negro folk songs, and in three years succeeded in raising $150,000, largely from voluntary contributions by members of the audiences. As other Negro institutes were founded, notably Hampton and Tuskegee, singers from their student bodies toured the country, and were equally successful. Aside from financial results, these widespread tours acquainted the nation, particularly the North, with the Negro's own songs.

In the programs of these groups, the emphasis was principally upon the so-called "Spirituals," or religious songs, of the Negro. This was owing to the fact that the Institutes themselves derived their support largely from religious groups and home missionary movements. The religious fervor of the Negro awoke sympathy among wealthier church-going people, and the Negro's primitive interpretation of Bible stories and characters appealed to the imagination of members of the white denominations. Moreover, religion exerted a strong appeal to the Negro in bondage, for during the darker moments of his slavery he had learned to cling to the idea of an after life as his ultimate deliverance from human suffering. Thus the crossing of the river Jordan, Daniel's deliverance from the lions' den, Moses leading the children of Israel to the Promised Land, all had a personal promise for the enslaved Negro.

II. The origin of the Negro's melodies is a controversial subject, particularly as to whether any appreciable number of them have an African background. Comparison is made between the music of African primitives and that of the American Negro. The pentatonic scale is common to both, and each has a decided tendency toward syncopation. The Negro has also a love for complex and involved rhythmic combinations, which some students claim derives from a tribal background. Other authorities, notably George Pullen Jackson in his *White Spirituals from the Southern Uplands* (1933), claim a white origin for many of the Negro songs, and point to many convincing examples [see *Jig]. It is true,

also, that white evangelists and "revival-
ists" traveled among the southern Negroes, and sang to them many of the
gospel songs from their own hymnbooks.
The most tenable theory, perhaps, is that
the Negro brought with him from Africa
his own musical characteristics, and that
association with white men and exposure
to their customs and their music tempered
and molded his native idioms into
something that represented a combination of the two. In other words, he took
what he learned from his white masters,
repeated it in his own manner and style,
and, no doubt, often added something of
his own.

Many of the Negro songs are of group
origin; improvised first by leaders at religious gatherings, and answered and
added to by the congregations. Others
are probably the creation of individual,
unnamed singers. The choruses and
quartets from the Institutes sang in parts,
using harmonies largely improvised by
themselves. This has led to the supposi-
tion that part-singing is natural to the
Negro, and is part of his African heritage.
Such a theory, however, is not universally
accepted; documents exist which indicate
that originally the Negroes sang in unison, which may suggest that their part-
singing was developed by listening to
musically-tutored white men.

III. The emphasis on the religious
songs of the Negro delayed for many
years recognition and general knowledge
of his secular songs, which cover a wide
range, both in type and in mood. These
have been collected and distributed only
in recent years, when interest in folklore
and balladry has become something of a
science among American scholars and research workers. There are work songs
— for cotton picking, corn shucking,
stevedoring; railroad songs of the section
gang; steamboat songs; and prison songs
of the chain gang and the rock pile. The
Negro's love of balladry is responsible for
many songs of the narrative type —
"Frankie and Johnnie," Negro versions
of "Casey Jones," the story of "John
Henry," and many other legends. In addition there are bad men's songs; un-

printable "devil's" songs; as well as
numerous tunes for Negro dances.

A type of Negro sorrow-song known
as the "blues" has become extremely
popular and has been adopted and imitated widely in the current Broadway
song-literature. The typical "blues" is
often based on self-pity, yet it generally
embodies a carefree philosophy which
keeps it far from the depths of despair.
Melodically, the "blues" song is characterized by a flat seventh and sometimes a
flat third, which have become known as
"blue" notes. The "blues" were first
popularized by W. C. Handy, a Negro
musician who composed the "Memphis
Blues" in 1912, and later the "St. Louis
Blues." The authentic folk "blues" and
the modern, composed species are sometimes indistinguishable. So many mil-
lions of phonograph records of blues
songs have been distributed that Negroes
who hear these records accept them as
their own songs and add new stanzas, or
often change the words and alter the
tunes to transform them into many local
variants. As Odum and Johnson, in
Negro Workaday Songs (1926), have observed: "The folk creative process operates upon a song, the origin of which
may already be mixed, and produces in
turn variations that may later become
the bases of other formal blues" [see also
*Jazz II].

The effect of Negro folk music on the
art music of America, as well as the work
of serious Negro composers, is discussed
under *American Music II, IV. See also
*Jazz.

Lit.: R. N. Dett, *Religious Folk-Songs
of the Negro as Sung on the Plantations*
(1926); T. F. Seward, *Jubilee Songs, as
Sung by the Jubilee Singers of Fisk Uni-
versity* (1872); W. F. Allen, C. P. Ware,
L. M. Garrison, *Slave Songs of the United
States* (1867, reprinted 1927); N. C.
Burlin, *Hampton Series of Negro Folk-
Songs* (1918–19); R. E. Kennedy, *Mel-
lows: Negro Work Songs, Street Cries,
and Spirituals*; G. P. Jackson, *White and
Negro Spirituals* (1943); H. E. Krehbiel,
Afro-American Folk Songs (1914); J. B.
T. March. *The Story of the Jubilee Sing-*

ers (1880); H. W. Odum and G. B. Johnson, *The Negro and His Songs* (1925); id., *Negro Workaday Songs* (1926); J. Tiersot, *Chansons nègres* (1933); S. Grew, in *ML* xvi, no. 2; P. Laubenstein, in *MQ* xvi; J. Lomax, in *MQ* xx; E. Andrews, in *MQ* xxiii.   J. T. H.

Neighbor-tone. Same as appoggiatura; see *Nonharmonic tones II.

Neo-Bechstein. See *Electronic musical instruments I.

Neo-classicism. A movement of 20th-century music which is characterized by the inclusion into contemporary style of features derived from the music of the Bach era and of still earlier periods. It represents the latest and strongest expression of the general reaction against the unrestrained emotionalism of the late Romanticism [see *New Music]. Particularly distinct is the influence of Bach which makes itself felt in the emphasis on contrapuntal texture; in the revival of early forms such as the suite (not the ballet-suite of the late 19th century), toccata, passacaglia, ricercare, concerto grosso, ground; in the reduction of orchestral resources and colors; in the abandoning of program music; and in a general tendency towards an objective and detached style. The music of Scarlatti, Couperin, Lully has also left imprints on contemporary works, particularly of French and Italian composers who supplemented the "back-to-Bach" movement with the motto "Clarté latine."

The first neo-classicist was, no doubt, the German-Italian composer-pianist Ferruccio Busoni (1866–1924). His "German" enthusiasm for Bach and Mozart, together with his "Italian" penchant for the 18th-century *commedia* with its dry and unsentimental buffoonery, led him to an outspoken aversion against Romantic music. This attitude appears in a number of his compositions in which a neo-classical vocabulary is used to express a visionary mysticism [Comedy Overture (1897); First Sonatina (1910); Second Sonatina (1912); Fantasia Contrappuntistica (1912); Sonatina in Diem Nativi-

tatis Christi (1917); Toccata (1921)]. Perhaps it was the sublimity and incorporeality of these works which prevented them from serving as an inspiration for other, younger, musicians. At any rate, neo-classicism as a general movement did not start until 1923 when Igor Stravinsky, a much more dynamic personality than Busoni, startled the musical world with his Octet for Wind Instruments written in what was then interpreted as an "18th-century mannerism," but what proved to be the beginning of a new era in contemporary music. The same idiom prevails in his Sonata (1922), Piano Concerto (1924), and Serenade (1925) for piano [see Example under *Pandiatonicism]. With the opera-oratorio *Oedipus Rex* (1927) and the ballet *Apollo Musagetes* (1927) Stravinsky's style adopted a distinct tinge of archaic Grecianism.

Still closer in spirit to Bach than Stravinsky is Paul Hindemith who, from *c.* 1925 on (Four Concertos, op. 36; Piano Studies, op. 37), has systematically developed a new contrapuntal style, deliberately impersonal and sometimes mechanical, which may well be characterized as a 20th-century version of Bach. Certain features point to a still more distinct relationship, namely, to the dissonant linearity of 14th-century composers such as Machaut [see reference under *Ars nova]. Hindemith is only one of a number of composers who, around 1925, arrived at neo-classicism as their "third period," after previous periods of impressionism and of a rather anarchic mixture of primitivism and jazz. Among this group we find Alfredo Casella, Francesco Malipiero, Walter Piston, and others. See also *Pandiatonicism; *Gebrauchsmusik; *Opera XI.

The denomination neo-classicist is sometimes extended to late 19th-century composers such as Brahms, Bruckner, Franck, Reger. Although the works of these composers do show the result of their studies of the early masters they can in no way be considered forerunners of the 20th-century neo-classicism, particularly owing to their entirely different attitude towards Romanticism.

Lit.: K. R. Heyman, *The Relation of Ultramodern to Archaic Music* (1921); A. Lourié, "Neogothic and Neoclassic" (*MM* v); A. G. Browne, "Hindemith and the Neo-classic Music" (*ML* xiii, no. 1).

Neo-romanticism. See *Romanticism. Term sometimes applied to late-nineteenth-century *Romanticism. See also *Neuromantik.

Netherlands music. A description of the history of Netherlands music cannot be given without taking into account the political changes which have been taking place during the last five hundred years in the northwestern corner of Europe. This was successively a part of France, Burgundy, and Spain until it became an independent state in 1581 (William of Nassau) which, until 1830, also included the present-day Belgium. Nineteenth-century historiographers, such as Kiesewetter, Fétis, Ambros, v. d. Straeten, naturally included the latter country in their studies of Netherlands music, and even expanded their scope to some bordering provinces of northern France (Cambrai) which in the 15th and 16th centuries were politically or culturally related to the Netherlands. Modern scholars have adopted racial and religious demarcations as a more stable basis, drawing a line of distinction between the northern (now Protestant) part and the southern (Catholic) part of the Low Countries, the former being considered as Netherlands or Dutch countries, the latter as Belgium or, with reference to early history, Flemish countries. If this distinction is adopted, the early history of Netherlands music loses much of that glory with which it has been surrounded by the above-mentioned writers [see *Netherlands Schools], and the continuous history of Netherlands music begins around 1600 with the great organ master Jan Pieterszon Sweelinck (1562–1621) whose organ playing at Amsterdam was an attraction of European fame, and who numbered among his pupils nearly all the leading German organists and organ composers of the early Baroque (Samuel Scheidt,

Heinrich Scheidemann, Melchior Schildt, Paul Siefert, Jacob Praetorius), a fact which gave him the name "Der deutsche Organistenmacher" (the maker of German organists). A successor of Sweelinck was Anthony van Noordt who, in 1659, published a *Tabulatur-Boeck* which has been re-edited by the Vereeniging for Nederlandsche Muziekgeschiednis. The editions of this society [see *Editions XXIX] contain practically everything — little of real importance — the Netherlands has produced from the 16th through the 18th century.

As late as the 19th century, creative musical activity was slow in coming to the fore in the Netherlands. While Johannes Verhulst (1816–91) imitated Schumann and Mendelssohn, and opposed any progress beyond this level, Alphons Diepenbrock (1862–1921), the most important Netherlands composer, was able to absorb the influence of Wagner and Mahler as well as of Debussy without losing the personal stamp of a subjective mysticism. In striking contrast to the incorporeality of his music stands that of his contemporary Cornelis Dopper (1860–1939), the "National" composer of the Netherlands, whose program symphonies (Rembrandt, Zuyderzee) show a typically "Dutch" mixture of dispassionate sturdiness, robust humor, and broad colors. The younger composers show a greater inclination towards an internationalism of either German or, more frequently, French derivation, e.g., Alex Voormolen (b. 1895) and Daniel Ruyneman (b. 1886). Still more advanced in idiom are Willem Pijper (b. 1894) and Bernard van Dieren (1884–1936) who, living in London since 1909, identified himself with English music.

During the past fifty years the Netherlands has played a prominent role in the field of reproductive music. In addition to internationally known singers such as Joh. Meschaert (1857–1922) and Julia Culp (b. 1881), the world-famous orchestra of the *Concertgebouw* [see *Orchestras] under its conductor Willem Mengelberg (b. 1871) must be mentioned. Cf. *AdHM*, 1081–87 (bibl.).

Netherlands Schools. A designation introduced by R. G. Kiesewetter, in his *Die Verdienste der Niederländer um die Tonkunst* (1826), for the long series of 15th and 16th-century musicians in the Low Countries. He distinguished a first, a second, and a third Netherlands School, which were headed respectively by Dufay (1400–74), Ockeghem and Obrecht (b. 1430), and Josquin (b. 1450). Today, these terms are being discarded, chiefly on account of the fact that among the host of "Netherlands" masters only one, namely Obrecht, came from the Netherlands proper, while all the others came either from the southern Lowlands (Belgium), from northern France (Cambrai), or from Burgundy (Dijon). A more appropriate designation for the first Netherlands School is *Burgundian School, while the musicians from Ockeghem to Lasso can be grouped best in various generations of the *Flemish School. Cf. P. Láng, in *MQ* xxv.

Nettement [F.]. Clearly.

Neue Musik [G.]. See *New music.

Neuma. (1) [from Greek *neuein*, to nod]. See *Neumes. — (2) [from Greek *pneuma*, breath, spirit]. Medieval term for extended melismatic passages of plainsong, sung to one syllable or simply a vowel [see *Vocalization]. In the early Middle Ages, when the Christian service had the character of boundless exultation rather than of restrained devotion, the *neuma* (already through the name itself) had a symbolic significance as an expression of mystic feeling which could not be put into words. After the reform of St. Gregory (*c.* 600) it survived chiefly in connection with the *alleluia, under the name of *jubilus. — (3) In the later Middle Ages the name *neuma* was given to instructive melodies devised in order to indicate the special characteristics of each mode [cf. *GD* iii, 481]. By a misuse, these melodies were introduced into the office, and sung before or after the antiphons (in Paris as late as 1873). They also served, under the name *Neuma*, as tenors for 13th-century motets [cf. P.

Aubry, *Recherches sur les "ténors" latins* (1907), p. 13].

Neumatic style. See *Gregorian chant II.

Neumes [from Gr. *neuma*, nod, sign; see also *Neuma]. The notational signs of the Middle Ages (8th–14th centuries) which were used for the written fixation of plainsong. The term denotes chiefly the signs used for the music of the Western Church (Gregorian chant), but is also used for other systems of a similar character, such as the Byzantine neumes or the Armenian neumes. The following explanations refer only to the first type.

I. The neumatic notation consists of a great number of signs for single tones as well as for groups of two, three, or more tones. The accompanying table shows the most important neumes as they occur in the MSS of St. Gall (9th–10th centuries), together with their modern forms used in the present-day *liturgical books (Solesmes edition, Vatican edition), and with a rendition in ordinary notation.

From the systematic point of view the neumes may be divided into two main groups, the "normal" neumes (A) and the "special" neumes (B). The former indicate melodic motion only, while the latter indicate in addition special manners of performance. The category A.1 of our table includes the so-called "simple" neumes, i.e., those having up to three notes. For these, individual names are used, while the neumes with more than three notes (A.2, "compound" neumes) are designated by compound names which, however, differ in various sources. The first three signs under B.1 indicate single notes to be sung in a special manner. The *strophicus* occurs as a single sign (*apostropha*) or, more frequently, in a group of two (*distropha*) or three (*tristropha*), and is thought to have called for some sort of staccato or *tremolo. The *oriscus* is always joined to the end of a neume and is sung more lightly than the other notes. The *quilisma* usually occurs between two notes forming a minor third and probably called for a *vibrato performance. Still another special neume of the early MSS is the *trigon*, consisting of three dots forming a triangle, and indicating staccato performance for three tones such as c–b–c or e–f–e. The signs given here under B.2 are the "lique-

A. 1.	Punctum
	Virga
	Podatus or Pes
	Clivis
	Scandicus
	Climacus
	Torculus
	Porrectus
2.	Scandicus flexus
	Porrectus flexus
	Torculus resupinus
	Pes sub-punctis
B. 1.	Strophicus
	Oriscus
	Quilisma
	Salicus
	Pressus
2.	Epiphonus
	Cephalicus
	Ancus

scent" neumes (*semivocales*). They usually occur on a diphthong or where there are two consonants in succession, such as *ng* (*angelus*), *lm*, *rn*, etc. They are thought to have called for a particularly smooth transition by means of an interpolated *e*, as for instance, *in(e)fer(e)ni* instead of *inferni*. The *epiphonus* is the liquescent variety of the podatus, the *cephalicus* that of the clivis, the *ancus* that of the climacus. See the accompanying example, from the introit "Circum-

inferni　circum-

dederunt." Early writers mention numerous other "ornamenting" neumes under names such as *notae vinnulae* ("neighing" notes) or *tremulae* which, we are told, the Frankish were unable to sing [cf. C. Vivell, "Les Sons répercutés dans le chant grégorien," *TG* xviii; see *Ornamentation].

II. Various theories have been offered for the origin of the neumes. The one most generally accepted today considers the neumes as an outgrowth of grammatical accents of Greek and Latin literature, signs which indicated not so much accentuation in the modern sense of the word, but rather an inflection of the voice, the acutus (a), a raising, the gravis (b), a lowering of the pitch. The former became the virga (which, as a rule, is

a	b	c	d	e

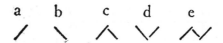

used for a higher note), the latter, the punctum (which usually indicates a lower tone). Combinations of these accents (c, d, e) lead to neumes of two or more notes, the podatus, clivis, porrectus, etc. Therefore, all these neumes (group A of the complete table) are called "accent neumes" [G. *Akzentneumen*]. Most of the neumes shown in group B belong to the category called "hook neumes" [G. *Hakenneumen*] because their graph includes a rounded hook which may have come from the Greek apostrophe: '.

In the earliest sources and in many later MSS (9th–11th centuries) the neumes are written in such a manner as to give only the general outline of the melodic motion, but no evidence of the actual intervals. Thus, the podatus may mean an ascending second, third, fifth, etc. Evidently these signs served only as a mnemonic aid for the singer who knew the melodies by heart, or for the choir leader who may have interpreted them to his choir by appropriate movements of the hand. These neumes are called *cheironomic, staffless, oratorical, or *in campo aperto* ("in the open field," that is, without clear orientation). Around 1000 we find the earliest traces of a more careful arrangement of the neumatic signs so as to give at least some indication of pitch. Particularly the 11th-century MSS of Italy, written in the so-called Longobardian or Beneventan character, are remarkable for their early use of "heighted" (intervallic, diastematic) neumes, i.e., neumes which are written on a staff, either imagined or really indicated by one, two, or finally four lines. Slightly later than the Beneventan neumes are the Aquitanian (or Proven-

I	II	III	IV	V
.	. ~	.	♦ .	♦
ſ	𝟷 𝟺	⌐	⌐	∫
ſ	♪	✓	⊐	⌐
⌐	♫	⌐:	⌐	⌐
ſ	♩	./	≡	••∫
::	⌐	: ⅃	⌐••	∫••
⌐	⌐	⌐ ⌐	⌐	⌐
⌐	♪	✓:✓	⌐	⌐

çal) neumes which are important because their shapes approximated, and finally led to, the square-shaped characters of the 13th century. These were quickly adopted everywhere, except in Germany where a peculiar variety, the Gothic neumes, remained in use as late as the 16th century. The square-shaped neumes are still used today in the liturgical books of the Roman Catholic Church [see *Plainsong notation]. The accompanying illustration shows the eight "simple" neumes in five different styles: I. Messine neumes (Monastery of Metz, 9th–10th centuries; G. *Metzer Neumen*); II. Beneventan neumes (Monastery of Benevent in Southern Italy, 11th–12th cent.); III. Aquitanian neumes (southern France, 12th–13th cent.); IV. Square neumes from Sarum, England (13th cent.); V. Gothic neumes, also called *Nagelschrift (German MSS of the 14th–15th cent.). These may be compared with the St. Gall neumes shown in the table on p. 487.

The cheironomic neumes as such cannot be deciphered [for a futile attempt in this direction, cf. O. Fleischer, *Die germanischen Neumen* (1923)]; they can only be compared with those of the later sources which, owing to the conservatism of Gregorian chant, have preserved the old melodies in a clearer system of notation, with the neumes written on an imaginary or real staff of one to four lines. For material showing the development of the neumes see *Editions XXIII, A, 2/3.

III. The question as to the rhythmic meaning of neumatic notation is infinitely more difficult. It has been the subject of the most painstaking research and of sharp controversies which still continue today. See *Gregorian chant V.

The neumatic signs in their final shape (square shapes of the 13th century) were also adopted for the notation of two other bodies of early music, namely, for secular monophonic melodies (troubadours, trouvères) and for polyphonic music (organa, clausulae of the School of Notre Dame). In both cases they present problems of rhythmic interpretation which are entirely different from those of the neumes in Gregorian chant. See *Plainsong notation and *Square notation; also *Notation.

Lit.: G. Suñol, *Introduction à la paléo-*

graphie musicale grégorienne (1935); P. Wagner, *Neumenkunde* (1905, 2d ed., 1912); H. M. Bannister, *Monumenti Vaticani* (1918; extensive tables of neumes); see also the lit. under *Gregorian chant and in *ReMMA*, 440–442.

Neuromantik [G.]. Neo-Romanticism. However, the German term is usually applied to the group Wagner, Brahms, Wolf, Bruckner, rather than to the neo-Romanticists of the 20th century.

Neutöner [G., inventors of new sounds]. A derogatory term which has been applied around 1890 to Wagner, Richard Strauss, and other "radicals" of bygone days.

New Music. A term which in the last few years has been gradually adopted as a general designation for the various radical or progressive trends in 20th-century music (the corresponding German term *Neue Musik* has been in use since about 1925). In distinction from designations such as "Modern Music" [see this] or "Contemporary Music," this term excludes composers who continue more or less along the traditional lines of the late 19th century, expounding the ideas and technical resources of *Romanticism, *Impressionism, *Nationalism, etc. (e.g., Sibelius, Strauss, Debussy). The term New Music has also an interesting historical significance, as similar names were used for somewhat similar movements 300 and 600 years ago, namely, *Nuove musiche and *Ars nova [see also *History of music].

New Music is, briefly stated, anti-Romanticism. The reaction against the Romanticism of the 19th century is usually understood as a pull-away from the Germanic tradition which held an almost unlimited supremacy during the 19th century. Thus, National composers such as Moussorgsky are credited with the initiative which finally led to the radical break of the early 20th century. Neither Moussorgsky, however, nor any other National composer succeeded in freeing himself from the fundamental conceptions or from the technical vocabu-

lary of the Romanticism. Even Debussy's impressionism, though much more definitely anti-German in spirit and style, stands before us as the final embodiment rather than the negation of the tradition of the 19th century. If it is understood that Romanticism is, ideally, subjectivism and, technically, 19th-century harmony, then the credit for the initiative belongs, in the former respect, to Erik Satie (1866–1925) and Ferruccio Busoni (1866–1924), in the latter, to Arnold Schönberg (b. 1874). As early as 1900 Satie wrote pieces which, though artistically insignificant and trifling, clearly show the tendency of distancing himself, by irony and whimsicality, from the exhibitionism and the ostentatiousness of the late Romanticism. Details such as the use of fourth-chords, the omission of bar-lines, the replacement of the traditional expression marks by plainly satirizing directions ("Comme un rossignol qui a mal de dent"), or the use of idiotic titles such as "Pièces froides" (1897), "Pièces en forme de poire" (1903), "Embryons desséchés" (1910), are significant, not as such, but as indications of a mentality which was bent on "shocking the bourgeois," including the bourgeois-musician. Busoni's opposition against the Romantic style was of a quite different nature and background. It was determined by his congeniality to Bach, Mozart, and by a general penchant towards detachment and distance — qualities which made him the father of one of the most important currents of New Music, i.e., *neo-classicism. Of still greater consequence was the activity of Schönberg. Ideally, i.e., from the point of view of feeling and expression, Schönberg was — at least up to 1920 — much less anti-Romantic than the other two, a fact which has caused many writers to deny him the role as a leader in the new movement and even to consider him a Romanticist. Such a view overlooks the fact that the break with a tradition involves not only a spiritual, but also a technical aspect. It was in the latter field that Schönberg's radicalism fully achieved what so many composers before him had only approximated: the complete break with the harmonic system, with the stylistic and formal principles of the 19th century. Completely casting away the harmonic and formal considerations of the tradition, he arrived at a novel style which has become known as *atonality (Drei Klavierstücke, op. 11, 1909). See also *Expressionism. Until after World War I, Schönberg's influence remained restricted to a few friends and pupils, notably Alban Berg (1885–1935) and Anton von Webern (b. 1883). In the meantime, another potent factor had appeared on the scene of European music, namely, rhythm. As early as 1910 the Hungarian Béla Bartók (b. 1881) had, in his piano piece Allegro Barbaro, arrived at a type of "barbaric" rhythm compared to which the percussive qualities of Igor Stravinsky's (b. 1882) much more famous Petrouchka (1911) sound almost conventional and suave [see also *Futurism]. Nonetheless, Stravinsky, perhaps owing to his more versatile personality, was destined to play a considerably greater role in the subsequent development than the Hungarian composer. Shortly after the war, jazz reached the Continent and created a sensation, not only among the dancing fans, but also among the composers. One of the first to use it was Stravinsky, in his Ragtime (1918) [see the list at the end of the article *Jazz].

The post-war period proved a most fertile soil for all these innovations, not only because it opened the communications between the various countries, but also because it left the whole of Europe, whether victorious or defeated, in a state of inner destruction and despair which threw the doors open to radicalism and anarchy. As a matter of fact, the period from 1918 to 1925 can hardly be termed other than anarchic. Scores of young composers appeared, particularly in Germany and France, who offered a confusing variety of solutions, of new ways out of the vacuum which the general negation of the tradition had created. *Atonality, *Twelve-tone technique, barbarism, *Bruitism, *Futurism, Gregorianism (Malipiero), *jazz, machine-music,

*satire, *Gebrauchsmusik, *quarter-tone music, are some of the most prominent traits of this period. Zóltan Kodaly (b. 1882), Francesco Malipiero (b. 1882), Alfredo Casella (b. 1883), Arthur Honegger (b. 1892), Darius Milhaud (b. 1892), Paul Hindemith (b. 1895), Ernst Krenek (b. 1900), may be mentioned here among the many who made contributions to the spotted picture of this period.

A third period of New Music began around 1925, when, after so many interesting experiments, so many futile efforts, a new name appeared on the scene: Bach. This great name was the magic word which was strong enough to dispel the destructive instincts, to make an end to so many sensational efforts, and to unite practically all the prominent composers in a new spirit of seriousness and constructive coöperation. Much as it might seem regrettable that, after all the radicalism of the previous years, music had to turn back to "history" in order to proceed to a new future, yet there was apparently no other solution. Around 1925, almost all the composers mentioned above entered what is usually termed their "third period," i.e., the neo-classic period after the "impressionistic" and the "anarchic." Up to the present day the movement known as *Neo-classicism has gradually gained impact and a foothold in practically every country. Only the immediate followers of Schönberg have remained aloof from what they believe to be a sterile historicism and have tried to remain true to the ideals of a radically new music (e.g., Krenek). In twenty years we shall know who pursued the right path.

A quarterly magazine dedicated to ultramodern music is published under the name New Music (founded in 1927 by H. Cowell).

Lit.: G. Dyson, The New Music (1924); H. Cowell, New Musical Resources (1930); E. Krenek, Über Neue Musik (1937); id., Music Here and Now (1939); A. Copland, Our New Music (1941); N. Slonimsky, "Modern Music . . ." (Introduction to D. Ewen, Book of Modern Composers, 1942); E. Blom,

"The Truly Modern in Music" (*ML*, iv, no. 3); R. W. Wood, "Modern Counterpoint" (*ML* xiii, no. 3); G. Dyson, "The Texture of Modern Music" (*ML* iv, no. 3); E. Wellesz, "Problems of Modern Music" (*MQ* x); H. Cowell, "New Terms for New Music" (*MM* v); W. Apel, "Die Neue Klaviermusik" (*DM* 1931/32, i, ii). See also under *Modern music, *Neoclassicism, *Atonality, *Twelve-tone technique, etc.

Nibelungenring. See *Ring des Nibelungs, Der.

Nicht schleppen [G.]. Do not drag.

Niederstrich [G.]. Down-bow; see *Bowing.

Ninth-chord. A chord which consists of the third, fifth, seventh, and ninth above the root. It occurs usually as the dominant of the key (dominant ninth-chord), e.g., in C major: g–b–d'–f'–a'. Frequently the root (g) is omitted in which case the chord can also be interpreted as the seventh-chord of the seventh degree (b). The principle of superposed thirds which leads from the triad to the seventh chord and to the ninth chord can be carried on still farther, resulting in the eleventh chord (g–b–d'–f'–a'–c'') and the thirteenth (g–b–d'–f'–a'–c''–e''). This build-

ing-up principle is used as a climactic means of great impressiveness in the first movement of Bruckner's Symphony no. 7 [see illustration]. Usually, the chords mentioned above occur in a reduced form and in exchanged position of the higher notes. In such case they can usually be interpreted as appoggiaturas of simpler chords (e.g., g–f'–b'–e'' as an appoggiatura of g–f'–b'–d'').

Nocturne [F., night piece]. The name is usually employed for Romantic *char-

acter pieces for the pianoforte, written in a somewhat melancholy or languid style, with an expressive melody over a broken-chord accompaniment. The first nocturnes were written by the Irishman John Field (1782–1837) from whom Chopin adopted the idea and the name. See *Notturno; *Nachtstück.

Nocturnes. Three *Symphonic poems by Debussy.

Nocturns [L. *nocturnum, horae nocturnae*]. See *Office hours.

Node. In a vibrating string the points of rest or of minimum amplitude. Such points occur not only at the two fixed ends of the string but also in regular distances in between, owing to the fact that the string vibrates not only as a whole, but also in segments of ½, ⅓, ¼, ⅕, etc., which are the physical cause of the harmonics. Similarly, in a vibrating air column (pipe), nodes are the points of highest density, where the air particles do not move. The intermediate points of maximum amplitude (string) or movement (pipe) are called loops or antinodes. See *Acoustics V.

No-drama. See *Japanese music I.

Noeane. Syllables of unknown meaning which appear in various treatises of the 10th century in connection with short melodies designed to give the characteristics of the various modes. They are probably derived from the Byzantine enechemata [see *Echos]. See also *Anenaiki; *Solmization. Cf. *ReMMA*, 173; *RiHM* i.2, 57; H. Riemann, in *ZIM* xiv; E. Werner, in *MQ* xxviii.

Noël [F., Christmas]. Popular Christmas songs, particularly those of French origin [see *Carols]. In 1553 Nicolas Denisot published two books *Cantiques et Noëls*, the second of which includes 13 melodies. Another important early publication is F. Colletet, *Noëls nouveaux et cantiques spirituels* (1660). Courvoy's *Meslanges* (1610) contain polyphonic settings of noëls. During the 17th to the 19th centuries innumerable noëls were published (frequently as sheet-music) in which a semi-religious text was set to profane melodies, dancing songs, drinking songs, vaudevilles, etc. In the 17th century the name was applied to organ pieces designed to be played during the Christmas service. Most of these are simple variations on popular Christmas melodies. Collections of such noëls were published by Le Begue [cf. *HAM*, no. 231], Nicolas Gigault, Jean Fr. Dandrieu, Claude Daquin, Boely, Balbastre, etc. See *Editions I; H. Expert, †*Maîtres français du clavecin*; F. Raugel, †*Les Maîtres français de l'orgue*.

Noire [F.]. See *Notes.

Nomos [Gr., law, rule]. In early Greek culture, particularly in the Homeric epoch, the traditional melodies which the singer (*aoidos*) used for the recitation of the epics, to the accompaniment of the phorminx. See *Greek music I; *Melody types.

None. (1) German term for the interval of the ninth; *Nonenakkord*, i.e., ninth-chord. — (2) See *Office hours.

Nonet [G. *Nonett*; It. *nonetto*]. Chamber music for nine instruments, e.g., string quartet and five winds. There exist a few examples, by Rheinberger, Stanford, and Ravel (*Poèmes*).

Nonharmonic tones. In *harmonic analysis, generic designation for tones which are foreign to the momentary harmony and which occur as melodic "ornamentations" in one of the voice parts. They may be classified into two main categories:

I. Rhythmically weak notes occurring between two "harmonic" notes (i.e., notes which are part of the harmony). There are five types, four of which are found between harmonic notes of different pitch [in our illustration, Examples 1–4, at the interval of a second], and one between harmonic notes of the same pitch [Ex. 5]. These are called: (1) *passing tone*; (2) *anticipation*; (3) *échappée*; (4) *cambiata*; (5) *auxiliary tone* (upper or

lower auxiliary; also called embellishment, returning note, alternating note).

The first four of these may, of course, occur between harmonic notes forming any larger interval, in descending as well as ascending motion. The difference between échappée and cambiata is that in

the former the motion to the ornamenting tone is contrary to the motion to the harmonic tone, while in the latter these two motions are similar. Thus, with an ascending progression of harmony notes, e.g., E–G, the nonharmonic note D would be an échappée (E–D–G), the nonharmonic note A a cambiata (E–A–G).

II. Rhythmically strong notes occurring in the place of a harmonic note. These are called *appoggiatura* [from It. *appoggiare*, to lean; also neighbor-tone]. An appoggiatura is usually the upper or lower second of a harmonic tone, played instead of this tone on the beat and resolved afterwards into the proper tone. The plain triad already offers many possibilities for appoggiatura formations [Ex. 6] which are interesting and important as sources for dissonant chordal combinations. If the "wrong" note appears in the preceding chord, one speaks of a *prepared appoggiatura* [Ex. 7], otherwise, the appoggiatura is unprepared. The former type is the more orthodox, because the previous appearance of the "wrong" note somewhat weakens its dissonant character. This character is still more weakened, in fact almost eliminated, if the preparing tone is tied to the appoggiatura. This formation is called *suspension* (sometimes retardation) [Ex. 8]. The derivation of the suspension from the appoggiatura does not imply a statement regarding the origin and the proper nature of the former which actually results from "suspending" the progression of the tone beyond the moment of change of the harmony. If two or more appoggiaturas occur simultaneously one speaks of an appoggiatura chord [Ex. 9, Tchaikovsky, Symphony no. 4, last movement]. A characteristic idiom of modern music is the extended use of "unresolved appoggiaturas" [Ex. 10, Debussy, Pelléas et Mélisande, end of Act I].

III. It should be noted that the above classification and terminology (based on W. Piston's *Harmony*, 1941) differs in particulars from that used by other authors. This is especially true in respect to the term appoggiatura which is frequently restricted to those cases in which the "wrong" note is approached by leap, as in Ex. 11, the cases of stepwise approach being called *accented passing tone* [Ex. 12]. The advantage of this terminology would seem to lie chiefly in its application to historical studies, since accented passing tones occur in practically all periods of music history, while the "free" appoggiatura was not much used before *c.* 1750 [it forms a characteristic feature of the *Empfindsamer Stil* of Ph. Em. Bach; cf. *SchGMB*, p. 458]. Other terms frequently used are: *free passing tone* for a passing tone approached by leap [Ex. 13]; *changing notes* for the upper and lower auxiliary in succession [Ex. 14]. Cf. E. Walker, "The Appoggiatura" (*ML* v, no. 2).

Nonnengeige [G., nun's fiddle]. German name for the *tromba marina.

Non Nobis Domine. A celebrated canon which is usually, but without demonstrable evidence, attributed to William Byrd. It is frequently sung at English banquets as a grace. It is remarkable for the great number of solutions it admits, solutions which differ according to the number of parts, and to the intervals and distance of the imitating voices. Cf. *GD* iii, 642.

Non tanto, non troppo [It.]. Not too much. *Non troppo allegro*, not too fast.

Norddeutsche Schule. See *Berlin School.

Norwegian music. The rise of art music in Norway went hand in hand with that of an independent political life which began in 1814, with the separation from Denmark. Waldemar Thrane's Singspiel *Fjeld-eventyret* (1824) may be said to mark the beginning of Norwegian music. Hafdan Kjerulf (1815–68) wrote numerous small piano pieces and songs in the style of Schumann, though not without that special touch of Norwegian lyricism which became known all over the world in the "Lyrical Pieces" of Norway's greatest composer, Edvard Grieg (1843–1907). Grieg replaced the somewhat "effeminate Scandinavianism" of the Danish composer Gade and others by a more vigorous style, reminiscent of the ruggedness of his country and the strong individualism of its inhabitants. Grieg's contemporaries Johan Svendsen (1840–1911) and Christian Sinding (1856–1941) are both exponents of the international Romanticism rather than of national Norwegian music, although traits of the latter are by no means missing. Both cultivated mainly the larger forms of symphonic and chamber music. Among the younger Norwegian composers no remarkable talent has as yet appeared. Cf. the article in *AdHM*, 1113ff.

Notation. I. The art of expressing music in writing. A fully developed system of notation must be so designed as to clearly indicate the two main properties of a musical sound: its pitch and its duration. The most satisfactory of the numerous symbols which have been devised for this purpose is the note, i.e., a point-like sign which indicates pitch by its position on a *staff provided with a *clef, and duration by a variety of shapes, such as hollow or black heads with or without stems, flags, etc. [see *Notes]. Additional symbols of modern notation are the *accidentals, the *key-signature, the *time signature, *dynamic marks, *tempo marks, *expression marks, the *tie, the *slur, etc. The modern system of notation dates back to the early 17th century. Previously, systems of notation had been used which differ more or less radically from the present one regarding either the fixation or rhythm (as in mensural notation) or that of pitch (as in the tablatures). Here follows a brief conspectus of the evolution of notation (in Europe), with reference to special articles.

II. Greek music was notated by means of *letters*. Two such systems were in use: an older one (used chiefly for instrumental music and evidently devised for the kithara) which included certain ancient symbols (Phoenician letters?) and which used these symbols in different positions, upright, reversed, etc. [see under *Pyknon]; and a more recent one (used chiefly for vocal music) which employed the Ionic alphabet together with a few additional signs [cf. *ReMMA* 26, 27; O. Sachs, in *ZMW* vi, vii]. This method left no immediate traces in the musical notation of the Christian era, probably because its "Hellenistic" clarity and preciseness did not lend itself to the "Oriental" exuberance of early Christian recitation and psalm-singing [for an 8th-century revival, see *Daseian notation]. The ensuing development and, for that matter, our modern system of notation, is rooted, not in the notational signs of Greek music, but in the much vaguer symbols of Greek and Oriental (Jewish) speech recitation, the grammatical *accents* of the second century B.C. and similar signs known generically as *ekphonetic notation*. These developed (around 500?) into a more elaborate system of stenographic symbols vaguely indicating the outlines of the melodic movement, the *neumes*. The neumes, far from being "primitive" (as they are frequently designated) represent a very sensitive and sup-

ple means of recording the innumerable finesses of ancient singing, involving special techniques which today survive only in Oriental tradition. On the other hand, owing to their failure to clearly indicate pitch as well as rhythm, they are not a fully-developed notation, but only a mnemonic aid for the oral handing-down of the chant. As early as the 8th century various methods were designed to remedy the indefiniteness of the neumes, chiefly by the addition of letters [see *Letter notation; *Romanian letters]. More important were the modifications of the graph of the neumes which took place during the 11th century, leading from the vague cheironomic symbols to shapes which corresponded more accurately to the rise and fall of the melody, the *diastematic* neumes. This evolution was stabilized by the adoption of *staff lines in increasing numbers, first one, then two, and finally four. Around 1200, the neumes acquired those square-shaped forms which are still used in the liturgical books of the Roman Catholic Church. See *Neumes.

III. These shapes [see Ex. 1] were soon adopted for the notation of monophonic secular melodies [see *Plainsong notation] as well as of polyphonic music, where they are known as *ligatures*. In

the latter field their introduction was accompanied, shortly before 1200, by the establishment of definite rhythmic values, on the basis of the rhythmic *modes. The resulting system is known as *square notation* [Ex. 2]. There followed, during the 13th and 14th centuries, an extremely rapid development, involving frequent changes and innovations: the introduction of two different note values, called *longa* and *brevis* (*c.* 1225), which became necessary for the notation of the texted parts of the motet [Ex. 3]; around 1250, the introduction of a smaller note-value, called *semibrevis*, two or three of which could be used in the place of a brevis; around 1260, the unequivocal rhythmic interpretation of the ligatures, independent of the modes (Franco of Cologne;

usually considered as the beginning of *mensural notation*); around 1280, the introduction of more than three semi-

Organum triplum *Descendit*
Wolfenbüttel *Helmst. 1099*

breves (up to seven) in the place of a brevis (Petrus de Cruce). Shortly after 1300, the restriction to modal meter, i.e., to ternary rhythm, which prevailed throughout the 13th century [*Ars antiqua] was abandoned and the basic principles of rhythm and of notation were

Motet *Ave beatissima*
Montpellier, Fac. des Méd. *H 196*

radically revised by Philippe de Vitry who must be considered the "father of modern notation," much more so than Franco of Cologne. The new system, expounded

in his treatise *Ars nova* (*c.* 1320), recognized duple and triple rhythm as equally important and applied this dichotomy to all the note-values in the different mensurations: *modus* (longa-brevis), *tempus* (brevis-semibrevis), and *prolatio* (semibrevis-minima). The notational principles of this period remained virtually unchanged until the end of the 16th century, the only modification being the transition, around 1450, from black notes (black mensural notation) to white notes (white mensural notation). The explanations of the latter system, to be found in the article *mensural notation, therefore cover also the principles (though not the details) of black mensural notation. Simultaneously with Vitry's system, however, there developed a different notational system in Italy (*Italian notation*) which retained to a greater extent the principles of the late 13th century (particularly, the Petronian groups of semibreves). After 1350 this system adopted features from the contemporary and more progressive French system, thus leading to a system (*Mixed notation*) which was used by Landini and other composers of

Francesco Landini, *Nessun ponga speranca*
Paris, Bibl. Nat. *ital. 568*

the second half of the 14th century [Ex. 4]. Toward the end of this century, notation took on features of spectacular difficulty and mannerism which make the pieces of this period the most interesting problems, the "études transcendentales" of the study of notation (*Mannered notation*).

IV. In the first half of the 15th century (Dufay) these complications were largely abandoned. There resulted what might be called the "classical" system of mensural notation (*c.* 1450–1600), character-

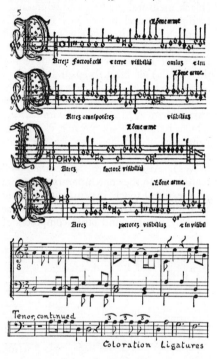

Pierre de la Rue, *Missa L'homme armé*, "Patrem"
Misse Petri de la Rue (Petrucci, 1503)

ized by the use of white instead of black notes (*White mensural notation*; Ex. 5). Its principles are the same as those of the French notation of the Machaut period, except for the addition of the *proportions as a notational device (hence the rather misleading term "proportional notation") and for the occasional use of riddle canons [see *Canon II]. This is the notation of the *Flemish masters, Ockeghem, Obrecht, and their numerous successors. In the later part of the 16th century the use of triple mensura-

tion (*tempus perfectum, prolatio perfecta*) as well as that of the ligatures was largely discarded, together with other special methods of mensural notation (proportions). Thus, the system of notation became virtually that of the present day, particularly after the general acceptance of *bar-lines and of score arrangement [see *Score; *Choir book; *Part books]. Throughout the 17th century, however, remnants of the older system still lingered on, particularly the use of blackened notes (coloration) and of proportional signs [see *Time-signatures]. Of all these the *alla-breve sign is the only one to survive to the present day. The accompanying example illustrates the development of the main notational signs in six periods.

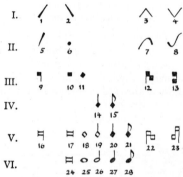

I. *Greek accents:* 1. Accentus acutus; 2. Acc. gravis; 3. Acc. circumflexis; 4. Hypothetical. II. *Neumes:* 5. Virga; 6. Punctum; 7. Podatus; 8. Clivis. III. *Black mensural notation (1250):* 9. Longa; 10. Brevis; 11. Semibrevis; 12. Descending ligature; 13. Ascending ligature. IV. *Additional signs of the 14th century:* 14. Minima; 15. Semiminima. V. *White mensural notation (1450):* 16.=9; 17.=10; 18.=11; 19.=14; 20.=15; 21. Fusa; 22.=12; 23.=13. VI. *Modern notation (after 1600):* 24. Breve or double-whole note; 25. Whole-note; 26. Half-note; 27. Quarter-note; 28. Eighth-note.

V. Side by side with the system of mensural notation there existed, particularly in the period 1450–1600, special notational methods known as *tablatures. These were used for the writing down of keyboard and lute music (generally of soloist music, i.e., for a single performer, while mensural notation was used for ensemble music; see *Ensemble). Some of these systems employ the ordinary mensural notes, differing from mensural notation only in that the parts are written in score, as in the modern piano score or the modern partitura. These may be designated as *keyboard scores* or *keyboard partituras*, in contradistinction to the tablatures proper, which use letters, figures, or other symbols instead of notes.

A survey of modern attempts at reform is given in A. Eaglefield-Hull, *A Dictionary of Modern Music* (1924). See also: Accidentals; Braille; Chevé; Chiavette; Clef; Daseian notation; Ekphonetic notation; Griffschrift; Letter notation; Ligatures; Mensural notation; Musica ficta; Nagelschrift; Neumes; Notes; Part books; Partial signature; Plainsong notation; Plica; Proportions; Punctus; Romanian letters; Score; Square notation; Staff; Staffless notation; Tablature; Tie; Time signatures; Tonic-Sol-fa.

Lit.: J. Wolf, *Handbuch der Notationskunde* (2 vols., 1913–19); *id.*, †*Musikalische Schrifttafeln* (facsimiles; 1922); *id.*, *Die Tonschriften* (1924); W. Apel, *Notation of Polyphonic Music* (1942; 2d edition 1944); H. Riemann, *Studien zur Geschichte der Notenschrift* (1878); *id.*, *Notenschrift und Notendruck* (1896); W. Apel, "The Importance of Notation . . ." (*PAMS*, 1938). See also under *Mensural notation; *Tablature; *Square notation; *Plainsong notation.

Notes. The signs by means of which music is fixed in writing [see *Notation]. The term is also used for the sound indicated by a note, and even for the key of

o [≡] whole-note
♩ [≡] half-note
♩ [𝄼] quarter-note
♪ [𝄽] eighth-note
♪ [𝄾] sixteenth-note
♪ [𝄿] thirty-second-note
♪ [𝅀] sixty-fourth-note

Whole-note: E., semibreve; G., Ganze (Note); F., ronde [pause]; I., semibreve. *Half-note:* E., minim; G., Halbe (Note); F., blanche [demi-pause]; I., minima or bianca. *Quarter-note:* E., crotchet; G., Viertel (Note); F., noire [soupir]; I., semiminima or nera [sospiro]. *Eighth-note:* E., quaver; G., Achtel (Note); F., croche [demi-soupir]; I., croma. *Sixteenth-note:* E., semiquaver; G., Sechzehntel; F., double-croche [quart de soupir]; I., semicroma. *Thirty-second-note:* E., demisemiquaver; G., Zweiunddreissigstel; F., triple-croche [huitième de soupir]; I., biscroma. *Sixty-fourth-note:* E., hemidemisemiquaver; G., Vierundsechzigstel; F., quadruple-croche [seizième de soupir]; I., semibiscroma.

the pianoforte which produces this sound. However, a clear distinction between the terms tone and note is strongly recommended. Briefly, one sees a note, and hears a tone.

The illustration shows the note values with their American terminology. English, German, French, and Italian terminology are given below. The signs and names in brackets are those of the corresponding rests. The German names for the rests are: *Ganze* (*halbe, viertel,* etc.), *Pause;* the Italian: *pausa di semibreve* (*minima,* etc.).

Note sensible [F.]. *Leading tone.

Notre Dame, School of. See *Ars antiqua; *French music II. Cf. J. Handschin, in *ZMW* vi, vii, and in *AM* iv, nos. 1–3; M. Schneider, in *ZMW* xiv.

Notturno [It., night piece]. (1) Italian designation for *nocturne. — (2) Eighteenth-century name for compositions similar to the *serenade, designed to be played as an evening entertainment. Haydn's Notturnos of 1790, for 2 lire (*hurdy-gurdies), 2 clarinetti, 2 viole, 2 corni, e violoncello, consist of three movements (new ed. by E. F. Schmidt, 1935ff). Similar pieces were written by Mozart (K.V. 286) and Gyrowetz.

Novachord. See *Electronic musical instruments I.

Novellette. A designation introduced by R. Schumann (op. 21) for a certain type of romantic piano piece [*Character piece] which is meant "to tell a story." It contains a number of contrasting sections, suggestive in a way of the various chapters of a narrative.

Nozze di Figaro, Le ("The Marriage of Figaro"). Opera buffa in four acts by

W. A. Mozart, libretto by Da Ponte (after Beaumarchais's play *Le Mariage de Figaro*, succeeding his *Le Barbier de Seville*, the source of Rossini's *Barbiere di Siviglia), composed 1786. *Count Almaviva* (Baritone), tired of his wife, the *Countess* (soprano; the Rosina of Rossini's opera), tries to console himself with other women, but *Figaro* (Bass), now his valet, no longer assists him (as in the *Barbiere*), but plots against him in order to punish him for his infidelity. Around this basic idea is woven a complicated plot of love affairs the details of which are not always clear. The Count flirts with the gardener's daughter *Barbarina* (Soprano) and with the Countess' maid *Susanna* (Soprano). The page *Cherubino* (Soprano) is attached to Barbarina as well as to the aging Countess, and Figaro has promised to marry *Marcellina* (Contralto) but is in love with Susanna. Figaro's difficulties are cleared up by the discovery (Act III) that Marcellina is his mother, and the Count's intrigues are brought to a stop by a plot which involves the writing of a fictitious love letter by Susanna (dictated to her by the Countess); the use of a pin to fasten this letter (to be sent back by the Count in token that he has received the letter); the loss of this pin by the messenger (Barbarina); an exchange of clothes between Susanna and the Countess, etc.

The looseness and confusion of the plot, far from being detrimental, actually enhance the value of the opera, because they bestow on it a charming quality of Rococo lightness and, above all, because they quickly cause the listener to give up all effort to "follow the plot" and induce him to accept the music as the central element of the opera. Needless to say, only music of such outstanding charm and artistic perfection as Mozart's could lead to this very desirable result.

Nuances [F.]. Subtle modifications of intensity, tempo, touch, phrasing, etc., such as make musical performance alive and interesting. The term is also used as a translation of the Greek *chroai, and for other microtonic intervals.

Number opera [G. *Nummernoper*]. An opera written in single "numbers," i.e., in separate pieces, such as arias, duets, ensembles, ballets, interspersed with recitativo or spoken dialogue. This type of opera prevailed until the early 19th century. It was vehemently opposed by Wagner who supplanted it by a continuous music which follows the action without interruption. His procedure has been adopted by practically all operatic composers up to the present. It must be noted, however, that the replacement of the "number-style" by continuous writing began as early as the operas of Jommelli, Traetta, Gluck, and, particularly, Mozart whose late operas (*Le Nozze di Figaro*, *Don Giovanni*) contain several lengthy movements in which various numbers are linked together by transitional passages into a complete, well-rounded, and unified musical whole. This tendency is still more pronounced in the operas of Beethoven, Weber, and Meyerbeer, while French and Italian composers such as Auber, Rossini, Bellini, Donizetti, generally adhered to the number opera. See *Opera VIII; XI.

Nunc Dimittis. See *Canticum.

Nuove musiche [It., new music]. (1) Title of a publication of 1602 by Giulio Caccini (*c.* 1550–1618) containing arias and madrigals in the then new style of *monodic recitativo with thorough-bass accompaniment. — (2) The term is used today to designate the whole period around 1600 which forms one of the most important landmarks in the history of music, since it marks the origin of the opera, the oratoria, the cantata, and of the *Baroque period in general [see *History of music]. The leading idea of the new movement was to abolish the Flemish tradition of the 16th century with its emphasis on contrapuntal style and artful elaboration. A particular point of objection and resentment was the obscuring of the text which resulted from the polyphonic treatment and from the motet style with its characteristic *points of imitation. A reaction arose which, in the course of a few decades, led to a complete reversal of the relationship between music and text, as was clearly expressed by Monteverdi (*Scherzi musicali*, 1607) in the words: "L'orazione sia padrona dell' armonia e non serva" (The text should be the master, not the servant, of the music). The main result was the replacement of the polyphonic a-cappella style by accompanied solo song (*aria, *recitativo).

These tendencies found a strong support in the antiquarian studies of Greek music which, around 1580, were pursued by Vincenzo Galilei (1533–91) and others known as the *camerata. Although not sufficiently equipped to decipher the remnants of Greek music, these men formed a rather adequate picture of the role which music had played in the ancient Greek drama, and instinctively felt the close relationship of Greek music — always a monophonic rendering of the text — to their own problem. Although accompanied solo songs in a rather plain homophonic style were cultivated in Spain as early as 1530 (lute songs by Milan, Valderrabano), it was not until the last years of the century that the open break with the tradition occurred, in the earliest operas of Peri and Caccini [see *Opera III] which were based exclusively on the principle of *monody (*stile rappresentativo*; see also *Recitative). Caccini, in his above-mentioned book of 1602, applied the new style to short lyrics, imparting to it a more subtle and more expressive design [cf. *HAM*, nos. 182–185; *SchGMB*, nos. 171–173]. His pieces, some of which are quaintly termed "madrigals," form the point of departure of the *aria and the *cantata, which in the

early 17th century are much the same thing. Cavalieri, another pioneer of the new style, used it for his *La Rappresentazione di anima e di corpo* of 1600 [see *Oratorio II], a work which, on account of its inclusion of choral passages [cf. *SchGMB*, no. 169], is less radical but actually more progressive than those of Peri and Caccini. In fact, the limitation of the *stile rappresentativo* soon became patent. Music could not, for any length of time, be completely subjugated to the role of a mere servant, and musicians began to resume some of the threads which had too abruptly been cut off. As early as 1607 Monteverdi's *Orfeo* showed that mixture of old and new ideas upon which the imposing structure of the musical Baroque was to be built. For literature see *Baroque; *Camerata.

Nut. (1) Of the violin. A slightly projected ridge fastened to the upper end of the neck of stringed instruments (violin, etc.), over which the strings pass in order to keep them from touching the finger board. — (2) Of the bow. The lower end of the bow at which it is held. It is adjusted by a screw mechanism in order to keep the hair in proper tension. Earlier bows (Bach) did not have this contrivance, the tension of the hair being adjusted by the varying pressure of the thumb. See *Bow.

Nutcracker Suite. An orchestral suite in six movements by Tchaikovsky (op. 71a, 1891), arranged from his ballet of the same title ("Casse-noisette"), which was based on E. T. A. Hoffmann's fantastic story *The Nutcracker and the Mouse King*. See *Ballet III.

O

O, or similar signs (circle; zero), occur in the following meanings: (1) In music for violins, etc., as an indication of the open string. — (2) In English *fingering for keyboard, as a sign for the thumb. — (3) In thorough-bass parts, for *tasto solo. — (4) In *mensural notation, as a

sign for *tempus perfectum* (circle). — (5) In medieval tonaries, it denotes the fourth church-mode.

Obbligato [It.]. Obligatory, usually with reference to instruments (*violino obbligato*) or parts that must not be omitted; the opposite is *ad libitum*. Unfortunately, by some queer misunderstanding or thoughtlessness, the term has come to adopt the meaning of a mere accompanying part which may be omitted, if necessary. The consequence is that one has to decide in each single case whether obbligato means "obbligato" or "ad libitum," the chances being in favor of the former meaning in the case of early music; of the latter, in more recent pieces. For *accompanimento obbligato*, see under *Accompaniment.

Obbligo [It.]. In the learned counterpoint of the 17th and 18th centuries *con obbligo* denotes a manner of writing which includes certain "self-imposed obligations," such as canon, double counterpoint, inversion, etc.

Oberdominante [G.]. Dominant, in contradistinction to *Unterdominante*, subdominant.

Oberstimme [G.]. Upper part.

Obertas [Polish, turning around]. A Polish round dance in quick triple meter and of a rough character, like a wild waltz. Examples exist in Wieniawski's *Mazurka Charactéristique* No. 1 (for violin) and in the first act of Boito's *Mefistofele*. Chopin's Mazurka op. 56, no. 2 is in the character of an obertas. A modern example occurs in A. Tansman's *Four Polish Dances* (1931) for orchestra.

Obertaste [G.]. See *Taste.

Oberton, Obertöne [G.]. Upper harmonic(s).

Oberwerk [G.]. Swell organ.

Obligat [G.]. See *obbligato.

Oblique motion. See *Motion.

Oboe family. The term is adopted here as a convenient collective designation for a large group of *wind instruments characterized by the use of a double reed [see *Reed; *Mouthpiece]. This group forms the contrast to the *clarinet family which includes the wind instruments using a single reed. In sci-

entific classification the oboe, English horn, bassoon, etc., are considered as constituting families of their own, since each of these instruments existed in various sizes [see N. Bessaraboff, *Ancient European Musical Instruments* (1941), p. 111]. From the point of view of the present article such distinctions are hardly necessary. The instruments of the present-day orchestra are discussed under I, others of rare use or obsolete, under II, while a historical survey is given under III. All these instruments (with the exception of some old types) have a conical bore, in contrast to the cylindrical bore of the clarinets. [See illustrations on p. 816.]

I. *Present-Day Forms.* A. The Oboe [F. *hautbois*, high wood]. The oboe consists of a conical pipe made of wood (usually in three parts, top joint, lower joint, and bell) to the upper end of which a double reed is fixed. The natural scale of the oboe is D (as is that of the flute), but it is not treated as a transposing instrument. Owing to its conical bore the oboe overblows at the octave, as do also all the other members of the family. For the difference in timbre between the oboe and the clarinet, see *Clarinet family I.

B. The English horn [F. *cor anglais*; G. *Englisch Horn*; It. *corno inghlese*]. This is an alto oboe, pitched a fifth below the oboe. In order to facilitate the handling of the rather long instrument a small metal tube is attached to its upper end and is bent back to meet the player's mouth. It is built with a pear-shaped bell [see II, A], which largely accounts for its soft and somewhat melancholic timbre. It is treated as a transposing instrument, the parts sounding a fifth lower than written. Early instruments of this size had a curved form reminiscent of that of an animal's horn, a fact which partly explains its name, the meaning of the denomination "English" being obscure [for a possible explanation, see II, B]. In the early part of the 19th century the English horn gradually replaced the older *oboe da caccia* (alto oboe). The general acceptance of the English horn into the orchestra dates from 1830 when Rossini used it in his *Guillaume Tell* (1829) and Meyerbeer in *Robert le diable* (1831).

C. Bassoon [F. *basson*; G. *Fagott*; It. *fagotto*]. This is the bass of the family. On account of the great length of the tube, this is bent back upon itself, first descending and then ascending. The instrument

RANGES
a. Oboe. b. English horn. c. Bassoon.
d. Contra-bassoon.

is made of five pieces: the *crook*, a narrow, curved metal tube to which the reed is attached; the *wing*, which forms the descending section of the pipe; the *double-joint* or *butt*, the bottom section in the shape of a U; the *long joint* which forms the ascending pipe; and the *bell*. The instrument is remarkably even in tone color, although the lowest fifth of its range tends to be rather thick and reedy and the highest fifth is somewhat "pinched" and terse. It has a wide dynamic range and performs all manner of legato and staccato figures with facility. It blends well with the French horns with which it is often used, but is equally valuable as a solo instrument or as a bass to the woodwind section. See *Phagotus. Cf. L. G. Langwill, "The Bassoon: Its Origin and Development" (*PMA* lxvi).

D. Contra-bassoon or Double-bassoon [F. *contrebasson*; G. *Kontrafagott*; It. *contrafagotto*]. This instrument, the modern form of which was developed by Heckel, has a tube of over sixteen feet in length, doubled on itself four times. The bell points downward, instead of upward, as in the bassoon. It is notated an octave above the actual sound (in Wagner's *Parsifal* it is written at its true pitch). The lowest as well as the highest tones of its range are rather unsatisfactory and therefore less frequently used. It is best suited for passages of from slow to moderate speed. The double bassoon (naturally in an older form) was used by Handel in the Coronation Anthem (1727) and in *L'Allegro* (1740). Haydn scored

for it in *The Creation*, and Beethoven used it in his Fifth and Ninth Symphonies.   W. W. D.

II. *Rare and Obsolete Forms*. It should be noted that the oboes of the 18th and early 19th centuries were much more strident and piercing in sound than the modern instruments, a statement which is even more true of the still earlier instruments [see remark under *aulos].

A. Oboe d'amore. This is a mezzo-soprano instrument with the same characteristic pear-shaped bell (*Liebesfuss*) which exists today with the English horn. The name probably refers to the sound of the instrument which was a good deal "sweeter" than that of the other oboes of its day. It was created about 1720, one of its earliest occurrences being in Bach's cantata no. 37, Wer da glaubet (1725). In a reconstructed form it has been used in R. Strauss's Sinfonia Domestica to characterize the "dreaming child."

B. Oboe da caccia ("hunting oboe"). This was a straight alto oboe with an expanding bell or, more frequently, a pear-shaped bell which rendered the sound less strident. The instrument also occurred in the shape of a half-circle and was then called *cor anglais* (English horn; originally *cor anglé*, "angled horn"?), a name which persisted after the straight form had been generally readopted.

C. Tenoroon [F. *basson quinte*; G. *Quintfagott, Tenorfagott*; It. *fagottino*]. A tenor instrument in the shape of a small bassoon, pitched a fifth above this. It was invented and used in the first half of the 19th century.

D. Quartfagott. A large bassoon pitched a perfect fourth lower than the standard instrument, and used mainly in Germany.

E. Heckelphone. A baritone oboe pitched an octave below the normal oboe, invented by Heckel in 1904. In spite of its full and rich sound it has been little used (R. Strauss, *Salome*; Delius).

F. Sarrusophone. A whole family of instruments made from metal and used only in military bands. It exists in six sizes (from soprano to double bass), pitched alternately in B-flat and E-flat. It was introduced by the French bandmaster Sarrus, about 1860. The only sarrusophone used in the orchestra is a contrabass size in C which has the same compass as the contrabassoon and which has been preferred by many French composers over the contrabassoon.

III. *History.* Double-reed instruments are very ancient and widespread, much more so than single-reed instruments (clarinets). They usually occur in pairs (double oboe), a fact which should not be construed as an evidence of "two-part music 3000 years ago," as the longer pipe was used to provide a drone or, perhaps, some tones missing in the other one. Sumerian double oboes are documented as far back as 2800 B.C., and similar instruments were frequent in Egypt, Israel (*halil*, see *Jewish music I), Greece (*aulos*), and Rome (*tibia*). They occur in practically all the countries of the Far and Near East, usually provided with a metal disk against which the lips of the player are stretched; he takes the reed entirely in his mouth — not, as in European practice, between his lips. Egyptian oboe players are trained to blow continuously without pausing for respiration, the breathing being done exclusively through the nose [see *Launedda]. The aboriginal oboe of China (*kuan*) and Japan (*hichiriki*) is cylindrical while a conical type is an importation from India, where "oboe music is in great demand . . . and expert performers are paid fabulous sums" [cf. *SaHMI*, 230].

The early European instruments with double reeds are collectively referred to as *shawms*. The French name is *bombarde*; the German, *Pommer* (*Bomhart, Pumhart*), except for the highest member of the group which was known as *Schalmei.* The earliest reference to such instruments is in French literary sources of the 13th century. In the 15th and 16th centuries they existed in all sizes, from sopranino (Praetorius' *Klein-Schalmey*) to double-bass (*Gross-Bass-Pommer*). The largest sizes (all straight tubes) were soon discarded in favor of shortened shapes which go back to a 16th-century type called *curtall* (the name is derived from

G. *Kortholt*, i.e., "short wood," referring to the shortened form of the instrument). These instruments differed from the modern bassoon mainly in that they were made from one solid block of wood with two bores, one descending and one ascending. Another name for a similar instrument, apparently of soft timbre, was *dolcian* (*dolcino, Dulzian*).

Numerous other types of double-reed instruments are described by Praetorius under names such as *Sordune, Schryari, Kortholt, Bassanelli.* The Sordune [F. *sourdines*] had a channel running down and up two or three times within the same piece of wood and ending in a lateral hole [cf. *SaHMI*, 317f]. More important are the *cromornes* [G. *Krummhorn*, so called on account of their slightly curved shape] which are shown on paintings of the 15th and 16th centuries in the hands of angels. They are interesting not only because their tube was nearly cylindrical, but also because they had a pierced wind cap which covered the reed so that the player was not able to touch the reed [see illustr. in *SaHMI*, 320]. Thus the reed was set in vibration by indirect wind pressure as in the reed pipes of the organ, and consequently the tone was just as unchangeable as that of organ pipes. Naturally, over-blowing was impossible also. One of the queerest instruments of all times is the *rackett* (*rankett*), a short, thick cylinder of solid wood pierced lengthwise by ten cylindrical channels which were connected so that they formed a continuous tube. In France it was known as *cervelas* (sausage), hence the name "sausage-bassoon" [G. *Wurstfagott*].

Ocarina. A popular instrument in the shape of an egg, a bird, a "sweet potato" (hence the colloquial name), with a mouthpiece and a number of fingerholes. Scientifically it is to be classified as a globular flute, a type which has an interesting ancestry in China and Africa [cf. *SaHMI*, 166f].

Octave. (1) The eighth tone of the diatonic scale [see *Intervals]. Acoustically, the tone with twice the frequency of the home tone (ratio 1:2; e.g., a = 440; a' = 880). The octave is the most perfect consonance, so perfect indeed that it gives the impression of a mere duplication of the original tone, a phenomenon for which no convincing explanation has ever been found and which may well be called "the basic miracle of music." Its peculiarity becomes apparent from a comparison of the acoustical frequencies with the series of color-frequencies (spectrum) which does not show any such duplication [see *Color and music]. The fundamental importance of the octave appears also from the fact that it is the only interval which is common to practically all the scales ever evolved, regardless of the number or pitch of the intermediate steps. For the designation of the various octaves, see *Pitch names.

(2) In ecclesiastical terminology, Octave denotes the continued observation, for eight (or seven) days, of the greater feasts.

Octave flute. *Piccolo flute.

Octave species [G. *Oktavgattungen*]. See *Greek music II (c).

Octavier [F.]. See *Wind instruments III.

Octet. Chamber music for eight instruments, either all strings (Mendelssohn, Gade, Enesco), all winds (Beethoven, op. 103; Stravinsky), or mixed (Schubert, Spohr).

Octobass. See *Violin family (j).

Octoechos. See *Echos.

Oddonic letters. See *Letter notation.

Ode. In ancient Greek and Latin as well as in modern poetry, a poem in free meter and verse structure, frequently addressed to a deity. Odes are usually composed in a free form, similar to that of the cantata, including several movements or sections for chorus, soloist, and orchestra. Dryden's "Ode on St. Cecilia's Day" (set by Purcell) and Schiller's "Ode to Joy" (set by Beethoven, Ninth Symphony) are well-known examples.

In the 16th century the Horatian odes were frequently set to music in strict chordal style and in a rhythm dictated by the poetic meter, e.g.:

Mae-ce-nas a-ta-vis e-di-te re-gi-bus

This practice was inaugurated by Konrad Celtis, professor of poetry at the university of Ingolstadt, 1492–97. Among the earliest publications of such odes are: Petronius Tritonius, *Melopoeia . . . super 22 genera carminum Horatii* (1507); Paulus Hofhaimer, *Harmoniae poeticae* (1539; new ed. by Achleitner, 1868); Ludwig Senfl, *Varia carminum genera . . .* (1532); Claude Goudimel, *Q. Horatii Flacci . . . odae . . . ad rhythmos musicos redactae* (1555). Examples for the lute occur in Judenkunig's *Ain schöne kunstliche Underweisung . . . 1523* [cf. *DTOe* 18.ii; *ApMZ* i]. In France, this poetic modification of musical rhythm [see *Rhythm II (b)] led to the *vers mesuré. In the collections of *frottole, published by Petrucci, the name *ode* is given to strophic songs in iambic heptameters and with the following scheme of rhymes: a a a b / b b b c / c c c d /, etc. See *Renaissance; *Humanism.

Lit.: R. v. Liliencron, in *VMW* iii; P. Masson, in *RMC* vi; H. J. Moser, *Paul Hofhaimer* (1929), Notenanhang, pp. 112ff.

Ode-Symphonie. French name for Beethoven's Symphony no. 9 (*Choral symphony). See under *Ode.

Odhecaton [from Gr. *ode*, song; *hekaton*, hundred]. Title (complete form: *Harmonice musices Odhecaton A*) of a printed collection of "100 songs" (actually only 99) published by Petrucci in 1501. The book is interesting as the earliest printed publication of polyphonic music [see *Printing of music], and of great importance as a collection of secular polyphonic music of the period from c. 1470 to 1500. Similar collections, *Canti B* and *Canti C*, appeared in 1502 and 1503. Among the composers are Heyne van Gizeghem [see *Burgundian

School], Ockeghem (1430–95), Obrecht (1430–1505), Isaac (1450–1517), Alexander Agricola (d. 1506), Josquin (1450–1521), and many others [cf. *RiML*, 1376]. The fact that only a few of the pieces have text does not necessarily prove that the contents of these books were instrumental music in the strict sense of the word; indeed, a considerable number of the compositions are preserved in other sources (manuscripts) with a text, at least in the discantus. On the other hand, the omission of the texts, although conditioned perhaps by merely external considerations (typographic difficulties), throws an interesting light upon the latitude of 16th-century musical practice, which readily admitted instrumental performance of vocal pieces. It is impossible, of course, to assume that Petrucci could have supposed all the prospective buyers of his books to be familiar with the texts of more than 300 compositions [cf. Cauchy].

Lit.: †*Odhecaton* (facsimile ed. by Bolletino bibliografico musicale, 1931); M. Hewitt, †*The Odhecaton* (1942; transcr.); G. Reese, in *MQ* xx; M. Cauchie, "L'Odhecaton, recueil de musique instrumentale" (*RdM*, nos. 16, 26); J. Marix, in *RdM*, no. 56.

Odoistic notation. See *Letter notation.

Oeuvre [F.]. *Opus.

Offertorium, offertory. In the Catholic liturgy, the fourth item of the Proper of the Mass, accompanying the placing upon the Altar of the Elements (Bread and Wine). Originally it was a psalm with antiphon (*antiphona ad offerendum*); today only the antiphon is left. Beginning with the 15th century, musical compositions (motets) were admitted instead of or in addition to the plainsong, in order to fill in the time consumed by the sacred rites. In 1593 Palestrina published a complete collection of such motets under the title *Offertoria per totum annum*. During the 17th century many Offertoria for the organ with or without instruments were composed by Le Bègue,

Grigny, F. Couperin, and others. An early instance is Frescobaldi's **Toccata avanti l'elevazione** [see *Toccata].

Office, officium. In the Catholic liturgy, the service of the hours [see *Office hours] as distinct from that of the *Mass. See *Gregorian chant I.

Office hours [Canonical hours, Daily hours, Divine office; G. *Stundenofficium*]. In the Roman Catholic Church, the hours at which service is held, eight times a day: 1. Matins [L. *matutinum*; G. *Mette*], during night, includes three Nocturns; 2. Lauds [L. *laudes*], at sunrise; 3. Prime [L. *ad primam*], c. 6 A.M.; 4. Terce [L. *ad tertiam*], c. 9 A.M.; 5. Sext [L. *ad sextam*], midday; 6. None [L. *ad nonam*], c. 3 P.M.; 7. Vespers or Evensong [L. *ad vesperam*], at sunset; 8. Compline [L. *completorium*], nightfall. Mass is sung after Terce, except on ordinary weekdays when it is sung after Sext; and on fast days, when it is after None.

From the musical point of view the most important services are those of Matins, Vespers, and Compline. That of Matins is now held regularly only in monastic churches; therefore only a limited number of these services are given in the common books of plainsong, namely that for the Office of the Dead (*AR* [152]–[176]), for *Tenebrae, and for the great feasts (*LU* 368, 765, etc). The chants of Matins include chiefly *responsoria and certain special chants which are interesting because they have retained the complete structure of ancient Gregorian psalmody, e.g., the *Invitatorium and the responsorium Libera me [see *Psalmody II].

The service of Vespers includes the *Magnificat; it is the only Office for which music other than Gregorian chant (motets, organ music) is admitted. The service of Compline includes the four Antiphons B.M.V. [see *Antiphon (2)], one for each season of the year. The complete service for the hours of an ordinary Sunday is given in *AR*, 1–69.

Oiseau de Feu, L' ["The Firebird"]. Ballet by Stravinsky; see *Ballet III.

Oketus. See *Hocket.

Oktave [G.]. Octave. In connection with instruments it denotes sizes either an octave above the normal size (e.g., *Oktavflöte,* i.e., piccolo flute), or below it (e.g., *Oktavfagott,* i.e., contrabassoon). *Oktavgattung,* *Octave species.

Oktavieren [G.]. See *Wind instruments III.

Oktoechos. See *Echos.

Old Hall MS. See *Sources, no 25.

Old Hundred. An old hymn tune which was used in Béza's *Genevan Psalter* (1554) for the 134th Psalm, in Knox's *Anglo-Genevan Psalter* (1556) for the third Psalm, and in Sternhold and Hopkins' *Psalter* (1562) for the 100th Psalm, hence the name.

Olé. See *Polo.

Oliphant [Old English for elephant]. A medieval instrument for signaling, made from an elephant's tusk, often beautifully carved. They are of no musical importance. Illustration in *GD* iv, 496.

Ombra scene [It. *ombra,* shade]. In early operas, designation for scenes which take place in Hades or in similar surroundings. Every opera dealing with the subject of *Orpheus has, of course, an ombra scene.

Ondeggiando [It.], **ondulé** [F.]. Undulating, swaying. In violin playing, an undulating movement of the bow. It is used for arpeggio-like figures but also on one note in order to produce a slight fluctuation of intensity. In earlier music (*c.* 1650–1750; Purcell, Stamitz) the latter effect, which must be classified as a *tremolo, was rather frequent, being indicated by a wavy line [see the table, p. 545]. See also *Bowing (o) and under *Vibrato.

One-step. American dance of the *jazz period (*c.* 1910–20) in quick duple meter, similar to the *fox-trot. It was superseded, around 1920, by the slower two-step (slow-fox).

Ongarese, All' [It.]. In Hungarian style.

Onion-flute. Same as *Eunuch flute. See *Mirliton.

Onzième [F.]. The interval of the eleventh.

Op. Abbreviation for opus.

Open fifth, open triad. A triad without the third, e.g., c–g–c'.

Open graces. See under *Grace.

Open harmony. See *Spacing.

Open notes. (1) On wind instruments, same as *natural notes. — (2) On stringed instruments, the tones which are produced on the *open strings.

Open pipe. See *Wind instruments III.

Open strings. The unstopped strings of violins, lutes, etc. Their use is sometimes prescribed by the figure o.

Opera [from It. *opera in musica,* a "work in music"; F. *opéra;* G. *Oper*]. "A drama, either tragic or comic, sung throughout, with appropriate scenery and acting, to the accompaniment of an orchestra" (*GD*). This definition requires modification in the case of *comic operas which (except for the Italian *opera buffa*) usually have spoken dialogue; there are also a few serious operas (e.g., Mozart's *Magic Flute,* Beethoven's *Fidelio,* Weber's *Freischütz*) which admit spoken dialogue.

I. *General.* The opera is the most important of the forms resulting from the combination of music and theatrical representation. It is a highly complex form, enlisting many different arts in its service: music (both instrumental and vocal), drama, poetry, acting, dance, stage-design, costuming, etc. — and this fact accounts in part for both its widespread appeal and for the equally widespread criticism directed against it on the score of its artistic impurity; the classic statement of this critical attitude being Saint-Evremonde's definition of opera as "a bizarre affair of poetry and music in which the poet and the musician, each equally obstructed by the other, give themselves no end of trouble to produce a wretched result." The fact that opera is, of all musical or dramatic forms, the most difficult and expensive to produce, has caused it almost always to be associated with the upper strata of social life, thus making it a "prestige symbol" for the public as well as an object of particular attraction for many ambitious composers and singers. It is noteworthy that most operas have been composed by specialists in this form. The number of composers who have distinguished themselves equally in opera and other branches of music is exceedingly small: Monteverdi, Handel, Mozart, and R. Strauss are outstanding in this respect. On the other hand, composers such as Bach, Haydn, Schubert, Schumann, Mendelssohn, Brahms, and Bruckner either did not venture into the operatic field at all, or did so without conspicuous success, while the achievements of Beethoven and Debussy are limited to one work each, albeit a masterpiece in both cases.

Like all art forms, the opera is founded on certain conventions, the most important of which is that the persons of the drama express their thoughts and feelings by means of song rather than speech. Criticism of this feature as "unnatural" is, of course, beside the point, since no work of art is intended to be a mere imitation of nature. While it is undeniable that people in real life do not continuously sing, it is equally undeniable that they do not continuously speak in blank verse, as do Shakespeare's characters. In both cases a conventional mode of expression must be accepted as a basis for the form. Even the most "realistic" drama has its conventions, and all movements toward realism in opera have resulted only in substituting a different set of conventions for those to which objection was made. Indeed, it may be questioned whether attempts at closer imitation of "real" life on the operatic stage do not defeat their purpose by merely emphasizing the inescapable distinction between the art-work and the object which it represents.

Another basic convention of opera is a consequence of the fact that a musical idea usually takes longer for its development than the time which would be required merely to speak the words with which it is connected. This results in either or both of the following devices: (1) a noticeable stretching-out, and consequent slow pace of the action (as in Wagner's music dramas); or (2) alternating periods of action and repose: the action being carried on in *recitative (with a minimum of music) and being periodically interrupted by musical "numbers" (arias, ensembles, ballets, etc.; see *Number opera) all of which are, from the dramatic standpoint, likely to be merely episodic, or at best unnecessarily long elaborations of certain moments of the action. Such a slow tempo of the drama, or such frequent interruptions, would be regarded as serious defects in a spoken play; but in an opera they are hardly avoidable. From this basic necessity arise many of the features of opera which persons unaccustomed to the form find difficult to accept, such as the frequent text-repetitions, the prolonged emotional scenes, dying speeches, and so on. While it is true that many operas are cheaply emotional, silly, or melodramatic, the same charge may be made against many plays. These faults are not inherent in the form, though the skillful use of music may cause the ordinary listener to forgive their presence in opera more readily than in a play.

II. *Prehistory*. Although the first work now known as an opera dates from 1597, the combination of music with dramatic performances is undoubtedly of very early origin. The drama of the Greeks, as it developed out of the ceremonies of the Bacchus cult, incorporated the choral songs and dances of the earlier rites. The tragedies of Aeschylus, Sophocles, and Euripides all give a large place to the chorus, and it is known from theoretical treatises (e.g., Aristotle's *Poetics*) that music was one of the essential elements of the form, though unfortunately only a single mutilated specimen of Greek dramatic music has survived (fragment of a chorus from the *Orestes* of Euripides).

In the Middle Ages the church fostered dramatic music in the *Liturgical Dramas (11th–13th centuries) and the *Mysteries (14th–16th centuries). The medieval religious drama had no direct historical connection with the earliest operas, but its tradition may still be traced in some of the operas on religious subjects at Rome and in Germany during the 17th century.

The immediate predecessors of opera are to be sought in the various types of secular dramatic entertainment with music which appeared during the sixteenth century. These may be grouped under two heads: (1) Works in which music served as an adjunct to scenery and dancing; the definitive form in this class is the *Ballet, which was brought from Italy into France where it later exercised a determining influence on the form of the French opera (see below). (2) Works in which music served as a diversion with spoken drama, i.e., in which the musical portions appeared usually as *Intermezzi between the acts of a play. However, the creation of opera itself had to await the discovery of a kind of drama which should lend itself to the continuous use of music, and the discovery of a kind of music which should be capable of dramatic expression. The necessary poetic form was found in the Pastorale, which toward the end of the 16th century displaced practically all earlier dramatic types in Italy, and culminated in Tasso's *Aminta* (1573) and Guarini's *Pastor fido* (1581–90). The earliest opera poems are pastorales on the model of these two works [see also *Eclogue]. The development of a musical style suitable for opera was the work of the Florentine *Camerata [see also *Nuove musiche; *Monody]; the *Madrigal comedies of Vecchi, however, which are frequently mentioned as pre-operatic types, have no place in the history of the opera.

The history of opera may be divided into five periods:

1590–1680. Development of dramatic style in music and of apppropriate dramatic and musical forms (III–VII).

1680–1760. Utilization of established style and forms in operas of a standard type: the Neapolitan opera (VIII).

1760–1850. Introduction of new subject-matter and loosening of traditional forms, in the interest of a more direct connection between dramatic content and musical expression (IX).

1850–1920. Abandonment of set forms and formal divisions in favor of continuous music, with recurrence of characteristic motifs: the music-drama (X).

1920–the present. Reaction against subject-matter, size, and musical amorphousness of the music-drama; return to 18th-century forms (the "number" opera) in modern musical idioms (XI).

III. *Florentine and Roman Opera.* The earliest operas, all performed at Florence, are: *Dafne*, poem by Rinuccini, music by Peri (1597; music lost); *Euridice*, poem by Rinuccini, music by Caccini (1600; in *Editions XXVI, 10); *Euridice*, music by Peri (1600; in *Editions II, 6 and VI, 24). (A. Tirabassi, in *MQ* xxv, makes a claim for Domenico Belli's *Orfeo dolente* as the earliest opera, but without convincing evidence). The music of the Florentine operas consists mostly of recitative over a thorough-bass, the somewhat colorless harmonies of which were realized by a small orchestra. Conformable to the ideal of imitation of Greek drama, the vocal line aims at close adherence to the natural rhythm and accent of the spoken word; therefore, although flawless in declamation and occasionally expressive in detail, it is lacking in any distinct melodic character or any principle of musical organization. Exceptions to this style occur in the occasional metrical songs and choruses, usually with dancing, which are placed at the end of the principal scenes; but the almost total exclusion of counterpoint and the neglect of instrumental music resulted, as soon as the novelty of the new "stile recitativo" had worn off, in an unbearable monotony of effect. It was the achievement of Monteverdi to begin the practice of introducing into opera the full resources of the art of music. His *Orfeo* (Mantua, 1607; poem by Alessandro Striggio) is on the same subject, and in the same general style, as the earlier Florentine *Euridice* operas; but it shows notable advances both in dramatic characterization and in musical form. Monteverdi's harmony is incomparably richer and more varied than that of Peri or Caccini. The recitative is more expressive, and is frequently organized by means of repetitions, sequential passages, etc., into distinct musical patterns. The remarkable aria "Possente spirto" in Act III consists of four strophes of elaborately "colored" solo, each with a different orchestral accompaniment. The large orchestra is another feature of this work, as well as the number of instrumental pieces (26 in all), including the introductory "toccata" (the earliest operatic *overture) and the frequent ritornelli which by their recurrence serve to give musical unity to long sections of the opera.

With the third decade of the 17th century the center of operatic interest shifts to Rome (chief composers: Stefano Landi, Domenico Mazzochi, Michelangelo Rossi, Luigi Rossi). Landi's *S. Alessio* (perf. 1632; cf. *Editions II, 5) shows a stage in the differentiation between recitative and aria, with the use of tuneful melodies in the latter, as well as continued progress toward formal clarity. In this work also the "canzona" type of overture appears, while the "sinfonia" before the second act is an early example of the three-movement arrangement (fast-slow-fast) of the later Italian overture. The Roman operas are distinguished by extensive use of the chorus. This school was also the first to produce *comic operas.

IV. *Venetian Opera.* The rise of the Venetian school begins in 1637, with the opening of the first public opera house ("Teatro S. Cassiano"). The first composers are: Monteverdi (*Il Ritorno d'Ulisse*, 1641; *L'Incoronazione di Poppea*, 1642), Cavalli (*Giasone*, 1649, in *Editions XXVI, 12; *Serse*, 1654), and Cesti (*La Dori*, 1662, in *Edi-

tions XXVI, 12; *Il Pomo d'oro*, 1667 at Vienna). The recitative of Monteverdi's *Incoronazione* is the apotheosis of the Florentine monodic style, and is combined with more regular aria forms to make one of the most beautiful operatic scores of the entire 17th century. The works of Cavalli and Cesti show the influence of public taste on the operatic form in their greater size, more lavish staging (see especially Burnacini's stage designs for *Il Pomo d'oro* in *DTOe* 3.ii and 4.ii), greater number of characters, plot-complications, and use of burlesque-comic episodes. Musical effects become less subtle than in earlier works. The virtuoso soloist begins to be featured. Recitative and aria become completely distinct and the latter crystallizes into standard forms (strophic, ostinato-bass, da capo). There are many arias in light, popular, melodic style, as well as more serious types. The use of an orchestral introduction to the aria, repeated at the close ("ritornello" principle), as well as short orchestral interludes between the sections, is established. There are important orchestral overtures and sinfonias, but the chorus is much less prominent than in the operas of the Roman school.

The course of Venetian opera after Cesti is difficult to follow owing to the unavailability of sources. There was a flourishing branch of comic-satirical opera, while serious works were composed by Legrenzi (*Eteocle e Polinice*, 1675), C. Pallavicino (*La Gerusalemme liberata*, 1687 at Dresden; cf. *DdT* 55), and Stradella.

The climax of the 17th-century Italian opera is seen in the works of Agostino Steffani (*Alarico*, 1687; *Henrico Leone*, 1689; cf. *DTB* 11.ii, 12.ii), a native of Venice but whose musical activity took place entirely in Germany. In Steffani the perfect reconciliation of the monodic and contrapuntal principles is achieved and the foundation firmly laid for the operatic style of Handel.

In the 18th century the Venetian school is represented by Lotti, C. F. Pollarolo, Vivaldi, and Galuppi, the last being distinguished for his "buffo" operas.

The historical importance of Venice lies in the establishment of opera as a public spectacle, the development of an appropriate musical style and forms, and furthermore in its widespread influence on the formation of opera in Germany and France.

V. *French Opera.* French national opera was founded by Robert Cambert (*Pomone*, 1671) and Jean-Baptiste Lully (*Cadmus et Hermione*, 1673; Atys, 1676; *Amadis de Gaule*, 1684; *Armide et Renaud*, 1686). Although there had been performances of Italian opera in Paris between 1645 and 1662 (notably Luigi Rossi's *Orfeo* in 1647), the French were slow to adopt the form, partly because in their own classical tragedy (Corneille, Racine) and in the Ballet they had already perfected two types of stage production with which they were satisfied and which they did not believe could be successfully merged. It is a tribute to Lully's skill that he was able to take certain features of each of these established forms, along with some elements of the Pastorale, and combine them in the opera. As compared with contemporary Italian works, the French opera is distinguished by (1) the relatively greater importance of the drama in the total scheme, (2) the exceptionally large place given to ballets, choruses, and spectacular scenes in general, (3) the greater use of instrumental music, (4) the use of short and simple songs, mostly of a dance-like character (*airs) rather than elaborate arias, (5) a special type of *recitative, and (6) a special type of *overture, known as French overture. This type of opera remained essentially unchanged in the works of Lully's successors, including Rameau (*Hippolyte et Aricie*, 1733; *Castor et Pollux*, 1737), whose operas represent the high-point of this form in France before Gluck. For reprints of French operas see *Editions IV.

VI. *English Opera.* As French opera grew out of the Ballet, so English opera developed from the *Masque, though not without difficulty owing to the prejudice during the Commonwealth (1649–60) against stage entertainments. John Blow's *Venus and Adonis* (*c.* 1685), although entitled "a masque," is the first genuine opera to be produced in England. The only great figure of English opera is Henry Purcell, whose *Dido and Aeneas* (*c.* 1689) is a masterpiece in miniature. Though not free of French influence (form of overture, care for clear text-declamation, certain rhythmic mannerisms, prominence of dancing, instrumental pieces, and choruses), it nevertheless combines these features with highly original and characteristically English melodies, rhythms, and harmonies, together with a degree of tragic expressiveness (Dido's lament, "When I am laid in earth") which has hardly been surpassed in opera. These same qualities may be found in much of Purcell's other theater music, which is in the form of incidental music to plays (*Dioclesian*, 1690; *King Arthur*, 1691). With Purcell's early death, the history of English serious opera may be said to end, so far as any works of first rank are concerned.

VII. *German Opera.* With the exception of Schütz's *Daphne* (1627 at Torgau; music lost), the early history of opera in Germany is predominantly the history of Italian composers at German courts: Pallavicino at Dresden, A. Draghi at Vienna, Steffani at Munich and Hanover, and a host of others. Their influence was such that for the next hundred years even native German masters were content to write in the Italian style, and to Italian texts (Fux, Hasse, Gluck, Mozart). The only important native German school was at Hamburg, where the titles of the first Singspiele (e.g., Theile's *Adam und Eva*, 1678) show the connection with the tradition of School-dramas on sacred themes. (An earlier example is Staden's "Spiritual pastorale" *Seelewig*, Nuremberg, 1644; see *MfM* xiii; *SchGMB*, no. 195.) German operas on secular subjects, both serious and comic, soon made their appearance. The chief composer of the Hamburg school was Reinhard Keiser, of whose reputed 120 operas but 18 have been preserved (*Croesus*, 1711, revised 1730; in *DdT* 37/38; *Octavia*, 1706; in Handel Gesellschaft, Supplement; *Prinz Jodelet,* 1726; in *Editions XXVI, 18). Keiser's importance lies not only in his position as the best composer of early German opera, but also in his direct influence on Handel, whose first four operatic works were produced at Hamburg in 1705–06. Keiser's style is essentially like that found in the operas of Steffani and (to a higher degree of development) in Handel. An outstanding feature of his style is the skill of the orchestral parts of the arias, and the variety of combinations of concertizing instruments which he employs. After Keiser, German opera degenerated and by the middle of the 18th century had entirely disappeared.

VIII. *Neapolitan Opera.* The prevailing type of 18th-century serious opera is known as "Neapolitan," from the name of the city where many of its early composers chiefly worked [see *Neapolitan School]. This type was cultivated in all countries (except France) by native and Italian composers alike, and the word "Neapolitan" has been generally applied to operas which vary widely from one another both in technical treatment and in artistic merit. By some historians the term is restricted to operas the music of which is in a popular, tuneful style with simple harmonic accompaniments, characteristic of the period 1710–50 [see *Gallant style].

Much of the usual criticism of the Neapolitan opera rises from lack of understanding of the principles of the form or from concentrating on its abuses while ignoring its virtues. Its foundation was a rationalistic ideal of drama, realized through the reforms of Zeno and his more famous successor Metastasio, who purged the chaotic 17th-century opera libretto of irrelevant elements (e.g., comic and fantastic episodes) and created a unified, closely-knit three-act dramatic structure, with characters and subjects drawn principally from classical history or legend (seldom from mythology). Formally, each scene consists of two distinct parts, the first comprising the action and the second devoted to the expression of the reflections, feelings, or resolves of the principal character, which are a consequence of the action just preceding. Thus the libretto presents a constant alternation of active and reflective portions, the former being interpreted musically as recitative (mostly *recitativo secco*) and the latter as aria. Choruses are practically non-existent. As for the orchestra, its function (except for the overture [see *Italian overture] and an occasional march or other incidental piece) is decidedly subordinate, though in the hands of an able composer the ritornellos and accompaniments to the arias may be of considerable interest and importance. But the center of attention and the basic unit in the structure of these operas was the aria, of which many different types existed (*aria cantabile, aria parlante, aria di bravura,* etc.), though practically all were in the Da Capo form. Fairly rigid conventions prevailed as to the number and order of the different types of aria and their distribution among the members of the cast, and the popularity of Metastasio (his 27 librettos were set to music over 1000 times in the 18th century) is in large part attributable to his ability to meet the peculiar requirements of the form without undue sacrifice of dramatic force and continuity. Corollary to the conception of the aria as the essential unit of form were two phenomena characteristic of 18th-century opera: (1) The high development of vocal technique [see *Bel canto], particularly by the *castrati; (2) The prevalent custom of borrowing arias from one opera for use in another, whether or not by the same composer [cf. *Pasticcio]. Since there were no printed scores, and no copyright restrictions, an opera was seldom performed the same way in two different places or at two different times, and the changes were sometimes so extensive as to make it impossible any more to reconstruct the original version.

The reputed founder of the Neapolitan school is Alessandro Scarlatti, of whose 114 operas not one exists complete in any modern edition. The degree of stylization evident in later composers is not seen in Scarlatti, though the works of his last period clearly foreshadow the tendency. The chief representatives of the Neapolitan school in the early 18th century are Porpora, L. Vinci, Leo, and J. A. Hasse. But unquestionably the greatest composer of Italian opera in this period is Handel, who from 1711 to 1740 produced at London a series of works some of which have never been surpassed for nobility of style or profundity of dramatic insight (*Giulio Cesare*, 1724; *Tamerlano*, 1724; *Rodelinda*, 1725). Later composers of serious opera in the Neapolitan tradition include Latilla, Piccini, Sarti, Sacchini, Salieri, Gluck (early works), and Mozart (*Idomeneo*, 1781). Growing criticism of the rigidity of the form and of the abuses consequent on the overbearing vanity of the singers (cf. Marcello's satire *Il Teatro alla moda, c.* 1720) led to efforts at reform, in which Jomelli (*Fetonte*, 1751; in *DdT* 32/33) and Traëtta (in *DTB* 14.i, 17) were prominent. Credit for the final reform of the Neapolitan opera is generally given to Gluck, in spite of the fact that of his "reform" operas only two (*Orfeo*, 1762; *Alceste*, 1767) were composed originally to Italian librettos, and these were later revised and adapted to French texts at Paris; while the others (*Iphigénie en Aulide*, 1772, *Armide*, 1777, *Iphigénie en Tauride*, 1779) were on French poems, were designed for and performed at Paris, and moreover embodied many of the features which had been characteristic of French opera from the time of Rameau and Lully: comparative subordination of music to drama, avoidance of mere vocal display, flexibility of musical forms, closer approximation of style between recitative and aria, and general simplicity both of subject and treatment. (These are the points stressed in the famous dedicatory preface to *Alceste*.) To these may be added another detail which is common to Rameau and Gluck, and not common in Neapolitan opera: the use of large choral and ballet scenes connected with the action. In short, the direct reform of Gluck lay in his injection of renewed dramatic vigor into French opera; though indirectly, his success at Paris and the subsequent stead-

ily growing influence of the French capital in operatic affairs made later Italian composers more ready to adopt practices calculated to assure a favorable Parisian hearing of their works, and thus led to a closer *rapprochement* of the two national styles. Other influences working toward a reform of the Neapolitan opera in the later 18th century were the cult of naturalness as set forth in the writings of Rousseau, and the increasing significance of popular "comic" operas, which by the end of the century in all countries had attained artistic equality with serious opera. See *Comic opera; *Number opera.

IX. *From Mozart to Wagner.* The climax of later 18th century Italian opera is in the works of Mozart (*Le Nozze di Figaro*, 1786; *Don Giovanni*, 1787; *Così fan tutte*, 1790), and it is significant that his three Italian masterpieces were of the "buffo" variety (the "opera seria" *La Clemenza di Tito*, 1791, is of less importance), though the designation then no longer had the narrow significance which it possessed in the early part of the century. Mozart's operas are outstanding in sharpness and subtlety of characterization, integration of vocal and instrumental factors, and the adaptation of the classical symphonic style in their ensemble finales. His *Entführung aus dem Serail* (1781) is one of the finest examples of the *Singspiel, and *Die Zauberflöte* (1791) is an important forerunner of 19th-century German Romantic opera.

The influence of Gluck was evident in a school of large-scale "heroic" opera centering at Paris, represented by such works as Sacchini's *Dardanus* (1784) and *Oedipe à Colone* (1786), Salieri's *Danaïdes* (1784), Cherubini's *Médée* (1797), Spontini's *Vestale* (1807), and Méhul's *Joseph* (1807). The continuation of this school was the 19th-century "grand opera" of which the most famous examples are Rossini's *Guillaume Tell* (1829), Halévy's *La Juive* (1835), Meyerbeer's *Huguenots* (1836) and *Prophète* (1849), Wagner's *Rienzi* (1842), and Berlioz' *Troyens* (comp. 1856–58; never performed in its entirety). In contrast to this style was the opera on more realistic, often melodramatic, subjects, one characteristic form of which was the "rescue opera" (Cherubini's *Deux journées*, 1800; Beethoven's *Fidelio*, 1805, '06, '14). The works so far mentioned constitute what may be called the international opera of the early 19th century. Less pretentious at first in scope and subject-matter, but of greater eventual importance historically were the various national schools.

In *Italy* the leading composers were Rossini (best known for his comic opera *Il Barbiere di Siviglia*, 1816); Bellini (*Norma*, 1831); Donizetti (*Lucrezia Borgia*, 1833; *Lucia di Lammermoor*, 1835); and Verdi (*Rigoletto*, 1851; *Il Trovatore*, *La Traviata*, 1853; *Aida*, 1871; *Otello*, 1887; *Falstaff*, 1893). The crowning-point of Italian opera with melodramatic plots, popular type melodies, and concentration on "effective" vocal numbers [see *Number opera] is reached in Verdi's works of the 1850's. *Aida*, a work in the "grand opera" tradition, shows unmistakable signs of the changes in style which were fully realized in *Otello* and *Falstaff*: better librettos, continuity of presentation, a more flexible rhythm, more expressive harmony, and closer approach to equality between vocal and instrumental elements — though still retaining the classical Italian qualities of clarity, dramatic simplicity, and profound comprehension of the expressive possibilities of the solo voice.

In *France*, aside from "grand opéra," the early 19th century was taken up with the *opéra-comique, a form and style inherited from the preceding period, but which gradually developed into the lyric opera of Gounod (*Faust*, 1859) and Thomas (*Mignon*, 1866), in both of whom Italian influence is manifest. Later 19th-century French opera is represented by Bizet (*Carmen*, 1875), Delibes (*Lakmé*, 1883), Chabrier (*Gwendoline*, 1886, obviously indebted to Wagner's *Tristan*), Massenet (*Manon*, 1884), d'Indy (*Fervaal*, 1889–95), and other composers (see below).

A national school of opera began in *Russia* with the performance of Glinka's *Life for the Tsar* in 1836. Its chief composer was Moussorgsky, who in *Boris Godunov* (perf. 1874) created a score which combined nationalistic subject-matter and musical material with originality and great dramatic power. Among the composers of Russian opera should also be mentioned Borodin (*Prince Igor*, perf. 1890) and Rimsky-Korsakov (*The Snow Maiden*, 1882; *Sadko*, 1897). Tchaikovsky's works in operatic form (*Eugen Oniegin*, 1877; *The Queen of Spades*, 1890) are in the Romantic style, but do not belong in the nationalistic category.

The background of Romantic opera in *Germany* is to be found in the *Singspiel of the late 18th and early 19th centuries. An important early composer is Spohr (*Faust*, 1818; *Jessonda*, 1823). Weber's *Freischütz* (1821) and *Euryanthe* (1823) established the fundamental characteristics of the school, which are: (1) the Romantic treatment of subjects derived from national legend and folklore; (2) a deep feeling for nature and the use of natural phenomena as an essential element in the drama; (3) the acceptance of supernatural agencies as a means of dramatic development; and (4) the direct or implied glorification of the German land, culture, and people. Musically, *Der Freischütz* marks an important stage in the discovery of Romantic expressive effects (introduction to the Overture, the Wolf's Glen scene), as well as in the use of folk-song-like melodies, side by side with more conventional operatic arias. The operas of Marschner (*Der Vampyr*, 1828; *Hans Heiling*, 1833) continue the general type established by Weber, and the latter's influence is strongly evident in Wagner's *Der fliegende Holländer* (1843), and even in *Lohengrin*.

X. *The Music Drama*. Wagner's next two operas after *Der fliegende Holländer* are steps in the evolution toward the Music Drama. *Tannhäuser* (1845) still retains the old-fashioned division into "numbers," and has some unessential display scenes; but with *Lohengrin* (comp. 1847) these irrelevancies are dismissed. Music and drama are more closely unified, greater continuity is achieved, and the symbolic meaning of the drama is made clearly evident. The vocal line becomes emancipated from the older periodic rhythm, approaching the free melodic style of the late works. Wagner employed the early years of his exile (1849–64) in completing the poem and part of the music of *Der Ring des Nibelungen* and in writing various essays, of which the most important is *Oper und Drama* (1851). In this work he developed the theoretical basis for the Music Drama, the practical application of which appears in the four dramas of the *Ring* (first complete performance at Bayreuth, 1876), *Tristan und Isolde* (comp. 1857–59), *Die Meistersinger von Nürnberg* (comp. 1862–67), and *Parsifal* (comp. 1877–79).

These works are all based on a conception of the Music Drama as a super-artform (Gesamtkunstwerk) in which all the constituent arts are transfigured, sacrificing their individual identity and some of their special characteristics for the larger possibilities of development opened up by the new association. The myth is held to be the ideal subject, not merely because it is entertaining but also because it is significant; its meaning is expressed in poetry (speech), but it is inevitably impelled to song, since only music is capable of conveying the intensity of feeling to which the ideas of the poem give rise. This song is flexible (non-periodic rhythm) and free (no formal divisions into recitative, aria, etc.); it implies a polyphonic substructure which is realized by the orchestra, and which embodies the "inner action" of the drama (i.e., the feelings) as the words embody its "outer action" (i.e., the precise ideas with which the feelings are connected). The orchestral music is continuous throughout an act, the technical concomitant of this being the avoidance of double bars and perfect cadences and the continual shifting of the tonal center; it is unified by the use of "*leit-motifs," musical themes each connected with a particular person, thing, or idea (or all three, as in the case of Siegfried's horn-call), and recurring, varying, or developing musically in accord with the recurrence,

variation, or development of the corresponding object in the drama. Wagner's music is the incarnation of the full, rich sound-ideal of the late Romantic period, deriving a peculiar intensity of expression from the skillful orchestration, the freedom and variety of the harmonic progressions, and the effective employment of suspensions and appoggiaturas. That his works continue popular is undoubtedly due more to their musical qualities and their sheer dramatic effectiveness than to any general acceptance of the theory of the Gesamtkunstwerk, with its manifold implications.

XI. *The Modern Opera.* Wagner's musical style and his ideal of "continuous melody" influenced all composers of opera in the late 19th and early 20th centuries, particularly Richard Strauss (*Salome*, 1905; *Der Rosenkavalier*, 1911). At the same time, the Music Drama provoked reactions in favor of so-called "realism" in subject-matter and compression and simplicity of musical treatment, evident in the Italians Mascagni, Leoncavallo, and Puccini (*La Bohème*, 1896; *Tosca*, 1900) and in the French Bruneau (*Messidor*, 1897) and Charpentier (*Louise*, 1900). Debussy's *Pelléas et Mélisande* (1902) is a unique application of the impressionist technique to opera, and comes closer than any other modern work to realizing the original Florentine ideal of music as an almost imperceptible support and setting for the poetry.

Recent composers of opera, despite the diversity of musical idioms, are united in the search for objectivity of expression and clarity of musical form. This is evident in three of the most significant operatic works of the period following the first World War: Berg's *Wozzeck* (perf. 1925), with its deliberate employment of classical forms (suite, passacaglia, sonata, etc.); Hindemith's *Cardillac* (1926), a straight "number" opera, in a style which Slonimsky has aptly called "neo-Handelian"; and Milhaud's *Christophe Colomb* (1930), which in its use of large choral and spectacular effects recalls the age of Lully and Rameau. Other phenomena of the post-war period are the jazz-operas

(Weill, Krenek), topical operas (Hindemith's *Neues vom Tage*, 1929) and Shostakovich's propaganda-opera *Lady Macbeth* (perf. 1934). A recent development in England and the United States is the rise of interest in "chamber opera," short works suitable for performance by small or semi-professional groups.

See also *Comic opera; *Operetta; *Ballet in opera; *Singspiel; *Ballad opera; *Libretto.

Lit. (selected): *A. Lexicons:* H. Riemann, *Opern-Handbuch* (1893); Clément and Larousse, *Dictionnaire Lyrique* (1905); Dassori, *Opere operisti* (1903); U. S. Library of Congress, *Catalogue of opera librettos printed before 1800*, 2 vols. (1914); W. Altmann, *Katalog der theatralischen Musik seit 1863* (1934); A. Loewenberg, *Annals of Opera 1597–1940* (1943).

B. Plots of Operas: G. Kobbé, *The Complete Opera Book* (1922, '24); H. E. Krehbiel, *A Book of Operas* (1919); O. Downes, *The Home Book of the Opera* (1937).

C. General History: E. Dent, *History of the Opera* (1942); W. Brockway and H. Weinstock, *The Opera* (1941); H. Kretzschmar, *Geschichte der Oper* (1919; useful for the period before 1800); O. Bie, *Die Oper* (1914); M. Graf, *The Opera and its Future in America* (1941).

D. Special History: A. Solerti, *Gli albori del melodramma*, 3 vols. (1904ff); H. Goldschmidt, *Studien zur Geschichte der italienischen Oper im 17. Jahrhundert*, 2 vols. (1901–04); R. Rolland, *Histoire de l'opéra en Europe avant Lully et Scarlatti* (1895); H. Prunières, *L'opéra italien en France avant Lully* (1914); *id.*, *Cavalli et l'opéra vénétien au xviie siècle* (1931); P.-M. Masson, *L'opéra de Rameau* (1930); E. Dent, *Alessandro Scarlatti* (1905); *id.*, *Foundations of English opera* (1928); *id.*, *Mozart's Operas* (1913); H. Schletterer, *Das deutsche Singspiel* (1863); H. Leichtentritt, *Reinhard Keiser in seinen Opern* (1901); H. Abert, *Niccolo Jommelli als Opernkomponist* (1908); F. Florimo, *La scuola musicale di Napoli*, 4 vols. (1880–83); A. B. Marx, *Gluck und die Oper*, 2 vols.

(1863); L. Schiedermair, *Die deutsche Oper* (1930); R. Newmarch, *The Russian Opera* (1914); E. B. Hill, *Modern French Music* (1924); A. Lorenz, *Das Geheimnis der Form bei Richard Wagner*, 4 vols. (1924–33).

E. Periodical Literature (grouped according to the paragraphs of the preceding article): II: A. Solerti, in *RMI* x. — III: O. G. Sonneck, in *SIM* xv (*Dafne*); A. Tirabassi, in *MQ* xxv (*Orfeo dolente*); W. J. Lawrence, in *MQ* x (Monteverdi); P. Epstein, in *ZMW* x (Monteverdi); L. Torchi, in *RMI* i, ii (instrumental accompaniment). — IV: A. Sandberger, in *JMP* xxxi; H. Kretzschmar, in *VMW* viii and in *JMP* xiv, xvii, xviii; H. C. Wolff, in *ZMW* xvi; A. Solerti, in *RMI* ix (1571–1605); H. Hess, in *Beihefte der IMG* ii.3 (Stradella). — V: D. J. Grout, in *ML* xxii, no. 1; Numéro Spécial, *RM* 1925 (Lully); P. Masson, in *RdM* xi (Rameau). — VI: E. J. Dent, in *PMA* lii; J. Mark, in *ML* v, no. 3 (Dryden). — VII: L. Schiedermaier, in *JMP* xvii; S. Schmidt, in *ZMW* v, vi (1627–1750); A. Sandberger, in *AMW* i (Nürnberg, *c.* 1700); A. Merbach, in *AMW* vi (Hamburg); Kleefeld, in *SIM* i (Hamburg, 1718–50). — VIII: W. Vetter, in *AMW* vi and in *ZMW* vii (Gluck); K. Wörner, in *ZMW* xiii (Gluck); H. Welti, in *VMW* vii (Gluck); W. Vetter, in *ZMW* xiv (Vienna, 1750); M. Callegori, in *RMI* xxvi, xxviii (Metastasio). — IX: H. Abert, in *ZMW* i (Joh. Chr. Bach); H. Kretzschmar, in *JMP* xii (Mozart); H. Strobel, in *ZMW* vi (Méhul); H. Leichtentritt, in *MQ* xiv (Schubert); W. Altmann, in *SIM* iv (Spontini); G. Schünemann, in *ZMW* v (Mendelssohn); S. Goddard, in *ML* x, no. 3 (*Boris Godunov*).   D. J. G.

Opera buffa. See *Comic opera.

Opera comique. See *Comic opera.

Opera houses. The first opera house was the *Teatro San Cassiano* in Venice, founded 1637; previously, opera performances had been given in private rooms and for invited guests only. There followed foundations in London (1656),

[514]

Paris (1669), Rome (1671), Hamburg (1678). After 1700, opera houses became common in all the musical centers of Europe. The most important opera houses of the present day are listed below.
I. America, United States. New York: *Metropolitan Opera House.* — Boston: *Opera House.* — Chicago: *Opera House.*
II. Latin America. Buenos Aires: *Opera*; *Teatro Colón.* — Rio de Janeiro: *Teatro Municipal.*
III. Austria. Vienna: *Staatsoper*; *Volksoper.*
IV. England. London: *Royal Covent Garden.*
V. Germany. Berlin: *Staatsoper*; *Städtische Oper* (Charlottenburg). — Dresden: *Sächsisches Staatstheater.* — Hamburg: *Stadttheater.* — Munich: *Bayrisches Staatstheater.* — Bayreuth: *Festspielhaus* (Wagner operas). — There exist about 30 more opera houses in smaller German cities [cf. A. Einstein, *Das Neue Musiklexikon* (1926), p. 464].
VI. France. Paris: *Théâtre National de l'Opéra*; *Opéra-Comique.*
VII. Italy. Rome: *Teatro Costanzi*; *Teatro Adriano.* — Milan: *Teatro alla Scala.* — Venice: *Teatro la Fenice.* — Torino: *Teatro Regio.* — Bologna: *Teatro Communale.* — Naples: *Teatro San Carlo.* — Genoa: *Teatro Carlo Felice.*
VIII. Spain. Madrid: *Teatro Real.*
For more detailed information see Pierre Key's *Music Year Book.*

Operetta [It., little opera]. In the 18th century the term is used for a short opera. In the 19th and 20th centuries it denotes a theatrical piece of light and sentimental character in simple and popular style, containing spoken dialogue, music, dancing scenes, etc. The modern operetta originated in Vienna with Franz von Suppé (1819–95; 31 operettas between 1834 and 1894) and in Paris with Jacques Offenbach (1819–80; *c.* 90 operettas between 1855 and 1879). The latter's *Orphée aux Enfers* ("Orpheus in the Underworld") and *La Belle Hélène* are famous for their satirical treatment of Greek mythology. Johann Strauss, Jr. (1825–99), raised the Viennese operetta to inter-

national fame with *c.* 30 operettas written between 1871 and 1895, among which *Die Fledermaus* ("The Bat," 1874) has remained on the repertory to the present day. At the same time Arthur Sullivan (1842–1900) wrote English operettas (mostly on librettos by W. S. Gilbert) which represent the highest point attained in English dramatic music since Purcell.
In the United States the operetta was cultivated mainly by Victor Herbert (1859–1924), composer of *The Wizard of the Nile* (1895) and many other operettas, and by Reginald de Koven (1859–1920), remembered mainly from his first operetta *Robin Hood* (1890). Among the more recent contributions *Firefly* (1912), by Rudolf Friml (b. 1884), *The Student Prince*, by Sigmund Romberg (b. 1887), and *Show Boat* (1929), by Jerome Kern, may be mentioned.
Lit.: M. S. Mackinley, *Light Opera* (1926); A. F. Beach, *Preparation and Presentation of the Operetta* (for Public Schools); K. R. Umfleet, *School Operettas and their Production*; O. Keller, *Die Operette in ihrer geschichtlichen Entwicklung* (1925). Cf. *MoML*, 583.

Ophicleide. See *Brass instruments V (c).

Opus [L., work; F. *oeuvre*], abbreviated op., indicates in conjunction with figures (op. 1, op. 2) the chronological position of a composition within the entire output of a composer. The opus-numbers are not always reliable owing to the fact that they are usually applied in the order of publication, rather than of composition. One of the first composers to use opus-numbers was Biagio Marini (op. 1, 1617). Bach never numbered his compositions, and with Haydn as well as with Mozart the opus-numbers are applied so inconsistently and haphazardly (frequently by the publisher rather than by the composer) that they are practically valueless. Beethoven was the first to use opus-number with a sufficient degree of consistency, at least for his greater works.

Orageux [F.]. Stormy.

Oratio [L.]. See *Mass A.

Oratoric. Oratoric rhythm [see
*Rhythm II (c)]. Oratoric(al) neumes,
same as staffless neumes [see *Neumes
II].

Oratorio. I. *Definition.* The composition of an extended libretto of religious
or contemplative character performed in
a concert hall or church, i.e., without
scenery, costumes, or action, by solo
voices, chorus, and orchestra. This explanation should be understood as a general description rather than a definition
which would cover every single example.
Especially in the early history of the
oratorio one encounters many exceptional
features, e.g., the earliest oratorios were
usually performed in an operatic manner,
with scenery and costumes. In such a
case, the more contemplative and less
dramatic character of the libretto is the
chief mark of distinction. Characteristic
features of musical style distinguishing
the oratorio from the opera are the greater
emphasis on the chorus, the absence of
quick dialogue (question and answer in
quick succession), and, frequently, the
narrator [It. *testo*] who introduces the
personalities and connects their parts.
Compositions of a similar character but
based on a scriptural or liturgical text
(Mass, Requiem, Passion) are usually not
included under the category oratorio.
There exist, however, Passion oratorios,
in which the story of the Passion is freely
told. From the sacred cantata (Bach)
the oratorio is distinguished by its
greater extension and by the more narrative and continuous character of the
libretto.

II. *History to 1650.* Early types of dramatic music in the character of an oratorio are the *liturgical dramas of the
later Middle Ages and the *mysteries of
the 14th/15th centuries. More properly,
the history of the oratorio began in the
mid-16th century when Filippo Neri inaugurated, in Rome, a special order called
"oratoriani" and founded a building
called "oratorio" (oratory, chapel) in
which regular services of a popular char-

acter — similar in a way to those of the
Salvation Army — were held. These included reading from the Scriptures, ser-
mon, and the singing of *laude. A special type of the latter were the "dialogue-
laude," i.e., religious poems in the form
of a dialogue between God and the Soul,
Heaven and Hell, etc. These were performed by different singers or, more accurately — considering their polyphonic
style — by different groups of singers who
might have dressed according to the characters they represented. It is from these
presentations (called "rappresentazione,"
"storia," "esempio," "misterio") that the
oratorio proper developed. Palestrina as
well as other famous 16th-century composers is reputed to have written music
for such occasions, but nothing has been
preserved prior to Emilio Cavalieri's (*c.*
1550–1602) *Rappresentazione di anima
e di corpo* (1600; see *Editions VI, 10;
also *SchGMB*, 169, 170; *HAM*, no. 182),
a work which regarding both date and
style is close to the earliest operas (Peri,
Caccini). In fact, some modern writers
(Alaleone) have denied it a place in the
history of the oratorio and, mainly on
account of its elaborate stage production
(including the simultaneous [*sic*] representation of Heaven, Earth, and Hell,
splendid costumes and ballets; cf. *GD*
iii, 709), have placed it in the category of
"sacred opera," a later example of which
is Steffano Landi's *Il San Alessio* (1632).
At any rate, it would seem as though this
work were an isolated attempt which
failed to establish a tradition. More successful in this respect was the *Teatro
Armonico Spirituale* (1619) of Giov.
Francesco Anerio (1567–1620) in which
a refined madrigal style is used for the
choral portions, alternating with monody
for the solistic parts among which we
already find the narrator. Steffano Landi
(*c.* 1590–1658) wrote an oratorio *Daniel*
[see *Editions II, 5]. Another important
work, greatly celebrated in its day, was
Domenico Mazzocchi's (1592–1665)
Querimonia di S. Maria Maddalena (*c.*
1640?). It is an example of the *oratorio
volgare,* i.e., an oratorio written in the
vernacular, not in Latin.

III. *1650–1800*. Around the middle of the 17th century the oratorio entered a new phase, owing to the activity of Giac. Carissimi (1605–74) who, in his *Jephtha, Judicium Salomonis, Jonas, Extremum Judicium* [see *Editions VI, 5], etc., created the first oratorios which, according to their extension and diversity of treatment, would seem to be fully deserving of this name [example in *HAM*, no. 207]. Carissimi's successors in the field of the oratorio were Antonio Draghi (1635–1700; c. 40 oratorios), Alessandro Stradella (1645–82) with his oratorios *S. Giovanno Battista* and *Susanna* [cf. *SchGMB*, no. 230], and Alessandro Scarlatti (1659–1725) who wrote a great number of oratorios (eighteen are preserved with the music) which approximate rather closely the style of his operas but are, on the whole, much less successful than these. The oratorios of Antonio Lotti (1667–1740) and Antonio Caldara (1670–1736), both representatives of the Roman-Venetian tradition, are more reserved in style, combining a noble dignity with a slightly sentimental pathos, while Leonardo Leo (1694–1744), Johann Adolph Hasse (1699–1783; *La Conversione di San Agostino, DdT* 20), and Niccolo Jommelli (1714–74; *La Passione*, see *Editions VI, 15) continued the Neapolitan type of virtuosity and vocal display, thus removing the oratorio even farther from its ideal.

At the beginning of the German oratorio stands Heinrich Schütz with his *Historia der Auferstehung* (1623) and his Christmas Oratorio (*Historia von der . . . Geburt Christi*, 1664), a work the artistic significance of which is no less than that of Bach's Christmas Oratorio written one century later. Oratorios by Selle (1642), Theile (1672), and Sebastiani (1672) belong to the special category of the Passion [see *Passion B], and later composers such as Weckmann, Buxtehude, Rosenmüller preferred the smaller form of the cantata. Thus J. S. Bach would seem to have been the first to take up again the tradition of Schütz in his great *Christmas Oratorio* (1733/34) and in the less important *Easter Oratorio*

(1736?). There followed Johann Ernst Eberlin with *Der blutschwitzende Jesus* (*DTOe* 28.i), Georg Ph. Telemann (1681–1767) with his highly dramatic *Der Tag des Gerichts* of 1761 (*DdT* 28), and Johann Christoph Friedrich Bach (1732–95) with *Die Kindheit Jesu* and *Die Auferweckung des Lazarus* (*DdT* 56). This development came to a fitting close with the truly remarkable oratorios of C. P. E. Bach (*Die Israeliten in der Wüste*, 1775; *Die Auferstehung und Himmelfahrt Jesu*, 1787) which, in a typical mixture of styles, look back to the works of his father as well as forward to Haydn [cf. the study by W. H. Hadow, in *OH* iv].

The English oratorio is represented by Handel who, after a few early works (*La Resurrezione*, 1708), turned to oratorio writing mainly after his dissatisfaction with his operatic activity and whose *Israel in Egypt* (1737), *Messiah* (1742), *Judas Maccabeus* (1746), and *Jephtha* (1751) stand out as lasting monuments of his greatness. In contradistinction to Bach's devotional attitude, Handel approached the oratorio from a boldly subjective point of view, making it the expression of his own dynamic personality and incorporating the elements of his dramatic opera style. It is interesting to note that Handel's oratorios were designed to be performed during the period of Lent, at which period theatrical performances were forbidden by law. These Lenten oratorios were continued by John Christopher Smith (1712–95), Charles John Stanley (1713–86), and others. While Thomas Arne (1710–78), in his *Abel* (1744) and *Judith* (1764), succeeded in saving himself from complete submission to the Handelian domination, the English oratorio entered, with Arne's death in 1775, "on a century of artistic darkness, over which brooded from first to last the elephantine shadow of Handel, to which was added in the final thirty years the almost equally universal though less ostentatiously ponderous shadow of Mendelssohn. The composers of these tons of oratorios were 'all honourable men'; but . . . their music is nothing worse than intolerably dull" (*GD* iii, 721f).

An important, though little known, development of the oratorio took place in France, beginning with Carissimi's pupil Marc-Antoine Charpentier (1634–1704) whose oratorios ("Histoires sacrées": *Judicium Salomonis; Filius prodigus, Le Reniement de St. Pierre*, etc., all with Latin text) combine masterly technique with depth of feeling and dramatic expression [cf. *HAM*, no. 226]. Unfortunately he found no successors in his country.

IV. *1800–Present.* Joseph Haydn (1732–1809), after his *Il Ritorno di Tobia* (1775; said to be "the finest example of 18th-century Italian oratorio that exists" [*GD* iii, 718]) and his highly expressive **Seven Words on the Cross* (1797), wrote the two works which inaugurated a new era in oratorio writing, *Die Schöpfung* ("The Creation," 1797) and *Die Jahreszeiten* ("The Seasons," 1801), the latter of which, though authentically named "Oratorio," belongs to the secular rather than the religious field. Compared with these master works which stand at the summit of a long life of creative activity, Beethoven's early *Christus am Ölberg* ("Mount of Olives," op. 85, composed 1800, publ. 1811) is insignificant. In the first half of the 19th century Germany was passing through a period of oratorio worship similar to that of England, and the works of Ludwig Spohr (1784–1859: *Das letzte Gericht*), Friedrich Schneider (1786–1853), and Karl Loewe (1796–1869: *Hiob*, 1848) enjoyed a popularity which is hardly justified by their artistic merits but which lasted undiminished until Mendelssohn (1809–47) appeared with his *St. Paul* (1836) and *Elijah* (1846), oratorios which, with their romantically colored Bach-Handel style, have retained a lasting place of honor, particularly in England.

After Mendelssohn quite a number of composers have ventured into the field of the oratorio (Wagner, *Das Liebesmahl der Apostel*, 1844; Liszt, *The Legend of St. Elizabeth*, 1862, and *Christus*, 1866;

Dvořák, *St. Ludmila*, 1886; Berlioz, *L'Enfance du Christ*, 1854; Franck, *Les Béatitudes*, 1879; *Rebecca*, 1881, etc.; d'Indy, *La Légende de Saint-Christophe*, properly a stage work) but, on the whole, with conspicuous lack of success. The only great contribution of this period is Brahms's *Deutsches Requiem* (op. 45, 1857–68), a work which, although not an oratorio in the strict sense of the word (it is based, not on a free text, but on scriptural passages), cannot be omitted in a description of this form. In England there occurred, after more than a century of utter mediocrity, a notable revival, in oratorios such as Hubert Parry's *Judith* (1888), *Job* (1892), and *King Saul* (1894); Elgar's *The Dream of Gerontius* (1900), *The Apostles* (1903), and *The Kingdom* (1906); Walford Davies' *Everyman* (1904); and William Walton's *Belshazzar's Feast* (1931), compositions practically all of which were written for and performed at one of the British Festivals. Among the American oratorios Horatio Parker's *The Legend of St. Christopher* and *Hora novissima*, as well as Paine's *St. Peter*, must be mentioned.

Recently Arthur Honegger has opened new possibilities for the oratorio in his *Le Roi David* (1923) by abandoning the "lyrical emotionalism" of the romantic oratorio, and by incorporating archaic idioms which bestow upon the work an impressive touch of "biblical greatness." Other living composers have cultivated the secular oratorio, e.g., Stravinsky in his *Oedipus Rex* (1927, with stage action), Hindemith in *Das Unaufhörliche* (1931), Hermann Reutter in *Der grosse Kalender* (1933).

Lit.: A. Schering, *Geschichte des Oratoriums* (1911); A. Patterson, *The Story of the Oratorio* (1909); *LavE* i.3, 1546ff (French oratorio); E. Vogl, *Die Oratorientechnik Carissimi's* (Diss. Prague 1928); D. Alaleone, *Studi della storia dell oratorio musicale in Italia* (1908); A. Schering, in *JMP*, 1903 and in *SIM* viii; K. Meyer, "Das Offizium und seine Beziehung zum Oratorium" (*AMW* iii); M. Brenet, "Les Oratoires de Carissimi"

(*RMI* iv); H. Vogel, "Das Oratorium in Wien, 1725–40" (*StM* xiv).

Orchésographie. See under *Dance music II.

Orchestra and orchestration [Gr., literally "dancing place," i.e., that portion of the Greek theater — situated between the auditorium and the stage, as in the modern opera — which was reserved for the dancing of the chorus and also for the instrumentalists].

I. *General.* In the common meaning of the term, a large ensemble of instruments, as distinct from small ensembles (one player to the part) used for chamber music or from ensembles consisting of special instruments, called *band. The modern orchestra (symphony orchestra) consists of about 100 instruments which are divided into four groups: strings (*c.* 60), wood winds (*c.* 15), brass (*c.* 15), and percussion (*c.* 10). To the first group belong the violins, divided into first and second violin, the violas, the celli, and the double-basses — also the harp; to the second, the flutes, oboes, English horn, bassoons, and clarinets; to the third, the horns, trumpets, trombones, and tubas; to the fourth, the kettledrums, side drums, glockenspiel, celesta, xylophone, tambourin, triangle, cymbals, etc. The Boston Symphony Orchestra included in 1944 the following: three flutes and piccolo; three oboes and English horn; three clarinets and bass clarinet; three bassoons and double bassoon; seven horns, four trumpets, four trombones, tuba; two timpanists, three percussion players, eighteen first violins, sixteen second violins, twelve violas, ten violoncellos, nine double basses, two harps.

The *strings* are the backbone of the orchestra and, in general, are given the most important melodic parts of the score. Highly expressive, adaptable, and not too "individual," they never become tiring and are, therefore, used throughout the composition with only short interruptions. Next in importance as melody instruments are *wood winds* each of which has a very characteristic timbre and one which, although highly attrac-

tive at first, tends to tire the listener's ear if it continues too long. The wood winds must, therefore, be used sparingly as color effects imposed upon the basic drawing of the violins. In the *brass* group, the horns (French horn) are rather similar in character and in use to the wood winds. Particularly in early symphonies (Haydn, Mozart) they are usually combined with the oboes. The trumpets and trombones, the "heavy artillery" of the orchestra, chiefly serve as a reinforcement for the climaxes of massed sound. They are, however, also valuable for soft effects and as soloist instruments, the trombones to express solemn grandeur, the trumpets for brilliant passages of a military or similar character. The *percussion* group contributes rhythmic life to the orchestra and also special effects (triangle, cymbals, celesta) which are the more effective the more sparingly they are used.

II. *History up to 1700.* While instruments must have been played together ever since their invention, any systematic combination in larger groups which takes into consideration questions of balance, capabilities, and individual characteristics was but slowly realized. What music of the Middle Ages and the Renaissance can be identified as "instrumental" [see *Instrumental music; *Instruments, history] was chamber rather than orchestral music. This does not mean to say that larger ensembles did not exist; they were, however, used mainly for ceremonial and festive purposes (fanfares, etc., for royal welcomes, banquets) which fell outside the scope of the composer. It is perhaps no coincidence that the first composer to utilize orchestral resources, Giovanni Gabrieli (1557–1612), worked in Venice, then the wealthiest and most cosmopolitan city of Europe, where ceremonial receptions and other celebrations were the order of the day. His *Sacrae symphoniae*, written *c.* 1600, are the first compositions to use a specific instrument for each part, namely, in addition to voices, cornetti, trombones, bassoons, and violins [see *Editions XIV, 2 (nos. 6, 11, 12, 16); cf. also *HAM*, no. 173]. Little distinction, however, is made between the capabilities of the various instruments. Claudio Monteverdi's *Orfeo* (1607) is a landmark of even greater interest in the early history of the orchestra, as it shows the attempts to treat the instruments individually and to achieve special orchestral effects. His orchestra consisted of: two harpsichords (*gravicembano*), two double bass viols (*contrabasso de viola*), ten viols (*viola da brazzo*), one harp (*arpa doppia*), two violins (*violino piccolo alla Francese*), two bass lutes (*chitarone*), two organs with wooden pipes (*organo di legno*), three bass viols (*basso da gamba*), four trombones, one *regal, two *cornetts, one small recorder (*flauto alla vigesima seconda*), one high trumpet (*clarino*), and three "soft" trumpets (*trombe sordine*). Although, in conformity with the then novel practice of *thorough-bass, the score consists, in the main, of the vocal parts and the bass part only, written directions are supplied from which an idea of the desired orchestral effects can be obtained. For instance, in Act III, Caronte (Charon) is always accompanied by the regal, Orfeo by the organo di legno [cf. *HAM*, no. 187].

While Monteverdi's individual use of the instruments probably represents an innovation, his orchestra as such is not at all as novel as the modern viewer is inclined to believe. In its emphasis on wind instruments and on strongly contrasting groups it is a Renaissance rather than a Baroque orchestra, and this interpretation explains the fact that his precedence remained entirely without succession. The Baroque favored the bowed instruments with their expressive qualities [see *Instruments, history], and it is only in the use of a relatively strong string section that Monteverdi's orchestra is progressive.

The 17th-century emphasis on the bowed instruments and the prevailing practice of thorough-bass scoring (melody and bass only) were not conducive to progress in the use of orchestral resources. Lully's famous orchestra was significantly called "les vingt-quatre violons du Roi," but, around 1700, included a well-defined group of wind instruments, flutes, oboes, and horns in addition to the violins which, by this time, had replaced the earlier viols.

III. *18th Century*. By the time of Bach (1685–1750), instruments and the technique of performance on them had been improved, and various effective combinations had been worked out. Bach's Cantata no. 119 (1723) utilizes the following: 4 voice parts, 4 trumpets, 2 timpani, 2 flutes, 3 oboes, 2 oboi da caccia, first violins, second violins, violas, and continuo, the last to be played by violoncelli and an organ (or harpsichord). An impartial distribution of interchangeable parts between string and wind instruments is the sum of Bach's method of orchestration; each of the four fundamental parts — as opposed to the three or five of the 17th century — is independent, melodic, essential, and conceived in general, not individual, instrumental terms. Thus a part, whether for the voice, a flute, an oboe, violins, or even brass, can scarcely be identified save by range. Wholesale duplication of the fundamental parts is common. In the arias, where smaller groups of instruments are used, these, as well as special effects such as pizzicato and con sordino, are carried through the entire number, the contrast being from number to number, rather than occurring within a piece, as in 19th-century practice.

Handel, appealing to a wider public and possessing a keener sense for orchestral effect, treated his instrumental forces in a more broadly contrasting style than does Bach, yet he did not depart from the "contrapuntal orchestration." His occasional use of the small recorder, contrabassoon, trombone, and harp in his operas and cantatas is exceptional for the period, while his purely instrumental compositions are often for groups much more restricted than those of Bach. For evidence of the fact that the make-up of the orchestra was not as yet standardized, one has but to examine the four Orchestral Suites of Bach.

While the orchestra as such remained largely unchanged throughout the 18th century, important progress was made in its treatment. Perhaps the first composer to give each instrument a distinct part of its own was Rameau (1683–1764). He introduced interesting and unexpected passages on the flutes, oboes, and bassoons and thus opened the path to the coloristic treatment of the modern orchestra. Johann Stamitz (1717–57), the leader of the famous Mannheim orchestra [see *Mannheim School], developed the dramatic resources of the orchestra, chiefly the string section, by the use of dynamic varieties such as sudden ff and pp, sustained crescendos, etc. C. P. E. Bach's four symphonies, written about 1776, may be said to represent the final phase of orchestration prior to the masterworks of Haydn and Mozart. They are scored for two flutes, two oboes, one or two bassoons, two horns, and the usual group of strings. The strings give melodic activity and figuration while the winds provide harmony and body. The interchangeable instrumental part of the past gives way to a part characteristic of the instrument for which it is written, though features of the older style remain in the frequent unison of the first and second violins and the near identity of viola, cello, and bass parts including the harpsichord [cf. the example in *GD* v, 207].

IV. *From Haydn to the Present.* During the period of Haydn and Mozart the stringed instruments assumed their position as the foundation of the orchestra, and their numbers grew larger in proportion to the number of performers in the entire group. Each wind instrument is regarded as capable of assuming the main melodic line if the occasion demands, as well as aiding in the supplying of the harmonic background, since the keyboard instrument is no longer used for that purpose. Instruments are no longer omitted from entire movements of a work, except in the trio of the minuet, and the orchestral color changes on a moment to moment basis, emphasizing the changes of subjects and the alternation of motifs. The instrumental group has become standardized: late symphonic works by Haydn, Mozart (with exceptions), and

the majority of those by Beethoven call for two flutes, two oboes, two clarinets, two bassoons, two horns, two trumpets, two timpani, and the standard group of strings, consisting of first violins, second violins, violas, violoncellos, and double basses.

The 19th century owes much to Berlioz regarding the use of instruments for their particular tonal quality, and his ambitious and imaginative compositions have greatly influenced later composers such as Liszt, Wagner, and Strauss. Berlioz seems to rise suddenly as an innovator during the 1830's, but if one considers the works of earlier composers, largely of the French School, one will realize that his apparently original work is well founded on the coloristic efforts of Gluck, Cherubini, Méhul, Spontini, Boieldieu, and Weber.

For an example of the extreme in the development of the orchestra which took place prior to approximately 1914 it will be interesting to consider the resources demanded by Gustav Mahler (1860–1911) in his Eighth Symphony: piccolo, four flutes, four oboes, English horn, E-flat clarinet, three B-flat clarinets, bass clarinet, four bassoons, contrabassoon; eight horns, four trumpets, four trombones, tuba, timpani, bass drum, cymbals, tam-tam, triangle, chimes, glockenspiel, celesta; piano, harmonium, organ, two harps, mandolin; four trumpets and three trombones as a fanfare group; first and second soprano, first and second alto, tenor, baritone, and bass soloists, two mixed choruses, boys' choir; first violins, second violins, violas, violoncellos, and double-basses. While such methods represent the acme as well as the end of the 19th-century development, there have been, in the past forty years, important tendencies towards new goals. Debussy introduced into the orchestra new methods of utter refinement and a highly developed coloristic technique for which the characteristic name "orchestral palette" has been widely adopted [see *Impressionism]. The musical revolution known as *New music has naturally brought with it many changes in the orchestral technique. The giant orchestra of the Mahler period is replaced by small groups, frequently approaching the size of a chamber orchestra, a change which may be illustrated by comparing two works of Stravinsky (b. 1882): the one, his *Rite of Spring* (1911–13), utilizes an instrumental group even larger than the above list (though without vocalists), while his *Histoire du Soldat* (1918) is scored for one violin, one double-bass, one clarinet, one bassoon, one cornet, one trombone, and eight percussion instruments handled by one player. While this may be an extreme case, the tendency has been to score for the instruments on the basis of musical requirements, rather than of availability in the so-called standard orchestra. The reaction against the 19th-century principles of orchestration appears also in the current method, frequent in Stravinsky, of "perverted orchestration," e.g., giving the melody to the brass and using the strings for percussive effects. Although this method was originally devised for parodistic purposes, it has become fairly generally accepted into the present orchestral technique.

V. *The Reading of Orchestral Scores.* From early in the 19th century it has been the practice to lay out an orchestral score in the following order, starting at the top of the page: wood wind, brass, percussion, strings. If a harp is used it is placed immediately above the strings, but should voices and organ be also used, these are written between the harp and the strings. In general, the instruments of each group are arranged in the order of from high to low pitch, though this is not always the case. The accurate reading of a modern orchestral score is rendered extremely difficult — unnecessarily difficult, indeed — by the use of two special notational devices, viz., the "ancient" clefs (alto and tenor) and the transposed writing for numerous wind instruments, devices both of which go back to earlier practice but have persisted to the present day with a reactionary tenacity which has but few counterparts in modern life [see *Clefs; *Transposing instruments].

While these difficulties can be mastered only by long study, the musical amateur who merely wishes to "follow" a performance with a score may well disregard them and content himself with acquiring facility in glancing quickly over the page and catching the momentarily leading melody from its general melodic contour and rhythm.

See also the special articles for the different instruments as well as those on *Conducting; *Score. Numerous examples illustrating the history of the orchestral score are contained in the article "Strumentazione" of the *Enciclopedia Italiana*.

Lit.: P. Bekker, *The Story of the Orchestra* (1936); A. Elson, *Orchestral Instruments and Their Use* (1923); Johnstone and Stringham, *Instruments of the Modern Symphony Orchestra* (1928); K. Schlesinger, *Instruments of the Modern Orchestra* (1910); V. Bakaleinikoff, *The Instruments of the Band and Orchestra* (1940); C. Forsyth, *Orchestration* (1935); S. Lockwood, *Elementary Orchestration* (1926); E. Wellesz, *Die neue Instrumentation* (1928); N. Rimsky-Korsakov, *Principles of Orchestration* (1922); M. Bernstein, *Introduction to Orchestration* (1942); A. Carse, *The History of Orchestration* (1925); L. A. Coerne, *The Evolution of Modern Orchestration* (1908); C. S. Terry, *Bach's Orchestration* (1932); W. Kleefeld, "Die Orchester der Hamburger Oper, 1678–1738" (*SIM* i); H. Goldschmidt, "Das Orchester der italienischen Oper im 17. Jahrhundert" (*SIM* ii); K. Nef, "Zur Instrumentation im 17. Jahrhundert" (*JMP* xxxv); J. Lawrence, "The English Theatre Orchestra . . ." (*MQ* iii); A. Carse, "17th Century Orchestral Instruments" (*ML* i, no. 4); R. Haas, "Zur Frage der Orchesterbesetzung in der zweiten Hälfte des 18. Jahrhunderts" (*KIM*, 1909, p. 159); A. Carse, "Brass Instruments in the Orchestra, Historical Sketch" (*ML* iii, no. 4); G. F. Malipiero, in *RMI* xxiii, xxiv.   W. D. D.
(II and III with additions by W. A.)

Orchestras. Following is a selected list of important orchestras (with date of foundation and present conductor): I. United States: Los Angeles Philharmonic O. (1919; Alfred Wallenstein). — Baltimore Symphony O. (1916; Reginald Stewart). — Boston Symphony O. (1881; Serge Koussevitzky). — Chicago Symphony O. (1891; Desiré Defauw). — Cincinnati Symphony O. (1895; Eugene Goossens). — Cleveland Symphony O. (1918; Erich Leinsdorf). — Detroit Symphony O. (1913; Karl Krueger).—Indianapolis Symphony O. (1930; Fabien Sevitzky. — Minneapolis Symphony O. (1903; Dmitri Mitropoulos). — New York, Philharmonic-Symphony O. (1842; Arthur Rodzinski). — Philadelphia O. (1900; Eugene Ormandy). — Pittsburgh Symphony O. (1895; Fritz Reiner). — Rochester Philharmonic O. (1922; José Iturbi). — St. Louis Symphony O. (1880; Vladimir Golschmann). — San Francisco Symphony O. (1909; Pierre Monteux). — Washington, National Symphony O. (1931; Hans Kindler).

II. Latin America: Bogotá (Colombia), Orquesta Sinfónica Nacional (1936, Guillermo Espinosa). — Buenos Aires (Argentina), Orguesta del Teatro Colon (1908, Juan José Castro). — Caracas (Venezuela), Orquesta Sinfónica (1935, Emilio Sojo). — Guatemala, Orquesta Progesista (1936, Gaston Pellegrini). — Havana (Cuba), Orquesta Filarmónica (1924, Massimo Freccia).—Lima (Peru), Orquesta Sinfónica Nacional (1938, Theo Buchwald).—Mexico, Orquesta Sinfónica de Mexico (1928; Carlos Chavez). — Montevideo (Uruguay), Orquesta Sinfónica del Servicio Oficial de Dufusión Radio Electrica, abbr. Ossodre (1931, Lamberto Baldi). — Rio de Janeiro (Brazil), Orquestra del Teatro Municipal (various conductors); Orquestra Brasileira (1940, Eugene Szenkaz). — Santiago (Chile), Orquesta Sinfónica de Chile (1922, Armando Carvajal).

III. Europe: Amsterdam, Concertgebouw Orchestra (1883; Willem Mengelberg). — Berlin, Philharmonisches Orchester (1882; Wilhelm Furtwängler). — Dresden, Orchester der Staatsoper (Karl Böhm). — Leipzig, Gewandhauskonzerte (1781; Wilhelm Furtwängler).

— London, Philharmonic Orchestra (1932; Sir Thomas Beecham); British Broadcasting Company Orchestra, B. B. C. O. (1930; Sir Adrian C. Boult). — Munich, Bayrisches Staatsorchester (1911; Clemens Kraus).—Munich, Konzertverein or Philharmoniker (Oswald Kabasta). — Paris, Concerts du Conservatoire (1792; Charles Munch); Concerts Colonne (1874; Paul Paray); Concerts Pasdeloup (1918; Albert Wolf). — Rome, Concerti dell Augusteo (1908; Bernardo Molinari). — Vienna, Wiener Philharmonische Konzerte (1842; guest conductors).

Lit.: M. Grant and H. S. Hettinger, *American Symphony Orchestras* (1940); Pierre Key's *Music Year Book*; A. Eaglefield-Hull, *Dictionary of Modern Music* (1924), article "Orchestras"; A. Einstein, *Das Neue Musiklexikon* (1926), article "Orchester."

Orchestrion. See *Mechanical instruments III.

Ordinary (Ordinarium), and Proper (Proprium). In the Catholic rites, the Ordinary (also called *Common*) is that portion of the service which remains the same for the different days, whereas the Proper includes all the variable texts and chants. The distinction is particularly important with the Mass [see *Mass A]. Other services, however, also comprise invariable and variable portions. For instance, the *Magnificat forms a part of the Ordinary of Vespers. For another application of the terms, see *Gregorian chant I.

Ordo [L., pl. *ordines*]. See *Modes, rhythmic.

Ordre [F.]. In F. Couperin's *Pièces de Clavecin* (1713–30), name for his suitelike collections of pieces in the same key. An ordre usually begins with a few pieces in the style of an allemande, courante, and sarabande, but also includes a great many other pieces with fanciful or descriptive titles. See *Suite III.

Organ. I. *General Description*. The organ is a keyboard instrument consisting of a series of pipes placed on a *wind chest supplied with valves operated by the keys through the medium of a purely mechanical apparatus or through the agency of pneumatics or electrical intermediaries. Means are also provided for delivering a constant supply of compressed air at a steady pressure. This is accomplished by bellows having manually operated *feeders, or they may be worked by hydraulic or electrical means. In recent years the feeders have been replaced by a suitably designed rotary blower, in which case the bellows consist of a reservoir, the top of which is weighted or sprung to ensure a steady pressure being supplied to the pipes through a wind pipe connecting the reservoir with the wind chest. The simplest organ consists of one set of pipes, there being but one pipe per note of the keyboard. To enable a variety of tone color to be available for use by the performer organs usually have several sets (ranks) of pipes, technically known as stops, which can be brought into play or retired at will.

II. *Mechanism*. In the older organs the sounding of a desired pipe, say, the pipe c of the *rank (*register, *stop) Principal, or, in other words, the admission of wind to this particular pipe, was effected by a combination of two mechanisms operating crosswise, the sliders and the pallets. Assuming a miniature organ with three ranks and seven keys, there will be twenty-one pipes and, consequently, twenty-one holes arranged in three lines of seven each, in the upper board of the wind chest. To each rank there corresponds an oblong board (slider) bored with seven holes which can be moved sideways by drawing or pushing a knob (stop, draw stop) located at the sides of the keyboard. To each key there belongs a hinged lid (pallet) crossing the sliders, which is operated by the key through the "action" (corresponding in a way to the action of the pianoforte; older organs have a mechanical action consisting of a series of rods called trackers and stickers, while in modern organs this is usually replaced by

a pneumatic or electric action). In order to obtain the desired tone, the player draws the knob Principal, thus causing the corresponding slider to move sideways so that its holes come to coincide with those of the chest board. He then depresses the key C thus causing the corresponding pallet to move downward in its hinge. The hole "C on Principal" is now open to the wind and the pipe sounds. In the modern organ the sliders are dispensed with and an individual valve is provided for each pipe on the chest. In this case the stop control is by means of electrical switches or some form of pneumatic action, and the drawing stops are replaced by balanced slips of ivory which are simply tipped over.

III. *Keyboards and Divisions*. An organ which can be considered as having the minimum requirement for a proper rendition of the literature of the instrument will comprise two keyboards (*manuals) each controlling a separate division with five or six stops each, and a clavier for the feet (pedal) commanding two to five stops. Organs having four manuals and a pedal with fifty to one hundred stops, however, are common, and even five to seven keyboards have been employed. The divisions or "organs" connected with the various keyboards are called: Pedal Organ, Great Organ, Swell Organ, Choir Organ, Solo Organ, and Echo Organ. Their allotment to the various manuals varies a great deal (except, of course, for the Pedal Organ), and so does the selection of pipes connected with each of them. The latter statement is particularly true if organs of different periods are considered. The specification given in section XI of this article may be studied for additional information on this point. Some of these divisions, particularly the Swell organ, are included in a swell box [see VII].

IV. *Couplers, etc*. Practically every organ possesses devices which make the various divisions available on other keyboards than their own. These are the so-called couplers. For instance, Coupler Swell-to-Great makes the Swell Organ available on the manual for the Great

Organ, so that stops from the former can be sounded together with stops from the latter. Similarly, any manual can be coupled to the Pedal and the Pedal can be coupled to the main manuals or to all of them. Sub-octave couplers and super-octave couplers connect one manual with the lower or higher octave of another manual. See also *Divided stops.

Modern organ playing requires many changes of *registration within a composition, frequently at places where the hands of the player are too occupied on the keyboard to manipulate a number of stops. To facilitate such changes, special stops, usually in the shape of small round buttons (called pistons), are provided, the so-called combination stops (composition stops). Each of these controls an ad libitum selection of ranks which the player can arrange in advance and which are brought into play by merely touching the button. These can also be made available on stops operated by the feet, the combination (or composition) pedals.

V. *Compass.* The compass of the organ manual is sixty-one notes or five complete octaves extending from C to c'''. That of the pedal clavier is thirty-two notes or two and one-half octaves extending from C_1 to g'. Actually, the compass of the organ is much larger than that of its keyboards, owing to the fact that there exist, in addition to the pipes of normal pitch (comparable to that of the pianoforte), others the pitch of which is one or two octaves lower or higher. The normal pitch is called unison and is indicated by the symbol 8′ [read eight-foot; see *Foot (2)], the sub-octave pitch is 16′, and three super-octave pitches exist, designated 4′, 2′, and 1′. On the pedal the normal pitch, being an octave below than of the manual, is known as 16′ pitch, its sub-octave being 32′. The frequency of 32′ C is approximately 16 vibrations per second while that of the top C of a manual 2′ stop is over 8000. It will, therefore, be realized that the real compass of the instrument extends over nine complete octaves.

VI. *Mutation and Mixture Stops.* In addition to the various octave pitches, called foundation stops, there are the so-called mutation stops the pitch of which corresponds to one of the harmonics of the unison pitch. For instance, a mutation stop $2\frac{2}{3}'$ is tuned to the third harmonic (twelfth), hence will sound g' if the key of c is depressed [see explanation under *Foot (2)]. The purpose of such stops is not to be played alone (which would result in transposition) or with a unison stop of about the same loudness (which would result in parallel fifths), but together with a unison stop of considerably greater force, in which case the mutation stop ceases to be heard individually and merely serves as an artificial harmonic, thus modifying the timbre of the unison stop. Finally there are mixture stops (also called compound stops), i.e., stops which combine a selection of unison and mutation ranks. These serve the same purpose and must also be drawn together with a sufficiently strong unison stop. Mutation and mixture stops, if properly used, are among the most valuable resources of the organ player. In early organs (15th–17th centuries) they were particularly prominent, a fact which has given considerable encouragement to the view, generally held in the 19th century, that the music of these periods must have been "crude and primitive." Their function was completely misunderstood by 19th-century musicians (Berlioz) and writers who objected to the parallel fifths and "unbearable dissonances" which resulted from "playing in C and in G simultaneously." On their behalf it may be said that 19th-century organ builders and organ players also misunderstood these devices, so that Percy C. Buck was perhaps justified in saying, as late as 1927, "the effect is distressing in the extreme to all but hardened organists." Early organists, including those of the Bach period, clearly visualized and judiciously exploited the potentialities of mixtures and mutation stops, and the return to the organ ideal of the Baroque has brought with it a new cultivation of these stops which are particularly useful in the performance of contrapuntal music [see IX (e) and (f)].

VII. *Expression.* The organ pipe

speaks on a steady air pressure; this cannot be varied because to increase the pressure would sharpen and to lower it would flatten the pitch. It, therefore, follows that when a pipe is sounding it speaks at a constant dynamic level and a crescendo or diminuendo is impossible. Expression in the organ is thus limited to (1) adding or retiring stops progressively (a mechanical device for this is the Crescendo pedal), or (2) by using a device known as the swell box or expression chamber. The swell box is a large room built around one or more divisions of the instrument, the front of the box being provided with a series of shutters similar to a Venetian blind. By means of a pedal (Swell pedal) the player can open or close the shutters, and thus obtain expressive control over the pipes contained therein. While the affair is somewhat crude, very fine musical effects can be obtained which are peculiar to the instrument. It would seem obvious that the complete instrument should be provided with this method of control, but there are musical reasons discussed more fully later [see under XI] why it is highly desirable to limit the expression boxes to certain divisions and to leave the rest in the open.

VIII. *Organ Pipes in General.* The pipes of the organ fall into two distinct classes — Flue and Reed. The flue pipe closely resembles the ordinary tin *whistle in which a vibrating air sheet sets up vibrations in the column of air surrounded by the pipe. The complete flue pipe comprises the following component parts: The cylindrical portion which encloses the column of air just mentioned and which is known as the "body"; the "foot" which is usually a tapered cone connecting the body to the wind supply from the chest; the "mouth" which consists of a rectangular opening cut from the body at the point where the foot joins it. At the location of the mouth the body of the pipe and the conical foot are flattened and the straight edge thus formed at the top of the mouth is called the "lip." The "languard" consists of a flat piece of metal located internally at the top of the foot at the point where it joins the body.

The front edge is beveled and arranged so as to form a narrow slit through which the wind sheet issues. The slit is known as the "flue." Lugs soldered to the pipe at the sides of the mouth are known as "ears" and assist in controlling the wind sheet.

Flue pipes are tuned by lengthening or shortening the pipe. In the modern organ this is usually accomplished by providing a sliding sleeve situated at the top of the pipe.

The type of reed pipe used almost exclusively in the organ is known as the beating reed, and must not be confused with the free reed employed in the harmonium and reed organ [see *Reed]. The beating reed comprises a vibrating curved tongue which rolls down the flattened surface of a brass tube called a "shallot." In this flattened surface an opening is cut communicating with the interior of the tube so that, as the tongue vibrates, it opens and closes this opening and thus sets up a sympathetic disturbance of the air column contained within a conical or cylindrical resonator which communicates with the upper end of the shallot. The shallot, tongue, and resonator are all held firmly by a heavy block of metal and the shallot and tongue are enclosed in a socket which has the function of conveying wind from the chest. Tuning is obtained at two points, first by lengthening or shortening the resonator at its upper end, and secondly, by means of a tuning wire which can be adjusted to control the free vibrating length of the tongue.

IX. *Flue Pipes.* Flue pipes may be either open or stopped [G. *gedackt*], that is to say, the top of the body may be completely open to the surrounding air or a stopper or plug may be inserted at the top of the pipe. The stopping of the open end causes the pipe to speak a note one octave lower than it would if left open; that is to say, a pipe having a normal speaking length of 4′ C would sound 8′ C if closed or stopped. The stopping also causes the even-numbered harmonics of the tone to be suppressed [see *Acoustics V].

All flue pipes fall into one of the following classes of tone: Principal or Diapason; Flute; String. There is one other class which may be termed a hybrid since the tone may lie midway between that of Principal and Flute, or Flute and String.

a. *Principal or Diapason.* Principal tone is characteristic of the organ, and does not exist in any other instrument. It is produced by open cylindrical pipes of medium to large scale [see *Scale, Scaling], and the tone has a strong fundamental accompanied by a chord of at least eight easily audible upper partials. In the best examples the unison harmonics (octaves) are prominent, while the 2d, 5th, 6th, and 7th are much less assertive and diminish in strength successively. Principals are used in manual and Pedal divisions at sub-unison, unison, octave, and super-octave pitches. They are also employed to furnish a mutation rank at $5\frac{1}{3}'$ or $2\frac{2}{3}'$ pitches and to form the individual ranks of mixture stops [see d, e].

There are many varieties of Principal tone, that is to say, the harmonics may be developed strongly or may be suppressed, causing the tone to have a flavor of string tone or flute tone as the case may be. Thus a Violin Diapason will tend towards the string side, while a Diapason phonon will possess a tone more fluty in character.

b. *Flute Tone.* Flutes fall into two main classes — open and stopped. The open Flutes, such as the Melodia, Claribel Flute, and Concert Flute, usually made of wood and rectangular in cross section, are characterized by a broad mellow flute tone. The open metal Flute inclines toward Principal tone in the bass and tenor. The treble portion may have harmonic pipes, i.e., pipes in which the body is double the normal length, and a hole is bored below the center to assist the pipe in speaking its octave. Such pipes (called Harmonic Flute) have a tone closely resembling the flute of the orchestra. Stopped Flutes may be of wood or metal, and owing to the fact that only the odd-numbered upper partials are present the tone is often light and transparent in texture. Typical examples are called Bourdon or Gedackt, and the term

Stopped Diapason is sometimes employed. The Quintaten (properly, *Quintadena*) falls into this class of pipe and is characterized by having the third harmonic developed equally with the fundamental. A quaint tone results which has considerable value in combinational use.

The Rohr Flute and Koppel Flute belong to a family of Flutes that are half stopped, a small cylindrical chimney or cone-shaped extension open at the top being inserted in the stopper. Such pipes have a high harmonic development in relation to the fundamental, imparting considerable brightness to the tone. They are valuable for use as mutation ranks in addition to being employed at unison and octave pitches. All Flutes are found at various pitches in the modern organ.

c. *String Tone.* String toned stops, such as the Cello, Viola, Gamba, Dulciana, and Viole d'Orchestre, have an extremely high harmonic development causing the tone to be thin and cutting. Many varieties are now in use, varying from quite a broad string tone to a highly pungent quality. String toned pipes are much smaller scale than other varieties of pipes; e.g., the low 8′ C may be as little as 2″ in diameter, whereas an 8′ Diapason pipe may be from 6″ to $6\frac{3}{4}$″. String toned stops are usually employed to form sub-unison, unison, and octave ranks only on manual and Pedal.

d. *Hybrids.* The hybrids already referred to are stops such as the Spitzflute and Gemshorn. The body of these pipes takes the form of an inverted cone. This construction brings into prominence the second harmonic, and according to the amount of taper employed the tone lies either between the Diapason and Flute or the String and Flute. This class of tone besides being useful in sub-unison, unison, and octave pitches is particularly valuable to form mutation stops of $2\frac{2}{3}'$, $1\frac{3}{5}'$, and $1\frac{1}{3}'$ pitches.

e. *Mutation Stops.* The mutation stop is characteristic of the organ, its chief office being for use with a unison or octave rank or a combination of such stops to change the tonal character by artificially bringing into prominence a particular overtone. These ranks greatly increase the tonal variety of the instrument since a wide range of synthetic qualities is possible. The most common examples employed comprise the Nazard $2\frac{2}{3}'$, Tierce $1\frac{3}{5}'$, Larigot $1\frac{1}{3}'$, and the Septieme $1\frac{1}{7}'$. Sometimes three or five ranks of mutations are drawn together by a single drawstop to form a powerful synthetic horn-like tone called a Cornet [see under f]. The ranks employed in a five rank Cornet would be a unison 8', octave 4', Nazard $2\frac{2}{3}'$, Blockflöte 2', and a Tierce $1\frac{3}{5}'$. The Sesquialtera (II Ranks) comprises a Nazard $2\frac{2}{3}'$ and a Tierce $1\frac{3}{5}'$.

f. *Mixture Stops.* Mixtures, also known as compound stops, comprise from two to seven ranks of principal pipes to each note arranged to speak harmonics of the fundamental of the note. There are a great many varieties of Mixtures, but usually the intervals employed are confined to unison and fifth sounding ranks. The Mixtures in common use are the Fourniture, Plein Jeu, and the Cymbel.

An important feature of Mixtures is the "breaks," i.e., changes of the arrangement of harmonics occurring at certain points of the keyboard. E.g., a rank which, at the lower end, starts out two octaves above normal, will break back at some higher point to the twelfth, and at still higher points to the octave, fifth, and finally unison. Corresponding breaks occur in the other ranks, and the result is that point and definition are added to the bass and tenor sections, breadth and fullness to the middle and treble. A typical layout of the ranks of a Fourniture IV Rks. with breaks is as follows:

	I	II	III	IV
C_1 to f:	15	19	22	26
f♯ to f':	12	15	19	22
f♯' to f'':	8	12	15	19
f♯'' to c'''':	1	8	12	15

The numbers 15, 19, etc., refer to diatonic tones counted from the fundamental; e.g., 15 is the second octave, 22 the third octave. The accompanying example serves as a further illustration; the white notes indicate the keys; the black notes the pitches of the first rank (I).

High Mixtures such as Cymbel may be used as a secondary Mixture to the Fourniture or may appear as the only

Mixture of a Positive division. They are useful musically not only as an ensemble register, but as a means of adding color to an 8' Flute or Flutes 8' and 4'. A sparkling effect can be produced in this way which is of distinct value for rapidly moving passages. In two-part playing on the same manual the combination just described helps to differentiate the tone color of the two parts due to the many breaks in the ranks.

The Cornet and like stops, such as the Sesquialtera, have already been referred to under "Mutation Stops." They are, strictly speaking, compound registers, but as a synthetic tone quality is aimed at in the voicing and owing to the fact that the ranks run through the compass without breaks, they are employed in a similar manner to mutations.

X. *Reed Pipes.* Reeds are of three categories: Chorus reeds, Semi-chorus reeds, and Solo or orchestral reeds. Chorus reeds belong chiefly to the Trumpet family, and appear in the modern organ on both Manual and Pedal divisions at sub-unison, unison, and octave pitches. Posaunes, Trombone, Trumpets, Cornopeans, and Clarions fall within this class. While the names employed suggest orchestral tones, they differ in quality considerably from their orchestral prototypes. They are purely organ voices and are used to add power and vigor to the ensemble. They may also be employed for solo work. The Trumpet family have conical resonators of full length, i.e., 8' C has a resonator of approximately 8' length.

Semi-chorus reeds come to us largely from the Baroque period, and are not imitative, although their names may suggest an orchestral background. The Cromorne, Schalmei, and the Rankett may be taken as typical examples. The term semi-chorus is used because they may function as chorus reeds, solo stops, or merely timbre creators in combination with other voices. The resonators of this class of reed are often cylindrical and of short length. They may be half, quarter, or even an eighth length.

The Solo or orchestral reeds are largely imitative of various orchestral instruments, such as the Bassoon, English Horn, Clarinet, and Orchestral Oboes. They are used largely as solo stops, and modern voicers have used considerable skill in producing faithful imitations of the real thing.

XI. *Tonal Structure of the Organ.* Owing to the mechanical perfection of the instrument by the use of electricity around the turn of the present century, the organ passed through a period of rapid development. Its size in regard to both numbers of manuals and stops increased greatly, and efforts were made to imitate as closely as possible the tonal effect of the symphony orchestra.

While many new voices were developed during this period, particularly in regard to orchestral and string timbres, the characteristic tone of the organ was badly neglected and the general effect became hard and overbearing. The instrument was no longer suited for the proper rendition of the best music from the organ literature, clarity, transparency, and purity of tone having given way to powerful and dull effects together with some fine solo voices and sentimental qualities nice enough in themselves but of limited usefulness.

Happily in recent years there has been a strong reaction, and the organ of the Bach period (Baroque organ) has been re-created with fine results. While some purely classical designs have been produced which have created great interest, such instruments are far from ideal for playing the organ literature of the Romantic and modern periods. The real solution of the problem is to combine the best of the classical and modern tonal ideals in one instrument, each being modified to fit into a perfect whole. This has

been accomplished very successfully in recent years, and the idea is being developed further, and a very fruitful era of organ building may be expected.

Organs of the Bach period were usually small — two or sometimes three manuals with a pedal organ and about 12 to 35 stops were considered sufficient. The pipes were voiced on light wind pressure imparting a delightful mellowness to the tone. It was a chorus instrument in which the blending of the various stops one with another and into a clear ringing ensemble was considered essential. The Pedal was not merely looked upon as a bass to the whole but was designed to be capable of carrying a melodic line independent of the manuals. The manual divisions were contrasted tonally, as was necessary for polyphonic music which demanded independence and clarity from all sections. Therefore, it is not surprising to find in these instruments an abundance of delightful principals and flutes, together with a good sprinkling of mutations and mixture stops. Of course, there was no swell box.

In reproducing these qualities in the modern organ it was found undesirable to enclose all divisions in a swell box for not only was the type of expression obtained by this means unnecessary, but the enclosure marred the clarity and intimacy of the tonal effect of these light pressure voices when heard singly or combined.

The most important divisions for the classical literature comprise a Pedal, Great, and Positive, and in the case of the music of the Romantic period it is necessary to have the modern Swell containing strings and reeds, and a second organ under separate expressive control to form an accompanimental Choir department. Modern music with its complex harmony is admirably suited to the transparency of the classical toned organ, and provided the Swell and Choir are present, we have an ideal arrangement for its rendition.

The following specification for a moderate sized instrument may be of help to the student in understanding how the best tonal features both classical and modern can be combined to make an adequate and complete whole suited to the musical requirements of all periods:

GREAT ORGAN (Unenclosed)
Middle Manual
16' Quintaten
8' Principal
8' Spitz Flute
8' Bourdon
4' Principal
4' Rohr Flute
2⅔' Quint (Principal tone)
2' Super Octave (Principal tone)
Fourniture (III to V Ranks)

SWELL ORGAN (Enclosed)
Top Manual
8' Viole-de-Gambe
8' Viole Celeste
8' Stopped Diapason
4' Principal
4' Lieblich Flute
2' Fifteenth
Plein Jeu (IV Ranks)
16' Contra Hautbois
8' Trompette
4' Clarion

POSITIVE (Unenclosed)
Lower Manual
8' Gedackt
4' Koppel Flute
2⅔' Nazard
2' Nachthorn
1⅗' Tierce
1' Octave
1⅓' Larigot
Cymbel (III Ranks)

CHOIR ORGAN (Enclosed)
Played from Positive Manual
8' Viola
8' Melodia
8' Dulciana
8' Unda Maris
4' Flute Harmonique
8' Cromorne

PEDAL ORGAN
16' Principal
16' Rohr Bourdon
16' Quintaten (derived from Great)
8' Principal
8' Gedackt
5⅓' Quint
4' Choral Bass
4' Nachthorn
2' Block Flute
Mixture (III Ranks)
16' Posaune
8' Trompette
4' Schalmei

XII. *History*. Legend traces the origin of the organ back to the "Syrinx" (pan-pipes) of the god Pan, or to Jubal "the father of all such as handle the harp and the organ," and up to the present day writers repeat these naïve stories more or less credulously. Factual evidence, however, points to a much more recent origin of the instrument. The invention of the Greek organ, the *hydraulis*, is ascribed (in Heron's *Pneumatika, c.* 120 B.C.) to the engineer Ktesibios who worked in Alexandria around 250 B.C., and it has been pointed out [*SaHMI*, 144] that this ascription is credible because Alexandria was at that time a center of engineering art and because the hydraulis with its complicated and amazingly perfect mechanism actually presupposes a high degree of technical skill and experience. This does not rule out the possibility that it had primitive ancestors, such as pan-pipes combined with arm-operated bellows [cf. *SaHMI*, pl. VIII, opp. p. 144], but these can hardly be considered as organs, since the mechanical wind supply as well as its mechanical admission to the pipes — by means of keys — is missing. The *magrepha* of the Jews was, no doubt, an imitation of the hydraulis and certainly was not used until near the end of Israel's national existence.

The hydraulis had a loud and penetrating tone, noisy rather than musical, and was therefore used chiefly in Rome as an accompaniment for popular entertainments (gladiator fights) and, quite significantly, for orgiastic cults. In the first centuries of the Christian era these instruments apparently still increased in size. They required not only several men to work at the wind supply (which, as early as the 4th century, was provided pneumatically, by bellows), but also several performers working with their arms at the heavy slides. St. Hieronymus (d. A.D. 420) tells of an organ at Jerusalem which could be heard at the Mount of Olives, nearly a mile distant. Such costly and elaborate machines were frequently sent as gifts by potentates and high church dignitaries (e.g., in 757 by the Byzantine Emperor Copronymus to the Frankish

King Pippin). This development culminated in monster organs such as that
erected in the 10th century at Winchester
in England. It had, we are told by the
monk Wulstan, 26 bellows which were
worked by 70 strong men "labouring with
their arms, covered with perspiration,
each inciting his companions to drive the
wind up with all its strength, that the
full-bosomed box may speak with its 400
pipes." It was played by two organists on
two keyboards each of which consisted of
twenty slides, and its effect was such that
"everyone stops with his hands his gap-
ing ears, being in no wise able to draw
near and bear the sound."

Organs of this period and up to the
13th century had several ranks of pipes
(up to twenty) forming a powerful mixture, but lacked any means of registration, such as stops. On the other hand, a
certain variety of timbre resulted from
the fact that the pipes of any rank all had
the same width, hence, a scale [see
*Scale, scaling] varying from narrow in
the low registers (long pipes) to wide in
the high registers (small pipes) so that
the bass possessed a somewhat harsh
String tone, the upper octaves a soft Flute
tone. In the 13th century the former
slides (*linguae*, i.e., tongues) were supplanted by keys controlling pallets. At
this time the organs had a keyboard of
three octaves with a number of semitones,
particularly in the middle range. The
earliest preserved examples of *organ
music, dating from about 1325, require a
complete chromatic middle-octave.

After 1300 the development of the organ made rapid strides, not only towards
increased size (in 1429, the organ of the
cathedral of Amiens had 2500 pipes, the
lowest of which were of a truly gigantic
size), but also towards refinement of
sound and technique. In addition to the
monster instruments which necessarily
remained somewhat crude, small organs
were developed, the *portative organ and
the *positive organ. The portative organ
(called *organetto* in Italy) was a small
portable instrument used for processions,
but also cultivated by outstanding musicians, notably Francesco Landini (1325–

97; see *Italian music), the blind master
whose playing on his beloved organetto
is most vividly and touchingly described
in Giovanni da Prato's *Paradiso degli
Alberti*. Fourteenth-century painters frequently show it in the hands of angels
[cf. *SaHMI*, pl. XVIII, opp. p. 304].
Still better known is the positive organ,
a stationary chamber organ of moderate
size, from the famous painting of van
Eyck (Altar of Ghent). It is probably
the latter type which must be considered
as having been instrumental in the development of polyphonic organ music.
In the 15th century solo stops were gradually added to the basic mixture tone:
flutes, stopped diapasons, and reeds. Simultaneously the pedal was developed as
a more or less complete keyboard and,
around 1500, an instrument emerged
which had all the basic contrivances of a
real organ. A detailed description of this
type of organ (Gothic organ) is given in
A. Schlick's *Spiegel der Orgelmacher und
Organisten* (1511). It seems that the development of this "polyphonic" organ
with contrasting timbres of strongly individual sonorities, several manuals, and
a pedal took place mainly in Germany,
while Italy and England developed a
more "homophonic" type of organ, of a
less varied and much softer tonal structure and without pedal (Renaissance organ), apparently a continuation of the
15th-century portative organ. A special
type of 16th-century organ, utilizing
reeds only, is the *regal.

In the 17th century there developed
that type of organ which, owing mainly
to its association with the work of Bach,
has become a model for contemporary
tendencies in progressive organ building,
the Baroque organ or Praetorius organ,
as it is called after Michael Praetorius
who, in his *Syntagma musicum* of 1615/
20, described it in detail. It retained the
contrasting qualities of the Gothic organ
of Schlick, but in softer and lighter
timbres. The great achievement of this
period was a tonal structure which combined individuality with homogeneity or,
as we might say, the "horizontal" and the
"vertical" aspects of the texture, as did the

organ music of the Baroque, above all that of Bach. Small wonder, then, that organ building is now turning back to this instrument in order to make possible the proper performance of the greatest organ music ever written. The climax of Baroque organ building is represented by Gottfried Silbermann (organs in Freiberg, Dresden) whose instruments, though still retaining the essential qualities of the true Baroque organ, foreshadow the trend towards increased expressiveness which characterizes the period from 1750 to 1900.

In this period the efforts of organ builders were governed by two ideals both of which are essentially extraneous to the organ, i.e., Romantic expressiveness and 19th-century orchestra. Abbé Vogler's organ of c. 1800 had various crescendo devices and was designed to give "a true picture of a well-organized orchestra." It made ample use of *differential tones, a method which resulted in a considerable reduction in the number of pipes but also in a very unsatisfactory tonal quality (for a similar attempt of recent date, see *Unit organ). During the 19th century there ensued the development leading to the admirable technical achievements, the stupendous sizes, and the questionable (to put it mildly) artistic merits of the modern organ. Organists naturally boast of, and revel in, that multiplicity of devices: couplers, swells, pistons, crescendo pedal, combination pedals, etc., which, in connection with overpowering or sentimental stops (Trumpet, Stentorphone, Tuba mirabilis, Vox angelica, Unda maris, Tremulant), enable them to pass instantly from the softest whisper to a roar far surpassing the fff-effects of the biggest orchestra, to imitate all conceivable colors of the orchestra, and to produce a great variety of sensational effects. Musicians and amateurs of cultivated taste frequently take a somewhat different view and consider this instrument as one which is at its best with the poorest type of organ music, and vice versa. The 19th-century development of the organ has been topped by the cinema organ a description of which

will certainly not be expected in a book dealing with music. Under these circumstances the progressive trend back to the organ of earlier days, which is outlined in section XI, must be highly welcomed, the more so as it is accompanied by a new rise in the quality of the music written for this instrument.

Lit.: W. H. Barnes, *The Contemporary American Organ* (1937); Walter and Thomas Lewis, *Modern Organ Building* (1939); G. A. Audsley, *The Art of Organ Building*, 2 vols. (1905); E. J. Hopkins, *The Organ . . .* (1887); E. M. Skinner, *The Modern Organ* (1917); R. Foort, *The Cinema Organ* (1932); A. Gray, "The Modern Development of the Organ" (*PMA* xxxix); G. D. Harrison, "The Classical Organ in the Germanic Museum" (Harvard University, *Germ. Mus. Bull.* i); C. F. A. Williams, *The Story of the Organ* (1903); N. Dufourq, *Esquisse d'une histoire de l'orgue* (1935); G. Frotscher, *Orgeldispositionen aus 5 Jahrhunderten* (1939); Ch. Mahrenholz, *Die Berechnung der Orgelmensuren . . .* (1938); C. F. A. Williams, "Evolution of the Organ" (*ML* v, no. 3); M. Raghib, "Description d'orgues pas des auteurs turcs et persans" (*RdM*, nos. 30, 36, 45, 46); A. G. Hill, "Mediaeval Organs in Spain" (*SIM* xiv). See also *Organ music; *Organ playing.

For additional literature see J. H. Burn, *Dictionary of Organs and Organists* (1923); *MoML*, 591f; N. Dufourq, "Essai d'une bibliographie de l'histoire de l'orgue en France" (*RdM*, 1934).

G. D. H.
(XII by W. A.)

Organ chorale. Polyphonic compositions for the organ based upon the melody of a *chorale (excluding simple harmonizations such as are used for the accompaniment of congregational singing). Although the term is commonly used for the polyphonic settings of the German Protestant chorales only, a complete study of the field must necessarily include the preceding development which took place under the auspices of the Catholic church and which is represented by a highly remarkable repertory of organ settings of Latin hymns (including the four *antiphons B.M.V.).

I. *The Catholic Organ Hymn.* Around 1500, numerous items of the service which theretofore were performed in the traditional plainsong were replaced by organ pieces. To these belong psalmverses [see *Verset], the *Magnificat, and large portions of the mass [see *Organ mass]. The hymns also were included in this process which, although it contributed to the rapid decline of Gregorian chant, was the chief impulse to the development of organ music. After a somewhat obscure starting period, represented by a few primitive examples in 15th-century German organ tablatures (Paumann, 1452), we find the organ hymn fully developed with Hofhaimer (1459–1537) and, particularly, in Arnolt Schlick's *Tabulaturen* (1512). Their settings all belong to that type which is usually referred to as cantus-firmus chorale, i.e., with the hymn melody in long notes (one or two to the measure, usually in the tenor) as the basis of a contrapuntal weave — a treatment which had a long ancestry reaching back to the *clausulae and *motets of the 13th century and which, on the other hand, was to become one of the standard procedures of the Protestant organ chorale. Schlick's composition of the verse "Eya ergo" from the "Salve regina" already shows the *Vorimitation so frequent in Bach's organ chorales, whilst his "Maria zart" (the only hymn with a German text) is a uniquely early example of what may be called the "Protestant approach," in that it has the melody, expressively designed and beautifully ornamented, standing out throughout the entire piece in the soprano [cf. *HAM*, nos. 100, 101]. The cantus-firmus treatment with *Vorimitation* is more clearly represented in the numerous settings of Buchner (MS tablature from *c.* 1525) who also has examples of the chorale canon (cantus firmus in canon). In this connection, an anonymous "In dulci jubilo" from Sicher's tablature [in Moser, *Frühmeister* (1930)] may be mentioned, because its canonic

treatment is remarkably similar to that in Bach's setting of the same hymn.

The hymns in Cavazzoni's *Intavolatura* (1542) already make deliberate use of the Flemish motet-style (imitation of the hymn melody in all the voices), usually in alternation with cantus-firmus treatment. Fully developed chorale-motets (imitative treatment of all the lines of the hymn in succession) are found in the compositions of John Redford (*c.* 1485–1545; cf. *HAM*, no. 120). Such pieces have frequently been interpreted as organ transcriptions of vocal motets. Actually, however, they are original organ pieces in the style of a motet (the extremely wide range of Redford's pieces clearly excludes vocal performance). The later English composers, including the Virginalists, cultivated particularly the figured chorale (contrapuntal parts in stereotyped keyboard figures), a treatment which remained rather barren and monotonous under their hands. A peak of outstanding artistic significance is reached in the organ hymns of Antonio de Cabezon (1510–66), most of which use the cantus-firmus technique.

In the early 17th century the development of the organ hymn came to fitting climax in the extended works of John Bull (1563–1628), Sweelinck (1562–1621), Jean Titelouze (1563–1633; cf. *HAM*, no. 180), Michael Praetorius (1571–1621), and Samuel Scheidt (1587–1654), among which those of Praetorius stand out as great, but almost unknown, masterworks of musical art.

II. *The Protestant Organ Chorale.* In the Protestant church the organ chorale held a position quite different from that which it occupied in the Roman service. In the latter, it served as a substitute for the plainsong from which it inherited its liturgical function as well as that spirit of mystic aloofness and transcendentality which pervades the whole Catholic ritual and its music. In the Protestant church the singing of the chorale became the cherished privilege of the congregation, and it was the organist's duty, not only to accompany this singing, but also to play the chorale beforehand on the organ as an introduction: hence the name *chorale prelude* by which the German organ chorales are usually designated. This novel function of the organ chorale naturally allowed for a greater freedom of treatment and stimulated the fancy of the composers towards the development of new methods of composition. No longer had the chorale to be mysteriously concealed as a tenor in incomprehensibly long notes, but it was made to stand out as a real melody in the soprano, recognizable to every member of the congregation. It must be noted, however, that the older methods of treatment, the cantus-firmus chorale and the chorale motet, were continued alongside the more recent methods, and that in Bach these two types still represent the most elaborate methods of composition.

At the outset of the development of the Protestant organ chorale stands Scheidt whose Fantasia (actually a chorale motet) "Ich ruf zu Dir," one of the greatest works of the entire literature, anticipates in form, style, and expression such works as Bach's chorale motet "Jesus Christus unser Heiland" (Ed. Peters vi, no. 31). The historical development between Scheidt and Bach followed along two lines, a North-German and a Middle-German [for the composers, see *Organ music II (a); the South-German organ composers, being Catholics, naturally made no contribution to the repertory of the organ chorale]. In North Germany we find a distinct preference for extended treatment and for a free, rhapsodic type known as *chorale fantasia. The choral preludes of the Middle-German masters are in shorter forms and in simpler style, chiefly melody chorales or chorale variations (partitas) [cf. *HAM*, no. 190].

Bach utilized all the forms of the past and, needless to assert, bestowed on them new qualities of expression and artistic perfection. The following types can be clearly distinguished: (a) *Cantus-firmus chorale:* the chorale melody in long notes usually in the bass (Ed. Peters, nos. 17, 30, 36); (b) *Chorale motet:* each line of the chorale is treated in imitation thus

resulting in a succession of "fugues" (nos. 31, 58); (c) *Chorale fugue:* the first line or the initial phrase of the chorale is treated as a fugue (nos. 10, 33, 41); (d) *Melody chorale* or *Figured chorale:* the chorale appears as a continuous melody in the soprano, accompanied by contrapuntal parts which usually proceed in definite figures (most of the chorales from the *Orgelbüchlein*); (e) *Ornamented chorale:* the chorale is used in the soprano with elaborate and expressive ornamentations (nos. 45; *Orgelb.* no. 51); (f) *Chorale canon* (*Orgelb.* nos. 15, 35); (g) *Chorale fantasia:* free, "North-German" treatment (nos. 15, 22); (h) *Chorale variations* (*partitas*); a number of variations (corresponding to the number of stanzas of the text) of the chorale melody (no. 48; also the Partitas, vol. v). Naturally, the above methods of treatment frequently overlap, e.g., the chorale prelude "Nun komm der Heiden Heiland" (no. 45) and many others combine the principle of imitation, as in the motet, with the ornamented treatment for the final statement of the "subject."

Among recent contributions to the repertory the chorale preludes of Brahms (op. 122) must be mentioned particularly.

Lit.: G. Kittler, *Geschichte des Protestantischen Orgelchorals* (1931); F. Dietrich, *Geschichte des deutschen Orgelchorals im 17. Jahrhundert* (1932); A. Scheide, *Zur Geschichte des Choralvorspiels* (1930); W. H. Frere, "Bach's Vorspiele of 1739" (*ML* i, no. 3); Ch. Macpherson, "Choral-Preludes" (*PMA* xxxix); E. Fischer, "Johann Crügers Choralbearbeitungen" (*ZMW* xiv). Also under *Organ music.

Organetto. Fourteenth-century name for a small portable organ (*portative organ); see *Organ XII.

Organ hymn. See *Organ chorale I.

Organicen, organoedus [from L. *canere*, Gr. *oidein*, to sing]. Humanistic names for organ player, organist.

Organista [L.]. Organ player, organist. However, the designation "optimus organista," conferred on Leoninus (c. 1200; see *Ars Antiqua) by the late 13th-century Anonymous IV of CS i, characterizes this master as a "great composer of organa" [see *Organum], not as a "very able organist," a misinterpretation frequently encountered in modern writings.

Organistrum [L.]. Medieval Latin name for the *hurdy-gurdy.

Organ Mass [G. *Orgelmesse*]. Polyphonic compositions of the Ordinary of the *Mass for the organ. Crude two-part settings of the Kyrie, Sanctus, Patrem, are contained in the tablature of Ludolf Wilkin from 1432 [cf. W. Apel, in *MQ* xxiii]. More advanced examples, usually in motet-style, occur in Attaingnant's books of 1528/29 [new ed. by Y. Rokseth], in Buchner's tablature of c. 1525 [cf. *VMW* v], in Redford [cf. C. Pfatteicher, *John Redford* (1934)]. Complete organ Masses are contained in Cavazzoni's *Intavolatura* of 1542 (Missa Apostolorum, Missa de Beata Virgine, etc.; cf. *HAM*, no. 117). Similar compositions, though of lesser artistic perfection, were published by Claudio Merulo in his *Misse d'organo* (1590?). Bach wrote what one might call a "German organ Mass," in his *Clavierübung*, part III.

Mention must be made here of a theory advanced by A. Schering (*Die Niederländische Orgelmesse*, 1912) according to which numerous Masses of the Flemish masters, which are commonly regarded as vocal compositions, were actually meant as organ music. That this theory is untenable appears from a glance at Schering's renditions for organ [cf. his *Alte Meister der Frühzeit des Orgelspiels* (1913); also *SchGMB*, no. 57] the highly complex texture of which is in an irreconcilable contradiction to the genuine organ style of the 15th century (Paumann, *Buxheim organ book).

Lit.: L. Schrade, "The Organ in the Mass of the 15th Century" (*MQ* xxviii); *id.*, "Die Messe in der Orgelmusik des 15. Jahrhunderts" (*AMF* i); A. Schering, "Zur alternierenden Orgelmesse" (*ZMW* xvii); A. Tessier, "Les Messes d'orgue de Couperin" (*RM* vi, no. 1).

Organ music. I. *Middle Ages and Renaissance*. Prior to 1300, organ playing was probably restricted to a monophonic duplication of plainsong and, perhaps, to the performance of the long-held notes of the tenor in *organa. The fact that the organs of this period had the sonority of a mixture-stop with very prominent harmonics practically rules out polyphonic music, perhaps with the exception of the note-against-note organum of the 9th to the 11th century. The earliest preserved examples of organ music (c. 1325) are *intabulations of motets and *estampies contained in the MS Add. 28550, the so-called Robertsbridge Codex, of the British Museum [cf. *WoHN* ii, 5ff; *ApMZ* ii; *ApNPM* 37ff]. They are usually assumed to be of English origin, although certain features, particularly the notation, would seem to point to Italy. A gap of more than 100 years separates these pieces from the next-oldest sources, various German tablatures of the mid-15th century [cf. L. Schrade, *Die ältesten Denkmäler der Orgelmusik* (1927); W. Apel, in *MQ* xxiii], among which the Ileborgh tablature of 1448 [cf. W. Apel, in *ZMW* xvi] is remarkable for its free *preludes, Paumann's *Fundamentum organisandi* of 1452 for its elaborations of German songs and for its instructive pieces [see *Counterpoint III], and the *Buxheim organ book of c. 1470 for its numerous intabulations of *Burgundian chansons [Ex. in *ApMZ* i]. Towards the end of the 15th century Paulus Hofhaimer was famous for his organ playing and improvisation, but only two or three pieces of his have come down to us, along with compositions of his pupils Kotter, Sicher, Buchner, Kleber [cf. H. J. Moser, *Frühmeister des deutschen Orgelspiels* (1930)]. German organ music reaches its first culmination point in the great master Arnolt Schlick whose *Tabulaturen etlicher Lobgesangk* . . . (1512; new ed. by G. Harms, 1924) contain chiefly *organ chorales. The German tradition of this period is continued in some extensive tablatures of Polish origin, written around 1550, which show particularly the influence of Buchner [see *Polish music].

In the 16th century other important developments take place in Italy, Spain, England, and France. Cavazzoni's *Intavolatura cioè ricercari, canzoni, himni, magnificati* (1542; see *Editions II, 3 and VI, 6) contain genuine organ *ricercares of high perfection, as well as the earliest organ canzonas [see *Canzona (5)]. Andrea Gabrieli (1510–86) contributed the first *toccatas, a form the artistic possibilities of which were more fully exploited by Claudio Merulo (1533–1604). For other Italian composers of this period cf. Torchi's volume [*Editions II, 3]. The Spanish organ music is known to us only by the works of the great master Antonio de Cabezon (1510–66), contained in the posthumous publication *Obras de musica* (1577; *Editions XIII, 3, 4, 7, 8), in which we find organ hymns, *tientos, *variations, and instructive pieces of rare excellence. In England there flourished before 1550 a very remarkable, but little known, school of organ composers, represented chiefly by John Redford (*c.* 1485–1545; cf. C. Pfatteicher, *John Redford*, 1934) whose numerous liturgical pieces (organ hymns) include some outstanding pieces in motet-style, compared with which the hymn settings, etc., of Tallis, Byrd, Bull [see *Virginalists], are a step backward rather than forward. Finally, two French publications of 1530 (Attaingnant; new ed. by Y. Rokseth, *Deux livres d'orgue* . . . , 1925) give evidence of an early activity the later traces of which are unfortunately lost for nearly 100 years, the next-oldest document of French organ music preserved being the organ books by Titelouze (1563–1633) issued in 1623 and 1626 [*Editions I, i; also in E. Kaller, *Liber Organi*, vols. i, ii].

II. *Baroque.* While Titelouze's organ hymns, together with the grandiose pieces of Michael Praetorius (1571–1621), represent the acme of the organ music of the Renaissance, the works of another composer of the 1560-generation, Jan Pieters Sweelinck (1562–1621), lead to the organ music of the Baroque, owing particularly to its new stylistic resources in the field of figuration and variation which Sweelinck borrowed from the virginalists.

a. *Germany.* Among Sweelinck's numerous pupils Samuel Scheidt (1587–1654) is the most outstanding [*Tabulatura nova* of 1624; new ed. *DdT* 1]. Although somewhat less imaginative than his teacher, particularly in the field of variation, his fugal compositions, liturgical pieces (Magnificats, etc.), and, particularly, organ chorales mark the beginning of a new development in German organ music which was to last and grow until the death of Bach, 100 years his junior. The ensuing development of German organ music may be divided into three branches, a North-German, a Middle-German, and a South-German. In the first, we find Sweelinck's pupil Melchior Schildt (1593–1667), Delphin Strungk (1601–94), Franz Tunder (1614–67), Matthias Weckmann (1621–74), Adam Reinken (1623–1722), Dietrich Buxtehude (1637–1707), Vincent Lübeck (1654–1740), Georg Böhm (1661–1733), and Nicolas Bruhns (1665–97) — composers who cultivated particularly the large and free forms of organ music — toccata, chorale fantasia, prelude, and fugue — and developed a free and highly imaginative style which has been termed *Gothic. The Middle-German composers, Thuringians and North Bavarians, worked with more modest and intimate means and contributed chiefly to the development of the melodic chorale prelude and of the variation [see *Partita]. This line is fittingly opened by Bach's grandfather Heinrich Bach (1615–92) and uncles Joh. Christof (1642–1703) and Johann Michael (1648–94; organ chorales in Ritter), and continues with Johann Krieger (1651–1735; *DTB* 18), Joh. Pachelbel (1653–1706; *DTB* 4.i), Joh. Kuhnau (1660–1722), Johann Heinrich Buttstedt (1666–1727), and Joh. Walther (1684–1748; *DdT* 26/27). An early South-German School of organ music is represented by Hans Leo Hassler (1564–1612; *DTB* 4.ii), Christian Erbach

(1570–1635; *DTB* 4.ii), Johann Ulrich Steigleder (1593–1635; interesting variations on the *Vaterunser*, new ed. by Emsheimer, 1928), Wolfgang Ebner (1610–65), and Johann Erasmus Kindermann (1616–55; *DTB* 23). Italian contrapuntal style and Italian forms such as the ricercare and the canzona figure largely in their works. A new development started with Johann Jacob Froberger (1616–67) who, as a pupil of Frescobaldi and a friend of French lutenists and clavecinists (Gaultier, Chambonnieres), instilled into the German organ music many new ideas derived from Frescobaldi's novel forms (toccata, variation canzona, *capriccio) and free, idiomatic keyboard style [see *Freistimmig], while the French influence benefited chiefly the development of his harpsichord music (*suite). The repertory of the later South-German composers, such as Johann Kaspar Kerll (1627–93; *DTB* 2.ii), Georg Muffat (1645–1704), Georg Reutter (1656–1738), Franz Xaver Murschhauser (1663–1738; *DTB* 18), Johann Kaspar Ferdinand Fischer (*c.* 1670–*c.* 1740; new ed. by E. v. Werra, 1901), and Gottlieb Muffat (1690–1770; *DTOe* 29.ii), also falls into an "Italian" division of ricercares, canzonas, toccatas, versets, and a "French" division of harpsichord music.

b. *Italy.* The Italian organ music of the Baroque started with the *Neapolitans Giov. Maria Trabaci and Ascanio Mayone who are important links between Cabezon and Frescobaldi [cf. W. Apel, in *MQ* xxiv]. The latter, a unique combination of intellectual scholar and highly imaginative artist, is one of the greatest and most fascinating figures of organ music. Unfortunately, he did not inaugurate an Italian school worthy of his merits. His pupil Michelangelo Rossi is only a mediocre imitator [cf. his toccatas in *TaAM* vi; an "Andante" in Rococo style which has been reprinted under his name in numerous collections of early keyboard music is the work of an 18th-century Lorenzo de Rossi]. Domenico Zipoli (*c.* 1675–?) is practically the only Italian organ composer after Frescobaldi worthy of note [see *Editions VI, 36].

c. *France.* The French organ music of the 17th century is represented by Henry Dumont (1610–84), Guillaume Nivers (*c.* 1617–after 1701), Nicolas Gigault (1625–*c.* 1707), Nicolas Le Begue (1630–1702), André Raison (publ. in 1687, 1714), and Louis Marchand (1669–1732) — whose compositions are much better than his inglorious encounter with Bach would make one expect — Jean-François Dandrieu (*c.* 1684–1740), and Louis Claude Daquin (1694–1772). Most of their compositions are liturgical pieces in a style which grew increasingly secular and "operatic" during the course of the period. They are noteworthy for their emphasis on registration which is usually carefully indicated [see *Editions I].

d. *Other Countries.* While the English organ music of the 17th century, represented by *voluntaries and similar pieces of John Blow (1648–1708), H. Purcell (1658–95), Jeremiah Clarke (*c.* 1659–1707), and William Croft (1678–1727), is rather insignificant, the Iberian peninsula produced a number of important, though little known, organ composers. Manuel Coelho (b. 1583; *Flores de musica*, 1620), Correa de Araujo (*Libro de tientos*, 1626), and Aguilera de Heredia (b. 1570?) wrote impressive organ pieces, mostly *tientos, in the style of Cabezon, intermingled with figurations borrowed from Sweelinck. A "Spanish Frescobaldi" arose in Juan José Cabanilles (1644–1712) whose several hundred organ compositions display a fascinating command of a great variety of forms and of styles [new ed. by H. Anglès, 3 vols., 1927–36; cf. also *LavE* i.4, 2091ff]. Later organ composers such as Pablo Bruna, Francisco Llissa, and Josep Elias are known only through a few pieces (reproduced in collections by Pedrell and Villalba).

e. *Bach.* In the field of organ music even more than in others Bach represents the consummate peak of Baroque music and, for that matter, of organ music in general. Here, as well as elsewhere, his achievements were in the direction of artistic perfection rather than of innovation.

Building upon the forms and methods of his predecessors, he bestowed upon the chorale preludes an incomparable expressiveness, on the toccatas and fugues a unique greatness of architectural structure, while his organ sonatas represent the most perfect realization — as well as idealization—of three-voice counterpoint.

III. *From 1750 to Present.* After Bach, organ music suffered a collapse from which it did not recuperate until around 1840. The low ebb of organ music around 1800 is beyond description (for examples, cf. an article by H. Müller, in *KJ*, 1901). Mendelssohn was one of the first to again write organ music of artistic significance. However, his six Sonatas (1839–44), although incorporating elements of Bach's style (fugues, chorales), clearly show the deteriorating influence which the Romantic thought had on organ composition. Franz Liszt's organ works opened a new period of organ composition, owing to their exploitation of the orchestral and coloristic resources of the instrument. This path was pursued further by the French Alexandre Guilmant (1837–1911), Charles-Marie Widor (1845–1937), and Louis Vierne (1870–1937), outstanding organ virtuosos who wrote veritable symphonies for the organ. César Franck's organ pieces, particularly his *Three Chorales* of 1890, are in a similar style, modified by the spiritual influence of Bach. Much closer to Bach in style and spirit are Brahms's *Chorale Preludes* of 1896. With Max Reger (1873–1916) Romantic organ music came to an imposing close. Cyclopic forms are filled with an exuberance of ideas and a profusion of technical display, but bound by a tremendous contrapuntal skill steeped in the tradition of Bach. The neo-classical tendencies of the 1920's brought along a more sincere revival of the polyphonic tradition of the Baroque. Heinrich Kaminski's (b. 1886) compositions are pervaded by a truly Gothic mysticism, while Kurt Thomas (b. 1904) and Hindemith (two organ sonatas, 1937) represent the present-day tendencies toward objectivism and linear design.

Lit.: A. De Brisay, *The Organ and its*

Music (1935); G. Frotscher, *Geschichte des Orgelspiels und der Orgelkomposition*, 2 vols. (1934/5); *LavE* ii.2, 1181–1374; A. Ritter, *Zur Geschichte des Orgelspiels* (1884); O. Kinkeldey, *Orgel und Klavier im 16. Jahrhundert* (1910); Y. Rokseth, *La Musique d'orgue au XVe siècle* . . . (1930); M. Fischer, *Die organistische Improvisation im 17. Jahrhundert* (Diss. Kassel 1929); H. Grace, *The Organ Works of Bach* (1922); H. Kelletat, *Zur Geschichte der Orgelmusik in der Frühklassik* (Diss. Königsberg 1933); J. Wolf, "Zur Geschichte der Orgelmusik im 14. Jahrhundert" (*KJ*, 1899, p. 14); W. Apel, "Du nouveau sur la musique française pour l'orgue au XVIe siècle" (*RM* xviii); E. West, "Old English Organ Music" (*PMA* xxxvii); F. Raugel, "The Ancient French Organ School" (*MQ* xi); K. G. Fellerer, "Zur italienischen Orgelmusik des 17/18. Jahrhunderts" (*JMP* xlv); O. Mansfield, "Mozart's Organ Sonatas" (*MQ* viii); H. Grace, "Modern French Organ Music" (*PMA* xliv); N. Dufourq, "Panorama de la musique d'orgue française au XXe siècle" (*RM* xix, xx).

Collections of Old Organ Music: H. J. Moser, *Frühmeister der deutschen Orgelkunst* (1930); O. Gauss, *Orgelkompositionen*, 4 vols. (1913ff); H. Redlich, *Meister des Orgelbarock* (new ed. of F. Commer's *Musica Sacra*); K. Straube, *Alte Meister des Orgelspiels* i, ii (1906; *Neue Folge* i, ii, 1929); M. Seiffert, *Organum*; W. Stahl, *150 Choralvorspiele alter Meister*; John E. West, *Old English Organ Music*; E. Kaller, *Liber Organi* (selected from A. Guilmant's *Archives*; see *Editions I); F. Raugel, *Les Maitres français de l'orgue*, 2 vols.; F. Pedrell, *Antologia de organistas clásicos españoles*; L. Villalba Muñoz, *Antologia de organistas clásicos españoles* (1914). See also *Organ chorale; *Organ Mass.

Organ playing (registration, accompaniment, etc.). The literature on this subject is extensive, but not up-to-date [see the remarks under *Organ XII (near end)]. A selected list follows.

Lit.: G. A. Audsley, *Organ Stops and*

their Artistic Registration (1921); Ch. N. Boyd, *Organ Registration and Accompaniment*, 2 vols. (1932); Cl. Dickinson, *The Technique and Art of Organ Playing* (1922); H. F. Ellingford, *The Art of Transcribing for the Organ* (1922); H. Grace, *The Complete Organist* (1920); A. Eaglefield-Hull, *Organ Playing* (1912); N. A. B. Hunt, *Modern Organ Stops* (1923); C. Locher, *An Explanation of the Organ Stops* (1888); G. B. Nevin, *A Primer of Organ Registration* (1920); E. E. Truett, *Organ Registration* (1919); J. I. Wedgwood, *Dictionary of Organ Stops . . .* (1905); H. Westerby, *The Complete Organ Recitalist* (1927); H. Gleason, "Organ Instruction before Bach" (*BAMS* iv). See also the literature under *Organ.

Organ point. See *Pedal point.

Organ stops. See *Organ VIII–XI. For literature see under *Organ and *Organ playing.

Organ tablature. (1) The various notational systems which were used for the writing down of early organ music (prior to 1600). They are usually distinguished as Italian, Spanish, etc., organ tablature. However, in Italy, as well as in France and England, organ music was notated in virtually the same way as it is today, except for minor details, such as variations in the number of the staff lines. Only in Germany and in Spain was organ music (more generally, keyboard music) written in systems which deserve the name tablature. See *Tablatures. — (2) The manuscripts and printed books of early organ music. As under (1), the name should properly be restricted to the German and the Spanish sources. Practically complete lists of organ tablatures (French, Italian, English, German, and Spanish) are given in *WoHN* ii, 32ff, 270ff, 278. Cf. also the article "Orgeltabulaturbuch" in *RiML*, where the name is restricted to the sources written in German tablature.

Organum. (1) Latin for organ. (2) The earliest type of polyphonic

music, from the 9th till the mid-13th century. In spite of the identity of names, the organum has no connection with the organ. Possibly, the word *organare* was used in the meaning of "to organize," i.e., different parts, a meaning which still persists in Paumann's **Fundamentum organisandi* (1452). In the broadest sense of the word, organum is a composition consisting of a liturgical (plainsong) tenor to which one or more contrapuntal parts (*duplum, triplum, quadruplum*) are added. In the earlier period of organum (prior to 1150) there was (judging from the relatively few preserved examples) no restriction as to the type of plainsong chosen as the basis for organum; simple syllabic hymns seem to have been preferred. Therefore, in this period, organum denotes a general technique of composition. In the School of Notre Dame, organum treatment became restricted to a few types of plainsong, mainly graduals, alleluias, and responsoria, resulting in a much narrower significance of the term [see V]. The following phases of the development can be distinguished:

I. *Parallel Organum* (9th and 10th centuries). The duplum (or *vox organalis*) accompanies the tenor (*vox principalis*) in the lower fifth or fourth, note against note. However, particularly in the organum at the fourth, the parallelism of the parts is strictly observed only in the middle of a phrase, while for the beginning and the close oblique motion may be used, starting and ending in unison [see under *Tritone]. Both voices could be duplicated at the octave, thus leading to a performance in four parts, probably by men's and boys' voices. The chief source for this type of organum is the *Musica Enchiriadis* (9th century; Ex. 1 and 2). A somewhat later type of parallel organum is that known as "organum in thirds," more properly called *gymel.

II. *Free Organum* (11th and early 12th centuries). The duplum still follows the tenor note against note, but without being restricted to parallel motion. There is an increasing emphasis on contrary motion (*occursus*). The two parts frequently cross, and the tenor now becomes generally the lower part. Occasionally we

find a group of notes (two to four) in the duplum against a single note of the tenor, an important foreshadowing of the next phase. The main treatises for this period are Guido's *Micrologus* (*c.* 1040; Ex. 3), Cotton's *Musica* (*c.* 1100), and the treatise *Ad organum faciendum* (*c.* 1150). A musical source is the 11th-century Winchester troper which, being written in neumes, makes exact reading of the intervals impossible but, nevertheless, shows clear evidence of contrary motion. A unique example of 11th-century free organum, notated in letters, is the two-voice "Ut tuo propitiatus" [cf. *ApNPM*, 205ff].

III. *Melismatic Organum* (12th century). The duplum, now regularly above the tenor, consists of groups of notes sung against a single note of the tenor, the extension of such a group varying from a few notes to long melismatic passages. This procedure, of course, greatly lengthens the compositions. A

Benedicamus domino composed in this style may easily be ten or twenty times as long as if sung in plainsong. Some of the pieces of this period have sections in note-against-note style interspersed between the melismatic sections [cf., e.g., *ApNPM*, 209ff]. A great number of compositions of this type are preserved in the MSS from Compostela [Ex. 4] and St. Martial (*c.* 1150) as well as in the sources of the School of *Notre Dame (*c.* 1200). Theorists of the 13th century refer to this type of organum as "organum duplum" or "organum purum" and emphasize the rhythmically free character of the upper part, in contradistinction to the measured performance of the *organa tripla* and *quadrupla* of the ensuing period [cf. *ApNPM*, 266ff].

IV. *Measured Organum* (before and after 1200). Around 1175, the rhythmically free dupla of the St. Martial style were supplanted by others written in strict rhythm, according to the rhythmic *modes. This epochal innovation is the work of Leoninus, the "optimus *organista," whose organa [see *Magnus liber organi] combine sections in melismatic style alongside with others in measured style [Ex. 5]. The latter style was exclusively adopted by Perotinus, the "optimus discantor" [see *Discant]. This procedure was necessitated (or, at least, accompanied) by his introduction of one or two additional contrapuntal parts, the triplum and quadruplum, moving in the same rhythm as the duplum above the longer notes of the tenor [for an example see *Notation, Ex. 2]. In addition to numerous *organa tripla* Perotinus composed three gigantic *organa quadrupla* which represent the acme as well as the end of the history of organum [cf. beginning of his "Viderunt omnes" in *AdHM* i, 229; complete transcription of his "Sederunt principes" by R. v. Ficker (1930); various organa tripla in *OH* i, 209ff].

V. In the School of Notre Dame (partly already in the earlier schools) polyphonic treatment and, therefore, the term organum, was restricted to certain types of plainsong, mainly graduals, alleluias, responsoria, and the *Benedicamus domino [see *Magnus liber organi]. It is important to notice that the liturgical melody of such a chant was never used in its entirety as a basis of polyphonic composition, but only those sections which, in Gregorian chant, are given to the soloist. E.g., in a gradual only the *incipit* and the entire vers, except for its conclusion, were composed polyphonically, the remaining portions being supplied, of course, by the choir in plainsong [for the structure of the graduals, see *Psalmody II]. This practice strongly suggests that the organum (i.e., polyphonic) sections were performed by a small number of soloists, not by a full chorus. The subsequent scheme illustrates the performance of Perotin's Christmas-Gradual "Viderunt" in the Cathedral of Notre Dame, around 1200 (S = soloists; Ch = choir).

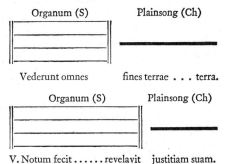

The history of organum is illustrated by examples in *HAM*, nos. 25–31.

Lit.: *OH* i, throughout; *ReMMA*, passim, bibl. 451–456; H. Husmann, *Die dreistimmigen Organa der Notre Dame Schule* . . . (1935); H. Schmidt, *Die drei- und vierstimmigen Organa* (1933); F. Ludwig, in *Riemann Festschrift* (1909); J. Handschin, in *ZMW* viii; H. Husmann, in *JMP* xlii. See also *Ars antiqua.

Organ vers. See *Verset.

Orgatron. See *Electronic musical instruments I.

Orgel- [G.]. Organ. *Orgelmesse*, (1) name of two masses by Haydn in which the organ plays an important solo role, one in E-flat, 1766 (*Grosse O.M.*), the other in B-flat, 1770 (*Kleine O.M.*); — (2) see *Organ mass. *Orgelpunkt*, pedal point. *Orgelwalze*, barrel organ [see *Mechanical instruments I].

Orgue [F.]. Organ. *Orgue de barbarie*, the street organ of the Italian organ-grinder, consisting of one or two rows of small organ pipes in a small portable case, operated by turning a handle. The word *barbarie* is a corruption of the name of an 18th-century Italian instrument-maker, Barbieri. *Orgue expressif*, *Harmonium. *Orgue plain*, full organ. *Orgue positif*, choir organ.

Oriental music. The music of the Orient: China, Japan, Indo-China, Polynesia, India, Arabia, North Africa, represents a vast treasure of musical art the significance and artistic values of which are just becoming apparent to the Western mind. We begin to see that the music of these nations, far from being primitive [see *Exotic music], represents a stage of cultural development which is entirely comparable to that of our music, the basic difference being that their efforts were almost exclusively directed towards melody and rhythm, while Western music has been interested primarily in the development of counterpoint and harmony. It is but natural, then, that the East should have developed subtleties of melody, rhythm, ornamentation, and tonal nuances (microtones) in comparison with which the Western achievements in these fields seem trifling and pedantic. "Polyphonic" traits are not rare in Oriental music, but are limited to rhythmic accompaniment, drones, and *heterophonic elements.

The chief difficulty encountered in the study of Oriental music is the lack of written sources, a lack which, in turn, is explained by the lack of adequate notational systems. It must be understood, however, that this lack is an intrinsic feature of Oriental music whose irrational character forestalls recording in exact symbols. In this respect, as in others also, Oriental music can be compared only to the ancient tradition of Gregorian chant, which was essentially dependent upon oral tradition and which began to decline at the time when the first attempts towards a more accurate fixation were made.

Oriental music has influenced Western music chiefly through two channels: via the Jews and the early Christian church, and via the Arabs in Spain. The former influence persists in the particular character of Gregorian chant (which is basically "un-European"); the latter in many musical instruments and in certain elements of theory and acoustics [see *Arabian music].

See the entries for the various nations mentioned above.

Lit.: Endo Hirosi, *Bibliography of Oriental and Primitive Music* (Tokyo, 1929); R. Lachmann, *Musik des Orients* (1929); *id., Ausser-Europäische Musik* (in *Bücken's Handbuch*, 1929); separate articles in *LavE*. See also the special entries (*Arabic, *Chinese, etc.).

Ornamentation. Musical ornamentation arose as a spontaneous act on the part of the interpreter who, in performing a written or traditional melody, enlivened it, expanded it, or varied it through his technique of improvisation. The more or less stereotyped melodic figures which, in this process, have been substituted for or added to the original notes of the melody are known as ornaments. Throughout the history of music three kinds of ornamentation have existed: I. that which is left entirely to the improvisation of the interpreter; II. that in which definite ornaments are indicated by some sort of stenographic sign; and III. that in which the ornaments are written out in notes.

I. *Historic Survey.* There is evidence that the early singers of Gregorian chant indulged in extemporary ornamentation of the traditional melodies, and that some of the variations created in this manner were eventually incorporated in the MSS [cf. A. Gastoué, *L'Origine du chant romain*]. In connection with polyphonic music improvised ornamentation occurred first in the *discantus supra librum*

of the 14th century. In the 16th century improvised ornamentation, known as *diminutio*, had its center at the Papal Chapel in Rome, where the singers ornamented and completely transformed works by Willaert, Lassus, Palestrina, etc. The technique of this practice was taught methodically in the theoretical works of the period [cf. M. Kuhn, *Die Verzierungskunst in der Gesangmusik des 16.–17 Jahrh.*]. All the voices of a polyphonic composition were susceptible to ornamentation. Hermann Finck, in his *Practica Musica* (1556), states that "the character of the coloratura depends upon the skill and the individuality of the executant. My own view is that *all* voices must be ornamented, but not simultaneously, so that each voice will be brought out in turn." Zacconi (*Pratica di musica*, 1592) writes that the art of diminution, also known as *gorgia*, "charms the listener, especially when in 4, 5, or 6-part pieces two voices stand out and sing solos together. It is a delight when one part of the piece is sung with improvised diminutions and the rest played upon instruments." The accompanying example, showing diminutions

by dalla Casa to Palestrina's madrigal "Vestiva i colli," illustrates the latter treatment [Ex. 1]. Diminutions (known in Spain as *glosas*, in England as *divisions*) were also used in purely instru-

mental performance. The fame of Merulo, the two Gabrielis, and Cabezon
rested largely upon the free and vivid
manner of improvising with which they
inspired seemingly dry pieces.

In many of the 16th-century treatises
on improvised ornamentation specific
names are attached to certain small melodic formulas which are made up either
of the repetition of a single note or of the
rapid alternation of two (or at most
three) adjacent notes. To the former
type belongs the Italian *trillo* (an accelerated *tremolo); to the latter (*trills), the
tremolo, *groppo*, and *ribattuta*, as well as
the Spanish *redoble* and *quiebro*, and the

English *relish [see Ex. 2]. Caccini,
Cavalieri, and other 17th-century Italian
musicians urged the cultivation of these
small ornaments, which they call *effetti*,
as a special means of expression. It was
in France, however, and under the name
of *agréments*, that these ornaments finally
became stereotyped and were systematized to the extent that it was possible to
indicate them in the music by signs or
abbreviations and to establish definite
rules for introducing them extemporaneously.

Improvised ornamentation and divisions continued to play a large part in
musical performance throughout the 17th
and 18th centuries. During this period
singers probably never executed a solo
part as it was written. The individual
qualities of operatic virtuosi led to "custom-composed" roles, written by the composer expressly for the range and style
of a certain singer who was engaged
for the part. Many composer-conductors
sketched out the ornamentation in advance and practiced it with the singers,
although no hint of this interpretation
appears in the published scores that have
come down to us. Corelli, Handel, Tartini, and their contemporaries made their

written parts of sonatas for strings mere
sketches of what the player should do.
The accompanying fragments from Handel's *Messiah* [Ex. 3] and a flute sonata

by Quantz [Ex. 4] illustrate typical 18th-
century practice.

Beginning with Gluck, composers
gradually suppressed most improvised
ornamentation except the agréments and
*cadenzas. One important relic of the
earlier practice, which persists even in
the operas of Mozart and Gluck, is the
appoggiatura in recitative. From the
time of Alessandro Scarlatti it was customary for composers to write the appoggiatura which appears at the end of
almost every phrase of recitative as a harmony note, in order to make the underlying harmony clear to the accompanist,
as in Ex. 5 the upper system of which
shows the customary notation, the lower,
the correct performance.

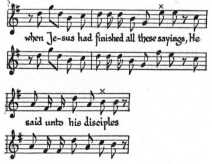

II. *Ornamentation as Indicated by
Signs.* Some musical ornaments are so
subtle and flexible in rhythm and pitch
that they defy expression in ordinary

musical notation and can only be represented by signs. The MSS of Gregorian chant contain certain special signs (sometimes appearing as modifications of the neumes), which indicate stressed notes (*pressus*), vibratos (*vinnula*), portamentos (*quilisma*), and smothered notes (liquescent neumes; see *Neumes I). According to the early theoretical writers the Gauls and Germans were incapable of performing some of these ornaments. Guido d'Arezzo (10th cent.) recommends that those who cannot execute "these sounds that the Italians produce naturally" should sing the simple note. The only frequently recurring sign for an ornament in the music of the later Middle Ages is the *plica, which was derived from the liquescent notes.

During the 16th century the indication of ornaments by sign was restricted almost entirely to keyboard music. The Germans used special signs for the *mordent, and in the English *virginal books there is a profusion of single and double oblique strokes through the stem of the note, denoting ornaments the exact nature of which has not been established. The Italian *groppo* and *tremolo* are sometimes indicated by abbreviations (the letters *g* and *t*) in the keyboard pieces of Valente [cf. *ApNPM*, facs. no. 16], Mayone, Trabaci, and Frescobaldi. Since the melodic forms of these ornaments were not yet definitely stereotyped the composers always wrote out the tremolo or groppo in notes the first time it occurred in a given piece or section, using the abbreviation only when the same melodic form was desired again.

By far the most important of all stenographic signs for ornaments are those of the French *agréments which were systematized during the 17th century and remained in continuous use by all European musicians until the beginning of the Romantic period. The correct interpretation of these signs constitutes a considerable problem in the execution of music of this period owing to the fact that the nomenclature and signs used for the individual agréments lacked uniformity and consistency. Identical ornaments

were often called by different names and represented by different signs, while the same name and sign were sometimes given to different agréments. The agréments, in general, may be divided into the following categories: 1. Appoggiaturas (also Double Appoggiaturas); 2. Trills; 3. Turns; 4. Mordents; 5. Nachschläge; 6. Arpeggios; 7. Vibratos. Each of these seven types of agrément receives fuller treatment under its own heading. The first three categories (Appoggiaturas, Trills, and Turns) were regarded as *essential* agréments, in the sense that their use was obligatory in certain positions of the musical phrase whether their signs appeared in the score or not. The others were arbitrary, and were often left to the discretion of the performer. It is significant that the only signs to be found in the works of Mozart and Beethoven are the tiny note representing the appoggiatura, the ~ for the turn, and the tr or t with a wavy line, indicating the trill. The other agréments had by that time become absorbed in the ordinary notation. Rossini was probably the first composer who — much to the indignation of Stendhal — deliberately abandoned the signs for agréments, writing out what he considered necessary in notes (in his opera *Elisabetta*, 1815).

For a detailed study of the Baroque ornaments the tables of signs given with a number of publications are indispensable [e.g., d'Anglebert, in *TaAM* vii, 111; F. Couperin, in *TaAM* x, 78; Kuhnau, in *TaAM* x, 2; Georg Muffat, in *DTOe* 2.ii, p. 52; Gottlieb Muffat, in *DTOe* 3.iii, p. 89]. Very helpful also are the realizations given in the modern edition of Loeillet [*Editions XVII, 1] and in an article by F. Dolmetsch (theme of Bach's Goldberg Variations, cf. *BSIM* viii, no. 2, p. 27). The accompanying table shows (without claim to completeness) a variety of signs used for the different types of ornamentations.

III. *Written-out Ornamentation.* The embellishment of a simple melody took its place, at an early date, among the regular procedures of composition. Frequently melismatic chants of the Gregorian repertory have been interpreted as ornamented versions of simpler skeleton melodies, e.g., of monotones [cf. *GD* iv, 369]. Definite evidence of ornamentation technique has been found in the music, mono-

I. Dashes.

⌐⌐⌐	Appoggiatura; Nachschlag
	Mordent; Double mordent
	Double appoggiatura
	Trill
	Appoggiatura
	Trill; Mordent; Appoggiatura
	Arpeggio

II. Zigzag Lines.

	Trill; Schneller
	Double appoggiatura
	Mordent
	Trill
	Trill (beginning with lower auxiliary note)
	Double mordent

III. Curved Lines.

	Appoggiatura
	Mordent
	Double appoggiatura
	Nachschlag
	Turn; Inverted turn
	Arpeggio
	Bebung (Clavichord)
	Ondulé (Violin)

IV. Letters.

t	Trill; Schneller
tr tw	Trill

phonic or polyphonic, of the 12th/14th centuries [cf. J. Handschin, "Zur Frage der melodischen Paraphrasierung im Mittelalter" (*ZMW* x)]. The upper voice of a 15th-century *discant Mass (by Dunstable, Dufay, Liebert, etc.) is usually an ornamented version of a Gregorian chorale or a folk tune [cf. R. Ficker, *Die Kolorierungstechnik der Trienter Messen,* wherein an example of this

technique dating as early as the 13th century is cited]. This practice reached its culmination in J. S. Bach's treatment of the Protestant chorale in his Organ Preludes (for example: "Wenn wir im höchsten Nöthen sein").

The transcription of vocal works for instrumental performance upon the keyboard, lute, or ensembles of melodic instruments is another field in which written-out ornamentation played an important role, especially during the 16th and 17th centuries [see *Intabulierung]. Furthermore, almost every 16th-century piece destined for keyboard or lute performance (whether transcription or independent composition) contains *groppi, tremoli, minute, *tirate,* etc. — ornaments which were customarily improvised by singers and by players of melodic instruments but which, in the case of keyboard and lute music, were written out in groups of rapid notes, as in the accompanying example from Sweelinck's Chro-

matic Fantasia. Some of these formulas gradually became more and more stereotyped in melodic form until finally they were incorporated in the system of agréments as *trills, relishes, double cadences, turns, mordents,* etc., and were henceforth indicated by means of stenographic signs or left to the improvisation of the performer.

Between 1650 and 1750 the practice of writing ornaments in notes was frowned upon as detrimental to the visual clarity of the melodic lines. J. S. Bach, for instance, was severely criticized by at least one contemporary musician, on the ground that "he writes down in actual notes the ornaments and embellishments that performers are accustomed to supply instinctively, a habit which not only sacrifices the harmonic beauty of his music but also makes the melody totally indistinct" (J. A. Scheibe, in *Der Critische Musicus* for May 14, 1737). The example here given shows how a passage from the Andante of the Italian Concerto would appear had it been written in the more conventional notation of Bach's time [(a) Doppelschlag (turn); (b) Schleifer

(double appoggiatura); (c) mordent; (d) passaggio; (e) tirata]. It must be noted, however, that Bach did not invariably adhere to this unorthodox practice; his keyboard suites, for instance, are provided with a goodly number of the traditional signs for agréments.

Since the late 18th century the pendulum has swung in the other direction, and composers have endeavored to indicate their intentions as precisely as possible on paper, using a minimum of signs and expressing all complex ornaments in such a way that there can be no doubt as to what notes are to be performed, even though, in certain cases, the rhythm of those notes be free, as in the so-called "cadenzas" written in tiny grace notes by Chopin and other Romantic composers.

Lit.: E. Dannreuther, *Musical Ornamentation*, 2 vols. (1893); A. Dolmetsch, *The Interpretation of the Music of the 17th and 18th Centuries*, 2 vols. (1915); E. Fowles, *Studies in Musical Graces* (1907); J. P. Dunn, *Ornamentation in the Works of Frederick Chopin* (1921); G. C. Hamilton, *Ornaments in Classical and Modern Music* (1930); M. Kuhn, *Die Verzierung in der Gesangsmusik des 16.–17. Jahrhunderts* (1902); H. Goldschmidt, *Die Lehre der vokalen Ornamentik* (1907); H. Ehrlich, *Die Ornamentik in Beethovens Klaviersonaten* (1896); P. Brunold, *Traité des signes et agréments employés par les clavecinistes français des 17. and 18. siècles* (1935); Jane Arger, *Les agréments . . . dans la musique vocale française du 18e siècle* (1920). — A. Dechevrens, in *SIM* xiv (Gregorian chant); J. Handschin, in *ZMW* x (Middle Ages); R. von Ficker, in *StM* vii (Trent Codices); J. Dodge, in *SIM* ix (lute tablatures); A. Moser, in

ZMW i (Corelli); H. Prunières, in *RM* xiii (Baroque, vocal); P. Aldrich, in *The Inchoirer*, Sept. 1939–Feb. 1940 (Bach's organ works); S. Salter, in *MQ* vi (same); E. Lockspeiser, in *ML* xvi, no. 4 (Bach-French); A. Schering, in *SIM* vii (18th century); H. Lungershausen, in *ZMW* xvi (same); M. Seiffert, in *SIM* viii (Messiah); F. Salzer, in *ZMW* xii (C. P. E. Bach); H. Mersmann, in *AMW* ii (pre-classical).   P. A.

Orphéon. French male choral societies, similar in character to the American *Apollo clubs or the German *Männergesangverein. The members consist chiefly of farmers, workers, and middle-class people. The movement started around 1835 and spread rapidly. By 1910 there were about 1200 orphéons in France. A system of public competitions, called "Concours Orphéoniques," was inaugurated by Bocquillon-Wilhelm in 1842. Gounod conducted the Orphéon of Paris from 1852 to 1860.

Orpheus and Euridice. The touching fable of the "inventor of music" recovering his beloved Euridice from Hades and losing her again in the moment of their reunion has been used more frequently than any other subject as an operatic libretto. Among the numerous operas based on this story, Monteverdi's *Orfeo* (1607), Gluck's *Orfeo ed Euridice* (1762; French version *Orphée*, 1774), and Offenbach's parody *Orphée aux Enfers* (1858) are immortal. It is interesting to note the difference between the tragic, but heroic, close of Monteverdi's opera and the "happy ending" of Gluck's. In the former, Orpheus loses Euridice, but, as a reward of his great love, is transferred to the stars by Apollo; in the latter, Amor appears and restores Euridice to life once more and for good.

Osanna. See *Hosanna.

Ossia [It., or] indicates an alternative version, usually one of easier execution.

Ostinato [It., obstinate]. A clearly defined melodic phrase which is repeated persistently, usually in immediate succession, throughout a composition or a section thereof. From other devices of repetition, such as *imitation and *sequence [see *Repetition], the ostinato is distinguished by the fact that it is reiterated in the same voice and at the same pitch. It is this feature which bestows upon the ostinato that peculiar character which is expressed in its name.

The earliest examples of ostinato occur in compositions of the 13th century, e.g., in the tenor of the motet *Amor potest conqueri* (Montpellier, no. 328) [Ex. 1].

A much better-known example from the same period is the *pes of the *Sumer canon. That the ostinato-technique is by no means restricted to the bass is shown in several organ pieces by John Redford (1485–1545) in which a short ostinato motive keeps recurring in the soprano [cf. C. Pfatteicher, *John Redford* (1934), p. 40; *HAM*, no. 120 b]. Another example of "soprano ostinato" is Frescobaldi's Capriccio sopra il cucco [*TaAM* iv, 64]. See also *Romanesca.

In the 16th century the ostinato technique received a fresh impulse from dance music, possibly from Oriental dances in which it is still prominent today. The Oriental element is particularly conspicuous in a Fantasia for two lutes by Valderrabano in which the second lute plays a one-measure ostinato throughout the entire composition [Ex. 2; cf. W. Apel, in *MQ* xx, 300]. Another early example of a dance-like ostinato occurs in "Mylady Carey's Dompe" of the Brit. Mus. *Roy. App. 58* (*c.* 1525; Ex. 3; see *Dump), while Hugh Aston's *Hornepype from the same MS utilizes the alternation of tonic and dominant as a harmonic basis without strict ostinato; thus the Dump and the Hornepype are early representatives of those two types of continuous variation [see *Variation] which are commonly distinguished as passaca-

glia and chaconne. The *Tratado de glosas* of the Spaniard Diego Ortiz (1553; new ed. by M. Schneider, 1912) contains the first examples of more extended bass melodies, in the character of the 17th-century *ground [Ex. 4].

The *New music of the 20th century has brought about an interesting and significant revival of the ostinato. Modern composers such as Hindemith and Bartók have been attracted by its polyphonic and rhythmic possibilities as well as by its anti-Romantic precision and straightforwardness [Ex. 5, Hindemith, Konzert, op. 38]. Ostinato technique has also been introduced into modern jazz under the name "riff" [see *Jazz IV]. For literature see *Ground.

Otello ("Othello"). Opera in four acts by Giuseppe Verdi (1813–1901), text by A. Boito after Shakespeare, produced 1887. The scene is 16th-century Cyprus where the Moor *Otello* rules as governor. The crafty *Iago* (Baritone), his secret enemy, devises a plot to convince Othello that his beloved and loving wife *Desdemona* (Soprano) is in love with the young officer *Cassio* (Tenor), a plot in which Desdemona's handkerchief, stolen from her and craftily slipped into Cassio's hand, serves as "convincing" evidence. In the last act, Othello strangles Desdemona who in vain pleads her innocence, and stabs himself after *Emilia* (Mezzo-Soprano), Iago's wife, has revealed the latter's treachery.

Otello, together with *Falstaff* (1893), represents the climax of Verdi's operatic work. In these operas Verdi abandoned the aria-style of his earlier operas (*Aida, etc.; see *Number opera) and adopted something like Wagner's principle of continuous composition without, however, sacrificing the "Italian" peculiarities of his personal style.

Ôtez [F.]. Take off (a stop).

Ottava [It.]. Octave, frequently abbreviated *8va* (*8*). *All'ottava, ottava alta, ottava sopra,* or simply *8va* written above the notes, indicates playing one octave higher than it is written; *ottava bassa,* *ottava sotta*, or *8va* written below the notes (usually in the bass part), calls for the lower octave. *Coll'ottava* means doubling in the higher (or lower) octave.

Ottavino [It.]. The piccolo flute.

Ottoni, or **stromenti d'ottone** [It.]. Brass instruments.

Ouvert [F., open]. (1) French term for the open strings of violins, etc. — (2) In the *ballades, *estampies, *virelais of the 14th century, *ouvert* and *clos* [L. *apertum, clausum*; It. *aperto, chiuso*] indicate different endings for repeated sections, corresponding to the modern *prima volta, seconda volta*. Cf. ApNPM, 349.

Ouverture [F.]. See *Overture.

Overblowing. See *Wind instruments II, III.

Overtones. See *Acoustics IV.

Overture. I. *The Operatic Overture.* Instrumental music composed as an introduction to an opera, oratorio, or similar work. The earliest operas, which usually began with a *prologue, had no overture or, at most, a flourish of instruments such as the "Toccata" of Monteverdi's *Orfeo* (1607). One of the first overtures of a more complex nature is that of Steffano Landi's *Il San'Alessio* (1632) which consists of a "Preambulum" in slow, pompous style followed by a "Canzona" in three sections. This opera also has elaborate *"Sinfonias" before the second and third acts, each in three-movement form (fast, slow, fast), like the later "Italian" overture [cf. H. Goldschmidt, *Studien zur Geschichte der italienischen Oper* i, pp. 230ff; HAM, no. 208]. The "canzona"-overture [see *Canzona (5)] was a favorite type in the Venetian opera, where it usually occurs in the form of an introductory slow movement in duple rhythm followed by a fast movement in triple rhythm (Cavalli, *Giasone*, 1649). Other overtures, hardly different in form, are called Sonata (e.g., Cesti, *Il Pomo d'oro*, 1667). There can be no doubt that the Venetian type of overture was the model for Lully's famous *French overture*

(earliest example in his ballet *Alcidiane*, 1658) which became the first standard type of overture. It consists of a slow introduction in pompous style with dotted rhythm, followed by an allegro in imitative style on a short canzona-like subject, though the imitative treatment is not strictly maintained and the "fugal" character of this movement is more illusory than real [cf. *HAM*, no. 224]. Sometimes the second movement of the French overture ends with a broad adagio passage which has led to the erroneous statement that this is a three-movement form; this statement is not in accordance with the actual examples in which the closing section (if present at all) is an "allargando" coda to the allegro rather than a separate movement. There exist, however, later examples of French overture in which the closing passage is extended into a "third movement," i.e., that which opens Bach's so-called *French Overture* (really, a French overture followed by a suite; see II). Handel's overture to *Rinaldo* (1711; cf. SchGMB, no. 278) illustrates other methods of amplification, merging with the sonata da chiesa.

In the late 17th century Al. Scarlatti introduced another type of overture, the "Italian overture" (earliest example in *Dal malo i bene*, 1681 or 1686), consisting of three sections, allegro, adagio, and allegro, an early adumbration of the three movements of the sonata. These sections are all in simple homophonic style except the first which introduces some imitative treatment for the entrances of the voices. The usual name for this type is "sinfonia" [see *Sinfonia; Ex. in *HAM*, no. 259]. During the first half of the 18th century both the French and the Italian types existed side by side. Cases of Italian operas and oratorios having a French overture — which excelled the other as regards artistic quality — are not rare (e.g., Handel). The French overture disappeared around 1750, as a result of the rapidly growing importance of the symphony and the sonata as standard forms.

An important feature of the ensuing development was the emphasis on a closer connection of the overture with the opera itself, mainly by incorporation into the overture of material from the opera. Examples of such a procedure occurred in Cesti's *Il Pomo d'oro* and in Rameau's *Castor et Pollux* (1735), but did not lead to an accepted practice until after 1750. Of still greater significance is the tendency to use the overture as an expression of mood preparatory to the first scene of the play. Perhaps the first example is the overture to Gluck's *Iphigénie en Tauride* (1778) in which the overture announces the approaching thunderstorm of the opening scene. Famous examples of an overture as a piece designed to set the emotional background for the plot are those to Haydn's *Creation*, Mozart's *Don Giovanni* and *The Magic Flute*, Beethoven's **Leonora-Overtures* (not the final Fidelio-Overture), Weber's *Freischütz*, and practically all the overtures by Wagner and his successors. Wagner abandoned the sonata-like structure of the overture in favor of a free "Vorspiel" directly leading into the first scene. His precedent is followed in most of the recent operas. In a strong contrast to this Romantic type is the overture to the 19th century "grand opéra" of French derivation (Rossini, Boildieu, Auber, Meyerbeer), which usually is merely a potpourri of the most important melodies of the opera.

II. *The French Overture as a Suite.* See *Suite V.

III. *The Concert-Overture* of the 19th century is an independent orchestral composition written along the same lines as the operatic overture, either as a single movement in sonata-form, or as a free

"Vorspiel." Well-known examples are Mendelssohn's *Hebrides Overture*, Berlioz' *Le Carnaval Romain*, Brahms's *Academic Festival Overture*. Under this category may also be included the overtures written as an introduction to spoken plays and frequently performed as concert pieces, such as Beethoven's overture to Goethe's *Coriolan* and Mendelssohn's overture to the *Midsummer-Night's Dream*.

Lit.: H. Botstiber, *Geschichte der Ouverture* (1913); A. Heuss, "Die Venetianischen Opernsinfonien" (*SIM* iv); H. Prunières, "Notes sur l'origine de l'ouverture française" (*SIM* xii).

Oxford Symphony. Haydn's Symphony no. 92 in G, composed in 1788. It was performed in Oxford in 1791 when Haydn was there to receive his honorary doctor's degree from the university.

Oxyrynchos hymn. The earliest Christian hymn (*c.* A.D. 300) for which the music is preserved. It takes its name from the place Oxyrynchos in Middle Egypt, where the papyrus was found on which it is written. The text is in Greek, and the melody is written in the Greek vocal notation [see *Notation]. The melody [cf. *BeMMR*, 45] shows certain traits of ancient Greek music (large intervals, rhythmic accentuation) as well as others of Oriental character (numerous small coloraturas) which on the whole would seem to predominate.

Lit.: A. S. Hunt, *The Oxyrynchos Papyri* (1928); H. Abert, in *ZMW* iv; O. Ursprung, in *BUM* iii (1923); *id.*, in *Theologie und Glaube* xviii (1926).

P

P. Abbreviation for piano; for pedal (in organ and piano music); or for [F.] *positif*, i.e., choir organ.

Pacato [It.]. Peaceful, placid.

Padiglione [It.]. The bell of a wind instrument. *Padiglione cinese*, i.e., Chinese *crescent.

Padovana, paduana. A 16th-century term which it is difficult to distinguish from the contemporary term *pavane. Etymologically, pavana may be a deterioration of paduana (dance from Padua), or paduana may be a corruption of pavana (peacock dance). The earliest source for both terms, Dalza's *Tabulatura de lauto* of 1508, contains four dances inscribed "Pavana," while the book title mentions "Padoane diverse." Similarly, in G. Morlaye's *Premier livre de tabelature* (1553), pieces inscribed "Paduanes" are listed under this name in the index, while the book title mentions "Pavanes." In Rotta's *Intabolatura de lauto* (1546) and in Waisselius's *Tabulatura* (1573) the name padovana appears in connection with dances in quick 6/8-meter. In the interest of clarity, it is recommended that this name be reserved for such dances, and the name pavane for dances in slow duple (or, occasionally, triple) meter. Dalza's dances are pavanes.

Paean [Gr., the healing]. Originally a name of Apollo, the term denotes a song in praise of this god, or a song of praise in general.

Pagan Poem, A. See *Symphonic poem IV.

Pagliacci (i.e., The Players; G. *Der Bajazzo*). Opera in two acts and prologue by Ruggiero Leoncavallo, to his own libretto, produced 1892. The scene is in a village in Calabria, 1865, where a comedy troupe consisting of *Canio* (Tenor), his wife *Nedda* (Soprano), *Tonio* (Baritone), and *Beppe* (Tenor) arrive to give a performance. Nedda, in love with the handsome villager *Silvio* (Baritone), refuses the urgent attentions of the ugly Tonio who, swearing revenge, calls Canio to surprise the lovers, but Silvio escapes unrecognized. In the second act the performance takes place. Canio, in terrible excitement, confuses play and reality, demands in vain from his wife the name of her lover, and losing all control, stabs Nedda to death as well as Silvio who rushes to her aid.

Together with Mascagni's *Cavalleria rusticana*, *Pagliacci* is the outstanding example of the movement known as *Verismo. Large portions of the text are composed in a speech-like recitation which contributes to making the opera a dramatic and exciting representation of "true life." Particularly famous is the prologue in which Tonio explains the

idea of the plot — a conscious revival of the *prologue of 17th-century opera.

P'ai hsiao. See *Panpipes.

Paléographie musicale. See *Editions, Historical, XXIII.

Palestrina style. A polyphonic a-cappella style based upon the principles of counterpoint, imitation, melodic movement, consonance and dissonance, such as are shown in the music of Palestrina. As early as the 17th century this style, under names such as *stile antico*, *stile osservato* [see *Stile], had become "classical" in the *Roman school. In the early 19th century it was revived by Baini (1775–1844) and, later, by the protagonists of the *Cecilian movement. Pope Pius X, through his *motu proprio*, raised it to new authority in the field of church composition, and in the recent teaching of counterpoint there is a tendency to make the Palestrina style, rather than that of Bach, the point of departure [cf. K. Jeppesen, *Counterpoint* (1939); A. T. Merritt, *Sixteenth-Century Polyphony* (1940)].

Lit.: K. Jeppesen, *The Palestrina Style and the Dissonance* (1927); O. Ursprung, *Restauration und Palestrina-renaissance in der katholischen Kirchenmusik der letzten zwei Jahrhunderte* (1924); K. G. Fellerer, *Der Palestrinastil und seine Bedeutung in der vokalen Kirchenmusik des 18. Jahrhunderts* (1929); H. J. Moser, in *KJ*, 1930.

Pallet. See *Organ II.

Palotache, palotas. See *Hungarian music II.

Pandean pipes. See *Panpipes.

Pandiatonicism. A recent term introduced by N. Slonimsky to denote an important trend in contemporary music, namely, the return to the diatonic scale as the basic tonal material, though without the harmonic restrictions implied in the common practice of such composers as Haydn and Mozart. The accompanying example [Stravinsky, Piano Concerto] illustrates this style in which usually the absence of functional harmony results in a certain tonal staticity, offset

by a greater interest in counterpoint, rhythm, and chord spacing. From a methodical point of view, pandiatonicism might be considered as the "diatonic" counterpart of *atonality which applies the same principle of "harmonically un-restricted combination" to the chromatic scale. Historically, however, pandiatoni-cism represents a reaction against the "pan-chromaticism" of atonality as well as against the "harmonic chromaticism" of the late 19th century. In fact, a page from, e.g., Stravinsky's Serenade (1925) or Poulenc's Suite (1920) with their C major appearance offers a most striking contrast to the piling up of sharps and flats in a page from Ravel or Schönberg.

Pandiatonic style is clearly present in many of the whimsical pieces by Satie, written around 1910 (e.g., Embryons desséchés), and in portions of Stravin-sky's Petrouchka (1911). It became more fully established around 1925 as a con-comitant of the *neo-classical movement. Cf. N. Slonimsky, *Music Since 1900* (1937), p. xxii.

Pandora, pandore, pandura, ban-dora, etc. These terms are used with-out clear distinction for several instru-ments: (1) A long-necked lute of ancient Greece (*pandura*) [see *Lute II]. — (2) A small bottle-shaped fiddle used in the Caucasus (*panduri, fandur*). — (3) A queer-shaped guitar of the 17th century (*pandora, pandore*, also *bandura*) [see *Guitar family].

Panharmonicon. See *Mechanical in-struments III.

Panorgue. See *Harmonium.

Panpipes, pandean pipes. A primi-tive wind instrument consisting of a num-ber of pipes (vertical flutes; see *Instru-ments III) of different size which are bound or glued together, usually in the form of a raft. It is played by moving it in front of the mouth, similar to the mouth-harmonica. See illustration on p. 272. The panpipes is one of the most ancient instruments. It occurs in ancient Greece where it was called *syrinx* and attributed to the god Pan, as well as in China, Rumania, and South America. The Peruvian panpipes is called *antaras*, that of Ecuador (made of 33 pipes of cane) *rondador*.

The Chinese panpipes, called *pai hsiao*, consists of sixteen (formerly twelve) pipes which are arranged in two whole-tone scales [see Ex.]. It is a ritualistic

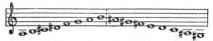

and symbolic instrument representing, by its shape, the outspread wings of the mystic bird phoenix, and by the arrange-ment of its pipes in two groups, the male and female element (the tones of the left half are the "yang lü," i.e., masculine tones; those of the right half, the "yin lü," i.e., feminine tones). See *Chinese music. Cf. A. H. Fox-Strangways, in *ML* x, no. 1; J. Tregenna, *The Pipes of Pan* (1926); E. M. von Hornbostel, in *Festschrift für P. W. Schmidt* (1928).

Pantaleon, pantalon. An enlarged *dulcimer invented around 1690 by Pan-taleon Hebenstreit who also was a virtu-oso on this instrument. It had 185 strings in all, and was played by means of two small hammers. The frequently-told story that the pantalon led to the inven-tion of the pianoforte is only partly true [see *Pianoforte II]. The last virtuoso on the instrument was one Georg Nölli (Noel) who gave performances in Eng-land (1767) on an instrument with 276 strings. Towards the end of the 18th century the name was transferred to a variety of the pianoforte in which the hammers struck from above.

Pantomime [Gr., everything imi-tated]. A dramatic performance without words, the action being revealed merely by gestures, to the accompaniment of music. From the *ballet the pantomime is distinguished by its emphasis on dramatic movements, rather than on stylized dancing; however, the *ballet d'action* is much the same thing as pantomime. Pantomimic representations played an important part in ancient Greece. Towards the end of the pre-Christian era they developed into a virtuoso show, in which a single actor performed entire plays, representing different personages in masques. Throughout the 18th century, pantomimes were extremely popular. At first they were of a mythological character, but soon changed into comedies, acted by Harlequin, Pantaloon, Clown, the Old Man and his Pretty Daughter, and similar characters. To such popular entertainments music was occasionally written by composers of some renown, such as the two Arnes, Dibdib, etc. [for more details, cf. the article in *GD*]. A revival of greater significance from the musical point of view was inaugurated by André Wormser's *L'Enfant prodigue* (1890). More recent examples are R. Strauss's *Josephslegende* (1914) and *Schlagobers* (1924), as well as Bartók's *Der wunderbare Mandarin* (1926). Cf. R. J. Broadbent, *A History of Pantomime* (1901).

Papadike. See *Byzantine chant III.

Papillons [F., butterflies]. A fancy title used by R. Schumann for his op. 2, a collection of twelve short piano pieces, "butterflies of different colors," as it were.

Parallel chords. The successive sounding of a fixed chordal combination, consonant or dissonant, through various degrees of the scale. In classical harmony this device is admissible only for the sixth-chord [see *Fauxbourdon (1)], and strictly prohibited in connection with triads, seventh-chords, etc., on account of the parallel fifths which would result in these cases. In deliberate violation of these principles, French composers, particularly Debussy, introduced parallelism

for triads and seventh-chords as well as for any dissonant combination involving seconds, fourths, etc. [Ex. 1, *Danse sacrée*, 1904; Ex. 2, *Et la lune descend*,

1907]. This technique, which is one of the most characteristic features of *impressionistic music, is in opposition to traditional harmony not only because it violates the rule of parallel fifths or because it introduces unresolved dissonances, but chiefly because it rejects the fundamental concept of traditional harmony, namely, the functional character of the chords. Instead, it establishes the chord as a mere sensuous and sonorous factor. Recent composers such as Stravinsky, Bartók, Casella, have exploited the percussive quality of parallel chords, by using them in rapid succession and in pronounced rhythm [Ex. 3, *Petrouchka*].

Although Debussy's name is rightfully connected with the establishment of parallelism as a technique, occasional examples are to be found with numerous 19th-century composers (Rossini, Moussorgsky, Lalo, Délibes; cf. *LavE* ii.1, 72ff, 632ff). Parallel *fourth-chords occur in Satie's *Le Fils des étoiles* of 1891 [Ex. 4], and "percussive" parallelism prevails in the introduction to Act II of Puccini's *La Bohème*, 1896 [Ex. 5]. In the 16th century, parallel triads were used parodistically in the *villanella*, and a "serious" example of remarkable boldness occurs in Monteverdi [cf. H. Leichtentritt, in *MM* v, 16]. The aesthetic and technical connection of the modern parallelism with the parallel fifths of the 10th-century *organum (writers frequently speak of an "organum technique") is very slight, the historical connection is nil.

Parallel (consecutive) fifths, octaves. These result if the melodic progression of a part (e.g., c–d) is duplicated by another part at the distance of a fifth (g–a) or octave (c′–d′). Such voice-leading [see Ex. 1] is considered faulty,

and is strictly prohibited in classical counterpoint. Its avoidance is a basic feature of the contrapuntal style from the 15th to the 19th century.

Naturally, a study of the music of this period reveals numerous exceptions to this rule, in Ockeghem and Josquin as well as in Bach and Mozart [see Ex. 2, from Bach's organ chorale *Nun hilf uns*]. This is something perfectly natural in music, which, after all, is an art, not an exact science, and in which there is no rule without legitimate exceptions. It would scarcely be necessary to dwell upon this point, were it not for the fact that theorists and writers of the 18th and 19th centuries have bestowed upon this rule the character of a "strict law." Equipped with this infallible instrument, they not only discovered many "stylistic faults" in Bach, but also condemned as "unbearably crude" early musical styles, such as the parallel *organum of the 9th century, or the motets of the 13th century, some-

times even going so far as to raise objections against the mixture stops of the organ [see *Organ VI]. Today, this narrow point of view has been largely abandoned.

A fifth (or octave) which is reached, not in parallel, but in similar motion, is referred to as a "hidden (covered) fifth" (or octave). This kind of voice-leading is usually admissible, except for certain extreme cases, e.g., when large skips are involved in both voices, e.g., $\begin{smallmatrix} g-c' \\ B-f \end{smallmatrix}$. Particularly frequent (and entirely proper) is the progression illustrated in Ex. 3. This is called horn fifths, since it forms a characteristic feature of the writing for natural horns. See also *Parallel chords.

Regarding a reputed medieval practice of "singing in parallel seconds," cf. E. Ferand, in *MQ* xxv.

Lit.: F. T. Arnold, "J. S. Bach and Consecutives in Accompaniment" (*ML* xiv, no. 4); F. E. Gladstone, in *PMA* viii; H. W. Nicholls, "Bach's Non-Observance of Some Fixed Rules" (*SIM* iii); M. G. Sewall, "Hucbald, Schoenberg and Others on Parallel Octaves and Fifths" (*MQ* xii); A. Schönberg, in *DM*, 1910/ 11, vol. xxx.

Parallel key. See *Key relationship.

Parallel motion. See *Motion.

Paralleltonart [G.]. Relative (not parallel) key.

Paramese, paranete. See *Greek music II (a).

Paraphonia, paraphonista. *Paraphonia* denotes, in late Greek and in early medieval theory, the intervals of the fifth and fourth, in contradistinction to *symphonia*, the unison, and *antiphonia*, the octave. The fact that certain early liturgical books (*Ordo Romanus I*, 7th century) mention singers called *paraphonistae* has been adduced as an evidence of parallel *organum long before Hucbald's *Musica enchiriadis*. Cf. R. Wagner, in *RdM*, nos. 25, 29; A. Gastoué, in *RdM*, no. 26; *ReMMA*, 252.

Paraphrase. The general meaning of the term is that of free rendition or elaboration. It is used to denote: (1) a textual paraphrase, i.e., a free rewriting of a text; e.g., a psalm paraphrase is a new wording of a psalm, usually in poetic language (metrical psalm; see *Psalter). See remark under *Contrafactum. — (2) A musical paraphrase, e.g., a free arrangement of operatic melodies (Liszt's paraphrases on Wagnerian operas); or polyphonic elaborations of liturgical cantus-firmus melodies (cf. the chapter "Das paraphrasierte Kirchenlied" in RiHM ii.1); or melodic modifications, ornamentations, etc., of pre-existing melodies (cf. J. Handschin, "Die melodische Paraphrase im Mittelalter," ZMW x). Cf. R. Köppel, Die Paraphrase (Diss. Vienna 1936).

Pardessus de viole. See *Dessus.

Parhypate. See *Greek music II (a).

Parlando [It., speaking]. In singing, an indication that the voice must approximate speech: in a way, "spoken music," as distinguished from the "musical speech" of the *recitative. Parlando occurs particularly in rapid tempo when the syllables of the text change with every note; see *Patter song. In connection with instrumental music, parlando (parlante) calls for an expressive declamation, suggestive of speech or song.

Parody. In present-day usage parody means a satirical imitation, such as may be created in music either by supplanting the original words by a textual parody, or by changing the composition as such in a comical manner [see *Satire]. In connection with earlier practice the term denotes: (a) replacement of text in general, with or without the implication of caricature [see *Contrafactum]; (b) specifically, a particular type of borrowing which plays an important role in 16th century composition of the mass [see *Parody Mass].
Lit.: D. F. Grout, "17th-Century Parodies of French Opera" (MQ xxvii); R.

Haas, "Wiener deutsche Parodieopern um 1730" (ZMW viii); G. Cucuel, "Les Opéras de Gluck dans les parodies du XVIIIe siècle" (RM iii); see also *Paraphrase; *Parody mass; *Satire; *Villanella.

Parody Mass [L. missa parodia]. The term refers to an important practice of 16th-century Mass composition, namely the use of musical material borrowed from pre-existent pieces (motets, chansons, madrigals) for the composition of the Mass. Usually the term is understood not to include the mere borrowing of a *cantus firmus, i.e., of a single melody used as a tenor, although, possibly, this widespread practice formed the point of departure for the procedure encountered in Parody Masses. Occasionally, the process of borrowing went so far as the taking over in toto of the entire musical substance of, e.g., a motet, the words of which were simply replaced by the text of a Mass item, a procedure which is equivalent to *contrafactum. Usually, however, more subtle methods of borrowing were used, the most common being the breaking up of the model into several passages or sections and their use in free modification and in alternation with newly composed sections. In the 15th century the borrowing was made from chansons. Early examples are Ockeghem's Missa Fors seullement (based on his own chanson of the same name) and Agricola's Missa Le serviteur (based on a chanson by Busnois). In the 16th century, particularly after Josquin (d. 1521), motets served most frequently as a model. About three-quarters of the Masses of Palestrina and Lassus are Parody Masses. For an example, cf. HAM, no. 146. Cf. also Hassler's motet "Ecce quam bonum" (DdT 2) and his Mass of the same name (DdT 7).
Lit.: W. H. Rubsamen, "Some First Elaborations of Masses from Motets" (BAMS iv); P. Pisk, "Das Parodieverfahren in den Messen des I. Gallus" (StM v); J. Schmidt-Görg, "Vier Parodiemessen des 16. Jahrhunderts" (KJ, 1930).

Parsifal. Opera in three acts by Richard Wagner, to his own libretto, produced at Bayreuth in 1882, for the dedication of the Festspielhaus [see *Bühnenweihfestspiel], and performed there exclusively for twenty years. First performances outside of Bayreuth were at New York in 1903 and (in Europe) at Zurich, 1913. *Amfortas* (Baritone), guardian of the Holy Grail (the vessel from which the Saviour drank at the Last Supper) and of the Holy Spear, has succumbed to the beguilements of *Kundry* (Soprano), a beautiful maiden who is torn between "evil and good," i.e., between the service of the enchanter *Klingsor* (Bass) and that of the Grail. The Spear has fallen in the hands of Klingsor who has afflicted Amfortas with a wound which will not heal. The deliverer appears in the person of the "guileless fool" *Parsifal* (Tenor) who (Act II) resists the temptations of Kundry (scene in the Magic Garden) and, seizing Klingsor's lance, destroys the latter's power. In years of wandering he learns wisdom and, returning to the Castle of the Grail as a knight in armor (Act III), delivers Amfortas and Kundry from their sin.

Parsifal, Wagner's last work, is written according to the principles of the Music Drama [see *Opera X]. The musical style is, in the passionate scenes (Kundry), similar to that of Tristan, but the basic expression is one of solemn dignity which does not always escape the danger of monotony.

Part. (1) In orchestral or chamber music, the music for the single instruments, such as violin, flute, pianoforte, etc. — (2) In contrapuntal music, the single melodic line of the contrapuntal web (fugue in three, four parts). The modern names for such parts, also called voices, are soprano, alto, tenor, and bass. Early names are: *vox principalis and organalis (9th–11th centuries); *tenor, *duplum (motetus), triplum, quadruplum (13th century); *discantus, tenor, *contratenor (1300–1450); cantus, altus, tenor, bassus, quinta vox, sexta vox, *vagans (1450–1600). See also *Treble;

*Meane. — (3) A section of a composition, as in three-part song form.

Part books [G. *Stimmbücher*]. The manuscript or printed books of the 15th and 16th centuries, each containing the music for an individual voice of a polyphonic composition [see under *Score II]. The usual number of part books is four: *Cantus* (*Discantus, Superius*); *Altus*; *Tenor*; *Bassus* (*Basis*), abbreviated: *C* (*D, S*); *A*; *T*; *B*. Books for additional parts were marked either *Cantus I*, *Cantus II*, or *Quinta Vox* (*V*), *Sexta Vox* (*VI*), etc.

Publication in part books clearly indicates that the music thus written or published is *ensemble music, either vocal, or instrumental, or mixed.

Parte [It.]. (1) Voice-part [see *Colla parte]. — (2) 17th-century term for variation [see *Partita; *Parthie].

Parthenia. A printed collection of *virginalistic music, published in 1611 (1613, 1635, and many later editions). According to the title, it was "the first musicke that euer was printed for the Virginalls." It contains 21 compositions "by three famous Masters William Byrd, Dr. John Bull and Orlando Gibbons." New editions from the old plates were made in 1847 (Rimbault) and in 1908. — A companion work is the *Parthenia Inviolata* which contains anonymous pieces ("dances and tunes") for virginal and bass-viol (only preserved copy in the New York Public Library).

Parthie, Partie [G.]. German 17th-century spelling for *partita. The French word *partie* usually has the meaning of part, voice (*fugue à 3 parties*).

Partials. See *Acoustics IV.

Partial signature. The use of a signature, practically always b-flat, in some but not all of the voices of a polyphonic composition. Prior to 1500 such signatures are extremely frequent, much more frequent in fact than "full" signatures. As a rule, the highest part carries no signature, the b-flat being indicated only with the lower parts. Typical combinations are: ♮, ♭ for two-voiced pieces (13th century); ♮, ♮, ♭, or ♮, ♭, ♭ for three-voiced pieces (13th, 14th centuries); ♮, ♮, ♭, ♭ for four-voiced pieces (15th century). This method of notation is not, as has frequently been assumed, a mere negligence or a meaningless tradition, but the adequate expression of a contrapuntal *polytonality in which the melody-carrying parts tend towards the tonal realm of the B-natural (Lydian), the lower parts towards that of the B-flat ("F-major or G-minor"). Cf. W. Apel, in *AM* x; *ApNPM*, 102ff, 140.

Partie [G., F.]. See under *Parthie.

Partimento [It.]. A 17th/18th-century practice of improvising melodies and complete pieces above a written bass, thus a broadening of the practice of *thorough-bass in which the bass as well as the melody is given. The English *"divisions upon a ground" belong to the field of partimento playing, which was extensively cultivated in the later Baroque period as a means of musical instruction. Gaetano Greco (b. 1680), Francesco Durante (1684–1755), and Giacomo Tritto (1733–1824) wrote partimenti. Cf. K. F. Fellerer, *Der Partimento-Spieler* (1940); *id.*, "Gebundene Improvisation" (*DM* xxxi.6).

Partita [It.]. A 17th- and 18th-century term which signifies either a suite or a series of variations. The original and proper meaning of the word is variation. In Trabaci's *Ricercate, canzone, . . . partite diverse* (1615) as well as in Frescobaldi's *Toccate e partite d'intavolatura* (1614) and in other early Italian publications, partita always means a series of variations, not a suite [cf. the erroneous statement in *RiML*, 1790], as it does also with Pachelbel (1699), Boehm, and in Bach's Chorale partitas for the organ. How the term came to adopt the meaning of suite is not entirely clear. Possibly the denomination *Parthien (for suites), which appears in the publications of Froberger (1693), Kuhnau (1692), Krieger (1697; here also in the version partita), Theo-

phil Muffat (1726), is derived, not from It. *partita*, but from F. *partie* (movement), a term which may have denoted suite-like compositions. Bach uses the designation partita for his six suites for harpsichord, published in the *Clavierübung* i (1731) and for those for violin solo. Several of the harpsichord partitas show Italian features, such as the Italian names "sinfonia" and "burlesca," and the preference for the *corrente instead of the *courante.

Partition [F.], **Partitur** [G.], **partitura** [It.]. *Score. See also under *Intavolatura.

Part-song. A choral composition in *homophonic style, i.e., with the top part as the sole carrier of melodic interest. The term is commonly understood in contrast to the madrigal with its emphasis on polyphonic texture and, therefore, applies chiefly to choral works of the 19th century, such as were written by Schumann, Mendelssohn, Parry, Stanford, Elgar, and many others. See also *Glee. In recent writings on music history the term is used in quite a different meaning, i.e., for the truly polyphonic songs of the pre-madrigal period. Thus, Isaac's *Innsbruck ich muss dich lassen* is designated as a "German part-song." Cf. A. Vogel, "The English Part-Song around 1500" (*BAMS*, 1940).

Pasacalle [Sp., make rounds of the street]. A Latin American dance which has adopted different traits in various countries. In Bolivia it is a gay, carefree serenade in slow duple meter; in Ecuador, a quick dance in 3/4- or 6/8-meter; in Peru, a march in 2/4-meter, a type which also occurs under the same name in Spain. None of these dances shows a demonstrable relationship to the old *passacaglia.

Paso doble [Sp.]. A kind of one-step (though the name means "double-step") in 6/8-meter which became popular about 1926.

Paspy. Anglicism for *passepied.

Passacaglia [It.], **passacaille** [F.]. See *Chaconne and passacaglia.

Passage. A term which is loosely used to refer to a short section of a composition, much in the same way as in literature (a passage from the Bible). More specifically, passages or passage work is a denomination for sections which contain brilliant display of virtuosity, rather than important musical ideas. Thus, one speaks of "scale passages," "arpeggio passages."

Passaggio [It.]. (1) Transition, modulation. — (2) Passage work. — (3) In the 16th-century art of diminution [see *Ornamentation] a generic term for improvised ornaments, usually other than plain scale passages or trill-like figurations.

Passamezzo, pass'e mezzo [It. *passo*, step; *mezzo*, half]. A dance of the second half of the 16th century, in duple meter and in moderately quick tempo [see *Dance music II]. Among the various explanations of the name ("pace-and-a-half feature in the dance steps"; "dance through the middle of the room"; "dance music in halved note values") only the last is worth attention. Very likely, the word "mezzo" refers to the diminution (halving) of the note values which is indicated by the alla-breve sign: ¢ [see *Proportions, proportio dupla]. The term, then, simply means that the dance is about twice as fast as the earlier *pavane. In fact, Arbeau, in his *Orchésographie* of 1585, explains the passamezzo as a "pavane, moins pesamment et d'une mesure plus légère." It may also be noted that the expression "pavane passemaize" occurs in Gervaise's *Sixième livre de danseries* (1550). The passamezzo is usually followed by the *saltarello, a combination which around 1550 superseded the combination pavane-gaillard.

The early passamezzos were not entirely free and original compositions, but were written as "variations" of a standard melody which occurs first in Spanish lute books under the name of *Guardame las vacas* or *Romanesca*. These passa-

mezzos are sometimes designated as "passamezzo antico." The melodies of two examples, (a) from Phalèse, 1571 [cf. *RiML*, 1352], (b) from Caroso's *Il Ballerino*, 1581 [cf. *GD* iv, 71], are shown here, together with their common skele-

ton melody [cf. also *HAM*, no. 154a, b; *BeMMR*, 308]. The later passamezzos, sometimes designated as "passamezzo nuovo," are usually in a major mode, with quicker *harmonic rhythm and more tonic-dominant harmonies [cf. Ammerbach's "Passamezzo d'Angleterre" in *ApMZ* i, 11].

Passecaille [F.]. Passacaglia.

Passepied [F., pass-foot; Anglicized, paspy]. A dance in rather quick ⅜- or ⅝-meter and of a gay and spirited character which was greatly in vogue at the French court under Louis XIV and Louis XV [see *Dance music III]. It is

said to have come from the Bretagne. Examples occur in the French operas (e.g., Campra, *L'Europe galante*, 1697; see Ex.) and in the suites of German composers (J. K. F. Fischer; J. S. Bach, English Suite no. 5).

Passing tone [F. *note de passage*; G. *Durchgangsnote*]. See *Nonharmonic tones I.

Passion music. A musical setting of the text of the Passion (Passio Domini nostri Jesu Christi) from one of the four Evangelists. In the Catholic rites the Passion according to St. Matthew is read on Palm Sunday, those of St. Mark and St. Luke on the following Tuesday and Wednesday, that of St. John on Good Friday.

A. *The Plainsong Passion* [G. *Choralpassion*; hence the English translation Choral Passion, cf. *GD* iv, 78; see remark under *Choral, chorale]. In the 12th century it became customary to have the Passion performed as a sort of play, the parts of Christ (*Vox Christi*), the Narrator (*Evangelista*; *Chronista*), and the Crowd (*Turba Judaeorum*) being sung each by one priest, and in a distinct manner. The part of Christ was sung in the lowest register (c–f) in a slow and solemn recitation; that of the *Evangelista* in a middle register (f–c'), in normal speed and character; that of the *Turba Judaeorum* in a high range (c'–f'), and with pronounced speed and agitation. In the old liturgical books these parts are indicated by the letters *t* (*tarde*, slowly), *c* (*celeriter*, quick), and *s* (*sursum*, high), or, later, by *b*, *m*, and *a* (*bassa, media, alta voce*), whereas in more recent books the signs † (Christ), C (Chronista), and S (Synagogue) are used. This dramatized performance was evidently designed to aid the congregation in following the Latin narrative. Most of the text was sung in a simple inflected monotone, except the Saviour's cry: *"Eli, Eli, lama sabachthani,"* for which a more expressive melody was used. The recitation-tones for the Passion are given in the *Cantorinus Vaticanus*.

B. *The Polyphonic Passion.* The dramatic story of the Passion has naturally attracted a great many composers who have set it to music in various styles, in the motet-style of the polyphonic era, or in the oratorio-style of the 17th century. Probably the earliest procedure was to compose only the turbae which naturally suggested performance by a chorus. On account of the dramatic effect resulting from the contrast of soloist and choral performance, this type of passion is called "Scenic Passion" (*GD*), or "Dramatic Passion" (*MoML*). The earliest existing examples are in the codex Modena Est. lat. 454/55 (*c.* 1480) and in the Eton MS (by Davy; *c.* 1490). Others are by Sermisy (1534), Lassus (St. Matthew, 1575; St. John, 1580; St. Mark, 1582; St. Luke), Asola, Vittoria, Francisco Guerrero, Byrd (St. John, 1607). In most of these Passions the treatment is in polyphonic (motet) style, with the original plainsong as a tenor. In Germany, Luther's reform led to the adoption of the vernacular as well as to the use of a plain homophonic style (*stile famigliare*), instead of the more elaborate polyphonic treatment usually found with the above-named composers. The earliest Passion of this type, that by Johann Walther (St. Matthew, 1530; cf. *GD* iv, 74) had a remarkable vogue and was still performed in 1806 at Nürnberg. Among the long list of composers, Protestant as well as Catholic, who used the same method, we find: A. Scandello (*c.* 1550), Jacob Mailand (St. John, 1568; St. Matthew, 1570), Thomas Mencken (1610; cf. *GD* iv, 73), Matthias Vulpius (1612), Christian Schultze-Delitzsch (1653), and Christian Flor (1667).

Side by side with this tradition, there existed another treatment of greater musical elaboration, that is, the composition of the entire text of the Passion in motet-style. Notable examples of this type are the Passions by Obrecht (*c.* 1500; new ed. D. de Lange, 1894; cf. *GD* iv, 73), Galliculus (1538), Cypriano de Rore (1557), Joachim a Burgk (1568; see *Editions XXVI), Jacobus Gallus (1587), and Leonard Lechner (1594). As a rule, the liturgical plainsong is preserved as a cantus firmus in these polyphonic settings, at least in the earlier works, while later composers adhered less strictly to this principle and occasionally abandoned it altogether.

The 17th century sees the application to the Passion of all the dramatic innovations of the Baroque era, such as the *stile recitativo*, the aria, the orchestra, etc., together with a freer treatment of the authentic text which was either paraphrased or broadened by free poetic interpolations, thus approaching the *oratorio (Passion-Oratorio). An early work indicative of the new tendencies is the Passion after St. John by Thomas Selle, of 1643 [see *Editions V, 26]. Interesting features are the recitativo passages, the introduction of "intermedii," i.e., choral settings of interpolated texts (psalms and Protestant chorales), the use of different instrumentation for the Evangelist and for Christ. The great figure of this period is Heinrich Schütz (1585–1672). His Passion-Oratorio *Sieben Worte Jesu Christi am Kreuz* from about 1645 uses the recitativo for the Evangelist, and a three-part instrumental accompaniment for the words of Christ, a treatment which was adopted by Bach in his Matthew Passion. Late in life (*c.* 1665–72) Schütz composed the *Historia des Leidens und Sterbens unseres Herrn und Heylandes Jesu Christi*, which contains four settings of the Passion story according to each of the four Evangelists. It shows the return to that austere archaism which is characteristic of the late Schütz [cf. *SchGMB*, no. 192]. Other Passions of this period are interesting chiefly for their progressive tendencies, such as the use of the orchestra and the introduction of chorales and arias [Chr. Flor, 1667; J. Sebastiani, 1672; J. Theile, 1673; cf. *DdT* 17]. After 1700 the authentic text of the Bible was abandoned in favor of rhymed paraphrases in the sentimental and allegorical style of the day. Particularly popular were Chr. F. Hunold-Menante's *Der blutige und sterbende Jesus* and Brockes' *Der für die Sünden der Welt gemarterte und sterbende Jesus*. The latter was set to music by more than twenty composers, among them Keiser, Telemann, Handel, and Mattheson. Hand in hand with this textual deterioration went a decline in musical taste leading to a style which approximates that of the opera rather than of the oratorio.

Against this background, Bach's *St. John Passion* (1723) and, particularly, his *St. Matthew Passion* (1729) represent a return to proper and dignified Passion style which is no less remarkable than their artistic superiority. Both Passions use the biblical text as a basic narrative, set in recitative or (for the turbae) in short choruses. Poetic texts (by Brockes for the St. John Passion, by Picander for the St. Matthew Passion) are used for the arias and for the large choruses. The form may be described as a succession of cantatas, each closing with a chorale. According to the earliest catalogue of Bach's works (1754), he wrote five Passions. However, aside from the two above, only portions of the *St. Mark Passion* remain in the *Trauer-Ode* of 1727. A *St. Luke Passion*, published in *B.-G.* xlv, is spurious.

The ensuing history of the Passion may be characterized by Telemann's *St. John Passion* (1741), Johann Ernst Bach's (1722–77) *Passionsoratorium* [*DdT* 48], two Passions by C. P. E. Bach (1787 and 1788), and by oratorios dealing with the Passion story, such as K. H. Graun's *Der Tod Jesu* (1755), Haydn's *Die sieben Worte am Kreuz* (1785), Beethoven's *Christus am Oelberg* (1803), Spohr's *Des Heilands letzte Stunden* (1835). Compositions of the *Stabat mater also fall under this category.

The recent Bach-renaissance has brought about a remarkable revival of the true Passion spirit in works such as the *Markus-Passion* of Kurth Thomas and the *Choralpassion* of Hugo Distler.

Lit.: O. Kade, *Die ältere Passionskomposition bis zum Jahre 1631* (1893); F. Spitta, *Die Passionen von Heinrich Schütz* (1886); Ph. Spitta, *Die Passionsmusiken von Bach and Schütz* (1893); W. Lott, "Zur Geschichte der Passionskomposition von 1650–1800" (*AMW* iii, vii); P. Epstein, "Zur Geschichte der deutschen Choralpassion" (*JMP*, 1929); *id.*, in *BJ*, 1930; K. Nef, "Schweizerische Passionsmusiken" (*Schweizer Jahrbuch für Musikwissenschaft* v); H. J. Moser, "Aus der Frühzeit der deutschen Generalbasspassion" (*JMP* xxvii); H. M. Adams, "Passion Music before 1724" (*ML* vii, no. 3); C. S. Terry, "The Spurious Bach Lucaspassion" (*ML* xiv, no. 3); R. Haas, "Zu Walthers Choralpassion nach Matthäus" (*AMW* iv); K. Nef, "Die Passionsoratorien Jean-François Lesueurs" (in *Editions XXIV B, 3/4); *id.*, "Beiträge zur Geschichte der Passion in Italien" (*ZMW* xvii). See also under *Oratorio.

Passy-measure. Old English for *passamezzo.

Pasticcio [It., pie, pastry]. A musical work, usually operatic, which includes contributions of various composers. Examples are the opera *Muzio Scevola* (1721) to which Mattei, Bononcini, and Handel contributed one act each; the oratorium *Die Schuldigkeit des ersten Gebots* which was written jointly by Mozart, Adlgasser, and Michael Haydn; the *Diabelli-variations; or the violin sonata for J. Joachim of which Schumann, Brahms, and Dietrich each wrote one movement. — More specifically, the term applies to operatic medleys of the 18th century the music of which was selected by the arranger or producer from the compositions of famous composers, for the purpose of entertaining the audience with an uninterrupted succession of their favorite songs, a procedure which immensely pleased the pleasure-seeking public of the 18th century. See also *Opera VIII. Cf. O. G. Sonneck, *Miscellaneous Studies in the History of Music* (1921), pp. 111–179; also in *SIM* xii.

Pastorale. (1) Instrumental or vocal pieces written in imitation of the music of shepherds, their shawms and pipes. Through the biblical shepherds who attended the birth of Christ, the pastorale acquired the character of an idyllic Christmas music. Typical features are the 6/8- or 12/8-meter in moderate time, suggestive of a lullaby, a tender, flowing melody, and long-held drones. The native country of the pastorale (as well as of the almost identical *siciliano) is Italy where there existed an old tradition among the rural shepherds (*pifferari) of coming to town on Christmas morning and playing on their shawms. Among the many beautiful examples of this class of composition (one of the earliest being by Frescobaldi)

it suffices to mention Bach's Pastorale for the organ, the Sinfonia which opens the second part of his Christmas Oratorio, the Sinfonia Pastorale in Handel's Messiah, and the last movement of Beethoven's *Pastoral Symphony.

(2) In the 16th century, dramatic performances based on an idyllic plot. These were among the most important forerunners of the *opera. In the 17th century this genre was particularly cultivated in France. Several of the early French operas, e.g., Cambert's *Les Peines et les plaisirs de l'amour* (1671) and Lully's *Les Festes de l'Amour et de Bacchus* (1672), bear the title Pastorale. Cf. L. de la Laurencie, "Les Pastorales . . . avant Lully . . ." (*KIM*, 1911, p. 139).

Pastoral Symphony. Beethoven's Symphony no. 6 (op. 68) in F, published in 1809 under the title: "Sinfonia Pastorale, No. 6." The four movements portray, according to Beethoven's inscriptions: The awakening of cheerful feelings on arrival in the country; A Scene at the Brook; A Merry Meeting of Country Folk, followed by Thunderstorm and Tempest; and, finally, Song of the Shepherds, Glad and Thankful Feelings after the Storm. This symphony is, no doubt, the greatest example — perhaps, the only really great example — of *program music. In this connection it is interesting to note that Beethoven expressly distinguished this work from the cheaper type of program music which prevailed in his day (battle pieces, etc.; see *Battaglia) by the remark: "Mehr Ausdruck der Empfindung als Mahlerei" (Expression of feelings rather than portraying).

Pastoso [It.]. With pomp, with ostentation.

Pastourelle [F.], **pastorela** [Provençal]. Chansons of the troubadours and trouvères which deal with rural love scenes, frequently with the inclusion of licentious allusions. The term is of purely literary significance. See *Madrigal.

Pathétique. Popular name of Beethoven's Pianoforte Sonata op. 13 (1799).

Tchaikovsky chose the name Symphonie Pathétique for his last symphony, no. 6, op. 74 (1893).

Patter-song. "A kind of song the humour of which consists in getting the greatest number of words uttered in the shortest possible time" (*GD*). This rapid *parlando-style has been frequently used for comical effects in operas (Mozart's *Don Giovanni*, "Catalogue Aria"; Rossini's *Barbiere di Siviglia*, "Largo al factotum"), and plays an important part in the comic operas of Sullivan.

Pauke [G.]. *Kettledrum. The term occurs in the popular names of three compositions by Haydn, namely: (a) *Paukenmesse*, a Mass in C, composed 1796, inscribed by Haydn: Missa in tempore belli, i.e., War-time Mass, a title which sufficiently explains the conspicuous role played by the kettledrums in this work; (b) *Paukenschlag Symphonie*, i.e., Drumstroke Symphony in G (1791), so called with reference to the sudden stroke of the timpani in the middle of the slow movement (a more common name is "Surprise Symphony"); (c) *Paukenwirbel Symphony*, i.e., Drum-roll Symphony, in E-flat (1795), so called because of the kettledrum roll which opens the introduction.

Pause [F. *point d'orgue*; G. *Fermate*; It. *fermata*]. The sign ⌢, also known as hold or fermata, which indicates that the note (or rest) over which it appears is to be prolonged. As a rule, a duration of approximately (but not exactly) the double of the normal value will prove satisfactory and appropriate. — It must be noted that the foreign terms *pause* [F.], *Pause* [G.], and *pausa* [It.] always mean a rest.

Pavane [Anglicized pavan, paven, pavin]. A court dance of the early 16th century, probably of Spanish origin [see *Dance music II]. It was executed in slow, solemn movements and with dignified gestures, imitating, in a way, the proud deportment of the *pavo*, i.e., peacock (for a different derivation of the name, see *Padovana). The international adoption of the Spanish pavane as the ceremonial court dance, instead of the earlier (French) *basse danse, is a characteristic symptom of the shift in cultural leadership which took place around 1500. The pavane is usually in slow duple meter [see illustration, A. de Cabezon (1510–

66)]; in the earliest Spanish sources, however, examples in slow triple meter are not infrequent (Milan, *Il Maestro*, 1535; cf. *ApMZ* ii; *TaAM* i). If in duple meter, it is frequently followed by the galliarde in quicker triple meter [see *Nachtanz; cf. *HAM*, no. 137; *SchGMB*, no. 134]. After 1550, the pavane and galliarde went out of dance fashion, being superseded by the *passamezzo and saltarello. They were perpetuated, however, by the English virginalists as an idealized type of music, and reached a most remarkable height of artistic perfection under the hands of William Byrd, John Bull, Orlando Gibbons, and John Dowland [cf. *HAM*, nos. 178, 179]. Gibbons' "Pavane the Earl of Salisbury" is, indeed, one of the most glorious examples of idealized dance music, comparable to the sarabande in Bach's Partita no. 6, and to the march ("alla Marcia") of Beethoven's Pianoforte Sonata op. 101. After 1600 the pavane was adopted (usually under the name *paduana) into the early German suite in which it serves as a slow introductory movement. Modern examples have been written by Ravel (*Ma mère l'Oye*; *Pavane pour une infante défunte*), Vaughan Williams (ballet *Job*), and others.

Paventoso [It.]. Timid.

Pavillon [F.]. The bell of wind instruments. *Pavillon chinois* is the *Crescent.

Peal. See *Change ringing.

Pedal [from L. *pes*, foot]. (1) In musical instruments, an action which is operated by the feet. See *Organ III, XI, XII;

*Pianoforte; *Harpsichord; *Harp. —
(2) Short for *pedal point.

Pedal clarinet. Older name for the double-bass clarinet.

Pedal clavicymbel. See *Pedal piano.

Pedalflügel [G.]. See *Pedal piano.

Pedal harp. The modern chromatic *harp.

Pedalier [F.]. (1) The pedal board of the organ, or a similar apparatus attached to a pianoforte. — (2) See *Pedal piano.

Pedalklavier [G.]. See *Pedal piano.

Pedalkoppel [G.]. The pedal coupler of the organ; see *Organ IV.

Pedal note. Same as *Pedal tone.

Pedal organ. See *Organ III.

Pedalpauke [G.]. Kettledrums tuned by pedals. See *Percussion instruments A, 1.

Pedal piano [F. *pedalier pianoforte*; G. *Pedalflügel*]. A pianoforte which is equipped with a pedal board, similar to that of the organ, so that the bass can be played with the feet. The *Pedalflügel*, which had but passing success, is known chiefly through the series of "Studien" and "Skizzen" which Schumann wrote for it (opp. 56, 58). There also exist compositions for this instrument by Alkan and Gounod [cf. *GD* iv, 95]. J. S. Bach had a two-manual harpsichord with hand stops and with a full pedal board. This was chiefly a practicing instrument for organists. The oft-repeated statement that his six trio-sonatas and even his passacaglia were written for this instrument is erroneous. All these pieces are genuine organ music, as appears, for instance, from the long-held notes which occur in most of the slow movements. It should also be noted that single bass notes which seem to be out of the reach of the hand (end of the Sonata in D, *B.-G.* xxxvi, 19; two fugues in A, *ibid.*, pp. 169, 173) by no means necessarily point to a pedal-harpsichord (nor to the organ) since they

can easily be played on a manual instrument with the *short octave arrangement. Cf. J. Handschin, "Das Pedalklavier" (*ZMW* xvii).

Pedal point [F. *point d'orgue*; G. *Orgelpunkt*; It. *pedale*]. Pedal point or, simply, pedal means a long-held note, normally in the bass, sounding against changing harmonies in the other parts. From the harmonic point of view, the interesting feature of the pedal point is that it represents one of the most natural sources of dissonance, inasmuch as the held note blends easily with every chordal combination (e.g., low C with a D-flat or a B-flat triad; see illustration). Accord-

ing to the scale degree of the held note, a distinction is made between tonic pedal, dominant pedal, and subdominant pedal (long note on the tonic, dominant, or subdominant of the key). The terms "inverted pedal" and "internal pedal" denote pedal points which appear, not in the bass, but in the soprano, or in a middle part.

The pedal point (also called *bourdon or *drone) is one of the earliest devices of polyphony, perhaps the earliest, as may already be concluded from its extended use in Oriental and primitive music [see *Oriental music]. In Western music it makes its first appearance in the *organa of the 12th and 13th centuries (Schools of St. Martial and Notre Dame; see *Ars antiqua) in which the notes of the original plainsong are frequently extended as long-held tones, one each serving as a basis for an entire section. A monumental example of a 13th-century pedal point is the beginning of Perotinus' organum quadruplum *Viderunt omnes* [cf. *AdHM* i, 229] which has been called the "F-major toccata of the 13th century" (with reference to the like-named composition of Bach). It may be noted that the term *punctus organicus* (organ point, *Orgel-punkt*) is probably to be explained as referring to these organa, rather than to the organ. As an organ device, the pedal point appears first in certain compositions of Frescobaldi, e.g., his *Pastorale*. Its importance in the organ works of Buxtehude, Bach, etc., is well known. Among modern composers Tchaikovsky has shown a particular predilection for pedal-points.

Pedal tone. See *Wind instruments II; *Horn I.

Peer Gynt Suite. See *Suite II; *Incidental music.

Pelléas et Mélisande. Opera in five acts by Claude Debussy (1862–1918), text from Maeterlinck's play of the same name, produced in 1902. Scene: a medieval castle. *Golaud* (Baritone) finds the beautiful *Mélisande* (Soprano) in a forest, marries her, and brings her to the gloomy castle of his grandfather *Arkel* (Bass) where she and *Pelléas* (Tenor), Golaud's younger half-brother, fall in love with each other. Golaud, thoughtful and friendly, encourages what he believes to be a childish sympathy, but, upon discovering the truth, rages with jealousy and kills Pelléas (Act IV). In the last act Mélisande dies. This story is told in a succession of scenes filled with mystic and symbolic significance, scenes which are not meant to form a continuous plot and which stand to the closely-knit action of Wagner opera in about the same relationship as Debussy's aphoristic *impressionism to the sweep and pathos of Wagner's musical style.

Pelléas et Mélisande, being the only significant opera which the impressionism has produced, stands in a class by itself. In opposition to the Wagnerian opera, Debussy has written a score which deliberately avoids emotional stress, providing only a "tonal envelope" of pale colors and of incorporeal transparency. Nonetheless, the opera shows a degree of unification and identification between the poet, the composer, and their characters which renders it a *Gesamtkunstwerk* in

the same sense as with Wagner's music dramas. See reference under *Recitativo.

Pelog. See *Javanese music.

Penillion. An ancient form of Welsh music practice [see *Bards], executed by a harper and a singer, with the former playing a well-known harp-air and the latter extemporizing words and a somewhat different melody to fit with the harper's tune and harmonies. The harper can change his tune as often as he wishes; the singer, after a measure or two, is expected to join with proper words and music, in accordance with the dictates of tradition. The penillion is probably the last relic of those legendary contests in which the heroes fought against one another not only with their weapons, but also with their wits, solving puzzles and competing with musical instruments. Cf. W. S. Gwynn Williams, †*Penillion in English* (1925).

Penitential psalms. Psalms 6, 32, 38, 51, 102, 130, and 143 in the Authorized Version; 6, 31, 37, 50, 101, 129, and 142 in the Vulgate [see *Psalm]. In music history the penitential psalms are famous particularly through Orlando di Lasso's composition of the whole series of texts (*Psalmi penitentiales*, 1565). The same project was carried out by L. Lechner (1587) and others. Later composers have been particularly attracted by the dramatic greatness of Ps. 130, *De profundis*, and Ps. 51, *Miserere*.

Pentatonic scale [the shorter form "penta-scale" may be used]. A scale which consists of five different tones, the octave being already reached at the sixth degree. Theoretically there exists, of course, an infinite variety of such scales. The following types are of special importance: (a) The *tonal penta-scale*, i.e., a five-tone scale which has no semitones (the German term is *anhemitonisch*). Properly speaking, there exists only one such scale (transpositions apart), namely: c d . f g a . c'. However, by using different tones as a tonic, five different "modes" can be derived from it, for instance: c d . f g a . c', or: f g a . c' d' . f', etc. On the pianoforte, such scales can easily be reproduced by playing the black keys only. The tonal penta-scale, usually in its "first mode" (on c), occurs in nearly all the early musical cultures, in China (as far back as 2000 B.C.), Polynesia, Africa, as well as with the American Indians, the Celts, and the Scots. It must be considered the prototype of all scales. The ancient Chinese already construed it as a succession of fifths and descending fourths: f–c′–g–d′–a [see *Chinese music]. — (b) The *semitonal* [G. *hemitonisch*] *penta-scale.* Such a scale results by omitting the second and the sixth, or the second and the fifth, degrees of the diatonic scale: c . e f g . b c′, or: c . e f . a b c′. Since these scales include two major thirds (*ditonus*) they are also called "ditonic." The second form is of especial interest since this is the scale which, in descending motion, prevailed in ancient Greece: e′ . c′ b a . f e. Semitonal penta-scales occur frequently in modern *Japanese music. — (c) A penta-scale with equidistant steps is the Javanese *salendro* [see *Javanese music]. This has been used, under the name "pentaphonic" scale, by Alaleone [cf. A. Eaglefield-Hull, in *Monthly Musical Record*, Sept. 1922].

Percussion instruments. Generic name for those instruments of the *orchestra which are sounded by striking or shaking. They can conveniently be divided into two groups, those which produce a sound of definite pitch and those which do not.

A. *Of Definite Pitch.* 1. *Kettledrum* [F. *timbale*; G. *Pauke*; It. *timpani*]. The kettledrum (seldom used singly) is the most important of the percussion instruments. It consists of a hemispherical shell of copper or some alloy, across which is stretched a "head," ordinarily of calfskin, which is held in place by a metal ring through which pass hand screws fixed to the shell, thus allowing the tension of the skin to be varied. The instrument is played by two sticks which have wooden handles and a head made ordinarily of hard felt covered with a layer of soft felt, although for special effects the

material used may differ. The number of kettledrums used by the classical school was two, one small and one large, which were tuned to the tonic and dominant of the key of the composition. A third drum of intermediate size was added about the middle of the 19th century and toward the end four were often demanded, though various composers, notably Berlioz and Mahler, have been more extreme in their desires. Example 1

shows the composite compass of the instruments in ordinary use, although this range is at times exceeded. Each of the drums is best confined to a range of about a perfect fifth; Ex. 2 shows that of the largest and Ex. 3 that of the smallest; the two others are in between. While the kettledrums are primarily rhythmic instruments, their tone color is of great value to an ensemble, and they are especially important as a regulating factor in orchestral dynamics. They may be muffled or muted [see *Mute]. Various methods of tuning the drums mechanically by means of a controlling pedal [*Pedalpauke*] or some such device have been invented. Such instruments, which allow the pitch to be changed quickly, are required, e.g., in *Salome's Dance* by R. Strauss and in d'Indy's *Summer Day on the Mountain.* Although their tone quality is less resonant than that of the ordinary instrument, they are generally in use nowadays.

The introduction of the kettledrums into the orchestra took place around 1670, John Locke with his opera *Psyche* (1673) and Lully with his *Thesée* (1675) being the rivals for a priority which is difficult to fix exactly. The frequent use of the timpani in Bach's cantatas for the expression of joy and truimph is well known.

Lit.: P. R. Kirby, "Kettledrums: An Historical Survey" (*ML* ix, no. 1); P. A. Browne, "The Orchestral Treatment of the Timpani" (*ML* iv, no. 4).

2. *Glockenspiel* [E.; G.] or *Bells* [F. *carillon, jeu de timbres*; It. *campanetta*].

An instrument composed of a series of horizontal rectangular steel plates of varying length, with or without resonators, which are arranged roughly in the same manner as a pianoforte keyboard, and are struck by two wooden or composition hammers. It is made in two sizes, one with a chromatic range as in Ex. 4, the other as in Ex. 5. The part for the glock-

enspiel is written in treble clef two octaves below the actual pitch. It is wise to keep within the range of the smaller instrument, since the larger is not universally used. Its most notable characteristic is its bright, penetrating tone color, and because of this it should be used sparingly. Wagner used the glockenspiel in the Dance of the Apprentices from *The Mastersingers*; Tchaikovsky in the Chinese Dance of his *Nutcracker Suite*.

3. *Xylophone.* An instrument resembling the glockenspiel in essential construction, save that the bars are made of wood. The instrument, pitched an octave lower than the glockenspiel, and therefore larger, is mounted on a frame, and the player stands while performing. Its sounding compass is one octave below that of the glockenspiel, notated at the actual pitch. In tone quality it is dry and "wooden." See also *Xylophone.

4. *Celesta.* An instrument resembling in appearance a small upright pianoforte. It may be considered as a "keyboard-glockenspiel," as the tone is produced by the striking of steel bars with hammers which are connected to a keyboard by a simplified pianoforte action. The range of the celesta is as shown in Ex. 6, and it is written for on two bracketed staves at an octave below the actual pitch. It is best adapted to light and graceful effects, whether chordal or arpeggiated. Melodic lines may be given to the instrument provided they do not contain notes of great length, since the sustaining power is limited. Owing to its light character, accompaniments to a celesta melody should

be thinly scored. The instrument was introduced by Tchaikovsky for the "Danse de la Fée Dragée" of his *Nutcracker Suite* (1891).

5. *Chimes.* A set of metal tubes, normally 18, suspended from a metal frame, tuned chromatically from c' to f'', and struck with a hammer. They are employed to produce the effect of church bells, hence the alternative name *tubular bells*. They are used in the finale of Tchaikovsky's "1812" Overture, in Mahler's Symphony no. 2, in Sibelius' Symphony no. 4 (fourth movement), and in many operas.

Other percussion instruments of rare occurrence are the *anvils, the *marimba, and the *dulcitone.

B. *Of Indefinite Pitch.* 1. *Side drum* or *Snare drum* [F. *petite caisse*; G. *Kleine Trommel*; It. *tamburo militare*]. A small cylindrical drum with two heads stretched over a shell of metal. The upper head, which is struck by the player with his two drumsticks, is called the batter-head; the lower, across which are stretched the taut snares (strings, in appearance not unlike violin strings), is called the snare-head. The brilliant tone quality of the side drum is largely dependent on the vibrations of the snare-head against the snares. The instrument may be "muffled" by loosening the snares. In addition to the roll, which produces a tremolo, there are two other strokes commonly used on the side drum: the Flam, consisting of two notes [Ex. 7], and the drag, which

7   8

♫   ♫♫

is a series of strokes fused into a sort of instantaneous roll, preceding an accented note [Ex. 8].

2. *Tenor drum* [F. *caisse roulante*; G. *Rührtrommel*; It. *cassa rullante*]. A drum of large size, with a wooden shell which is deeper in relation to its diameter than is the side drum.

3. *Bass drum* [F. *grosse caisse*; G. *grosse Trommel*; It. *gran cassa*]. A large drum which varies considerably in size, both in depth and diameter. The heads are thicker and their tension is much less

than with the two smaller drums. It has no snares and is played with a large soft-headed stick. The sound produced is low and heavy. Single strokes should be used at moderate speed, but a roll, performed by two timpani sticks, is also effective. The bass drum was used by Mozart in his *Entführung* and by Beethoven in the finale of his Ninth Symphony.

4. *Tambourine.* A small single-headed drum, the shell of which is pierced at intervals to allow the insertion of loosely-hanging "jingles" (circular metal plates), usually in pairs connected by a wire which passes through the holes of the shell. The instrument is played (a) by striking the head with knuckles, which gives detached sounds and simple rhythmical figures, (b) by grasping the shell firmly and shaking it, which gives a "roll" of the jingles, and (c) by rubbing the thumb on the head, which gives a tremolo of the jingles.

5. *Triangle.* A small round bar of steel bent in the shape of a triangle, open at the upper end, struck with a beater of the same material. Because of its penetrating tone quality it should be used sparingly, single widely-spaced strokes being the most effective manner of writing for the instrument, although it can perform complex rhythmic figures and rolls. It was used first in Gluck's *Iphigénie en Tauride* (1779) and in Mozart's *Abduction from the Seraglio* (1782) in order to obtain an exotic, Turkish, atmosphere [see *Janizary music]. Beethoven used it in the finale of his Ninth Symphony for the "Turkish" variation of the theme; Haydn in his "Military Symphony." For a prominent solo part see the Piano Concerto in E-flat by Liszt.

6. *Cymbals* [F. *cymbales*; G. *Becken*; It. *piatti* or *cinelli*]. Two large circular brass plates of equal size, made slightly convex so that only the edges will touch when they are struck together. In the center of each cymbal is a deep saucer-like depression, pierced by a hole, through which a strap is attached, enabling the player to hold it. They are played in the following ways: (a) by clashing them together with a sideways movement — the ordinary way of playing single notes;

(b) by striking a single cymbal with a hard snare-drum stick or a soft timpani stick; (c) by clashing the two cymbals against each other as fast as possible, a rather unsatisfactory effect; (d) by suspending one cymbal and performing a roll on it with two hard snare-drum sticks or two soft timpani sticks; (e) by fastening one cymbal to the shell of the bass drum, thus enabling the player to play both instruments at the same time. See also *Cymbals.

7. *Tam-tam* or *Gong.* A broad circular disk of metal, slightly convex, with the edges turned, giving it the appearance of a shallow plate with low vertical sides. It is suspended in a frame so as to hang freely, and is struck with a heavy bass-drum beater.

8. Other instruments of this class, rarely used in orchestral scores, are the *anvil, *castanets, *rattle, *thunder machine. Modern radicalists have devised percussive and noise-producing effects compared with which Richard Strauss's thunder machine is mere child's play [see *Futurism]. Primitive instruments, such as the Cuban *maracas* (a gourd filled with dry seeds; see *Rattle) and the *guiro* (a serrated gourd scraped with a stick), have been used by Prokofiev (*Alexander Nevsky*) and Stravinsky (*Le Sacre du Printemps*). An interesting instance of a purely percussive score is Edgar Varèse's *Ionisation* (1931).

In scientific classification, the various drums [see *Drums] are grouped under *membranophones*; the other instruments under *idiophones* [see *Instruments I and II].

Lit.: Ch. Bairn, *The Percussion Band from A to Z* (1936). W. D. D.

Perdendo(si) [It.]. Gradually dying away.

Perfect, imperfect. See *Cadence; *Intervals; *Mensural notation. It may be noticed that the *modus perfectus, imperfectus* of mensural notation is something entirely different from the *modus perfectus, imperfectus* of the 13th-century theory of rhythmic *modes. While, in the former case, the terms indicate the ternary or binary value of the *longa* ($L =$ 3 *B* or $= 2$ *B*), they refer, in the latter case, to the final note in the pattern of a mode, this final note being present in the modus perfectus, absent (replaced by a rest) in the modus imperfectus. The modi imperfecti, although discussed at length by theorists (Anon. IV; cf. *ReMMA*, 280), are entirely devoid of practical significance [cf. *ApNPM*, 231].

Period. A term frequently used to denote a group of measures comprising a natural division of the melody. Usually considered as comprising two *phrases.

Periodicals, Musical. I. *Historical Survey.* Among the earliest periodicals of music (leaving out of account periodical publications of music, etc.) are Scheibe's *Critischer Musicus* (1737–40), the *Journal de musique française et italienne* (1764–68), and J. A. Hiller's *Wöchentliche Nachrichten* (1766–70). Following are the most important of the subsequent enterprises: *Allgemeine musikalische Zeitung* (Breitkopf und Härtel, 1789–1848, 1863–82); Fétis' *Revue musicale* (1827–80; merged with *Gazette musicale de Paris* and became the *Revue et Gazette musicale de Paris*); *Le Ménestrel* (Paris, 1833–); *Neue Zeitschrift für Musik* (founded by Robert Schumann, 1834; now issued as *Zeitschrift für Musik*; see IV); *Signale für die musikalische Welt* (Leipzig, 1843–); *The Musical Times* (London, 1844–); *Dwight's Journal of Music* (Boston, 1852–81); *Le Guide Musicale* (Brussels, 1855–1914, 1917–18); *The Musical Standard* (London, 1862–1933); *Music* (Chicago, 1891–1902).

There follows a selected list of periodicals still issued (or issued until recently), classified according to countries, with a special group (VII) reserved for musicological publications.

II. *United States. The Musical Courier* (New York, 1880–; semimonthly). — *The Etude* (Philadelphia, 1883–; monthly). — *The Musician* (New York, 1895–; monthly). — *Musical America* (New York, 1898–; fortnightly). —

Music Educator's Journal (Chicago, 1914–; bimonthly). — *The Musical Quarterly* (New York, 1915–; quarterly; see also VII). — *Modern Music* (New York, 1924–; quarterly). — *American Music Lover* (New York, 1935–; monthly).

III. *England. The Musical Times* (London, 1844–; monthly). — *The Monthly Musical Record* (London, 1871–; monthly). — *Musical Opinion* (London, 1877–; monthly). — *The Strad* (London, 1890–; monthly). — *Music and Letters* (London, 1920–; quarterly; see also VII). — *Music Review* (London, 1939–; quarterly; see also VII).

IV. *Germany, Austria, Switzerland. Zeitschrift für Musik* (Regensburg, 1834–; monthly). — *Signale für die musikalische Welt* (Leipzig, 1843–; weekly). — *Allgemeine Musikzeitung* (Berlin, 1874–; weekly). — *Neue Musikzeitung* (Stuttgart, 1880–; monthly). — *Die Musik* (Berlin, 1901–15; fortnightly; 1922–; monthly). — *Anbruch* (Vienna, 1919–37; monthly). — *Melos* (Mainz, 1920–36; monthly). — *Der Auftakt* (Prague, 1920–38; monthly). — *Schweizerische Musikzeitung* (Zurich, 1861–; monthly).

V. *France, Belgium. Le Ménestrel* (Paris, 1833–1940; weekly). — *Revue musicale* (Paris, 1901–40; monthly; see also VII). — *La Revue musicale Belge* (Brussels, 1924–; weekly). — *La Revue Grégorienne* (Tournai, 1911–; monthly). — *La Revue internationale de musique* (Brussels, 1938–; bimonthly).

VI. *Italy. Rivista musicale italiana* (Torino, 1894–; quarterly; see also VII). — *La Rassegna musicale* (Torino, 1928–; monthly). — *Musica d'oggi* (Milano, 1919). — *Rassegna Gregoriana* (Rome, 1902–). — *Il Pensiero musicale* (Bologna, 1921–). — *Bollettino bibliografico musicale* (Milan, 1926–). — *Il Musicista* (Rome, 1934). — *Rivista nazionale di musica* (Rome, 1935–).

VI. *Other Countries. La Revista Musical* (Buenos Aires, 1925–34). — *Revista Brasileira de Musica* (Rio de Janeiro, 1934–; quarterly). — *Revista Musical Mexicana* (Mexico, D.F., 1942–; semimonthly). — *Musica Viva* (Rio de Janeiro, 1940–42). — *Musicalia* (Havana,

1927–). — *Boletino Latino-Americano de música* (Montevideo, 1935–; annually). — *The Canadian Journal of Music* (Toronto, 1914–; monthly). — *De Muziek* (Amsterdam, 1926–).—*De Muziekwereld* (Amsterdam, 1936–). — *Sovietskaya Musica* (Moscow, 1933–41). — *Revista musical Catalana* (Barcelona, 1904–37).

VII. *Musicological Periodicals.* Most of the periodicals belonging to this group are listed on pp. viii f, with their abbreviations as used in this Dictionary. Additional publications are: *The Journal of Musicology* (Greenfield, Ohio, 1939–; quarterly); *Note d'archivio* (Rome, 1924; quarterly).

For additional lists of periodicals cf. *GD* iv, 110–121 and Suppl. Vol., 504–507; A. Einstein, *Das neue Musiklexikon* (1926), 720–724.

Lit.: A. *General:* F. Crome, *Die Anfänge des musikalischen Journalismus in Deutschland* (Diss. Berlin 1897); H. Koch, *Die deutschen musikalischen Fachzeitschriften des 18. Jahrhunderts* (Diss. Halle 1923); W. Freystätter, *Die musikalischen Zeitschriften* (1884); E. van der Straeten, *Nos Périodiques musicaux* (1893); O. Sonneck, "Die musikalischen Zeitschriften-Literatur . . ." (*ZIM* i); E. O'Meara, "Music in the 17th and 18th Century Periodicals" (*Music Libr. Ass. Notes* iv); J. T. Windle, "Report on the Project for Indexing Music Periodicals . . ." (*M.L.A. Notes*, ix); H. E. Johnson, "Early New England Periodicals devoted to Music" (*MQ* xxvi).

B. *Indices to periodical literature:* D. H. Daugherty, *A Bibliography of Periodical Literature in Musicology* . . . (annual, 1940ff); *Bibliographie des Musikschrifttums* (Leipzig, 1936–; annual); E. Refardt, *Verzeichnis der Aufsätze über Musik in den nichtmusikalischen Zeitschriften* . . . (1925). Current indices are contained in *ZIM* and *ZMW*.

Permutatio. See *Hexachord.

Perpetuum mobile [L., perpetual motion]. A term used by Paganini (op. 11), Weber (last movement of Piano Sonata op. 19), and others to denote pieces which proceed from the beginning to the end in the same rapid motion, e.g., 16th-notes in presto. Pieces of this type, although not labeled thus, occur also in Chopin's Études.

Persian music. See *Arabian music. Cf. *LavE* i.5, 3065–83.

Peru. In pre-Hispanic times Peru was the center of the vast Incan empire which dominated most of the northwestern section of the South American continent. The Incas, or "people of the sun," probably settled in the valley of Cuzco (the city of that name was their capital) in the 13th century, the country having been ruled before then by the Aymarás. Although the civilization of the Incas was in some ways less advanced than that of the Mayas of Central America, they appear to have had a more highly developed musical system. Many musical instruments from ancient Peru have been preserved, chiefly *panpipes and flutes (*quena*), and from these it is evident that the Incas could produce elaborate melodies. It is a moot point as to whether they used scales with semitones in addition to the tonal penta-scale [see *Pentatonic], but considerable evidence has been assembled to indicate that the use of semitones was not unknown. Besides various kinds of panpipes and flutes (generally made of canes), the ancient Peruvians also had rattles and bells, drums, endblown shell trumpets, and tubular trumpets of wood or clay.

After the Spanish conquest, which began in 1526 and was marked by much internal strife among the *conquistadores*, Peru became the most important center of Spanish power in South America, and the new colonial capital, Lima, was the seat of a brilliant viceregal court (the first viceroy was appointed in 1544) in which cultural activities flourished. Music was cultivated not only in the churches, but also in the theaters, where Spanish dramas were performed with the customary musical settings.

In the early period of independence an outstanding figure was Bernardo Alzedo (1798–1878), who composed the Peruvian

National Hymn (1821). He lived for many years in Santiago de Chile, becoming choirmaster of the cathedral there. In 1864 he returned to Lima. He was the author of a didactic work entitled *Filosofía elemental de la música* (Lima, 1869), an introduction to musical theory and one of the earliest books of its kind to be published in South America. Alzedo also composed much religious music.

The study and utilization of Peruvian folk music, upon which the modern national school is based, was initiated by Claudio Rebagliati (1843–1909), an Italian musician who settled in Lima in 1863. His Peruvian Rhapsody, *Un 28 de Julio*, was the first attempt to obtain local atmosphere in an orchestral medium. Rebagliati made a revision of the National Hymn which was approved by Alzedo and officially accepted. The gathering of folk music was carried on assiduously by Daniel Alomias Robles (1871–1942), whose collection (mostly unpublished) consisted of some 1200 tunes. He lived in the United States for many years, and at the time of his death was head of the Fine Arts section in the Ministry of Public Education at Lima. He composed the opera *Illa-Cori*, several symphonic poems, many songs, and piano pieces. The late Theodoro Valcárcel (1902–42) also cultivated Peruvian folk idioms in his compositions, which include the ballet-opera *Suray-Surita*, the ballet *Chori Kancha*, and *Suite autóctona* for violin and piano. He published several collections of folk music from Peru.

Andrés Sas (b. Paris, 1900) has made a special study of Peruvian Indian music, whose characteristic scales and rhythms he has utilized in several compositions, such as *Suite Peruana* and *Himno y Danza* for piano. Manuel Aguirre is known chiefly for his piano pieces of folkloristic coloring, such as the suite *De mis montañas* (orchestrated by Sas). Pablo Chavez Aguilar (b. 1898), choirmaster of Lima Cathedral, has published *Seis Preludios Incaicos* and *Ocho Variaciones sobre un tema incaico*, for piano.

On the whole, Peru now has a flourishing contemporary school, whose younger representatives include Carlos Sánchez Málaga (b. 1905), Roberto Carpio (b. 1900), Raoul de Verneuil (b. 1901), and Alfonso de Silva (1903–37). Peruvian composers have been held back chiefly by lack of adequate technical training, but they have a rich tradition upon which to draw and a definite national school of considerable promise seems now to be emerging.

Lit.: R. and M. d'Harcourt, *La Musique des Incas et ses survivances* (1925); R. Klatovsky, "Music in the Realm of the Incas" (*Musical Times*, lxxv, 696ff); C. Vega, "Tonleitern mit Halbtönen in der Musik der alten Peruaner" (*AM* ix); A. Sas, "Ensayo sobre la musica Inca" (*Boletin latino-americano de musica* i); C. Raygada, "Panorama musical del Perú" (*ibid.*, ii).   G. C.

Pes [L., foot]. (1) Same as podatus; see *Neumes I. — (2) Name for the iterated bass motive of the *Sumer canon [see also *Ostinato].

Pesante [It.]. Weighing, heavy.

Pescia [It.]. See under *Caccia.

Petrouchka. See *Ballet III.

Pezzo [It.]. Piece, composition.

PF. In orchestral scores, etc., short for pianoforte. As a dynamic sign, short for "piano followed by forte."

Pfeife [G.]. Fife; organ pipe.

Pfundnoten [G. *Pfund*, pound]. The long notes (each, as it were, "weighing a pound") which occur in the *cantus firmus of innumerable polyphonic compositions, from the 13th-century *organa to Bach's "cantus-firmus" chorales [see *Organ chorale].

Phagotus. A curious instrument of the 16th century which is worth mentioning only because it has erroneously been considered the predecessor of the *fagot, i.e., bassoon. Actually it was a fanciful and impracticable modification of the bagpipe. Cf. L. F. Valdrighi, *Il Phagotus di Afranio* (1881). *GD* iv, 131 (illustration); F. W. Galpin, in *PMA* lxvii.

Phantasie [G.]. See *Fantasia. *Phantasiestücke, Phantasiebilder,* etc., are romantic titles for pieces of an imaginative, fanciful character, with a slight programmatic connotation. See *Character piece. *Phantasieren* is "to improvise."

Phantasy. Title of English chamber music pieces which were written for the Cobbett Competitions, established in 1906. According to the statutes of the competition, they have to be in one movement. Over forty of these compositions were written between 1905 and 1930. R. Vaughan Williams, W. H. Hurlstone, Frank Bridge, John Ireland, Thomas Dunhill, were among the contributors. Cf. Ch. Maclean, in *ZIM* xii.

Philharmonic pitch. See *Pitch.

Philharmonie. Name of two famous concert halls and orchestras, one in Berlin, the other in Vienna. See *Orchestras II.

Philidor, Collection. A large MS collection of 17th-century music (chiefly French), compiled by André Philidor (*c.* 1647–1730; proper name Danican; father of the famous chess-player François Philidor). The collection contains innumerable dance tunes, airs, military signals, as well as all the ballets and operas of Lully and of a few other composers; finally, all the sacred music in use at the French court chapel. A large part of the collection is now at St. Michael's College in Tenbury (England; see *Libraries III, D), another in the library of the Paris Conservatoire. Cf. J. W. Wasielewski, in *VMW* i; E. H. Fellowes, in *ML* xii, no. 2; A. Tessier, in *RM* xii, no. 114.

Phonograph and recorded music. The phonograph traces its origin to Thomas A. Edison, who in 1877 produced a record made of tin foil from which his own voice could be heard reciting *Mary had a little lamb.* This record was a cylinder, as were all the commercial records made by Edison for many years. The invention of the disk record (patented in 1896) and the surmounting of the problems of mass production and marketing of recordings were the work of Emil Ber-

liner, whose factory was the beginning of the Victor Company, the largest producer in the field. The reproduction of sound by the passage of a needle or stylus through the grooves of a record, whether a cylinder or a disk, has been accomplished by two methods. By far the more common of these is the "lateral cut," used from the early days by Victor, Columbia, and other companies, in which the sound is produced by variations on the sides of the groove through which the needle passes. The other method, adhered to by Edison, and by the Pathé Frères in Paris, was called "vertical cut," or "hill and dale," because the motion of the needle (or the Edison diamond point and the Pathé sapphire ball) is up and down rather than sidewise. Though this latter method is considered by many experts to be superior, it has been abandoned in recent years, because its adoption by one of the major companies would mean the scrapping of all present equipment. In the early phonograph the sound was amplified by means of a mica sound box, which held the needle, and a large horn.

The types of phonographs and records remained generally the same until 1925, when the Orthophonic Victrola and electric recording were introduced. These instruments, with more sonorous sound chambers than were found with the earlier machines, were able to bring more music from the records than had been heard before; and the new method of recording, utilizing the microphone which had come into being with the radio, marked a tremendous advance in the range and faithfulness of reproduction. The next few years saw the development of the electric phonograph, in which the sound is reproduced entirely by electricity, and of "higher fidelity" recording, in which the frequency range has been increased still further. A modern record played on a modern machine is amazingly lifelike, and even early acoustical recordings can be made to sound remarkably well. Certain problems are still to be solved, such as that of surface noise, or the hissing sound which the needle makes in passing through the record grooves. Commercial phonographs, turned out in mass, are very often unsatisfactory because of inequalities in the materials used: a record can sound its best only on a good reproducing equipment.

The repertoire of the phonograph has undergone considerable change since the early days. Edison's original intention was to produce literally a talking machine, and the musical possibilities of the new instrument were not at first apparent. The earliest repertoire, therefore, of the commercial phonograph was made up mostly of vaudeville sketches and monologues. These were gradually supplemented with band records and sentimental songs; for it was possible to reproduce wind instruments with reasonable clarity, and the singing voice emerged recognizably from the wax. Celebrated singers early began to play with recording their voices, and by the nineties the stunt was quite fashionable. About the year 1900 the record companies in Europe began to see the commercial possibilities of this idea, and a new period in phonograph history began. The first American celebrity recordings were announced in 1903 by the Columbia Company, the list including disks by Marcella Sembrich, Edouard de Reszke, Ernestine Schumann-Heink, Giuseppe Campanari, Antonio Scotti, Charles Gilbert, and Suzanne Adams. Victor was not slow to follow by building up an impressive "red seal" catalogue, to which most of the feted vocalists and instrumentalists of the day contributed. The singers recorded mostly operatic arias, occasionally branching out into the song repertoire, and the violinists, cellists, and pianists gave their versions of the lighter classics. At first all accompaniments were played on the piano, but about 1905 many of the singers were busy remaking their selections with orchestra. Owing to the limitations of reproduction at that time, all kinds of alterations were made in the orchestrations of arias, and the instruments were necessarily few in number, but the voices as recorded were unmistakably those of their famous prototypes. Today the collecting of early celebrity recordings has become a major hobby,

and several societies have been formed for the purpose of re-recording or re-pressing old masters on a subscription basis.

In 1913 the Gramophone Company in Europe experimented with orchestral recording, securing the services of Arthur Nikisch, who conducted the Berlin Philharmonic Orchestra in Beethoven's *Fifth Symphony*, and the London Symphony Orchestra in a series of standard works. In the United States the Columbia Company engaged Felix Weingartner the same year and enlarged their staff orchestra for several recordings under his direction. The first of these were cut versions of the "Liebestod" from *Tristan* and the conductor's arrangement of Weber's "Invitation to the Dance." Several years later (1917) Columbia engaged the Chicago Symphony, conducted by Frederick Stock, the Cincinnati Orchestra under Kunwald, and the New York Philharmonic under Stransky. Victor followed a year later with a series of recordings of Dr. Karl Muck and the Boston Symphony, and shortly thereafter Leopold Stokowski began his long series with the Philadelphia Orchestra. The year 1919 saw the first serious attempts at recording chamber music in this country when the Flonzaley Quartet made for Victor a series of abbreviated movements from their repertoire.

The issuing of complete symphonies and other larger works received its greatest impetus in Europe. As long ago as 1907 and 1908 Victor was issuing here complete performances of operas (including *Pagliacci* made under the direction of the composer) recorded by La Scala Company in Milan, but it was not until the establishment of electrical recording that the American catalogues began to fill up with records made for the sake of the music rather than that of the artist. After a period of depression, attributed to the competition of the radio, records began to enjoy a new popularity comparable to that they had known in the great days of celebrity disks. Within the first decade of electric recording the usual repertoire of standard works, both instrumental and vocal, was pretty well covered, and the enterprise of some of the companies, particularly in Europe, made it possible for the phonograph owner to come to know a great deal of music he might never otherwise have had a chance to hear. This fact has certainly been in no small measure responsible for the general rebirth of interest in the music of the sixteenth and seventeenth centuries. Societies were formed for the recording of music whose appeal was expected to be limited, but many of the sets so issued proved sufficiently popular to be given release subsequently in the regular commercial catalogues. The music of such men as Delius, Hugo Wolf, Sibelius, Kilpeinen, and Purcell was issued in such society sets, as well as the Sonatas of Beethoven, various works of Bach, and several operas of Mozart. A further development has been the issuance of records of chamber music with one of the instrumental parts missing, and of accompaniments to songs, for the benefit of amateurs who lack the necessary partners for musical performance.

The amazing growth of interest in records is illustrated by the amount of literature published on the subject. *The Gramophone*, in England, and *The American Music Lover*, in the United States, are magazines devoted entirely to recorded music, and various dealers publish critical bulletins. Many general magazines and newspapers have instituted record review columns, and in 1936 The Gramophone Shop in New York published an *Encyclopedia of Recorded Music* (a new edition of which appeared in 1943). Most modern books on music include lists of records, and several critical surveys of recorded music have been brought out.

Another important development has been the introduction of record collections in libraries throughout the world. A project of the Carnegie Corporation has been the assembling of "music sets" for colleges and schools, and the free distribution of these records, books, and scores to selected institutions. Steps are being taken to establish record archives in connection with various libraries in order not only to provide the public with a place to listen to

music, but to preserve many of the important disks no longer on the market. The voices of such singers as Caruso, Eames, Lilli Lehmann, Victor Maurel, Adelina Patti, Melba, Tamagno, De Lucia, Tetrazzini, and Fremstad, and the playing of Paderewski, Kreisler, Ysaye, De Pachmann, and many others will thus be preserved for posterity.

The output of recorded music includes, needless to say, the entire standard repertoire of our concerts and many compositions which are very seldom heard in the concert hall. Particularly worth mentioning is the attention which has been given to the music of Bach and of the masters of still earlier periods. Most of the latter have been recorded in sets covering the entire history of music or special phases thereof. The most important of these are: *L'Anthologie Sonore* (Parlophone-Odeon; ed. by C. Sachs); *History of Music by Eye and Ear* (Columbia; ed. by P. Scholes); *Seven Centuries of Sacred Music* (Lumen); *Éditions de l'Oiseau-Lyre*; *Trois siècles de musique d'orgue* (Pathé). For recordings of medieval music, cf. the Record List in *ReMMA*, 465ff. See also *Music Education III.

Lit.: *Bibliography of Music Records* (Minneapolis Board of Education, 1940); R. D. Darrell, *Encyclopedia of Recorded Music* (1936).   P. L. M.

Phonola. See *Mechanical instruments IV.

Phorminx. Homeric name for the *kithara, or *lyra.

Phrase. A natural division of the melodic line, comparable to a sentence of speech. The term is used with so little exactness and uniformity that a more specific description can scarcely be given. The accompanying example (Beethoven,

Piano Sonata op. 2, no. 2) merely serves to illustrate the principle (P = Phrase; M = *Motive). In music of the classical

period (Bach to Brahms) a phrase usually includes, according to the tempo, two, four, or eight measures; however, in the 17th century, phrases of three, five, and seven measures are very frequent [e.g., the two *grounds in Purcell's *Dido and Aeneas*]. See *Vierhebigkeit.

Phrasing. The clear rendering in musical performance of the *phrases of the melody. This is achieved by the interpolation of a slight rest (breathing-rest) with the last note which, therefore, will have to be shortened in some sort of portato or staccato (depending upon the speed and loudness of passage).

The study of phrasing has been evolved, in the late 19th century, chiefly by German writers such as R. Westphal (1880) and H. Riemann (1884). Riemann in particular has contributed to its establishment as a topic of musical analysis. In his *Analysen von Beethoven's Klaviersonaten* (3 vols., 1917) phrasing is practically the only stylistic consideration, and his numerous "Phrasierungsausgaben" of compositions by Bach, Beethoven, and other masters are provided with a great number of minute phrase marks.

Unfortunately, Riemann, as well as many other writers and editors, has done ill service to a good cause by exaggeration and dogmatism. Not only are Riemann's Phrasierungsausgaben practically worthless (in fact, illegible) by the confusing number and variety of phrase marks, but also in cases of greater moderation the fact is usually overlooked that "in music of high artistic quality there is not always just one single way of phrasing but several possibilities which overlap and balance one another" [cf. *MoML*, 626]. For

instance, in Schubert's "Death and the Maiden" there exist at least three different types of phrasing, each of which has its

special significance and justification [Ex. 1]. It would be nonsensical, of course, to indicate all these minute nuances by slurs. In the above melody all the three manners of phrasing actually merge into what might be called a "breathing legato"; thus, Schubert very wisely (that is to say, with the unconscious wisdom of the artist) indicated none of them. In fact, upon closer consideration one might well arrive at the conclusion that the old masters who were not "phrase-minded" came a good deal closer to artistic truth than the modern editors with their phrase-consciousness.

The above considerations apply also to one particular "law" of phrasing, namely, Riemann's *Auftaktigkeit*, according to which every musical phrase begins with an "Auftakt," i.e., an upbeat. Undoubtedly, this is a principle of basic importance and one the consideration of which is particularly necessary for the initiating performer, who is likely to regard each barline as a barrier. Once more, however, a sound principle has been carried *ad absurdum* by exaggeration and dogmatism. Examples 2 (by Combarieu) and 3 (by

Schweitzer) will sufficiently illustrate this point. Particularly in the case of Bach the fact cannot be too strongly emphasized that his melodies are so highly complex in structure, so rich in relationships of various degrees, that any indication of phrasing is bound to be one-sided and therefore misleading.

Phrygian. (1) See *Greek music. — (2) In the system of the *Church modes, the Phrygian is represented by the segment e–e' of the diatonic scale, with e as the tonic (*finalis*). From the modern point of view, it appears as a variety of minor (E minor), the characteristic distinguishing feature being the minor second: e f g a, instead of e f♯ g a. In compositions in the Phrygian mode, this characteristic step appears most conspicuously

in the cadences (Phrygian cadence; see Ex.). To the harmonically minded, such formulae seem to be not so much a full close in E (VII–I) as a half-cadence in A (IV–V). In this meaning the Phrygian cadence is frequently found in the sonatas of Corelli, Handel, and others, as a transition from one movement to the next. For an example of Phrygian in modern music see *Modality.

Physharmonica. See under *Harmonium.

Piacevole [It.]. Agreeable.

Pianamente [It.]. Softly.

Piangendo [It.]. Plaintive.

Pianino [G.]. The upright piano.

Piano. (1) Short for *Pianoforte. — (2) Soft; *pianissimo,* very soft. See *Dynamic marks.

Piano concerto. See *Concerto II, III (c).

Piano duet. A composition for two piano players playing on either one or two instruments. Such compositions are also called "for four hands" [F. *à quatre mains*; G. *vierhändig*].

(a) *Duets for One Piano.* An isolated early example is an early-17th-century piece by Nicholas Carlton entitled: "A Verse for two to play on one Virginal or Organ" (Brit. Mus. MS 29996; cf. H. Miller, in *MQ* xxix, no. 4). A continuous tradition did not begin until the late 18th century. A famous picture of 1762 shows the young Mozart and his sister playing four-hand. Among the earliest extant compositions are a Sonata by Joh. Christian Bach (1735–82) [cf. A. Prosniz, *Handbuch der Klavierliteratur* (1908), p. 128], Mozart's four-hand Sonata in D (K.V. 381; 1772?), Burney's *Four So-*

natas or *Duets for two performers on one Pianoforte or Harpsichord* (1777), Haydn's *Il maestro e lo scolare, variazioni a quadri mani per un clavicembalo* (1778), and five more compositions (four sonatas and one set of variations) by Mozart, composed between 1780 and 1791. Besides Mozart the only great composer who was seriously interested in four-hand music was Schubert. Brahms wrote a set of variations on a theme by Schumann (op. 23).

(b) *Duets for Two Pianos.* Isolated early compositions for two harpsichords are a "Verse for two Virginals" by Giles Farnaby (late 16th century; cf. Fitzwilliam Virginal Book, i, 202), a Fancy by Thomas Tomkins (1573–1656) in Brit. Mus. Add. 29996, several sonatas by Pasquini (*Deux sonates pour 2 clavecins,* Paris), an Allemande, by F. Couperin (new ed. by Brahms-Chrysander, vol. ii, 160; other examples in vol. iii), and two fugues in Bach's *Art of Fugue. A sonata for two harpsichords reproduced in the complete works of Bach (B.-G. vol. 43.i, p. 47), but actually composed by his son W. F. Bach, has been little noticed. The present-day repertory begins with Mozart, who, in his Sonata in D (K.V. 448; 1781), has written one of the most famous pieces for two pianos. Other original compositions are his Fugue in C minor (K.V. 426; 1783), two Sonatas by Clementi, Schumann's Variations op. 46, a Rondo by Chopin in C, Variations by Sinding, and several compositions by Busoni. More numerous are arrangements for two pianos, among which those made by the composers themselves are particularly worth mentioning (Brahms, F Minor Quintet and Variations on a Theme by Haydn; Busoni, *Fantasia contrappuntistica,* originally written for piano solo). Important contributions to the repertory of four-hand music are the arrangements of the organ works by Bach, for one or for two pianos. Cf. A. M. Henderson, in *PMA* lii; F. Niecks, in *ZIM* v; H. Miller, in *MQ* xxix, no. 4.

Pianoforte. I. The pianoforte may be described briefly as a stringed instrument, the strings being struck by hammers which are put into motion from keys by means of a connecting mechanism called action. In the scientific classification, which is based upon the consideration of the sound-producing agent, it is classified as a zither, i.e., as a stringed instrument the strings of which are stretched over a board, the sounding-board [see *Instruments IV, A, 1 (b)]. Its most interesting and most complicated part is the *action* which, in its present form, is a highly involved mechanism, in fact one of the triumphs of 19th-century technical ingenuity. Its complexity is caused mainly by the so-called *repetition*, i.e., a mechanism which makes it possible to strike the hammer for a second time (and more times) before the key has returned to its original position. It is this device which makes possible the rapid iteration of one and the same note. Passing over a detailed explanation of this mechanism with its various parts (hopper, check, escapement, etc.) which can be successfully studied only from a model, the device to be mentioned next is the *dampers*, i.e., small lengthy pieces of wood covered with felt which lie above the strings and which, by means of connecting wires, move up and down together with the action, thus making the string free for vibration in the moment in which the hammer strikes and checking it when the key is released. Finally, the pianoforte has two (or frequently three) *pedals*, the damper pedal to the right, the soft pedal to the left, and the sostenuto pedal in the middle. The *damper pedal*, upon being depressed, raises all the dampers, thus allowing the strings to vibrate after the keys have been released. It therefore is, properly speaking, a "non-damper pedal." The *soft pedal* causes the entire keyboard, action and hammers, to shift a little to the left (hence the German name *Verschiebung*) so that the hammers strike only two instead of, as normally, all the three strings assigned to them [see *Course] or, in the lower registers, only one instead of two [see *Mute; *Una corde]. The *sostenuto pedal* is an ingenious modification of the damper pedal. It raises the dampers, not from all the strings, but from only that note or chord which is held in the moment in which it is put into action, leaving the other notes free for playing with or without the dampers. Thus it permits the sustaining of single notes, e.g., a pedal-point in the bass, but also permits numerous coloristic effects which have been little exploited by modern composers, probably owing to the fact that it is seldom found on European instruments and may have been unfamiliar to composers such as Debussy or Ravel. One such effect is to depress the keys of, e.g., the C major chord without producing a sound, then to depress the sostenuto pedal, and after this to execute a scale-glissando (without the ordinary damper pedal), which will then resound as a C major chord.

II. *History.* The origin of the pianoforte or, at least, of its distinguishing device, the hammer action, is usually traced back to the activity of Pantaleon Hebenstreit who toured Europe as a virtuoso of the *pantalon, i.e., a large dulcimer played with hammers, like the cimbalom of the Hungarian gypsies [see also under *Echiquier]. In fact, one of the various "inventors" of the pianoforte, Gottlieb Schröter, admitted in 1717 that Hebenstreit's playing had inspired his invention of a hammer mechanism which, however primitive, made it possible to play "soft and loud" on the harpsichord. Several years earlier, however, in 1709, a much more perfect hammer mechanism had been invented by Bartolommeo Cristofori (1655–1731) of Florence, very likely without any knowledge of the performances of Hebenstreit, who is not known to have played in Italy. Cristofori's action, as well as that of the most famous of early piano makers, Gottfried Silbermann — who evidently took up Cristofori's ideas — already had a hopper (escapement), similar to the repetition of the modern piano, a feature which was abandoned by the later German makers until Johann Andreas Stein (1728–92) reintroduced it in 1770, giving a separate escaper to each key, instead of a long rail which had been used theretofore. It was this action, known as *German action* or

Viennese action, which delighted Mozart when he visited Stein's workshop, in 1777. Under the hands of Stein's son-in-law, Johann Andreas Streicher (1761–1833), this became the typical Viennese instrument of the Hummel-period. It was similar in shape to the harpsichord, elegant in appearance as well as in sound, and had a very light action.

In the meantime, another country had taken up the making of pianos, England. Here the instrument acquired, mainly under John Broadwood (1732–1812), various features which were destined to be of great consequence for its further development, and which separated it finally from its ancestor, the harpsichord. Among these was a much heavier structure, allowing for a greater tension of the strings which thus became more sonorous; also the two pedals of the present pianoforte (patent from 1783); and an action, known as *English action*, which was much heavier than the Viennese action but also more expressive and dynamic. Small wonder that Beethoven much preferred his Broadwood to the Viennese instruments. Around 1800, piano makers experimented a good deal trying to introduce new shapes [see *Giraffe piano] and special devices operated by stops or pedals (*Janizary stop; cf. R. Harding, "Experimental Pianofortes," *PMA*, lvii). At the same time important steps were made towards the modern pianoforte by the introduction of iron frames (first full cast-iron frame by A. Babcock, Boston, 1825) and by the invention (Séb. Érard, Paris, 1821) of the *double escapement* which causes the hammer to fall back immediately to an intermediate position, and to its final resting position only after the key is released. The last step in the evolution of the piano was the introduction of *cross-stringing*, i.e., the arrangement of the higher strings in the form of a fan, spreading over the largest part of the soundboard, and with the bass strings crossing them at a higher level. Cross-stringing was invented by Babcock around 1830, but was not generally adopted until 1855 when Steinway and Sons of New York gave it its definite form. Modern attempts at improvement

have been made mainly with regard to the keyboard [see *Keyboard III]. See also *Pedalier; *Sostenente pianoforte; *Electronic musical instruments I (*Neo-Bechstein*; *Solovox*).

Lit.: R. E. M. Harding, *The Pianoforte* (1933; bibl.); E. A. Wier, *The Piano* (1941); Ph. James, *Early Keyboard Instruments . . . to the Year 1820* (1930); E. Blom, *The Romance of the Piano* (1928); L. Nalder, *The Modern Piano* (1927); W. Spillane, *History of the American Pianoforte* (1890); H. Brunner, *Das Klavierklangideal Mozarts und die Klaviere seiner Zeit* (1933); R. Harding, "Experimental Pianofortes . . ." (*PMA* lvii); *id.*, in *KIM*, 1930; C. Parrish, "Criticisms of the Piano when it was New" (*MQ* xxx).

Pianoforte music. The literature proper for the pianoforte starts with the sonatas which Clementi, Haydn, and Mozart wrote from *c.* 1775 on, and thereafter includes among its contributors practically all the great and lesser composers of the 19th and 20th centuries. Nobody would think of excluding from this repertory the works of J. S. Bach although these were written for different instruments, the *harpsichord and the *clavichord. During the last decades there has been a noticeable increase of interest in the music of still earlier keyboard composers, and it is mainly on account of this tendency (which deserves all possible encouragement) that the scope of the present article is extended to cover the entire repertory of keyboard music, except that which, owing to its church affiliation, is clearly designed for the organ. Since, however, throughout the 16th and 17th centuries it is frequently impossible to draw a clear distinction between music for the organ, harpsichord, and clavichord, the article on *organ music should be consulted for additional information. Regarding the attempts to distinguish between the repertories for the harpsichord and clavichord, see *Keyboard music. For a related repertory see *Lute music.

I. *Renaissance* (–1600). While most keyboard music written prior to 1600 belongs primarily to the field of organ music [see *Organ music I], a special literature for the stringed instruments exists in the numerous dances of the 16th century. The earliest examples occur in the MS book of Kotter (*c*. 1515), in P. Attaingnant's *Quatorze gaillards* ... (1529), and in certain English MSS of *c*. 1525 [see *Dump; *Hornpipe]. Towards the end of the century a large repertory occurs in the books of the German *colorists*. Another secular form of the period is the variations which figure prominently in the repertory of the *virginalists* who were the first to develop an idiomatic style based on ʻuick "pianistic" figurations (broken chord passages, parallel thirds, quick scales, etc.). See also *Basse danse, *Passamezzo, *Pavane; *Variations IV.

II. *Baroque* (1600–1750). As in the preceding period, the pianistic literature consists mainly of dances, now arranged in *suites, and of variations. Gradually certain types of organ music, such as the *toccata and the fugal forms (*ricercare, *canzona, *capriccio, *fugue), take on stylistic features which make them suitable for the stringed keyboard instruments also. In Italy we find, around 1600, a school of composers working in Naples who were the first to emphasize the harpsichord over the organ. Antonio Valente published, in 1576, an *Intavolatura de cimbalo*, and Giov. Maria Trabaci says, in his publication of 1615, that "the harpsichord is the sovereign of all the instruments in the world, and upon it all music can be played easily" [cf. W. Apel, in *MQ* xxiv, 425]. These Neapolitan masters form the transition to Frescobaldi (1583–1643) whose numerous *partitas (variations) are outstanding in the pianistic literature of the Baroque. Frescobaldi abandoned the strictly contrapuntal texture of the earlier period for a freer and more idiomatic keyboard style in which the voices are allowed to pass out and enter freely [see *Freistimmigkeit]. His pupil Froberger (1616–67) went even farther in this direction, being influenced by the free style of French lute music (Denis Gaultier). Johann Kaspar Kerll

(1627–93), Alessandro Poglietti (d. 1683), and Johann Jacob Kuhnau (1660–1722) contributed some amusing *program pieces, the last-named being particularly known for his *Biblical Stories* (1700) and his attempts to transfer the trio-sonata to the harpsichord (*Clavierübung* ii, 1692). A large repertory of preludes, fugues, suites, toccatas, etc., exists in the works of numerous 17th-century German composers mentioned under *organ music II. Bach's compositions include such immortal works as the *Inventions, the *Well-tempered Clavier, the English and French Suites, the *Partitas, the Chromatic Fantasy and Fugue, the Italian Concerto [see *Concerto grosso], the French Overture [see *Overture II], and the *Goldberg Variations.

An important school of harpsichord composers (clavecinists) existed in France, extending from Chambonnières (1602–72) to Rameau (1683–1764) [see *French music III]. François Couperin (1668–1733) created the pianistic *character piece in *gallant style, a type which Rameau endowed with startling traits of ingenious characterization. In England Henry Purcell (1658–95) and Handel (1685–1759) made important contributions, mainly in the field of the suite. In Italy the toccata took on features of a somewhat superficial virtuosity with Bernardo Pasquini (1637–1710) and Alessandro Scarlatti (1659–1725), while Domenico Zipoli (b. 1675) pursued a more serious line in his toccatas, fugues, and suites. The greatest Italian keyboard composer of this period is Domenico Scarlatti (1685–1757) who wrote over 400 pieces, called sonatas, in which he exhibited a highly remarkable display of ingenuity, introducing special pianistic devices such as the crossing of the hands and extended rapid scales. His style was imitated by the Spanish padre Antonio Soler (1729–83). A contemporary of Scarlatti, Francesco Durante (1684–1755), represents, in his *studii* and *esercizi*, the transition to the *Rococo style of the 18th century.

III. *Rococo* (1730–80). While Bach was writing his sublime masterworks, the apotheosis of a glorious tradition, other composers eagerly adopted the facile methods of the *gallant style and produced quantities of mediocre works which even today fill the volumes euphemistically called "The Early Masters of the Piano." Mainly Italian composers, such as Durante, Porpora, Antonio Rossi (frequently confused with Frescobaldi's pupil Michelangelo Rossi), Paradisi, Galuppi, Grazioli, Sacchini, Rutini, wrote numerous sonatas which, however slight in quality, are historically important as the precursors of the classical sonata [see *Sonata B, III; also *Haffner Collection]. Padre Martini's (1706–84) sonatas are of a more serious nature, but suffer somewhat from academic anemia. At the same time compositions of great significance were written by the sons of J. S. Bach. Philipp Emanuel's sonatas were the immediate point of departure for Haydn, while those of Johann Christian served Mozart as a model. Wilhelm Friedemann's compositions (fugues, *polonaises) remained without succession, but stand out for themselves as great, though entirely forgotten, masterworks of the pianistic literature.

The close of this period marks the emergence of the pianoforte as the victorious rival of the harpsichord and the clavichord. The earliest known pieces for the pianoforte (though written in true harpsichord style) are by Lodovico Giustini who, in 1732, published sonatas for the "cembalo di piano e forte detto volgaramente dei martellati" (. . . "commonly called the one with hammers") [cf. R. Harding, in ML xiii; new ed. by R. Harding]. These, however, remained as isolated as Cristofori's instrument [see *Pianoforte II], and it was not until about 40 years later that the pianoforte began its triumphal career. One of its first champions was Johann Fr. Edelmann (1749–94) in Paris. Clementi's first sonatas of 1773 are perhaps the earliest pieces to make use of the distinctive powers of the instrument. Of C. P. E. Bach's six publications "für Kenner und Liebhaber" the first (1779) is called "Sechs Clavier-Sonaten," probably indicating an ad-

libitum use of the three keyboard instruments, while the others (1780–87) expressly call "fürs Forte-piano." On the other hand, it is interesting to note that the original editions of almost all the Beethoven sonatas up to op. 27 (including the Moonlight Sonata) bear the inscription "Pour le clavecin ou pianoforte," an inscription for which the publishers rather than the author would seem to be responsible [see *Harpsichord II].

IV. *Classicism* (1780–1830). This, the greatest, period of piano music is too well known to be described here. Suffice it to point to some of the most obvious advances in the exploitation of the resources of the instrument, such as the amazing degree of virtuosity attained in Beethoven's Waldstein Sonata, Appassionata, and Piano Concertos, the transcendental technique of his latest sonatas (op. 106ff) which narrow-minded virtuosos have termed "unpianistic," and the "orchestral coloring" which makes its appearance in Schubert's great, but little known, sonatas. Beethoven's Bagatelles mark the beginning of an important type of 19th-century piano music, the *character piece.

V. *Romanticism* (1830–1910). The remark made at the beginning of the previous paragraph applies here too. The piano pieces by Schumann, Chopin, Liszt, Brahms, form the standard repertoire of the pianists and, indeed, overshadow many other pieces which would be equally or more worthy of their attention (particularly Schubert). Mendelssohn, who was the most favored composer of former generations, has fallen into a not entirely deserved eclipse from which he seems to emerge again. Weber's sonatas also could be put to use as a relief from the monotony of our pianistic programs.

Around 1870 the national composers began to make their novel contribution to the pianistic repertory, with Edvard Grieg as the pioneer. Relatively easy to play and yet highly effective, his pieces as well as those of Dvořák, Smetana, MacDowell, Albeniz, Granados, Falla, are greatly favored by players and listeners. A contrary statement can be made with regard to Max Reger and Ferruccio Busoni. Cyclopic compositions such as the former's Variations on a Theme by Bach or the latter's Fantasia Contrappuntistica, though extremely interesting, make requirements on the technical and mental capacities of the player which are not in relation to their appeal to the general public. Alexander Scriabin's Etudes and Sonatas fall largely into the same category. Debussy, on the other hand, was highly successful in developing a pianistic style of great attractiveness and in exploiting entirely novel resources of the instrument [see *Impressionism]. His coloristic technique has left its imprint on the works of Ravel as well as of numerous other composers of the 20th century.

VI. *New Music* (1910–). At the outset of this period stand Arnold Schönberg's Drei Klavierstücke (1909) the *atonality of which shocked the musical world of the 1910's, as did also the miniature form of his Sechs kleine Klavierstücke (1911). The pianistic production of the ensuing three decades reflects, of course, the general trends which characterize this extremely tumultuous development and which are outlined in the article on *New music. On the other hand, this production affords a very convenient survey over the confusing maze of experiments and tendencies [see Lit. VI, W. Apel]. The recent sonatas of Hindemith stand out as works of superior artistic significance. See also *Sonata B, IV.

Lit.: H. Westerby, *The History of Pianoforte Music* (1924); C. G. Hamilton, *Piano Music — its Composers and Characteristics* (1925); M. Seiffert, *Geschichte der Klaviermusik* i (up to 1750; 1899); A. Prosniz, *Handbuch der Klavierliteratur* (1907ff); G. Tagliapietra, †*Anthologie alter und neuer Musik für Klavier*, 18 vols. (German ed. by W. Apel, 1934). — *To I:* O. Kinkeldey, *Orgel und Klavier im 16. Jahrhundert* (1910); W. Merian, †*Der Tanz in den deutschen Tabulaturbüchern* (1927); H. Halbig, †*Klaviertänze des 16. Jahrhunderts*; W. Apel, †*Musik aus früher Zeit*, 2 vols. (1934); *id.,* "Early Spanish Music . . ." (*MQ* xx); *id.,* "Early German Keyboard Music" (*MQ* xxiii); *id.,* "Neapolitan

Links between Cabezon and Frescobaldi" (*MQ* xxiv). See also *Colorists; *Virginalists. — *To II:* G. Pannain, *Le Origini e lo sviluppo dell' arte pianistica in Italia dal 1500 fino al 1730 circa* (1917; also in *RMI* xxi to xxii); L. Oesterle, †*Early Keyboard Music*, 2 vols.; R. Buchmayer, †*Aus historischen Klavierkonzerten*, 5 vols.; P. Epstein, †*Alte Meisterstücke*, 4 vols.; W. Apel, †*Concord Classics for the Piano* (1938); G. Abraham, "Handel's Clavier Music" (*ML* xvi, no. 4); J. S. Shedlock, "The Harpsichord Music of Al. Scarlatti" (*SIM* vi); Ch. van den Borren, "La Musique de clavier au XVIIe siècle" (*RM* ii, no. 6). — *To III:* F. Torrefranca, *Le Origini italiani del romanticismo musicale* (1930); R. Harding, "The Earliest Pianoforte Music" (*ML* xiii, no. 2); G. de St. Foix, "Les premiers pianistes parisiens" (*RM* iii–vii, ix); C. Parrish, *The Early Pianoforte . . .* (diss. Harvard 1939); G. Benvenuti, †*Cembalisti italiani del settecento*; M. S. Kastner, †*Cravistas Portuguezes.* — *To IV:* H. Abert, "Joseph Haydn's Klavierwerk" (*ZMW* ii); *id.,* "Joseph Haydn's Klaviersonaten" (*ZMW* iii); John P. Porte, "Mozart's Pianoforte Works" (*ML* vii, no. 4). — *To V:* K. Westphal, "Der romantische Klavierstil" (*DM* xxii, no. 2). — *To VI:* W. Apel, "Die neue Klaviermusik" (*DM* xxiv, nos. 3 and 7); E. J. Dent, "The Pianoforte and its Influence on Modern Music" (*MQ* ii). — See also under *Organ music; *Sonata; *Suite; *Concerto; *Character piece.

Pianoforte playing. The inclusion in this Dictionary of an article on piano playing (while similar topics, such as "Violin playing," are omitted) is justified by the general interest in this subject as well as by the fact that the technique of the piano, more than that of any other instrument, is sufficiently "rational" to permit of a summary description. Although there exist various points of contention amongst professional artists and teachers as to just how the piano should be played, a vast field of knowledge has been systematically organized so that we are able to ascertain many basic and universally accepted laws which govern the art of pianism.

Considering this situation it is surprising that among the rank and file of piano teachers (and, as a consequence, of piano players) there are still a great number who are ignorant of some of these basic principles, particularly of those which have been developed and accepted within the last fifty or seventy years. The subsequent explanations are chiefly meant as a contribution towards correcting this deplorable and dangerous state of affairs.

I. *The Pianistic Apparatus.* The playing apparatus of the pianist is a flexible system of levers connected by four joints, as follows (joints in parentheses): fingers — (knuckles) — hand — (wrist) — forearm — (elbow) — upper arm — (shoulder) — torso. As a consequence there are four different ways of producing a sound: (a) by moving the fingers from the knuckles; (b) by moving the hand from the wrist; (c) by moving the forearm from the elbow; (d) by moving the upper arm from the shoulder. The first of these, the *finger action*, is, of course, by far the most important and actually forms the very basis of piano playing. The second (*wrist action*) is useful for the playing of passages in light and quick staccato, e.g., rapid octaves. The elbow is important mainly because it permits of a rocking action of the forearm to be used for tremolos and *Alberti bass figures. In the older school a straight downward movement of the forearm was taught under the name of "elbow staccato," but this is of practically no value since it causes the fingers to make a wasteful circular movement. Such waste is eliminated in the last method of playing, known as *arm action*, in which the whole arm is moved from the shoulder, thus enabling the hand to rise vertically above the keys and to drop down from a lesser or greater distance. This action is important in modern piano music for the execution of powerful fortissimo chords. It should be noticed that the arm action differs from the others in that these involve muscular activity while the former is properly made through a passive relaxation of the muscles which brings the weight of the arm into play.

II. *The Basic Piano Technique.* In addition to the above-described actions there is still another method of producing a sound, which might be characterized as a "minimized arm action": the finger is placed immediately on the key, the arm is slightly raised and then relaxed as in the visible arm action. The advantage of this method is that it produces a "singing" tone and allows for a minute control of dynamic nuances such as is not obtained otherwise. The usefulness of this method is by no means restricted to the production of single tones, as might seem to be the case. It can be used for the most rapid passages if combined with a "minimized finger action" (the fingers keeping in constant touch with the depressed and rising keys) and with a process of transferring the weight of the arm from one finger to the next. This "close technique" (which, by the way, is much easier learned than described) can be said to be the basic technique of truly accomplished piano playing.

It is only by this method of playing that melodies can be made to sound as a "living organism," rather than as the dead sum of so many single notes, as is the case if the pure finger action is used. If combined with a rotating movement of the hand, it renders easy the execution of rapid figures (e.g., quick turns) which are difficult and unsatisfactory if played by the fingers alone. In fact, all the other movements of the levers and joints easily and naturally find their proper place within the basic frame of this technique. Thus the stiffness which so frequently attends the older methods of playing is eliminated at the very outset.

Although the systematic teaching of the close-finger technique and of arm-weight methods is of a relatively recent date, there can be no doubt that the great pianists of the earlier periods employed it to a large extent. Particularly informative in this respect is the description which Forkel gives of J. S. Bach's playing (*Ueber Johann Sebastian Bachs Leben, Kunst und Kunstwerke*, 1802; new ed. 1925, pp.

28ff): "According to Bach's manner . . . the five fingers are curved so that . . . each of them is placed immediately above its respective key. This position requires that the finger should not *fall down* on the key nor (as is frequently done) be *thrown*, but merely should be *carried* through the movement with a certain feeling of security and mastery."

The discovery of the arm-weight playing and of its revolutionizing possibilities has led certain pedagogues to an extreme reaction against the pure finger method of the older school. Such a radical point of view is, however, extremely dangerous. Finger development is a most important factor, after all, in piano playing, and the finger exercises of the old school still have their legitimate place in modern piano instruction, although their ultimate purpose is different. While formerly they were considered as representing the proper method of piano playing, their main function within the new system is to develop that independence and strength of the fingers which enables them to support the weight of the arm and to direct it into the individual key. There are, however, cases in which a more active participation of the fingers (i.e., acting from a certain distance) is desirable, mainly in order to bring out the crispness and brilliancy required by Mozart, or the dry and percussive sound called for in modern music of, e.g., Bartók, Hindemith, Stravinsky. The trill is perhaps the only pianistic figure which calls for a pure finger action. Its brilliant execution is, therefore, one of the most difficult feats of piano playing.

III. *The Wrist.* The proper use of the wrist in piano playing is often neglected. One of the most important playing conditions to be set up is that of the supple, flexible wrist with prehensile fingers. These conditions are to a certain degree opposed to each other, but their smooth combination and coöperation are indispensable in piano playing. One of the most useful functions of the wrist is its role in shaping the musical phrase. In general one may follow the principle of beginning the phrase with the wrist at keyboard level, gradually lifting the wrist

as the phrase develops, and dropping it again as the phrase comes to an end. With a tapering phrase, however, the wrist should be lifted towards the end. Sideways motions are another extremely important function of the wrist, to be used mainly for widely spaced broken-chord figures, as, e.g., in Chopin's A-flat Etude. Here the principle is to move the wrist (almost ahead of the fingers) in such a way that each finger, if called into action, forms the straight prolongation of the arm. In playing chords the wrist assumes the function of a shock absorber. Sometimes a stiff wrist, resulting in a percussive and harsh effect, may be desired, but as a rule the wrist should be flexible and elastic in order to make the sound full and sonorous. In octave-playing the wrist may be employed in one of two ways. Light, quick octaves are executed by a pure up-and-down movement of the flexible wrist (particularly for octave repetitions on the same keys). Octave passages in f or ff call for arm action combined with a fixed wrist.

IV. *The Sense of Touch.* Many difficulties encountered in elementary piano instruction result from the failure of the teacher to develop the pupil's sense of touch as applied to the keys of his instrument. Beginners, trying to find a note, fall into the habit of looking at the keyboard, so that their eyes are constantly shifting up and down between the music sheet and the keyboard. The numerous interruptions which mar the playing of otherwise promising students are a common fault resulting from this habit. Told by the teacher to play without such interruptions they fall into the even more detrimental habit of playing from memory, usually in a haphazard way which is neither fish nor flesh. The only remedy to this deplorable situation is to show the pupil how to play "blind," i.e., to find the intervals (third, fifth, octave, etc.) by using his sense of touch, without being allowed to look at the keys. Wide jumps (which, for this very reason, should be avoided in the first two or three years of piano playing) are an exception to an otherwise infallible rule. How much a fully developed sense of touch contributes to facilitate sight-reading need hardly be pointed out ⌊see *Sight-reading III⌋.

V. *Touch and Tone Quality.* The word "touch" is widely used in piano teaching in order to denote (somewhat vaguely, no doubt) the physical approach to the key as the conditioning factor to obtain a variety of tone qualities, ranging from the soft and lyrical to the harsh and percussive. The basic idea of the theory of touch is that piano playing permits not only of dynamic gradations of sound (pp, p, mf, etc.), but, within a given intensity, of additional variations of timbre, so that a mf may be either "lyrical," or "decisive," or "percussive," etc. Whether this is possible or not is a hotly contested problem among modern pianists. The affirmative group holds that the percussive noise accompanying the inception of tone attack determines its quality (timbre) and proposes that, by varying the degree of finger action, different timbres can be produced in each dynamic register. The negative group ("a piano key struck by Paderewski and the same key struck by an umbrella sound absolutely the same") holds that no such variation is possible with the single sound and that the varieties of timbre which are clearly noticeable in the playing of accomplished pianists result only from the relationship of varying intensities produced either simultaneously (as in chords) or successively (as in melodies). At any rate, the perception of tone-quality, even if not tenable from the scientific point of view, should be retained as a mental factor of prime importance. While it may not have a *de facto* basis, it has an "as-if" value which no piano player can afford to neglect.

VI. *Piano Playing and Brains.* The picture of modern pianism would be sorely incomplete without pointing to the importance of certain mental processes which go hand in hand with the purely technical methods. "Brains as well as hands play on the piano" [cf. Th. Fielden, in *PMA* lix] is a truism which should find a place on the front page of every pianist's study book. Most of this mental training consists of a "look-ahead" attitude, of a proc-

ess of mental preparation which anticipates the actual playing of the fingers. The "blind playing" described in a previous paragraph forms the first step in this direction. Of basic importance in the mastering of difficult passages is the "positioning" of the hand, i.e., an analysis of the passage as to the changing positions of the hand, and the use of preparatory "in-between" movements which lead the hand to the new position while the fingers are still occupied in the old one. Another realization of the same basic principle is the so-called "long hand," involving the "pre"-formation of wide skips such as are frequently encountered in the accompaniment of the left hand [see remark under *Technique].

VII. *Historical Conspectus.* Interesting information regarding the technique of the 16th-century keyboard (clavichord, organ) players is contained in Tomas de Santa Maria's *Arte de tañer fantasia* (1565; cf. O. Kinkeldey, *Orgel und Klavier in der Musik des 16. Jahrhunderts,* 1910) and in Girolamo Diruta's *Il Transilvano* (1593, 1609). Extremely difficult pianistic passages occur in the works of the *virginal composers, particularly those of John Bull (rapid scales in parallel thirds, iterated notes, etc.). J. S. Bach played a leading part in the development of the modern system of fingering [see *Fingering]. His contemporary Domenico Scarlatti (1685–1757) explored the virtuoso resources of the harpsichord to the fullest (crossing of the hands, wide skips, far-flung arpeggios), while C. P. E. Bach, in his *Versuch über die wahre Art das Klavier zu spielen* (1753), treated chiefly the clavichord as a melodic instrument.

The "old school" of piano playing (emphasis on finger technique) is represented by Muzio Clementi (1752–1832), Johann Nepomuk Hummel (1778–1837), and Carl Czerny (1791–1857). Great pianists such as Beethoven, Chopin, Liszt, Rubinstein were, of course, in full command of all the advanced methods of modern pianism, but Ludwig Deppe (1828–90) was the first to point out the importance of a deliberate use of the arm and its weight [cf. Amy Fay, *Music Study in Germany*, 1880]. Theodor Leschetitzky (1830–1915) established the methodical training in the new style of playing. Rudolf Breithaupt (b. 1873) introduced the principles of relaxation, Rollung (rolling and rotating movements of the hand), positioning, coördination of finger and arm, not without a dangerous tendency towards underestimating the importance of finger training. The same statement applies to the modern Relaxation School, represented mainly by Tobias Matthay (b. 1858) who, by his one-sided emphasis on freedom and suppleness, has to some extent discredited a good cause. Willy Bardas (1887–1924) made important contributions towards our understanding of the mental processes involved in piano playing. See *Fingering.

Lit.: H. Klose, *Die Deppesche Lehre des Klavierspiels* (1886); M. Brée, *The Groundwork of the Leschetizky Method* (1905); R. M. Breithaupt, *Natural Pianotechnic* (1909; German original ed. 1905); F. A. Steinhausen, *Ueber die physiologischen Fehler und die Umgestaltung der Klaviertechnik* (1905); T. A. Matthay, *The Act of Touch in all its Diversity* (1903, '24); id., *Visible and Invisible in Pianoforte Technique* (1932); W. Bardas, *Zur Psychologie der Klaviertechnik* (1927); O. R. Ortmann, *The Physiological Mechanics of Piano Technique* (1929); M. Levinskaya, *The Levinskaya System of Pianoforte Technique and Tone-colour* . . . (1930); Arnold Schultz, *The Riddle of the Pianist's Finger* . . . (1936); Y. Bowen, *Pedalling the Modern Pianoforte* (1936); C. A. Martienssen, *Die individuelle Klaviertechnik* . . . (1930); Th. Fielden, "The History of the Evolution of Pianoforte Technique" (*PMA* lix).

Pianola. See *Mechanical instruments IV.

Piano-violin. See *Sostenente pianoforte.

Piatti [It.]. Cymbals.

Pibgorn (pibcorn). See *Clarinet IV; *Reed II. Cf. H. L. Balfour, in *Journal of the Anthropological Institute* xx, 142.

Pibroch [Anglicized form of Gaelic *piobaireachd*, pipe tune]. An interesting type of Scotch bagpipe music, consisting of highly ornamented variations on a theme called *urlar*. They were formerly written down in a curious notation called *canntaireachd*, in which syllables such as "em, en, dari, dili . . ." denote tones or stereotyped motives. Cf. T. P. Grant, in *ML* vi, no. 1; A. Mackay, *A Collection of Ancient Piobaireachd* (1907).

Picardy third [F. *tierce de Picardie*]. The major third as used for the final chord of a composition in a minor key. This practice originated around 1500 when, for the first time, the third was admitted in the final chord of a piece. (The statement, found in some recent reference books, that the major third was "a common idiom from the beginning of harmonic composition, about A.D. 1000" is erroneous since prior to 1500 the final chord was practically always without the third, consisting of root, fifth, and octave only [see *Cadence].) When, around 1500, the third was admitted into the final chord, the major variety was preferred, probably because, from the point of view of contemporary theory, it is more consonant than the minor [see *Consonance and dissonance]. The picardy third continued to be used till the end of the Baroque period (*c.* 1750). No plausible explanation for the name "tierce de Picardie" which occurs for the first time in J. J. Rousseau's *Dictionnaire de musique* (1764) can be given.

Piccolo [It., small]. Short for piccolo flute, see *Flute I (b).

Pickelflöte [G.]. Older name for the piccolo flute. The modern name is *Kleine Flöte*.

Piedi [It., feet]. See under *Ballata.

Pien. In *Chinese music *pien* denotes certain degrees of the scale which are considered as subordinate in importance to others and which, therefore, are treated as mere ornamental or passing tones. These are the two "leading-tones" of the diatonic scale, that is, e and b, both of which form a semitone upwards. They represent later additions to the original pentatonic scale of Chinese music, c–d–f–g–a–c′. The term is also used by modern writers with reference to other musical provinces, e.g., to plainsong, in which the leading-tones frequently appear as auxiliary degrees. See, however, *Gregorian chant V (c).

Pieno [It.]. Full. E.g., *organo pieno*, full organ; *a voce piena*, with full voice.

Pietoso [It.]. Kindly, sympathetic.

Piffero [It.]. Old term for various popular Italian wind instruments such as the shawm, fife, bagpipe, all of which were used by the shepherds. Hence, the name *pifferari* for the rustic people who, in the 18th century, went to Rome every Christmas morning to play there in imitation of the Biblical shepherds. See *Pastorale.

Pincé. See *Mordent.

Pines of Rome. See *Symphonic poem IV.

P'ip'a. A Chinese short lute, with the neck leading into the body, in the shape of a bottle. It has four silk strings, tuned variously, and twelve or more frets the upper four of which have the form of convex ledges. It is used today chiefly by street singers and beggars. The early form of the Chinese lute is represented by a Japanese instrument, the *biwa*, which was introduced into Japan as early as the 17th century. This instrument has retained a much higher position than the Chinese p'ip'a and, as a consequence, is played with great refinement and artistic perfection. To withstand the strong blows of the plectrum (*batsi*) a band of leather or, in smaller instruments, of lacquer is laid across the soundboard. It has only the four ledges of the p'ip'a, without the additional inlaid frets. The delicate trill of the strings vibrating against these ledges is a characteristic feature of biwa playing. Cf. *SaHMI*, 189ff. Illustration on p. 413.

Pipe. (1) A small instrument of the recorder type which was held and played with the left hand only, while the right hand played the *tabor*, a diminutive drum. The playing of the "pipe and tabor" [F. *galoubet* and *tambourin*; Sp. *flaviol* and *tamborino*] was popular as early as the 13th century, as is shown by the famous miniatures of the Cantigas-MSS of the Escorial [illustration in *GD* iv, 184; ii, 260]. It was the usual accompaniment to the *farandole and to the English *Morris dance, and is still used for the Spanish *sardana. — (2) Generic name either for all the *wind instruments, or for certain classes, e.g., the wood winds, or the flutes, or the pipes of the organ, or primitive instruments in the shape of a simple tube.

Piqué [F.]. See *Bowing (d).

Piston. I.e., piston valves [see *Valves].

Pitch. (1) [F. *accordé*; G. *Tonhöhe*; It. *intonazione*]. The location of a musical sound in the tonal scale, proceeding from low to high, comparable to the temperature which indicates the location of a body in the thermal scale proceeding from cold to warm. The exact determination of pitch is by the frequency (number of vibrations) of the sound; see *Acoustics I. [Scientifically speaking, pitch, as the physiological sensation of acuteness and gravity, depends also to a small degree upon other factors (e.g., intensity) which are, however, negligible from the musical point of view; cf. Stevens and Davis, *Hearing* (1938).]

(2) [F. *diapason*; G. *Kammerton, Stimmung*; It. *diapason*]. The absolute pitch of one specific note, standardized for the purpose of obtaining identical pitches on all instruments. The present-day standard of pitch is a′ = 440 (double) vibrations in the United States, 435 in Europe. The latter pitch, known as International pitch, Concert pitch, New Philharmonic pitch, *Diapason normal* [F.], *Kammerton* [G.], was fixed by the Paris Academy in 1858 and was internationally adopted at a conference held at Vienna in 1889.

Prior to this agreement there existed a confusing variety of pitches, and the question of pitch has become a real problem particularly in connection with the works of Bach who frequently had to transpose his orchestral and choral parts on account of the different tuning of the organs in different churches, or who had to score wood-wind parts in, e.g., C while the parts for the organ, voices, and strings were scored in A (for the voices and strings a different scoring was obviously unnecessary since these could adapt themselves to the pitch of the organ). These discrepancies were caused by the fact that, throughout the Baroque period, different pitches were in use for different ensembles, namely the *Kammerton* (chamber pitch) for domestic instrumental music, the *Chorton* (choir pitch, organ pitch) for church organs and, consequently, for sacred choral music, and the *Cornett-ton* which the town-musicians used for their brass instruments. The confusion in this matter has been greatly increased by numerous erroneous or one-sided statements in modern writings which usually concern themselves with terms rather than with facts [see, e.g., the contradictory statements in *RiML*, 316 and 856]. By far the clearest account is found in N. Bessaraboff's *Ancient European Musical Instruments* (1941), pp. 357ff, 377f, and 442. Following his suggestion, the different pitches are represented here by keys (disregarding microtonic deviations), the standard pitch of the present day being represented by the key of C. The pitches used during the Baroque period and the various names by which they were referred to appear from the following tabulation:

	Praetorius (*Organographia*, 1619)	Common designation after Praetorius
Bb	Tertia minore	Tief Kammerton
B	Chorton	Hoch Kammerton
C#	Kammerton	Chorton
D	Cornett-ton	Cornett-ton

(The designations of the left column are used subsequently.)

The *Hoch Kammerton* must be regarded as the "standard instrumental pitch" from 1600 to *c*. 1820. Thus, Bach's instrumental compositions as well as the symphonies of Haydn, Mozart, and Beethoven sounded a semitone lower than they are performed today [see reference

under *Absolute pitch]. On the other hand, his organ works and cantatas (which involved the participation of the organ) sounded a semitone or even a whole-tone higher than today. Following is a list of some characteristic data covering the period from *c*. 1500 to 1850:

Pitch		Date	Source
A	a' = 377	1511	Arnold Schlick's "low organ"
	374	1700	Lille, Organ of the Hospice Comtesse
Bb	393	1713	Strasbourg, Silbermann organ
B	422	1751	Handel's tuning fork
	422	1780	Mozart's tuning fork
	423	1618	Praetorius' *Chor-ton*
	427	1811	Paris, Grand opera
C	440	1834	Scheibler (Stuttgart pitch)
	446	1856	Paris, Grand opera
C#	475	1618	Praetorius' *Kammerton*
D	503	1511	Arnold Schlick's "high organ"
	506	1495	Halberstadt organ
E	563	1636	Mersenne's Ton de chambre

It may be noted that recently the accuracy of Ellis' calculations of the Halberstadt organ and of Schlick's pitches has been questioned. According to R. Kendall, Schlick's "high organ" was a quarter-tone below present-day pitch (*c*. 435) while his "low organ" pitch was merely theoretical.

Lit.: A. J. Ellis, *The History of Musical Pitch* (1880; also in *Journal of the Society of Arts*, 1880); N. Bessaraboff [see above]; R. Kendall, "Notes on Arnold Schlick" (*AM* ix).

Pitch names. I. Following is a tabulation of the English, German, French, and Italian names for the tones of an octave:

English:	C	D	E	F	G	A	B
German:	C	D	E	F	G	A	H
French:	ut	ré	mi	fa	sol	la	si
Italian:	do	re	mi	fa	sol	la	si

English:	C-sharp	C-flat
German:	cis	ces
French:	ut dièse	ut bémol
Italian:	do diesis	do bemolle

English:	C-double-sharp	C-double-flat
German:	cisis	ceses
French:	ut double-dièse	ut double-bémol
Italian:	do doppio diesis	do doppio bemolle

N.B. The German terminology denotes a sharp by the suffix -is, a flat by the suffix

-es, a double-sharp by -isis, and a double-flat by -eses. Irregular formations are: *B*, i.e., B-flat, instead of *Hes*; *Es*, i.e., E-flat, instead of *Ees*; *As*, i.e., A-flat, instead of *Aes*. Note, particularly, that the English B is in German *H* (pronounced hä), and that the English B-flat is in German *B*.

II. As regards the indication of different octaves, there exists, unfortunately, no uniform practice. The accompanying table shows the system employed in this book and most widely used elsewhere (1), together with two others, (2), and (3). The chief source of confusion arises from the fact that some writers designate mid-

Pivot chord. See under *Modulation.

Pizzicato [It., plucked; abbr. *pizz.*]. In violin- (cello-) playing, indication that the string is to be plucked with the finger, as regularly in guitars, harps, etc. Early instances of this technique occur in Reinhold Keiser's *Adonis* (1697), and in Handel's operas *Agrippina* (1709) and *Il Pastor Fido* (1712). Paganini introduced the virtuoso technique of plucking the strings with the left hand, in alternation or simultaneously with bowed tones.

Placido [It.]. Peaceful.

	Contra	Great	Small	One-line		Two-line	Three-line	Four-line
1.	C₁	C	c	c′		c″	c‴	c⁗
2.	CCC	CC	C	c		c′	c″	c‴
3.	C₂	C₁	C	c		c¹	c²	c³

dle c (the C in the middle of the keyboard) by c′, others by c. The method (3) is, perhaps, the simplest and most logical; however, it has not been widely accepted. Cf. R. W. Young, in *Journal of Musicology* i.

For other systems of pitch designation, see *Solmization, *Letter notation.

Pitch pipe. A device used since the 18th century as an aid in tuning instruments. It consists of a wooden pipe with a movable stopper which, if pushed out or in, emits sounds of various pitches which are indicated on a graduated scale. It was largely discarded after the introduction of the tuning fork.

Più [It.]. More; e.g., *più allegro*, quicker. *Piuttosto allegro*, rather quick.

Piva [It.]. (1) Ancient name for the *bagpipe, shawm, or similar instruments. — (2) An early 16th-century dance in quick triple meter, apparently an imitation of music played on the instrument piva. Dalza's lute book of 1508 (Petrucci, *Intavolatura de lauto*, iv) contains several "suites" consisting of pavane, saltarello, and piva.

Plagal cadence [G. *Plagalschluss*]. The cadence with the subdominant preceding the tonic: IV–I. This cadence, also known as *Amen-cadence* because of its traditional use for the "Amen" at the end of hymns, was prominent in early music (15th, 16th centuries), became obsolete or archaic during the 18th and 19th centuries, but begins once more to play an important role in contemporary music, particularly in the works of Hindemith. This revival is concomitant with the modern aversion to the leading tone which is the characteristic note of the authentic cadence. See *Cadence.

Plagalis, plagius [L., from Gr. *plagios*, slanting, i.e., collateral]. A plagal mode. E.g., *primus plagius*, first plagal mode. See *Church modes.

Plainchant. Same as *plainsong, *Gregorian chant.

Plain-chant musical [F.]. A 17th-century French type of plainsong, characterized by the use of more "expressive" melodic progressions than are found in Gregorian chant, of accidentals (leading tone), and of strictly measured note-values (half- and quarter-notes) in the free arrangement of "measured rhythm" [see *Rhythm II (b)]. The rhythmic principles used in the plain-chant musical are obviously derived from the *vers mesuré of the 16th century. The plain-chant musical started around 1620 and spread all over France in the 17th and 18th centuries, but is now extinct. Henry Dumont (*Messes en plainchant*, 1669), Bourgoing, Chastelain, Nivers, wrote many melodies (all monophonic) in this style [see illustration]. Cf. A. Gastoué, in *TG* ix, 81ff;

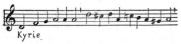

Kyrie

id., in *Cours ... de chant grégorien* (1917), pp. 84ff; H. Quittard, *Henry du Mont* (1906), pp. 175ff.

Plainsong. The term is derived from L. *cantus planus*, a 13th-century name for the *Gregorian chant. It is used synonymously with the latter, but also in a wider sense, as a general denomination for the ancient style of monophonic and rhythmically free melody which is the common possession of the various Western liturgies (Gregorian chant, *Ambrosian chant, *Gallican chant, *Mozarabic chant) as well as of those of the East (Byzantine chant, Syrian chant, Armenian chant). It may also be applied to similar bodies of non-Christian liturgical music (Jewish, Hindu) in order to indicate that this music is neither harmonic nor strictly measured.

Plainsong notation. This term is used here as the English equivalent of G. *Choralnotation* (*Choral*, i.e., *Gregorianischer Choral*, i.e., plainsong). Properly speaking, both terms denote the notation of Gregorian chant, i.e., the notation in *neumes. Actually, however, the German term is used preferably with reference to a considerably later stage of monophonic notation, starting around 1200 when the four-line staff had been generally accepted and the neumes had been replaced by those square-shaped forms which are still used today in the liturgical books [see *Nota-

tion II; *Neumes II]. The rhythmic problems of this system are the same as those presented by the neumes [see *Gregorian chant VI], unless melodies of a more recent date (hymns, sequences) are considered or the possibility of a deteriorated practice is taken into account. Cf. *WoHN* i, 146–171.

The term *Choralnotation* is also used with reference to the large repertory of 13th to 15th-century secular monophonic music for which the same notational symbols (essentially those of the present-day liturgical books) were employed, i.e., the melodies of the troubadours, trouvères, Minnesinger, Meistersinger, the Italian laude, the Spanish cantigas, etc. [cf. *WoHN* i, 172–197]. It goes without saying that, thus used, the term and, as a consequence, its English synonym are entirely inappropriate designations. No better terms, however, have as yet been suggested. In the secular repertory the use of metrically indefinite symbols — lacking, e.g., a clear distinction between long and short values — for the writing down of (presumably) measured melodies has given rise to various contrasting theories, most of which are based on a consideration of the poetic meter of the text. While Riemann forced the melodies into his scheme of *Vierhebigkeit*, J. Beck and others applied the principle of modal interpretation [G. *Modaltheorie*] according to which each melody follows the pattern of one of the rhythmic *modes. The latter method has been generally accepted for the melodies of the troubadours and trouvères [see *Trouvères] but seems of questionable value in the case of Minnesinger melodies. It is interesting to note that J. Beck, who was the first to expound this theory, in 1907, turned against it in 1927. As a matter of fact, the whole problem is still far from being solved. Even the textual meter is by no means as clear a guide as it is usually assumed to be [see *Text and music; *Poetic meter III]. A thorough study of the whole field, unbiased by modern prejudice in favor of "correct" accentuation, measure, strict meter, etc., is sorely needed.

Lit.: *WoHN* i, 146–71; 172–97; *RiHM*

i.2, 245ff, 260ff; J. B. Beck, *Die Melodien der Troubadours* (1908; see the footnote in *WoHN* i, 200); *id., Le Chansonnier Cangé* (1927); H. Riemann, in *JMP* xii; J. Handschin, in *AM* x and in *Medium Aevum* iv (1935); H. J. Moser, in *ZMW* vii, 367ff; E. Jammers, in *ZMW* vii.

Plainte [F.]. (1) See *Tombeau. — (2) See *Planc. — (3) A Baroque ornament, either a *portamento (in 17th-century viol music) or a *Nachschlag.

Plaisanterie [F.]. Name for playful movements in the suites of the 18th century; also for collections of pieces in the light style of the *Rococo.

Planc, planh [Provençal]. Troubadour songs of a mournful character. The term carries no particular connotation of musical form.

Plantation songs. See *Negro music.

Plaqué [F.]. Played simultaneously and deliberately, as opposed to *arpeggio.

Plateau [F.]. Plate, i.e., of the *cymbals.

Platerspiel [old G. *Plater*, bladder]. *Bladder pipe.

Player piano. See *Mechanical instruments IV.

Plectrum. A small piece of horn, tortoise-shell, wood, ivory, metal, etc., used for the playing of certain stringed instruments, such as the Greek lyra and the modern mandolin and zither. The quills of the harpsichord are a mechanized form of plectrum.

Plein-jeu [F.]. Full organ. Also name for pieces written for the full organ. *Demi-jeu*, half organ, i.e., softer registration.

Plica [L., fold, plait]. A notational sign of the 13th century calling for an ornamental tone to be inserted between written notes. The sign for the *plica* is an upward or downward dash which is attached to single notes (longa, brevis) as well as to the final note of a ligature (*ligatura pli-*

cata). The direction of the dash indicates whether the grace note is higher or lower than the main note (usually a second or, more rarely, a third, depending upon the position of the next-following note). The accompanying example shows three *plicae*

longae (1,2,4), characterized by a longer dash to the right side, two *plicae breves* (3,7), characterized by a longer dash to the left side or two dashes of about equal length, and two *ligaturae plicatae* (5,6) [cf. *ApNPM, passim*].

The *plica* developed from the liquescent *neumes of the Gregorian chant. According to 13th-century theorists (Pseudo-Aristoteles; cf. *GS* i, 173) it was sung in a special manner, probably a tremolo [see *Tremolo (3)]. The theory, advanced by H. Riemann (*Mus. Wochenblatt*, 1897) and utilized by P. Runge (*Die Colmarer Liederhandschrift*, 1896), that the plica played a prominent part in the music of the Minnesinger is erroneous. The German scribes of the 14th and 15th centuries used notational characters which are similar in shape to the plica notes of 13th-century music, without having their meaning. See *Ornamentation II.

Plut. See under *Magnus liber organi.

Pmo. Short for *pianissimo.

Pneuma. See *Neuma (2).

Pneumatic action. See *Organ II.

Pochette [F.]. *Kit.

Poco [It.]. Little. Diminutive forms are *pochetto, pochettino, pochissimo*.

Podatus. See *Neumes I.

Poetic meter. I. Poetic meter, with its regular alternation of accented (strong) and unaccented (weak) syllables or, in ancient Greek terminology, of *thesis* and *arsis, is very similar to musical meter with its various schemes of accented and unaccented notes. The terminology of ancient Greek poetry is, therefore, frequently used to denote corresponding schemes of musical rhythm. The chief patterns (called "feet") of the Greek system are:

	Poetic	Musical
Iamb:	.│.│	$\frac{3}{4}$ ♩│♩ ♩│♩
Trochee:	│.│.	$\frac{3}{4}$ │♩ ♩│♩♩ │
Dactyl:	│..│..	$\frac{4}{4}$ │♩ ♩♩│♩ ♩♩│
Anapaest:	..│..│	$\frac{4}{4}$ ♩♩│♩ ♩♩│♩ ♩♩│
Amphibrach:	.│..│.	$\frac{4}{4}$ ♩│♩ ♩♩│♩ ♩

(In the musical examples each thesis is rendered as a half-note, each arsis as a quarter-note.)

This terminology is used particularly in connection with the 13th-century system of rhythmic modes in which, however, nearly all the musical schemes differ in some detail from those indicated above [see *Modes, Rhythmic].

II. According to the number of feet contained in one line of the poem, one distinguishes between *dimeter* (two feet), *trimeter* (three), *tetrameter* (four), *pentameter* (five), and *hexameter* (six). For instance, the dactylic hexameter (Homer) consists of six dactyls the last of which is usually one arsis short (*katalectic*): │..│..│..│..│..│.. . In the case of an iambic or trochaic foot, however, the numbering proceeds in pairs of feet (*dipody*, i.e., two feet). Thus, a line including four iambs, .│.│.│.│, is called an iambic dimeter (not tetrameter). In hymnody certain standard meters have distinct names and designations, e.g., the *common meter*, indicated thus: 8 6. 8 6 (the figures give the numbers of syllables in each line). Here each line usually is an iambic dimeter, the lines "8" complete, the lines "6" katalectic, with one arsis and thesis missing at the end.

III. As regards the application of the metrical schemes to words (versification), there are two principles determining which syllables fall on the thesis and which on the arsis, one ancient and one modern. In ancient poetry the division of lines into feet was quantitative, based on the recurrence of long syllables (G., *Silbenmes-*

sung), whereas in modern poetry the division is qualitative, based on the recurrence of stressed syllables (G., *Silbenwägung*).

In modern poetry the thesis- and arsis-syllables are essentially the same as they are in prose; in other words, the poetic accentuation follows the natural accent of the words, e.g.:

│ . . │.│ . │.│ .
Meantime we shall express our darker purpose

In Greek and Latin poetry, however, the poetic accentuation differed essentially from that of prose, as the following example shows:

Prose accent: . │ . │.. │.. │ . .
Maecenas atavis edite regibus
Poetic accent: │ .│ ..│ │..│ .│

(For the rules governing ancient poetry cf. any Greek or Latin grammar.)

While ancient Greek and Latin poetry was exclusively quantitative, the modern principle of quality originated in Syrian poetry of the 4th century (Ephrem, d. 373) and was introduced into the Latin Church by St. Ambrose and St. Augustine. It prevails in most of the Latin poetry of the Middle Ages, e.g., in the *Ambrosian hymns and in the *sequences of the 12th and 13th centuries (Adam de St. Victor). In the 8th century, however, there was, under the influence of Byzantine poetry, a return to the ancient system, though less rigidly applied. In fact, with many medieval Latin poems it is questionable whether they should be read quantitatively (a) or qualitatively (b), e.g.:

(a) │ ..│ ..│ ..│
Conditio naturae defuit,
(b) . │.│ .│. │.│
(a) │ ..│ . .│ ..│
In filio quem virgo genuit
(b) . │.│ . │.│.│

Similar problems arise with medieval French poems, owing to the peculiar indifference of the French language towards accentuation (in contrast to English or German), e.g.:

(a) │ . .│ . .│ . . │
Quar eusse je cent mile mars d'argent
(b) . │.│ . │.│ . │

These ambiguities present great difficulties in the interpretation of medieval monophonic songs, particularly those of the troubadours and trouvères [cf. J. B.

Beck, *Die Melodien der Troubadours* ..., pp. 132, 138; see *Plainsong notation]. Cf. also *MoML*, 11.

Lit.: C. F. Abdy Williams, "The Aristoxenian Theory of the Rhythmic Feet" (*MA* ii); I. Krohn, "Der metrische Taktfuss in der modernen Musik" (*AMW* iv); F. Rosenthal, "Probleme der musikalischen Metrik" (*ZMW* viii).

Poggiato [It.]. "Leaned upon," dwelt upon.

Poi [It.]. Then, afterwards. *Poi la coda,* "then the coda," usually given at the end of the Trio to indicate that the resumption of the Scherzo is to be followed by the Coda: S – T – S – C.

Point. (1) The upper end of the violin bow. — (2) Point of perfection, of division, etc. [see *Punctus]. — (3) In the motets of the 16th century, point of imitation denotes a section of the polyphonic texture in which a single subject, connected with a small division of the text, is treated in imitation. These points are the structural cellules of the motet which consists of a succession of a considerable number of points. In the classical motet of the Josquin period the points are usually marked off, not vertically, but diagonally, so that the conclusion of one point overlaps the beginning of the next. For an example cf. *HAM*, no. 89; *SchGMB*, no. 107.

Point d'orgue [F.]. (1) The *pause and its sign. — (2) *Pedal-point. — (3) A *cadenza in a concerto, so called because its beginning is customarily indicated by a pause sign placed above the preceding chord of the composition proper.

Pointing. See under *Anglican chant.

Polacca [It.]. *Polonaise.

Polish music. I (–1600). Poland possesses a famous war song, *Bogarodzica,* dating from the 13th century, which is preserved in 11 copies [cf. *LavE* i.5, 2572]. The earliest known Polish composer is Nicolaus of Radom (after 1400) of whom a number of Mass compositions are preserved [cf. F. Ludwig, in *AMW* vii, 430].

A continuous development of Polish music started in the 16th century with Sebastian Felsztyn who wrote motets, hymns, and a Mass, — all in Flemish style — and published several theoretical books between 1519 and 1544. He was followed by Vinceslas Szamotuly (psalms), Martinus Leopolita (Martin Lwowczyk; 1540–89), Thomas of Szadek, and Nicolas Gomolka (1539–1609), all brought up in the tradition of the Flemish School or, later on, of Palestrina [cf. Lit., *Monumenta* i–iii]. German influence (Johannes Buchner) is patent in two extensive organ tablatures of *c.* 1540 [cf. *WoHN* ii, 27ff] which contain a great number of hymns and motets arranged for the organ, but also interesting preludes. Towards the end of the 16th century Polish dances made their appearance at the Saxon court, as is shown by a number of pieces ("Polnischer Tantz") contained in the tablature of Nörmiger of 1599 [see *Colorists]. Their music, however, does not show any specific national traits. A center of musical culture was the chapel of the Roratistes which, founded in 1543, continued to the end of the 18th century.

II (1600–1900). Under King Sigismund III (1587–1632) an opera, directed by Marco Scacchi of Rome, was established at the court of Warsaw, but the ensuing political collapse of Poland brought musical life to an almost complete standstill for more than 150 years. The Polish opera came to new life under Matheus Kamienski (1734–1821) who composed numerous operas between 1780 and 1800, in the style of the *Singspiel. Josef Kozlowski (1757–1821) is interesting mainly as a composer of numerous *polonaises, as is also his pupil Count Michael Oginski (1765–1833). Joseph Elsner, known mainly as the teacher of Chopin, wrote numerous operas of which only the titles have been preserved and, besides, symphonies, chamber music, songs, and a famous Passion oratorio. He also founded the first conservatory at Warsaw (1821–30), of which Chopin was a pupil. Even more important was Charles Kurpinski (1785–1857), as a composer of operas, conductor, and teacher. The foremost instrumental composer of the "classical" period of Polish music was Ignace-Félix Dobrzynski (1807–67; two symphonies, chamber music).

Frédéric Chopin (1810–49), son of a French father and a Polish mother, put all these achievements into eclipse and carried the fame of Polish music into all parts of the world. Together with Schumann and Mendelssohn he founded the musical *Romanticism to which he imparted a distinct tinge of national expression, particularly in his polonaises and *mazurkas. Stanislav Moniuszko (1819–72) wrote numerous songs many of which became a part of the national treasure of Poland. His opera *Halka* (1858) is the first Polish national opera. Five of the 15 operas he wrote belong to the permanent repertory of Polish opera houses. His most important successor was Ladislas Zelenski (1837–1921) who composed operas of some merit, but deserves mention mainly as a composer of chamber music in a moderately Romantic style, influenced by Schumann and Brahms. Henrik Wieniawski (1835–80) became world-famous as a violin virtuoso, and composed two well-known violin concertos as well as other pieces for his instrument. Ignaz Paderewski (1860–1940) occupied a similar place in piano music, to say nothing about his outstanding position in the political life of Poland.

III (1900–). The "young-Polish" group is represented mainly by Karol Szymanowski (1883–1937), one of the outstanding composers of modern music. Successively influenced by Richard Strauss, Scriabin, and, after World War I, Debussy, he arrived, about 1920, at a mature style of his own, a mixture of Romantic and impressionistic elements, but consciously Polish at the same time and, in his latest works, tending towards atonality and constructivism. Among his most important works are a Stabat mater, a ballet *Harnasie* (1926), a Symphonie Concertante for piano and orchestra, and his Second Violin Concerto (1930). Other modern composers of significance are Alexander Tansman (b. 1897) and Karol Rathaus (b. 1895), both of whom follow

the radical trends of *New music, and Jerzy Fitelberg (b. 1903), who writes in a strongly neo-classical idiom. Both Tansman and Fitelberg are now in America.

Lit.: E. Rayson, *Polish Music and Chopin its Laureate* (1916); LavE i.5, 2568–85; AdHM ii, 1144–51 (modern music); A. Wieniawski, *La musique polonaise* (1937); H. Opienski, *La musique polonaise* (1918, '29); M. Glinski, *Muzyka polska* (1927); H. Jachimecki, *Historjy muzyki polskiej* (1920); J. Surczynski, †*Monumenta musices sacrae in Polonia*, 4 vols. (1887); Z. Jachimecki, "Polish Music" (*MQ* vi); F. Starczewski, "Die polnischen Tänze" (*SIM* ii); T. Norlind, "Zur Geschichte der polnischen Tänze" (*SIM* xii). To I: J. Surczynski, in *KJ*, 1890; A. Chybinski, in *Riemann Festschrift* (1909); id., in *SIM* xiii; id., in *ZIM* xiii; J. W. Reiss, in *ZIM* xiii; Z. Jachimecki, in *ZMW* ii. — To II: H. Opienski, in *RdM*, 1929, no. 30 (opera); id., in *RdM*, 1934, no. 52 (symphony). — To III: Z. Jachimecki, "Karol Szymanowski" (*MQ* viii). Cf. also *RiHM* ii.1, 342f.

Polka. A Bohemian dance in quick duple meter and characteristic rhythms. It originated around 1830 in Bohemia, and soon spread to the European salons, causing a real "polkamania" which lasted until the end of the century. The polka was introduced into art music by Smetana (*The Bartered Bride*; *From my Life*; *Bohemian Dances*), Dvořák, and others. See *Dance music IV.

1. Polka. 2. Polo

Polo. An Andalusian (north Spanish) dance in moderate ⅜-meter, with frequent syncopations of the *hemiola-type [see Ex.], and with rapid coloraturas sung to syllables such as "Ay," "Ole," etc. The dance movements show Oriental influence, being movements of the body rather than of the feet. Two famous polos were written by Manuel Garcia (1805–1906), "Yo soy el contrabandista" and "Cuerpo bueno" [cf. LavE i.4, 2293ff], the latter of which was used by Bizet in the prelude to the fourth act of Carmen. A good modern example is found in Falla's Seven Spanish Popular Songs (no. 7).

Polonaise. A Polish national dance of a stately and festive character. The music is always in moderate triple meter, with rhythms such as those illustrated [Ex. 1],

and shows a number of characteristic features, e.g., feminine ending of the phrases; repetition of short and precise motives, frequently three times within a measure; characteristic accompanying rhythms, traits which can all be seen in the accompanying example [Ex. 2] by Beethoven (op. 89).

The polonaise is not a folk dance, but developed from courtly ceremonies and processions, records of which go back as far as the late 16th century [cf. GD iv, 218]. Although in this period Polish dances make their appearance in various musical manuscripts and printed books, none of them bears any resemblance to the polonaise. The earliest known examples of the polonaise proper are those written by Bach (Brandenburg Concerto no. 1; French Suite no. 6; Orchestral Suite no. 2, in B minor; also pieces in the Notenbüchlein der Anna Magd. Bach) and Handel (Concerto Grosso no. 3). Around the middle of the 18th century the polonaise became very popular, probably as the result of political changes (election of the Saxon Elector Augustus III to the Polish throne, 1733). A great number of vocal polonaises are contained in Sperontes' Singende Muse [DdT 25/26]. J. Th. Goldberg (for whom Bach wrote his *Goldberg Variations) wrote 24 polonaises, and W. Fr. Bach, in his 12 polonaises, raised the dance to an idealized type of extraordinary imagination and artistic perfection (new ed. Peters, no. 750), whereas Mozart (Pianoforte Sonata in D major; K.V. 284) furnished a charming example in a much simpler style. During the first half of the 19th century the polonaise continued to attract the interest of composers such as Beethoven, Schubert (polonaises for four hands), Weber (opp. 21 and 72), Liszt (Deux Polonaises, 1852), and, above all, Chopin who, preceded by his countrymen Josef Kozlowski (1757–1821) and Count Michael Oginski (1765–1833; see *Polish music II), made the polonaise the symbol of the heroism and chivalry of the Polish nation. See *Dance music III.

Polska. A Swedish dance, probably of Polish origin, similar in character to the mazurka rather than to the polonaise. For an example cf. GD iv, 219; also Niemann, in SIM v, 99.

Polychoral style. The term is used with reference to compositions in which the ensemble (chorus with or without the orchestra) is divided into several (usu-

ally two or three) distinct groups singing and playing in alternation. This technique, which is also known as *antiphonal style, was exploited chiefly by Giov. Gabrieli (1557–1612; see illustration). It forms a characteristic feature of the *Venetian School and persisted throughout the Baroque period, particularly in Rome (Orazio Benevoli; see *Roman School), in the English Services where the two choruses are designated *Dec.* and *Can.* (i.e., *Decani* and *Cantoris*, signifying respectively the south side and the north side of the cathedral, according to the seats usually occupied by these officers), and in Germany (Handl, Hassler, Schütz), the latest examples being found in Bach (first movement of the St. Matthew Passion). Early adumbrations of polychoral treatment occur in the works of Josquin des Près who frequently interrupts the full-voiced writing in four parts (S,A,T,B) by "antiphonal" passages in which two half-choruses (S,A and T,B or S,A,T and A,T,B) perform a short phrase twice, in an echo-like manner [Ex. under *Echo; also in *BeMMR*, 250]. Zarlino, in his *Istituzioni harmoniche* of 1558, credits Willaert with the introduction of the polychoral style in its more explicit form. Its development during the second half of the 16th century was furthered by the alternate playing on the two organs of St. Mark's at Venice which were installed in the two apses of the cathedral. Accordingly, different choruses were placed with the organs and elsewhere in the building (*cori spezzati*; G. *Apsidenchöre*).

Lit.: L. Reitter, *Doppelchortechnik bei Heinrich Schütz* (Diss. Zürich 1937); E. Hertzmann, in *ZMW* xii.

Polychronion. See *Acclamation.

Polymetric. See *Polyrhythm.

Polyphonic, polyphony [Gr. *polys*, many; *phonos*, voice; G. *Mehrstimmig, Vielstimmig*]. Music written as a combination of several simultaneous voices (parts) of a more or less pronounced individuality. Hence, the term polyphony is practically synonymous with *counterpoint. It should be noted that the word "poly" must not be taken literally, since as few as two parts can make perfect polyphony, better, indeed, than six or eight.

Although, according to definition, there is no difference between polyphony and counterpoint, the former term is used preferably with regard to early music (Medieval polyphony) as well as for broad classification (polyphonic, monophonic); the latter for the styles of, e.g., Palestrina and Bach, and, consequently, in teaching where these serve as models. See also *Contrapuntal; *Texture.

Numerous theories have been advanced regarding the "origin of polyphony," but none of these can be said to be more than hypothetical. Some scholars have ventured to regard the earliest extant examples of polyphony (*c.* 800), not as a beginning, but as a "first culmination point" of a development, traces of which they believe to exist in Oriental and primitive music [cf. *ReMMA*, 249ff]. See *Primitive music IV.

Lit.: M. Schneider, *Geschichte der Mehrstimmigkeit*, i, ii (1934–35); P. Wagner, "Ueber die Anfänge des mehrstimmigen Gesanges" (*ZMW* ix); E. Steinhard, "Zur Frühgeschichte der Mehrstimmigkeit" (*AMW* iii); F. Ludwig, "Studien über die Geschichte der mehrstimmigen Musik im Mittelalter" (*SIM* v); M. Schneider, "Kaukasische Parallelen zur mittelalterlichen Mehrstimmigkeit" (*AM* xii); for additional bibliography cf. *ReMMA*, 451f.

Polyrhythm. The simultaneous use of strikingly contrasting rhythms in different parts of the musical fabric, also known as cross-rhythm. Properly speaking, all truly contrapuntal or polyphonic music is polyrhythmic, since rhythmic variety in simultaneous parts more than anything else contributes to giving the voice-parts that quality of individuality which is essential to polyphonic style [see *Texture]. Generally, however, the term is restricted to those examples in which rhythmic variety is introduced, not as a means to enhance contrapuntal life, but for its own sake (cross rhythm). A distinction can be made between two types: contrasting rhythms within the same scheme of accents (meter) [Ex. 1, a and b]; contrasting rhythms involving a conflict of meter or accents [Ex. 1, c and d]. The latter type is sometimes termed "polymetric." Twice in the history of music have poly-

metric designs played a prominent role: around 1400, and in present-day music [see *New music]. A passage from the 15th-century song "Amans ames secrete-

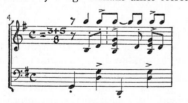

ment" [Ex. 2; cf. *ApNPM*, 175] and one from Hindemith's *Klaviermusik*, op. 37 [Ex. 3] serve as illustrations.

Polymetric passages can also be written in such a way that different meters are avoided, in which cases one of the two voice-parts will necessarily be in *synco-pation [Ex. 1 (d)]. This manner of writing is frequently preferred for the sake of easier reading, but it actually obscures the true rhythmic life, in modern editions of early music as well as in jazz [Ex. 4]. See also *Imbroglio.

Polytonality. The simultaneous use of different tonalities (usually two: bi-tonality) in different parts of the musical fabric, e.g., of B-flat minor in the left hand against F-sharp minor in the right hand of a pianoforte piece [see Ex. 1, from Prokofiev's *Sarcasmes*]. This technique has been used to quite an extent by con-temporary composers seeking new means of tonal design. Among the earliest ex-amples are passages in Stravinsky's *Pe-trouchka*, 1911 (Ex. 2) and in Busoni's

Sonatina seconda, 1912 (see *Cadence, Ex. 27). The combination C against F-sharp or, in terms of the pianoforte key-board, "white against black," has become known as the "Petrouchka chord." This device has been exploited, somewhat fa-cetiously, by numerous other composers, particularly in pieces which they consid-ered suitable for children (Casella, *Pezzi infantili*). In these cases, as in others as well, the jocose character of the device is patent. In this respect it is interesting to note that occasionally earlier composers have used polytonal schemes for satirical purposes, e.g., Hans Newsidler in a lute piece *Der Judentantz* (The Jew's dance)

of 1535 [cf. *ApMZ* i], and Mozart in his *Ein musikalischer Spass* (A Musical Jest), composed in 1787 (K.V. 522). See also *Partial signature.

Lit.: J. Deroux, "La Musique polytonale" (*RM* ii); D. Milhaud, "Polytonalité et atonalité" (*RM* iv, no. 4); A. Machabey, "Dissonance, polytonalité, atonalité" (*RM* xii).

Pomhart, Pommer. Old German for *Bombarde [see *Oboe family III].

Ponticello [It.]. The bridge of stringed instruments. *Sul ponticello*, see *Bowing (k).

Pontificale. See *Liturgical books I.

Porrectus. See *Neumes I.

Port. A term formerly in use in Scotland to denominate an instrumental piece, usually for the harp. Cf. *GD.*

Portamento [It., carrying]. A special manner of singing, with the voice gliding gradually from one tone to the next through all the intermediate pitches. A similar effect, frequently but erroneously called *glissando, is possible on the violin and on the trombone. In vocal compositions the portamento is indicated by a slur connecting two notes of different pitch. See *Portato.

Portative organ [G. *Portativ*]. A small portable organ of the Middle Ages which was used for processions and for domestic music. An Italian 14th-century name is *organetto*. See *Organ XII. There exists a movement in Germany to revive this instrument. Cf. H. Hickmann, *Das Portativ* (1936); H. Wolff, in *ZMW* xv, 318.

Portato [It., carried]. A manner of performance halfway between legato and staccato [see *Legato]. The use of the name *portamento for this is misleading and should be avoided.

Port de voix [F.]. (1) In modern French usage, same as *portamento. — (2) One of the most important French *agréments* of the 17th and 18th centuries. Essentially it is an upward-resolved suspension or appoggiatura, generally expressed by sign or a particular notation [see *Appoggiatura]. Usually, however, both appoggiatura and resolution are repeated, so that the ornament consists of four notes, the last three forming a *pincé* (*mordent). In keyboard music this fuller execution is usually indicated by combining the sign for the *port de voix* with

that for the pincé, as illustrated. In music for the voice and all other instruments the pincé was taken for granted.   P. A.

Portée [F.]. Staff.

Porter (portez) la voix. See *Port de voix (1).

Portuguese hymn. The hymn *Adeste fideles* (O come, all ye faithful), so called because it was frequently used, around 1800, in the Portuguese chapel at London.

Portuguese music. I (–1700). In the 13th century the Portuguese Kings Affonso III (1248–79) and Dinez (Denis) I (1279–1325) attracted Provençal troubadours to their courts. Very likely these instigated interest and succession among native musicians one of whom, Martin Codax, is known to us through seven songs which were discovered in 1914 in the binding of a 14th-century MS of Cicero's *De officiis* [cf. *ML* v, 29f; I. Pope, in *Speculum* ix (1934)]. João I (1385–1433) was a munificent and lavish ruler who entertained a large orchestra at his court for festivities and ceremonial occasions. The rule of João III (1521–57) saw the rise of Flemish polyphony in Portugal, with Damião de Goes (1502–53, well known as a historian and traveler; a motet "Ne laetaris" in Glareanus' *Dodekachordon*) and Manuel Cardoso (d. 1595) as the first native representatives.

In the 17th century a splendid school of Portuguese polyphonic music emerged, known as the School of Évora. To this belong Manuel Mendes (d. 1605), Duarte Lobo (*c.* 1565–1643), its greatest master, Frei Manuel Cardoso (1569–1650), Felipe de Magalhães (publications 1631, '42), João Lourenço Rebello (1610–61), and

Diego de Melgaço (1638–1700). To these must be added the Portuguese King John IV (1604–56), who studied music under Rebello, composed many works for church use (of which two motets are preserved), wrote a book and pamphlet in defense of Palestrina, and founded the world-famous library the destruction of which, in the Lisbon earthquake of 1755, entailed the loss of innumerable priceless musical works. A contemporary of Lobo was Manuel Coelho (b. 1583) who, in 1620, published an interesting collection of organ music (*Flores de musica*), containing *tentos (ricercares) in the style of Cabezon and Sweelinck (new ed. of 5 tentos by S. Kastner). A similar collection was published in 1626 by F. Correia de Araujo (*Libro de tientos*).

II (1700–Present). Under the dissolute and fanatic King John V (1706–50) Portuguese music came under the influence of Italian musicians. Domenico Scarlatti stayed at the Portuguese court from 1721 to 1729, and his influence is patent in the works of the "Portuguese Scarlatti," José de Seixas (1709–42), who wrote hundreds of "sonatas" in his master's style [cf. M. S. Kastner, *Cravistas Portuguezes*]. Even more penetrating was the Italian influence in the field of the opera which came entirely under the domination of the Neapolitan composers. Among the first Portuguese composers of operas was Francisco de Almeida (*La Pazienza di Socrate*, 1733). He was followed by João de Sousa Carvalho (1709–98) whose pupil Marcos Portugal (1762–1830) became the greatest Portuguese opera composer, while João Domingos Bomtempo (1775–1842) was the first symphonist of Portugal, writing orchestral works in the style of Haydn and Mozart. Unfortunately he had no followers of note.

The father of modern Portuguese music is José Vianna da Motta (b. 1868) who is a champion of nationalism (*The Lusiads* for chorus and orchestra). Freitas Branco (b. 1890) combines impressionistic idioms with national elements. Ruy Coelho (b. 1891) has written several operas and symphonic poems in the national tradition. Frederico de Freitas (b. 1902)

is the author of orchestral and instrumental pieces in the impressionist vein.

Lit.: G. Chase, *The Music of Spain* (1941), chapter XVIII; *LavE* i.4, 2401ff; A. Soubis, *La Musique à Portugal* (1890); S. Kastner, *Contribución al estudio de la música española y portuguesa* (1941); A. Pinto, *Musica moderna portuguesa* (1930); E. Vieira, *Diccionario biographico dos musicos portuguezes* (1891); Julio Eduardo dos Santos, †*A Polifonia classica portuguesa* (1938); S. Kastner, †*Cravistas portuguezes*. For folk music see under *Fado.

Pos. Short for *position, or [F.] *positif, or [G.] *Posaune.

Posaune [G.]. Trombone.

Posé [F.]. Steady, sedate.

Positif [F.]. Choir organ.

Position. (1) With reference to chords (close, wide position), see *Spacing. — (2) On the violin, etc., positions are the different places on the finger board occupied by the left hand. Thus, on the G-string the first position covers the fifth from g to d', g being the open string and the successive four notes a, b, c', d' being stopped by the four fingers. The second position starts with the first finger on b and ends with the fifth finger on e', etc. The moving from one position into another is known as shift. For the history of this technique cf. *GD*, article "Shift." Both terms apply also to the trombone with reference to the varying position of the slide. The home position is called the first, and each successive position lowers the pitch a semitone.

Positive organ [G. *Positiv*]. In the Middle Ages, name for a small chamber organ which was stationary, as opposed to the portable *portative organ. It had mostly soft flute-stops. A famous illustration is found on van Eyck's Altar of Ghent [cf. *AdHM*, 574]. Later the name was applied to a special section of the church organ in which also flue-stops (Principal, etc.) prevail, such as are suitable for the accompaniment of the choir; hence, synonymous with *choir organ. See *Organ XII. Cf. F. W. Galpin, in *MA* iv.

Postlude. An organ piece played at the conclusion of the service, during the exit of the congregation. It is usually improvised. The term is also used in the meaning of *coda.

Potpourri [F.]. A medley of popular tunes, operatic airs, patriotic songs, etc., which are played in succession, being connected by a few measures of introduction or modulation. The name, which properly denotes a dish mixed of many ingredients (literally "rotten-pot"), occurs as early as in Ballard's collection of *brunettes of 1711. J. B. Cramer was the first to use it for the 19th-century type of drawing-room piece.

Poussé [F., pushed]. Up-bow; see *Bowing.

Poussez [F.]. Push on, speed up.

Pp. Pianissimo. Sometimes ppp, pppp, are used to denote the ultimate degree of softness.

P.R. In French organ music, abbreviation of *Positif-Récit*, i.e., choir organ and swell organ coupled.

Prachtvoll [G.]. Grand, pompous.

Praeambulum [L.]. Sixteenth-century name for *prelude.

Praefatio [L.]. See *Preface.

Praeludium. See *Prelude.

Prague Symphony. Mozart's Symphony in D (K.V. 504), composed in 1786 and enthusiastically received in Prague in 1787.

Pralltriller [G.]. Modern term for the "inverted mordent." See under *Schneller.

Préambule [F.], **preambulum** [L.]. See *Prelude.

Precentor. The director of music in a cathedral or monastic church.

Precipitando [It.]. "With precipitation," impetuously.

Preface [L. *Praefatio*]. A solemn ascription of praise sung at Mass, and leading without a break into the Sanctus [see *Mass A]. It includes short solo verses and choral responses [see *GR*, 118*; also *LU*, 3, 109].

Preg(h)ando [It.]. "Praying," devotionally.

Prelude [F. *prélude*; G. *Praeludium, Vorspiel*; It. *preludio*]. Properly, a piece of music designed to be played as an introduction, for instance, to a liturgical ceremony or, more usually, to another composition, such as a fugue or a suite. This connotation, which prevails throughout the entire early history of the prelude (see below), was lost in the 19th century, when Chopin and his followers (Scriabin, Debussy) used the word merely as one of the numerous noncommittal titles of Romantic pianoforte pieces [see *Character piece]. How completely the term has lost its proper meaning appears from the fact that even the most pedantic listeners seem never to have objected against twenty-four preludes being played in succession.

The history of the prelude is of particular interest since it represents not only one of the earliest types of keyboard music, but *the* earliest type of idiomatic keyboard music, as distinct from the vocally-influenced types such as *Intabulierungen, the ricercar or the canzona. The history of the prelude can be divided into three periods which may be designated, somewhat fancifully, as the periods of I the unconnected, II the connected, and III the disconnected prelude. In the first period (*c.* 1450–1650) the prelude is a single composition which may be used for any suitable purpose, either in the church or in the home; in the second period (*c.* 1650–1750) the prelude becomes the "first movement" of a special composition with which it is inseparably connected; in the third period (19th century) it becomes an independent piece to which no function or other composition is attached.

I. The preludes of the 15th and early

16th centuries are short pieces (10 to 20 measures) which are remarkable for their free keyboard style, mixed of passages and chords, and which thus offer a marked contrast to the strict contrapuntal style of contemporary vocal music. This repertory includes about 50 pieces in the Ileborgh tablature (1448); in Paumann's *Fundamentum (1452); in the *Buxheim Organ Book (c. 1460); in Kotter's tablature (c. 1520); and in Kleber's tablature (c. 1520) [Ex. in HAM, no. 84; MQ xxiii, 213; ApMZ i]. Of a similar character, though frequently more extended, are the lute preludes preserved in the tablatures of Spinaccino and Dalza (Petrucci, Intavolatura de lauto i, ii, 1507), Judenkunig (1523), Hans Neusiedler (1536), Gerle (1552), and others. The preludes of the first-mentioned publication are called ricercari [see *Ricercar II] or tastar de corde [Ex. in HAM, nos. 98, 99; SchGMB, nos. 63b, 93; ApMZ ii]. Toward the end of the century William Byrd and John Bull wrote a number of preludes which are noteworthy for their virtuoso character (Fitzwilliam Virginal Book), and to which the simultaneous lute pieces by Besardus (Thesaurus Harmonicus, 1602; cf. ApMZ ii) offer a striking contrast of style and expression.

II. Around 1650, composers began to combine the prelude with a special composition. The prelude as an introduction to suites or suite-like series of pieces occurs with Louis Couperin who created a unique type of prelude, completely free in rhythm and, therefore, notated without the conventional note-values [cf. TaAM vii, 40; the "Transcription" offered on p. 43 completely obscures the basic character of the composition; for a similar prelude by d'Anglebert, cf. HAM, no. 232]. Particularly remarkable are the preludes to the lute suites of E. Reusner (1636–79; Ex. in HAM, no. 233 and in RiMB; cf. also H. Riemann, in SIM vi). Handel preferred for his suites a prelude in a free and improvisatory style, while the introductory pieces to Bach's suites and partitas are full-sized concerto grosso movements, overtures, toccatas, or sinfonias. The combination of the prelude

with a fugue which received its classical codification by Bach can be traced back to organ preludes of the early 17th century which, after a section in free style, continue and close with a short fugal section. A piece such as the 9th Praeludium of Heinrich Scheidemann (c. 1595–1663) in the collection Organum (Vierte Reihe, Heft 1, ed. by M. Seiffert) or the Praeludium by Tunder in HAM, no. 215, may be considered as indicating the point of departure of this interesting development which, half a century later, led to the monumental "Praeludium and Fuga" of Buxtehude [Ex. in HAM, no. 234], and finally to those of Bach. For a closely related form of keyboard music see *Toccata.

III. The "disconnected" prelude is represented by the preludes of Chopin and those of his numerous imitators, chiefly Scriabin (85 preludes), Debussy (24 in two books), and Rachmaninov (op. 23). As explained above, these are pianistic character pieces, usually based on a short figure or motive which is exploited by means of harmonic modulations.

Prélude à l'Après-midi d'un Faune. See *Symphonic poem IV.

Premier temps [F.]. See *Chronos protos.

Preparation. A dissonant note is said to be prepared if it occurs immediately before as a consonant note with the preceding chord. In the strict counterpoint of the Palestrina style dissonant notes always are prepared, while in that of Bach this principle is largely discarded. See *Nonharmonic tones, particularly appoggiatura.

Presa [It.]. In canons a sign, usually like an S, which indicates the place at which the imitating voice or voices enter.

Pressus. An ornamenting neume; see *Ornamentation II.

Presto [It.]. Very quick, i.e., quicker than allegro. Prestissimo denotes the highest possible degree of speed. See *Tempo marks.

Priamel. Sixteenth-century German misspelling for *Praeambel* [see *Prelude]. The explanation given in Brenet's *Dictionnaire de musique* is erroneous.

Prick song [Old Engl., to prick, i.e., to mark]. A 16th/17th-century English term for written or printed music, i.e., for composed music as distinguished from the oral tradition of plainsong, folk song, popular dance music, etc., as well as from improvised music.

Prim [G.]. *Prime (1).

Prima donna [It., first lady]. Originally, the singer of the principal female role of an opera, as distinguished from the *primo huomo*, the leading male singer, and the *seconda donna*, the second female singer. These designations played a basic role in the construction of the plots of 18th-century operas, as can be seen, e.g., from Mozart's *Don Giovanni* and *Figaro* [see *Neapolitan School]. In the 19th century the term adopted the somewhat derogatory meaning of a conceited, jealous, and capricious operatic star, a meaning which is also extended to the male examples of the species, including its performing and conducting varieties. Cf. H. S. Edwards, *The Prima Donna* (1888).

Prima vista [It., at first sight] means unprepared playing with previous study. See *Sight-reading.

Prima volta, seconda volta [It., the first time, the second time]. The different endings for the first and the second performance of a repeated section. In musical scores, abbreviations such as: ⌐1. and ⌐2. are used. See *Ouvert (2).

Prime [G. *Prim, Prime*]. (1) The interval "zero," i.e., unison. — (2) See *Office hours.

Primgeiger [G.]. First violinist, also concertmaster.

Primitive music. I. *General.* Primitive music might be defined as the folk music of social groups which do not possess a tradition of art music, such a lack being, of course, explained by the absence of a higher cultural development in general. Wherever cultural progress has resulted in the development of an art music among the higher classes, this invariably reflects upon the folk music of the "lower classes" and shapes it in such a way that it cannot be considered primitive. This does not, of course, rule out the possibility that occasionally remnants of primitive music may be found in certain remote places in civilized countries where they have escaped the standardizing influence of art music. For instance, the oldest strata of Hungarian folk music show features of irregularity, rhythmically as well as tonally, which might justify their classification as primitive music, and a similar statement could be made with regard to certain primitive manners of performance, e.g., the Tyrolean *yodeling or the blowing of the Swiss *alphorn. As a rule, however, primitive music is found mainly among the indigenous tribes of Africa, America, and Australia — much less frequently in the Orient where most nations possess a long-established tradition of art music [see under *Exotic music].

The study of primitive music is the most recent branch of musicology, and is known as *comparative musicology. Owing to the fact that primitive music is always transmitted orally and that its irregularities of rhythm, intonation, performance, etc., defy exact reproduction in our system of musical notation, a successful study of this field was not possible until the phonograph had been put into service (*c.* 1900). Equipped with this invaluable device of research, scholars have traveled everywhere and have brought together a vast amount of records which form the basis of the study. According to a survey made by G. Herzog (*Primitive and Folkmusic in the United States*, 1936) there are well over 14,000 records of primitive music in the principal collections of the United States alone.

The subsequent explanations are not meant to represent a cross section of the whole field, but only to bring out some of the most important characteristics and aspects.

II. *Performance.* It must be said at the

outset that perhaps the most characteristic earmark of primitive music is one which is entirely lost in the written fixation, namely, the manner of performance as practiced in the various tribal or racial provinces. Two melodies, one from Ceylon, the other from Brazil, may look pretty much alike "on paper," but will sound very different in real performance. The intonation may be exact in one case and fluctuating in another; similarly, the one performance may be full of strong accents, the other flowing; one timbre nasal, the other throaty; the rhythm steady in one case and free in the other, etc. More than any other feature, the manner of delivery characterizes and distinguishes racial groups, and, moreover, connects the music of such a group with its general anthropological characteristics, such as posture, bodily movement, emotional characteristics, etc. Thus, African music as well as motor behavior is characterized by an unbridled emotionalism which is essentially different from the restrained dignity of the American Indians and of their music.

III. *Melody.* A basic consideration is the distinction between melodies in conjunct and disjunct motion, i.e., between songs which move largely along the degrees of the scale and those employing wider intervals, thirds, fourths, fifths, etc. As a rule, melodies of the former type are dynamic and strongly emotional, full of excitement and tension, while those of the latter type are more "static" and restrained. There is reason to assume that, in general, the latter type represents a more advanced stratum than the former. (It may be remarked here that this statement also applies to civilized music; Chinese music, e.g., with its four thousand years of culture, shows a striking preference for wide intervals, while in younger Oriental traditions of music, such as the Japanese, scalic motion is prevalent; European music, likewise, shows a gradual increase in the use of larger intervals, as a comparison of the "scalic" Gregorian chant with the "chordal" design of classical music readily shows; see *Motion; *Melody IV.) Another important char-

acteristic is the range of the melodies. The songs of the Patagonian Indians and of the Weddas of Ceylon employ only two neighboring notes in alternation, while songs of more advanced tribes embrace a full octave, more or less. Regarding motion as well as range, Ex. 2, a song of the

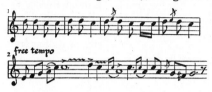

Hopi Indians, offers a striking contrast to the Wedda song of Ex. 1. A tendency towards descending rather than ascending motion has frequently been noticed as a characteristic of primitive music in general and of Indian songs in particular. (Here again, it may be pointed out that the ancient Greeks read the scale downwards, not upwards as we do.)

IV. *Rhythm.* From the rhythmic point of view the repertory of primitive music falls into two clearly separated classes, one of which employs free recitation, the other strict rhythm. The former type is found, among others, with the ceremonial songs of the medicine-men (shamans) who use it to exert magic, to dispel evil spirits, to cure by hypnotic influence. Such "incantations" are similar in function to the *chant of the Christian Churches, and it is very interesting to see that this similarity of function leads to a certain likeness in the musical character, with respect to rhythm as well as melodic motion and intonation. The strictly rhythmical type is represented mainly by the music for dance. Here the rhythmic background is usually provided by drums, which, however, are used in different ways by different people. The Indians use a very simple type of drum-beating consisting of single strokes of equal force and at equal intervals. In Africa, on the other hand, drumbeating is developed to a high degree of refinement, involving complicated crossrhythms between two and more drums and dynamic shades produced by using the fingers in alternation with the palm, etc. In striking contrast to the European conception of dance rhythm, the beats of the drum frequently do not correspond to the natural accent of the melody but occur in syncopated position, as in modern jazz. Still more interesting is the fact that the dance steps and movements themselves frequently occur in a rhythm which overlaps that of the melody and that of the drums so that a very complex rhythmic phenomenon results.

V. *Polyphony.* Primitive music is commonly thought to consist of a melody only, and the absence of harmony and polyphony is frequently considered one of the most characteristic earmarks of non-European music. Recent investigations, however, have shown that polyphonic elements play quite an important part in primitive music, particularly in that of Africa. *Heterophony is, of course, very frequent. As has been mentioned above, the beating of the drums is frequently so elaborate that it assumes the character of an "added part" rather than of a mere rhythmic accentuation. A polyphonic element is still more clearly noticeable if percussion instruments possessing gradation of pitch are employed, such as *xylophones [see Ex. 3, from the South African

Pangwe]. Finally, examples of singing in two distinct parts have been found in surprising number by recent investigators. Among the devices of primitive polyphony we find drones, parallel fourths and fifths [Ex. 4; East-African Bantu], antiphonal singing with overlapping of the two parts, and even canonic imitation of short motives [Ex. 5; from Malaka].

Lit.: Hirosi Endo, *Bibliography of Oriental and Primitive Music* (Tokyo, 1929); G. Herzog, *Primitive and Folk Music in*

the *United States* (1936); R. Wallaschek, *Primitive Music* (1893); C. Sachs, *The Rise of Music* (1943); *id., The History of Musical Instruments* (1940); *id., A World History of the Dance* (1937); E. M. von Hornbostel, *African Negro Music* (1929); D. H. Varley, *African Native Music: An Annotated Bibliography* (1936); M. Schneider, "Ethnologische Musikforschung" (in Th. Preuss, *Lehrbuch der Völkerkunde*, 1937); R. Lachmann, "Musik der aussereuropäischen Völker" (in *BüHM*); M. Schneider, *Geschichte der Mehrstimmigkeit* i (1934); C. Stumpf, *Anfänge der Musik* (1911); O. Seewald, *Beiträge zur Kenntnis der steinzeitlichen Musikinstrumente Europas* (1934); *LavE* i.5, 3197–3225 (Africa); A. Schaeffner, *Origine des instruments de musique* (1936); St. Chauvret, *Musique nègre* (1929); Ch. S. Myers, "The Study of Primitive Music" (*MA* iii).

For special periodical articles (which number over a thousand) the bibliographies contained in most of the above books should be consulted. Cf. also D. H. Daugherty, *A Bibliography of Periodical Literature in Musicology . . .* (1940), pp. 102ff. See also under *Comparative musicology; *American Indian music.

Primo [It.]. First. *Primo violino,* first violin; *primo uomo,* see *Prima donna.

Principal. In German organs, the "open diapason," in 8', 16', 32', and 4' [see *Foot]. In American and British organ parlance it means a 4'-open diapason only, or an 8'-open diapason on the pedal.

Printing of music. The printing of music followed quickly upon that of ordinary letter types (Gutenberg's Bible, c. 1455). The earliest method used for music books was *double printing,* i.e., the staff lines and the notes were printed in two different processes, usually the former in red, the latter from types in black. Various printers of the 15th century used this method for liturgical books (missals), e.g., Ulrich Hahn (Rome, 1476); Jörg Reyser (Würzburg, 1481); Octavianus Scotto (Venice); J. Sensenschmidt (1485); Erhardt Ratdolt (1487). In the early 16th century it was brought to highest perfection by Ottaviano dei Petrucci (first printed book the *Odhecaton, 1501), the only music printer who can be compared to Gutenberg. He found an emulator equal to his rank in Peter Schoeffer who printed the beautiful publication of Arnolt Schlick's *Tabulaturen* (1512). Most printers, however, found double printing too difficult and replaced it by two other methods which, with many variations and improvements, have persisted side by side until the present day, namely (a), *block* or *sheet printing* and (b), *type printing*.

(a) In *block printing*, the block for the entire page of music is prepared as a total. While woodcuts, such as used in N. Burtius' *Musices Opusculum* (1487), gave extremely clumsy results [illustration in *GD* iv, 254], hand-engraved metal plates (used first by A. de Antiquis, 1516) proved very satisfactory, as is shown by the beautiful prints of Simone Verovio in Rome (*Diletto spirituale*, 1586; Cl. Merulo's *Toccatas*, 1598, 1604), of Nicola Borbone, Rome (*Toccatas* of Frescobaldi), by the *Parthenia*, etc. Not infrequently the composers themselves engraved their music, as, for instance, Ulrich Steigleder (*Ricercar Tabulaturen*, 1624). Throughout the 17th and 18th centuries, engraving was the most common method of printing. American publishers imported engraved plates from England (as early as 1690), Paul Revere being the first American to engrave music (*c.* 1760). An important advance was made in the early 18th century by John Walsh who around 1710 (1730?) mechanized the process of engraving by the use of punches, i.e., long tools having a note, etc., at one end, the other end being struck by a hammer. A combination of punching and hand-engraving (e.g., for long lines) is still usual today. Around 1800, Senefelder's lithographic process (writing on a smooth stone with a greasy ink) was used for music publications; C. M. von Weber participated actively in the perfection of this method, and lithographed his opus 2 himself in 1800. Later the stone was replaced by a copper plate covered with beeswax on which the musical signs were scratched. When the plate was then etched with acid the signs appeared as grooves in the copper plate. In the modern *offset-process* (also called *photo-lithography*) the notes, etc., are first hand-engraved (with the aid of punches, of course) on a lead plate from which a clear proof on paper is drawn. Eight or 16 such proofs are pasted on a large sheet and a negative photograph of this is made. This is reproduced photographically on a sensitive zinc plate (covered with a photographic emulsion) which, after treatment with an acid, shows the signs engraved.

(b) In *type printing*, movable types, comparable in size to the letter types, are put together in order to prepare the block for the printing. In the 16th century these types consisted of a note combined with a small section of the staff, as illustrated. $\stackrel{=}{\underline{\diamondsuit}}$ $\stackrel{=}{\bar{\diamond}}$ Although this method proved successful for the printing of *partbooks (vocal music), in which each staff carried only one melodic line, it was very tedious and costly in the case of keyboard music which frequently called for chords. Examples of keyboard music printed in this manner are Attaingnant's books of 1529. Type-printing was largely abandoned after 1600, but was reintroduced, in a greatly improved manner, by Gottlob Immanuel Breitkopf (1755) who used tiny pieces of type, one each for note-heads, stems, flags, etc., which were put together in a complicated mosaic. This troublesome method is used today chiefly for short musical examples inserted in printed books.

Lit.: W. Gamble, *Music Engraving and Printing* (1923); W. A. Fisher, *150 Years of Music Publishing in the United States* (1934); W. B. Squire, *Notes on Early Music Printing* (1896); R. R. Steele, *The Earliest English Music Printing* (1903); K. Meyer, "The Printing of Music, 1473–1934" (*The Dolphin*, 1935); G. Reese, in *MQ* xx; O. Kinkeldey, *Music and Music Printing in Incunabula* (1932; repr. from

Papers of the Bibliographical Society of America, xxvi); M. Foss, in *ML* iv, no. 4; W. H. Cummings, in *PMA* xi; A. Thürlings, in *VMW* viii; H. Springer, in *KIM,* 1906, p. 37. H. Riemann, "Notenschrift und Notendruck" (*Festschrift . . . der Firma C. G. Roeder,* 1896). *WoHN* ii, 475ff.

Prix de Rome. See *Scholarships, Fellowships, and Prizes II.

Prizes. See *Scholarships, Fellowships, and Prizes.

Processional (e). See *Liturgical books I.

Prodanà Nevesta. See *Bartered Bride, The.

Profession of music. I. *Teaching.* This is the field in which the greatest number of opportunities exist, and must be regarded as the surest and steadiest method of earning an income. The following branches of teaching exist:

a. Public Schools. The requirements for teachers in the public grade and high schools vary greatly, according to state and city regulations. The B.A. (or B.S.) degree is usually presupposed in larger cities and better schools. Many larger high schools are demanding an M.A. degree. A teacher's certificate alone is sufficient to secure and hold a position in some smaller or musically less progressive communities. A teacher's certificate, involving knowledge of public school music methods, is required in all states, regardless of degrees. Very often the teacher must be able to give instruction in one or more subjects besides music.

b. Private Schools, Elementary and Secondary. The requirements for teachers in private schools vary greatly, according to the school in question. Most private schools require a B.A., often an M.A. degree. In some instances a single teacher is employed for all classroom teaching — theory, history, solfeggio, appreciation, etc. He may also be required to teach an instrument or voice, direct a chorus or band, etc. Some schools, especially smaller ones, require that the music master be

able to teach another subject in addition to music.

c. Colleges and Universities. The B.A. degree is presupposed (or B.S., or B.Mus.). The M.A. is highly desirable and is coming more and more to be required. The Ph.D. is valuable for obtaining positions in the top-ranking colleges and universities. A balance of musical knowledge (theory and history) with performing ability is ideal, the one or the other being stressed according to the teacher's special abilities. A knowledge of the other arts is receiving ever wider recognition as an important part of the understanding of music.

d. Music Schools. Here the emphasis is apt to be more specifically on performance. Although the better music schools include on their staff teachers of theory and history, they have a place also for the sheer virtuoso, whose interest is primarily in performance and the training of performers.

e. The Private Music Teacher. Except for a few "stars," who have often distinguished themselves first as performers, the private music teacher has a difficult time of it. Unassociated with any school, he depends for his living upon the students he may attract (or lure) to his studio. Anyone so minded may open a studio, with a result that many incompetents do so — to the detriment of the cause of music. The number of private music teachers has decreased in recent years and is likely to continue to decrease. Private teaching as a side line is a different matter. The church organist, the symphonic player, in some cases the school music teacher, may be able to increase their earnings by taking private pupils. It goes without saying that recognized concert artists and figures in the public eye will not lack for pupils nor for high fees.

II. *Performing.* The variety of opportunities for performing musicians is great, and only a few possibilities can be mentioned here. Frequently performance is combined with teaching, as mentioned above. The number of musicians who earn their living from appearances on the concert or operatic stage is comparatively small, despite the considerable number of students who aspire to such a career. Many of those who are in the public eye, moreover, consider their concert appearances as a kind of professional advertisement. It is probable that there may be a good future for local concert artists — performers who appear principally in a given region, in which region they also participate, as teachers or otherwise, in the musical life of the community.

Symphony orchestras (and a few opera and ballet companies) provide employment for good instrumental players, and the growth in recent years of good orchestras in the smaller cities has created new opportunities. Musical shows, operettas, and musical comedies, offer employment to orchestral players, but seldom on a permanent basis. Many musicians find semi-permanent work in small groups playing popular and dance music.

Conducting offers a limited field for those who have this particular ability. Orchestras, choruses, and glee clubs pay various salaries, ranging from very little to very much for the first-rate organizations.

The churches employ a large number of musicians, singers, organists, and choirmasters. The singers usually do not receive enough salary to constitute a living; only a very few metropolitan churches pay more than a few dollars a week for soloists. A considerable number of churches, however, pay a sufficient salary to their organist and choirmaster to enable him (usually with the help of private lessons) to support himself from this income.

III. Various other special activities are open to professional musicians. Some of them, such as composition, offer little in material returns. Others, such as writing and arranging for motion pictures or for the radio, recording for the phonograph, acting as commentator for radio programs, or making arrangements of popular music for "name bands," pay in general very handsomely but employ a very small number of persons. Newspaper criticism pays very little, with a few important exceptions. Opportunities for music librarians have increased during the past few years, and it may be that this field will become even broader in the future.

Lit.: W. R. Anderson, *Music as a Career* (1939); E. B. Helm, *Music (Vocational Monographs*, no. 6, 1940); W. Martin, *The Conditions of Life and Work of Musicians,* 2 vols. (1924); K. Singer, *Diseases of the Music Profession* (1937); H. Taubman, *Music as a Profession* (1939). E. B. H.

Program chanson. See *Chanson (3); *Program music III.

Program music. I. *General.* Music inspired by, and suggestive of, a program, i.e., an extramusical idea indicated in the title of the piece and sometimes substantiated in explanatory remarks or in a preface. Thus, program music is the opposite of *absolute music. Although examples of program music are found in nearly all periods of music history from at least the 14th century, it was not until the 19th century that it assumed an importance which enabled it to appear as a serious rival of absolute music, even to oust the latter — at least temporarily — from its dominating position. Around 1900 there were many people, particularly writers on music, who believed that music, in order to be understandable, ought to "express something" or to "tell a story," and who, in pursuit of this idea, provided Bach's Forty-eight with descriptive titles (Queen Carmen Sylva of Rumania) or maintained that the word *giocoso* at the head of a sonata movement was indicative of a particular mood of the composer, hence of a program (F. Niecks). Today such views are a thing of the past, at least among serious musicians and educated amateurs. It is generally agreed that music is basically an art in its own right and of its own substance; that its fundamental purpose is to work with its own material, and that too great a reliance on outside program is likely to weaken rather than to enhance the artistic merit of a composition [see *Aesthetics III]. As a matter of fact, one cannot help feeling that a good deal of the interest which composers have taken in program music is but the avowal of a lack of truly musical imagination and constructive ideas, a lack for which they hoped to make up by an interesting program. In the final analysis, there are two types of program music: that which is good music regardless of the program; and that which is poor music even with a "good" program. While in the former class there are such outstanding works of musical art as Beethoven's *Pastoral Symphony* and Berlioz' *Symphonie fantastique,* together with remarkable compositions such as Richard Strauss's *Till Eulenspiegel,* Dukas' *L'Apprenti sorcier,* and Debussy's *L'Après-midi d'un faune,* the great majority of modern program pieces fall, no doubt, under the latter category.

Champions of program music have derived satisfaction and encouragement from the fact that programmatic ideas are frequently found in the works of 17th- and 18th-century composers. François Couperin with his numerous program pieces [see below] and Bach with his word-painting in arias and choral preludes have been frequently cited in this connection. It must be noted, however, that the old masters approached the problem in an entirely different manner. Far from identifying themselves with the programmatic thought, they used it only as a point of departure from which they

So schnell — ein rau—

schend Wasser schiesst

derived not much more than the general design of the initial theme. A comparison between Bach's aria "So schnell ein

rauschend Wasser fliesst," from the cantata *Ach wie flüchtig,* no. 43 [Ex. 1], and Debussy's "Reflets dans l'eau" [Ex. 2] — both using "water" as their source of inspiration — illustrates very clearly this difference, a difference which might be briefly described as the difference between the transforming imagination of a painter and the reproductive skill — an admirable skill, to be sure — of a photographer. Finally, it is important to realize that early program pieces in which the programmatic idea is pursued with a thoroughness comparable to that found in modern examples are usually rather poor from the musical point of view and, therefore, disprove rather than strengthen the position of the champions of program music. This is particularly true of the program chansons of Jannequin, or of the battle pieces [see *Battaglia] by Byrd, Kerll, and others — Beethoven's "Battle of Victoria" being no exception.

II. *Methods.* In the development of program music, a general trend leading from the pictorial to the psychological can be seen. Prior to 1600, musicians limited themselves to the imitation of natural sounds (birds, battle-cries, thunder, trumpet fanfares, etc.), of bodily movements (flight, running, hobbling, throwing, falling, stopping), or of words which immediately associate themselves with movements (e.g., heaven = high; death = fall; see *Word painting). Beginning with the 17th century we find an increased portraying of simple psychological phenomena which are "translated" into music by means of associated movements or sounds. For instance, anguish is portrayed by a trembling or staggering motion, confidence by secure and wide steps, joy by a melody reminiscent of laughter, sorrow by descending steps in chromatic succession [see *Chromaticism], etc. It appears, then, that there exist only two possibilities of illustrative program music, namely, imitation of sounds and imitation of movements, and that these may be used either directly, or indirectly by way of association. These devices are also the chief vehicles of 19th-century program music, in which, however, they are used with much greater subtlety and refinement. In addition, the orchestral palette of modern music opened possibilities for convincing portrayal and faithful imitation which greatly enlarged the potentialities of program music. While Beethoven's *Pastoral Symphony* introduces the musical cry of the nightingale, the cuckoo, and the quail, Wagner imitated very skillfully the toad and the serpent (in *Rhinegold*), and Richard Strauss a flock of sheep in his *Don Quixote*. The climax of this trend and, one might say, the *reductio ad absurdum* of program music occurs in Respighi's *The Pines of Rome* where the problem of imitating the nightingale is solved by simply turning on a record taken from "real life."

III. *History.* Several of the Italian *caccias of the late 14th century show the attempt to imitate in music the vivid scenes described in their texts, e.g., street cries, sounds of horns, and the general commotion of a hunting scene, a fishing trip, a fire. From the same time dates a "bird-motet" by Jean Vaillant which recurs, with a German text, among the compositions of Oswald von Wolkenstein [Ex. 3; cf. *DTOe* 9.i, p. 181]. More

deliberate in approach, but much less imaginative, are the program chansons by Jannequin (1529): "Le Chant des Oyseaux," "La Chasse," "L'Alouette" (The Swallow), "La Guerre," the last of which, suggested by the famous battle of Marignano (1515), was followed by a host of imitations [cf. *Editions XVI, 7; HAM*, no. 107]. Newsidler's *Der Judentanz* (1535; *ApMZ* i) is an amusing example of caricature [see *Satire in music], and Byrd's *The Bells* is remarkable for its artistic ingenuity, far superior to the naïve attempts of John Munday to imitate "Lightning," "Thunder," and "Faire Wether" [cf. *Fitzwilliam Virginal Book* i, 274 and 23]. Passing over the numerous instances of programmatic portraying in operas, oratorios, etc., it may suffice to

mention some outstanding examples of instrumental program music of the Baroque period, such as Froberger's beautiful *Lamento sopra la dolorosa perdita della R. Maestà di Ferdinando IV* [cf. *HAM*, no. 216; see also *Lamento; *Tombeau], Poglietti's fun-making *Aria allemagna con variazioni . . .* [*DTOe* 13.ii; also *TaAM* viii], Johann Kuhnau's *Biblische Historien* (depicting the fight between David and Goliath, the marriage of Jacob, etc.; cf. *DdT* 4; *HAM*, no. 262), the numerous descriptive pieces by François Couperin (*Pièces de clavecin*, 1713–30; cf. *HAM*, no. 265) including an interesting anticipation of Schumann's *Carnaval [see *Ménestrandise], Rameau's "La Poule" and "Les Cyclopes" (*Pièces de clavecin*, 1706; cf. *HAM*, no. 277), and Bach's "Capriccio sopra la lontananza del suo fratello dilettissimo" (Capriccio on the Departure of his beloved Brother, *c.* 1704), a successful imitation of Kuhnau's program pieces. Perhaps the most startling example of Baroque program music is a "Tableau de l'opération de la taille" for viol and harpsichord by Marais (1717), describing the painful details of a surgical operation [reproduced in *LavE* ii.3, p. 1776]. Between 1750 and 1800, mediocre musicians served an easily satisfied audience with the cheapest kind of battle pieces [see *Battaglia].

Beethoven's Pastoral Symphony of 1808 marks the beginning of the program music of the 19th century. His remark "Expression of feelings rather than portraying" [see *Pastoral Symphony] characterized also Schumann's approach to program music (Scenes from Childhood, etc.), except for pieces such as the *Carnaval with its realistic references to the scenes of a masked ball. There followed Berlioz with his autobiographical Symphonie fantastique (1830–31) and Franz Liszt who, in his numerous symphonic poems, created that type of program music which was to become dominant in the ensuing decades of the 19th century [see *Symphonic poem]. The contemporary development known as *New Music brought about a sharp reaction against program music as a goal in itself and exploited the potentialities of musical portraying chiefly as a means of caricature and jest [see *Satire in music]. See *Word-painting.

Lit.: F. Niecks, *Programme Music in the last Four Centuries* (1907);W. Klatte, *Zur Geschichte der Programm-Musik* (1905); O. Klauwell, *Geschichte der Programm-Musik* (1910); A. Wellek, *Doppelempfinden und Programm Musik* (Diss. Vienna 1928); W. P. James, "Music Pure and Applied" (*ML* ii, no. 4); H. Antcliffe, in *PMA*, 37; M. D. Calvocoressi, "Esquisse d'une esthétique de la musique à programme" (*SIM* ix); M. Brenet, "Essai sur les origines de la musique descriptive" (*RMI* xiv, xv); K. Schubert, †*Die Programm Musik* (1933).

Prolation [L. *prolatio*]. See *Mensural notation II. In the early 14th century the term had a somewhat different significance, denoting all the mensurations (*modus, tempus,* and *prolatio*), or else the four combinations of *tempus* and *prolatio* (Vitry's "quatre prolacions"). Cf. *ApNPM, passim.*

Prologue. In early operas and ballets an introductory scene in which one or several narrators, representing deities, virtues, etc., give a brief exposé of the following opera, a description of its symbolic meaning, or of its dedicatory significance. The prologues sometimes developed into a small play with an entirely independent action, designed to serve as a dedication to, or a eulogy of, the royal or princely patron. An example is the prologue of Lully's *Phaeton* (1683) which consists of 12 different pieces. The simple narrative prologue of the earliest operas (Caccini's and Peri's *Euridice,* 1600; Monteverdi's *Orfeo,* 1607) has been successfully revived by Leoncavallo, in his *I *Pagliacci* (1892). Cf. H. Leichtentritt, in *PAMS,* 1936.

Prolongement [F.]. The sostenuto pedal of the pianoforte.

Prometheus. (1) A ballet by Beethoven (op. 43, 1801); see *Ballet II. — (2) A *symphonic poem by Scriabin (op. 60, 1911).

Pronto [It.]. Quick.

Pronunciation. Cf. A. J. Ellis, *Pronunciation for Singers* (1877; E., F., G., It.); C. J. Brennan, *Words in Singing;* E. Wilcke, *German Diction in Singing* (1930).

Prooemium [L.]. Humanistic (16th-century) name for prelude.

Proper, proprium. See *Ordinary.

Proportional notation. Same as *Mensural notation. The term is misleading, to say the least, since the *proportions form only a part of the mensural system, and one the importance of which has been greatly overemphasized. Moreover, it is unfortunate since it tends to perpetuate the apparently ineradicable idea that 15th-century composers such as Ockeghem and Isaac did nothing but "indulge in proportional subtleties," and that the composers of the "Golden Age" (Palestrina) finally succeeded in "casting away the fetters of the proportional system."

Proportions. (1) In *mensural notation, the diminution or (more rarely) augmentation of the normal note values in arithmetic ratios. For instance, the sign $\frac{4}{3}$ indicates that, in the subsequent passage, each note is reduced to three-fourths of its normal value (the so-called *integer valor*), or, in other words, that four notes of this passage equal in duration three notes of the preceding passage [Ex. 1].

The most important proportions are *proportio dupla, tripla,* and *sesquialtera,* which call respectively for a diminution of the note values in the ratios of 1:2, 1:3, and 2:3. The first is usually indicated by a vertical dash drawn through the sign of mensuration, thus: ¢, ø [Ex. 2,a], the others by figures [Ex. 3,a; 4,a]. In the accompanying illustrations, Ex. 2 shows *proportio dupla* (2 S *prop.* = 1 S *int. val.*); Ex. 3, *proportio tripla* (3 S *prop.* = 1 S *int. val.*); Ex. 4, *proportio sesquialtera* (3 S *prop.* = 2 *S int. val.*). In Ex. 2 it appears that under the sign ¢ the beat (**tactus*,

rendered as a quarter-note) is represented by the *brevis*, while under the normal signs of mensuration, c, o, it falls on the *semibrevis*. Therefore, the latter were called *alla semibreve*, the former, **alla breve*, a name which still persists, the only remnant of the proportional system. The reduction indicated by sesquialtera could also be produced by *coloration. Regarding *proportio tripla*, see also *Proportz. See also *Time signatures.

The system of proportions, although relatively simple in principle, presents certain difficulties for which the reader is referred to the special studies on mensural notation (*WoHN*; *ApNPM*). Occasionally composers went quite far in the devising of proportional tricks, combined with canonic riddles. Nonetheless, these cases are, on the whole, not numerous and typical enough to justify the sweeping statements, current in many history books, regarding the speculative and "purely intellectual" character of early Flemish music. The proportions, in their normal use, were by training and experience just as familiar to the choir singer of the 15th century as are the operatic roles to a singer of today. In their more tricky application they offered him a combination of intellectual and artistic enjoyment for which our time has no analogy [see under *Proportional notation].

(2) In early treatises on musical acoustics the proportions are used to indicate the Pythagorean relationships of vibrating strings and, consequently, to denote intervals. For instance, *dupla* 2:1 is the octave, *tripla* 3:1 the twelfth (compound fifth), *sesquialtera* 3:2 the fifth, *sesquitertia* 4:3 the fourth. See *Acoustics III.

Proportz, Proportio. In the German dance literature of the 16th century a **Nachtanz* in quick triple time, following a main dance in slower duple time. Both dances have the same melody in different meters. This is actually implied in the name which indicates the application of a *proportion to the original melody. Nominally, this proportion was *proportio tripla* (another name for such a *Nachtanz* was *Tripla*); actually, however, it was — for reasons which cannot be considered here — *proportio sesquialtera*. Therefore, three notes of the Proportz equal in duration two notes of the main dance. The accompanying example shows the

exact rhythmic relationship between the two [cf. W. Merian, *Der Tanz in den deutschen Tabulaturbüchern* (1927), 77]. Cf. H. Riemann, "Tänze des 16. Jahrhunderts à double emploi" (*DM* vi.3).

Proposta [It.]. Term for the subject (*dux*) of a fugue, in contradistinction to *risposta*, the answer (*comes*).

Proprietas. See *Ligatures.

Proprium missae [L.]. Proper of the Mass. See under *Ordinary.

Prosa [L.], **prose** [F.]. A term, used particularly in France, for the medieval *sequence. The name, which is in a somewhat puzzling contradiction to the fact that the texts of the sequences are poetic, has been explained by the remark that they are more like prose than are the strictly metrical poems of the Latin hymns. Another explanation, more plausible, derives the name from *Pro s'a*, i.e., *Pro s(equenti)a* [cf. *RiHM* i.2, 116].

Proslambanomenos [Gr., the added]. The lowest tone A (not G!) of the Greek scale, which was added beneath the lowest tetrachord. See *Greek music II(a).

Protestant church music (German). See *Church music III. For literature cf. *MoML*, 399.

Ps. Short for psalm or, in German scores, for *Posaune*, i.e., trombone.

Psalm [F. *psaum*; G. *Psalm*; It. *salmo*]. The Book of Psalms has been, no doubt, the most influential single source of text in all musical history. There is ample evidence that even in their original form the psalms were not pure poetry but songs, perhaps with an instrumental accompaniment. Some information regarding the ancient Hebrew method of psalm singing is contained in the inscriptions given with many psalms. According to modern Biblical scholarship, these do not indicate "classification according to instruments," but classification according to standard melodies. For instance, the inscription commonly translated "To the chief musician upon Gittith (Shoshannim, Alamoth, etc.)" [cf. Ps. 8, 45, 46] actually means: "To be sung to the strain 'Wine-press' ('Lilies,' 'Maidens,' etc.)," these terms denoting *melody-types similar to the Arabian maqams [cf. *SaHMI*, 124ff].

In its present state, the Book of Psalms consists of 150 poems; in the Latin version of the Bible (Vulgate) which is used in the Roman rites, the numbering is one less between no. 10 and no. 147, since the English nos. 10 and 11 are united into one (no. 10) of the Vulgate, and the Vulgate nos. 146 and 147 are united into one (no. 147) of the English version.

The psalms are written in a style of "poetic prose." Each psalm consists of a number of verses (designated ℣ in the liturgical books of the Catholic Church) which frequently fall into halves expressing the same thought in two different ways (*parallelismus membrorum*). The psalms were accepted by almost all the Christian Churches as the textual foundation of their music, with the exception of the German Protestant Church, whose music is based on the *chorale. For the psalm music of the Catholic Church see *Psalmody, *Psalm tones; for that of the Anglican, see *Anglican Chant; for that

of the Reformed Churches see *Psalter; for the polyphonic composition of psalm texts see *Psalm composition. See also *Penitential psalms.

Psalm composition. Aside from their strictly liturgical use, the psalms have been used innumerable times as texts for musical compositions. Numerous *motets of the 15th and 16th centuries are settings of Latin psalms, and most of the *anthems use psalm texts in English translation [see also *Psalter]. A high-point of psalm composition is the composition of all the *penitential psalms by Lassus, while the fame of Allegri's *Miserere would seem to be less well-deserved. In the 17th and 18th centuries paraphrased psalm texts were composed, e.g., in Benedetto Marcello's *Estro poetico-harmonico* (8 vols., 1724, '27). Among the modern psalm compositions those by Schubert (Psalm 23, op. 132), Mendelssohn, and Liszt are outstanding. See also *Bay Psalm Book.

Lit.: M. Cauchie, "Les Psaumes de Jannequin" (in *Editions XXIV B, 3/4); B. Widmann, "Die Kompositionen der Psalmen von Statius Olthof" (*VMW* v).

Psalmody, Gregorian. The *psalms are by far the most important texts used in Gregorian chant [see *Gregorian chant II]. In the early days of Christian worship the service consisted only of psalm singing, and in spite of the many and fundamental changes which took place in the ensuing centuries the psalms have retained their dominant position in the Catholic liturgy. This development, which may have taken place between the years 400 and 800, led to a variety of forms and types for the different items of the chant, each item receiving that structure which was proper for it from the point of view of the liturgy. All these forms go back to three original types, namely: I. direct psalmody, II. responsorial psalmody, and III. antiphonal psalmody. The last two terms originally refer to two different methods of performance, one in which there was alternation between a soloist and the chorus (responsorial), the other in which there was alternation between two half-choruses (antiphonal). It must be noted, however, that this distinction is no longer valid [see *Responsorial] and that the terms, therefore, have only historical and structural significance.

I. *Direct Psalmody* means the singing of a psalm (or a number of verses thereof) straight, without any textual addition or modification. This method survives in two types, one belonging to the Mass, the other to the Office. The former is the *tract. The latter is known as *psalmus directaneus* (*in directum, indirectum*) and means the singing of a psalm to a psalm tone, but without antiphon [see under III; also *Psalm tone]. For this method, which is rarely used, special psalm tones are provided, under the name *tonus in directum* [cf. *AR*, 30*; also *LU*, 118, 1776].

II. *Responsorial Psalmody*. This method of psalm-singing was directly taken over from the Jewish service. Originally, the entire psalm was sung by a soloist (*cantor*), with the chorus (congregation or, eventually, the church choir, *schola*) responding after each verse with a short affirmative sentence such as Amen, Alleluia, etc. (A direct model for this exists in the Psalm 136, in which each verse ends with the sentence: "For his mercy endureth forever.") The resulting form may be indicated as follows:

$$\underline{(R)} \; \underset{\cdots}{V} \; \underline{R} \; \underset{\cdots}{V} \; \underline{R} \; \underset{\cdots}{V} \ldots \underline{R}$$

(R is the recurrent response, V stands for the verses of the psalm; straight underlining indicates choral performance; dotted lines, solo performance). Although originally the singing of the cantor was but a simple recitation in the style of an inflected monotone, similar to that of the psalm tones, there developed, probably in the 3d and 4th centuries, more elaborate methods of singing which finally led to a highly melismatic style in the singing of the psalm verses. A similar development took place with the responses which, originally sung by the congregation, soon passed over to the trained chorus (*schola*) and grew considerably longer, both in text and in music. Naturally the increase in length of the single sections, verses as well as response, necessitated a drastic

reduction in the number of sections [for a similar development, see the one leading from the *canzona to the *sonata]. Instead of singing an entire psalm, single verses were selected, varying in number from four to only one. Cuts were also made in the response in such a way that this was not repeated in full after each verse, but in a reduced form, its initial half (or third) being omitted.

It is in these more or less radically reduced forms that responsorial psalmody entered into the Gregorian collection. In only a few special chants does the original scheme survive to some extent. An unusually full-shaped example is the *responsorium *Aspiciens a longe* [responsorium for Matins on the First Sunday in Advent; cf. *GD* iv, 370]. Its scheme is:

$$\underline{R} \; \underset{\cdots}{V_1} \; \underline{R'} \; \underset{\cdots}{V_2} \; \underline{R''} \; \underset{\cdots}{V_3} \; \underline{R'''} \; \underline{D} \; \underset{\cdots}{R''''}.$$

R is the respond: *Aspiciens a longe ecce video dei potentiam venientem, et nebulam totam terram tegentem.* * *Ite obviam ei, et dicite:* † *Nuncia nobis si tu es ipse,* ‡ *qui regnaturus es* § *in populo Israel.* In the four repetitions of the respond, this is successively shortened from the beginning, as is indicated by the signs *, †, ‡, §, the last repetition R'''' being only: *in populo Israel.* The verses V_1, V_2, V_3 are taken from three different psalms, and are sung, not to a specially composed melody, but to the seventh psalm tone (this is an archaic feature not to be found in any of the other chants of responsorial psalmody). The letter D stands for the minor *doxology, the first part of which, *Gloria patri et filio et spiritui sancto*, is frequently added in the forms of responsorial (and of antiphonal) psalmody as a final "verse." A chant of almost equal completeness of structure is the responsorium *Libera me*, which is sung at Exequies (*GR*, 103*; *LU*, 1767; *HAM*, no. 14). Following is its scheme:

$$\underline{R} \; \underset{\cdots}{V_1} \; \underline{R'} \; \underset{\cdots}{V_2} \; \underline{R''} \; \underset{\cdots}{V_3} \; \underline{R} \; . $$

The text of the full respond is: *Libera me, Domine,* * *de morte aeterna, in die illa tremenda: *quando caeli movendi sunt et* *terra:* † *Dum veneris judicare saeculum per ignem.* Here the second * as well as the † indicates the cuts for the two middle responds (R': *Quando-terra*; R'': *Dum-ignem*) while the first asterisk, somewhat confusingly, indicates a different practice found with all the responsorial chants, i.e., the soloist opening (*Incipit) of the first (and last) choral response. In our schemes, this method is indicated by the symbol: ·—, instead of the plain: —. Likewise a choral ending of a solo section is indicated thus: ···—. Still another responsorium showing the rondo structure of the early responsorial psalmody is the *Subvenite* of the Requiem Mass [*GR*, 106*; *LU*, 1765].

Aside from such isolated examples, the surviving categories of responsorial chant are still more reduced. The most important of these types are the *responsorium* (*prolixum*), the *responsorium breve*, the *gradual*, and the *alleluia*. The following table shows the usual form of these chants:

(1) Responsorium: R̲ V̲ R̲′ or R̲ V̲ R̲′ R̲
　　　or R̲ V̲ R̲′ D̲ R̲

(2) Responsorium breve: R̲ R̲ V̲ R̲′ D̲
　　　R̲ V̲ R₁

(3) Alleluia: R̲′ R̲ V̲ R̲

(4) Gradual: R̲ V̲ (R)

Examples for (1) are found in *LU*, 726, 722, 375. The *responsorium breve* has a

1 R·Christe fili Dei vi-vi *Mi-se-re- re nobis
2　"　"　"　"　　"　　"
6　"　"　"　"　4　"　"

3 V. Qui se-des ad dex-te-ram Patris

5 D.Glo-ri-a Pa-tri, et fi-li-o, et Spiri tu-i Sancto .

7 V.　Ex-surge, Christe, ad-ju-va nos
8 R.　Et libera nos propter nomen tuum.

fairly extended (somewhat variable) scheme, but short and simple melodies in

each section. The final V and R are sung to a new melody in repetition. The accompanying example of a *responsorium breve* [*AR*, 19; *LU*, 229] will also help to clarify the structure of the other, more melismatic chants. In the Alleluias the response consists of the word "Alleluia" only. This is sung first by the soloist (R'), after which the chorus repeats it and continues with the *jubilus on (allelui)a— (R). Actually, the structure of the alleluias is somewhat more complex than our scheme suggests, since the melody for the verse practically always closes with that of the jubilus, thus leading to the following scheme: A, A+j, B+j, A+j. With the graduals the repetition of the response is optional [cf. *LU*, 320].

III. *Antiphonal Psalmody* originally consisted in the singing of the psalms by two alternating half-choruses. This method was introduced into the Western Church by St. Ambrosius (333–397), in imitation of Syrian models. The exact procedure in the early antiphonal psalmody is not known; there may have been alternating performance for the two halves of each single verse, or (more likely) for each pair of verses [see *Antiphon (History)*].

The antiphonal method of psalm singing was at an early time enriched by the addition of a short sentence which was sung by the whole chorus (or, perhaps, the congregation) after each two verses, and which was called antiphon (A). There resulted a rondeau-like scheme: A V₁ V₂ A V₃ V₄ A ... A, similar in structure to that of the early responsorial psalmody. As in the case of the latter, the extended scheme survives only in certain special chants, such as the *invitatorium, which is sung at matins in the Office of the Dead and in which Ps. 94 *Venite exultemus Domino* (Ps. 95, O come, let us sing unto the Lord, of the English numbering) is sung according to the following scheme [cf. *AR*, (152)]: A̲ A̲ V₁ V₂ A̲ V₃ V₄ A̲′ V₅ V₆ V₇ A̲ V₈ V₉ A̲′ V₁₀ V₁₁ A̲ V₁₂ A̲′A. A is the antiphon *Regem cui omnia vivunt*, *Ve-*

nite adoremus; A′ stands for its second half alone; the verses of the Latin text (Vulgate) do not always agree with the divisions of the English version; the last verse is: *Requiem aeternam dona eis Domine: et lux perpetua luceat eis* (replacing the Gloria Patri in the Office of the Dead). A similarly extended structure (A V₁ A V₂ A V₃ A V₄ A D A) occurs with the antiphon *Lumen ad revelationem gentium* which is sung in alternation with the verses of the canticle *Nunc dimittis* during the distribution of the candles on the feast of Purification [*LU*, 1357].

Aside from such special chants, there are four standard types of chants which are considered as derivatives of antiphonal psalmody, the *office-psalms* and the *introit, *offertorium, and *communion of the Mass. The office-psalms are complete psalms sung to a psalm tone (the same for each verse) and introduced and closed by a short antiphon: A V₁ V₂ .... Vₙ A [see *Psalm tones]. The form of the introitus is: A V D A. (D is the minor doxology, see above.) In the offertorium and communion the verse has been entirely lost, so that only the antiphon: A remains.

Psalm tones. In Gregorian chant, the recitation melodies which are used for the singing of the (complete) psalms during the Office [see *Psalmody III]. There are eight such tones, one for each church mode, and all in the character of an inflected *monotone. The main note of the recitation, called *tenor* (repercussio, tuba, reciting note), is always the dominant of the mode [see *Church modes]. According to the binary structure of the psalm verses, the psalm tone falls into halves, the former consisting of *initium* (*in-*

ceptio), *tenor*, and *mediatio*; the latter of *tenor* and *terminatio*. If the former half

is too long to be sung in one breath, there appears another slight inflection at the breathing point, the *flexa*. The accompanying example (verse 1 of Ps. 1: Beatus vir, qui non abiit in consilio impiorum, † et in via peccatorum non stetit, * et in cathedra pestilentiae non sedit; cf. *LU*, 771) shows all these details.

Each psalm is sung with an enframing *antiphon which occurs in full at the end, and is reduced to its first word or two (*incipit* only, that is) at the beginning; except on greater feasts ("Doubles") when the antiphon is sung entire before as well as after. The antiphon determines not only the psalm tone, which has to be in the same mode as the antiphon, but also its ending (*terminatio*), for which a number of different formulae, called *differentiae* (differences), are provided. The one to be chosen is so designed as to lead back smoothly to the initial note of the antiphon, as sung after the last verse of the psalm. It is indicated, e.g., as follows: Ant. 8.c (mode 8 with the ending on c). Since the *Gloria patri ... seculorum amen* [see *Doxology] invariably serves as a last verse of the psalm, the liturgical books give the *differentia* with the syllables *E u o u a e (= *seculorum Amen*). The antiphon *Beatus populus* with some verses of the psalm 143 serves as an example (it must be noticed that the *initium* is sung with the first psalm verse). Cf. also *HAM*, no. 11.

An exceptional psalm tone is the *tonus peregrinus* which has a different tenor for its first and second half. It is used only for the psalm *In exitu Israel* [*AR*, 28*; *LU*, 160]. Cf. H. Gaïsser, in *TG* vii. For *tonus directaneus* see *Psalmody I.

Psalter. Name for the Book of Psalms translated into the vernacular (English, French, Dutch Psalter), frequently in rhymed versions (metrical Psalter), and provided with music for congregational singing [for a Psalter of the 3d century, see *Hymns].

To all branches of the Christian faith as well as to the Jewish congregation, the Book of Psalms has been a perennial resource; and it was natural, therefore, that the Reformed Churches should, with one exception [see *Chorale; *Protestant music], turn to it for the texts which were to supply them with material for congregational song. The fact that the words of the Lutheran Chorales were not "inspired," that is, were not drawn from the Bible, but from the poetic and religious feeling of ordinary human beings, caused them to be rejected outside of Germany. Instead, the other Reformed Churches turned to the Psalters. The most important and influential of the Psalters was the French, the completed form of which appeared in 1562, the metrical versions of the texts being supplied by Marot and Beza. Bourgeois and Dubisson were successively the musical editors. About Dubisson's comparatively brief connection with the work little is known, and it is to Bourgeois that credit is generally assigned for the excellence of the music. Bourgeois' contributions consist of adaptations of existing melodies, some of them drawn from secular sources, and of composed tunes which are assumed to be his own. In conformity with the Protestant trend toward musical simplification, the settings are almost uniformly one note to a syllable. Calvin was opposed to the setting of the Psalter melodies in parts, but it was inevitable, of course, that they should be so treated. In this connection it is interesting to compare the part settings of Chorales by German Reformation composers with similar settings of the French psalm tunes. In both instances the chief voice is in the tenor; but where the Chorale theme seems to generate a somewhat stiff and ungrateful counterpoint in the surrounding parts, the Psalter lends itself readily to a homogeneous musical treatment. The root of the difference is not to be found in the texts, for both the French and the German were based on quantity

and not accent; rather does it lie in the greater flexibility and contrapuntal adaptability of the French melodies which were close enough in nature to Plainsong to render them inviting to composers long trained in the Roman tradition of polyphony. Among the composers who cultivated part settings of the French Psalter were Bourgeois, Goudimel, Jannequin, Le Jeune, and the Dutchman Sweelinck [Ex. in HAM, nos. 126, 132]. The French Psalter was adopted in the Netherlands in 1566, replacing here the collection of *Souterliedekens of 1540.

During the persecutions under Queen Mary, about the middle of the 16th century, many English Protestants fled to Geneva where they came under the influence of the French Psalter. The result was the so-called Anglo-Genevan Psalter with the publication of which both Englishmen and Scotchmen were connected. The French style is strongly represented in this work, and after the return of the refugees to Britain the Scottish Psalter of 1564 continued to perpetuate the French influence, while the English Psalter pursued a quite different course with regard to both verse and music. Among the better-known English Psalters are Sternhold and Hopkins, completed and published by Day in 1562; Ravenscroft (1621); Playford (1677); and Tate and Brady (1696). The English type of psalm tune consists of a number of shorter notes lying between two longer ones. Such an invariable pattern is bound, after many repetitions, to prove monotonous and it compares most unfavorably with the free flowing and infinitely varied melodies of the French prototype.

Another group of refugees was to come under the influence of the French form, this time in Amsterdam, where Henry Ainsworth in 1612 brought out a Psalter for the benefit of the English "Separatists." Thence it traveled to America with the Pilgrims in 1620. Its hold on its devotees must have been remarkable, for though the highly influential *Bay Psalm Book appeared in 1640, Ainsworth's Psalter was not entirely displaced for many years after that date.

It is significant that in the early 18th century in both England and America the grace or ornament became popular in psalm singing. The clerical protests which were made against this use are characteristic of more than one attempt in the history of music to preserve a medium which was becoming outmoded. In the first place, the Psalter, while its range of expression is certainly wide, is the language and the feeling of another day. The worshiper cannot be blamed for wishing to sing words more expressive of religious feeling cast in terms of contemporary thought. Second, the music was formally monotonous, and while it was praiseworthy for its pervading dignity, the manner of its performance was such as to inspire revolt and encourage any relief from its monotony. Aside from the fact that the pace was probably painfully slow, the custom of *"lining-out" the psalm disrupted the sense of the text and destroyed musical continuity. In the 18th century the *hymn began to make its way among English-speaking Protestant congregations in general. Its eventual adoption with a corresponding neglect of psalm singing was neither completely profitable nor wholly to be deplored. It is noteworthy that Scotch devotion to the Psalter was so strong that it was not until 1861 that the Established Church of Scotland authorized the singing of hymns.

Lit.: A. C. Welch, *The Psalter in Life, Worship and History* (1926); E. B. Cross, *Modern Worship and the Psalter* (1934); C. C. Keet, *A Liturgical Study of the Psalter* (1928); W. S. Pratt, *The Music of the French Psalter of 1562* (1939); J. Warrington, *Short Titles of Books Relating to the History of Psalmody in the United States, 1620–1820* (1898); G. R. Woodward, "The Genevan Psalter of 1562 . . ." (*PMA* xliv); W. Truron, "The Rhythm of Metrical Psalm Tunes" (*ML* ix, no. 1); W. S. Pratt, "The Importance of the Early French Psalter" (*MQ* xxi); articles "Psalter" and "Bourgeois" in *GD*; article "Hymn and Hymn Tunes" in P. C. Scholes, *The Oxford Companion to Music* (1940).   A. T. D.

Psaltery. Name for ancient and medieval instruments consisting of a flat soundboard over which a number of strings are stretched which are plucked with the fingers. This manner of playing distinguishes the psaltery from the *dulcimer which is similar in construction, but struck with hammers. The term is also used in scientific classification of instruments for a group which includes, among others, the harpsichord, a keyed psaltery [see *Instruments IV, A, 1 (a)].

The name *psalterion* is encountered in Greek literature, possibly denoting a harp [cf. *SaHMI*, 136, also 115f]. In a letter attributed to St. Jerome (*c.* 330–420) a *psalterium decacordum* (ten-stringed psalterium) is depicted which has the shape of a rectangle and which the writer interprets symbolically, relating the strings to the Ten Commandments and the four sides of the frame to the four Gospels. From the 14th to the 16th century psalteries were used in various shapes. The normal type had the shape of a symmetrical trapezoid, sometimes with the slanting sides curved inwards. Such instruments were called *caño, canon*, after their Arabic model, the *ḳanûn*. In another type the shape was one-half of the above trapezoid (thus with a rectangle to the left side), and this was called *medio canon* or *micanon* (sometimes perverted into *medicinale*). This shape, which persisted in the winged form of the harpsichord and of the pianoforte, had a certain likeness to that of a pig's head, hence the name *istromento di porco* given by Praetorius (*Syntagma Musicum* ii, 1620). Among the more recent types of psalteries are the Austrian *zither, the Finnish *kantele, and the Russian *gusli. See also *Bell harp. See the illustrations on p. 823.

Public school music. See *Music Education I. Cf. also article in O. Thompson, *The International Cyclopedia of Music and Musicians* (1939); bibl. pp. 2270f.

Publications of music. See *Editions, historical.

Publishers, Music.

I. *Publishers of the Present Day.* Following is a selected list of important firms, arranged alphabetically according to countries.

Argentina: Ricordi, Buenos Aires. *Austria:* L. Doblinger, Vienna. — Universal Edition, Vienna (amalgamated with Wiener Philharmonischer Verlag). *Belgium* (all Brussels): Schott Frères. — A. Cranz. — Bosworth & Co. *Brazil:* Arthur Napoleão, Rio de Janeiro. — Carlos Wehrs, Rio. — Ricordi, São Paulo. *Czechoslovakia* (all Prague): Hudebni Matice. — Fr. A. Urbanek. *Denmark:* Wilhelm Hansen, Copenhagen. *England* (all London): Augener, 18 Great Marlborough St., W. — Boosey & Hawkes, 295 Regent St., W. 1. — Chappell & Co., 50 New Bond Street, W. — J. & W. Chester, 11 Great Marlborough St., W. — J. Curwen & Sons, 24 Berners St., W. — Ernst Eulenburg, 36 Dean St., W. 1. — Murdoch & Co., 463 Oxford St., W. 1. — Novello & Co., 160 Wardour St., W. — Oxford Press, Amen House, Warwick Sq. — Schott & Co., 48 Great Marlborough St., W. 1. — Stainer & Bell, 58 Berners St., W. *France* (all Paris): P. de Choudens. — Durand & Cie. — Max Eschig. — H. Heugel. — A. Leduc. — H. Lemoine fils. — Rouart, Lerolle et Cie. — M. Sénart et Cie. *Germany:* C. F. Peters, Leipzig. — B. Schott's Söhne, Mainz. — Breitkopf und Härtel, Leipzig. — Bote & Bock, Berlin. — Adolph Fürstner, Berlin. — C. F. Kahnt, Leipzig. — Georg Kallmeyer, Wolfenbüttel. — Kistner & Siegel, Leipzig. — Bärenreiter Verlag, Kassel. — Simrock Verlag, Berlin. — Litolff Co., Braunschweig. — Steingräber, Leipzig. *Holland:* G. Alsbach Co., Amsterdam. *Hungary:* Rosznyai, Budapest. — Rözsavölgyi Co., Budapest. *Italy* (all Milan): G. Ricordi Co. — Sonzogno. — A. Carisch. *Mexico:* Wagner y Levien Co. *Norway:* Norsk Musikforlag, Oslo. *Peru:* Guillermo Brandes, Lima. *Russia:* Russian State Music Publishing Department (known as Musgiz), Moscow. — Triton, Leningrad. *Scotland:* Paterson & Sons, Edinburgh. *Spain:* Unión Musical Española, Madrid. — Ildefonso Alier, Madrid. — J. B. Pujol & Co., Barcelona. *Sweden* (all Stockholm): Lundqvists Förlag. — Abr. Hirschs Förlag. — Carl Gehrmans Musikförlag. *Switzerland:* Foetisch, Lausanne. — Henn, Geneva. — Hug, Zurich. — Chouet & Gaden, Geneva. *United States:* Associated Music Publishers, New York (sales agents for foreign publications). — Arrow Music Press, New York (Copland, Piston, Harris, Sessions). — Carl Fischer, Inc., New York (Bloch, Godovsky, Kreisler, etc.). — C. C. Birchard Co., Boston (school music; also Cadman, Chadwick, Hanson, Jansen, etc.). — Theodore Presser Co., Philadelphia (*The Etude*; educational publications). — E. C. Schirmer Music Co., Boston (choral and a-cappella music). — G. Schirmer, New York (editions of the classics; also Loeffler, Harris, Bloch, S. Barber, W. Schumann). — Elkan Vogel (agent for French publishers). *Uruguay:* Editorial Cooperativa Interamericana de Compositores, Montevideo.

For a more complete list see the article in O. Thompson, *The International Cyclopedia of Music and Musicians* (1943). Also Pierre Key's *Music Year Book* and *Who is Who in Music* (Lee Stern Press, 1941), p. 673.

II. *History.* The musical publishing business started with Octavianus Scotus of Venice (1480) and Ottaviano dei Petrucci of Venice who, in 1498, obtained from the Seignory a twenty years' monopoly for the printing of music (other than plainsong). His first publication was the famous *Odhecaton* of 1501 which was followed by a score of most important books of masses, motets, and frottolas [cf. *GD*, "Petrucci"]. Thirty years after Petrucci, the French Pierre Attaingnant founded a publishing house at Paris which, from 1529 to 1549, issued books of lute music, organ music, motets, masses, and 35 books of chansons. In the later part of the 16th century quite a number of music publishers were at work, as a result of the generally rising economic conditions and the rise in music production and consumption: Gardano in Venice (1538–1619); Verovio in Rome (1586–1604; the first publisher of engraved music; see *Printing of music); Jacques Moderne at Lyons (1532–67); Pierre Phalèse at Antwerp (1545–after 1650); Tielman Susato at Antwerp (1543–60 and later); and the establishment of Ballard and Le Roy at Paris which, founded in 1551, continued to exist until after 1776, using their first type for over 200 years. In England Tallis and Byrd were granted a monopoly for music printing in 1575 which, in 1598, was transferred to Morley. The publishing, however, was done by Thomas and Michael Este (East) who issued practically all the books of English madrigals, from 1587 till 1638. There followed Playford, from c. 1650 to 1700, and, in the 18th century, the house of Walsh (c. 1705–66), the first music publisher to use "high-pressure" methods, including a good deal of pirating [see Lit., Pincherle]. At the same time the house of Roger flourished in Amsterdam, that of Haffner in Nürnberg [see *Haffner collection]. About 1750 the world-famous house of Breitkopf (later Breitkopf & Härtel) published its first music books, using a new typographical method which revolutionized the printing of music [see *Printing of music (b)]. In 1773 the house of Schott (Mainz) was founded which, together with Artaria (1778, Vienna), published many of the works of Beethoven. There followed Simrock, of Berlin (1790), Peters, of Leipzig (1814), Bote and Bock, of Berlin (1838), and Steingräber, of Leipzig (1878). Modern music publishing in England started with Novello (1811), and continued with Augener (1853), Chester (1860), and many others.

Music publishing in the United States started in the last two decades of the 18th century. Publishing houses known to have existed before 1790 were John Aitken (1785), Thomas Dobson (1785), and Alexander Reinagle (1787), in Philadelphia; Thomas Dobson (1787) and George

Gilfert (1787), in New York. In the following decade about twenty more names were added to the list, e.g., Joseph Carr (1794), in Baltimore, and Gottlieb Graupner (1800), in Boston. [Cf. H. Dichter and E. Shapiro, *Early American Sheet Music* (1941), pp. 165ff.] The first publishing house of importance was Ditson, in Boston (1835). There followed Schirmer, of New York (1861), Carl Fischer, of New York (1872), Theodore Presser, of Philadelphia (1888), and many others.

Lit.: G. Dunn, *Methods of Music Publishing* (1931); F. Kidson, *British Music Publishers* (1900); W. Arms Fisher, *One-hundred-and-fifty Years of Music Publishing in the United States . . .* (1933); R. Eitner, "Verzeichnis der Musikhändler und Musikdrucker" (*MfM*, 1909, Beilage); F. Kidson, "John Playford . . ." (*MQ* iv); id., "Handel's Publisher John Walsh . . ." (*MQ* vi); R. S. Hill, "The Plate Numbers of C. F. Peters Predecessors" (*PAMS*, 1938); K. Meyer, "Artaria Plate Numbers" (in *Notes for the Music Library Association*, no. 15); W. B. Squire, "Publisher's Numbers" (*SIM* xv); M. Brenet, "La Librairie musicale en France de 1653 à 1790" (*SIM* viii); A. Cucuel, ". . . la librairie musicale au xiiie siècle" (*SIM* xiii); M. Pincherle, "De la piraterie . . . aux environs de 1700" (*RdM*, no. 47). See also *Printing of music.

Pui. See *Puy.

Pumhart. Old German for *bombarde; see *Oboe family III.

Punctum. (1) See *Neumes I. — (2) Same as *punctus.

Punctus [L., dot]. (1) In *mensural notation, a sign like the dot of modern notation, but used in the meaning of the modern dot as well as in a function somewhat similar to that of the modern barline. In the former meaning it is called *punctus additionis* or *augmentationis*, and is used for binary (imperfect) notes to which it adds one-half of their value. In the latter meaning it is called *punctus* *divisionis*, and is used only in triple meter (tempus perfectum, prolatio perfecta), in order to mark off groups of perfections (i.e., of three semibreves, or three minims) whenever this is desirable or necessary for the sake of clarity. In the accompanying example, the second, third, and fifth

dot are *puncti additionis*, the others are *puncti divisionis*.

The system of puncti has been unnecessarily complicated by early theorists who deal in detail with a number of other puncti, such as *punctus perfectionis, imperfectionis, alterationis, syncopationis*, etc. The three first-mentioned puncti are nothing but the *punctus divisionis*, the various names indicating only certain secondary effects upon the neighboring notes. For instance, the first punctus of the above example makes the preceding brevis perfect, and therefore is called a *punctus perfectionis*. The fourth punctus, however, may be called either a *punctus imperfectionis* or a *punctus alterationis*, according to whether its effect upon the preceding or the following notes is considered. Unfortunately these unnecessary complications have been perpetuated by modern writers. Especially misleading is the "simplified" explanation [see Lit., Warner] which distinguishes only between the *punctus divisionis* and the *punctus perfectionis*, since a further distinction must be made between the *punctus perfectionis* in perfect mensuration and the *punctus* "perfectionis" — properly, *additionis* — in imperfect mensuration. Finally, the *punctus syncopationis*, which occurs only in music prior to 1450, is a *punctus divisionis* in displaced position, occurring somewhere in the middle of a measure. The details are too complicated to be briefly explained [cf. *ApNPM, passim*; S. T. Warner, in *PMA* xlv].

(2) In the *estampies of the 13th and 14th centuries the various sections, each of which is repeated, are called *punctus* (*primus punctus, secundus punctus*, etc.).

Punto, punta [It.]. Point. *A punta d'arco*, with the point of the bow (of the violin); *punto d'organo*, the pause and its sign.

Purfling. The inlaid border of violins, etc., consisting of three small slips of wood, the middle one black, the outer two white. Aside from its ornamental value it serves to prevent the chipping of the edges.

Puritans and music. See under *American music I. Also: P. Scholes, *The Puritans and Their Music in England and New England* (1934); W. S. Pratt, *The Music of the Pilgrims* (1901).

Puy, pui. Medieval French festivals of literary and musical guilds, held regularly with competitions and prizes. They are documented as far back as the 11th century (earliest troubadours), and existed as late as the 16th century. The most famous was the *Puy d'Évreux*, held annually from 1570 till 1614, on St. Cecilia's Day. Among its laureates (*roy de puy*) were Orlando di Lasso, Titelouze, du Caurroy. The puys of the troubadours served as a model for similar competitions of the German Minnesinger, such as the "Sängerkrieg auf der Wartburg," which forms the background of Wagner's *Tannhäuser*. See also *Meistersinger III; *Tenso.

Pyknon [Gr., density]. In the Greek scale [see *Greek music II (b)] the places of the greatest density, i.e., the two successive semitones of the chromatic scale, or the two successive quarter-tones of the enharmonic scale. For instance, the Hypodorian chromatic scale (read downwards) contains the following two pykna: a — f♯-f-e — c♯-c-b — a. In each pyknon the highest of the three tones involved was called *oxypyknon*, the middle *mesopyknon*, and the lowest *barypyknon*. On the kithara these three degrees were performed on the same string, the barypyknon on the open string (e, b), the other two by stopping at the first or second semitone. This method is reflected in the Greek instrumental notation, in which (as a rule) one and the same sign serves for all the three degrees, but in different positions, e.g., K, ⊻, Ↄ, for b, c, and c♯. Cf. C. Sachs, in *ZMW* vi, 289.

Pythagorean scale. A scale, invented by Pythagoras (*c.* 550 B.C.), which derives all the tones from the interval of the pure fifth, $\frac{3}{2}$ [see *Acoustics III]. The tones of the diatonic scale are obtained as a series of five successive upper fifths and one lower fifth:

$$\begin{array}{cccccc} F & c & g & d' & a' & e'' & b'' \\ \frac{2}{3} & 1 & \frac{3}{2} & \left(\frac{3}{2}\right)^2 & \left(\frac{3}{2}\right)^3 & \left(\frac{3}{2}\right)^4 & \left(\frac{3}{2}\right)^5 \end{array}$$

By reducing these tones into one and the same octave (c–b), the following scale results:

	c	d	e	f	g	a	b	c'
Frequency:	1	$\frac{9}{8}$	$\frac{81}{64}$	$\frac{4}{3}$	$\frac{3}{2}$	$\frac{27}{16}$	$\frac{243}{128}$	2
Intervals:		$\frac{9}{8}$	$\frac{9}{8}$	$\frac{256}{243}$	$\frac{9}{8}$	$\frac{9}{8}$	$\frac{9}{8}$	$\frac{256}{243}$

(For the calculation of the frequencies and the intervals, see *Intervals, Calculation of, I–III; see also the tables under *Intervals, p. 362, and *Temperament). It appears that the Pythagorean whole-tone is slightly larger than that of the well-tempered scale (204 cents instead of 200), while the semitone is considerably lower (90 instead of 100). Likewise, the Pythagorean third is 8 cents higher than the well-tempered third which, in turn, is higher than the "pure" third (408, 400, and 386 cents).

The succession of the Pythagorean fifths can be continued beyond the tone b, leading to chromatic tones, f♯, c♯, etc., and finally back to c, in the well-known *circle of fifths which, in the Pythagorean system, actually is a "spiral of fifths" since the twelfth fifth is 24 cents higher than the seventh octave ($12 \times 702 - 7 \times 1200 = 24$). This difference is the *Pythagorean comma* [see *Comma]. The difference between the (Pythagorean) whole-tone and semitone was called *apotome:* $\frac{9}{8} : \frac{256}{243} = \frac{3^7}{2^{11}} = \frac{2187}{2048} = 114$ cents. In the Greek scale it appears as the interval between b♭ and b (a-b minus a-b♭). The Pythagorean semitone $\left(\frac{256}{243}\right)$ was called *limma* (leftover), because it could be obtained as the difference between the tetrachord (fourth) and two whole-tones. Another name for the same interval was *diesis.*

Q

Qanun. See *Kanûn.

Q.-L. Customary abbreviation for R. Eitner's *Quellen-Lexikon* [see under *Libraries].

Quadratnotation [G.]. See *Square notation.

Quadrible. See under *Treble.

Quadrille [F.]. (1) A French dance of the early 19th century performed by two or four couples moving in a square. The dance consisted of five figures ("Le Pantalon," "L'Été," etc.), the music for which, alternately in $\frac{6}{8}$- and $\frac{2}{4}$-meter, was usually chosen from popular tunes or operatic airs. The dance was very popular during the Napoleonic era and remained fashionable until it was replaced by the *polka. — (2) In the 17th-century French ballet (Campra, Lully) *quadrille* is the name of each of the dance figures which make up an *entré.* See *Dance music IV.

Quadrivium [L., four ways]. In the medieval system of education, the four "mathematical arts," namely: arithmetic, geometry, music, and astronomy, as opposed to the *trivium* of the "rhetorical arts," i.e., grammar, dialectics, and rhetoric. In this scheme music was, of course, considered not as an art in the modern sense of the word, but as a science bordering on mathematics and physics (acoustics).

Quadruple counterpoint. See *Double counterpoint.

Quadruple-croche [F.]. See *Notes.

Quadruple fugue. A fugue with four different subjects, such as the last (unfinished) piece of Bach's *Art of Fugue. See *Double fugue.

Quadruplet. A group of four notes, to be played in the time of three.

Quadruple meter, time. See *Meter.

Quadruplum. See *Duplum.

Quality. (1) Tone quality, see *Timbre. — (2) As opposed to quantity, see *Poetic meter III.

Quantity. See *Poetic meter III.

Quart, Quarte [G.]. The interval of the fourth. As a prefix to instruments the term indicates that the instrument is a fourth higher (*Quartflöte, Quartgeige*) or a fourth lower (*Quartfagott; see *Oboe family II, E) than the normal instrument.

Quartal harmony. Recent term for a harmonic system based on the *fourth, as distinguished from the common system of *tertian harmony, based on the third. Quartal harmonies have been recommended to replace tertian harmonies in harmonizations of Gregorian chant [cf. J. Yasser, *Mediaeval Quartal Harmony* (1938); also in *MQ* xxiii, xxiv]. See *Accompaniment V.

Quarter-note. See *Notes.

Quarter-tone. An interval equal to one-half of the semitone, there being 24 to the octave. There has been a good deal of experimentation with quarter-tone music within the past fifty years. A quarter-tone piano was patented first in 1892 (G. A. Behrens-Senegalden). In 1923 A. Förster, in Prague, built an instrument with two manuals, the second a quarter-tone higher than the first, which

has given considerable encouragement to the protagonists of quarter-tone music, foremost among whom is Alois Hába. He composed a considerable number of pieces (op. 7–op. 26) in the new idiom for string quartet for violin alone (op. 9), for pianoforte, for orchestra, for chorus,

etc. (Cf. the list of his works in *GD* ii, 489.) Other composers are Hans Barth (Concerto for quarter-tone piano and strings, 1930), who also built a quarter-tone piano [cf. N. Slonimsky, *Music Since 1900*, p. 336]; I. Vyschnegradsky (*Dithyramb*, 1926; *Prelude and Fugue*, 1929); and the Mexican Julian Carrillo, who uses eighth- and sixteenth-tones. The accompanying example shows the usual notation of quarter-tones and the beginning of Hába's op. 9.

The use of quarter-tones is far from being new. The enharmonic system of Greek music, which gained an ephemeral importance in the period of Euripides (c. 400 B.C.), included quarter-tones [see *Greek music II(b)]. In the 11th century this system was revived in theory (Guido, Regino of Prüm) and possibly in practice (missal of Montpellier, *H. 159*; cf. *WoHN* i, 44; for a negative position in this question cf. Baralli, in *Rassegna Gregoriana*, 1911). Another attempt at revival was made by N. Vicentino [see *Arcicembalo]. Finally, the microtonic intervals of Hindu and of Arabian music may be mentioned. In all these cases quarter-tones appear, however, only at certain points of the scale as *pien-tones not equally distributed throughout the octave, as in the modern system. See *Microtones.

Lit.: A. Haba, *Von neuer Musik* (1925); *id., Neue Harmonielehre* (1927); J. Wyschnegradsky, in *RM* xviii; A. Wellek, in *MQ* xii; A. A. Holde, in *MQ* xxiv; C. C. Pratt, in *The Pedagogical Seminary*, vol. 35 (1928), p. 286.

Quartet [F. *quatuor*; G. *Quartett*; It. *quartetto*]. A composition for four instruments or voices. By far the most important combination is the *string-quartet. Piano quartets (for piano, violin, viola, and cello) exist in a limited number: 2 by Mozart, 4 by Beethoven, 3 by Mendelssohn, 1 by Schumann, 2 by Brahms, 2 by Dvořák, etc.

The "vocal quartet," i.e., polyphonic composition for four voices, was established around 1450 by the early *Flemish composers, isolated earlier examples such as Perotinus' *organa quadrupla* [see *Organum; *Ars Antiqua] and Guillaume de Machaut's Mass notwithstanding. Much of the music of the 16th century (motets, masses, madrigals, chansons, etc.) is written in four parts although there was a tendency towards increasing the number of parts to five, six, and more. In the 17th century, four-part writing was limited chiefly to the English *Glee and the German *Chorale. In the 19th century the a-cappella quartet was extensively cultivated by Glee Clubs, Liedertafel, etc. Four-part writing has always been considered the proper medium for studies in harmony and counterpoint.

Quartfagott, Quartflöte, Quartgeige [G.]. See under *Quart.

Quartole [G.], **quartolet** [F.]. Quadruplet.

Quartsextakkord [G.]. The second inversion of the triad (six-four chord).

Quasi [It.]. "As if," "almost." E.g., *allegro quasi presto*: allegro, almost presto. *Quasi niente*, "as if nothing," i.e., ppp.

Quatreble. See under *Treble.

Quattro [It.]. Four. *Quattro mani*, four hands; *quattro voci*, four voices.

Quatuor [F.]. Quartet.

Quaver. See *Notes.

Quempas. Abbreviation of L. *Quem pastores adorabant* (He, whom the shepherds worshiped), a Christmas song which was popular in Germany in the 16th century. The term was used as a generic designation for Christmas songs,

particularly in the connection *Quempas Singen*, that is, the singing of carols by the students of Latin schools, an activity in which Luther is known to have participated. The alms earned by singing from house to house were a welcome addition to the meager income of many students [see *Currende]. *Quempasheft* was the collection of carols which every student used to copy for himself.

Querelle des bouffons [F.]. See *Guerre des bouffons.

Quer- [G.]. *Querflöte* (transverse), flute; *Querpfeife*, fife; *Querstand*, *false relation.

Queue [F., tail]. The stem of a note. *Piano à queue*, i.e., grand piano.

Quick-step. In military parlance, a march in quick steps (*c.* 108 per minute). Also the music for such a march.

Quiebro. See *Ornamentation I.

Quilisma [from Gr. *kylindein*, to roll]. See *Neumes I; *Ornamentation II.

Quindezime [G.]. The interval of the fifteenth, i.e., the double octave.

Quinible. See under *Treble.

Quinta falsa [L.]. False, i.e., diminished fifth.

Quintatön [G.]. Perversion of *Quintadena*, an old mixture stop [see *Organ IX b].

Quinta vox [L.]. See *Part (2); *Part books.

Quinte, Quint [G.]. Fifth. *Quintenparallelen*, parallel fifths. *Quintenzirkel*, *Circle of fifths.

Quinte [F.]. (1) Interval of the fifth. — (2) French name for the viola (*quinte de viol*), or for the *quinton.

Quinterne. German 16th/17th-century name for the guitar or similar instruments. Cf. K. Geiringer, in *AMW* vi.

Quintet [F. *quintette, quintuor*; G. *Quintett*; It. *quintetto*]. Chamber music for five players. The string quintet is usually for two violins, two violas, and cello (18 by Boccherini, 12 by Dittersdorf, 6 by Mozart, 3 by Beethoven, 2 by Mendelssohn, 2 by Brahms, 1 by Bruckner, 1 by Vaughan Williams, 1 by Reger, etc.). The less usual combination of two violins, viola, and two celli prevailed in Boccherini (113), but survived only in Schubert's famous Quintet in C, op. 163. A piano (clarinet, etc.) quintet is a composition for piano (clarinet, etc.) and string quartet. The list of piano quintets includes Schubert's op. 114 (Trout Quintet), Schumann's op. 44, Brahms's op. 34, and compositions by Dvořák, Franck, Reger, Pfitzner, Fauré, Elgar, Hindemith, Bloch (in quarter-tones), Shostakovitch, etc.

Vocal quintets are usually for two S, A, T, and B. A large literature of vocal music in five parts exists in the madrigals, ballettos, etc., of the late 16th century (Lasso, Lechner, English madrigalists).

Quintfagott [G.]. See *Oboe family II, C.

Quintieren [G.]. See *Wind instruments III.

Quintole [G.], **quintolet** [F.]. Quintuplet.

Quinton [F.]. An 18th-century French violin (not viol) with five strings tuned g–d′–a′–d″–g″ [cf. SaHMI].

Quintoyer [F.]. See *Wind instruments III.

Quintsaite [G.]. E-string of the violin.

Quintsextakkord [G.]. See under *Seventh chord.

Quintuor [F.]. Quintet.

Quintuple time. The measure of five beats. Quintuple time can usually be considered as a compound of a duple and a triple measure or, less frequently, of a triple and a duple measure. Well-known examples occur in Chopin's Sonata op. 4, in Tchaikovsky's Symphony no. 6 [Ex. 1], and in Wagner's *Tristan*, Act III,

Scene 2 [Ex. 2]. To those mentioned in GD iv, 310 the cavatina in Auber's *La Dame blanche*, Act II, may be added.

Probably the earliest composition in this meter is a *Felix namque in the English MS, Brit. Mus. *Roy. App. 56* (*c.* 1530). Quintuple time was common in ancient Greek music under the name Cretan rhythm [cf. *AdHM* i, 63] and forms a characteristic feature of certain folk dances, such as the *Zortziko* and the *Kochersberg*.

Quintuplet. A group of five notes played in the place of four.

Quire. Obsolete spelling for choir.

Qui tollis [L.]. Section of the *Agnus dei of the Mass [see *Mass B, III]. Medieval settings of the Agnus dei frequently begin with these words, the initial words being sung in plainsong.

Quodlibet [L., what you please]. A humorous type of music characterized by the quotation of well-known melodies or texts which are combined in an advisedly incongruous manner. The following types can be distinguished:

I. *The Polyphonic Quodlibet.* In this type, which is easily the most interesting one, different melodies or snatches thereof are used simultaneously in different voice-parts of a polyphonic composition. This method appears in some 13th-century motets in which refrains of trouvère songs occur in the upper voice against the liturgical melody (borrowed from Gregorian chant) in the tenor [see *Refrain III; also *Motet III]. In the 15th and 16th centuries numerous quodlibets were written in which different folk tunes were combined contrapuntally, the only license being that the time-values may be lengthened or shortened, according to the requirements of consonance. One of the earliest examples, contained in the *Glo-*

gauer Liederbuch of *c.* 1460 [see *Lieder-buch], contrasts the then famous "O rosa bella" melody with snatches of German folk songs [cf. *HAM*, nos. 80, 82]. An outstanding composer of such quodlibets was Ludwig Senfl [cf. *SchGMB*, no. 110], and comprehensive collections were published by Wolfgang Schmeltzl (*Guter, seltzamer und künstreicher teutscher Gesang . . .*, 1544) and by Melchior Franck (*Musikalischer Grillenvertreiber*, 1622). These pieces proved extremely valuable as sources of 16th-century German folk song [see *Lied II]. An example by Göldel, in which five chorales are skillfully combined, is quoted in *GD* iv, 311; for another (by Kindermann), using three chorales, cf. *DTB* 21/24, 13. The best-known example of this type is the final variation of Bach's *Goldberg Variations, in which two popular melodies of his day: (a) "Ich bin so lang nicht bei dir g'west" (Long have I been away from thee) and (b) "Kraut und Rüben" (Cabbage and turnips) are artfully combined within the harmonic frame of the theme [see illustration].

(a) Jch bin so lang nicht bei dir g'west

(b) Kraut und Rü- ben haben mich vertrieben

II. *The Successive Quodlibet.* A simpler type of quodlibet is that in which various melodies are quoted in succession, much in the manner of a potpourri. To this category belong various pieces contained in the collections mentioned above.

III. *The Textual Quodlibet.* The term quodlibet is also applied to pieces which show an incongruous mixture of borrowed *texts*, without involving the borrowing of musical material. As in the musical quodlibet, these texts may occur simultaneously or successively. The polytextual motet of the 13th century is frequently cited as an example of the textual quodlibet, but it should be observed that in all these motets (aside from the special type of the refrain motet) the texts of the upper parts are not borrowed, but freely invented, while the tenor has no full text, but only an *incipit; and that the element of incongruity is present only in the "French" motets which use a French text (mostly amorous) against the liturgical melody of the tenor and (frequently) against a Latin text in the middle part. More clearly under the category of the textual quodlibet fall a number of 18th-century pieces whose fun consists in the succession of jocose and deliberately incongruous texts. To this type belongs a "quodlibet" which is believed to be an early work of J. S. Bach [publ. by M. Schneider, in *Veröffentlichungen der Neuen Bach-Gesellschaft*, xxxii.2]. It consists of a great number of short texts [the "seafaring allusions" which C. S. Terry mentions in an article in *ML* xiv, no. 1, have a clearly obscene side-meaning] set to music evidently without using pre-existing melodies. There is a distinct possibility that this piece, rather than the truly polyphonic quodlibet from the *Goldberg Variations*, illustrates the "improvised quodlibet singing" which, according to C. P. E. Bach, was traditional in his family for many generations. Numerous examples of the same type occur in Valentin Rathgeber's *Augsburger Tafelkonfekt* of 1733 [repr. in E. O. Lindner, *Geschichte des deutschen Liedes . . .* (1871)]. Cf. also Moser, *Corydon.*

The Italian terms *misticanza* and *messanza* would seem to denote potpourris rather than quodlibets [see *Ensalada]. The term *centone is also used for quodlibets. Cf. K. Jeppesen, in *Papers Read at the International Congress of Musicology* (New York, 1939), 1944, p. 62. See also *Pasticcio. For Quodlibet Mass see *Mass B, II (b).

Lit.: W. Bienenfeld, in *SIM* vi; R. Eitner, "Das deutsche Lied des 15/16. Jahrhunderts," i (*MfM* viii, ix, Beilage); H. J. Moser, †*Corydon*, 2 vols. (1931/34).

R

R. In early orchestral music, *ripieno; in French organ music, *recit; in Gregorian chant (℞), *responsorium.

Rackett. See *Oboe family III.

Raddolcendo [It.]. Becoming dolce.

Raddoppiare [It.]. To double, usually in the lower octave.

Radel [G., from *Rad*, wheel]. German 14th-century name for a canon or *round. Cf. *ReMMA*, 377; also *Rota (2).

Radical bass. Same as *fundamental bass.

Radio broadcasting of music. The transmission of sound through space by radio, or wireless, telephony is used (1) to convey messages to specific receivers (*radio communication*) and (2) to send out information or entertainment intended for general reception (*radio broadcasting*). This article seeks to describe, in terms suited to the musician and music lover, the transmission and reproduction of musical sound in broadcasting.

When music performed before a microphone is heard by listeners many miles away, a double transformation has taken place. Sound waves have been converted into electromagnetic waves, and these, after traveling through space at incredible speed, have been converted back into sound waves. In order to understand how this is accomplished it is necessary to know something of the nature of sound; therefore, the article on *Acoustics should be read by way of preface to the following one.

I. *Electromagnetic Waves*. Wave motion is a phenomenon with which we are all familiar, at least in one manifestation. When water is disturbed, waves travel outward in concentric circles from the point of disturbance, gradually diminishing in amplitude (i.e., the height of their crests and depth of their troughs) as the energy which created them is dissipated. Since water is not compressible, waves travel only over its surface in the form of alternate ridges and depressions. Sound waves travel through air in the form of alternate areas of compression and rarefaction, expanding in all directions as concentric spheres. Their velocity (in warm air) is about 1100 feet per second. The precise nature of electromagnetic waves is still a scientific mystery, though their behavior is fairly well understood. They travel in all directions, as do sound waves, expanding as concentric spheres through a hypothetical medium, the ether. Their velocity is about 186,000 miles per second. In radio transmission they are generated by oscillations of high-frequency alternating current in a *transmitting antenna*. This is usually a wire or tower located in the open at some point from which the waves can radiate with a minimum of interference or adsorption by conductors such as power transmission lines or steel-framed buildings. As the current flows along the antenna, first in one direction and then in the other, it generates waves of electromagnetic energy in the surrounding "ether," just as a vibrating piano string generates waves of acoustic energy in the surrounding air [for more details, see, e.g., J. Langdon-Davies, *Radio*, ch. IV]. In both cases the waves have the same frequency, or rate of occurrence per second, as the oscillations which produce them; e.g., a piano string vibrating at the rate of 1000 oscillations, or cycles, per second generates 1000 sound waves per second, and current in a transmitting antenna alternating at the rate of 100,000 cycles per second generates 100,000 electromagnetic waves per second.

The waves currently used for radio transmission in the United States range in frequency from 10 kilocycles (10,000 cycles) to 300 megacycles (300,000,000 cycles) per second. These waves are divided into bands which are allocated by governmental authority to various services. The lowest bands (from 10 kc to

540 kc) are assigned chiefly to communication services, and the highest (from 1610 kc to 300 mc), to additional communication services, short wave broadcasting, ultra-short wave broadcasting, television, and facsimile transmission. Standard wave broadcasting utilizes the frequencies between 550 kc and 1600 kc, with stations spaced at intervals of 10 kc.

II. *Transmission of Sound.* Let us now follow the progress of a musical tone from its birth in a broadcasting studio to its reproduction in the home of a distant radio listener. To reduce the problem to its simplest musical terms we may assume that the original sound is Middle C, a "pure" tone produced by a tuning fork vibrating at the frequency of 261.63 cycles per second. The first step in radio transmission is to change the acoustic waves generated by the vibrations of the tuning fork into electrical vibrations. This is done by a *microphone*, which is a specially sensitive telephone transmitter. Early microphones operated on the same principle as the telephone transmitter, which consists of a diaphragm with a quantity of granular carbon behind it. As pressure of a sound wave forces the diaphragm backward the carbon granules are pressed together and their resistance to the current flowing through the microphone is lowered; as the diaphragm moves in the opposite direction the granules tend to separate, thus increasing their resistance. The result is a series of electrical impulses corresponding in frequency and amplitude to the sound waves. This is called *audio-frequency* current, since its frequency is the same as that of audible waves. A later microphone, now widely used in the United States, is the so-called *velocity* type. Instead of a diaphragm, this microphone has a thin metallic ribbon suspended between the poles of powerful magnets. As sound waves cause the air molecules to move back and forth at velocities that vary according to the frequency and amplitude of the sound vibrations, the ribbon oscillates in the magnetic field of the magnets, thus generating by electromagnetic induction an audio-frequency current.

The first step in the conversion process having been accomplished by the microphone, the sound of the tuning fork is now represented by electrical current alternating at the frequency of 261.63 cycles per second. This current is too weak to perform the tasks required of it; therefore it is conducted by wire to the *amplifiers*, a series of vacuum tubes which increases its strength. The amplified current then continues through wires to the *control panel*, where its volume is regulated by an engineer, and thence to the transmitter. Up to this point the electrical vibrations are still at *audio frequencies*, but electromagnetic waves of such comparatively low frequencies do not radiate satisfactorily. Consequently, the transmitter sends out a continuous high-frequency wave, called the *carrier*, which is *modulated* by the audio-frequency current received from the microphone. This means that the current generated by a sound wave is imposed on the carrier in such a way that the latter undergoes a series of changes corresponding in frequency to the vibrations of the sound wave. Thus Middle C becomes a series of variations, at the rate of 261.63 per second, in a series of electromagnetic waves of much higher frequency. The resulting phenomenon may be likened to the numerous small ripples which are imposed on the big waves of the sea.

The carrier may be varied, or modulated, either in amplitude or in frequency. The former method is used by all transmitters in the standard broadcast band and is called *amplitude modulation* (Ex. 1). The other method is called *frequency modulation* (Ex. 2) and is used only in ultra-high-frequency transmission.

The carrier, modulated by the audio frequency of 261.63 cycles, radiates from the transmitting antenna at the speed of light. When it encounters the antenna of a *receiver* the process which took place at the transmitter is reversed; i.e., a current of the same frequency and having the same modulations is induced in the receiving antenna. The effect is analogous to the sympathetic vibrations of an undamped piano string when the pitch to which it is tuned is sounded near by. In one respect, however, the receiving antenna resembles an entire piano, rather than a single string, for it responds to any

frequencies called *sidebands*. One sideband frequency is equal to the carrier frequency *plus* the audio frequency, the other sideband frequency is equal to the

1

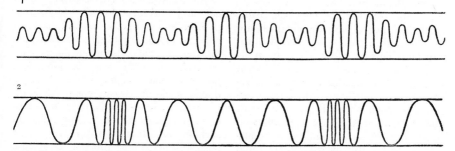

2

frequency of the radio scale; and since it is usually intercepting waves from many different transmitters at the same time, the receiver circuit is provided with a *detector*, or tuning device, which selects the frequency of the desired station and excludes all others.

As the energy picked up by the receiving antenna is only a tiny fraction of that sent out by the transmitter, the receiver circuit also includes amplifiers which bring the antenna current up to the required strength. The current is then *demodulated* — that is, the modulations of the carrier frequency are translated into audio-frequency current, and this current operates the diaphragm of a telephone receiver or loudspeaker, causing it to vibrate at the same frequency. The motions of the diaphragm generate sound waves in the air, and the radio listener hears a more or less faithful reproduction of the tone produced in the studio by the tuning fork.

III. *Fidelity.* The fidelity of sound reproduction by radio depends on various factors, chief of which is the efficiency of broadcasting equipment. Faithful reproduction of music requires a system free of noise and distortion throughout an adequate range of audio frequencies, and the transmitter must have room in the radio spectrum to utilize its full frequency range. When the carrier wave of an amplitude-modulation system is modulated by audio-frequency current, its original frequency is supplemented by additional

carrier frequency *minus* the audio frequency. For example, if a carrier wave of 1000 kilocycles is modulated by a frequency of one kilocycle, one sideband will have a frequency of 1001 kilocycles, the other a frequency of 999 kilocycles. The transmitter will then require a channel two kilocycles wide. Modulation of the carrier wave by the full frequency range of musical sound produces sidebands of at least 15,000 cycles each and necessitates a channel at least 30,000 cycles wide. As standard-wave channels are only 10,000 cycles wide, transmitters in that band are limited to an audio-frequency range of 5000 cycles. If they exceed it their sidebands overlap those of other stations, causing *interference*. Consequently, standard-wave receivers are not ordinarily designed to reproduce frequencies above 5000 cycles.

A range of 5000 cycles is sufficient to reproduce all fundamental pitches of the orchestral instruments but not all of their harmonics. The oboe and violin, for example, produce harmonics above 15,000 cycles, and nearly all musical instruments have harmonics above 5000 cycles. Failure to reproduce any portion of the harmonic components of a tone causes, of course, a proportionate loss of realism in its timbre. However, experience shows that the characteristic qualities of musical instruments are adequately conveyed by a reproducer limited to 5000 cycles, provided it is efficient in other respects. In any case, it is doubtful whether the average listener in a concert hall hears very many of the higher harmonics, owing to their low intensity, their rapid attenuation in air, and the blanketing effect of other sounds.

In the ultra-high-frequency band (above 40 megacycles) the channels are wide enough for full-range sound transmission. This is often referred to as "high-fidelity" transmission, but the term is somewhat misleading, for realistic reproduction of music involves various factors other than pitch. Perhaps the most important difference between music as it is heard in the studio and the reproduction of that music heard by the radio listener is that the latter is *monaural*. A normal human being hears *binaurally*; i.e., his two ears receive sound vibrations from slightly different angles, and usually at slightly different distances. This enables him to sense the direction from which a sound comes, and gives it a *stereophonic* (three-dimensional) quality comparable with that of a stereoscopic photograph. Broadcasting as yet employs only one "ear." Sounds, whether picked up by a single microphone or by several, are fed into a single system of wires and amplifiers, radiated on a single carrier wave, and reproduced by a single loudspeaker. The result is equivalent to what would be heard in the studio by a person deaf in one ear.

In order to broadcast stereophonically, the sounds in the studio must be picked up by two or more microphones and fed through separate systems of lines and amplifiers to separate transmitters operating on separate wave-lengths; and in order to receive such a broadcast stereophonically the listener must have separate receivers tuned to the several transmitters and so placed that the position of each loudspeaker corresponds to the position of the microphone whose output it receives. Stereophonic transmission has been successfully demonstrated under laboratory conditions, where wire lines could be used instead of radio transmitters, but the difficulty of obtaining dual channels has hitherto prevented its application to broadcasting in the standard band. De-

velopment of the ultra-high-frequency band, where congestion is less acute, may remove that impediment to stereophonic radio transmission.

For technical reasons it is sometimes necessary to control the volume of music transmitted by radio. *Pianissimo* passages may have to be amplified to enable them to override the extraneous noises that sometimes interfere with reception, and *fortissimo* passages may have to be reduced in volume to prevent overloading of circuits. In the early days of broadcasting, volume had to be controlled to such an extent that often there was noticeable distortion of musical dynamics. This gave rise to a controversy as to whether the controls should be operated by an engineer or by a musician. Since, it was argued, the man at the controls had the power to alter dynamic effects planned by the musician, he should be qualified by training to perform the task with musical taste and judgment.

However, improved equipment has so increased the volume range of broadcasting that this issue has virtually ceased to exist. Current practice among studio engineers is to find, during rehearsal, a control setting which will accommodate both the loudest and the softest passages in the music, thereby obviating the necessity for changing the volume controls during the broadcast. "Editing" of the performer's dynamics is thus eliminated, and, at the same time, the man at the controls is left free to attend to the various important technical duties which only an engineer is qualified to perform.

One of the most important factors relating to fidelity of transmission is *microphone placement*. In concert halls there are points which are specially advantageous acoustically. Experienced concertgoers are well aware of this and often go to considerable lengths to secure "the best seat in the house." The microphone will probably "hear" best at a point much nearer the source of sound than the human listener would select. This is partly due to the fact that the microphone picks up and transmits, along with the music, extraneous noises which the human being hears but disregards. In the quietest auditorium there is usually a considerable amount of noise. Chairs creak, programs rustle, people cough, and traffic or other noises filter in from the outside. The listener is surrounded by noises but, thanks to his stereophonic hearing, he is able to concentrate his attention on the musical sounds coming to him from one direction and ignore the noises coming from other directions. The radio listener, to whom music and noise come from the same direction — that is, from his loud-speaker — finds it much more difficult to dissociate them. Consequently, it is essential that the microphone be located near enough to the source of sound to maintain a high ratio of music to noise.

Acoustical conditions at the point of origin may affect the transmission of music in various ways. Excessive reverberation is detrimental to clarity. Excessive adsorption tends to damp the sound waves prematurely, causing a loss of resonance and richness. Unequal adsorption of different frequencies may result in loss of brilliance. The clothing of an audience, for example, is adsorbent to high frequencies. Consequently, when an orchestra broadcasts from a crowded auditorium the high-pitched instruments may sound less brilliant than they do when no audience is present.

In this connection it may be noted that broadcasting studios are usually less "live" — i.e., reverberant — than concert halls, the reason being that a greater proportion of reflected sound is tolerated by the listener in the concert hall than by the radio listener. The former, hearing binaurally, has no difficulty in distinguishing direct from reflected sound, while the latter, hearing a monaural reproduction of the music, receives both direct and reflected sound from the same direction and hence is unable to discriminate between them.

There are no hard-and-fast rules of studio technique. So many variable factors enter into the problem that each situation must be studied individually and dealt with empirically; but a working knowledge of the principles governing

microphone placement is essential to the production director who supervises the placement of the microphone and valuable to the musician who performs before it. To the listener, an understanding of those principles may be helpful as a guide to the selection and efficient use of receiving equipment. Published literature on this subject is not extensive. However, some material pertaining to it will be found in items 3, 10, and 11 of the bibliography.

Lit.: 1. G. L. Archer, *History of Radio to 1926* (1938); 2. *id., Big Business and Radio* (1939); 3. K. Henney, *Radio Engineering Handbook* (1941); 4. J. Jeans, *Science and Music* (1937); 5. J. Langdon-Davies, *Radio* (1935); 6. John Mills, *A Fugue in Cycles and Bels* (1935); 7. *id., Letters of a Radio Engineer to his Son* (1922); 8. A. Morgan, *Getting Acquainted with Radio* (1940); 9. W. and E. Watson, *Understanding Radio* (1940); 10. E. La Prade, "The Technique of Broadcasting Instrumental Groups" (*Proceedings, Music Educators Natl. Conf.,* 1935); 11. *id.,* "Problems in Microphone Placement" (*ibid.,* 1938). E. P.

Radleyer [G.]. *Hurdy-gurdy.

Rätselkanon [G.]. Riddle canon.

Raffrenando [It.]. "Putting on the brakes," checking the speed.

Raga. See *Hindu music; *Melody types.

Ragtime. See *Jazz I.

Rakoczy March. The Hungarian national air [see *National anthems], named after the national hero Francis Rakoczy (1676–1735), composed (possibly after an older folk-tune) by Janos Bihari in 1809. The melody has been used by Liszt in one of his *Hungarian Rhapsodies* (no. 15) and by Berlioz in his *Marche Hongroise* and *The Damnation of Faust.* See *Tarogato.

Rallentando, abbr. *rall.* Same as ritardando.

Range. See *Voices, Range of.

Rank. In organ parlance, a complete set of pipes of the same type, controlled by one *stop. A *mixture-stop, however, has several ranks, according to the number of pipes combined in the production of a single tone. See *Organ II; *Register.

Rankett. See *Oboe family III.

Rant. A name of a 17th-century dance occurring, e.g., in the fantasies (suites) of John Jenkins and in Matthew Locke's *Melothesia* (1673). Judging from the type of the music, the term may well be an abbreviation of *corranto*, i.e., *courante.

Ranz des vaches [F.; G. *Kuhreigen, Kuhreihen*, cow procession]. A type of Swiss mountain melody sung or played on the *alphorn by the herdsmen to call the scattered cows. There exist about fifty such melodies which are traditionally kept in the various districts of the Alps. They all show that irregularity of rhythm and of melodic design which is the earmark of ancient folk music. Indeed, one of them, beginning with the words "Loba, Loba," occurs as early as 1545, in Rhaw's *Bicinia*.

The ranz des vaches has been repeatedly used in operas dealing with Swiss subjects, e.g., in the overtures of Gretry and of Rossini's *William Tell*, and in Kienzl's *Der Kuhreigen*. Cf. A. Glück, in *VMW* viii.

Rappresentativo. See under *Stile.

Rasgado [Sp., scraping]. In guitar playing, sweeping the strings with the thumb to produce an arpeggio.

Rasoumofsky Quartets. See *Russian Quartets.

Ratisbon Edition. See *Liturgical books II.

Ratsche [G.]. *Rattle.

Rattenando, rattenuto [It.]. Holding back.

Rattle. An instrument of the *percussion family, similar to the well-known children's toy. It consists of a wooden cogwheel which is revolved against a hard flexible spring of wood or metal. It is used in Richard Strauss's *Till Eulenspiegel*. — In scientific classification the term rattle is used to denote shaken idiophones [see *Instruments I, B]. Such instruments, which represent almost the earliest stage in the making of instruments, are extremely frequent in primitive cultures. An example is the Cuban *maracas*, consisting of a gourd filled with pebbles or dry seeds and shaken by means of a wooden handle [see *Percussion instruments B 8].

Rauschend [G.]. "Rustling," exuberant.

Rauscher [G.]. German 18th-century term for the French *batterie* [see *Batterie (3)] or quick figures involving repeated notes.

Ravvivando [It.]. Quickening.

Razor Quartet [G. *Rasiermesser-quartett*]. Popular name of Haydn's string quartet no. 61 (op. 55, no. 2) in F minor, so called because it is said to have been given by Haydn to his publisher in exchange for a new razor which he needed badly.

Re. See *Solmization.

Reading Rota. Name for the *Sumer canon, a *rota supposedly composed by a monk from Reading.

Real answer, real fugue. See *Tonal and real.

Rebab. Name for various bowed string instruments found in Moslem countries. They occur in a great variety of strange shapes with one to three strings. See the illustration, p. 800 (also *SaRM*, 317; *SaHMI*, 245; *GD* v, 514). It is used in the *Javanese orchestra as a conductor's instrument. The European descendants are the *rebec and the rubeba.

Rebec, rebeck. A medieval bowed string instrument shaped like a long slender pear, also known as *rubeba, lyra, gigue*. See the illustration on p. 800 (also *SaRM*, 318; *GD* v, 514; *AdHM*, 593).

About its relationship to the Arabic *rebab, cf. *SaRM*. The rubeba, which some scholars believe to be a larger type of rebec, has been described by Johannes de Moravia (*CS* i, 152). A 15th-century rebec is preserved in Bologna; cf. B. Disertori, in *RMI* xlii.

Rebute [F.]. *Jew's harp.

Recapitulation. See under *Sonata form.

Recercada, recercar. See *Ricercar.

Récit [F.]. Seventeenth-century term, derived from *recitativo, for a vocal solo piece, usually in aria style; e.g., *récit de basse*, bass aria. In organ parlance, the term was used in similar connotations, i.e., for a solo organ stop and the entire solo organ (*clavier de récit*); also as a title for organ pieces with a distinct melodic part (in distinction from the earlier contrapuntal type of organ music). See also under *Taille.

Recital. The term, which denotes public performances by one player (in distinction from concert), was first used in connection with performances given by F. Liszt in London, around 1840.

Recitative [It. *recitativo*]. I. A vocal style designed to imitate and to emphasize the natural inflections of speech. It is usually employed in connection with prose texts of a more or less narrative character, particularly in operas in which it serves to carry on the action from one aria (ensemble, chorus) to another. In accordance with its declamatory character, the purely musical principles of vocal melody, phrase, and rhythm are largely disregarded in the recitative; instead of beautifully designed lines one finds speech-like reiteration of the same note, slight inflections, short groups of quick notes in irregular rhythms, purely syllabic treatment of the text, etc. The recitative is sung either to a *thoroughbass accompaniment, or to a written-out accompaniment of a more fully developed character. The former type is known as *recitativo secco*, the latter as *recitativo accompagnato* or *stromentato*.

In spite of the intrinsic limitation of recitative style its evolution shows quite a variety of types which are far from being adequately covered by the conventional classification just mentioned, as will appear from the subsequent historical survey.

II. The recitative originated around 1600 as the most startling innovation of the *Nuove Musiche, and in immediate connection with the development of the *opera [see also *Monody]. The earliest operas (Peri's, Caccini's *Euridice*, 1600) are written throughout in a carefully and impressively designed declamation, which is quite different from the later "parlando" style. The accompanying example from Caccini's *Euridice* (1600) is typical of this early Florentine recitative [Ex. 1]. During the 17th century this style of singing evolved in three different directions:

(a) Taking on more distinct phrasing, melodic character, and definite form, it grows into the aria, of which examples are to be found in Monteverdi, the Roman and Venetian composers, though not yet fully set apart from the recitative portions (e.g., Cavalli's *Giasone*, 1649).

Nin-fa, deh sii contenta ridir perchè t'af-
fanni, che ta-ciu lo marti troppo tor-men-ti.

G: A-mi-co, che ti par?
L: Mi par chabbiate un

Vá là, che sei gran gonzo
a-ni-ma di bronzo.

(b) With the rise of the aria as a distinct type, the recitative begins to assume a more rapid, less melodic character. Examples of this style are already to be found in Cesti (*Pomo d'oro*, 1667) and Pallavicino (*La Gerusalemme liberata*, 1687). It was not until the 18th century, however, that this "parlando style" attained general importance, under the name of *recitativo secco* (*secco*, dry — with reference to the unexpressive character of the declamation, not to the lack of an elaborate accompaniment). This type remained in use throughout the period of the Neapolitan opera as well as in the operas of Mozart and Rossini [see Ex. 2, from Mozart's *Don Giovanni*].

(c) While the early Florentine as well as the secco recitative were sung to a thorough-bass accompaniment only, a fuller accompaniment (including strings) was introduced for recitatives of special importance. Monteverdi was one of the first to use this method in the closing measures of the famous "Possenti spirti" in his *Orfeo* (1607) and Schütz used it consistently for the part of the Evangelist in his *Auferstehungs Historie* (1623). The use of an ensemble accompaniment naturally led a more strictly measured type of recitative, dramatic rather than declamatory, the *recitativo accompagnato* or *stromentato*. It assumed considerable importance in 18th-century opera where it is usually reserved for the climactic scenes

of the drama, and serves to introduce the most brilliant arias of the work. Bach, in his *St. Matthew Passion*, uses it consistently for the part of Christ and for

the recitatives preceding an aria [Ex. 3].

(d) A special type of recitative, characterized by the frequent change of meter (⁴⁄₄, ³⁄₄, ²⁄₄), developed in France under Lully [Ex. 4] and spread, with necessary adaptation to the language, to England (Purcell). This recitative presents the attempt to set down in exact note values the rhythm, accentuation, and inflections of the French language, on a principle similar to the *vers mesuré of the 16th century [see also *Rhythm II (b)].

(e) Finally, it may be mentioned that Schütz, in his latest works, the Passions, developed a highly impressive type of "archaic" recitative, entirely unaccompanied, a Baroque revival of the Gregorian psalm tones [cf. *SchGMB*, no. 192].

(f) The most outspoken adversary of the Italian opera and its stereotyped parlando recitative, namely, Richard Wagner, was destined to bring about a new flowering of the truly musical recitative: his "unending melody" is indeed nothing but a recitative of the highest expressiveness and dramatic significance. An interesting contrast to the emotionalism of Wagner's recitative is formed by the mysteriously vague recitative of Debussy's *Pelléas et Mélisande*.

The free character of the recitative has repeatedly been imitated in instrumental music. Examples occur in Kuhnau's *Biblische Historien* (1698), in Bach's *Chromatic Fantasie*, in Beethoven's Piano Sonata op. 30, 1 (first movement, recapitulation) and op. 110 (slow movement), in Schumann's *Scenes from Childhood* (The Poet Speaks), etc. See also *Arioso.

Lit.: Ch. Spitz, "Die Entwicklung von Stile Recitativo" (*AMW* iii); S. Wilson, "The Recitatives of the St. Matthew Passion" (*ML*, xvi, no. 3); E. Borrel, "L'Interprétation de l'ancien récitatife français" (*RdM*, no. 37). D. J. G. and W. A.

Reciting note. See under *Psalm tones.

Recorded music. See *Phonograph and recorded music.

Recorder [F. *Flûte douce*, *Flûte à bec*; G. *Blockflöte*, *Schnabelflöte*; It. *flauto* *dolce, flauto diritto*]. The most important type of whistle (or fipple) flute, i.e., end-blown, with a "whistle" mouthpiece [see *Whistle flute]. Its tone-quality is highly individual, soft, and slightly reedy, in part produced by an inverted conical bore smallest at the lower end. The recorder attained very nearly its final form in the late Middle Ages; in the 16th century it formed a complete family of instruments from treble to bass which played an important part in the music of the late Renaissance. By the early 18th century only one size, with a range from f′ to g‴, remained in common use. This was called "Flauto" by J. S. Bach and most of his contemporaries; the transverse flute (the modern instrument) is normally distinguished as "Traverso." Bach and Handel very occasionally made use of a "Flauto Piccolo," a small recorder usually an octave higher in pitch than the Flauto; the statement that this was a *flageolet is erroneous. After 1750 the recorder passed gradually out of use.

In the early 20th century a revival took place, begun by Arnold Dolmetsch in England, to be followed after 1918 by German manufacturers using large-scale methods, and finally, on a much smaller scale, by makers in the United States. Modern instruments are generally made in four sizes, named by German and English makers as follows:

German	English	Range
Soprano	Descant	c″ — d⁗
Alto	Treble	f′ — g‴
Tenor	Tenor	c′ — d‴
Bass	Bass	f — f″

Two systems of boring the fingerholes have been used in modern instruments; that used by certain German makers to simplify the fingering of the first octave, usually called "German fingering," has not gained wide acceptance, and the 18th-century system, today called "English fingering," is now most used. The Alto (Treble), owing to its widespread popularity as a chamber-music instrument in the 18th century, possesses an important literature written expressly for it by composers of nearly every nationality; much

of this music has been reprinted. See the illustrations on p. 272.

Lit.: Chr. Welch, *Six Lectures on the Recorder* (1911); C. Sachs, *Handbuch der Musikinstrumentenkunde* (2d ed., 1930); *id., The History of Musical Instruments* (1940); F. J. Giesbert, *Schule für die Altblockflöte* (Mainz); Sebastian Virdung, *Musica getutscht* (1511, repr. 1882); Michael Praetorius, *Syntagma Musicum II* (1618, repr. 1884); Sylvestro Ganassi, *Opera intitulata Fontegara* (1535, facs. ed. 1934); Jaques Hotteterre, *Principes de la flûte . . . à bec* (1707); H. Fitzgibbon, "Of Flutes and Soft Recorders" (*MQ* xx); C. F. Dolmetsch, in *ML* xxii, no. 1; A. Carse, "Fingering the Recorder" (*MR* i); Ch. Welch, "Literature Relative to the Recorder" (*PMA* xxiv).   J. F. O.

Recoeuilli [F.]. Collected, reserved.

Recoupe [F.]. See under *Basse dance.

Recte et retro [L.]. See *Retrograde.

Redobles [Sp.]. See *Ornamentation I.

Redowa, rejdowak. A Bohemian dance in moderately quick triple meter, similar to the mazurka. It attained popularity around 1850. Cf. the example in *GD* iv, 340.

Réduction [F.]. Arrangement. *Piano réduction*, arrangement for piano.

Reed [F. *anche*; G. *Zunge, Blatt, Rohrblatt*; It. *ancia*]. I. A small elastic piece of thin reed (cane) or metal which is fixed at one end and is free to vibrate, by means of blown air, at the other end. The reed is the sound-producing agent in various musical instruments, chiefly oboes, clarinets, saxophones, bagpipe, harmonium, accordion, mouth harmonica, and the reed stops of the organ. Those of the first four instruments are made from cane, the others from metal. The best cane reeds are made from *Arundo donax*, a tall grass growing in the south of France (Fréjus).

Two basically different types of reeds must be distinguished, namely *idiophonic* and *heterophonic* reeds [G. *harte* and *weiche Zungen*]. The idiophonic [Gr., own sound] reeds are made of a heavy and hard substance, usually metal, and are capable of producing a sound of one pitch only, this being determined by their length and thickness (similar to, e.g., a tuning fork). Such reeds are used in the *harmonium, the *accordion, the *mouth harmonica, the Chinese *sheng, the *regal, and the organ reed stops. In the latter they are combined with a pipe which, however, serves only to reinforce the sound [see *Organ VIII]. A heterophonic [Gr., other sound] reed is made of a light and soft substance, usually cane, and is capable of producing a wide range of pitches, but only if it is attached to a pipe, the length of which determines the pitch of the sound. In instruments such as the oboe or clarinet the sounding length of the pipe can be varied by covering different holes, so that a whole scale can be obtained from the reed. It is this type of reed that the term usually refers to.

II. Heterophonic reeds occur in two varieties, i.e., *single reeds* (clarinet, saxophone) and *double reeds* (oboe, bassoon). In the former type there is only one reed which vibrates against a slot of the pipe, while in the latter type there are two reeds, separated by a slight opening, which vibrate against each other. It may be remarked that the lips of the trumpet and horn player form, from the acoustical point of view, a pair of heterophonic double reeds.

Another distinction of somewhat lesser importance (referring chiefly to the idiophonic class) is that between *free reeds* and *beating reeds*. In the former type, which is used in the harmonium, the reeds move outside and inside of a slot which is just wide enough to let the reed pass "freely"; in the other type, used chiefly in the organ, the opening of the slot is somewhat smaller than the reed so that this "beats" against the frame of the slot. The reed of the clarinet also is a beating reed.

A special type of reed is the *covered reed*, i.e., a (single or double) reed which is enclosed in a cap perforated by a hole into which the player blows, thus con-

trolling the reed indirectly. This device which excludes expressive and dynamic nuances was used in various early instruments, e.g., in the *cromornes, while in the *pibgorn the reed is enclosed in a funnel-shaped mouthpiece which is pressed tightly around the lips.

Reed pipes, stops. See *Organ VIII, X.

Reel. A dance performed by two or more couples standing in a circle and describing a series of figures each in the time of eight measures. It is common in Scotland, Ireland, and America, the American variety being known as the Virginia reel. The music consists of four or eight measures in moderately quick duple meter which are repeated over and over again. See under *Strathspey.

Réexposition [F.]. Recapitulation.

Refrain. I. A term of poetry, equivalent to burden, thus denoting one or two lines of identical text which occur at the end of each stanza of a strophic poem. In musical composition the refrain is naturally set to the same melody, so that the term adopts the meaning of both textual and musical repetition. A popular name for the refrain is chorus, referring to the common practice of singing the refrain in full chorus, the stanzas (verses) solo.

II. The principle of the refrain was already present in the antiphonal and responsorial singing of the early Christian Church in which an exclamation such as Amen, Alleluia, etc., was repeated by the congregation or the choir after each verse or pair of verses of a psalm [see *Psalmody II, III]. The refrain poem developed particularly in the 12th and 13th centuries under the *troubadours and *trouvères, leading to various refrain-forms, the simplest of which is the *ballade, usually a poem of three stanzas of eight lines each, the last two of which are a refrain. Its musical scheme is a a b R for the stanza (refrains are usually printed in italics and, in schematic presentations, indicated by capital letters). Another refrain-form of the 13th century is the *virelai with the structure A b b a A for the stanza, the closing refrain serving also as the initial refrain for the next stanza. (In these schemes one letter, whether small or capital, always denotes identical music.) The situation is somewhat different with the medieval rondeau: A B a A a b A B [see *Rondeau (1)] since this has normally only one stanza within which the textual and musical reiteration takes place. In the Italian 14th-century *ballata the refrain is called *ripresa; in the Spanish *villancico, *estribillo.

III. The refrain lines, particularly of the rondeaux, are frequently borrowed material, i.e., sentences which were taken over from earlier poems and which, owing to their popularity, were in common use so that their "quotation" was a matter of courtly education. Thus, the term refrain adopts the meaning of a line of text taken over from some other literary product. There existed in the first half of the 13th century a whole stock of well-known refrains, usually of amorous character, such as "Eai! ke ferai? Je mur d'amourette" or "En ma dame ai mis mon cuer, et ma pensée," which were freely borrowed for new songs as well as for the upper parts of French motets [cf. HAM, nos. 19b and 32d]. Three such usages may be mentioned here: (a) The chanson avec des refrains was a strophic song each stanza of which concluded with a "different refrain" — if this self-contradictory term be permitted [Ex. in AdHM i, 195f]. (b) The refrain motet, i.e., a motet which includes refrain-quotations in the text of the upper parts, usually at the end. This was a very common procedure in the French motets from about 1250. (c) The motet enté which begins with the first half of a refrain and ends with its conclusion, with new material in between [see *Enté]. There are even a few motets (and one conductus) the text of which consists entirely of refrains [Ex. in AdHM i, 240, E], in the manner of a *cento. While the textual aspect of the borrowing in motets has been fully investigated by philologists, the question as to what extent musical borrowing went with it is much less clear. In quite a few instances, however, it has been shown that the refrain was incorpo-

rated into the motet together with a melody. In such cases the technique is that of the *quodlibet since the tenor-melody is always borrowed (from plainsong). Frequently the method of borrowing was the reverse of that just described, i.e., the initial phrase of a motet duplum became a refrain. The custom of refrain quotation persisted till the late 15th century [cf. M. F. Bukofzer, in MQ, 1942, p. 33].

The principle of alternation between variable and reiterated portions of a composition reappears in the instrumental *ritornelli of the 17th century, as well as in the rondeaux of the French clavecinists [see *Rondeau (2), and *Rondo].

Lit.: H. Orenstein, Die Refrainformen im Chansonnier de l'Arsenal (Diss. Vienna 1937); F. Gennrich, Musikwissenschaft und Romanische Philologie (1918).

Regal. A portable organ invented probably around 1450 and much used during the 16th and 17th centuries, which had reed pipes only [see *Reed]. The reproduction in GD iv, 344 furnishes a good view of the construction. The explanation of the name is uncertain [cf. the conjectures in GD iv, 344; SaHMI, 308; SaRM, 318]. In the 16th century, the reed pipes of the regal were incorporated into the organ which theretofore had possessed only flue pipes. Thus, the reed stops of the later organs are frequently called "regal" in general, many of them bearing names such as Geigenregal, Trichterregal (from the funnel-like shapes of the pipes), etc. On the other hand, regals themselves were also enlarged by the addition of flue pipes. Monteverdi prescribed the regal in his Orfeo (1607) to accompany the song of Charon [see *Orchestration I].— A particularly small type of regal was the bible regal, so called because it could be folded together like a book. Cf. SaHMI, 309.

Regisseur. German designation for the artistic or technical director of an opera. In German, "Regie" corresponds generally to "production." The Regiebuch contains the operatic text with the indication of the stage setting.

Register. (1) In organ parlance, the full set of pipes controlled by one stop; hence, practically identical with organ stop. A register may include one or (in mixture stops, etc.) several *ranks. — (2) The different ranges of the human voice are distinguished, according to the method of their production and sound quality, as "head register," "chest register," etc. As in most matters concerning singing, there is considerable disagreement among singers and voice teachers regarding the question of the vocal registers. Some say the voice has two registers, high and low. Many claim three registers, high (head), middle (throat), and low (chest). Others subdivide still further. While formerly the registers played a most prominent part in the teaching of, and writing on, singing, there is a strong tendency at present to ignore the whole idea as of little importance and value. R. Y. R.

Registration [G. *Registrierung*]. The art of using and combining the organ registers in playing on the organ. While modern organ composers frequently indicate the registration of their compositions (at least in a general way), such indications are rare in the literature of the Bach period. Authentic details regarding Bach's registration are available in a few pieces, notably the chorale preludes "Ein feste Burg" (Peters VI, no. 22: *piano* and *forte*), "Christ lag in Todesbanden" (Peters VI, no. 15: *piano* and *forte*), and the Dorian Toccata (Peters III: *Oberwerk* and *Positiv*). It should be noted that French organ composers of the 17th century were much more detailed in the indication of stops than German and Italian [see *Organ music II (c)]. For literature see under *Organ playing.

Regola dell' ottava (the rule of the

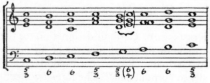

octave). In the *thorough-bass practice of the 18th century a scheme according

to which each tone of the octave is provided with a suitable chord, as in the accompanying example. Such schemes proved helpful for the realization of simple basses which had no figures indicating more elaborate chords. Cf. E. Borrel, in *TG* xxi, 175.

Rehab. Same as *rebab.

Reigen [G.]. Round dance.

Reimofficium [G., rhymed office]. Rhymed versions of the liturgical texts for the offices of Saints. They were very popular during the 11th through the 16th centuries, until they were abolished by the Council of Trent (1545–63). Cf. *AdHM* i, 89; P. Wagner, *Einführung in die Gregorianischen Melodien*, i, 300; K. Meyer, in *AMW* iii.

Reimsequenz [G.]. The rhymed *sequences of the 12th century.

Reine Stimmung [G.]. *Just intonation.

Rejouissance [F.]. In 18th-century music (Bach, Orchestral Suite no. 4), name for light and playful pieces, generally in quick triple meter.

Related key. See *Key relationships.

Relative keys. See *Key relationships.

Relative pitch. (1) Acoustically, the pitch of a tone (e.g., E) in relation to a standard tone or to a given key (e.g., C). It may be expressed either as an interval (major third), or by means of solmization syllables (mi), or by relative frequencies $(\frac{5}{4})$. — (2) Psychologically, the faculty to recognize and to indicate the relative pitch, e.g., to recognize the tone E as the major third above C, or to sing this tone, if the major third above C is demanded. This faculty is one of the most fundamental requirements of a musician, much more important, in fact, than the *absolute pitch.

Relish. An ornament used in the performance of early English music for lute, viol, and keyboard. The term *Single Relish* was applied to any ornament formed by the alternation of two adjacent notes. The *Double Relish*, a complex ornament similar to the French *double cadence*, consists essentially of a trill upon each of two successive notes, as follows:

P. A.

Remettez [F.]. In French organ music, indication to take off a stop.

Renaissance, Music of the. The counterpart in music of the Renaissance in the Fine Arts and in literature. Although the term is universally used, there will hardly be found even two interpreters who entirely agree as to its proper meaning and to its temporal as well as spatial limitations. If Renaissance means — as it originally did in the other arts — the rediscovery of ancient Greek culture, then Renaissance music can hardly be said to exist; phenomena such as the composition in the Horatian meters [see *Ode; also *Humanism] are, indeed, of a very subordinate importance and the efforts towards a revival of the Greek drama were purely imaginative, not to mention the fact that they led to a musical style (monody, opera, oratorio) which is generally agreed upon as already representing the beginning of the *Baroque period. If the term means the liberation of music from the bondage to the Church and the rise of a secular aestheticism, then the music of the 14th century rather than that of the 15th might be termed Renaissance music. As a matter of fact, even in the Fine Arts there has recently been a tendency towards dating back the beginning of the Renaissance as early as 1300 ("Proto-Renaissance" of Giotto, etc.). A musical "proto-Renaissance" might be said to begin as early as 1250 (secular motets) and to continue throughout the 14th century (*Ars Nova); however, a special difficulty, not paralleled in the Fine Arts, is presented by the even earlier existence of a markedly secular musical

tradition, namely, that of the troubadours and trouvères (12th to 13th century).

The most satisfactory definition may be obtained on the basis of stylistic qualities, i.e., internal musical evidence. Clarity, balance, self-reliance, euphony, expressiveness within well-regulated limits, finally the development of artistic standards [see *Maniera], and of rational methods of composition (imitation, treatment of dissonances), are among the characteristic features of what is usually understood to constitute Renaissance style. If this view is accepted, the beginning of the musical Renaissance can scarcely be dated earlier than 1500, the time when Josquin, Isaac, Hofhaimer (all born about 1450), reached maturity of style. This leaves an unaccounted-for gap of 50 years between the beginning of the Renaissance and the end of the Gothic period (1450), a half-century which comprises the work of the earliest Flemish composers, Ockeghem and Obrecht (both born 1430). Of these the former will have to be considered as continuing the Gothic tradition, the latter as preparing the style of the Renaissance. See *History of music; *Flemish Schools; *Humanism; *Musica reservata; and the various countries.

Renforcer [F.]. To reinforce, to increase.

Renversement [F.]. Inversion (of intervals, chords, subjects).

Renvoi [F.]. Sign of *Da capo.

Repeat. The signs ‖: at the beginning, and :‖ at the end of a section, which call for repetition of this section. If the latter sign alone appears, the repetition is meant to start from the beginning of the composition (e.g., the exposition of sonata-form).

Repercussa, repercussio [L.], **Reperkussion** [G.]. See under *Psalm tone.

Repetition. (1) A special device of the pianoforte-action which permits the quick repetition of a tone (invented by S. Erard). See *Pianoforte.

(2) As a device of musical composition, repetition is one of the most important, if not the most important, principles of musical construction. This will be realized if it is remembered that the repetition of a musical idea or motive includes among its subspecies: sequential treatment, imitation, ostinato, variation, and repetition of entire sections. This last is the basic principle of nearly all the musical *forms (A B A; A A B A; A B A C A D A; etc.). In a wider sense, repetition is also present in the equal length and comparable rhythm of phrases (four measures); in fact, the very presence of a uniform meter throughout a piece already constitutes an element of repetition. It will easily be seen that this basic factor of music has no counterpart in painting, while in architecture it appears, with more restricted significance, as symmetry.

In contrapuntal music, four devices of repetition are used which may be distinguished as follows:
Repetition in the same part at the same pitch: *ostinato;
Repetition in the same part at a different pitch: *sequence;
Repetition in a different part at the same pitch: *Stimmtausch;
Repetition in a different part at a different pitch: *imitation.

Lit.: C. A. Harris, "The Element of Repetition in Nature and the Arts" (*MQ* xvii); R. Lach, "Das Konstructionsprinzip der Repetition" (*Sitzungsberichte der Wiener Akademie der Wissenschaften*, Bd. 201, 1925).

Répétition [F.], **repetizione** [It.]. Rehearsal. *Répétition général*, dress rehearsal.

Replica [It.]. Repeat. *Senza replica* indicates omission of the repeats as is usual with the repetition of the menuet or scherzo after the trio.

Répons [F.]. *Responsorium.

Réponse [F.]. Fugal answer.

Reports. A 17th-century English term for *points of imitation or, at least, for some sort of contrapuntal treatment.

Thus, in Playford's *Introduction to the Skill of Music* (12th edition, 1694) reference is made to "imitation or reports," and the Scottish psalter of 1635 contains tunes treated in the style of an anthem and inscribed: "Psalmes in Reports."

Reprendere [It.]. To take up again (the tempo).

Reprise [E., F., G.]. (1) Repetition. The term is particularly used in connection with *sonata-form, unfortunately in two different meanings. Originally, it refers to the repetition of the exposition before the development usually indicated by the "repeat"-sign. This meaning exists in the case of Ph. Em. Bach's *Sonaten mit veränderten Reprisen* in which the repetition of the exposition is written out in a varied form. In present-day nomenclature, however, the term usually means the recapitulation, i.e., the repetition of the exposition after the development section [see under *Durchführung]. — (2) In 17th-century French music the second section of pieces in binary form is called *reprise*, e.g., in practically all the dances in the suites of d'Anglebert. See also under *Ripresa (4).

Reprisenbar [G.]. See *Barform II.

Reproaches. See *Improperia.

Requiem [from L. *requies*, rest]. A composition of the text of the Mass for the Dead (Missa pro defunctis), so called because it begins with the Introit "Requiem aeternam dona eis Domine" (Give them eternal rest, O Lord). The liturgical structure of this Mass is essentially the same as that of any other *Mass, the main difference being that the joyful portions of the Ordinary (Gloria and Credo) are omitted, that the Alleluia is replaced by a Tractus and that, after the Tractus, the sequence *Dies irae* (by Thomas a Celano, 13th century) is added. For the plainsong music of this Mass, cf. *GR*, 95*.

The polyphonic composition of the Mass for the Dead differs from that of the normal Mass chiefly because it includes not only the invariable portions of the Ordinary (Kyrie, Sanctus, Agnus Dei), but also, and in fact more prominently, the items of the Proper (Introit, Gradual, etc.). The reason for this procedure is, of course, that in this special Mass these items have a fixed text, like those of the Ordinary. Compositions of the Requiem are not very numerous, but among them are works of the highest artistic significance. The earliest settings are from the 16th century: Pierre de la Rue [*Editions V, 11], Johannes Prioris (publ. by Attaingnant, 1532), Antoine de Fevin, Cristobal Morales [*Editions XIII, 1], Francisco Guerrero (*Liber primus missarum . . . , 1566), Palestrina (*Missarum liber primus*, 1591), Lassus (1589), and finally Tomaso Vittoria's great *Officium defunctorum*, written in 1603 for the death of the Spanish Empress Maria. In all of these works the Dies irae is not composed, but sung in plainsong, as are the opening intonations of the various portions, while the composed sections use the liturgical melodies more or less freely as a cantus firmus. The dramatic mind of the 17th century was captivated particularly by the tremendous words of the Dies irae. The 17th-century requiems of Christian Straus (fl. 1616–27), Heinrich Franz Biber (1644–1704), and Joh. Kaspar Kerll (1627–93), reproduced in *DTOe* 30.i, all use tremolo effects for the words "Quantus tremor." Among the orchestral settings of the 18th century, Jommelli's and, above all, Mozart's Requiem are outstanding. The list of 19th-century composers of the Requiem includes Cherubini, Berlioz, Dvořák, Bruckner, Verdi, Saint-Saëns, and Fauré. Brahms, in his *Deutsches Requiem* (op. 45, 1868), created an impressive work based on German texts freely chosen from the Scriptures [see *German Requiem]. Cf. Ch. W. Fox, "The Polyphonic Requiem before 1615" (*BAMS* vii).

Reservata. See *Musica reservata.

Res facta [L., completed work]. With reference to 15th-century music, a composition fully written out in all its parts, as distinguished from improvised *fauxbourdon.

Resolution. In harmonic analysis, the following-up of a dissonant note, e.g., an appoggiatura, by the corresponding consonant note [Ex. 1]; or of a dissonant

chord, e.g., a seventh-chord, by a consonant chord. If the seventh-chord is followed by the tonic, the resolution is regular [Ex. 2]; otherwise, irregular [Ex. 3]. The last of our examples illustrates the resolution into another dissonance, a very frequent and important means of obtaining "harmonic flow."

Resonance. The transmission of vibrations from one vibrating body to another. This acoustical phenomenon takes place only when the two bodies are capable of vibrations of the same frequency. If, e.g., two tuning forks of the same frequency (i.e., of the same pitch) are placed close together and if one of them is struck with a hammer, the other will immediately begin to vibrate and to emit the same sound, as can be shown by silencing the former. In the case of vibrating strings the possibilities of resonance are considerably larger, owing to the existence of harmonics. On the pianoforte, e.g., the string C sets up resonant vibrations in the strings c, g, c′, e′, etc., as can be shown by an experiment described under *Acoustics IV. The resonance in the numerous strings of the pianoforte is the cause of the change in timbre which results if, by means of the right pedal, the dampers are lifted from all the strings. See also *Sympathetic strings. Still more important in musical instruments are the so-called "general resonators," i.e., bodies which react with sounds of any frequency or pitch. To this type belong the sounding-board of the piano and the belly and back of the violin which co-vibrate with any sound produced on the strings and reinforce it by resonance. Some writers, however, do not consider this phenomenon as resonance but as "transmission by contact." In true resonance, then, transmission is effected only by the air. Resonance is one of the various factors which enter into the study of *architectural acoustics [see this and *Acoustics for literature]. Cf. M. Seiffert, in *ZMW* xi.

Resonanzsaiten [G.]. *Sympathetic strings.

Resonator. Acoustical implements, usually in the shape of a hollow vessel, which serve to reinforce sounds by resonance. Resonators in the form of a glass globe with a small opening were used by Helmholtz to prove the existence of the harmonics. Others, in the shape of hollow cylinders, are used with the Javanese xylophones and with the *marimba. The use of the term to denote globular flutes results from (or, at least, leads to) a confusion with Helmholtz' scientific implements.

Respond. Used in the meaning of *responsorium, or, occasionally, of *response.

Response. In the Anglican service, the replies of the choir to the prayers or statements of the priest, such as "Amen," or "And grant us thy salvation." They are not derived from the *responsoria of the Roman Church, but from the *toni versiculorum* (*AR*, 32*) and the *toni orationum* (*AR*, 49*), simple recitations for the psalm verses or the prayers with responding sentences or words. In Merbecke's *Booke of Common Praier Noted . . .* of 1549, the English texts are given with the plainsong recitations of their Latin models. Tallis, shortly after, wrote two harmonized versions of these, one in four parts with the melody in the treble, and one in five, with the plainsong melody in the tenor. These are known today as *Festal responses.* For weekdays and ordinary Sundays, the *Ferial responses* are used which are modern harmonizations having the plainsong in the soprano.

Responsorial. (1) In Gregorian chant, responsorial singing is the performance of a chant in alternation between a soloist and the chorus (**schola*). This method of performance is in opposition to that by two alternating half-choruses, known as *antiphonal singing. Although originally each method was restricted to special types of chant [see *Psalmody II, III], they are used today more or less indiscriminately according to existing conditions. Antiphonal performance (North Choir and South Choir) is the most normal. For responsorial psalmody see *Psalmody II. — (2) Older name for *Graduale* [see *Liturgical books] or, more specifically, for a collection of the solo sections of the chants of Mass.

Responsorium (responsory, respond). In the Roman service, name of various chants which grew out of the ancient form of *responsorial psalmody, consisting of an alternation of solo verse and choral refrain: R V R V . . . R [see *Psalmody II]. Originally the *Gradual (*responsorium graduale*) as well as the *Alleluia belonged to this class; the Gradual is even today called "Responsorium" in the liturgical books of the Dominicans. More specifically, the name applies to two special categories of chants, the melismatic *responsoria prolixa* and the much simpler *responsoria brevia* [regarding their form, see under *Psalmody II]. The former are sung at Matins or Nocturnes of high feasts, such as Christmas, Corpus Christi, Easter, etc., or, occasionally, introductory to the Mass (e.g., "Ingrediente Domino," on Palm Sunday). Being chants of Matins, etc., they are not included in the *Antiphonale*, but are found in the *Liber Usualis* [see *Liturgical books]. The responsoria brevia are sung during the daily hours and elsewhere. They are not indexed in the *Liber Usualis*.

Rest [F. *pause, silence*; G. *Pause*; It. *pausa*]. See *Notes.

Restatement. Same as recapitulation in *Sonata-form.

Resultant bass. Name of organ pipes in which the acoustical phenomenon of resultant (differential) tones is used for the production of the lowest registers. See *Combination tones.

Resultant tones. Same as *Combination tones.

Retardation. A rare term for *suspension, or, particularly, the suspension revolving upwards.

Retenant [F.]. Holding back (immediately).

Retrograde. The term denotes the backward reading of a melody, i.e., beginning with the last note and ending with the first one. Synonymous terms are: crab motion [L. *cancrizans*; G. *Krebsgang*], *al rovescio*, and *recte et retro*. Ex. 1 serves as an illustration.

Although this procedure (unlike the effect produced by *inversion) completely obscures, from the listener's point of view, the original melody, it has been not infrequently used by composers as a constructive device. The earliest instance is a 13th-century clausula "Nusmido" the tenor of which has the liturgical melody "Dominus" in retrograde motion [cf. F. Ludwig, *Repertorium* (1910), p. 80]. Retrograde motion is one of the most frequent tricks in the riddle canons of the 14th and 15th centuries in which it is indicated by inscriptions such as: "Ma fin est mon commencement" (Machaut), "Ubi α ibi ω" (with reference to the first and last letters of the Greek alphabet), "Cancriza" (walk like a crab), "Canit more Hebraeorum" (sing as the Hebrews read, i.e., from the right to the left), "Vade retro Satanas" (Retreat, Satan), by backward spelling such as "Ronet" or "Nusmido," etc. An example of outstanding ingenuity is Byrd's motet *Diliges Dominum* [cf. Hawkins, *History*, chapter 96]. Bach has used retrograde motion only in some of the canons of his *Musical Offering*, in which it is called for by the clefs placed at the end as well as at the beginning of the piece. Another example, humorous rather than scholarly,

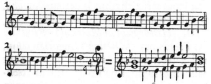

is the "Menuetto al rovescio" of Haydn's Sonata no. 4 for PF. and violin [cf. GD

iv, 456; see *Rovescio]. Beethoven revived crab motion as a device of fugal style in the final fugue of the Hammerklavier Sonata, op. 106. More recently, Schönberg has introduced retrograde motion as a basic feature of his *twelve-tone technique.

Retrograde inversion is the combination of retrograde motion and inversion. This can be achieved by turning the music sheet upside down, a possibility which has occasionally been used in jest canons showing one melody which is to be played by two players reading from the two opposite sides of the sheet (Mozart). Ex. 2 illustrates this musical joke.

Réunis [F.]. In orchestral music, unison (after *divisés). In organ music, coupled.

Revidiert [G.]. Revised.

Rf., rfz. Short for *rinforzando.

Rhapsody [Gr. *rhaptein*, to tear; *ode*, song]. A Greek term denoting a portion of an epic (e.g., the *Iliad*), as well as a free medley of such portions sung in succession. Musicians have adopted this name in different meanings, chiefly for free fantasies of a somewhat epic, heroic, or national character (F. Liszt, Rhapsodies Hongroises; Raff; Lalo; Dvořák; Bartók). In Brahms's Rhapsodien for PF. (op. 79 and op. 119, 4) the name would seem to refer to their ballade-like character, whereas, in his Rhapsodie in C, op. 53, for alto, male chorus, and orchestra, the title may have been chosen with regard to the fact that it is written to a portion only of Goethe's *Harzreise im Winter*. The free, "rhapsodic" element appears to be prominent in Gershwin's Rhapsody in Blue.

Rheingold. See *Ring des Nibelungen.

Rhumba. See *Rumba.

Rhythm. I. *General*. It would be a hopeless task to search for a definition of rhythm which would prove acceptable even to a small minority of musicians and writers on music. In view of this situation it is desirable to adopt, at least for the purpose of this article, a definition as inclusive as possible, i.e., the following: *Rhythm is everything pertaining to the temporal quality (duration) of the musical sound.* Thus rhythm forms the counterpart of *motion, i.e., everything pertaining to the pitch quality of the musical sound. Each melody can be separated into a rhythm skeleton and a motion skeleton, as is illustrated under *Melody.

There is, however, an additional element of musical rhythm which enters into the picture as a fundamental factor, i.e., accent. In fact, one and the same rhythm pattern has entirely different meanings depending upon where the accent or dynamic stress falls [see Example].

II. *Classification.* On the basis of a consideration of temporal values and of accent, the following categories of rhythm may be distinguished:

(a) Metrical rhythm, i.e., rhythm in which every time value is a multiple (or fraction) of a fixed unit of time, called beat, and in which the normal accent recurs in regular intervals, called measure. The basic scheme of time-values within each measure is called *meter. In modern notation, the measures are marked off one from another by bar-lines. See the above Example, a–d. This is, aside from exceptions mentioned below, *the* rhythm of European music. For more details see under III.

(b) Measured rhythm, i.e., a rhythm in which every time value is a multiple (or fraction) of a fixed unit of time, but

which lacks regularly recurrent accent. Since, in modern notation, accent is indicated by bar-lines (the understanding being that the first note after the bar-line receives an accent), this rhythm leads to a free alternation of different measures [see Example, e]. This type of rhythm is much more important in music history than is generally recognized. Gregorian chant, in its Solesmes rendering as well as in the interpretation of the "mensuralists" [see *Gregorian chant VI], belongs to this category (the common reference to Gregorian rhythm as being "free" is actually misleading; a certain freedom of performance, involving ritardandos and accelerandos, may be applied to any type of rhythm). So does modern *Russian and *Syrian chant as well as the humanistic *ode and the *vers mesuré of the 16th century, the *plainchant musical, and the French *recitative of the 17th century. Measured rhythm has gained considerable importance in the works of recent composers such as Stravinsky, Bartók, and Hindemith, in which it frequently is notated as *syncopation, i.e., as a temporary displacement of regular meter and accent.

(c) Free rhythm, i.e., the use of temporal values which have no common metrical unit (beat). The existence of such rhythm cannot be disputed, as appears from a study of (recorded) Oriental, Indian, etc., songs and certain ancient types of European folk music, e.g., Hungarian [see *Primitive music]. Obviously, such a rhythm cannot be expressed in our musical notation which is essentially based upon the idea of a common unit of time (quarter-note or eighth-note). For an interesting attempt to escape the rhythmic fetters of our notation, see *Prelude II (Louis Couperin). Free rhythm is also actually present whenever a striking deviation from strict rhythm is demanded, e.g., by rallentando, accelerando, rubato.

III. *History of (Metrical) Rhythm.* (a) Prehistory. Whether Gregorian chant had a free, oratoric rhythm or an essentially measured rhythm is still an open question. At any rate, it is now generally agreed upon (in contrast to earlier theories, e.g., by Riemann) that it was not in metrical rhythm, i.e., that it had no regularly recurrent accents. A different situation is encountered in the case of the earliest poetic texts, the *hymns. As early as the 4th century the *Ambrosian hymns had strictly metrical melodies, as we know from St. Augustine's testimony. The numerous office hymns of the 10th to the 12th century as well as the rhymed *sequences of, e.g., Adam de St. Victor (d. 1192) introduced strictly metrical poetry, e.g.: O sálutáris hóstiá, Quae cáeli pándis óstiúm, etc. This, however, was not immediately accompanied by the introduction of metrical rhythm, as the accompanying example shows, the rhythmic rendering of which leaves room for conjecture, but is certainly not "metrical" (as indicated below the staff).

(b) Modal Rhythm. It was not until shortly before 1200 that strict metrical rhythm became definitely established in the modal rhythm [see *Modes, rhythmic] of the organa, clausulae, etc., of the

School of Notre Dame. This epochal innovation must be credited to Magister Leoninus. While his organa (dupla) would seem to represent an intermediate type, including sections in modal rhythm alongside with others in the free rhythm of the earlier period (*St. Martial), his successor Perotinus established the exclusive use of modal, hence metrical, rhythm [see *Organum; also *Ars antiqua]. At the same time modal rhythm appears in the songs of the trouvères although its application to this repertory is conjectural to some extent [see *Plainsong notation]. The system of the six rhythmic modes, which developed shortly after 1200, is the first attempt towards a methodical treatment of rhythm. It prevailed throughout the rest of the century, being broadened later by the introduction of smaller values (two to six *semibreves*) in the place of one *brevis* (the quarter-note of ¾-meter).

(c) Rhythm of the Polyphonic Era,

1300–1600. Around 1250 the first attempts were made to introduce duple meter. An interesting remark in a contemporary treatise (Pseudo-Aristotle; cf. *CS* i, 271) not only refers to this daring innovation, but also indicates the strength of the opposition it met: "... If somebody were to ask whether a song can be formed by imperfect (i.e., duple) *longae* (i.e., half-notes) exclusively just as it can be formed by perfect *longae* (i.e., triple or dotted half-notes), the approved answer is no; since nobody can sing a succession of pure imperfect *longae*." In order to understand this position, it must be remembered that, to the 13th-century musician, triple meter was something "perfect," because it had "beginning," "middle," and "end"; duple meter, on the other hand, had "beginning" and "middle," but no "end," and was, therefore, "imperfect" in the true meaning of the word [cf. *ApNPM*, 292]. Progress did not stop, however, before such scholastic reasoning, and shortly after 1300 duple and triple meter were recognized as of equal right in all degrees, from the *maxima* to the *semiminima* or, as we would say, from the whole-note to the quarter-note, so that all meters, ²⁄₄, ³⁄₄, ⁶⁄₈, ⁹⁄₈, became available. This system, which is the basis of the *mensurations of *mensural notation, was established by Philippe de Vitry (*c.* 1320). Hand in hand with this freedom of meter went a rapid advance in the use of rhythmic subtleties and finesses, such as dotted rhythm (the 13th century had given preference to the iambic, i.e., inverted dotted rhythm, at least in the smaller values), *syncopation, and *polyrhythms Toward the end of the 14th century, polyphonic music achieved a complexity of rhythm which has never been paralleled in all history [see *Polyrhythm, Ex. 1]. These complexities largely disappeared in the *Burgundian School (Dufay) and in the subsequent *Flemish Schools (Ockeghem, Obrecht, Josquin). While the 15th century preferred ternary meter, the 16th adopted binary meter as its standard meter and, within this general frame, developed the technique of contrapuntal rhythms which is the very essence of true counterpoint [see *Texture].

(d) Classical Rhythm. With the abandoning of polyphonic music and the introduction of accompanied melody (1600; see *Baroque) the rhythmic life of music became greatly simplified. There developed what might be called the classical type of rhythm, i.e., a simple rhythm combined with strong accents in regular recurrence (meter) which pervade and regulate uniformly the entire fabric. This rhythm, which is most clearly realized in the dance, becomes the rhythmic basis of all music from c. 1600 to 1900, Bach being practically the only one who succeeded in imbuing it with contrapuntal life. Around 1700 there developed, particularly with Antonio Vivaldi (d. 1743), a precise and energetic rhythm in quick notes which is well known from many fugal themes of Handel and, especially, from the Brandenburg Concertos of Bach. After 1750, the development of music offers little interest from the rhythmic point of view until Brahms who, familiar with the music of earlier periods, made ample use of rather complicated cross-rhythms, syncopated formulae, unusual triplet formations, change of accent [particularly from $\frac{6}{4}$ to $\frac{3}{2}$; see *Hemiola], etc.

(e) The 20th Century. The 20th century has seen a tremendous rise of interest in rhythm as an essential factor of the musical life. Slavic dances with their lively rhythms, jazz with its complicated syncopations, the modern machine with its relentless motorism, the neo-classicism with its return to polyphonic styles, and the general tendency to explore to the limit whatever was neglected in the 19th century, all these factors contribute to giving rhythm a place in contemporary music such as it had not had for many centuries [see *New music]. For more details see *Jazz; *Syncopation; *Polyrhythm.

Related articles: Agogic; Beat; Measure; Mensuration; Meter; Modes, Rhythmic; Poetic meter; Polyrhythm; Proportions; Rubato; Tactus; Tempo; Tempus; Time signature; Syncopation.

Lit.: M. H. Glyn, *Rhythmic Conception of Music* (1907); E. Jacques-Dalcroze,

Rhythm, Music and Education (1921); M. Lussy, *Short Treatise on Musical Rhythm* (1909); Th. Taig, *Rhythm and Metre* (1930); C. F. A. Williams, *Rhythm of Modern Music* (1909); H. D. Cowell, *New Musical Resources* (1930); H. Riemann, *System der musikalischen Rhythmik und Metrik* (1903); G. Becking, *Der musikalische Rhythmus als Erkenntnisquelle* (1928); R. Dumesnil, *Le Rhythme musicale* (1921); C. Avogadro, *Teoria musica del ritmo* (1910); K. Wilson, in *ML* viii, no. 1; M. Lussy, in *VMW* i; H. Cowell, in *MM* v, no. 4.

Rhythmic modes. See *Modes, Rhythmic.

Ribattuta [It.]. See *Ornamentation I.

Ribeba, ribeca. Same as *rebec.

Ribible. Chaucerian spelling of *rebec.

Ribs. The sides of instruments of the violin family, connecting the back and the table.

Ricercar(e), ricercata [from It. *ricercare*, to search.] A term which, during the 16th and 17th centuries, was applied to various types of instrumental music for which it is difficult to find a common denominator since they differ widely in style and purpose. By far the most important of these is the "imitative ricercar" discussed below under I. The other connotations, however, should not be overlooked in order fully to understand the meaning of this rather puzzling term, which, perhaps, can be best understood as the equivalent of our term "study," either contrapuntal (I), or technical (II).

I. *The Imitative Ricercar.* This is the instrumental counterpart of the (vocal) motet of Josquin and his successors. Its chief characteristic is, therefore, the imitative treatment of several themes in succession, corresponding to the *points of imitation of the motet. Such pieces were written for *ensemble performance and for the organ. Since the former (called here "instrumental ricercar") differ in certain details of style and form from the latter, they are here treated separately.

(a) The Instrumental Ricercar. Instrumental pieces in the style of the motet occurred as early as with Isaac (*c.* 1450–1517), Hofhaimer (1459–1537), and other contemporary composers. Some of the former's "Instrumentalsätze" [e.g., *DTOe* 14.i, nos. 42, 51] and of the latter's *carmina* [cf. H. J. Moser, *Paul Hofhaimer, Werke*, p. 102] might well be considered the point of departure of the ricercar. It may, however, be noticed that some of Isaac's instrumental pieces approach the character of the *canzona rather than that of the ricercar [cf. *HAM*, no. 88]. The earliest ensemble pieces named ricercar (to be found in publications by Jacques Buus, 1547; Willaert, 1549, '59; Tiburtino da Tievoli, 1549; Annibale Padovano, 1556) can also be characterized as textless motets, although some of them exceed the confines of proper motet style owing to their considerable extension or to a somewhat scholarly treatment (augmentation, stretto), traits which frequently render these pieces rather unenjoyable, if not boring — an extreme example being a piece by Buus in which one single theme is made the basis of a monotonous contrapuntal texture of nearly 300 measures (Wasielewski, no. 18). Others however, particularly those by Willaert (new edition by H. Zenck), are exquisite examples of 16th-century chamber music [cf. *HAM*, no. 114; *SchGMB*, no. 56]. It must be noticed that all the above publications are printed in part books, like the vocal music of that time. As a matter of fact, their relationship to vocal practice is emphasized by inscriptions such as: "da cantare e suonare," inscriptions which doubtless indicate that these ricercares could be sung (i.e., in *vocalization) as well as played on viols, recorders, cornetts, etc. At any rate, it is a fundamental mistake to interpret and to present these pieces as organ music, as has been done in the case of Padovano (ed. by N. Pierront, 1934) [see *Ensemble].

A much-discussed problem is that of the distinction between the 16th-century ricercar and the contemporary *fantasia*. The theory, advanced by M. Seiffert (Seiffert-Weitzmann, *Geschichte der Kla-*

viermusik, 1899, p. 33), according to which the fantasia is mono-thematic, the ricercar poly-thematic, does not stand the test of thorough investigation. Probably no clear distinction can be made, since the term fantasia was used for a variety of types some of which approximate the much more clearly defined ricercar [see *Fantasia (5)].

(b) The Organ Ricercar. The history of the imitative ricercar for the organ begins with Girolamo Cavazzoni's *Intavolatura cioè recercari canzoni himni magnificati* of 1542/43. The four ricercars contained in this publication [cf. *HAM*, no. 116] are remarkable because they exhibit certain peculiarities of style and form which make the organ ricercar a form in its own right, not a mere "textless motet" as is largely the case with the instrumental ricercar. The most important difference is their sectional construction which forms a marked contrast to the numerous short and overlapping "points of imitation" of the motet. As a consequence, there are usually many fewer "themes" in an organ ricercar, but each of these is awarded fuller treatment in a lengthy section which frequently closes with coloratura-like runs in toccata style. There resulted around 1550 (Andrea Gabrieli) a type of organ ricercar which has remained relatively stable throughout the 200 years of its existence and which is characterized by the elaborate and learned treatment of one theme (monothematic ricercar) or several themes in succession, the themes being slow, and lacking rhythmic as well as melodic individuality (the fugues in C-sharp minor and E major from Bach's *Well-tempered Clavier* I and II may well serve as an example of 18th-century ricercar style). After 1600 the organ ricercar was cultivated chiefly in Germany (Froberger, Kerll, Buxtehude, J. Krieger [cf. *HAM*, no. 249b]), until Bach closed the development with his famous ricercar (acrostic title: R–egis I–ussu C–antio E–t R–eliqua A–rte C–anonica R–esoluta: Upon the King's Demand, the Theme and Additions Resolved in Canonic Style) from the *Musical Offering*, 1748.

II. *The Non-Imitative Ricercar*. The

earliest pieces bearing the name ricercar as well as numerous later examples from the 16th and 17th centuries show traits of style and form which set them clearly apart from the type just described. It is difficult to find a common denominator for all these pieces. Perhaps they might be described as being designed to exploit the idiomatic resources of the various instruments for which they were written, somewhat in the character of our etude.

(a) For the Lute. The numerous lute ricercars contained in Petrucci's *Intabolatura de lauto* i, ii, iv (1507/8; iii is lost) are the earliest pieces bearing this name. They show no connection with the motet, being short pieces in free lute style, and consisting chiefly of passages and chords, much like a prelude. Counterpoint is reduced to a bare minimum, and imitation is practically absent [cf. *HAM*, no. 98; *SchGMB*, no. 63b]. It must be noted, however, that a flat identification of these pieces with preludes (as suggested by various writers) is obviated by the fact that several pieces in Petrucci's book iv (Dalza) consist of a "*Tastar de corde" (touching of the strings) and a "Recercar dietro" (ricercar thereafter). Here the tastar evidently takes the place of prelude proper; in fact, the ricercar is, by comparison, a good deal more "constructed" [cf. *HAM*, no. 99]. In the later literature for the lute [Francesco da Milano (1547; cf. *SchGMB*, no. 115); Simon Gintzler (1547; cf. *DTOe* 18.ii); Valentin Bacfarc (1552); Vincenzo Galilei (*Il Fronimo*, 1563); see *Editions XIV, 4] the lute ricercar more and more approaches the style of the imitative ricercar, apparently owing to an increased ability of the lute players who by then regarded the polyphonic style as idiomatic to their instrument.

(b) For the Organ. The earliest organ pieces called ricercar are found in Marcantonio da Bologna's *Ricercari moteti canzoni* (1523). Like the lute pieces, they have no connection with the motet. They are lengthy pieces written in the chordal and scalic style of the toccata rather than in the contrapuntal style of the motet. In spite of their length they apparently served

somewhat in the function of a prelude, because each of the two ricercars is followed by a piece in the same key, a *Salve virgo* and an *O stella maris* — evidently the "motets" of the title.

(c) For Viols, etc. Theoretical writers such as Ganassi (*Regola Rubertina*, 1542; new ed. by M. Schneider, 1924) and Diego Ortiz (*Tratado de glosas*, 1553; new ed. by M. Schneider, 1913) use the term ricercar for instructive pieces designed to demonstrate the skillful playing of the viola da gamba. Ganassi's pieces are interesting for the extensive use of double-stops [cf. *HAM*, no. 119], while those by Ortiz serve to illustrate the art of variation and ornamentation. Clearly to the same category belong 17th-century ricercars for violoncello solo (without accompaniment), much in the character of a concert etude, by Giambattista degli Antoni and by Domenico Gabrielli (1689; cf. *SchGMB*, no. 228).

(d) For Voices. The instructive connotation is clearly indicated in an extensive repertory of 17th-century "ricercare a due voci" [Guami (1588); Metallo (1614, later editions till 1885); Gentile (1642); Piochi (1671)], i.e., of two-voice untexted compositions in imitative counterpoint. These pieces seem to be designed primarily for use by singers, since in several of the above publications they are referred to as vocal exercises — to be performed, of course, in *vocalization. Orlando di Lasso's "Cantiones sine textu" [cf. Cpl. Ed. i, 8ff] belong to the same category. In this connection it is interesting to note that, as late as 1774, Padre Martini in his *Esemplare ossia saggio* ... (p. 295) speaks of "the masters who compose ricercars and solfeggios." These pieces are particularly interesting as potential predecessors of Bach's two-voice *inventions.

Lit.: W. Wasielewski, *Geschichte der Instrumentalmusik im 16. Jahrhundert* (1878), Beilage (nos. 12–15 for lute, 17–18 for ensemble, 20, 21, 24 for organ); O. Kinkeldey, *Orgel und Klavier in der Musik des 16. Jahrhunderts* (1910; examples); G. Frotscher, *Geschichte des Orgelspiels* (1935), *passim*; H. Opienski, "Quel-

ques considerations sur l'origine des ricercares pour luth" (in *Editions XXIV,
B, 3/4); A. Einstein, "Vincenzo Galilei
e il duetto didattico" (*LRM* xi).

Ricochet [F.]. See *Bowing (e).

Riddle canon. See *Canon (1) II.

Ridotto [It.]. Reduced, i.e., arranged
(for PF., etc.).

Riduzione [It.]. Arrangement.

Rigaudon, rigadoon. A Provençal
dance of the 17th century [see *Dance
music III] used in the operatic ballets of
Campra, Rameau, and also adopted into
the optional group of the suite (Pachelbel,
Bach). Among the earliest extant exam-

ples is a Rigadoon by Purcell (1658–95;
see illustration). The rigaudon also occurs in the suites of modern composers
(Grieg, *From Holberg's Time*; Ravel, *Le
Tombeau de Couperin*). Cf. V. Alford,
in *MQ* xxx, no. 3.

Rigo [It.]. Staff.

Rigoletto. Opera in three acts by Giuseppe Verdi (1813–1901), text by F. M.
Piave (after Victor Hugo's drama *Le Roi
s'amuse*), produced 1851. The scene is
16th-century Italy where the handsome
and profligate *Duke* (Tenor), aided by
the humpbacked jester *Rigoletto* (Baritone), pursues the wives and daughters
of his courtiers who resolve to take vengeance on Rigoletto for his sneering in-
vectives (Act I). They succeed in ab-
ducting Rigoletto's daughter *Gilda* (Soprano) into the Duke's palace where he
easily wins her love (Act II). Thirsting
for revenge, Rigoletto hires the professional assassin *Sparafucile* (Bass) to murder the Duke who (Act III) comes to
Sparafucile's inn in order to amuse himself with the latter's sister *Maddalena*

(Mezzo-Soprano). Implored by his sister, Sparafucile agrees to murder, instead
of the Duke, the first person who will
enter the inn, and Gilda, overhearing this,
sacrifices herself. Rigoletto receives from
Sparafucile a sack which he believes to
contain the corpse of the Duke until finally, opening it, he discovers that of his
own daughter.

Its gruesome plot places *Rigoletto* in
the category of the "horror-opera" which
had a great vogue around 1850. However, the action is full of moments of genuinely dramatic tension, and the music,
in particular, elevates the opera far beyond
the level of, e.g., Meyerbeer's *Robert le
Diable*. Together with *Il Trovatore*
(1853) and *La Traviata* (1853) it represents the crowning-point of the Italian
opera with melodramatic plots, popular
type melodies, and concentration on "effective" vocal numbers.

Rilasciando [It.]. "Releasing," slowing.

Rimettendo [It.]. Resuming the old
tempo.

Rinforzando [It., reinforcing], abbrev.
rf, rfz, rinf. A sudden stress applied to a
single note or chord, practically synonymous with *sforzando. In early orchestral music (Stamitz) the term is used in
the meaning of a short but strong crescendo.

Ring des Nibelungen, Der ("The
Ring of the Nibelung"). Trilogy by
Richard Wagner, consisting actually of
four operas (hence also referred to as a
tetralogy); *Das Rheingold* ("The Rhine
Gold," 1853–54; designated by Wagner
as Vorspiel, i.e., prologue), *Die Walküre*
("The Valkyrie," 1854–56), *Siegfried*
(1856–71), and *Götterdämmerung* ("The
Dusk of the Gods," 1869–74). The libretto is by Wagner, after legends from
the Scandinavian Edda. First performance of the whole Ring in Bayreuth, 1876,
for the dedication of the Bayreuth Festspielhaus.

Without even attempting a summary
of the plots of these four operas, their col-

lective basic idea may be said to be the ancient Germanic conception of the world consisting of three realms struggling against each other: the light realm of the gods (Walhalla, with Wotan, his wife Fricka, the Fire God Loge); the realm of men (Earth, represented by Siegmund, Sieglinde, Siegfried, Hunding, Hagen, Gunther, Gutrune), and the dark realm of the Nibelungs, a race of dwarfs living beneath the earth (Alberich, Mime). In addition there are the Valkyries, Wotan's daughters (Brünnhilde and her sisters), the Giants (Fasolt and Fafner), and the Norns, goddesses who represent the eternal destiny to which even the gods are subjected. Two basic plots are merged in the libretto. The first is a legendary plot centering around the magic ring which, forged by Alberich, falls successively into the hands of Wotan, of Fafner (who guards it as a dragon), of Siegfried, who gives it to Brünnhilde as a sign of his love (in *Siegfried*) but, in the *Götterdämmerung*, takes it again away from her. The second is a human plot centering, in *Die Walküre*, around the incestuous love of Siegmund and Sieglinde and, in *Siegfried*, around the love of their son Siegfried and Brünnhilde, while, in the *Götterdämmerung*, Siegfried, blinded by a love potion, falls in love with Gutrune until immediately before his end, when he once more remembers Brünnhilde and calls her name with his last breath.

In order to forge together this gigantic plot Wagner relies here more than in any other of his operas upon the *leitmotif as a means of unification. Not only has each of the characters his own characteristic motive, but also basic ideas, such as "the curse," "the ring," "the sword," are thus represented. Moreover, in contradistinction to earlier operas such as *Tannhäuser* and *Lohengrin*, Wagner completely discards here the last remnants of the aria or the lied as an ingredient of operatic structure, replacing it by an "unending melody" which, purposely avoiding definite cadences and sectional construction, continues almost from the beginning to the end of each act in an un-

interrupted flow [see *Opera X; *Recitative; *Leitmotif].

Ripieno [It., filled up]. In 17th- and 18th-century orchestral music, particularly in the *concerti grossi, the term denotes the "reinforcing section" of the orchestra, comparable to the "rear section" of the violins, etc., in the modern orchestra. Therefore, "ripieni" indicates the full orchestra (*tutti, concerto grosso*), as distinguished from the soloists (*concertino*). The term "senza ripieni," however, is not identical with "orchestra silent," but calls for the leading members only of the orchestra, i.e., for a smaller ensemble used for the accompaniment of the soloists (concertino). *Ripienista* (Ripienist) is an orchestral player.

Riposato [It.]. With a feeling of repose.

Riprendere [It.]. To take up (the original tempo).

Ripresa [It.]. (1) Repeat or repetition (also of a performance, opera, etc.). — (2) Recapitulation (in sonata form). — (3) In the 14th-century *ballata (and in its descendant, the *frottola) the *refrain. — (4) In 16th-century dances, a repetition in varied form [cf. Th. Norlind, in *SIM* vii]. See also *Reprise.

Riservata [It.]. See *Musica reservata.

Risoluto [It.]. Resolute.

Risposta [It.]. Fugal answer.

Ris-qolo. See *Syrian Chant; also *Melody types.

Ristringendo [It.]. Quickening.

Risvegliato [It.]. "Wakened up," animated.

Ritardando [It.], abbr. rit., ritard. Gradually slackening in speed, also indicated by rallentando. Ritenuto properly indicates a different effect, i.e., immediate reduction of speed.

Ritenuto [It.]. See under *Ritardando.

Ritmo [It.]. Rhythm. Beethoven's indication "ritmo di tre (quattro) battute"

(Ninth Symphony, Scherzo), indicates groups of three (four) measures, the speed of the piece being so fast that there is one beat only to the measure.

Ritornelle, ritournelle [F.], **ritornello** [It.]. (1) In the 14th-century *madrigal, the last two lines of the stanza. This ritornello is not a refrain; as a matter of fact, the madrigal never has a refrain, in contradistinction to the *ballata and its later derivative, the *frottola, the refrain of which is called *ripresa.— (2) In early 17th-century operas [Monteverdi, *Orfeo* (1607)] an instrumental interlude preceding or following after an aria, scene, etc. Aside from the *sinfonias which serve a somewhat different purpose, the ritornelli are the only instrumental pieces in the early operas. Later there is frequently thematic relationship between the ritornello and the aria.— (3) In the German 17th-century strophic songs, called *aria (Erasmus Kindermann, cf. *DTB* 21/24; Adam Krieger, cf. *DdT* 19), an instrumental interlude of four to eight measures played after each stanza; thus, an instrumental *refrain [cf. *HAM*, no. 228; *SchGMB*, nos. 209a, 210].— (4) Modern writers occasionally use the term for the recurrent tutti portions of the concerto grosso or of the rondo. — (5) The ritournelle is a 17th-century dance in quick triple time, by far the most frequent dance type in the ballets of Lully. — (6) Ritornello also denotes a type of Italian popular poetry, consisting of three-line stanzas, the first and last in rhyme (similar to Dante's *terza rima*).

Riverso, rivolto [It.]. Terms denoting properly *inversion (of intervals, chords, or parts), but also used in the meaning of *retrograde motion. See *Rovescio.

Rivolto [It.]. Inversion (of intervals, chords, and subjects).

Rococo [from F. *rocaille*, shell]. In the Fine Arts and applied arts (interior decoration, cabinetmaking) a designation for the 18th-century outgrowth of the *Ba-

roque, characterized by an abundance of merely decorative scroll and shell work and by a general tendency towards elegance, hedonism, and frivolity. These traits are also patent in 18th-century music, in which Rococo designates the period of the "gallant style," which, with its emphasis on pleasantness and prettiness, forms a marked contrast to the impressive grandeur of the true Baroque style. The main period of Rococo may be said to extend from 1725 to 1775. It must be noted, however, that the movement started at a considerably earlier time in France, where François Couperin (1668–1733) represents the musical counterpart of the first Rococo painter, Watteau (1684–1721). From France it spread to Germany (Telemann, 1681–1767; Mattheson, 1681–1764) and Italy (Domenico Scarlatti, 1685–1757). The wholehearted adoption of the Rococo style resulted in a deterioration of artistic standards under musicians such as Balbastre, Daquin, Nichelmann, Grazioli, Sacchini, and many others who fill the volumes euphemistically called "The Old Masters of the Pianoforte." Although as early as 1740 Johann Stamitz, the founder of the *Mannheim School, established a novel style of a more vigorous nature, Rococo elements are still present in the works of C. P. E. Bach, Haydn, and Mozart. See *Gallant style; *Empfindsamer Stil. Cf. *LaMWC*, 530ff.

Rogue's March. A tune of English origin which was used when a soldier was expelled from the army. Cf. *GD* iv, 416, and iii, 316.

Rohrblatt [G., strip of cane]. The *reed of the clarinet, oboe, etc., instruments which are called *Rohrblattinstrumente*.

Rohrstimmen, Rohrwerk [G.]. The reed department of the organ.

Rolle [G.]. German 18th-century term (Türk) for the *turn.

Rollschweller [G.]. The crescendo pedal of the organ.

Romance [F.], Romanze [G.], Romanza [It.]. In French (Italian) *romance* (*romanza*) means a lyrical and usually sentimental song; *romances sans paroles*, i.e., songs without words. The German term is used chiefly for instrumental pieces of a particularly tender character (Mozart, Pianoforte Concerto D minor; Beethoven, *Romanzen*, op. 40, 50) or (probably with reference to the medieval origin of the word romance) for songs in which an adventure as if "of olden times" is told (e.g., Pedrillo's Romanza in Mozart's *Abduction from the Seraglio*). *Romancero* (the Spanish word for troubadour) is used as a designation for a collection ot songs, such as might have been sung by a romancero.

Roman chant [L. *cantus Romanus, cantilena Romana*]. That branch of Christian chant which developed in Rome. It is usually called *Gregorian chant, after Pope Gregory I (*c.* 540–604), who put it in final order. It was gradually adopted in almost all the Western places of Christian worship. See under *Chant.

Roman de Fauvel. See *Sources, no. 8.

Romanesca. A famous melody of the 16th century which appears first in Spanish lute-books [Narvaez (1538); Mudarra (1546); Valderrabano (1547)], under the name "O guardame las vacas" or "Romanesca O guardame las vacas" as a theme for continuous variations [see *Variations I] in the character of a cha-

conne or passacaglia. It was used by numerous later composers (Trabaci, 1603; Mayone, 1609; Frescobaldi, 1615) for the same purpose (*Partite sopra la Roma-*

nesca; cf. *HAM*, no. 192). The basic melody is the descending tetrachord (which, in the 17th century, was widely used as a *ground), this motive coming to a tonic close in the repetition: a–g–f–e–a–g–fe-d [see the accompanying example, by Valderrabano]. The Romanesca, therefore, belongs to the category of *soprano ostinato* [see *Ostinato] rather than *basso ostinato* (ground) as it is usually interpreted [cf. *MoML*, 702; *RiML*, 1539]. In 17th-century examples the structure is frequently obscured by the then customary barring in duple meter, as, e.g., in the Romanesca by Marini [see *Editions II, 7; cf. *HAM*, no. 199]. Cf. also *RiHM* ii.2, 88f (Rossi), and 353f (Kittel); †*RiMB*, no. 81 (Rossi). The Romanesca melody is also used in numerous *passamezzos.

Roman Festivals. See *Symphonic poem.

Romanian letters [G. *Romanus-buchstaben*]. A system of letters said to have been invented by a legendary 8th-century papal singer called Romanus. The system is explained by Notker Balbulus (*GS* i, 95) and others, and is used in various neumatic MSS from St. Gall, Metz, and Chartres. These letters were designed to be used in connection with the neumes in order to clarify certain details of pitch, rhythm, or performance not indicated by the neumes themselves. Among the numerous letters mentioned by Notker only a few gained practical significance, chiefly those which refer to temporal values: *c* (*celeriter*, quick), *t* (*tenere*, slow), and *m* (*mediocriter*). They play a central part in the present-day discussion of Gregorian rhythm [see *Gregorian chant VI]. Cf. *WoHN* i, 140; *ReMMA*, 140ff.

Roman music. For a full account of what little is known about the music of the ancient Romans see *ReMMA*, 51ff and *GéHM*, 114ff. See also *Hydraulis; *Lituus (1); *Tuba (2); *Buccina.

Roman School. The term is used to denote the tradition of *a cappella* church music which was established in Rome by Palestrina (1525–94) [see *Palestrina style] and was continued, with incorporation of the polychoral elements of the *Venetian style, by a long series of strongly conservative musicians, mostly in Rome, such as Giov. M. Nanini (1545–1607), Francesco Suriano (1549–1621), Ruggiero Giovanelli (c. 1550–1625), Felice Anerio (1560?–1614), Gregorio Allegri (1582–1652), Domenico Mazzochi (1592–1665), Orazio Benevoli (1605–72), Francesco Foggia (1605–88), Ercole Bernabei (1620–87), Tommaso Baj (1650–1714), Giuseppe Pitoni (1657–1743), Johann Fux (1660–1741), Antonio Lotti (1667–1740), Antonio Caldara (1670–1736), and others. These musicians rejected, in general, the current styles and forms of Baroque music (aria, recitative, oratorio, cantata, opera, sonata, toccata, etc.) and devoted themselves to the composition of strictly liturgical music: Masses, motets, requiems, psalms, etc. Based on the principles of vocal style of the Palestrina period, their technique tended to scholarly treatment (canonic contrivances) as well as to pompous display: Masses in 16, 24, and more voices are no rarity in what has aptly been called "colossal style," and some composers used up to eight choruses, which were placed all over the huge building of St. Peter's [cf. the 53-voice mass by Benevoli in DTOe 9.i]. For the continuation of this style throughout the 18th century, leading to Palestrina's well-known biographer Giuseppe Baini (1775–1844), cf. G. Fellerer, Der Palestrinastil im 18. Jahrhundert (1928); also O. Ursprung, in ZMW vii. See *A cappella; *Palestrina style.

Romanticism [F. romantisme; G. Romantik; It. romanticismo]. Designation for an important movement embracing the last three-quarters of the 19th century, and following after the Viennese *classical school. Foreshadowed in the late works — particularly the piano sonatas — of Beethoven (1770–1827), it found its first champions in Weber (1786–1826) and Schubert (1797–1828), both of whom died too young to carry the new ideas to their fullest realization. This was achieved by five composers born shortly after 1800, namely, Berlioz (1803–69), Mendelssohn (1809–47), Schumann (1810–56), Chopin (1810–49), Liszt (1811–80), and Wagner (1813–83). There followed Franck (1822–90), Bruckner (1824–96), Brahms (1833–97), and Tchaikovsky (1840–93), composers whose work represents a certain reaction against the full-fledged Romanticism of the earlier group, as is indicated by their return to the great forms of the classical symphony and sonata, as well as by their emphasis on absolute music. In fact, some of them are sometimes labeled as classicists (GD iv, 420) or as *neo-classicists. Among them Tchaikovsky would seem to be the most Romantic, Bruckner the least. The Romantic movement was continued with renewed emphasis by a great number of composers born between 1850 and 1880, who are sometimes called neo-romanticists or post-romanticists [G. Neuromantiker; see *Modern music]. It will suffice to characterize this group by a few names such as Edward Elgar (1857–1934), Edward MacDowell (1861–1908), Richard Strauss (b. 1864), Jean Sibelius (b. 1865), Max Reger (1873–1916), Gustav Holst (1874–1934).

The Romantic movement as well as the term Romantic originated in a German literary school of the late 18th century, formed by writers such as Wackenroder (1773–98), Ludwig Tieck (1773–1853), Novalis (1772–1801), who, in search for relief from the supposed or real prosiness and shallowness of their surroundings, went back to the literature and culture of the Middle Ages, with its valiant knights, gracious ladies, and pious monks, adopting the term romantisch as an expression of the spirit of the Romanesque [G. romanisch] era (11th, 12th centuries). From this movement, musicians took over the general feeling of "longing for something non-existent," a propensity for dream and vision, for the fanciful and emotional. In fact, music soon proved to be a much more fertile ground for these tendencies than literature or any of the other arts, owing, no doubt, to the intangible character of its material, i.e., sounds. E. T. Hoffmann, writer as well as musician, declared music to be *"the* Romantic art" and others added that "music is always Romantic."

Musical Romanticism may, therefore, be characterized as an art which emphasizes the subjective and the emotional possibilities of music and neglects the formal and structural point of view. This does not mean to imply that non-Romantic music lacks in emotional appeal. However, while a composition by Bach or Mozart stimulates the emotions through its musical qualities, Romanticism tries to cut short the road from the composer to the listener by eliminating what is believed to be mere "unnecessary formalism" in the expectation of increasing by that much the emotional volume. Not unlike a real short circuit, music has by this method immensely gained in "high tension," but, as might well be expected, at the expense of sustaining power. It is a common experience that the appeal of much truly Romantic music (Schumann, Chopin, Liszt) wears out rather quickly upon repeated listening, while the greatest works of the Romantic era are, no doubt, those which derive substance and balance from the classical principles of form and structure, such as the symphonies of Brahms and Bruckner. Shortly after 1900 there began a reaction against Romanticism which has continuously gained impetus. While Debussy's *impressionism, directed largely against the "Teutonic" element of Romantic music, did not achieve much more than to supplant this by a "Gallic" Romanticism, the movement known as *New Music was a radical negation of Romanticism in all its aspects, technical as well as ideal.

In spite of all its limitations, Romanticism has, of course, brought about results of the greatest importance. There is no need here to point to the many outstanding compositions of Romantic composers which still supply the greater half of the repertory of our pianists and conductors. Suffice it to say that, in the province of musical forms, Romanticism

has made two outstanding additions, the *character piece for piano, and the *symphonic poem for orchestra, both true images of the all-pervading subjectivism of Romantic composers. While the melodies of Romantic music are frequently of inferior quality (Bruckner being a noteworthy exception), the development of harmony and of orchestral colors has been greatly furthered. Finally, it may be noticed that many features of Romantic music can be understood as the result of a general tendency to what might be called blurring of border lines. Among these is the amalgamation of literature and music which shows itself in such general designations as "symphonic poem" or "tone poem," in the choice of literary subjects for program pieces (*Mazeppa, Till Eulenspiegel*), and, most clearly, in Wagner's conception of the opera as a *Gesamtkunstwerk*. Technical concomitants of this trend are found in the blurring of melodic, rhythmic, and harmonic contours, examples of which are frequent in many Romantic pieces.

In the first part of this article a remark was quoted to the effect that "all music is romantic." Although such a statement is either a falsification or a triviality, depending upon how seriously the term "Romantic" is taken, there have been earlier periods of music history which bear an unmistakable resemblance — in their general character — to 19th-century Romanticism and which, therefore, might well be termed "Romantic," in contrast to others which must be considered as "classical" periods [see *Classicism]. See also *Modern music.

Lit.: D. G. Mason, *The Romantic Composers* (1930); W. H. Hadow, *Studies in Modern Music*, 2 vols. (1894–95); *LaMWC*, 734ff; E. Istel, *Die Blütezeit der musikalischen Romantik in Deutschland* (1909); R. Dumesnil, *Musiciens romantiques* (1928); Cl. Laforêt, *La Vie musicale au temps romantique* (1929); E. Kurth, *Die romantische Harmonik und ihre Krise in Wagner's Tristan* (1920); P. Roeseling, *Die Grundhaltung romantischer Melodien* (Diss. Cologne 1928); H. Eckardt, *Die Musikauffassung der französischen Romantik* (Diss. Heidelberg 1932); E. J. Dent, "The Romantic Spirit in Music" (*PMA* lix); P. Láng, "Liszt and the Romantic Movement" (*MQ* xxii); A. Schering, "Kritik des romantischen Musikbegriffs" (*JMP* xliv); V. Basch, "Le Romantisme de Schumann" (*RM* v); A. Coeuroy, "Debussy et l'harmonie romantique" (*RM* ii); A. Farinelli, "Il romanticismo e la musica" (*RMI* xxxiii).

Romanus-buchstaben [G.]. See *Romanian letters.

Romanze, Romanzero. See *Romance.

Rondador. See *Panpipes.

Ronde [F.]. See *Notes and rests.

Rondeau. (1) An important form of medieval French music, frequent in the monophonic songs of the trouvères (13th century) as well as in the polyphonic music of the 14th and 15th centuries. The musical structure of the rondeau is always A B a A a b A B (capital letters indicating the *refrain), except in the earliest period

1. 4. 7. En ma dame ai mis mon cœur 2. 8. Et mon pen- ser
3. N'en par- ti- roi a nul fuer 6. ri-ant et clair
5. Si mont sorpris si vair oeil

when the shorter scheme, a A a b A B, i.e., without the initial refrain, prevailed. The accompanying example shows the complete rondeau.

Monophonic rondeaus exist in the Codex Florence, plut. 29.1 [cf. *AdHM* i, 183], and in the various *chansonniers of the trouvères. Polyphonic settings (accompanied solo songs) were composed by Adam de la Halle (1220–87), Machaut (1300–77), Baude Cordier (*c.* 1400), Dufay (1400–74), Binchois (1400–60), and still figure prominently in the collections of the late 15th century (*Kopenhagener Chansonnier*, ed. by K. Jeppesen; *Odhecaton; Petrucci's collections of *Frottole). Examples in *HAM*, nos. 17c, 19b, 36, 48, 68, 69, 71, 72. See *Rondellus (1).

Lit.: F. Gennrich, *Rondeaux, Virelais,*

Balladen; P. Aubry, "Refrains et rondeaux du XIIIe siècle" (*Riemann Festschrift*, 1909); *ReMMA*, 221ff, 322ff; *RiHM* ii.1, 57ff.

(2) An instrumental form of the 17th century, consisting of a reiterated *refrain and different "couplets": A B A C A D . . . A. Whether this form is an outgrowth of the medieval rondeau is, to say the least, doubtful; no connecting links exist between the old and the new form. This rondeau is the most frequent form of the French clavecinists (Chambonnières, Louis Couperin, d'Anglebert, François Couperin, Rameau), as well as of contemporary orchestral and operatic music (Lully). The refrain as well as each couplet is a well-marked strain of 8 or 16 measures. Each couplet usually emphasizes a different key, e.g., the first, tonic; the second, dominant; the third, relative minor; etc. [examples in *HAM*, no. 277]. In the late 18th century, the 17th-century rondeau developed into the *rondo form of the sonata.

Rondellus. Medieval Latin term designating (1) the monophonic *rondeau [cf. *HAM*, no. 17c] or (2) a canonic form similar to the *Round.

Rondeña. See *Fandango.

Rondo, rondo form, rondo-sonata form. A form frequently used in the classical sonatas, symphonies, concertos, for the final movement. It was developed from the *rondeau of the French clavecinists by cutting down the number of "couplets" to three, by using the same material for the first and the third couplet, and by elaborating the middle couplet in the style of the development section of the *sonata form, so that the following scheme results: R A R B R A' R. It appears that in this form the principle of the rondeau merges with that of the sonata form, inasmuch as A and A' correspond to exposition and recapitulation, B to the development. The recurrent section is usually called *rondo*, the intermediate sections, *episode* or *diversion*. The rondo form has frequently been used for the last movements of sonatas and concertos when a joyful and playful conclusion was desired. Numerous examples of rondo form exist in the final movements of Beethoven's earlier pianoforte sonatas (op. 2, no. 3; op. 13, etc.) and in practically all the concertos of the Viennese classics. Earlier less-developed examples occur in the sonatas of Johann Christian Bach (e.g., no. 6 of the new ed. by L. Landshoff), in the independent rondos of Ph. Em. Bach (e.g., *Clavier-Sonaten nebst einigen Rondos fürs Pianoforte,* 1780), and in the early works of Haydn (e.g., Sonata no. 24, op. 17, 3). See *Sonata B III (b).

The term rondo form is also used, particularly by English writers, for shorter alternation schemes than the true rondo, namely the ternary form A B A and the five-part form A B A B A (or A B A C A), these being called respectively "first" and "second" rondo form, in distinction from the "third rondo form" explained above. This terminology is objectionable mainly on historical grounds, as only the "third rondo form" developed from the rondeau. The "first rondo form" constitutes a form in its own right, the ternary form [see *Binary and ternary form], while the "second rondo form" represents a broadening thereof. See *Forms, Musical.

Lit.: W. Chrzanowski, *Das instrumentale Rondo und die Rondo-formen des 18 Jahrhunderts* (Diss. Leipzig 1911); F. Piersig, †*Das Rondo*; C. F. Abdy Williams, in *PMA* xvii; G. Clercx, "La Forme du rondo chez C. P. E. Bach" (*RDM,* no. 55).

Room acoustics. See *Architectural acoustics.

Root. The generating note of a triad or any of its inversions and modifications

(seventh-chord). For instance, in the following chords the root is always C:

A triad, seventh-chord, etc., is said to be in root position if the root is the lowest note; otherwise, it is in *inversion. See *Harmonic analysis IV.

Rosalia. A disparaging term denoting the schematic and unimaginative application of sequential treatment, such as occurs frequently in the works of second-class composers of the period 1750–1850. The word applies in particular to sequences which, owing to the exact repetition of the intervals, involve modulation of the key to the higher second, e.g., G–C–A–D–B–E, etc. The poor effect of

such passages is probably due to the facile symmetry of melody, harmony, and phrasing. The German equivalent of the term is *Schusterfleck* (cobbler's patch).

Rose. Ornamental scutcheon inserted in the circular soundhole of instruments such as lutes, guitars, and early harpsichords, frequently serving as the maker's trade mark. See *Soundholes.

Rosin, resin [F. *colophane,* G. *Kolophonium*]. A preparation made from turpentine which is applied to the hair of the violin bow in order to give it the necessary grip upon the strings.

Rota [L., wheel]. (1) Medieval name for a round, particularly the *Sumercanon, probably with reference to the "turnover" of the melody in the different parts [see also *Round]. — (2) Name for the *hurdy-gurdy which is operated by a wheel. — (3) See *Rotta.

Rote. See *Rotta.

Rotrouenge, rotruenge [possibly from L. *retroientia,* repetition]. A type of medieval French poetry and music which seems to have been current chiefly among the popular singers (jongleurs) of the 12th century. Seven poems, consisting of from three to seven stanzas, can be definitely identified as rotrouenges, on the basis of textual references such as

"Ma rotruenge finira . . . ." Only one of these, *Chanter m'estuet* (Raynaud, no. 636), is preserved with music and shows the following structure: a a a B c, B being an internal refrain "Oiés pour quoi." From this evidence it has been construed that the musical form of the rotrouenge was characterized by the repetition of the same melody for all the lines of the stanza, except for the two last, or the last, e.g.: a a a a B [cf. *AdHM*, 195]. The same structure occurs in the *laisse. Other pieces, probably belonging to the same category (though not originally referred to as rotrouenge), anticipate the refrain melody for the last line of the body, e.g.: a a a b B [cf. *HAM*, no. 19d] or a a b B [*ReMMA*, 220]. The latter type, which is relatively frequent, approaches the *ballade (a a b); in fact, various pieces which have been reproduced as rotrouenges are clearly ballades, e.g., "J'a nus hons pris" of Richard the Lion-hearted [cf. *HAM*, no. 19a]. Cf. F. Gennrich, *Die altfranzösische Rotrouenge* (1925): *id.*, "Das Formproblem des Minnesangs" (*Deutsche Vierteljahrsschrift für Literaturgeschichte* ix, 306).

Rotta, rotte, rota. A medieval instrument usually identified with a *lyre (in some books even with a lute!). According to recent studies, however, it was more likely a harp [cf. *SaHMI*, 262; also *GD* ii, 542 and iv, 450]. See also under *Crwth. — The name *rotta* also appears as a denomination for a dance (*Nachtanz) of the 14th century [cf. *SchGMB*, no. 28; also *BeMMR*, 155].

Roulade. A disparaging name for meaningless coloraturas, such as occur in operatic arias of the 18th and 19th centuries. Originally, the term denoted an ornament, consisting of rapid passing notes inserted between two principal melodic notes.

Round. Common name for a circle canon, i.e., a canon in which each singer returns from the conclusion of the melody to its beginning, repeating it *ad libitum*. The result of a three-voice round is indicated in the following scheme:

```
I    a  b  c ‖ a  b  c ‖
II      a  b ‖ : c  a  b :
III        a ‖ b  c  a ‖
```

It appears that the melody of a round always consists of sections of equal length which are so designed as to make good harmony with each other. Accompanying is an example (by M. Praetorius, 1571–1621) together with the resulting harmony. The earliest and most famous

Vi - va vi va la Musica

round is the *Sumer-canon of the 13th century which is designated as *rota* (wheel). The *rondellus of the 13th century was much the same thing, possibly lacking the initial imitation, i.e., with all the voices starting simultaneously (after the repeat sign); cf. *OH* i, 319. For a 14th-century example, notated in the form of a circle, cf. *RiHM* i.2, 352; also P. Aubry, *Les plus anciens monuments de la musique française* (1903; facsimile). Rounds enjoyed an extreme popularity in England, particularly in that variety known as *catch.

Rounded chanson. See *Barform II.

Roundelay. A 14th-century Anglicism for F. *rondelet*, i.e., *rondeau (1).

Rovescio [It.]. Retrograde motion or inversion. E.g., "Menuetto al rovescio" in Haydn's Sonata no. 4 for pianoforte and violin (identical with the Piano Sonata no. 26, B.a.H.) is to be played backwards, in retrograde motion [cf. *GD* iv, 456; see also *Retrograde], while that in Mozart's Serenade K.V. 388 uses imitation in the inversion.

Royal counterpoint. See under *Diaphonia.

Rubato [It., robbed]. The term denotes a certain elasticity and flexibility of tempo consisting of slight accelerandos and ritardandos which alternate according to the requirements of the musical expression. There has been a great deal of discussion regarding the nature of the tempo rubato, and writers have gone so far as to maintain that the term rubato is the most difficult to define of all musical terms. Actually, all the supposed difficulties and perplexities disappear if it is remembered that there exist two types of rubato, one which affects the melody only, and one which affects the whole musical texture.

The existence of the former type does not have to be demonstrated to anybody familiar with modern jazz. It is surprising, however, to see that it was also universally known in the second half of the 18th century, as appears from remarks in the writings of Tosi (1723), Quantz (1752), C. P. E. Bach (1753), Leopold Mozart (1756), and D. G. Türk (1789), all of whom maintain that the rubato applies only to the melody and should not affect the accompaniment. Chopin is also reported to have practiced and taught this type of rubato, which, naturally, is restricted to the limits of one or two measures, after which the accents of melody and harmony will again coincide.

The second type of rubato, i.e., that which affects the whole musical fabric, would hardly need any further comment were it not for the fact that several writers, studying the above-mentioned books, have applied the "give-and-take" principle of the 18th- (and 20th-) century type to the "full" rubato of Liszt or Chopin, maintaining that here also the accelerandos and ritardandos must compensate each other so that, after six or seven measures of free tempo, the player arrives in exactly the same moment as if he had played in rigid tempo. This misinterpretation has given rise to one of the most heated controversies in music, continuing to the present day. Once its source is understood it should be allowed to fall into oblivion rather than to be perpetuated as a "problem."

The preface to Frescobaldi's *Fiori musicali* (1630) contains interesting remarks regarding the rubato-performance of his toccatas [cf. *TaAM* iv, p. x]. The earliest examples of tempo change as a

means of expression occur in the lute fantasias of Luis Milan's *El Maestro* (1535), in which alternation of quick and slow is prescribed by *a priesa* and *a espazio* [cf. *ApNPM*, 190].

Lit.: Henry T. Finck, *Musical Progress* (1923), chapter vi; John B. McEwen, *Tempo Rubato or Time-variation in Musical Performance* (1928); J. A. Johnstone, *Rubato* (1931); B. Bruck, *Wandlungen des Begriffs tempo rubato* (Diss. Erlangen 1928); L. Kamienski, "Zum tempo rubato" (*AMW* i).

Rubeba, rubible. Same as *rebec, or possibly an instrument of the same design but of a larger size.

Rückpositif [G.]. In German organs of the 16th to the 18th century, a small structure located at the back of the organist, screening him from the nave.

Rücksichtslos; ohne Rücksicht [G.]. Without consideration. *Rücksichtsloser Kontrapunkt*, the modern "reckless" counterpoint, without regard to harmonic considerations.

Rueda. A Spanish (Castilian) round dance in fast quintuple time. See *Zortziko. Cf. H. Collet, "La Musique espagnole moderne" (*BSIM* iv).

Rührtrommel [G.]. The tenor drum; see *Percussion instruments B, 2.

Ruggiero. A melody used by numerous 17th-century composers as a *ground for arias or instrumental pieces; see Ex. 1. One may reasonably assume that originally the name *Ruggiero* referred not to

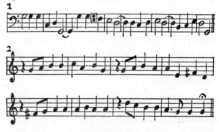

this rather unmelodic bass-line but to a popular song melody for which it served as a bass. As a matter of fact, in a collection of 17th-century *laude (*Corona di sacre canzoni o laude spirituali* . . . 1710), a melody called "Aria dell' Ortolano o Ruggieri" is given which fits perfectly with the famous bass melody [Ex. 2; cf. Alaleona, in *RMI* xvi, 26]. Probably the earliest extant Ruggiero composition is that by Diego Ortiz (1553). Later examples include variations by Gio. Macque (*c*. 1580; see *Editions XVII, 4), a "Sonata" by Salomone Rossi (1613; cf. *RiHM* ii.2, 94), a two-voice aria by Antonio Cifra (*Scherzi*, 1613), keyboard variations (*partite*) by Frescobaldi (1615; cf. *TaAM* iv), a "Canzon Ruggiero" by Tarquinio Merula (1637; cf. H. Riemann, *Old Chamber Music* III), and a virtuoso solo aria by Kaspar Kittel (*RiHM* ii.2, 349), the latter in the extended form of the *strophic bass.

According to A. Einstein, the name Ruggiero refers to a stanza "Ruggier qual sempre fui . . ." from Ariosto's *Orlando furioso*. At some time in the 17th century the term must have been used as a generic term for variations in general, since Johann Kindermann (1616–55) has a piece called "Ruggiero sopra Fillis" [cf. *DTB* 21/24, p. 94] which is a set of variations on the 17th-century tune "Fillis sass in einen Bötgen" [cf. *ApMZ* i; *ApNPM*, 36]. Cf. A. Einstein, in *SIM* xiii, and in *RMI* xli.

Ruhelos [G.]. Restless.

Ruhig [G.]. Quiet.

Ruins of Athens, The. See *Incidental music.

Rumanian music. The main representative of present-day Rumanian music is Georg Enescu (b. 1881), well known as a violin virtuoso and composer of orchestral and chamber music.

Lit.: *LavE* i.4, 2656ff; *AdHM* ii, 1182ff; article "Rumania" in P. A. Scholes, *The Oxford Companion to Music* (1938); B. Bartók, "Die Musikdialekte der Rumänen von Hunyad" (*ZMW* ii).

Rumba. A Cuban dance which, around 1930, became incorporated into jazz [see

*Jazz III]. It is of African character, with a strong emphasis on rhythm, complicated syncopations, and indefinite repetitions of an eight-measure theme, while melody and text are of subordinate importance. The dancing consists of movements of the body, rather than of the feet.

Rundkanzone [G.]. See *Barform II.

Russian bassoon. An obsolete instrument which has no connection with the bassoon, but is a brass instrument similar to the bass horn. See *Brass instruments V.

Russian horns. Hunting horns, straight or slightly bent in form, which were used from about 1750 to about 1825 in groups of from 30 to 60, each horn playing a single note only, i.e., without making use of the overblown tones. These unique orchestras, which have been compared to a living organ, were established by a Czech horn player, Marech, in 1751 and attained a high degree of perfection, as appears from the rather complicated pieces they played. Two examples are reproduced in *LavE* i.5, 2499.

Russian music. I. Prior to *c*. 1700 musical activity in Russia was, aside from folk music, restricted mainly to the Church. The adoption of the Christian faith by Prince Vladimir (988) and his son Jaroslav (1016–54) brought with it an influx of elements of Byzantine chant, probably through the intermediation of Bulgarian monks. There ensued, from the 12th century, a development which gradually led away from the Byzantine models and resulted in the establishment of the Russian chant, also known as *Znamenny chant, the classical period of which embraced the 13th and 14th centuries. Chants from this period are preserved in a number of liturgical MSS which have so far withstood all attempts at deciphering. They are written in neumatic symbols, called kriuki (= hooks), which are evidently derived from the Byzantine neumes but which developed into a complicated system comprising a great number of different signs (more than 80), most of which apparently denote melodic formulae. In certain MSS two rows of symbols appear, which have tentatively been interpreted as indicative of singing in two parts [see also *Kondakarion]. In the 16th century this notation was improved by Shaidurov, who added letters in red ink (hence the name "cinnabar letters") which fixed the intervallic meaning of the kriuki symbols, a development comparable to that leading from the staffless to the intervallic neumes of Gregorian chant [see *Neumes II]. Unfortunately, at the same time the Znamenny chant deteriorated, through the interpolation of meaningless vowels, syllables, and unauthentic coloraturas resulting from the license and rivalry of ambitious singers [see *Anenaiki]. A reform was carried out by Mesenetz, who in 1668 codified the chant and adopted for its fixation the five-line staff with distinctive notes ("Kiev signs"; cf. WoHN i, 120 f). At about the same time, polyphonic singing was officially adopted by the Russian church. All these reforms were rejected, however, by the raskolniki (Old Believers), among whom the old chant and the kriuki notation survive to this day. The majority of the Russian chants are based upon a system of eight echoi [see *Echos] each of which consists of melodic figures (called popievki) which form the basis of all the chants written in that particular echos [see *Melody types].

Peter the Great, the "civilizer" of Russia, was active in the introduction of Western operatic music. Under Catherine II (1762–96) Italian composers dominated in St. Petersburg, among them Manfredini, Galuppi, Traetta, and Paisiello, who reigned supreme over the imperial opera from 1776 to 1794. The earliest Russian composers, such as Maximus Beresovsky (1745–77), Dimitri Bortnianski (1751–1825), and J. Fomin (1761–1800), all studied with Italians and wrote operas in the Italian style, while Alexei Titov (1769–1827) imitated Mozart to some extent. His son Nikolai Titov (1800–75) and Alexander Varlamoff (1801–48) wrote a great number

of highly popular songs, and the latter is still remembered as the composer of "The Red Sarafan." Alexei Verstovsky (1799–1862) deserves mention as a forerunner of the first great Russian composer, Glinka.   W. A.

II. Michael Glinka (1804–57) is the acknowledged father of Russian music. The pre-Glinka composers were feeble imitators of the Italians or Germans. In Glinka's music, however, there is a new element of nationalism, revealed particularly in his patriotic opera A Life for the Czar (1836), produced in Soviet Russia under the title Ivan Susanin; his second opera, Russlan and Ludmilla (1842), has some Oriental elements. Alexandre Dargomizhsky (1813–69), a younger contemporary of Glinka, was the precursor of the modern period of national Russian music. His operas Russalka (1856) and The Stone Guest (1867) are remarkable for the realism of their music. Alexandre Serov (1820–71) wrote in the Western tradition. His opera Judith (1862) is conceived in the monumental style of Meyerbeer, but his later operas Rogneda (1865) and Evil Power (1870) are imbued with Russian song element. Anton Rubinstein (1829–94) was chiefly known as a great pianist, but his numerous operas (Dmitri Donskoy, Feramors, Nero, The Maccabees), written in the conventional style, were very popular. The opera Demon (1871) still survives in the Russian operatic repertoire.

Glinka, Dargomizhsky, Serov, and Rubinstein were operatic composers par excellence. The first great Russian symphonist was Tchaikovsky (1840–93). Of his six symphonies, the last three are widely known, although lately the Second and Third symphonies have been revived. The somberness of Tchaikovsky's personal philosophy is revealed in these symphonies, which are marked by a feeling of tragic helplessness and despair. Tchaikovsky's operas on Pushkin's subjects, Eugene Onegin (1879) and Pique Dame (1890), are extremely popular in Russia. The continuator of Tchaikovsky's tradition was Rachmaninov

(1873–1943). Close to Rachmaninov in musical philosophy stands Nicolas Medtner (b. 1880), who writes chiefly for piano and whose style veers toward neo-classicism. Anton Arensky (1861–1906) and Vasily Kalinnikov (1866–1901) also followed in the Tchaikovsky tradition.

Contemporaries of Tchaikovsky were Mily Balakirev (1837–1910), Nicolas Rimsky-Korsakov (1844–1908), Alexander Borodin (1833–87), and Modest Moussorgsky (1839–81). With a secondary composer, Cesar Cui (1835–1918), these names are known as the Mighty Five, so described by the music critic Vladimir Stassov (1824–1906), or, more broadly, as founders of the Russian National School. Moussorgsky, although inferior in technique to his colleagues, towers above them in sheer genius. His opera *Boris Godunov* (1872) exercised profound influence on new music everywhere. The unfinished opera *The Wedding* foreshadows the modern development of short opera. Balakirev wrote two symphonies and a symphonic poem, *Tamara*, the latter in an orientalistic style. Borodin is the author of two symphonies and an opera, *Prince Igor*. The "Polovtzian Dances" from *Prince Igor* exemplify Russian orientalism at its best. Rimsky-Korsakov, the most prolific of the Five, composed nine operas. The last three, *Kastshei the Immortal* (1902), *The Invisible Town of Kitezh* (1907), and *The Golden Cockerel* (1908), constitute an introduction to the modern period of Russian music. His symphonic poem *Scheherezade* (1888) is an outstanding example of modern orchestral colorism. Cesar Cui is a romantic composer, whose association with the Russian National School is a historic accident. His opera *William Ratcliff* takes for its subject an early drama by Heine from Scottish legends.

The continuator of the Russian national tradition in the symphonic field was Alexandre Glasunov (1865–1936). He wrote eight symphonies but no operas. Ipolitov-Ivanov (1859–1935), Reinhold Glière (b. 1875), Alexandre Gretchaninov (b. 1864), Nicolas Tcherepnin (b. 1873),

and Sergei Vasilenko (b. 1872) have written symphonic and operatic music in the manner of the Russian National School.

Alexandre Scriabin (1872–1915), a composer-mystic, is an isolated phenomenon in Russian music. His musical style stems from Wagner and Chopin, and in his symphonic and piano works he reaches the threshold of atonality. His symphonic poem *Prometheus* (1910) is based on a six-tone chord, derived from the upper harmonics of the natural scale.

The greatest of Russian modernists, Igor Stravinsky (b. 1882), is the legitimate successor of the Rimsky-Korsakov line, his symphonic poem *The Firebird* (1910) being closely related to Rimsky-Korsakov's last period. Stravinsky's *Le Sacre du Printemps* (1913) has exercised profound influence on the development of modern music. Stravinsky abandoned the Russian style in favor of *neo-classicism in 1924. He lived in Western Europe from 1914 to 1939, and since then has settled in America. Serge Prokofiev (b. 1891) has, since 1933, associated himself with Soviet music. His music is optimistic, with a considerable admixture of sarcasm and irony. He has written ten operas (*Love for Three Oranges*, 1921; *War and Peace*, 1941), symphonies, several concertos for piano and violin, seven piano sonatas, etc. His symphonic fairy tale *Peter and the Wolf* (1936) has been extremely successful. Nicolai Miaskovsky (b. 1881) belongs to the Moscow school of neo-romantic composers; he is the author of twenty-four symphonies.

Of the post-revolutionary composers, the greatest star is unquestionably Dmitri Shostakovitch (b. 1906). His operas (*The Nose*, 1930; *Lady Macbeth of the District of Mzensk*, 1934), were severely criticized in Russia, but his symphonies received great acclaim. The Seventh Symphony, written in Leningrad under siege in 1941, is regarded as the greatest single work issued from the present war, and its performances in Russia, England, and America were sensational events. The Eighth Symphony, composed in 1943, has aroused as much enthusiasm as the Seventh, a fact which demonstrates the powerful hold which Shostakovitch exercises in the musical world. Among other Soviet composers to be mentioned are Ivan Dzerzhinsky (1909), Alexandre Mossolov (1900), Aram Khatchaturian (1903), Tikhon Khrennikov (1913), Leo Knipper (1898), Alexandre Krein (1883), his brother Gregory Krein (1880), Julian Krein (1913), son of Gregory, Michael Gniessin (1883), Vissarion Shebalin (1902), Michael Starokadomsky (1901), and Dmitri Kabalevsky (1904).

Lit.: G. Abraham, *Studies in Russian Music* (1935); *id., On Russian Music* (1939); M. D. Calvocoressi and G. Abraham, *Masters of Russian Music* (1936); M. Montague-Nathan, *A History of Russian Music* (1914); *id., Contemporary Russian Composers* (1917); R. Newmarch, *The Russian Opera* (1914); L. Sabaneyeff, *Modern Russian Composers* (1927); *id., Geschichte der russischen Musik* (1926); *LavE* i.5, 2486ff, ii.1, 159ff (modern), ii.4, 2355ff (church music), ii.5, 2745ff (folk music); P. Panoff, *Die altslavische Volks- und Kirchenmusik* (*BüHM*, 1929); G. Abraham, "The Elements of R. Music" (*ML* ix, no. 1); *id.,* "The Foundation Stone of R. Music" (*ML* xviii, no. 1); R. Newmarch, "The Development of Russian Opera" (*PMA* xxviii–xxxi); N. Findeisen, "The Earliest Russian Operas" (*MQ* xix); *id.,* in *SIM* ii; E. Oliphant, "A Survey of Russian Song" (*MQ* xii); A. Lourie, "The Russian School" (*MQ* xviii); L. Sabaneev, "Music and Musicians in the U.S.S.R." (*ML* xv, no. 1); W. J. Birbeck, "Some Notes on Russian Ecclesiastical Music" (*PMA* xvii); V. Belaiev, "The Folk Music of Georgia" (*MQ* xix); P. Panoff, "Die Volksmusik der Grossrussen" (*DM* xxi, no. 5). For detailed bibliography cf. Orlov's *Musicalnaya Literatura* (Leningrad, 1935).   N. S.

Russian Quartets. Beethoven's string quartets op. 59, nos. 1–3, composed in 1807, also known as "Rasoumofsky Quartets" because they were commissioned by the Russian Count Rasoumofsky. In nos. 1 and 2 Beethoven has used a "Thème Russe" which he took from a collection of 150 songs published by Ivan Pratch in 1790. — The name is also applied, for an unknown reason, to Haydn's quartets nos. 37–42, following after the *Sonnenquartette*, nos. 31–36.

Rute [G., rod]. A sort of birch brush used by R. Strauss and others to obtain a peculiar effect on the bass drum.

S

S. (1) Short for *segno, *sinistra, *subito. — (2) In liturgical books, short for *schola, i.e., choir. — (3) In Riemann's system of harmonic analysis, short for subdominant. — (4) In 16th-century *part books, short for *superius* (i.e., soprano).

Sacbut, sackbut, sagbut, saqueboute. The medieval type of the trombone. See *Trombone II.

Saccadé [F.]. "Jerked," sharply accented.

Sackgeige [G., pocket fiddle]. The *kit.

Sackpfeife [G.]. Bagpipe.

Sacre du Printemps. See under *Ballet III.

Saeta, saeto [Sp., arrow]. A southern Spanish (Andalusian) type of song, sung in improvised coloraturas to texts such as "Lord, pity us" by young girls during the procession on Good Friday. The girls remain unseen in their rooms. The name of this type of song obviously refers to its deeply touching effect upon the hearers. Cf. F. Pedrell, †*Cancionero musical popolare español* i, 119ff.

Sagbut. See *Sacbut.

Sainete. A Spanish type of comic opera, approaching the character of low comedy, and portraying scenes from everyday life. Among the composers of sainetes were Antonio Soler (1729–83), Blas Laserna (1751–1816), and others.

St. Anne's Fugue. Popular designation of Bach's great organ fugue in E-flat major (ed. Peters, vol. iii), on account of the similarity of its theme to the beginning of a 17th-century hymn known as St. Anne's tune [cf. *GD* iv, 499]. The fugue appears at the end of Bach's *Clavierübung*, part III (1739) and is

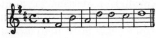

usually played together with the magnificent prelude in the same key which opens the publication. The statement that Bach "used the St. Anne's tune" is, needless to say, misleading, as is also the contention that the tune is "based upon a motet by Palestrina." Subjects of such a simple and natural design are bound to recur in different works, without any intention on the part of the composer. See *Double fugue.

St. Martial, School of. An important music school of the 10th to the 12th century domiciled at the abbey of St. Martial in Limoges (southern France), also known as the School of Limoges. Aside from a remarkable activity in the field of *sequences and *tropes (chiefly 10th and 11th centuries), its main importance lies in its contribution to the development of *organum, in which the polyphonic School of St. Martial (*c.* 1100–50) immediately precedes that of *Notre Dame. Cf. *ReMMA, passim*; *ApNPM*, 209ff; *AdHM*, 177ff.

Saite [G.]. String. *Saitenchor*, *course of strings. *Saiteninstrument*, stringed instrument.

Salendro. See *Javanese music.

Salicus. See *Neumes I.

Salmo [It.]. Psalm, psalm composition.

Salomon Symphonies. See *London Symphonies.

Salpinx. See *Brass instruments V (a).

Saltarello [from It. *saltare*, to jump]. An Italian 16th-century dance in quick triple meter which usually appears as a *Nachtanz of the *passamezzo (*passamezzo con il suo saltarello*) or of other dances in even meter. Sometimes both dances use the same melody in different rhythm [cf. *SchGMB*, 95, 119; W. Merian, *Der Tanz in den deutschen Tabulaturbüchern*, p. 92; see also *Proportz]. The saltarello continued as a popular dance throughout the 19th century, but came to be executed much more rapidly and violently than the older dance. It is from this later type that Mendelssohn borrowed the idea for the last movement of his Italian Symphony (op. 90). Dances named saltarello occur as early as the 14th century; these are even slower than those of the 16th century [cf. *SchGMB*, no. 28].

Saltato, saltando [It.]. Same as *Sautillé.

Saltbox. A popular noise-producing instrument in the form of a box with a revolving mechanism. It was used by the English clowns of the 18th century.

Salterio [It.]. *Psaltery. *Salterio tedesco* is the *dulcimer.

Salve regina. One of the four antiphons B.V.M. [see *Antiphon (2)], probably written and composed by Hermannus Contractus (1013–54). The chant, which really is a hymn with a free poetic text sung to a Dorian melody of great beauty [*LU*, 276], became quickly famous and popular, particularly among the religious societies of the 14th to the 16th century which had as their main object the worship of the Virgin (Salve Societies). Polyphonic compositions of the text, with or without utilization of the plainsong melody, are fairly numerous (e.g., Dunstable, cf. *DTOe* 27.i, pp. 39ff; Ockeghem, cf. *BeMMR*, 238; Obrecht; Josquin). Of particular interest are the compositions for organ (Hofhaimer, Kotter, Schlick; cf. H. J. Moser, *Frühmeister des deutschen Orgelspiels*) which usually include only the odd-numbered verses (Salve regina; Ad te clamamus; Eia ergo; O clemens; O dulcis), the others (Vita dulcedo; Ad te suspiramus; Et Jesum; O pia) being sung *alternatim* in plainsong. Cf. *HAM*, nos. 100, 139.

Lit.: J. Maier, *Beiträge zur Geschichte der Marienantiphon Salve Regina* (1934); K. Dèzes, in *ZMW* x; P. Runge, in *Liliencron Festschrift* (1910).

Samba. A Brazilian dance in square time, derived from the *maxixe, frequently used for the Carnival festivities. It appeared in New York in 1938. There also exists a rural type which is faster and more violent.

Sambuca. An ancient Greek instrument, harp or psaltery, probably of Phoenician or Hebrew origin. The name was also used for a small flute made from the elder bush [L. *sambucus*] and in the Middle Ages for the *hurdy-gurdy (*sambuca rotata; sambuca* probably corrupted from *symphonia).

Sambute [F.]. *Sacbut.

Samisen. See *Japanese music V; *Guitar family.

Sampogna. Same as *zampogna.

Sanctus. The fourth of the five items of the Ordinary of the *Mass. In the 15th century it was frequently composed as a single movement [cf., e.g., the numerous examples in the *Old Hall MS*, new ed. by Ramsbotham, vol. 3].

Sanft [G.]. Soft, gentle.

Sanglot [F., sigh]. French 18th-century name for an appoggiatura or passing tone sung to plaintive words such as "Oh" or "Hélas."

Sangsaite [G.]. See *Cantino.

Saqueboute [F.]. See *Sacbut.

Saraband [F., G. *Sarabande*]. A 17th- and 18th-century dance [see *Dance

music III] in slow triple meter and of dignified expression, usually without upbeat, frequently with an accent or prolonged tone on the second beat and with feminine endings of the phrases.

The saraband probably came from the Orient (Persia) and appeared in Spain in the early part of the 16th century. Originally it must have been a wild and even lascivious love dance, since it is described and severely attacked as such by various writers, among them Cervantes. Particularly characteristic is the following passage from a *Tratado contra los Juegos Publicos* (Treatise against Public Amusements) of Mariana (1536–1623): ". . . a dance and song, so lascivious in its words, so ugly in its movements, that it is enough to inflame even very honest people." The dance was actually suppressed in Spain, *c.* 1590, by Philip II, but continued to exist under the name *zarabanda* throughout the 17th and 18th centuries as a quick dance with a characteristic alternation of ¾ and ⅜ meter. [Cf. *LavE* i.4, 2098, 2247.] As late as 1676, Thomas Mace, in his *Music's Monument*, says that "Sarabandes are of the shortest triple time, but are more toyish, and lighter than corantes."

About 1600 the saraband made its appearance in France and England. Orlando Gibbons wrote a "Sarabrande" which is the earliest preserved example and which, being quicker in speed and gayer in character than the classical type,

may be considered as representing the transition from the original character of the dance to its later dignity (similar examples appear in Praetorius, *Terpsi-*

chore, 1612). Examples of the slower type occur in Chambonnières (*c.* 1650). At the same time (Froberger) it was introduced into the *suite as the third of its four standard dances. The accompanying example [from Handel's Suite no. 7] illustrates the normal type of the saraband, whereas the saraband from Bach's sixth Partita shows it in its final stage of artistic idealization.

Sardana. The national dance of Catalonia (northeastern Spain), usually in quick ⁶⁄₈-meter and danced in a circle to the accompaniment of the *pipe and tabor. Cf. *LavE* i.4, 2379.

Sarinda. See *Violin II.

Sarrusophone. See *Oboe family II, F.

Sarum use. The practice of the cathedral of Salisbury [L. *Sarum*] in England which differed in details from that of the Roman liturgy. It prevailed during the later Middle Ages throughout a great part of England, until it was abolished by decree in 1547. Two plainsong MSS, dating from the 13th century, have been published in facsimile by W. H. Frere under the titles *Graduale Sarisburiense* (1894) and *Antiphonale Sarisburiense* (1901–25). Cf. his *The Sarum Gradual and the Gregorian Antiphonale Missarum* (1896).

Sassofono [It.]. Saxophone.

Satire in music. Satire, irony, and caricature are by no means as foreign to music as one might think at first. While fifty years ago writers of philosophical and aesthetic dissertations were able to "prove" that such things had no place in musical expression, the development of the past 30 years has brought forth abundant evidence of the contrary. In fact, satirizing is one of the most characteristic features of 20th-century music, and no account of the revolutionary movement known as *New Music would be complete without pointing to the important place which satire, irony, and caricature played in the efforts to overthrow the tradition of the 19th century. French composers particularly have used ridicule as

a weapon, notably Erik Satie in the numerous whimsical and barren sketches in which he seems to deride the *impressionism of Debussy. The new harmonic style with its unlimited exploitation of discords naturally offered unprecedented opportunities for caricaturing effects. Examples are Debussy's *Golliwogg's Cakewalk* with its allusion to the Tristan theme; Stravinsky's *Petrouchka* with the caricaturing Valse; Casella's *Puppazetti;* Goossens' *Kaleidoscope;* Shostakovitch's *Polka* (from *The Golden Age*) which satirizes the Geneva disarmament conference.

Perhaps the first example of musical caricature (usually acomplished by deliberately "wrong" harmonies, rhythm, etc.) is Hans Neusiedler's *Judentanz* of 1536 [cf. *ApMZ* i, 10]. In the late 16th century parallel fifths were deliberately used in the *villanella, as a means of enhancing the parodying nature of the text. Aside from the innumerable examples of operatic scenes the comical nature of which usually lies mainly in the text and in the action, further examples of truly musical satire exist in Mozart's charming *Ein musikalischer Spass* (1787, K.V. 522), with its good-natured mockery of peasant music, in the Beckmesser Scene of Wagner's *Meistersinger,* and in Berlioz' *Symphonie phantastique* in which the distorted presentation of the *Dies irae portrays hellish despair and fiendish laughter. One of the first modern composers to write satirical music for its own sake was Enrico Bossi (*Pezzi satirici*).

Lit.: H. F. Gilbert, "Humor in Music" (*MQ* xii); R. D. Chennevière, "Eric Satie and the Music of Irony" (*MQ* 1919); A. Einstein, "Die Parodie in der Villanella" (*ZMW* ii).

Satz [G.]. (1) Movement (of a sonata, symphony, etc.); e.g., *erster Satz,* first movement. However, *Hauptsatz, Seitensatz (Nebensatz)* denote the first and second theme within a movement. — (2) Style, manner of writing; e.g., *strenger (freier) Satz,* strict (free) style.

Saudade. Portuguese term for longing, nostalgia; hence, denomination for Brazilian dances of such character (Villa-Lobos, Milhaud).

Sautillé [F.]. See *Bowing (d).

Savart. The unit of a system of logarithmic pitch-determination introduced by the Frenchman Savart (1791–1841). It is based upon the facts that the logarithm of 2 (frequency of the octave) is 0.30103 and that, therefore, the logarithmic frequencies of all the intervals lie between 0 and 0.30103. For greater convenience all figures are multiplied by 1000, so that the octave measures 301 Savart. This system is very convenient, particularly since for all practical purposes the figure 301 can be replaced by 300, so that each semitone equals 25 Savart. It was later supplanted by Ellis' system of *Cents, in which all the figures are four times as large (exact relationship: 1 Savart = 3.99 Cents). See *Intervals, Calculation of, V.

Saxhorn. See *Brass instruments III (f).

Saxophone. A family of hybrid instruments invented by Adolphe Sax of Brussels in 1840. They are played by a single beating reed, as are the clarinets, but are conical in bore, as are the oboes. The body of the instrument is of metal, as in the brass instruments. The saxophones are especially valuable in bands, in which they blend well either with the wood winds or the brass. The complete family numbers six instruments, alternately in E-flat and B-flat, as follows: (1) Sopranino in E-flat; (2) Soprano in B-flat; (3) Alto in E-flat; (4) Tenor in B-flat; (5) Baritone in E-flat; (6) Bass in B-flat. All are treated as transposing instruments, written in the treble clef, and with the written chromatic compass shown.

matic compass shown. The Sopranino sounds a minor third higher than written, the Soprano a major second lower than written, etc. Nos. 1 and 6 are rare,

and nos. 3 to 5 are most commonly seen. Illustration on p. 152.

The sound of the saxophone is extremely variable. Being intermediate between the timbres of wood and brass, it passes from the softness of the flute over the broad, mellow tone of the cello to the metallic strength of the cornet. These properties together with its great flexibility have given it a prominent place in jazz bands. The principal member of the family is the alto saxophone (also made in F), which has been employed for solos by many French composers, first by Kastner in *Le Dernier Roi de Juda* (1844), subsequently by Délibes, Thomas, Saint-Saëns, Bizet, and d'Indy. Richard Strauss introduced a quartet of saxophones in his *Domestic Symphony*, and Hindemith used the saxophone in his opera *Cardillac*.

Lit.: J. Kool, *Das Saxophon* (1931); E. Rosenkaimer, "Das Saxophon in seinen Frühzeiten" (*DM* xx.12).   W. D.

Sax(o)tromba. A modification of the *saxhorn, with a less conical bore, approaching that of the trumpet (tromba). Now little used.

Saxtuba. The bass of the *saxhorns.

Scala, La. See *Opera houses VII.

Scala enigmatica. An arbitrary scale, c–db–e–f#–g#–a#–b–c', used by Verdi in his *Ave Maria* (1898).

Scale [F. *gamme*; G. *Tonleiter*; It. *scala*]. I. The term, which properly means "ladder," denotes the tonal material of music arranged according to rising pitches. Since the tonal material varies greatly in the different phases of music history as well as in different countries (particularly, *Oriental), there exist a great number of scales. The basic scale of European music is the *diatonic scale*, comprising the tones c d e f g a b c' (plus octave extensions), i.e., the tones given by the white keys of the pianoforte. It consists of whole-tones (t) and semitones (s) in the following arrangement: t t s t t s. This scale is usually referred to as *major scale* (properly C-major scale; see III) as distinguished from the *minor scale* in which the arrangement of intervals is: t s t t t t s, e.g.: c d eb f g a b c' (for more details see *Major and minor scale). Both the major and minor scales occur also in "transposition," i.e., starting with another tone than c, e.g.: d e f# g a b c'# d', or d e f g a b c'# d'. Thus there are 12 major scales and 12 minor scales, one in each *key. All the tones found in any of the above scales can be combined in one scale, the *chromatic scale*, which consists of twelve semitones. This all-inclusive scale, also known as *duodecuple scale, forms the tonal foundation of modern music, the other scales now being considered as selections thereof [see *Gapped scales]. Naturally, numerous other selections are possible and have occasionally been employed, particularly the *whole-tone scale*, the so-called *gypsy-scale*, and the *pentatonic scale*. The accompanying table illustrates the details of construction:

Chromatic:	c	c#	d	d#	e	f	f#	g	g#	a	a#	b	c'
Major:	c		d		e f		g		a		b	c'
Minor, melodic:	c		d eb	f		g		a		b	c'
descending:	c		d eb	f		g ab		bb		c'
Minor, harmonic:	c		d eb	f		g ab			b	c'
Whole-tone:	c		d		e	f#		g#		a#		c'
Gypsy:	c		d eb		f# g	ab			b	c'
Pentatonic:	c		d		f	g		a			c'

Recently attempts have been made to broaden the tonal material of music by the introduction of *quarter-tones, resulting in a quarter-tone scale of 24 tones to the octave.

II. All the scales explained above can be derived from the diatonic scale which was already used by the ancient Greeks. Upon closer examination, however, it appears that this scale underwent minute changes owing to the different systems of intonation (tuning) used in the various phases of music history from about 500 B.C. to A.D. 1750. Thus, the Greek diatonic scale was based on the*Pythagorean system, while in the Middle Ages certain intervals of *just intonation crept in [particularly, the *third], a fact which, in turn, necessitated the adoption of various systems of *temperament the last and final of which was that of equal temperament, established in the time of Bach.

For more details reference may be had to the separate entries. Tables showing the difference between these scales are found under *Temperament and *Intervals (p. 362). Still greater deviations are met with in the numerous Oriental scales, such as the *Javanese *salendro* and *pelog*, the *Hindu *sa-grama*, the *Arabian 17-tone scale, the *Japanese scales, etc.

III. In the preceding explanations the term scale was used in the sense as explained in the initial definition, i.e., as an ordered arrangement of pitch material. Usually, however, another consideration enters into the conception of "scale," namely *center tone* (tonic, home tone). This means that the various tones of the scale are not considered as equally important, but are related and subordinated to one of them. Thus, the diatonic scale is usually interpreted as a "C-major scale," in consideration of the fact that C is its initial tone [for an ingenious method of constructing the diatonic scale without preference given to one tone, see *Hexachord]. Actually, any of the tones of the diatonic scale (as well as of the other scales) can be designated as the center tone, a possibility which is the basis of the system of the medieval *church modes. In the interest of clarity, the term "scale" should be avoided for these "centralized scales." Thus, what is frequently called "Lydian scale" is properly termed "Lydian mode," or, more exactly, "Lydian mode (or F-mode) of the diatonic scale." The so-called C-major scale is the "C-mode of the diatonic scale," the other major scales being transpositions thereof. The same terminology can be applied to the other scales, e.g., "D-mode of the pentatonic scale," etc.

Actually, the medieval modes (as well as the Greek "scales") included another element of limitation, i.e., *ambitus. Thus, the medieval Hypolydian is the "c–c' segment of the F-mode of the diatonic scale."

Lit.: A. H. Fox-Strangways, in *ML* vii, no. 4; V. de Rubertis, in *RMI* xxix.

Scale, scaling [G. *Mensur*]. The term is used in organ parlance to indicate the ratio of the length to the width of a pipe. Thus, pipes are said to have wide or narrow scaling [G. *weite* or *enge Mensur*] depending upon whether their length is (in the extreme cases) 24 or 10 times their width. Wide scaling (used in the Principal flue stops) gives a soft sound with few overtones, whereas narrow scaling (used in Gamba, Violin, etc.) makes the sound thin, sharp, and rich in overtones. A term such as "Diapason of 6″ scale" means that the C of this stop has a diameter of 6″, the other pipes being larger and smaller in proportion to their length.

Scale degrees. Special names and signs used in *harmonic analysis to denote the various tones of the scale as they occur as the roots of triads, seventh chords, etc. These names are: tonic (I), supertonic (II), mediant (III), subdominant (IV), dominant (V), submediant or superdominant (VI), subtonic (VII). The most important of these are the *tonic, the *dominant, and the *subdominant.

Scampanio [It.]. Chimes.

Scampata [It.]. Same as *charivari.

Scandicus. See *Neumes I.

Scanning [G. *Skandieren*]. See *Poetic meter.

Scat singing. See *Jazz IV.

Scemando [It.]. Diminishing.

Scenario. A skeleton libretto of a play or an opera showing the characters, number, and general nature of the scenes, etc. The German word *Scenarium*, on the contrary, denotes a full libretto with detailed directions for the scenery.

Schablone [G.]. Stencil; hence, cliché, conventionalism.

Schachtbret. Old German for *echiquier.

Schalkhaft [G.]. Roguish, joking.

Schall [G.]. Sound, chiefly acoustical. *Schallbecken*, cymbals. *Schalloch*, sound hole. *Schallplatte*, record. *Schallwellen*, acoustical waves.

Schalmei [G.]. See *Oboe family III.

Scharf betont [G.]. Strongly accented.

Schaurig [G.]. Ghastly, gruesome.

Schelmisch [G.]. Roguish, joking.

Schellen [G.]. Tambourine. *Schellenbaum*, Turkish *crescent. *Schellentrommel*, tambourine.

Scherzando [It.], **Scherzhaft** [G.]. Playful.

Scherzo [It., joke, play]. (1) A movement, usually the third, of sonatas, symphonies, quartets (rarely in concertos), which was introduced by Beethoven to replace the *minuet. Like this, the scherzo is followed by a *trio after which the scherzo is repeated. Occasionally (e.g., Beethoven, Seventh Symphony) the scheme of alternation is extended to S T S T S. The distinguishing features of the scherzo are rapid speed in ¾-meter, vigorous rhythm, a certain abruptness of thought involving elements of surprise and whim, and a character of bustling humor which may veer from the playful to the ominous (e.g., in Beethoven's Fifth Symphony). It goes without saying that the line of demarcation between the minuet and the scherzo is by no means always clear. Some minuets of the late Haydn approximate the scherzo, as do also minuets by Beethoven such as that of his first PF. Sonata; on the other hand, Haydn used the term scherzo in some of his earlier works (Russian Quartets, nos. 37–42) for pieces which are hardly different from his minuets. The great masters of the true scherzo are Beethoven, Schubert, and Bruckner. The Nationalist composers have frequently used it as a vehicle for the introduction of national dance types, a procedure which has enabled many composers to write a moderately good scherzo as the high light of an otherwise mediocre symphony. Regarding the internal structure of the scherzo, see *Binary and ternary form II.

(2) Chopin and Brahms (op. 4) have employed the term for independent pieces in which sections of a highly dramatic

and somewhat gloomy character (scherzo) alternate with others of a more lyrical expression (trio).

(3) In the Baroque period the term scherzo was used for vocal pieces in a lighter vein [Monteverdi, *Scherzi musicali* (1607); Cifra, *Scherzi sacri* (1613); Marini, *Scherzi e canzonette a 1 e 2 voci*, 1622], as well as for instrumental pieces of a somewhat fanciful character similar to the *capriccio [A. Troilo, *Sinfonie, scherzi* . . . (1608); Johannes Schenk, *Scherzi musicali* (*c.* 1700) for viola da gamba and bass [see *Editions XXIX, 28]; J. S. Bach, in Partita no. 3].

Lit.: G. Becking, *Beethoven's Scherzothema* (1921).

Schiettamente [It.]. Sincerely, simply.

Schisma. See under *Comma.

Schlag [G.]. Beat. *Schlaginstrumente, Schlagzeug,* percussion instruments.

Schlagzither [G.]. The modern *zither (not the dulcimer), in contradistinction to earlier types which were bowed (so-called *Streichzither*).

Schlangenrohr [G.]. Rare name for *serpent.

Schlegel [G.]. Drumstick.

Schleifer [G.]. See under *Appoggiatura, Double II.

Schleppend [G.]. Dragging.

Schlüssel [G.]. Clef.

Schlummerlied [G.]. Slumber song.

Schluss [G.]. Conclusion, cadence. *Schluss-satz,* final movement.

Schmachtend [G.]. Languishing.

Schmeichelnd [G.]. Coaxing.

Schmelzend [G.]. "Melting," i.e., very lyrical.

Schmerzhaft [G.]. Painful, grievous.

Schmetternd [G.]. Blared. See under *Horn I.

Schnabel [G., beak]. The mouthpiece of the clarinet and the recorder; see *Mouthpiece (b), (d).

Schnabelflöte [G., beak flute]. Old name for *recorder.

Schnadahupfl [from Bavarian *schnadern,* to prattle, and *Hupf,* jump]. A type of Bavarian-Austrian folk song, frequently with improvised humorous texts between an iterated refrain. Cf. K. Rotter, *Der Schnadahupfl-Rhythmus* (1912).

Schnarre [G.]. Rattle. *Schnarrtrommel,* snare drum. *Schnarrwerk,* old term for the reed department of the organ.

Schneidend [G.]. "Cutting," i.e., with utmost precision.

Schnell [G.]. Quick.

Schneller [G.]. An 18th-century ornament consisting of the alternation of the written note with the note immediately above it, and to be performed in the manner of a short, rapid trill beginning on the beat. The *Schneller* was not one of the French agréments, having been introduced after 1750 by K. P. E. Bach, who always indicated it by means of two small grace notes, as under (a). Later composers often designated the Schneller by the short wavy line (b), which originally indicated a somewhat different ornament, called *Pralltriller.* This is, properly speaking, a rapid trill of four notes, beginning with the upper auxiliary, as was customary with trills in that period. This trill was used only on the *lower* note of a descending second and tied to the preceding note, a fact which sometimes gives the erroneous impression that the Pralltriller begins with the main note. The Schneller, on the other hand, can only occur on a detached note, that is, the *upper* note of a descending second, so that the position of the sign (b) usually indicates whether a Schneller (c) or a Pralltriller (d) is meant.

After 1800 the Pralltriller dropped out of use so that the sign (b) always indicates the Schneller. Simultaneously, however, the name Schneller dropped out of use and the ornament illustrated under (c) became known as Pralltriller which is the current German term for it. The

common English denomination is "inverted mordent." The former restriction regarding its position on the first note of a descending second has, of course, been long abandoned, and the Pralltriller is frequently found in connection with skips to which he adds a tinge of crispness and determined attack [last movement of Beethoven's Hammerklavier Sonata op. 106]. Around 1830 (Hummel, Moscheles) the Pralltriller began to be performed *before* the main note, and today this is generally considered the proper manner of execution. As late as in Chopin, however, examples abound in which the old method, upon closer examination, appears to be preferable, owing to its greater expressiveness [Ex. (e), Valse in A–flat].   P. A.

Schöpfung, Die [G.]. German title of Haydn's oratorio *The Creation*.

Schöpfungsmesse [G.]. Haydn's Mass in B-flat (1801), so called on account of the similarity of a theme in the Qui tollis with one in his oratorio *The Creation* [G. *Die Schöpfung*].

Schola (cantorum) [L., school of singers]. Originally and properly, the papal choir and singing school said to have been founded by Pope Sylvester (314–335) and reorganized by St. Gregory (590–605), who made it the central body for the propagation of Roman chant, by sending his singers to other churches and monasteries [see *Sistine choir]. By the bull *Motu proprio* of Pope Pius X (1903) a new impetus has been given to the establishment of *scholae cantorum*

even in the smallest churches. The name has also been adopted by certain institutions outside the church, of which that founded by Vincent d'Indy in Paris in 1896 is the most important. Originally planned as an institution for church music, it developed around 1900 into a general music school with an intensive training based on Gregorian chant and counterpoint. The name Schola has come into use as a general denomination for the conservative and academic trends in French music, represented by César Franck and his spiritual successors.

Scholarships, Fellowships, and Prizes. I. *United States.* Scholarships and fellowships are awards of money granted by institutions or corporations to applicants of unusual ability, for the purpose of further study, research, or composition. The general distinction between the two is one of degree. A fellowship is usually of higher monetary value and greater honor to the recipient than a scholarship. Also, in awarding scholarships the financial need of the applicant is generally considered in addition to his merit, while the same considerations do not usually enter into decisions regarding fellowships.

Scholarships and fellowships divide themselves roughly into two classes: those which are maintained by funds from a specific bequest (usually bearing the name of the donor); and those of which the funds are supplied from a general fund and are administered according to prevailing policy or circumstances. The former sometimes contain definite stipulations as to the qualifications of the applicant and the use to which the scholarship or fellowship is to be put. For example, the John Doe Fellowship of $1100 may be awarded only to graduates of X college for the purpose of studying piano in Paris; or the like. One of the most common stipulations of larger fellowships in music is that the recipient shall go abroad to work.

1. Scholarships and Student Aid. These terms are often used synonymously to designate grants of money for study in

the institution granting the awards. A common way of administering such funds is in "tuition scholarships," which take the form of a remission of part or all of the student's tuition costs. Unfortunately such a practice has led to abuse in some instances; the granting of tuition scholarships has been only a means of reducing prices to compete with other schools. The fairest method of awarding scholarships is by competition, and this method is used, especially in applied music, by some of the larger schools. In some instances, especially in the larger schools, certain comparatively small sums are given as scholarships for specific studies, such as piano, voice, violin (e.g. Eastman School, New England Conservatory). The Juilliard School of Music, however, grants full tuition fellowships to all students who are admitted to the Graduate School (not to those studying in the Institute of Musical Art), while making no provision for the students' living expenses in New York. The same is true of the Curtis Institute in Philadelphia.

2. Fellowships. These are granted principally by universities or by corporations. Generally they bear a name, have a fixed value, and specify in what field the holder shall work. Most fellowships carry a large enough stipend to enable the holder to live modestly. They are awarded for advanced work in various fields of music — musicology, composition, performance, pedagogy, etc. Resident fellowships are given for work in a specific institution; traveling fellowships often require the recipient to go abroad. Most fellowships are granted primarily to enable an advanced student to continue his education. Some of these are:

Pulitzer Travelling Scholarship (about $1500), given by Columbia University for composition. *Charles H. Ditson Fellowship* (about $2000), given by Yale University for graduate study abroad. *John Knowles Paine Travelling Fellowship* (about $1500), given by Harvard University for musicology or composition (open only to Harvard students). *Beebe Fund Scholarships*, for sending abroad one or more young and talented men or women who intend to pursue a professional career in music. *Matthay Scholarship* (about $1000), to enable pianists to study in London with Matthay.

The fellowships granted by the *Guggenheim Foundation* are of a different sort. They are usually granted to persons who have passed the student stage, and are given in composition or in musical research.

The *American Academy in Rome* offers several fellowships in music. These are granted to young composers of unusual promise. They require that the candidate reside at the Academy in Rome. At present (1942) they have been discontinued and $1000 prizes in composition are offered instead.

II. *Other Countries*. 1. *Prix de Rome*. Awarded by the Académie des beaux arts of Paris annually (since 1803) after severe competitive examination, including the composition of a cantata. The first prize consists of a four-year stay in the Villa Medici in Rome, the second is a gold medal. Among the winners of the "Grand Prix de Rome" have been Halévy (1819), Berlioz (1830), Bizet (1857), Debussy (1884), Charpentier (1887), Florent Schmitt (1900). Ravel was among those who failed to win it. Belgium has also a Prix de Rome, awarded every second year.

2. The most important English prize is the *Mendelssohn Scholarship*, founded in 1847, awarded annually for composition, and valued at present from about £150 per annum. Except for A. S. Sullivan (1856–60) and Eugen d'Albert (1881–82) no outstanding composer appears on the list of the holders [cf. *GD*; also Suppl. Vol.].

3. For the German prizes cf. the articles "Preise" in *RiML* and *MoML*.

E. B. H.

Scholia enchiriadis. See *Musica enchiriadis.

Schools of music. See *Education.

Schottische [G., Scotch]. A round dance of the mid-19th century in the character of a slow polka, not to be confused with the much quicker *écossaise. It was also known in England under the name "German polka."

Schrammelquartet [G.]. A type of instrumental ensemble, inaugurated in 1877 by the Viennese violinist Johann Schrammel, which has become very popular in Vienna and elsewhere for the performance of light music (waltzes, etc.). The original quartet consisted of two violins, clarinet, and guitar; the clarinet was later replaced by the accordion. A Schrammel orchestra is an enlarged ensemble of a similar type.

Schrittmässig [G.]. As if walking.

Schuhplattler [G.]. A dance of Bavaria, the characteristic feature of which is clapping of the knees and shoe soles with the hands. The music is that of the *Ländler or similar dances.

Schusterfleck [G.]. See under *Rosalia.

Schwärmer [G.]. See *Tremolo (1).

Schwankend [G.]. Staggering, uncertain.

Schwebelpfeif [G.]. See under *Schwegel.

Schwebungen [G.]. *Beats.

Schwegel, Schwegelpfeife [G.]. Obsolete word for the military *fife [see also *Flute III]. In Poglietti's *Aria allemagna con alcuni variazoni* (*c.* 1680; cf. *TaAM* viii) it occurs, in the misspelling *Schwebelpfeif*, as a designation for a variation in which the quick and high passages of the fife are imitated.

Schweller [G.]. *Swell.

Schwellkasten. Swell box. *Schwellwerk*, swell organ.

Schwermütig [G.]. Heavy-hearted, melancholic.

Schwindend [G.]. "Disappearing," i.e., dying away.

Schwingung [G.]. Vibration.

Schwungvoll [G.]. With *élan*.

Scialumo [It.]. See Chalumeau (2).

Scintillante [It.]. Sparkling.

Sciolto [It.]. In a free and easy manner. Also used in the sense of non legato. In earlier writings it occurs as an indication of free style of composition, e.g., *fuga sciolta*, i.e., a fugue with license.

Scivolando [It.]. Sliding, glissando.

Scordatura [It., mis-tuning]. Abnormal tuning of a stringed instrument for the purpose of obtaining unusual chords, facilitating difficult passages, or changing the tone color. Scordatura was frequently used in the lute music of the 16th and 17th centuries, the most common method being the lowering of the lowest string from A to G (*Laute im Abzug, bordone descordato*; cf. *WoHN* ii, 63). A remarkable piece showing an unusual scordatura is the "Judentantz" in Hans Neusiedler's *Ein newgeordnet künstlich Lautenbuch*, 1536 [cf. the differing transcriptions in *DTOe* 18 and in *ApMZ* i; cf. also *ApNPM*, 78]. In the early part of the 17th century a normal tuning for the lute was practically non-existent; consequently it is rather difficult in this period to consider any tuning as a scordatura. As a matter of fact, the particular tuning to be used with a given piece, and indicated at the beginning, was called *accord (accordatura)*.

Scordatura was also much used in the violin music of the 17th century, particularly by Heinrich Biber [cf. *DTOe* 5.ii and 12.ii; also *SchGMB*, no. 238; *WoHN* ii, 237]. The accompanying example

(beginning of Bach's Sonata no. 5 for cello solo) illustrates the notational method. The "accord" at the beginning shows that the A-string is to be lowered one tone. The notes indicate, not the actual sound, but the position of the fingers in the usual manner, and the natural in the signature directs the player always to play g–a–b♭ on the highest string, a succession which sounds f–g–a♭. In violin music of a more recent period the most common instance of scordatura is the tuning of the lowest string a semitone or a tone lower in order to increase the compass, or a tone higher in order to increase the brilliancy of the sound.

Lit.: T. Russel, in *MQ* xxiv; A. Moser, in *AMW* i; M. Schneider, in *ZIM* viii, ix; E. Lesser in *AM* iv, nos. 3 and 4.

Score [F. *partition*; G. *Partitur*; It. *partitura, partizione*]. I. A manner of writing music which shows all the parts of an ensemble (orchestra or chamber music) arranged one underneath the other on different staves (full score, orchestral score). A vocal score is a score of a choral work (opera, oratorio) which shows the vocal parts on separate staves, but the instrumental parts in a piano reduction. A piano score is the reduction of an orchestral score to a version for piano, on two staves. For the arrangement and reading of a modern orchestral score see *Orchestra and orchestration V.

Score-reading is the facility of grasping from a chamber-music, vocal, or orchestral score the essential features of the melodic and harmonic structure and, if possible, of reproducing these on the piano. This task, not easy in itself, is rendered still more complicated by the customary use of different *clefs for different voices or instruments and, in the case of orchestral scores, by the custom of notating a number of the wind instruments as *transposing instruments. Cf. H. Gàl, *Directions for Score-Reading* (1924); M. Bernstein, *Score Reading* (1932).

II. Score arrangement, i.e., a notational scheme showing simultaneous tones in a vertical alignment, was used exclusively for the writing down of polyphonic music prior to 1225. All the organa, conductus, clausulae, in short the entire repertory of the Schools of St. Martial and Notre Dame, were notated in this fashion. With the rise of the motet (*c.* 1225) this arrangement was discarded for the so-called choir-book arrangement [see *Choir book], in which the parts are notated

separately on one or, usually, on two opposite pages of the opened book [cf., e.g., *ApNPM*, 283]. This method was

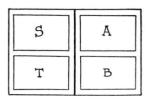

more economical of space owing to the great difference in length between the texted upper parts of the motet and the textless tenor with its few and long notes written in ligatures. The accompanying drawing illustrates the arrangement of music in four parts (15th, 16th centuries). The choir-book arrangement persisted until the middle of the 16th century but was gradually superseded by the arrangement in *part books [G. *Stimmbücher*], i.e., separate books for the soprano, alto, etc. The earliest manuscript part books date from *c.* 1450 (*Glogauer, Münchner *Liederbuch*). This method was particularly advantageous for printing and, in fact, was almost exclusively employed in the printed books of 16th-century vocal music. Around 1600 the rise of orchestral music (G. Gabrieli) led to the adoption of the modern score with bar-lines (earliest example in Cipriano de Rore's *Madrigali*, 1577). It is interesting to note that the largest score ever written is that of a 53-voice Mass by Benevoli from *c.* 1650 [*DTOe* 9.i; see *Roman School]. The arrangement in part-books survives, e.g., in the four volumes containing the parts of Beethoven's string quartets. Cf. R. Schwartz, "Zur Partitur im 16. Jahrhundert" (*AMW* ii); *ApNPM*, p. xx.

Scoring. The art and process of orchestration.

Scorrevole [It.]. Freely flowing.

Scotch snap. See *Dotted notes III.

Scottish music. Probably the earliest extant information about musical activity in Scotland comes from Giraldus

Cambrensis (*c.* 1147–1220) who in his famous *Topographia Hibernica* (*c.* 1190) states that "in the opinion of many, Scotland has not only equalled Ireland, her teacher in music, but has . . . surpassed her." While, prior to this time, music was exclusively in the hands of the *bards, there now developed folk music of a more popular character, and polyphonic music was cultivated in at least one place, the monastery of St. Andrews. It was here that the *MS Wolfenbüttel 677* (*c.* 1250) was written, the earliest preserved book containing the **Magnus liber organi* and the additional repertory of the School of **Notre Dame. Although the bulk of its contents is of French origin, its last fascicle (11th) contains a collection of two-part pieces which is very probably of insular origin, although not necessarily Scottish [see *English music II]. It is not until the 16th century that sources of Scottish music are encountered, viz., a MS incorrectly labeled "Antiphonarium" in the Advocates Library of Edinburgh, and a MS set of four part books known as the St. Andrews Psalter (or Wood's Psalter) now scattered in Edinburgh, Dublin, and London. The former contains masses, motets, and magnificats, several of these by Robert Carver (b. *c.* 1491); the latter, dated 1566, contains psalm tunes, Latin motets, and canticles, by Robert Johnson, the most important composer of Scotland until recently [cf. the article in *GD*], David Peebles (d. 1579), and others. Another composer of this period was Patrick Douglas of whom a few motets remain in a MS at Christ Church, Oxford.

The scarcity of Scotch 16th-century church music and the complete lack of secular compositions (madrigals) offers a striking contrast to the wealth of English music during the same period. Since there is much evidence in contemporary documents (Court records, etc.) showing that music played a prominent part in the cultural life of Scotland, it is assumed that destruction of sources went much farther here than in England. No Scottish composers of note are known until the end of the 19th century when A. C. MacKenzie

(1847–1935), J. B. McEwen (b. 1868), and William Wallace (b. 1860) participated in the recent rise of English music. See *Strathspey; *Lament; *Pibroch.

Lit.: D. Baptie, *Musical Scotland: Dictionary of Scottish Musicians from about 1400* (1894); J. Love, *Scottish Church Music* (1891); J. Glen, *Early Scottish Melodies* (1900); H. G. Farmer, *Music in Mediaeval Scotland* (1930; also in *PMA* 56); N. Diem, *Beiträge zur Geschichte der schottischen Musik im 17. Jahrhundert* (Diss. Berlin 1919); A. Carmichael, *Musica gadelica*, 4 vols. (1900–41); H. G. Farmer, "Some Early Scotch Composers" (*MA* ii); J. Beveridge, "Two Scottish 13th-century Songs" (*ML* xx, no. 4); G. Abrahams, "Burns and the Scottish Folksong" (*ML* iv, no. 1).

Scriptores [L., writers]. A term used as a short reference to two important publications of medieval treatises on music, namely: (a) *Scriptores ecclesiastici de musica sacra potissimum*, 3 vols., ed. by M. Gerbert in 1784 (facs. ed. 1931); and (b) *Scriptorum de musica medii aevi nova series*, 4 vols., ed. by E. Coussemaker in 1864–76 (facs. ed. 1931). The collections are usually designated as *Gerbert Scriptores* (abbr. *G.S.*, *GS*, or *G.Scr.*) and *Coussemaker Scriptores* (*C.S.*, *CS*, or *C.Scr.*). Both collections are indispensable reference books of musicological research in the Middle Ages. The *Gerbert Scriptores* contain chiefly the earliest treatises (9th–11th centuries), the *Coussemaker Scriptores* those of the 13th and 14th centuries [see *Theory]. The contents are given in full in *GD* iv, 704ff. A collection of writers on Greek music has been published by K. v. Jan under the title: *Musici scriptores graeci* (1895, 1899).

Scrittura [It.]. The commission to write an opera for the next season, granted by the opera company.

Scucito [It.]. "Unsewed," i.e., disconnected.

Sdrucciolando [It., sliding]. Same as *glissando.

Sea trumpet. Erroneous translation of *tromba marina.*

Seashore tests. See *Tests.

Seasons, The. See *Oratorio IV.

Secco [It.]. Dry. See also under *Recitative.

Sechzehntel [G.]. See *Notes.

Second [F. *seconde*; G. *Sekunde*]. See *Intervals.

Secondary dominants. See *Dominant (1).

Seconda volta [It.]. See *Prima volta.

Seele [G., properly, soul]. *Sound post (of the violin).

Seelenamt [G.]. *Requiem Mass.

Seelenvoll [G.]. Soulful.

Segno [It., sign]. A sign in the form of an S which is used to indicate the beginning (*dal segno, dal S.*) or the end (*al segno, al S.*) of a section to be played or to be repeated.

Segue [It., follows]. Request to join up the following movement without break (*segue l'aria, segue la coda*). It is also used to mean: continue in the same manner, for instance, with a certain pattern of broken chords which is written out in full only at the beginning [see under *Abbreviations].

Seguidilla. A national dance from Andalusia (southern Spain) in fast triple time, similar to the *bolero but quicker. It is sung and danced to the accompaniment of the castanets and the guitar, with four bars of castanet rhythm recurring after each verse (*copla*). In the first act of Bizet's *Carmen* there is a *Seguidille* which unfortunately is not a very good example of the species. Statements regarding the "Moorish origin" of this dance are without foundation.

Sehnsuchtsvoll [G.]. Yearning.

Sehr [G.]. Very; e.g., *sehr schnell,* very fast.

Seikilos Song. One of the few remnants of ancient Greek music, a short lyrical song from the 2d century B.C. at the earliest [see *Greek music III]. Cf. *HAM,* no. 6c; *SchGMB,* no. 1.

Seises [Sp. *seis,* six]. A group of six (or more) choir boys who perform dances with singing and clapping of castanets before the high altar of the Cathedral of Seville on great festival days (formerly also in other churches of Spain). Vittoria, Guerrero, Morales, and others have written music for these liturgical dances. However, the music now used is of a recent date and of mediocre quality. Cf. R. H. Stein, "Die Kirchentänze in Sevilla" (*DM* xv.1).

Seiten- [G., side]. *Seitenbewegung,* oblique motion. *Seitenthema, Seitensatz,* the second theme of a movement in sonata form, or of other forms.

Sekunde [G.]. Second. *Sekundakkord* [see under *Seventh-chord].

Semi- [L., half]. *Semibiscroma, semibreve* (*semibrevis*), *semicroma, semifusa, semiminima, semiquaver,* see *Notes; also *Mensural notation. *Semichorus,* half-chorus. *Semidiapente,* Latin term for the diminished fifth. *Semiditonus,* Latin term for the minor third. *Semiditas,* in *mensural notation (*proportions), same as *proportio dupla.*

Semiseria [It.]. Eighteenth-century term for an opera seria which contained a number of comic scenes.

Semitone [L. *semitonium*]. The half of a whole-tone, the smallest interval of European music. The octave consists of twelve semitones and the diatonic scale includes two semitones [see *Scales]. The exact measurement of a semitone varies slightly according to the system of tuning. In equal temperament [see *Temperament] each semitone equals exactly 100 *cents, while in the other systems various semitones occur. For instance, in the *Pythagorean system the "diatonic" semitone (e–f, b–c′, called *limma*) is equivalent to 90 cents, the "chromatic" semitone (bb–b, called *apotome*), 204 − 90 = 114 cents. In *Just intonation, these values are almost reversed, namely, 112 and 92 cents ($\dfrac{16}{15}$ and $\dfrac{135}{128}$ in relative frequencies).

Semplice [It.]. Simple.

Sempre [It.]. Always; e.g., *sempre legato*, always legato.

Senkung [G.]. See under *Arsis and thesis.

Sennet, also written *Senet, Sennate, Synnet, Cynet,* etc. A word which occurs in stage directions in the plays of the Elizabethan dramatists, and is used to denote "that a particular fanfare is to be played" (*GD* iv, 715). The term is derived, not from seven, as is suggested in various dictionaries, but, very probably, from sonata [see *Sonata B, I]. An indication such as "Trumpets sound a florish, and then a sennate" (Dekker, *Satiromastix*), therefore calls for a flourish (fanfare) followed by a somewhat longer piece played on brass instruments. For a similar word formation see *Tucket.

Sensible [F.]. The leading tone.

Sentito [It.]. "Felt," with expression.

Senza [It.]. Without. *Senza tempo, senza misura,* without strict measure. For *senza sordini* see *Sordini.

Sepolcro [It.]. See *Sepulchrum play.

Septet. Chamber music for seven players, usually strings and wind mixed. Aside from Beethoven's well-known Septet op. 20 there are others by Spohr, Hummel, Saint-Saëns, d'Indy, Ravel, Schönberg.

Septième [F.], **Septime** [G.]. The interval of the seventh.

Septimenakkord [G.]. Seventh chord.

Septimole, Septole [G.], **septuplet.** A group of seven notes to be played in the time of four or six.

Septuor [F.]. Septet.

Sepulchrum play [It. *sepolcro*]. A medieval play showing the burial of Christ. See *Liturgical drama; *Mysteries.

Sequela. A term used by some modern writers for the pre-existing melodies of sequences [see *Sequence (2)], the term sequence being used for the combination of these melodies with the text. Cf. A. Hughes, *Anglo-French Sequelae* (1934).

Sequence [G. *Sequenz*]. (1) In musical composition, the repetition in one and the same part of a short musical phrase at another pitch, usually at the second above or below, more rarely at the third [see *Repetition]. A sequence is called *melodic* when the repetition occurs in the melody only (as in monophonic music or when the lower parts do not partake of the sequential procedure), *harmonic* if similar repetitions occur in all the parts. If the repetitions are made without accidentals (change of key) the sequence is called *tonal* or *diatonic* [Ex. 1]. This

procedure necessarily implies that some of the intervals come out larger or smaller by a semitone (minor instead of major third, diminished instead of pure fifth, etc.). If, on the other hand, the intervals of the model pattern are preserved exactly, the sequence is called *real* [Ex. 2; see *Tonal and real]. Most sequences, as occur in actual music, belong to a mixed type, called *modulatory* or *chromatic*, as is illustrated in Ex. 3.

In spite of its stereotyped construction, the sequence is of high artistic significance as an element of logical continuation. This is particularly true of the tonal sequence (in its exact or slightly modified form) which combines unity of key with variety of intervallic repetition. From the point of view of *harmonic analysis, the sequence is interesting because it often produces chordal combinations which otherwise are not admitted in strict style (diminished fifths, secondary seventh-chords, etc.).

The melodic sequence is not infrequent in plainsong, and plays a rather prominent part in the Italian polyphonic music of the 14th century [cf., e.g., the example in *ReMMA*, 365], as well as in the works of the Flemish masters (Obrecht, Isaac, and successors). The harmonic sequence became an important means of formal development and continuation in many compositions of the 17th through the 19th centuries, being used frequently in the episodes of the fugue and in the development section of the sonata. In the late 18th century mediocre composers made abundant use of a cheap type of sequence known as *rosalia.

Lit.: All books on Harmony; H. A. Mishkin, *The Function of the Episodic Sequence in Baroque Instrumental Music* (unpubl. diss. Harvard 1938); M. G. Dann, "Elgar's Use of the Sequence" (*ML* xix).

(2) In early liturgical music (plainsong), sequence denotes the oldest and most important type of tropes [see *Trope (4)], namely, literary and musical accretions to the Alleluias (alleluia trope). The invention of the sequence is usually attributed to Notker Balbulus, a German monk of St. Gall (d. 912) who, according to his own report, conceived the idea of providing suitable texts to the long vocalizations over the final vowel of the Alleluia (the so-called *jubilus), in order to facilitate memorizing them. However, recent investigations (H. M. Bannister, C. Blume) have made it probable that before Notker there existed sequences in northern France (Jumièges) as well as in Provence (*St. Martial at Limoges). The term sequence [from L. *sequi*, to follow] is probably explained by the fact that the sequence "follows" immediately after the alleluia, replacing its verse [see

*Mass A]. An equivalent term, used preferably in France, is *prosa (prose). In order to clearly understand the sequence it is advisable to deal separately with the textual and the musical aspect, although in the actual development both are closely interlocked.

(a) *Text.* The sequence texts are lengthy poems in a free style, and usually cast in the form a, b b, c c, d d, ... i i, k; i.e., they begin and end with a single line (a, k) between which there are a number (from 4 to 10 or more) of double-line stanzas. The two lines of each stanza are identical in the number and accentuation of syllables, but usually there is a marked variation from one stanza to the next. For instance, Notker's sequence *Puella turbata* shows the following scheme of numbers of syllables: 13; 18, 18; 23, 23; 38, 38; 23, 23; 16, 16; 16, 16; 17, 17; 20, 20; 16, 16; 61 [cf. H. J. Moser, *Geschichte der deutschen Musik*, p. 93]. The irregular length of the stanzas and the absence of strict poetic meter suggest Byzantine rather than Latin origin of this type of poetry [for an example of early medieval Latin poetry see *Ambrosian hymns]. The French sequences for which the name *prosa* became customary show an additional feature of poetry, namely, rhyme. In many of them, each line ends on *a*, in assonance with the final vowel of the preceding alleluia.

(b) *Music.* The sequence texts are set to music in a rather strict syllabic style, and with identical music for the two lines of a couplet. The relationship of these melodies to those of the alleluias is by no means as clear and simple as Notker's remarks (underlaying of a text to a pre-existing vocalization) would cause us to expect. Frequently it is only the beginning of the sequence which shows a certain relationship to the alleluia, the continuation being free [for an example of an unusually close agreement, cf. *BeMMR*, 85 and Schubiger, no. 18; also *HAM*, no. 16a]. Moreover, the style of the sequence melodies is quite different from that of the older chants, owing to their wider range as well as to the much larger use of formal devices such as repetition of motives, sequential treatment [see *Sequence (1)], variation-like elaboration of standard phrases, etc. In a way, the sequences may be said to open a new phase in European music, i.e., the beginning of "composition" in the proper sense of the word [cf., e.g., the sequence *Adducentur* in Hughes].

In Germany, Wipo (*c.* 1000–50) was an important successor of Notker [cf. *HAM*, no. 16b], while in France, Adam of St. Victor (d. 1192) introduced a new type, that of the rhymed sequence (*Reimsequenz*). His poems are hymns, practically always in six-line stanzas of trochaic dimeters. Although the elegance of his Latin was and still is greatly admired, the music is rather formalistic and inferior to that of the older sequences [cf. *HAM*, no. 16c]. His procedure led to an enormous output of rhymed sequences which in the ensuing centuries threatened to overshadow the traditional repertory of Gregorian chant. A drastic step was taken at the Council of Trent (1545–63) which abolished all of them but four: Wipo's Easter sequence *Victimae paschali laudes* (the only remnant of the older type); the sequence for Whitsunday *Veni sancte spiritus* (Golden Sequence, attributed to Innocent III, late 12th century); Thomas Aquinas's sequence for Corpus Christi, *Lauda Sion* (*c.* 1261); and Thomas a Celano's sequence for the *requiem mass, Dies irae (c.* 1200). In 1727 a fifth sequence was adopted into liturgical use, namely, Jacopone's celebrated *Stabat mater*. The Christmas sequence *Laetabundus* [cf. *ZMW* xi, 274f] is still being used in the service of the Dominican monks. Derivatives of the sequence are the *estampie and the *lai.

The sequences have frequently been composed polyphonically, either as a cantus-firmus elaboration of the plainsong melody [example, by Willaert, in *HAM*, no. 113], or in free style [example, by Jommelli, in *HAM*, no. 306].

Lit.: G. M. Dreves, *Analecta hymnica*, vols. 7, 50, 53, 54 (collection of texts); F. Wolf, *Über die Lais, Sequenzen, und Leiche* (1840); A. Schubiger, *Die Sänger-*

schule von St. Gallen (1858); A. Hughes, *Anglo-French Sequelae* (1934); P. Aubry-Misset, †*Les Proses de St. Adam de Victor* (1900); Cl. Blume, "Vom Alleluia zur Sequenz" (*KJ*, 1911); A. Gastoué, "Sur les origines de la form 'sequentia' . . . " (*KIM*, 1906, p. 165); J. Handschin, in *ZMW* xii, xiii; P. Aubry, in *TG* v, vi, vii; J. Wolf, in *RMI* xlii; A. Hammerich, *Mediaeval Musical Relics of Denmark* (1912); C. A. Moberg, *Über die schwedischen Sequenzen* (1927).

Séraphine. See under *Harmonium.

Serbian chant. See *Yugoslavian music.

Serenade. Evening music, vocal or instrumental. The former type (song of a lover beneath his lady's window) is frequent in operatic music (Mozart, Don Giovanni's aria "Deh vieni") and in the song repertory. The contrast is *aubade, i.e., morning music.

More important is the instrumental serenade which, losing its "utilitarian" affiliation, developed, around 1770, into a purely musical type similar to the *cassation, the *divertimento, and the *notturno. As a form, the serenade is characterized by the mixture of elements taken from the suite, particularly marches and minuets, and from the sonata. The style, likewise, is about midway between that of the suite and that of the symphony. Serenades are written for a small ensemble consisting of a limited number of strings and a few wind instruments, such as would seem to be suitable for an open-air performance. The most famous examples are Mozart's *Haffner Serenade (K.V. 250) and Eine kleine Nachtmusik (K.V. 525). Others are by Haydn, Beethoven (op. 8, 25; also op. 41, 42, which are arrangements of the two former), Brahms (op. 16), Dvořák (op. 22, 90, 44), Elgar (op. 20).

Serenata [It.]. Not only the Italian term for *serenade, but specifically a designation for 18th-century short operatic works written as a complimentary offering for the birthdays of royal persons (particularly at the Viennese court) and performed (in the evening?) in a reception room with costumes and modest scenery. They are described best as dramatic cantatas. A well-known example is Handel's *Acis and Galatea* (1720) and his earlier *Aci, Galatea e Polifemo* (Naples, 1709).

Sereno [It.]. Serene.

Serinette [F.]. A miniature barrel organ used formerly in teaching canaries (*serin*) to sing, by the frequent repetition of the same tune.

Serpent. See under *Cornett; also *Brass instruments V (b).

Serrando [It.], **serré** [F.]. Pressing, getting quicker.

Serva padrona, La. See under *Comic opera; *Bouffons.

Service. In the Anglican Church, the whole of the musical compositions of the canticles and other invariable items (Kyrie, Creed) contained in the Book of Common Prayer, as distinct from the simple harmonization of plainsong (preces, responses, chants for the psalms) and from the *anthems. The settings of the Service are grouped under three main headings: the Morning Prayer (including the *Invitatory Psalm Venite exultemus, the *canticles *Te Deum, Benedictus es, Dominus Deus Israel, and the alternatives Benedicite and Jubilate); the Evening Prayer (including the canticles *Magnificat and Nunc dimittis, with the alternatives Cantate Domino and Deus misereatur); and the Communion (including the Kyrie, the Creed, the Sanctus, and the Gloria in excelsis; today also the Benedictus and the Agnus Dei). All these items were taken over from the Roman Catholic rites, as appears from the fact that they are traditionally referred to by their original Latin designations, although the texts themselves are, of course, in English [see *Canticum; *Mass]. A "Full Service" includes all (or nearly all) the items listed above, usually composed in one and the same

key and therefore commonly referred to by names such as "Stanford in B-flat" (i.e., a Full Service by Stanford in B-flat). There are, however, numerous Services which include only one of the three above groups (Morning Service; Evening Service; Communion Service) or even single items only. The terms Short Service and Great Service, used chiefly in the 16th and early 17th centuries, would seem to refer chiefly to the more or less elaborate style of composition, the former being chiefly in straight chordal (syllabic) style, the latter (also called High Service) in a richer contrapuntal style, with repetition of text phrases and various contrapuntal devices.

The history of the Service begins with Christopher Tye (*c.* 1500–72) and Thomas Tallis (*c.* 1505–85) [for some pre-Reformation Mass compositions with English texts, cf. *GD* iv, 725]. Tye's Evening Service as well as Tallis' Short Service (written probably before 1550) are in the simple homophonic style which was demanded by Archbishop Cranmer. Apparently the musicians were not enthusiastic about this injunction, for it was not long before William Byrd (*c.* 1542–1623), the first great master of Service music, reverted to the polyphonic tradition of the Flemish masters in his magnificent *Great Service*. In his *Second Service with verses to the organs* and in the *Third Service* (repr. in *Editions XXVIII, 2) he introduced important novel methods of performance: in the former the contrast between solo singers accompanied by the organ ("Verse") and chorus ("Full"); in the latter, half-choruses in alternation with the full chorus ("Can.," "Dec.," "Full"; see *Polychoral style). The most important writers of Services after Byrd are Weelkes, Tomkins, and Orlando Gibbons. Weelkes wrote 10 settings of the Evening Service, to 6 of which there is a corresponding Morning Service. Most of these, however, are incompletely transmitted. Tomkins wrote 5 settings of the Morning and 7 of the Evening Service. It should be noted that the Communion Service quickly lost the importance which its model, the Mass, has always maintained in the Catholic Church, and that, therefore, the interest concentrated upon the other Services, chiefly the Morning Service. The Services of Weelkes and Tomkins as well as Gibbons' two Services make use of the chorus as well as of solo voices accompanied by the organ. In some of them there are alternate sections of accompanied solo ("verse") and of chorus.

After these masters there begins a long period of stagnation and deterioration of the Service. The "Great Service" was almost completely neglected and the "Short Service" became the accepted model for composers such as William Child (1606–97), Benjamin Rogers (1614–98), Henry Aldrich (1647–1710), John Blow (1649–1708), Henry Purcell (1659–95), William Croft (1678–1727). This lack of interest is all the more surprising in view of the remarkable advance of the anthem in the same period, notably under Blow and Purcell. In this connection it should be noted that neither Purcell's Te Deum in D nor those of Handel belong to the category of the Service since they were written for special occasions, not for daily use. The standard of the Service reached its lowest point in 18th-century composers such as Charles King (1687–1748), James Kent (1700–76), William Boyce (1710–79), James Nares (1715–83), and Benjamin Cooke (1734–93).

A turn for the better occurred around 1800 with Th. Attwood (1765–1838), a pupil of Mozart, and Samuel Wesley (1766–1837). But it is to Thomas A. Walmisley (1814–56) and Samuel Sebastian Wesley (1810–76) that credit goes for the re-establishment of an artistic standard of Service music. Among the characteristic features of their Services are the imaginative use of the organ and the introduction of Romantic harmonies. Later composers, such as John Stainer (1840–1901), Arthur Sullivan (1842–1900), and Charles Stanford (1852–1924), made important contributions among which Stanford's *Service in B-flat* excels as a work of high artistic signifi-

cance. For literature see under *Cathedral music. Also A. Hughes, "16th-Century Service Music" (*ML* v, nos. 2 and 4).

Sesqui- [L., from *semique*, plus one half]. Latin prefix used to denote fractions the numerator of which is larger by one than the denominator, e.g., *sesqui-altera*: $\frac{3}{2}$ (one plus one half), *sesquitertia*: $\frac{4}{3}$, *sesquiquarta*: $\frac{5}{4}$, etc. In early musical theory these terms were used to denote either ratios of vibrations (i.e., *intervals), or ratios of time-values (i.e., *proportions). For instance, sesquialtera means, in discussions of the intervals, the fifth [see *Acoustics III], while, in treatises dealing with proportions, it denotes temporal values corresponding to our triplet notes (three triplet notes equal two normal notes). The former meaning occurs also in the organ stop called Sesquialtera, originally a mixture stop combining the octave with the fifth, but usually including also other harmonics, such as the third in various octaves. Another term for sesquialtera is *hemiola.

Sestetto [It.]. Sextet.

Setzart [G.]. Style of composition.

Seufzend [G.]. Sighing.

Seven (Last) Words, The. The seven last words of Christ (compiled from the four Gospels) have occasionally been used as a text for *Passion music, e.g., by Heinrich Schütz (*c.* 1645), Haydn (1785), and Gounod (*Les sept paroles de Jesus*). Haydn's composition, commissioned by the Bishop of Cadiz, is not a choral setting of the text, but a series of seven instrumental "sonatas" each to be played after the recitation of one of the "words." It is particularly interesting because it appeared in three versions: first, for orchestra (op. 47), then for string quartet (op. 48), and finally for pianoforte (op. 49). There also exists a choral version in the form of a cantata, probably by Haydn's brother Michael.

Seventh. See *Intervals. Also *I.

Seventh chord. A chord consisting of the third, fifth, and seventh above the fundamental. In a given key there are seven such chords, one on each degree of the scale, e.g., in C Major: c–e–g–b (I⁷), d–f–a–c′ (II⁷), e–g–b–d′ (III⁷), etc. By far the most important of these is that on the fifth degree, the so-called dominant seventh chord: g–b–d′–f′ (V⁷). Each seventh chord is capable of three inversions, according to whether its lowest tone is the third, the fifth, or the seventh. Below are the dominant seventh chord and its three inversions, together with their designations in *harmonic analysis and with the corresponding German terms:

Root Position g–b–d′–f′		Septimenakkord
	V⁷	

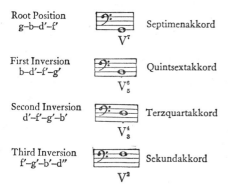

First Inversion b–d′–f′–g′		Quintsextakkord
	V⁶₅	

Second Inversion d′–f′–g′–b′		Terzquartakkord
	V⁴₃	

Third Inversion f′–g′–b′–d″		Sekundakkord
	V²	

It may be noticed that the dominant seventh chord is enharmonically identical with the so-called "German" augmented sixth chord [see *Sixth chord], e.g.: g–b–d′–f′ = g–b–d′–e♯′. The natural resolution of the former chord is into the triad on C; of the latter, into that on F-sharp.

While each of the seven "diatonic" seventh chords contains major as well as minor thirds (in various arrangements), there also exists an important type of seventh chord consisting of minor thirds only, the *diminished seventh chord*. This usually appears on the seventh degree of the scale, e.g., b–d′–f′–ab′ in C (major or minor). The normal resolution of this chord is into the tonic triad (c′–e′–g′). On account of its dominant character, it is frequently explained as a dominant ninth chord (g–b–d′–f′–ab′) with the

root (g) omitted. Owing to its equidistant construction, any of its tones can be considered as the home tone, so that one and the same chord may serve as a dominant to four different keys. In each case the chord must, of course, be written differently, as is shown in Ex. 1. Still other resolutions result from the fact that the chord can also be interpreted as the seventh chord of the raised supertonic, as illustrated in Ex. 2. Owing to its Protean

nature the diminished seventh chord is frequently used for quick modulation into far distant keys, e.g., from G into C-sharp [Ex. 3]. See *Harmonic analysis III.

Sext. (1) See *Office hours. — (2) German term (also *Sexte*) for the interval of the sixth. *Sextakkord*, see under *Triad.

Sextet [F. *sextette, sextuor*; G. *Sextett*; It. *sestetto*]. Chamber music for six performers, in various combinations, e.g., two violins, two violas, and two cellos (Brahms, op. 18, op. 36; Dvořák, op. 48), string quartet and two horns (Beethoven, op. 81b), two clarinets, two horns, two bassoons (Beethoven, op. 71), etc. A vocal sextet is a composition for six singers with or without instrumental accompaniment.

Sextolet [G. *Sextole*; It. *sestina*]. A group of six notes played in the time of

From top to bottom:
Grove, Scholes, Riemann, Moser

four ordinary notes. There should be a clear indication in writing as to whether the six notes are meant to form three groups of two each, or two groups of three each. Unfortunately, there is no agreement regarding the proper way of doing this, as appears from the accompanying table showing what the authors of four dictionaries consider correct.

Sfogato [It.]. Light and easy.

Sfoggiando [It.]. Flaunting, ostentatious.

Sforzando, sforzato [It.], abbr. *sf*, *sfz*. Forcing, i.e., with a sudden and strong accent on a single note or chord. *Sfp* means *sforzando* followed immediately by *piano*.

Shake. Older name for the trill. For closed and open shake, see the remark under *Grace. Shaked beat is a reiterated inferior appoggiatura, shaked cadent a reiterated Nachschlag.   P. A.

Shank. See *Wind instruments IV (b).

Shanty, chanty, chantey. Working songs of the English and American sailors, sung when engaged in pulling the ropes or any other kind of work calling for concerted effort. Well-known shanties are: The Wide Missouri; The Banks of Sacramento; The Rio Grande. Cf. F. Rickaby, *Ballads and Songs of the Shanty-Boy* (1926); R. R. Terry, in *ML* i, nos. 1 and 3; *id.*, in *PMA* xli; H. Whates, in *ML* xviii, no. 3.

Shape-note. See *Fasola.

Sharp [F. *dièse*; G. *Kreuz*; It. *diesis*]. The sign ♯ which indicates the raising of a note by a semitone, e.g., from C to C-sharp. For its origin and its use in early music, see the article on *B. In the notation of the 16th to the 18th century, the sharp frequently has the form of a recumbent double cross [see *Accidentals II]. There also was a practice of using the term sharp to denote the "sharped," i.e., the major third of a key. For instance Burney used the term "key E-sharp" in the meaning of "key E major," and Beethoven inscribed his Leonora Overture no. 1 (in C major) "Ouverture in C♯."

The foreign terms for C-sharp, etc., are given under *Pitch names.

Shawm [F. *chalumeau*; G. *Schalmei*; It. *cialamello*]. See *Oboe family III.

Sheng (frequently but wrongly spelled *Cheng). A peculiar Chinese wind instrument, consisting of a bowl-shaped air reservoir made from a gourd or wood, into the top of which are thrust a number (12–17) of bamboo pipes. The pipes each contain a free reed made of thin brass which is set in motion by suction and, less frequently, by aspiration through a mouthpiece attached to the side of the cup. Each pipe has a small hole which must be covered by the finger in order to make the pipe sound. See the illustration on p. 272. The special interest of the sheng lies in the fact that, after its importation (around 1800) into Europe, it led to the invention of the *harmonium. The music played on the sheng is interesting because it usually moves in parallel fifths or triads. Example in R. Lachmann, *Musik des Orients* (1929), p. 108.

Shift. In violin playing, see *Position.

Shimmy. See *Jazz III.

Shivaree. American corruption of *charivari.

Shofar. An ancient Jewish instrument made from a ram's horn and used up to the present day in the Jewish worship, at the celebration of the New Year. The statement, found in a recent reference book, that it has a recorded history of 60 centuries is, to put it mildly, a slight exaggeration — 30 being nearer to the truth — as is also the statement that it produces a natural scale. Actually, it produces only two crude and awe-inspiring sounds, roughly corresponding to the second and third harmonic.

Short octave. A special arrangement of the keys in the lowest octave of early organs, harpsichords, etc. The fact that the lowest chromatic tones (C♯, D♯, F♯, G♯) were almost never needed in keyboard music prior to, say, 1700 naturally led to the omission of the corresponding pipes or strings, a procedure which was particularly desirable in view of the great cost of the large organ pipes. On the keyboard, instead of omitting the four corresponding black keys, the keys for the remaining eight tones were arranged in a "shortened" octave which extended only to the key normally occupied by E. The keys for the tones F, G, A, Bb, and B were usually left in their normal position, and the three remaining keys (normally E, F#, G#) were allotted to the tones C, D, and E in arrangements such as:

	(a)		(b)	
Black		C D Bb		D E Bb
White	E F G A B		C F G A B	

An additional advantage of this arrangement was the possibility of playing certain widely spaced chords, e.g., E B e g# with the left hand alone [cf. *Fitzwilliam Virginal Book* 1, pp. xvii and 287]. As a matter of fact, in the arrangement (b) this chord is produced by the keys G# B e g#, which are within the easy reach of the hand. It may be noticed that the often discussed tenth E–g which occurs at the end of J. S. Bach's harpsichord toccata in E minor is no proof of Spitta's and Schweitzer's contention that this toccata is an organ piece (the theory being that the low E calls for the organ pedal), since it can easily be played with the left hand on the short octave (b). Similar widely spaced chords occur in the works of Froberger. A later (19th century) arrangement on pianofortes was the *broken octave*. Here the lowest octave was complete with 12 keys, except that the C-sharp was replaced by the more useful note A_1 from below. See also *Pedal piano.

Lit.: *GD* iii, 748 (organ) and v, 92ff (almost a doctoral dissertation on the topic); G. Kinsky, in *ZMW* ii.

Short Service. See *Service.

Si. See *Pitch names; *Solmization.

Siamese music. The music of Siam (Thai) is similar to that of Java [see *Javanese music].

Siciliano. A 17th- and 18th-century dance type of Sicilian origin, in very moderate ⅜ or ¹²⁄₈ meter, usually with a flowing broken-chord acompaniment and a soft, lyrical melody with dotted rhythms — similar if not identical in character to that of the *pastorale. It occurs as a slow movement in early sonatas (Corelli, Bach, Padre Martini) as well as in vocal music (operas, cantatas) whenever soft rural scenes are to be rendered in music.

Side drum. Same as snare drum; see *Percussion instruments B, 1.

Siegfried. See *Ring des Nibelungen, Der. *Siegfried Idyll* is the scene, frequently played in symphonic concerts, in which Siegfried, having tasted the dragon's blood, becomes able to understand the language of the birds and silently listens to them (Act II).

Sight. See *Fauxbourdon (2).

Sight-reading (singing). I. The ability to read and perform music at first sight, i.e., without preparatory study of the piece. Naturally, no finished result is expected in such performance, the aim being to obtain or to give a satisfactory general impression of the piece. This type of playing (to exemplify on the piano) puts entirely different demands on the performer than the ordinary type of finished playing. In fact, from the technical as well as the psychological point of view, it is its very opposite, so that accomplished pianists and virtuosos are frequently very poor at sight-reading. Unfortunately, this situation exists not only among concert-pianists who can, perhaps, afford to neglect sight-reading, but also among numerous students and amateurs who greatly suffer from their inability to play even the simplest piece without having studied it for weeks or months. Thus, in the course of years of study, they acquire nothing but a limited "repertory" and fail entirely to attain that broad knowledge of musical literature which is the precondition of all genuine accomplishments in the field of music. This is, no doubt, a serious fault of our present musical education, the blame for which lies with the music teachers the great majority of whom do not realize the importance of sight-reading and do not know how to teach it.

The problems of sight-reading are somewhat different in the various fields of musical activity. In singing, not much more is required than a thorough acquaintance with the elements of musical melody and rhythm and with their notation. In recent years this basic study has been emphasized in a number of music schools where it is taught under the name of *solfege. Another important means of obtaining facility in sight-singing is the participation in a choral group. Recently, there has been a considerable movement to facilitate sight-singing by the use of *solmization-systems in the place of the ordinary musical notation. Methods such as the English *Tonic Sol-fa avoid many of the complications inherent in the traditional system of musical notation (clefs, signatures, accidentals, etc.), but they restrict the student to a limited field of music, while, on the other hand, familiarity with the foundations of the ordinary notation opens to the student the entire field of music, choral as well as instrumental and orchestral.

II. The situation of the violin player is not very different from that of the singer since his music is, in the main, also restricted to melodic progression in one line. As in singing, the facility of grasping immediately the significance of intervals and of rhythmic figures is prerequisite for playing at sight. As in the case of the singer, group performance is of the highest importance, either with an accompanying pianist, or in a chamber ensemble, or in a student's orchestra.

III. The pianist's problems of sight-reading are of a different nature. Here the difficulties are considerably greater, owing to the greater complexity of the music he is concerned with. At the outset it must be said that the greatest enemy of sight-playing is playing by heart. The latter method, which is today considered indispensable for any kind of "finished performance" — with doubtful justification, by the way — causes the player to rely on his memory and on the control of

his fingers by his eyes. In sight-reading, however, the player is expected to rely, not on his memory, but on his faculty of immediate and quick apperception; moreover, his eyes must be fixed not on his hands, but on the music page. This latter technique constitutes the very basis of any success in playing at sight on the piano. The student must be taught to fix his eyes unerringly on the music and to make his fingers rely exclusively on touch, "feeling their way" through the keyboard as a blind man does with his stick. Simple exercises such as playing an octave, a fifth, a triad, a seventh chord without looking at the keys will gradually give that feeling of tactile security which is the basis of sight-playing on the pianoforte, and which is also an important factor of pianoforte playing in general [see *Pianoforte playing IV].

Still greater are the intellectual demands in the case of playing from score of chamber or orchestral music. See *Score. Cf. W. G. McNaught, "The Psychology of Sight-Singing" (*PMA* xxvi).

Signal. See *Fanfare; *Military band.

Signature. Signs placed at the beginning of a composition, indicating the key [see *Key signature] or the meter [see *Time signature].

Signet. Same as *Sennet.

Silence [F.]. Rest.

Sillet [F.]. (1) *Nut (of the violin). — (2) *Fret (of the lute).

Similar motion. See *Motion.

Simile, simili [It.]. Indication to continue "in a similar way," e.g., with the same kind of bowing, or with the same type of broken chord figure, etc.

Sin'al fine (segno) [It.]. Until the end (sign). See *Segno.

Sincopa [It.]. *Syncopation.

Sincopas. See *Cinque-pace.

Sinfonia. (1) Italian for *symphony. — (2) A name chosen by Bach for his three-voice *inventions.— (3) In the early Baroque period (1600–1750), name for orchestral introductory pieces of Italian origin. These were short pieces designed to serve as an introduction to an opera or an operatic scene (Monteverdi, *Orfeo*, 1607; Stefano Landi, *Il San Alessio*, 1634 [cf. *HAM*, no. 208; *RiHM* ii.2, 255, 263]; Michelangelo Rossi, *Erminia del Giardano*, 1637; Monteverdi, *L'Incoronazione di Poppea*, 1640, etc.); an orchestral suite (Salomone Rossi, *Sinfonie e gagliarde* . . . , 1607, '08, '13; Johann Jakob Löwe, *Sinfonien, Gagliarden, Arien* . . . , 1658; Johann Rosenmüller, *Sonate da camera cioè Sinfonie Alemande, Correnti* . . . , 1670; Johann Fux, *Concentus*, cf. *DTOe* 23.ii); or a cantata (e.g., two cantatas by Provenzale, cf. *RiHM* ii.2, 386; Bach, *Christ lag in Todesbanden*). Bach also transferred the Sinfonia to the harpsichord, in his Partita no. 2.

No fixed form or style attaches to these pieces. In this period, Sinfonia is simply one of the various names used for introductory instrumental pieces [see *Overture], others being Sonata, Toccata, etc. On the other hand, independent canzonas and sonatas were also designated as Sinfonias [see *Sonata B, I, II]. Possibly the latter term carried the connotation of orchestral performance, not necessarily implied by the others. It was not until *c.* 1690 that the operatic Sinfonia became standardized (by Alessandro Scarlatti; cf. *HAM*, no. 259) into what is usually called "Italian overture" [see *Overture] which is one of the ancestors of the modern *symphony. Examples of 17th-century Sinfonias in *SchGMB*, nos. 151, 191, 211, 220, 223, 224, 229. The last of these shows the merging of the Sinfonia with the trio-sonata. For an unusually early example of "symphonia" (15th century), strikingly similar in style and form to the Toccata in Monteverdi's *Orfeo*, cf. *RiHM* ii.1, 42 and 207.

Sinfonia Domestica. See *Symphonic poem III.

Sinfonietta. A small symphony, usually also for a smaller orchestra.

Sinfonische Dichtung [G.]. *Symphonic poem.

Singakademie. A society for concert-giving founded at Berlin in 1791 by Christian Fasch. Today it is mainly known through its concert hall.

Singing. I. Singing is, no doubt, the most ancient and widespread type of music making, being the only one (except for whistling) which does not depend upon an instrument. For the historian, this fact has, unfortunately, the disadvantage of leaving him without any information regarding the early practice of singing while, in the case of instrumental practice, the numerous pictorial representations or literary descriptions of instruments enable him to form at least a general idea of the music in, e.g., Babylon, Egypt, Greece, etc. Many people will be inclined to take it for granted that the human voice and the way it is used in singing must have been the same in remote periods as it is today. This, however, is certainly a mistaken belief. It suffices to point to the Oriental cultures (Chinese, Japanese) or to the singing of primitive tribes (Indians, Africans) to see that the human vocal apparatus can be used in very different ways. Such differences are partly due to anatomic peculiarities of the various races but also to a large extent to training and taste. Even in the European history of music the "timbre" of the voice has not remained unchanged. Although, of course, statements in this matter are necessarily somewhat hypothetical, there is reason to assume that the singers of ancient Gregorian chant preferred an Oriental, somewhat nasal timbre (as is still frequently heard in Catholic churches). The strikingly high range of much 14th- and 15th-century music is explained by the extensive use of the *falsetto. The celebrated *castrati of the 17th and 18th centuries probably possessed a vocal timbre which few people today would consider ideal. Around 1850 the purity and brilliance of the *bel canto were abandoned in favor of the "dramatic" voice of present-day opera, and in modern jazz we are witnessing the cultivation of special manners of singing which, although not recognized as artistic, help to illustrate the variability of the vocal timbre.

II. There is an infinitely greater amount of variability if questions of style and performance are taken into consideration. Particularly interesting is the ample use which, from pre-Christian times down through the 17th century and later, was made of *vocalization. The singing of Gregorian chant involved numerous vocal ornaments such as *vibrato, *tremolo, *portamento, some of which were indicated by special neumatic signs [see *Neumes]. In the 13th century, Magister Lambert (Pseudo-Aristotle) tells us that the *plica, a derivative of the "liquescent" neumes, is to be performed "by the partial closing of the epiglottis combined with a subtle repercussion of the throat." In this respect it may be mentioned that some writers explain the Jewish word "alleluia" as a phonetic formation derived from the trilling of the tongue against the roof of the mouth (l-l-l), a vocal technique which is still widely used in the Orient. Among the most striking features of early vocal music, Gregorian as well as polyphonic, is the seeming indifference in matters of correct underlaying of the text, frequently leading to wrong accentuation. In many cases, however, a closer examination shows that this procedure was not mere indifference but the result of principles which, although different from or opposed to those of modern music, nonetheless are logical and aesthetically justified. See *Text and music.

III. Another interesting point of view is that concerned with the vocal ranges. Although there always existed voices of the same ranges, high, medium, or low, as we have them today, in early periods these were far from being used to the full extent that they are today. The average range of Gregorian chant is from c to e', that is, the range of the tenor voice. Practically all polyphonic music of the 13th century still is within this range in all its parts (usually three) while much music of the 14th century (Machaut,

Landini) and of the early 15th century (Dufay) is even higher, from f to c", thus calling for the use of falsetto in the melody. An important change took place around 1450 with the rise of the *Flemish School. The bass voice was "discovered," and it was here for the first time that the texture of polyphonic music became separated into four different ranges, corresponding to that of the bass, tenor, contralto, and mezzo-soprano. Since practically all the music of this period is sacred, the performance was, of course, by men's voices exclusively, perhaps occasionally with the help of boy singers. Even in the secular repertoire of the Middle Ages and the Renaissance there is nothing to indicate performance by women, aside from exceptional pieces such as the liturgical drama of the Resurrection (c. 1100) in which there is a dialogue between the angel and the women watching the tomb [cf. SchGMB, no. 8]. The rise of the opera in the 17th century brought about the decisive change in this matter, the various roles now being given to voices of a characteristic range. The leading hero (primo huomo) is a castrato, the leading heroine (prima donna) a high soprano, while the secondo huomo is a bass and the seconda donna a contralto — a scheme which, of course, admits of modifications [see *Prima donna]. As an illustration of the astonishing range of operatic stars in the heyday of the opera it may be mentioned that a bass-part in Handel's Acis et Galatée (1708), written for the celebrated bass Giuseppe Boschi, shifts, within one measure, from a' to C, more than 2½ octaves, and that the soprano Lucrezia Agujari (1742–83) could reach c''''.

IV. The 19th century brought about the "scientific" study of the vocal apparatus and of its use in singing. Manuel Garcia (1805–1906) laid the foundation for this study in his Mémoire sur la voix humaine which he presented to the French Institut in 1840 and which was followed in 1847 by his Traité complet de l'art du chant. Among his pupils were Jenny Lind, Mathilde Marchesi, Julius Stockhausen, and others who, in turn, became the teachers of more recent generations of celebrated singers. As Garcia lived to the age of 101 years he saw practically all the great singers of the 19th and 20th centuries appear and many of them disappear from the opera stage or the concert hall. His personal teaching, however, seems to have been much more successful and influential in the end than his scientific studies. Although the scientific study of the vocal apparatus and its acoustic functions has been immensely widened and deepened, it has benefited the physiologist rather than the singer. As a matter of fact, the advance in research has brought about a widespread tendency among singing teachers to abandon the scientific method altogether and to rely on personal experience, influence, and imagination rather than on physiological or scientific "facts."

For more details about the technical aspect of voice production, see *Voice. Related articles: Voice; Voices, Range of; Register (2); Bel canto; Castrati; Falsetto; Vocalization; Solfège; Song; Tremolo; Vibrato; Text and music; Vocal music; Word painting.

Lit.: A. Historical: W. J. Henderson, Early History of Singing (1921); id., The Art of Singing (1938); G. Fantoni, Storia universale del canto (1873); H. Biehle, Die Stimmkunst, i (1931); Th. Gérold, Zur Geschichte der französischen Gesangskunst (Diss. Strassburg 1909); B. Ulrich, Die Grundsätze der Stimmbildung 1474–1640 (Diss. Berlin 1910); M. Högg, Die Gesangskunst der Faustina Hasse . . . (Diss. Berlin 1931); H. Buhle, "Die aesthetischen Grundlagen der französischen Gesangskunst im 17/18. Jahrhundert" (ZMW xii). See also *Bel canto; *Castrati. For early literature, cf. MoML, 265.

B. Practical: A. B. Bach, Principles of Singing (1902); J. F. Cooke, Great Singers on the Art of Singing (1921); D. Dossert, Sound Sense in Singing (1932); W. S. Drew, Voice Training (1924); Fucito and Beyer, Caruso and the Art of Singing (1922); H. P. Plunket, Interpretation in Song (1912); Y. Guilbert, How to Sing a Song (1918); W. J. Henderson,

Art of the Singer (1906); G. Henschel, Articulation in Singing (1926); Lilly Lehmann, How to Sing (1929); M. P. Marafiotti, Caruso's Method of Voice Production (1922); M. Ryan, What Every Singer Should Know; Ch. Santley, Art of Singing (1908); W. Shakespeare, Art of Singing (1910); id., Plain Words on Singing (1929); D. Stanley, The Science of the Voice (1932); D. C. Taylor, Psychology of Singing (1908); E. G. White, Science and Singing (1938); J. C. Wilcox, The Living Voice (1935); H. Witherspoon, Singing (1925); H. J. Wood, Gentle Art of Singing, i–iv (1925; abridged ed. in one vol.). See also *Pronunciation.

Singing saw. An ordinary handsaw, held between the knees and set in vibration by either a violin bow or by drumsticks. Its special effect is a gradual modification of pitch (similar to the *portamento of the violin) obtained by the bending of the free end of the blade with the left hand. The instrument has been used lately in jazz and in other popular musical presentations (radio).

Singspiel [G.]. Around 1700, the German equivalent for "dramma per musica" (drama with music), i.e., opera, applied alike to serious and comic operas (e.g. Keiser's Croesus, 1711). Later (c. 1750) the term was restricted to comic operas with spoken dialogue, written on the models of the English *ballad opera or the French *opéra-comique. Coffey's ballad operas, The Devil to Pay (1728) and The Merry Cobbler (1735), were translated by Christian Weisse (Der Teufel ist los and Der lustige Schuster) and set to music by Johann Standfuss (c. 1750). Johann Adam Hiller (1728–1804) composed the same two librettos and many others (Die Jagd, 1770), bringing the Leipzig Singspiel to its highpoint. From Leipzig the movement spread to other places, chiefly Berlin and Vienna. Most of the members of the *Berlin School wrote Singspiele, notably Georg Benda (Der Jahrmarkt, 1775). In Vienna, where as early as 1751 the young Haydn wrote Der neue krumme Teufel (lost; cf. *DTOe* 33.i), the Singspiel attained its artistic peak in Mozart's *Entführung aus dem Serail* (1782), other important examples being Ignaz Umlauff's *Die Bergknappen* (1778; *DTOe* 18.i), Dittersdorf's *Doktor und Apotheker* (1786), Johann Schenk's *Der Dorfbarbier* (1796; *DTOe* 34), and Schubert's *Die Zwillingsbrüder* (1819). The *Singspiel* is the ancestor of the German Romantic opera of the 19th century. Operatic works with spoken dialogue occur as early as the 17th century, e.g., S. G. Staden's *Seelewig* (1644) [cf. *MfM* xiii], Wolfgang Briegel's *Das Triumphierende Siegesspiel* (1673), and W. Franck's *Die drey Töchter Cecrops* (1679) [cf. *AMF* iv]. See *Opera VII; *Comic opera II (e).

Lit.: H. M. Schletterer, *Das deutsche Singspiel* (1863, '79); H. Graf, *Das Singspielrepertoire Berlins 1771–86* (1934); G. Calmus, *Die Singspiele von Standfuss und Hiller* (1908, *BIM*); E. O. Beer, *Mozart und das Wiener Singspiel* (Diss. Vienna 1932); R. Krott, *Die Singspiele Schuberts* (Diss. Vienna 1921); R. Eitner, in *MfM* xiii (Seelewig); G. Schmidt, in *AMF* iv (Cecrops); W. Stauder, in *AMF* i (Joh. André); P. Nettl, in *ZMW* vi (Singballett); V. Helfert, in *ZMW* v (Wiener Singspiel); F. Brückner, in *SIM* v (Benda).   D. J. G.

Sinistra [It.]. Left (hand).

Sink-a-pace, sinqua-pace. See *Cinque-pace.

Sirventes [Prov., song of service]. A type of *troubadour poetry, usually of considerable length and of heroic, political, or moral content. There is no specific musical form for these poems which were probably recited to some well-known short melody repeated for many lines [see *Chanson de geste].

Si segue [It.]. It follows.

Sistine choir (chapel). The present name of the Papal choir of 32 singers who provide the music for the services in which the Pope officiates in person. It developed from the ancient *schola can-

torum and received its present name from the *Cappella Sixtina*, the chapel built by Pope Sixtus IV in 1471–84. Since 1480 there has existed another choir, the *Cappella Giulia* (richly endowed by Pope Julian II), which is domiciled at St. Peter's and which has frequently, but incorrectly, been called Sistine choir. Both bodies have been greatly admired for the excellence of their vocal technique, involving long crescendi and decrescendi, and many refined shades of sound. However, from a musical and historical point of view, their performances of Palestrina, etc., are decidedly in mediocre taste, overladen with romantic sentimentality, and much inferior to those of other bodies, such as the *Schola Cantorum* of Paris.

Lit.: F. X. Haberl, *Die römische Schola Cantorum* . . . (1887; also in *VMW* iii); R. R. Terry, in *MA* iii; E. Celani, in *RMI* xiv; K. Weinmann in *AMW* ii; R. Casimiri, "I Diarii Sistini" (*Note d'Archivio* i [1924] to date).

Sistrum. An ancient Egyptian rattle used especially in the worship of Isis. It consisted of a metal frame with loose metal bars, the frame attached to a handle. In modern writings the term sistre sometimes occurs as a wrong spelling for *cistre.

Si tace [It.]. It keeps silent.

Sitole. Same as *cistre, etc.

Six, Les; The Group of Six. A group of six French composers, associated about 1918 and comprising: Louis Durey (b. 1888); Arthur Honegger (b. 1892); Darius Milhaud (b. 1892); Germaine Tailleferre (b. 1892); Georges Auric (b. 1899); and François Poulenc (b. 1899). The group made its first public appearance under the name *Les Nouveaux Jeunes*, but later adopted the name *Les Six* [cf. N. Slonimsky, *Music Since 1900* (1937), pp. 181, 201]. Although they do not represent a School in the proper sense of the word, a common bond exists in their attachment to Erik Satie whom they considered as their spiritual father, and in their stand against the impressionistic style of Debussy and Ravel [see *New Music]. A later group of a similar character was the *École d'Arcueil. Cf. E. Vuillermoz, in *MM* i; R. Manuel, in *MM* ii.

Six-four chord. The second inversion of the triad, e.g., g–c–e', indicated I$_4^6$ II$_4^6$, etc., in modern harmonic analysis, $^6_4$ in figured-bass parts. It occurs normally in strong position followed by the dominant V, as shown in measure 4 of the accompanying example, but may also occur

I   I^6 II   I$_4^6$ II^6 II   I$_4^6$ V   I

in weak position, as in measure 2. Cf. G. Haydon, *The Evolution of the Six-four chord* (1933); L. Matossi, in *DM* x.6.

Sixteen-foot. See *Foot (2).

Sixth [F. *sixième*, G. *Sexte*]. See *Intervals.

Sixth chord. The first inversion of the triad, e.g.: e–g–c', indicated I^6, II^6, etc., in modern harmonic analysis, 6 or $^6_3$ in figured-bass parts. In four-part harmony, doubling of the fundamental is generally avoided (e–c'–g'–c'', not e–e'–g'–c'') because the e can only be resolved upward to the f so that, with doubled e, parallel octaves (e–f, e'–f') would result. The sixth chord is used on every degree of the scale, and occurs frequently in parallel progression [see *Fauxbourdon, Ex. 1]. A specially interesting chord is the *Neapolitan sixth*, f–ab–db' in C major, which is usually explained as the first inversion of the triad on the lowered supertonic, db–f–ab [see, however, *Functional harmony]. One of the earliest instances of its use is in the Frost Scene of Purcell's *King Arthur*, 1691 [Ex. 1]. See also reference under *Temperament II (Schlick). Among the numerous chromatic varieties encountered with the chord of the sixth (e.g., f–ab–d', instead of f–a–d') those containing an *augmented sixth*, e.g., ab–f#', deserve special mention. There are four common ones: the

IV   IV^{*+}V   IV^7 IV$_3^{4+}$ V   II^7 II$_3^{4+}$ I$_4$

II^7. II$_3^{4+}$. I$_4$

augmented sixth, the augmented six-five-three, the augmented six-four-three, and the doubly augmented six-four-three. The first three of these are, rather pointlessly, distinguished as "Italian," "German," and "French" sixth. Their derivations and common resolutions are shown in Ex. 2 (+ and ++ indicate augmented and doubly augmented intervals). Cf. P. Miller, "The Augmented Sixth Chord" (*Journal of Musicology* i). See also *Added sixth.

Skala [G.]. Scale.

Slancio, Con. With impetuosity.

Slargando, slentando [It.]. Slowing up.

Slavic music. See *Bulgarian, *Czech, *Rumanian, *Russian, *Serbian music.

Slide. (1) In violin playing a slight *portamento used to pass quickly from one note to another, usually at the distance of a third or a fourth. It serves to attain a matchless legato as well as a special effect of expressiveness. Paganini introduced a virtuoso type of slide, by executing chromatic passages, singly or in thirds, entirely with the same finger. — (2) The movable portion of the *trombone. See also *Wind instruments IV (a); *Slide trumpet. — (3) An ornamentation consisting of two or more notes approaching the main note by conjunct motion; see *Appoggiatura, Double II.

Slide trumpet. See *Trumpet II.

Slider. See *Organ II.

Slur. (1) A curved line placed above or below a group of notes to indicate that they are to be played legato, e.g., with one stroke of the violin bow, or with one breath in singing. If the notes to be found under the slur have staccato dots, the meaning of the combined signs is *portato. A slur connecting two notes of equal pitch is properly called *tie or bind. — (2) An ornamentation resembling the French *tierce coulée* [see *Appoggiatura, Double II].

Smanioso [It.]. Frenzied.

Smarfioso [It.]. "Mincing," affected.

Sminuendo [It.]. Diminishing.

Smorzando [It.]. Dying away.

Snare drum. See *Percussion instruments B, 1.

Snello [It.]. Nimble, quick.

Soave [It.]. Suave, gentle.

Societies, Musical. I. *America.* Some of the more important musical organizations of national scope are the following:
1. A.G.O. (American Guild of Organists). A national association of church organists (founded in 1896), having as its purposes: (1) the improvement of music in the churches; (2) the maintenance of high standards among organists; and (3) the exchange of views and information among members through periodic meetings. In regard to (2), examinations covering performance and general knowledge of music are given for the certificates of associate (A.A.G.O.) and fellow (F.A.G.O.), which is the highest rank. Members are admitted as "colleagues" without examination. To promote (3), the Guild is subdivided into numerous regional chapters (close to 100), which hold local meetings and administer the examinations.
2. A.M.S. (American Musicological Society). An organization for "the advancement of research in the various fields of music as a branch of learning" (from the constitution). The Society is divided into regional chapters which hold

regular meetings at which papers of musicological interest are read. A national convention is traditionally held each year in connection with the M.T.N.A. convention [see (6)]. Two yearly publications, *Papers Read by the Members of the A.M.S.* (*PAMS*) and *Bulletin of the A.M.S.* (*BAMS*), are issued.
3. I.S.C.M. (International Society for Contemporary Music). The Society was begun in Europe in 1922; the United States Section was founded in 1923. The purpose of the Society is to discover and encourage talent in composition and to provide opportunities for performance of contemporary works. To this end, annual Festivals of Contemporary Music are held, at which works are performed which have been selected by an international jury. See III, 3.
4. League of Composers. An organization (founded in 1923) for promoting modern music through the performance and commissioning of new works, and through its official organ *Modern Music.* The League was for a number of years primarily a New York organization; more recently other chapters have been founded in various sections of the country.
5. M.E.N.C. (Music Educators National Conference). This organization began in 1907 as the Music Supervisors National Conference. The present name was adopted in 1936. Its purpose is to foster coöperation among public school teachers, especially supervisors, with a view to raising standards of music in the schools, and to securing a better place for music in the curriculum of the schools. Much has been accomplished by the organization in the way of developing bands, orchestras, and choruses, and in promoting instrumental instruction in the public schools.
6. M.T.N.A. (Music Teachers' National Association). An organization (founded in 1876) interested primarily in the practical problems of musical education. The chief activity of the M.T. N.A. is its annual convention, at which papers are read and discussions carried on by educators from all sections of the

country and from all branches of music education. A volume of Proceedings is published annually, containing reprints of the papers read at the conventions.

7. N.A.S.M. (National Association of Schools of Music). An organization of professional music schools the aim of which is to unify the curriculum, maintain the standards, and serve as an accrediting organization for music schools. Annual meetings are held in conjunction with the M.T.N.A. [see 6]. Much of the credit for the N.A.S.M.'s development belongs to Howard Hanson, its present president.

II. *Europe.* 1. Allgemeiner Deutscher Musikverein. Founded 1861 by Franz Liszt and Franz Brendel, having as its purposes: (1) the furthering in a progressive sense of musical life in Germany; (2) to look after the interests of the professional musicians and composers; (3) to support needy composers and their survivors. The Society has given over 60 festivals (Tonkünstlerfeste) in various cities of Germany.

2. Bach-Gesellschaft. A German society founded in 1850 (the centenary of Bach's death) with the object of publishing a complete critical edition of Bach's works. This edition, which includes 46 volumes, is referred to by the abbreviation B.-G. The society was dissolved in 1900, after the last volume had been issued. Simultaneously, a "Neue Bach-Gesellschaft" was founded to carry on the work of completing the original edition by publishing corrected revisions and practical scores. Since 1904 this society has issued an annual *Bach-Jahrbuch* containing articles on Bach and related subjects. See *Bach-Gesellschaft.

3. British Music Society. Founded in 1918 by Dr. Eaglefield-Hull, reorganized in 1921. The object of the Society is the furthering of the interests of musicians throughout Great Britain. Primarily it is an organizing and educative, not a concert-giving, institution. It has more than 50 centers with over 3500 members and an even greater number of associates. The Society is the British section of the

International Society for Contemporary Music [see III, 3].

4. Gesellschaft der Musikfreunde. The oldest and most important musical society of Austria (Vienna), founded 1813, largely through the efforts of Joseph von Sonnleithner. It has been active in various directions: (a) Conservatory, founded 1817, first director Salieri; (b) Singverein, an amateur choral society of outstanding rank, founded 1859; (c) Gesellschaftsorchester (today Orchester Verein), an orchestral society, first amateur, later professional, founded in 1859, first conductor Hellmesberger, present conductor Furtwängler; (d) Music library, founded 1819 [see *Libraries C, Vienna]; (e) Museum, containing autographs, letters, pictures, musical instruments (Haydn's piano), and musical curios (Beethoven's ear trumpets).

5. Incorporated Society of Musicians. An English society founded in 1882 by James Dawber and Dr. Henry Hiles for the furtherance of the following objects: (1) the union of the musical profession in a representative Society; (2) the provision of opportunities for discussion; (3) the improvement of musical education; (4) the organization of musicians; and (5) the obtaining of legal recognition of qualified teachers of music. Meetings are held periodically in several sections and an annual conference is held in one of the large cities. The Society, which has a membership of 3800 professional musicians, is generally recognized and consulted by Government Departments.

6. Maatschappij tot Bevordering der Toonkunst. The largest musical society in Holland, founded in 1829 and located in Amsterdam. It includes more than 40 branches with over 8000 members which are mainly active in choral singing. The choir of the Amsterdam Toonkunst, conducted by Mengelberg, is particularly well known. The Society has also been active in the editing of old music [see *Editions XXIX].

7. Société des Concerts du Conservatoire. Founded by Habeneck in Paris, probably 1792, for the purpose of giving concerts [see *Concert II]. It was defi-

nitely established in 1828 and has, from then, continued to the present day to give concerts with conservative programs.

8. Société Nationale de Musique. Founded in Paris, 1871, by Romaine Bassine and Saint-Saëns, for the purpose of giving performances of living French composers. At the first concert a trio by César Franck was performed.

III. *International*. 1. Internationale Gesellschaft für Musikwissenschaft (International Society for Musical Research). A society founded in 1927 to further musicological activities, in place of the former Internationale Musikgesellschaft [see III, 2]. The headquarters are at Basle. Congresses are arranged every few years [see under III, 2] and a periodical, *Acta Musicologica* (*AM*), has been published since 1930.

2. Internationale Musikgesellschaft (International Musical Society). A society founded in 1899 by O. Fleischer which had for its object a federation of the musicians and musical connoisseurs of all countries, and which has been instrumental mainly in the furthering of musicological research. It issued: a monthly periodical, *Zeitschrift der Internationalen Musikgesellschaft* (*ZIM*; see *Periodicals VII); a quarterly magazine, *Sammelbände der Internationalen Musikgesellschaft* (*SIM*) for larger articles; and book publications issued under the collective title *Beihefte der Internationalen Musikgesellschaft*. Congresses were held in 1904 (Leipzig), 1906 (Basle), 1909 (Vienna), 1911 (London), and 1914 (Paris), and reports were published under titles such as *Kongress der Internationalen Musikgesellschaft* (*KIM*; see p. viii). The Society ceased to exist in September, 1914.

3. International Society for Contemporary Music, founded at Salzburg in 1922, with headquarters in London since 1923 (president, E. Dent). The object is the furthering of contemporary music. See under *Festivals III. National societies were formed in various countries; see I, 3 and II, 3.

See also *Accademia; *Academy; *Apollo Club; *Männergesang verein; *Orphéon; *Singakademie. For more

complete and more detailed information regarding the American societies see Pierre Key's *Music Year Book*; regarding the others, see A. Einstein, *Das neue Musiklexikon* (1926), article "Vereine," and *RiML*, 1920ff.   E. B. H.

Soggetto [It.]. Subject or theme. In 18th-century theory the term is used in a more special sense to denote a fugal theme of a more or less orthodox character (somewhat similar to the subjects of the 16th-century *ricercar), as distinguished

1. Soggetto. 2. Andamento

from *andamento*, which is a longer theme, usually falling into two phrases, and from the *attacco* which is a short motive such as are used in motets or in the episodal sections of fugues. The subjects of the fugues in C-sharp minor and in G major from *Wt. Cl.* i may serve to illustrate the difference between a *soggetto* and an *andamento*. See *Tonal and real.

Soggetto cavato [from It. *cavare*, to hollow out; see *Cavata]. According to 16th-century theory [Zarlino, *Istituzioni harmoniche* (1588)] a musical subject which is derived by "carving out" vowels from a literary sentence and by transforming these vowels into a melody by means of the solmization syllables of the Guidonian hexachord. An example is furnished by Josquin's Mass, *Hercules Dux Ferrarie* (dedicated to Hercules, Duke of Ferrara), the main subject of which is: e–u–e–u–e–a–i–e or, in corresponding solmization syllables: re–ut–re–ut–re–fa–mi–re, or, in modern notes: d–c–d–c–d–f–e–d. Another example is the motto "Vive le roi" (V = u, i.e., ut) the musical realization of which (ut–mi–ut–re–re–sol–mi, i.e., c–e–c–d–d–g–e) is the tenor of an instrumental piece by Josquin which was written for a festive occasion, possibly for Louis XII's ascendancy to the throne of France, in 1498 [cf. *SchGMB*,

62]. See *Mass B, II (b). Cf. A. Thürlings, in *KIM*, 1906, p. 183.

Sogitha. See under *Syrian music.

Sol (soh). See *Pitch names; *Solmization.

Soléa. An Andalusian type of folk song, with stanzas of three 8-syllable lines, the first and third in rhyme. For an example cf. *LavE* i.4, 2394.

Solemn Mass. See *Missa solemnis.

Solennel [F.]. Solemn.

Solesmes. The Benedictine monks of Solesmes (a village near Le Mans in France) have become famous through their activity on behalf of the restoration of Gregorian chant. Their main achievements are two: First, the edition of a correct text of Gregorian chant at its highpoint of development (9th, 10th centuries). This edition was officially adopted in 1904 under the name *Editio Vaticana*, to supplant the corrupt versions of the *Editio Medicea* (16th century) and the similar *Ratisbon Edition* of the late 19th century [see *Liturgical books II]. Second, the first serious attempt toward a solution of the problem of the rhythm of Gregorian chant. The Solesmes interpretation of Gregorian rhythm has won wide acclaim and was recognized officially by Pope Leo XII; however, it has also met with serious criticism on the part of various musicologists [see *Gregorian chant VI]. The leading personalities in the musical activities of the Solesmes Benedictines were Dom Guéranger (1805–75), Dom Pothier (1835–1923), and Dom Mocquereau (1849–1930), who inaugurated the publication of early neumatic MSS, called *Paléographie Musicale* [see *Editions XXIII] and who was also the chief champion of the Solesmes theory of Gregorian rhythm (*Le Nombre musical grégorien ou rhythmique grégorienne*, 1908). The present leader is Dom Gajard. A periodical, *Revue grégorienne*, is published bi-monthly.

Lit.: N. Rousseau, *L'Ecole grégorienne de Solesmes* 1833–1910; C. Bellaigue, "A

l'abbaye de Solesmes" (*Revue des Deux Mondes*, Nov. 15, 1898).

Sol-fa. See *Tonic sol-fa.

Solfège [F.], **solfeggio** [It.]. (1) Vocal exercises sung to a vowel or to the syllables of *solmization: ut (do), re, mi . . . , these being used instead of a text. The latter method, which was the original one, combines the purpose of acquiring vocal technique with one of elementary instruction [see (2)] since the student is supposed to recognize the notes and intervals, a requirement which is of basic importance, particularly from the point of view of *sight-reading. Vocal exercises sung to a vowel, a, o, u . . . , are properly called *vocalises* [F.], *vocalizzi* [It.], but the name solfeggio also has become more common for this type, which includes virtuoso exercises of the greatest difficulty and frequently involves passages much too rapid to be "sol-fa"-ed.

Vocal exercises without text occur in great number throughout the 17th century under the name "ricercari" [see *Ricercar II]. In 1786 a volume *Solfèges d'Italie* was published in Paris which contained exercises by Scarlatti, Porpora, Caffaro, and others, to be treated either as solfeggi or vocalizzi. A famous collection is the *Solfèges du Conservatoire*, which contains contributions by Cherubini and other professors of the Paris Conservatoire. An outstanding collection of recent date is the *Répertoire moderne de vocalises-études* which includes contributions by Fauré, d'Indy, Ravel, and others.

(2) The term has been adopted to denote instruction in the rudiments of music, i.e., the study of intervals, rhythm, clefs, signatures, etc. Extensive courses in "Solfège," sometimes covering four years of study, were first introduced in France and Belgium and have been adopted recently by some American institutions. Cf. R. Longy-Miquelle, *Principles of Musical Theory* (1925); A. Danhauser, *Théorie de la musique* (1872 and many later editions).

Solfeggietto [It.]. Title used by some composers (C. P. E. Bach) in the meaning of "little study."

Sollecitando [It.]. Hastening, forward.

Solmization (from sol-mi). I. General term for systems of designating the degrees of the scale, not by letters, but by syllables. The syllables mostly used today are: *do* (or *doh*), *re, mi, fa, sol, la, si* (*ti*). There are two current methods of applying these syllables to the scale degrees, known as "fixed do" and "movable do." In the former, the syllables are applied to "fixed" notes, i.e., to those of the C major scale (do = C; re = D; etc.). In the latter, they are applicable to any major scale, so that do, re, mi, etc., denote tonic, supertonic, mediant, etc. (e.g., in D major: D, E, F♯, etc.). The former system is, of course, essentially identical with the current system of tone letters, as there is an exact and unchangeable correspondence between the letters (C, D, E . . .) and the sylables (do, re, mi, . . .). The syllables have, however, certain advantages, chiefly that they lend themselves better for singing purposes [see *Solfège] and that they have more "individuality." They are used chiefly in France and Italy. The movable syllables are of a much wider application and can be used with great advantage in elementary studies, such as scales, different clefs, intervals, simple modulations, etc. A modern system of "movable do" is the *Tonic-sol-fa. This is widely used in England. See *Sight-reading.

II. The use of syllables for the designation of tones is very old. The Chinese had such a system and tone-syllables are still used in *Hindu music. The ancient Greeks employed the syllables *tah, tā, toh, teh* (τα, τη, τω, τε) for the tones of the descending tetrachord (e.g., a, g, f, e). It is probably from similar syllables (*va, vη, vω, vε*) that the Byzantine *enechemata* [see *Echos] and the *Noeane* of Western medieval theory were derived. The inventor of the modern system of solmization was Guido of Arezzo (980–1050) who used the syllables *ut re mi fa sol la* as

movable names, to be used with the hexachord on G (G A B-c d e), on c (c d e-f g a), and on f (f g a- b♭ c d; the hyphen indicates the semitone *mi-fa); for more details on this system see *Hexachord. The name solmization [L. *solmisatio*] is derived from the combination sol-mi which, however, denotes, not g–e, but g–a, the syllable mi (i.e., a) being understood as belonging to the hexachord on f. Thus, it denotes, properly speaking, not so much the Guidonian syllables as such, but the concomitant principle of mutation (change from one hexachord into another). It is interesting to note that the Guidonian syllables were also used as the basis of a "fixed do" terminology, that is, in the compound terms *C–fa–ut, D–sol–re,* etc. [see *Hexachord].

III. Guido's system remained unaltered until the end of the 16th century when the more and more extended use of chromatic tones and transposed keys rendered it more and more unsuitable. About 1600, French musicians began to use the Guidonian syllables in a fixed position, ut for C, etc. In order to complete the octave, the syllable *si* (probably derived from the last words S-ancte I-oannes of Guido's hymn) was introduced, and around 1650 the rather unsingable syllable ut was replaced by *do* (Otto Gibelius, *Seminarium modulatoriae vocalis,* 1645; cf. *RiML,* 2097). Simultaneously, various attempts were made to introduce new systems, e.g., the "*voces belgicae*" of Hubert Waelrant (1517–95): *bo ce di ga lo ma ni* (known as "Bocedization"), or Daniel Hitzler's (1576–1635) "Bebezation" *la be ce de me fe ge,* or Heinrich Graun's (1701–59) "Damenization" *da mi ni po tu la be* — all ephemeral attempts which are occasionally classified as "Bobizations." In the United States a simplified system of solmization, known as *Fasola, was widely used during the 18th century. More recently, attempts at reform have been made in England and in Germany, with the idea of making the solmization syllables more useful for the purpose of elementary instruction and of sight-singing [see *Tonic Sol-fa; *Tonika Do; for two other German systems, *Tonwort* and *Zale*, cf. *MoML*, 199 and 534].

Lit.: G. Lange, "Zur Geschichte der Solmisation" (*SIM* i); F. Ring, "Zur altgriechischen Solmisations-lehre" (*AMF* iii); Ch. E. Ruelle, "La Solmisation chez les anciens Grecs" (*SIM* ix); H. Müller, "Solmisations-silben in der Medicäischen Choralausgabe" (*AMW* i); *RiHM* i.2, 167–187.

Solo [It., alone]. (1) Designation for pieces executed by one performer, either alone (piano solo; violin solo, e.g., Bach's Sonatas for violin solo), or with accompaniment of the piano, organ, orchestra, etc. — (2) In orchestral scores the term is used for passages which are intended to stand out in relief. — (3) In concertos, designation for the soloist, in distinction from the orchestra (tutti). — (4) In the early concerto (Bach, Handel) the term is also used in the orchestral parts for passages which are to be played "senza ripieni" [see *Ripieni]. See also *Ensemble.

Solo organ. See *Organ III.

Solo pitch. A pitch slightly higher than normal; it is used occasionally in order to obtain greater brilliancy of tone.

Solovox. See *Electronic musical instruments I.

Soltanto [It.]. Solely, only.

Sommesso [It.]. Subdued.

Sonante [It.]. Sounding, resonant.

Sonata [from It. *suonare*, to sound]. A. *General*. The term sonata, in its present-day meaning, denotes an instrumental composition for piano (piano sonata), or for violin, cello, etc., with piano accompaniment (violin sonata, cello sonata), which consists of three or four independent pieces, called movements, each of which follows certain standards of character and form, to be explained subsequently. It must be noted, however, that practically all the features of the sonata are also found in certain other types of instrumental music, namely, the symphony, the various species of chamber

music (quartet, trio, quintet, etc.), and, with certain modifications, the concerto. The difference lies only in the performing bodies, the symphony being a "sonata" for orchestra, the quartet a "sonata" for four strings, the concerto a "sonata" for a soloist plus orchestra, etc. From this it appears that the sonata is by far the most important form of 19th-century music, since it includes practically all the great master works of the present-day concert repertory, from Haydn and Mozart to Brahms, Bruckner and more recent composers.

The normal scheme for the movements of a sonata (symphony, etc.) is: Allegro, Adagio, Scherzo (or Minuet), Allegro. While the terms Allegro (Allegro molto, Presto) and Adagio (Largo, Lento) merely mean "quick," "slow," the term Scherzo or Minuet has a specific implication, namely that of a dance-like character. This movement is sometimes missing, particularly in the sonatas of Mozart and in most of the concertos. Symphonies frequently open with a slow Introduction. The above scheme is observed in the great majority of sonatas (symphonies, etc.). Notable exceptions are Beethoven's *Moonlight Sonata* (deliberately designated by Beethoven as *Sonata quasi una fantasia*) which consists of Adagio, Scherzo, Presto; his op. 111, consisting of Introduction, Allegro, Adagio; and Liszt's Sonata in B minor, consisting of one movement with contrasting sections.

Not only the sonata as a whole, but its single movements also are subject to certain principles of form which are usually adhered to by composers — more strictly, needless to say, by Mozart and Beethoven than by César Franck or Hindemith. The first movement (Allegro) is practically always in what is somewhat misleadingly called "*sonata-form"; the second (Adagio) is usually in sonata-form or in *ternary form, but may also be in *binary form or in variation form; the third movement is normally in the ternary form Scherzo–Trio–Scherzo [see *Scherzo]; the last movement (Allegro, Presto) is in sonata-form or *rondo-form (occasionally variation form). The fact that, certain exceptions notwithstanding, the above scheme is rather strictly adhered to in all sonatas, symphonies, quartets, written between 1780 and 1880 is the strongest possible argument against recent trends to minimize the importance of form in music [see *Forms, Musical].

B. *History*. I. Until 1650. The history of the sonata as a musical type is not identical with the history of the term sonata. The latter means "sound-piece" and is frequently contrasted with *toccata* (touch-piece) and *cantata* (sing-piece) as denoting instrumental music in contrast to keyboard music and vocal music. For over 100 years (*c.* 1530–1650) it was applied to all sorts of instrumental music, until it came to denote something definite. Luis Milan, in his lute book *El Maestro* (1535), mentions "villancicos y sonadas," the latter being instrumental pieces such as dances (pavanes) or fantasias. Giovanni Gabrieli's well-known *Sonata pian'e forte* [*HAM*, no. 173] is another piece which has a merely nominal connection with the sonata as we understand it. It seems to be more closely related to the "sonatas" of the field trumpeters and of other brass ensembles, such as the German *Turmsonaten or the English *sennets.

The sonata proper can be traced back to the French chanson of the early 16th century [see *Chanson (3)], a type of vocal polyphonic music which is distinguished from the contemporary motet, among others, by its clearer sectional structure, frequently involving repetition schemes such as AAB, ABB, etc. In Italy, this vocal form was transferred, around 1540, to the organ and, around 1580, to instrumental ensembles and was called here *canzona d'organo* and *canzona da sonare* respectively [see *Canzona (5)]. The latter type must be considered as the real ancestor of the sonata. Between 1600 and 1650 an enormous number of instrumental ensemble pieces, entitled *Canzone, Canzone da sonar, Sonate* (the simplified term *Sonate* appears first in publications by Giov. Croce, 1580; Andrea Gabrieli, 1586; and Cesario Gussago, 1608), *Sinfonie*, etc., were pub-

lished. These can be characterized as one-movement pieces which fall into a number (from five to ten or more) of short sections (approximately from four to twenty or more measures each) in contrasting styles, frequently alternating from slow sections in homophonic style to fast sections in fugal style, the latter usually more extended than the former. A frequent feature of these pieces is the reiteration of thematic material in different sections, a procedure which anticipates the *cyclical treatment of the late 19th century [cf., e.g., Viadana's *Canzon francese* (1602) in H. Riemann, *Old Chamber Music* (*OCM*) i]. Around 1635 there begins a tendency to decrease the number of sections and, as a recompense, to enlarge their extension. An early example is Tarquinio Merula's canzona *La Gallina* which falls into three distinct movements, the first and the last based on the same theme [cf. *OCM* iii]. Other composers to be mentioned in this connection are Salomone Rossi, Biagio Marini, Carlo Fontana, Massimiliano Neri, Gio. Batt. Buonamente, all of whom published between 1625 and 1650 [Ex. in *RiMB*, nos. 98, 99; Wasielewski, †*Instrumentalsätze*; *Editions II, 7]. It is interesting to note that, outside of Italy, the canzona with its somewhat loosely defined aggregation of numerous sections in an essentially polyphonic style persisted until the end of the 17th century. Examples are the sonatas by Purcell (1683, '97) in which the fugal movements are labeled "canzona," and Buxtehude's sonatas op. 1 (1696; cf. *DdT* 11), the sixth of which falls into 13 sections, alternately slow and quick [cf. also the Symphonies by Pez, in *DTB* 27/28].

II. 1650–1730. After 1650 there develops, chiefly in Venice under Legrenzi (1626–90), a certain standard structure consisting of two fugal allegro movements at the beginning and the end, frequently with identical or related thematic material, and a homophonic movement in dance-like triple meter in the middle, a three-part scheme which is usually enlarged to four or five movements by the insertion of shorter adagios before or/

and after the slow movement. A piece such as Legrenzi's Sonata "La Valvasona" of 1655 (*OCM* iv), with its four movements, Allegro–Adagio–Allegretto scherzando–Allegro (the inscriptions are not original), comes surprisingly close to the form of the classical sonata [for another example cf. *RiMB*, no. 102]. Needless to say, there is no historical connection between this "Venetian sonata" and the Viennese classical form. The "symmetrical" construction of this sonata type is even more conspicuous in many sonatas by the Bolognese [see *Bologna school] Gio. Batt. Vitali (1644–92), written in five movements: Allegro–Adagio–Scherzo–Adagio–Allegro (the term "scherzo" is adopted here for the sake of short reference); cf. his Sonata from 1667 in *OCM* iv. Vitali's compatriot Gius. Torelli (*c.* 1650–1702) introduced, in his *Sinfonie a 2, 3, 4 istromenti* (1687), a novel form in four movements, Adagio–Allegro–Adagio–Allegro, a form which, under the name *sonata da chiesa*, was adopted by all the later composers, notably Arcangelo Corelli (1653–1713) in his 24 *Sonate da chiesa a tre* (1683, '89). A sonata by Tommaso Vitali (*c.* 1665–1750) of 1693 [reproduced in *SchGMB*, no. 241], written in this form, still shows the "archaic" cyclical treatment of the first and last movement. It should be noted that Corelli's second "adagio" retains the triple meter and the homophonic style of the central "scherzo" of the earlier type, but usually in a slower speed, adopting the character of a sarabande. The final movement also shows dance-like rhythm, in the character of a gigue, minuet, gavotte, etc. This observation is important because it serves to correct the current distinction between the *sonata da chiesa* (church sonata) and the *sonata da camera* (chamber sonata; see under *Suite IV) on the basis of the absence or presence of dance-like movements. It is only in the later examples of the sonata da chiesa that the dance character of the last two movements tends to disappear. Numerous examples of the pure chiesa-type, i.e., sonatas in four idealized movements, slow–fast–slow–fast, occur in the works of non-Italian

composers, such as Bach, Handel, Jean-Marie Leclair (1697–1764; see *Editions XXVI, 27), while the Italian composers of this generation frequently preferred enlarged or shortened schemes. E.g., the violin sonatas by Veracini (1685–1750) have from five to eight movements [see *Editions VI, 34], those of Tartini (1692–1770) usually three: slow–fast–very fast [see *Editions VI, 32], those of Locatelli always three: andante–allegro–minuet (or aria con variazioni).

According to medium the repertory of the Baroque sonata falls into four categories: those written in one part, in two parts (*a due*), in three parts (*a tre*), and in four or more parts. The most famous examples of the first category are Bach's Sonatas for violin solo and for cello solo [for earlier compositions of this type see *Violin music; *Violoncello]. The "sonatas a due" usually call for three performers, one for the melody part (mostly violin) and two for the realization of the thorough-bass part [see *Thorough-bass]. This type, usually referred to as "violin sonata" (sometimes, somewhat misleadingly, as "solo violin sonata"), was cultivated as early as 1617 by Marini (*Affetti musicali*) in a strikingly virtuoso style employing trills, rapid runs, double-stops, etc. [cf. *SchGMB*, 183; *RiHM* ii.2, 96]. The virtuoso element is even more prominent in the sonatas of the Germans Joh. H. Schmelzer (1623–80) and Franz H. Biber (1644–1704; cf. *SchGMB*, no. 238). The "sonata a trè" or *trio sonata*, the most important type of all, was executed by one, two, or four performers, practically never by three [see *Trio sonata], while the "sonata a quatro" or "a cinque," cultivated mainly in the 1650–80 period, probably was for small orchestral ensemble [see *Sinfonia (3)]. Johann Jakob Kuhnau (1660–1722) was the first to write sonatas (da chiesa) for the harpsichord alone, in his *Klavierübung* ii and *Frische Klavierfrüchte* (both 1692).

III. 1730–80. The emergence of the "Viennese classical sonata" of Haydn, Mozart, and Beethoven is one of the most difficult chapters of music history and, in fact, one of the least explored. This surprising fact is due, not so much to lack of material or to negligence on the part of scholars, but mainly to the exceptional complexity of the phenomenon. The change from the Baroque sonata to the classical sonata involves much more than the change from a four-movement scheme Adagio–Allegro–Adagio–Allegro to a three-movement scheme Allegro–Adagio–Allegro or another four-movement scheme Allegro–Adagio–Scherzo–Allegro. It involves also, and chiefly, changes of style and of formal structure of the single movements. Furthermore, the repertory now becomes divided into the three species of soloist sonata (piano sonata), chamber sonata (quartet), and orchestral sonata (symphony), each of which follows a separate line of development, though within the same general frame. It is clearly impossible to describe this complex phenomenon within the limitations of a reference book, all the more since, in spite of numerous special studies, no comprehensive survey has as yet been made. Only the briefest outlines can be given and these, for the sake of clarity, under three points of view: (a) form-at-large; (b) form of the single movement; (c) style.

(a) Form-at-large. The three-movement form Allegro–Adagio–Allegro originated with the Italian overture of Alessandro Scarlatti [see *Overture I]. Antonio Vivaldi (c. 1680–1743) established it as the standard form of the concerto [see *Concerto III (b)] for which it has been retained to the present day, without the addition of a minuet or scherzo. Bach employed this form not only for his Brandenburg Concerti and his well-known Italian Concerto, but also for his six organ sonatas, probably the first sonatas written in this form (although, of course, in the strictly contrapuntal style of the Baroque). The Italian composers of harpsichord sonatas (Sammartini, 1701–75; Galuppi, 1706–85; Paradisi, 1710–92; Rutini, 1730–97; see *Editions VI) reduced the sonata to three or, frequently, two movements (Sammartini, op. 7: allegro-minuet) — not to mention the one-movement "sonatas" of Domenico Scarlatti

(1685–1757). It will suffice to mention schemes such as Andantino – Allegro – Presto; Larghetto – Allegro – Minuetto; Allegro – Minuetto [cf. the *Haffner collection] in order to illustrate the situation in the period from c. 1730 to 1760. Haydn's (1732–1809) early sonatas still belong to this loose type. The introduction of the four-movement scheme Allegro – Adagio – Minuet – Allegro must be credited to the founder of the *Mannheim School, Johann Stamitz (1717–57), who used it in all his symphonies and chamber pieces as did also most of his successors, Anton Filtz, Anton Stamitz, Ignaz Holzbauer, and others [cf. DTB 3.i; 7.ii; 8.ii; 15; 16]. Practically all the symphonies and quartets by Haydn and Mozart are in four movements, while their sonatas are in three movements only. With Beethoven, the four-movement scheme became the standard type for all the categories of the sonata, and the minuet was replaced by the *scherzo.

(b) Form of the single movements. In the Rococo sonatas of the mid-18th century (Sammartini, Rutini) practically all the movements — except, of course, the minuets — are in binary form A B, with both sections repeated. The development leading from this form to the sonata-form of the first movement is described under *sonata-form. The development of the other movements has been little investigated. Suffice it to mention that in the *Haffner collection of c. 1760 there is one example of ternary form for a slow movement (Sonata 8 by Paradies, Aria) and one example of *rondo-form (Sonata 16 by Serini). The slow movements in the sonatas of C. P. E. Bach are usually in a free form, sometimes involving elements of ternary construction. Haydn seems to have been the first to make frequent use of the rondo form for the final movement.

(c) Style. The development of style is, of course, even more difficult to describe than that of form. The tendency away from the contrapuntal texture of the Baroque sonata towards a homophonic texture already appears in the final movements of Corelli's sonatas. This tendency was supported by the brilliant and rhythmically incisive style of Vivaldi as well as by the facile melody-style of the Rococo composers [see *Gallant style] which, in turn, was largely derived from operatic models. The change towards a more dramatic manner of writing is usually credited to the Mannheim School, although Italian composers (particularly Sammartini, 1701–75) worked in the same direction [see *Mannheim School]. C. P. E. Bach cultivated a highly expressive style [see *Empfindsamer Stil] which exercised considerable influence on the young Haydn, while his younger brother Johann Christian Bach represents the link between the Italian gallant style and Mozart. Muzio Clementi's sonatas anticipate many of the dramatic elements of the Beethoven sonatas.

IV. 1780–Present. The Viennese classical sonata, as represented by the piano sonatas, quartets, and symphonies of Haydn, Mozart, and Beethoven, forms a climax of the whole development known to every music lover. In referring the reader to the articles on *String quartet and *Symphony we restrict ourselves to a general outline of the development of the sonata, mainly for pianoforte.

Although the sonatas by Mozart, piano as well as violin, are the earliest normally considered by the amateurs, students, and virtuosos of these instruments, the piano sonatas by C. P. E. Bach and those by Haydn may be expressly mentioned here because they represent an artistic treasure of great significance, many of them being definitely superior to some of the early Mozart sonatas. In his late sonatas, however, written after 1780, Mozart reached a beauty and truthfulness of expression as well as a balance of form which make these compositions unsurpassed masterworks. It may be remarked that there is no justification for connecting his C minor Fantasy K.V. 475 with the C minor Sonata K.V. 457. Beethoven's 32 sonatas (to which four early sonatas, composed in Bonn, must be added) are conspicuous and famous, above all, for the unique individuality which makes each of them a work in its own right, rather than a representative of a species. It is interesting

to note that, except for the last eight sonatas (opp. 79, 81, 90, 101, 106, 109, 110, 111), these sonatas were all composed from 1795 to 1805. Beethoven's successor in the field of the piano sonata was Franz Schubert. The general neglect of his sonatas is just as deplorable and unpardonable as is that of Bruckner's symphonies. Schumann's sonatas demonstrate, in general, the incapacity of this composer to master the large forms, while Chopin's two sonatas in B-flat minor and in B minor, together with Liszt's B Minor Sonata, are the outstanding examples of the Romantic sonata, a category to which Moscheles' Sonate Mélancolique may be added. Brahms's three piano sonatas, opp. 1, 2, and 5, stand out among the small number of important piano sonatas written after 1850. The noval trends of the early 20th century [see *New music] evoked a distinct aversion against the sonata as a typical representative of the 19th-century tradition. Some composers such as Busoni and Ravel took refuge in the less pretentious type of the *sonatina, but it was not until after the emerging of *neo-classicism (around 1920) that Stravinsky and Hindemith turned again to the form of the sonata. Particularly the latter's three piano sonatas would seem to open a period of new life for this form with its imposing history of 300 years.

Lit.: General: W. H. Hadow, Sonata Form (190–); J. S. Shedlock, The Pianoforte Sonata (1895); O. Klauwell, Geschichte der Sonate (1899); B. Selva, La Sonate ... (1913); R. Refouté, La Sonate de piano (1922). — To I and II: J. W. von Wasielewski, Die Violine im 17. Jahrhundert und die Anfänge der Instrumentalcomposition (1874); id., †Instrumentalsätze vom Ende des 16. bis zum Ende des 17. Jahrhunderts (1874, 1905); A. Schlossberg, Die Italienische Sonate ... im 17. Jahrhundert (Diss. Heidelberg 1932); E. H. Meyer, Die deutsche Sonate für mehrere Instrumente (1930); G. Beckmann, Violinspiel in Deutschland vor 1700 (1918); D. Iselin, Biagio Marini (Diss. Basle 1930); E. Kuri, "Die Triosonate ... bis Haydn" (Zeitschrift für

Hausmusik iii, p. 37); A. Schering, "Zur Geschichte der Solo Sonata . . ." (*Riemann Festschrift*, 1909); S. Clercx, "Johann Kuhnau et la sonate" (*RdM* xv). — *To III:* M. Lange, *Beiträge zur Entstehung der südwestdeutschen Klaviersonate im 18. Jahrhundert* (Diss. Giessen 1930); F. Torrefranca, *Le Origine italiane del romanticismo musicale* (1930); B. Studeny, *Zur Geschichte der Violinsonate im 18. Jahrhundert* (Diss. Munich 1911); A. Stauch, *Clementi's Klaviersonaten* . . . (Diss. Cologne 1929); E. Stilz, *Die Berliner Klaviersonate zur Zeit Friedrichs des Grossen* (Diss. Greifswald 1929); H. Michel, *La Sonate pour clavier avant Beethoven* (1907); V. Helfert, "Zur Entwicklungsgeschichte der Sonatenform" (*AMW* vii); F. Tutenberg, "Die Durchführungsfragen in der vorneuklassischen Sinfonie" (*ZMW* ix); E. Bosquet, "Origine . . . de la sonate . . . de 1698 à 1742" (*La Revue Internationale de Musique*, 1939, p. 853); F. Torrefranca, "La Creazione della sonata dramatica moderna" (*RMI* xvii). — *To IV:* P. Eger, *Zur Geschichte der Klaviersonate nach Beethoven* (Diss. Munich 1929); O. Mayer, *Die romantische Klaviersonate* (Diss. Greifswald 1929); F. Salzer, "Die Sonatenform bei Schubert" (*StM* xv); V. Urbantschetsch, "Die Entwicklung der Sonatenform bei Brahms" (*StM* xiv). See also *Symphony.

Sonata-form. A term which, unfortunately, does not designate what the name implies, i.e., the form of the sonata [see *Sonata A], but the form used frequently for single movements of the sonata (symphony, quartet, etc.). Since this form is practically always used for the first movement of a sonata, it is also designated as first-movement form. This term, however, is also misleading since the same form is frequently employed also for the slow and for the final movements of sonatas. Both terms designate a form which is of fundamental importance in music from Haydn and Mozart to the contemporary composers of sonatas or symphonies although, after 1900, it was so freely treated that sometimes only traces of it

are discernible. It is probably correct to say that 80 per cent of all the movements found in the sonatas, symphonies, quartets, concertos, trios, etc., from 1780 to the present day, are written in sonata-form, strictly or freely applied.

I. A movement written in sonata-form falls into three sections, called exposition, development, and recapitulation (also called statement, fantasia section, and restatement), the last being usually followed by a shorter or longer coda. In the exposition the composer introduces his musical ideas, consisting of a number of themes; in the development section he "develops" this material, and in the recapitulation he repeats the exposition, though with certain modifications. In practically all the sonatas of the earlier period the exposition is repeated, as is indicated by the repeat-sign at its end, a sign which is also helpful for the reader in finding the end of the exposition and the beginning of the development section. Accordingly, the structure of sonata-form is indicated by the scheme A A B A. There can be no doubt that composers, when they wrote the repeat-sign at the end of the exposition, wanted this section to be played twice, the more so since they frequently took the trouble to write two different endings (*prima* and *seconda volta*) for this purpose. In fact, the repetition of the exposition finds its justification not only in historical facts [see II] but also, and mainly, in artistic considerations, since it helps to impress into the hearer's mind the themes on which the whole movement is based. The prevailing concert practice of omitting the repetition is to be deplored; at any rate, it cannot serve as a reason for interpreting sonata-form as a plain ternary form A B A, as is usually done. It was not until *c.* 1870 that the repetition was consistently discarded, mainly on account of the ever-growing dimensions of each section, by such composers as Brahms, Bruckner, Franck, Mahler, and all their successors.

The exposition contains a number of themes and connecting passages (bridge passages) which fall into two groups, first and second group or, as they are also called, first and second theme, the other melodies occurring in each group being considered as continuations of these two. There is usually a noticeable difference in character between the first and the second themes, the former being, e.g., dramatic, the latter lyrical. Furthermore, the second theme is in another key, normally in the key of the dominant if the tonic is major, and in the relative key if the tonic is minor. Towards the end of the second group one frequently finds a "closing theme" which stands out for its individual character. In later sonatas or symphonies (Brahms, Bruckner) this adopts a significance equal to that of the two other themes, and Bruckner, particularly, regularly uses three themes in three distinct groups of the exposition.

The development is the central section of the movement, on account of its position as well as its character. The style and treatment here differ radically from that in the exposition. A great number of devices and procedures are used to produce that special character of "development," "dynamic tension," "increased temperature," "fighting forces," etc., which is proper to this section [see *Development]. Probably the two most important means of development technique are melodic segmentation and rapid harmonic *modulation. Other devices are contrapuntal imitation of melodic motives (fugal style), contrapuntal combination of different motives, use of themes or motives in *inversion or *diminution. There are, of course, no set rules as to any of the details of procedure. In the development section more than anywhere else the composer is free to use his ingenuity in forming a dynamic body from the building material at his disposal. Some composers have occasionally used new themes and new material in the development sections, but most of them seem to have taken pride in showing what they can accomplish without doing this.

The recapitulation normally contains all the material of the exposition, although usually with certain modifications, particularly in the bridge passages. One modification is obligatory, namely, that which makes the second theme appear in

the tonic (not, as formerly, in the dominant) so that the whole movement comes to a close in the tonic. In modern symphonies (Sibelius) the recapitulation is frequently drastically reduced, e.g., to a restatement of the principal theme only.

The coda which, in many instances, is only a closing sentence of moderate length, assumes, in others, considerable proportions and sometimes spreads out into another development section (e.g., in the first movement of Beethoven's *Eroica*).

Sonata-form may be diagramed thus:

$\|$: Exp.   :$\|$ Dev.   Recap.   Coda
  I II (III)   I II (III)
  T D   T T

II. *History*. Sonata-form emerged in the early part of the 18th century as an amalgamation of formal and stylistic traits encountered in several earlier forms, notably the dance movements of the suite, the da capo aria, the concerto grosso, and the first movement of the Neapolitan operatic sinfonia. As is explained under *Binary and ternary form, the "rounded binary form" $\|$: A :$\|$: B A :$\|$ was well established around 1720, in the movements of the suite as well as in other types of composition. Its scheme is identical with that of sonata-form, the main difference being the use of two contrasting themes (for A) in the latter, as against the continuous style in the former. The root of this important principle is found in the contrast style of the concerto grosso, with its alternation between tutti and solo sections. The carrier of the development which led to the adoption and amalgamation of these principles was the Neapolitan operatic sinfonia [see *Sinfonia (3); *Overture (1)]. The first movement of the Overture (Sinfonia) to Francesco Conti's opera *Pallade trionfante* of 1721 is a fully developed example of sonata-form [cf. *AdHM* ii, 797]. The same form was applied to chamber music by Maria Veracini (1721) and Giov. Batt. Pergolesi (*c.* 1730), to the piano sonata by C. P. E. Bach ("Prussian" Sonatas, 1742), and, at about the same time, by Giovanni Platti (b. *c.* 1700). The changes which, between 1725 and 1775, led from the "Rococo" sonata-form to the "classical" sonata-form are, above all, changes of style, from the stereotyped brilliance of the early Neapolitans (A. Scarlatti) to a pre-Mozartian style of lively or singable melody (Pergolesi, J. Chr. Bach), a pre-Beethovian style of dynamic abruptness (Stamitz; see *Mannheim School), and to the "*empfindsamer Stil" of C. P. E. Bach and the early Haydn. In addition, the scheme of sonata-form underwent various changes, two of which may be singled out here: first, the abandoning of the repetition for the second section, i.e., the change from ‖: A :‖: B A :‖ to ‖: A :‖ B A; and second, the dropping out of the main theme at the outset of the development section. Both features, which are left-overs from the binary form of the dance movements, are still found in most of Haydn's sonatas (e.g., op. 42, no. 8 in A-flat), the former also in a number of sonatas by Mozart, as well as in Beethoven's Piano Sonata in F♯ (op. 78).

The above survey will suffice to show that the emergence of sonata-form is the result of a gradual development carried on by a great number of composers, not the achievement of any single "inventor of sonata-form" such as have been presented by various scholars (Riemann: Stamitz; Adler: Monn; Helffert: Bohemian composers; Torrefranca: Platti). Riemann's claims in favor of Johann Stamitz as the originator of sonata-form are definitely unjustified since in practically all his symphonies Stamitz uses a mosaic-like alternation of recurring fragments which is somewhat similar to the construction of Domenico Scarlatti's sonatas. A symphony from 1740 by the Viennese Monn (*DTOe* 16.i), on the other hand, shows the essential features of sonata-form, exposition, development, and recapitulation, as well as two distinct themes in the exposition. It is interesting to note that the basic structure of sonata-form also occurs, on a much smaller scale, in the scherzos or minuets of the sonata, as well as in many folk songs; see *Binary and ternary form II. For literature see under *Sonata (Lit.: *To III*).

Sonatina. A diminutive sonata, with fewer and shorter movements than the normal type, also usually of lighter execution, designed for instruction (Clementi, Kuhlau). Recent composers, however, such as Busoni, Ravel, have written sonatinas of considerable technical difficulty and artistic aspiration. See under *Sonata B IV.

Song. A song may be defined as a short composition for solo voice, usually but not necessarily accompanied, based on a poetic text, and composed in a fairly simple style so designed as to enhance rather than to overshadow the significance of the text.

Just as *singing is the most ancient and most widespread kind of music-making, so song stands out among all the forms and types of music for the age of its tradition and for the largeness of its repertory. Referring the reader to the article on *folk song we restrict ourselves here to a consideration of the art-song, i.e., song as a personal creation aiming at artistic perfection.

I. Up to 1600. While most of the few remnants of Greek vocal music fall outside the category of song, owing to their liturgical affiliation, a charming lyrical song has been preserved in the *Seikilos song. A few examples of medieval Latin lyric songs have been preserved, notably the 10th-century love song "O admirabile Veneris ydolum" [cf. *BeMMR*, 72], the melody of which is interesting on account of its clear G major tonality. The "Planctus Karoli," a mourning song for the death of Charlemagne, 814, is written in neumes which cannot be deciphered [cf. the fascimile and the abortive attempt at transcription in *GD* v, 1f]. Around 1100 a great flowering period of song started with the French *troubadours and *trouvères, and continued with the German *Minnesinger and *Meistersinger. The devotional songs of Italy and Spain, known as *laude and *cantigas, may also be mentioned in this connection. While all the previously mentioned songs are unaccompanied, songs with instrumental accompaniment figure prominently in the musical literature of the 14th century in France and in Italy [see *Ars nova; *ballade, *ballata; *madrigal I; *rondeau; *virelais]. This development reached a wonderful climax in the chansons of the *Burgundian masters Dufay and Binchois (both born *c.* 1400). Around 1450 the rise of the *Flemish school with its emphasis on polyphonic and sacred music put the lyrical song into an eclipse from which it emerged again in the 16th-century lute songs [see *Villancico] of the Spanish Luis de Milan (*El Maestro,* 1535), Valderrabano (*Silva de Sirenas,* 1547), and others. Whether the early 16th-century *frottole were accompanied solo songs or choral music remains open to question. A large number of beautiful lute songs (*ayres) were written in England around 1600 by John Dowland, Thomas Morley, and many others [see *Editions XI]. At the same time the *air de court was cultivated in France. It was supplanted, during the 17th and 18th centuries, by the more popular types known as *vauxdevilles, *pastourelles, *bergerettes, and *brunettes.

II. *Baroque.* The rise of *monody, about 1600, brought with it fresh impetus for the composition of songs, by its emphasis on good and careful declamation as well as by the reduction of the accompaniment to its bare essentials. It is interesting to note that in Italy, where this movement originated, it did not lead to a lasting tradition of song writing, the reason being that all the interest was focused on the opera which demanded a more pretentious and elaborate type of vocal music than simple lyrical songs, the *aria. In Germany, however, the new tendencies led to a flowering period of genuine songs which opens the glorious tradition of the German *lied* which is treated separately under the heading *lied.

III. *Modern Song.* It was not until long after the German lied had reached its high-point under Schubert that a new activity in the field of art-song started among the other nations, particularly in France, where composers of rank, inspired by the refined poetry of Verlaine and Baudelaire, inaugurated a typically

French tradition of song. Among the earliest and most impressive examples are the sixteen songs by Duparc (1848–1933), composed between 1868 and 1877. About the same time Fauré (1845-1924) began to write songs, mostly in cycles such as *La bonne chanson* (1892), *La Chanson d'Eve* (1907–10), *Le Jardin clos* (1915–18), *L'Horizon chimérique* (1922). In the meantime Debussy (1862–1918) had appeared with his sensational *Chansons de Bilitis* (1897) which marked a decisive turn away from German models towards a typically French (impressionistic) style and expression. The songs of Ravel and Albert Roussel follow the same general trend. The more recent development of French vocal writing shows a shift from impressionism towards neo-classicism or towards a sophisticated type of pseudo-popular chanson.

The Russians, beginning with Glinka, have evolved a highly effective type of romance, usually in symmetrical (ternary) song-form. Thus, the songs of Tchaikovsky, Rachmaninov, Gretchaninov, Glière, are mostly lyrical and somewhat sentimental, with texts taken from mediocre contemporary poets. Moussorgsky created a vigorous and un-academic type of song, often employing an expressive and realistic recitative — a style which influenced not only the Russian but also French and Spanish song-writers. Rimsky-Korsakov, Balakirev, and Borodin wrote numerous songs in a strongly nationalistic idiom, with emphasis on an elaborate accompaniment. The Soviet school largely follows the Moussorgsky-Borodin tradition, but Tchaikovsky's influence is also apparent.

The Italian song literature of the 19th century consists of a great number of popular and sentimental songs of an appallingly low level of taste. Here the preoccupation with the opera, together with the lack of a tradition of Italian folk music, proved fatal for the song, and it was not until the reversal of these trends, around 1910, that Italian composers took a serious interest in songs. While the songs of Ottorino Respighi are written in the sensuous and hedonistic style of the

[699]

late Romanticism, there has been recently a trend towards simplification and towards archaism, based on the study of old Italian song types (Casella, Malipiero, Petrassi).

In England, also, hardly any song of importance was written during the 19th century. Among the modern English composers who have been active in this field, Vaughan Williams, Holst, Bax, Goossens, John Ireland, and Roger Quilter may be mentioned.

In the United States Stephen Foster was the creator of a national type of song, and many of his songs have become genuine folk songs. In the development of art-song Henry F. Gilbert and Horatio Parker were pioneers. The Romantic type is represented by MacDowell, Hadley, Carpenter, Cadman, and others; the impressionistic by Loeffler and Griffes; the modern song has found an impressive representative in Charles Ives.

Lit.: H. T. Finck, *Songs and Song Writers* (1900); J. J. Geller, *Famous Songs and Their Stories* (1931); G. Kobbé, *Famous American Songs* (1906); W. T. Upton, *Art-Song in America* (1930); H. C. Colles, *Voice and Verse* (1928); F. Kidson, *English Songs of the Georgian Period*; H. P. Greene, "Stanford's Songs" (*ML* ii, no. 2); *id.*, "The Future of the English Song" (*ML* i, no. 1); M. Cooper, "Liszt as a Song Writer" (*ML* xix, no. 2); E. Walker, "Songs of Schumann and Brahms" (*ML* iii, no. 1); H. Bedford, "Unaccompanied Song" (*ML* iii, no. 3); E. Oliphant, "A Survey of Russian Song" (*MQ* xii). See also *Ayre, *Ballad, *Folk song; *Lied; *Shanty; *Text and music.

Song cycle [G. *Liederkreis*]. A string of songs of related thought and character, designed to form a musical entity. Famous examples are Beethoven's *An die ferne Geliebte*, op. 98 (composed 1816 to the words of A. Jeitteles); Schubert's *Die schöne Müllerin* (1823) and *Winterreise* (1827); Schumann's *Frauenliebe und Leben* (1840; poems by Chamisso), and *Dichterliebe* (1840; poems by Heine); Brahms's *Magelone* (1861–68; poems by

Tieck); Fauré's *La bonne chanson* (1892; poems by Verlaine); Debussy's *Chansons de Bilitis* (1897; poems by Pierre Louys).

Song-form [G. *Liedform*]. A generally accepted, though not very fortunate, designation for the simple ternary form A B A, a form which, as a matter of fact, is much more frequent in instrumental (particularly piano) music than in songs. The term was used first (by B. Marx; cf. *GD* iv, 195) to designate the M T M form of the minuet with trio, a species for which the term ternary form is, no doubt, preferable, in view of the wide discrepancy in style between these dance-like pieces and a song.

In modern writings, the term song-form is also used for *binary form, a distinction being made between ternary song-form and binary song-form. Actually, the word "song" might just as well be omitted here, unless it is taken to indicate that the sections in each of these forms are simple and small enough to be suggestive of a song. However, it would be quite difficult to carry through such a distinction, e.g., in the case of the dances (all binary) in Bach's suites, where the term "song"-form might perhaps be applied to the minuets or bourrées, but is rather out of place for the elaborate allemandes or gigues.

Songs Without Words. See *Lieder ohne Worte.

Sonnenquartette. See under *Russian quartets.

Sonneries [F.]. Signals given by trumpets or by church bells.

Sons bouchés [F.]. The stopped notes in horn playing. See *Horn I.

Sopra [It.]. Above. *Come sopra*, as above. *M.d.* (or *M.s.*) *sopra* means right (or left) hand above the other (in pianoforte playing); see *Sotto.

Soprano [G. *Sopran*]. The highest female voice; see *Voices, Range of. Soloists are classified as dramatic, lyric, or coloratura. Voices of similar range are the unchanged boy's voice, "boy soprano," and the "male soprano," i.e., either a *falsettist or, formerly, a *castrato. The term is also used in connection with certain instruments, to denote the highest member of a family, e.g., the soprano recorder.

Soprano clef. See *Clefs.

Sorcerer's Apprentice, The ("L'apprenti sorcier"). See *Symphonic poem IV.

Sordamente [It.]. Subdued, muffled.

Sordino [It.]. (1) See *Mute.— (2) Old Italian name for the *kit or the *clavichord.

Sordun. See *Oboe family III.

Sospirando [It.]. Sighing, plaintive.

Sostenente (sostinente) pianoforte. Generic name for a pianoforte which produces a sustained sound, as the violin or the organ. A great number of such instruments, all more or less ephemeral, have been invented. There are four principal means of obtaining the desired effect: (1) by currents of air directed against the strings; (2) by repeating hammers; (3) by a bowing mechanism; (4) by means of electricity. The first method was used in Schnell's *Anémochord* [see under *Aeolian harp]. The second, in which rapidly striking hammers produce a tremolo, was invented by Hawkins in 1800, improved in the *Melopiano* of c. 1873, and patented, in a new form, by E. Moor in 1931 and by Cloetens in 1932. The third is realized in a great number of instruments, generically called *pianoviolin* [G. *Bogenklavier*; *Streichklavier*; *Geigenwerk*], of which the *hurdygurdy may be considered the ancestor. Usually, the ordinary violin bow is replaced by one or several wheels bearing rosined strings, and set in rotation by a foot-mechanism, while the strings are pressed against the wheel by a mechanism connected with the keys. The first perfect instrument of this type was Hans Haiden's *Gambenwerk* (c. 1575; described in Praetorius *De Organographia*, 1619 and *Teatrum Instrumentorum*,

1620). Later constructions frequently used complete violins, violas, etc., which are placed inside a big circular bow and pressed against this, in different positions, by a mechanism connected with the keyboard. Regarding the fourth category, see *Electronic musical instruments. Cf. *SaRM*, 360; *GD* v, 82; *GD*, Suppl. Vol., 598ff.

Sostenuto, sostenendo [It.]. Sustaining the tone or slackening the tempo. *Andante sostenuto* calls for a slow andante.

Sostenuto pedal. See *Pianoforte I.

Sotto [It.]. Under. *Sotto voce* (under the voice) means performance, vocal or instrumental "in an undertone," i.e., with subdued sound. *M.d.* (*M.s.*) *sotto* means right (left) hand underneath the other (in pianoforte playing); see *Sopra.

Soubrette [F., a young servant]. The term has been adopted into German usage to denote operatic sopranos of a light and somewhat comical type, e.g., the Zerlina in Mozart's *Don Giovanni*. The corresponding French term is *dugazon*, after a famous singer Louise Dugazon (1755–1821) who excelled in such roles.

Sound board [F. *table d'harmonie*; G. *Resonanzboden*]. In pianofortes, the wooden surface expanding beneath the strings which serves as a resonator (also called *belly). Most defects in sound, such as usually develop in pianos after a number of years, are due to the cracking or bending of the sound board.

Sound-film. See *Electronic musical instruments VII.

Soundholes [F. *ouïe*; G. *Schalloch*; It. *occhi*]. The apertures in the shape of an *f* (F-holes) which are cut in the table of violins, etc. Their function is to give greater freedom of movement to the central segment of the table, thus making it more serviceable for its purpose of reinforcing the tones produced by the strings. Savart (1791–1841) has shown by experiments that in violins, violas, etc., the traditional *f*-form of the holes is superior to any other form. In earlier instruments of the violin type (viols) the holes were in the shape of a sickle or half-moon (C-holes). The apertures of lutes and guitars are in the form of a full circle in the center of the table [see *Rose]. Their particular shape and position bring about prolongation of the sound while the soundholes of the violins have rather the opposite effect.

Sound ideal. A recent term (translation of G. *Klangideal*) used by music historians to refer to the characteristic "sonorities" of the various periods of music, particularly the earlier ones. For instance, the *Burgundian sound ideal (early 15th century) is that of a light, multicolored combination of vocal sound with many instrumental timbres of a somewhat nasal character, extremely rich in overtones, indeed rather harsh and piercing. To this sonority that of the early *Flemish School (late 15th century) forms a most striking contrast, being darker in color, lower in range, relatively uniform in timbre, and preferably vocal. Cf. A. Schering, in *JMP* xxxiv; G. Pietsch, in *AM* iv, nos. 2 and 3; K. G. Fellerer, in *JMP* xliv; H. Brunner, *Das Klavierklangideal Mozarts* (1933).

Sound post [F. *ame*; G. *Seele, Stimmstock*; It. *anima*]. In violins, etc., a small pillar of pine wood fixed between the table and the back. It serves not only to counter the heavy pressure exercised by the bridge upon the table (a purpose for which it was originally introduced), but chiefly to convey the vibrations of the table to the back of the instrument and to bring the various vibrating sections into conformity with each other. The correct position of the sound post is slightly behind the right foot of the bridge. Attempts to change the material or the shape of the sound post have proved unsuccessful. Cf. W. Huggins, *On the Function of the Sound-post* (1883).

Soupir [F.]. See *Notes.

Soupirant [F.]. Sighing, plaintive.

Sources, Musical, prior to 1450. These can be grouped under four catego-

ries: Gregorian chant; Secular monophony; Organ music; Polyphonic music. For the first category, see *Editions XXIII; for the second, see under *Trouvères, *Minnesinger, *Laude, *Cantigas; for the third, under *Organ music I. The most important sources of polyphonic music prior to 1450 are listed below.

Before 1100. Theoretical treatises dealing with *Organum; *Winchester Troper* [see under *Troper].

12th Century. 1. MSS of *St. Martial, *c.* 1150: Paris B.N. *lat. 1139, 3719, 3549.* London, Br. Mus. *Add. MS 36881.*

2. *Codex Calixtinus* of Santiago de Compostela, *c.* 1150 [cf. P. Wagner, *Die Gesänge der Jakobusliturgie* (1931)].

13th Century. 3. Various MSS containing the repertory of the School of Notre Dame. The three most important of these are indicated under *Magnus liber organi. For the others cf. F. Ludwig, *Repertorium organorum . . . et motetorum . . .* (1910).

4. *Codex *Montpellier,* Montpellier, Fac. des Médecins *H 196 (Mo).* Contents: motets. New ed. in Y. Rokseth, *Polyphonies du XIIIe siècle,* 4 vols. (facsimile, transcriptions, commentary), 1936–39.

5. *Codex Bamberg,* Bamberg, Kgl. Bibl. *Ed. IV.6 (Ba).* Contents: motets, *In seculum-compositions. New ed. in P. Aubry, *Cent motets du XIIIe siècle,* 3 vols. (facs., transcr., comm.), 1908.

6. *Codex Huelgas* or *Burgos,* Monastery of Las Huelgas near Burgos *(Hu).* Contents: motets and monophonic hymns. New ed. in H. Anglès, *El Codex musical de Las Huelgas,* 3 vols. (facs., transcr., comm.), 1931.

7. *Codex Torino,* Turin, Bibl. Reale, *man. var. N. 42.*

14th Century. 8. *Roman de Fauvel,* Paris, Bibl. Nat. *fr. 146 (c.* 1315). Contents: motets and monophonic songs inserted in a continuous narrative. New ed. in P. Aubry, *Le Roman de Fauvel* (facs.), 1907.

9. *Codex Ivrea,* Ivrea (Italy), Library of the Chapter. Contents: French compositions of the early 14th century. Cf. *AMW* vii, 185.

10. *Machaut MSS* of the Bibl. Nat., Paris. Contents: complete works of G. de Machaut (1300–77). New ed. in F. Ludwig, *G. de Machaut, Musikalische Werke*, 3 vols., 1926–29.

11. Florence, Bibl. Nac. *Panciatichi 26.* Contents: madrigals, caccias, ballatas, of early Italian composers. Cf. *WoGM* i, 244 (for corrections of the various lists of contents given in *WoGM*, cf. F. Ludwig, in *SIM* iv).

12. London, Brit. Mus. *Add. 29987.* Contents: Italian compositions of the 14th century, also instrumental *estampies. Cf. *WoGM* i, 268.

13. *Codex Squarcialupi*, Florence, Bibl. Laurenziana *Pal. 87.* Contents: works of Francesco Landini and of numerous other 14th-century Italian composers (madrigals, ballatas, caccias). Cf. *WoGM* i, 228. Partly repr. in L. Ellinwood, *The Works of Francesco Landini*, 1939.

14. Paris, B.N. *ital. 568.* Contents: Italian compositions of the 14th century. Cf. *WoGM* i, 250.

15. *Codex Reina*, Paris, B.N. *fonds fr. nouv. acq. 6771.* Contents: (1) Italian 14th-century pieces; (2) French 14th-century pieces; (3) compositions of the period of Dufay. Cf. *WoGM* i, 260.

16. Modena, Bibl. Estense *L. 568.* Contents: French and Italian compositions of the late 14th century. Cf. *WoGM* i, 335.

17. Chantilly, Musée Condé *1047.* Contents: French compositions of the late 14th century. Cf. *WoGM* i, 328.

18. Torino, Bibl. Naz. *J II 9.* Contents: French and Italian compositions of the late 14th century. Cf. *AMW* vii, 210.

19. *Codex Apt*, Apt (France), Library of the Chapter, *c.* 1400. Contents: chiefly Mass items. Cf. *AMW* vii, 201. New ed. in A. Gastoué, *Le Codex d'Apt* [see *Editions XXIV, A 10; cf. the review by G. de Van, in *AM* xii, 64].

15th Century. 20. Bologna, Lic. Mus. *37.* Contents: Compositions by Dunstable and many composers of the early Burgundian School. Cf. *WoGM* i, 197.

21. Modena, Bibl. Estense *471.* Con-

tents: similar to that of 20. Cf. *AMW* vii, 236.

22. Bologna, Bibl. Univ. *2216.* Contents: similar to that of 20. Cf. *WoGM* i, 199.

23. Oxford, Bodl. Libr. *Selden B. 26.* Contents: English 15th-century pieces. Cf. *WoGM* i, 368. Facs. in Stainer, *Early Bodleian Music* i, 37–97.

24. *Canonici MS*, Oxford, Bodl. Libr. *Ms. Can. misc. 213* (*c.* 1450). Contents: Mass items, motets, chansons. New ed. of the secular pieces in Stainer, *Dufay and His Contemporaries* (1898); of the sacred in Ch. van den Borren, *Polyphonia sacra*, 3 vols. (1935).

25. *Old Hall MS*, Catholic College of St. Edmunds, Old Hall, England (*c.* 1450). Contents: Mass compositions, hymns. New ed. by A. Ramsbotham and H. B. Collins, 3 vols., 1935–38.

26. *Trent Codices.* See separate entry.

27. *Cancionero musical*, Madrid, Bibl. del Palacio, MS 2, 1–5 (*c.* 1500). Contents: 459 Spanish accompanied songs, mostly *villancicos. New ed. in F. A. Barbieri, *Cancionero musical del los siglos XV y XVI* (1890).

See also *Chansonnier; *Liederbuch. For more complete lists cf. *ApNPM*, 201ff (12th–14th centuries); *WoHN* i, 351ff and 444ff (14th–16th centuries); *AMW* vii, 245 (14th–15th centuries).

Sourd [F.]. Muffled. *Pédale sourde*, soft pedal.

Sourdine [F.]. (1) *Mute (*sordini*). — (2) An obsolete wind instrument of muffled sound; see *Oboe family III. — (3) *Kit.

Sousaphone. See *Brass instruments III (e).

Souterliedekens [Neth., psalter songs]. A 16th-century Netherlands collection of 158 monophonic psalm tunes, published in 1540 and reprinted in more than thirty editions. From the literary standpoint the publication is interesting as the earliest complete translation (rhymed) of the psalms into the vernacular [see *Psalter]. Its musicological importance lies in the fact that the melodies are not newly composed, but taken from popular folk melodies of the period, and that the editor has indicated with each melody the beginning of the original secular text, thus preserving to posterity a wealth of early folk melodies, mostly from the Netherlands. In 1556–57 Clemens non Papa published the same melodies in a three-voice setting [cf. Ex. in BeMMR, 259], while his pupil Gherardus Mes made an edition in four parts (1561).

Lit.: E. Mincoff-Marriage, *Souterliedekens (1922; facs. ed.); D. F. Scheurleer, De Souterliedekens (1894); K. P. Bernet Kempers, in Tijdschrift der Vereeniging voor Nederlandsche Muziek Geschiedenis, xii (1928); H. Commer, *Collectio operum musicorum Batavorum, xi (Clemens non Papa).

South American music. See *Latin American music.

Soviet music. See *Russian music.

Sp. [G.]. Short for *Spitze.

Spacing. The arrangement of the notes of a chord according to the demands of the single voices. When the three upper voices are as close together as possible, the spacing is described as close position or close harmony [Ex. 1, 2]; sometimes

the term is reserved for positions not exceeding a twelfth [Ex. 3, 4]. The other arrangements, frequent in vocal music, are called open position or open harmony [Ex. 5, 6].

Spandendo [It.]. Expanding (i.e., in power).

Spanish music. Spain has an ancient and extremely interesting tradition of music. Unfortunately many phases of its

musical history are still obscure, owing partly to the lack of source material, partly to the fact that the extant material has been jealously guarded by narrow-minded state and town authorities. Only during the last decade has a somewhat more obliging attitude been taken.

I (Until 1500). The Christianization of Spain which took place during the 4th century led to the establishment of the so-called Visigothic chant, the Spanish counterpart of the Gregorian (Roman) chant. It persisted until about the 11th century when it was superseded by the Gregorian chant. Since it remained in use during the Arab domination (711–1085) it is usually referred to as *Mozarabic chant [see also *Chant]. In the pre-Arabic period Seville, Toledo, and Saragossa were great centers of musical culture, particularly under the bishops St. Leander (d. 599) and St. Isidore (d. 636). The latter's writings contain valuable information concerning contemporary practice of church music [cf. ReMMA, 110]. There also exist a number of secular songs, unfortunately notated in neumes which cannot be deciphered. One of the most discussed problems of early Spanish music is the Arabic element which, according to some scholars (Farmer), exercised a basic influence not only on Spanish music but also on European music in general. Few of these sweeping claims have stood up under the scrutiny of unbiased examination [see *Arabian music I]. A highly important source of devotional songs is preserved in the 13th-century MSS of cantigas, written for (and partly by) King Alfonso X (1252–82). These volumes are also of the highest importance as a unique source of information on medieval instruments of which they contain numerous reproductions [see *Cantiga]. In the 12th century the monastery Santiago de Compostela in the Pyrenees was a leading center of polyphonic music, side by side with the School of *St. Martial [Codex Calixtinus; see *Sources 2; cf. ReMMA, 267f; AdHM, 181; ApNPM, 212f]. Very likely one of the most important sources of the repertory of the French

School of Notre Dame, the MS Madrid, Bibl. Nat. *Hh167* (formerly *20486*), was written in Spain. The influence of French polyphonic music is also apparent in the *Codex Huelgas* (or *Codex Burgos*) [see *Sources, no. 6], which contains original Spanish pieces, monophonic as well as polyphonic, and in which Johan Rodriguez is repeatedly mentioned as a composer.

From 1300 till 1450 we have very scant information about the music in Spain, and musical sources are entirely lacking. Fortunately, an invaluable collection compiled shortly after 1500, the *Cancionero musical del palacio* [see *Sources, no. 27], contains, among its 459 compositions, a vast number of pieces by 15th-century Spanish composers such as Johannes de Cornago (also represented in the *Trent codices), Juan Urrede, Fernando della Torre (fl. around 1450), composers who wrote secular polyphonic compositions in the styles of Dufay and Ockeghem and in the French forms of the *ballade and the *virelai. The latter form was widely adopted, under the name of *villancico, by the later composers of the Cancionero, notably the poet-musician Juan dell Encina (1469–1529?) [for a list of other composers cf. *RiHM* ii.1, 284]. A famous theorist of the same period was Ramos de Pareja (1440–1521; see *Theory II).

II (1500–1800). The 16th century is the golden period of Spanish music. In the fields of sacred vocal polyphony as well as of organ and lute music it has produced masters of the highest rank. In the first group we find Cristobal Morales (c. 1500–53), his pupil Francisco Guerrero (1528–99), the "Spanish Palestrina" Tomas Luis de Victoria (c. 1540–1611), and Juan Ginés Perez (1548–1612). Morales particularly stands out as a great genius who sometimes even surpasses a master like Josquin in a typically Spanish expression of dark-glowing ecstasy, and whose motet "Emendemus in melius" is one of the greatest works in all music history. The Spanish organ music of the 16th century is represented by Antonio de Cabezon (1510–66; *Obras de musica*, 1577; see *Editions XIII) whose *tientos and *diferencias rank among the most im-

portant organ pieces written before Bach. No less outstanding are the Spanish lute composers Luis Milan, Luis de Narvaez, Enriquez de Valderrabano, Miguel de Fuenllana, Diego Pisador, and Esteban Daza, who published lute music between 1535 and 1576 [see *Vihuela]. The above list may be completed by the names of musicians who were active mainly in the field of theory: Juan Bermudo, Tomas de Santa Maria [cf. O. Kinkeldey, *Orgel und Klavier* . . . (1910)], Diego Ortiz (*Tratado de glosas* . . . , 1553, new ed. by M. Schneider, 1913), and Francisco Salinas (1513–90) whose *De musica libri VII* (1577) is a valuable, yet little explored, source of information [see *Temperament II]. See also *Madrigal IV; *Ensalada.

After 1600 the polyphonic tradition was continued mainly by Aguilera de Heredia (b. 1570?), Joan Pujol (1573–1626; complete works ed. by H. Anglès, 1926–32), Mateo Romero (d. 1647), Carlos Patino (d. 1647), and Joan Rebello (1609–61). The School of Montserrat, entirely unknown until recently, has stepped into the foreground, owing to the publication of the works (motets, Masses, villancicos) of Joan Cererols (in D. Pujol, *Mestres de l'escolania de Montserrat*, 3 vols., 1930). For the organ music of this period see *Organ music II (d).

The middle of the 17th century saw the rise of the *zarzuela, the Spanish type of opera, which, however, differs essentially from that of the other countries. After 1750 it was replaced by more popular types of lyric theater, the *tonadilla and the *sainete. During the 18th century Italian influence became more and more predominant in Spain, owing mainly to the unlimited power which the Italian castrato Farinelli, favorite of King Philip V, held. Operas of Neapolitan composers were performed at the royal theater and, on the other hand, two Spanish musicians were absorbed completely by the Italian opera, Domingo Terradellas (Italianized name Domenico Terradeglias, 1713–51) who came to Naples as a boy, and Martin y Soler (1756–1806; frequently confused with the organ composer Antonio Soler) who, from 1780 on, spent his life in Florence, Vienna, and St. Petersburg. He is remembered mainly as the composer of the opera *Una cosa rara* (1786) from which Mozart quoted an entire section in the final scene of his *Don Giovanni*, a fact which is all the more remarkable as Soler's opera had completely eclipsed for a time Mozart's *Figaro*. The Spanish harpsichord music of the Rococo is represented chiefly by Antonio Soler (1729–83). He wrote a great number of harpsichord pieces in the style of Domenico Scarlatti who was active in Madrid from 1729 to 1754.

III (1800–present). During the first half of the 19th century musical production came to an almost complete standstill. Bellini, Donizetti, Rossini, reigned supreme on the operatic stage, until the popular zarzuela, in the form of short comic operas with spoken dialogue, was revived by F. A. Barbieri (1823–94). Felipe Pedrell (1841–1922), Tomas Bretón (1850–1923), Ruperto Chapí (1851–1909), gradually worked towards a more artistic type of Spanish opera.

The founder of modern Spanish music is Isaac Albéniz (1860–1909) who became famous mainly through his "Iberia" (1906–09), a collection of 12 piano pieces in which Spanish dance rhythms are presented with a most colorful imagination and a virtuoso piano technique. His brother-in-arms was Enrique Granados (1867–1916) whose numerous piano pieces, notably the "Goyescas" (1912–14), though lacking the dash and exuberance of Albéniz' music, are actually closer to the national soul of Spain in their aristocratic grace and elegance. Even more "Spanish" in its tense passion and ardent severity is the music of Manuel de Falla (b. 1876), author of two important operas, *La Vida breve* (1907) and *El Retablo de Maese Pedro* (1922, after an episode from Don Quixote), and of the ballet *El Sombrero de tres picos* (*The Three-cornered Hat*, 1919). Similar in approach, though much weaker in substance, is the music of Joaquin Turina (b. 1882). The main representatives of the modern school are Ernesto Halffter

(b. 1905), whose neo-classical tendencies are apparent in his Sinfonietta (1923–27), a polytonal revival of Haydn's symphony; and his brother, Rodolfo (b. 1900, now living in Mexico), composer of numerous ballets in an acrid modernistic vein, as well as a virtuoso type of instrumental music in the national Spanish manner (Violin Concerto, 1942). The Catalonian composer Jaime Pahissa (b. 1880, now living in Buenos Aires) has developed a personal system of composition, based exclusively on unisons and multiple octaves producing a polyphonic effect through contrary motion (Intertonal Suite). Oscar Esplà (b. 1886) is distinguished in Spanish music as a theorist as well as a composer. Julian Bantista (b. 1901, now living in Buenos Aires) is the composer of modernistic pieces outside of the national tradition.

More than any other country Spain is conspicuous for its wealth of national dances which, time and again, have inspired the fancy of composers, Spanish as well as foreign. See Alalà; Alborado; Aurrescu; Bolero; Cante hondo; Fandango; Flamenco; Folia; Guajira; Habanera; Jaléo; Jota; Muñeira; Murciana; Pavane; Polo; Rueda; Saeta; Sarabande; Sardana; Seguidilla; Seises; Soléa; Zortziko. Also Auto; Mystery; Sainete; Tonadilla; Zarzuela; Madrigal IV.

Lit.: G. Chase, *The Music of Spain* (1941; bibl.); *LavE* i.4, pp. 1913–2400; A. Soubis, *Histoire de la Musique: Espagne*, 3 vols. (1900).— *To I:* J. B. Trend, *The Music of Spanish History to 1600* (1926); P. Aubry, "Iter Hispanicum" (*SIM* viii, ix); I. Pope, in *Speculum ix* (13th-cent. song); O. Ursprung, in *ZMW* iv (14th-cent. songs); H. Angles, in *Kroyer-Festschrift*, 1933 (15th-cent. song); G. Chase, "Juan del Encina ..." (*ML* xx, no. 4). See also under *Mozarabic chant; *Cantigas; *Villancico. — *To II:* H. Collet, *Le Mysticisme musical espagnol au xvie siècle* (1913); M. Eslava, †*Lira sacrohispanica* (1869ff); F. Pedrell, †*Hispaniae schola musica sacra*, 7 vols. (1894–98; see *Editions XIII); D. Pujol, *Mestres de l'escolania de Montserrat* (1934, '36); H. Angles, *Johannis Pujol ... opera omnia*,

2 vols. (1926, '32); F. Pedrell, †*Antologia de organistas clásicos españoles* (1908); L. Villalba Muñoz, †*Antologia de organistas clásicos españoles*; H. Angles, *Musici organici J. Cabānilles opera omnia* (1927–36); W. Apel, "Early Spanish Music for Lute and Keyboard Instruments" (*MQ* xx). See also *Tonadilla; *Vihuela; *Zarzuela. — *To III:* Van Vechten, *Music of Spain* (1933); H. Collet, *L'Essor de la musique espagnole au xxe siècle* (1929); *id.*, in *SIM*, 1908 and *RdM*, 1936. — *Folk music:* K. Schindler, †*Folk Music of Spain and Portugal* (1941); F. Pedrell, †*Cancionero musical popular español*, 4 vols. (1918–22; new ed. in two vols., 1936); M. Torner, *Cancionero musical* (1928); C. Rice, *Dancing in Spain*; H. Angles, "Das Spanische Volkslied" (*AMF* iii); J. B. Trend, "Salinas and 16th-Century Folksongs" (*ML* viii, no. 1); F. Pedrell, "Folk-lore musical castillan du xvie siècle" (*SIM* i).

Sparte [G.]; **sparta, spartita** [It.]. Partition score. *Spartieren* means to write a partition score. The term is used specifically with reference to early vocal music (prior to 1600) which is originally written in single parts. Therefore, it is synonymous with "transcribing of early music," a process which demands a knowledge of *mensural notation. See also under *Intavolatura.

Spasshaft [G.]. Jocular.

Spatium [L.]. The space between two lines of a staff.

Speaker key. In wind instruments a key which facilitates the production of tones by overblowing. It opens a small hole which causes the air column to vibrate in one-half or one-third of its entire length. The oboe usually has two such keys, producing the first and second octave respectively, while the clarinet has only one, producing the twelfth.

Speaking stops. On organs, all the stops which produce sounds, as distinct from others which merely operate couplers, etc.

Sperdendosi [It.]. Fading out.

Spezzato [It.]. See *Cori spezzati.

Spianato [It.]. "Leveled," i.e., smooth, even.

Spiccato [It.]. See *Bowing (d).

Spiegando [It.]. "Unfolding," becoming louder.

Spiegelfuge [G.]. *Mirror fugue.

Spieldose [G.]. Musical box.

Spieloper [G.]. Name for German 19th-century *comic operas (Lortzing, Marschner).

Spinet [from L. *spina*, thorn]. Originally, a name for the *harpsichord (with reference to the thorn-like points of leather or quills which pluck the strings), particularly the smaller variety in square form and with one manual only, thus practically identical with the virginal. The Italian spinets usually had a pentagonal case. In the 18th century the name designated harpsichords in the form of a short triangle, in which the strings ran out from the keyboard at an angle of about 45 degrees, while in the older type they ran parallel to it. Today the term is sometimes incorrectly used for the small, oblong pianofortes of the early 19th century.

Spiritoso [It.]. Spirited.

Spirituals. See *Negro music I, II.

Spitze [G.]. Abbr. *Sp.* indicates in violin music the point of the bow; in organ music the toe of the foot.

Spitzig [G.]. Pointed, sharp.

Sponsus play. See *Liturgical drama.

Sprechgesang [G. *sprechen*, to speak]. German term for *recitative; also for the "elevated" speech used in the *melodrama (more properly called *Sprechstimme*).

Springbogen [G.]. Sautillé, spiccato; see *Bowing (d).

Springer. An agrément used in 17th-century English lute and viol music and belonging to the class of the *Nachschlag.

Squarcialupi, Codex. See *Sources, no. 13.

Square notation [G. *Quadratnotation*]. The German term has been introduced by F. Ludwig to designate the notation of the School of *Notre Dame (*c.* 1175–1250) which, for the first time, shows square shapes of the notes and ligatures, as distinguished from the less definitely drawn, neume-like symbols of the preceding periods (School of *St. Martial). The chief sources of square notation are the three MSS containing the *Magnus liber organi.*

Recent writers have frequently replaced the term square notation by modal notation, a substitution whose suitability is questionable. The term square notation has the advantage that it merely states an undeniable feature of external appearance, while the term modal notation implies that the notational signs are to be interpreted in modal meter, i.e., in the scheme of the rhythmic *modes, a presupposition which does not hold good in a general sense. Actually, the pieces written in square notation fall into several categories, only one of which — the most important one, no doubt — deserves the name modal notation, i.e., the repertory of the organa tripla, quadrupla, and clausulae. With others, such as the earlier organa dupla (Leoninus), the conductus, the monophonic songs, modal interpretation is at least doubtful. For an example see *Notation, Ex. 2. Cf. *ApNPM*, 215–281; *WoHN* i, 198–250.

Stabat mater [L.]. A 13th-century *sequence (*Stabat mater dolorosa;* There stood the Mother) of the Roman Catholic liturgy, probably written by the Franciscan Jacopone da Todi (*c.* 1228–1306), and still sung today at the feast of the Seven Dolours (Sept. 15). For the text and the liturgical melody cf. *GR*, 445. The famous text has also been composed by Josquin, Palestrina, Astorga (ed. by R. Franz), Steffani, Al. Scarlatti, Caldara (cf. *DTOe* 13.i), Pergolese, Haydn, Schubert, Rossini, Verdi, Dvořák, Stanford, and Szymanovski.

Lit.: Bitter, *Studie zum Stabat Mater*

(1883); E. Schmitz, *Das Madonnenideal in der Tonkunst* (1910); B. E. Clifford, in *SIM* ii; P. Mies, in *KJ*, 1932; W. Baeumker, in *KJ*, 1883, p. 59.

Stabreim [G.]. *Alliteration.

Staccato [It., detached]. A manner of performance indicated by a dot or the sign ▼ placed over the note, calling for a reduction of its written duration with a rest substituted for half or more of its value. Thus, a quarter-note will be reduced to perhaps a sixteenth-note, followed by three sixteenth-rests. In piano- and violin-playing as well as in singing there exist various types of staccato produced by different touch, bowing, attack, etc. [see *Bowing (g)]. Earlier composers, such as Ph. Em. Bach, Haydn, Beethoven, indicated staccato normally by the wedge [cf., Schencker's edition of Beethoven's piano sonatas], reserving the dot for a less rigid staccato (portato), preferably in slow movements. Today the dot is used as the normal sign, and the dash for a more pronounced staccato. Cf. A. Kreutz, "Die Staccatozeichen in der Klaviermusik" (*Deutsche Tonkünstlerzeitung* 1937/38, p. 127).

Ständchen [G.]. *Serenade.

Staff or **stave** [F. *portée*; G. *Liniensystem, System*; It. *rigo*]. A series of horizontal lines, now invariably five in number, upon and between which the musical notes are written, thus indicating (in connection with a *clef) their pitch. The positions of the notes on the staff give a satisfactory image of the pitches, although one not entirely correct, in so far as they fail to indicate the difference between whole-tones and semitones, as well as the modifications of pitch produced by accidentals (e.g., C-double-sharp is actually higher in pitch, but lower in staff location, than D-flat).

The use of horizontal lines for the representation of pitches occurs first in the *Musica enchiriadis* (9th century). However, only the spaces between the lines are used here, with the syllables of the text written in at their proper place [cf.

ApNPM, facs. 42]. The invention of the staff proper is ascribed to Guido of Arezzo (*c.* 1000) who, in his *Regulae de ignotu cantu* [*GS* ii, 34], recommends the use of three or four lines, denoting f a c' or d f a c' (the use of one or two lines, red for f and yellow for c', occurred in slightly earlier MSS). The four-line staff has been preserved to the present day for the notation of Gregorian chant. For the writing down of polyphonic music the five-line staff was used as early as 1200 [cf. *ApNPM*, facs. 47]. For compositions in simple note-against-note style (*conductus) the different staves were frequently written so closely that they give the impression of a single staff of ten or more lines [cf. *ApNPM*, facs. 46]; however, the fact that on such a staff the same clef letter (c') is used simultaneously in different positions clearly shows that this is a juxtaposition of several staves, not one single staff. It was not until the 16th century that real staves with more than five lines came into general use, for the writing down of keyboard music [cf. *ApNPM*, facs. 1, 3, 4, 5].

In the lute music and in the Spanish keyboard music of the 16th century series of lines are used which are identical in appearance with the staff but have an entirely different significance. In the former case they represent the strings of the lute, in the latter the voice parts of a composition. See *Tablature. For modern reforms of the staff, cf. *WoHN* ii, 347ff (*passim*).

Staffless neumes. See *Neumes II.

Staffless notation. General term for methods of notation in which the tones are indicated, not by notes written on a staff, but by letters or similar symbols. An ancient method of this type is the German organ- and the German lute-tablature [see *Tablature], a recent one the *Tonic Sol-fa.

Stahlspiel [G. *Stahl*, steel]. The military *Glockenspiel [see *Lyra (3)].

Stampita, stantipes. See *Estampie.

Stark anblasen [G.]. Blow strongly.

Star-Spangled Banner, The. The *national anthem of the United States of America, officially adopted by a Bill passed on March 3, 1931. The words were written by Francis Scott Key in September, 1814, while he watched, from the cartel-ship "Minden," the British bombardment of Fort McHenry, near Baltimore. It is sung to a tune by the English John Stafford Smith, composed originally for a poem "To Anacreon in Heaven." It is not known whether Key had this tune in mind when he wrote his words, or whether text and music were united later, possibly by Joseph Hopper Nicholson. Cf. O. Sonneck, *The Star-Spangled Banner* (1914); J. Muller, *The Star-Spangled Banner* (1935).

Statement. Same as exposition in *Sonata-form.

Steel guitar. See *Electronic musical instruments III.

Steg [G.]. Bridge of the violin, etc. See *Bowing (k).

Stegreif [G.]. Improvisation, or performance without preparation. *Stegreif-komödien*, i.e., farcical plays with improvised dialogue, were extremely popular in Vienna toward the end of the 18th century. Cf. *DTOe* 33.i.

Stendendo [It.]. "Extending," i.e., rallentando.

Stentando [It.]. "Laboring," i.e., retarding.

Sterbend [G.]. Dying away.

Steso [It.]. Same.

Sticheron. In the *Byzantine church music of the 8th century and later, poetic intercalations between the verses (*stichos*) of a psalm; in other words, psalm-*tropes. A collection of such hymns was called *sticherarion*.

Stickers. See *Organ II.

Stil [G.], **stile** [It.]. *Style. *Stile antico* (*obbligato, grave, osservato, romano*), the strict contrapuntal style of the older

period (Palestrina) which was continuously cultivated during the 17th century
in Rome [see *Roman School]. *Stile
concertante (moderno)*, the style of con-
certo-like treatment, i.e., of rivaling instruments [see *Concerto III]. *Stile concitato*, style of dramatic expression and
excitement (Monteverdi, "Il Combattimento di Tancredi e Clorinda," 1624; cf.
W. Kreidler, *H. Schütz und der Stile
concitato von Monteverdi*, Diss. Bern
1933). *Stile nuovo (espressivo, rappresentativo, recitativo)*, the *monodic style
of the early 17th century [see *Nuove
musiche], in which *recitative is used
for the purpose of heightened expression
and "representation" of feelings. *Stile
galante*, the "*gallant" style of the 18th
century [see *Rococo]. *Stile sueto*, the
"*freistimmige" style of the late 18th
century (Haydn, Mozart).

Stimm- [G., voice]. *Stimmbänder, vo-*
cal chords; *Stimmbildung*, voice training;
Stimmbruch, mutation; *Stimmbücher*,
part-books; *Stimmgabel*, tuning fork;
Stimmhorn, a tool in the shape of a hollow cone used in the tuning of organ pipes
(widening or narrowing of the mouth);
Stimmführung, *voice-leading; *Stimm-
brücke*, *tuning wire; *Stimmpfeife*,
*pitch pipe; *Stimmritze*, glottis; *Stimmstock*, sound post; *Stimmumfang*, range;
Stimmwechsel, mutation (of the voice);
Stimmzug, slide (of trombones).

Stimme [G.]. (1) Voice. — (2) Voice
part. — (3) Sound post.

Stimmen [G.]. To tune.

Stimmenkreuzung [G.]. Crossing of
voice parts.

Stimmtausch. The execution of a passage in contrapuntal style by exchanged
voices, so that, e.g., the soprano sings the

part of the alto and vice versa (without
the octave transposition, found in *in-

vertible counterpoint). This method was
practiced in the 13th century, suggested
and facilitated by the fact that in the organa tripla and quadrupla of this period
(Perotinus) the two or three parts above
the tenor move in the same range. The
accompanying example, from Walter
Odington's treatise [cf. *CS* i, 247], serves
as an illustration. Cf. also **HAM*, nos.
32c and 33b. Better known, though not
usually recognized as such, is the strict
application of Stimmtausch in all the
*rounds (circle canons). See also *Repe-
tition. Cf. J. Handschin, in *ZMW* x, 535.

Stimmung [G.]. (1) Mood; thus,
Stimmungsbild, title for pieces meant to
express some definite mood. — (2) Tuning, intonation, e.g., *reine Stimmung*,
just intonation; also the process of tuning
an instrument. — (3) Pitch.

Sting. See under *Vibrato (1).

Stinguendo [It.]. Fading out.

Stirando, stiracchiando [It.]. Retarding (lit. "stretching").

Stockhorn. *Pibgorn.

Stollen [G.]. See under *Barform.
Sometimes used as a term for exposition
which, in sonata-form, corresponds to the
Stollen of the medieval Bar.

Stop. On the organ, the handle by which
the organ-player can draw on or shut off
the various registers. The term is also
used to denote the *registers themselves
[see *Organ II, III]. The stops acting on
pipes are more specifically called sounding
(speaking) stops, as distinct from those
which control couplers and similar mechanical devices. A stop is called short-
stop (half-stop) if the pipes governed by
it do not go through the whole compass;
in particular, it is called a divided stop if
the whole rank of pipes is divided into a
lower and upper half, each having a separate stop. — Stops also occur in a limited
number on *harpsichords.

Stopped notes. See *Horn I.

Stopped pipe. See *Organ IX; also
*Wind instruments III.

Stopping. (1) On stringed instruments (violins, lutes), the placing of the tips of the fingers of the left hand so that they shorten the vibrating length of the string. See *Double stops. — (2) On the natural horn, see *Horn.

Stracciacalando [It.]. Prattling.

Stradivarius violins (frequently abbreviated Strad). See *Violin.

Straff [G.]. Tense.

Strambotto. A type of 15th-century Italian poetry, written in stanzas of eight lines in iambic pentameters, with the rhyme scheme ab ab ab ab or, more frequently, ab ab ab cc (the latter type is known as *ottava rima*; cf. Byron's "Don Juan"). In Petrucci's *Frottole* (1504–14) strambotti are composed in strophic form, the music of the first two lines being repeated four times [Ex. in *RiHM* ii.1, 356]. Later examples are through-composed, in the manner of the madrigal. For literature see under *Frottola.

Strascinando [It.]. Dragging, slurring.

Strathspey. A slow Scottish dance in 4/4-meter, with many dotted notes, frequently in the inverted arrangement of the *Scotch snap. The name, derived from the strath (valley) of the Spey, was originally coterminous with *reel; later, the term reel was given to somewhat quicker dances in a more smoothly flowing rhythm, lacking dotted notes. Important early collections of strathspeys (reels) are: A. Cummings, *A Collection of Strathspeys or Old-Highland Reels ...* (Strathspey, 1780); Niel Gow, *A Collection (A Second ..., Sixth Collection) of Strathspey Reels* (Dunkeld, 1784–1822). Niel Gow (1727–1807) was the most famous performer of strathspeys and reels.

Stravagante [It.]. Extravagant, fantastic.

Stravaganza [It., extravagance]. General term for pieces in free style or involving some sort of fanciful treatment. As early as the end of the 16th century the

name was used by Giov. Macque (d. 1614) for a prelude in free style [see *Editions XVII, 4, pp. 60, 69].

Strawfiddle. See *Xylophone.

Straziante [It.]. "Tearing," piercing.

Street organ, hand organ. A *mechanical instrument of the barrel-and-pin principle in which the pins operate reed pipes similar to those of the organ. A crank turns the barrel and also operates a bellows which furnishes the air to set the reeds into vibration. The instrument, which is associated with the Italian street musician and his monkey, is popularly but erroneously called *hurdy-gurdy.

Streich- [G. *streichen*, to bow]. *Streich-instrumente*, bowed instruments. *Streich-quartett* (*-quintett*), string quartet (quintet). *Streichklavier*, piano-violin [see *Sostenente pianoforte].

Strepitoso [It.]. Noisy.

Stretta [It.]. Same as *stretto (2).

Stretto [It., close]. (1) In a fugue, the imitation of the subject in close succession, with the answer coming in before the subject is completed [G. *Engführung*]. The resulting dovetailing of the subject with its imitation brings about an increase of intensity which is particularly suitable for a climactic conclusion of the fugue [see the illustration, from the fugue in D,

Wt. Cl. ii]. — (2) In non-fugal compositions *stretto* (*stretta*) means a concluding section in increased speed, as, e.g., at the end of the last movement of Beethoven's Fifth Symphony.

Strich [G.]. Bow stroke.

Stringed instruments. Instruments in which the sound-producing agent is a stretched string. The scientific name is chordophone [see under *Instruments IV for their classification]. The most important members of this large group are the violin (and its family), the harp, and the piano. In each of these instruments a different manner of sound generation is used, namely, bowing, plucking, or striking by hammer. Ordinarily, the name stringed instruments ("strings") denotes the members of the violin family or of the violin type. Cf. H. Panum, *The Stringed Instruments of the Middle Ages* (1941); A. Rühlmann, *Geschichte der Bogeninstrumente* (1882).

Stringendo [It.]. Quickening, accelerando.

String quartet [F. *quatuor à cordes*; G. *Streichquartett*]. Chamber music for four strings, practically always first and second violin, viola, and cello. The string quartet is the chief type of *chamber music and is frequently considered, by serious musicians as well as by cultured amateurs, the ideal type of music, because "it always says what is necessary, and never too much." For its form, see the explanations given under *Sonata.

I. *The Present Repertory*. The present-day repertory of string quartets begins with the later quartets of Haydn (written between 1780 and 1790) and with those by Mozart written in the same decade. In these works Haydn and Mozart established the string quartet not only as a definite ensemble and form, but also stylistically as the realization of that ideal perception of "foursome companionship" which — in spite of all stylistic changes and a certain amount of side-stepping in the late 19th century — has always remained the basic principle of quartet writing. Their heritage was taken over by Beethoven whose earlier works (op. 18, nos. 1–6, 1801; op. 59, *Russian quartets, 1808) are what might be called "Haydn quartets in Beethoven's language," while his late quartets (opp. 127, 130–133, 135) lead far away from "distinguished entertainment" into a realm of sublime thought and of transcendental subjectivism. Beethoven's successor was Franz Schubert whose late quartets (A

minor, D minor) deserve much more recognition (and performance) than is generally awarded them. While the quartets of the immediately following period (Cherubini, Schumann, Mendelssohn) are of secondary importance, a new peak is reached in the quartets of Brahms (op. 51, op. 67) who filled the traditional form with a new expression of restrained Romanticism. The Romantic period of the string quartet came to its conclusion with the works of Dvořák (eight quartets, 1874–1895), Franck (D minor, 1889), d'Indy (op. 35, 1890; op. 45, 1897; op. 96, 1930), and Max Reger (opp. 54, 74, 109, 121, 133).

The French impressionism with its emphasis on coloristic effects and the turbulent decades of the early 20th century with their complete disintegration of all previous standards [see *New music] were not particularly favorable to the cultivation of so traditional a form as the quartet. Nonetheless, the quartets of this period are interesting documents showing the attempt to utilize the medium of strings as a vehicle for impressionistic methods (Debussy, Ravel); for atonality (Schönberg, Alban Berg, Webern); for twelve-tone technique (Schönberg, op. 30); for motoric and percussive rhythms (Bartók, nos. 3 and 4); for neo-classical texture (Stravinsky, Sessions, Piston); for an archaic folklorism (Malipiero, *Rispetti e strambotti*); for quarter-tone technique (Bartók, no. 6, Burletta), etc.

II. *History*. The string quartet is one of the most recent types of music. To trace it back to the 16th or early 17th century, as is occasionally done, is somewhat amateurish, not only because the four-voice chamber music of this period (*ricercares and similar pieces by Isaac, Hofhaimer, Senfl, Willaert, and Padovano; instrumental *canzonas by Maschera and many others) is, needless to say, entirely different from the modern quartet in form and style but, particularly, because it has no historical connection with the latter, since the medium of four strings was almost completely abandoned in the Baroque period, except in England where the *fancy was cultivated until *c.*

1680. Still more amateurish is the attempt, made in a recent reference book, to single out a special composition (by Allegri, 1582–1652) as "the first work for four stringed instruments" [see also A. Eaglefield-Hull, in *MQ* xv]. Even before Allegri was born a great number of such pieces had been written any one of which might just as well be called "the first string quartet." During the first half of the 17th century quite a number of four-voice instrumental pieces were written in Italy and Germany; these, however, would seem to have been destined for small string orchestras rather than for a quartet [see *Sonata B, II, close]. Around 1675 the four-part ensemble was largely abandoned, and the *trio sonata became the chief type of chamber music during the later Baroque period.

Certain sonatas by Alessandro Scarlatti (1659–1725) bear the (authentic?) remark *per due violini, violetta, e violoncello*, the earliest extant indication of the medium of the modern string quartet. Its history proper, however, does not begin much before 1750. The question of precedence is very difficult to settle since various claimants lived at the same time (Tartini, 1692–1770; Sammartini, 1705–75; Franz Xaver Richter, 1709–89; cf. *DTB* 15), while others (Starzer; cf. *DTOe* 15.ii; Pugnani; Boccherini; Canales; Karl Stamitz; Anton Stamitz; Gyrowetz) belong to the generation of Haydn (b. 1732). In general, it can be said that the earliest string quartets (including those of the young Haydn) are orchestral rather than chamber music, as they were performed by several players to the part. Their form is frequently that of the *divertimento. Haydn wrote 83 quartets, Boccherini 91, Gyrowetz 60.

Lit.: W. Altmann, *Handbuch für Streichquartett-Spieler* (1928); J. Lener, *The Technique of String Quartet Playing*; M. D. H. Norton, *String Quartet Playing* (1925); E. Heimeran and B. Aulich, *The Well-Tempered String Quartet* (1938); J. de Marliave, *Beethoven's String Quartets* (1928); M. Pincherle, "On the Origins of the String Quartet" (*MQ* xv); A. Sandberger, "Zur Geschich-

te des Haydn'schen Streichquartetts" (in *Gesammelte Aufsätze* i, 224ff); M. Scott, "Haydn's '83'" (*ML* xi, no. 3); E. Goossens, "The String Quartet since Brahms" (*ML* iii, no. 4). See also *Chamber music.

String quintet. Chamber music for five strings. See *Quintet.

Strings. Colloquial abbreviation for the stringed instruments of the orchestra (string section) or of the string quartet, quintet, etc.

String trio. Chamber music for three strings. See *Trio.

Strisciando [It.]. Smooth, slurred; also glissando.

Strohfiedel [G.]. *Strawfiddle [see *Xylophone].

Stroh violin (cello). Instrument invented by Charles Stroh in 1901 for the purpose of recording, in which the usual body is replaced by an aluminum plate connecting with an amplifying horn.

Stromento [It.]. Instrument. *Stromentato*, instrumented, accompanied by instruments; see *Recitative. *Stromenti a corde*, stringed instruments; *d'arco*, bowed instruments; *di legno*, wood-wind instruments; *d'ottone* or *di metallo*, brass instruments; *a percossa*, percussion instruments; *a fiato* or *di vento*, wind instruments; *da tasto*, keyboard instruments.

Strophenbass [G.]. See *Strophic bass.

Strophenlied [G.]. Strophic song.

Strophic [from Gr. *strophe*, stanza]. A song is termed strophic if all the stanzas of the text are sung to the same music. The opposite treatment, with new music to each stanza, is called *durchkomponiert* or *through-composed. Generally the former method is preferred for simple lyrical texts, the latter for texts of a dramatic character and for more refined lyrics involving subtle shades of mood and expression.

Strophic bass. The term refers to a method, frequent in the early cantatas, of using the same bass line for all the stanzas of a song, with varying melodies in the upper part. From the *ground proper (*basso ostinato*) the strophic bass is distinguished by its considerably longer extension and by the fact that it comes to a definite close at its end. Briefly, basso ostinato and strophic bass are examples of continuous and sectional *variation, respectively. A typical example of strophic bass (by Alessandro Grandi, 1620) is reproduced in *RiHM* ii.2, 39–45. See *Cantata I; *Aria III; *Ruggiero.

Strophic song. See under *Through-composed.

Strophicus. See *Neumes I.

Strumento d'acciaio. See under *Glockenspiel.

Stück [G.]. Piece, composition.

Stürmisch [G.]. Stormy, passionate.

Stürze [G.]. Bell of the horn. *Stürze hoch*, i.e., the bell turned upward.

Stufe [G.]. Degree (of the scale).

Stundenofficium [G.]. *Office hours.

Stutzflügel [G.]. Baby grand piano.

Style [F. *style*; G. *Stil*; It. *stile*]. "Distinctive or characteristic mode of presentation, construction, or execution in any art" (Webster). Musical style, therefore, means "characteristic language" or "characteristic handwriting," particularly with reference to the details of a composition, as distinguished from its large outlines, i.e., *form. By and large, form and style stand in the relationship of "fixed" and "fluid," there being many pieces in the same form, but differing in style (e.g., sonatas by Beethoven and by Brahms). Each style, however, also has its "fixed" features which recur in different forms (e.g., the style in all the works of Mozart).

There exists a full "scale" of stylistic points of view leading from the more limited ones to those of widest application. The term style may be applied: to single works (e.g., the style of *Tristan* as compared with that of the *Meistersinger*: work style); to composers (e.g., the style of Wagner as compared with that of Beethoven: personal style); to types of composition (operatic style, symphonic style, motet style, church style); to mediums (instrumental style, vocal style, keyboard style); to methods of composition (contrapuntal style, homophonic style, monodic style); to nations (French style, German style); to periods (Baroque style, Romantic style); etc. Naturally, several such points of view may be combined into one, as, e.g., "Beethoven's symphonic style," "German Romantic style," "instrumental style of the Baroque," etc.

The stylistic point of view was introduced into music by the Italian writers of the 17th century who invented a remarkable vocabulary to denote various "languages" of music [see *Stile]. The founder of the modern stylistic analysis is Guido Adler (1855–1940).

Lit.: G. Adler, *Der Stil in der Musik* (1911); *id.*, *Prinzipien und Arten des musikalischen Stils* (2d ed., 1929); E. Katz, *Die musikalischen Stilbegriffe des 17. Jahrhunderts* (Diss. Freiburg 1926); G. Adler, "Style-Criticism" (*MQ* xx); E. Closson, "Du style" (*AM* iii, no. 3); K. Meyer, "Zum Stilproblem in der Musik," (*ZMW* v); A. Schering, "Historische und nationale Klangstile" (*JMP* xxxiv).

Style galant [F.]. *Gallant style.

Suave [It.]. Sweet.

Subdiapente; subdiatessaron. See *Diapente; Diatessaron.

Subdominant. The fourth degree of the scale (f in C major or C minor), so called because this tone is a fifth below (*sub*) the tonic, just as the dominant is a fifth above it [see *Scale degrees]. In harmonic analysis the triad of the subdominant is indicated IV or S. It occurs chiefly in the combination IV V I, i.e., as the antepenultimate chord in cadences. In early music it frequently occurs as the penultimate chord IV I, a combination known as plagal cadence. More than any other triad, the subdominant is capable of modifications which, in the current system of *harmonic analysis, are considered and labeled as different chords with dif-

ferent roots [cf. Ex.], although from a functional point of view they are essentially identical [see *Functional harmony].

Subito [It.]. Suddenly.

Subject [F. *sujet, thème*; G. *Thema*; It. *tema, soggetto*]. A melody which, by virtue of its characteristic design, its prominent position, or its special treatment, becomes a basic factor in the structure of the composition. The subject (or, if there are several, the main subject) is always stated at the outset of the composition. In *sonata-form there are normally two subjects or, in more extended examples, two groups of subjects. A fugue usually has only one subject, except in special types such as double or triple fugues.

The development of music shows an ever-increasing importance of musical subjects as the staple of the composition and as an element of unification. Early music (prior to 1500) has no subjects proper, unless the borrowed *cantus firmi, which form the basis of numerous compositions (motets), are considered as such. During the second half of the 15th century (Ockeghem, Isaac) characteristic figures (motives) were gradually adopted as material for short passages, in imitation, sequential treatment, or occasionally as *ostinati. The use of identical or similar motives for the beginning of all the movements of a Mass may also be mentioned as indicative of a certain tendency towards unification [see *Mass B, II]. The fully developed imitative style of the Josquin period used numerous subjects in succession, one for each *point of imitation. The contemporary *ricercares usually reduce the number of such sub-

jects, and make more extensive use of each one. In fact, they can already be considered as "fugues in several sections," each fugue being based on one theme. An important step forward occurs in the *variation-canzonas (-ricercares) of Frescobaldi, which use rhythmic modifications of one and the same subject for the different sections of the piece [see *Canzona (5) I]. The development of the monothematic fugue is described under *Fugue. Bach brought this form to its peak of perfection, and also created the "ideal type" of fugal subjects [see *Soggetto]. New efforts had to be made in order to develop that different type of subjects which suited the needs of the sonata. The details of the development leading from the "continuous melody" of the sonata da chiesa (Bach, Handel) to the incisive and individualized subjects of the late Haydn and Mozart (*c*. 1780) are too involved to be indicated in a brief summary. Suffice it to mention D. Scarlatti, Pergolesi, J. Stamitz, Johann Christian Bach, as landmarks on this road.

Submediant. See *Scale degrees.

Subsemitonium. The "semitone below the tonic," an older term for the leading tone (e.g., f#–g), in contradistinction to the *subtonium*, i.e., the whole-tone below the tonic (e.g., f-g). These terms are important in the theory of the *church modes, all of which have the subtonium, except for the Lydian and Ionian. The replacement, in any of the other modes, of the subtonium by the subsemitonium (e.g., the use of f# in Mixolydian) was considered as *musica ficta.

Subsidiary subject. A *subject of lesser importance, particularly one of those subjects which, in the fully grown examples of sonata-form, follow after the "first subject" or the "second subject," thus forming the "first group" or the "second group."

Subtonic. The tone "below the tonic," i.e., the leading tone, a semitone below the tonic [see *Scale degrees]. In 16th-century theory, however, *subtonium* means "whole-tone below the tonic," in distinction from *subsemitonium.

Suite. An important instrumental form of Baroque music, consisting of a number of movements, each in the character of a dance, and all in the same key.

I. *The Suite of Bach.* The standard scheme of the suite as it occurs with Bach is A–C–S–O–G, where A stands for *allemande, C for *courante, S for *sarabande, G for *gigue, and O for what is called optional dance or optional group, i.e., one or several dances of various types, chiefly *minuet, *bourrée, *gavotte, *passepied, *polonaise, *rigaudon, *anglaise, *loure, *air. Bach wrote for the harpsichord, aside from some single suites, six "English Suites," six "French Suites," and six "Partitas." Only the last term, borrowed from Italian terminology, has a certain significance since some of the movements show Italian features [see *Partita]. The English suites and the Partitas are preceded by an introductory piece (prelude). The preludes of the English suites are (except for the first) in the character of a *concerto-grosso movement. Those of the first three partitas are modeled after the *Inventions (as are also numerous preludes of the *Well-tempered Clavier), that of the fourth is a French overture [see *Overture I], and the last two borrow their style from the *toccata. The dance movements are invariably in binary form, either symmetrical (i.e., with both sections of about the same length) or asymmetrical, i.e., with the second section expanded in a manner foreshadowing the sonata-form [see *Binary and ternary; *Sonata-form]. Stylistically the dances of the optional group form a contrast to the others, being usually simpler in style and more clearly suggestive of dance types. The reason for this important difference is that the allemande, courante, sarabande, gigue, are much older types which originated in the 16th century and which, at the time of their adoption as the constitutional elements of the suite (*c.* 1650) had already lost their dance connotation and had become idealized types, rhythmically weakened but

elaborate in texture and style. The optional dances, on the other hand, originated in the French ballets of the late 17th century (Lully) and retained, even in the latest suites (Bach, *c.* 1735) their character as actual dance music.

II. *The Modern Suite.* The suite became practically extinct after 1750, leaving only traces in the *divertimento and *cassation as well as in the minuet of the classical *sonata (symphony). An antiquarian attempt at revival was made by Franz Lachner (1803–90) in his eight orchestral suites, written in a learned contrapuntal style. Of greater importance was the establishment of a modern type of suite in which the traditional scheme of dances is replaced by a free succession of movements of different character, frequently in the character of national dances or ballet dances. This type of orchestral music gained favor in the 1880's and 1890's. Particularly frequent are orchestral arrangements from operas and ballets, e.g., Bizet's *Arlésienne Suite* (from the play with incidental music, *L'Arlésienne,* 1872), Grieg's *Peer Gynt Suite* (from the incidental music to Ibsen's play, 1875), Tchaikovsky's *Nutcracker Suite* (from the ballet, 1892), Stravinsky's *Petrouchka Suite* (from the ballet, 1911). In the period from 1915 to 1930 the "back-to-Bach" movement led to a somewhat demonstrative revival of the abstract (non-operatic) suite, and Bach's example served as welcome pretext for the introduction of jazz dances into the field of art music (Hindemith, *Suite 1922;* Krenek, Schulhoff, Conrad Beck).

III. *The Suite before Bach.* The development leading to the suites of Bach presents an interesting picture of international coöperation. Briefly stated, Italy contributed the early development (16th century), England the gigue, Spain the sarabande, France the great wealth of dance types (early 17th century), and Germany the conception of the suite as a unified and definite musical form.

The origin of the suite is usually looked for in the frequent combinations of two dances, one in duple time, the other in triple time, such as occur throughout the 16th century, e.g., Pavane – Galliard or Passamezzo – Saltarello [see *Nachtanz]. More important than these somewhat irrelevant combinations are the combinations, not infrequent in 16th-century lute books, of three or more dances played in succession. Examples are the combination Basse danse – Recoupe – Tordion which occurs in the lute books of Attaingnant (1529), Passamezzo – Gagliarda – Padovano in that of Rotta (1546), or Passamezzo – Padovano – Saltarello – Ripresa in that of Waisselius (1573). After 1600 this course was further pursued by German composers such as Paul Peuerl, Isaak Posch (both in *DTOe* 36.ii), Samuel Scheidt (1587–1654), and Hermann Schein (1586–1630), each of whom established his own standard form, e.g., Paduana – Intrada – Dantz – Gagliard (Peuerl, 1611; cf. *EiBM*, no. 26), or Pavana – Galliarde – Courante – Allemanda – Tripla (Schein, *Banchetto musicale*, 1617; cf. *HAM*, no. 199). While the idea of the suite as a unified musical form is clearly present in these compositions, it is lacking in the works of French composers such as Jean-Baptiste Besard (1567–?), Chambonnières (1602–72), Louis Couperin (1626–61), d'Anglebert (1635–?), who merely arranged the dances either according to types (Besard, *Thesaurus harmonicus*, 1603: one "Livre" of allemandes, another of courantes, etc.) or, later, according to keys, but in such large numbers as to exclude the idea of a definite form. E.g., a "suite" by Chambonnières, as contained in the Bauyn-MSS (*c.* 1650) includes 5 allemandes, 11 courantes, 4 sarabandes, 2 gigues, 5 courantes, 1 chaconne — all in C major. This loose aggregation still exists in the harpsichord works of François Couperin (publ. 1713–30) who, perhaps deliberately, avoids the name suite — then long established — and prefers the more suitable name "Ordre" which might well be applied in the case of the earlier French composers likewise.

If the French failed to grasp the idea of the suite as a musical form, they made other important contributions to its de-velopment. Not only did they transform the allemande, courante, gigue, sarabande, from their 16th-century plainness to Baroque refinement (the *courante is particularly interesting in this respect), but they also enlarged the repertory by those numerous dances which were adopted, around 1700, into the optional group of the suite.

To the best of our knowledge the creation of the classical suite must be credited to Johann Jacob Froberger (1616–67) who, born in Stuttgart, educated partly in Rome and spending the late time of his life in France, was eminently suited for the task of imbuing the German "Renaissance"-suite of Peuerl and Schein with the stylistic achievements of the French Baroque. It must be noted that, around 1650, the prevailing type of suite was one in three movements only: A–C–S. Many suites of Froberger have this scheme, as do also all those by Kindermann (*c.* 1645; cf. *DTB* 21/24) and nearly all the instrumental suites of the Kassel MS (ed. by Écorcheville). The gigue was introduced at a slightly later time as an "optional" dance, either before or after the courante, with the sarabande retaining its position as the concluding movement: A–C–G–S or A–G–C–S. In Froberger's autograph MSS his four-movement suites invariably close with the sarabande, as do also, e.g., Rosenmüller's *Sonate da camera* of 1670 and the suites in M. Locke's *Melothesia* (1673). One will hardly go wrong in interpreting this arrangement, which reserves the slow dance for the conclusion, as an evidence of that "Romantic" spirit which so frequently steps forth in Baroque music [see remark under *Classicism]. It was not until after Froberger's death that the positions of the sarabande and the gigue were exchanged, as appears from the earliest printed edition of his suites (published posthumously in 1693) which bears the remark: "mis en meilleur ordre" (put in better order). Other examples of the A–C–S–G arrangement occur in the suites of Georg Böhm (1661–1733).

Around 1700 we find the earliest examples of the "complete suite," e.g., in Johann

Krieger's suites (*Sechs Musikalische Partien*, 1697; *DTB* 18; see *Partita) which follow the scheme A–C–S–G–O and in those of Pachelbel (1699; *DTB* 2.i) which have the arrangement A–C–O–S–G.

J. S. Bach seems to have been the first to place the O-group before the gigue.

IV. *The Sonata da Camera.* Side by side with this "central development" there were others of a somewhat freer character, chiefly in the field of chamber and of orchestral music. In Italy the suite was cultivated mainly as a chamber music type, under the name of *sonata da camera* (chamber sonata) as opposed to the sonata da chiesa [see *Sonata B, II]. As early as 1629 and 1637 we encounter instrumental suites such as Sinfonia – (Brando) – Gagliarda – Corrente in publications by G. B. Buonamente [cf. P. Nettl, in *ZMW* ix]. The earliest extant record of the term sonata da camera is in a publication (from 1667) of the German Johann Rosenmüller (1620–84) which contains pieces mostly in the form Sinfonia – Allemanda – Corrente – Intrada – Ballo – Sarabande [cf. *DdT* 18; *HAM*, no. 218]. After Buonamente no other Italian sonate da camera are known until Corelli's op. 2 (1685) and op. 4 (1694), containing twelve suites each, mostly in four movements such as Preludio – Allemanda – Corrente (or Sarabanda) – Giga (or Gavotta) [Ex. in *HAM*, no. 253]. Veracini's *Sonate da camera* (op. 1) show the tendency towards amalgamation with the sonata da chiesa, by the inclusion of free movements, e.g., Fantasia – Allegro – Allemanda – Pastorale – Giga.

V. *The French Overture.* Still another type of suite, designed for orchestral performance, originated (we may assume) in a practice similar to that exemplified by, e.g., Tchaikovsky's Nutcracker Suite, i.e., the performance of Lully's operas or stage ballets "in abstracto," as a succession of their most successful dance numbers preceded by the operatic overture. This idea was taken over by numerous German composers who wrote orchestral suites consisting of a French overture [see *Overture I] followed by a series of "modern" dances, such as rigaudon,

marche, chaconne, bourré, traquenard, and many others. Such suites, briefly called "Ouverture," were written by Johann S. Kusser (*Composition suivant la méthode française*, 1682), Georg Muffat (*Florilegium*, 1695/96; *DTOe* 1.i, 1.ii), J. K. F. Fischer (*Le Journal de Printemps*, 1695; *DdT* 10), J. A. Schmierer (*Zodiacus musicus*, 1698; *ibid.*), Joh. Jos. Fux (*Concentus musico-instrumentalis*, 1701; *DTOe* 23.ii), Telemann (*Musique de table*, 1733; *DdT* 61/62), and J. S. Bach (4 Orchestral Suites). Bach also transferred this type to the harpsichord in his *Französische Ouverture* (contained in the *Clavierübung* iii, 1739) as did Georg Böhm before him [see his *Sämtliche Werke* i (1927), no. 2]. In its use of "modern" dances this suite comes much closer to the 19th-century type than the idealized "classical" suite.

Lit.: K. Nef, *Geschichte der Sinfonie und der Suite* (1921); F. Blume, *Studien zur Vorgeschichte der Orchester-suite im 15/16. Jahrhundert* (1925); G. Condamin, *La Suite instrumentale* (1905); *AdHM* i, 563ff; E. Noack, "Ein Beitrag zur Geschichte der älteren deutschen Suite" (*AMW* ii); T. Norlind, "Zur Geschichte der Suite" (*SIM* vii); G. Adler, in *RMI* iii (Gottlieb Muffat); B. Wojcikowna, in *ZMW* v (Joh. Fischer).

Suivez [F.]. Same as *colla parte.

Sul [It.]. On, at. *Sul G*, on the G-string of the violin. *Sul ponticello* indicates bowing near the bridge; *sul tasto, sulla tastiera*, bowing near the finger board. See *Bowing (k), (l).

Sumer is icumen in. A famous composition of *c.* 1310 [see Addenda, p. 825], preserved in MS Brit. Mus. *Harleyan 978* (facs. reprod. in *GD* v, frontispiece; in *OH* i, 333, and elsewhere) written in the form of two simultaneous circular canons, the upper in four parts, the lower (called *pes* in the original) in two. This piece, called *rota in the original, is remarkable not only as the oldest existing canon, but also for its charming and folk-like character in melody as well as in harmony. Its artistic and historic significance, however, is frequently grossly over-rated. Regarding the former point it may be noticed that its very structure as a circular canon excludes really great artistic excellence, much in the same way as is the case with the innumerable rounds of the 18th and 19th centuries, even including those by Haydn, Mozart, or Beethoven. Regarding the latter point it suffices to mention that a canon-like exchange of parts (*Stimmtausch) is encountered frequently in the *organa quadrupla* of Perotinus (*c.* 1160–1220; see *Ars antiqua) who treats this device with much more imagination than the "monk of Reading." A statement such as that quoted in *GD* v, 191 (". . . artistically we may say that nothing written for two hundred years afterwards can touch it") shows so clearly a preponderance of enthusiasm over historical knowledge that it cannot be taken seriously.

Brahms has imitated the construction of the Sumer canon in his op. 113 (*Kanons*), no. 13.

Summation(al) tones. See *Combination tones.

Superdominant. See *Scale degrees.

Superius. See *Part books.

Supertonic. See *Scale degrees.

Surprise Symphony. Haydn's Symphony in G major (no. 3 of the Salomon Symphonies; no. 94 of the current enumeration), composed in 1791; so called on account of the "surprise" caused by the sudden ff-chord in the middle of the peaceful theme of the slow movement. Another name, referring to the same effect, is Drum Stroke Symphony.

Suspension. (1) See *Nonharmonic tones II. — (2) An 18th-century agrément, in which the written note is slightly delayed by a short rest:

$$\hat{P} = \gamma \, \int \! P$$

Suspirium [L.]. Old name of the rest of the value of a *minima*, the equivalent of the modern half-note. The modern

French term *soupir*, however, denotes a quarter-note rest. See *Notes.

Sussurando [It.]. Whispering.

Sustaining pedal. The sostenuto pedal (middle pedal) of the *pianoforte. Sometimes used for the damper pedal (right pedal).

Svegliando [It.]. Brisk, alert.

Svelto [It.]. Smart, quick.

Svolgimento [It.]. Development.

Sw. Abbreviation for Swell Organ.

Swedish music. The tradition of Gregorian chant led, in the 13th century, to a national production of sequences [see Lit., Moberg]. Aside from this, very little is known about the music in Sweden prior to the 17th century. Dietrich Buxtehude was born in the Swedish town of Helsingborg, but his German parentage, his life (mostly in Lübeck), and his work definitely classify him as a German composer. Another German, Gustav Düben (1624–90), who became court conductor in 1640, is important as the compiler of a famous MS collection of music, now in the possession of the library of Upsala. His sons succeeded him in his position at the court. The first native composer of Sweden was Johan Helmich Roman (1694–1758), who studied in London under Ariosti and Pepusch, possibly also under Handel. He became director of the court music in 1729 and wrote a considerable number of instrumental and vocal pieces in the style of Handel [cf. *RiML*, 1538]. Johann Joachim Agrell (1701–63) spent most of his life in Germany (Kassel, Nürnberg) while, on the other hand, the German Johann Gottlieb Naumann (1741–1801) is worth mentioning for the success of his operas *Amphion* (1776) and *Gustav Vasa* (1783), both produced in Stockholm. Other Germans who played a role in the musical life of Sweden were G. J. Vogler (Abbé Vogler, 1749–1814; opera *Gustav Adolf och Ebba Brahe*, 1788) and his pupil J. Martin Kraus (1756–1792; symphonies). Particularly successful was the French-Swiss

Jean-Baptiste du Puy (1770–1822) with his opera *Ungdom og Galskab* (1806) which was on the repertoire of the Copenhagen and Stockholm operas throughout the 19th century.

Johan Fredrik Palm (1753–1821) and Olof Ahlström (1756–1838) were among the first to write Swedish songs and were also active in collecting Swedish folk songs. Bernard Crusell (1775–1838), a native of Finland, wrote chamber music for the clarinet, and songs to Tegner's *Frithiof*. Passing over numerous other composers of minor importance, Franz Adolf Berwald (1796–1868) deserves mention as a composer of valuable symphonies, string quartets, and other chamber music. Ivar Hallström (1826–1901) gained a reputation as a composer of operas some of which show clearly national idioms, a fact which has earned him the title of "The Swedish Glinka." August Söderman (1832–76) encouraged the national movement by his orchestral ballades and solo songs. This movement, although widely supported by the public and by musical societies, did not, however, find a champion comparable in stature to the Norwegian Grieg. Andreas Hallén (1846–1925) wrote operas (*Harold the Viking*, 1881) and symphonic poems in the styles of Wagner and Liszt, but without lasting success. Emil Sjögren (1853–1918) wrote piano pieces and songs in Romantic style, with a certain admixture of national idioms. Wilhelm Stenhammer (1871–1927) and Hugo Alfvén (b. 1872) followed the direction inaugurated by Hallén, the former in symphonic poems, the latter in operas (also chamber music and songs).

The Swedish music of the present day is represented mainly by Natanael Berg (b. 1879), Edwin Kallstenius (b. 1881), Ture Rangström (b. 1884), and Kurt Atterberg (b. 1887), whose works show the influence of Richard Strauss and Pfitzner.

Lit.: *LavE* i.5, 2587ff; *AdHM* ii, 1118ff (modern); A. A. Moberg, *Die schwedischen Sequenzen* (1927); K. Valentin, *Studien über die schwedischen Volksmelodien* (1865); A. Soubies, "La Musique scandinave avant le xixe siècle"

(*RMI* viii); C. A. Moberg, "Der gregorianische Gesang in Schweden" (*KJ*, 1932); *id.*, "Essais d'opéras en Suède sous Charles XII" (in *Editions XXIV, B, 3/4*); T. Norlind, "Die Musikgeschichte Schwedens in den Jahren 1630–1730" (*SIM* i); *id.*, in *SIM* ii; *id.*, in *Festschrift für Johannes Wolf* (1929). For Swedish literature cf. *MoML*, 774.

Swell. In organs a contrivance to obtain a gradation of sound, crescendo and diminuendo. It consists of a large room (swell box) built around one or more divisions of the pipes, and provided with shutters similar to those of Venetian blinds — hence the name Venetian swell [G. *Jalousieschweller*]. The enclosed division is called swell organ, a name which also applies to the manual from which it is played. The swell box is opened and closed by a swell pedal, operated by the feet. The swell mechanism was invented in 1769 by Shudi, and was applied to harpsichords before it was adopted for the organ. See *Organ III and VII.

Swing. See *Jazz V.

Swiss music. In the early Middle Ages the monastery of St. Gall was one of the chief centers of Gregorian chant. Its MSS, written in the so-called St. Gall neumes [see *Neumes I], are among the most valuable sources of Gregorian chant [see *Editions XXIII A 1, B 1, 2] although their former position as the "true source of the chant" is no longer recognized (P. Wagner). In the 9th and 10th centuries St. Gall became foremost in the writing of *sequences (Notker, Tuotilo) while Hermannus Contractus (d. 1054) and Berno (d. 1048), both monks of the abbey of Reichenau, wrote important treatises (*GS* i, ii). In the 15th century organ building and organ playing flourished in Switzerland, and in the early 16th century we find here a highly important group of organ composers, Hans Kotter in Bern, Fridolin Sicher in St. Gall, and Johannes Buchner in Basle [see *Organ music I]. Above all stands Ludwig Senfl (1490–?), born in Zurich, and Henricus Glareanus (Heinrich Loris, 1488–1563), the author of the *Dodekachordon (1547). Benedictus Appenzeller [cf. W. Barclay Squire in *SIM* xiii], Sixtus Dietrich (*c.* 1490–1548), Gregor Meyer (frequently mentioned and quoted in the Dodekachordon), are other Josquin pupils of rank, while Johann Wannenmacher (d. 1551) is noteworthy particularly for his *Bicinia germanica* (1553). After 1550 the impulse of the *Humanism faded out, and musical activity declined considerably in Switzerland. Johann Melchior Gletle (d. before 1684) was a prolific composer of Masses, psalms, motets, and is interesting as the composer of some pieces for the *tromba marina. Heinrich Binswang (fl. 1700) from Weissenburg, better known as Albicastro, wrote trio sonatas and concertos.

The inborn Swiss penchant for community life and festive gatherings found an expression in the foundation of numerous choral societies — a movement which was inaugurated by Hans Georg Nägeli (1773–1836) and which brought about a remarkable repertory of outstanding compositions for male chorus, notably by Karl Attenhofer (1837–1914) and Friedrich Hegar (1841–1927). The two outstanding representatives of modern German-Swiss music are Othmar Schoeck (b. 1886), chiefly known as a writer of lyrical songs, and Hermann Suter (1870–1926), who wrote string quartets and symphonies. The connection with France and with the novel tendencies of the 20th century (*New music) is represented by Frank Martin (b. 1890) and Ernst Levy (b. 1895, now in the United States), while the Germanic influence appears in Konrad Beck (b. 1901). The Swiss-born Ernest Bloch (b. 1880, now in the United States) is a champion of national Jewish music.

Lit.: *LavE* i.5, 2665ff; *AdHM* ii, 1038ff, 1077ff; G. Becker, *La Musique en Suisse* (new ed. 1923); A. Geering, *Die schweizerischen Komponisten in der 1. Hälfte des 16. Jahrhunderts* (Diss. Basle 1933); K. Nef, †*Musikalische Werke schweizerischer Komponisten des 16.–18. Jahrhunderts*, 3 vols. (1927-·34). For additional bibl. cf. *MoML*, 777.

Syllabic style. See *Gregorian chant III.

Sympathetic strings. Strings which are not played upon but which merely serve to reinforce the sound of the bowed or plucked strings to which they run parallel at a close distance, and to whose pitch they are tuned in unison or octave [see *Resonance]. Various old instruments had such strings, e.g., the *viola d'amore, the *viola bastarda, the *baryton, the *tromba marina. They have also been added, under the name of *aliquot strings, to the highest register of pianos. Cf. T. L. Southgate, in *PMA* xlii.

Symphonia [Gr., simultaneous sound]. (1) Ancient Greek term for unison, as distinguished from *antiphonia*, the octave [see *Antiphon] and *paraphonia*, the fifth; also for consonance. — (2) In the Middle Ages the term was applied to various instruments, the drum (Isidorus de Sevilla, 7th century), the *hurdy-gurdy, also called *cinfonie* (Joh. de Muris, *c.* 1300), the bagpipe (hence the modern name *zampogna), and a type of clavichord (16th century). — (3) Beginning with the 17th century the name was used for various types of orchestral music which gradually led to the modern *symphony, but which, for the sake of clarity and distinction, are discussed in this book under the heading of *sinfonia.

Symphonic poem. I. Symphonic poem or tone poem is the name given to a type of 19th-century symphonic music which is based upon an extramusical idea, either poetic or descriptive. Thus the symphonic poem belongs to the general category known as *program music of which it represents the most recent and most thorough embodiment. The term is usually restricted to compositions in one movement, while a programmatic composition which follows the scheme of the four-movement symphony is called program symphony. Beethoven's *Pastoral Symphony*, Berlioz' *Symphonie fantastique*, Liszt's symphonies *Dante* (1855) and *Faust* (1854–57), and Dvořák's symphony *From the New World* (1893) belong to this category. The symphonic poem proper was inaugurated by Liszt in his one-movement compositions *Ce qu'on entend sur la montagne* (1848, after a poem of Victor Hugo), *Tasso* (1849, after Byron), *Les Préludes* (after Lamartine's Méditations poétiques), *Mazeppa* (1851, after Hugo), *Die Ideale* (1857, after Schiller), *Hunnenschlacht* (after a painting by Kaulbach, showing the slaughter of the Huns), *Hamlet* (1858), etc. Usually these compositions follow, in a somewhat free manner, the form of the first movement of a symphony [see *Sonata-form]. A composition such as Beethoven's *Coriolanus Overture* (1807) may be considered as a predecessor of the symphonic poem.

II. Liszt's innovation was eagerly seized upon by a great number of composers to whom literary, pictorial, and other ideas revealed a new source of inspiration. Particularly favored were works descriptive of national life and scenery, and it was a happy circumstance that the symphonic poem came into being at the same time that *nationalism was awakening in music. The first contribution in this particular province were Smetana's six symphonic poems *Mà Vlast* ("My Fatherland"), composed in 1874–79 [earlier symphonic poems of his were *Richard III* (1858), *Wallenstein's Camp* (1858), and *Hakon Jarl* (1861)]. His example was followed by a host of successors, and there is scarcely one country which has not been described in music. Compositions such as Borodin's *Steppes of Central Asia* (1880), Saint-Saëns's *Africa* (1891), Sibelius' *Finlandia* (1899), Vaughan Williams' *A London Symphony* (1914), Respighi's *Fontane di Roma* (1917), F. Grofé's *Grand Canyon*, E. Bloch's *America* (1928), illustrate the scope of the "musical atlas" which, perhaps not by mere chance, includes few, if any, pictures from Germany and France where the national movement had but little following.

The poetic type inaugurated by Liszt was continued, among others, by Tchaikovsky who wrote the symphonic poems *Romeo and Juliet* (1870), *Francesca da Rimini* (1876), and *Hamlet* (1885); by Saint-Saëns with *Omphale's Spinning*

Wheel (1871) and *Phaeton* (1873), and by Franck with *Les Éolides* (1876), *Le Chasseur maudit* (1882), *Les Djinns* (1885), and *Psyché* (1886, with chorus).

III. A new period of the symphonic poem began in 1895 when Richard Strauss, after some preliminary works of lesser importance (*Aus Italien*, 1887; *Macbeth*, 1887; *Don Juan*, 1888), made an outstanding contribution in his *Tod und Verklärung* ("Death and Transfiguration"). It was particularly the realistic approach and the extremely bold and skillful handling of the orchestra which made this work famous, although it met with violent criticism on the part of the professional writers and of a large section of the public. In 1895 he wrote *Till Eulenspiegel*, by far his most spontaneous and best work. There followed: *Also sprach Zarathustra* ("Thus Spake Zoroaster," after Nietzsche, 1896); *Don Quixote*, a series of free variations which include such realistic effects as the bleating of sheep and a wind machine to represent an imaginary flight through the air; *Ein Heldenleben* ("A Hero's Life," 1898), a musical autobiography including among its scenes one called "The Hero's Battlefield" in which the artist fights his critics who, as may well be imagined, do not fare too well. His *Sinfonia domestica* (1903) describes, with realistic rather than musical success, a day in the composer's family life, and his *Alpensinfonie* (1915) is a detailed description of a day's experience in climbing the Alps.

IV. Shortly before 1900 two important symphonic poems were written in France, Debussy's impressionistic *L'Après-midi d'un faune* (1895) and Paul Dukas' realistic *L'Apprenti sorcier* (1897). Both of them have the distinction, not shared by many other works of the category, of possessing outstanding musical qualities even apart from the realization of the programmatic idea. Sibelius wrote a number of tone poems, mostly based on the Kalevala, the Finnish national epic: *En Saga* (1892), *Kullervo* (1892), *The Swan of Tuonela* (1893), *Lemminkäinen and the Maidens* (1895), *Lemminkäinen in Tuonela* (1895), *The Return of Lem-*

minkäinen (1895), *Pohjola's Daughter* (1906), *Nightride and Sunrise* (1909), *The Bard* (1913), *Luonnotar* (1913), *The Oceanides* (1914), *Tapiola* (1925). To the list of 20th-century symphonic poems may be added Debussy's *La Mer* (1903–05), consisting of three pieces ("De l'aube à midi sur la mer"; "Jeux de vagues"; "Dialogue du vent et de la mer") in which atmospheric sensations are captured with consummate skill; Stravinsky's *Fireworks* (1908); Loeffler's *A Pagan Poem* (1909), based on an Eclogue by Vergil; Elgar's *Falstaff* (1913), perhaps the most detailed musical description of a literary subject; Respighi's Roman Trilogy *Fontane di Roma* ("The Fountains of Rome," 1917), *Pini di Roma* ("The Pines of Rome," 1924), and *Feste Romane* ("Roman Festivals," 1929). A. Honegger's *Pacific 231* (1923) and *Rugby* (1928), realistic glorifications of the modern age, indicate, in their subject-matter — the machine and active sport — as well as in their percussive and motoric idiom, an attempt to instill new lifeblood into the symphonic poem which, with its sensuousness and over-refinement, had outlived its time. On the whole, this attempt has not proved successful. The neo-classical tendencies of the present day with their emphasis on purely musical forms and styles would seem to have brought the development of the symphonic poem to its conclusion.

Lit.: R. Mendl, "The Art of the Symphonic Poem" (*MQ* xviii).

Symphonie Fantastique. A symphony by Hector Berlioz (1803–69), composed in 1831, which holds a prominent place in the symphonic literature of the 19th century owing to its outstanding artistic qualities as well as to its historic importance in the field of program music [see also *Symphonic poem] and in the development of the *leitmotif. The five sections of the symphony (with its subtitle "Episodes from an Artist's Life") are headed: "Reveries-Passions," "A Ball," "Scene in the Country," "March to the Scaffold," "Dreams of a Witch's Sabbath," and are held together by the use of a recurring theme, called *idée fixe*. In the "March to the Scaffold" the caricatured appearance of the *Dies irae* melody is worth mentioning.

Symphony. A symphony may be defined as a sonata for orchestra. For all the details of form, the reader is referred to the explanations given under *sonata, *sonata-form, etc. Naturally, the use of a large orchestral body instead of a single instrument (pianoforte sonata) or a small group of performers (trio, quartet) leads to a broadening of the form (the symphony is normally in four movements of considerable extension, frequently preceded by an introduction) and also accounts for differences in style, for greater richness in texture and variety of colors, for a greater emphasis on climactic effects, for stronger contrasts within a single movement as well as between one and the other.

I. *The Present-day Repertoire.* This begins with the latest symphonies of Mozart and Haydn. Mozart, although the younger man by nearly a quarter of a century, was the first to write truly great symphonies, namely the *Prague Symphony (D major, K.V. 504, written in 1786) and his last three symphonies, in E-flat major (K.V. 543), G minor (K.V. 550), and C major (*Jupiter Symphony, K.V. 551), written in June, July, and August 1788. Among Haydn's symphonies, which number more than one hundred, only the twelve written in 1790–95 for Salomon, his London impresario, show the same maturity of style as those by Mozart [see *London Symphonies]. The advance of these works over the earlier ones is chiefly threefold: thematic invention, development technique, and *obbligato* accompaniment. Not until after 1785 did Haydn and Mozart succeed in creating that special type of instrumental melody which is comparable in greatness, although different in character, to the melodies and themes of the Bach-period; a melody which is unified and individual enough to serve as an impressive motto and yet which lends itself to all the manipulations demanded in the development section. Hand in hand with this goes an increasing emancipation of the lower instruments from their former servant role as a mere chordal background, leading to their active participation in the statement as well as in the development of the themes [see *Accompaniment].

Beethoven, in limiting himself to nine symphonies — as compared with the several score written by his predecessors — established the character of the symphony as an "individual," rather than as an "example of a type." His first two symphonies (op. 21, in C, 1800; op. 36, in D, 1802) already show, if compared with those of Haydn and Mozart, a greater seriousness of purpose, a more dynamic vitality, larger dimensions, and a more advanced orchestration. The later ones, particularly the nos. 3 (*Eroica, op. 55, 1804), 5 (C minor, op. 67, 1809), 6 (*Pastoral Symphony, op. 68, 1809), and 9 (*Choral Symphony, op. 125, 1817–23), stand out as unparalleled peaks of symphonic literature. Beethoven's heir to the symphonic tradition was Franz Schubert (eight symphonies), mainly with his lyrico-dramatic Unfinished Symphony (B minor, 1822) and the magnificent C major Symphony, no. 7 (1828). Of equal artistic rank is Hector Berlioz' *Symphonie fantastique [see also *French music] while the four symphonies of Mendelssohn (C minor, 1824; Scotch Symphony, 1830–42; Italian Symphony, 1833; Reformation Symphony, 1830–32) and the four symphonies of Schumann (B-flat, "Spring," 1841; C major, 1846; E-flat, "Rhenish," 1850; D minor, 1841, revised 1851) are noticeably weaker in substance and expression.

Although in the subsequent decades the novel type of the *symphonic poem absorbed the interest of composers, the symphony arrived at a new peak around 1880, mainly with the four symphonies of Brahms (op. 68, 1875; op. 73, 1877; op. 90, 1883; op. 98, 1885) and the nine symphonies of Anton Bruckner (particularly no. 4, 1874; no. 5, 1876; no. 6, 1879; no. 7, 1883; no. 8, 1885; no. 9, 1894). Brahms took over the basic idea as well as the form of the Beethovian symphony, modifying

its style from a straightforward dynamism to a pliable and Romantic lyricism of great impressiveness. Bruckner, on the whole a more truly creative genius than Brahms, established a symphonic form and style of his own the artistic significance of which is even today far from being understood or recognized. Scarcely second to Beethoven in the greatness of melodic invention, he created an "architectural" type of symphony whose huge dimensions are matched by a deeply religious ethos and an almost superhuman pathos. His movements, as compared with those of Beethoven, are the realization, not so much of one continuous thought, but of changing visions, each represented as a painting in its frame, with the result that a static (sectional) element is interpolated between the dynamic forces of the single sections (first, second, third theme, etc.) and the huge arch of the whole movement.

Much better known than Bruckner's symphonies are those by Tchaikovsky, although only the sixth (Pathetic Symphony, 1893) can be included in the list of truly great works. Its highly subjective, even autobiographical, nature forms a most interesting contrast to the almost liturgical character of Bruckner's symphonies. Dvořák wrote nine symphonies the last of which is the popular "From the New World" (op. 95, 1893). Other works of this period are the D minor Symphony by Franck (1888), and d'Indy's "Symphonie sur un chant montagnard français" (1886).

Gustav Mahler, one of the first admirers of Bruckner, followed, in his nine symphonies (written from 1888 to 1909), the latter's trend toward huge symphonic dimensions, but from a more subjective and Romantic standpoint. Taking the modern position that "the contents should shape the form," he largely discarded the traditional forms (sonata-form, ternary form, etc.) of the single movements, making his symphonies deeply moving expressions of his spiritual experiences, messages of a life filled equally with tragic desperation and with never diminishing hope. A characteristic feature is the frequent use of solo instruments as well as (in nos. 2, 3, 4, 8) of solo voices, to say nothing about the masterly orchestration in general. Frequently the massive chording of the Romantic era is replaced by a thin linear texture, a procedure which foreshadowed the neo-classical return to polyphonic style. Sibelius wrote seven symphonies of which the first three (1899, 1901, 1904–07) are conceived in an idiom mixed of Romantic, national, and impressionistic elements, while with his Fourth Symphony (1911) there occurred a decided change towards purely musical purpose and design. His symphonies, though extremely popular in England and in the United States, have never gained a foothold in continental Europe.

The radicalism of the movement known as *New music led to a rather general neglect of the symphony, the huge form and dramatic emotionalism of which did not agree with the novel tendencies of the 20th century. Nonetheless, composers of more conservative affiliation continued to cultivate the symphony, e.g., Roussel (four), Vaughan Williams (five), Rachmaninov (three), Prokofiev (five, including the "Classical Symphony," op. 25, 1917), Howard Hanson (four). Around 1930, however, progressively minded composers also turned their interest to the symphony, frequently in a compact one-movement form or with choral participation. Among this group we find Stravinsky ("Symphony of Psalms," with chorus, 1930), Honegger (1930), Roy Harris (five symphonies, 1929–35, one a cappella, one for chorus and orchestra), Malipiero (1934, '36), Piston (1938, '44). A special place must be reserved for the Russian Dmitri Shostakovich who, at the age of 38, could boast of a record of eight symphonies among which the 1st, 5th, and 7th have been particularly successful, owing mainly to a skillful blending of modernistic and popularizing elements. The most prolific symphonist of the present day is, no doubt, Nicolas Miaskovsky (b. 1881), composer of 24 symphonies.

II. *The Early History.* The symphony developed during the 18th century side by side with the *sonata, its counterpart in the field of chamber music. It developed in particular from the Italian operatic overture which was called *Sinfonia avanti l'opera* and which, around 1700, had been standardized as a composition consisting of three sections in the succession: fast — slow — fast (for the earlier Italian sinfonia, see *Sinfonia; see also *Overture I). Although examples of such sinfonias occur as early as in the works of Alessandro Stradella (*c.* 1645–92; operatic cantata *Il Barcheggio,* 1681) the type became established under Alessandro Scarlatti (1659–1725), who used it first in his opera *Dal male di bene,* of *c.* 1696. It should be noted that in Scarlatti's sinfonias the slow section is always short and transitional in character; that the first as well as the second section usually closes with a half-cadence; and that the third section is in the character of a minuet or gigue [for an example cf. *HAM,* no. 259]. While this type was perpetuated in a rather unimaginative manner by the later composers of the Neapolitan opera [see *Neapolitan School], the tendency towards a more developed type appears in the sinfonia of the opera *Pallade trionfante* (1722) of Francesco Conti (1681–1732) who worked in Vienna. Here the first and the third sections are independent movements in sonata-form, with two themes, development and (shortened) recapitulation, while the middle movement still is transitional in character [reprint in H. Botstiber, *Geschichte der Ouverture* (1913); also *AdHM,* 797]. The operatic sinfonias were frequently played in concert performance, a practice which, around 1730, led to the composition of independent orchestral pieces in the same style, the first symphonies proper. Locatelli (1693–1764), Rinaldo di Capua (*c.* 1700–*c.* 80), and G. B. Sammartini (1701–75) were the pioneers in this field. Particularly Rinaldo's compositions are remarkable for their relatively large form and their "dynamic" style resembling that of the *Mannheim group. German composers such as Georg Monn (1717–50) and Georg Wagenseil (1715–77) in Vienna, Franz Xaver Richter (1709–89) and Johann Stamitz (1717–57) in Mannheim developed the symphonic dualism (first and second theme) and cultivated a style of dynamic and militant conciseness which the later Mannheimers (Beck, Cannabich, Anton Stamitz) mitigated by the inclusion of melodic and lyrical elements, thus preparing the way for the symphonies of Haydn (1732–1809) and Boccherini (1743–1805). See also *Sonata; *Sonata-form.

Lit.: *To I:* O. Downes, *Symphonic Masterpieces* (1935); P. Goetschius, *Masters of the Symphony* (1919); Ch. O'Connell, *The Victor Book of the Symphony* (1934); P. Bekker, *Die Sinfonie von Beethoven bis Mahler* (1918). — *To II:* K. Nef, *Geschichte der Sinfonie und der Suite* (1921); Flueler, *Die Norddeutsche Sinfonie* (Diss. Berlin 1910); F. Tutenberg, *Die Sinfonik J. Chr. Bach's* (1927); R. Sondheimer, *Die Theorie der Sinfonie im 18. Jahrhundert* (1925); R. Sondheimer, "Die formale Entwicklung der vorklassischen Sinfonie" (*AMW* iv); *id.,* "Die Sinfonien Franz Becks" (*ZMW* iv); *id.,* in *ZMW* iii (Sammartini); *id.,* in *RMI* 1920 (Boccherini); H. Kretzschmar, "Die Jugendsinfonien Josef Haydns" (*JMP* xv); P. Gradenwitz, in *MR* i (Stamitz); J. Tiersot, "La Symphonie en France" (*ZIM* iii); G. de Saint-Foix, "Contribution à l'histoire de la symphonie française vers 1750" (*L'année musicale,* 1911); *id.,* in *RMI* xxxi (Clementi); A. Casella, in *RdM* xvii (Clementi); R. Viollier, in *RdM* xvii, no. 60 (Jean Mauret); F. Torrefranca, "Le Origini della sinfonia" (*RMI* xx, xxi, xxii).

Syncopation. Syncopation is, generally speaking, any deliberate upsetting of the normal pulse of meter, accent, and rhythm. Our system of musical rhythm rests upon the grouping of equal beats into groups of two and three, with a regularly recurrent accent on the first beat of each group [see *Rhythm II (a)]. Any deviation from this scheme is felt as a disturbance or contradiction between the underlying (normal) pulse and the actual (abnormal) rhythm.

Ex. 1 shows the three most common methods of shifting the accent to the nor-

mally weak beats of the measure, namely: (a) by holding on over the strong beat; (b) by having rests on the strong beats;

(c) by placing a stress on the weak beat. The examples given under Ex. 2 show the practical application of these methods [(a): Beethoven, Piano Sonata op. 28, no. 1; (b): Beethoven, Appassionata; (c): Brahms, Symphony no. 4, Scherzo].

Normally, syncopation is only "partial," i.e., it occurs in one part only (either the melody or the bass), while other parts maintain and emphasize the normal pulse of the meter. In the late works of Beethoven, however, there occur the earliest

examples of "complete syncopation," i.e., the displacement of accents in the entire texture [Ex. 3, Piano Sonata, op. 101]. This procedure brings about a complete unbalance of our feeling of rhythmic security, an effect which occurs in Romantic music (Schumann) as a means of blurring, while, in modern music (jazz), it rather has the effect of a shock. Still another type of syncopation, resulting not from a displaced accent in unchanged meter, but from a sudden change of the meter itself, is frequent in the pieces of modern composers, particularly those of Stravinsky [Ex. 4].

Syncopation appears first in the French Ars nova (G. de Machaut), and reached its all-time peak of complication in the music of the late 14th century (Cunelier, Grimace, Cordier, Solage, and others). It should be observed that, in 14th-century theory, syncopation is explained, not as it is today (such an explanation being impossible since accent or strong beat is a

concept foreign to early theory), but as a separation of a normal group of notes by the insertion of larger values, e.g. as in Ex. 5a. Instead of rendering this rhythm by tied notes in unchanged meter (b), a rendition similar to the methods employed by contemporary composers [see Ex. 4] is preferable in order to convey the true meaning of early syncopation, as in 5c. For still another method of rendering and for the original notation of 14th-century syncopation (*punctus syncopationis*) cf. *ApNPM*, 395ff.

Synemmenon. See *Greek music II (a).

Syntagma musicum. See *Theorists.

Syntonic comma. See *Comma.

Syrian Chant. Syria, being one of the first countries to be Christianized, has a long and interesting history of church music. Christian poetry reached an early peak in the hymns, still in use today, of St. Ephrem (d. 373) which represent the beginning of Christian hymn writing and which were imitated by St. Hilarius, bishop of Poitiers (d. 366), and by St. Ambrose, bishop of Milan (d. 397; see *Am-

brosian hymns). Ambrosius also imported from Syria the practice of *antiphonal singing. Important successors of Ephrem were Narses of Edessa (end of the 5th century), Jacob of Serugh (451–528), and Simeon of Gesir, the Potter (after 500). They founded a novel principle of poetry, based upon a given number of accents in a line, with a changeable number of weak syllables in between, similar to doggerel verse. The two chief types of ancient Syrian poetry are the *madrashe* (ode), consisting of a number of stanzas for a soloist with a refrain for chorus, and the *sogitha* (hymn), which was performed antiphonally by two choruses, with soloist leaders.

Since no early MSS of Syrian chant (if it was ever written down) have been preserved, the present practice of Syrian chant is the only material available for investigation. Modern Syrian chant is based on measured rhythm [see *Rhythm II (b)], as appears from the accompanying example. It is a good deal more rhythmic and

syllabic — thus, in a way, less "Oriental" — than Gregorian chant. To what degree the Syrian chant of today is representative of the early chant is a matter of conjecture and dispute. Contentions to the effect that Syrian chant shows Hellenic influence [cf. *BeMMR* 48] would seem to be rather far-fetched. Such rational features as are evident in Syrian chant may well be the result of 18th- and 19th-century Occidental influence [cf. *ReMMA*, 70]. A characteristic trait of Syrian church music is the use of standard melodies for a number of different poems of a similar verse-pattern. Such standard melodies (which allow for a certain amount of rhythmic modification) are known as *risqolo* (for similar methods used in other musical traditions, see *Melody types). In a Syrian MS of *c.* 515, the *Plerophoriai*, we find the earliest mention of the *oktoechos* [see *Echos].

Lit.: Dom J. Jeannin, *Melodies liturgiques syriennes et chaldéennes*, 2 vols.

(1926, '28); A. Z. Idelsohn, "Der Kirchengesang der Jakobiten" (*AMW* iv);
L. Bonvin, "On Syrian Liturgical Chant"
(*MQ* iv); Dom J. Jeannin, "L'Octoechos
syrien" (*Oriens Christianus*, New Series
iii, 82, 277). Cf. *ReMMA*, 432.

Syrinx. The Greek name for the *panpipes (also for a single flute).

System. The collection of staves, two or
more, as used for the writing down of
keyboard, chamber, or orchestral music.

T

T. Abbreviation of tonic, tutti, toe (in
pedal parts of organ pieces), trill (in 17th-
century music, usually a mordent only),
tasto, talon (in violin music). In 16th-
century *part-books, abbreviation of tenor.

Tabatière de musique [F.]. See *Mechanical instruments III.

Tablature [G. *Tabulatur*; It. *intavolatura*]. (1) General name for the various
early (15th–17th centuries) systems of
notation (for keyboard instruments, lute,
guitar, viol, flute, etc.), in which the tones
are indicated, not by notes on a staff (as in
the contemporary *mensural notation for
vocal music), but by letters, figures, or
other symbols. The most important ones
are the organ tablatures (more properly
keyboard tablatures) and the lute tablatures. There exist two types of keyboard
tablature, the German and the Spanish,
and three types of lute tablature, the Italian (also used in Spain), the French (used
everywhere after 1600), and the German.
It may be noticed that what are frequently
called "French, Italian, and English organ tablatures" (e.g., in *WoHN* ii) are
not tablatures in the sense defined above,
since they are written entirely in notes on
two staves, in practically the same manner
as the modern piano score. Although
they were called *intavolatura* in the 16th
century, they are omitted from the following consideration.

   I. *German Keyboard Tablatures.* The
Examples 1 and 2 illustrate what is called
"old" and "new" German keyboard tablature. The former, which employs notes
for the upper part, letters for the lower
parts, was in use prior to 1550; the latter,
written in letters exclusively, after 1550
(as late as 1720 Bach reverted to this sys-

tem in his *Orgelbüchlein* when there was
not sufficient space on the page to complete the piece in ordinary staff notation;

1. *Buxheim Organ Book, c. 1460*

cf. *ApNPM*, facs. no. 13). The letters
a, b, c, etc., have their present-day significance; it must be noted, however, that
in German terminology b means B-flat,
while the B-natural is indicated by the
letter h [see *B]. Chromatic alterations

2. *B. Schmid, Tabulatur Buch, 1607*

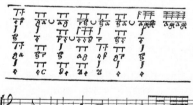

are indicated by affixing to the letter a
graph in the form of a loop or hook. This
was the stenographic sign for the Latin

syllable *is* (e.g., *arbor-is*) so that *c* with this loop means *cis*, the German term for C-sharp. The tones of the higher octave (usually from c′ to b′; in some sources from a to g′) are marked by a dash above the letter: c̄ (one-line c). Rhythmic values are indicated by the signs illustrated,

. | ſ ſ

denoting successively a *semibrevis*, *minima*, *semiminima*, and *fusa*. The transcription with Ex. 1 and 2 will help to clarify additional details of the notation.

II. *Spanish Keyboard Tablature*. Here a number of lines (three, four, five) represent the different voice-parts of a composition. The figures 1 to 7 stand for the notes of the diatonic scale beginning with f (1=f; 2=g; 3=a; 4=b or b♭, according to whether the sign ♮ or B is given at

3. *Cabezón, Obras de Musica, 1578*

the beginning of the piece; 5=c′, etc.). Higher and lower octaves are marked by special signs, e.g., a tick on the 3=A (cf. the third symbol on the bottom line of Example 3); the plain figure 3=a; a dot beside it=a′; a prime beside it, a″. A comma (,) indicates tying of the preceding note, a diagonal dash (/) indicates a rest.

III. *Italian (Spanish) Lute Tablatures*. All lute tablatures are based upon the idea, revived in certain modern instruments (ukulele, zither, guitar), of directing the fingers of the players to the position necessary for the desired tone or chord. Thus they avoid the entire matter of "solfège" (pitch, interval, scale, key, accidentals, etc.). They are a "finger-notation" [G. *Griffschrift*], as distinguished from the usual "pitch-notation." In the Italian system six horizontal lines represent the six strings of the lute, tuned G–c–f–a–d′–g′, in reversed order, so that

the highest line represents the string G (only in Milan's *Il Maestro*, 1535 is the highest line used for the highest string; see also under IV). On each line, figures from 0 to 9 appear which indicate the fret on which the player is supposed to put his finger, with 0 signifying the open string, 1 the first fret, etc. Since these frets proceed in semitones, the figures 1, 2, 3 . . . represent tones which are one, two, three . . . semitones higher than the open string. E.g., 3 on the second line from above indicates c (second open string) plus 3 semitones, i.e., d♯ or e♭. The rhythmical values are indicated above the staff by the accompanying signs, the first of which

| ſ ſ ſ

represents the *semibrevis* (usually transcribed as half-note). In spite of the contrapuntal character of 16th- and 17th-century lute music, no differentiation is ever made between the different temporal values of simultaneous sounds, e.g., between an eighth-note in the upper part as against a simultaneous half-note in a lower part. The rhythmic signs merely give the shortest of all the simultaneous notes, e.g., the eighth-note. The two transcriptions of Example 4 illustrate the "exact" rendition

4. *Fuenllana, Orphenica lyra, 1554*

together with the contrapuntal interpretation usually preferred in modern editions (as to this point, cf. *ApNPM*, 6off).

IV. *French Lute Tablature*. This system differs from the Italian merely in details. The staff has only five lines which represent the five highest strings in their natural order (as in Milan), while the lowest string is represented underneath on short ledger lines. Instead of the ciphers 0, 1, 2, 3 . . ., the letters a, b, c, d . . . are used, with a standing for the open string. See Ex. 5. After 1600 this system

5. *H. Bataille, Airs, 1611*

of notation underwent various modifications which, around 1650, led to a new system, based on Denis Gaultier's novel method of tuning (*nouveau ton*) A–d–f–a–d′–f′. Here, the Italian staff of six lines is used for the six strings which cross the frets, while the signs

$$\bar{a}, \quad \bar{\bar{a}}, \quad \overset{=}{a}, \quad \overset{\equiv}{a}, \quad 4$$

written underneath the staff indicate the bass-courses tuned (normally): G, F, E, D, C, which are unalterable in pitch.

V. *German Lute Tablature.* This system is much more awkward than the others, mainly because it was originally designed for a (15th-century) lute with only five strings, and was broadened later (16th century) by the inclusion of signs for the sixth (lowest) string. Our table shows the most common system of designation: figures 1–5 for the open strings (read from bottom to top); the letters of

		Frets						
		0	1	2	3	4	5	6	7
Strings	g′	5	e	k	p	v	9	ē	k̄....
	d′	4	d	i	o	t	7	d̄	ī....
	a	3	c	h	n	s	z	c̄	h̄....
	f	2	b	g	m	r	y	b̄	ḡ....
	c	1	a	f	l	q	x	ā	f̄....
	G	1	2	3	4	5	6	7	8....

the alphabet (completed by two special signs designated here 7 and 9) for the frets 1–5; the same letters with dashes for the higher frets. These tabulations show that, e.g., the sign h denotes the tone b (two semitones above a), and the sign x the tone f (five semitones above c). See Ex. 6.

6 *H. Gerle, Lautenbuch, 1552*

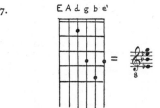

VI. *Modern Tablatures.* Tablature notation is used today for several popular instruments the playing of which is greatly facilitated by a notation which directs

7.

the fingers of the player immediately to the desired place, avoiding the cumbersome medium of musical notes and the study of pitch, intervals, accidentals, scales, etc. The accompanying Example 7 illustrates the notation of the modern guitar which is similar to the 16th-century lute tablatures. The vertical lines represent the six strings of the guitar, tuned E–A–d–g–b–e′; the horizontal lines the frets in chromatic progression. The dots indicate the position of the fingers. A similar method is used for the four-stringed ukulele.

Lit.: *ApNPM,* 21–81; *WoHN* ii, 1–247; *GD,* article Tablature.

(2) The set of rules which regulated the musical activities of the *Meistersinger.

Tabor, taboret, tabourin, tabret. See *Tambourin.

Tabulatur [G.]. See *Tablature.

Tace [It.], tacet [L.]. "Is silent," given with orchestral parts which are not wanted for a movement or a long section thereof.

Tact [G.]. See *Takt.

Tactus. The 15th- and 16th-century term for beat, in its temporal significance as well as in the meaning of "conductor's beat." There is, however, an essential difference between the tactus and the modern beat in so far as the former is a relatively fixed duration of time, about M.M. 50–60 (one second), while the latter may take on any value between large limits, according to the tempo and character of the composition. This means that in the period of Flemish music there existed a uniform "normal tempo" from which only slight deviations were possible. Since the tactus was normally represented by the *semibrevis* (*S*), the proper tempo of the motets of Ockeghem, Josquin, Palestrina, can be expressed by the metronomic mark: *S* = M.M. 50–60. For certain complications, caused chiefly by the use of the alla-breve sign ¢ instead of the "alla-semibreve" sign ℂ, cf. *ApNPM*, 188–195. See also *Tempo marks.

In the 13th and 14th centuries there existed similar units of time, called *tempus* (e.g., Franco of Cologne) which, however, were considerably shorter of duration and which changed somewhat during the course of these centuries. There also was a successive shift in the note values used to represent the "normal beat," namely from the *longa* (around 1200, School of Notre Dame) to the *brevis* (13th century), the *semibrevis* (14th–16th centuries), the *minima* (around 1550), and finally the *semiminima*, i.e., our quarternote (during the 17th century). For a tentative table of the changes in tempo prior to 1400 cf. *ApNPM*, 343.

Lit.: E. Praetorius, *Die Mensuraltheorie des Franchinus Gafurius* (1905), pp. 68ff; A. Chybinski, *Beiträge zur Geschichte des Taktschlagens* (Krakau, 1908); G. Schünemann, *Handbuch des Dirigierens* (1913), Kapitel III.

Tändelnd [G.]. Bantering.

Tafelmusik [G.]. Table music, i.e., music designed to be performed at a banquet. Cf., e.g., Telemann's *Musique de table* in *DdT* 61/62, and J. A. Reutter's *Servizio di tavola* in *DTOe* 15.ii.

Tagliato [It.]. An obsolete term for the *alla-breve sign.

Tagelied [G., day song]. See *Alba.

Taille [F.]. Old name for a middle voice, particularly the tenor. The term was also used for instruments performing such parts, e.g., *taille de basson*, tenor oboe; *taille de violon* or simply *taille*, viola. The indication "taille" in some of Bach's cantatas would seem to always call for the tenor oboe (oboe da caccia, English horn). In French 17th-century organ music an inscription such as *Récit de tierce en taille* means solo-passage (*récit*) in a middle part (*taille*) for the left hand, played on the organ stop *Tierce*. *Haute taille* and *basse taille* denote higher and lower tenor parts.

Takt [G.]. (1) Beat (*schwerer, leichter Takt*, i.e., strong, weak beat); (2) measure (*nach 10 Takten*, after 10 measures); (3) meter, time (¾-*Takt*, ¾-meter). *Im Takt*, in strict tempo and meter; *Taktmässig*, in strict meter; *Taktmesser*, metronome; *Taktstock*, baton; *Taktstrich*, bar-line; *Taktvorzeichnung*, time signature; *Taktwechsel*, change of meter; *Taktzeichen*, time signature; *taktieren*, to indicate the beat.

Talea. See *Isorhythmic.

Talent. See *Tests and Measurements.

Tales of Hoffmann, The. See *Contes d'Hoffmann, Les.

Talon [F.]. The *nut of the violin bow.

Tambour [F.]. Drum; also a drum player. *Tambour militaire*, snare drum.

Tambourin [F.]. An oblong, narrow drum (about double as deep as wide) of Provençal origin, also called *tambour de Basque, tambour the Provence* (English tabor). It is usually played together with the galoubet, a small flute (English: pipe and tabor; see *Pipe). In the 18th century the word also denoted dances ac-

companied by the galoubet and tambourin. Several examples occur in Rameau's
opera *Fêtes d'Hébé*, one of these also in
his works for harpsichord. If found in
modern scores, the term always denotes
the *tambourine.

Tambourine. See *Percussion instruments B, 4. If occurring with reference
to early music the term denotes the *tambourin.

Tamburin [G.], **tanburino** [It.].
Both terms usually denote the modern
*tambourine, rarely the obsolete *tam-
bourin. Note that words such as *tambur,
tambura, tampur* are likely to be designations for the *tanbur or similar Oriental
lutes.

Tamburo [It.]. Drum; *t. grande, grosso*, old name for the bass drum; *t. rullante*,
tenor drum; *t. militaire*, snare drum.

Tampon [F.]. Two-headed drumstick
used to produce a roll on the bass drum.
It is held in the middle and moved by
shaking the wrist.

Tamtam. Same as *Gong. Not to be
confused with *tom-tom.

Tanbur (also called *tanburi, tambur,
tamboura, tampur*, etc.). A lute with a
long neck and a small round body, found
in Persia, Arabia, India, etc. See *Lute II.

Tañer [Sp.]. See *Tastar.

Tangent [G. *Tangente*]. See *Clavichord.

Tango. A modern dance which originated around 1900 in the suburbs of
Buenos Aires from elements of the *habanera and the *milonga. After 1905 it
adopted syncopation as its characteristic
trait. It was soon imported into the ballrooms of the whole world, creating a sensation and shocking the Church and educators into open denunciation of the dance
as utterly immoral [see *Forlana]. Later
it became more tame and was widely cultivated in good society. About 1920 the
tango made its way into the realm of art
music, especially in the modern suites of

German composers, e.g., Hindemith,
Krenek, Conrad Beck, Erwin Schulhoff

[see Ex., by Schulhoff]. For a plausible
explanation of the name, i.e., as a Negro
onomatopoetic for drumbeat (tan-gó), cf.
Vicente Rossi, *Cosas de Negros* (1926).

Tannhäuser, or *Der Sängerkrieg auf
der Wartburg* ("The Singers' Contest at
the Wartburg"). Opera in three acts, text
(after a medieval legend) and music by
Richard Wagner, first produced in 1845.
The plot centers around the *Minnesinger
Tannhäuser (Tenor) who, after a year
of sinful life spent in the Venusberg, the
abode of *Venus* (Soprano), longs for freedom (Scene 1) and breaks the unholy
spell by imploring the Virgin Mary. In
Scene 2 he is found by the *Landgrave*
(Bass) and his knights — among them
Wolfram von Eschenbach (Baritone) —
who take their long-lost associate to the
Wartburg, where the Landgrave's niece,
Elizabeth (Soprano) has been waiting
faithfully for his return. Act II shows the
Sängerkrieg in which Elizabeth's hand is
to be the prize of the contest [see *Puy].
While Wolfram and the other Minnesinger praise virtuous love, Tannhäuser
in shameless defiance extols the sensuous
pleasures of love lust. Indignantly all the
ladies leave the hall, and only Elizabeth
remains. Deeply touched by her faithful
love, Tannhäuser expresses his penitence,
and joins a procession of pilgrims, to obtain forgiveness from the Pope. In Act III
the pilgrims return from Rome, but without Tannhäuser, and Elizabeth, who has
been waiting for him, goes away broken-
hearted. Finally Tannhäuser appears,
seeking again the cavern of Venus, since
the Pope has not forgiven his sin. In this
moment a funeral procession arrives, carrying the body of Elizabeth, and Tannhäuser, overwhelmed with emotion, joins
her in death. Pilgrims enter carrying

Tannhäuser's staff which has put forth fresh leaves in evidence that God has forgiven him.

The score of *Tannhäuser* shows Wagner working with the tools of the "grand opéra" of Meyerbeer and Bellini, but trying to create with them a new work of higher artistic and human significance. The formal structure is essentially that of the traditional *number opera, with distinct arias, numerous choruses, and even a ballet (first scene), although the actual numbering of the different items is abandoned. The harmonic style also is fairly traditional. It is by reason of its expressive and emotional qualities that *Tannhäuser* opens a new period in the history of opera. Wagner's "eternal theme," salvation through love, is presented here with a stirring emotionalism hardly less than that of his *Tristan* and *Parsifal*.

Tanto [It.]. Much, so much. *Non tanto*, not too much.

Tanz [G.]. Dance.

Tap box. Same as *Clog box.

Tapiola. See *Symphonic poem IV.

Tarantella. A Neapolitan dance in rapid ⁶⁄₈-meter, named probably after Taranto in South Italy or, according to a widespread legend, after the spider *tarantula* whose poisonous bite the dance was believed to cure. In the mid-19th century it was frequently composed (Chopin, Liszt, St. Heller, Auber, Weber, Thalberg) in the style of a brilliant *perpetuum mobile*.

Tarbouka. A North African drum which Berlioz used in the Slave Dance of his *Les Troyens*.

Tardo, tardamente [It.]. Slow, slowly. *Tardando*, slowing.

Tarogato. Hungarian instrument of ancient origin, originally a wooden trumpet having only natural tones. Such instruments were used for the sounding of military signals such as occur in the well-known melody of the *Rakoczy march. Later, the name was used for a wooden

shawm (oboe mouthpiece) with five or more holes. The modern tarogato, built by W. J. Schunda, is a wooden saxophone, i.e., with a clarinet mouthpiece. It has a somewhat darker timbre than the normal saxophone. See *Clarinet II. Illustration on p. 152.

Tartini's tones. Same as *differential tones.

Taschengeige [G., pocket fiddle]. *Kit.

Tasso. See *Symphonic poem I.

Tastar [It.]. Italian 16th-century term for lute pieces in the style of a free prelude (*tastar de corde*, "touching of the strings"). Examples in *HAM*, no. 99, and in *ApMZ* i. The Spanish synonym was *tañer* (Luis de Milan). See *Ricercar II (a).

Taste [G.]. Key (of the piano, organ, etc.). *Untertaste*, white key; *Obertaste*, black key.

Tastiera [It.]. The finger board of the violin, also called *tasto. Sulla tastiera (sul tasto)*, see *Bowing (1).

Tasto [It.]. (1) The key of a keyboard. For *tasto solo* (*t.s.*) see *Thorough-bass 6. — (2) On the violin, same as *tastiera.

Tattoo [F. *rappel*; G. *Zapfenstreich*]. The military signals sounded on bugles and drums by which the soldiers are recalled to their quarters at night.

Technique [G. *Technik*]. The mechanical skill which is the foundation of the mastery of an instrument or, in other words, the complete coördination of all the bodily movements required. It should always be remembered that such a coördination is not only a matter of the fingers, wrist, arm, etc., but also of psychological discipline. Many technical problems (e.g., big leaps on the pianoforte) are chiefly a problem of mental coördination and preparation. In fact, it would not be too much to say that most of the problems of advanced technique may be conquered by the precept: "think even faster than you play" [see *Pianoforte playing VI]. The desire for acquiring a perfect technique has led to a tremendous output of "technical studies" which intentionally neglect the musical element (still preserved to a certain degree in most *etudes) and provide only training for the fingers, etc. Daily practice for this routine material is generally recognized to be necessary for the improvement and the maintenance of technique, even by the most advanced virtuoso. It should hardly be necessary to warn the student against overrating technique and technical studies, which are nothing but the indispensable basis upon which to build up interpretation.

Tecla [Sp.]. The Spanish 16th- and 17th-century term for key and keyboard. *Musica para tecla* (e.g., Cabezon's *Obras*, 1578) is music for keyboard instruments.

Tedesca [It., German, i.e., dance]. In the 17th century, name for the *allemande. Around 1800, name for the *Ländler and similar dances in rather quick triple meter [cf. Beethoven, op. 79 and op. 130].

Te deum laudamus [G. usually *Te-deum*]. A celebrated hymn of praise and rejoicing which has been erroneously attributed to St. Ambrose (hence the designation Ambrosian Hymn), but which was probably written, both text and music, by Nicetas (c. 400), Bishop of Remesiana (now Nish, Serbia). In the Roman liturgy it is sung at matins of greater feasts of a joyful character [cf. *AR*, 66**]. Its present form is the result of several additions and intercalations such as are very uncommon in the tradition of Gregorian chant [for the structure cf. *GD* v, 295; also *RiHM* i.2, 42 (in wrong rhythmic interpretation); P. Wagner, *Einführung in die Gregorianischen Melodien*, iii, 225].

The *Te deum* has been widely used outside of the service as a text for compositions designed for occasions of thanksgiving, e.g., after great victories. Composers of the 16th century (Palestrina, Anerio, de Vaet) used the plainsong melody as a basis of contrapuntal elaboration, while later examples are free compositions in a grandiose style, frequently for double chorus with orchestra (Purcell, 1694;

Handel, for the peace of Utrecht, 1712, and for the victory of Dettingen, 1743; Graun, 1756, performed at the close of the Seven Years' War; Berlioz, for the Paris Exhibition of 1855; Bruckner, 1884; Dvořák, 1896; Verdi, 1898; Sullivan, for Queen Victoria's Diamond Jubilee, 1897).

The English translation is "We praise Thee, O God"; the German (by Luther) "Herr Gott wir loben Dich." Under the latter title J. S. Bach wrote an extended organ piece (hardly to be classified as a "Chorale prelude") in which he exhibits a great ingenuity in providing different polyphonic settings for the frequently repeated phrases of the (somewhat simplified) plainsong melody.

Telharmonium. See *Electronic musical instruments.

Telyn. The Welsh harp. See *Harp III.

Tema [It.]. Theme, subject.

Temperament [G. *Temperatur*]. I. *General.* The term denotes those systems of tuning in which the intervals deviate from the "pure," i.e., acoustically correct intervals as used in the *Pythagorean system and in *Just intonation. These deviations represent adjustments necessitated by the fact that the two systems just mentioned, although perfect within a small range of tones (mainly those of the C major scale), become increasingly inadequate with the successive introduction of the chromatic tones. For instance, the acoustically perfect fifth [see *Acoustics III] might well be used to obtain a succession of five or six fifths, c, g, d, a, e, b. If, however, tones such as f#, c#, g#, d# are added in the same manner, the resulting tones cannot be satisfactorily used for melodies such as d e f# g, or d# f g g# (meaning eb f g ab). Moreover, the twelfth tone of the succession of fifths, b#, is noticeably higher than the tone c which it would represent in our system of notation [see *Circle of fifths]. It follows that compromise methods are necessary which, instead of being perfect in the simple keys and intolerably wrong in the others, spread the inevitable inaccuracy over all the tones and keys. The most consistent realization of this principle is the *equal temperament* which is universally used today. Prior to its general acceptance various other systems of tempered intervals, generally referred to as "unequal temperament," were in use, among which the *mean-tone system* was the only one to attain practical significance.

II. *The Mean-Tone System.* This system, which was in use around 1500 (A. Schlick, *Spiegel der Organisten* ..., 1511) and fully discussed by F. Salinas (*De musica libri VII*, 1577), is based on a fifth which is one-fourth of the syntonic *comma (*c.* 20 *cents) smaller than the perfect fifth (697, instead of 702 cents), the result being that four such fifths, if taken in succession (c–g–d'–a'–e''), lead to a perfect third (e''). In the simple keys with one or two sharps or flats, the mean-tone scale is very satisfactory from both the melodic and the harmonic point of view. In fact, owing to the presence of a perfect third and an almost perfect fifth, the triads sound much purer than in equal temperament. However, the continuation of the series of mean-tone fifths leads to a very noticeable discrepancy between the sharp and flat tones, namely to a difference of almost a quarter-tone (41 cents) between any two enharmonic tones (e.g., G♯ = 773, A♭ = 814), a difference known as the "wolf." Having to choose between these two tones (the corresponding choice between C♯ and D♭, or between D♯ and E♭, being relatively easier, namely, in favor of C♯ and of E♭), Schlick interestingly enough preferred the A♭, in order to obtain the "süss und fremd lautende Konkordanz" (the sweet and strange-sounding consonance) of the Neapolitan sixth c–e♭–a♭, which actually occurs in his "Da Pacem" [cf. the new edition by G. Harms, p. 37; all the pieces are transposed here a fourth below]. Since this tone could not be used to represent G♯, Schlick recommends avoiding the G♯ or covering it up by a *coloratura [cf. G. Frotscher, *Geschichte des Orgelspiels*, I, 94]. A better expedient out of this dilemma is afforded by the use of divided keys, which, as a matter of fact, were not infrequently used

in organs of the 16th century. However, even this improvement was insufficient to satisfy the needs of the more fully developed system of harmonies, modulations, and keys as it arose during the 17th century. The increased use of keys with 3 to 6 sharps and flats necessarily led to the system of equal temperament.

III. *Equal Temperament.* The principle of equal temperament is to divide the octave into twelve equal semitones. Since the frequency of the octave is 2, the frequency s of this semitone is given by the equation: $s^{12} = 2$; $s = \sqrt[12]{2} = 1.05946$. The successive powers of this figure give the frequencies for the tones of the chromatic scale, e.g., $c = 1$; $c♯ = 1.05946$; $d = 1.05946^2 = 1.1225$; $d♯ = e♭ = 1.05946^3 = 1.14973$, etc. Usually a logarithmic measurement is used in which the whole octave equals 1200 *cents, each semitone 100 cents [see *Intervals, Calculation of, IV, V].

In equal temperament no interval other than the octave is acoustically correct or pure. The deviation of the fifth (2 cents) is too small to be noticed at all. With the thirds, the difference is considerably greater, the well-tempered third (400 cents) being 14 cents (one-eighth of a semitone) larger than the pure third (386 cents). However, our ear has become completely accustomed to this "error," and the advantages of the system far outweigh its flaws. The following table shows the actual frequencies of the Pythagorean system (P), of just intonation (J), and of the tempered tones (E).

	c	d	e	f	g	a	b	c
P:	520	585	658	693	780	877	987	1040
J:	520	585	650	693	780	867	975	1040
E:	520	584	655	694	779	874	982	1040

The accompanying drawing illustrates the difference between E and J in cents.

Equal Temperament

Just Intonation

Equal temperament is usually said to have been invented by Andreas Werkmeister around 1700. This statement is not in accordance with the facts. The history of equal temperament can be traced back to 1518, when H. Grammateus recommended dividing the octave into 10 equal semitones and two of somewhat smaller size. V. Galilei, in his *Dialogo* (1581), proposed to use a semitone of the frequency $^{18}\!/_{17}$ (99.3 cents) which is a very good approximation of the well-tempered semitone. The principle of equal temperament was clearly expounded by the Chinese prince Tsai-yu in 1596, and by Mersenne in 1635. Contrary to common belief, Werkmeister never stated equal temperament correctly. The introduction of equal temperament into musical practice was a very slow process. Whether Bach's famous collection of pieces in all the major and minor keys, the *Well-tempered Clavier* (1722), or its less complete predecessor, J. K. F. Fischer's *Ariadne Musica* (*c.* 1710), referred to equal temperament or merely to a sufficiently close approximation, is not entirely clear. At any rate, the system was not universally adopted in Germany until *c.* 1800, in France and England until *c.* 1850. Other systems of temperament, such as that of the mathematician Leonard Euler (1707–83) and of Kirnberger (1721–83), never attained practical significance. See also *Just intonation.

Lit.: P. Garnault, *Histoire et influence du temperament* (1929); C. Dupont, *Geschichte der musikalischen Temperatur* (1935); J. M. Barbour, *Equal Temperament, its History from Ramis (1482) to Rameau (1737)* (unpubl. diss. Cornell University, 1932); H. J. Watt, in *ML* iv, no. 3; L. S. Lloyd, in *ML* xix, no. 4, xx, no. 4, xxi, no. 4; *id.*, in *MR* v, no. 4 (Mean-tone tuning); J. Handschin, in *Schweizer Jahrbuch für Musikwissenschaft* ii; K. Hasse, in *ZMW* xiii.

Temperatur [G.].   *Temperament. *Gleichschwebende, ungleichschwebende T.*, equal, unequal temperament.

Tempo. The rate of speed of a composition or a section thereof, ranging from the slowest to the quickest, as is indicated by tempo marks such as largo, adagio, andante, moderato, allegro, presto, pres-

tissimo. More accurate are *metronome indications, such as $\bm{\downharpoonleft}$ = M.M. 100, i.e., the quarter-note lasts one one-hundredth of a minute. The practical limits for the duration of the beat are M.M. 50 and M.M. 120. M.M. 60–80 represents a "normal" tempo which agrees with various natural paces, e.g., that of moderate walking or of the human pulse. The question of the "right tempo" for a piece is, as is well known, one of the favorite topics among musicians, listeners, and critics. The discrepancy in tempo encountered in two performances of, e.g., the second movement of Beethoven's Seventh Symphony is simply appalling, as is also the unyielding pertinacity with which each conductor and his disciples usually defend their position. Such discrepancies are frequently explained as being conditioned by external factors, e.g., the size and reverberations of the concert hall, the sonority of the instruments, the size of the orchestra. Such an explanation, however, would account only for minute modifications, not for the startling differences found between a performance by, e.g., Toscanini and Stokowski. These are purely a matter of interpretation, and the differences encountered in the interpretation of the tempo are not more considerable — though perhaps more striking for the amateur listener — than those encountered in matters of style, phrasing, and orchestral treatment. The observations to be made with regard to *interpretation in general apply, equally, to the particular topic of tempo. See also *Tempo marks. — For the tempo in early music, see under *Tactus.

Lit.: E. O. Turner, "Tempo Variation" (*ML* xix, no. 3); R. Kolisch, "Tempo and Character in Beethoven's Music" (*MQ* xxix); H. Gal, "The Right Tempo" (*Monthly Musical Record* lxix, 174). See also under *Metronome.

Tempo giusto [It.]. Normal, proper speed.

Tempo marks. In order to indicate the tempo of a piece, a number of Italian terms are used the most important of which are given here, proceeding from

8:45

the slowest to the quickest: *largo* (broad), *lento* (slow), *adagio* (slow; literally, at ease), *andante* (walking), *moderato* (moderate), *allegretto, allegro* (quick; literally, cheerful), *presto* (very fast), *prestissimo* (as fast as possible). In addition to these, there exist terms calling for gradual change of speed, mainly *ritardando* (slackening) and *accelerando* (quickening), while a deliberate unsteadiness of tempo is indicated by **rubato*.

By the use of the different tempo marks the duration of any given note value becomes variable within large limits. In actual practice the range of variation is still considerably larger than one might assume, owing to the practice of writing quick pieces in the larger values (whole- to eighth-notes), and slow pieces in the smaller ones (quarter- to sixty-fourth-notes). Our two examples (1: Mozart, Piano Concerto, A major, last movement; 2: Beethoven, Piano Sonata, op. 10, no. 3, slow movement) show that the duration of the half-note may vary from less than half a second to four seconds. It is not easy

to find a satisfactory explanation for the above-mentioned practice which might be rooted in a general tendency of "overstating the case." How much it helps to emphasize the impression of "extremely quick" and "extremely slow" appears if the two examples are written according to the "natural" principle of using small values for quick notes, large values for long notes [see Ex. 3 and 4]. If this principle were accepted, tempo marks would become largely superfluous since the duration of the sound could be expressed by choosing from a series of approximately unchangeable note-values.

This consideration is not meant as a recommendation for reform of the prevailing practice, but rather to clarify its significance, particularly in contrast to the earlier practice which indeed was of the type just described. Prior to 1600, tempo marks were practically unknown, since the pace of a composition was expressed in the notation itself, the note-values then used having absolute durations which were variable only within small limits [see **Tactus*]. An isolated early example of tempo indication occurs in the lute book *El Maestro* (1536) of Luis de Milan [see **Editions* XXV, 2] who points out that certain sections of his lute fantasias must be played "apriessa" (quick), others "espacio" (slow). One of the first composers to use the modern tempo marks was Adriano Banchieri (*c.* 1567–1634) who, in his *Organo suonarino* (1611, '22), prescribes *Adagio, Allegro, Veloce, Presto, Più presto,* and *Prestissimo* [cf. *ApMZ* i]. It may be noticed that in the 17th and 18th centuries presto did not have the present-day meaning of "extremely quick," but only meant "quick." Thus, players of Bach's E minor Prelude from *Wt.Cl.* i commit a grave error if they try to play its final section in a speed comparable to that of a presto-etude by Chopin. It was not until the time of Mozart that presto was used in its present-day significance.

Temps [F.]. Beat; *temps fort (faible),* strong (weak) beat. *Temps premier,* see **Chronos protos.*

Tempus [L., time]. In 13th-century theory the unit of musical time, comparable to the **tactus* of the 16th century. Franco of Cologne describes it very accurately as "minimum in plenitudine vocis," i.e., as the smallest time in which a "full sound" can be conveniently produced (*c.* M.M. 80). In the 13th century this duration was represented by the *brevis* while, with the beginning of the Ars nova, the *semibrevis* was used instead. However, the term tempus remained connected with the brevis in another sense, i.e., as the indication of its mensuration, signifying whether the brevis was equal to three or to two semibreves (tempus perfectum, imperfectum). See **Mensural notation* II.

Ten. Short for *tenuto*.

Tenebrae [L., the dark, *sc.* hours]. The service of Matins and Lauds on the Wednesday, Thursday, and Friday (Good Friday) of Holy Week, preceding Easter, so called owing to the gradual extinction of the candles which accompanies the celebration in an impressive ceremony. At the first Nocturn the *Lamentations of Jeremiah are sung (*LU* 626, 669, 715), at other occasions the *Miserere (Psalm 50) and the *Improperia.

Tenendo [It.]. Sustaining.

Teneramente [It.]. Tenderly.

Tenete [It.]. Hold out.

Tenor [from L. *tenere*, to hold]. (1) The highest natural voice of men [see *Voices, Range of]. — (2) In part music, the part above the lowest [see *Part (2)]. — (3) Instruments of about the same range as the vocal tenor are referred to as tenor trombone, *tenor horn, tenor sax-horn, *tenor violin, etc. — (4) In plain-song psalmody, same as *repercussion. — (5) In early polyphonic music (*c.* 1150–1500 and later) tenor denotes that part (of about the same range as the modern tenor) which served as the point of de-parture of the composition, the other voices being added above it as *duplum, triplum, etc. In sacred works (organa, motets, Masses) the tenor was practically always taken from plainsong, or, in the 15th century, borrowed from secular mel-odies (*cantus firmus). It usually con-sists of a succession of long notes (*Pfund-noten) such as still occur in many chorale preludes of Bach, here usually in the bass. See *Tenor Mass. Cf. P. Aubry, *Recher-ches sur les "tenors" français (latins) dans les motets du XIIIe siècle* (1907).

Tenorhorn [G.]. Baritone; see *Brass instruments III (c).

Tenor Mass. A polyphonic Mass based upon a cantus firmus which is used as a tenor. Most Masses of the 15th and 16th centuries are of this type [see *Mass B, II (b)]. See also *Discant Mass.

Tenoroon. See *Oboe family II, C.

Tenorschlüssel [G.]. Tenor clef. See *Clefs.

Tenor violin. See *Violin family (f).

Tenso. A type of troubadour and trou-vère poetry, in the nature of a (real or feigned) dialogue or debate referring to political events or other "debatable" mat-ter. A similar type was the *jeu parti*, i.e., an actual dialogue, usually on a question of love [cf. *ReMMA*, 213f]. No special musical form attached to these types. They played an important part in the competi-tions of the troubadours and of the *Min-nesinger, the *puys and *Sängerkriege*.

Tenth. See *Intervals.

Tento [Sp., Port.]. See under *Tiento.

Tenue [F.], tenuto [It.]. Held, sus-tained.

Tepido [It.]. "Lukewarm," unimpas-sioned.

Teponaztli. See *Mexico.

Terce. See *Office hours.

Teretism. See under *Anenaiki.

Ternary form. See *Binary and ter-nary form.

Ter Sanctus [L., Thrice Holy]. Used with reference to the "Sanctus, sanctus, sanctus" ("Holy, holy, holy") of the *Trishagion, of the Sanctus of the Mass, or of the *Te Deum.

Tertian harmony. A harmonic system based on the third, i.e., on the triad; hence, our common system of harmony as op-posed to, e.g., *quartal harmony. See also under *Third.

Terz [G.]. Third. *Terzdezime*, a 13th, i.e., upper sixth. *Terzquartakkord*, see under *Seventh-chord. *Terzverwandt-schaft*, the relationship between keys a third apart, e.g., C and E, or C and Eb. *Terzflöte (Terzfagott)*, a flute (oboe) in E.

Terzett [G.], terzetto [It.]. A vocal piece for three voices. See *Trio.

Terzina [It.]. Triplet.

Terzo suono. Tartini's name for the *combination tones discovered by him.

Tessitura [It., texture]. The general "lie" of a vocal part, whether high or low in its average pitch. It differs from *range in that it does not take into account a few isolated notes of extraordinarily high or low pitch.

Testo [It., text]. *Narrator (in oratorios, passions, etc.).

Tests and measurements in music. Psychological tests in all fields had their inception at the time of World War I. Tests in music have been devised to measure efficiency of teaching, general musical knowledge and achievement, musical taste or preference, and innate musical capacity. They may be divided into two groups: (a) tests and measurements of musical capacities, and (b) tests and measurements of musical abilities. The former are independent of training while the latter are dependent on capacity and training. (Capacity means undeveloped, innate, native talent, receptive powers, i.e., potentiality for development; ability denotes acquisition of knowledges, skills, and technics, i.e., development of a capacity.)

Tests and Measurements of Musical Capacities: Research in music tests began with experiments by C. E. Seashore in the Psychological Laboratory at the University of Iowa at the beginning of the 20th century. In 1919 the original phonograph recordings known as the Seashore Measures of Musical Talent were released for use. This set of six records purports to measure innate sense for the following musical factors: pitch, intensity, time, consonance, tonal memory, and rhythm. The 1939 revision consists of two series. Series A is suggested for group surveys to discover talent. Series B constitutes an individual measurement where greater reliability is desired and is suggested as a basic entrance requirement for admission to music schools, assignment to musical instruments, and diagnosis of special prob-

lems. Both revised series measure the same factors: pitch, loudness, time, timbre, rhythm, and tonal memory.

The Kwalwasser-Dykema Music Test developed by J. Kwalwasser and P. Dykema has been available since 1930. It consists of phonograph records measuring the following abilities and capacities: tonal memory, quality discrimination, intensity discrimination, feeling for tonal movement, time discrimination, rhythm discrimination, pitch discrimination, melodic tastes, and rhythm imagery.

All the capacity tests are measures of auditory perception and may be given in groups or individually for the purpose of individual diagnosis and prognosis. They can be given to those musically trained or untrained, to adults and to children as young as nine years or in the fifth grade. Early researches substantiated by later investigations proved that records of musical capacities do not vary with age, training, and general intelligence. A high Intelligence Quotient is no assurance of keen pitch discrimination or superior talent in any other musical factor. Training is effective in developing the power to use a fixed capacity. Variation with age may be attributed to maturation, and may therefore mean that there is no improvement in the physiologic limit of pitch discrimination itself.

As would be expected, ratings as determined by capacity measures have been high for successful musicians or students who have made satisfactory or outstanding progress in music. This and other reasons have been considered evidence of the validity of the measures of musical capacity and justify their use in vocational and avocational guidance in music. The reliability and the validity of all psychological measures depend upon the training and experience of the examiner. It is generally agreed that no one should assume responsibility for the administration, interpretation, and application of tests and results without knowledge of the nature of the psychology of music, principles of testing, principles of musical interpretation and guidance.

Tests and Measurements of (*Musical*

Abilities: Tests in this group may be classified as (a) those measuring appreciation and information, and (b) those measuring performance. Tests of appreciation and information based on knowledge acquired in elementary school, high school, and college measure general information, recognition, and comprehension of music from notation, musical symbols, terms, musical instruments, composers, artists, melodies, etc. These are largely paper and pencil tests in the form of completion, multiple choice, true and false, or answer to a direct question. Tests measuring performance include tests of sight-singing ability, melodic and rhythmic dictation (writing in musical notation what one has heard played), and the analysis of musical performances directly or from phonograph recordings by means of the recent developments in phonophotography [cf. *The Vibrato* by Seashore]. Many college music departments have devised placement tests in music which are given to applicants for the purpose of estimating the extent and quality of the student's previous musical training. These tests often combine tests of appreciation and information and tests of performance.

Lit.: C. E. Seashore, *The Psychology of Musical Talent* (1919); *id., Psychology of Music* (1938); *id., The Vibrato* (1935); H. M. Stanton, *Measurement of Musical Talent* (1935); J. L. Mursell, *Psychology of Music* (1937); C. W. Flemming and M. Flagg, *Descriptive Bibliography of Prognostic and Achievement Tests in Music* (1936); S. K. Gernet, *Musical Discrimination at Various Ages and Grade Levels* (1939); V. R. Ross, *Relationship between Intelligence, Scholastic Achievement and Musical Talent* (1937); H. Lowery, in *PMA* lxvii; C. E. Seashore, in *MQ* i; J. C. Moos, "The Yardstick Applied to Musical Talent" (*MQ* xvi).
                                                    D. D.

Testudo [L., turtle]. (1) The ancient Greek *lyra which was frequently made from a tortoise shell. — (2) A 16th-century humanistic name for the lute (e.g., L. Fuhrmann, *Testudo Gallo-Germanica*, 1615).

Tetrachord. In ancient Greek music a succession of three descending wholetones, followed by a descending semitone, e.g., e′–d′–c′–b, a–g–f–e. By joining several such tetrachords the entire diatonic scale from e′ down to A was obtained [see *Greek music]. It should be noted that, in Greek theory, a tetrachord always has the above structure; groups of four tones with a semitone at another place (e.g., d′–c′–b–a, c′–b–a–g, etc., sometimes designated in modern writings as Phrygian, Lydian, etc., tetrachord) did not exist in the Greek system. There existed, however, chromatic modifications of the tetrachord, the chromatic tetrachord e′–c′♯–c′–b and the enharmonic tetrachord e′–c′–x–b (x designating the quarter-tone between c′ and b).

Tetrardus. See *Church modes II.

Text and music. In vocal music, particularly in songs, the consideration of the text is one of the prime concerns of the modern composer. Correct accentuation, clarity of pronunciation, emphasis of important words, etc., are the basic requirements of good vocal style, but only the indispensable premises to the main objective, i.e., to convey in musical language the general character of the text as well as its fluctuating shades or contrasts. Any song, from Schubert to the present day, will readily show the attention given by composers to this matter. In fact, from 1880 on, one finds a tendency to emphasize the text at the expense of the musical melody which is frequently reduced to a mere "recitation" (Hugo Wolf, Debussy, Schönberg). It may also be noted that modern composers have been very careful in the selection of poetic texts for their songs, choosing only poems of outstanding literary value, and that, on the other hand, the 19th-century development of poetry in which one encounters such outstanding figures as Goethe, Mörike, Baudelaire, Mallarmé, has given a great impetus to the rise and development of the song. On the other hand, it cannot be denied that occasionally matters have been carried to the extreme, and it is well to remember that Bach has written some of his greatest arias to notoriously inferior texts.

The above-mentioned principles of textual treatment developed gradually in the 16th century, and were fully recognized first by English composers [see *Just note and accent]. Throughout the early history of music, however, examples abound showing that composers were less strongly interested in these matters and frequently considered them as of secondary importance. Two such examples may be mentioned: an Ave regina by Dufay in which the following declamation occurs: ra-dix, an-ge-lo-rum, re-gi-na: and a motet from the Roman de Fauvel (c. 1300) in which an almost deliberately absurd declamation is used with the Ovidian hexameter: In nova fert animus [cf. *ApNPM*, 118, 336]. It was not until the *musica reservata of the 16th century (Josquin) that a different attitude towards accentuation was adopted. Naturally, the introduction of the vernacular into polyphonic music (c. 1550) contributed considerably to the abandoning of the earlier indifference in this matter. Byrd's anthems contain many examples of a most careful interpretation of the text, and the declamation in Purcell's dramatic works is generally admired as a model. German composers, however, were less quick to adopt the new point of view. A striking example of mis-declamation — not lacking, however, a certain forcefulness of expression — occurs at the end of Schütz's Christmas Oratorio (1664) where the accentuation "mit Schalle" is consistently used instead of the correct "mit Schalle." Such deviation should not be considered as mere negligence or faultiness, but rather as a deliberate means to avoid the weakness of feminine endings. The same procedure can be observed in Bach, e.g., in the tenor aria, "Geduld, Geduld" of the St. Matthew Passion, where the accentuation "rächen" is used instead of "rächen. There are, however, other cases in Bach in which incorrect declamation can be explained only as the result

of his preoccupation with purely musical (melodic) considerations, e.g., in his cantata no. 105: "Herr gehe nicht ins Gericht," instead of Herr, gehe nicht ins Gericht."

Two additional problems of textual treatment may be briefly considered, viz., word painting and text repetition. The expression in music of characteristic words such as "heaven," "laughter," "to run," etc., occurs as early as in Obrecht (c. 1430–1505) and Josquin (c. 1450–1521), and became a well-established method of composition in the 17th century [see *Word painting; *Affectenlehre]. Repetition of words or short phrases also started with the Flemish masters (Obrecht and others; cf. *HAM*, no. 76), particularly in their motets [see, however, below regarding textual repetition in Masses]. Towards the end of the 16th century it was also adopted for secular pieces in the vernacular (Italian and English madrigals; German polyphonic songs) and in the vocal compositions of the Baroque one finds numerous examples of a phrase being repeated ten or more times, either in order to provide a basis for the display of vocal virtuosity (Italian operatic arias) or as an expressive means of emphasis designed to bring out to the fullest the significance of the words (Schütz, Handel, Bach). The former method persisted in the "grand opéra" of the 19th century (Meyerbeer, Verdi), but Schubert's *lied* and the operatic reform of Wagner led to the abandonment of such external routine methods.

For the numerous problems arising in connection with the text (more properly, with the absence or scarcity of text) in the Masses of the 15th century, reference must be made to special studies. Here it must suffice to say that the modern editorial practice of repeating words for passages lacking a text in the original (e.g., "Kyrie eleison" ten times, instead of once or, perhaps, thrice) is of very doubtful authenticity. Long *vocalizations (on the syllable e of Kyrie) are much more probable from the musical as well as from the liturgical point of view. See also *Odhecaton.

Lit.: H. E. Wooldridge, "The Treatment of Words in Polyphonic Music" (*MA* i); H. Monro, "Words to Music" (*ML* i, no. 1); G. Adler, "Über Textunterlegung in den Trienter Codices" (*Riemann Festschrift*); K. Jeppesen, "Textlegung in der Chansonmusik des späteren 15. Jahrhunderts" (*KIM*, Vienna, 1927); for extended bibl. cf. *BeMMR*, 319.

Texture. This term, which generally denotes "characteristic disposition of interwoven threads, filaments, etc." (Webster), is very useful in referring to a number of phenomena resulting from the fact that music is two-dimensional in character, consisting of *horizontal* as well as *vertical* elements. The former are represented by the successive sounds forming melodies, the latter by the simultaneous sounds forming harmonies [see also *Counterpoint I]. The analogy between music and the warp and woof of a fabric is particularly obvious in the case of part-music, i.e., music written in a given number of parts. Here each part represents a horizontal line of individual design, but connected with the other lines by the (vertical) relationship of consonance or of harmony. Such music is said to be of *contrapuntal* or *polyphonic* texture. A different situation exists in that type of music commonly referred to as "accompanied melody." Here the texture is primarily vertical, being based on a succession of chordal blocks which are horizontally connected by a top melody. Such texture is called *chordal* or *homophonic*. Ex. 1, (a) and (b), illustrates the two

methods, applied to the same melody. In chordal style the accompanying chords are frequently spread out in the form of

broken chords, a modification which of course does not alter the basic character of the texture.

Between the anti-poles of strictly polyphonic and strictly homophonic music there exists, of course, a large variety of intermediate types of textures. Ex. 2

[Beethoven, Piano Sonata op. 106] illustrates a mixture of horizontal and vertical elements which is particularly frequent in 19th-century piano music of high standing (Beethoven, Brahms). As early as the 17th century the strictly contrapuntal texture of the polyphonic era was mitigated into a pseudo-contrapuntal texture known as *freistimmig. In contrapuntal music a distinctive feature of prime importance is the rhythmic relationship between the parts. There exist two opposite types of polyphonic texture, one in which the four parts move in identical rhythm (as in a church hymn), the other in which they show complete rhythmic independence (as frequently in Palestrina or Bach). Only the latter texture, known as *polyrhythmic, is contrapuntal in the true sense of the word while the former, known as *familiar style, borders on chordal texture and is, indeed, frequently referred to as *strict chordal style* (in contradistinction to *free chordal style* in which there is no restriction to a given number of parts and usually no horizontal movement except for the top melody).

Another interesting aspect is the distinction between "light" and "heavy" textures. To the latter category belong, e.g., Gabrieli's *polychoral compositions and Sibelius' symphonies; to the former the chansons by Dufay [see *Burgundian School] and Stravinsky's *L'Histoire du soldat*. A preference for light texture is a significant characteristic of *New music.

Occasionally the two-dimensional texture of music is reinforced by diagonal threads. The most important phenome-

non of this type is the *canon in which
there is a consistent diagonal relationship
between the two parts, owing to the imitation of every motive at a fixed distance.
It is the co-existence of horizontal, vertical, and diagonal relationships which
creates the impression of special intensity
in canonic writing as well as in fugal
styles in general. Melodic *anticipation
might also be considered as a diagonal
formation, e.g., those bold and persistent
anticipations which are characteristic of
*Japanese music. See A. Dyson, "The
Texture of Modern Music" (*ML* iv,
no. 3).

Theme [F. *thème*; G. *Thema*; It. *tema*].
In sonatas and fugues, same as subject.
For theme with variations, see *Varia-
tions.

Themenaufstellung [G.]. Exposition.

Theorboe [G. *Theorbe*]. See *Lute III.
Cf. H. Quittard, "L'accompagnement au
théorbe" (*BSIM*, 1910).

Theory, Musical. I. *General.* The
theory of music as commonly taught today includes elementary studies usually
classified as *solfège, and advanced studies in harmony [see *Harmonic analysis],
*counterpoint, *form, and *orchestration.
In this curriculum at least one important
study is missing, that of *melody. Other
aspects of musical theory, closely bound
up with that of melody, are *rhythm and
*phrasing. More on the scientific side is
the study of *acoustics, *intervals (calculation of), *scales, etc., while the philosophical and speculative aspect falls under
the province of musical *aesthetics. See
also *Musicology.

II. *History.* The fourteen centuries of
European musical theory (*c.* 500–1900)
may be briefly indicated by the following
names:

A (Until 1200). Boethius, *c.* 480–524
[see *Aesthetics II; *Letter notation]. —
Hucbald, *c.* 840–930 [see *Musica en-
chiriadis; *Dasia notation]. — Oddo of
Cluny, d. 942 [see *Letter notation]. —
Guido d'Arezzo, *c.* 995–1050 [see *Staff;
*Micrologus; *Organum II; *Letter nota-

tion]. — John Cotton, fl. *c.* 1100 [see *Organum II]. The treatises of this group
are reprinted in *GS* i, ii.

B (1200–1500). *Discantus positio vulgaris, c.* 1225. — Johannes de Garlandia,
c. 1190–after 1245 [see *Discant]. —
Franco of Cologne, fl. *c.* 1250 [see *Notation III; *Tempus]. — Anonymous IV of
Coussemaker's *Scriptores* i, fl. *c.* 1280
[see *Ars antiqua]. — Walter Odington,
fl. *c.* 1300 [see *Modes, Rhythmic; *Consonance and dissonance II; *Third]. —
Johannes de Grocheo, *c.* 1300 [*Theoria,
repr. by J. Wolf in *SIM* i; see *Estampie].
— Philippe de Vitry, *c.* 1290–1361 [see
*Ars nova; *Notation III]. — Unknown
author (Jacobus of Liège?) of *Speculum
musicae, c.* 1330 [see *Ars nova I]. —
Johannes de Muris, d. after 1350. — Marchettus de Padua, fl. after 1300 [see *Ars
nova I; *Italian music I]. — Simon Tunstede, fl. after 1350 [see *Discantus supra
librum]. — Guilelmus Monachus, *c.* 1480
[see *Fauxbourdon (2)]. — Ramis de
Pareia, 1440–1521 [*Musica practica, c.*
1490, new ed. by J. Wolf; see *Spanish
music I]. — Johannes Tinctoris, *c.* 1446–
1511. Most of the treatises in this group
are reprinted in *CS* i–iv.

C (1500–1700). Franchinus Gafurius,
1451–1522 [*Practica musicae*, 1496, cf. E.
Praetorius, *Die Mensuraltheorie des Franchinus Gafurius . . .* (1906)]. — Martin
Agricola, *c.* 1500–56 [*Musica instrumentalis deudsch*, 1529; new ed. 1896]. —
Henricus Glareanus, 1488–1563 [see *Dodekachordon; *Swiss music]. — Adria-
nus Coclicus, *c.* 1500–63 [see *Musica
reservata]. — Niccolò Vicentino, 1511–72
[see *Arcicembalo]. — Diego Ortiz, fl.
1547–65 [*Tratado de glosas*, 1553, repr.
by M. Schneider, 1913; see *Spanish music II; *Ricercar II (c)]. — Gioseffo Zarlino, 1517–90 [*Istituzioni*, 1558, cf. *GD* v,
776ff; see *Dualism; *Ornamentation I].
— Vincenzo Galilei, 1533–after 1589
[*Dialogo*, 1581; see *Nuove musiche]. —
Lodovico Zacconi, 1555–1627 [*Prattica di
musica*, 1592–1619, cf. *GD* v, 772f]. —
Thomas Morley, 1557–1603 [*Plaine and
Easie Introduction to Practicall Musicke*,
1597, repr. 1937]. — Girolamo Diruta, *c.*
1560–? [*Il Transilvano*, 1597 and later,

cf. *GD* ii, 69; repr. by C. Krebs, in *VMW*
viii]. — Michael Praetorius, 1571–1621
[*Syntagma musicum*, 3 vols., 1615–19, cf.
GD iv, 243f; vol. ii, *Organographia* repr.
in *Editions XXVI, 13 and by W. Gurlitt
(facs.)]. — Marin Mersenne, 1588–1648
[*Harmonie universelle*, 1636; see *Temperament III].

D (1700–present). Jean-Philippe Rameau, 1683–1764 [*Nouveau système de
musique theorique*, 1726; see *Fundamental bass; *Dualism]. — Johann Mattheson, 1681–1764 [cf. *GD* iii, 352]. —
Friedrich W. Marpurg, 1718–95 [cf. *GD*
iii, 327f]. — Among the modern contributions to musical theory the writings by
Hugo Riemann (1849–1919; see *Phrasing; *Vierhebigkeit) and by Heinrich
Schenker, 1868–1935 [see *Urlinie] are
outstanding.

Lit.: H. Riemann, *Geschichte der Musiktheorie im 9. bis 19. Jahrhundert*
(1898); G. Pietzsch, *Studien zur Geschichte der Musik-Theorie im Mittelalter*
(Diss. Freiburg 1928); A. Hughes, in *OH*
1928, Introductory Volume; *AdHM* ii,
1244ff (bibl.); *LavE* i.1, 556ff; *ReMMA*,
17ff (Greek) and 125ff (medieval);
ApNPM, 201ff; J. Wolf, "Early English
Musical Theorists" (*MQ* xxv); *id.*, "Die
Musiktheorie des Mittelalters" (*AM* iii;
bibl.); U. Kornmüller, "Die alten Musik-
theoretiker" (*KJ*, 1891, '99, 1903); D. von
Bartha, "Studien zum Musikalischen
Schrifttum des 15. Jahrhunderts"(*AMF* i).

Theremin. See *Electronic musical instruments VI.

Thesis. See *Arsis and thesis.

Third [F. *tierce*; G. *Terz*; It. *terza*]. The
third degree of a scale, and the interval
thus formed [see *Intervals]. The third
is the most characteristic interval of our
harmonic system which, indeed, might be
called the system of *tertian harmony
(*c.* 1400–1900), as distinguished from an
earlier period (pre-tertian harmony, *c.*
900–1400) in which the third was not
fully admitted, and from a recent one
(post-tertian harmony, *c.* 1900–) in which
it has lost its former dominant position
[see *Harmony II].

Passages in parallel thirds occur occasionally in the 13th-century organa [cf.
J. Handschin, in *Festschrift für Guido
Adler*, p. 57] and form the basis of the
English *gymel. As an integral element
of harmony the third appeared in the
sixth-chord style [see *fauxbourdon] in
the 14th century; of melody, in the works
of Dunstable, *c.* 1400 [cf., e.g., *SchGMB*,
nos. 34, 35; see also *Burgundian School].
An interesting early example of a tertian
and, at the same time, pentatonic melody
is Neithart von Reuenthal's Minnesinger
melody "Der May hat" (*c.* 1225; cf. *DTOe*
37.i, p. 33). Regarding the emergence of

the third as a consonant interval, see *Consonance and dissonance III. It may be
noticed that, prior to 1500, the third was
not admitted in the final chord [see *Picardy third].

The third is also interesting from the
point of view of theoretical acoustics. In
the Pythagorean system the major third
is obtained as the fourth consecutive fifth
$(c–g–d'–a'–e'')$, with the frequency $\frac{81}{64}$,
the minor third as the third consecutive
fourth $(c–f–bb'–eb')$ with the frequency
$\frac{32}{27}$. Owing to the complex formation of
these fractions, both thirds were regarded
as dissonances. This interpretation persisted throughout the Middle Ages, al-
though the consonant (pure) third $\frac{5}{4}$, i.e.,
the third of *just intonation, was already
known to Aristoxenos (*c.* 354–300 B.C.).
The first medieval writer to consider a
third as a consonance was the Englishman
W. Odington (*c.* 1300) [see *Consonance
and dissonance III]. This fact is interesting, since singing in parallel thirds (*gymel) was actually practiced in England
much earlier than anywhere else. The
difference (in *cents) between the thirds

of the various systems appears from the following table.

	Minor Third	Major Third
Pythagorean	294	408
Just Intonation	315	386
Mean-tone system	315	386
Equal temperament	300	400

The difference between the tempered and the pure major third can easily be demonstrated on an organ by playing on one manual the tone e″ with a normal 8′-register (principal), and on the second manual the tone c with a tertia-stop ($5\frac{1}{3}'$), which produces the fifth harmonic e″ in just intonation.

Thirteenth, Chord of the. See under *Seventh chord.

Thirty-second note. See *Notes.

Thirty-two foot stop. See *Foot (2).

Thorough-bass, figured bass [F. *basse chiffré*; G. *Generalbass, bezifferter Bass*; It. *basso continuo*. Thorough (old spelling for "through") is the translation of *continuo*, i.e., continuing throughout the piece].

I. A method of indicating an accompanying part by the bass notes only, together with figures designating the chief intervals and chords to be played above the bass notes. This stenographic system was universally used in the *Baroque period (1600–1750) for which it is so significant that the name "Thorough-bass period" is frequently used for that era. The chief principles for the developed system (*c.* 1700) are as follows:

1. A figure given with a bass note calls for the corresponding interval above this note in the key indicated by the signature. For instance, in Ab major, a 6 written underneath (or above) g indicates Eb, and the figures $\frac{6}{5}$ indicate Db and Eb.

2. The intervals of the third, fifth, octave, are frequently not indicated by figures (3, 5, 8), the understanding being that these are to be added where suitable.

3. Chromatic alterations are indicated by a sharp or flat placed in front of (or, occasionally, behind) the figure. A sharp

or flat without figure calls respectively for the major or minor third. The natural sign is used in a similar way. Sharping is frequently indicated by a diagonal stroke through the figure, or by an apostrophe.

4. A horizontal dash following a figure or a vertical group of figures indicates that the notes of the right hand are to be held, although the bass proceeds to other tones.

5. A small diagonal dash indicates repetition of the same figures above a changed bass note, i.e., sequential transposition of the chord.

6. The figure o indicates *tasto solo*, i.e., no accompaniment other than the bass note.

7. Frequently, two or more successive figures do not indicate chords proper, but only voice leading, appoggiaturas, or passing tones, e.g., 4 3, or 9 8, or 5 4 3. The accompanying examples illustrate these principles.

II. It goes without saying that the above principles constitute only the rudiments of an art the full mastery of which is not easily acquired. A good thorough-bass accompaniment is considerably more than a mere translation of the figures into musical notes. At the proper places, the musical material used in the solo parts (voice, violin) should be incorporated into the accompaniment, in free imitation, or in doubling thirds, or in contrapuntal contrast. How far to go in this direction is the most difficult and the most controversial issue of the whole matter. Obviously, this question cannot be answered categorically, as different situations are presented by different compositions and by works from different periods. Within the course of time from 1600 to 1750 the style of improvised accompaniment changed from simple homophony to real counterpoint. Such elaborately contrapuntal realizations as have been given by H. Riemann for arias of the mid-17th century [cf. his *Kantatenfrühling*] are entirely out of place. They are the result of editorial ostentatiousness, rather than of scholarly conscientiousness. On the other hand, realizations such as appear in some recent editions (Bärenreiter Verlag, Nagel) are decidedly too poor and uninteresting.

It is important to note that Bach himself has left two records of his own practice of thorough-bass improvisation, one in the second aria of the solo-cantata *Amore traditore*, the other in the second movement of his sonata in B minor for flute and harpsichord. Although both parts are designated as Cembalo obbligato, their style differs markedly from that of other written-out parts and may be regarded as an indication of his style of thorough-bass improvisation [cf. M. Schneider, in *JMP* xxi/xxii]. Another informative example of written-out thorough-bass accompaniment exists in a sonata by Handel for viola da gamba and harpsichord [B.-H. edition, vol. 48, p. 115].

The realization of a thorough-bass part, in addition to the accompanying harpsichordist, calls for a violoncello or a viola da gamba which reinforces the bass line. It would be entirely in keeping with the *Aufführungspraxis of the Baroque if the players of such instruments would somewhat simplify the written part whenever this includes rapid figures, underlining intelligently the contours, rather than disturbing the equilibrium by a forced display of virtuosity.

III. The thorough-bass practice of the Baroque grew out of the improvisation methods of the 16th century. Towards the end of this century motets were occasionally accompanied on the organ by means of a *bassus pro organo*, i.e., a separate bass part from which the organist played the harmonies. The earliest known instance of this method is in a motet by A. Striggio of 1587 [cf. M. Schneider, p. 67]. A similar bass part, printed for Giovanni Croce's *Motetti* of 1594, has ♯ and ♭ above the notes in order to indicate major or minor triads (thirds). The earliest examples of a basso continuo with figures are Cavalieri's *Rappresentazione* and (less completely) Peri's and Caccini's operas *Euridice*, all from 1600. Here, as well as in numerous later works, different figures are used for the different octaves, e.g., 10 for the tenth (upper third), 15 for the double octave [cf., e.g., *WoHN* ii, 315]. See also *Partimento.

Lit.: F. T. Arnold, *The Art of Accompaniment from a Thorough-Bass* (1931); H. Keller, *Schule des Generalbass-spiels* (1931); E. Ulrich, *Studien zur deutschen Generalbass-Praxis des 18. Jahrhunderts* (1932); M. Schneider, *Die Anfänge des Basso continuo und seiner Bezifferung* (1918); L. Landshoff, in *Sandberger Festschrift* (1918); *RiHM* ii.2, 72ff; E. Stilz, in *ZMW* xiii; L. Torchi, in *RMI* i, ii; A. Toni, in *RMI* xxvi; *GD* v, article "Thorough-bass"; *WoHN* ii, 314ff.

Through-composed. This term, which is widely accepted as a translation of G. *durchkomponiert*, denotes songs in which new music is provided for each stanza. Its opposite is "strophic song," i.e., a song every stanza of which is sung to the same melody. The latter method is frequently used for simple lyrics, while the former is preferred for texts of a dramatic or narrative character in which the situation changes with every stanza as, e.g., in Schubert's "Erlkönig." Early examples of through-composed songs are the *vers of the troubadours and the *aria of the Baroque period. In the 19th century F. Schubert and Carl Löwe [see *Ballade (G.)] were among the first to employ the through-composed style. This has been universally accepted by recent composers (Debussy) for their lyrical songs.

Thunder machine. A device called for in R. Strauss's Alpine Symphony and elsewhere, which usually consists of a big drum with hard balls inside. The drum can be rotated and the balls then strike against the parchment.

Thus Spake Zoroaster. See *Symphonic poem III.

Tibetan music. Some information is found in: *LavE* i.5, 3084ff (examples doubtful); C. G. Bruce, *The Assault on Mount Everest*, ch. XIV; Jacques Bacot, *Le Tibet révolté* (1912), pp. 44ff; L. A. Waddell, *Lamaism* (1939), p. 433; T. H. Somervell, in *Musical Times*, 1923, p. 107. Particularly interesting is the Tibetan musical notation, consisting of elaborate scrolls of a highly ornamental design.

Tibia. Latin name for the Greek *aulos; see *Oboe family III. *Tibicen*, flute player.

Tie or **Bind.** A curved line, identical in appearance with the *slur, which connects two successive notes of the same pitch, and which has the function of uniting them into a single sound equal to the combined durations. The tie is used (1) to connect two notes separated by a barline, (2) to produce values which cannot be indicated by a single note, e.g., the value of seven eighth-notes: ♩♩. (7 = 4 + 3).

The tie has a remarkable historic significance since it represents, together with the bar-line, the most conspicuous achievement of modern notation over the earlier system of *mensural notation in which it does not exist (the earliest known instance occurs in a keyboard score of 1523, Marcantonio da Bologna's *Ricercari motetti canzoni*; cf. *ApNPM*, 5). It is interesting to observe that, owing to the non-existence of the tie in mensural notation, a note equaling five units has never been used in duple meter (*tempus imperfectum*) in any vocal composition prior to *c.* 1600; only in triple meter (*tempus*

perfectum) could such a value be obtained, by subtracting one from six (imperfection).

In *GD* v, article "Tie," examples of piano music (Beethoven, Chopin) are cited in which the tie would seem to call not for complete tying-over, but for a subtle repetition of the note, a manner of playing erroneously referred to as *Bebung.

Tiento [Sp.]. Spanish 16th-century name for organ compositions in strict imitative counterpoint, practically synonymous with the *ricercar (not with the toccata, as has been wrongly stated). The main source is A. de Cabezon's *Obras de musica*, 1578 [see *Editions XIII, 3/4 and 7/8]. *Tento* is the Portuguese version of the term, used, e.g., by Manuel de Coelho, *Flores de musica*, 1620 [new ed. of 5 Tentos by S. Kastner, 1936].

Tiepido [It.]. See *Tepido.

Tierce [F.]. Third. *Tierce de Picardie*. see *Picardy third.

Till Eulenspiegel. See *Symphonic poem III.

Timbale [F.], **timballo** [It.]. Kettledrum.

Timbre [G. *Klangfarbe*]. (1) The quality or "color" of a tone, i.e., the difference between tones of the same pitch if produced on various instruments, e.g., a violin and a flute. As has been shown by Helmholtz and others, the timbre of a given tone is determined by its harmonics, i.e., by the greater or lesser prominence of some of these harmonics over the others. The accompanying diagram shows that, although the c of the violin and the c of the horn have the same series of harmonics (c', g', c'', e'', g'' . . .), their quotas in the total intensity differ widely.

The sound of a tuning fork and of the stopped diapason of the organ are practically without harmonics; the "pure sound" of the flute is the result of its lacking practically all the harmonics except for the first (octave); the rich and mellow timbre of the clarinet is the result of the fact that the even-numbered har-

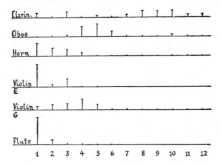

monics (c′, c″) are absent but that the odd-numbered harmonics (g′, e″ . . .) are quite prominent. The pungent and nasal sound of the oboe is due to the presence of practically all the harmonics which also appear, in different degrees, in the tones of the violin.

The classical theory of timbre, as outlined above, has been modified to some extent by the recent theory of the *formant.* According to the older theory, the characteristic constituents of, e.g., a tone sounded on a violin are in a fixed relation to the fundamental tone and, therefore, are shifted up or down if the fundamental changes. E.g., if for the violin-tone g the characteristic partials are g″ and b″, the violin-tone d′ would have the (much higher) characteristic partials d‴ and f‴. According to more recent investigations, however, the characteristic partials of a violin-tone lie within an absolutely fixed range of rather narrow limits, regardless of the higher or lower pitch of the fundamental. This characteristic "absolute range of partials" is called formant. In most violins the formant lies between 3000 and 6000 frequencies. The formant theory also plays an important part in the explanation of the different "timbre" of the vowels in singing. For each vowel, the human voice represents a different "instrument" with the formant in a different region. Cf. the modern books on *acoustics; SaHMI,* 354; W. T. Bartholomew, "Voice Research" (*BAMS* vi).

(2) French term for pre-existing melodies used for new texts, or for standard

motives used variously as building material for a longer melody or for a composition. See *Melody types.

(3) The term is also used as an equivalent for the German term *Klangideal* [see *Sound ideal].

Time. The term is used loosely to indicate *meter, tempo, or the duration of a given note.

Time signatures. The time (meter) is indicated at the beginning of a piece in the form of a fraction the denominator of which indicates the chosen unit of measurement (half-note, quarter-note, etc.), while the numerator indicates the number of such units comprised in a measure. See *Meter.

The early time signatures and their proportional modifications are explained under *mensural notation II and *proportions. Two of these survive to the present day, namely the sign c for $\frac{4}{4}$, and the sign ¢ for $\frac{2}{2}$ (*alla breve). In the sources of the 17th century more complicated signs such as c3, c$\frac{3}{2}$ are still frequent and puzzling to the modern reader to whom a combination of c ($\frac{4}{4}$) and $\frac{3}{2}$, $\frac{6}{4}$, $\frac{6}{9}$ (sic), seems contradictory and senseless. The explanation is found in the fact that such signs combine two meanings, the older proportional meaning with the more recent, metrical. E.g., the sign c$\frac{6}{4}$ (cf. Froberger, Suite no. 4) means (a) that each measure contains six quarter-notes, and (b) that these six notes are equal in duration to the four notes of the preceding section. It appears that these signs have a strictly metronomic significance (relative to the normal tempo of the piece), a fact which is usually overlooked by modern readers. Particularly noteworthy is the signature c3 (3, $\frac{3}{1}$) which is very frequently used for sections containing three whole-notes to the measure. Although this manner of writing suggests to the modern student a very slow tempo, the correct speed of such pieces is moderately quick, since these three whole-notes will have to be played in the time normally consumed by one whole-note:

$$c_o | \flat\flat || c_3{}_{ooo} | o\cdot\flat_o | =$$
$$c_o | \flat\flat || \flat\flat\flat | \flat\cdot\flat\flat |$$

If, however (as usually in 16th-century vocal music; Palestrina), the composition is notated in alla breve, then the relationship is, not 3:1, but 3:2 [cf. *ApNPM*, 193ff].

Around 1700 the symbol ꜀Ɔ was used to indicate measures of double length, i.e., ⁶⁄₄ instead of ⁴⁄₄ (cf. Bach, Partita no. VI, gigue), a method of designation which still survived in the ₵Ɔ (= ⁶⁄₂) of Schubert's Impromptu op. 90, no. 3.

Timoroso [It.]. Timid, fearful.

Timpan. Old E. for tympanon, i.e., *dulcimer or, perhaps, *psaltery. Also for drum [cf. timpani].

Timpani [It.]. *Kettledrums. *Timpani coperti* or *sordi*, muffled kettledrums.

Tintant [F.], **tintinnando** [It.]. Tinkling.

Tintinnabulum [L.]. Medieval term for bell.

Tiorba [It.]. *Theorboe.

Tiple [Sp.]. Soprano, upper voice. Also a small guitar. The meaning of titles such as "Tiple a tre" (Falconiero, c. 1620; cf. Torchi, *L'Arte musicale in Italia* vii, 128) is not clear.

Tipping. See *Tonguing.

Tirade [F.], **tirata** [It.]. A Baroque ornament consisting of a scale passage of more than three notes that serves as a transition between two principal melody notes. It was written out or indicated by

the sign illustrated in Ex. 1, but frequently improvised to fill in large intervals. Tirades are a typical feature of the French overture style [see Ex. 2, from Bach's Goldberg Variations]. A late ex-

ample occurs in the fourth measure of Beethoven's Piano Concerto in G. P. A.

Tirana. A special type of Andalusian dance-song. Blas de Laserna (1751–1816; see *Tonadilla) wrote a "Tirana del Trípili" which was famous all over Europe throughout the 19th century.

Tirare [It.]. To draw. *Tira tutti* (draw all), full organ. *Tirarsi* (to be drawn) designates the sliding mechanism of the *trombone. *Tirando* means slowing of tempo.

Tirasse [F.]. Originally, the pedals of a small organ which had no separate pipes, but were mechanically connected with manual keys. Hence, a pedal coupler of the organ, e.g., *Tirasse du Positif* (*Tir. P.*), coupler "Choir to Pedal."

Tirer, tirez, tiré [F.]. Indicates the down-stroke of the bow [see *Bowing], the drawing of organ stops, or a slowing down of tempo.

Toccata [from It. *toccare*, to touch, with reference to the "touching" of the keys, as contrasted with the "sounding" of strings in the sonata, and the "singing" of voices in the cantata]. (1) A keyboard (organ, harpsichord) composition in free, idiomatic keyboard style, employing full chords and running passages, with or without the inclusion of sections in imitative style (fugues). The earliest toccatas, by A. Gabrieli [*Editions II, 3], consist of full chords and interlacing scale passages only. To consider them as mere virtuoso pieces (as is frequently done) is scarcely appropriate, since the passages have a decidedly expressive significance, particularly if played in the free tempo which is typical of the toccata [see reference to Frescobaldi under *rubato]. With Claudio Merulo (1533–1604) the toccata became organized into an alternation of free (toccata-like) and of fugal sections, usually in the arrangement T F T F T. Frescobaldi's (1583–1643) toccatas, if compared with those of Merulo, clearly illustrate the difference between the grandiose pomp of the late Renaissance and the sensitive disintegration of the early Baroque period. They are written in a succession of quickly changing "scenes," an interesting exhibition of overflowing imagination without any restraining and binding principle of form. A special type (already to be found with his predecessors Trabaci and Mayone; cf. W. Apel in *MQ* xx) is the short liturgical toccata (e.g., "Toccata avanti l'elevazione," i.e., to be played before the elevation of the host; see *Offertorium), which is a short prelude in dignified style. With Bernardo Pasquini (1637–1710) and Alessandro Scarlatti (1659–1725) the Italian toccata became the arena for empty pianistic virtuosity and soon declined into a *perpetuum mobile type which is very close to the etudes of the 19th century (Clementi).

The development of the toccata in Germany falls into two branches. The South-German composers (Froberger, Kerll, Muffat) followed the Italian model (Frescobaldi), not without enriching its stylistic resources and enlivening its contents. More important is the North-German development which led to an entirely novel type of toccata of a free and rhapsodic character, a type which, owing to its unbounded irrationalism and transcendental greatness, has not inappropriately been termed "*Gothic." This new style appeared first in the toccatas of Matthias Weckmann (1621–74), and developed to great artistic height in those of Dietrich Buxtehude (1637–1707), Nicolaus Bruhns (*c.* 1665–97), and J. S. Bach (1685–1750). Most of these toccatas, particularly those of Bach, retain the Merulo-scheme of five sections, alternating between free and contrapuntal style. Bach's great organ toccata in F major, however, combines the huge dimensions of the North-German type with the rhythmic precision of the late Italian toccata (Pasquini). The toccata style is also frequently used for the preludes of fugues, as, e.g., for Bach's organ fugue in A minor.

Both the North-German and the Italian type of the toccata were also cultivated in modern music. Examples of the perpetuum mobile type are the toccatas by Schumann, Debussy (in *Pour le Piano,* 1911), Honegger, Prokofiev, and Casella, while the free, rhapsodic style is used in the toccatas of Busoni (1921) and Petyrek (1934).

(2) Around 1600, the name toccata was also used for brass music in the character of a festive fanfare, e.g., in the introduction of Monteverdi's *Orfeo* (1607). Why the same name was applied to pieces so different in character is not clear. Possibly the latter connotation is bound up with the use of kettledrums for the bass part of such pieces [see *Toccato; *Toccatina; *Tucket; *Touche (4); *Tusch].

Lit.: E. Valentin, *Die Entwicklung der Tokkate im 17–18. Jahrhundert* (1930); L. Schrade, "Ein Beitrag zur Geschichte der Toccata" (*ZMW* viii); O. Gombosi, "Zur Vorgeschichte der Tokkate" (*AM* vi, no. 2); L. Torchi, †*L'Arte musicale in Italia* iii; F. Boghen, †*Toccate italiani*; E. Kaller, †*Liber organi* v.

Toccatina. A small toccata, serving as a prelude to a suite. Examples occurring in Fischer, Murschhauser, show a style which is closer to that of the orchestral *toccata (2) than to the free style of the keyboard toccata (1).

Toccato. In the 17th-century literature for trumpets, the bass part of a trumpet piece, so called probably because it was originally played on, or together with, kettledrums. See the literature under *Clarin trumpet. See also *Toccata (2).

Tod und Verklärung. See *Symphonic poem III.

Tokkate [G.]. See *Toccata.

Tombeau [F., tombstone]. Compositions written in memory of one deceased. A great number of very beautiful examples exist in the French literature of the 17th century, e.g., one by Denis Gaultier for the Seigneur de Lenclos [cf. *ApMZ* ii], by Raquette for Gaultier, by L. Couperin and by d'Anglebert for their teacher Chambonnières, two (in the form of a cantata, called Apotheose) by F. Couperin for Lully and for Corelli. *Lamentos and plaintes (Froberger; cf. *TaAM* vi, 142) complete the list of a repertory in which the Romanticism of the 17th century has expressed itself most beautifully [see under *Classicism]. Cf. M. Brenet, in *RMC* iii.

Tom-tom. American-Indian or Oriental drums of indefinite pitch, imitations of which are occasionally used in dance bands.

Ton [F.]. (1) Pitch (*donner le ton,* to give the pitch). — (2) Key or mode (*ton d'ut,* key of C; *ton majeur,* major key; *ton d'église,* church mode). — (3) Wholetone, as distinct from *demiton,* semitone. — (4) Sound (*ton doux,* sweet sound). — (5) Crook (*ton du cor, ton de rechange,* crook of the horn). — (6) *Ton bouché,* stopped tone (of a horn); *ton ouvert,* open (natural) tone of a wind instrument.

Ton [G.]. *Tone, chiefly in the meanings (1) and (3).

Tonabstand [G.]. Interval.

Tonada. Spanish term for song in general; also used in the Latin American countries.

Tonadilla [Sp.]. A short Spanish comic opera of popular type, for one to four characters, consisting of solo song and, occasionally, choruses. Its origins were short scenic interludes performed between the acts of a play or serious opera but (like the Italian *opera buffa) it later became an independent piece, and flourished from about the middle of the 18th to the early 19th century. One of the first tonadillas is a comic musical dialogue between a woman innkeeper and an itinerant Bohemian written by Luis Misón in 1757. Chief composers are Misón, Pablo Esteve, and Blas de Laserna (1751–1816). The tonadilla superseded the *zarzuela which was an elaborately staged serious opera, mostly based on mythological subjects.

Lit.: *LavE* i.4, pp. 2227–57; J. Subira, *La Tonadilla escénica* (2 vols., 1928); F. Pedrell, *Teatro lirico español* . . . (5 vols., 1897–98); M. Hamilton, *Music in Eighteenth-Century Spain* (1937); J. Subira, in *Editions XXIV, B, 3/4.   D. G.

Tonal and real. In a fugue, an *answer is called real if it is an exact (diatonic) transposition of the subject. It is called tonal if certain steps are modified. Such modifications frequently take place if the subject contains the interval of the fifth (d–a), this being answered not by the transposed fifth (a–e'), but by the fourth (a–d'), as is illustrated by the accompanying example from Bach's *The

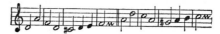

Art of Fugue. The reason for this method is the desire to avoid sudden oscillations between the keys of the tonic and of the dominant. In fact, with the theme in question the "real answer" a–e'–c' . . . would bring about a somewhat irritating clash between the low d in the subject and the high e in the answer. It is difficult to summarize rules as to when tonal and real answer is properly used. In general it may be noticed that the fugal themes called *soggetto lend themselves more easily to tonal treatment, while the more recent types of subjects called *andamento are frequently too "individual" and well-defined to admit any modification.

The dichotomy tonal-real has also been applied to entire fugues, a fugue being called tonal if the answer is tonal; real, if it is real. This distinction is, however, rather absurd. Obviously, it implies that in a fugue one or the other type of answer is strictly maintained. Although there exist examples of "real fugue" (chiefly those based on an andamento-subject, e.g., *Wt. Cl.* i, G major, or the organ fugue in A minor), there hardly exists an example of "tonal fugue," since, in the further context of the fugue — unless it is of the student's type — the answers are likely to waver between tonal and real.

The terms tonal and real are also used in connection with imitation at intervals other than the fifth, particularly with the imitation at the higher or lower second which occurs in sequential passages [see *Sequence (1)]. This is called real if the intervals are imitated exactly, thus involving modulation; tonal if it stays within the key.

Tonale [L.]. Same as *tonarium.

Tonalität [G.]. *Tonality in the sense of "loyalty to a key," but admitting modulations into another key which are not necessarily included in the German term "Tonart." Thus, the beginning of Beethoven's Waldstein Sonata shows the "Tonarten" of C, G, B-flat, F, and C in quick succession but has only one "Tonalität," C major.

Tonality. While the general meaning of this term is rather obvious, its exact ramifications are difficult of definition. Numerous attempts have been made to clarify its significance, some of which show the tendency to preserve a certain vagueness of meaning. This tendency appears particularly in the efforts to make a distinction between key and tonality, somewhat in the manner of the distinction between "clear facts" and "general feeling." It is probably some such distinction which the following words (quoted from *GD*, Suppl. Vol., article "Key," p. 313) are meant to express: "The quality called tonality might indeed be usefully nicknamed 'Keyishness,' to distinguish it from all the musical joys of Key itself, just as a bather might distinguish the elemental joy of wetness from the act of swimming." Other authorities, however, take a simpler point of view, declining to make a distinction between tonality and key. Even so, there remain difficulties, and these would seem to be caused mainly by the fact that, within the last half-century, the "tonality" of music has undergone so radical changes that a definition put forward 30 years ago is, by necessity, outdated at the present time. From the present-day point of view it seems best to interpret tonality as "loyalty to a tonic" in the broadest sense of the word, or, as Vincent d'Indy puts it, as "the ensemble of musical phenomena which human understanding is able to appreciate by direct comparison with a constant element — the tonic." This definition expresses what might well be

called one of the most striking phenomena of music, viz., the fact that throughout its evolution, in primitive and Oriental cultures as well as in Gregorian chant and in harmonized music, practically every single piece gives preference to one tone (the tonic), making this the tonal center to which all other tones are related — the only exception being the "atonal" music of the 20th century in which such preference is studiously avoided.

Although (with the just-mentioned exception) all music is tonal, the means of achieving tonality have, of course, greatly changed during the various phases of musical history. While in Gregorian chant and similar bodies of monophonic music the relationships are of a purely melodic character, a much more complex situation is encountered in the field of harmonized music. Passing over the earlier phases of this development it will suffice to mention that, around 1700, a system of tonal functions became generally accepted which was based on the establishment of three main chords, the tonic, the dominant, and the sub-dominant triads as the carriers of the harmonic as well as of the melodic movements. Broadened by the ample use of chromatic alterations and of modulation into other keys, it prevailed throughout the 18th and 19th centuries, and, after a short eclipse caused by the radicalism of atonality, made its comeback in that modification frequently referred to under the name of "tonal center." In this modern type of tonality the constituent triads of the older system have lost their former prerogatives, and the relationships to the tonic are made through dissonant (though not atonal) chords which frequently result from an emphasis on linear (polyphonic) texture.

A short explanation is necessary in order to clarify the relationship between the terms tonality and modality. In current usage these are mutually exclusive terms, the former referring to music written in a "key" (major or minor mode), the latter to pieces written in, or showing the influence of, the church modes [see *Modality]. It goes without saying that this usage is not compatible with the above broad definition of tonality which includes all tonal relationships, whether "tonal" or "modal." If the explanation of mode as the constituent scale is accepted [see *Mode (1)], then tonality exists in different "modal" varieties, based, e.g., on the church modes, the major and minor modes, the pentatonic mode, the whole-tone mode, the diatonic mode [see *Pandiatonicism] or, as in some modern music, the chromatic mode. Tonality also exists in the quarter-tone mode (e.g., in the Greek enharmonic genus), although modern quarter-tone music tends towards atonality.

The above explanations are made with a view towards clarification of some fundamental facts rather than to establish a new terminology which, at any event, has little expectation of being accepted. Other usages of the term tonality, e.g., in the sense of "tonal system" (almost synonymous with what has been termed above modality), or in the sense of major-and-minor tonality (as opposed to modality in the accepted meaning of the term), have became firmly entrenched in current usage, as a perusal of the literature on this topic clearly shows.

Lit.: J. Yasser, *A Theory of Evolving Tonality* (1932); I. S. Tovey, "Tonality" (*ML* ix, no. 4); J. Yasser, "The Future of Tonality" (*MM* viii); H. Reichenbach, "The Tonality of English and Gaelic Folksong" (*ML* xix, no. 3); W. H. Frere, "Key-Relationships in Early Mediaeval Music" (*SIM* xiii; also in *KIM*, 1911, p. 114); M. Touze, "La Tonalité chromatique" (*RM* iii).

Tonarium, Tonale. Medieval books of Gregorian chant in which the melodies (chiefly the Antiphons of the Office) are arranged according to their modes, a practice which, no doubt, originated in the desire to facilitate the memorizing of music notated only in neumes. An example is the *Antiphonary of Montpellier* which has been published in vols. vii, viii of the *Paléographie musicale* [see *Editions XXIII]. Theoretical writings of a similar character are the *Tonarius Ber-*

nonis (*GS* ii, 79), and the *Commemoratio brevis de tonis et psalmis modulandis* (*GS* i, 213), both of the 10th century. Cf. F. X. Mathias, *Die Tonarien* (1903); M. Runge, in *MfM* xxxv.

Tonart [G.]. Key [see under *Tonalität].

Tonbuchstaben [G.]. Tone letters [see *Letter notation].

Tondichtung [G.]. Tone poem; also any composition of a poetic character.

Tone [F. *ton*; G. *Ton*; It. *tono*]. (1) A sound of definite pitch and duration, as distinct from noise and from less definite phenomena, such as the violin *portamento. Tone, therefore, is the building material of music. — (2) The interval of a major second, i.e., a whole-tone, as distinct from a semitone (minor second). This is the usual meaning of the term in English parlance in which the word "note" is used for the meaning (1). — (3) In the connections Gregorian tone, Psalm tone, it means standard recitation formulae used for the singing of the psalms or other liturgical texts [see *Tonus (3); *Psalm tones].

Tone color. See *Timbre.

Tone poem. See *Symphonic poem.

Tone row [G. *Tonreihe*]. See *Twelve-tone technique.

Tonfarbe [G.]. Timbre.

Tongeschlecht [G.]. Distinction of a chord or key, whether major or minor.

Tonguing. In playing wind instruments, the use of the tongue for greater speed and accurateness of intonation. It consists of a momentary interruption of the wind-stream by an action of the tongue as if pronouncing the letter t or k. Three types of tonguing are distinguished: single tonguing (t–t . . .), double tonguing (t–k t–k . . .), and triple tonguing t–k–t t–k–t . . .). The first is employed in slower passages, the last two in rapid passages in groups of two or three notes. Tonguing is used on practically all the wind instruments, but is particularly important and indispensable for the flute player. A special type of tonguing, called *Flatterzunge* or flutter-tonguing, has been introduced by R. Strauss. It calls for a rolling movement of the tongue, as if pronouncing d–r–r–r. Double-tonguing is also called tippling.

Tonhöhe [G.]. *Pitch.

Tonic. The first and main note of a key, hence, key-note. See *Scale degrees; *Key; *Tonality.

Tonic accent. An *accent consisting in a change (raising) of pitch, rather than in a stress, e.g., *Domine*, not *Dómĭnĕ*, the latter method being called dynamic accent. Tonic accentuation was used in ancient Greek poetry (Homer) in which it was occasionally indicated by the *accents known as acute (high), grave (low), and circumflex (high followed by low). The term is also used in connection with a melody in order to indicate that a strong syllable of the text receives a note of higher pitch than the surrounding weak syllables. The tonic accent plays an important role in the discussion of Gregorian and other chants [cf. *ReMMA, passim*].

Tonic Sol-fa. An English method of solmization designed primarily to facilitate sight-singing. It was developed from earlier methods (Lancashire system) by Miss S. A. Glover and perfected about 1840 by John Curwen (1816–80). It is widely used for teaching purposes in England, and has also become known in some other countries, e.g., in Germany (under the name Tonika-Do).

Tonic Sol-fa is a system of "movable Do," i.e., the tone-syllables *doh, ray, me, fah, soh, lah, te* are used with reference to the key of the piece or any section thereof where there is a change of key. The syllables or, more properly, their initial consonants *d r m f s l t* are also used for the notation of the music in a manner reminiscent of the German keyboard *tablatures of the 16th century. Octave repeti-

tions are indicated for the higher octave thus: *d̄ r̄ m̄* or *d′ r′ m′*, for the lower octave thus: *d̲ r̲ m̲* or *d, r, m,*. For the minor scale the third degree becomes *doh*, owing to the changed intervals of this scale: *l t d r m f s l*. Actually this succession represents the Aeolian scale (white keys from A, or any transposition). In order to arrive at the minor scale, the sixth and seventh degrees must be sharpened. Sharpened tones are indicated by changing the vowel to *e* (*de, re, fe, se, le*), flattened tones by changing it to *a* (*ra, ma, la, ta*). For the sixth degree of the ascending minor scale a separate syllable *ba* is introduced, since the use of *fe* would suggest a half step to the next note, while actually a whole step follows (to *se*). Therefore we have the following designation of the melodic minor scale (up and down): *l t d r m ba se l; l s f m r d t l*. The tones and their relation to each other are shown in a chart called *Modulator*.

If the piece modulates into another key this key is indicated (in different ways), and the tone syllables are now to be reckoned in the new key. For the indication of meter and rhythm additional signs (horizontal strokes, single dots, colons, commas, etc.) are used.

Lit.: J. Curwen, *The New Standard Course of Lessons and Exercises on the Tonica Sol-fa Method* (1900 and later); W. R. Phillips, *Dictionary of the Tonic Sol-fa System* (1909); W. G. Whittaker, in *ML*, no. 4, and in *MQ* viii; J. Taylor, J. C. Ward, in *PMA* xxiii; C. A. Harris, in *MQ* iv; J. A. Fuller-Maitland, in *MQ* vii.

Tonika [G.]. Tonic. *Tonika-Do*, German modification of *Tonic Sol-fa. Cf. A. Hundoegger, *Leitfaden der Tonika-Do-Lehre* (1929).

Tonkunst [G.]. Music; *Tonkünstler*, composer.

Tonleiter [G.]. Scale.

Tonlos [G.]. Toneless.

Tonmalerei [G.]. Word painting or descriptive music.

Tono [It.]. Tone; whole-tone; key; mode. *Primo* (*secondo*, etc.) *tono*, first (second, etc.) church mode.

Tonos, pl. **tonoi** [Gr.]. See *Greek music II (d).

Tonsatz [G.]. Composition. *Tonsetzer*, composer.

Tonschlüssel [G.]. Clef.

Tonschrift [G.]. Notation.

Tonsystem [G.]. System of tones, i.e., *tonality, used mainly in combinations such as "Europäisches Tonsystem," "Javanisches Tonsystem," "Pythagoräisches Tonsystem." Cf. A. v. Hornbostel, "Musikalische Tonsysteme" (in H. Geiger, *Handbuch der Physik*, 1928).

Tonus [L.]. (1) Whole-tone. — (2) Church mode, e.g., *primus tonus*, first mode; *tonus authenticus* (*plagalis*), authentic (plagal) mode. — (3) Psalm tone or other recitations (*tonus lectionis*, etc.).

Tonus in directum (indirectum), or **directaneus**. See *Psalmody I.

Tonus mixtus. See *Church modes III.

Tonus peregrinus [L., the foreign mode]. See *Psalm tones.

Tonverschmelzung [G.]. See *Consonance and Dissonance I (d).

Tonwort [G.]. A method of solmization invented, in 1892, by C. Eitz, and designed with particular reference to chromatic progressions and enharmonic changes. Cf. *MoML*, 199; A. Einstein, *Das neue Musiklexikon* (1926), 647.

Torculus. See *Neumes I.

Tordion. See under *Basse dance.

Tornada [Sp.]. Refrain of a song.

Tosto [It.]. Rapid; or immediately. *Tostissimo*, very rapid.

Tost Quartets. Twelve quartets by Haydn, written 1789–90 and dedicated to Johann Tost, Viennese merchant and violin player. They comprise op. 54, nos. 1–3; op. 55, nos. 1–3; op. 64, nos. 1–6.

Touch [G. *Anschlag*]. See *Pianoforte playing (particularly IV and V).

Touche [F.]. (1) Key of the pianoforte. — (2) Finger board of the violin [see *Bowing (I)]. — (3) 16th-century term for fret (of a lute, guitar). — (4) 17th-century term (also used in English sources) for the "orchestral" toccata [see *Toccata (2)].

Tour de force [F.]. A strikingly difficult passage.

Tour de gosier [F., turn of the throat]. A vocal ornament of the 17th and 18th centuries, consisting of a turn composed of five notes. The term is also applied to the closing notes of the trill.   P. A.

Tourdion [F.]. See under *Basse danse.

Tourte bow. The violin bows made by F. Tourte (1747–1835), the most famous bow-maker. See *Bow. Cf. *GD* v, 366.

Toye. Title of short and light compositions of the virginalistic period.

Tp. Abbr. of timpani.

Tr. Abbr. of trumpet or trill.

Tracker. See *Organ II.

Tract [L. *tractus*]. In Gregorian chant an item of the Proper of the *Mass, used instead of the alleluia mainly for feasts of a somber character, during Lent, Ember days, and at Requiem Mass. It consists of a number, usually three or four, of psalm verses, without the addition of an antiphon or response, and thus represents one of the few remaining examples of "direct psalmody [see *Psalmody I]. All the tracts are in either the 2d or the 8th mode, a restriction not elsewhere encountered in Gregorian chant. Actually, the restriction goes much farther since most of the tracts are sung to a limited number of standard melodies (or, more properly, standard phrases) which are used, with minor modifications, for a great number of texts. The principle may be illustrated by the two subsequent schemes, the first for the tract *Attendite caelum*, the second for *Sicut cervus* (I, II, etc., indicate the different verses; a, b, etc., various musical phrases; c and c′ the same phrase with different ending):

(a) I   II   III   IV   V
     a b   c c′ b   c′ b   c c′ b c d

(b) I   II   III
     a b   c c′ b d   c c′ b d

This method is reminiscent of the use of *melody types in many branches of Oriental music, and may well be considered as indicative of a very early stage in the development of the chant. In fact, the tracts are believed to be an early type of plainsong which was later replaced by the alleluia, except for those occasions for which the joyful character of the latter was not proper. The tract *Qui habitat in adjutorio* is the only remaining instance of an entire psalm (Ps. 90) in the Mass. Cf. H. Riemann, in *SIM* ix.

Tradolce [It.]. Very sweet.

Traduction [F.], **traduzione** [It.]. (1) Arrangement. — (2) Transposition. — (3) Translation. *Traduisé, tradotto,* arranged.

Träumerisch [G.]. Dreamy.

Traîné [F.]. Dragged, held back.

Trait [F.]. *Tract.

Trakt [G.]. *Tract.

Traktur [G.]. *Trackers.

Transcription. See *Arrangement.

Transformation of themes. See *Metamorphosis.

Transient modulation. Same as passing *modulation.

Transition. The term is used in different meanings: (1) as synonymous with passing modulation; (2) for a lasting change of key effected with abruptness rather than by regular modulation; (3) for a passage (bridge) which leads from one main section to another, e.g., from the first to the second theme of a movement.

Transposing instruments. Instruments for which the music is written in another key or in another octave than that of their actual sound. This method is widely used for wind instruments, such as the clarinet in B♭, the natural tones of which are the harmonics of B♭. Since the player of such an instrument naturally considers B♭ his simplest key, it has become customary to present this key to him in the simplest notation, i.e., as C major. The transposition to be made from the written part to the actual sound is indicated by the interval from C to the pitch note of the instrument, e.g., to B♭ in the case of the B♭-clarinet, or to A in that of the A-clarinet [see Ex.: Bruckner, Seventh Symphony]. With certain instruments the transposition includes a change to the lower octave, e.g., for the horn in E♭.

1. A-clarinet as written. 2. As it sounds.

The use of transposing instruments or, more accurately, of transposing notation, dates back to the period (18th century) when only the natural tones were available. With the introduction of valves and keys the difference of facility in playing in the various keys was greatly diminished, and eventually almost completely eliminated. Therefore, from the present point of view, the transposed notation must be considered as inappropriate and antiquated. Its abolishment is particularly desirable from the standpoint of the orchestral conductor and, still more so, from that of the layman for whom the presence of six or seven different types of transposed notations offers the chief obstacle to the study of orchestral scores. Yet, contrary to the general progressiveness of our time, the transposed notation has successfully maintained its traditional place.

Nearly all the wind instruments, not pitched in C, are transposing instruments, with the exception of the trombones which, although pitched to E♭, B♭, etc., are written as they sound. The term is also applied to instruments such as the piccolo flute which is, quite sensibly, notated an octave lower than it sounds, merely to avoid ledger lines. Here, only a special clef such as $\substack{\phi \\ 8}$ (see *Clefs) would be necessary in order to exclude such instruments from the category of transposing instruments proper.

Transposition. The rewriting or the *ex tempore* performance of a composition at another pitch, i.e., in another key, e.g., in E-flat instead of the original D, etc. This practice is particularly frequent in songs, in order to accommodate the range of the different voices. A good accompanist should be able to extemporize transposition. The easiest transposition is that of a semitone, e.g., from F to F-sharp, or from E to E-flat, since here most of the written notes remain unaltered, and only a different signature has to be imagined. Transposition of a third, fourth, calls for a full acquaintance with harmonies, intervals, etc., and becomes, of course, increasingly difficult in the case of music involving many modulations, chromatic alterations, etc.

Transverse flute [F. *flute traversière*; G. *Querflöte*; It. *flauto traverso*]. The modern *flute, in contradistinction to the *recorder.

Traps. In jazz parlance the various noise-producing devices attached to the drum (trap drum) and played by the trap drummer. See *Jazz III.

Traquenard. A dance type not infrequent in German orchestral suites [see *Suite V] of the late 17th century, e.g., by Muffat [cf. *DTOe* 2.ii, p. 188], J. K. F. Fischer [cf. *DdT* 10, p. 54], Erlebach, Krieger, and others. The term denotes properly a defective ambling of a horse, and the dotted rhythm of the music, usually in alla breve, evidently imitates this movement. Cf. P. Nettl, in *StM* viii, 93.

Trascinando [It.]. Dragging, holding back.

Trattenuto [It.]. Held back or sustained.

Trauermusik [G.]. Funeral music. *Trauermarsch*, funeral march.

Traurig [G.]. Sad.

Trautonium. See *Electronic musical instruments VI.

Traversa [It.], **traversière** [F.], **Traversflöte** [G.]. Same as *transverse flute.

Traviata, La ("The Erring One"). Opera in three acts by Giuseppe Verdi, text by Piave after Dumas' *La Dame aux camélias*, produced 1853. The scene is contemporary Paris with the courtesan *Violetta* (Soprano) as the central figure. Falling in love with *Alfred Germont* (Tenor), she gives up her life of pleasure and marries him (Act II) but, implored by Alfred's father, *Old Germont* (Baritone), leaves his home and resumes her former life (costume ball, Act II). Alfred, not knowing that her change of mind is only a pretext, insults her at the ball, but in Act III he and the dying Violetta are united in love.

Traviata is one of the earliest instances of the use of a contemporary plot in opera, a practice which became established, around 1890, by the *verismo movement. Musically it follows the tradition of the "grand opéra," a mixture of lyrical and pathetic elements, with popular type melodies and concentration on effective vocal numbers. *Rigoletto* and Il *Trovatore* belong to the same musical category.

Traynour. According to the 14th-century theorist Philippus de Caserta, the use of conflicting rhythmic groupings in different voice-parts, e.g., nine or three notes against two, four notes against three, etc. [cf. *CS* iii, 123]. This was a common practice towards the end of the 14th century [cf., e.g., *ApNPM*, 403ff]. H. Riemann's interpretation of 17th-century examples of *hemiola as traynour [cf. *RiHM* ii.2, Index] and his explanation of traynour as syncopation [*RiML*, 1875] are misleading.

Tre [It.]. Three. *A tre voci*, in three parts. *Tre corde*, see *Una corde.

Treble [from L. *triplum*]. The highest part of a choral composition, hence synonymous with soprano. However, treble clef is not the same as soprano clef [see *Clefs]. For treble viol, recorder, see under *Descant.

The old English terms treble, quatreble (quadrible), and quinible, derived from L. *triplum, quadruplum, quintuplum,* would seem to have originated about 1400 in connection with a then current method of improvised five-voice *fauxbourdon (properly, English discant), in which the two upper parts of the normal (three-voice) fauxbourdon were doubled at the higher octave, similar to the octave-doubling used in the 9th century parallel organum. The two lowest parts were called tenor and *meane (replacing the L. *duplum*). Thus, if the tenor with its plainsong melody would start on d, the meane, treble, quatreble, and quinible would start on a, d', a', d'' respectively [cf. the articles "Quatreble" and "Quinible" in J. A. H. Murray, *New English Dictionary* (1888ff)]. After this the voices would continue according to the principles of fauxbourdon, in doubled sixth-chords. The explanation (given in a recent reference book) of quadrible and quinible as "singing in parallel fourths and fifths" is without foundation. Actually, the starting interval of the quatreble is a twelfth (higher fifth), that of the quinible a double octave, and in the further course these intervals change into (higher) thirds and sixths. Cf. M. Bukofzer, *Geschichte des englischen Diskants und des Fauxbourdons . . .* (1936), passim. Also *RiHM* i.2, 165f.

Tredecime [G.]. The interval of the thirteenth, i.e., the compound sixth.

Treibend [G.]. "Driving," hurrying.

Tremando, tremante [It.]. With tremolo.

Tremblement. The most important of the French agréments of the 17th and 18th centuries, more commonly known as *trill.   P. A.

Tremendo [It.]. Tremendous.

Tremolo [It., trembling]. (1) On stringed instruments the quick reiteration of the same tone, produced by a rapid up-and-down movement of the bow, indicated as in (a) [see *Bowing (j)]. The string tremolo is an important orchestral effect which is widely used for passages of dramatic expression or for the purpose of orchestral coloring. It appeared in some of the earliest compositions for the violin (Biagio Marini, *Affetti musicali*, 1617; cf. *RiHM* ii.2, 101). Monteverdi, in his *Combattimento di Tancredi e Clorinda* (1624), used it as a pictorial means to express excitement and danger, as which it has been used innumerable times, e.g., in Bach's *St. Matthew Passion* ("Und der Vorhang zerriss"), in the oracle scene of Gluck's *Alceste*, etc. The term is also used for the rapid alternation between two notes of a chord, usually in the distance of a third, as in (b), this being called a fingered tremolo. Eighteenth-century names for the string tremolo are *bombo* [It.] and *Schwärmer* [G.].

In violin music of the 18th century (Stamitz, Gluck, Haydn) a special type of tremolo, known as "undulating tremolo" [It. *ondeggiando*; F. *ondulé*] is much used [see *Bowing (o)]. It produces a series of dynamic pulses in moderate speed, usually four to a note. It was indicated by a wavy line extending over repeated eighth- or quarter-notes [see *Ornamentation, table p. 545], a sign which has been misinterpreted in recent reference books as indicating a vibrato. It may be noticed that the undulating tremolo of the strings has also been imitated on keyboard instruments. Probably the earliest example is the "imitatio violistica" in S. Scheidt's *Tabulatura nova* (1624), while the latest examples occur in certain passages of Beethoven and Chopin which have been erroneously referred to as *Bebung. Bebung is a fluctuation of pitch (not of intensity), hence, a *vibrato. It cannot be produced on any keyboard instrument except the clavichord.

(2) On the pianoforte the string tremolo is imitated by the rapid alternation of a tone and its octave or with another harmonic interval (third, fifth). It occurs frequently in piano arrangements of orchestral music, but is rarely used in original compositions.

(3) In singing the term tremolo is unfortunately used in a different meaning, to denote a slight fluctuation of pitch which is comparable to what the string players correctly call vibrato [see *Vibrato (2)]. The true vocal tremolo, i.e., the quick reiteration of the same pitch, is an effect which is practically never used today. In early music, however, it was one of the most important ornamentations. Terms such as *notae vinnulae* ("neighing notes") or *notae tremulae*, mentioned by early writers on Gregorian chant, indicate rather clearly vocal tremolos. Whether neumatic signs such as the *bistropha* and *tristropha* [see *Neumes I] were performed as a tremolo or a vibrato is not entirely clear [cf. *AdHM* i, 94], but 13th-century terms such as *repercussio gutturis* [see *Plica] and *reverberatio* [cf. *CS* i, 91] would seem to indicate a vocal tremolo. In the early part of the 17th century the vocal tremolo was widely used under the name *trillo*, and was usually written out in quick notes [see Ex. (c), from Benedetto Ferrari's *Varie musiche*, 1633ff; cf. also *GD* v, 20 (Caccini); *GD* iv, 234 (Porter); *RiHM* ii.2, 28, and 297 (Caccini, Saracini)]. It should be noticed that, in this period, the term *tremolo* denoted a trill; see *Ornamentation I, III.

In the 18th century the vocal tremolo fell into disuse and was henceforth referred to under derogative names such as *chèvrotement* [F.] and *Bockstriller* [G.; cf. *MoML*, 82], both of which liken it to the bleating of a goat [F. *chèvre*, G. *Bock*].

Tremulant. A mechanical organ device operated by a stop which produces alternating increase and decrease of wind pressure, thus producing mechanical pulsations of tone which are sometimes euphemistically compared to the violinist's vibrato. The tremulant is, no doubt, one of the most detestable inventions of modern organ building.

Trenchmore. An English countrydance of the 16th and 17th centuries, in lively triple meter with dotted rhythms. An amusing description from 1689, showing that its only rival in popularity at the court of King Charles was the cushion dance, is quoted in *GD* v, 377.

Trent Codices [G. *Trienter Codices*]. Seven MS volumes of 15th-century polyphonic music, the first six of which were discovered by F. X. Haberl in the library of the cathedral of Trent (in Southern Tyrol, also famous through the *Council of Trent) and first described in his *Dufay* (1885). In 1891 they were purchased by the Hofbibliothek of Vienna but became Italian state property in the treaty of St. Germain of 1918. The first six volumes (Codd. 87–92) contain 1585 compositions, mostly from the middle of the 15th century, while a recently discovered seventh volume contains mostly duplicates. The major part of the collection was written by Johannes Wiser for the bishop Johannes Hinderbach. This collection, which is by far the most important source of 15th-century music, contains compositions of about 75 composers, French, English, Italian, and German, e.g., Dunstable, Lyonel Power, Reginald Liebert, Ciconia, Brasart, Dufay, Binchois, Ockeghem, Busnois, and Isaac. A large selection has been published in the following 6 volumes of the *DTOe* [see *Editions VII, Collective Volumes]: 7 and 11.i (all the French, Italian, and German secular songs); 19.i (5 complete Masses); 27.i (Mass of Reginald Liebert, motets, antiphons, hymns); 31 (Masses and Mass movements by various composers); 40 (sacred and secular motets by Dunstable, Dufay, Brasart, de Vitry, and others).

Lit.: G. Adler, "Ueber Textlegung in den Trienter Codices" (*Riemann Festschrift*, 1909); R. v. Ficker, "Die Kolorierungstechnik der Trienter Messen" (*StM* vii); A. Orel, "Einige Grundformen der Motettkomposition im 15. Jahrhundert" (*StM* vii); R. Wolkan, "Die

Heimat der Trienter Musikhandschriften" (*StM* viii).

Trepak. A Cossack dance in quick duple time.

Trésor musicale. See *Editions, Historical, XXVII.

Trezza. A dance movement occurring in some German suites of the 17th century, e.g., in the ballets of J. H. Schmelzer [cf. *DTOe* 28.ii, p. 9]. It is similar in character to the courante or gagliarde.

Triad [G. *Dreiklang*]. A chord of three tones obtained by the superposition of two thirds, i.e., consisting of a third and a fifth above the root. There are four species of triad, major (major plus minor third), minor (minor plus major third), diminished (minor plus minor third), and augmented (major plus major third). The former two are consonant, the latter two dissonant chords. Each triad (e.g.,

Triads: (a) major; (b) minor; (c) diminished; (d) augmented.

c–e–g) admits of two inversions, the *sixth-chord (e–g–c′; G. *Sextakkord*), and the *six-four chord (g–c′–e′; G. *Quartsextakkord*).

The triad is the basis of our harmonic system, a place from which even the radical developments of the past thirty years [see *New music] have not completely ousted it, although its position is much less dominant than it formerly was. See *Harmony; *Harmonic analysis II.

Triangle [G. *Triangel*; It. *triangolo*]. See *Percussion instruments B, 5.

Trias [L.]. Triad.

Tricinium [L.]. A 16th-century name for vocal compositions in three parts. A large repertory exists in publications such as G. Rhau, *Tricinia . . . Latina, Germanica, Brabantica, et Gallica . . .* (1542); J. Montanus and A. Neuber, *Selectorum triciniorum discantus . . .* (1559); Sethis

Calvisius, *Tricinia* (1603; expl. in *SchGMB*, no. 160); Melchior Franck, *Tricinia nova* (1611); Michael Praetorius, *Musae Sionae* (1605–10; complete ed. vol. ix); and elsewhere. Particularly the latter's three-voice elaborations of chorale melodies are true gems of musical art.

Trienter Codices [G.]. *Trent Codices.

Trigon. See *Neumes I.

Trill [formerly *shake*; F. *cadence, tremblement*; G. *Triller*; It. *trillo*]. A musical ornament consisting of the rapid alternation of a given note with the diatonic second above it.

I. The trill originated in the 16th century as an ornamental resolution of a suspension dissonance at a cadence. Example 1 shows various forms of the 16th-century trill: (a) and (b) represent the typical vocal cadence as it is found in the works of Palestrina, Lassus, etc. The other variants occur frequently in instrumental transcriptions of vocal works and in independent keyboard compositions. It is probable, however, that even in vocal

performances the singers of this period were accustomed to embellish the simple written cadence in this more elaborate manner.

It will be noted that the cadence formulas given above have the following characteristics in common: (1) the trill begins on the penultimate strong beat of the phrase, with a dissonant note (suspension or appoggiatura); (2) it consists chiefly in the alternation of that dissonant note with its resolution; (3) the dissonant note receives the accent throughout, since it coincides with the accented subdivisions of the beat; (4) the note below the resolution may be introduced, either near the beginning or near the end of the trill.

These characteristics remain to form the basis of the most important *agrément* of the 17th century, the French *cadence* or *tremblement*, which was adopted in Germany as the *Triller*, in England as the *shake*, and in Italy as the *trillo* [for the early meaning of this term, see *Tremolo (3)]. As its French name implies, the ornament was at first (i.e., in the early 17th century) invariably associated with cadences. Later it was freely introduced at other positions in the musical phrase, retaining, however, until the end of the 18th century, its primary function as the ornamental resolution of a dissonance. G. F. Wolf, writing in 1783 (*Unterricht im Klavierspiel*) that: "The trill is a series of superior appoggiaturas repeated one after another . . . one should note that the lowest tone of the trill is always the main note and that it is not this note but its upper neighbor which begins the trill" was only repeating a definition previously formulated in almost these identical terms by Loulié in 1698 and by Marpurg in 1755.

II. In music of the 17th and 18th centuries the trill, instead of being written out in notes or being left to the improvisation of the performer (as had hitherto been the case), is usually indicated in the score by one of the following signs:

tr   t   tᴧᴧᴧ   ᴧᴧ   ᴧ   +

These signs are exactly synonymous; the use of one rather than another has no relation to the performance of the ornament and reveals nothing but the composer's personal preference. Since the sign is always placed over the harmony note the accent must always fall upon the upper auxiliary which, as the dissonance, requires the greater emphasis. Apart from this factor, which is constant throughout the period, the execution of the trill was varied considerably in individual cases by adding prefixes or terminations and by varying the number and rhythm of the notes comprising the ornament. At the time of Bach and Handel three ways of ending the trill were almost equally popular [Ex. 2]. The use of a simple sign (t, tr) for the trill left the performer free to choose interpretation (a), (b), or (c). If the composer especially desired an execution as at (b) or (c) he used one of the notations shown at (b) or (c).

The number and rhythmic distribution of the notes comprising the trill were generally left entirely to the discretion of the performer. Ex. 3 shows several realizations of a cadence formula that is particularly common in the works of J. S. Bach and his contemporaries. All these interpretations are equally correct according to the traditions of Bach's time; the choice between them should depend upon the tempo and character of the passage in which the trill occurs. A greater number of notes should obviously be used for a trill on a long note than for one on a short note. Interpretations (d) and (e) are therefore more appropriate for a rapid tempo; (a) and (c) for a slow tempo. It is also evident that the most expressive interpretations are those which give the most weight to the initial dissonance, as at (c) and (d). This dwelling upon the introductory note of the trill, known in French as *tremblement appuyé*, in German as *vorbereiter Triller*, is sometimes expressly indicated by the composer (1) by inserting the sign for an appoggiatura, (2) by prefixing a vertical stroke to the sign for the trill, or (3) by writing the introductory appoggiatura as an ordinary note. The excerpts given in Ex. 4 illustrate J. S. Bach's use of all three procedures.

In the music of this period, trills on very short notes are best rendered as four notes of equal value. If the tempo is too rapid to permit the clear execution of four notes the trill should rather be abbreviated to two notes, i.e., a single appoggiatura, with which it is, in a sense, synonymous. In no

case must the trill be reduced to a triplet beginning with the main note, for the accent would then fall on the wrong note. [See also remark under *Turn.]

III. The beginning of a trill is often varied by the addition of a prefix, which may be indicated by one or more small notes, or by a modification of the ordinary sign for the trill. The number of small notes used in the notation of the prefix does not affect the interpretation. A hook extending downwards from the beginning of the trill sign indicates a prefix starting below the main note; a hook extending upwards represents an introductory turn beginning with the upper auxiliary [Ex. 5]. The prefix from below is

especially common; indeed, it was customary, throughout the 18th century, to start a long trill with such a prefix, even when not indicated, whenever the main note was approached conjunctly from be-

low, as in the illustrated passage from Beethoven's Piano Sonata op. 10, no. 3 [Ex. 6].

IV. The modern trill, which begins with the main note, was first introduced early in the 19th century by the Viennese pianists, Hummel, Czerny, and Moscheles. It is usually played with a two-note

termination [G. Nachschlag]. This trill no longer fulfills the appoggiatura-function with which the ornament had been associated for nearly two centuries; it is an effect of virtuosity and serves merely to accentuate the main note or to add brilliance or color to the performance, as shown in Example 7 [a, Chopin (Bolero); b, Liszt (Hungarian Rhapsody no. 14)].

The "main note" trill did not entirely supplant the traditional form, which often appears in the works of Chopin, Schumann, and Liszt. It is customary, however, in the music of the Romantic and Modern periods, for the composer to indicate the first note of the trill by means of a small grace note. In the absence of such indication the trill should begin on the main note.   P. A.

Triller [G.]. Trill. *Trillerkette*, chain, series of trills.

Trillo [It.]. Trill. In the 17th century usually the true vocal tremolo [see *Tremolo (3)]. *Trillo del Diavolo* (The Devil's Trill), a famous sonata for violin with accompaniment by Tartini (1692–1770), so called on account of the trills in the last movement.

Trilogie [G.]. See *Ring des Nibelungen.

Trinklied [G.]. Drinking song.

Trio [It.]. (1) Originally and properly a contrapuntal composition in three parts. This meaning exists in Bach's six sonatas for the organ [see *Trio sonata] as well as in the three-voice pieces in Hindemith's *Reihe kleiner Stücke*, op. 37.

(2) In the Scherzo or Minuet movement of the sonata (symphony, quartet, etc.), the middle section played between the scherzo (minuet) and its repetition [see *Scherzo]. The designation *trio* comes from the 17th-century custom of writing minuets and other dances in three parts, frequently for two oboes and bassoon (Lully), a treatment which was used particularly for the second of two dances played alternately, so that the arrangement *Menuet, Menuet en trio, Menuet* resulted. A good instance exists in Bach's Brandenburg Concerto no. 1, in which the minuet is fully orchestrated, while the trio is written for two oboes and bassoon. The accompanying example, from

Bach's French Suite no. 6, shows the use of the same trio-style in harpsichord music. As late as Haydn, Mozart, and Beethoven (e.g., Symphony no. 7) the trio usually retained the lighter texture and the wood-wind character of Lully's trio. Schubert and others adopted the term as a designation for the middle section of compositions in ternary form. Cf. E. Blom, in *ML* xxii, no. 2.

(3) Chamber music for three players. The most important type is the pianoforte trio, for piano, violin, and cello. In most of Haydn's 35 trios the violin and cello are chiefly reinforcements of the piano part. Mozart's 7 trios show greater individuality of the parts and pave the way for such great works as Beethoven's Trios op. 70, op. 97, and Schubert's op. 99 and op. 100. The list of the classical repertoire is completed by Schumann's three, Men-

delssohn's two, Brahms's three, and Dvořák's four trios. The string trio, usually for violin, viola, and cello, has been much less attractive to composers. After Haydn's 20 trios (for two violins and cello) there is only one divertimento by Mozart (K.V. 563), Beethoven's opp. 3, 9, 87, and a few later compositions.

Triole [G.], **triolet** [F.]. Triplet.

Trionfale [It.]. Triumphant.

Trionfo di Dori, Il. See *Triumphes of Oriana, The.

Trio sonata. The most important type of Baroque chamber music, written in three parts, two upper parts of similar range and design and a supporting figured-bass part [see *Thorough-bass]. The trio sonata is usually performed on four instruments, two violins (or, in the earlier period, viols, cornetti) for the two upper parts, a cello (viola da gamba, violone) for the bass part, and a harpsichord (organ, theorboe) for the bass part together with the realization of the thorough-bass accompaniment. Other performing bodies were occasionally employed, e.g., in Biagio Marini's Sonatas for violin and organ op. 8 (1626) in which the organ has two written parts, in Bach's six organ trios written for the organ alone in three parts without thorough-bass figures, or in G. B. Bononcini's op. 4 (1686), for which there are five part books, 1st and 2d violin, cello, theorboe, and organ. Towards the end of the 17th century there occur trio sonatas written in four voices, the cello part becoming somewhat different from the bass part for the harpsichord [cf. Tommaso Vitali, *Sonate da chiesa a tre*, 1693]. There even exist orchestral trio sonatas, usually called Sinfonia. In all these cases, however, the writing is essentially in three parts, and it is this texture which is indicated in the customary designation "*a trè*."

Early three-voice compositions, written mostly in the form and style of the instrumental *canzona, are by Salomone Rossi (*Varie Sonate*, 1622), Buonamente (4th, 5th, 7th book of *Sonate*, 1626–37),

Tarquinio Merula, Biagio Marini, and others [see *Editions II, 7]. Towards the end of the 17th century the trio sonata became established in two types, known as *sonata da chiesa* (church sonata) and *sonata da camera* (chamber sonata). Regarding the former, see *Sonata B, II; regarding the latter, see *Suite IV. The trio-style was cultivated particularly in France, under the name of *sonate en trio* [see *Trio (2)]. The medium persisted into the classical period, the last examples being those by Gluck (1746), the *Mannheimers, and Haydn [*Six sonates à deux violons et basse*, op. 8, c. 1762]. Thereafter it changed into the classical trio for three instruments, and with a fully written-out part for the pianoforte [see *Trio (3)].

The literature of the trio sonata includes all the illustrious names of the Baroque, such as Corelli (48, opp. 1–4, 1683–94), Purcell (12, 1683), Buxtehude (1696), Handel (21, six of which are for two oboes and bass), François Couperin (14), Antonio Vivaldi (12, 1737). Bach wrote only a few trio sonatas of the normal type (i.e., for two melody instruments and thorough-bass accompaniment), namely, that from the *Musical Offering and three others [*B.-G.* vol. ix, pp. 221, 231, 260]. His sonatas for violin and harpsichord as well as his organ sonatas represent the trio sonata with three obbligato parts, i.e., without thorough-bass accompaniment. The fact, however, that the opening measures of the movements in the violin sonatas have thorough-bass figures suggests (together with some other considerations) that a second, "accompanying" harpsichord was used which played the main notes of the bass part and improvised the chordal accompaniment.

Lit.: H. Hoffmann, *Die Norddeutsche Triosonate* ... (1929); E. Kuri, "Die Trio-Sonate von ihren Anfängen bis zu Haydn und Mozart" (*Zeitschrift für Hausmusik* iii, 37); see also under *Sonata.

Tripla. (1) In mensural notation, i.e., *proportio tripla*, see *Proportions. — (2) Same as *Proportz. — (3) Plural of *triplum.

Triple concerto. A concerto for three solo instruments, such as Bach's two concertos for three harpsichords.

Triple counterpoint. See *Double counterpoint.

Triple-croche [F.]. See *Notes.

Triple fugue. See *Double fugue.

Triplet [F. *triolet*; G. *Triole*; It. *terzina*]. A group of three notes to be performed in the place of two of the same kind, indicated by a 3 and, usually, a slur:

$$\text{♪♪♪}_3 \qquad \text{♪♪♪}_3$$

For the indication of a certain triplet rhythm by dotted notes, see *Dotted notes.

Triple time. See *Meter.

Triplum. See *Duplum.

Tris(h)agion [Gr. *tris*, thrice; *hagios*, holy]. The oldest form of the Sanctus, written in the Greek language (as is also the Kyrie). In the Roman rites it occurs in the *Improperia of Good Friday, in which each Greek phrase (*Agios o Theos*) is answered antiphonically (to the same melody) by its Latin translation (*Sanctus Deus*, ...) [cf. *GR*, 198]. The text is also known as the Cherubic Hymn and has been set to music various times by Russian composers.

Tristan und Isolde. Opera in three acts by Richard Wagner, to his own libretto, after a medieval legend of Celtic origin; produced 1865. The main characters are *Isolde* (Soprano), an Irish princess, and *Tristan* (Tenor), a knight who is escorting her from Ireland to Cornwall, to be married to the English King *Marke* (Bass). Isolde, torn between hatred and love, orders her companion *Brangäne* (Mezzo-soprano) to prepare a poisoned drink for Tristan and herself, but Brangäne mixes a love potion instead (Act I). The lovers, meeting while the king goes hunting (opening of Act II), are spied upon by *Melot* (Baritone), who wounds Tristan in combat. Tristan, brought to his own castle by his servant

Kurvenal (Baritone), dies, and Isolde, her heart breaking, follows him.

Tristan is, without doubt, the truest and fullest incarnation of love passion ever presented on the stage. Practically the whole second and third acts are an "unending love duet" in which every feeling and sensation, ranging from the tenderest to the most passionate, is portrayed. Owing to the relative simplicity and unimportance of the "story," the *leitmotif plays a secondary role in this opera (if compared with the *Ring), and the most conspicuous features of the music are the "unending melody" and a harmonic vocabulary full of daring chromatic progressions and bold appoggiaturas. In fact, so conspicuous are these traits that "Tristan melody" and "Tristan harmony" have become common technical terms.

Triste. An Argentine type of love song, slow and melancholic. It is a mixture of Indian and European elements, musically as well as textually.

Tristopha. See *Neumes I.

Trite [G.]. See *Greek music II (a).

Tritone [L. *tritonus*]. The interval of three whole tones, i.e., the augmented fourth (e.g., f–b). As a melodic progression it sounded awkward, and was hence forbidden in plainsong and in early polyphonic music under names such as *diabolus in musica* (the devil in music) or *mi contra fa*. The rule prohibiting the tritone is still observed in students' counterpoint. However, the progression becomes much less objectionable if the b resolves upwards as a leading tone: f'–b–c', a progression which is not infrequent in arias of Mozart.

The avoidance of the tritone as a chordal combination plays an important part in the early organum (*Musica enchiriadis, c.* 900) where it leads to certain modifications of the strictly parallel movement

[Ex. 1a instead of 1b]. The sources of 13th- and 14th-century polyphonic music,

however, show clearly that the tritone chord b–f'–b' was considered a legitimate combination, although it had to be resolved into a full consonance such as a–e'–a' or c–g'–c'' [Ex. 2]. In classical harmony the tritone is admitted only in combination with other intervals, mainly in the seventh chord and its derivatives. The third inversion of the seventh chord, b–f'–g'–d'', is sometimes called tritone.

Trittico [It.]. A triptych, i.e., a painting on three panels such as is common over altars. The name was used by Puccini for a group of three short independent operas, *Il Tabarro* (The Cloak), *Suor Angelica* (Sister Angelica), and *Gianni Schicchi* (composed 1918), which are to be performed together.

Triumphes of Oriana, The. A collection of English madrigals, published by Morley in imitation of an Italian collection of madrigals, *Il trionfo di Dori* (1592), and dedicated to Queen Elizabeth. The book was scheduled to appear in 1601, but was not published until 1603, after the Queen's death. It contains 29 madrigals in five or six parts, by Morley, Weelkes, E. Gibbons, and others, all of which close with the refrain "Long live fair Oriana" (an imitation of the refrain "Viva la bella Dori" in the *Trionfo*), except for the last three which have the refrain "In Heaven lives Oriana." List of contents in *GD* v, 385; reprint see *Editions X, 32.

Trochee, trochaic. See *Poetic meter I; *Modes, Rhythmic.

Tromba [It.]. Trumpet. *T. cromatica (a macchina, ventile*), valve trumpet. *T. bassa,* bass trumpet. *T. da tirarsi,* slide trumpet [see *Trumpet II]. *T. spezzata* (pieced trumpet), trombone.

Tromba marina [marine trumpet, sea trumpet, nun's fiddle; F. *trompette marine*; G. *Trumscheit, Nonnengeige*]. An instrument of the later Middle Ages, but still in use in the 18th century, which consisted of a long tapering body (5 to 6 feet) over which a single string was stretched. The string was not stopped, as in violin playing, but slightly touched to produce harmonic notes, the bow playing above the touching finger near the upper end. Inside the long soundbox a great number (up to fifty) of sympathetic strings were fixed which were tuned in unison with the playing string [see illustration, on p. 800]. The most peculiar detail of construction was the "trembling bridge," i.e., a bridge in the shape of a wide inverted U the right leg of which was placed directly under the string, while the other was free to vibrate against the soundboard so that a drumming noise resulted, hence the German name *Trumscheit* (drum log). At the same time the sound of the instrument is strikingly like that of a trumpet, thus leading to another possible explanation of the name trumpet (*tromba*). More difficult is the explanation of the adjective "marina" which appears after 1600. It has led to various fanciful explanations, the most amusing of which is that the instrument was used for signaling purposes in the Navy. A plausible explanation derives the word from "Mary"; as a matter of fact, the instrument was frequently used by nuns under the name *Nonnengeige* (nun's fiddle). Antonio Vivaldi (*c.* 1680–1743) wrote solo parts for two tromba marinas in one of his concertos [cf. A. Schering, *Geschichte des Instrumentalkonzerts* (1905), p. 62], and the Swiss Johann Gletle (d. before 1684) wrote duets for the instrument (new ed. in A. Stern and W. Schuh, *Schweizer Sing- und Spielmusik* (Hug), vol. 6). A *Mémoire* by J.-B. Prin of 1742 is reprinted in *BSIM* iv (1908). For a detailed description of the instrument cf. N. Bessaraboff, *Ancient European Musical Instruments* (1941), 317ff; also *SaHMI* 291, 304f, and *GD* v, 386f.

Lit.: F. W. Galpin, "Monsieur Prin and his Trumpet Marine" (*ML* xiv, no. 1); *LavE* ii.3, 1757ff (bibl.); P. Garnault, *La Trompette marine* (1926).

Trombetta [It.]. Old name for a small trumpet.

Trombone [G. *Posaune*]. I. The modern orchestral trombone is a brass instru-

ment with a cylindrical bore except for the lower third of its length which gradually expands into the bell, and with a cup-shaped mouthpiece. It consists of two separate pieces, one being formed by the mouthpiece and the bell, held together by a crossbar, the other by a U-shaped middle piece which, by means of another crossbar, can be moved away and towards the player and which, therefore, is called slide. This sliding mechanism takes the place of the valves used with the other brass instruments and, like these, serves to fill in the gaps of the natural tones [see *Wind instruments IV (a)]. There are seven recognized positions (six plus the original one) of the slide, each a semitone lower and thus changing the natural tuning of the trombone successively from, say, B-flat into A, A-flat, etc. The range for each position is one of about two octaves ($B_1b–Bb–f–bb$ for the normal position), but the lowest note of this series, called *pedal tone, is difficult to produce in the three lowest positions. Since the movement from position to position requires a certain amount of time, a true legato is not possible on the trombone. On the other hand, a *glissando (properly termed *portamento) is possible, and this effect, although musically bad, has been used by some modern composers for the purpose of caricature.

The trombone can be regarded as the bass of the trumpet although its tone is more dignified and solemn, less brilliant than the latter's. This difference in tone color is due mainly to the larger mouthpiece of the trombone. Trombones have been made in many sizes ranging from soprano to contra-bass, and in many keys. The four types used in the modern orchestra are the tenor trombone, the bass trombone, the tenor-bass trombone, and the double-bass trombone.

(a) Tenor trombone. This is pitched in B-flat and has a complete chromatic

compass as shown in (a), in addition to which four pedal tones, as shown in (b), are available. It is notated at its sounding pitch (not transposing as, e.g., the horn). See the illustration on p. 97.

(b) Bass trombone. This is pitched in F, although instruments pitched in G or E-flat occur in England. Its compass is a fourth below that of the tenor trombone. Owing to the great length of the pipe the slides are difficult to handle, and the instrument is nowadays replaced by the tenor-bass trombone.

(c) Tenor-bass trombone. This has the size (and pitch) of the tenor trombone, but a wider bore which facilitates the playing of the pedal tones and renders the sound similar to that of the bass trombone. It is furnished with a single valve which lowers the pitch a fourth, i.e., to that of the bass trombone. The tenor-bass trombone has virtually supplanted the bass trombone in the present-day orchestra.

(d) Double-bass trombone. This is pitched an octave below the tenor trombone (English instruments are sometimes pitched in C). The difficulty caused by the great length of its pipe was overcome in 1816 (Gottfried Weber) by the invention of the "double slide," the pipe being bent into four parallel tubes. Wagner introduced it into his *Ring*, and other composers have followed his example (e.g., d'Indy in *A Summer Day in the Mountains*). It is, however, very tiring to play, owing to the great strain on the player's lungs and lips.

Occasionally valve trombones have been made (used by d'Indy in *Le Chant de la cloche*). Their tone, however, is less noble than that of the slide trombone.

II. *History.* The trombone was the first of all our orchestral instruments to appear in its present shape. It developed in the 15th century out of a large trumpet (hence the name *trombone*, i.e., large *tromba*) by the addition of a slide, and the earliest representations, on paintings of the late 15th century, show all the essentials of the present instrument. The German name *Posaune* points to another line of descent, the large and straight *buysine*, a name which in turn goes back to L. **buccina.* The medieval name for

the trombone was *sacbut* (derived from an old Spanish word *sacabuche,* "draw tube," or from old French *sacqueboute,* "pull-push"). Trombones were common throughout the 16th century in the ceremonial bands of princes and of large cities as well as in churches. Their sliding mechanism made them suitable for the rendering of art music at a time when the horns and trumpets were still limited to the performance of military signals. Owing to the less expanded bell of the old trombones their sound was relatively soft and therefore combined well with the strings. Among the earliest compositions prescribing trombones are G. Gabrieli's *Sacrae symphoniae* of *c.* 1600, scored for cornetti, trombones, bassoons, and strings [see *Orchestra II]. Michael Praetorius, in his *Theatrum instrumentorum* (1620), gives reproductions of Alto, Tenor, and Bass trombones, called *Alt-Posaun, Rechte gemeine* (right common) *Posaune,* and *Quart-Posaune,* respectively. Bach and Handel used the instrument occasionally, but mostly in unison with voices for the sake of greater sonority. Gluck was perhaps the first to make effective use of the trombone for accompanying chords, e.g., in the aria "Divinité du Styx" of his *Alceste,* and Mozart gave the trombones a prominent place in his *The Magic Flute* and *Don Giovanni.* Beethoven introduced the trombones into symphonic music in the final movement of his Fifth Symphony, but it was not until after 1850 that, owing to the precedence of Berlioz and Wagner, the trombone became firmly established as a member of the orchestra.

Trommel [G.]. Drum [see *Percussion instruments B, 1–3]. *Trommelschlegel,* drumstick.

Trommelbass [G.]. Derogative name for stereotyped bass figures, such as the pianoforte tremolo in octaves.

Trompete [G.], **trompette** [F.]. Trumpet.

Trompetengeige [G.]. *Tromba marina.

Troparion. See *Byzantine chant II.

Troparium [L.]. Troper. See *Liturgical books I.

Trope [L. *tropus*]. (1) In certain medieval treatises, synonym for *modus, tonus,* i.e., *church mode. — (2) Same as *differentiae. — (3) See *Twelve-tone technique (Hauer).

(4) In the Roman liturgy of the 9th to the 13th century a textual addition to the authorized texts as they were set down by St. Gregory (*c.* 600). There was, in the above period, an extensive activity of this kind, springing from the natural desire toward continued creative contribution to the authorized repertory of texts. The tropes range from a few amplifying words interpolated between the Kyrie eleison (e.g., Kyrie–*fons bonitatis*–eleison: *farced Kyrie) to lengthy explanatory sentences (e.g., Surge–*infida gens, dejecta perfidia, quem demonstravit stella regem regum venerare*–et illuminare–*cogita, spera et suspira, coelestia contemplate*–Jerusalem), and even to entire poems placed between two words of an authentic text [cf., e.g., O. Ursprung, *Katholische Kirchenmusik*, 68]. As regards the musical treatment of the tropes, two categories must be distinguished: (a) Troped texts which were adapted to a pre-existing melisma, occurring in the original chant at the place of the trope (e.g., in a Kyrie on the syllable *e*). Here the new text was underlaid to the single notes of the melisma, so that a syllabic setting resulted. Most of the shorter tropes belong to this class [cf. *HAM*, no. 15; also 26b, 37]. A particularly important type of this group are the tropes to the final melisma of the Alleluia, the Alleluia tropes or *sequences which underwent a special development. (b) Tropes which were sung to new melodies. The musical material for such new melodies was occasionally derived from the original melody in a free variation technique [cf. *BeMMR*, 90].

The origin of the tropes is still obscure. Tutilo of St. Gall (d. *c.* 915; cf. *HAM*, no. 15) would seem to have played in this field a role similar to that of his contemporary Notker in the field of the se-

quence, i.e., that of an early master rather than of an inventor. His Christmas trope "Hodie cantandus est" [*SchGMB*, no. 3], written in the form of a dialogue (dialogue trope), is considered a forerunner of the *liturgical drama. Troping was used most frequently with the items of the Ordinary of the Mass (Kyrie tropes; Sanctus tropes; Gloria tropes, also called *laudes*), and with the Benedicamus domino (Benedicamus tropes). All the tropes were abolished by the *Council of Trent, and the five sequences which were retained are the only remnant of a once flourishing production. Traces of the tropes survive, however, in the present names of many Kyries [see *Kyrie].

In musicological research, the term troping is also used in connection with the polyphonic elaborations of liturgical chants. For instance, the early motet may be considered a "polyphonic trope" (or "vertical trope"), since here a new text, elaborating upon the idea of the original chant in the tenor, is used for the upper parts. Finally, the process of troping can also be observed in trouvère music in which new texts were interpolated between the two halves of a refrain, a procedure which is believed to have been the origin of the *rondeau (Gennrich), and which is clearly noticeable in the *motets entés* [see *Enté].

Lit.: See under *Sequence (2); also J. Handschin in *ZMW* x.

Troper. English for *troparium, i.e., a liturgical book containing tropes [see *Liturgical books I]. Cf. W. H. Frere, *The Winchester Troper* (1894); J. Handschin, "The two Winchester Tropers" (*Journal for Theological Studies* xxxvii).

Troppo [It.]. Too much. *Allegro non troppo*, not too quick.

Tropus. See *Trope (1), (2), (4).

Troubadours. The aristocratic poet-musicians of the Middle Ages in southern France (Provence). It was here, *c.* 1100, that a movement started which in the mid-12th century spread to northern France (*trouvères*) and Germany (*Minne-

singer), and which presents a unique picture of high nobility devoting themselves to the cultivation of poetry and music in a romantic service of chivalrous love [G. *Minnedienst*]. There is no complete agreement among scholars regarding the roots of this movement. Arabic-Spanish models as well as Carolingian love-lyrics and the adoration of the Virgin Mary have been cited as sources of origin. Very likely, these all contributed certain impulses. Another much-discussed question (of somewhat secondary importance) is to what extent the noblemen were assisted in their creative or reproductive activities by individuals of minor birth, the so-called jongleurs. Probably the practice varied in different cases [see *Minstrels*]. Among the troubadours who are known to us by their melodies we find Guillaume de Poitou (1070–1127), Marcabru (a commoner, d. *c.* 1150), Bernart de Ventadorn (d. 1195), Peïre Vidal (d. 1215), Rambault de Vaqueiras (d. 1207), Folquet de Marseille (d. 1231), Raimon de Miraval (d. *c.* 1220), Aimeric de Peguillan (1205–75), and Guiraut Riquier (d. 1294), the "last of the troubadours."

Of more than 1000 troubadour poems 323 are preserved with their melodies in the so-called *chansonniers [see under *Trouvères]. From the textual point of view these poems fall into classes such as *sirventes (songs of service, usually of political or moral contents), *plancs (plainte, song of mourning), *albas (song of dawn), and others. The two chief musical forms are the *canzo and the *vers. The melodies of the troubadours (as well as of the trouvères) are all monophonic, and were never accompanied in the modern sense of the word. Instrumental participation in the performance, such as is suggested by some pictures showing a singer holding a fiddle or being assisted by an instrumentalist, was restricted to a strict or slightly varied unison duplication of the melody [see *Heterophony] or, perhaps, to some short extemporization in the manner of a prelude, interlude, or postlude. For the notation and rhythmic interpretation of

the troubadour songs, see under *trouvères; also for literature. Examples in *HAM*, no. 18.

Trouvères. The aristocratic poet-musicians of the Middle Ages in northern France, where the movement, spreading from the Provence [see *Troubadours], started in the mid-12th century with Blondel de Nesles (*c.* 1150–1200) and Quesnes de Béthune (1150–1224), continued with Thibaut IV, King of Navarre (1208–53), and Perrin d'Angecourt (fl. *c.* 1250), and closed with the commoner Adam de la Halle (1220–87). Regarding the general features of the movement, see *Troubadours. About 800 songs are preserved with their melodies. The chief sources of trouvère and troubadour melodies are *Chansonnier de St. Germain* (Paris, Bibl. Nat. *20050*; facs. ed. by G. Raynaud and P. Meyer, 1892); *Chansonnier de l'Arsenal* (Paris, Bibl. de l'Arsenal, *1598*; new ed. by Pierre Aubry, 1909ff); *Chansonnier du Roy* (Bibl. Nat. *844*; new ed. by J. B. Beck, 1938); *Chansonnier Cangé* (Bibl. Nat. *846*; new ed. by J. B. Beck, 1927); Bibl. Nat. *25566* (publ. in E. de Coussemaker, *Oeuvres complètes du trouvère Adam de la Halle*, 1872); *Chansonnier de Noailles* (Bibl. Nat. *12615*); *Chansonnier d'Arras* (facs. ed. by A. Jean, roy, 1925); Bibl. Nat. *845, 847*, and *nouv. acqu. 1050* [cf. *AdHM* i, 193; *ReMMA*, 448].

The melodies of the trouvères, all monophonic as those of the troubadours, show a considerably greater emphasis on formal structure than those from the Provence. As a matter of fact, it is here for the first time that musical forms proper were developed some of which proved of long-lasting importance [see *Barform; *Virelai]. The through-composed type, called simply *chanson* (corresponding to the Provençal *vers, not the *canzo), is relatively rare as compared with various strict forms (*formes fixes*) such as the *rotrouenge, the *rondeau, the *virelai, and the *ballade [regarding a not very convincing genealogy of these forms, cf. F. Gennrich, *Grundriss einer Formenlehre des mittelalterlichen*

Liedes (1932); also *ReMMA*, 219ff]. Earlier forms of a more narrative type are the **chanson de geste*, and the **lai* or *descort*. Other classifications, such as *chanson de court*, **chanson de toile*, **tenso*, or *jeu-parti*, are made chiefly with reference to subject matters.

The melodies of the trouvères (and troubadours) are practically all notated in the symbols of **square notation*, i.e., with only one character for the single note (a square, usually with a tiny tail) and short ligatures for a group of notes in place of a single one (in German writings this notation is usually referred to as *Choralnotation*; see **Plainsong notation*). The rhythmic interpretation of this notation has been a subject of much investigation and controversy. The early attempts to apply the principles of mensural notation (particularly, the Franconian rules of ligatures; cf. *RiHM* i.2, 225) were abandoned around 1890 (Runge) in favor of a rhythmic interpretation based on the meter of the text, a principle which was considerably modified by Beck and Aubry around 1905 by the introduction of modal, i.e., ternary, rhythm [see **Modes, rhythmic*]. The modal interpretation has been rather generally accepted for the melody of the trouvères, while its applicability to those of the troubadours and the Minnesinger would appear to be much more open to question. More recently Beck, who was one of the first champions of modal interpretation, has taken quite a different position in his edition of the *Chansonnier de Noailles* (1927). Examples in *HAM*, no. 19; *SchGMB*, nos. 13, 14; *EiBM*, no. 7.

Lit.: (a) *General:* P. Aubry, *Trouvères et troubadours* (1909; Engl. transl. by C. Aveling, 1914); J. B. Beck, *La Musique des troubadours* (1910); *ReMMA*, 204ff; *AdHM* i, 188ff; *GéHM*, 258ff; B. Smythe, "Troubadour Songs" (*ML* ii, no. 3); P. Aubry, "L'Oeuvre mélodique des trouvères et troubadours" (*RMC* vii). — (b) *Special:* J. B. Beck, *Die Melodien der Troubadours* (1908); P. Aubry, *La Rhythmique musicale des troubadours and trouvères* (1907); P. Aubry, "Refrains et rondeaux du XIIIe siècle" (*Rie-*

mann Festschrift, 1909); *id.,* "Quatre poesies de Marcabru" (*TG* x); H. J. Moser, "Zu Ventadorns Melodien" (*ZMW* xvi). See also the literature for special articles (e.g., **Rotrouenge*, **Lai*, **Modes, Rhythmic*, etc.). — (c) *Publications of music:* Various chansonniers (see text); P. Aubry, †*Lais et descorts français du XIIIe siècle* (1901); F. Gennrich, †*Rondeaux, Virelais und Balladen*, 2 vols. (1921, '27). — (d) *Philological studies:* H. J. Chaytor, *The Troubadours* (1912); R. Croft-Cooke, *Troubadours* (1930); A. Jeanroy, *Bibliographie sommaire des chansonniers français du moyen-âge* (1918); A. Jeanroy, *Bibliographie sommaire des chansonniers provencaux* (1916). For additional literature cf. *ReMMA*, 445ff.

Trübe [G.]. Grievous.

Trugschluss [G.]. Deceptive cadence.

Trumbscheit [G.]. **Tromba marina.*

Trumpet [F. *trompette*; G. *Trompete*; It. *tromba*]. I. The modern orchestral trumpet is a **brass instrument with a narrow tube which is cylindrical for about three-quarters of its length, then widening out into a moderate-sized bell; and with a cup-shaped mouthpiece. These characteristics distinguish it from the horn which has a prevailingly conical bore and a funnel-shaped mouthpiece. They account for the different timbres of the two instruments, this being bright, brilliant, and penetrating in the case of the trumpet, mellow and full in that of the horn. The difference in shape, circular with the latter and oblong with the former, is of secondary importance although it is the most striking characteristic for the casual viewer. The trumpet has three **valves* (rotary or piston) which, taken singly or in combination, lower the natural pitch of the instrument by one to six semitones; hence, the name valve trumpet [F. *trompette-à-pistons* or *chromatique*; G. *Ventiltrompete*; It. *tromba ventile, cromatica, a macchina, a pistoni*] in distinction from the earlier natural trumpet [see II]. See the illustration on

p. 97. The basic principles of tone-pro-
duction on the trumpet are explained
under *Wind instruments.

The modern orchestral trumpet is
pitched in B-flat, and has the chromatic
compass shown. It is now usually no-

tated at the actual pitch, i.e., as a non-
transposing instrument, but this is a relatively recent practice. In earlier scores
(Beethoven, Brahms) it was usually notated as a transposing instrument, either
in B-flat throughout, or in different transpositions according to the crooks [see II],
these being indicated in the score.

At the end of the 19th century a larger
trumpet, pitched in F (or, for military
bands, in E-flat), was in vogue. This
corresponds in length of tubing and in
actual pitch to the horn and has a much
nobler tone than the B-flat trumpet. It
lacks, however, the latter's agility and is
now practically abandoned.

Bass trumpets, pitched in low E, D, or
C, were demanded by Wagner for his
Ring, but have proved impracticable.
The instruments thus called and used as
substitutes are really valve trombones,
pitched in C.

II. *History.* The following explanation
deals only with the immediate predecessors of the modern trumpet, the earlier
types being treated under the general
article on *brass instruments. Prior to
c. 1800 the trumpet existed only in the
form known as natural trumpet [G.
Naturtrompete], i.e., as a plain tube without any devices such as side-holes, crooks,
slides, valves, designed to bridge the gaps
of the natural scale of harmonics. From
the 14th century on the trumpet became
associated with military and ceremonial
functions. It was among the carefully
guarded privileges of the nobility and
only the official court trumpeters were
allowed to play it [see *Feldtrompeter].
After 1600 the trumpet began to be used
in art music, the "clarino" and "trombe
sordine" of Monteverdi's *Orfeo* (1607;
see *Orchestra II) being an early, though

isolated instance. In 1638 there appeared
a *Modo per imparare a sonare di tromba*
(Method of learning to play the trumpet)
by Fantini. Towards the end of the 17th
century the trumpets were quite frequently used in operas, cantatas, etc., for
scenes of a military character or for the
expression of joyful triumph (Purcell,
Buxtehude). At this time there developed the art of playing the highest register of the trumpet where the harmonics
form a full scale, while formerly only the
low and middle registers had been used
in which fanfare-like motives only are
possible [see *Clarin trumpet; *Bach
trumpet].

During the 18th century various attempts were made to overcome the limitation in compass of the natural trumpet.
As early as Bach's time crooks were used,
i.e., additional lengths of tubing which
were inserted between the mouthpiece
and the instrument and which lowered
its pitch by several semitones or whole-
tones. This, of course, was only an expedient to make one and the same instrument useful for pieces in a variety of keys,
but in any such key only the natural tones
were available. More drastic steps were
taken toward the end of the 18th century,
by the introduction of side-holes covered
with keys and of a sliding mechanism.
Key trumpets were invented in 1770 by
Kölbel of St. Petersburg, but were soon
abandoned since side-holes, though fairly
satisfactory on conical instruments such
as cornets and bugles (key bugle), are
really not applicable to instruments with
a cylindrical bore.

More successful was the application of
the sliding mechanism which had always
been used for the trombones. In an
earlier construction (17th, 18th centuries)
the slide was at the mouthpiece which
was provided with a long "throat," long
enough to be pulled out so that all the
gaps in the natural scale could be filled
up. It is this instrument which Bach prescribes under the name *tromba da tirarsi*
(Cantatas nos. 5, 20, 46, 77). The terms
tromba ò corno da tirarsi (Cantata no. 46)
and *corno da tirarsi* (Cantatas 67, 162)
probably indicate the same instrument

[cf. *SaHMI*, 384f]. At the end of the 18th century another construction was made by John Hyde (or by Woodham, *c.* 1810?) in which the U of the upper coil was transformed into a movable slide, similar to that of the trombone, and provided with springs to bring it back into its normal position. This instrument has been in constant use in England throughout the 19th century [cf. *GD* v, 395f]. Although it has the fine sound of the natural trumpet it lacked the agility demanded in modern scores and was, therefore, finally given up in favor of the valve trumpet.

The invention of the valves (1813) opened the way for the permanent establishment of the trumpet in the orchestra. The first example of a part for the valve trumpet would seem to be that in Halévy's *La Juive* (1835) in which two valve trumpets are used side by side with two crooked natural trumpets. The recent development of a brilliant trumpet technique has enabled composers to use the trumpets as melody instruments equal and occasionally superior in importance to the wood winds. The scores of Stravinsky, Shostakovitch, and others contain many interesting trumpet passages, frequently of a caricaturing character.

Trumscheit. *Tromba marina.

T.s. Abbreviation for *tasto solo.

Tuba. (1) In ancient Rome the name for a straight trumpet [see *Brass instruments V (a)].

(2) In modern usage the term tuba is loosely and without clear definition applied to any sort of bass-pitched brass instrument other than the trombones. They exist in a great variety of shapes, differing according to countries and makers, a fact which is partly explained by their extensive use in military and other bands. The most important of these, such as the Euphonium, Helicon, Sousaphone, Baritone, are briefly described under *Brass instruments III.

The tubas of the modern orchestra are bass instruments which combine the conical bore of the horn with the oblong shape

and the cupped mouthpiece of the trumpet. They have four or five valves and exist in three sizes: (a) Tenor tuba [G. *Baryton*] in B-flat, a fifth below the horn; (b) Bass tuba, pitched either in E-flat (E-flat or EE-flat bass tuba) or in F (F bass tuba); (c) Double-bass tuba (usually called BB-flat bass tuba or BB-flat bass), piched an octave below the tenor tuba.

Wagner tuba is the name given to instruments designed for Wagner's *Ring.* They have a somewhat narrower bore (corresponding to that of the *cornet) and are provided with a funnel-shaped mouthpiece like that of the horns. Wagner employed two tenor and two bass instruments of this type, together with a normal double-bass tuba for the lowest part. The Wagner tubas combine the agility of the cornet with the mellow timbre of the true tubas. They have also been used by Bruckner and R. Strauss (Elektra). Illustrations on p. 97.

(3) In Gregorian chant, see under *Psalm tones.

Tucket, tuck. Elizabethan name for a trumpet flourish. Evidently this word is an Anglicization of toccata [see *Toccata (2)]. Cf. the German version *Tusch*, and the French version *touche*.

Tudor Church Music. See *Editions, Historical, XXVIII.

Tune. Popular term for any clear-cut and easily retained melody, such as appears in folk songs, operatic arias, and also in many works of the classical and Romantic schools.

Tuning. The adjustment of the strings of stringed instruments to their proper pitch. The term is used particularly with reference to the pianoforte which, owing to its great number of strings, presents a special problem in tuning. The modern method of pianoforte tuning is based on the pure octave and the well-tempered fifth. The former is tuned so as to give no *beats, while the latter is obtained empirically by lowering the pure fifth (no beats) to the point at which it gives one beat per second. In this manner, a succession of fifths (with their lower octave): a, e, b, f♯ . . . is tuned. As soon as a third is available (a–c♯ being the first), this is used for testing. After the middle section of the keyboard (the ground work) has been tuned, the higher and lower registers are tuned by octaves. More recently, another system of tuning has been introduced (by O. C. Faust) and widely accepted (outside of the piano factories), which starts with c and uses major thirds upwards and fifths downwards. The accompanying scheme illus-

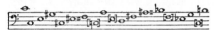

trates the general procedure. Even more radical is a method advocated by E. Neugebauer, which has pure fifths but slightly sharp fourths and octaves. Tests have shown it to be superior to the older methods. Cf. J. Redfield, *Music: A Science and an Art* (1928).

Tuning fork [F. *diapason*; G. *Stimmgabel*; It. *corista*]. A two-pronged piece of steel used to indicate absolute pitch. The modern tuning forks give the international pitch for the tone *a* (440 vibrations per second). The instrument was invented by John Shore in 1711, and improved by Rudolph König, Paris, around 1850. For the purpose of acoustical demonstration entire sets of tuning forks are built. They have great permanence in retaining their pitch, and produce almost pure tones, without harmonics. Cf. E. A. Kielhauser, *Die Stimmgabel* (1907).

Tuning slide. In organ building, a movable metal clip or cylinder, attached to the upper end of an open flue pipe. By lowering or raising it the tuning of the pipe can be adjusted.

Tuning wire. In organ building, a wire by which the tuning of reed pipes can be adjusted.

Tuono [It.]. See *Tono.

Turba [L., crowd]. In oratorios, passions, etc., name for the choral movements representing the Jewish or heathen

population. They are usually allegros in fugal style using short motives in close imitation. Numerous examples exist in Bach's *St. Matthew Passion*. Cf. G. Adler, in *Liliencron Festschrift* (1910).

Turca, Alla [It.]. In the Turkish style, i.e., in imitation of the Turkish military music (Janizaries) which became popular in Europe in the late 18th century. See *Janizary music.

Turkish crescent (hat, pavillon). See *Crescent.

Turkish music. I. *Theory.* The classical music of Turkey, as practiced at the court and the great monasteries at Constantinople, is based on a fundamental scale containing 24 notes to the octave. This scale is derived from the chief instrument of Turkish music, the long-neck lute, *tanbur, which has 24 frets. The various tones of the scale are calculated mostly on the basis of the Pythagorean system (consecutive fifths) and differ therefore from those of the European *quarter-tone system [cf. *LavE* i.5, 3016]. From this fundamental scale selections are made for the purpose of practical music-making and about one hundred different "modes" are distinguished. Among these are the mode *Tchariguiah*, which is the Pythagorean scale of C, and the mode *Raste*, the most frequent of all, in which the E and the B are those of *just intonation ($\frac{5}{4}$ and $\frac{15}{8}$), i.e., a comma lower than the corresponding tones in the former mode. Thirty such modes are illustrated in *LavE* i.5, 2997ff. No less elaborate is the Turkish system of rhythm, called *Oussoul*. This is derived from the playing of the kettledrum, on which two kinds of drum strokes are distinguished, one in the center (called *Dum*, i.e., muffled) and one at the side (called *Tek*, i.e., clear). About fifty standard combinations of these beats are known and they correspond to our meters, each combination being repeated throughout the entire composition. Rhythmic schemes involving nine or seven beats are frequent [Ex. 1, *Sofian*; 2, *Devri-Hindi*].

II. *Practice*. The religious music "consists of *Ilahi*, hymns for all the months of the Moslem year, *Tevchih*, or praises of the Prophet, and *Ayni Cherif*, or offices of the whirling Dervishes. All these together make up an important body of music, in which are found many masterpieces of Turkish music. To them must be added the famous *Nat* by Itri, the magnificent *Bayram Tekbiri*, also by him, the *Sala*, the *Temdjid*, the *Sabah essalati*, the *Miradjiye*" [cf. E. Borrel, in *GD*, Suppl. Vol., 633]. The secular art music is derived largely from Arabian practice. The most important type is the *Fasl*, a sort of suite composed of several pieces, instrumental and vocal, all in the same "key," i.e., in the same maqam [see *Arabian music II]. The instruments (*tanbur, oud, keman,* *kanun*) are also those used in Arabian music. Of particular interest is the music of the *Janizaries.

Lit.: *GD*, Suppl. Vol., 633ff (bibl.); H. G. Farmer, *Turkish Instruments of Music in the 17th Century* (1937); *LavE* i.5, 2845–3064; V. Belaiev, "Turkish Music" (*MQ* xxi); R. Yekta, "Musique orientale" (*RMC* vii, viii).

Turmsonaten [G. *Turm*, tower]. A type of German 17th-century *Gebrauchsmusik which was sounded on brass instruments from the tower of the town hall or a church, as a time signal, at noontime, sunset, etc. It consisted of harmonized chorales, plain tunes, military signals, or "sonatas" [see *Sonata B, I]. Interesting collections of such pieces are Johann Christoph Petzold's (Petzel) *Hora decima* (1670) and *Fünfstimmigte blasende Musik* (1685). New ed. in *DdT* 63; cf. also *SchGMB*, no. 157.

Turn [F. *double cadence, doublé, brisé*; G. *Doppelschlag*]. An ornament consisting of a group of four or five notes which wind around the principal note. The most common form of turn in the music of the 17th and 18th centuries is indicated by a curved line, contains four notes, and begins on the beat with the note above the written note [Ex. 1]. It is important to note that the melodic form of the turn is identical with that of a trill with closing notes. The turn, in the 17th and 18th centuries, was for this reason regarded as synonymous with the short trill; it may be substituted for the latter whenever the tempo is too fast to permit the clear execution of a greater number of notes.

The sign for the turn was originally used only for the first trill of the compound ornament known as a *double cadence*. The formula, illustrated in Ex. 2, occurring frequently in the works of J. S. Bach and his contemporaries, actually constitutes a single ornament; there should be no break between the turn and the ensuing trill. So closely was the sign in question associated with this formula that it was retained for the isolated turn, as was also its name, *double cadence*.

It will be noted that in Ex. 2 the sign for the turn is placed slightly to the right of the written note instead of directly

above it, showing that the main note should be sounded first. In Bach's works this occurs only when another ornament (generally a trill) is to be played immediately afterward, as in the double cadence. Later, however, this practice became quite common, as it appears in the accompanying examples by Mozart [Ex. 3] and Beethoven [Ex. 4].

Until about 1750 the turn was regularly performed as four equal notes, taking up the whole time-value of the written note. J. S. Bach frequently writes out this execution in ordinary notes [see Ex. 5, from *Wt. Cl.* ii, no. 24]. K. P. E. Bach introduced the custom of playing the first two notes of the *Doppelschlag* (as the turn was now called) more rapidly than the last, as in Ex. 6 [Mozart, Violin Sonata G minor]. This execution does not apply, however, to a turn that is played after the written note or to a turn on a very short note.

The practice of indicating the turn by means of small grace notes (which became popular during the classical period) is more ambiguous than the use of the sign, since it is not always easy to determine whether a turn upon a note or a

turn between two notes is intended. Examples 7 and 8 show that the turn upon

the note requires three small notes, while the turn after the note requires four.

The turns of the Romantic composers often contain five or six notes. Their rhythm is exceedingly flexible, the only definite rule being that they are to be performed in the time-value of the preceding note [Ex. 9 and 10: Chopin, Nocturnes op. 37, no. 1 and op. 48, no. 1].

Among the exceptional forms of turn are: (1) the *geschnellter Doppelschlag*, a rapid five-note turn beginning with the main note [Ex. 11, C. P. E. Bach]; this was known in Italy as *gruppo* (*groppo*) or *gruppetto*, in Germany as *Rolle*. (2) The *prallender Doppelschlag*, a turn combined with an appoggiatura and short trill [Ex. 12, C. P. E. Bach]. (3) The *inverted turn*, which is sometimes indicated by the ordinary sign upside down or in a vertical position but is more often repre-

∽ ᎓

sented by tiny notes as in Ex. 13 [Mozart, Rondo in A minor]. P. A.

Tusch [G., from F. *touche, i.e., toccata]. A fanfare played on brass instruments. See *Tucket.

Tutti [It., all]. In orchestral works, particularly in concertos, the parts for the whole orchestra as distinct from that for the soloist.

Tuyau [F.]. Tube, pipe. *T. à anche*, reed pipe; *t. à bouche*, flue pipe.

Twelfth. See *Intervals.

Twelve-tone technique [G. *Zwölf-ton-system*]. A novel system of composition, devised mainly by Arnold Schönberg as an attempt to arrive at constructive methods to take the place of the traditional principles of chord-construction, chord-relationship, tonality, etc. The negation, in *New music, of these principles, already foreshadowed in Debussy's impressionistic devices (*parallel chords; *whole-tone scale, etc.) and, still more so, in the "synthetic chords" of Scriabin (e.g., his *mystic chord), led Schönberg, around 1910, to a type of music which is usually referred to as *atonal, although Schönberg himself strongly resented the use of this term. No matter how it is called, it certainly represents a musical style in which all the tonal principles of 19th-century music are radically denied. Neither the chordal combinations nor the melodic contours show any traces of "tonality" in the broadest sense of the word. The most striking examples of this style are his *Drei Klavierstücke*, op. 11 (1908) and his *Sechs kleine Klavierstücke*, op. 19 (1911). Their amorphous character as well as the expression of high-strung and nervous tension to be found in them has frequently misled observers into considering them as "Romantic" pieces, a designation which, although not entirely without justification, puts them into a wrong place. Actually, they became the point of departure for efforts to arrive at constructive methods of composition, comparable in function and serviceability to the orthodox principles of tonality, form, thematic material, development, etc. These new methods were developed in the second decade of the century and found their first definite expression in the fourth movement of Schönberg's Serenade op. 24 (composed in 1923) and in his Piano Suite op. 25 (1924). The principles of this technique are as follows:

1. Every composition is based upon an arbitrary arrangement of the twelve chromatic tones, called *tone-row* or *series* [G. *Grundgestalt*]. The chosen succession of tones remains unchanged throughout the composition, except for the modifications explained subsequently.

2. The octave position of any tone of the series can be changed at will.

3. In addition to its original form (S) the series is available also in its inversion (S^i), in its retrograde form (S^r), and in its retrograde inversion (S^{ri}).

4. The above four forms of the series can be used in transposition to any step of the chromatic scale. Thus the series becomes available in 48 (12 x 4) modifications.

5. From this basic material melodic progressions and chordal combinations can be formed, the main principles being that the tones, whether arranged hori-

zontally or vertically, must always occur in the arrangement of the series, and that its twelve tones must be presented in full, before the series can be used again. The beginning of the Trio from Schönberg's Suite op. 25 illustrates the practical application of these principles. The example

Schönberg, Suite op. 25

cation of these principles. The example also shows the series of this piece, together with its three basic modifications. The composition starts out with four full statements of the series, the third and fourth in transposition. The continuation is based, not so much on the full series, but on sections of four tones each, marked 1, 2, 3. This method of working with fixed sections of the series constitutes a deviation, or rather a modification, of the principle previously mentioned. It may be noticed that, in the series under consideration, the section 3 is identical (aside from transposition) with its retrograde inversion, 3^{ri}. In the Klavierstück, op. 33a, the three sections of the series are treated even more individually. Meas. 1 brings the entire series in three chords of four tones each, and meas. 2 applies the same treatment to the retrograde inversion of the series, transposed a semitone below. In the following three measures the ri-form of the

Schönberg, Klavierstück op. 33a

series appears in the right hand, but with the succession of the tones changed in each section (11, 10, 9, 12 instead of 12, 11, 10, 9, etc.), and in the left hand a similar treatment is applied to the sections of the original series (2, 3, 4, 1 instead of 1, 2, 3, 4, etc.).

Schönberg's twelve-tone technique has been adopted by Alban Berg first in several movements of his *Lyric Suite* for string quartet (1925–26), and in all his later works, the concert aria *Der Wein* (1929), the *Violin Concerto* (1935), and the opera *Lulu* (1928–35). His Violin Concerto is interesting because its tone-row abandons the "traditional" association of this device with atonality, since it is constructed in such a manner as to include major and minor triads as well as the whole-tone scale [see illustration]. In fact, it should

be noted that, while Schönberg studiously avoids the use of common triads, there is nothing in the twelve-tone technique that

precludes tonal organization. N. Slonimsky has experimented with the "tonal application of the twelve-tone technique," in rows of four mutually exclusive triads [cf. his paper "Plurality of Melodic and Harmonic Systems" in *PAMS*, 1938]. Other composers who have worked with the twelve-tone technique are Anton Webern and, more recently, Ernst Krenek (opera *Karl V*, 1932; Sixth String Quartet, op. 78; Twelve Short Piano Pieces, op. 83).

A different twelve-tone technique was developed by Josef Hauer who starts from the fact that there exist 479,001,600 (i.e., 1.2.3.4... .12 = 12!) different combinations of twelve tones, a number which is reduced to its 12th part (11!) by disregarding transpositions. Each such series is divided into halves of 6 notes each, and all series which have the same notes in their first as well as their second half are put into one group, called *trope*, of which there exist, according to Hauer, 44 [a calculation shows that there actually are $77 \left(\dfrac{11!}{6! \times 6!} \right)$ such groups]. Each trope, then, represents in a way a key with two fundamental chords, and the movement from one trope to another is comparable to modulation.

Lit.: E. Krenek, *Studies in Counterpoint* (1940); R. S. Hill, "Schoenberg's Tone-Rows . . ." (*MQ* xxii); G. Perle, "Evolution of the Tone-Row" (*MR* ii); A. Weiss, "The Lyceum of Schönberg" (*MM* 1932); *GD*, Suppl. Vol., 635ff (bibl.); E. Krenek, in *MR* iv.

Two-step. See under *One-step.

Tymbalon, tymbal. An early Provençal kettledrum [see *Timbale].

Tympanon, tympanum. Greek, Roman, and humanistic name for big drums or kettledrums. Medieval writers (e.g., Giraldus Cambrensis) also used the name instead of *cymbalon*, i.e., dulcimer. In modern writings tympani occurs as a misspelling of timpani.

Tyrolienne. A Tyrolean type of folk song, in the rhythm of a *Ländler, and sung with that sudden change from the chest voice to the falsetto known as *Yodel. The name is also used for operatic ballets (e.g., Rossini, *Guillaume Tell*, Act III) and popular pieces written in the style of Tyrolean folk dance.

U

U.C. *Una corde.

'Ud [Arabic, wood]. See *Lute, history.

Über- [G., over, above]. *Überblasen*, to overblow; *Übergang*, transition; *übergreifen*, to cross the hands (in piano playing); *Überleitung*, transition; *übermässig*, augmented (for intervals); *überschlagen*, to cross the hands; *übersetzen*, to put over (in piano fingering).

Übung [G.]. Exercise, study.

Uilleann pipes [from Irish *uillean*, elbow]. The Irish *bagpipe the name of which was later corrupted into *union pipes*.

Ukulele. A Hawaiian instrument of the guitar family, with four strings and a long finger board, usually with frets. It developed from a Portuguese guitar, called *machete* [see *Guitar family] and became popular in the United States about 1920. The notation for this instrument follows the principles used in the lute tablatures of the 16th century, but was invented independently [see *Tablatures VI]. Illustration on p. 314.

Umfang [G.]. Compass, range (of a voice, etc.).

Umkehrung [G.]. Inversion (of intervals, chords, or melodies).

Umstimmen [G.]. To change the tuning, e.g., of kettledrums.

Una corda [It., one string]. In piano playing, a direction (abbr. *u.c.*) to use the left pedal (soft pedal; F. *petite pédale*; G. *Verschiebung*) which, by moving the entire action, keyboard and hammers, a little to the right side, causes the hammer to strike a single string (in modern instruments usually two strings) instead of all

three. The indication is canceled by "tre corde" or "tutte le corde" (*t.c.*). Beethoven, who was the first to indicate the use of *una corda*, not only calls for a gradation in three steps: *una corda, due, e poi tre corde* (G major Concerto, op. 58, slow movement), but even for a gradual execution of the shift: *poco a poco due corde* (Piano Sonata op. 101, slow movement). The latter request represents, no doubt, an unattainable ideal. See *Mute.

Unda maris. See under *Vox angelica.

Undezime [G.]. Eleventh.

Unequal temperament [G. *Ungleichschwebende Temperatur*]. A *temperament which stands midway between pure intonation and equal temperament, i.e., any system of tuning in which the pure intervals are still retained for some keys (C, G, F), adjustments being made for the more remote keys, with the result that the most remote keys (G-sharp, C-sharp) cannot be used. Various systems were in use prior to the general acceptance of equal temperament, e.g., the mean-tone system (which by some writers is not considered an unequal temperament; cf. *GD* v, 301), and the systems of Euler, Kirnberger. See *Temperament.

Unequal voices. Mixed male and female voices.

Unfinished Symphony. Schubert's Symphony no. 8 in B minor, so called because only the first two movements exist. These were written as early as 1822, six years before the composer's death. The work had its first performance in 1865.

Ungebunden [G.]. Unconstrained, free.

Ungeduldig [G.]. Impatient.

Ungezwungen [G.]. Easy going, natural.

Ungrader Takt [G.]. Uneven, i.e., triple meter.

Unheimlich [G.]. Uncanny.

Union pipes. See *Uillean pipes.

Unison [from It. *unisono*, one sound; F. *unisson*; G. *Einklang*]. (1) Playing of the same notes or the same melody by various instruments or by the whole orchestra, either at exactly the same pitch or in a different octave, e.g., violin and cello in unison (*all' unisono*). — (2) The pseudo-interval formed by a tone and its duplication [G. *Prime*], e.g., c–c, as distinguished from the second, c–d, etc.

Unit organ. A modern type of organ in which one rank of pipes is arranged to do duty for several stops through the medium of an electric couple device. Thus an extended rank of 85 Principal pipes can be employed to form 16′ Principal, 8′ Principal, and 4′ Octave. In the straight organ 183 pipes would be necessary to form these three stops, 61 for each. Unification, or *Extension* as it is sometimes called, is extensively used for cinema organs, and is also useful for very small organs where space is at a premium, or on a Pedal department. Its general acceptance is prohibited chiefly by the fact that in the playing of contrapuntal music there occur numerous gaps, e.g., whenever a C in a lower part sounds against its octave in a higher part.

Unmerklich [G.]. Imperceptibly.

Un peu [F.]. A little.

Unruhig [G.]. Restless.

Unter- [G., below, under]. *Unterdominante*, subdominant; *Untermediante*, submediant; *untersetzen*, to put under (the thumb in piano playing); *Unterstimme*, lower, or lowest part; *Untertaste*, white key; *Unterwerk*, choir organ.

Up-beat [G. *Auftakt*]. One or several initial notes of a melody which occur before the first bar-line. The up-beat plays a central part in a theory of Riemann and others, according to which every melody or phrase begins with an up-beat (real or imaginary). This is a gross exaggeration of the pertinent observation that the beginning or ending of a phrase frequently does not coincide with the bar-line (particularly in the music of Bach). See *Phrasing ("Auftaktigkeit").

Urlinie, Ursatz [G.]. Terms coined by the German musicologist Heinrich Schenker (1868–1935) which may be translated "fundamental line," "fundamental structure." They represent the attempt to discover, in any composition, an underlying skeleton structure and to show that the skeleton structures of all compositions written by the great masters — roughly from Bach to Brahms —follow certain fundamental principles and patterns of structure. By a process of stepwise reduction Schenker's analysis leads from the actual composition, the "foreground," to the structural tone pattern in the "background," i.e., the *Ursatz*. Its treble line is the *Urlinie*, which Schenker in his earlier studies considered exclusively, but which he later discarded completely as an independent phenomenon, replacing it by the full Ursatz.

The analysis of the theme from the last movement of Beethoven's Ninth Symphony may serve as an example. The well-known melody itself is the "foreground," and Ex. 1a shows the "middleground" which represents the first phase of the reduction of the actual music to its basic structure (the Arabic numerals refer to the measures of the original melody). The reduction leads from this stage to the "background" which is shown in Ex. 1b; this is the Ursatz. Important elements of this, as of every, structural pattern are the "motions" (*Züge*) of the upper part, or parts [in our example it is a "motion of a third" (*Terz-Zug*); the numerals 3̂, 2̂, 1̂, signify scale degrees] and the "breaking-up" of an otherwise continuous tonic by a î–ŝ–î movement of the bass (*Bassbrechung*).

It is not the purpose of this kind of analysis to show that all the various compositions can be reduced to a few types of "fundamental structures." Naturally, the analysis has to proceed from the foreground to the background, but its results should be read in the opposite direction. Schenker's analysis does not seek to prove that ultimately all compositions are more or less alike; it seeks to demonstrate how a few basic patterns miraculously unfold into the infinite variety, the broad and rich life, of the actual compositions. Accordingly, its main interest does not lie in the background itself, but in the point where it shows *how* background and foreground are connected: the middleground. For instance, an analysis of the second song from Schumann's "Dichterliebe" leads to the same Ursatz as Beethoven's melody. The difference lies in the middleground, which appears more complex here — so complex indeed that two successive reductions become necessary, resulting in two levels of middleground.

It is the middleground where hidden relations are revealed and the secret meaning of many a detail finds its explanation. It is the middleground where the work of the genius can be distinguished from the work of the lesser talent. An Ursatz can be found in any music, be it great or poor; without such a skeleton music would not move at all. In poor music, however, the relation between foreground and background will appear primitive, without interest. Only the creation of the genius has the density of organic structure which in turn produces such interesting middleground pictures as the one in Ex. 2 (Bach, 12 Little Preludes, no. 3).

By no means should the development from background through middleground

to foreground be interpreted in a temporal sense, as if the actual creation of a

composition proceeded from one to the other as through successive stages. The relation between the actual music and its Ursatz is completely subconscious to the composer and has nothing whatsoever to do with the creative process.

Schenker applied the Ursatz analysis mostly to compositions of the period from Bach through Brahms (excluding Wagner). His pupils have shown that the results are equally satisfactory when the method is applied to medieval music; there is no doubt that only slight modifications are necessary to make it equally applicable to late Romantic music (Wagner, Bruckner). No attempts have been made as yet to study the Ursatz problem in relation to 20th-century music.

Lit.: H. Schenker, *Der Tonwille* (pamphlets); *id.*, *Das Meisterwerk in der Musik*, 3 vols. (1926–29); *id.*, †*Fünf Urlinie-Tafeln* (1932); A. T. Katz, in *MQ* xxi; R. Sessions, in *MM* xii, no. 4; W. Riezler, in *DM* xxii, no. 7.   V. Z.

Ut. The first of the Guidonian syllables of solmization [see *Hexachord]. In French and Italian nomenclature, name for C [see *Pitch names]. Ut-re-mi-fa-sol-la is used as a title for pieces (Sweelinck, and others) based on the tones of the hexachord.

Utility music. See *Gebrauchsmusik.

Ut supra [L.]. As above, as before.

V

V. Abbr. for (1) *vide*, i.e., "see." (2) Violin (also V°); VV, violins. (3) Voci, e.g., 3 v, for three voices. (4) In liturgical books, V̸ means *verse.

Va. Abbreviation for viola.

Vacillando [It.]. Wavering.

Vagans [L., rambling, i.e., part]. In 15th- and 16th-century polyphony, name for a *part which is designed chiefly to fill in the harmony and which, therefore, has a less natural design than the others, frequently jumping up and down in sevenths, octaves, etc. In compositions of the early Burgundian school (Cesaris, Dufay), the contra-tenor usually is a *vagans*. For other explanations of the term, cf. the articles in *RiML* and *GD*.

Vaghezza, Con [It.]. With charm.

Vago [It.]. Charming, graceful.

Valkyrie, The. See *Ring des Nibelungen.

Valor [L., value]. In mensural notation, same as *integer valor* [see *Proportions].

Valse [F.]. Waltz.

Valve [F. *piston*; G. *Ventil*; It. *pistone*]. A mechanism, invented by Blühmel in 1813, by which all the tones of the chromatic scale become available on brass instruments. The principle of the construction is to add to the proper pipe of the instrument short additional pieces of tubing which are connected with the main pipe in such a manner that, upon depressing a knob, the wind is compelled to make the detour through this additional tubing so that the sounding length of the pipe is increased and the instrument, normally, for example, in B-flat, is momentarily changed to one pitched in A or A-flat. Usually horns and trumpets have three valves which lower the pitch a semitone, a wholetone, and a minor third respectively. By combining two or all three valves the pitch

can be lowered by six semitones, resulting in a complete chromatic scale [see *Wind instruments IV (c)]. It should be noted that the simultaneous use of two (even more, of three) valves produces tones which are somewhat too sharp, since an additional tubing which is calculated to lower the normal pipe by a semitone is, of course, a little too short to produce the same effect on a pipe which is already lengthened by another tubing. This drawback is corrected in the "compensating valves" (numerous patents; cf. *GD* v, 438) and avoided in Adolphe Sax's "ascending valves" which shorten the original pipe. Neither method, however, has gained acceptance.

For the closing and opening of the by-path two types of valves are in use, piston valves and rotary (or cylinder) valves. In the former a piston works up and down in a casing. The latter, which is preferred in the United States and on the Continent, though not in England, is a four-way stop-cock turning in a cylindrical case in the plane of the instrument, two of its four ways forming part of the main pipe, the other two, on its rotating through a quadrant of the circle, admitting it to the bypath. The practical results are the same in both types. See *Horn; *Trumpet; *Tuba; *Wind instruments IV (c).

Valve instruments. Brass instruments provided with a *valve mechanism. Today all the brass instruments (trumpets, horns, tubas, etc.) are built with valves except the trombone. The terms valve horn, valve trumpet, etc., distinguish the modern types from the earlier natural or keyed types.

Vamp. An extemporized accompaniment consisting of simple chords. Hence, vamping tutor, a book of instruction in this type of accompaniment.

Vamphorn. A speaking tube of 2 to 8 feet in length which was used as a megaphone in English churches during the 18th and 19th centuries, to give out notices.

Vaporeux [F.]. "Vaporous," hazy.

Variante [G.]. In H. Riemann's system of harmonic analysis, term for parallel key (substitution of minor for major, or vice versa).

Variation canzona. See *Canzona (5), I.

Variations. The variation or, more fully, the theme with variations, is a musical form based upon the principle of presenting a musical idea (theme) in an arbitrary number of modifications (from 4 to 30 or more), each of these being a "variation." Variations appear as independent compositions (Bach's Goldberg Variations; Beethoven's Diabelli Variations) or as a movement of a sonata, usually the slow movement (Beethoven's Appassionata, Ninth Symphony).

I. *Theme.* The theme is usually a simple tune in binary form, ranging in length between 16 and 32 measures and frequently borrowed from other composers (e.g., Beethoven's variations on a theme by Diabelli, or Brahms's variations on a theme by Handel). There exists, however, a special class of variations whose theme is not a complete tune but is only a four- or eight-measure scheme of harmonies or a bass line of the same length. Under this class fall the examples known as *chaconne, passacaglia, *ground, and *basso ostinato. To consider these forms as different from or even opposed to "theme with variations," as is done by some writers, is scarcely justifiable, since variation technique is basic for one as for the other. The fundamental difference between the two classes of variations might be fittingly expressed by the terms *sectional variations* and *continuous variations.* The former term applies to those examples in which the theme is a full-grown and complete tune calling for a stop at its end and consequently at the end of each variation (aside from exceptional cases in which the composer pre-

scribes *segue subito* for the purpose of a special effect); the latter, to those in which the theme is only a short succession of harmonies to be repeated over and over again without any interruption. Another important difference between the two classes is that in the former a theme always has a distinct melody while in the latter it consists only of a scheme of harmonies which is frequently, but not necessarily, represented by a reiterated bass. To distinguish between the two classes as "variations of a melody" and "variations of a bass" is not very fortunate, since there exist numerous chaconnes and passacaglias which are lacking a clearly designed bass line [see *Chaconne and passacaglia]. At any rate, the length or shortness of the theme and its sectional or continuous character are more pertinent marks of distinction than the presence or lack of a bass. Border cases are the *strophic basses of the 17th century, whose theme is a bass of such extension and completeness that a sectional structure results. The subsequent explanations refer chiefly to the normal (sectional) type of "theme with variations."

II. *The Fixed Elements.* It is evident that a variation of a theme will always have some features in common with the theme, and also that it will deviate from the theme in other traits. As regards the former point of view, a distinction is frequently made between variations in which the original melody is preserved, these being called *melodic variations,* and those in which the original harmonies are preserved, these being called *structural* or *harmonic variations* [cf. the article in *GD* which, however, is not always consistent in the use of the last two terms]. This distinction is unsatisfactory for various reasons. First, the terminology is unfortunate, since the adjectives "melodic" and "harmonic" are used with reference to the fixed (i.e., unchanged) features while similar terms such as "rhythmic variation," "contrapuntal variation," "canonic variation" are naturally and generally understood to refer to the variable and distinctive features of the variation. As a matter of fact, the terms "melodic variations" and "harmonic variations" are frequently used in the exact opposite meaning, a usage which deserves preference and which is adopted in the present explanations [see below]. Second, aside from the ambiguity of meaning, the dichotomy as such has little value, since the two types — whatever they are called — are not really of similar or comparable importance. Stability of the harmonic scheme (at least in its main outlines) is a prerequisite for practically all variations, except the entirely free variations of modern composers (since Brahms). Stability of the melody is an additional restriction which was traditionally observed in the early period of variation (16th, 17th centuries) but is the exception rather than the rule with composers such as Mozart, Beethoven, Schubert, Brahms.

In studying the question of the fixed elements it is essential to bear in mind that the main bond of connection between the theme and any variation is the scheme of harmonies. Starting from the harmonically fixed variation as the normal type, we find two others, one showing a greater, the other a lesser degree of restriction to the theme. The former is that in which, in addition to the harmonies, the melody of the theme is kept more or less intact (a mere ornamentation of the melody, which is one of the most frequent devices of variation, is not considered as a new melody, so that all examples of "ornamenting variation" would fall in the present category). The latter is that in which the harmonies deviate deliberately from the original scheme so that only its larger outlines are preserved, such as the number of measures, the structure of sections and phrases, the cadential endings. For the sake of convenience these three categories, (1) the harmonically and melodically fixed, (2) the harmonically fixed, and the (3) structurally fixed, will be referred to here as the *categories A, B, C*. In order to make the classification complete, a fourth *category, D*, should be reserved for the entirely free variations of recent date in which even the structural outlines of the theme are no longer recognizable.

As is natural to assume, these four categories are not only of methodical but also of historical significance. Generally speaking, category A prevails throughout the 16th and 17th centuries, category B throughout the classical period, category C is frequent among the Romantic composers, and D is characteristic of the most recent style (d'Indy, Reger, R. Strauss). It should be noted, however, that all the variations of the class referred to previously [see I] as continuous variations belong to the category B (not A), since here the thematic substance does not include a melody so that by necessity each variation will be melodically independent. Since this type of variations prevailed mainly during the Baroque era, it appears that, in this period, two categories of variations existed side by side, category A for the sectional variations (such as Scheidt's variations on a Passamezzo), and category B for the continuous variations (passacaglias, chaconnes, grounds).

It may be mentioned that there is still another category of fixation, which would have to be termed "melodically fixed," and which includes variations in which the melody is retained but the harmonies are altered. In the classical period this occurs only exceptionally as a "trick," an instance in point being the variation no. 6 of Beethoven's Eroica Variations, op. 35, in which the original melody is harmonized in C minor instead of E-flat major. This method attains a somewhat greater significance, however, in the contrapuntal variations of the Baroque, in which the melody is treated as a cantus firmus [cf., e.g., variation no. 4 of Samuel Scheidt's *Wehe Windgen wehe*; *DdT* 1].

III. *The Variable Elements*. Taking the consideration of the fixed elements as a point of departure, the interest now turns to the question as to how variety is achieved in a variation. Although it is difficult to generalize, certain standard procedures of composers can be singled out. In the strictest category, A, the most frequent procedure is to ornament the melody (*ornamenting variation*; see Ex. 1). Another method, particularly frequent in the 17th century, is to modify the contrapuntal web by the introduction of characteristic figures, or by placing the melody in one of the lower parts (*contrapuntal variation*; see Ex. 2). Under cate-

gory B we find practically all the variations of the classical period, except for the ornamenting variations. Within this large field — the center-piece of the whole pic-

ture, as it were — some typical procedures may be singled out as follows: (a) *melodic variations*, i.e. those in which a new melody is invented to the original scheme of harmonies [Ex. 3]. Perhaps the earliest instances of the full-scale application of this method are Bach's Goldberg Variations. Another striking example is the first variation in the final movement of Beethoven's Piano Sonata, op. 109. Other types are (b) the *figural variation* in which a characteristic figure is employed throughout [Ex. 4]; the *canonic variation* [Ex. 5]; the *harmonic variation* [Ex. 6]; the *tempo variation* involving a change of tempo; the *modal variation* involving a change from the major to the minor mode or vice versa; and the *character variation* which bestows upon the variation a special character such as that of a dance, a military march, etc. The last three methods may be summarily illustrated by our Ex. 7. Naturally, most of these procedures may occur in any of the four categories, except for the ornamenting variation which is restricted to category A, the melodic variation which cannot occur in this category, and the harmonic variation which belongs to category C.

IV. *History.* a. (−1600). Of all the forms of present-day music none has a longer and more continuous history than the variation. The earliest extant example of a theme with variations is a composition of the late 14th century, "Di molen van pariis" (The Windmills of Paris). [Cf. R. Haas, *Musikalische Aufführungspraxis*, pp. 103f.] This, however, is an isolated specimen. The history proper of variations starts with the rise of lute and keyboard music in the early 16th century. Judging from the preserved examples, Spain and England have about an equal claim to precedence, the latter country in the field of continuous variations (Aston's *Hornepype, Mylady Carey's *Dompe, both c. 1525; see *Ostinato), the former in this field as well as in that of the sectional variations based on a fully developed theme (lute variations by Narvaez, 1538; cf. *HAM*, no. 122; *ApMZ* ii). The advanced style of the Hornepype as well as of Narvaez' variations points to a prehistory of considerable length, all traces of which are lost. By 1550 the evolution of the Spanish variations had come to its peak and close in the masterworks of Antonio de Cabezon (1510–66; cf. *HAM*, no. 134). Cabezon's variations, called *diferencias [see also *Glosa], are mostly of the contrapuntal type which, needless to say, prevails also in the variations of the later masters (Sweelinck, Scheidt, Frescobaldi). Toward the end of the 16th century the English virginalists (Byrd, Bull, Munday, Gibbons) established a novel trend in variation technique by exploring the figural variation, frequently in a brilliant virtuoso style (rapid scales, broken chord figures, figures in parallel thirds, etc.; cf. *HAM*, no. 177). While with Byrd the technical and the musical interest are well in balance, Bull's variations are conspicuous for their exploitation of the former aspect, frequently at the expense of the latter. Another great master of the variation arose in Sweelinck who took over the technical achievements of the virginalists, but used them with superior ingenuity. His variations on "Mein junges Leben hat ein End" [*TaAM* iii] figure among the dozen of the greatest masterworks in this form. Measured by this standard, the variations of his pupil Scheidt frequently appear somewhat dull and monotonous [cf. the examples by Sweelinck and Scheidt in *RMC* v, 199ff] although a certain reservedness and simplicity raises them beyond the level of showy display which is characteristic of John Bull [cf. *HAM*, no. 196].

b. (1600–1750). In Italy the traceable history of variations starts with the Neapolitan composers Valente, Trabaci, and Mayone who, probably influenced by Cabezon, wrote *partitas on popular tunes such as *Romanesca, *Ruggiero, Zefiro, etc. [see also *Folia]. Their tradition was continued, with greater artistic inspiration, in the numerous partitas of Frescobaldi which, owing to their intellectual refinement, are likely to interest the connoisseur rather than the average listener [cf. *HAM*, no. 192; also 199]. In Froberger's (1616–67) partitas "Auff die Meyerin" we encounter the first examples of character variations, in the style of a courante or sarabande. These are indicative of a trend towards merging the form of variations with that of the *suite which is quite frequently encountered in the music of the Baroque. For instance, Wolfgang Ebner's 36 "Variazioni sopra un' aria dell' Imperatore Ferdinando III" [*c*. 1660; *TaAM* vii] fall into three groups of twelve variations each, the first dozen containing those in the style of an allemande, the second and third those in the styles of the courante and sarabande [regarding the absence of the gigue, see under *Suite III]. A remarkable specimen is Alessandro Poglietti's "Aria allemagna" (1677; *TaAM* viii) which consists mainly of programmatic character variations such as Lyra, Böhmisch Dudlsackh, Holländisch Flageolett, Bayrische Schalmei, Alter Weiber Conduct, Gaugler Seiltantz, Französische Baiselemens (French Kiss-the-hand). Although not of a very refined taste, these pieces are amusing portrayals or caricatures forming together a sort of pageant in honor of the Austrian Empress Maddalena Theresa to whom the work was dedicated in 1677. Of particular importance is the German 17th-century tradition of variations based upon a chorale [see *Chorale partita]. For other types, see *Chaconne and passacaglia; *Ground; *Strophic bass; *Noel. At the end of the Baroque period stand as a fitting climax Bach's *Goldberg Variations in which, as has been pointed out previously, the variation type referred to as category B prevails for the first time.

c. (1750–1900). In comparison to the rather elaborate variation technique of the Baroque, that of Mozart's pianoforte variations appears simple and somewhat schematic although the results certainly do not lack in charm all their own. Mozart usually sets out with a group of ornamenting variations in triplets and sixteenth-notes, then turns to some more special methods such as pianistic or contrapuntal devices, follows up with a slow variation and concludes with a quick variation in changed meter (duple instead of triple or vice versa). Haydn's greatest contributions to the repertory are found in his symphonies and, particularly, in his late quartets, above all the Emperor Quartet (op. 76, no. 4) with its variations on "Gott erhalte Franz den Kaiser." With Beethoven the variation form reached its all-time peak. He replaced the more conventional methods, particularly that of ornamentation, by a wealth of individual treatments and ideas which evades all attempts at summary description. He also was the first to organize the mere succession of variations into contrasting groups, a procedure which is particularly patent in his "continuous" variations in C minor op. 32 (sometimes described as a chaconne). In his "Eroica" Variations op. 35 he prefaces the theme by a short group of "negative variations," so to speak, which are based on the bass motive only. His Diabelli Variations op. 120 (1823) are an incomparable treasure of ingenuity, while in the variations of his late quartets and pianoforte sonatas technical methods are sublimated into a new realm of transcendental vision, so that even the most conventional methods attain a new significance. Nowhere is this transformation more clearly patent than in the "ornamenting" variations of the pianoforte sonatas opp. 106 and 111.

Hardly second to Beethoven is Franz Schubert in such great though little known works as his variations for four hands in B minor and in A-flat major, compositions which are quite superior to his more popular variations for two hands in B-flat major. Schumann's most remarkable contributions are the Études Symphoniques which open the field of free variations since some of them derive not more from the theme than a germinating motive. In his Andante and Variations for two pianos, on the other hand, he falls into his habit of exploiting *ad nauseam* a somewhat obtrusive figure or rhythm, as he so frequently does in his later works.

Franz Liszt made very frequent and, needless to say, effective use of a brilliant and highly virtuoso-like variation technique in many of his Rhapsodies and, particularly, in his variations on the theme by Paganini (Paganini Etudes, no. 6) which was also used by Brahms as a theme

for a series of extremely difficult and extremely interesting variations. The fame of Brahms as a master of this form rests, however, on his Variations on a Theme by Handel (op. 24) for pianoforte, and on his orchestral Variations on a Theme by Haydn op. 56 (also for two pianos). His variations belong mostly to our category C, owing to the freedom with which he treats the harmonies without giving up the structural outlines of the theme. Following the precedent of Beethoven's Eroica and Diabelli Variations he usually climaxes the series of variations with an elaborate fugue (in the case of the Haydn variations this is replaced by a passacaglia).

d. (1900–present). Shortly before 1900 two important examples of "free variation" were written, Vincent d'Indy's Istar Variations (1896) and Richard Strauss's Don Quixote (1897). The former are "variations in the reverse" in so far as the "theme" (properly, two thematic motives) appears at the end, a procedure of "disrobing" which is insinuated in the title, Istar being the Egyptian goddess of Sin. In comparison with these two works, the treatment of Elgar's *Enigma Variations is considerably more conventional, approximately along the lines of Schumann's Études Symphoniques. The last composer to work along these lines was Max Reger, who wrote numerous variations for pianoforte, organ, and orchestra, among which the Pianoforte Variations on a Theme by Bach (op. 81, 1904) and the Orchestral Variations on a Theme by Mozart (op. 132, 1912?) are outstanding, while his Pianoforte Variations on a Theme by Telemann (op. 134, 1914) show the attempt, not very successful, to revert to the tradition of the Mozart period. The composers of the youngest generation have shown comparatively more interest in the Baroque type of the chaconne (Busoni, Krenek) than in the traditional type of 19th-century variation.

Lit.: R. Gress, *Die Entwicklung der Klavier-Variation von A. Gabrieli bis zu J. S. Bach* (1929); E. Reichert, *Die Variations-Arbeit bei Haydn* (Diss. Vienna

1926); V. Luttmann, *Brahms' Werke in Variationsform* (Diss. Vienna 1926); W. Schwarz, *Robert Schumann und die Variation* (1932); P. Mies, in *AMF* ii (Mozart); V. Luythlen, in *StM* xiv (Brahms).

Varsovienne. A Polish dance, named after the city of Warsaw, in slow mazurka rhythm, usually with an accented dotted note on the first beat of each second and fourth measure. It was popular in the ballrooms from about 1850 to 1870.

Vater unser [G., father our]. German version of the Lord's Prayer [*Pater noster*]. It is sung as a hymn (*Choral*) to a 16th-century melody (by Luther?), which has been used as a basis of compositions by Hans Leo Hassler (10 choral settings in *Psalmen und Christlich Gesäng*, 1607; new ed. by Saalfeld), Ulrich Steigleder (*Tabulaturbuch, Das Vaterunser ... vierzigmal variiert*, 1627), Bach (organ chorales), and others. Cf. *HAM*, no. 190a–e.

Vatican Edition (Editio Vaticana). See *Liturgical books II.

Vaudeville [F., from *vaux de Vire*, the valley of Vire, birthplace of a 15th-century poet who is said to have been the originator of the vaudeville; another, less favored, etymology is *voix de ville*, voices of the town, or *à vau de ville*, all about the town]. In the 17th and 18th centuries, a short satirical poem sung to a melody of popular character. One and the same melody commonly served for many different texts written in the same poetic meter. The vaudeville was the principal type of song in the early opéra-comique (1715–c. 1735). A large collection of such songs may be found in *Le Théatre de la foire* (Paris, 1734–37) and in *La Clé du Caveau* (4th ed., 1872). In the 19th century, vaudeville was the name given in France to short comedies interspersed with simple popular songs.   D. J. G.

Vcl. Abbreviation for violoncello.

Velato [It.]. Veiled.

Veloce [It.]. Quick.

Venetian School. A 16th-century school of Flemish and Italian composers working in Venice. It was inaugurated by Adriaen Willaert (c. 1485–1562) and included, among others, Andrea Gabrieli (c. 1510–86), Cypriano de Rore (1516–65) — both pupils of Willaert — Joseffo Guami (c. 1540–1611), Giovanni Gabrieli (1557–1612), Giovanni Croce (c. 1557–1609), the organ composers Jacques Buus (–1565), Annibale Padovano (1527–75), Vincenzo Bell'Haver (c. 1530–88), Claudio Merulo (1533–1604), and the theorists Niccola Vicentino (1511–72) and Gioseffo Zarlino (1517–90).

While the contemporary *Roman School represents the final high-point of a long development of polyphonic music, the Venetian School is important mainly on account of its novel ideas and progressive tendencies which, together with the Florentine *monody, paved the way for the 17th century. Among these contributions are Willaert's chromaticism and freer use of modulations, the toccata style of A. Gabrieli and Merulo, Vicentino's daring speculations and experiments with quarter-tones [see *Arcicembalo], Zarlino's investigations of *just intonation, *dualism, and, to some extent, equal temperament; finally and above all, Giovanni Gabrieli's magnificent "Venetian style" with its broad masses of sound, *polychoral treatment, *echo effects, and progressive use of instruments which makes him the "father of orchestration" [see *Orchestration]. The movement spread particularly to Germany where Jacob Gallus (Handl, 1550–91), Hieronimus Praetorius (1560–1629), Hans Leo Hassler (1564–1621), and Michael Praetorius (1571–1621) are the most important representatives of the Venetian style (*Deutschvenezianer*).

Although the novelty of the Florentine monody (c. 1600) for some time put the Venetian School into an eclipse, the latter continued to exercise a lasting influence throughout the Baroque period, a period which, in fact, is rooted equally in Florence (vocal music) and in Venice (instrumental music) [see *Baroque].

Lit.: C. von Winterfeld, *Johannes Gabrieli und sein Zeitalter* (1834).

Venetian swell. See *Swell.

Venezuela. During the Colonial period and the early years of Independence, Venezuela had what was probably the most homogeneous and most flourishing school of music in the whole of South America. It was, moreover, a school of music in the strictest sense of the term, since its representative figures were pupils of the same teacher and followed the same general style. The founder of this school was Juan Manuel Olivares, who founded a philharmonic society in the capital around 1750. Olivares was also the director of a music academy founded by Pedro Palacios y Sojo (d. *c.* 1800), another eminent figure in the early musical life of Venezuela. Other notable members of this school were José Francisco Velásquez, José Antonio Caro de Boesi, José Cayetano Carreño, José Lorenzo Montero, and José Luis Landaeta (who in 1811 composed the Venezuelan National Anthem). The greatest composer of this period, and the most famous produced by Venezuela, was José Angel Lamas (d. 1814), author of the celebrated "Popule meus" (1806) which the Venezuelans regard as a sort of unofficial national hymn. Lamas, like the other composers mentioned above, was primarily a composer of church music. Many MS compositions by these musicians have been preserved in the archives of the Escuela de Música of Caracas. They display an admirable technique, with strong Italian influences. Mention should also be made of Lino Gallardo who from 1819 was director of the Music Academy of Caracas and conductor of the concerts of the Philharmonic Society.

During the 19th century the outstanding composers were José Angel Montero (1839–81), choirmaster of Caracas Cathedral, who composed, in addition to religious music, 15 zarzuelas and the opera *Virginia* (1873); Felipe Larrazábal (1816–73), pianist and composer of a celebrated trio for piano, violin, and cello; and Federico Villena (1835–*c.* 1900), a prolific composer of Romantic tendencies.

Turning to the contemporary scene we find that the composers of today have carefully cultivated their musical heritage, in both its artistic and folklore aspects. Juan Bautista Plaza (b. 1898), archivist of the Escuela de Música, has made a special study of Colonial music and has produced a copious amount of original work in both secular and sacred forms. Vicente Emilio Sojo (b. 1887) is director of the choral society, "Orfeón Lamas," of the Escuela de Música, and of the Orquesta Sinfónica. He has composed church and chamber music, choral works, and songs, and has also collected and harmonized Venezuelan folk songs. Juan Lecuna (b. 1898), for several years a diplomatic attaché in Washington, has published four pieces for piano based on Venezuelan traditional dances, and has in MS various chamber music works. María Luisa Escobar (b. 1903) has specialized in stylizations of Venezuelan folk music. Other composers who may be mentioned are Moisés Moleiro, José Antonio Calcaño, Eduardo Plaza, José Antonio Estévez, and Evencio Castellanos. Reynaldo Hahn (b. 1875), though a native of Caracas, was taken to France as a child and is generally considered French.

Venezuela has produced one of the world's greatest pianists in the person of Teresa Carreño (1853–1917), the teacher of Edward MacDowell. She composed a festival hymn for the Bolivar centenary (1883), also many pieces for piano, a string quartet, etc.

The most characteristic Venezuelan folk dance is the *joropo, in lively tempo and ¾ rhythm, strongly accented. In the coastal region of Venezuela the joropo and other popular forms have undergone considerable Negro influence.

Lit.: José A. Calcaño, *Contribución al estudio de la música en Venezuela* (Caracas, 1939); Baltasar de Matallāna, *La música indígena Taurepan* (Caracas, 1939); M. de Lara, "Ritmo y melodía nativos de Venezuela" (*Boletin latinoamericano de musica*, vol. iii, 1937); J. B. Plaza, "Music in Caracas . . . (1770–1811)" (*MQ* xxix, no. 2). G. C.

Veni Sancte Spiritus. See *Sequence (2).

Venite exultemus. See *Psalmody III.

Vent [F.]. Wind. *Instruments à vent*, wind instruments.

Ventil [G.], **ventile** [It.]. Valve. *Ventilhorn*, i.e., valve horn.

Veränderungen [G.]. Variations.

Verbunko. *See Hungarian music II.

Verdoppeln [G.]. To double. See *Doubling.

Vergleichende Musikwissenschaft [G.]. Comparative musicology.

Vergnügt [G.]. Gay.

Vergrösserung [G.]. Augmentation.

Verhallend [G.]. Fading away.

Verismo [It., realism]. An Italian operatic school of the late 19th century which represents the musical counterpart of the literary "realism" of Zola, Flaubert, Ibsen, and others. Instead of the heroic, exalted libretti of the preceding operas which practically always dealt with mythological or historical matters, realistic subjects from everyday life were chosen. As a matter of course coloratura arias and other features of the earlier Italian opera were abandoned in favor of a melodramatic recitative which is frequently much more naturalistic than Wagner's "unending melody." Mascagni's *Cavalleria Rusticana* of 1890 (dealing with scenes from peasant life) and Leoncavallo's *Pagliacci* of 1892 (circus life) were the first products of the new movement, which were followed, in 1900, by the Frenchman Charpentier's *Louise.* Puccini's *La Bohème* (1896) represents a somewhat modified verismo of a more lyrical character. Cf. M. Rinaldi, *Musica e verismo* (1932).

Verkaufte Braut, Die [G.]. See *Bartered Bride, The.

Verklärt [G.]. Transfigured, supernatural.

Verkleinerung, Verkürzung [G.]. Diminution (of a fugal subject).

Verlierend [G.]. "Losing," fading out.

Verlöschend [G.]. "Extinguishing," fading out.

Vermindert [G.]. Diminished (interval).

Vers [F., G.]. (1) See *Verse. — (2) In the tradition of the Provençal *troubadours, *vers* denotes a very ancient type of song characterized by the absence of formal structure, such as exists with the canzo, rondeau, ballade, virelai; in other words, a through-composed melody, which was repeated with the various stanzas of the poem. Examples in *HAM*, no. 18a; *BeMMR*, 106; *ReMMA*, 229.

Verschiebung [G.]. Soft pedal. See *Una corda; *Mute.

Verschwindend [G.]. Disappearing, i.e., fading out.

Verse [L. *versus*; F. *vers*; G. *Vers*; It. *verso*]. (1) In poetry a line or — less correctly — a stanza of a poem. In German terminology *Vers* always means a stanza, the single line being called *Zeile.* — (2) In Gregorian chant the term (abbreviated ℣) denotes a verse of a psalm or canticle, or a sentence from other scriptural texts. Single verses of this sort occur chiefly in the graduals, alleluias, and introits (in which they are indicated Ps., i.e., psalm) [see *Psalmody II, III]. They are always sung by the soloist (though usually with a short choral opening). The soloist connotation of the plainsong verse survived in the *Verse Service* and *Verse Anthem* of the English church. These terms denote settings which include sections for solo voices, as distinguished from the purely choral Full Service and Full Anthem. — (3) For organ verse, see *Verset.

Verset [G. *Versett, Versettl*; It. *verso, versetto*; Sp. *versillo*]. Organ verse, i.e., a short organ piece, usually in fugal style, designed to be played in the place of a plainsong *verse of a psalm, canticle, etc., or of other short items of the service (section of a Kyrie). In the 16th to the 18th centuries it was customary to have the

even-numbered verses of a psalm or canticle replaced by organ versets, in alternation with plainsong performance for the
others [see *Magnificat]. This practice
was designed to relieve the monotony of
the traditional method of psalm singing.
Although, from the liturgical point of
view, it represents an abuse and decline,
it has been a great stimulus in the field
of organ composition. Organ composers
usually provided a number (from four to
eight) of versets for each church mode
(*Versi octo tonorum*). The vast repertory of such versets includes contributions
by Johannes Buchner (*Fundamentum,*
c. 1530); Antonio Valente (*Versi spiritu-*
ali, 1576); Antonio de Cabezon (*Obras*
de musica, 1578; cf. *HAM,* no. 133);
Christian Erbach (after 1600; cf. *DTB*
4.ii); Erasmus Kindermann (*Harmonia*
organica, 1645); Georg Muffat (*Appa-*
ratus musico-organisticus, 1690; new ed.
by S. de Lange, 1888); Johann Speth
(*Ars magna organistica,* 1693); F. X.
Murschhauser (*Octitonium,* 1696; *DTB*
18); J. K. F. Fischer (*Blumenstrauss,*
c. 1700; new ed. E. von Werra, 1901);
and Gottlieb Muffat (*72 Versettl samt 12*
Toccaten, 1726; *DTOe* 29.ii). In the more
recent of these collections the first verset
is frequently in a freer style and therefore designated Toccata. For the versets
designed especially for the Magnificat,
see *Magnificat.

The practice of replacing plainsong by
organ playing still exists today, particularly in France, and is known as "supplying." While the organist plays, the
clergy and choir merely repeat the words
to themselves. Pius X, in his *Motu
Proprio* of 1903, abolished a good deal of
this practice.

Versetto [It.]. *Verset.

Versetzung [G.]. Transposition. *Ver-*
setzungszeichen, accidental.

Versicle. In the Roman or Anglican
service a *verse spoken or chanted by the
priest.

Versillo [Sp.]. *Verset.

Versmaass [G.]. Poetic meter.

Vers mesuré. The term denotes a late
16th-century French practice of setting
poetic texts to music in a rhythm which
reproduces exactly the strong and weak
syllables of text, by giving the former the
exact double duration of the latter. This
procedure which is observed, e.g., in the
Chansonettes mesurées of Jacques Mauduit (1557–1627) and in Claude le
Jeune's *Le Printemps* (1603; see *Editions XVI, 11, 12; Ex. in *HAM,* no. 138)
is the continuation of earlier methods applied to the Horatian *odes. See also
*Air de cour; *Rhythm II (b). Cf.
LaMWC, 253ff; P.-M. Masson, "L'Hu-
manisme musical en France . . ." (*KIM,*
1906, p. 170).

Verso [It.]. *Verse; *verset.

Verstärken [G.]. To reinforce.

Versus alleluiaticus. See under *Alleluia.

Vertical. See under *Texture.

Verwechslung, Enharmonische
[G.]. Enharmonic change.

Verweilend [G.]. Delaying.

Verzierung [G.]. Ornamentations indicated by signs or small notes.

Vesperal, vesperale [L.]. See *Liturgical books I (1).

Vespers. The last but one of the
*Office hours. The service consists of the
Deus in adjutorium, 5 psalms each preceded by an antiphon, a hymn, and the
*Magnificat. It is particularly important
from the musical point of view because
it is, outside of the Mass, the only service
for which music other than plainsong is
admitted. Beginning with the 16th century the evening psalms were frequently
treated in four-voice harmony (so-called
*fauxbourdon), and the Magnificat, par-
ticularly, has been composed very elaborately by numerous great composers.
The motets also find their place chiefly
at Vespers. Mozart wrote two Vespers
(K.V. 321 and 339) for voices, orchestra,
and organ, each comprising five psalms
and the Magnificat.

Via [It.]. Away. *Via sordini*, remove the mutes.

Vibrations. See *Acoustics I.

Vibrato. (1) On stringed instruments a slight fluctuation of pitch produced on sustained notes by an oscillating motion of the left hand. Violin and violoncello players use it freely in order to increase the emotional quality of the violin tone. Some great violinists have strongly objected to the consistent application of this technique, insisting that it be reserved for moments of heightened expression. Sensible as such advice seems to be to every musician and listener to music, the vibrato has been adopted by most players as a basic technique, but is usually applied with sufficient moderation to produce no noticeable fluctuation of pitch.

Lute players of the 17th century made a distinction between a vibrato produced by a motion of the finger [F. *langeur*; E. *closed shake*, see under *Grace; It. *ondeggiamento*] and one performed with the aid of a second finger which lightly beats the string as close as possible to the stopping finger [F. *battement*; E. sting]. A particularly striking vibrato is possible on the clavichord [see *Bebung].

(2) Among singers there exists not only uncertainty as to what vibrato means but also confusion with the term *tremolo. According to some authorities the vocal vibrato is the quick reiteration of the same pitch produced by a quickly intermittent stream of breath with fixed vocal chords. This effect corresponds to what the string players correctly term tremolo. As explained under this heading, it is never used in modern singing. Most singers use the term vibrato for a scarcely noticeable wavering of the tone, an effect which would correspond to the moderate vibrato of the violinist, since it increases the emotional effect of the sound without resulting in a noticeable fluctuation of pitch. Cultivated by many singers, it is avoided by others as likely to degenerate into a real wobble, caused by a lack of control over the vocal chords which may be due either to an insufficient technique or to extreme overuse of the voice. This unwelcome effect the singers call tremolo, thus using the term in a sense altogether different from its proper one.

The vocal vibrato, whether in its moderate or exaggerated form, constitutes a danger for the singer, since most singers use it without being aware of doing so. Apparently the reason for the perpetual use of a mannerism which every serious music lover detests is not so much lack of taste on the part of the singers as their lack of control of the vocal chords.

A scientific study of the vibrato has been made by C. Seashore: *The Vibrato* (1932), and *Psychology of the Vibrato in Voice and Instrument* (1936).

Victimae paschali laudes. See *Sequence (2).

Vide [F.]. Empty. *Corde à vide*, open string. — [L.]. See. The term is used, with its syllables *Vi—–de* placed at separate places of the score, to indicate an optional shortening, the player being permitted to proceed from the place marked *Vi—* immediately to the place marked *–de.*

Viella, vielle. The most important string instrument of the 12th–13th centuries, mentioned by numerous writers and described in detail by Hieronymus de Moravia, according to whom it had a drone string and four fingered strings [cf. *WoHN* ii, 220]. Its prominent role is also attested in the inscription "In seculum viellatoris" found with instrumental pieces of the 13th century [see *In seculum]. Later (15th century) the name was applied to the *hurdy-gurdy, properly called *vielle à roue* (wheel viol). Illustration on p. 800.

Vielstimmig [G.]. For many voices, polyphonic.

Viennese Classics [G. *Wiener Klassiker*]. Collective designation for the Viennese masters of classical music, Haydn, Mozart, and Beethoven. See *Classicism. The term Viennese School may be used in a wider sense, including predecessors such as Georg Reutter

(1708–72), Georg Chr. Wagenseil (1715–77), and Matthias Monn (1717–50). Regarding the latter two, see *Mannheim School.

Vierhebigkeit [G. *vier*, four; *Hebung*, stress]. A term introduced by H. Riemann for musical phrases involving four accents (four measures) or multiples thereof. The great majority of all melodies and themes belong to this class, a fact which was strongly emphasized by Riemann, who claimed for it almost universal validity throughout the entire history of music. Such a contention goes much too far. It was not until the end of the 17th century that the four-measure phrase became established as a principle of structural organization of music other than dance music and simple songs. Composers such as Cesti and Carissimi seem to have been among the first to use it with some degree of consistency, thus bestowing upon their music a novel touch of "popularization." It must be noticed that the somewhat obvious and facile regularity which attaches to music written in four-measure phrases is not without danger, a danger of which the great masters have usually been aware, but which lesser composers have not always escaped. The accompanying example

from Haydn's Quartet op. 20, no. 5 is one of the most striking proofs against the idolization of four-measure phrases.

Riemann was particularly unfortunate in his attempts to draw upon Vierhebigkeit as a scholarly principle in interpreting medieval monophonic music. He has not hesitated to apply truly procrustean methods in order to force rhythmically free melodies into patterns of four beats and four measures [cf. his interpretations

of Gregorian chants, *RiHM* i.2, pp. 32ff; or of the two-voice "Ut tuo propitiatus," *ibid.*, p. 141, which may be compared with that in *ApNPM*, 205]. Riemann's principle has recently been adopted, with equally unfortunate results, by F. Liuzzi in his edition of the 14th-century *laudas. See also *Plainsong notation.

Viertel [G.]. Quarter. *Viertelnote*, quarter-note; *Viertelton*, quarter tone.

Vihuela [Sp.]. Early Spanish name (1) for the viola (*vihuela de arco*; cf. *GD* iii, 260). — (2) More frequently, for the Spanish "lute" of the 16th century (*vihuela da mano*). Actually, this instrument had the flat and waisted body of a guitar [see *Guitar family]. Since, however, the number and tuning of the strings as well as the notation and manner of playing were the same as those of the ordinary lute, it is usually classified as such. An impressive repertory of music for the vihuela has come down to us in a number of Spanish lutebooks [see *Lute music; *Spanish music II].

A repertory for the vihuela is also indicated in the titles of the two remaining books of Spanish 16th-century organ music, by Hinegas de Vinestrosa (1557) and Antonio de Cabezon (1578), both of which bear the remark: "para tecla, harpa y vihuela" (for keyboard, harp and lute). However, they do not contain specific compositions for the last two instruments, but only strictly polyphonic organ music most of which could not be played on a harp or a lute without considerable adaptation.

Lit.: J. B. Trend, *Luis Milan and the Vihuelistas* (1925); G. Morphy, †*Les Luthistes espagnols* (1902); L. Schrade [see *Editions XXV, 2]; E. Torner, †*Colección de vihuelistas españoles del siglo XVI* (1923); W. Apel, "Early Spanish Music for Lute and Keyboard Instruments" (*MQ* XX); G. Chase, in *BAMS* vi.

Villancico [Sp., from *villano*, rustic]. In the 15th and 16th centuries a type of Spanish poetry, idyllic or devotional as to subject-matter, consisting of several

stanzas (*copla*) linked by a reiterated refrain (*estribillo*). A considerable number
of such poems, set for three or four voices
in a simple note-against-note style (*familiar style), occur in the *Cancionero del
Palacio* (*c.* 1500; see *Sources, no. 27).
Most of these pieces show the form A B
B A (derived from the French *virelai)
which, in the case of several stanzas, is
extended to A B B A B B A . . . A [cf.,
e.g., *Cancionero*, no. 14; other examples
in *HAM*, no. 98; *OH* ii (1905), 308;
RiHM ii.1, 201; *SchGMB*, no. 96b; *LavE*,
i.4, 2007ff]. After 1500 the villancico was
also cultivated as a solo song with lute
accompaniment. Luis Milan, Diego Fuenllana, Alonso Mudarra [see *Lute
music], wrote a number of Spanish and
Portuguese villancicos which are outstanding for their grace and finish and
which, in fact, might be considered the
earliest examples of song in the modern
sense of the word [cf. G. Chase, *The
Music of Spain* (1941), pp. 47ff; also A.
Geiger, in *ZMW* iv].

After 1600 the villancico adopted an
entirely different significance, i.e., of a
composition resembling a cantata or an
anthem, based on a religious text and
written in several movements for chorus,
soloists, and orchestra. These villancicos
usually open or/and close with a choral
movement called *estribillo*, between which
there are a number of solo movements
(arias) called *coplas*. (This terminology
points to a connection, otherwise obscure,
with the 16th-century villancico in which
the estribillo could be sung by a chorus,
the coplas by a soloist.) Among the composers of such villancicos are Carlos Pa-
tiño (d. *c.* 1680) and Fray Juan Romero
(fl. *c.* 1670) [cf. *LavE* i.4, 2050ff]. A
number of villancicos are preserved in
MSS at the library of Munich [cf. the
catalogue by J. J. Maier]. The scarcity
or inaccessibility of sources makes it
difficult to obtain a correct idea of this
phase of Spanish music. Fortunately the
gap has been filled in to some extent by
the recent publication of the villancicos
by Joan Cererols, a member of the School
of Montserrat, who died in 1676. His
villancicos consist of a choral estribillo

and one copla in the form of a short
strophic song with from 6 to 9 stanzas
[cf. D. Pujol, *Mestres de l'escolania de
Montserrat*, vol. iii, 1930; example in
HAM, no. 227].

Villanella, villanesca [It., properly
canzon villanesca, rural song]. A 16th-
century type of vocal music which originated in Naples (*v. alla Napolitana*) and
which regarding text as well as musical
style forms a sharp contrast to — probably a reaction against — the refinements
of the contemporary madrigal. M. Praetorius' characterization of the villanella
as "eine Bäurisch Music zu einer Bäu-
rischen Matery" is less appropriate than
Morley's designation as a "clownish musick to a clownish matter," since the villanella, although suggested by folk music,
had as little in common with the Italian
peasants as had the "style galant" of the
18th century with the shepherds of
France. The sophisticated and parodistic
character of the villanella appears particularly in its frequent use of "forbidden" parallel fifths [see Ex.]. The earli-

Dol-ce mi-se-ri - a u-scir di af-fann'e pe — ne

est collections of villanellas are by Gio.
Dom. Nola (1541), Thomaso Cimello
(1545), A. Willaert (1545), Baldassare
Donati (1550). The *stile villanesco* spread
particularly to Germany where it was
adapted to drinking songs, jesting songs,
etc., not without losing a good deal of its
Italian flavor, and becoming either more
civilized (Orlando di Lasso), or simply
dull.

The *villota* represents a somewhat
earlier type of dance song, more genuinely
folk-like, lacking the parodistic character
of the villanella, and chiefly of North-
Italian provenance. Its local character is
indicated in titles of publications such as
Villote alla veneziana (1535), *Villote
padovane* (1550), *Villote alla napoletana*
(1550), *Villote mantovane* (1583). Expl.
in *BeMMR*, 299. The recent attempt
made by F. Torrefranca to elevate the vil-

lota to the rank of a "missing link" between the Italian music of the 14th century [see *Ars Nova] and that of the 16th century (*frottola) rests on very weak ground. Cf. O. Kinkeldey, "F. Torrefranca's Theory of the Villota" (*BAMS* vi).

Subspecies of the villanella are the *greghesca*, the *justiniana*, the *mascherata*, and the *moresca*. The *greghesca* is a villanella alla napolitana, in 3 parts, and with a text mixed of Venetian and Greek elements. Its creator was the Venetian-Levantine poet-musician Antonio Molino whose texts in such dialects were composed by many Venetian composers, from Willaert to Bel' Haver. The *justiniane* are a type of villanella (always in three parts) the text of which is a ridicule of the enfeebled and stuttering Venetian patrician. The poems have no relationship whatsoever to the choice lyrics also called "giustiniani" of the early 15th-century poet Leonardo Giustiniani (1385–1446). The *mascherata* is a type of villanella designed to be sung during a masked ball or procession [Ex. by Nola in *EiBM*, no. 18]. Collections of such songs were published by G. Scotto (*Primo libro delle justiniane*, 1570), A. Gabrieli (*Greghesche et justiniane*, 1571; *Mascherate et justiniane*, 1601), O. Vecchi (*Selva di varia ricreatione*, 1590), and others. The *moresca* is a type in which the singers represent Moorish girls (examples in Lasso, cpl. ed., vol. x). It has no relationship to the dance *morisca*. See also *Maggiolata.

Modern composers, such as Berlioz, Chabrier, Dukas, Granados, Loeffler, have used the term villanelle or villanesca for instrumental pieces in the style of a rustic dance, usually in quick $^6/_8$-meter. An early example of such villanelles occurs in a suite by Telemann (no. 5 of the six *Ouvertures*, *c.* 1725).

Lit.: W. Scheer, *Die Frühgeschichte der Villanella* (Diss. Cologne 1935); G. M. Monti, *La Villanella alla napolitana* . . . (1925); A. W. Ambros, *Geschichte der Musik* iii, 526ff; K. Somborn, *Die Villota* (1901); H. Springer, "Villota und Nio" (*Liliencron Festschrift*, 1910); *id.*,

in *SIM* xi; A. Einstein, "Die Parodie in der Villanella" (*ZMW* ii).

Villota, villotta. See under *Villanella.

Vina. See *Hindu music II. Illustration on p. 823.

Vingt-quatre violons. A band of 24 violinists, in the service of the French kings Louis XIII, Louis XIV, and Louis XV (*c.* 1650–1761), which became particularly famous under its leader Lully who first (1655) obtained the direction of a smaller group of 16 players, called "petite bande," but later became the conductor of the "grande bande." Their main function was to play at the court-balls, at the king's levee, dinner, etc. Lully organized the band into a string orchestra which became famous all over Europe and which was imitated by various sovereigns, e.g., by Charles II, under the name "King's Music."

Vinnula. See *Neumes I; *Tremolo (3).

Viol. I. *General Characteristics.* Name for a family of stringed instruments which were in use mainly during the 16th and 17th centuries, following after the various types of medieval fiddles (*rebec, *vielle) and being superseded in turn by the *violin family. The viols stand in about the same relationship to the violins as the harpsichord to the piano, the recorder to the flute. They are very delicate and soft in timbre, lacking the brilliance and the versatility of the modern instruments. Thus they are suited for the intimacy of a private room and for the musical amateur rather than for the concert hall and the professional virtuoso. The making and playing of viols has been revived to quite an extent, owing chiefly to the initiative of Arnold Dolmetsch in England.

The instruments of the viol family differ from those of the violin family in the following characteristics: (a) The shoulders slope from the neck instead of starting from it at right angles; (b) the back is usually flat, instead of bulging; (c) the ribs are deeper; (d) the normal number of strings is six, instead of four; (e) the finger board is provided with frets in the form of pieces of gut tied around the finger board; (f) the sound-holes have usually the shape of a *c* instead of an *f* [see *F-holes]; (g) the bridge is less arched thus facilitating the playing of full chords; (h) the strings are thinner and less tense; (i) the viol is played with an older type of bow the stick of which curves outward from the hair [see *Bow], and the hand is properly held under the bow, not over it as today; (j) the viols were not pressed against the shoulder but were held downward, resting on or between the legs of the player. Some of the above characteristics are frequently neglected in modern viol playing, e.g., the use of frets and the downward position.

II. *Standard Types.* In the 17th century, the classical period of the viols, these existed in three sizes, treble viol [F. *dessus de viole*], tenor viol (*taille de viole*), and bass viol (*basse de viole*), the last being known also as viola da gamba [modern G. *Gambe*; see *Viola (2)]. According to Th. Mace's *Musick's Monument* (1676) a good set of viols or, as it was called, "chest of viols" consisted of "two basses, two tenors and two trebles: all truly and proportionably suited." The tuning of these instruments followed that of the 16th-century lute, viz., in fourths with a third in the middle: bass viol D G c e a d'; tenor viol A d g b e' a'; treble viol d g c' e' a' d''. Towards the end of the 17th century French musicians added a small viol tuned a fourth above the treble viol and called it *pardessus de viole*. The corresponding English term is descant viol which, however, is used also for the treble viol.

III. *Viol Music.* Although instrumental ensemble music of the 16th century, such as the ricercares by Willaert, the canzonas by Maschera, etc., were doubtless played on viols (as well as on other melody instruments such as recorders or cornetts), it was in England that viol making, viol playing, and viol composition reached its "Golden Age," mainly in the period from *c.* 1625 to 1675. Pre-

ceded by the *Innomines and *Brownings, the English *fancy of the 17th century steps out as the chief representative of English viol music [see also *Consort]. Around 1660 the appearance of the violin in England quickly brought an end to this splendid period [see *English music V]. The bass viol, however, had a longer career as a solo instrument, beginning with the Recercadas for "violone" and organ in Diego Ortiz' *Tratado de glosas* (1553), continuing with famous players such as Christopher Simpson (d. 1669; *The Division Violist*, 1659ff), André Maugars (born *c.* 1600), Hautman or Hotman (d. 1663), Jean Rousseau (*Traité de la viole*, 1687), and with composers such as Marin Marais (1656–1728; 5 vols. of pieces for 1–3 viola da gambas, 1686–1725), his son Roland Marais (two books *Pièces de violes*, 1735, '38), Johann Schenk (*Scherzi musicali*, *c.* 1692; see *Editions XXIX, 28, also *SchGMB*, no. 245), Ernst Christian Hesse (1676–1762), August Kühnel (b. 1645?; *Sonate . . . ad una o due viole da gamba*, 1698; several republished by A. Einstein, Döbereiner, Bennat), Antoine Forqueray (1671–1745; *Pièces de viole*, edited by his son Jean-Baptiste; several republished by Carl Schröder), Louis de Caix d'Hervelois (*c.* 1670–*c.* 1760; 6 books *Pièces de viole*, 1725–52; several sonatas republished by Carl Schröder), and finally Karl Friedrich Abel, the last of the violists (1725–87; numerous MS pieces, one sonata published by R. Engländer; see Lit., Einstein). Bach wrote three wonderful sonatas for viola da gamba (B.-G. ix, 175ff) and the aria "Komm süsses Kreuz" of the *St. Matthew Passion* for viola da gamba and bass. There also exists an early sonata by Handel [see reference under *Thorough-bass II].

IV. *Special Types.* In addition to the aforementioned standard types there existed various other instruments of the same family.

1. Double-bass Viol [F. *contre-basse de viole*; It. *violone*]. A six-stringed instrument tuned an octave below the bass viol. This is the ancestor of the modern *double-bass which has retained some of

the features of the viol family, together with the alternative name bass viol. The *violone* frequently prescribed in Bach's cantatas probably was an intermediate instrument between the old type with six strings and the modern double-bass.

2. Division Viol. A slightly smaller bass viol which was preferred for the playing of *divisions upon a ground and for similar soloist performance.

3. Lyra Viol. An instrument still somewhat smaller than the division viol. Since its size was in between that of the bass viol and the tenor viol it was also called *viola bastarda*. The lyra viol, or "bass viol lyra-way" as John Playford calls it (1658), differed from the other viols in its tuning which was in fifths and fourths, e.g., C G c e a d' or A₁ E A e a d', and which was taken over from that of the older *lira da gamba*, hence the name lyraway. This manner of tuning, which greatly facilitated the playing of chords, was also known as "harp-way tuning" (Th. Mace). The music for this instrument was written, not in ordinary notation, but in *tablature [cf. the example in *WoHN* ii, 226f].

4. Viola d'amore [F. *viole d'amour*]. This instrument was the size of a treble viol, from which it was distinguished by the addition of *sympathetic strings made from thin wire which were stretched behind the bowed strings, thus producing a silvery resonance. In distinction from the viols proper it had no frets and was held like a violin. It must be noted, however, that alongside this type there existed viola d'amores without sympathetic strings, but with metal strings replacing the gut strings of the ordinary viols. Since this instrument had a metallic timbre, the name viola d'amore (love viol) is not likely to refer to a "loving" sound, but perhaps to the peculiar shape of the scroll which usually was fashioned as a blindfold face like that of the god Amor [cf. *SaHMI*, 366f]. The *English violet* mentioned by Leopold Mozart probably was a larger variety of viola d'amore with seven bowed and fourteen or fifteen sympathetic strings [cf. Bessaraboff, p. 286].

The literature for the viola d'amore is quite extensive, considering the peculiar traits of the instrument. It includes compositions by Attilio Ariosti (1666–*c*. 1740; 6 Sonatas, new ed., Augener, Durand); Jean-Baptiste Loeillet (1680–1730; 3 Sonatas, ed. by Beon); J. S. Bach (1685–1750; *St. John Passion*, Cantata no. 132); Michel Corrette (early 18th cent.; Sonata, new ed., Lemoine); Haydn (1732–1809; Divertimento, new ed., Nagel); and Karl Stamitz (1746–1801; *DTB* 16; also new ed., Schott). In 1782 Milandre published a *Méthode facile pour la viole d'amour*. In the 19th century the instrument was used by Meyerbeer (*Les Huguenots*), Charpentier (*Louise*), Puccini (*Madame Butterfly*), R. Strauss (*Sinfonia Domestica*), and Ch. Loeffler (*The Death of Tintageles*). In concert performance it has been revived by Louis van Waefelghem (1840–1908), Carli Zoeller (1840–89), Francis Casadesus (b. 1870), and others. Hindemith wrote a Sonata (op. 25, 2) and a Concerto (op. 46, 1) for viola d'amore.

5. Baryton. An 18th-century instrument which might be considered as a viola da gamba provided with sympathetic strings, or, in other words, a larger size of the viola d'amore. The neck was usually carved out beneath the finger board (leaving only an oblong frame) so that the sympathetic strings could also be reached from underneath, by plucking with the thumb of the left (!) hand [illustration in *SaRM*, 32; *SaHMI*, 368]. Quite a number of late-18th-century compositions for the baryton are extant. Most of them were written for Prince Nikolaus Esterhazy, who was a great lover of the instrument. Among them are *Partien auf die Viola Paredon* by J. G. Krause (*c*. 1700), 175 compositions by Haydn [cf. C. F. Pohl, *Haydn* i, 249], 24 divertimenti by Luigi Tommasini (1747–1806), pieces by Joseph Weigl (1766–1820), and others.

Lit.: *Viols in general:* N. Bessaraboff, *Ancient European Musical Instruments* (1941), pp. 255–89, 357–73; G. R. Hayes, *Musical Instruments . . . ;* vol. 2: *The Viols* (1930); *LavE* ii.3, 1753ff; E. van der Straeten, "The Revival of the Viols" (*The Strad*, May, 1908–June, 1912); J. Pulver, "The Viols in England" (*PMA* xlvii); Ch. Bouvet, "Les Pièces de viole de Couperin" (*RdM*, 1922, no. 2).— *Viola d'amore:* C. Zoeller, *The Viole d'amour* . . . (without date); R. Dolejší, *Modern Viola Technique* (1939), pp. 38ff, 133; E. de Bricqueville, *La Viole d'amour* (1908); *LavE* ii.3, 1781ff; W. Altmann and W. Borissowsky, *Literaturverzeichnis für Bratsche und Viola d'amore* (1937); W. E. Köhler, *Beiträge zur Geschichte und Literatur der Viola d'amore* (Diss. Berlin 1938); F. Scherber, in *Musikbuch aus Oesterreich* (1910); W. Altmann, in *Die Bratsche*, no. 4; D. Fryklund, in *Svensk Tidskrift för Musikforskning* iii (1921).— *Baryton: LavE* ii.3, 1779ff; W. O. Strunk, "Haydn's Divertimenti for Baryton, Viola, and Bass" (*MQ* xviii); L. Greilsamer, in *BSIM*, 1910; D. Fryklund, in *Svensk Tidskrift för Musikforskning* iv (1922).— *Viola da gamba and other types:* A. Einstein, *Zur deutschen Literatur für Viola da gamba im 16/17. Jahrhundert* (1905); E. Albini, "La Viola da gamba in Italia" (*RMI* xxviii); C. Sachs, "Die Viola bastarda" (*ZIM* xv).

Viola. (1) In modern usage, the second member of the violin family [G. *Bratsche*; F. *alto*]. It is tuned a fifth lower than the violin, c g d′ a′. Nonetheless, its size is only ⅐ larger than that of the violin, a disproportion which causes its timbre to become quite different from that of the violin and violoncello, rendering it more nasal and veiled. For modern constructions in deviating sizes, see *Violin family (c), (d). In contrast to the violin, the viola has been used almost exclusively as an ensemble instrument, in the orchestra or in chamber music [see *Quartet]. Notable exceptions are P. Hindemith's Sonatas for viola solo (op. 11, 5; op. 25, 1) and for viola and piano (op. 11, 4; op. 25, 4; without op. number, 1939).

Around 1600 the viola was called *violino* (*violino ordinario*), the smaller violin being called *violino piccolo* [see *Violin II]. Therefore the viola would seem to have been considered at that time the normal type of the violin family. In the 17th and 18th centuries it was frequently called *violetta*, the name viola being used for the viola da gamba [cf., e.g., Rosenmüller's Symphoniae, in *DdT* 18].

(2) In the Renaissance and Baroque periods *viola* is the generic Italian name for the entire group of bowed strings. This fell into two classes: *viole da gamba* (knee viols) and *viole da braccio* (arm viols). The former which were held on or between the knees are the *viols; the latter which were held against the shoulder (at least with the smaller sizes) are the immediate forerunners of the violins [see *Violin II]. Later, these collective terms became identified each with one special member of the group, the viola da gamba [G. *Gambe*] with the bass viol [see *Viol II], the viola da braccio [viola; G. *Bratsche*] with the alto violin.

Lit.: B. Tours, *The Viola*; R. Dolejší, *Modern Viola Technique* (1939); Cl. Meyer, †*Alte Meister des Violaspiels* (Ed. Peters); R. Clarke, "The History of the Viola in Quartet Writing" (*ML* iv, no. 1).

Viola alta. See *Violin family (d).

Viola bastarda. Italian name for the lyra viol [see *Viol IV, 3], not for the baryton [see *Viol IV, 5]. Cf. C. Sachs, in *ZIM* xv.

Viola da braccio, da gamba. See *Viola (2); also *Viol II.

Viola d'amore. See *Viol IV, 4.

Viola da spalla [It. *spalla*, shoulder]. An 18th-century variety of the cello which was carried by ambulant musicians across the chest suspended from a strap over the shoulder.

Viola di bordone, viola paredon. Same as baryton; see *Viol IV, 5.

Viola pomposa. An 18th-century instrument of the violin (not viol) family, the invention of which is erroneously credited to J. S. Bach (in unreliable sources dating from 1782 to 1792). Actually Bach never wrote for it, and the only clues for the identification of the instrument are two compositions by Telemann, a concerto by Graun, and a *Sonata per la Pomposa col Basso* by Cristoforo Gius. Lidarti from about 1760. From the nature of these pieces it has been concluded that the viola pomposa was a larger viola held on the arm (not under the chin) and with five strings, tuned c–g–d′–a′–e′. The *violino pomposo* found in some sources denoted the same instrument. Cf. F. W. Galpin, A. Dolmetsch, G. Kinsky, F. T. Arnold, in *ZMW* xiii, xiv; F. W. Galpin, in *ML* xii; *SaHMI*, 367f.

Viole. F. for *viol. *Viole d'amour*, viola d'amore [see *Viol IV, 4].

Violet. A name sometimes given to the viola d'amore [see *Viol IV, 4].

Viole-tenor. See *Violin family (g).

Violetta. (1) Name for 16th-century three-stringed instruments of the violin type [see *Violin II]. — (2) 17th/18th-century name for the viola, used by Rosenmüller, Bach, and other German composers. — *Violetta marina* is a name for the viola d'amore. — *Violetta piccola* was, according to Praetorius (*Syntagma musicum*, 1614–20), a small viol, but may also have denoted a violin.

Violin [F. *violon*; G. *Violine, Geige*; It. *violino*]. I. *General*. The most important of the stringed instruments, in the orchestra as well as in chamber and solo music. Its main parts are: (a) the body, consisting of the table (sound board), the back, and the ribs (side walls); (b) the finger board ending in the pegbox and the scroll; (c) the string holder (tail piece); (d) the bridge. Other details of the construction are shown in illustration on p. 799. Inside the body there is the *bass–bar glued to the table, reinforcing blocks glued to the corners of the bouts and to the back, and the *sound-post fixed between the table and the back. The violin has four strings tuned in fifths: g d′ a′ e″.

The prominent position which the violin holds in our music rests on its singular qualities, such as an expressiveness ranging from the softest lyricism to the highest dramatic excitement, an extremely soulful and sensitive timbre which comes closer than any other instrument to the sound of the human voice, crescendos and diminuendos unequaled by other instruments, and a great variability of performance which includes many types of *bowing as well as the *pizzicato and the use of *harmonics.

A singular glory surrounds the "old violins." While all the other modern instruments (except the organ) have reached their highest degree of perfection within the last fifty years, the great period of violin building followed very shortly after the emergence of the instrument as a definite type. From 1600 to 1750 there worked at Cremona the great masters of violin making, notably Nicolo Amati (1596–1684), Antonio Stradivari (1644–1737), and Giuseppe Guarneri, also known as Giuseppe del Gesù (1681–1742). Their instruments are priceless treasures for which fabulous sums have been paid. Although the craftsmanship and beauty of these instruments have never been equaled, modern makers have succeeded in producing instruments the sound of which cannot be distinguished from that of a genuine "Strad," as has been proved by actual tests in which old and new instruments were played behind a screen before outstanding authorities. In particular, the widespread opinion that the composition of the varnish has a decisive influence on the sound of a violin has been shown to be untrue. The incomparable luster of the old instruments adds greatly to their beauty, but nothing tangible to their tonal quality.

II. *History*. The violin, as the main representative of the class of "bowed stringed instruments" or, as they are scientifically termed, "fiddles" [see *Instruments IV, B, 2], has a relatively short prehistory and ancestry. There is no evidence of the use of the bow (which distinguishes the fiddles from the much earlier lutes and zithers) prior to the 9th century when it is mentioned in Persian and Chinese sources. There is some evi-

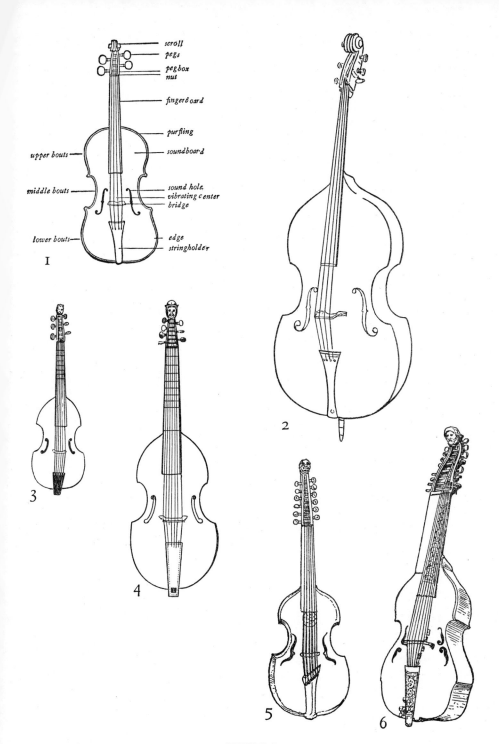

scroll

pegs

pegbox
nut

fingerboard

purfling

upper bouts

soundboard

middle bouts

sound hole
vibrating center
bridge

lower bouts

edge
stringholder

I

2

3

4

5

6

VIOLINS I

1. Violin. **2.** Double bass. **3.** Tenor viol. **4.** Bass viol. **5.** Viola d'amore. **6.** Baryton.

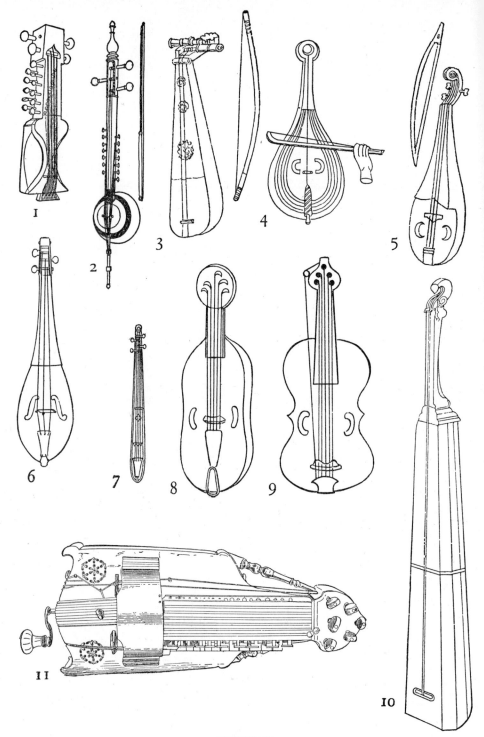

VIOLINS II

1. Sarinda. 2. Kemantche. 3. Rebab. 4. Gigue. 5. Rebec. 6. Rebec, 17th century.
7. Kit. 8. Vielle. 9. Lira da braccio. 10. Tromba marina. 11. Hurdy-gurdy.

dence in favor of the theory that the fiddle originated in Central Asia whence it spread to the Far East as well as to Europe. The Chinese have a fiddle called *hu ch'in* which has a small cylindrical soundbox made of bambo or some other material, covered at the front with snake-skin and pierced diametrically by a long neck in the form of a stick over which from two to four strings are stretched. The bow cannot be removed since it passes between the strings, rubbing some of them from below, the others from above. A similar instrument is the Persian *kemantche* [see *Arabian music II]. In India fiddles called *sarinda* have truly fantastic shapes such as only the Indian fancy could have produced [cf. SaHMI, 227]. Slightly less fantastic are the shapes of the Arabian *rebab* the name of which recurs in the *rebec* of medieval Europe.

The earliest European fiddles had the shape of a slender bottle or of a pear, and were known under various names: *rebec, *gigue, *lyra. The last of these names persisted with the Italian *lira da braccio* and *lira da gamba*. The slender fiddle (rebec) persisted in the *klein geigen* [see below] and in the *kit. The most important medieval fiddle was the *vielle* of the 13th century. The development during the ensuing two centuries is somewhat obscure. Suffice it to say that the violin developed between c. 1550 and 1600 out of several earlier types each of which contributed some of its essential features. Bearing in mind the characteristic differences between the violin and the earlier viols [see under *Viol] quite a number of "predecessors" of the violin can be singled out. The practice of leaning the instrument against the shoulder and bowing it palm-downward occurred with the vielle. The tuning in consecutive fifths is documented as early as 1533 (Lanfranco, *Scintille de musica*) and was consistently used with the three-stringed *klein geigen* (descendants of the slender rebec) throughout the 16th century (Agricola, *Musica deudsch*, 1528). The rectangle between the finger board and the upper end of the body occurs on a *lira designed by Rafael (c. 1510) as

well as with the *violettas* mentioned by Lanfranco and Ganassi (1543). The latter instruments which had no frets and three strings tuned in fifths came very close to the classical violin. A picture by Gaudenzio Ferrari from about 1535 shows violettas with shallow ribs, pointed corners, round shoulders, a depression running around the edge, *f*-holes, and a scroll [cf. SaHMI, 357]. Thus only the addition of a fourth string was necessary in order to arrive at what might be called "the first violin."

As is usually the case in historical evolutions, the emergence of a name does not coincide with the emergence of the thing itself. Thus throughout the 16th century names such as *violini, violons*, were applied to viols and similar instruments. Around 1600, *violino* denoted the *viola rather than the violin, as, e.g., in Giov. Gabrieli's *Symphoniae sacrae* (1597) and in Monteverdi's *Orfeo* (1607) in which *violino ordinario* means the viola, *violino piccolo* the violin [cf. SaHMI, 358].

The first known makers of true violins were Gasparo Bertolotti, called from his birthplace "da Salò" (1540–1609), Gio. Paolo Maggini (1581–1628), both working in Brescia, and the brothers Amati (Antonio, c. 1555–after 1640; Hieronymus, c. 1556–1630) who founded the fame of Cremona as the center of violin making. Hieronymus' son Nicolo (1596–1684) is the first of the great triad of violin makers. The Amatis created the classical shape of the violin by flattening the body which is deeply bulging in the instruments of Bertolotti, by deepening the middle bouts, sharpening the corners, rounding the holes in a more elegant shape, and improving the varnish.

Nicolo Amati's pupil Antonio Stradivari built the most famous of all violins. Working at first along the lines of his master, he created, in 1690, that model which has become known as the "Long Strad" (length 14³⁄₁₆ in., width 8 in.; ordinary length 14 in., width 8⅛ in.). In 1698 he returned to the shorter pattern of the earlier period, and made violins of about 14 in. in length, but with widths similar to those of the "Long

Strad." It was in this pattern that, from 1700 on, Stradivarius made his finest instruments, such as the "Betts" (1704), now in the Library of Congress, the "Viotti" (1709), the "Parke" (1711), the "Boissier" (1713), the "Dolphin" (1714), the "Messiah" (1716), the "Cessol" (1716), the "Maurin" (1718), the "Rode" (1722), the "Sarasate" (1724), the "Wilhelmj" (1725), the "Swan" (1735). All in all Stradivari is believed to have made 1116 instruments between 1666 and 1737; of these, 540 violins, 12 violas, and 50 violoncellos are actually known.

Guarneri's work is on a different line from that of Stradivari. He revived the bold and rugged outline, and with it the massive build and powerful tone of the earlier Brescian masters, Gasparo di Salò and Paolo Maggini. He was mainly interested in tone quality. In contrast to Stradivari he worked with no uniformity as to design, size, appearance, or finish, relying only on his intuition and on experimentation.

Other famous violin makers of Italy were the Ruggieri (Francesco, known as "il Per," Giovanni Battista, and others) whose instruments bear a general resemblance to the Amatis; the Rogeri (Giovanni and Pietro) of Brescia; and the Testore (Carlo Giuseppe, Carlo Antonio, and Paolo Antonio) of Milan. A famous German violin maker, scarcely second to the great Italians, was Jacob Stainer of Absam in Tyrol (1621–83) whose tradition was continued by the family of the Klotz of Mittenwald in Bavaria (Mathias, 1653–1743; Sebastian, 1698–?; and others). Nine-tenths of the violins which pass as "Stainers" were made by the Klotz family and their followers. In England violin making began with Thomas Urquhart (active from 1670 to 1690) and continued with Edward Pamphlon (b. c. 1680) and Barak Norman (1688–1740). A French maker of note was Nicolas Lupot (1758–1824), known for his valuable copies of Stradivari violins.

Lit. (selected): E. Heron-Allen, *De Fidiculis Bibliographia*, 2 vols. (1890, '93); A. Bachmann, *An Encyclopedia of the Violin* (1925); F. B. Emery, *The Vio-*

linist's Dictionary (1925); E. van der Straeten, *The History of the Violin*, 2 vols. (1933); H. Poidras, *Critical and Documentary Dictionary of Violin Makers*, 2 vols. (1924, '29); P. Stoeving, *The Story of the Violin* (1904); *id., The Violin . . .* 1929); W. M. Morris, *British Violin Makers* (1916); W. H. Hill, *Antonio Stradivari . . .* (1901); *id., The Violin-makers of the Guarneri Family* (1931); H. Petherick, *Antonio Stradivari* (1900); *id., Joseph Guarnerius* (1906); *id., The Repairing and Restoration of Violins* (1903); W. L. von Lütgendorff, *Die Geigen- und Lautenmacher . . .*, 2 vols. (1913, '22); O. Haubensack, *Ursprung und Geschichte der Geige* (1930); L. Grillet, *Les ancêtres du violon et du violoncelle . . .*, 2 vols. (1901, '05); A. Seiffert, "Eine Theorie der Geige" (*AMW* iv); A. Jarosy, "The Secret of the Italian Violin Makers" (*ML* xvi, no. 2).

Violin concerto. See *Concerto II, III (b).

Violin family. The chief members of this family are the *violin, the *viola, the *violoncello, and the *double-bass. These four instruments form the string section of the orchestra, the first three being used also in chamber music [*string quartet]. For more details see the separate articles.

A great number of in-between sizes have been constructed none of which achieved permanent importance. Among these are (arranged according to size):

(a) Violino piccolo [G. *Quartgeige*]. Bach scored for this instrument in his Cantata no. 140, and in his first Brandenburg Concerto. The *violini piccoli* of Monteverdi's *Orfeo* (1607), however, are true violins [see *Violin II; also *Viola].

(b) Contra-violin, introduced by H. Newbold (c. 1930), slightly bigger than the normal violin and designed to take the place of the second violin in chamber music.

(c) Contralto, a larger viola with a fuller tone, constructed by J.-B. Vuillaume, 1855.

(d) Viola alta, constructed by H. Ritter and used during the Bayreuth Festivals 1872–75. This was a larger viola (length 26 in.) and was later provided with a fifth string tuned e″.

(e) Violotta, constructed by A. Stelzner in 1891, a larger viola measuring 28 in., tuned G d a e′. F. Draeseke, Max Schillings (*Pfeifertag*), and others have scored for it.

(f) Tenor violin. General name for various instruments of the size between the viola and the violoncello (27 to 28 in. in length). They were used mainly around 1700, tuned F c g d′ or (if with five strings) F c g d′ a′. Numerous instruments of this type were built in the 19th century, by Vuillaume (1855), H. Ritter, A. Stelzner [see c, d, e], and others.

(g) Viole-ténor, constructed by R. Parramon in 1930; is held like a violoncello.

(h) Violoncello piccolo. An instrument of 36 to 38 in. in length which Bach frequently preferred over the violoncello because its smaller size facilitated the execution of soloist passages. It was tuned like the usual cello. The *violoncello à cinque cordes* which Bach prescribed in the sixth of his Suites for cello solo was probably only slightly smaller than the usual cello.

(i) Cellone, constructed by Stelzner [see (e)], a large violoncello (length 46 in.), tuned G_1 D A e and intended chiefly as a contrabass for chamber music.

(j) Octobasse, constructed by J. B. Vuillaume in 1849, a giant size double-bass about 13 feet high with three strings tuned C_2 G_2 C_1. The notes were stopped by a mechanical system of levers and 8 pedals. The Victoria and Albert Museum of London owns a double-bass which is over eight feet high. An American model made by John Geyer in 1889 measures almost 15 feet.

See also *Quinton.

Violin music. Very shortly after the establishment of the violin (*c.* 1600) its virtuoso potentialities, which distinguished it strikingly from the viols, were exploited, one of the earliest examples being the use of two solo violins in the

aria "Possente spirto" of Monteverdi's *Orfeo* (1607). Giov. Batt. Fontana from Brescia (d. 1630) may be considered as the first-known composer of violin music. His Sonatas (publ. 1641) show a clear understanding of true violin technique [cf. *RiHM* ii.2, 111f; also in Wasielewski, *Instrumentalsätze*, see Lit.]. Two composers living in Mantua treated the instrument with a striking degree of virtuosity, namely Biagio Marini (*c.* 1595–1665) and Carlo Farina (fl. 1635–37). Their sonatas and other pieces make use of double-stops, trills, tremoli [cf. *SchGMB*, nos. 182, 183], and in Farina's Capriccio stravagante (1627) these means as well as *pizzicato*, *col legno*, and harmonics are used to imitate, rather childishly, the barking of dogs, caterwauling, fifes and drums, etc. Double-stops and higher positions (up to the 5th) are frequent in the pieces of Marco Uccellini (fl. 1639–67; cf. Wasielewski, Torchi). While the virtuoso exploitation of the instrument continued in Germany under Joh. Heinrich Schmelzer (1623–80), Nikolas Adam Strungk (1640–1700), Heinrich Franz Biber (1644–1704; cf. *DTOe* 5.ii and 12.ii; *HAM*, no. 238; *SchGMB*, no. 238; see *Scordatura), and Joh. Jak. Walther (1650–?), Italian composers turned, after 1650, their attention to the true musical qualities of the violin and developed its "singing" style. Giov. Legrenzi (1626–90), Giov. Batt. Vitali (1644–92), Gius. Torelli (*c.* 1650–1702), and others led up to the "classical" simplicity of Arcangelo Corelli (1653–1713) who, in spite of his somewhat academic tendencies, nonetheless holds a central position in the history of violin music [see also *Bologna School]. Still another type of violin music, characterized by animated flow and rhythmic precision, was inaugurated by Antonio Vivaldi (1680–1743) whose violin concertos attracted the interest of Bach. Francesco Veracini (1685–1750), Giuseppe Tartini (1692–1770), and Pietro Locatelli (1693–1764) represent the acme of the Italian violin music of the Baroque. Their sonatas opened for the violin new possibilities of lyric and passionate expression while their concertos, particularly those of Tartini, are written in a highly virtuoso style.

Bach wrote an early suite (A major) and his well-known six sonatas for violin and harpsichord. His six sonatas for violin without accompaniment (actually three sonatas and three suites, one of which includes the celebrated chaconne) represent the peak of a rather extended literature for the violin solo, including pieces by Thomas Baltzer (*c.* 1630–63; cf. *SchGMB*, no. 237), J. J. Walther (*Hortus Chelicus*, 1688), Nicola Matteis (fl. *c.* 1670), Biber (1644–1704), Geminiani (1674–1762), Telemann (1681–1767), and Johann Georg Pisendel (1687–1755) [cf. A. C. Roncalio, in *The Journal of Musicology*, 1940, no. 3]. The violin pieces of the *Mannheimer group, particularly the sonatas of Schobert (d. 1767), are written in a dynamic style which foreshadows the idiom of Mozart and Beethoven [cf. *DdT* 39]. A happy amalgamation of this style with the achievements of the Italian school is represented by Giov. Batt. Viotti (1753–1824) among whose 29 violin concertos the 22d stands out as a landmark of violin literature (also 18 violin sonatas). Among his predecessors Antonio Lolli (1730–1802) and Gaeto Pugnani (1731–98) must be mentioned.

With Mozart and Beethoven begins a new period of violin music which needs no further description. For a list of violin concertos see under *Concerto.

Lit.: A. Moser, *Geschichte des Violinspiels* (1922); J. W. von Wasielewski, *Die Violine und ihre Meister* (1883, last ed. 1927; Engl. transl. 1894); id., *Die Violine im 17. Jahrhundert* (1874; Notenbeilage, published separately as *Instrumentalsätze*); S. Pfau, *Die Violinmusik in Italien*, 1600–50 (Diss. Berlin 1931); G. Beckmann, *Das Violinspiel in Deutschland vor 1700* (1918); B. Studeny, *Beiträge zur Geschichte der Violin-Sonate im 18. Jahrhundert* (1911); W. Lungershausen, *Das Violinkonzert der norddeutschen Schule* (1927); A. Pougin, *Le Violon, les violinistes et la musique du violon du xvie au xviiie siècle* (1924); L. de la Laurencie, *L'École française du*

violon, 3 vols. (1922–24); A. Bonaventura, *Storia del violino, dei violinisti e della musica per violino* (1926); F. David, †*Vorschule und hohe Schule des Violinspiels*; D. Alard, †*Les Maîtres classiques*; G. Jensen, †*Klassische Violinmusik*; H. Riemann, †*Old Chamber Music*; id., †*Collegium musicum*; A. Schering, †*Alte Meister des Violinspiels*; J. W. Wasielewski, †*Instrumentalsätze des 17. Jahrhunderts*; L. Torchi, †*L'Arte musicale in Italia*, vol. vii [see *Editions II]; M. Scott, "Solo Violin Sonatas" (*ML* x, no. 1); K. Gerhartz, "Die Violinschule bis Leopold Mozart" (*ZMW* vii); M. Pincherle, "La Technique du violon chez les premiers sonatistes français" (*SIM* xii).

Violoncello (abbreviated cello). The bass size of the violin, tuned an octave and a fourth below this: C G d a. It is about double the length of the violin (48½ in. as against 23½ in.) with the other measurements nearly in proportion, except for the higher ribs (5 in. as against 1¼ in.). The violoncello came into existence together with the violin and the viola, two instruments by Andrea Amati, made between 1560 and 1570 being the earliest preserved specimens. Throughout the 17th century it was used only for accompaniment [see *Thorough-bass]. Domenico Gabrielli (1659–90) seems to have been one of the first to cultivate it as a solo instrument. Particularly interesting are his pieces (called *Ricercare) for cello without accompaniment (MS of 1689; cf. *SchGMB*, no. 288) as they belong in the same category as Bach's celebrated six suites for cello solo. Another composer of "Ricercate" for the cello was Giamb. degli Antoni (1687, '90).

Giuseppe Jacchini's *Concerti . . . con violoncello obligato*, op. 4 (1701) open the repertory of the violoncello concerto which was also cultivated during the 18th century by Antonio Vivaldi, F. dall' Abaco (in *Concerti da chiesa*, op. 2, 1712–14), Leonardo Leo (6 concertos, 1737/38), Tartini (properly for viola da gamba), Anton Filtz, Matthias Monn, Johann G. F. Wassmuth (d. 1766), C. P. E. Bach, and Haydn (eight concertos, two of which are preserved). Domenico della Bella wrote 12 sonatas "a 2 violini e violoncello" (1704), G.-B. Bononcini (1665–after 1648) a sonata for two violoncellos and other solo pieces. Of greater importance is Jacopo Bassevi, called Cervetto (1682–1783), who brought the cello into favor in England and published *Twelve (Six) Solos for a Violoncello with a Thorough Bass for the Harpsichord* (c. 1747 and c. 1749), as well as pieces for two and three cellos. He was followed by his son James Cervetto (c. 1745–1837) who published *Six Solos* (c. 1775), *Six Duets* (c. 1792), etc. The Italian violoncello music of the 18th century culminated in L. Boccherini (1743–1805), composer of six concertos and a number of sonatas for the instrument, as well as 113 quintets with two cellos. An important method was published in 1741 by Michel Corrette, who devoted a full chapter to the higher thumb positions. The classical school of cello playing is the *Essai sur le doigté du violoncelle* . . . (before 1819) of Jean Louis Duport (1749–1819) who also composed sonatas, duets, and other pieces for the instrument.

The 19th- and 20th-century repertory includes concertos by Schumann (op. 129), Dvořák (in A, 1865), Robert Volkmann (c. 1860), Saint-Saëns (op. 33, 1873; op. 119, 1902), Lalo (1876), Elgar (op. 85), Toch (chamber orchestra, op. 35), Hindemith (chamber orchestra, op. 36, 1925), Ernest Bloch (*Voice in the Wilderness*, 1936; *Schelomo*, 1915), A. Tcherepnin (*Rhapsodie georgienne*), André Chaplet (*Epiphanie*, 1923), and Jaques Ibert (*Concertino*, 1925); sonatas by Beethoven (5), Brahms (op. 38 and op. 99), Saint-Saëns (op. 32, 1873; op. 123, 1905), Richard Strauss (op. 6, 1883), Lalo, Rachmaninov (1901), Huré (3; c. 1905), Ropartz (2; 1904, '19), Reger (4), Debussy (1915), Casella (1907, '27), Hindemith (A minor, 1922), Alexander Tcherepnin (3), and others. Pieces for cello solo were written by Reger, Ravel (with violin), Kodaly, Wellesz, and Hindemith.

Lit.: E. van der Straeten, *History of the Violoncello* (1915); A. Broadley, *The Violoncello* (1921); C. Schroeder, *Handbook of Violoncello Playing* (1894); D. Alexanian, *Theoretical and Practical Treatise of the Violoncello* (1932), J. W. von Wasielewsky, *The Violoncello and its History* (1894); M. Merseburger, *Das Violoncello und seine Literatur* (1920); B. Weigl, *Handbuch der Violoncello Literatur* (1929); L. Forino, *Il Violoncello* (1905); E. Rapp, *Beiträge zur Frühgeschichte des Violoncello-konzerts* (Diss. Würzburg 1933); H. Weber, *Das Violoncello-konzert des 18. und beginnenden 19. Jahrhunderts* (Diss. Tübingen 1932); F. Vatielli, "Les Origines de l'art du violoncelle" (*RM* iv, no. 4); E. Albini, "Domenico Gabrielli . . ." (*RMI* xli).

Violoncello piccolo. See *Violin family (h).

Violoncino. Old name for violoncello.

Violotta. See *Violin family (e).

Virelai [probably from F. *virer*, to turn around, and *lai*]. An important type of medieval French poetry and music, the standard structure of which is as follows:

text: $r_1 r_2 l_1 l_2 l_3 l_4 r_1 r_2$

music: A b b A A

(r, refrain; l, lines with varying text). The virelai, also called *chanson ballade*, originally was a dancing song and was performed in alternation of a chorus and a soloist, the chorus singing the refrain before and after each stanza in such a manner that the final refrain of the first stanza also served as the initial refrain of the

I II III

second, etc.: A b b a A b b a A b b a A. According to F. Gennrich, the virelai developed from the medieval *rondeau, the poetic structure of which may, for the sake of comparison, be indicated thus: $r_1 r_2 l_1 r_1 l_3 l_4 r_1 r_2$. It should be noted, however, that the rondeau invariably has only one stanza, while the virelai practically always has several stanzas, normally three. For another theory see *Zajal.

A number of monophonic virelais are preserved in the repertory of the *trouvères [cf. Gennrich i, nos. 49, 178, 387;

also *HAM*, no. 19c; *BeMMR*, 120]. G. de Machaut wrote virelai melodies strikingly similar in character to the popular French chanson of the present day, and also composed polyphonic virelais [cf. *HAM*, no. 46], a type which was cultivated throughout the 14th and 15th centuries [cf. *HAM*, nos. 74, 75; *ApNPM*, 151 and 412].

The virelai structure was also frequently used in Italy and in Spain. Many of the 13th-century *laude and *cantigas are written in this form, which also occurs with the 15th-century *bergerettes, *frottole, and *villancicos [for an example from 1525, cf. *SchGMB*, 89 a]. The Italian *ballata of the 14th century (Landini) is an exact duplication of the polyphonic virelai. Cf. E. Heldt, *Die Liedformen in der Chanson des 15. Jahrhunderts* (1916); F. Gennrich, †*Rondeaux, Virelais und Balladen*, 2 vols. (1921, '27).

Virga [L.]. See *Neumes I.

Virgil clavier. A practice piano invented by the American A. K. Virgil in 1892, which has no sound-producing parts but which, by means of a slight click accompanying the depression and the release of the key, gives perfect control over legato playing.

Virginal. A 16th-century type of harpsichord, described as early as 1511, in Virdung's *Musica getutscht*, a fact which clearly refutes the current interpretation of the name as referring to the "maiden Queen Elizabeth." Whether it is so called because "virgins play on them," or with reference to L. *virga* (rod, i.e., jack; cf. *SaHMI*), is uncertain. The earliest virginals had the shape of a small oblong box, to be placed on a table or even held in the player's lap. Towards the end of the 16th century the term was indiscriminately applied to all types of harpsichord, whether rectangular, wing-shaped, or trapezoidal [see *Harpsichord II]. The common denomination was "pair of virginals," an idiom the origin of which is unsettled (perhaps L. *virginalis* — virginals — pair of virginals?). A description

of a number of 17th-century virginals still in existence is given in *GD* v, 544f.

Virginal book. General name of various collections containing music of the *virginalists. The most important ones are (in approximate chronological order): (a) *My Ladye Nevells Booke* (1591), containing 42 compositions by William Byrd (new ed. by H. A. Andrews, 1926); (b) *Fitzwilliam Virginal Book* (also called erroneously *Queen Elizabeth's Virginal Book*), the most extensive and most important collection, containing 297 compositions by practically every composer of the virginalistic school (new ed. by J. A. Fuller Maitland and W. Barclay Squire, 1894–99; for a detailed list of contents see *GD* v, 545ff); (c) *Benjamin Cosyn's Virginal Book*, containing 98 pieces, chiefly by John Bull, Orlando Gibbons, and Benjamin Cosyns; (d) *Will Forster's Virginal Book*, containing 78 pieces, mostly by William Byrd. Numerous later MSS of lesser interest exist in the libraries of London and Paris. A printed collection is the *Parthenia. The *Mulliner Book* (c. 1550) described in *GD*, Suppl. Vol., 651 contains mostly liturgical organ pieces. Cf. M. L. Pereyra, "Les Livres de virginal de la Bibliothèque du Conservatoire de Paris" (*RdM* 1926–32, nos. 20, 21, 24, 28, 29, 37, 42, 45).

Virginalists. English composers of the late 16th and early 17th centuries who wrote music for the *virginal. The most important ones are, arranged in three generations: I. William Byrd (1543–1623); II. Thomas Morley (1557–1603), Peter Philips (1560–1633), Giles Farnaby (c. 1560–c. 1600), John Bull (1563–1628); III. Thomas Weelkes (c. 1575–1623), Thomas Tomkins (1573–1656), Orlando Gibbons (1583–1625). It is interesting to note that William Byrd lived longer than, or almost as long as, any of his successors, with the sole exception of Tomkins, and that the "three famous Masters William Byrd, Dr. John Bull and Orlando Gibbons," as they are called in the title of the *Parthenia, were born exactly 20 years apart. Although Byrd seems to have been the first to cultivate the virginal intensively (only a few scattered pieces, among them the famous *Hornepype by Hugh Aston, exist in earlier sources), he represents an artistic peak which dwarfs all the other virginalists except the last, Gibbons. Indeed, Byrd's natural charm and simplicity are just as great as Gibbons' refinement and sovereign mastery. They indicate the beginning and the end of a movement and development which, in a way, resemble that leading from Haydn and Mozart to the late Beethoven. John Bull's importance lies mainly in his virtuoso-like exploitation of the technical means of his instrument (rapid passages, scales in parallel thirds, broken chord figures, etc.), a contribution which left traces in the works of Sweelinck and Scheidt.

The repertory of the virginalist composers comprises dances (mainly *pavanes and gaillards), variations, *preludes, fantasias, liturgical pieces (*organ hymns; see also *Innomine), and transcriptions of madrigals.

Lit.: Ch. van den Borren, *Les Origines de la musique de clavier en Angleterre* (1912; Engl. 1913); M. Glyn, *About Elizabethan Virginal Music and its Composers* (1924). See also under *Virginal books.

Virtuoso. A performer who excels in technical ability; sometimes, one who excels in this only.

Visigothic chant. See *Mozarabic chant.

Vista [It.]. Sight. *A prima vista,* at sight [see *Sight reading].

Vite [F.]. Quick.

Vivace, vivamente, vivo [It.]. Quick, lively. *Vivacissimo,* very quick.

Vl. Abbreviation for violin. *Vla.,* viola. *Vlc.,* violoncello. *Vll.,* violins.

Vocalization [F. *vocalise;* G. *Vokalise;* It. *vocalizzo*]. An extended melody sung on a vowel, i.e., without text. The term is used chiefly with reference to vocal exercises (*solfeggio) and has, therefore, adopted a somewhat derogatory meaning, implying technical display for its own sake. The fact should not be overlooked,

however, that the absence of words enables the singer to utilize his "instrument" to a degree that is not possible in texted passages, and that throughout the early history of singing (i.e., prior to 1800) composers have shown full appreciation of this fact. Bach's and Handel's works contain numerous vocalizations (usually called *coloraturas) of a highly artistic character, and the untexted melismas of Gregorian chant are even more remote from any inference of virtuosity for its own sake [see *Neuma].

Particularly interesting, though generally misunderstood, is the role which vocalization played in the polyphonic music of the 13th to the 15th centuries. The tenors of the 13th-century motets, which, being textless, have frequently been interpreted as "instrumental tenors," are actually vocalizations on the vowel of the *incipit, as they are in their original form as melismas of a Gregorian chant [see *Clausula; *Motet A, I]. For an interesting example of a long vocalization in the upper parts of a 13th-century motet, cf. *ApNPM,* 315. Most of the accompanied songs (ballades, madrigals) of the 14th century contain extended passages lacking a text, passages which, no doubt, must be sung as vocalizations. Unfortunately, modern editors, such as Riemann and Schering, have interpreted such passages as "instrumental preludes" (or interludes, postludes), a procedure which frequently leads to an artificial interruption of a continuous melodic line [cf., e.g., *RiHM* i.2, pp. 306–34 and *SchGMB,* no. 19; for a correct rendition of G. de Florentia's "Nel mezzo a sei paon," cf. *WoGM* iii, 92]. See also *Text and music (reference to Kyrie); *Frottola.

There exists a considerable literature of pieces intended to be performed in vocalization throughout; in other words, of pieces in which the human voice is treated as an instrument, without a "disturbing" addition of words. This manner of performance is indicated in various 16th-century publications inscribed "*da cantare e sonare*" ("to sing and to play"), e.g., Willaert's *Ricercari* of 1549. Since these extended pieces (in three or four parts) have no text, they are meant (primarily, to judge from the precedence given to the word *cantare*) to be vocalized throughout in all the parts. It is interesting to note that this practice persisted in the numerous two-part ricercares of the 17th century, some of which are expressly designated as "vocal exercises" [see *Ricercare II (c)]. Spontini, in his opera *Nurmahal*, has chosen vocalization for the "Chorus of Heavenly Spirits," and several recent composers have written for vocalizing voices, e.g., Debussy (*Sirènes*, 1899), Ravel (*Vocalise en forme d'Habanera*, 1907), and Medtner (*Sonate-Vocalise*, op. 41a; *Suite-Vocalise*, op. 41b). Cf. M. Dange, "Essai sur la vocalise" (*RM* xvi).

Vocal music. Music written for voices, either solo or chorus (Choral music). Practically all music prior to 1500 is vocal, as is nine-tenths of the music of the 16th century. During the Baroque period vocal and instrumental music are about equal in quantity and prominence, while after 1750 instrumental music gains the upper hand [see *Instrumental music; also *Ensemble]. Following is a survey of the most important types of vocal music (italics indicate accompanied vocal music):

A. Period of superior importance (–1600): 6th–9th centuries: Gregorian chant. — 9th–12th (13th) centuries: Sequence; Trope; Organum. — 12th–13th centuries: Troubadours; Trouvères; Minnesinger. — 13th century: Clausula; Conductus; Motet. — 14th century: Motet; Mass items; *Ballade*; *Virelai*; *Rondeau*; *Madrigal*; *Ballata*; *Caccia*. — 15th century: Motet (Flemish); Mass; Chansons. — 16th century: Motet; Mass; Madrigal; Polyphonic lied; Chanson; Frottola; *Lute song*; Villanella.

B. Period of equal importance (1600–1750): *Cantata*; *Opera*; *Oratorio*; *Aria*; Anthem; Glee.

C. Period of inferior importance (1750–present): *Lied*; French, English, etc. *Song*; *Opera*.

Voce, pl. **voci** [It.]. Voice. *A due (tre)* **voci,** for two (three) voices. *Colla voce,*

see *Colla. *Voce di gola,* throat voice, guttural voice; *voce di petto,* chest voice; *voce di testa,* head voice, *falsetto. *Voci pari* or *eguali,* equal voices.

Voces [L.]. Voices. *Voces aequales,* equal voices. *Voces musicales,* medieval term for the tones and solmization syllables of the *hexachord [cf. *SchGMB,* no. 86]. *Voces belgicae,* the syllables of *Bocedisation.

Voice. The facts about the physical machinery of voice production are widely known, but usually only superficially understood. The larynx containing the "vocal cords" initiates the tone in much the same way that the lips start the tone in the mouthpiece of a brass instrument. The breath is pressed upward from the lungs through these "vocal lips" which are held closely together, at varying tensions according to the pitch desired, setting the lips and the breath into vibration. This resulting tone is modified and strengthened by contact with all of the inner surfaces of the mouth, nose, throat, and even the lungs. If the singer or speaker be relaxed yet vital, there will then be a balance of the different resonances resulting in an agreeable tone.

Singers will generally agree with the above statements. They also are in fair agreement upon what constitutes an agreeable tone. There is, however, a great difference of opinion as to how best to achieve this ideal; and the reason for this disagreement is not difficult to see, as will be pointed out later.

If it were always remembered that there can never be a clear description of the real center and essence of singing, the final understanding might be more easily attained. Let one consider how he would describe the process of raising his arm or closing his eyes: the real impulse can only be hinted at. Unfortunately the voice teachers' hints are usually wrongly taken as statements of fact; or in other words, what should be only sensation or imagination is confused with physical effort. One cannot, for example, really *throw* tone here or there to a localized point any more than one can throw a handful of air from place to place, since both are impalpable. To imagine doing so, however, is often helpful in achieving good tone production. Thus we are often more concerned with what appears to be the fact than with what actually is the fact.

When it is remembered how numerous are the muscles of the diaphragm, ribs, throat, tongue, jaw, larynx, and so forth, that are used in producing the voice, it is easy to see the impossibility of keeping a conscious control over all at the same time. A baby, on the other hand, uses these muscles with great efficiency even during the first days of life, when it obviously knows nothing about them. The fact that his tone is of bad quality is not of importance in this discussion as the baby quite evidently desires a disagreeable tone when crying. The tone can be pleasant enough when the baby is pleased and happy. The voice like the face expresses rather accurately what is in the mind. It is evident then that we are born with the instinctive ability to use the voice easily and freely and with good expression, without any instruction. This of course cannot be considered high art, but at least it has something to do with good free tone work.

Why then do we not all sing with good tone quality? Almost any singer will agree that muscular tension is the main cause of our bad tones; and also it is evident that undue pressure or restraint of the tone is the main cause of muscular tension, and the main cause of this forcing or holding the tone is some form of self-consciousness. This self-consciousness divides the attention, expressing, so to speak, two or more thought paths at the same time, which is confusing both to the singer and the listener. It could be said, then, that if the singer's mind were clearly, vitally concentrated upon the expression of his song, he would relax and sing well, and that the kernel of singing is mental control: concentration enough to rule out self-consciousness. This is probably true, but the practical objection to this point of view is the extreme difficulty of really clear concentration. For example, if one decides to think only of the phrase as he sings, his mind will in spite of himself

also be examining the result, and comparing it with his desires. This of course disturbs his concentration, and he sings unnaturally, into himself, instead of out to the audience, clearly expressing the very self-consciousness he seeks to eliminate. The body coördinates automatically to the thought. But if there are many conflicting thoughts, we are, in effect, trying to make several conflicting coördinations at the same time. This is simply confusion, as the muscles are working at cross purposes. The more the singer concerns himself with the lack of coördination the more his attention is distracted from the song itself, which further divides and complicates his problem.

To meet this situation teachers devise many exercises and imaginative concepts which result mostly in diverting attention from the disturbed areas. For example, the tongue under tension thickens and draws back, partly closing the throat. The back nasal passages become too stretched, or too relaxed; the jaw becomes set and stiff, and a corresponding distortion appears in the tone. If the pupil is taught to "place the voice" or imagine the vibration of the tone gently in the front mouth surfaces, and the nose, the attention is removed from the throat and tongue, which tend to relax, and the nasal passages become free of their own accord. Unfortunately, the attention then being drawn in the new direction, the singer will often feel he must push his tone into place, causing a new set of tensions. Various devices are then employed to teach the pupil to "support the breath," leading him to find the knack of avoiding this "forcing," and bringing coördination nearer. Thought now being upon the breath, the pupil tends to strain his breathing, feeling that he is aiding the process. Tension returns and he finds his throat closing again.

Here can be seen the reason for the great disagreement among singers. No single phase of singing will function well unless coördinated with other phases. If "placement" or focus is good, the breath will often coördinate to it with little or no conscious attention, so this individual will feel that attention to the breath is unnecessary. Another singer will find that if the breath is "correct" the relaxation and focus need little thought, and will teach his pupils accordingly, and moreover have success with many whose thought and problem happen to fit into the teacher's own pattern. Thus we find fads springing up among sincere people.

There are many ways to help the pupil arrive at the goal of good singing. Perhaps the best road is simply the one which he best understands. Anything that helps toward free, simple, vital, sincere, natural expression of a clear musical conception, without inhibiting counter effort, is good practice.

For a historical conspectus of the art of singing, for related articles, and for literature, see *Singing.   R. Y. R.

Voice leading [G. *Stimmführung*]. In contrapuntal music, the principles governing the progression of the various voice-parts (particularly of those other than the soprano) — not so much from the point of view of the resulting harmony, but with regard to the design of the individual lines. Principles such as preference of step-wise motion (at least in the three upper parts), contrary *motion in at least one part, avoidance of *parallel fifths and octaves, form the basis of voice leading. See Counterpoint.

Voices, Range of. The human voices are usually classified in six types: three female voices, soprano, mezzo-soprano, and contralto, and three male voices, tenor, baritone, and bass. In choral singing the middle voice of each group is omitted. The normal range of these voices may be approximately described as an octave

Bass Baritone Tenor Contralto Mezzo Soprano

(more safely, a seventh) below and above the notes d, f, a, and e′, g′, b′, as shown in the illustration. (It may be noticed that the indication of ranges differs markedly in books of different nationalities, e.g., English, Italian, German, Russian.)

Trained soloists frequently exceed these ranges. Particularly the singers of the 17th and 18th centuries possessed ranges which seem miraculous. The soprano Lucrezia Agujari (1743–83) could reach c″″, and a bass-part in Händel's *Acis et Galatea* (1708), written for Giuseppe Boschi, shifts, within one measure, from a′ to C♯, more than 2½ octaves. Russian basses are found who can sing down to F₁, a fifth below low C.

Among operatic singers further classifications are made mainly with regard to the character and timbre of the voice:

Dramatic soprano, with powerful voice and marked declamatory and histrionic ability; *Lyric soprano*, with lighter quality and pleasant cantabile style; *Coloratura soprano*, with great agility and a high range.

Tenore robusto (robust tenor), with full voice and vigor; *Lyric tenor*, corresponding to the Lyric Soprano; *Heldentenor* (heroic tenor), combining agility, brilliant timbre, and expressive power.

Basso profondo (*Basse profonde*, "deep bass"), with low range, powerful voice, and solemn character; *Basso cantante* (basse chantante, "singing bass"), with qualities similar to the lyric soprano; *Basso buffo*, comical, agile.

Voicing. In organ building, the adjustment of the timbre and the pitch of the pipes.

Voilé [F.]. Veiled, subdued.

Voix [F.]. Voice. *Voix de poitrine*, chest voice; *voix de tête*, head voice; *voix mixte*, the medium register. *Voix céleste*, see *Vox angelica.

Vokal [G.]. Vowel. *Vokalisieren*, to vocalize; *Vokalise*, vocalization.

Volante [It.]. "Flying," swift.

Volkslied [G.]. Folk song.

Volkstümliches Lied [G.]. A term for the German art song of the later part of the 18th century which, in reaction against the supposed artificiality of the coloratura aria (*Kunstlied*), reverted to a somewhat affected simplicity of expression and style approximating folk music. Representatives of this period were J. A. P. Schultz (1747–1800), J. Fr. Reichardt (1752–1814), C. F. Zelter (1758–1832), and F. Silcher (1786–1860). See *Lied IV; *Berlin School. Example in *SchGMB*, no. 309b.

Volles Werk [G.]. Full organ.

Vollstimmig [G.]. Full-voiced.

Volltönend [G.]. Sonorous.

Volta, volte [It., turn]. (1) A dance of the period around 1600, usually in dotted ⁶⁄₈-meter. It was extremely popular, probably on account of the rather indecent character of the dance, such as the lifting of the woman high into the air. Reynold Scot, in 1584, says that "night dansing witches brought out of Italy unto France that danse which is called Lavolta." English writers (Shakespeare) and musicians frequently called it *Lavolta* or *Levalto*. — (2) See *Ballata. — (3) In modern scores *prima* and *seconda volta* indicate the first and second ending of a section which has to be repeated: 1a :‖ 2a. See also *Ouvert and clos.

Volteggiando [It.]. Crossing the hands (in piano playing).

Volti [It.]. Turn over (the page); *volti subito* (abbr. *v.s.*), turn quickly.

Volubile [It.]. Flowing easily.

Voluntary. English organ pieces to be played in connection with the church service. As is suggested by the name, voluntaries originally were pieces in a somewhat freer style than was common in the period in question (for a term of similar connotation, see *Fantasia). Thus, Morley says in his *Plaine and Easy Introduction to Musicke* (1597): "To make two parts upon a plaine song is more hard than to make three parts into voluntarie." The earliest voluntaries (*Mulliner Book*, c. 1550) are short pieces in imitative counterpoint, not based upon a cantus firmus (plainsong). Three voluntaries by Byrd are preserved in *My Ladye Nevells*

Booke [see *Virginal book]; others occur in the keyboard works by O. Gibbons and Th. Weelkes [cf. the editions by M. H. Glyn]. During the 17th and 18th centuries the voluntary changed in pace with the general changes of style, incorporating elements of the prelude, toccata, operatic aria, suite, sonata, etc., and frequently exceeding by far the limitations of proper church style. Among the composers of voluntaries we find Benjamin Rogers (1614–98), John Blow (1648–1708), Purcell (1658–95), Thomas Roseingrave (1690–1766: *Fifteen Voluntaries and Fugues*), Jacob Kirkman (d. 1799: *A Collection of Six Voluntaries for the Organ, Harpsichord and Piano-Forte*, op. 9), Samuel Wesley (1766–1837; cf. *GD* v, 702), and numerous mediocre composers of the 18th and 19th centuries. More recently, determined efforts have been made to raise the artistic level of the voluntaries played in English churches. It goes without saying that voluntaries were frequently improvised.

Lit.: J. E. West, *Old English Organ Music*, nos. 14, 16, 20, 24, etc.; G. Frotscher, *Geschichte des Orgelspiels* (1935), *passim*.

Vom Blattspiel [G., playing from the sheet]. *Sight-reading.

Vorausnahme [G.]. Anticipation.

Vorbereiten [G.]. To prepare.

Vordersatz [G.]. First subject.

Vorhalt [G.]. Suspension (*vorbereiteter Vorhalt*) or appoggiatura (*freier Vorhalt*).

Vorimitation [G., anticipating imitation]. In *organ chorales or in vocal settings of chorales (as occur frequently as a

first movement in Bach's cantatas), the fugal treatment of a chorale line (or its initial motive), frequently in halved or quartered note-values (*diminution), as a preparation to the final appearance of the chorale line in its full note-values. Usually each line of the chorale is preceded by such a Vorimitation. The illustration is from Bach's organ chorale *Ach Gott und Herr*.

Vornehm [G.]. Noble, dignified.

Vorschlag [G.]. Appoggiatura (the ornament). *Kurzer, langer Vorschlag*, short, long appoggiatura.

Vorspiel [G.]. Prelude, overture. Also simple performance (*vorspielen*, to perform before an audience).

Vortrag [G.]. Interpretation; performance.

Vortragszeichen [G.]. Expression marks.

Vorwärts [G.]. "Forward," faster.

Vorzeichnung [G.]. Signature, both of the key and of the meter.

Vox [L.]. Voice. In early music, the Guidonian tone syllables; see *Hexachord, *Voces. In the 9th/11th centuries *vox principalis* and *vox organalis* are the main

and the added part in parallel *organum. See *Parts.

Vox angelica, coelestis, humana. Organ stops which are supposed to represent the voices of the angels, of Heaven, and of men, and which attract the interest of the public mainly, it would seem, owing to their failure to live up to their names. The *vox coelestis* (*voix céleste*; also known as *unda maris*) utilizes the principle of *beats in order to produce a waving effect; it consists of two ranks of soft flue stops one of which is tuned sharp. The *vox angelica* is usually the same, but also occurs as a single-rank stop of soft dulciana quality. The *vox humana* is a reed stop of the 17th century with very short capped pipes (about ⅛ of the normal length) which therefore reinforce only the higher harmonics. Its similarity to the human voice is most remote, unless it be "the cracked voice of an old woman of ninety," as Dr. Burney remarked.

V.s. Abbreviation for *Volti subito.

Vuoto [It.]. "Empty," toneless. *Corda vuota*, open string.

Vv. Violins.

W

Wachsend [G.]. "Growing," crescendo.

Wärme, Mit [G.]. With warmth.

Wagner tuba. See *Tuba.

Wait. Originally a watchman of an English town who (like the *Nachtwächter* in Wagner's *Meistersinger*) sounded the hours of the night. In the 15th and 16th centuries the waits developed into bands of musicians, paid by the town and beautifully uniformed, who provided music on ceremonial occasions. They also played or sang at Christmas before the houses of notables; it is in this meaning that the term survives, in present-day parlance, for

somebody making Christmas music in the streets. The term wait (wayte) was also used for their characteristic instrument, a shawm, as well as for the tunes played by the various local guilds, e.g., London Waits, Chester Waits. Many of these tunes are preserved in 17th- and 18th-century dance books, such as Playford's *Dancing Master* (1665). Cf. F. W. Galpin, "Shawms and Waits" (*ML* iv); J. C. Bridge, in *PMA* liv.

Waldhorn [G., forest horn]. The French horn, either natural or with valves.

Waldstein Sonata. Beethoven's Piano Sonata in C, op. 53, dedicated to his friend, Graf Waldstein,

Walküre, Die. See *Ring des Nibelungen.

Waltz [F. *valse*; G. *Walzer*]. A dance in moderate triple time which originated around 1800 and which not only has retained its popularity to the present day, but has also, time and again, inspired the imagination of composers. The waltzes by Beethoven [vol. xxv of the B.-H. edition; cf. also the well-known Walzer of the Diabelli Variations] still resemble the earlier *Ländler* or *Deutsche Tanz*, as do also to some extent the numerous waltzes by Schubert [vol. xii of the complete ed.]. Weber's "Aufforderung zum Tanz" (1819) for the first time shows that irresistible sway and characteristic accompaniment which have remained associated with the waltz. For the later history of the waltz in art music it suffices to mention the names of Chopin, Johann Strauss, father and son (see *DTOe* 32.ii and 35.ii), Berlioz (Symphonie Fantastique), Brahms (Liebeslieder Walzer), Richard Strauss (in *Rosenkavalier*), Ravel (Valses nobles et sentimentales; also La Valse, for orchestra).

The waltz developed from an Austrian peasant dance, the *Ländler (the theory of its French origin and its derivation from the *volta is discussed and properly refuted in *GD*). As early as 1700 its characteristic idiom appears in the ritornelle of a pastoral *Singspiel* [see the accompanying example]. The waltz was an

epoch in the history of the dance because it was the first dance in which the partners embraced each other. Naturally this evoked enthusiastic response as well as violent protest. Burney, in Reese's *Cyclopedia* (*c.* 1805), probably confusing *walzen* with *sich wälzen*, makes an allusion to "rolling in the dirt of mire" and speaks about the "familiar treatment" and the "obliging manner in which the freedom is returned by the females." Although the waltz was already popular in Vienna in the time of Haydn and Mozart — the English singer Kelly records its vogue in 1773 — statements found in a recent reference book to the effect that Haydn and Mozart wrote waltzes are misleading. The "Mouvement de Walze" found in a Haydn Sonata from about 1766 is a real minuet, and the above inscription is very likely the addition of one Demar who printed the work in his *Méthode* of 1806 [cf. the reprint in *BSIM* vi, 34ff]. Mozart's Deutsche Tänze (K.V. 509, 536, 567, etc.) are real Ländlers, as far as the musical style is concerned. It is interesting to note that Beethoven's name has been associated with a number of waltzes ("Beethoven's Last Waltz," "The Spirit Waltz," "Jubelwalzer") the utter triviality of which clearly marks such attribution as spurious.

Lit.: B. Weigl, *Die Geschichte des Walzers* (1910); F. Niecks, "Concerning the Waltz" (*ZIM* vi); J. Mendelssohn, in *StM* xiii; P. Nettl, in *BUM* iii.

Walze [G.]. (1) The crescendo pedal of the organ. — (2) In 18th-century parlance, term for stereotyped undulating figures, such as an *Alberti bass.

War of the Bouffons. See *Bouffons.

Wasserorgel [G.]. *Hydraulis.

Water Music. An orchestral suite by Handel, composed in 1715 for a festivity which took place in boats on the Thames. Cf. W. Michael, in *ZMW* iv.

Wa-wan Press. An American publishing firm, established by Arthur Farwell in 1901, which specialized in the publication of compositions based on Indian or Negro themes (A. Farwell, H. F. Gilbert, H. W. Loomis). It was sold to G. Schirmer in 1912.

Wechsel- [G., change]. *Wechseldominante*, the dominant of the dominant, i.e., the (major) supertonic. *Wechselgesang*, alternative or antiphonal singing. *Wechselnote* is somewhat loosely used to denote *nonharmonic tones involving a change of direction, e.g., cambiata, échappée, appoggiatura; *verlassene* or *Fux'sche Wechselnote* is always the cambiata, particularly in its combination with a suspension:

Wehmütig [G.]. Sorrowful.

Weihnachtsmusik [G.]. Christmas music.

Well-tempered Clavier. English for *Wohltemperiertes Clavier*, Bach's collection of forty-eight [see *Forty-eight] preludes and fugues, written in two parts (1722 and 1744) each of which contains 24 preludes and fugues, one for each major and minor key (C major, C minor, C♯ major, C♯ minor, etc.). The name refers to the then novel system of equal temperament [see *Temperament] which made it possible to play equally well in all the keys, and of which Bach's collection was the first complete realization. The first printed edition appeared in 1799 (Kollmann, London). The pieces in the two collections date from widely different periods of Bach's life. The most obvious difference of style between the first and second parts is found in the preludes in aria style and in binary form which do not occur in the first collection. A much discussed question is that of the "proper" instrument for these pieces, i.e., whether they are written for the harpsichord or for the clavichord. Usually this problem has been approached too much from that modern "either-or" point of view which has proved detrimental in so many problems of early music. Some scholars have gone so far as to maintain that certain preludes of the *Wt. Cl.* are written for the clavichord while the corresponding fugue is written for the harpsichord.

An important forerunner of Bach's work is the *Ariadne musica* of J. K. F. Fischer (*c.* 1700; new ed. by E. von Werra) which contains 20 preludes and fugues in 19 different keys. Particularly interesting is the unmistakable thematic similarity between some of Fischer's fugues

and those of Bach in the same key, e.g., those in G minor (*Wt. Cl.* i), E major (*Wt. Cl.* ii), and F major (*Wt. Cl.* i) — a similarity which is too striking to be incidental [cf. *HAM*, no. 248]. On the other hand, a collection of 24 preludes and fugues written by B. C. Weber under a title identical with that of Bach's first collection is not a forerunner, but an imitation of Bach's work (the date 1689, which appears on the MS of the Brussels Conservatory, is spurious; Weber lived from 1712 to 1758). Cf. W. Tappert, in *MfM* xx, 10 and xxi, 8; new edition in *Veröffentlichungen der Neuen Bach-Gesellschaft* xxxiv.1.

Lit.: J. A. Fuller-Maitland, *The "48," Bach's Wohltemperiertes Clavier* (1925); C. Gray, *The Forty-eight Preludes and Fugues of J. S. Bach* (1938); E. Prout, *Analysis of Bach's 48 Fugues.*

Welsh music. See *Bards.

Weltlich [G.]. Secular.

Whistle. A very small and simple flageolet (end-blown pipe) with only six holes, made from wood, cane, metal, or, recently, celluloid.

In scientific classification whistle flutes or fipple flutes denotes a category of flutes which are blown by means of a "flue" [see *Instruments III, B, 2 (c)]. The upper end of the pipe is stopped by a plug, called fipple or *Block* (hence the German name *Blockflöte* for the recorder), with a narrow slit left, through which the breath is led towards the sharp edge of a side opening. The same principle of sound generation is used in the "flue pipes" of the organ [see *Organ VIII]. To this category belong several families, mainly the *recorders and the flageolets. The latter differ from the recorder in certain details of construction, but mainly in the smaller number of finger-holes, four in front and two thumb-holes in the rear. Cf. N. Bessaraboff, *Ancient European Musical Instruments* (1941), pp. 6off.

Whole-note. See *Notes.

Whole-tone. The interval of the major second. See *Intervals.

Whole-tone scale [G. *Ganztonleiter*]. A scale consisting of whole-tones only, six to the octave. Only two such scales exist, namely: c–d–e–f♯–g♯–b♭–c′ and c♯–d♯–f–g–a–b–c♯′. The whole-tone scale lacks three of the most fundamental intervals of traditional music, i.e., the perfect fifth, the perfect fourth, and the leading tone. In fact, the exploitation of its resources has been, in the hands of Debussy, one of the most obvious indications of the 20th-century revolt against the harmonic system of the 19th century. Owing to the presence of only one interval the whole-tone scale completely lacks that feeling of "centralization" and "localization" which, in the normal scales or in church modes, is indicated by the term "tonic." Its inherent indecision and vagueness make it an appropriate vehicle of the impressionistic style, but put a definite limitation on its usefulness for a more constructive type of music. As a matter of fact, after a short vogue in the first decade of the 20th century, it has lost most of its glamour and is seldom used today. Rebikov's (1866–1920) "Les Démons s'amusent" is written entirely in the whole-tone scale, as are also sections of Debussy's "Voiles" (1910), while Busoni, in the second movement of his Sonatina seconda (1912), uses it for the passages of the right

hand [see Ex.]. Whole-tone formations in earlier compositions (Schubert (?), Rossini, Glinka, Berlioz) which have frequently been cited, are merely in the character of modulatory progressions within the conventional system of harmonies, not examples of a unified whole-tone tonality.

Whole-tube instruments. See *Wind-instruments II.

Wiegend [G.]. Swaying.

Wiener Klassiker [G.]. *Viennese classics.

Wie zuvor [G.]. As previously.

Winchester troper. See *Troper.

Wind band. See *Band.

Wind-chest. In organs, an air-tight box which receives the wind from the bellows and from which it passes to the pipes above it. See *Organ I.

Wind-gauge. In organs, a device indicating the supply of air in the bellows. In the modern electrically operated organs it is hardly necessary.

Wind instruments. Generic term for all instruments in which the sound-generating medium is an enclosed column of air. They are, in scientific terminology, usually referred to as Aerophones, although, strictly speaking, this latter category includes a subdivision, the "free aerophones" which usually are not included under the term Wind instruments [see *Instruments III A, B]. The main species of wind instruments are the *brass instruments (*trumpets, *horns, *tubas, etc.), the *flutes, the *clarinets, and the *oboes (the last three also called *Wood winds), each of which receives special treatment in this book. The subsequent explanations deal with their common acoustical properties.

I. In each wind instrument an enclosed column of air, cylindrical or conical (dependent on the bore of the instrument), is set into vibration [see *Acoustics V]. Neither the material (whether brass or wood) nor the shape (whether straight or wound) is important. The pitch of the produced sound depends only on the length of the pipe, its timbre mainly on the mouthpiece (single reed in the clarinets, double reed in the oboes, mouth-hole in the flutes, cupped mouthpiece in the trumpets, funnel mouthpiece in the horns, etc.), on the shape of the bore, the widening of the bell, etc.

II. Properly, a pipe of given length gives one tone only, e.g., a pipe of 8 ft. length approximately the tone C, of 4 ft. the tone c, etc. [see *Foot]. However, by proper control of the breath and the lips, called *overblowing*, a pipe can easily

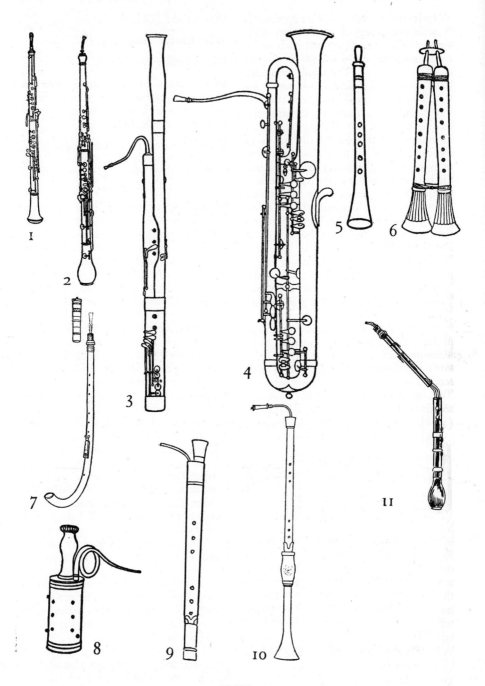

OBOES

1. Oboe. 2. English horn. 3. Bassoon. 4. Sarrusophone. 5. Tibia. 6. Indian double oboe.
7. Cromorne. 8. Ranket. 9. Dulcian. 10. Shawm, tenor. 11. Oboe de caccia.

be made to sound not only its normal tone, the *fundamental*, but also the higher *harmonics. These tones constitute what is called the "natural tones" of a wind instru-

$$\overset{\text{1 2 3 4 5 6 7 8 9 10}}{}$$

ment, e.g.: c c′ g′ c″ e″ g″ bb″ c‴ d‴ e‴, etc. Another term for the fundamental tone is *pedal tone*. On a number of instruments the pedal tone is practically unobtainable, and a distinction is made between *whole-tube instruments* in which the air column can be made to vibrate as a whole, thus producing the pedal tone, and *half-tube instruments* in which even the slightest air pressure is likely to set up vibrations of the half length, thus producing the first harmonic (c′). To the former category belong all the wood winds and the brass instruments of wide bore (tubas); to the latter, nominally, the brass instruments of narrow bore (trumpets, horns, trombones, higher saxhorns). It should be noted, however, that good players of the present day can obtain the pedal notes on trumpets and saxhorns, so that the French horn and the trombone in the lower positions of the slide remain, for all practical purposes, the only half-tube instruments.

III. The above explanations refer to the so-called *open pipes*, i.e., pipes which are open at their lower end. If a pipe of the same length is closed at the lower end (*stopped pipe*), its fundamental is an octave lower than in the open pipe [see *Acoustics V for an explanation] and, in addition, the odd-numbered partials only above this fundamental are obtainable. If an open pipe and a stopped pipe of half the length are compared the fundamentals will be the same, but the natural series will differ as follows:

$$\overset{\text{1 2 3 4 5 6 7 8 9 10}}{}$$

Open 4′ pipe: c c′ g′ c″ e″ g″ bb″ c‴ d‴ e‴
Stopped 2′ pipe: c   g′   e″   bb″   d‴

Stopped pipes are frequently used in organ building, to obtain lower tones from relatively short pipes [see *Organ IX]. Wind instruments with a cylindrical bore usually act as stopped pipes, although they are not actually stopped at the lower end. The most important instrument of this class is the clarinet which

is said to "overblow at the fifth" (correctly, at the tenth), while the instruments with a conoidal bore (oboes, horns, etc.) overblow at the octave. In German terminology the former class is called *quintierend* [F. *quintoyer*], the latter *oktavierend* [F. *octavier*].

IV. On a wind instrument which consists of merely a pipe the natural tones are the only ones available (e.g., on the "natural" horn or trumpet). In order to obtain the numerous tones between the gaps of the natural series, means must be provided to temporarily shorten or lengthen the pipe. These are chiefly four in kind: (a) slides; (b) crooks; (c) valves; (d) sideholes.

(a) Slide. This means that the instrument consists of two separate portions of tubing, one sliding within the other so that it can be drawn out. Thus the tube is actually lengthened, and in each position a new series of natural tones, beginning respectively with C, B, Bb, etc., becomes available. Since the largest gap in the series of overtones is the fifth (c–g′), a complete chromatic scale can be obtained by the combined tones of seven series of overtones, e.g., from c–g–c′ . . . down to F#–c#–f#. . . . This principle is used with the *trombone.

(b) Crook or Shank. This is an additional piece of tubing which is inserted by the player when demanded. Since this manipulation consumes time it does not really serve to fill in the gaps of the natural scale, but only serves to give the instrument a different (lower) tuning for different pieces or different sections of a piece. This method was used with trumpets in the 18th century [see *Trumpet II].

(c) Valves. This name is misleading. What is really meant are crooks attached permanently to the instrument, but to be opened and closed momentarily by means of a valve. Normally three valves (I, II, III) are provided which lower the pitch respectively by 1, 2, or 3 semitones, while through their combined use a lowering of 4 (I+III), 5 (II+III), and 6 (I+II+III) semitones can be obtained. Thus seven series of overtones become available, resulting in a complete chromatic scale, as explained under (a). For more details, see *Valve.

(d) Side-holes. These are holes bored in the side wall of the instrument (today, of the wood winds only; formerly also of trumpets and cornets: key trumpet, key bugle) which can be opened and closed by the fingers, usually with the help of a key mechanism [see *Key (1)]. If all the holes are closed, the pipe sounds its fundamental. If some of the holes are opened, the acoustical length of the air column is shortened, and higher tones are produced. The details of this process are too complicated to be briefly described.

On the horns a limited alteration of pitch can be obtained by "stopping" [see *Horn].

Lit.: A. Carse, *Musical Wind Instruments* (1939); *GD* v, 737ff; R. Dunstan, in *PMA* xliv.

Wind machine. A device designed to imitate the sound of wind, occasionally used for descriptive purposes (R. Strauss, *Don Quixote*). It consists of a barrel framework covered with silk and revolved so that the silk is in friction against cardboard or wood.

Wirbel [G.]. (1) The peg of a violin; *Wirbelkasten*, pegbox. — (2) A drum roll.

Wohltemperiertes Clavier [G.]. See *Well-tempered Clavier.

Wolf. Generally, any disagreeable effect produced by the imperfect tuning of instruments, e.g., by organ pipes not quite in tune. Specifically: (1) The slight difference in pitch between the G♯ and the A♭ of the *mean-tone system, and similar roughnesses in other systems of unequal temperament [see *Temperament II]. — (2) In violins and cellos the term Wolfnote is given to certain tones which differ markedly both in intensity and in quality from those in adjoining parts of the compass. This undesirable effect is particularly noticeable near the F♯ on the D-string of the cello, a tone which has a poor and somewhat wobbling sound. In

the violin a similar effect occurs near the C♯ on the A-string. The wolf is found in practically all instruments, regardless of their quality. In fact, it becomes the more obtrusive the more sonorous is the general sound of the instrument. The wolf is usually attributed to some defect in the construction of the particular instrument, either the uneven thickness of the belly, the unequal elasticity of the wood, etc. However, more recent investigations have shown that it is a defect inherent in the design of the violin and the other instruments of the same family. It results from certain particularly strong vibration patterns of the belly. Cf. C. V. Raman in *Nature* 97 (1916, '17), pp. 362–363 and in *Philosophical Magazine* 32 (1916); J. A. Kessler, *The Wolfnote* (unpubl. diss. Harvard 1941).

Wood winds. See *Orchestra I. Cf. R. W. Wood, "The Woodwind Ensemble" (*ML* xv, no. 1).

Word-painting [G. *Wortmalerei*]. The expression through music of the ideas resident in or suggested by the words of a song or other vocal piece. The term is usually taken to refer to the portraying of single words or phrases which lend themselves to specific treatment, rather than to the more subtle method of capturing in music the "general mood" of the text. Modern composers usually reject the somewhat naïve device of word painting which, however, plays a prominent role in earlier music, particularly of the Baroque period. It is hardly an exaggeration to say that, in the entire vocal literature of the Baroque, it will be difficult to find the word "Heaven" or "water" without an ascending or an undulating motion in the music. As is explained under *Program music II, the methods of direct word painting are mainly of two kinds: imitation of natural sounds (laughing, fanfares, birds), or of bodily movements (running, falling, ascending, descending). Both may, of course, occur with associated words, such as "war" (fanfare), "Heaven" (ascending), "Death" (fall). The accompanying examples from Bach's Cantatas nos. 8, 26, and 12 illustrate the descriptive treatment of the words "Ruhstatt" (resting place), "Tropfen" (drops), and "Ich folge" (I

follow). There are, of course, other associations which can be "translated" into music. For instance Weelkes in *As Vesta Was Descending* successively uses voices to the number of two, three, six, and one for the words, "First two by two, then three by three to-gether, Leaving their Goddess all alone."

More subtle and more interesting are those types of word-painting which belong within the area of indirect suggestion achieved mainly through scoring. Some of the most telling examples of this are found in the works of Josquin, in the period of the *musica reservata, when words and music were first forming an intelligent partnership. For instance, in his motet *In pauperum refugium* the harmonic and contrapuntal treatment is orthodox up to the point where the words "via errantium" (the life of the erring ones) occur; here the

succeeding aimlessness of the lines and the absence of harmonic agreement between them result in a startlingly vivid depiction of the idea expressed in the text, a depiction which is strengthened by the clear and obviously appropriate harmonic implications of the music at the words "veritas et vita" (truth and life).

Countless instances of word-painting of one sort or another might be cited in every period from the time of Josquin through our own. Some contemporary composers, to be sure, seem not to be greatly concerned with this matter, perhaps because the idiom which they employ is better suited to the conveyance of abstract musical ideas expressed instrumentally. Many stimulating examples, however, may be found in the vocal works of such composers as Milhaud, Honegger, Walton, Thompson, Vaughan Williams, Pizzetti, and Holst.

Word repetition. See *Text and Music.

Wt. Cl. Customary abbreviation for Bach's *Well-tempered Clavier.*

Wuchtig [G.]. Forceful, heavy.

Wurstfagott [G., sausage bassoon]. The rankett [see *Oboe family III].

Würdig [G.]. With dignity.

Wütend [G.]. Furious.

X

Xylophone [from Gr. *xylos*, wood, and *phone*, sound]. A percussion instrument consisting of graduated bars of hardwood which are struck with a stick. For the modern orchestral instrument see *Percussion instruments A, 3. A jazz-band variety is the *marimba. Xylophones are frequently used in primitive cultures, particularly in Africa, and have attained a high degree of perfection in the *Javanese orchestra. Around 1500 they became known in Europe under the

name *hültze glechter* ("wooden percussion"; Arnolt Schlick, *Spiegel der Orgelmacher und Organisten*, 1511) and *Strohfiedel* ("strawfiddle," so called because the bars were lying on straw). Still other names are *Holzharmonika* [G.], *gigelira* [It.], and *ligneum psalterium* [L.]. Around 1830 a Russian Jew, J. Gusikow, became famous as a player of the Strohfiedel and aroused the special interest of Mendelssohn (cf. *GD* v, 765). The instrument has been em-

ployed by H. C. Lumbye in his "Traum-
bilder," by Saint-Saëns in his Danse
Macabre (1874), to describe the rattling

of skeletons, and in several modern symphonies, e.g., Shostakovich's Fifth Symphony.

Y

Yankee Doodle. A popular American
tune which, in the course of 150 years,
has been used for a great number of texts
of a humorous character. The origin of
the tune is just as mysterious as that of
the words "Yankee" and "Doodle." Its
first recorded appearance is in James
Aird's *Selection of Scotch, English, Irish
and Foreign Airs* (c. 1775), where it is
given, with the title "Yankee doodle,"
as an instrumental tune, without text.
This has led to the theory that it originally was a tune for the flute, and that the
word "doodle" imitates the specific sound
of the flute if played in *tonguing. The
tune has been used as a theme for variations by Anton Rubinstein, Henri Vieuxtemps (Caprice burlesque, op. 17), and
Daniel G. Mason ("In the Styles of Various Composers"). It also occurs, in a
perfectly recognizable modification, in
the last movement of Dvořák's symphony
"From the New World."

Yodel. A special type of singing among
the mountain population of Switzerland
and Austria (Tyrol) and characterized
by the frequent and quick passing from
a low chest-voice to a high falsetto. The
"Jodler" is a vocalization appended to a

song, with low vowels (a, o) used for the
low tones, and high vowels (e, i) for the
high ones. Cf. E. v. Hornbostel, "Entstehung des Jodelns" (*KIM*, 1924).

Yüeh ch'in. A Chinese guitar. See
*Guitar family.

Yugoslavian music. The Yugoslavs
(formerly Serbs) possess an ancient tradition of epic poems which are recited
by itinerant musicians to the accompaniment of the *gadulka*, a zither similar to
the Russian gusla [Ex. in Panoff, pp. 8f].
Of special interest is the history of Serbian
liturgical chant which to the present day
has preserved the ancient system of the
octoechos [see *Echos]. The modern development of Yugoslavian music started
with Davorin Jenko (1835–1914), composer of the national hymn and of 39
operas. The leading composer of the
present day is Bozidar Sirola (b. 1889)
who wrote operas and an oratorio in
archaic style, *Cyrill und Methodus* (1927).
A modernist is Josip Slavensky (b. 1896).
   Lit.: A. Dobronic, "A Study of Yugo-
slav Music" (*MQ* xii); *AdHM* ii, 1168;
ML, 785; P. Panoff, in *BüHM*; E. Wellesz, "Die Struktur des serbischen Oktoechos" (*ZMW* ii).

Z

Zählzeit [G.]. Beat.

Zajal. A type of medieval Arabian
poetry characterized by the appearance of
a refrain before and after each stanza.
It attained a high degree of perfection in
the first half of the 12th century. Many
songs of the Spanish *cantigas are written in this form which may also have

served as the model for the French
*virelai and other refrain forms. Cf.
ReMMA, 245f.

Zaleo. Same as *Jaleo.

Zampogna [It.]. A *bagpipe or a
*shawm. Also *Hurdy-gurdy.

Zanfonia [Sp.]. *Hurdy-gurdy.

Zapateado [Sp.]. A Spanish solo dance in triple time the rhythm of which is marked by stamping of the heels, frequently in syncopation and in many other rhythms in contrast to that of the melody.

Zapfenstreich [G.]. A *Tattoo; at special occasions, however, the *Zapfenstreich* is a much more elaborate performance of military music, including signals as well as marches played by a large band.

Zarabanda [Sp.]. See *Sarabande.

Zarge [G.]. The ribs of the violin.

Zart [G.]. Tender, delicate.

Zarzuela [Sp.]. The most important type of Spanish opera. It is distinguished from the opera proper by the fact that it has music intermingled with spoken dialogue, so that it belongs to the category of *Comic opera. Its subjects, however, are not restricted to the comic type. It takes its name from the Palace of La Zarzuela (a royal country seat near Madrid, comparable to Versailles) where festive representations, called "Fiestas de Zarzuela," were given, the earliest on record being Lope de Vega's *eclogue, *La Selva sin amor* (The Forest without Love), of 1629. The earliest known composer of zarzuelas was Juan Hidalgo whose *Los Celos hacen estrellas* (text by Velez; produced 1644 ?) shows the use of the recitative [cf. *LavE* i.4, 2066] as well as of choruses in the style of the madrigal. He also composed Calderon's *Ni amor se libra de Amor* (1640; cf. F. Pedrell, *Teatro lirico espanol*, vols. iv, v) and *Celos aun del aire matan* (1660; first act published by Subira, 1933). In the later part of the 17th century the zarzuela approached the French *ballet de cour*, by the emphasis on elaborate stage production and the addition of ballets and of popular dances accompanied by the guitar and castanets (Conde de Clavijo, *c.* 1700). This type of "aristocratic opera," based largely on mythological subjects, reached its high-point with Sebastien Durón (d. 1716) and Antonio Literes (d. after 1752). At the same time there arose

a "popular" reaction against the zarzuela in the *tonadilla, a development parallel to the "guerre des bouffons." The increasing influence of the Italian opera — clearly present in the works of José de Nebra (*c.* 1685–1768) — also contributed to the decline of the zarzuela, a decline which went hand in hand with that of the Spanish drama.

An attempt at revival in a more popular form, made around 1770 by the dramatist Ramón de la Cruz in collaboration with the composer Antonio Rodriguez de Hita (d. *c.* 1787), had only temporary success. It was not until the middle of the 19th century that a forceful national movement led to a new era of the zarzuela. This renascence began chiefly with Francisco Barbieri (1823–94; *Jugar con Fuego*, 1851) and Pascual Arrieta (1823–94; *Marina*, 1871). In 1865 the *Teatro de la Zarzuela* was founded, and the movement found numerous collaborators, e.g., Ruperto Chapí (1811–1909), M. Fernandez Caballero (1835–1906), Tomas Breton (1850–1923), Joaquín Valverde (d. 1910), Amadeo Vives (1871–1933). The modern zarzuelas are classified as "zarzuela grande" in three acts, and "genero chico" or "zarzuelita" in one act. The former deal preferably with subjects of a serious and dramatic character, while the latter are essentially comic. Breton's *La Dolores* (1895) and *La Verbena de la Paloma* (1894) are outstanding examples of each type. In the most recent times the "zarzuela grande" has been cultivated chiefly by Francisco Alonso (b. 1887) and Federico Moreno-Torroba (1891); the "genero chico" (with features derived from the Viennese operetta and even of American jazz), by Jacinto Guerrero, Rosillo, and others.

Lit.: G. Chase, *The Music of Spain* (1941), *passim* (bibl.); E. Cotalero y Mori, *Historia de la Zarzuela* i (1934); *LavE* i.4, 2052ff; A. Salazar, "Music in the Primitive Spanish Theatre" (*PAMS*, 1938); G. Chase, "Origins of the Lyric Theatre in Spain" (*MQ* xxv); *id.*, "Barbieri and the Spanish Zarzuela" (*ML* xx, no. 1); J. Subira, in *AM* iv, no. 2; A. Pedrell, in *SIM* iv.

Zauberflöte, Die ("The Magic Flute"). German opera in two acts by W. A. Mozart, libretto (concocted of Oriental fairy-tale and Freemasonry) by E. Schikaneder, produced 1791. *Tamino* (Tenor), seeing a picture of *Pamina* (Soprano), the daughter of the evil *Queen of the Night* (Soprano), falls in love with her and, on orders of the Queen, goes out — accompanied by the bird-catcher *Papageno* (Baritone) — to rescue her from the temple of the High-Priest *Sarastro* (Bass) where she is held captive, guarded and pestered by the Moor *Monostatos* (Tenor). Sarastro who holds Pamina only in order to "guide her to wisdom" finds Tamino worthy and also promises that Papageno will find a companion—*Papagena* (Soprano)—but various ordeals (injunction against speaking; passing through fire and water) are necessary before the lovers are united.

The *Zauberflöte*, Mozart's last opera, indicates a decided change in Mozart's approach to opera, a change which, unfortunately, was cut short by his death, in 1792. The Italian opera buffa idea, which prevails in *Figaro and *Don Giovanni, is replaced here by a seriousness of purpose and sincerity of feeling which presage Beethoven. On the other hand, the process of purification is not carried to its full end so that, on the whole, the opera would seem to be a somewhat less perfect example of its type than is the case with *Figaro* and *Don Giovanni*.

Zeitmass [G.]. Tempo.

Zeitmesser [G.]. Metronome.

Zeunertanz [G.]. Old German for *Zigeunertanz*, i.e., gypsy dance (in H. Newsidler, 1535).

Ziehharmonika [G.]. *Accordion.

Ziemlich [G.]. Rather.

Zigeunermusik [G.]. Gypsy music.

Zimbalon. See *Cimbalom.

Zingaresa, Alla [It.]. In the style of gypsy music.

Zink(en). German for the *cornett.

Zirkelkanon [G.]. Circular canon.

Zither. (1) A modern instrument used chiefly by the Bavarian and Austrian peasants (and their imitators), consisting of a flat wooden soundbox over which from 30 to 45 strings are stretched. Four or five melody strings, nearest to the player, can be stopped on a fretted finger board and are plucked by a plectrum. The other strings are plucked by the fingers and are used for accompaniment. Cf. Ch. Maclean, in *ZIM* x. — (2) Scientific name for a large class of stringed instruments also called *Psalteries [see *Instruments IV, A, 1 (a)]. Illustrations on p. 823. — (3) Sometimes wrong spelling for *cither.

Zitternd [G.]. Trembling.

Znamenny chant. Name for the chant of the Russian Church, as used from the 12th through the 17th century. The name is derived from *znamia*, i.e., sign, neume. The oldest extant musical monuments date from *c.* 1200, and are notated in signs which are very similar to those of the early Byzantine notation. Later sources (11th to 17th centuries) are written in the so-called kriuki (or znamenny) notation, a system including over 90 different signs for single notes as well as for stereotyped melodic formulae. They have not yet been deciphered. Eventually the number of signs was reduced and certain auxiliary symbols were added, usually in red ink (hence the name Cinnabar letters), by Schaidurov (16th century). At about the same time the simple outlines of the original chant were amplified into rich and ornamental contours, and the two types were distinguished as "lesser" and "greater" chant. Beginning with the 17th century there were abuses [see *Anenaiki] which finally led to the decline of the chant. See also *Russian music I.

Lit.: A. J. Swan, "The Znamenny Chant of the Russian Church" (*MQ* xxvi; also in *PAMS*, 1938); *ReMMA*, 97ff (bibl. p. 435); P. Panoff, *Die altslavische*

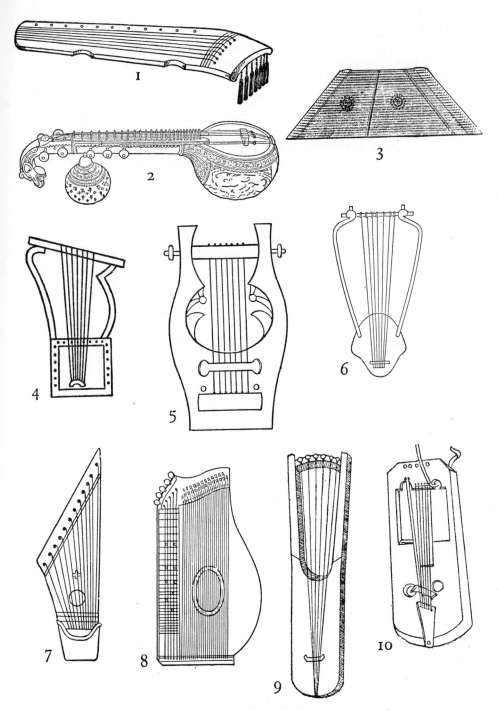

ZITHERS AND LYRES

1. Ch'in. 2. Vina. 3. Psaltery. 4. Egyptian Kithara. 5. Greek Kithara. 6. Greek Lyra.
7. Kantele. 8. Zither. 9. Rotte. 10. Crwth.

Kirchenmusik (in *BüHM*); *WoHN* i, 89; O. v. Riesemann, *Die Notation des altrussischen Kirchengesangs* (1909); *AdHM* i, 141.

Zögernd [G.]. Hesitating.

Zopf, Zopfstil [G., pigtail]. A derogative term applied to the conventional style of the period in which pigtails were the fashion, i.e., particularly the later part of the 18th century.

Zoppa, alla [It., in a limping manner]. Italian term for the inverted dotted rhythm [see *Dotted notes III]. The term *Zoppa* also occurs for 17th-century dance movements in syncopated rhythm, e.g., by Vitali [cf. *Editions II, 7].

Zortziko. A Basque folk dance in quick ⅝-time and in dotted rhythm. The Castilian *rueda is also in quintuple time, but without dotted notes. Cf. the examples in *LavE* i.4, 2363.

Zuffolo [It.]. General name for primitive shepherd pipes, shawms, flageolets, etc.

Zug [G.]. Slide. *Zugposaune,* slide trombone, the ordinary trombone. *Zugtrompete,* slide trumpet.

Zunge [G.]. Reed. *Zungenpfeife,* reed pipe.

Zurückhalten [G.]. To hold back.

Zutraulich [G.]. Confiding.

Zwerchflöte [from old G. *zwerch,* across]. Old name for the transverse flute.

Zwischensatz [G.]. The middle section in ternary form, also used for the development section in sonata-form.

Zwischenspiel [G.]. Interlude, particularly the instrumental interludes between the stanzas of a song [ritornello], or the tutti sections in a concerto. Also denomination for fugal episodes [see *Durchführung], or the episodes in rondo-form.

Zwölftonsystem [G.]. See *Twelvetone technique.

Zyklische [G.]. *Cyclic, always in the sense explained under (1).

Zymbel [G.]. *Cymbal.

Accidentals. The sign for the double-sharp is used in Giov. M. Trabaci's *Il secondo libro de ricercare . . .* of 1615.

Acoustics. Lit.: Charles A. Culver, *Musical Acoustics* (1941).

Aesthetics of Music. III (b): An early "autonomist" is M. de Chabanon, who in 1785 published *De la musique considerée en elle même.*

Affektenlehre. Lit.: E. Katz, *Die musikalischen Stilbegriffe des 17. Jahrunderts* (1926).

Ambrosian hymns. Lit.: Emilio Garbagnati, *Gli inni del breviario ambrosiano* (1897).

American music. P. 34, col. 2: *for* Schumann *read* Schuman.

Anche. Also reed instrument, e.g., in *Trio d'anches.*

Aria. Lit.: L. Torchi, "Canzoni ed arie . . . nel secolo XVII" (*RMI* i).

Arpeggio. P. 53, col. 1, ex. 2, measure 2: first quarter note on each staff should be dotted.

Ars nova. P. 56, col. 2: *for* Liège *read* Liége.

Aufführungspraxis. Lit.: H. Albrecht, *Die Aufführungspraxis der italienischen Musik des 14. Jahrhunderts* (Diss. Berlin, 1924); F. Dorian, *The History of Music in Performance* (1942).

Australia. Composers of Australian descent include Percy A. Grainger (b. 1882, now a citizen of the United States), Alfred Hill (b. 1870), Roy Agnew (b. 1893), and Margaret Sutherland (b. 1897). Fritz Bennicke Hart (b. 1874 in England) settled in Australia in 1909 and is now director of the Melbourne Conservatory. Australia's most outstanding contribution in the field of music has been made by Mrs. Louise B. Dyer through the foundation of the Lyre Bird Press. The magnificent and invaluable publications of this press include, among others, the complete edition of the Montpellier Codex [see *Sources, no. 4], and the complete works of François Couperin. Cf. Marks Levine, "Musical Life in Australia and New Zealand" (in Pierre Key's *Music Year Book,* 1926/27, p. 178); V. A. Rucroft, "A Survey of Music in New Zealand" (*PMA,* 1943, p. 56); Dai-kong Lee, "Music Down Under" (*MM* xxii, no. 4).

B-A-C-H. Correct: W. Piston, *Chromatic Study on the Name of Bach.* Add: A. Casella, *Due Ricercari sul nome di Bach.*

Ballet. II. Adolphe Ch. Adam wrote a number of ballets, the most successful of which was *Giselle* (1841). Danish ballets were written by J. P. E. Hartmann (*Valkyrien, Thrymskviden*) and his son E. Hartmann (*Fjeldstuen*).
III. P. 70, col. 2, lines 11-12: *for* Marc Blitzstein *read* Arthur Bliss.

Barbershop harmony. P. 73, col. 2, musical example: insert figure 8 beneath the treble clef.

Basse danse. All the early sources, theoretical as well as practical, clearly indicate that the basse danse is in slow triple meter. Only in the latest sources do examples in duple meter occur.

Cancionero. An important recent publication is R. Mitjana, J. Bal y Gay, and I. Pope, *Cancionero de Upsala* (Mexico, 1944).

Canon. Change the first sentence to read as follows: "A polyphonic composition in which one part is imitated strictly and for its entire length in another part, or in all the parts." The term canon is also used for the short "canonic" imitations properly termed *stretto.

Cantiga. Lit.: J. Ribera, †*La musica de las cantigas* (1922); G. Sunyol, *Cantigues de Montserrat . . . (Publicaciones del Monasterio de Montserrat).*

Canzona. (5): Instrumental canzonas (though not named thus) occur in the works of Obrecht and Isaac. Cf. *HAM*, nos. 78, 88.

Carnival of Venice. Omit reference to Liszt.

Chamber music. Lit.: H. Mersmann, *Kammermusik* (4 vols., 1930ff).

Chapel. P. 132, col. 1: *for* Gratton *read* Grattan.

Chinese music. Lit.: C. Sachs, *The Rise of Music* (1943), pp. 105ff.

Chorus. Add: (3) Same as refrain.

Chroai. Cf. C. Sachs, *The Rise of Music* (1943).

Clarin trumpet. Lit.: Joh. Ernst Altenburg, *Versuch einer Anleitung zur heroisch-musikalischen Trompeten und Pauken Kunst* (1795, new ed. 1912); W. Menke, *History of the Trumpet of Bach and Handel* (1934).

Classicism. F. Torrefranca, "Le Origini dello stile mozartiano" (*RMI* xxvii, xxxiii, xxxiv, xxxvi).

Clausula. P. 156, col. 1, line 27: *for* vers *read* verse.

Clavichord. The "bundfreie" clavichord is expressly called for in the preface to Johann Speth's *Ars Magna Consoni et Dissoni* of 1697.

Color and music. Lit.: Arthur Lange, *Spectrotone System of Orchestration* (1943); A. László, *Die Farblichtmusik* (1925); *id.,* †*Kompositionen für Klavier und Farblicht* (1926).

Comic opera. Lit.: F. Vatielli, "Opere comiche di G. B. Martini' (*RMI* xxxix).

Composition. P. 169, col. 1: *for* Ernst Bloch *read* Ernest Bloch.

Concerto. Lit.: H. Engel, *Die Entwicklung des Klavierkonzerts von Mozart bis Liszt* (1927); Th. Stengel, *Die Entwicklung des Klavierkonzerts von Liszt bis zur Gegenwart* (1931); C. M. Girdlestone, *Mozart et ses concerts pour piano* (1939); M. Brusotti, "Di alcuni inediti 'Klavierkonzerte' di J. Haydn" (*RMI* xxxviii).

A violin concerto by Schumann has recently been discovered.

Copyright. P. 187, col. 1, line 18: *for* proclamation *read* proclamations.

Coronation Concerto. There are two Coronation Concertos by Mozart, K. V. 459 in F major (1784) and K. V. 537 in D major (1788); the latter is the more famous. Both were played by Mozart at the coronation of the Emperor Leopold at Frankfurt in 1790.

Council of Trent. Lit.: H. Leichtentritt, in *MQ* xxx, no. 3.

Counterpoint. Lit.: J. J. Fux, *Steps to Parnassus* (1944; transl. by A. Mann of the *Gradus ad Parnassum* of 1725); R. O. Morris, *Introduction to Counterpoint* (1944); *id., Contrapuntal Technique in the Sixteenth Century* (1922).

Courante. Cf. C. Sachs, *World History of the Dance* (1937), pp. 361ff.

École d'Arcueil. The followers of Satie never actually convened in his home at Arcueil.

Editions, Historical. V. 50: J. Georg Kühnhausen, Deutsche Mattheus-Passion. — 51: Lambert de Sayve, Deutsche Liedlein. — 52: Augustin Pfleger, Passionsmusik.

XXIII A. *Plain-song and Mediaeval Music Society.* Selection of publications; numbering (chronological) not original. (1) The Musical Notation of the Middle-Ages (facsimiles). — (2) A Collection of (English) Songs and Madrigals . . . of the . . . 15th Century. — (3) Madrigals by English Composers of the . . . 15th Century. — (4) Graduale Sarisburiense (facsimile, ed. W. H. Frere). — (5) Early English Harmony, 2 vols. (facs. and transcr., ed. H. Hughes). — (6) Antiphonale Sarisburiense (facs., ed. W. H. Frere). — (7) Theodoric Petri, *Piae cantiones ecclesiasticae et scholasticae,* 1582 (Swedish source, ed. G. R. Woodward). — (8) Worcester Mediaeval Harmony (ed. A. Hughes). — (9) *Missa O quam suavis* (ed. H. B. Collins). — (10) The Old Hall Manuscript, 3 vols. (ed. A. Ramsbotham). — (11) Anglo-French Sequelae (ed. H. M. Bannister).

XXV. 10: Das Madrigal als Formideal (H. Schultz). — 11: Die drei- und vierstimmigen Notre-Dame Organa (Husmann).

XXVI A. *Smith College Archives.* (1) Geminiani, 12 Sonatas for violin and pianoforte (R. L. Finney; I). — (2) J. J. Fux, *Costanza e Fortezza* (G. P. Smith; Op). — (3) L. Boccherini, Concerto for Cello (M. DeRonde; I). — (4) Andrea Antico (publ.), *Canzoni Sonetti Strambotte et Frottole, Lib.* 30, 1517 (A. Einstein; V). — (5) The Chansons of Jacques Arcadelt, vol. I (E. B. Helm; V).

Egyptian music. Lit.: C. Sachs, *The Rise of Music* (1943), pp. 71ff.

English music. Lit.: Correct: *Early English Harmony,* vol. i, facsimiles, by H. E. Wooldridge (1897); vol. ii, transcriptions, by H. V. Hughes (1913). Add:

J. Stainer, †*Early Bodleian Music,* 2 vols. (1901); Ch. van den Borren, *Sources of Keyboard Music in England* (1913).

Estampie. There also exist two-voice examples of estampie (or ductia); cf. *HAM,* no. 41. Monophonic examples are given in *HAM,* no. 40.

Ethos. Lit.: C. Sachs, *The Rise of Music* (1943).

Exotic music. Cf. G. Knopf, "Essai d'harmonie exotique" (*RMI* xxxviii).

Exposition. The term is also used for the subsequent imitative sections of a fugue. See the explanation under *Fugue I (d), (f).

Film music. Lit.: L. L. Sabaneev, *Music for the Films* (1935); K. London, *Film Music* (1936).

Flemish school. P. 269, col. 1, line 15: *for* Adriaen *read* Adrian.

Flute. Lit.: D. C. Miller, *Catalogue of Books . . . Relating to the Flute* (1935).

Folia. See below under Passamezzo.

Form. K. Westphal, *Der Begriff der musikalischen Form* (1933).

Fourth. P. 280, col. 1: *for* successive fourths *read* superimposed fourths.

Frottola. The full refrain (*ripresa*) is given only at the beginning of the poem, while between the stanzas (*piedi*) it occurs in a shortened form (*volta*), consisting of the first half of the initial ripresa:

	Ripresa	Piedi	Volta	Piedi	Volta . . .
Text:	r r	s s s	r	s s s	r . . .
Music:	a b	a a b	a–	a a b	a– . . .

a– indicates a coda-like extension of a. Frequently the second half of a (music for the second single line) is identical with the first half of b (third single line). In the case of eight-line stanzas (s s s s) their musical scheme is a a b b.

German music. P. 294, col. 2, line 14. 1587, not 1586.

Goliard songs. A number of the songs are preserved with decipherable melodies in the Notre Dame MSS. [*Sources, no. 3].

Gregorian chant. II: An invaluable help for the study of the Gregorian texts is C. Marbach, *Carmina Scripturarum* (1927), which gives the sources for the Scriptural texts of the Gregorian chant.
IV. (a): In the tracts the repetitions are essential to the form. — Lit.: G. Stevens, "Gregorian Chant" (*MQ* xxx, no. 2).

Ground. Lit.: L. Propper, *Der basso ostinato* (Diss. Berlin, 1926).

Harmonic rhythm. P. 319, col. 2, musical example, measure 4, last chord: bottom note should be f-natural.

Heterophony. For examples of heterophonic style see *HAM*, nos. 2 (Japanese) and 3 (Siamese).

Hindu music. Lit.: C. Sachs, *The Rise of Music* (1943), pp. 158ff.
A survey of the historical development is given in Fox-Strangway, pp. 83ff. Cf. also *HAM*, no. 4.

History of music. P. 339, col. 1, lines 6-8: Of the *Historical Anthology of Music* by A. T. Davison and Willi Apel, Vol. I. was published in 1946, Vol. II in 1950.

Hydraulis. Lit.: H. Degering, *Die Orgel . . . bis zur Karolingerzeit* (1905).

Hymn, English. Lit.: H. W. Foote, *Three Centuries of American Hymnody* (1940); W. H. Frere, *Hymns Ancient and Modern;* with Introduction (1909).

Imitation. P. 349, col. 2, example 2: the last note in the lowest voice in measure 4 should be connected by a slur with the first note in the same voice in measure 5.

Instrumental music. Regarding the problem of instrumental versus vocal style in early music, see under *Ensemble. Cf. also L. Hibberd, in *MQ* xxii, no. 2.

Invitatorium. P. 366b, lines 3 and 6, read "Office of the Dead" for "Requiem Mass."

Japanese music. Lit.: C. Sachs, *The Rise of Music* (1943), pp. 105ff.

Jewish music. P. 382, col. 2, line 16: *for* Spickler *read* Spicker.
Lit.: C. Sachs, *The Rise of Music* (1943), pp. 79ff.; O. Kinkeldey, "A Jewish Musician of the 15th Century" (A. S. Freidus Memorial Volume).

Keyboard. P. 386, col. 2, example 1: the key (C) at the right end of the diagram should be notched to indicate the adjoining black key.

Keyboard music. Lit.: E. Bodky, *Der Vortrag alter Klaviermusik* (1932).

Krakowiak [G.], Cracovienne [F.]. A Polish dance named after the city of Cracow. The music is in 2/4-time and employs simple syncopated patterns. The krakowiak was danced by large groups, with shouting, improvised singing, and striking of the heels together. It was in vogue in the early part of the nineteenth century and became known all over the world through the stage performances of Fanny Elssler. Chopin wrote a "Krakowiak" for piano and orchestra (op. 14).

Lamentations. Omit sentence p. 392b, lines 3 and 2 from bottom, "The . . . (1474)."

Latin America. Lit.: N. Slonimsky, *Music of Latin America* (1945).

Lauda. P. 395, col. 1, line 4: for *Lauda* read *Laude*.

Leonora Overtures. Cf. H. Braunstein, *Beethoven's Leonore-Ouvertüren* (1927).

Libraries. P. 403b, insert:
  Oxford. Bodleian Library and *Christ Church Library.* Catalogue of MSS, by G. E. P. Arkwright (1915); of printed music, by Aloys Hiff (1919).

Lied. Additional lit. in *MoML*, 452.

Liturgical books. Add under *Processionale: The Processionale monasticum . . .* Ordinis Sancti Benedicti (1893) contains many important responsoria, e.g., the *Aspiciens a longe* mentioned on p. 610.

Madrigal. Lit.: G. Cesari, "Le Origini del madrigale cinquecentesco" (*RIM* xix).
  Lit.: E. H. Fellowes, *The English Madrigal Composers* (1921); *id., The English Madrigal* (1925).

March. W. D. Allen, *Our Marching Civilization* (1943).

Mass. P. 427, col. 1, line 2: for *méssa* read *messa*.

Mechanical composition. Lit.: J. Ph. Kirnberger, *Der allezeit fertige Polonoisen- und Menuettenkomponist* (1757); A. László, *The Dice Composer* (1941).

Mechanical instruments. Lit.: R. Mosoriak, *The Curious History of Music Boxes* (1943).

Metamorphosis. Omit the last sentence.

Middle Ages. Lit.: G. S. Bedrook. "The Nature of Mediaeval Music" (*ML* xxvi, no. 2).

Monody. Lit.: O. Kinkeldey, *Orgel und Klavier im 16. Jahrhundert* (1910).

Motet. Lit. A: H. Tischler, "The Motet in 13th-Century France" (unpubl. diss. Yale, 1942); *id.,* in *MQ* xxx — Lit. B: O. Strunk, "Some Motet-Types of the 16th Century" (*Papers Read at the International Congress of Musicology* [New York, 1939], 1944).

Music criticism. I. No less important than Schumann is E. T. A. Hoffmann (1776–1822), whose reviews, written for the *Allgemeine musikalische Zeitung* (Leipzig, 1809ff.), include some admirable analyses of Beethoven's C-minor Symphony, Coriolan Overture, Trios op. 70 and *Egmont* (cf. the cpl. ed. by W. Harich, vol. xii). — Lit.: I. Kolodin, *The Critical Composer* (1940); T. Stege, *Bilder aus der deutschen Musikkritik* (1936).

Music education. Lit.: Ch. W. Hughes, *Chamber Music in American Schools* (1933).

Mute. Muted cellos and double-basses are used very effectively at the beginning of Stravinsky's Firebird Suite. Mutes are also made with two or five prongs.

National Anthems. "God Save the King" is definitely not by H. Carey. Cf. P. A. Scholes, *God Save the King* (1942).

Neapolitan School. Cf. E. J. Dent, "The Nomenclature of Opera" (*ML* xxv).

Notation. Lit.: J. Wolf, *Geschichte der Mensuralnotation* (3 vols., 1904).

Nuove musiche. P. 498, col. 2, line 2: 1601, not 1602.

Ode-symphonie. The term is also used for other French compositions employing an orchestra and a chorus, e.g., Bizet's *Vasco da Gama.*

Odhecaton. P. 504, col. 1, line 27: Helen Hewitt, not M. Hewitt; *Harmonice Musices Odhecaton: A,* not *The Odhecaton.*

Opera. Lit. A: J. Towers, *Dictionary-Catalogue of Operas . . .* (1910). — Lit. B: Ernest Newman, *Stories of Great Operas* (1928; 2d vol. 1943). — Lit. E: E. J. Dent, "Nomenclature of Opera" (*ML* xxv).

Oratorio. Lit.: C. H. Bitter, *Beiträge zur Geschichte des Oratoriums* (1872).

Orchestra. P. 520b: Handel's "piccolo" is, of course, a small recorder, not the modern piccolo flute. — Lit.: A. Carse, *The Orchestra in the 18th Century* (1940).

Organ. Lit.: Adlung, *Musica mechanica organoedi* (1768; new ed. 1931); H. Degering, *Die Orgel . . . bis zur Karolingerzeit* (1905).

Organ chorale. Lit.: Stainton de B. Taylor, *The Chorale Preludes of J. S. Bach* (1942); H. E. Huggler, *J. S. Bach's Orgelbüchlein* (Diss. Bern, 1930).

Organ Mass. Cavazzoni's organ Masses are not completely for the organ, but for alternating organ and choir.

Oriental music. Lit.: C. Sachs, *The Rise of Music* (1943).

Ornamentation. For the example given on p. 546 the writer of this article is indebted to W. Landowska, *Music of the Past* (1924), p. 131ff.

Ostinato. A modern example of the tonic-dominant ostinato exists in Chopin's Berceuse. For another example of soprano ostinato in English 16th-century music (Taverner) see *HAM, no.* 112.

Parthenia. Rimbault's edition is not made from the original plates. A facsimile edition of the original appeared in 1943.

Partial signature. Cf. also E. E. Lowinsky, in *MQ* xxxi, no. 2.

Partimento. De Nardis, †*Partimenti dei maestri Cotumacci . . .* (Ricordi, 1933).

Passamezzo. According to some scholars (O. Gombosi, M. F. Bukofzer) the "theme" used for numerous passamezzos

is to be found, not in the melody, but in the bass line: G-F-D-B flat-F-G (C-D-) G. The same remark applies to the Folia and the Romanesca. Cf. O. Gombosi, "Italia: Patria del basso ostinato" (*LRM* vii).

Phonograph and recorded music. P. 572, col. 1, line 17: *for* Kilpeinen *read* Kilpinen.
Lit.: D. Hall, *The Record Book* (1940).

Piano duet. (a): Beethoven wrote several piano duets, e.g., a Sonata op. 6, Three Marches op. 45, and op. 134, a four-hand arrangement of his Great Fugue in B-flat for string quartet (op. 133). — (b): Hindemith and Stravinsky each wrote a sonata for two pianos (1942, 1944). — Lit.: A. Rowley, *Four Hands, One Piano* (1940); K. Ganzer and L. Kusche, *Vierhändig* (1937).

Pianoforte. The first American pianofortes were built by John Brenet in Philadelphia, *c.* 1774.

Polymetric. The term is also used for modern editions of 16th-century vocal music in which the bar-lines are placed in irregular intervals, according to the requirements of the musical and textual phrases.

Prelude. A considerable number of preludes from the Buxheim Organ Book and from Kleber's tablature are reproduced in *MfM* 1888/89, Beilage.

Primitive music. Lit.: C. Sachs, *The Rise of Music* (1943).

Psalm tones. P. 612, col. 2, musical example: first words of verses 1, 2, 10, and 11 are, respectively, *Deus canticum; Qui das; Gloria; Sicut.*

Publishers, Music. *United States: for* Schumann *read* Schuman.
Add: A. P. Schmidt Company, Boston (MacDowell).

Quer-. P. 620, col. 2: after *Querflöte* insert comma, and delete comma at end of line.

Quodlibet. The term is also used for pieces whose only distinction is a somewhat nonsensical text, e.g., one dealing with the different kinds of "noses."

Ranz des vaches. A Kuhreigen of 1710 is reproduced in the B.-H. edition of Franz Liszt, *Pianoforte Werke,* vol. iv, p. iv. It shows the augmented fourth which is another characteristic trait of these melodies.

Resonance. P. 638, col. 1, line 4: *for* M. Seiffert *read* A. Seiffert.

Retrograde. For another retrograde minuet, by C. P. E. Bach, cf. *Nagel's Musik Archiv* Nr. 65 (O. Vrieslander), no. 6a.

Ricercare. The *neo-classical movement of the 20th century has led to a revival of the ricercare, e.g., in B. Martinu's *Tre Ricercari* and in A. Casella's *Due Ricercari sul nome di Bach.*

Romanesca. F. Liszt wrote a modern composition on the Romanesca theme (1860). See remark above under Passamezzo.

Rubato. Around 1800 the term rubato was used to indicate free modifications, not of temporal but of dynamic values, e.g., forte-accents on normally weak notes, such as the second and fourth beat of a 4/4-measure (Türk, 1789; H. Ch. Koch, 1808; cf. Lit., Bruck). It is entirely possible that Chopin had this manner of performance in mind when he prescribed "rubato" in his compositions. It should be noticed that he used this term almost exclusively in his mazurkas or for melodies in the character of a mazurka (F minor Concerto, last movement), the very nature of which would seem to exclude modifications of tempo but readily admits unexpected accents on the second or third beat.

Rumanian music. P. 655, col. 1: *for* Georg Enescu *read* Georges Enesco.

Russian horns. Lit.: Joh. Christian Hinrichs, *Entstehung, Fortgang und jetzige Beschaffenheit der russischen Jagdmusik* (Petersburg, 1796).

Russian music. P. 658, col. 1, line 17: *for* Montague-Nathan *read* Montagu-Nathan.

Schneller. Mr. Aldrich's implied (and intended) statement that, in music before 1750, the sign (b) always indicates the four-note ornament (*Pralltriller*), not the three-note ornament (*Schneller*), is open to doubt. Aesthetic considerations make it difficult to believe that the four-note execution should be used in cases like J. S. Bach's Preludes 6 and 12 of *Wt. Cl.* ii, or the fugal theme of the Toccata of his Partita no. 6, or D. Scarlatti's Sonata in F minor (*TaAM* xi, p. 144). All these examples show the sign in question on a "detached" note, as in Ex. (c), a position which, regardless of the period, would seem to call for the "rhythmic" Schneller rather than the "melodic" Pralltriller. In the fugal theme of Buxtehude's Toccata in G (*Orgelkompositionen,* ed. by Spitta, pp. 116f) the speed of motion makes the use of the Pralltriller almost impossible.   W. A.

Sequence. P. 674, col. 2, line 3: for *de St. Adam de Victor read d'Adam de St. Victor.*

Sonata. End of II, p. 693b: Sonatas for cembalo occur in Gregorio Strozzi's *Capricci da sonare* of 1687. Similar compositions by Pasquini may well be of an even earlier date [cf. M. Seiffert, *Geschichte der Klaviermusik* (1899), p. 278].

Sonata-form. P. 697, col. 2: *for* Maria Veracini *read* F. M. Veracini.

The symphony by Monn mentioned in the second paragraph of p. 698 is found in *DTOe* xix, 1, p. 1. It is, however, a less perfect example of sonata-form than is the first movement of a Trio by Pergolesi (d. 1736), which is reprinted in H. Riemann's *Collegium musicum*, No. 30.

Spanish music. Lit.: P. Aubry's "Iter Hispanicum" articles appeared also as a book (1908).

Style. Lit.: E. Katz, *Die musikalischen Stilbegriffe des 17. Jahrhunderts* (1926).

Suite. P. 717b, line 35: read "some of the suites" instead of "the suites"; p. 718a, lines 6 and 7: Suites with the scheme P-A-C-S-O-G (P = Prelude) are found in Draghi's *Six Select Suites of Lessons* (*c.* 1700).

Sumer is icumen in. P. 718, col. 2: *for* Harleyan *read* Harleian.
M. F. Bukofzer, in a recent study, *Sumer is icumen in* (1944), has conclusively shown that the piece dates from the early 14th century, approximately 1310.

Tenebrae. The Improperia do not belong to Tenebrae, but to the Good Friday morning service.

Tetrachord. P. 740, col. 2, line 2: *for* three *read* two.

Thorough-bass. Lit.: G. Ph. Telemann, *Sing-, Spiel- und Generalbassübungen* (1734; ed. M. Seiffert, 1914).

Tonguing. P. 754, col. 1, line 8: Double-tonguing is also called tipping.

Tromba marina. The tenor, marked "Trompette," in Pierre Fontaine's chanson "J'aime bien celui" (*c.* 1400) is probably written for the tromba marina. Cf. P. Aubry, in *SIM* viii, 526.

Trouvères. Lit.: A. Restori, "Per la storia musicale dei trovatori procenzali" (*RMI* ii, iii).

Twelve-tone technique. P. 777, col. 1, last musical example: the second note should be b-flat. Lit.: E. Krenek, "New Developments of the Twelve-Tone Technique" (*MR* iv).

U. C. P. 778, col. 1: *for* corde *read* corda.

Urlinie. In the opening paragraph, replace the sentence "They represent . . . patterns of structure" by the following one: They are essential elements of Schenker's theory and represent the attempt to reveal the organic structure of music by showing that every composition ultimately follows some simple structural tone pattern which acts as its secret skeleton and guarantees its continuity and coherence.
Lit.: H. Schenker, *Musikalische Theorien und Phantasien*, vol. 3: *Der freie Satz* (1935); F. Salzer, *Sinn und Wesen der abendländischen Mehrstimmigkeit* (193?); O. Jonas, *Das Wesen des musikalischen Kunstwerks* (193?).

Variations. IV. The composition mentioned at the beginning of this section can hardly be considered a theme with variations. It is a three-voice rondeau, "Amis tout dous," for the upper part of which two ornamented versions have been preserved. The title given in the text, "Di molen van Pariis," actually refers to the composer, Pierre Moulins of Paris. Cf. F. Kammerer, *Die Musikstücke des Prager Kodex XI E 9* (1931), p. 145.

Venezuela. Lit.: A collection has been started under the title *Archivo de Musica Colonial Venezolana* (1942ff.).

Villanella. E. Kiwi, *Villanella und Canzonetta im 16. Jahrhundert* (Diss. Heidelberg, 1936).

Violin family. (b). P. 802, col. 2: Newbould (not Newbold); 1917 (not *c.* 1930).

Violoncello. P. 804, col. 2, line 16 from bottom: *for* 288 *read* 228.

Vocal music. Regarding the problem of vocal versus instrumental style, in early music, see under *Ensemble. Cf. also L. Hibberd, in *MQ* xxii, no. 2.

Voices, Range of. Cf. A. T. Davison, *The Technique of Choral Composition* (1945), p. 17.

Wa-wan Press. Cf. article by E. Waters, in G. Reese, *A Birthday Present to C(arl) E(ngel)* (1943).

Yankee Doodle. Cf. O. G. Th. Sonneck, *Report on . . . Yankee-Doodle* (1909).

NEW ENTRIES

Ballad meter. This term is commonly employed to designate the most usual poetic meter of English and American ballads, namely that also known as *common meter* [cf. *Ballad, *Poetic meter II].

Choral music. Cf. A. T. Davison, *The Technique of Choral Composition* (1945).

Chôros (properly, *Chôro,* singular). The name originally applied to a musical ensemble of guitars, flutes, and drums, employed for entertainment at popular festivals in Brazil, but now meaning the music played by chôro bands, and resembling the *samba or *maxixe. Villa-Lobos has extended the meaning of chôros to designate any piece in the Brazilian manner, and has composed twelve Chôros, varying from a solo for guitar to a choral symphonic poem.

Conflicting signatures. Same as *partial signatures.

Convertible counterpoint. Same as *invertible counterpoint.

Dice music. See *Mechanical composition.

Eoliphone [F.]. *Wind machine (e.g., in Ravel's *Daphnis and Chloe*).

Harpa [It.]. (1) Harp. — (2) Harpsichord, e.g., in Handel's *Concertos for . . . Harpa o Organo.*

Limoges, School of. Same as School of *St. Martial.

Luftpause [G.]. Breathing rest.

Orpheoreon, orpharion. An instrument described by M. Praetorius (*Organographia,* 1619), and others, similar to the *pandora. Cf. *GD* iii, 773.

Round O. Seventeenth-century Anglicism for *rondo.

Supplying. See under *Verset.